A BIBLICAL AND THEOLOGICAL DICTIONARY

Volume I: A to I

With Illustrated Maps and Charts

BY RICHARD WATSON.

[REVISED BY THE AMERICAN EDITORS.]

NEW-YORK,

PUBLISHED BY B. WAUGH AND T. MASON,

FOR THE METHODIST EPISCOPAL CHURCH, AT THE CONFERENCE

OFFICE, 14 CROSBY-STREET.

J. Collord, Printer.1832.

PREFACE BY THE AUTHOR.

In the following Dictionary, compiled from the best sources ancient and modern, with the addition of many original articles, the selections have been made with reference to what was thought most useful; and thus many things of minor importance, usually found in similar works, have been excluded. Every article too, taken from preceding Dictionaries, has been carefully weighed, and in a great number of instances modified, corrected, or enlarged; and numerous other writings variously illustrative of the Holy Scriptures have been made to contribute a portion of their information under different heads. This general acknowledgment renders a particular reference to the works made use of unnecessary. The fact is, that many of the most valuable of them are compilations from preceding compilations, and so have no title to be referred to as original authorities; while in other instances the articles in this Dictionary have been collected from several sources, and so altered, or combined with original corrections or enlargements, that it would be difficult to assign each portion to its proper original. Where, however, any particulars of fact or history required confirmation, the authority has been given.

It will be observed that all the places and persons mentioned in the Bible have not been noticed, for this would only have made the same unprofitable display of proper names which is seen in several other Dictionaries; but those have been selected on which any thing important for the right understanding of the Scriptures seemed, more or less, to depend. The same rule has been observed as to the natural history of the Bible, on which department great light has been thrown by Dr. Harris, whose learned work has been rather freely used. The leading sects and heresies, ancient and modern, have also been introduced; but with no design to embody a complete account of religious opinions: those only, therefore, have been inserted with which it is most necessary that the theological student should have a general acquaintance.

All that is important in those useful modern works which have been published upon the manners and customs of the east will be found embodied under different heads so far as it tends to elucidate the sacred volume; and many interesting extracts are given from the most intelligent of our modern travellers in Palestine, and neighbouring countries, pointing out the present condition of places celebrated in sacred geography, and especially when the account illustrates and renders remarkable the fulfilment of prophecy.

At the close of the whole, a complete alphabetical list of proper names occurring in the Bible, with their significations and right pronunciation, is appended.

London, AUGUST 20, 1831.

Contents

AARON, the son of Amram and Jochebed, of the tribe of Levi. Aaron was three years older than his brother Moses; and when God appeared in the burning bush, Moses having excused himself from the undertaking committed to him, by urging that he was slow of speech, Aaron, who was an eloquent man, was made his interpreter and spokesman; and in effecting the deliverance of the Hebrews we therefore find them constantly associated. During the march of the children of Israel through the wilderness, Aaron and his sons were appointed by God to exercise for ever the office of priests in the tabernacle. Moses having ascended the mountain to receive the law from God, Aaron, his sons, and seventy elders, followed him, Exod. xxiv, 1, 2, 9–11; not indeed to the summit, but "afar off," "and they saw the God of Israel," that is, the glory in which he appeared, "as it were the paved work of a sapphire stone, and as it were the body of heaven for clearness;"--a clear and dazzling azure, a pure, unmingled splendour like that of the heavens. "And upon the nobles of Israel," Aaron, his sons, and the seventy elders, "he laid not his hand,"--they were not destroyed by a sight which must have overwhelmed the weakness of mortal men had they not been strengthened to bear it; "and they did eat and drink,"--they joyfully and devoutly feasted before the Lord, as a religious act, upon the sacrifices they offered. After this they departed, and Moses remained with God on the very summit of the mount forty days.

During this period, the people, grown impatient at the long absence of Moses, addressed themselves to Aaron in a tumultuous manner, saying, "Make us gods which shall go before us: for, as for this Moses, the man that brought us up out of the land of Egypt, we wot not what is become of him." Aaron sinfully yielded to the importunities of the people; and having ordered them to bring the pendants and the ear-rings of their wives and children, he melted them down, and then made a golden calf, probably in imitation of the Egyptian Apis, an ox or calf dedicated to Osiris. In this instance the image was dedicated to Jehovah the true God; but the guilt consisted in an attempt to establish image worship, which, when even ultimately referring to God, he has forbidden. Neither are images to be worshipped, nor the true God by images;--this is the standing unrepealed law of Heaven. The calf was called a golden calf, as being highly ornamented with gold. Having finished the idol, the people placed it on a pedestal, and danced around it, saying, "These be thy gods, O Israel;" or, as it is expressed in Nehemiah, "This is thy God," the image or symbol of thy God, "which brought thee up out of the land of Egypt." Moses, having hastened from the mount by the command of God, testified to the people, by breaking the tables of the law in their presence, that the covenant between God and them was now rendered of none effect through their offence. He also indignantly reproved Aaron, whose sin indeed had kindled against him the anger of the Lord, so that he would "have destroyed him but that Moses prayed for him."

After the tabernacle was built, Moses consecrated Aaron to the high priesthood with the holy oil, and invested him with his priestly robes,--his garments "of glory and beauty;" but Aaron's weakness was again manifested in concurring with Miriam, his sister, to censure and oppose Moses, through envy. Aaron, as being the elder brother, could not perhaps brook his superiority. What the motive of Miriam might be does not appear; but she being struck with leprosy, this punishment, as being immediately from God, opened Aaron's eyes; he acknowledged his fault, and asked forgiveness of Moses both for himself and his sister.

Aaron himself became also the object of jealousy; but two miraculous interpositions confirmed him in his office of high priest, as of Divine appointment. The first was the destruction of Korah, who sought that office for himself, and of the two hundred and fifty Levites who supported his pretensions, Num. xvi. The second was the blossoming of Aaron's rod, which was designed "to cause the murmurings of the Israelites against him to cease," by showing that he was chosen of God. Moses having, at the command of God, taken twelve rods of an almond tree from the princes of the twelve tribes, and Aaron's separately, he placed them in the tabernacle before the sanctuary, after having written upon each the name of the tribe which it represented, and upon the rod of Aaron the name of Aaron. The day following, when the rods were taken out, that of Aaron "was budded, and brought forth buds, and bloomed blossoms, and yielded almonds." This rod therefore was laid up by the ark, to perpetuate the remembrance of the miracle, and to be a token of Aaron's right to his office.

Aaron married Elisheba, the daughter of Amminadab, of the tribe of Judah, by whom he had four sons, Nadab and Abihu, Eleazar and Ithamar, Exodus vi, 23. The two first were killed by fire from heaven, as a punishment for presuming to offer incense with strange fire in their censers, Lev. x, 1, 2. From the two others the succession of high priests was continued in Israel.

The account of the death of Aaron is peculiarly solemn and affecting. As he and Moses, in striking the rock at Meribah, Num. xvi, had not honoured God by a perfect obedience and faith, he in his wrath declared unto them that they should not enter into the promised land. Soon after, the Lord commanded Moses, "Take Aaron, and Eleazar his son, and bring them up to mount Hor; and strip Aaron of his garments,"--his splendid pontifical vestments,--"and put them upon Eleazar, his son; and Aaron shall be gathered unto his people, and shall die there." This command was carried into effect in the presence of all Israel, who were encamped at the foot of the mountain; and his son being invested with the father's priestly dress, Aaron died, and all the people mourned for him thirty days. His sepulchre was left unmarked and unknown, perhaps to prevent the superstitious reverence of future ages. In Deuteronomy it is said that Aaron died at Mosera; because that was the name of the district in which mount Hor was situated.

2. The PRIESTHOOD being established in Aaron and his family, the nature of this office among the Israelites, and the distinction between the high priest and the other priests, require here to be pointed out.

Before the promulgation of the law by Moses, the fathers of every family, and the princes of every tribe, were priests. This was the case both before and after the flood; for Cain and Abel, Noah, Abraham, Job, Abimelech, Laban, Isaac, and Jacob, themselves offered their own sacrifices. But after the Lord had chosen the family of Aaron, and annexed the priesthood to that line, then the right of sacrificing to God was reserved to that family only. The high priesthood was confined to the first-born in succession; and the rest of his posterity were priests simply so called, or priests of the second order. Both in the high priest and the second or inferior priests, two things deserve notice,--their consecration and their office. In some things they differed, and in others agreed. In their CONSECRATION they differed thus: the high priest had the chrism, or sacred ointment, poured upon his head, so as to run down to his beard, and the skirts of his garment, Exod. xxx, 23; Lev. viii, 12; Psa. cxxxiii, 2. But the second priests were only sprinkled with this oil, mixed with the blood of the sacrifice, Lev. viii, 30. They differed also in their ROBES, which were a necessary adjunct to consecration. The high priest wore at the ordinary times of his ministration in the temple, eight garments;--linen drawers--a coat of fine linen close to his skin--an embroidered girdle of fine linen, blue and scarlet, to surround the coat--a robe all of blue with seventy-two bells, and as many embroidered pomegranates upon the skirts of it; this was put over the coat and girdle--an ephod of gold, and of blue, purple, scarlet, and fine linen, curiously wrought, on the shoulders of which were two stones engraved with the names of the twelve tribes; this was put over the robe, and girt with a curious girdle of the same--a breastplate, about a span square, wrought with gold, blue, purple, scarlet, and fine linen, and fastened upon the ephod by golden chains and rings; in this breastplate were placed the urim and thummim, also twelve several stones, containing the names of the twelve tribes--a mitre of fine linen, sixteen cubits long, to wrap round his head--and lastly, a plate of gold, or holy crown, two fingers broad, whereon was engraved, "Holiness to the Lord;" this was tied with blue lace upon the front of the mitre. Beside these garments, which he wore in his ordinary ministration, there were four others, which he wore only upon extraordinary occasions, viz. on the day of expiation, when he went into the holy of holies, which was once a year. These were: linen drawers--a linen coat--a linen girdle--a linen mitre, all white, Exod. xxviii; Lev. xvi, 4. But the inferior priests had only four garments: linen drawers--a linen coat--a linen girdle--a linen bonnet. The priest and high priest differed also in their MARRIAGE RESTRICTIONS; for the high priest might not marry a widow, nor a divorced woman, nor a harlot, but a virgin only; whereas the other priests might lawfully marry a widow, Lev. xxi, 7.

In the following particulars the high priest and inferior priests agreed in their consecration: both were to be void of bodily blemish--both were to be presented to the Lord at the door of the tabernacle--both were to be washed with water--both were to be consecrated by offering up certain sacrifices--both were to have the blood of a ram put upon the tip of the right ear, the thumb of the right hand, and the great toe of the right foot, Exod. xxix, 20. In the time of consecration, certain pieces of the sacrifice were put into the priest's hand, which was called "filling his hand;" hence the Hebrew phrase, "to fill the hand," signifies consecration.

In the discharge of their offices, the high priest differed from the other priests in these particulars: the high priest only, and that but once a year, might enter into the holy of holies--the high priest might not mourn for his nearest relations by uncovering his head, or tearing any part of his garments, except the skirt; whereas the priest was allowed to mourn for these six,--father, mother, son, daughter, brother, and sister if she had no husband, Lev. xxi, 2, 10, 11; but they agreed in these respects: they both burnt incense and offered sacrifices--they both sounded the trumpet, either as an alarm in war, or to assemble the people and their rulers--they both slew the sacrifices--both instructed the people--and both judged of leprosy.

For the more orderly performance of these offices, the high priest had his sagan, who, in case of the high priest's pollution, performed his duty. The high priest and his sagan resembled our bishop and his suffragan.

3. Aaron was a TYPE of Christ, not personally, but as the high priest of the Jewish church. All the priests, as offering gifts and sacrifices, were in their office types of Christ; but Aaron especially, 1. As the high priest. 2. In entering into the holy place on the great day of atonement, and reconciling the people to God; in making intercession for them, and pronouncing upon them the blessing of Jehovah, at the termination of solemn services. 3. In being anointed with the holy oil by EFFUSION, which was prefigurative of the Holy Spirit with which our Lord was endowed. 4. In bearing the names of all the tribes of Israel upon his breast and upon his shoulders, thus presenting them always before God, and representing them to him. 5. In being the medium of their inquiring of God by urim and thummim; and of the communication of his will to them. But though the offices of Aaron were typical, the priesthood of Christ is of a different and higher ORDER than his, namely, that of Melchizedeck. See Calf, Priest, Type, Ephod, Breastplate, Urim.

AB, in the Hebrew chronology, the eleventh month of the civil year, and the fifth of the ecclesiastical year, which began with Nisan. This month answered to the moon of July, comprehending part of July and of August, and contained thirty days.

The first day of this month is observed as a fast by the Jews, in memory of Aaron's death; and the ninth, in commemoration of the destruction of the temple by Nebuchadnezzar, in the year before Christ 587. Josephus observes, that the burning of the temple by Nebuchadnezzar happened on the same day of the year on which it was afterward burned by Titus. The same day was remarkable for

Adrian's edict, which prohibited the Jews to continue in Judea, or to look toward Jerusalem and lament its desolation. The eighteenth day is also kept as a fast, because the sacred lamp was extinguished on that night, in the reign of Ahaz. On the twenty-first, or, according to Scaliger, the twenty-second day, was a feast called Xylophoria, from their laying up the necessary wood in the temple: and on the twenty-fourth, a feast in commemoration of the abolishing of a law by the Asmoneans, or Maccabees, which had been introduced by the Sadducees, and which enacted, that both sons and daughters should alike inherit the estate of their parents.

ABADDON, Heb. corresponding to APOLLYON, Gr. that is, DESTROYER, is represented, Rev. ix, 11, as king of the locusts, and the angel of the bottomless pit. Le Clerc and Dr. Hammond understand by the locusts in this passage, the zealots and robbers who infested and desolated Judea before Jerusalem was taken by the Romans; and by Abaddon, John of Gischala, who having treacherously left that town before it was surrendered to Titus, came to Jerusalem and headed those of the zealots who acknowledged him as their king, and involved the Jews in many grievous calamities. The learned Grotius concurs in opinion, that the locusts are designed to represent the sect of the zealots, who appeared among the Jews during the siege, and at the time of the destruction of Jerusalem. But Mr. Mede remarks, that the title Abaddon alludes to Obodas, the common name of the ancient monarchs of that part of Arabia from which Mohammed came; and considers the passage as descriptive of the inundation of the Saracens. Mr. Lowman adopts and confirms this interpretation. He shows that the rise and progress of the Mohammedan religion and empire exhibit a signal accomplishment of this prophecy. All the circumstances here recited correspond to the character of the Arabians, and the history of the period that extended from A. D. 568 to A. D. 675. In conformity to this opinion, Abaddon may be understood to denote either Mohammed, who issued from the abyss, or the cave of Hera, to propagate his pretended revelations, or, more generally, the Saracen power. Mr. Bryant supposes Abaddon to have been the name of the Ophite deity, the worship of whom prevailed very anciently and very generally.

ABANA. Naaman, the leper, on being directed to wash in the river Jordan, says, 2 Kings v, 12, "Are not Abana and Pharpar, rivers of Damascus, better than all the waters of Israel?" Probably the Abana is a branch of the Barrady, or Chrysorrhoas, which derives its source from the foot of mount Libanus, eastward; runs round and through Damascus, and continues its course till lost in the wilderness, four or five leagues south of the city. Benjamin of Tudela will have that part of Barrady which runs through Damascus to be the Abana, and the streams which water the gardens without the city, to be Pharpar; but perhaps the Pharpar is the same with Orontes, the most noted river of Syria, which, taking its rise a little to the north or north-east of Damascus, glides through a delightful plain, till, after passing Antioch, and running about two hundred miles to the north-west, it loses itself in the Mediterranean sea, 2 Kings v, 12.

ABBA, a Syriac word, which signifies FATHER. The learned Mr. Selden, from the Babylonian Gemara, has proved that slaves were not allowed to use the title abba in addressing the master of the family to which they belonged. This may serve to illustrate Rom. viii, 15, and Gal. iv, 6, as it shows that through faith in Christ all true Christians pass into the relation of sons; are permitted to address God with filial confidence in prayer; and to regard themselves as heirs of the heavenly inheritance. This adoption into the family of God, inseparably follows our justification; and the power to call God our Father, in this special and appropriative sense, results from the inward testimony given to our forgiveness by the Holy Spirit. St. Paul and St. Mark use the Syriac word ABBA, a term which was understood in the synagogues and primitive assemblies of Christians; but added to it when writing to foreigners the explanation, FATHER. Figuratively, abba means also a superior, in respect of age, dignity, or affection. It is more particularly used in the Syriac, Coptic, and Ethiopic churches as a title given to their bishops. The bishops themselves bestow the title abba more eminently upon the bishop of Alexandria, which occasioned the people to give him the title of baba, or papa, that is, grandfather; a title which he bore before the bishop of Rome.

ABEDNEGO, the Chaldee name given by the king of Babylon's officer to Azariah, one of Daniel's companions, Dan. i, 7. This name imports the servant of Nago, or Nego, which is supposed to signify the sun, or morning star, so called from its brightness. Abednego was thrown into a fiery furnace, at Babylon, with his two companions Shadrach and Meshach, for refusing to adore the statue erected by the command of Nebuchadnezzar. God suffered them not to be injured by the flames; but made the whole to redound to his own glory, and the shame of the idols of Babylon. One like unto the Son of God, or a Divine person, probably the Angel of the Divine presence himself, appeared in the midst of them; and they came out of the furnace, which had been heated seven times hotter than usual, so completely preserved from the power of the flames, that not even "the smell of fire had passed upon them." This was an illustrious instance of the courageous and hallowed spirit of martyrdom; and the interposition was no doubt designed to encourage the Jews while in captivity, living among idolaters, to hold fast their religion. It is an instance also of those gracious visitations to the old Heathen world, by which it was loudly called from its idolatries, and aroused to the acknowledgment of the true and only Jehovah, who, in various ways, "left not himself without witness" among them. A great temporary effect was produced by this and other miracles related in the book of Daniel; but the people relapsed again into idolatry, and justly brought upon themselves all those wasting judgments which in succession swept over the mightiest and most ancient states.

ABEL. He was the second son of Adam and Eve, and born probably in the second or third year of the world; though some will have it that he and Cain were twins. His name signifies VAPOUR, VANITY, and might be given either because our first parents now began so to feel the emptiness and vanity of all earthly things, that the birth of another son reminded them painfully of it, although in itself a matter of joy; or it was imposed under prophetic impulse, and obscurely referred to his premature death. His employment was that of a shepherd; Cain followed the occupation of his father, and was a tiller of the ground. Whether they remained in their father's family at the time when they brought their offerings to the Lord, or had establishments separate from that of Adam, does not clearly appear. Abel was probably unmarried, or had no children; but Cain's wife is mentioned. "At the end of the days,"--which is a more literal rendering than "in process of time," as in our translation, that is, on the Sabbath,--both brothers brought an offering to the Lord. Cain "brought of the fruit of the ground;" Abel "the firstlings of his flock, and of the fat thereof." "And the Lord had respect to Abel and to his offering; but unto Cain and his offering he had not respect." As Cain afterward complains that "he should be hid from the FACE or PRESENCE of the Lord," it is probable that the worship of the first family was performed before some visible manifestation of the glory of God, which thus consecrated a particular place for their services. Some have thought that this was at the east gate of Eden, where "Cherubim and a flaming sword were placed;" but this was a vengeful manifestation, and could only have inspired a dread of God inconsistent with the confidence and hope with which men through the promise of redemption were now encouraged to draw nigh to him. The respect which God was pleased to show to Abel's offering, appears from the account to have been sensibly declared; for Cain must have known by some token that the sacrifice of Abel was accepted, the absence of which sign, as to his own offering, showed that it was rejected. Whether this was by fire going forth from "the presence of the Lord," to consume the sacrifice, as in later instances recorded in the Old Testament, or in some other way, it is in vain to inquire;--that the token of acceptance was a sensible one is however an almost certain inference. The effect of this upon Cain was not to humble him before God, but to excite anger against his brother; and, being in the field with him, or, as the old versions have it, having said to him, "Let us go out into the field," "he rose up against Abel his brother, and slew him;" and for that crime, by which the first blood of man was shed by man upon the earth,--a murder aggravated by the relationship and the "righteous" character of the sufferer, and having in it also the nature of religious persecution,--he was pronounced by the Lord "cursed from the earth."

2. As the sacrifice of Abel is the first on record, and has given rise to some controversy, it demands particular attention. It was offered, says St. Paul, "in faith," and it was "a more excellent sacrifice" than that of Cain. Both these expressions intimate that it was EXPIATORY and PREFIGURATIVE.

As to the matter of the sacrifice, it was an ANIMAL offering. "Cain brought of the fruit of the ground; and Abel also brought of the firstlings of his flock, and of the fat thereof;" or, more literally, "the fat of them," that is, according to the Hebrew idiom, the fattest or best of his flock; and in this circumstance consisted its specific character as an act of FAITH. This is supported by the import of the phrase, ϖλείονα θυσίαν, used by the Apostle in the Epistle to the Hebrews, when speaking of the sacrifice of Abel. Our translators have rendered it, "a more excellent sacrifice." Wickliffe translates it, as Archbishop Magee observes, uncouthly, but in the full sense of the original, "a much more sacrifice;" and the controversy which has arisen on this point is, whether this epithet of "much more," or "fuller," refers to quantity or quality; whether it is to be understood in the sense of a MORE ABUNDANT, or of a BETTER, a MORE EXCELLENT sacrifice. Dr. Kennicott takes it in the sense of measure and quantity, as well as quality; and supposes that Abel brought a double offering of the firstlings of his flock, and of the fruit of the ground ALSO. His criticism has been very satisfactorily refuted by Archbishop Magee. The sacrifice of Abel was that of animal victims, and it was indicative not of gratitude but of "faith:" a quality not to be made manifest by the QUANTITY of an offering, for the one has no relation to the other.

3. This will more fully appear if we consider the import of the words of the Apostle,--"By FAITH Abel offered unto God a more excellent sacrifice than Cain, by which he obtained WITNESS that he was RIGHTEOUS, God testifying of his gifts; and by it, he, being dead, yet speaketh." Now what is the meaning of the Apostle, when he says that it was witnessed or testified to Abel that he was RIGHTEOUS? His doctrine is, that men are sinners; that all, consequently, need pardon; and TO BE DECLARED, WITNESSED, and ACCOUNTED RIGHTEOUS, are, according to his style of writing, the same as "to be justified, pardoned, and dealt with as righteous." Thus he argues that Abraham believed God, "and it was accounted to him for righteousness,"--"that faith was reckoned to Abraham for righteousness,"--"that he received the sign of circumcision, a SEAL," a visible confirmatory, declaratory, and witnessing mark "of the righteousness which he had by faith." In these cases we have a similarity so striking, that they can scarcely fail to explain each other. In both, sinful men are placed in the condition of RIGHTEOUS men; the instrument, in both cases, is FAITH; and the transaction is, in both cases also, publicly and sensibly WITNESSED,--as to Abraham, by the sign of circumcision; as to Abel, by a visible acceptance of his sacrifice, and the rejection of that of Cain.

Abel had faith, and he expressed that faith by the kind of sacrifice he offered. It was in this way that his faith "pleased God;" it pleased him as a principle, and by the act to which it led, which act was the offering of a sacrifice to God different from that of Cain. Cain had not this faith, whatever might be its object; and Cain, accordingly, did not bring an offering to which God had "respect." That which vitiated the offering of Cain was the want of this faith; for his offering was not significant of faith: that which "pleased God," in the case of Abel, was his faith; and he had "respect" to his offering, because it was the expression of that faith; and upon his faith so expressing itself, God witnessed to him "that he was righteous." So forcibly do the words of St. Paul, when commenting upon this transaction, show, that Abel's sacrifice was accepted, because of its immediate connection with his FAITH, for by faith he is said to have offered it; and whatever it might be, which made Abel's offering differ from that of Cain, whether ABUNDANCE, or KIND, or both, this was the result of his faith. So evident also is it from the Apostle, that Abel was witnessed to be "righteous," not with reference to any previous "habit of a religious life," as some say, but with reference to his FAITH; and to this faith as expressing itself by his offering "a more excellent sacrifice."

4. If, then, the faith of Abel had an immediate connection with his sacrifice, and both with his being accepted as "righteous,"--that is, JUSTIFIED, in St. Paul's use of the term,--to what had his faith respect? The particular object of the faith of the elders, celebrated in Hebrews xi, is to be deduced from the circumstances mentioned as illustrative of the existence and operation of this great principle, and by which it manifested itself in them. Let us explain this, and then ascertain the object of Abel's faith also from the manner of its manifestation,--from the acts in which it embodied and rendered itself conspicuous.

Faith, in this chapter, is taken in the sense of AFFIANCE in God, and, as such, it can only be exercised toward God, as to all its particular acts, in those respects in which we have some warrant to confide in him. This supposes revelation, and, in particular, promises or declarations on his part, as the ground of every act of affiance. When, therefore, it is said that "by faith Enoch was translated that he should not see death," it must be supposed that he had some promise or intimation to this effect, on which, improbable as the event was, he nobly relied; and in the result God honoured his faith in the sight of all men. The faith of Noah had immediate respect to the threatened flood, and to the promise of God to preserve him in the ark which he was commanded to prepare. The chapter is filled with other instances, expressed or implied; and from the whole, as well as from the nature of things, it will appear, that, when the Apostle speaks of the faith of the elders in its particular acts, he represents it as having respect to some promise, declaration, or revelation of God.

This revelation was necessarily antecedent to the faith; but it is also to be observed, that the acts by which the faith was represented, whenever it was represented by particular acts, and when the case admitted it, had a natural and striking conformity and correspondence to the previous revelation. So Noah built the ark, which indicated that he had heard the threat of the world's destruction by water, and had received the promise of his own preservation, and that of his family, as well as that of a part of the beasts of the earth. When Abraham went into Canaan at the command of God, and upon the promise that that country should become the inheritance of his decendants, he showed his faith by taking possession of it for them in anticipation, and his residence there indicated the kind of promise which he had received. Thus these instances show, that when the faith which the Apostle commends exhibited itself in some particular act, that act had a correspondency to the previous promise or revelation which was the ground of faith. We must therefore interpret the acts of Abel's faith so as to make them also correspond with an antecedent revelation. His faith had respect to some previous revelation, and the nature of the revelation is to be collected from the significant manner in which he declared his faith in it.

Now that which Abel did "by faith," was, GENERALLY, to perform an act of solemn worship, in the confidence that it would be acceptable to God. This supposes a revelation, immediate or by tradition, that such acts of worship were acceptable to God, or his faith could have had no warrant, and would not have been faith, but fancy. But the case must be considered more particularly. His faith led him to offer "a more excellent sacrifice" than that of Cain; but this as necessarily implies, that there was some antecedent revelation to which his faith, as thus expressed, had respect, and on which that peculiarity of his offering, which distinguished it from the offering of Cain, was founded; a revelation which indicated that the way in which God would be approached acceptably, in solemn worship, was by animal sacrifices. Without this, the faith to which his offering, which was an offering of the firstlings of his flock, had a special fitness and adaptation, could have had no warrant in Divine authority. But this revelation must have included, in order to its being the ground of faith, as "the substance of things hoped for," a promise of a benefit to be conferred, in which promise Abel might CONFIDE. But if so, then this promise must have been connected, not with the worship of God in general, or performed in any way whatever indifferently, but with his worship by animal oblations; for it was in this way that the faith of Abel specially and distinctively indicated itself. The antecedent revelation was, therefore, a promise of a benefit to be conferred, by means of animal sacrifice; and we are taught what this benefit was, by that which was actually received by the offerer,--"He obtained witness that he was RIGHTEOUS;" which must be interpreted in the sense of a declaration of his personal justification, and acceptance as righteous, by the forgiveness of his sins. The reason of Abel's acceptance and of Cain's rejection is hereby made manifest; the one, in seeking the Divine favour, conformed to his established and appointed method of being approached by guilty men, and the other not only neglected this, but profanely and presumptuously substituted his own inventions.

5. It is impossible, then, to allow the sacrifice of Abel, in this instance, to have been an act of FAITH, without supposing that it had respect to a previous revelation, which agreed with all the parts of that sacrificial action by which he expressed his faith in it. Had Abel's sacrifice been eucharistic merely, it would have expressed gratitude, but not faith; or if faith in the general sense of confidence in God that he would receive an act of grateful worship, and reward the worshippers, it did not more express faith than the offering of Cain, who surely believed these two points, or he would not have brought an offering of any kind. The offering of Abel expressed a faith which Cain had not; and the doctrinal principles which Abel's faith respected were such as his sacrifice visibly embodied. If it was not an eucharistic sacrifice, it was an expiatory one; and, in fact, it is only in a sacrifice of this kind, that it is possible to see that faith exhibited which Abel had, and Cain had not. If then we refer to the subsequent sacrifices of expiation appointed by Divine authority, and their

explanation in the New Testament, it will be obvious to what doctrines and principles of an antecedent revelation the faith of Abel had respect, and which his sacrifice, the exhibition of his faith, proclaimed: confession of the fact of being a sinner,--acknowledgment that the demerit and penalty of sin is death,--submission to an appointed mode of expiation,--animal sacrifice offered VICARIOUSLY, but in itself a mere type of a better sacrifice, "the Seed of the woman," appointed to be offered at some future period,--and the efficacy of this appointed method of expiation to obtain forgiveness, and to admit the guilty into the Divine favour.

"Abel," Dr. Magee justly says, "in firm reliance on the promise of God, and in obedience to his command, offered that sacrifice which had been enjoined as the religious expression of his faith; whilst Cain, disregarding the gracious assurances that had been vouchsafed, or at least disdaining to adopt the prescribed mode of manifesting his belief, possibly as not appearing to HIS REASON to possess any efficacy or natural fitness, thought he had sufficiently acquitted himself of his duty in acknowledging the general superintendence of God, and expressing his gratitude to the Supreme Benefactor, by presenting some of those good things which he thereby confessed to have been derived from his bounty. In short, Cain, the first-born of the fall, exhibits the first fruits of his parents' disobedience, in the arrogance and self-sufficiency of reason rejecting the aids of revelation, because they fell not within its apprehension of right. He takes the first place in the annals of Deism, and displays, in his proud rejection of the ordinance of sacrifice, the same spirit which, in later days, has actuated his ENLIGHTENED followers, in rejecting the sacrifice of Christ."

Abel was killed about the year of the world, 130.

ABEL-MISRAIM, the floor of Atad, beyond the river Jordan, where Joseph, his brethren, and the Egyptians mourned for the death of Jacob, Gen. l, 11. On this occasion the funeral procession was, at the command of Joseph, attended by "all the elders of Egypt, and all the servants of Pharaoh, and all his house, and the house of his brethren, chariots and horsemen, a very great company;" an affecting proof, as it has been remarked, of Joseph's simplicity and singleness of heart, which allowed him to give to the great men of Egypt, over whom he bore absolute rule, an opportunity of observing his own comparatively humble origin, by leading them in attendance upon his father's corpse to the valleys of Canaan, the modest cradle of his race, and to their simple burial places.

ABEL-SHITTIM, a city situate in the plains of Moab, beyond Jordan, opposite to Jericho, Num. xxv, 1, &c; xxiii, 49; Joshua xi, 1. Eusebius says it stood in the neighbourhood of mount Peor. Moses encamped at Abel-Shittim some time before the Hebrew army passed the Jordan. Here the Israelites fell into idolatry, and worshipped Baal-peor, for which God punished them by the destruction of twenty-four thousand persons in one day.

ABIAH, the second son of the prophet Samuel, and brother of Joel. Samuel having entrusted to his sons the administration of public justice, and admitted them to a share in the government, they behaved so ill, that the people demanded a king, 1 Sam. viii, 2. A. M. 2909.

ABIATHAR, the son of Ahimelech, and the tenth high priest among the Jews, and fourth in descent from Eli, 2 Sam. viii, 17; 1 Chron. xviii, 16. When Saul sent to Nob to murder all the priests, Abiathar escaped the massacre, and fled to David in the wilderness. There he continued in the quality of high priest; but Saul, out of aversion to Ahimelech, whom he imagined to have betrayed his interests, transferred the dignity of the high priesthood from Ithamar's family into that of Eleazar, by conferring this office upon Zadok. Thus there were, at the same time, two high priests in Israel, Abiathar with David, and Zadok with Saul. In this state things continued, until the reign of Solomon, when Abiathar, being attached to the party of Adonijah, was, by Solomon, divested of his priesthood, A. M. 2989; and the race of Zadok alone performed the functions of that office during the reign of Solomon, to the exclusion of the family of Ithamar, according to the word of the Lord to Eli, 1 Sam. ii, 30, &c.

ABIB, the name of the first Hebrew sacred month, Exod. xiii, 4. This month was afterward called Nisan; it contained thirty days, and answered to part of our March and April. Abib signifies green ears of corn, or fresh fruits, according to Jerom's translation, Exod. xiii, 4, and to the **LXX**. It was so named because corn, particularly barley, was in ear at that time. It was an early custom to give names to months, from the appearances of nature; and the custom is still in force among many nations. The year among the Jews commenced in September, and consequently their jubilees and other civil matters were regulated in this way, Lev. xxv, 8–10; but their sacred year began in Abib. This change took place at the redemption of Israel from Egypt, Exod. xii, 2, "This shall be to you the beginning of months." Ravanelli observes, that as this deliverance from Egypt was a figure of the redemption of the church of Jesus Christ, who died and rose again in this month, it was made the "beginning of months," to lead the church to expect the acceptable year of the Lord. On the tenth day of this month the paschal lamb was taken; and on the fourteenth they ate the passover. On the seven succeeding days they celebrated the feast of unleavened bread, on the last of which days they held a solemn convocation, Exod. xii, xiii. On the fifteenth they gathered the sheaf of the barley first fruits, and on the following day presented an offering of it to the Lord, which having done they might begin their harvest, Lev. xxiii.

ABIHU, the son of Aaron, the high priest, was consumed, together with his brother Nadab, by fire sent from God, because he had offered incense with strange fire, instead of taking it from the altar, Lev. x, 1, 2. This calamity happened A. M. 2514; within eight days after the consecration of Aaron and his sons. Some commentators believe that this fire proceeded from the altar of burnt offerings; others, that it came from the altar of incense. Several interpreters, as the Rabbins, Lyra, Cajetan, and others, are of opinion, that

Nadab and Abihu were overtaken with wine, and so forgot to take the sacred fire in their censers. This conjecture is founded on the command of God delivered immediately afterward to the priests, forbidding them the use of wine during the time they should be employed in the service of the temple. Another class allege, that there was nothing so heinous in their transgression, but it was awfully punished, to teach ministers fidelity and exactness in discharging their office. It had a vastly more important meaning,--this instance of vengeance is a standing example of that divine wrath which shall consume all who pretend to serve God, except with incense kindled from the one altar and offering by which he for ever perfects them that are sanctified.

ABIJAH, the son of Jeroboam, the first king of the ten tribes, who died very young, 1 Kings xiv, 1, &c, A. M. 3046.--2. The son of Rehoboam, king of Judah, and of Maachah, the daughter of Uriel, who succeeded his father, A. M. 3046, 2 Chron. xi, 20; xiii, 2, &c. The Rabbins reproach this monarch with neglecting to destroy the profane altar which Jeroboam had erected at Bethel; and with not suppressing the worship of the golden calves there after his victory over that prince.

ABILENE, a small province in Cœlo Syria, between Lebanon and Antilibanus. Of this place Lysanias was governor in the fifteenth year of Tiberius, Luke iii, 1. Abela, or Abila, the capital, was north of Damascus, and south of Heliopolis.

ABIMELECH. This seems to have been the title of the kings of Philistia, as Cæsar was of the Roman emperors, and Pharaoh of the sovereigns of Egypt. It was the name also of one of the sons of Gideon, who became a judge of Israel, Judges ix; and of the Jewish high priest, who gave Goliath's sword, which had been deposited in the tabernacle, and part of the shew bread, to David, at the time this prince was flying from Saul, 1 Sam. xxi, 1.

ABIRAM, the eldest son of Hiel, the Bethelite. Joshua having destroyed the city of Jericho, pronounced this curse: "Cursed be the man, before the Lord, that riseth up and buildeth this city, Jericho: he shall lay the foundation thereof in his first-born, and in his youngest son shall he set up the gates of it," Joshua vi, 26. Hiel of Bethel, about five hundred and thirty-seven years after this imprecation, having undertaken to rebuild Jericho, whilst he was laying the foundation of it, lost his eldest son, Abiram, 1 Kings xvi, 34; and Segub, the youngest, when they set up the gates of it: a remarkable instance of a prophetic denunciation fulfilled, perhaps on a person who would not credit the tradition, or the truth of the prediction. So true is the word of the Lord; so minutely are the most distant contingencies foreseen by him; and so exact is the accomplishment of Divine prophecy!

2. Abiram, the son of Eliab, of the tribe of Reuben, was one of those who conspired with Korah and Dathan against Moses in the wilderness, and was swallowed up alive, with his companions, by the earth, which opened to receive them, Num. xvi.

ABISHAG, a young woman, a native of Shunam, in the tribe of Issachar. David, at the age of seventy, finding no warmth in his bed, was advised by his physicians to procure some young person, who might communicate the heat required. To this end Abishag was presented to him, who was one of the most beautiful women in Israel, 1 Kings i, 3; and the king made her his wife. After his death, Adonijah requested her in marriage, for which he lost his life; Solomon perceiving in this a design upon the crown also. Adonijah was his elder brother, an intriguing man, and had aspired to be king before the death of David, and had had his life spared only upon the condition of his peaceable conduct. By this request he convinced Solomon, that he was still actuated by political views, and this brought upon him the punishment of treason.

ABISHAI, the son of Zeruiah, David's sister, who was one of the most valiant men of his time, and one of the principal generals in David's armies.

ABLUTION, purification by washing the body, either in whole or part. Ablutions appear to be almost as ancient as external worship itself. Moses enjoined them; the Heathens adopted them; and Mohammed and his followers have continued them: thus they have been introduced among most nations, and make a considerable part of all superstitious religions. The Egyptian priests had their diurnal and nocturnal ablutions; the Grecians, their sprinklings; the Romans, their lustrations and lavations; the Jews, their washings of hands and feet, beside their baptisms; the ancient Christians used ablution before communion, which the Romish church still retains before the mass, sometimes after; the Syrians, Copts, &c, have their solemn washings on Good Friday; the Turks their greater and less ablutions, &c.

Lustration, among the Romans, was a solemn ceremony by which they purified their cities, fields, armies, or people, after any crime or impurity. Lustrations might be performed by fire, by sulphur, by water, and by air; the last was applied by ventilation, or fanning the thing to be purified. All sorts of people, slaves excepted, might perform some kind of lustration. When a person died the house was to be swept in a particular manner; new married persons were sprinkled by the priest with water. People sometimes, by way of purification, ran several times naked through the streets. There was scarcely any action performed, at the beginning and end of which some ceremony was not required to purify themselves and appease the gods.

ABNER was the uncle of king Saul, and the general of his army. After Saul's death, he made Ishbosheth king; and for seven years supported the family of Saul, in opposition to David; but in most of his skirmishes came off with loss. While Ishbosheth's and David's troops lay near each other, hard by Gibeon, Abner challenged Joab to select twelve of David's warriors to fight with an equal number of his. Joab consented: the twenty-four engaged; and fell together on the spot. A fierce battle ensued, in which Abner and his troops were routed. Abner himself was hotly pursued by Asahel, whom he killed by a back stroke of his spear. Still he was followed by Joab and Abishai, till he, who in the morning sported with murder, was obliged at even to entreat that Joab would stay his troops from the effusion of blood, 2 Sam. ii.

Not long after, Abner, taking it highly amiss for Ishbosheth to charge him with lewd behaviour toward Rizpah, Saul's concubine, vowed that he would quickly transfer the whole kingdom into the hands of David. He therefore commenced a correspondence with David, and had an interview with him at Hebron. Abner had just left the feast at which David had entertained him, when Joab, informed of the matter, warmly remonstrated, asserting, that Abner had come as a spy. On his own authority he sent a messenger to invite him back, to have some farther communication with the king; and when Abner was come into Joab's presence, the latter, partly from jealousy lest Abner might become his superior, and partly to revenge his brother Asahel's death, mortally stabbed him in the act of salutation. David, to show how heartily he detested the act, honoured Abner with a splendid funeral, and composed an elegy on his death, 2 Sam. iii.

ABOMINATION. This term was used with regard to the Hebrews, who, being shepherds, are said to have been an abomination to the Egyptians; because they sacrificed the animals held sacred by that people, as oxen, goats, sheep, &c, which the Egyptians esteemed unlawful. This word is also applied in the sacred writings to idolatry and idols, not only because the worship of idols is in itself an abominable thing, but likewise because the ceremonies of idolaters were almost always of an infamous and licentious nature. For this reason, Chrysostom affirms, that every idol, and every image of a man, was called an abomination among the Jews. The "abomination of desolation" foretold by the Prophet Daniel, x, 27, xi, 31, is supposed by some interpreters to denote the statue of Jupiter Olympius, which Antiochus Epiphanes caused to be erected in the temple of Jerusalem. The second of the passages above cited may probably refer to this circumstance, as the statue of Jupiter did, in fact, "make desolate," by banishing the true worship of God, and those who performed it, from the temple. But the former passage, considered in its whole connection, bears more immediate reference to that which the evangelists have denominated the "abomination of desolation," Matt. xxiv, 15, 16; Mark xiii, 14. This, without doubt, signifies the ensigns of the Roman armies under the command of Titus, during the last siege of Jerusalem. The images of their gods and emperors were delineated on these ensigns; and the ensigns themselves, especially the eagles, which were carried at the heads of the legions, were objects of worship; and, according to the usual style of Scripture, they were therefore an abomination. Those ensigns were placed upon the ruins of the temple after it was taken and demolished; and, as Josephus informs us, the Romans sacrificed to them there. The horror with which the Jews regarded them, sufficiently appears from the account which Josephus gives of Pilate's introducing them into the city, when he sent his army from Cæsarea into winter quarters at Jerusalem, and of Vitellius's proposing to march through Judea, after he had received orders from Tiberius to attack Aretas, king of Petra. The people supplicated and remonstrated, and induced Pilate to remove the army, and Vitellius to march his troops another way. The Jews applied the above passage of Daniel to the Romans, as we are informed by Jerome. The learned Mr. Mede concurs in the same opinion. Sir Isaac Newton, *Obs. on Daniel* ix, xii, observes, that in the sixteenth year of the emperor Adrian, B. C. 132, the Romans accomplished the prediction of Daniel by building a temple to Jupiter Capitolinus, where the temple of God in Jerusalem had stood. Upon this occasion the Jews, under the conduct of Barchochab, rose up in arms against the Romans, and in the war had fifty cities demolished, nine hundred and eighty-five of their best towns destroyed, and five hundred and eighty thousand men slain by the sword; and in the end of the war, B. C. 136, they were banished from Judea upon pain of death; and thenceforth the land remained desolate of its old inhabitants. Others again have applied the prediction of Daniel to the invasion and desolation of Christendom by the Mohammedans, and to their conversion of the churches into mosques. From this interpretation they infer, that the religion of Mohammed will prevail in the east one thousand two hundred and sixty years, and be succeeded by the restoration of the Jews, the destruction of antichrist, the full conversion of the Gentiles to the church of Christ, and the commencement of the millennium.

In general, whatever is morally or ceremonially impure, or leads to sin, is designated an ABOMINATION to God. Thus lying lips are said to be an ABOMINATION to the Lord. Every thing in doctrine or practice which tended to corrupt the simplicity of the Gospel is also in Scripture called abominable; hence Babylon is represented, Rev. xvii, 4, as holding in her hand a cup "full of abominations." In this view, to "work abomination," is to introduce idolatry, or any other great corruption, into the church and worship of God, 1 Kings xi, 7.

ABRAM, אברם, A HIGH FATHER; and **ABRAHAM**, אברהם, FATHER OF A GREAT MULTITUDE, the son of Terah, born at Ur, a city of Chaldea, A. M. 2008. The account of this eminent patriarch occupies so large a part of the book of Genesis, and stands so intimately connected with both the Jewish and Christian dispensations,--with the one by a political and religious, and with the other by a mystical, relation,--that his history demands particular notice. Our account may be divided into his PERSONAL HISTORY, and his TYPICAL, AND MYSTIC CHARACTER.

I. Abraham's PERSONAL history.

1. Chaldea, the native country of Abraham, was inhabited by a pastoral people, who were almost irresistibly invited to the study of the motions of the heavenly bodies, by the peculiar serenity of the heavens in that climate, and their habit of spending their nights in the open air in tending their flocks. The first rudiments of astronomy, as a science, is traced to this region; and here, too, one of the earliest forms of idolatry, the worship of the host of heaven, usually called Tsabaism, first began to prevail. During the three hundred and fifty years which elapsed between the deluge and the birth of Abraham, this and other idolatrous superstitions had

greatly corrupted the human race, perverted the simple forms of the patriarchal religion, and beclouded the import of its typical rites. The family of Abraham was idolatrous, for his "fathers served other gods beyond the flood," that is, the great river Euphrates; but whether he himself was in the early period of his life an idolater, we are not informed by Moses. The Arabian and Jewish legends speak of his early idolatry, his conversion from it, and of his zeal in breaking the images in his father's house; but these are little to be depended upon. Before his call he was certainly a worshipper of the true God; and that not in form only, but "in spirit and in truth." Whilst Abraham was still sojourning in Ur, "the God of glory" appeared to him, and said unto him, "Get thee out of thy country and from thy kindred, and go into the land which I shall show thee;" and so firm was his faith in the providence and care of God, that although the place of his future abode was not indicated, nor any information given of the nature of the country, or the character of its inhabitants, he nevertheless promptly obeyed, and "went out, not knowing whither he went." Terah his father, Nahor his brother, and Lot his nephew, the son of Haran his deceased brother, accompanied him; a circumstance which indicates that if the family had formerly been idolatrous it had now received the faith of Abraham. They first migrated to Haran, or Charran, in Mesopotamia, a flat, barren region westward of Ur; and after a residence there of a few years, during which Terah had died, Abraham left Haran to go into Palestine, taking with him Sarah his wife, who had no child, and Lot, with his paternal property. Nahor appears to have been left in Haran. To this second migration he was incited also by a Divine command, accompanied by the promises of a numerous issue, that his seed should become a great nation, and, above all, that "in him all the families of the earth should be blessed;" in other words, that the Messiah, known among the patriarchs as the promised "seed of the woman," should be born in his line. Palestine was then inhabited by the Canaanites, from whom it was called Canaan. Abraham, leading his tribe, first settled at Sechem, a valley between the mountains Ebal and Gerizim, where God appeared to him and promised to give him the land of Canaan, and where, as in other places in which he remained any time, he built an altar to the Lord. He then removed to a hilly region on the north of Jericho; and as the pastures were exhausted, migrated southward, till a famine drove him into Egypt, probably the earliest, certainly the most productive, corn country of the ancient world.

2. Here it may be observed, that the migrations of Abraham and his sons show the manner in which the earth was gradually covered with people. In those ages some cities had been built, and the country to some extent about them cultivated; but wide spaces of unoccupied land lay between them. A part of society following therefore the pastoral life, led forth their flocks, and, in large family tribes, of which the parent was the head, uniting both the sovereign power and the priesthood in himself, and with a train of servants attached to the tribe by hereditary ties, pitched their camps wherever a fertile and unappropriated district offered them pasture. A few of these nomadic tribes appear to have made the circuit of the same region, seldom going far from their native seats; which would probably have been the case with Abraham, had he not received the call of God to depart to a distant country. Others, more bold, followed the track of rivers, and the sweep of fertile valleys, and at length some built cities and formed settlements in those distant regions; whilst others, either from attachment to their former mode of life, or from necessity, continued in their pastoral occupations, and followed the supplies afforded for their flocks by the still expanding regions of the fertile earth. Wars and violences, droughts, famines, and the constant increase of population, continued to impel these innumerable, but at first, small streams of men into parts still more remote. Those who settled on the sea coast began to use that element, both for supplying themselves with a new species of food, and as a medium of communication by vessels with other countries for the interchange of such commodities as their own lands afforded with those offered by maritime states, more or less distant. Thus were laid the foundations of commerce, and thus the maritime cities were gradually rendered opulent and powerful. Colonies were in time transported from them by means of their ships, and settled on the coasts of still more distant and fertile countries. Thus the migrations of the three primitive families proceeded from the central regions of Armenia, Mesopotamia, and Assyria; and in succession they established numerous communities,--the Phenicians, Arabians, Egyptians, Ethiopians, and Lybians southward;--the Persians, Indians, and Chinese eastward;--the Scythians, Celts, and Tartars northward;--and the Goths, Greeks, and Latins westward, even as far as the Peruvians and Mexicans of South America, and the Indians of North America.

3. Abraham, knowing the dissolute character of the Egyptians, directed Sarah to call herself his sister, which she was, although by another mother; fearing that if they knew her to be his wife, they would not only seize her, but kill him. This circumstance indicates the vicious state of morals and government in Egypt at this early period. In this affair Abraham has been blamed for want of faith in God; but it was perhaps no more than an act of common prudence, as the seraglio of the Egyptian monarch was supplied by any means, however violent and lawless. Sarah, upon the report of her beauty, was seized and taken into his harem; and God sent great plagues upon his house, which, from their extraordinary character, he concluded to be divine judgments. This led to inquiry, and on discovering that he

was detaining another man's wife by violence, he sent her back, and dismissed Abraham laden with presents.

4. After the famine Abraham returned to Canaan, and pitched his tents between Bethel and Hai, where he had previously raised an altar. Here, as his flocks and herds, and those of Lot, had greatly increased, and strifes had arisen between their herdsmen as to pasturage and water, they peaceably separated. Lot returning to the plain of the Jordan, which before the destruction of Sodom was as "the garden of God," and Abraham to Mamre, near Hebron, after receiving a renewal of the promise, that God would give him the whole land for a possession. The separation of Abraham and Lot still farther secured the unmingled descent of the Abrahamitic family. The territories of the kings of the cities of the plain were a few years afterward invaded by a confederacy of the petty kings of the Euphrates and the neighbouring countries, and Lot and his family were taken prisoners. This intelligence being brought to Abraham, he collected the men of his tribe, three hundred and eighteen, and falling upon the kings by night, near the fountains of Jericho, he defeated them, retook the spoil, and recovered Lot. On his return, passing near Salem, supposed to be the city afterward called Jerusalem, he was blessed by its king Melchizedec, who was priest of the most high God; so that the knowledge and worship of Jehovah had not quite departed at that time from the Canaanitish nations. To him Abraham gave a tithe of the spoil. The rest he generously restored to the king of Sodom, refusing, in a noble spirit of independence, to retain so much as a "shoe lachet," except the portion which, by usage of war, fell to the young native sheiks, Aner, Eschal, and Mamre, who had joined him in the expedition.

5. After this he had another encouraging vision of God, Gen. xv, 1; and to his complaint that he was still childless, and that his name and property would descend to the stranger Eliezer, who held the next rank in his tribe, the promise was given, that he himself should have a son, and that his seed should be countless as the stars of heaven. And it is emphatically added, "He believed in the Lord, and he counted it to him for righteousness." He was then fully assured, that he stood before God, a pardoned and accepted man, "whose iniquities were forgiven," and to whom "the Lord did not impute sin." Still the fulfilment of the promise of a son was delayed; and Sarah, perhaps despairing that it would be accomplished in her person, and the revelation which had been made merely stating that this son should be the fruit of Abraham's body, without any reference to her, she gave to him, according to the custom of those times, one of her handmaids, an Egyptian, to be his secondary wife, who brought forth Ishmael. Children born in this manner had the privileges of legitimacy; but fourteen years afterward, when Abraham was a hundred years old, and Sarah ninety, the Lord appeared to him again, established his covenant with him and with his seed, changed his name to Abraham, "the father of many nations," promised that Sarah herself should bring forth the son to whom the preceding promises had referred; instituted circumcision as the sign of the covenant; and changed the name of his wife from Sarai, MY PRINCESS, to Sarah, THE PRINCESS, that is, of many people to descend from her.

6. At this time Abraham occupied his former encampment near Hebron. Here, as he sat in the door of his tent, three mysterious strangers appeared. Abraham, with true Arabian hospitality, received and entertained them. The chief of the three renewed the promise of a son to be born from Sarah, a promise which she received with a laugh of incredulity, for which she was mildly reproved. As Abraham accompanied them toward the valley of the Jordan, the same divine person, for so he manifestly appears, announced the dreadful ruin impending over the licentious cities among which Lot had taken up his abode. No passage, even in the sacred writings, exhibits a more exalted view of the divine condescension than that in which Abraham is seen expostulating on the apparent injustice of involving the innocent in the ruin of the guilty: "Shall the city perish, if fifty, if forty-five, if forty, if thirty, if twenty, if ten righteous men be found within its walls?" "Ten righteous men shall avert its doom." Such was the promise of the celestial visitant; but the guilt was universal, the ruin inevitable; and the violation of the sacred laws of hospitality and nature, which Lot in his horror attempted to avert by the most revolting expedient, confirmed the justice of the divine sentence.

7. Sarah having conceived, according to the divine promise, Abraham left the plain of Mamre, and went south to Gerar, where Abimelech reigned; and again fearing lest Sarah should be forced from him, and himself be put to death, her beauty having been, it would appear, preternaturally continued, notwithstanding her age, he here called her, as he had done in Egypt, his sister. Abimelech took her to his house, designing to marry her; but God having, in a dream, informed him that she was Abraham's wife, he returned her to him with great presents. This year Sarah was delivered of Isaac; and Abraham circumcised him, according to the covenant stipulation; and when he was weaned, made a great entertainment. Sarah, having observed Ishmael, son of Hagar, mocking her son Isaac, said to Abraham, "Cast out this bondwoman and her son, for Ishmael shall not be heir with Isaac." After great reluctance, Abraham complied; God having informed him that this was according to the appointments of his providence, with respect to future ages. About the same time, Abimelech came with Phicol, his general, to conclude an alliance with Abraham, who made that prince a present of seven ewe lambs out of his flock, in confirmation that a well he had opened should be his own property; and they called the place Beer-sheba, or "the well of swearing," because of the covenant there ratified with oaths. Here Abraham planted a grove, built an altar, and for some time resided, Gen. xx, xxi.

8. More than twenty years after this, (A. M. 2133,) God, for the final trial and illustration of Abraham's faith, directed him to offer up his son Isaac. Abraham took his son, and two servants, and went toward mount Moriah. When within sight of the mountain, Abraham left his servants, and ascended it with his son only; and there having bound him, he prepared for the affecting sacrifice; but when he was about to give the

blow, an angel from heaven cried out to him, "Lay not thine hand upon the lad, neither do thou any thing to him. Now I know that thou fearest God, since thou hast not withheld thine only son from me." Abraham, turning, saw a ram entangled in the bush by his horns; and he offered this animal as a burnt offering, instead of his son Isaac. This memorable place he called by the prophetic name, JEHOVAH-JIREH, or THE LORD WILL SEE--or PROVIDE, Gen. xxii, 1–14, having respect, no doubt, to the true sacrifice which, in the fulness of time, was to be offered for the whole world upon the same mountain.

9. Twelve years afterward, Sarah, wife of Abraham, died in Hebron. Abraham came to mourn and to perform the funeral offices for her. He addressed the people at the city gate, entreating them to allow him to bury his wife among them; for, being a stranger, and having no land of his own, he could claim no right of interment in any sepulchre of that country. He, therefore, bought of Ephron, one of the inhabitants, the field of Machpelah, with the cave and sepulchre in it, at the price of four hundred shekels of silver, about forty-five pounds sterling. And here Abraham buried Sarah, with due solemnities, according to the custom of the country, Gen. xxiii. This whole transaction impressively illustrates the dignity, courtesy, and honour of these ancient chiefs; and wholly disproves the notion that theirs was a rude and unpolished age.

10. Abraham, having grown old, sent Eliezer, his steward, into Mesopotamia, with directions to obtain a young woman of his own family, as a wife for his son Isaac. Eliezer executed his commission with fidelity, and brought back Rebecca, daughter of Bethuel, grand-daughter of Nahor, and, consequently, Abraham's niece, whom Isaac married. Abraham afterward married Keturah; by whom he had six sons, Zimran, Jokshan, Medan, Midian, Ishbak, and Shuah; who became heads of different people, which dwelt in Arabia, and around it. He died, aged a hundred and seventy-five years, and was buried, with Sarah his wife, in the cave of Machpelah, which he had purchased of Ephron, Gen. xxiv, xxv, A. M. 2183, before Christ 1821.

II. From the personal history of Abraham we may now proceed to the consideration of the TYPICAL circumstances which were connected with it.

1. Abraham himself with his family may be regarded as a type of the church of God in future ages. They indeed constituted God's ancient church. Not that many scattered patriarchal and family churches did not remain: such was that of Melchizedec; and such probably was that of Nahor, whom Abraham left behind in Mesopotamia. But a visible church relation was established between Abraham's family and the Most High, signified by the visible and distinguishing sacrament of circumcision, and followed by new and enlarged revelations of truth. Two purposes were to be answered by this,--THE PRESERVATION OF THE TRUE DOCTRINE OF SALVATION IN THE WORLD, which is the great and solemn duty of every branch of the church of God,--and THE MANIFESTATION OF THAT TRUTH TO OTHERS. Both were done by Abraham. Wherever he sojourned he built his altars to the true God, and publicly celebrated his worship; and, as we learn from St. Paul, he lived in tents in preference to settling in the land of Canaan, though it had been given to him for a possession, in order that he might thus proclaim his faith in the eternal inheritance of which Canaan was a type; and in bearing this testimony, his example was followed by Isaac and Jacob, the "heirs with him of the same promise," who also thus "confessed that they were strangers and pilgrims," and that "they looked" for a continuing and eternal city in heaven. So also now is the same doctrine of immortality committed to the church of Christ; and by deadness to the world ought its members to declare the reality of their own faith in it.

2. The numerous natural posterity promised to Abraham was also a type of the spiritual seed, the true members of the church of Christ, springing from the Messiah, of whom Isaac was the symbol. Thus St. Paul expressly distinguishes between the fleshly and the spiritual seed of Abraham; to the latter of which, in their ultimate and highest sense, the promises of increase as the stars of heaven, and the sands of the sea shore, are to be referred, as also the promise of the heavenly Canaan.

3. The intentional offering up Isaac, with its result, was probably that transaction in which Abraham, more clearly than in any other, "saw the day of Christ, and was glad." He received Isaac from the dead, says St. Paul, "in a figure." This could be a figure of nothing but the resurrection of our Lord; and, if so, Isaac's being laid upon the altar was a figure of his sacrificial death, scenically and most impressively represented to Abraham. The PLACE, the same ridge of hills on which our Lord was crucified; the PERSON, an only son, to die for no offence of his own; the SACRIFICER, a father; the RECEIVING BACK, as it were, from death to life; the NAME impressed upon the place, importing, "THE LORD WILL PROVIDE," in allusion to Abraham's own words to Isaac, "the Lord will provide a lamb for a burnt offering;" all indicate a mystery which lay deep beneath this transaction, and which Abraham, as the reward of his obedience, was permitted to behold. "The day" of Christ's humiliation and exaltation was thus opened to him; and served to keep the great truth in mind, that the true burnt offering and sacrifice for sin was to be something higher than the immolation of lambs and bulls and goats,--nay, something more than what was MERELY human.

4. The transaction of the expulsion of Hagar was also a type. It was an allegory in action, by which St. Paul teaches us to understand that the son of the bondwoman represented those who are under the law; and the child of the freewoman those who by faith in Christ are supernaturally begotten into the family of God. The bondwoman and her son being cast out, represented also the expulsion of the unbelieving Jews from the church of God, which was to be composed of true believers of all nations, all of whom, whether Jews or Gentiles, were to become "fellow heirs."

III. But Abraham appears before us invested with a MYSTIC character, which it is of great importance rightly to understand.

1. He is to be regarded as standing in a FEDERAL or COVENANT relation, not only to his natural seed, but specially and eminently to all believers. "The Gospel," we are told by St. Paul, "was preached to Abraham, saying, In thee shall all nations be blessed." "Abraham believed in God, and it was accounted to him for righteousness;" in other words, he was justified. A covenant of gratuitous justification through faith was made with him and his believing descendants; and the rite of circumcision, which was not confined to his posterity by Sarah, but appointed in every branch of his family, was the sign or sacrament of this covenant of grace, and so remained till it was displaced by the sacraments appointed by Christ. Wherever that sign was it declared the doctrine, and offered the grace, of this covenant--free justification by faith, and its glorious results--to all the tribes that proceeded from Abraham. This same grace is offered to us by the Gospel, who become "Abraham's SEED," his spiritual children with whom the covenant is established, through the same faith, and are thus made "the heirs with him of the same promise."

2. Abraham is also exhibited to us as the REPRESENTATIVE of true believers; and in this especially, that the true nature of faith was exhibited in him. This great principle was marked in Abraham with the following characters:--An entire unhesitating belief in the word of God;--an unfaltering trust in all his promises;--a steady regard to his almighty power, leading him to overlook all apparent difficulties and impossibilities in every case where God had explicitly promised;--and habitual and cheerful and entire obedience. The Apostle has described faith in Heb. xi, 1; and that faith is seen living and acting in all its energy in Abraham.

A few miscellaneous remarks are suggested by some of the circumstances of Abraham's history:--

1. The ancient method of ratifying a covenant by sacrifice is illustrated in the account given in Gen. xv, 9, 10. The beasts were slain and DIVIDED in the midst, and the persons covenanting passed between the parts. Hence, after Abraham had performed this part of the ceremony, the symbol of the Almighty's presence, "a smoking furnace, and a burning lamp, passed between the pieces," verse 18, and so both parties ratified the covenant.

2. As the beauty of Sarah, which she retained so long as quite to conceal her real age from observers, attracted so much notice as to lead to her forcible seizure, once by Pharaoh in Egypt, and again by Abimelech in Palestine, it may appear strange, that, as in the east women are generally kept in seclusion, and seldom appear without veils, she exposed herself to observation. But to this day the Arab women do not wear veils at home in their tents; and Sarah's countenance might have been seen in the tent by some of the officers of Pharaoh and Abimelech, who reported her beauty to their masters.

3. The intentional offering up of Isaac is not to be supposed as viewed by Abraham as an act sanctioned by the Pagan practice of human sacrifice. The immolation of human victims, particularly of that which was most precious, the favourite, the first-born child, appears to have been a common usage among many early nations, more especially the tribes by which Abraham was surrounded. It was the distinguishing rite among the worshippers of Moloch; at a later period of the Jewish history, it was practised by a king of Moab; and it was undoubtedly derived by the Carthaginians from their Phenecian ancestors on the shores of Syria. Where it was an ordinary usage, as in the worship of Moloch, it was in unison with the character of the religion, and of its deity. It was the last act of a dark and sanguinary superstition, which rose by regular gradation to this complete triumph over human nature. The god, who was propitiated by these offerings, had been satiated with more cheap and vulgar victims; he had been glutted to the full with human suffering and with human blood. In general it was the final mark of the subjugation of the national mind to an inhuman and domineering priesthood. But the Mosaic religion held human sacrifices in abhorrence; and the God of the Abrahamitic family, uniformly beneficent, had imposed no duties which entailed human suffering, had demanded no offerings which were repugnant to the better feelings of our nature. The command to offer Isaac as "a burnt offering," was for these reasons a trial the more severe to Abraham's faith. He must therefore have been fully assured of the divine command; and he left the mystery to be explained by God himself. His was a simple act of unhesitating obedience to the command of God; the last proof of perfect reliance on the certain accomplishment of the divine promises. Isaac, so miraculously bestowed, could be as miraculously restored; Abraham, such is the comment of the Christian Apostle, "believed that God could even raise him up from the dead."

4. The wide and deep impression made by the character of Abraham upon the ancient world is proved by the reverence which people of almost all nations and countries have paid to him, and the manner in which the events of his life have been interwoven in their mythology, and their religious traditions. Jews, Magians, Sabians, Indians, and Mohammedans have claimed him as the great patriarch and founder of their several sects; and his history has been embellished with a variety of fictions. One of the most pleasing of these is the following, but it proceeds upon the supposition that he was educated in idolatry: "As Abraham was walking by night from the grotto where he was born, to the city of Babylon, he gazed on the stars of heaven, and among them on the beautiful planet Venus. 'Behold,' said he within himself, 'the God and Lord of the universe!' but the star set and disappeared, and Abraham felt that the Lord of the universe could not thus be liable to change. Shortly after, he beheld the moon at the full: 'Lo,' he cried, 'the Divine Creator, the manifest Deity!' but the moon sank below the horizon, and Abraham made the same reflection as at the setting of the evening star. All the rest of the night he passed

in profound rumination; at sunrise he stood before the gates of Babylon, and saw the whole people prostrate in adoration. 'Wondrous orb,' he exclaimed, 'thou surely art the Creator and Ruler of all nature! but thou, too, hastest like the rest to thy setting!--neither then art thou my Creator, my Lord, or my God!'"

ABRAHAMITES, reported heretical sects of the eighth and ninth centuries, charged with the Paulician errors, and some of them with idolatry. For these charges we have, however, only the word of their persecutors. Also the name of a sect in Bohemia, as late as 1782, who professed the religion of Abraham before his circumcision, and admitted no scriptures but the decalogue and the Lord's prayer. As these were persecuted, they too were probably misrepresented, and especially as their conduct is allowed to have been good, even by their enemies.

ABSALOM, the son of David by Maachah, daughter of the king of Geshur; distinguished for his fine person, his vices, and his unnatural rebellion. Of his open revolt, his conduct in Jerusalem, his pursuit of the king his father, his defeat and death, see 2 Sam. xvi-xviii, at large.

ABSOLUTION, in the church of Rome, is a sacrament, in which the priests assume the power of forgiving sins. The rite of absolution in the church of England is acknowledged to be declarative only--"Almighty God hath given power and commandment to his ministers to declare and pronounce to his people, being penitent, the absolution and remission of their sins: He pardoneth," &c. In this view it is innocent; and although any private Christian has a right to declare and pronounce the same doctrine to his neighbour, the OFFICIAL publication of the grace of the Gospel is the public duty of its ministers in the congregation, since they are Christ's "ambassadors."

ABSTINENCE, forbearance of any thing It is generally used with reference to forbearance from food under a religious motive. The Jewish law ordained that the priests should abstain from the use of wine during the whole time of their being employed in the service of the temple, Lev. x, 9. The same abstinence was enjoined upon the Nazarites, during the time of their Nazariteship, or separation, Num. vi, 3. The Jews were commanded to abstain from several sorts of animals. See Animal.

The fat of all sorts of animals that were sacrificed was forbidden to be eaten, Lev. iii, 17; vii, 23; and the blood of every animal, in general, was prohibited under pain of death. Indeed blood was forbidden by the Creator, from the time of the grant of the flesh of beasts to man for food; this prohibition was continued under the Jewish economy, and transmitted to the Christian church by Apostolic authority, Acts xv, 28, 29. (See BLOOD.) The Jews also abstained from the sinew which is upon the hollow of the thigh, Gen. xxxii, 25; because of the shrinking of the sinew of Jacob's thigh when touched by the angel, as though by that the part had been made sacred.

Among the primitive Christians, some denied themselves the use of such meats as were prohibited by the law; others treated this abstinence with contempt. St. Paul has given his decision on these questions in his epistles, 1 Cor. viii, 7–10; Rom. xiv, 1–3. The council of Jerusalem, which was held by the Apostles, enjoined the Christian converts to abstain from meats strangled, from blood, from fornication, and from idolatry, Acts xv, 20.

The spiritual monarchy of the western world introduced another sort of abstinence which may be termed RITUAL, and which consists in abstaining from particular meats at certain times and seasons, the rules of which are called rogations. The ancient Lent was observed only a few days before Easter. In the course of the third century, it extended at Rome to three weeks; and before the middle of the succeeding age, it was prolonged to six weeks, and began to be called quadragesima, or the forty days' fast.

ABYSS, or DEEP, ἄβυσσος, WITHOUT BOTTOM. The chaos; the deepest parts of the sea; and, in the New Testament, the place of the dead, Rom. x, 7; a deep place of punishment. The devils besought Jesus that he would not send them into the abyss, a place they evidently dreaded, Luke viii, 31; where it seems to mean that part of Hades in which wicked spirits are in torment. See Hell.

In the opinion of the ancient Hebrews, and of the generality of eastern people at this day, the abyss, the sea, or waters, encompassed the whole earth. This was supposed to float upon the abyss, of which it covered a small part. According to the same notion, the earth was founded on the waters, or at least its foundations were on the abyss beneath, Psalm xxiv, 2; cxxxvi, 6. Under these waters, and at the bottom of this abyss, they represented the wicked as groaning, and suffering the punishment of their sin. The Rephaim were confined there, those old giants, who, whilst living, caused surrounding nations to tremble, Prov. ix, 18; xxi, 16, &c. Lastly, in these dark dungeons the kings of Tyre, Babylon, and Egypt are described by the Prophets as suffering the punishment of their pride and cruelty, Isaiah xxvi, 14; Ezek. xxviii, 10, &c.

These depths are figuratively represented as the abodes of evil spirits, and powers opposed to God: "I saw," says St. John, "a star fall from heaven unto the earth, and to him was given the key of the bottomless pit. And he opened the bottomless pit; and there arose a smoke out of it, as the smoke of a great furnace; and the sun and the air were darkened by reason of the smoke of the pit. And there came out of the smoke locusts upon the earth. And they had a king over them, which is the angel of the bottomless pit," Rev. ix, 1, 2, 11. In another place, the beast is represented as ascending out of the bottomless pit, and waging war against the two witnesses of God, Rev. xi, 7. Lastly, St. John says, "I saw an angel come down from heaven, having the key of the bottomless pit, and a great chain in his hand. And he laid hold on the dragon, that old serpent, which is the devil, and Satan, and bound him a thousand years, and cast him into the bottomless pit, and shut him up, and set a seal upon him, that he should deceive the nations no more till the thousand years should be fulfilled: and after that he must be loosed a little season," Rev. xx, 1–3.

ABYSSINIAN CHURCH, a branch of the Coptic church, in Upper Ethiopia. The Abyssinians, by the most authentic accounts, were converted to the Christian faith about the year 330; when Frumentius, being providentially raised to a high office, under the patronage of the queen of Ethiopia, and ordained bishop of that country by Athanasius, patriarch of Alexandria, established Christianity, built churches, and ordained a regular clergy to officiate in them. The Abyssinian Christians themselves, indeed, claim a much higher antiquity, having a tradition, that the doctrine of Christ was first introduced among them by Queen Candace, Acts viii, 27; or even preached there by the Apostles Matthew and Bartholomew; but the former is supported by no collateral evidence, and the latter is in opposition to high authority. Some of them claim relation to the Israelites, through the queen of Sheba, so far back as the reign of Solomon.

The Abyssinian Christians have always received their abuna, or patriarch, from Alexandria, whence they sprang, and consequently their creed is Monophysite, or Eutychian; maintaining one nature only in the person of Christ, namely, the divine, in which they considered all the properties of the humanity to be absorbed; in opposition to the Nestorians.

On the power of the Saracens prevailing in the east, all communication being nearly cut off between the eastern and western churches, the Abyssinian church remained unknown in Europe till nearly the close of the fifteenth century, when John **II**, of Portugal, accidentally hearing of the existence of such a church, sent to make inquiry. This led to a correspondence between the Abyssinians and the church of Rome; and Bermudes, a Portuguese, was consecrated by the pope patriarch of Ethiopia, and the Abyssinians were required to receive the Roman Catholic faith, in return for some military assistance afforded to the emperor. Instead of this, however, the emperor sent for a new patriarch from Alexandria, imprisoned Bermudes, and declared the pope a heretic.

About the middle of the sixteenth century, the Jesuits attempted a mission to Abyssinia, in the hope of reducing it to the pope's authority; but without success. In 1588 a second mission was attempted, and so far succeeded as to introduce a system of persecution, which cost many lives, and caused many troubles to the empire. In the following century, however, the Jesuits were all expelled, Abyssinia returned to its ancient faith, and nothing more was heard of the church of Abyssinia, till the latter part of the last century.

After the expulsion of the Jesuits, all Europeans were interdicted; nor does it appear that any one dared to attempt an entrance until the celebrated Mr. Bruce, by the report of his medical skill, contrived to introduce himself to the court, where he even obtained military promotion; and was in such repute, that it was with great difficulty he obtained leave to return to England.

Encouraged, perhaps, by this circumstance, the Moravian brethren attempted a mission to this country, but in vain. They were compelled to retreat to Grand Cairo, from whence, by leave of the patriarch, they visited the Copts at Behrusser, and formed a small society; but in 1783, they were driven thence, and compelled to return to Europe. More recently, however, the late king of Abyssinia (Itsa Takley Gorges) addressed a letter to Mr. Salt, the British consul in Egypt, and requested copies of some parts of both the Old and New Testaments. Copies of the Psalms, in Ethiopic, as printed by the British and Foreign Bible Society, were also sent to him.

ACADEMICS, a name given to such philosophers as adopted the doctrines of Plato. They were so called from the ACADEMIA, a grove near Athens, where they frequently indulged their contemplations. Academia is said to derive its name from one Academus, a god or hero so called. Thus Horace,--

ATQUE INTER SYLVAS ACADEMI QUÆRERE VERUM.

[And in the groves of Academus to search for truth.]

The academics are divided into those of the first academy, who taught the doctrines of Plato in their original purity; those of the second or middle academy, who differed materially from the first, and inclined to skepticism; and those of the new academy. The middle school laid it down as a principle, that neither our senses, nor our reason, are to be trusted; but that in common affairs we are to conform to received opinions. The new academy maintained that we have no means of distinguishing truth, and that the most evident appearances may lead us into error; they granted the wise man opinion, but denied him certainty. They held, however, that it was best to follow the greatest probability, which was sufficient for all the useful purposes of life, and laid down rules for the attainment of felicity. The difference betwixt the middle academy and the new seems to have been this, that though they agreed in the imbecility of human nature, yet the first denied that probabilities were of any use in the pursuit of happiness; and the latter held them to be of service in such a design: the former recommended a conformity with received opinions, and the latter allowed men an opinion of their own. In the first academy, Speusippus filled the chair; in the second, Arcesilaus; and in the new or third academy, Carneades.

ACCAD, one of the four cities built by Nimrod, the founder of the Assyrian empire. (See NIMROD.) "And the beginning of his kingdom was Babel, and Erech, and Accad, and Calneh, in the land of Shinar," Gen. x, 10. Thus it appears that Accad was contemporary with Babylon, and was one of the first four great cities of the world.

It would scarcely be expected that any thing should now remain to guide us in our search for this ancient city, seeing that Babylon itself, with which it was coeval, is reduced to heaps; and that it is not mentioned under its ancient name by any profane author. But the discoveries of modern travellers may be brought to aid us in our inquiry. At the distance of about six miles from the modern town of Bagdad, is found a mound, surmounted by a tower-shaped ruin, called by the Arabs Tell Nimrood, and by the Turks Nemrood Tepasse; both terms implying the Hill of Nimrod. This gigantic mass rises in an irregularly pyramidal or turreted shape, according to the view in which it is taken, one hundred and twenty-five or one hundred and thirty feet above the gently inclined elevation on which it stands. Its circumference, at the bottom, is three hundred feet. The mound which constitutes its foundation is composed of a collection of rubbish, formed from the decay of the superstructure; and consists of sandy earth, fragments of burnt brick, pottery, and hard clay, partially vitrified. In the remains of the tower, the different layers of sun-dried brick, of which it is composed, may be traced with great precision. These bricks, cemented together by slime, and divided into courses varying from twelve to twenty feet in height, are separated from one another by a stratum of reeds, similar to those now growing in the marshy parts of the plain, and in a wonderful state of preservation. The resemblance of this mode of building to that in some of the structures at Babylon, cannot escape observation; and we may reasonably conclude it to be the workmanship of the same architects. The solidity and the loftiness of this pile, unfashioned to any other purpose, bespeak it to be one of those enormous pyramidal towers which were consecrated to the Sabian worship; which, as essential to their religious rites, were probably erected in all the early cities of the Cuthites; and, like their prototype at Babylon, answered the double purpose of altars and observatories. Here then was the site of one of these early cities. It was not Babylon; it was not Erech; it was not Calneh. It might be too much to say that THEREFORE it must be Accad; but the inference is at least warrantable; which is farther strengthened by the name of the place, Akarkouff; which bears a greater affinity to that of Accad than many others which are forced into the support of geographical speculations, especially when it is recollected that the Syrian name of the city was Achar.

ACCESS, free admission, open entrance. Our access to God is by Jesus Christ, the way, the truth, and the life, Rom. v, 2; Eph. ii, 18. Under the law, the high priest alone had access into the holiest of all; but when the veil of the temple was rent in twain, at the death of Christ, it was declared that a new and living way of access was laid open through the veil, that is to say, his flesh. By his death, also, the middle wall of partition was broken down, and Jew and Gentile had both free access to God; whereas, before, the Gentiles had no nearer access in the temple worship than to the gate of the court of Israel. Thus the saving grace and lofty privileges of the Gospel are equally bestowed upon true believers of all nations.

ACCHO, afterward called Ptolemais, and now Akka by the Arabs, and Acre by the Turks. It was given to the tribe of Asher, Judges i, 31. Christianity was planted here at an early period, and here St. Paul visited the saints in his way to Jerusalem, Acts xxi, 7. It is a seaport of Palestine, thirty miles south of Tyre, and, in the first partition of the holy land, belonged to the tribe of Asher; but this was one of the places out of which the Israelites could not drive the primitive inhabitants. In succeeding times it was enlarged by the first Ptolemy, to whose lot it fell, and who named it after himself, Ptolemais.

This city, now called Acre, which, from the convenience of its port, is one of the most considerable on the Syrian coast, was, during almost two centuries, the principal theatre of the holy wars, and the frequent scene of the perfidies and treacheries of the crusaders.

Among its antiquities, Dr. E. D. Clarke describes the remains of a very considerable edifice, exhibiting a conspicuous appearance among the buildings on the north side of the city. "In this structure the style of the architecture is of the kind we call Gothic. Perhaps it has on that account borne among our countrymen the appellation of 'King Richard's Palace,' although, in the period to which the tradition refers, the English were hardly capable of erecting palaces, or any other buildings of equal magnificence. Two lofty arches, and part of the cornice, are all that now remain to attest the former greatness of the superstructure. The cornice, ornamented with enormous stone busts, exhibiting a series of hideous distorted countenances, whose features are in no instances alike, may either have served as allusions to the decapitation of St. John, or were intended for a representation of the heads of Saracens suspended as trophies upon the walls." Maundrell and Pococke consider this building to have been the church of St. Andrew; but Dr. E. D. Clarke thinks it was that of St. John, erected by the Knights of Jerusalem, whence the city changed its name of Ptolemais for that of St. John d'Acre. He also considers the style of architecture to be in some degree the original of our ornamented Gothic, before its translation from the holy land to Italy, France, and England.

Mr. Buckingham, who visited Acre in 1816, says, "Of the Canaanitish Accho it would be thought idle perhaps to seek for remains; yet some presented themselves to my observation so peculiar in form and materials, and of such high antiquity, as to leave no doubt in my own mind of their being the fragments of buildings constructed in the earliest ages.

"Of the splendour of Ptolemais, no perfect monument remains; but throughout the town are seen shafts of red and grey granite, and marble pillars. The Saracenic remains are only to be partially traced in the inner walls of the town; which have themselves been so broken down and repaired, as to leave little visible of the original work; and all the mosques, fountains, bazaars, and other public buildings, are in a style rather Turkish than Arabic, excepting only an old, but regular and well-built khan or caravanserai, which might perhaps be attributed to the Saracen age. The Christian ruins are altogether gone, scarcely leaving a trace of the spot on which they stood."

Acre has been rendered famous in our own times by the successful resistance made by our countryman Sir Sydney Smith, aided by the celebrated Djezzar Pasha, to the progress of the French under Buonaparte. Since this period, the fortifications have been considerably increased; and although to the eye of an engineer they may still be very defective, Acre may be considered as the strongest place in Palestine.

Mr. Conner says, on the authority of the English consul, that there are about ten thousand inhabitants in Acre, of whom three thousand are Turks, and the remainder Christians, chiefly Catholics.

ACCUBATION, the posture used at table by the ancients. The old Romans sat at meat as we do, till the Grecian luxury and softness had corrupted them. The same custom, of lying upon couches at their entertainments, prevailed among the Jews also in our Saviour's time; for having been lately conquered by Pompey, they conformed in this, and in many other respects, to the example of their masters. The manner of lying at meat among the Romans, Greeks, and more modern Jews, was the same in all respects. The table was placed in the middle of the room, around which stood three couches covered with cloth or tapestry, according to the quality of the master of the house; upon these they lay, inclining the superior part of their bodies upon their left arms, the lower part being stretched out at full length, or a little bent. Their heads were supported and raised with pillows. The first man lay at the head of the couch; the next man lay with his head toward the feet of the other, from which he was defended by the bolster that supported his own back, commonly reaching over to the middle of the first man; and the rest after the same manner. The most honourable place was the MIDDLE couch--and the MIDDLE of THAT. Favourites commonly lay in the bosom of their friends; that is, they were placed next below them: see John xiii, 23, where St. John is said to have lain in our Saviour's bosom. The ancient Greeks sat at the table; for Homer observes that when Ulysses arrived at the palace of Alcinous, the king dispatched his son Laodamas to seat Ulysses in a magnificent chair. The Egyptians sat at table anciently, as well as the Romans, till toward the end of the Punic war, when they began to recline at table.

ACCURSED, in the Scriptures, signifies that which is separated or devoted. With regard to persons, it denotes the cutting off or separating any one from the communion of the church, the number of the living, or the privileges of society; and also the devoting an animal, city, or other thing to destruction. ANATHEMA was a species of EXCOMMUNICATION among the Jews, and was often practised after they had lost the power of life and death, against those persons who, according to the Mosaic law, ought to have been executed. A criminal, after the sentence of excommunication was pronounced, became ANATHEMA: and they had a full persuasion that the sentence would not be in vain; but that God would interfere to punish the offender in a manner similar to the penalty of the law of Moses: a man, for instance, whom the law condemned to be stoned, would, they believed, be killed by the falling of a stone upon him; a man to be hanged, would be choked; and one whom the law sentenced to the flames, would be burnt in his house, &c. MARANATHA, a Syriac word, signifying THE LORD COMETH, was added to the sentence, to express their persuasion that the Lord God would come to take vengeance upon that guilt which they, circumstanced as they were, had not the power to punish, 1 Cor. xvi, 22.

According to the idiom of the Hebrew language, ACCURSED and CRUCIFIED were synonymous terms. By the Jews every one who died upon a tree was reckoned ACCURSED, Deut. xxi, 23.

Excommunication is a kind of anathema also among some Christians; and by it the offender is deprived, not only of communicating in prayers and other holy offices, but of admittance to the church, and of conversation with the faithful. The spirit of Judaism, rather than that of the Gospel, has in this been imitated; for among the Hebrews, they who were excommunicated could not perform any public duty of their employments; could be neither judges nor witnesses; neither be present at funerals, nor circumcise their own sons, nor sit down in the company of other men, nearer than within the distance of four cubits. If they died under excommunication, they were denied the rites of burial; and a large stone was left on their graves, or a heap of stones was thrown over them, as over Achan, Joshua vii, 26. The Apostolical excommunication was simply to deny to the offender, after admonition, the right of partaking of the Lord's Supper, which was excision from the church of Christ.

ACELDAMA, a piece of ground without the south wall of Jerusalem, on the other side of the brook Siloam. It was called the Potter's Field, because an earth or clay was dug in it, of which pottery was made. It was likewise called the Fuller's Field, because cloth was dried in it. But it having been afterward bought with the money by which the high priest and rulers of the Jews purchased the blood of Jesus, it was called Aceldama, or the Field of Blood.

ACHAIA. This name is used to denote the whole of Greece, as it existed as a Roman province; or Achaia Proper, a district in the northern part of the Peloponnesus, on the bay of Corinth, and in which the city of that name stood. It appears to have been used in the former sense in 2 Cor. xi, 10; and in the latter, in Acts xix, 21.

ACHAN, the son of Carmi, of the tribe of Judah, who having taken a part of the spoils of Jericho, against the injunction of God, who had ACCURSED or devoted the whole city, was, upon being taken by lot, doomed to be stoned to death. The whole history is recorded, Joshua vii. It would appear that Achan's family were also stoned; for they were led out with him, and all his property, "And all Israel stoned him with stones, and burned them with fire, after they had stoned them with stones." Some of the critics have made efforts to confine the stoning to Achan, and the burning to his goods; but not without violence to the text. It is probable, therefore, that his family were privy to the theft, seeing he hid the accursed things which he had stolen in the earth, in his tent. By concealment they therefore became partakers of his crime, and so the sentence was justified.

ACHMETHA. See Ecbatana.

ACHOR, Valley of, between Jericho and Ai. So called from the trouble brought upon the Israelites by the sin of Achan; Achor in the Hebrew denoting trouble.

ACHZIB, a city on the coast of the Mediterranean, in the tribe of Asher, and one of the cities out of which that tribe did not expel the inhabitants, Judges i, 31. It was called Ecdippa by the Greeks, and is at present termed Zib. It is situated about ten miles north of Accho, or Ptolemais. Mr. Buckingham, who passed by this place, says that it is small, and situated on a hill near the sea; having a few palm trees rearing themselves above its dwellings.

ACRA, Ἄκρα. This Greek word signifies, in general, A CITADEL. The Syrians and Chaldeans use הקרא, in the same sense. King Antiochus gave orders for building a citadel at Jerusalem, north of the temple, on an eminence, which commanded the holy place; and for that reason was called Acra. Josephus says, that this eminence was semicircular, and that Simon Maccabæus, having expelled the Syrians, who had seized Acra, demolished it, and spent three years in levelling the mountain on which it stood; that no situation in future should command the temple. On mount Acra were afterward built, the palace of Helena; Agrippa's palace, the place where the public records were lodged; and that where the magistrates of Jerusalem assembled.

ACRABATENE, a district of Judæa, extending between Shechem (now Napolose) and Jericho, inclining east. It was about twelve miles in length. The Acrabatene had its name from a place called Akrabbim, about nine miles from Shechem, eastward. This was also the name of another district of Judea on the frontier of Idumea, toward the northern extremity of the Dead Sea.

ACTS OF THE APOSTLES. This book, in the very beginning, professes itself to be a continuation of the Gospel of St. Luke; and its style bespeaks it to be written by the same person. The external evidence is also very satisfactory; for besides allusions in earlier authors, and particularly in Clement of Rome, Polycarp, and Justin Martyr, the Acts of the Apostles are not only quoted by Irenæus, as written by Luke the evangelist, but there are few things recorded in this book which are not mentioned by that ancient father. This strong testimony in favour of the genuineness of the Acts of the Apostles is supported by Clement of Alexandria, Tertullian, Jerome, Eusebius, Theodoret, and most of the later fathers. It may be added, that the name of St. Luke is prefixed to this book in several ancient Greek manuscripts of the New Testament, and also in the old Syriac version.

2. This is the only inspired work which gives us any historical account of the progress of Christianity after our Saviour's ascension. It comprehends a period of about thirty years, but it by no means contains a general history of the church during that time. The principal facts recorded in it are, the choice of Matthias to be an Apostle in the room of the traitor Judas; the descent of the Holy Ghost on the day of pentecost; the preaching, miracles, and sufferings of the Apostles at Jerusalem; the death of Stephen, the first martyr; the persecution and dispersion of the Christians; the preaching of the Gospel in different parts of Palestine, especially in Samaria; the conversion of St. Paul; the call of Cornelius, the first Gentile convert; the persecution of the Christians by Herod Agrippa; the preaching of Paul and Barnabas to the Gentiles, by the express command of the Holy Ghost; the decree made at Jerusalem, declaring that circumcision, and a conformity to other Jewish rites and ceremonies, were not necessary in Gentile converts; and the latter part of the book is confined to the history of St. Paul, of whom St. Luke was the constant companion for several years.

3. As this account of St. Paul is not continued beyond his two years' imprisonment at Rome, it is probable that this book was written soon after his release, which happened in the year 63; we may therefore consider the Acts of the Apostles as written about the year 64.

4. The place of its publication is more doubtful. The probability appears to be in favour of Greece, though some contend for Alexandria in Egypt. This latter opinion rests upon the subscriptions at the end of some Greek manuscripts, and of the copies of the Syriac version; but the best critics think, that these subscriptions, which are also affixed to other books of the New Testament, deserve but little weight; and in this case they are not supported by any ancient authority.

5. It must have been of the utmost importance in the early times of the Gospel, and certainly not of less importance to every subsequent age, to have an authentic account of the promised descent of the Holy Ghost, and of the success which attended the first preachers of the Gospel both among the Jews and Gentiles. These great events completed the evidence of the divine mission of Christ, established the truth of the religion which he taught, and pointed out in the clearest manner the comprehensive nature of the redemption which he purchased by his death.

Œcumenius calls the Acts, the "Gospel of the Holy Ghost;" and St. Chrysostom, the "Gospel of our Saviour's resurrection," or the Gospel of Jesus Christ risen from the dead. Here, in the lives and preaching of the Apostles, we have the most miraculous instances of the power of the Holy Ghost; and in the account of those who were the first believers, we have received the most excellent pattern of the true Christian life.

ADAM, the name given to man in general, both male and female in the Hebrew Scriptures, Gen. i, 26, 27; v, 1, 2; xi, 5; Josh. xiv, 15; 2 Sam. vii, 19; Eccl. iii, 21; Jer. xxxii, 20; Hosea vi, 7; Zech. xiii, 7: in all which places mankind is understood; but particularly it is the name of the first man and father of the human race, created by God himself out of the dust of the earth. Josephus thinks that he was called Adam by reason of the reddish colour of the earth out of which he was formed, for Adam in Hebrew signifies red. God having made man out of the dust of the earth, breathed into him the breath of life, and gave him dominion over all the creatures of this world, Gen. i, 26, 27; ii, 7. He created him after his own image and resemblance; and having blessed him, he placed him in a delicious garden, in Eden, that he might cultivate it, and feed upon its fruits, Gen. ii, 8; but under the following injunction: "Of every tree of the garden thou mayest freely eat: but of the tree of the knowledge of good and evil, thou shalt not eat of it; for in the day thou eatest thereof, thou shalt surely die." The first thing that Adam did after his introduction into paradise, was to give names to all the beasts and birds which presented themselves before him, Gen. ii, 19, 20.

But man was without a fellow creature of his own species; wherefore God said, "It is not good for man to be alone; I will make him a help meet for him." And the Lord caused a deep sleep to fall upon Adam, and while he slept, he took one of his ribs, "and closed up the flesh instead thereof;" and of that substance which he took from man made he a woman, whom he presented to him. Then said Adam, "This is now bone of my bone, and flesh of my flesh: she shall be called woman, because she was taken out of man," Gen. ii, 21, &c.

The woman was seduced by the tempter; and she seduced her husband to eat of the forbidden fruit. When called to judgment for this transgression before God, Adam attempted to cast the blame upon his wife, and the woman upon the serpent tempter. But God declared them all guilty, and punished the serpent by degradation; the woman by painful childbearing and subjection; and the man by agricultural labour and toil; of which punishments every day witnesses the fulfilment. As their natural passions now became irregular, and their exposure to accidents was great, God made a covering of skins for Adam and for his wife; and expelled them from the garden, to the country without; placing at the east of the garden cherubims and a flaming sword, which turned every way, to keep the way of the tree of life. It is not known how long Adam and his wife continued in paradise: some say, many years; others, not many days; others, not many hours. Adam called his wife's name EVE, which signifies "the mother of all living." Shortly after, Eve brought forth Cain, Gen. iv, 1, 2. It is believed that she had a girl at the time, and that, generally, she had twins. The Scriptures notice only three sons of Adam: Cain, Abel, and Seth; and omits daughters; except that Moses tells us, "Adam begat sons and daughters;" no doubt many. He died, aged nine hundred and thirty, B. C. 3074.

Upon this history, so interesting to all Adam's descendants, some remarks may be offered.

1. It is disputed whether the name ADAM is derived from RED EARTH. Sir W. Jones thinks it may be from ADIM, which in Sanscrit signifies, THE FIRST. The Persians, however, denominate him Adamah, which signifies, according to Sale, RED EARTH. The term for woman is AISHA, the feminine of AISH, man, and signifies, therefore, maness or female man.

2. The manner in which the creation of Adam is narrated indicates something peculiar and eminent in the being to be formed. Among the heavenly bodies the earth, and above all the various productions of its surface, vegetable and animal, however perfect in their kinds, and beautiful and excellent in their respective natures, not one being was found to whom the rest could minister instruction; inspire with moral delight; or lead up to the Creator himself. There was, properly speaking, no intellectual being; none to whom the whole frame and furniture of material nature could minister knowledge; no one who could employ upon them the generalizing faculty, and make them the basis of inductive knowledge. If, then, it was not wholly for himself that the world was created by God; and if angels were not so immediately connected with this system, as to lead us to suppose that it was made for them; a rational inhabitant was obviously still wanting to complete the work, and to constitute a perfect whole. The formation of such a being was marked, therefore, by a manner of proceeding which serves to impress us with a sense of the greatness of the work. Not that it could be a matter of more difficulty to Omnipotence to create man than any thing beside; but principally, it is probable, because he was to be the lord of the whole and therefore himself accountable to the original proprietor; and was to be the subject of another species of government, a moral administration; and to be constituted an image of the intellectual and moral perfections, and of the immortality, of the common Maker. Every thing therefore, as to man's creation, is given in a solemn and deliberative form, and contains also an intimation of a Trinity of Persons in the Godhead, all equally possessed of CREATIVE power, and therefore DIVINE, to each of whom man was to stand in relations the most sacred and intimate:--"And God said, Let **US** make man in our image, after our likeness; and let them have dominion," &c.

3. It may be next inquired in what that image of God in which man was made consists.

It is manifest from the history of Moses, that human nature has two essential constituent parts, the BODY formed out of preëxisting matter, the earth; and a LIVING SOUL, breathed into the body by an INSPIRATION from God. "And the Lord God formed man out of the dust of the ground, and breathed into his nostrils (or FACE) the breath of life, (LIVES,) and man became a living soul." Whatever was thus imparted to the body of man, already "FORMED," and perfectly finished in all its parts, was the only cause of life; and the whole tenor of Scripture shows that this was the rational spirit itself, which, by a law of its Creator, was incapable of death, even after the body had fallen under that penalty.

The "image" or likeness of God in which man was made has, by some, been assigned to the body; by others, to the soul. It has, also, been placed in the circumstance of his having "DOMINION" over the other creatures. As to the body, it is not necessary to prove that in no sense can it bear the image of God; that is, be "LIKE" God. An upright form has no more likeness to God than a prone or reptile one; God is incorporeal, and cannot be the antitype of any thing material.

Equally unfounded is the notion that the image of God in man consisted in the "dominion" which was granted to him over this lower world. Limited dominion may, it is true, be an image of large and absolute dominion; but man is not said to have been made in the image of God's dominion, which is an accident merely, for, before creatures existed, God himself could have no dominion:--he was made in the image and likeness of God himself. Still farther, it is evident that man, according to the history, was made in the image of God IN ORDER to his having dominion, as the Hebrew particle imports; and, therefore, his dominion was consequent upon his formation in the "image" and "likeness" of God, and could not be that image itself.

The notion that the original resemblance of man to God must be placed in some one essential quality, is not consistent with holy writ, from which alone we can derive our information on this subject. We shall, it is true, find that the Bible partly places it in what is essential to human nature; but that it should comprehend nothing else, or consist in one quality only, has no proof or reason; and we are, in fact, taught that it comprises also what is so far from being essential that it may be both lost and regained. When God is called "the Father of spirits," a likeness is suggested between man and God in the SPIRITUALITY of their nature. This is also implied in the striking argument of St. Paul with the Athenians: "Forasmuch, then, as we are the OFFSPRING of God, we ought not to think that the Godhead is like unto gold, or silver, or stone, graven by art and man's device;"--plainly referring to the idolatrous statues by which God was represented among Heathens. If likeness to God in man consisted in bodily shape, this would not have been an argument against human representations of the Deity; but it imports, as Howe well expresses it, that "we are to understand that our resemblance to him, as we are his offspring, lies in some higher, more noble, and more excellent thing, of which there can be no figure; as who can tell how to give the figure or image of a thought, or of the mind or thinking power?" In SPIRITUALITY, and, consequently, immateriality, this image of God in man, then, in the first instance, consists. Nor is it any valid objection to say, that "immateriality is not peculiar to the soul of man; for we have reason to believe that the inferior animals are actuated by an immaterial principle." This is as certain as analogy can make it: but though we allow a spiritual principle to animals, its KIND is obviously inferior; for that spirit which is incapable of induction and moral knowledge, must be of an inferior order to the spirit which possesses these capabilities; and this is the kind of spirit which is peculiar to man.

The sentiment expressed in Wisdom ii, 23, is an evidence that, in the opinion of the ancient Jews, the image of God in man comprised IMMORTALITY also. "For God created man to be immortal, and made him to be an image of his own eternity:" and though other creatures were made capable of immortality, and at least the material human frame, whatever we may think of the case of animals, would have escaped death, had not sin entered the world; yet, without admitting the absurdity of the "natural immortality" of the human soul, that essence must have been constituted immortal in a high and peculiar sense which has ever retained its prerogative of continued duration amidst the universal death not only of animals, but of the bodies of all human beings. There appears also a manifest allusion to man's immortality, as being included in THE IMAGE OF GOD, in the reason which is given in Genesis for the law which inflicts death on murderers: "Whoso sheddeth man's blood, by man shall his blood be shed: for in THE IMAGE OF GOD made he man." The essence of the crime of homicide is not confined here to the putting to death the mere animal part of man; and it must, therefore, lie in the peculiar value of life to an immortal being, accountable in another state for the actions done in this, and whose life ought to be specially guarded for this very reason, that death introduces him into changeless and eternal relations, which were not to be left to the mercy of human passions.

To these we are to add the INTELLECTUAL POWERS, and we have what divines, in perfect accordance with the Scriptures, have called, "the NATURAL image of God in his creatures," which is essential and ineffaceable. Man was made capable of KNOWLEDGE, and he was endowed with liberty of WILL.

This natural image of God was the foundation of that MORAL image by which also man was distinguished. Unless he had been a spiritual, knowing, and willing being, he would have been wholly incapable of MORAL qualities. That he had such qualities eminently, and that in them consisted the image of God, as well as in the natural attributes just stated, we have also the express testimony of Scripture: "Lo this only have I found, that God made man UPRIGHT; but they have sought out many inventions." There is also an express allusion to the moral image of God, in which man was at first created, in Colossians iii, 10: "And have put on the new man, which is renewed in knowledge, after the image of Him that created him;" and in Ephesians iv, 24: "Put on the new man, which after God is created in righteousness and true holiness." In these passages the Apostle represents the change produced in true Christians by the Gospel, as a "renewal of the image of God in man; as a new or second creation in that image;" and he explicitly declares, that that image consists in "knowledge," in "righteousness," and in "true holiness."

This also may be finally argued from the satisfaction with which the historian of the creation represents the Creator as viewing the works of his hands as "VERY GOOD," which was pronounced with reference to each of them individually, as well as to the whole: "And God saw EVERY THING that he had made, and behold it was very good." But, as to man, this goodness must necessarily imply moral as well as physical qualities. Without them he would have been imperfect as MAN; and had they, in their first exercises, been perverted and sinful, he must have been an exception, and could not have been pronounced "very good." The goodness of man, as a rational being, must lie in devotedness and consecration to God; consequently, man was at first holy. A rational creature, as such, is capable of knowing, loving, serving, and living in communion with the Most Holy One. Adam, at first, did or did not exert this capacity; if he did not, he was not VERY GOOD,--not good at all.

4. On the intellectual and moral endowments of the progenitor of the human race, erring views appear to have been taken on both sides.

In knowledge, some have thought him little inferior to the angels; others, as furnished with but the simple elements of science and of language. The truth seems to be that, as to CAPACITY, his intellect must have been vigorous beyond that of any of his fallen descendants; which itself gives us very high views of the strength of his understanding, although we should allow him to have been created "lower than the angels." As to his ACTUAL KNOWLEDGE, that would depend upon the time and opportunity he had for observing the nature and laws of the objects around him; and the degree in which he was favoured with revelations from God on moral and religious subjects.

On the degree of moral excellence also in the first man, much license has been given to a warm imagination, and to rhetorical embellishment; and Adam's perfection has sometimes been fixed at an elevation which renders it exceedingly difficult to conceive how he could fall into sin at all. On the other hand, those who either deny or hold very slightly the doctrine of our hereditary depravity, delight to represent Adam as little superior in moral perfection and capability to his descendants. But, if we attend to the passages of holy writ above quoted, we shall be able, on this subject, to ascertain, if not the exact degree of his moral endowments, yet that there is a certain standard below which they cannot be placed.--Generally, he was made in the IMAGE of God, which, we have already proved, is to be understood MORALLY as well as NATURALLY. Now, however the image of any thing may be limited in extent, it must still be an accurate representation as far as it goes. Every thing good in the creation must always be a miniature representation of the excellence of the Creator; but, in this case, the "goodness," that is, the perfection, of every creature, according to the part it was designed to act in the general assemblage of beings collected into our system, wholly forbids us to suppose that the image of God's moral perfections in man was a blurred and dim representation. To whatever EXTENT it went, it necessarily excluded all that from man which did not resemble God; it was a likeness to God in "righteousness and true holiness," whatever the degree of each might be, and excluded all admixture of unrighteousness and unholiness. Man, therefore, in his original state, was SINLESS, both in act and in principle. Hence it is said that "God made man UPRIGHT." That this signifies moral rectitude cannot be doubted; but the import of the word is very extensive. It expresses, by an easy figure, the EXACTNESS of truth, justice, and obedience; and it comprehends the state and habit both of the heart and the life. Such, then, was the condition of primitive man; there was no obliquity in his moral principles, his mind, or affections; none in his conduct. He was perfectly sincere and exactly just, rendering from the heart all that was due to God and to the creature. Tried by the exactest PLUMMET, he was UPRIGHT; by the most perfect rule, he was STRAIGHT.

The "KNOWLEDGE" in which the Apostle Paul, in the passage quoted above from Colossians iii, 10, places "the image of God" after which man was created, does not merely imply the faculty of understanding, which is a part of the NATURAL image of God; but that which might be lost, because it is that in which we may be "RENEWED." It is, therefore, to be understood of the faculty of knowledge in right exercise; and of that willing reception, and firm retaining, and hearty approval, of religious truth, in which knowledge, when spoken of morally, is always understood in the Scriptures. We may not be disposed to allow, with some, that Adam understood the deep philosophy of nature, and could comprehend and explain the sublime mysteries of religion. The circumstance of his giving names to the animals, is certainly no sufficient proof of his having attained to a philosophical acquaintance with their qualities and distinguishing habits, although we should allow their names to be still retained in the Hebrew, and to be as expressive of their peculiarities as some expositors have stated. Sufficient time appears not to have been afforded him for the study of the properties of animals, as this event took place previous to the formation of Eve; and as for the notion of his acquiring knowledge by intuition, this is contradicted by the REVEALED fact, that angels themselves acquire their knowledge by observation and study, though no doubt, with great rapidity and certainty. The whole of this transaction was supernatural; the beasts were "brought" to Adam, and it is probable that he named them under a Divine suggestion. He has been also supposed to be the inventor of language, but his history shows that he was never without speech. From the first he was able to converse with God; and we may, therefore, infer that language was in him a supernatural and miraculous endowment. That his understanding was, as to its capacity, deep and large beyond any of his posterity, must follow from the perfection in which he was created; and his acquisitions of knowledge would, therefore, be rapid and easy. It was, however, in moral and religious truth, as being of the first concern to him, that we are to suppose the excellency of his knowledge to have consisted. "His reason would be clear, his judgment uncorrupted, and his conscience upright and sensible." The best knowledge would, in him, be placed first, and that of every other kind be made subservient to it, according to its relation to that. The Apostle adds to knowledge, "righteousness and true holiness;" terms which express, not merely freedom from sin, but positive and active virtue.

Sober as these views of man's primitive state are, it is not, perhaps, possible for us fully to conceive of so exalted a condition as even this. Below this standard it could not fall; and that it implied a glory, and dignity, and moral greatness of a very exalted kind, is made sufficiently apparent from the degree of guilt charged upon Adam when he fell: for the aggravating circumstances of his offence may well be deduced from the tremendous consequences which followed.

5. The salvation of Adam has been disputed; for what reason does not appear, except that the silence of Scripture, as to his after life, has given bold men occasion to obtrude their speculations upon a subject which called for no such expression of opinion. As nothing to the contrary appears, the charitable inference is, that as he was the first to receive the promise of redemption, so he was the first to prove its virtue. It is another presumption, that as Adam and Eve were clothed with skins of beasts, which could not have been slain for food, these were the skins of their sacrifices; and as the offering of animal sacrifice was an expression of faith in the appointed propitiation, to that refuge we may conclude they resorted, and through its merits were accepted.

6. The Rabbinical and Mohammedan traditions and fables respecting the first man are as absurd as they are numerous. Some of them indeed are monstrous, unless we suppose them to be allegories in the exaggerated style of the orientals. Some say that he was nine hundred cubits high; whilst others, not satisfied with this, affirm that his head touched the heavens. The Jews think that he wrote the ninety-first Psalm, invented the Hebrew letters, and composed several treatises; the Arabians, that he preserved twenty books which fell from heaven; and the Musselmen, that he himself wrote ten volumes.

7. That Adam was a type of Christ, is plainly affirmed by St. Paul, who calls him "the figure of him who was to come." Hence our Lord is sometimes called, not inaptly, the Second Adam. This typical relation stands sometimes in SIMILITUDE, sometimes in CONTRAST. Adam was formed immediately by God, as was the humanity of Christ. In each the nature was spotless, and richly endowed with knowledge and true holiness. Both are seen invested with dominion over the earth and all its creatures; and this may explain the eighth Psalm, where David seems to make the sovereignty of the first man over the whole earth in its pristine glory, the prophetic symbol of the dominion of Christ over the world restored. Beyond these particulars fancy must not carry us; and the typical CONTRAST must also be limited to that which is stated in Scripture, or supported by its allusions. Adam and Christ were each a public person, a FEDERAL HEAD to the whole race of mankind; but the one was the fountain of sin and death, the other of righteousness and life. By Adam's transgression "many were made sinners," Rom. v, 14–19. Through him, "death passed upon all men, because all have sinned" in him. But he thus prefigured that one man, by whose righteousness the "free gift comes upon all men to justification of life." The first man communicated a living soul to all his posterity; the other is a quickening Spirit, to restore them to newness of life now, and to raise them up at the last day. By the imputation of the first Adam's sin, and the communication of his fallen, depraved nature, death reigned over those who had not sinned after the similitude of Adam's transgression; and through the righteousness of the Second Adam, and the communication of a divine nature by the Holy Spirit, favour and grace shall much more abound in Christ's true followers unto eternal life. See Redemption.

ADAMA, one of the five cities which were destroyed by fire from heaven, and buried under the waters of the Dead Sea, Gen. xiv, 2; Deut. xxix, 23. It was the most easterly of all those which were swallowed up; and there is some probability that it was not entirely sunk under the waters; or that the inhabitants of the country built a new city of the same name upon the eastern shore of the Dead Sea: for Isaiah, according to the Septuagint, says, "God will destroy the Moabites, the city of Ar, and the remnant of Adama."

ADAMANT, שמיר, Ἀδάμας, Ecclus. xvi, 16. A stone of impenetrable hardness. Sometimes this name is given to the diamond; and so it is rendered, Jer. xvii, 1. But the Hebrew word rather means a very hard kind of stone, probably the SMIRIS, which was also used for cutting, engraving, and polishing other hard stones and crystals. The word occurs also in Ezek. iii, 9, and Zech. vii, 12. In the former place the Lord says to the Prophet, "I have made thy forehead as an adamant, firmer than a rock;" that is, endued thee with undaunted courage. In the latter, the hearts of wicked men are declared to be as adamant; neither broken by the threatenings and judgments of God, nor penetrated by his promises, invitations, and mercies. See Diamond.

ADAMITES, sects reputed to have professed the attainment of a perfect innocence, so that they wore no clothes in their assemblies. But Lardner doubts their existence in ancient, and Beausobre in modern, times.

ADAR, the twelfth month of the ecclesiastical, and the sixth of the civil, year among the Hebrews. It contains but twenty-nine days, and answers to our February, and sometimes enters into March, according to the course of the moon, by which they regulated their seasons.

ADARCONIM, אדרכונים, a sort of money, mentioned 1 Chron. xxix, 7, and Ezra viii, 27. The Vulgate translates it, GOLDEN PENCE, the **LXX**, PIECES OF GOLD. They were darics, a gold coin, which some value at twenty drachms of silver.

ADER. Jerom observes, that the place where the angels declared the birth of Jesus Christ to the shepherds, was called by this name, Luke ii, 8, 9. The empress Helena built a church on this spot, the remains of which are still visible.

ADDER, a venomous serpent, more usually called the viper. In our translation of the Bible we find the word adder five times; but without sufficient authority from the original.

שפיפון, in Gen. xlix, 17, is probably the cerastes; a serpent of the viper kind, of a light brown colour, which lurks in the sand and the tracks of wheels in the road, and unexpectedly bites not only the unwary traveller, but the legs of horses and other beasts. By comparing the Danites to this artful reptile, the patriarch intimated that by stratagem, more than by open bravery, they should avenge themselves of their enemies and extend their conquests.--פתן, in Psalm lviii, 4; xci, 13, signifies an asp. We may perhaps trace to this the Python of the Greeks, and its derivatives. (See ASP.)--עכשוב, עכשוב found only in Psalm cxl, 3, is derived from a verb which signifies TO BEND BACK ON ITSELF. The Chaldee Paraphrasts render it עכביש, which we translate elsewhere, SPIDER: they may therefore have understood it to have been the tarantula. It is rendered ASP by the Septuagint and Vulgate, and is so taken, Rom. iii, 13. The name is from the Arabic ACHASA. But there are several serpents which coil themselves previously to darting on their enemy; if this be a character of the asp, it is not peculiar to that reptile.--צפע, or צפעני, Prov. xxiii, 32; Isaiah xi, 8; xiv, 29; lix, 5; and Jer. viii, 17, is that deadly serpent called the basilisk, said to kill with its very breath. See Cockatrice.

In Psalm lviii, 5, reference is made to the effect of musical sounds upon serpents. That they might be rendered tame and harmless by certain charms, or soft and sweet sounds, and trained to delight in music, was an opinion which prevailed very early and universally.

Many ancient authors mention this effect; Virgil speaks of it particularly, *Æn.* vii, v, 750.

QUIN ET MARRUBIA VENIT DE GENTE SACERDOS,

FRONDE SUPER GALEAM ET FELICI COMPTUS OLIVA,

ARCHIPPI REGIS MISSU FORTISSIMUS UMBRO;

VIPEREO GENERI, ET GRAVITER SPIRANTIBUS HYDRIS

SPARGERE QUI SOMNOS CANTUQUE MANUQUE SOLEBAT,

MULCEBATQUE IRAS, ET MORSUS ARTE LEVABAT.

"Umbro, the brave Marrubian priest, was there,

Sent by the Marsian monarch to the war.

The smiling olive with her verdant boughs

Shades his bright helmet and adorns his brows;

His charms in peace the furious serpent keep;

And lull the envenom'd viper's race to sleep:

His healing hand allay'd the raging pain,

And at his touch the poisons fled again."

PITT.

Mr. Boyle quotes the following passage from Sir H. Blunt's Voyage into the Levant:--

"Many rarities of living creatures I saw in Grand Cairo; but the most ingenious was a nest of serpents, of two feet long, black and ugly, kept by a Frenchman, who, when he came to handle them, would not endure him, but ran and hid in their hole. Then he would take his cittern and play upon it. They, hearing his music, came all crawling to his feet, and began to climb up him, till he gave over playing, then away they ran."

The wonderful effect which music produces on the serpent tribes, is confirmed by the testimony of several respectable moderns. Adders swell at the sound of a flute, raising themselves up on the one half of their body, turning themselves round, beating proper time, and following the instrument. Their head, naturally round and long like an eel, becomes broad and flat like a fan. The tame serpents, many of which the orientals keep in their houses, are known to leave their holes in hot weather, at the sound of a musical instrument, and run upon the performer. Dr. Shaw had an opportunity of seeing a number of serpents keep exact time with the Dervishes in their circulatory dances, running over their heads and arms, turning when they turned, and stopping when they stopped. The rattlesnake acknowledges the power of music as much as any of his family; of which the following instance is a decisive proof: When Chateaubriand was in Canada, a snake of that species entered their encampment; a young Canadian, one of the party, who could play on the flute, to divert his associates, advanced against the serpent with his new species of weapon: on the approach of his enemy, the haughty reptile curled himself into a spiral line, flattened his head, inflated his cheeks, contracted his lips, displayed his envenomed fangs, and his bloody throat, his double tongue glowed like two flames of fire; his eyes were burning coals; his body, swollen with rage, rose and fell like the bellows of a forge; his dilated skin assumed a dull and scaly appearance; and his tail, which sounded the denunciation of death, vibrated with so great rapidity as to resemble a light vapour. The Canadian now began to play upon his flute, the serpent started with surprise, and drew back his head. In proportion as he was struck with the magic effect, his eyes lost their fierceness, the oscillations of his tail became slower, and the sound which it emitted became weaker, and gradually died away. Less perpendicular upon their spiral line, the rings of the fascinated serpent were by degrees expanded, and sunk one after another upon the ground, in concentric circles. The shades of azure, green, white, and gold, recovered their brilliancy on his quivering skin, and slightly turning his head, he remained motionless, in the attitude of attention and pleasure. At this moment, the Canadian advanced a few steps, producing with his flute sweet and simple notes. The reptile, inclining his variegated neck, opened a passage with his head through the high grass, and began to creep after the musician, stopping when he stopped, and beginning to follow him again, as soon as he moved forward. In this manner he was led out of their camp, attended by a great number of spectators, both savages and Europeans, who could scarcely believe their eyes, when they beheld this wonderful effect of harmony. The assembly unanimously decreed, that the serpent which had so highly entertained them, should be permitted to escape. Many of them are carried in baskets through Hindostan, and procure a maintenance for a set of people who play a few simple notes on the flute, with which the snakes seem much delighted, and keep time by a graceful motion of the head, erecting about half their length from the ground, and following the music with gentle curves, like the undulating lines of a swan's neck.

But on some serpents, these charms seem to have no power; and it appears from Scripture, that the adder sometimes takes precautions to prevent the fascination which he sees preparing for him: "for the deaf adder shutteth her ear, and will not hear the voice of the most skilful charmer." The threatening of the Prophet Jeremiah proceeds upon the same fact: "I will send serpents" (cockatrices) "among you, which will not be charmed, and they shall bite you." In all these quotations, the sacred writers, while they take it for granted that many serpents are disarmed by charming, plainly admit that the powers of the charmer are in vain exerted upon others.

It is the opinion of some interpreters, that the word שחל, which in some parts of Scripture denotes a lion, in others means an adder, or some other kind of serpent. Thus, in the ninety-first Psalm, they render it the basilisk: "Thou shalt tread upon the adder and the basilisk, the young lion and the dragon thou shalt trample under foot." Indeed, all the ancient expositors agree, that some species of serpent is meant, although they cannot determine what particular serpent the sacred writer had in view. The learned Bochart thinks it extremely probable that the holy Psalmist in this verse treats of serpents only; and, by consequence, that both the terms שחל and כפיר mean some kind of snakes, as well as פתן and תנין; because the coherence of the verse is by this view better preserved, than by mingling lions and serpents together, as our translators and other interpreters have commonly done; nor is it easy to imagine what can be meant by treading upon the lion, and trampling the young lion under foot; for it is not possible in walking to tread upon the lion, as upon the adder, the basilisk, and other serpents.

To **ADJURE**, to bind by oath, as under the penalty of a fearful curse, Joshua vi, 26; Mark v, 7. 2. To charge solemnly, as by the authority, and under pain, of the displeasure of God, Matt. xxvi, 63; Acts xix, 13.

ADONAI, one of the names of God. This word in the plural number signifies MY LORDS. The Jews, who either out of respect or superstition, do not pronounce the name of Jehovah, read Adonai in the room of it, as often as they meet with Jehovah in the Hebrew text. But the ancient Jews were not so scrupulous. Neither is there any law which forbids them to pronounce any name of God.

ADONIS. The text of the Vulgate in Ezek. viii, 14, says, that the Prophet saw women sitting in the temple, and weeping for Adonis; but according to the reading of the Hebrew text, they are said to weep for Thamuz, or Tammuz, the HIDDEN ONE. Among the Egyptians Adonis was adored under the name of Osiris, the husband of Isis. But he was sometimes called by the name of Ammuz, or Tammuz, THE CONCEALED, probably to denote his death or burial. The Hebrews, in derision, sometimes call him the DEAD, Psalm cvi, 28; Lev. xix, 28; because they wept for him, and represented him as dead in his coffin; and at other times they denominate him the image of jealousy, Ezek. viii, 3, 5, because he was the object of the jealousy of Mars. The Syrians, Phœnicians, and Cyprians, called him Adonis; and Calmet is of opinion that the Ammonites and Moabites designated him by the name of Baal-peor.

The manner in which they celebrated the festival of this false deity was as follows: They represented him as lying dead in his coffin, wept for him, bemoaned themselves, and sought for him with great eagerness and inquietude. After this, they pretended that they had found him again, and that he was still living. At this good news they exhibited marks of the most extravagant joy, and were guilty of a thousand lewd practices, to convince Venus how much they congratulated her on the return and revival of her favourite, as they had before condoled with her on his death. The Hebrew women, of whom the Prophet Ezekiel speaks, celebrated the feasts of Tammuz, or Adonis, in Jerusalem; and God showed the Prophet these women weeping for this infamous god, even in his temple.

Fabulous history gives the following account of Adonis: He was a beautiful young shepherd, the son of Cyniras, king of Cyprus, by his own daughter Myrrha. The goddess Venus fell in love with this youth, and frequently met him on mount Libanus. Mars, who envied this rival, transformed himself into a wild boar, and, as Adonis was hunting, struck him in the groin and killed him. Venus lamented the death of Adonis in an inconsolable manner. The eastern people, in imitation of her mourning, generally established some solemn days for the bewailing of Adonis. After his death, Venus went to the shades, and obtained from Proserpine, that Adonis might be with her six months in the year, and continue the other six in the infernal regions. Upon this were founded those public rejoicings, which succeeded the lamentations of his death. Some say that Adonis was a native of Syria; some, of Cyprus; and others, of Egypt.

ADOPTION. An act by which one takes another into his family, owns him for his son, and appoints him his heir. The Greeks and Romans had many regulations concerning adoption. It does not appear that adoption, properly so called, was formerly in use among the Jews. Moses makes no mention of it in his laws; and the case of Jacob's two grandsons, Gen. xlviii, 14, seems rather a substitution.

2. Adoption in a theological sense is that act of God's free grace by which, upon our being justified by faith in Christ, we are received into the family of God, and entitled to the inheritance of heaven. This appears not so much a distinct act of God, as involved in, and necessarily flowing from, our justification; so that, at least the one always implies the other. Nor is there any good ground to suppose that in the New Testament the term adoption is used with any reference to the civil practice of adoption by the Greeks, Romans, or other Heathens, and therefore it is not judicious to illustrate the texts in which the word occurs by their formalities. The Apostles in using the term appear to have had before them the simple view, that our sins had deprived us of our sonship, the favour of God, and the right to the inheritance of eternal life; but that, upon our return to God, and reconciliation with him, our forfeited privileges were not only restored, but greatly heightened through the paternal kindness of God. They could scarcely be forgetful of the affecting parable of the prodigal son; and it is under the same view that St. Paul quotes from the Old Testament, "Wherefore come out from among them, and be ye separate, saith the Lord, and touch not the unclean thing, and I will receive you, and I will be a Father unto you, and ye shall be my sons and daughters, saith the Lord Almighty."

Adoption, then, is that act by which we who were alienated, and enemies, and disinherited, are made the sons of God, and heirs of his eternal glory. "If children, then heirs, heirs of God and joint heirs with Christ;" where it is to be remarked, that it is not in our own right, nor in the right of any work done in us, or which we ourselves do, though it should be an evangelical work, that we become heirs; but jointly with Christ, and in his right.

3. To this state belong, freedom from a servile spirit, for we are not servants but sons; the special love and care of God our heavenly Father; a filial confidence in him; free access to him at all times and in all circumstances; a title to the heavenly inheritance; and the Spirit of adoption, or the witness of the Holy Spirit to our adoption, which is the foundation of all the comfort we can derive from those privileges, as it is the only means by which we can know that they are ours.

4. The last mentioned great privilege of adoption merits special attention. It consists in the inward witness or testimony of the Holy Spirit to the sonship of believers, from which flows a comfortable persuasion or conviction of our present acceptance with God, and the hope of our future and eternal glory. This is taught in several passages of Scripture:--

Rom. viii, 15, 16, "For ye have not received the spirit of bondage again to fear, but the Spirit of adoption, whereby we cry, Abba, Father. The Spirit itself beareth witness with our spirit that we are the children of God." In this passage it is to be remarked, 1. That the Holy Spirit takes away "fear," a servile dread of God as offended. 2. That the "Spirit of God" here mentioned, is not the personified spirit or genius of the Gospel, as some would have it, but "the Spirit itself," or himself, and hence he is called in the Galatians, "the Spirit of his Son," which cannot mean the genius of the Gospel. 3. That he inspires a filial confidence in God, as our Father, which is opposed to "the fear" produced by the "spirit of bondage." 4. That he excites this filial confidence, and enables us to call God our Father, by witnessing, bearing testimony with our spirit, "that we are the children of God."

Gal. iv, 4–6, "But when the fulness of the time was come, God sent forth his Son, made of a woman, made under the law, to redeem them that were under the law, that we might receive the adoption of sons; and because ye are sons, God hath sent forth the Spirit of his Son into your hearts, crying, Abba, Father." Here also are to be noted, 1. The means of our redemption from under (the curse of) the law,--the incarnation and sufferings of Christ. 2. That the adoption of sons follows upon our actual redemption from that curse, or, in other words, upon our pardon. 3. That upon our being pardoned, the "Spirit of the Son" is "sent forth into our hearts," producing the same effect as that mentioned in the Epistle to the Romans, viz. filial confidence in God,--"crying, Abba, Father." To these texts are to be added all those passages, so numerous in the New Testament, which express the confidence and the joy of Christians; their friendship with God; their confident access to him as their God; their entire union and delightful intercourse with him in spirit.

This has been generally termed the doctrine of assurance, and, perhaps, the expressions of St. Paul, "the full assurance of faith," and "the full assurance of hope," may warrant the use of the word. But as there is a current and generally understood sense of this term, implying that the assurance of our present acceptance and sonship implies an assurance of our final perseverance, and of an indefeasible title to heaven; the phrase, a comfortable persuasion, or conviction of our justification and adoption, arising out of the Spirit's inward and direct testimony, is to be preferred.

There is, also, another reason for the sparing and cautious use of the term assurance, which is, that it seems to imply, though not necessarily, the absence of all doubt, and shuts out all those lower degrees of persuasion which may exist in the experience of Christians. For, our faith may not at first, or at all times, be equally strong, and the testimony of the Spirit may have its degrees of clearness. Nevertheless, the fulness of this attainment is to be pressed upon every one: "Let us draw near," says St. Paul to all Christians, "with full assurance of faith."

It may serve, also, to remove an objection sometimes made to the doctrine, and to correct an error which sometimes pervades the statement of it, to observe that this assurance, persuasion, or conviction, whichever term be adopted, is not of the essence of justifying faith; that is, justifying faith does not consist in the assurance that I am now forgiven, through Christ. This would be obviously contradictory. For we must believe before we can be justified; much more before we can be assured, in any degree, that we are justified:--this persuasion, therefore, follows justification, and is one of its results. But though we must not only distinguish, but separate, this persuasion of our acceptance from the faith which justifies, we must not separate it, but only distinguish it, from justification itself. With that come in as concomitants, adoption, the "Spirit of adoption," and regeneration.

ADORATION, the act of rendering divine honours; or of addressing God or any other being as supposing it to be God. (See WORSHIP.) The word is compounded of AD, "to," and OS, "mouth;" and literally signifies to apply the hand to the mouth; MANUM AD OS ADMOVERE, "to kiss the hand;" this being in eastern countries one of the great marks of respect and submission. To this mode of idolatrous worship Job refers, xxxi, 26, 27. See also 1 Kings xix, 18.

The Jewish manner of adoration was by prostration, bowing, and kneeling. The Christians adopted the Grecian, rather than the Roman, method, and always adored uncovered. The ordinary posture of the ancient Christians was kneeling; but on Sundays, standing.

Adoration is also used for certain extraordinary acts of civil honour, which resemble those paid to the Deity, yet are given to men.

We read of adorations paid to kings, princes, emperors, popes, bishops, abbots, &c, by kneeling, falling prostrate, kissing the feet, hands, garments, &c.

The Persian manner of adoration, introduced by Cyrus, was by bending the knee, and falling on the face at the prince's feet, striking the earth with the forehead, and kissing the ground. This was an indispensable condition on the part of foreign ministers and ambassadors, as well as the king's own vassals, of being admitted to audience, and of obtaining any favour. This token of reverence was ordered to be paid to their favourites as well as to themselves, as we learn from the history of Haman and Mordecai, in the book of Esther; and even to their statues and images; for Philostratus informs us that, in the time of Apollonius, a golden statue of the king was exposed to all who entered Babylon, and none but those who adored it were admitted within the gates. The ceremony, which the Greeks called ϖροσκυνεῖν, Conon refused to perform to Artaxerxes, and Callisthenes to Alexander the Great, as reputing it impious and unlawful.

The adoration performed to the Roman and Grecian emperors consisted in bowing or kneeling at the prince's feet, laying hold of his purple robe, and then bringing the hand to the lips. Some attribute the origin of this practice to Constantius. They were only persons of rank or dignity that were entitled to the honour. Bare kneeling before the emperor to deliver a petition, was also called adoration.

It is particularly said of Dioclesian, that he had gems fastened to his shoes, that divine honours might be more willingly paid him, by kissing his feet. And this mode of adoration was continued till the last age of the Greek monarchy. When any one pays his respects to the king of Achen in Sumatra, he first takes off his shoes and stockings, and leaves them at the door.

The practice of adoration may be said to be still subsisting in England, in the custom of kissing the king's or queen's hand.

Adoration is also used in the court of Rome, in the ceremony of kissing the pope's feet. It is not certain at what period this practice was introduced into the church: but it was probably borrowed from the Byzantine court, and accompanied the temporal power. Dr. Maclaine, in the chronological table which he has subjoined to his translation of Mosheim's *Ecclesiastical History*, places its introduction in the eighth century, immediately after the grant of Pepin and Charlemagne. Baronius traces it to a much higher antiquity, and pretends that examples of this homage to the vicars of Christ occur so early as the year 204. These prelates finding a vehement disposition in the people to fall down before them, and kiss their feet, procured crucifixes to be fastened on their slippers; by which stratagem, the adoration intended for the pope's person is supposed to be transferred to Christ. Divers acts of this adoration we find offered even by princes to the pope; and Gregory **XIII**, claims this act of homage as a duty.

Adoration properly is paid only to the pope when placed on the altar, in which posture the cardinals, conclavists, alone are admitted to kiss his feet. The people are afterward admitted to do the like at St. Peter's church; the ceremony is described at large by Guicciardin.

Adoration is more particularly used for kissing one's hand in presence of another as a token of reverence. The Jews adored by kissing their hands, and bowing down their heads; whence in their language kissing is properly used for adoration. This illustrates a passage in Psalm ii, "Kiss the Son lest he be angry;"--that is, pay him HOMAGE and WORSHIP.

It was the practice among the Greek Christians to worship with the head uncovered, 1 Cor. xi; but in the east the ancient custom of worshipping with the head covered was retained.

ADRAMMELECH, the son of Sennacherib, king of Assyria. The king returning to Nineveh, after his unhappy expedition made into Judea against king Hezekiah, was killed by his two sons, Adrammelech and Sharezer, whilst at his devotions in the temple of his god Nisroch, Isaiah xxxvii, 38; 2 Kings xix. It is not known what prompted these two princes to commit this parricide; but after they had committed the murder, they fled for safety to the mountains of Armenia, and their brother, Esarhaddon, succeeded to the crown.

Adrammelech was also one of the gods adored by the inhabitants of Sepharvaim, who were settled in the country of Samaria, in the room of the Israelites, who were carried beyond the Euphrates. The Sepharvaites made their children pass through the fire in honour of this idol, and another, called ANAMMELECH, 2 Kings xvii, 31. The Rabbins say, that Adrammelech was represented under the form of a mule;

but there is much more reason to believe that Adrammelech meant the sun, and Anammelech the moon; the first signifying THE MAGNIFICENT KING, the second THE GENTLE KING,--many eastern nations adoring the moon as a GOD, not as a GODDESS.

ADRAMYTTIUM, a city on the west coast of Mysia, in Lesser Asia, over against the isle of Lesbos. It was in a ship belonging to this place, that St. Paul sailed from Cesarea to proceed to Rome as a prisoner, Acts xxvii, 2. It is now called EDREMIT.

ADRIA. This name, which occurs in Acts xxvii, 27, is now confined to the gulf lying between Italy on the one side, and the coasts of Dalmatia and Albania on the other. But in St. Paul's time it was extended to all that portion of the Mediterranean between Crete and Sicily. Thus Ptolemy says that Sicily was bounded on the east by the Adriatic, and Crete in a similar manner on the west; and Strabo says that the Ionian Gulf was a part of what, in his time, was called the Adriatic Sea.

ADULLAM, a city in the tribe of Judah, to the west of Hebron, whose king was slain by Joshua, Josh. xii, 15. It is frequently mentioned in the history of Saul and David; and is chiefly memorable from the cave in its neighbourhood, where David retired from Achish, king of Gath, when he was joined by the distressed and discontented, to the number of four hundred, over whom he became captain, 1 Sam. xxii, 1. Judas Maccabeus encamped in the plain of Adullam, where he passed the Sabbath day, 2 Mac. xii, 38. Eusebius says that, in his time, Adullam was a very great town, ten miles to the east of Eleutheropolis.

ADULTERY, the violation of the marriage bed. The law of Moses punished with death both the man and the woman who were guilty of this crime, Lev. xx, 10. If a woman was betrothed to a man, and was guilty of this infamous crime before the marriage was completed, she was, in this case, along with her paramour, to be stoned, Deut. xxii, 22–24.

When any man among the Jews, prompted by jealousy, suspected his wife of the crime of adultery, he brought her first before the judges, and informed them that, in consequence of his suspicions, he had privately admonished her, but that she was regardless of his admonitions. If before the judges she asserted her innocency, he required that she should drink the WATERS OF JEALOUSY, that God might by these means discover what she attempted to conceal, Num. v, 12, &c. The man then produced his witnesses, and they were heard. After this, both the man and the woman were conveyed to Jerusalem, and placed before the sanhedrim; the judges of which, by threats and other means, endeavoured to confound the woman, and make her confess. If she persisted in denying the fact, she was led to the eastern gate of the court of Israel, stripped of her own clothes, and dressed in black, before great numbers of her own sex. The priest then told her, that if she was really innocent, she had nothing to fear; but if guilty, she might expect to suffer all that the law had denounced against her, to which she answered, "Amen, amen." The priest then wrote the terms of the law in this form:--"If a strange man hath not come near you, and you are not polluted by forsaking the bed of your husband, these bitter waters, which I have cursed, will not hurt you: but if you have polluted yourself by coming near to another man, and gone astray from your husband,--may you be accursed of the Lord, and become an example for all his people; may your thigh rot, and your belly swell till it burst; may these cursed waters enter into your belly, and being swelled therewith, may your thighs putrefy."

After this, the priest filled a pitcher out of the brazen vessel, near the altar of burnt offerings, cast some dust of the pavement into it, mingled something with it as bitter as wormwood, and then read the curses, and received her answer of Amen. Another priest, in the meantime, tore off her clothes as low as her bosom--made her head bare--untied the tresses of her hair--fastened her clothes, which were thus torn, with a girdle under her breasts, and then presented her with the tenth part of an ephah, or about three pints, of barley meal. The other priest then gave her the WATERS OF JEALOUSY, or bitterness, to drink; and as soon as the woman had swallowed them, he gave her the meal in a vessel like a frying-pan into her hand. This was stirred before the Lord, and part of it thrown into the fire of the altar. If the wife was innocent, she returned with her husband, and the waters, so far from injuring her, increased her health, and made her more fruitful; but if she was guilty, she grew pale immediately, her eyes swelled; and, lest she should pollute the temple, she was instantly carried out, with these symptoms upon her, and died instantly, with all the ignominious circumstances related in the curses.

On this law of Moses, Michaëlis has the following remarks:--

"This oath was, perhaps, a relic of some more severe and barbarous consuetudinary laws, whose rigours Moses mitigated; as he did in many other cases, where an established usage could not be conveniently abolished altogether. Among ourselves, in barbarous times, the ORDEAL, or trial by fire, was, notwithstanding the parity of our married people, in common use; and this, in point of equity, was much the same in effect, as if the husband had had the right to insist on his wife submitting to the hazardous trial of her purity, by drinking a poisoned potion; which, according to an ancient superstition, could never hurt her if she was innocent. And, in fact, such a right is not altogether unexampled; for, according to Oldendorp's *History of the Mission of the Evangelical Brethren, in the Caribbee Islands*, it is actually in use among some of the savage nations in the interior parts of Western Africa.

"Now, when in place of a poisoned potion like this, which very few husbands can be very willing to have administered to their wives, we see, as among the Hebrews, an imprecation-drink, whose avenger God himself promises to become, we cannot but be struck with the contrast of wisdom and clemency which such a contrivance manifests. In the one case, (and herein consists their great distinction,) innocence can only be preserved by a miracle; while, on the other, guilt only is revealed and punished by the hand of God himself.

"By one of the clauses of the oath of purgation, (and had not the legislator been perfectly assured of his divine mission, the insertion of any such clause would have been a very bold step indeed,) a visible and corporeal punishment was specified, which the person swearing imprecated on herself, and which God himself was understood as engaging to execute. To have given so accurate a definition of the punishment that God meant to inflict, and still more one that consisted of such a rare disease, would have been a step of incomprehensible boldness in a legislator who pretended to have a divine mission, if he was not, with the most assured conviction, conscious of its reality.

"Seldom, however, very seldom, was it likely that Providence would have an opportunity of inflicting the punishment in question. For the oath was so regulated, that a woman of the utmost effrontery could scarcely have taken it without changing colour to such a degree as to betray herself.

"In the FIRST place, it was not administered to the woman in her own house, but she was under the necessity of going to that place of the land where God in a special manner had his abode, and took it there. Now, the solemnity of the place, unfamiliarized to her by daily business or resort, would have a great effect upon her mind. In the NEXT place, there was offered unto God what was termed an EXECRATION OFFERING, not in order to propitiate his mercy, but to invoke his vengeance on the guilty. Here the process was extremely slow, which gave her more time for reflection than to a guilty person could be acceptable, and that, too, amidst a multitude of unusual ceremonies. For the priest conducted her to the front of the sanctuary, and took holy water, that is, water out of the priests' laver, which stood before it, together with some earth off its floor, which was likewise deemed holy; and having put the earth in the water, he then proceeded to uncover the woman's head, that her face might be seen, and every change on her countenance during the administration of the oath accurately observed: and this was a circumstance which, in the east, where the women are always veiled, must have had a great effect; because a woman, accustomed to wear a veil, could, on so extraordinary an occasion, have had far less command of her eyes and her countenance than a European adulteress, who is generally a perfect mistress in all the arts of dissimulation, would display. To render the scene still more awful, the tresses of her hair were loosened, and then the execration offering was put into HER hand, while the priest held in HIS the imprecation water. This is commonly termed the BITTER WATER; but we must not understand this as if the water had really been bitter; for how could it have been so? The earth of the floor of the tabernacle could not make it bitter. Among the Hebrews, and other oriental nations, the word BITTER was rather used for CURSE: and, strictly speaking, the phrase does not mean BITTER WATER, but the WATER OF BITTERNESSES, that is, of curses. The priest now pronounced the oath, which was in all points so framed that it could excite no terrors in the breast of an innocent woman; for it expressly consisted in this, that the imprecation water should not harm her if she was innocent. It would seem as if the priest here made a stop, and again left the woman some time to consider whether she would proceed with the oath. This I infer from the circumstance of his speech not being directly continued in verse 21st, which is rather the APODOSIS of what goes before; and from the detail proceeding anew in the words of the historian, THEN SHALL THE PRIEST PRONOUNCE THE REST OF THE OATH AND THE CURSES TO THE WOMAN; AND PROCEED THUS.--After this stop he pronounced the curses, and the woman was obliged to declare her acquiescence in them by a repeated AMEN. Nor was the solemn scene yet altogether at an end; but rather, as it were commenced anew. For the priest had yet to write the curses in a book, which I suppose he did at great deliberation; having done so, he washed them out again in the very imprecation water, which the woman had now to drink; and this water being now presented to her, she was obliged to drink it, with this warning and assurance, in the name of God, that if she was guilty, it would prove within her an absolute curse. Now, what must have been her feelings, while drinking, if not conscious of purity? In my opinion she must have conceived that she already felt an alteration in the state of her body, and the germ, as it were, of the disease springing within her. Conscience and imagination would conspire together, and render it almost impossible for her to drink it out. Finally, the execration offering was taken out of her hand, and burnt upon the altar. I cannot but think that, under the sanction of such a PURGATORIUM, perjury must have been a very rare occurrence indeed. If it happened but once in an age, God had bound himself to punish it; and if this took place but once, (if but one woman who had taken the oath was attacked with that rare disease which it threatened,) it was quite enough to serve as a determent to all others for at least one generation."

This procedure had also the effect of keeping in mind, among the Jews, God's high displeasure against this violation of his law; and though some lax moralists have been found, in modern times, to palliate it, yet the Christian will always remember the solemn denunciations of the New Testament against a crime so aggravated, whether considered in its effects upon the domestic relations, upon the moral character of the guilty parties, or upon society at large,-- "Whoremongers and adulterers God will judge."

Adultery, in the prophetic scriptures, is often metaphorically taken, and signifies idolatry, and apostasy from God, by which men basely defile themselves, and wickedly violate their ecclesiastical and covenant relation to God, Hos. ii, 2; Ezek. xvi.

ADVOCATE, Παράκλητος, A PATRON, one who pleads the cause of any one before another. In this sense the term is applied to Christ our intercessor, 1 John ii, 1. It signifies also a COMFORTER, and AN INSTRUCTER; and is used of the Holy Spirit, John xiv, 16, and xv, 26.

ADYTUM is a Greek word, signifying INACCESSIBLE, by which is understood the most retired and secret place of the Heathen temples, into which none but the priests were allowed to enter. The ADYTUM of the Greeks and Romans answered to the SANCTUM SANCTORUM of the Jews, and was the place from whence oracles were delivered.

ÆRA, a series of years, commencing from a certain point of time called an EPOCHA: thus we say, the Christian æra; that is, the number of years elapsed since the birth of Christ. The generality of authors use the terms æra and epocha in a synonymous sense; that is, for the point of time from which any computation begins.

The ancient Jews made use of several æras in their computation; sometimes they reckoned from the deluge, sometimes from the division of tongues; sometimes from their departure out of Egypt; and at other times from the building of the temple; and sometimes from the restoration after the Babylonish captivity: but their vulgar æra was from the creation of the world, which falls in with the year of the Julian period 953; and consequently they supposed the world created 294 years sooner than according to our computation. But when the Jews became subject to the Syro-Macedonian kings, they were obliged to make use of the æra of the Seleucidæ in all their contracts, which from thence was called the æra of contracts. This æra begins with the year of the world 3692, of the Julian period 4402, and before Christ 312. The æra in general use among the Christians is that from the birth of Jesus Christ, concerning the true time of which chronologers differ; some place it two years, others four, and again others five, before the vulgar æra, which is fixed for the year of the world 4004: but Archbishop Usher, and after him the generality of modern chronologers, place it in the year of the world 4000.

The ancient Heathens used several æras:

1. The æra of the first olympiad is placed in the year of the world 3228, and before the vulgar æra of Jesus Christ 776. 2. The taking of Troy by the Greeks, in the year of the world 2820, and before Jesus Christ 1884. 3. The voyage undertaken for the purpose of bringing away the golden fleece, in the year of the world 2760. 4. The foundation of Rome, in 2856. 5. The æra of Nabonassar, in 3257. 6. The æra of Alexander the Great, or his last victory over Darius, in 3674, and before Jesus Christ 330.

AERIANS, a sect which arose about the middle of the fourth century, being the followers of Aërius, (who must be distinguished from Arius and Aëtius,) a monk and a presbyter of Sebastia, in Pontus. He is charged with being an Arian, or Semi-Arian; but the heaviest accusation against him is an attempt to reform the church; and, by rejecting prayers for the dead, with certain fasts and festivals then superstitiously observed, to reduce Christianity as nearly as possible "to its primitive simplicity; a purpose, indeed, laudable and noble," says Dr. Mosheim, "when considered in itself: though the principles from WHENCE it springs, and the means BY which it is executed, are sometimes, in many respects, worthy of censure, and MAY have been so in the case of this reformer." This gentle rebuke probably refers to a report that the zeal of Aërius originated in his being disappointed of the bishopric of Sebastia, (conferred on Eustathius,) which led him to affirm that the Scriptures make no distinction between a presbyter and a bishop, which he founded chiefly on 1 Tim. iv, 14. Hence he is considered by many, as the father of the modern Presbyterians.--"For this opinion, CHIEFLY," says Dr. Turner, "he is ranked among the heretics, by Epiphanius, his contemporary, who calls it a notion FULL OF FOLLY AND MADNESS. His followers were driven from the churches, and out of all the towns and villages, and were obliged to assemble in the woods, caverns, and open defiles."

AETIANS, another branch (as it is said) of Arians, so called from Aëtius, bishop of Antioch, who is also charged with maintaining "faith without works," as "sufficient to salvation," or rather justification; and with maintaining "that sin is not imputed to believers." It is added, that he taught God had revealed to him things which he had "concealed from the Apostles;" which, perhaps, is only a misrepresentation of what he taught on the doctrine of divine influences.

AFFINITY. There are several degrees of affinity, wherein marriage was prohibited by the law of Moses: thus the son could not marry his mother, nor his father's wife, Lev. xviii, 7, &c. The brother could not marry his sister, whether she were so by the father only, or only by the mother, and much less if she were his sister both by the same father and mother. The grandfather could not marry his granddaughter, either by his son or daughter. No one could marry the daughter of his father's wife; nor the sister of his father or mother; nor the uncle, his niece; nor the aunt, her nephew; nor the nephew, the wife of his uncle by the father's side. The father-in-law could not marry his daughter-in-law; nor the brother the wife of his brother, while living; nor even after the death of his brother, if he left children. If he left no children, the surviving brother was to raise up children to his deceased brother by marrying his widow. It was forbidden to marry the mother and the daughter at one time, or the daughter of the mother's son, or the daughter of her daughter, or two sisters, together.

It is true the patriarchs, before the law, married their sisters, as Abraham married Sarah, who was his father's daughter by another mother; and two sisters together, as Jacob married Rachel and Leah; and their own sisters, both by father and mother, as Seth and Cain. But these cases are not to be proposed as examples; because in some they were authorized by necessity; in others, by custom; and the law as yet was not in being. If some other examples may be found, either before or since the law, the Scripture expressly disapproves of them; as Reuben's incest with Balah, his father's concubine; and the action of Amnon with his sister Tamar; and that of Herod Antipas, who married Herodias, his sister-in-law, his brother Philip's wife, while her husband was yet living; and that which St. Paul reproves and punishes among the Corinthians, 1 Cor. v, 1.

AGABUS, a prophet, and as the Greeks say, one of the seventy disciples of our Saviour. He foretold that there would be a great famine over all the earth; which came to pass accordingly, under the emperor Claudius, in the fourth year of his reign, A. D. 44, Acts xi, 28.

Ten years after this, as St. Paul was going to Jerusalem, and had already landed at Cæsarea, in Palestine, the same prophet, Agabus, arrived there, and coming to visit St. Paul and his company, he took this Apostle's girdle, and binding himself hand and feet, he said, "Thus saith the Holy Ghost, So shall the Jews at Jerusalem bind the man that owneth this girdle, and shall deliver him into the hands of the Gentiles," Acts xxi, 10. We know no other particulars of the life of Agabus. The Greeks say that he suffered martyrdom at Antioch.

AGAG. This seems to have been a common name of the princes of Amalek, one of whom was very powerful as early as the time of Moses, Num. xxiv, 7. On account of the cruelties exercised by this king and his army against the Israelites, as they returned from Egypt, a bloody and long contested battle took place between Joshua and the Amalekites, in which the former was victorious, Exod. xvii, 8–13. At the same time, God protested with an oath to destroy Amalek, verses 14–16; Deut. xxv, 17–19, A. M. 2513. About four hundred years after this, the Lord remembered the cruel treatment of his people, and his own oath; and he commanded Saul, by the mouth of Samuel, to destroy the Amalekites. Saul mustered his army, and found it two hundred thousand strong, 1 Sam. xv, 1, &c. Having entered into their country, he cut in pieces all he could meet with from Havilah to Shur. Agag their king, and the best of their cattle, were however spared, an act of disobedience on the part of Saul, probably dictated by covetousness. But Agag did not long enjoy this reprieve; for Samuel no sooner heard that he was alive, than he sent for him; and notwithstanding his insinuating address, and the vain hopes with which he flattered himself that the bitterness of death was past, he caused him to be hewed to pieces in Gilgal before the Lord, saying, "As, כאשר, IN THE SAME IDENTICAL MODE AS, thy sword hath made women childless, so shall thy mother be childless among women." This savage chieftain had hewed many prisoners to death; and, therefore, by command of the Judge of the whole earth, he was visited with the same punishment which he had inflicted upon others.

AGAPÆ. See Love Feast.

AGAR, mount Sinai, so called, Gal. iv, 24, 25. But this reading is doubtful, many **MSS**. having the verse, "for this Sinai is a mountain of Arabia." Some critics however contend for the reading of the received text, and urge that AGAR, which signifies "a rocky mountain," is the Arabic name for SINAI.

AGATE, שבו, Exod. xxviii, 19; xxxix, 12. In the Septuagint ἀχάτης, and Vulgate, ACHATES. A precious stone, semi-pellucid. Its variegations are sometimes most beautifully disposed, representing plants, trees, rivers, clouds, &c. Its Hebrew name is, perhaps, derived from the country whence the Jews imported it; for the merchants of Sheba brought to the market of Tyre all kinds of precious stones, Ezek. xxvii, 22. The agate was the second stone in the third row of the pectoral of the high priest, Exod. xxviii, 19, and xxxix, 12.

AGE, in the most general sense of the term, denotes the duration of any substance, animate or inanimate; and is applied either to the whole period of its existence, or to that portion of it which precedes the time to which the description of it refers. In this sense it is used to signify either the whole natural duration of the LIFE of man, or any interval of it that has elapsed before the period of which we speak. When age is understood of a certain portion of the life of man, its whole duration is divided into four different ages, viz. infancy, youth, manhood, and old age: the first extending to the fourteenth year; the second, denominated youth, adolescence, or the age of puberty, commencing at fourteen, and terminating at about twenty-five; manhood, or the virile age, concluding at fifty; and the last ending at the close of life. Some divide the first period into infancy and childhood; and the last likewise into two stages, calling that which succeeds the age of seventy-five, decrepit old age. Age is applicable to the duration of things inanimate or factitious; and in this use of the term we speak of the age of a house, of a country, of a state or kingdom, &c.

Age, in CHRONOLOGY, is used for a century, or a period of one hundred years: in which sense it is the same with SECULUM, and differs from GENERATION. It is also used in speaking of the times past since the creation of the world. The several ages of the world may be reduced to three grand epochas, viz. the age of the law of nature, called by the Jews the void age, from Adam to Moses. The age of the Jewish law, from Moses to Christ, called by the Jews the present age. And the age of grace, from Christ to the present year. The Jews call the third age, the age to come, or the future age; denoting by it the time from the advent of the Messiah to the end of the world. The Romans distinguished the time that preceded them into three ages: the obscure or uncertain age, which reached down as low as Ogyges king of Attica, in whose reign the deluge happened in Greece; the fabulous or heroic age, which ended at the first olympiad; and the historical age, which commenced at the building of Rome. Among the poets, the four ages of the world are, the golden, the silver, the brazen, and the iron age.

Age is sometimes used among the ancient poets in the same sense as GENERATION, or a period of thirty years. Thus Nestor is said to have lived three ages, when he was ninety years old.

The period preceding the birth of Jesus Christ has been generally divided into six ages. The first extends from the creation to the deluge, and comprehends 1656 years. The second age, from the deluge to Abraham's entering the land of promise, A. M. 2082, comprehends 426 years. The third age from Abraham's entrance into the promised land to the Exodus, A. M. 2512, includes 430 years. The fourth age, from the Exodus to the building of the temple by Solomon, A. M.

2992, contains 480 years. The fifth age from the foundation of Solomon's temple to the Babylonish captivity, A. M. 3416, comprehends 424 years. The sixth age, from the Babylonish captivity to the birth of Jesus Christ, A. M. 4000, the fourth year before the vulgar æra, includes 584 years. Those who follow the Septuagint, or Greek version, divide this period into seven ages, viz. 1. From the creation to the deluge, 2262 years. 2. From the deluge to the confusion of tongues, 738 years. 3. From this confusion to the calling of Abraham, 460 years. 4. From this period to Jacob's descent into Egypt, 215 years; and from this event to the Exodus, 430 years, making the whole 645 years. 5. From the Exodus to Saul, 774 years. 6. From Saul to Cyrus, 583 years. 7. From Cyrus to the vulgar æra of Christians, 538 years; the whole period from the creation to this period containing 6000 years.

AGRIPPA, surnamed Herod, the son of Aristobulus and Mariamne, and grandson of Herod the Great, was born A. M. 3997, three years before the birth of our Saviour, and seven years before the vulgar æra. After the death of his father Aristobulus, Josephus informs us that Herod, his grandfather, took care of his education, and sent him to Rome to make his court to Tiberius. Agrippa, having a great inclination for Caius, the son of Germanicus, and grandson of Antonia, chose to attach himself to this prince, as if he had some prophetic views of the future elevation of Caius, who at that time was beloved by all the world. The great assiduity and agreeable behaviour of Agrippa so far won upon this prince, that he was unable to live without him. Agrippa, being one day in conversation with Caius, was overheard by one Eutychus, a slave whom Agrippa had emancipated, to say that he should be glad to see the old emperor take his departure for the other world and leave Caius master of this, without meeting with any obstacle from the emperor's grandson, Tiberius Nero. Eutychus, some time after this, thinking he had reason to be dissatisfied with Agrippa, communicated the conversation to the emperor; whereupon Agrippa was loaded with fetters, and committed to the custody of an officer. Soon after this, Tiberius dying, and Caius Caligula succeeding him, the new emperor heaped many favours and much wealth upon Agrippa, changed his iron fetters into a chain of gold, set a royal diadem on his head, and gave him the tetrarchy which Philip, the son of Herod the Great, had been possessed of, that is, Batanæa and Trachonitis. To this he added that of Lysanias; and Agrippa returned very soon into Judea, to take possession of his new kingdom. The emperor Caius, desiring to be adored as a god, commanded to have his statue set up in the temple of Jerusalem. But the Jews opposed this design with so much resolution, that Petronius was forced to suspend his proceedings in this affair, and to represent, in a letter to the emperor, the resistance he met with from the Jews. Agrippa, who was then at Rome, coming to the emperor at the very time he was reading the letter, Caius told him that the Jews were the only people of all mankind who refused to own him for a deity; and that they had taken arms to oppose his resolution. At these words Agrippa fainted away, and, being carried home to his house, continued in that state for a long time. As soon as he was somewhat recovered, he wrote a long letter to Caius, wherein he endeavoured to soften him; and his arguments made such an impression upon the emperor's mind, that he desisted, in appearance, from the design which he had formed of setting up his statue in the temple. Caius being killed in the beginning of the following year, A. D. 41, Agrippa, who was then at Rome, contributed much by his advice to maintain Claudius in possession of the imperial dignity, to which he had been advanced by the army. The emperor, as an acknowledgment for his kind offices, gave him all Judea, and the kingdom of Chalcis, which had been possessed by Herod his brother. Thus Agrippa became of a sudden one of the greatest princes of the east, and was possessed of as much, if not more territory, than had been held by Herod the Great, his grandfather. He returned to Judea, and governed it to the great satisfaction of the Jews. But the desire of pleasing them, and a mistaken zeal for their religion, induced him to put to death the Apostle James, and to cast Peter into prison with the same design; and, but for a miraculous interposition, which, however, produced no effect upon the mind of the tyrant, his hands would have been imbrued in the blood of two Apostles, the memory whereof is preserved in Scripture. At Cæsarea, he had games performed in honour of Claudius. Here the inhabitants of Tyre and Sidon waited on him to sue for peace. Agrippa being come early in the morning into the theatre, with a design to give them audience, seated himself on his throne, dressed in a robe of silver tissue, worked in the most admirable manner. The rising sun darted his golden beams thereon, and gave it such a lustre as dazzled the eyes of the spectators; and when the king began his speech to the Tyrians and Sidonians, the parasites around him began to say, it was "the voice of a god and not of man." Instead of rejecting these impious flatteries, Agrippa received them with an air of complacency; and the angel of the Lord smote him because he did not give God the glory. Being therefore carried home to his palace, he died, at the end of five days, racked with tormenting pains in his bowels, and devoured with worms. Such was the death of Herod Agrippa, A. D. 44, after a reign of seven years. He left a son of the same name, and three daughters--Bernice, who was married to her uncle Herod, her father's brother; Mariamne, betrothed to Julius Archelaus; and Drusilla, promised to Epiphanius, the son of Archelaus, the son of Comagena.

AGRIPPA, son of the former Agrippa, was at Rome with the emperor Claudius when his father died. The emperor, we are told by Josephus, was inclined to give him all the dominions that had been possessed by his father, but was dissuaded from it, Agrippa being only seventeen years of age; and he kept him therefore at his court four years.

Three years after this, Herod, king of Chalcis, and uncle to young Agrippa, dying, the emperor gave his dominions to this prince, who, notwithstanding, did not go into Judea till four years after, A. D. 53; when, Claudius taking from him the kingdom of Chalcis, gave him the provinces of Gaulonitis, Trachonitis, Batanæa, Paneas, and Abylene, which formerly had been in the possession of Lysanias. After the death of Claudius, his successor, Nero, who had a great affection for Agrippa, to his other dominions added Julias in Peræa, and that part of Galilee to which Tarichæa and

Tiberias belonged. Festus governor of Judea, coming to his government, A. D. 60, king Agrippa and Bernice, his sister, went as far as Cæsarea to salute him; and as they continued there for some time, Festus talked with the king concerning the affair of St. Paul, who had been seized in the temple about two years before, and within a few days previous to his visit had appealed to the emperor. Agrippa wishing to hear Paul, that Apostle delivered that noble address in his presence which is recorded, Acts xxvi.

AGUR. The thirtieth chapter of Proverbs begins with this title: "The words of Agur, the son of Jakeh;" and the thirty-first, with "the words of king Lemuel;" with respect to which some conjecture that Solomon describes himself under these appellations; others, that these chapters are the productions of persons whose real names are prefixed. Scripture history, indeed, affords us no information respecting their situation and character; but there must have been sufficient reason for regarding their works in the light of inspired productions, or they would not have been admitted into the sacred canon.

They are called MASSA, a term frequently applied to the undoubted productions of the prophetic Spirit; and it is not improbable that the authors meant, by the adoption of this term, to lay claim to the character of inspiration. A succession of virtuous and eminent men, favoured with divine illuminations, flourished in Judea till the final completion of the sacred code; and, most likely, many more than those whose writings have been preserved. Agur may then have been one of those prophets whom Divine providence raised up to comfort or admonish his chosen people; and Lemuel may have been some neighbouring prince, the son of a Jewish woman, by whom he was taught the Massa contained in the thirty-first chapter. These, of course, can only be considered as mere conjectures; for, in the absence of historic evidence, who can venture to pronounce with certainty? The opinion, however, that Agur and Lemuel are appellations of Solomon, is sanctioned by so many and such respectable writers, that it demands a more particular examination.

The knowledge of names was anciently regarded as a matter of the highest importance, in order to understand the nature of the persons or things which they designate; and, in the opinion of the rabbins, was preferable even to the study of the written law. The Heathens paid considerable attention to it, as appears from the Cratylus of Plato; and some of the Christian fathers entertained very favourable notions of such knowledge. The Jewish doctors, it is true, refined upon the subject with an amazing degree of subtilty, grounding upon it many ridiculous ideas and absurd fancies; yet it is unquestionable that many of the proper names in Scripture are significant and characteristic. Thus the names Eve, Cain, Seth, Noah, Abraham, Israel, &c, were imposed by reason of their being expressive of the several characters of the persons whom they represent. Reasoning from analogy, we may infer that all the proper names in the Old Testament, at their original imposition, were intended to denote some quality or circumstance in the person or thing to which they belong; and though many, from transference, have ceased to be personally characteristic, yet are they all significative.

As the custom of imposing descriptive names prevailed in the primitive ages, it is not impossible that Agur and Lemuel may be appropriated to Solomon, and Jakeh to David as mystic appellations significative of their respective characters. It is even some confirmation of this opinion, that Solomon is denominated Jedidiah (beloved of the Lord) by the Prophet Nathan; and that in the book of Ecclesiastes, he styles himself Koheleth, or the Preacher. Nevertheless, this hypothesis does not appear to rest upon a firm foundation. It is foreign to the simplicity of the sacred penmen, and contrary to their custom in similar cases, to adopt a mystic name, without either explaining it, or alleging the reasons for its adoption. In the names Eve, Cain, Seth, Noah, &c, before alluded to; in the appellation Nabal; in the enigmatical names in the first chapter of Hosea; in the descriptive names given to places, as Beersheba, Jehovah-jireh, Peniel, Bethel, Gilgal; and in many other instances, the meaning of the terms is either explained, or the circumstances are mentioned which led to their selection. When Solomon is called Jedidiah, it is added that it was "because of the Lord;" and when he styles himself Koheleth, an explanatory clause is annexed, describing himself "the son of David, the king of Jerusalem." But if Solomon be meant by the titles Agur and Lemuel, he is so called without any statement of the reasons for their application, and without any explanation of their import; a circumstance unusual with the sacred writers, and the reverse to what is practised in the book of Proverbs, where his proper name, Solomon, is attributed to him in three different places. Nor is anything characteristic of the Jewish monarchs discoverable in the terms themselves. Jakeh, which denotes OBEDIENT, is no more applicable to David than to Nathan, or any other personage of eminent worth and piety among the Israelites. The name of Agur is not of easy explanation; some giving it the sense of RECOLLECTUS, that is, recovered from his errors, and become penitent; an explanation more applicable to David than to Solomon. Simon, in his lexicon, says it may perhaps denote "him who applies to the study of wisdom;" an interpretation very suitable to the royal philosopher, but not supported by adequate authority; and in his Onomasticon he explains it in a different manner. Others suppose that it means COLLECTOR; though it has been argued, that, as it has a passive form, it cannot have an active sense. But this is not a valid objection, as several examples may be produced from the Bible of a similar form with an active signification. If such be its meaning, it is suitable to Solomon, who was not the collector or compiler, but the author, of the Proverbs. With respect to the name Lemuel, it signifies one that is for God, or devoted to God; and is not, therefore, peculiarly descriptive of Solomon. It appears, then, that nothing can be inferred from the signification of the names Agur and Lemuel in support of the conjecture, that they are appellations of Solomon. The contents, likewise, of the two chapters in question strongly militate against this hypothesis.

When all these circumstances are taken into consideration, together with the extreme improbability that Solomon should be denominated three times by his proper name, and afterward, in the same work, by two different enigmatical names, we are fully warranted in rejecting the notion, that the wise monarch is designed by the appellations Agur and Lemuel. And it seems most reasonable to consider them as denoting real persons.

AHAB, the son and successor of Omri. He began his reign over Israel, A. M. 3086, and reigned 22 years. In impiety he far exceeded all the kings of Israel. He married Jezebel, the daughter of Ethbaal, king of Zidon, who introduced the whole abominations and idols of her country, Baal and Ashtaroth.

2. Ahab the son of Kolaiah, and Zedekiah the son of Maaseiah, were two false prophets, who, about A. M. 3406, seduced the Jewish captives at Babylon with hopes of a speedy deliverance, and stirred them up against Jeremiah. The Lord threatened them with a public and ignominious death, before such as they had deceived; and that their names should become a curse; men wishing that their foes might be made like Ahab and Zedekiah, whom Nebuchadnezzar king of Babylon roasted in the fire, Jer. xxix, 21, 22.

AHASUERUS was the king of Persia, who advanced Esther to be queen, and at her request delivered the Jews from the destruction plotted for them by Haman. Archbishop Usher is of opinion that this Ahasuerus was Darius Hystaspes; and that Atossa was the Vashti, and Artystona the Esther, of the Scriptures. But, according to Herodotus, the latter was the daughter of Cyrus, and therefore could not be Esther; and the former had four sons by Darius, besides daughters, born to him after he was king; and therefore she could not be the queen Vashti, divorced from her husband in the third year of his reign, nor he the Ahasuerus who divorced her. Besides, Atossa retained her influence over Darius to his death, and obtained the succession of the crown for his son, Xerxes; whereas Vashti was removed from the presence of Ahasuerus by an irrevocable decree, Esther i, 19. Joseph Scaliger maintains that Xerxes was the Ahasuerus, and Hamestris his queen, the Esther, of Scripture. The opinion is founded on the similitude of names, but contradicted by the dissimilitude of the characters of Hamestris and Esther. Besides, Herodotus says that Xerxes had a son by Hamestris that was marriageable in the seventh year of his reign; and therefore she could not be Esther. The Ahasuerus of Scripture, according to Dr. Prideaux, was Artaxerxes Longimanus. Josephus positively says that this was the person. The Septuagint, through the whole book of Esther, uses Artaxerxes for the Hebrew Ahasuerus wherever the appellation occurs; and the apocryphal additions to that book every where call the husband of Esther Artaxerxes; and he could be no other than Artaxerxes Longimanus. The extraordinary favour shown to the Jews by this king, first in sending Ezra, and afterward Nehemiah, to relieve this people, and restore them to their ancient prosperity, affords strong presumptive evidence that they had near his person and high in his regard such an advocate as Esther. Ahasuerus is also a name given in Scripture, Ezra iv, 6, to Cambyses, the son of Cyrus; and to Astyages, king of the Medes, Dan. ix, 1.

AHAVA. The name of a river of Babylonia, or rather of Assyria, where Ezra assembled those captives whom he afterward brought into Judea, Ezra viii, 15. The river Ahava is thought to be that which ran along the Adabene, where a river Diava, or Adiava, is mentioned, and on which Ptolemy places the city Abane or Aavane. This is probably the country called Ava, whence the kings of Assyria translated the people called Avites into Palestine, and where they settled some of the captive Israelites, 2 Kings xvii, 24; xviii, 34; xix, 13; xvii, 31. Ezra, intending to collect as many Israelites as he could, who might return to Judea, halted in the country of Ava, or Aahava, whence he sent agents into the Caspian mountains, to invite such Jews as were willing to join him, Ezra viii, 16. The history of Izates, king of the Adiabenians, and of his mother Helena, who became converts to Judaism some years after the death of Jesus Christ, sufficiently proves that there were many Jews still settled in that country.

AHAZ succeeded his father Jotham, as king of Israel, at the age of twenty years, reigned till the year before Christ, 726, and addicted himself to the practice of idolatry. After the customs of the Heathen, he made his children to pass through fire; he shut up the temple, and destroyed its vessels. He became tributary to Tiglath-pileser, whose assistance he supplicated against the kings of Syria and Israel. Such was his impiety, that he was not allowed burial in the sepulchres of the kings of Israel, 2 Kings xvi; 2 Chron. xxviii.

AHAZIAH, the son of Ahab, king of Israel. Ahaziah reigned two years, partly alone, and partly with his father Ahab, who appointed him his associate in the kingdom a year before his death. Ahaziah imitated his father's impieties, 1 Kings xxii, 52, &c, and paid his adorations to Baal and Ashtaroth, the worship of whom had been introduced into Israel by Jezebel his mother. The Moabites, who had been always obedient to the kings of the ten tribes, ever since their separation from the kingdom of Judah, revolted after the death of Ahab, and refused to pay the ordinary tribute. Ahaziah had not leisure or power to reduce them, 2 Kings i, 1, 2, &c, for, about the same time, having fallen through a lattice from the top of his house, he was considerably injured, and sent messengers to Ekron to consult Baalzebub, the god of that place, whether he should recover, 2 Kings i, 1–17. Elijah met the messengers, and informed them he should certainly die; and he died accordingly.

2. Ahaziah, king of Judah, the son of Jehoram and Athaliah. He succeeded his father in the kingdom of Judah, A. M. 3119; being in the twenty-second year of his age, 2 Kings viii, 26, &c; and he reigned one year only in Jerusalem. He walked in the ways of Ahab's house, to which he was related, his mother being of that family. Joram, king of Israel, 2 Kings viii, going to attack Ramoth Gilead, which the kings of Syria had taken from his predecessors, was there dangerously wounded, and carried by his own appointment to Jezreel, for the purpose of surgical assistance. Ahaziah, Joram's friend and relation, accompanied him in this war, and came afterward to visit him at Jezreel. In the meantime, Jehu, the son of Nimshi, whom Joram had left besieging the fortress of Ramoth, rebelled against his master, and set out with a

design of extirpating the house of Ahab, according to the commandment of the Lord, 2 Kings ix. Joram and Ahaziah, who knew nothing of his intentions, went to meet him. Jehu killed Joram dead upon the spot: Ahaziah fled, but Jehu's people overtook him at the going up of Gur, and mortally wounded him; notwithstanding which, he had strength enough to reach Megiddo, where he died. His servants, having laid him in his chariot, carried him to Jerusalem, where he was buried with his fathers, in the city of David.

AHIJAH, the prophet of the Lord, who dwelt in Shiloh. He is thought to be the person who spoke twice to Solomon from God, once while he was building the temple, 1 Kings vi, 11, at which time he promised him the divine protection; and again, 1 Kings xi, 11, after his falling into his irregularities, with great threatenings and reproaches. Ahijah was one of those who wrote the history or annals of this prince, 2 Chron. ix, 29. The same prophet declared to Jeroboam, that he would usurp the kingdom, 1 Kings xi, 29, &c; and, about the end of Jeroboam's reign, he also predicted the death of Abijah, the only pious son of that prince, as is recorded 1 Kings xiv, 2, &c. Ahijah, in all probability, did not long survive the delivery of this last prophecy; but we are not informed of the time and manner of his death.

AHIKAM, the son of Shaphan, and father of Gedaliah. He was sent by Josiah, king of Judah, to Huldah the prophetess, 2 Kings xxii, 12, to consult her concerning the book of the law, which had been found in the temple.

AHIMAAZ, the son of Zadok, the high priest. Ahimaaz succeeded his father under the reign of Solomon. He performed a very important piece of service for David during the war with Absalom. While his father Zadok was in Jerusalem, 2 Sam. xv, 29, Ahimaaz and Jonathan continued without the city, xvii, 17, near En-Rogel, or the fountain of Rogel; thither a maid servant came to tell them the resolution which had been taken in Absalom's council: whereupon they immediately departed to give the king intelligence. But being discovered by a young lad who gave information concerning them to Absalom, that prince sent orders to pursue them: Ahimaaz and Jonathan, fearing to be taken, retired to a man's house at Baharim, in whose court-yard there was a well, wherein they concealed themselves. After the battle, in which Absalom was overcome and slain, xviii, Ahimaaz desired leave of Joab to carry the news thereof to David. But instead of him Joab sent Cushi to carry the news, and told Ahimaaz that he would send him to the king upon some other occasion; but soon after Cushi was departed, Ahimaaz applied again to Joab, praying to be permitted to run after Cushi; and, having obtained leave, he ran by the way of the plain, and outran Cushi. He was succeeded in the priesthood by his son Azariah.

AHIMELECH. He was the son of Ahitub, and brother of Ahia, whom he succeeded in the high priesthood. He is called Abiathar, Mark ii, 26. During his priesthood the tabernacle was at Nob, where Ahimelech, with other priests, had their habitation. David, being informed by his friend Jonathan that Saul was determined to destroy him, thought it prudent to retire. He therefore went to Nob, to the high priest Ahimelech, who gave him the shew bread, and the sword of Goliath. One day, when Saul was complaining of his officers, that no one was affected with his misfortunes, or gave him any intelligence of what was carrying on against him, 1 Sam. xxii, 9, &c, Doeg related to him what had occurred when David came to Ahimelech the high priest. On this information, Saul convened the priests, and having charged them with the crime of treason, ordered his guards to slay them, which they refusing to do, Doeg, who had been their accuser, at the king's command became their executioner, and with his sacrilegious hand massacred no less than eighty-five of them; the Septuagint and Syriac versions make the number of priests slain by Doeg three hundred and five. Nor did Saul stop here; but, sending a party to Nob, he commanded them to slay men, women, and children, and even cattle, with the edge of the sword. Only one son of Ahimelech, named Abiathar, escaped the carnage and fled to David.

AHITHOPHEL, a native of Giloh, who, after having been David's counsellor, joined in the rebellion of Absalom, and assisted him with his advice. Hushai, the friend of David, was employed to counteract the counsels of Ahithophel, and to deprive Absalom, under a pretence of serving him, of the advantage that was likely to result from the measures which he proposed. One of these measures was calculated to render David irreconcilable, and was immediately adopted; and the other to secure, or to slay him. Before the last counsel was followed, Hushai's advice was desired; and he recommended their assembling together the whole force of Israel, putting Absalom at their head, and overwhelming David by their number. The treacherous counsel of Hushai was preferred to that of Ahithophel; with which the latter being disgusted he hastened to his house at Giloh, where he put an end to his life. He probably foresaw Absalom's defeat, and dreaded the punishment which would be inflicted on himself as a traitor, when David was resettled on the throne. A. M. 2981. B. C. 1023. 2 Sam. xv, xvii.

AHOLIBAH. This and Aholah are two feigned names made use of by Ezekiel, xxiii, 4, to denote the two kingdoms of Judah and Samaria. Aholah and Aholibah are represented as two sisters of Egyptian extraction. Aholah stands for Samaria, and Aholibah for Jerusalem. The first signifies a TENT, and the second, MY TENT IS IN HER. They both prostituted themselves to the Egyptians and Assyrians, in imitating their abominations and idolatries; for which reason the Lord abandoned them to those very people for whose evil practices they had shown so passionate an affection. They were carried into captivity, and reduced to the severest servitude.

AI, called by the **LXX**, Gai, by Josephus Aina, and by others Ajah, a town of Palestine, situate west of Bethel, and at a small distance north-west of Jericho. The three thousand men, first sent by Joshua to reduce this city, were repulsed, on account of the sin of Achan, who had violated the anathema pronounced against Jericho, by appropriating a part of the spoil. After the expiation of this offence, the whole army of Israel marched against Ai, with orders to treat that city as Jericho had been treated, with this difference, that the plunder was to be given to the army. Joshua, having appointed an ambush of thirty thousand men, marched against the city, and by a feigned retreat, drew out the king of Ai with his troops; and upon a signal given by elevating his shield on the top of a pike, the men in ambush entered the city and set fire to it. Thus the soldiers of Ai, placed between two divisions of Joshua's army, were all destroyed; the king alone being preserved for a more ignominious death on a gibbet, where he hung till sunset. The spoil of the place was afterward divided among the Israelites. The men appointed for ambush are, in one place, said to be thirty thousand, and in another five thousand. For reconciling this apparent contradiction, most commentators have generally supposed, that there were two bodies placed in ambuscade between Bethel and Ai, one of twenty-five thousand and the other of five thousand men; the latter being probably a detachment from the thirty thousand first sent, and ordered to lie as near to the city as possible. Masius allows only five thousand men for the ambuscade, and twenty-five thousand for the attack.

AICHMALOTARCH, Ἀιχμαλοτάρχης signifies THE PRINCE OF THE CAPTIVITY, or CHIEF OF THE CAPTIVES. The Jews pretend that this was the title of him who had the government of their people during the captivity of Babylon; and they believe these princes or governors to have been constantly of the tribe of Judah, and family of David. But they give no satisfactory proof of the real existence of these Aichmalotarchs. There was no prince of the captivity before the end of the second century, from which period the office continued till the eleventh century. The princes of the captivity resided at Babylon, where they were installed with great ceremony, held courts of justice, &c, and were set over the eastern Jews, or those settled in Babylon, Chaldæa, Assyria, and Persia. Thus they affected to restore the splendour of their ancient monarchy, and in this view the following account may be amusing. The ceremonial of the installation is thus described: The spiritual heads of the people, the masters of the learned schools, the elders, and the people, assembled in great multitudes within a stately chamber, adorned with rich curtains, in Babylon, where, during his days of splendour, the Resch-Glutha fixed his residence. The prince was seated on a lofty throne. The heads of the schools of Sura and Pumbeditha on his right hand and left. These chiefs of the learned men then delivered an address, exhorting the new monarch not to abuse his power; and reminded him that he was called to slavery rather than to sovereignty, for he was prince of a captive people. On the next Thursday he was inaugurated by the laying on of hands, and the sound of trumpets, and acclamations. He was escorted to his palace with great pomp, and received magnificent presents from all his subjects. On the Sabbath all the principal people being assembled before his house, he placed himself at their head, and, with his face covered with a silken veil, proceeded to the synagogue. Benedictions and hymns of thanksgiving announced his entrance. They then brought him the book of the law, out of which he read the first line, afterward he addressed the assembly, with his eyes closed out of respect. He exhorted them to charity, and set the example by offering liberal alms to the poor. The ceremony closed with new acclamations, and prayers to God that, under the new prince, he would be pleased to put an end to their calamities. The prince gave his blessing to the people, and prayed for each province, that it might be preserved from war and famine. He concluded his orisons in a low voice, lest his prayer should be repeated to the jealous ears of the native monarchs, for he prayed for the restoration of the kingdom of Israel, which could not rise but on the ruins of their empire. The prince returned to his palace, where he gave a splendid banquet to the chief persons of the community. After that day he lived in a sort of stately oriental seclusion, never quitting his palace, except to go to the schools of the learned, where, as he entered, the whole assembly rose and continued standing, till he took his seat. He sometimes paid a visit to the native sovereign in Babylon (Bagdad.) This probably refers to a somewhat later period. On these great occasions his imperial host sent his own chariot for his guest; but the prince of the captivity dared not accept the invidious distinction, he walked in humble and submissive modesty behind the chariot. Yet his own state was by no means wanting in splendour: he was arrayed in cloth of gold; fifty guards marched before him; all the Jews who met him on the way paid their homage, and fell behind into his train. He was received by the eunuchs, who conducted him to the throne, while one of his officers, as he marched slowly along, distributed gold and silver on all sides. As the prince approached the imperial throne, he prostrated himself on the ground, in token of vassalage. The eunuchs raised him and placed him on the left hand of the sovereign. After the first salutation, the prince represented the grievances, or discussed the affairs, of his people.

The court of the Resch-Glutha is described as splendid. In imitation of his Persian master, he had his officers, counsellors, and cup-bearers; and rabbins were appointed as satraps over the different communities. This state, it is probable, was maintained by a tribute raised from the body of the people, and substituted for that which, in ancient times was paid for the temple in Jerusalem. His subjects in Babylonia were many of them wealthy.

AIJALON, a city of the Canaanites; the valley adjoining to which is memorable in sacred history from the miracle of Joshua, in arresting the course of the sun and moon, that the Israelites might have sufficient light to pursue their enemies, Joshua x, 12, 13. Aijalon was afterward a Levitical city, and belonged to the tribe of Dan; who did not, however, drive out the Amorite inhabitants, Judges i, 35.

AIR, that thin, fluid, elastic, transparent, ponderous, compressible body which surrounds the terraqueous globe to a considerable height. In Scripture it is sometimes used for HEAVEN; as, "the birds of the air;" "the birds of heaven." To "beat the air," and "to speak to the air," 1 Cor. ix, 26, signify to fatigue ourselves in vain, and to speak to no purpose. "The prince of the power of the air" is the head and chief of the evil spirits, with which both Jews and Heathens thought the air was filled.

ALABASTER, Ἀλάβαςρον, the name of a genus of fossils nearly allied to marble. It is a bright elegant stone, sometimes of a snowy whiteness. It may be cut freely, and is capable of a fine polish; and, being of a soft nature, it is wrought into any form or figure with ease. Vases or cruises were anciently made of it, wherein to preserve odoriferous liquors and ointments. Pliny and others represent it as peculiarly proper for this purpose; and the druggists in Egypt have, at this day, vessels made of it, in which they keep their medicines and perfumes.

In Matt. xxvi, 6, 7, we read that Jesus being at table in Bethany, in the house of Simon the leper, a woman came thither and poured an alabaster box of ointment on his head. St. Mark adds, "She brake the box," which merely refers to the seal upon the vase which closed it, and kept the perfume from evaporating. This had never been removed, but was on this occasion broken, that is, first opened.

ALBIGENSES. See Waldenses.

ALEPH, א, the name of the first letter in the Hebrew alphabet, from which the alpha of the Syrians and Greeks was formed. This word signifies, PRINCE, CHIEF, or THOUSAND, expressing, as it were, a leading number.

ALEXANDER, commonly called the Great, son and successor of Philip, king of Macedon, is denoted in the prophecies of Daniel by a leopard with four wings, signifying his great strength, and the unusual rapidity of his conquests, Dan. vii, 6; and by a one-horned he-goat running over the earth so swiftly as not to touch it, attacking a ram with two horns, overthrowing him, and trampling him under foot, without any being able to rescue him, Dan. viii, 4–7. The he-goat prefigured Alexander; the ram, Darius Codomannus, the last of the Persian kings. In the statue beheld by Nebuchadnezzar in his dream, Dan. ii, 39, the belly of brass was the emblem of Alexander. He was appointed by God to destroy the Persian empire, and to substitute in its room the Grecian monarchy.

Alexander succeeded his father Philip, A. M. 3668, and B. C. 336. He was chosen, by the Greeks, general of their troops against the Persians, and entered Asia at the head of thirty-four thousand men, A. M. 3670. In one campaign, he subdued almost all Asia Minor; and afterward defeated, in the narrow passes which led from Syria to Cilicia, the army of Darius, which consisted of four hundred thousand foot, and one hundred thousand horse. Darius fled, and left in the hands of the conqueror, his camp, baggage, children, wife, and mother.

After subduing Syria, Alexander came to Tyre; and the Tyrians refusing him entrance into their city, he besieged it. At the same time he wrote to Jaddus, high priest of the Jews, that he expected to be acknowledged by him, and to receive from him the same submission which had hitherto been paid to the king of Persia. Jaddus refusing to comply under the plea of having sworn fidelity to Darius, Alexander resolved to march against Jerusalem, when he had reduced Tyre. After a long siege, this city was taken and sacked; and Alexander entered Palestine, A. M. 3672, and subjected it to his obedience. As he was marching against Jerusalem, the Jews became greatly alarmed, and had recourse to prayers and sacrifices. The Lord, in a dream, commanded Jaddus to open the gates to the conqueror, and, at the head of his people, dressed in his pontifical ornaments, and attended by the priests in their robes, to advance and meet the Macedonian king. Jaddus obeyed; and Alexander perceiving this company approaching, hastened toward the high priest, whom he saluted. He then adored God, whose name was engraven on a thin plate of gold, worn by the high priest upon his forehead. The kings of Syria who accompanied him, and the great officers about Alexander, could not comprehend the meaning of his conduct. Parmenio alone ventured to ask him why he adored the Jewish high priest; Alexander replied, that he paid this respect to God, and not to the high priest. "For," added he, "whilst I was yet in Macedonia, I saw the God of the Jews, who appeared to me in the same form and dress as the high priest at present, and who encouraged me and commanded me to march boldly into Asia, promising that he would be my guide, and give me the empire of the Persians. As soon, therefore, as I perceived this habit, I recollected the vision, and understood that my undertaking was favoured by God, and that under his protection I might expect prosperity."

Having said this, Alexander accompanied Jaddus to Jerusalem, where he offered sacrifices in the temple according to the directions of the high priest. Jaddus is said to have showed him the prophecies of Daniel, in which the destruction of the Persian empire by Alexander is declared. The king was therefore confirmed in his opinion, that God had chosen him to execute this great work. At his departure, Alexander bade the Jews ask of him what they would. The high priest desired only the liberty of living under his government according to their own laws, and an exemption from tribute every seventh year, because in that year the Jews neither tilled their grounds, nor reaped their fruits. With this request Alexander readily complied.

Having left Jerusalem, Alexander visited other cities of Palestine, and was every where received with great testimonies of friendship and submission. The Samaritans who dwelt at Sichem, and were apostates from the Jewish religion, observing how kindly Alexander had treated the Jews, resolved to say that they also were by religion Jews. For it was their practice, when they saw the affairs of the Jews in a prosperous state, to boast that they were descended from Manasseh and Ephraim; but when they thought it their interest to say the contrary, they failed not to affirm, and even to swear, that they were not related to the Jews. They came, therefore, with many demonstrations of joy, to meet Alexander, as far almost as the territories of Jerusalem. Alexander commended their zeal; and the Sichemites entreated him to visit their temple and city. Alexander promised this at his return; but as they petitioned him for the same privileges as the Jews, he asked them if they were Jews. They replied, they were Hebrews, and were called by the

Phœnicians, Sichemites. Alexander said that he had granted this exemption only to the Jews, but that at his return he would inquire into the affair, and do them justice.

This prince having conquered Egypt, and regulated it, gave orders for the building of the city of Alexandria, and departed thence, about spring, in pursuit of Darius. Passing through Palestine, he was informed that the Samaritans, in a general insurrection, had killed Andromachus, governor of Syria and Palestine, who had come to Samaria to regulate some affairs. This action greatly incensed Alexander, who loved Andromachus. He therefore commanded all those who were concerned in his murder to be put to death, and the rest to be banished from Samaria; and settled a colony of Macedonians in their room. What remained of their lands he gave to the Jews, and exempted them from the payment of tribute. The Samaritans who escaped this calamity, retired to Sichem, at the foot of mount Gerizim, which afterward became their capital. Lest the eight thousand men of this nation, who were in the service of Alexander, and had accompanied him since the siege of Tyre, if permitted to return to their own country, should renew the spirit of rebellion, he sent them into Thebais, the most remote southern province of Egypt, where he assigned them lands.

Alexander, after defeating Darius in a pitched battle, and subduing all Asia and the Indies with incredible rapidity, gave himself up to intemperance. Having drunk to excess, he fell sick and died, after he had obliged "all the world to be quiet before him," 1 Macc. i, 3. Being sensible that his end was near, he sent for the grandees of his court, and declared that "he gave the empire to the most deserving." Some affirm that he regulated the succession by a will. The author of the first book of Maccabees says, that he divided his kingdom among his generals while he was living, 1 Macc. i, 7. This he might do; or he might express his foresight of what actually took place after his death. It is certain, that a partition was made of Alexander's dominions among the four principal officers of his army, and that the empire which he founded in Asia subsisted for many ages. Alexander died, A. M. 3684, and B. C. 323, in the thirty-third year of his age, and the twelfth of his reign. The above particulars of Alexander are here introduced because, from his invasion of Palestine, the intercourse of the Jews with the Greeks became intimate, and influenced many events of their subsequent history.

On the account above given of the interview between Alexander and the Jewish high priest, by Josephus, many doubts have been cast by critics. But the sudden change of his feelings toward them, and the favour with which the nation was treated by him, render the story not improbable.

ALEXANDRIA, a famous city of Egypt, and, during the reign of the Ptolemies, the regal capital of that kingdom. It was founded by Alexander the Great: who being struck with the advantageous situation of the spot where the city afterward stood, ordered its immediate erection; drew the plan of the city himself, and peopled it with colonies of Greeks and Jews: to which latter people, in particular, he gave great encouragement. They were, in fact, made free citizens, and had all the privileges of Macedonians granted to them; which liberal policy contributed much to the rise and prosperity of the new city; for this enterprising and commercial people knew much better than either the Greeks or the Egyptians how to turn the happy situation of Alexandria to the best account. The fall of Tyre happening about the same time, the trade of that city was soon drawn to Alexandria, which became the centre of commercial intercourse between the east and the west; and in process of time grew to such an extent, in magnitude and wealth, as to be second in point of population and magnificence to none but Rome itself.

Alexandria owed much of its celebrity as well as its population to the Ptolemies. Ptolemy Soter, one of Alexander's captains, who, after the death of this monarch, was first governor of Egypt, and afterward assumed the title of king, made this city the place of his residence, about B. C. 304. This prince founded an academy, called the Museum, in which a society of learned men devoted themselves to philosophical studies, and the improvement of all the other sciences; and he also gave them a library, which was prodigiously increased by his successors. He likewise induced the merchants of Syria and Greece to reside in this city, and to make it a principal mart of their commerce. His son and successor, Ptolemy Philadelphus, pursued the designs of his father.

In the hands of the Romans, the successors of the Macedonians in the government of Egypt, the trade of Alexandria continued to flourish, until luxury and licentiousness paved the way, as in every similar instance, for its overthrow.

Alexandria, together with the rest of Egypt, passed from the dominion of the Romans to that of the Saracens. With this event, the sun of Alexandria may be said to have set: the blighting hand of Islamism was laid on it; and although the genius and the resources of such a city could not be immediately destroyed, it continued to languish until the passage by the Cape of Good Hope, in the fifteenth century, gave a new channel to the trade which for so many centuries had been its support; and at this day, Alexandria, like most eastern cities, presents a mixed spectacle of ruins and wretchedness,--of fallen greatness and enslaved human beings.

Some idea may be formed of the extent and grandeur of Alexandria, by the boast made by Amrou: "I have taken," said he, "the great city of the west. It is impossible for me to enumerate the variety of its riches and beauty. I shall content myself with observing, that it contains four thousand palaces, four thousand baths, four hundred theatres or places of amusement, twelve thousand shops for the sale of vegetable foods, and forty thousand tributary Jews."

It was in Alexandria chiefly that the Grecian philosophy was engrafted upon the stock of ancient oriental wisdom. The Egyptian method of teaching by allegory was peculiarly favourable to such a union: and we may well suppose that when Alexander, in order to preserve by the arts of peace that extensive empire which he had obtained by the force of arms, endeavoured to incorporate the customs of the Greeks with those of the Persian, Indian, and other eastern nations, the opinions as well as the manners of this feeble and obsequious race would, in a great measure, be accommodated to those of their conquerors. This influence of the Grecian upon the oriental philosophy continued long after the time of Alexander, and was one principal occasion of the confusion of opinions which occurs in the history of the Alexandrian and Christian schools. Alexander, when he built the city of Alexandria, with a determination to make it the seat of his empire, and peopled it with emigrants from various countries, opened a new mart of philosophy, which emulated the fame of Athens itself. A general indulgence was granted to the promiscuous crowd assembled in this rising city, whether Egyptians, Grecians, Jews, or others, to profess their respective systems of philosophy without molestation. The consequence was, that Egypt was soon filled with religious and philosophical sectaries of every kind; and particularly, that almost every Grecian sect found an advocate and professor in Alexandria. The family of the Ptolemies, as we have seen, who after Alexander obtained the government of Egypt, from motives of policy encouraged this new establishment. Ptolemy Lagus, who had obtained the crown of Egypt by usurpation, was particularly careful to secure the interest of the Greeks in his favour, and with this view invited people from every part of Greece to settle in Egypt, and removed the schools of Athens to Alexandria. This enlightened prince spared no pains to raise the literary, as well as the civil, military, and commercial credit of his country. Under the patronage first of the Egyptian princes, and afterward of the Roman emperors, Alexandria long continued to enjoy great celebrity as the seat of learning, and to send forth eminent philosophers of every sect to distant countries. It remained a school of learning, as well as a commercial emporium, till it was taken, and plundered of its literary treasures by the Saracens. Philosophy, during this period, suffered a grievous corruption from the attempt which was made by philosophers of different sects and countries, Grecian, Egyptian, and oriental, who were assembled in Alexandria, to frame, from their different tenets, one general system of opinions. The respect which had long been universally paid to the schools of Greece, and the honours with which they were now adorned by the Egyptian princes, induced other wise men, and even the Egyptian priests and philosophers themselves, to submit to this innovation. Hence arose a heterogeneous mass of opinions, under the name of the ECLECTIC PHILOSOPHY, and which was the foundation of endless confusion, error, and absurdity, not only in the Alexandrian school, but among Jews and Christians; producing among the former that specious kind of philosophy, which they called their CABALA, and among the latter innumerable corruptions of the Christian faith.

At Alexandria there was, in a very early period of the Christian æra, a Christian school of considerable eminence. St. Jerome says, the school at Alexandria had been in being from the time of St. Mark. Pantænus, placed by Lardner at the year 192, presided in it. St. Clement of Alexandria succeeded Pantænus in this school about the year 190; and he was succeeded by Origen. The extensive commerce of Alexandria, and its proximity to Palestine, gave an easy entrance to the new religion, and when Adrian visited Egypt, he found a church composed of Jews and Greeks, sufficiently important to attract the notice of that inquisitive prince. The theological system of Plato was introduced into both the philosophical and Christian schools of Alexandria; and of course many of his sentiments and expressions were blended with the opinions and language of the professors and teachers of Christianity.

Alexandria was the source, and for some time the principal stronghold, of Arianism; which had its name from its founder, Arius, a presbyter of the church of this city, about the year 315. His doctrines were condemned by a council held here in the year 320; and afterward by a general council of three hundred and eighty fathers, held at Nice, by order of Constantine, in 325. These doctrines, however, which suited the reigning taste for disputative theology, and the pride and self-sufficiency of nominal Christians, better than the unsophisticated simplicity of the Gospel, spread widely and rapidly notwithstanding. Arius was steadfastly opposed by the celebrated Athanasius, bishop of Alexandria, the intrepid champion of the catholic faith, who was raised to the archiepiscopal throne of Alexandria in 326.

This city was, in 415, distinguished by a fierce persecution of the Jews by the patriarch Cyril. They who had enjoyed the rights of citizens, and the freedom of religious worship, for seven hundred years, ever since the foundation of the city, incurred the hatred of this ecclesiastic; who, in his zeal for the extermination of heretics of every kind, pulled down their synagogues, plundered their property, and expelled them, to the number of forty thousand, from the city.

It was in a ship belonging to the port of Alexandria, that St. Paul sailed from Myra, a city of Lycia, on his way to Rome, Acts xxvii, 5, 6. Alexandria was also the native place of Apollos.

ALEXANDRIAN LIBRARY. This celebrated collection of books was first founded by Ptolemy Soter, for the use of the academy, or society of learned men, which he had founded at Alexandria. Beside the books which he procured, his son, Ptolemy Philadelphus, added many more, and left in this library at his death a hundred thousand volumes; and the succeeding princes of this race enlarged it still more, till at length the books lodged in it amounted to the number of seven hundred thousand volumes. The method by which they are said to have collected these books was this: they seized all the books that were brought by the Greeks or other foreigners into Egypt, and sent them to the academy, or museum, where they were transcribed by persons employed for that purpose. The transcripts were then delivered to the proprietors, and the originals laid up in the library. Ptolemy Euergetes, for instance, borrowed of the Athenians the works of Sophocles, Euripides, and Æschylus, and only returned them the copies, which he caused to be transcribed in as beautiful a manner as possible; the originals he retained for his own library, presenting the Athenians with fifteen talents for the exchange, that is, with three thousand pounds sterling and upwards. As the museum was at first in the quarter of the city called Bruchion, the library was placed there; but when the number of books amounted to four hundred thousand volumes, another library, within the Serapeum, was erected by way of supplement to it, and, on that account, called the daughter of the former. The books lodged in this increased to the number of three hundred thousand volumes; and these two made up the number of seven hundred thousand volumes, of which the royal libraries of the Ptolemies were said to consist. In the war which Julius Cæsar waged with the inhabitants of Alexandria, the library of Bruchion was accidentally, but unfortunately, burnt. But the library in Serapeum still remained, and there Cleopatra deposited the two hundred thousand volumes of the Pergamean library with which she was presented by Marc Antony. These, and others added to them from time to time, rendered the new library more numerous and considerable than the former; and though it was plundered more than once during the revolutions which happened in the Roman empire, yet it was as frequently supplied with the same number of books, and continued, for many ages, to be of great fame and use, till it was burnt by the Saracens, A. D. 642. Abulpharagius, in his history of the tenth dynasty, gives the following account of this catastrophe: John Philoponus, surnamed the Grammarian, a famous Peripatetic philosopher, being at Alexandria when the city was taken by the Saracens, was admitted to familiar intercourse with Amrou, the Arabian general, and presumed to solicit a gift, inestimable in his opinion, but contemptible in that of the barbarians; and this was the royal library. Amrou was inclined to gratify his wish, but his rigid integrity scrupled to alienate the least object without the consent of the caliph. He accordingly wrote to Omar, whose well known answer was dictated by the ignorance of a fanatic: "If these writings of the Greeks agree with the Koran, or book of God, they are useless, and need not be preserved; if they disagree, they are pernicious, and ought to be destroyed." The sentence of destruction was executed with blind obedience: the volumes of paper or parchment were distributed to the four thousand baths of the city; and such was their number, that six months were barely sufficient for the consumption of this precious fuel.

ALGUM, אלגם or אלגומים, 1 Kings x, 11, 12. This is the name of a kind of wood, or tree, large quantities of which were brought by the fleet of Solomon from Ophir, of which he made pillars for the house of the Lord, and for his own palace; also musical instruments. See Almug.

ALLEGORY, a figure in rhetoric, whereby we make use of terms which, in their proper signification, mean something else than what they are brought to denote; or it is a figure whereby we say one thing, expecting it shall be understood of another, to which it alludes; or which, under the literal sense of the words, conceals a foreign or distant meaning. An allegory is, properly, a continued metaphor, or a series of several metaphors in one or more sentences. Such is that beautiful allegory in Horace, lib. i, Od. 14.

"O NAVIS, REFERENT IN MARE TE NOVI

FLUCTUS," *&c.*

[O ship, shall new billows drive thee again to sea, &c.]

Where the ship is usually held to stand for the republic; waves, for civil war; port, for peace and concord; oars, for soldiers; and mariners for magistrates. Thus, also, in Prior's Henry and Emma, Emma describes her constancy to Henry in the following allegorical manner:--

"Did I but purpose to embark with thee

On the smooth surface of a summer's sea,

While gentle zephyrs play with prosperous gales,

And fortune's favour fills the swelling sails;

But would forsake the ship, and make the shore,

When the winds whistle, and the tempests roar?"

Cicero, likewise, speaking of himself, in Pison. c. 9, tom. vi, p. 187, uses this allegorical language: "Nor was I so timorous, that, after I had steered the ship of the state through the greatest storms and waves, and brought her safe into port, I should fear the cloud of your forehead, or your colleague's pestilential breath. I saw other winds, I perceived other storms, I did not withdraw from other impending tempests; but I exposed myself singly to them for the common safety." Here the state is compared to a ship, and all the things said of it under that image, are expressed in metaphors made use of to denote the dangers with which it had been threatened. We have also a very fine example of an allegory in Psalm lxxx; in which the people of Israel are represented under the image of a vine, and the figure is supported throughout with great correctness and beauty. Whereas, if, instead of describing the vine as wasted by the boar from the wood, and devoured by the wild beasts of the field, the Psalmist had said, it was afflicted by Heathens, or overcome by enemies, which is the real meaning, the figurative and the literal meaning would have been blended, and the allegory ruined. The learned Bishop Lowth, *De Sacrâ Poesi Hebræorum, Præl.* 10, 11, has specified three forms of allegory that occur in sacred poetry. The first is that which rhetoricians call a continued metaphor. When several metaphors succeed each other, they alter the form of the composition; and this succession has very properly, in reference to the etymology of the word, been denominated by the Greeks αλληγορια, an allegory; although Aristotle, instead of considering it as a new species of figure, has referred it to the class of metaphors. The principle of allegory in this sense of the term, and of the simple metaphor, is the same; nor is it an easy matter to restrict each to its proper limit, and to mark the precise termination of the one, and the commencement of the other. This eminently judicious critic observes, that when the Hebrew poets use the congenial figures of metaphor, allegory, and comparison, particularly in the prophetic poetry, they adopt a peculiar mode of doing it, and seldom regulate the imagery which they introduce by any fixed principle or standard. Not satisfied with a simple metaphor, they often run it into an allegory, or blend with it a direct comparison. The allegory sometimes follows, and sometimes precedes the simile: to this is added a frequent change of imagery, as well as of persons and tenses; and thus are displayed an energy and boldness, both of expression and meaning, which are unconfined by any stated rules, and which mark the discriminating genius of the Hebrew poetry. Thus, in Gen. xlix, 9, "Judah is a lion's whelp;" this metaphor is immediately drawn out into an allegory, with a change of person: "From the prey, my son, thou art gone up," that is, to the mountains, which is understood; and in the succeeding sentences the person is again changed, the image is gradually advanced, and the metaphor is joined with a comparison that is repeated.

"He stoopeth down, he coucheth as a lion;

And as a lioness; who shall rouse him?"

A similar instance occurs in the prophecy, recorded in Psalm cx, 3, which explicitly foretels the abundant increase of the Gospel on its first promulgation. This kind of allegory, however, sometimes assumes a more regular and perfect form, and then occupies the whole subject and compass of the discourse. An example of this kind occurs in Solomon's well known allegory, Eccles. xii, 2–6, in which old age is so admirably depicted. There is also, in Isaiah xxviii, 24–29, an allegory, which, with no less elegance of imagery, is more simple and regular, as well as more just and complete, both in the form and the method of treating it. Another kind of allegory is that which, in the proper and more restricted sense, may be called a parable; and consists of a continued narration of some fictitious event, accommodated, by way of similitude, to the illustration of some important truth. The Greeks call these allegories αινοι or apologues, and the Latins FABULÆ, or fables. (See PARABLE.) The third species of allegory, which often occurs in the prophetic poetry, is that in which a double meaning is couched under the same words, or when the same discourse, differently interpreted, designates different events, dissimilar in their nature, and remote as to time. These different relations are denominated the literal and mystical senses. This kind of allegory, which the learned prelate calls mystical, seems to derive its origin from the principles of the Jewish religion; and it differs from the two former species in a variety of respects. In these allegories the writer may adopt any imagery that is most suitable to his fancy or inclination; but the only proper materials for this allegory must be supplied from the sacred rites of the Hebrews themselves; and it can only be introduced in relation to such things as are immediately connected with the Jewish religion, or their immediate opposites. The former kinds partake of the common privileges of poetry; but the mystical allegory has its foundation in the nature of the Jewish economy, and is adapted solely to the poetry of the Hebrews. Besides, in the other forms of allegory, the exterior or ostensible imagery is mere fiction, and the truth lies altogether in the interior or remote sense; but in this allegory each idea is equally agreeable to truth. The exterior or ostensible image is itself a reality; and although it sustains another character, it does not wholly lay aside its own. There is also a great variety in the use and conduct of the mystical allegory; in the modes in which the corresponding images are arranged, and in which they are obscured or eclipsed by one another. Sometimes the obvious or literal sense is so prominent and conspicuous, both in the words and sentiments, that the remote or figurative sense is scarcely permitted to glimmer through it. On the other hand, the figurative sense is more frequently found to beam forth with so much perspicuity and lustre, that the literal sense is quite cast into the shade, or becomes indiscernible. Sometimes the principal or figurative idea is exhibited to the attentive eye with a constant and equal light; and sometimes it unexpectedly glares upon us, and breaks forth with sudden and astonishing coruscations, like a flash of lightning bursting from the clouds. But the mode or form of this figure which possesses the chief beauty and elegance, is, when the two images, equally conspicuous, run, as it were, parallel throughout the whole poem, mutually illustrating and correspondent to each other. The learned author has illustrated these observations by instances selected from Psalms ii, and lxxii. He adds, that the mystical allegory is, on account of the obscurity resulting from the nature of the figure, and the style of the composition, so agreeable to the nature of the prophecy, that it is the form which it generally, and indeed lawfully, assumes, as best adapted to the prediction of future events. It describes events in a manner exactly conformable to the intention of prophecy; that is, in a dark, disguised, and intricate manner, sketching out, in a general way, their form and outline; and seldom descending to a minuteness of description and exactness of detail.

ALLELUIA, or Hallelu-jah, הללו־יה, PRAISE THE LORD; or, PRAISE TO THE LORD: compounded of הללו, PRAISE YE, and יה, THE LORD. This word occurs at the beginning, or at the end, of many Psalms. Alleluia was sung on solemn days of rejoicing: "And all her streets shall sing Alleluia," says Tobit, speaking of the rebuilding of Jerusalem, Tob. xiii, 18. St. John, in the Revelation, xix, 1, 3, 4, 6, says, "I heard a great voice of much people in heaven, who cried, Alleluia; and the four living creatures fell down, and worshipped God, saying, Alleluia." This expression of joy and praise was transferred from the synagogue to the church. At the funeral of Fabiola, "several psalms were sung with loud alleluias," says Jerom, in *Epitaphio Paulæ*, "The monks of Palestine were awaked at their midnight watchings, with the singing of alleluias." It is still occasionally used in devotional psalmody.

ALMAH, עלמה, a Hebrew word signifying properly A VIRGIN, a young woman unacquainted with man. In this sense it occurs in the famous passage of Isaiah, vii, 14: "Behold a virgin shall conceive and bear a son." The Hebrew has no term that more properly signifies a virgin than ALMAH. St. Jerom, in his commentary on this passage, observes, that the Prophet declined using the word BETHAUL which signifies any young woman, or young person, but employed the term ALMAH, which denotes a virgin never seen by man. This is the import of the word ALMAH, which is derived from a root which signifies TO CONCEAL. It is very well known, that young women in the east do not appear in public, but are shut up in their houses, and their mothers' apartments, like nuns. The Chaldee paraphrast and the Septuagint translate ALMAH "a virgin;" and Akiba, the famous rabbin, who was a great enemy to Christ and Christians, and lived in the second century, understands it in the same manner. The Apostles and Evangelists, and the Jews of our Saviour's time, explained it in the same sense, and expected a Messiah born of a virgin.

The Jews, that they may obscure this plain text, and weaken this proof of the truth of the Christian religion, pretend that the Hebrew word signifies a young woman, and not a virgin. But this corrupt translation is easily confuted. 1. Because this word constantly denotes a virgin in all other passages of Scripture in which it is used. 2. From the intent of the passage, which was to confirm their faith by a strange and wonderful sign. It surely could be no wonder, that a young woman should conceive a child; but it was a very extraordinary circumstance that a virgin should conceive and bear a son.

ALMIGHTY, an attribute of the Deity, Gen. xvii, 1. The Hebrew name, שדי, SHADDAI, signifies also ALL-SUFFICIENT, or ALL-BOUNTIFUL. See Gen. xxviii, 3; xxxv, 11; xliii, 14; xlix, 25. Of the omnipotence of God, we have a most ample revelation in the Scriptures, expressed in the most sublime language. From the annunciation by Moses of a divine existence who was "in the beginning," before all things, the very first step is to the display of his almighty power in the creation out of nothing, and the immediate arrangement in order and perfection, of the "HEAVEN AND THE EARTH;" by which is meant, not this globe only with its atmosphere, or even with its own celestial system, but the universe itself; for "HE MADE THE STARS ALSO." We are thus at once placed in the presence of an agent of unbounded power; for we must all feel that a being which could create such a world as this, must, beyond all comparison, possess a power greater than any which we experience in ourselves, than any which we observe in other visible agents, and to which we are not authorized by our observation or knowledge to assign any limits of space or duration.

2. That the sacred writers should so frequently dwell upon the omnipotence of God, has important reasons which arise out of the very design of the revelation which they were the means of communicating to mankind. Men were to be reminded of their obligations to obedience; and God is therefore constantly exhibited as the Creator, the Preserver, and Lord of all things. His solemn worship and fear were to be enjoined upon them; and, by the manifestation of his works, the veil was withdrawn from his glory and majesty. Idolatry was to be checked and reproved, and the true God was therefore placed in contrast with the limited and powerless gods of the Heathen: "Among the gods of the nations, is there no god like unto thee; neither are there any works like thy works." Finally, he is exhibited as the object of TRUST to creatures constantly reminded by experience of their own infirmity and dependence; and to them it is essential to know, that his power is absolute, unlimited, and irresistible, and that, in a word, he is "mighty to save."

3. In a revelation which was thus designed to awe and control the wicked, and to afford strength of mind and consolation to good men under all circumstances, the omnipotence of God is therefore placed in a great variety of impressive views, and connected with the most striking illustrations.

It is declared by the fact of CREATION, the creation of beings out of NOTHING; which itself, though it had been confined to a single object, however minute, exceeds finite comprehension, and overwhelms the faculties. This with God required no effort: "He spake and it was done, he commanded and it stood fast." The VASTNESS and VARIETY of his works enlarge the conception: "The heavens declare the glory of God, and the firmament showeth his handy work." "He spreadeth out the heavens, and treadeth upon the waves of the sea; he maketh Arcturus, Orion, and Pleiades, and the chambers of the south; he doeth great things, past finding out, yea, and wonders without number. He stretcheth out the north over the empty place, and hangeth the earth upon nothing. He bindeth up the waters in the thick clouds, and the cloud is not rent under them; he hath compassed the waters with bounds until the day and night come to an end." The EASE with which he sustains, orders, and controls the most powerful and unruly of the elements, arrays his omnipotence with an aspect of ineffable dignity and majesty: "By him all things consist." "He brake up for the sea a decreed place, and set bars and doors, and said, Hitherto shalt thou come and no farther, and here shall thy proud waves be stayed." "He looketh to the end of the earth, and seeth under the whole heaven, to make the weight for the winds, to weigh the waters by measure, to make a decree for the rain, and a way for the lightning of the thunder." "Who hath measured the waters in the hollow of his hand, meted out heaven with a span, comprehended the dust of the earth in a measure, and weighed the mountains in scales, and the hills in a balance." The descriptions of the divine power are often TERRIBLE: "The pillars of heaven tremble, and are astonished at his reproof; he divideth the sea by his power." "He removeth the mountains, and they know it not; he overturneth them in his anger; he shaketh the earth out of her place, and the pillars thereof tremble; he commandeth the sun and it riseth not, and sealeth up the stars." The same absolute subjection of creatures to his dominion is seen among the intelligent inhabitants of the material universe; and angels, mortals the most exalted, and evil spirits, are swayed with as much ease as the most passive elements: "He maketh his angels spirits, and his ministers a flame of fire." They veil their faces before his throne, and acknowledge themselves his servants: "It is he that sitteth upon the circle of the earth, and the inhabitants thereof are as grasshoppers," "as the dust of the balance, less than nothing and vanity." "He bringeth princes to nothing." "He setteth up one and putteth down another;" "for the kingdom is the Lord's, and he is governor among the nations." "The angels that sinned he cast down to hell, and delivered them into chains of darkness, to be reserved unto judgment." The closing scenes of this world complete these transcendent conceptions of the majesty and power of God. The dead of all ages rise from their graves at his VOICE: and the sea gives up the dead which are in it. Before his FACE heaven and earth fly away; the stars fall from heaven, and the powers of heaven are shaken. The dead, small and great, stand before God, and are divided as a shepherd divideth the sheep from the goats. The wicked go away into everlasting punishment, but the righteous into life eternal.

4. Of these amazing views of the omnipotence of God, spread almost through every page of the Scriptures, the power lies in their TRUTH. They are not eastern exaggerations, mistaken for sublimity. Every thing in nature answers to them, and renews from age to age the energy of the impression which they cannot but make on the reflecting mind. The order of the astral revolutions indicates the constant presence of an invisible but incomprehensible power. The seas hurl the weight of their billows upon the rising shores, but every where find a "BOUND fixed by a perpetual decree." The tides reach their height; if they flowed on for a few hours, the earth would change places with the bed of the sea; but, under an invisible control, they become refluent. The expression, "He toucheth the mountains and they smoke," is not mere imagery:--every volcano is a testimony of its truth; and earthquakes proclaim, that, before him, "the pillars of the world tremble." Men collected into armies, or populous nations, give us vast ideas of human power; but let an army be placed amidst the sand storms and burning winds of the desert, as, in the east; or, before "HIS FROST," as in our own day in Russia, where one of the mightiest armaments was seen retreating before, or perishing under, an unexpected visitation of snow and storm; or let the utterly helpless state of a populous country which has been visited by famine, or by a resistless pestilential disease, be reflected upon; and we feel that it is scarcely a figure of speech to say, that "all nations before him are LESS THAN NOTHING and VANITY."

5. Nor, in reviewing this doctrine of Scripture, ought the great practical uses made of the omnipotence of God, by the sacred writers, to be overlooked. By them nothing is said for the mere display of knowledge, as in Heathen writers; and we have no speculations without a subservient MORAL. To excite and keep alive in man the fear and worship of God, and to bring him to a felicitous confidence in that almighty power which pervades and controls all things, are the noble ends of those ample displays of the omnipotence of God, which roll through the sacred volume with a sublimity that inspiration only could supply. "Declare his glory among the Heathen, his marvellous works among all nations; for great is the Lord, and greatly to be praised.--Glory and honour are in his presence, and strength and gladness in his place.--Give unto the Lord, ye kindreds of the people, give unto the Lord glory and strength; give unto the Lord the glory due unto his name.--The Lord is my light and my salvation; whom shall I fear?--The Lord is the strength of my life; of whom shall I be afraid? If God be for us, who THEN can be against us? Our help standeth in the name of the Lord, who made heaven and earth.--What time I am afraid, I will trust in thee."--Thus, as one observes, "our natural fears, of which we must have many, remit us to God, and remind us, since we know what God is, to lay hold on his almighty power."

6. Ample, however, as are these views of the power of God, the subject is not exhausted. As, when the Scriptures speak of the eternity of God, they declare it so as to give us a mere glimpse of that fearful peculiarity of the divine nature, that God is the fountain of being to himself, and that he is eternal, because he is the "I am;" so we are taught not to measure God's omnipotence by the actual displays of it which we see around us. These are the MANIFESTATIONS of the fact, but not the MEASURE of the attribute; and should we resort to the discoveries of modern philosophy, which, by the help of instruments, has so greatly enlarged the known boundaries of the visible universe, and add to the stars which are visible to the naked eye, those new exhibitions of the divine power in the nebulous appearances of the heavens which are resolvable into myriads of distinct celestial luminaries, whose immense distances commingle their light before it reaches our eyes; we thus almost infinitely expand the circle of created existence, and enter upon a formerly unknown and overwhelming range of divine operation. But still we are only reminded, that his power is truly ALMIGHTY and MEASURELESS--"Lo, all these are parts of his ways; but how little a portion is known of him, and the thunder of his power who can understand?" It is a mighty conception that we form of a power from which all other power is derived, and to which it is subordinate; which nothing can oppose; which can beat down and annihilate all other power whatever; which operates in the most perfect manner, at once, in an instant, with the utmost ease; but the Scriptures lead us to the contemplation of greater and even unfathomable depths. The omnipotence of God is

inconceivable and boundless. It arises from the infinite perfection of God, that his power can never be actually exhausted; and, in every imaginable instant in eternity, that inexhaustible power of God can, if it please him, be adding either more creatures to those in existence, or greater perfection to them; since "it belongs to self-existent being, to be always full and communicative, and, to the communicated contingent being, to be ever empty and craving."

7. One limitation of the divine power it is true we can conceive, but it detracts nothing from its perfection. Where things in themselves imply a contradiction, as that a body may be extended and not extended, in a certain place and not in it, at the same time; such things cannot be done by God, because contradictions are impossible in their own nature. Nor is it any derogation from the divine power to say, they cannot be done; for as the object of the understanding, of the eye, and the ear, is that which is intelligible, visible, and audible; so the object of power must be that which is possible; and as it is no prejudice to the most perfect understanding, or sight, or hearing, that it does not understand what is not intelligible, or see what is not visible, or hear what is not audible; so neither is it any diminution to the most perfect power, that it does not do what is not possible. In like manner, God cannot do any thing that is repugnant to his other perfections: he cannot lie, nor deceive, nor deny himself; for this would be injurious to his truth. He cannot love sin, nor punish innocence; for this would destroy his holiness and goodness: and therefore to ascribe a power to him that is inconsistent with the rectitude of his nature, is not to magnify but debase him; for all unrighteousness is weakness, a defection from right reason, a deviation from the perfect rule of action, and arises from a want of goodness and power. In a word, since all the attributes of God are essentially the same, a power in him which tends to destroy any other attribute of the divine nature, must be a power destructive of itself. Well, therefore, may we conclude him absolutely omnipotent, who, by being able to effect all things consistent with his perfections, showeth infinite ability, and, by not being able to do any thing repugnant to the same perfections, demonstrates himself subject to no infirmity.

8. Nothing certainly in the finest writings of antiquity, were all their best thoughts collected as to the majesty and power of God, can bear any comparison with the views thus presented to us by divine revelation. Were we to forget, for a moment, what is the fact, that their noblest notions stand connected with fancies and vain speculations which deprive them of their force, still their thoughts never rise so high; the current is broken, the round of lofty conception is not completed, and, unconnected as their views of divine power were with the eternal destiny of man, and the very reason of creation, we never hear in them, as in the Scriptures, "the THUNDER of his power."

ALMOND TREE, לוז. Arabic, LAUZ. Translated HAZEL, Gen. xxx, 37; שקד, rendered ALMOND, Gen. xliii, 11; Exod. xxv, 33, 34; xxxvii, 19, 20; Num. xvii, 8; Eccles. xii, 5; and Jer. i, 11. The first name may be that of the TREE; the other, that of the FRUIT, or NUT.

A tree resembling the peach tree in its leaves and blossoms, but the fruit is longer and more compressed, the outer green coat is thinner and drier when ripe, and the shell of the stone is not so rugged. This stone, or nut, contains a kernel, which is the only esculent part. The whole arrives at maturity in September, when the outer tough cover splits open and discharges the nut. From the circumstance of its blossoming the earliest of any of the trees, beginning as soon as the rigour of winter is past, and before it is in leaf, it has its Hebrew name SHAKAD, which comes from a verb signifying TO MAKE HASTE, TO BE IN A HURRY, or TO AWAKE EARLY. To the forwardness of the almond tree there seems to be a reference in Jeremiah: "The word of the Lord came unto me, saying, Jeremiah, what seest thou? And I said, I see a rod of an almond tree. Then said the Lord unto me, Thou hast well seen: for I will hasten my word to perform it;" or rather, "I am hastening, or watching over my word to fulfil it," Jer. i, 11, 12. In this manner it is rendered by the Seventy; and by the Vulgate, VIGILABO EGO SUPER VERBUM MEUM. [I will watch over my word.] This is the first vision with which the Prophet was honoured; and his attention is roused by a very significant emblem of that severe correction with which the Most High was hastening to visit his people for their iniquity; and from the species of tree to which the rod belonged, he is warned of its near approach. The idea which the appearance of the almond rod suggested to his mind, is confirmed by the exposition of God himself: "I am watching over, or on account of, my word to fulfil it;" and this double mode of instruction, first by emblem, and then by exposition, was certainly intended to make a deeper impression on the mind both of Jeremiah and of the people to whom he was sent.

It is probable that the rods which the princes of Israel bore, were scions of the almond tree, at once the ensign of their office, and the emblem of their vigilance. Such, we know from the testimony of Scripture, was the rod of Aaron; which renders it exceedingly probable, that the rods of the other chiefs were from the same tree.

The hoary head is beautifully compared by Solomon to the almond tree, covered in the earliest days of spring with its snow white flowers, before a single leaf has budded: "The almond tree shall flourish, and the grasshopper shall be a burden, and desire shall fail," Eccl. xii, 5. Man has existed in this world but a few days, when old age begins to appear, sheds its snows upon his head, prematurely nips his hopes, darkens his earthly prospects, and hurries him into the grave.

ALMUG TREE, a certain kind of wood, mentioned 1 Kings, x, 11; 2 Chron. ii, 8; ix, 10, 11. Jerom and the Vulgate render it, LIGNA THYINA, and the Septuagint ξύλα πελεκητὰ, WROUGHT WOOD. Several critics understand it to mean GUMMY WOOD; but a wood abounding in resin must be very unfit for the uses to which this is said to be applied. Celsus queries if it be not the sandal; but Michaelis thinks the particular species of wood to be wholly unknown to us. Dr. Shaw supposes that the almug tree was the cypress; and he observes that the wood of this tree is still used in Italy and other places for violins, harpsichords, and other stringed instruments.

ALOE, עלר, a plant with broad leaves, nearly two inches thick, prickly and serrated. It grows about two feet high. A very bitter gum is extracted from it, used for medicinal purposes, and anciently for embalming dead bodies. Nicodemus is said, John xix, 39, to have brought one hundred pounds' weight of myrrh and aloes to embalm the body of Jesus. The quantity has been exclaimed against by certain Jews, as being enough for fifty bodies. But instead of ἑκατὸν it might originally have been written δέκατον, TEN pounds' weight. However, at the funeral of Herod there were five hundred ἀρωματόφορους, SPICE BEARERS; and at that of R. Gamaliel, eighty pounds of opobalsamum were used.

The wood which God showed Moses, that with it he might sweeten the waters of Marah, is called ALVAH, Exod. xv, 25. The word has some relation to aloe; and some interpreters are of opinion that Moses used a bitter sort of wood, that so the power of God might be the more remarkable. Mr. Bruce mentions a town, or large village, by the name of Elvah. It is thickly planted with trees; is the OASIS PARVA of the ancients; and the last inhabited place to the west that is under the jurisdiction of Egypt. He also observes that the Arabs call a shrub or tree, not unlike our hawthorn, either in wood or flower, by the name of elvah. "It was this," say they, "with which Moses sweetened the waters of Marah; and with this, too, did Kalib Ibn el Walid sweeten those of Elvah, once bitter, and give the place the name of this circumstance." It may be that God directed Moses to the very wood proper for the purpose. M. Neibuhr, when in these parts, inquired after wood capable of this effect, but could gain no information of any such. It will not, however, from hence follow that Moses really used a bitter wood; but, as Providence usually works by the proper and fit means to accomplish its ends, it seems likely that the wood he made use of was, in some degree at least, corrective of that quality which abounded in the water, and so rendered it potable. This seems to have been the opinion of the author of Ecclesiasticus, xxxviii, 5. That other water, also, requires some correction, and that such a correction is applied to it, appears from the custom in Egypt in respect to that of the Nile, which, though somewhat muddy, is rendered pure and salutary by being put into jars, the inside of which is rubbed with a paste made of bitter almonds. The first discoverers of the Floridas are said to have corrected the stagnant and fetid water they found there, by infusing in it branches of sassafras; and it is understood that the first inducement of the Chinese to the general use of tea, was to correct the water of their ponds and rivers.

The Lign-Aloe, or agallochum, Num. xxiv, 6; Psalm xlv, 9; and Cantic. iv, 14. אהלת, masculine, אהל, whose plural is אהלים, is a small tree about eight or ten feet high. That the flower of this plant yielded a fragrance, is assured to us in the following extract from Swinburne's Travels, letter xii: "This morning, like many of the foregoing ones, was delicious. The sun rose gloriously out of the sea, and all the air around was perfumed with the effluvia of the aloe, as its rays sucked up the dew from the leaves." This extremely bitter plant contains under the bark three sorts of wood. The first is black, solid, and weighty; the second is of a tawny colour, of a light spongy texture, very porous, and filled with a resin extremely fragrant and agreeable; the third kind of wood, which is the heart, has a strong aromatic odour, and is esteemed in the east more precious than gold itself. It is used for perfuming habits and apartments, and is administered as a cordial in fainting and epileptic fits. These pieces, called calunbac, are carefully preserved in pewter boxes, to prevent their drying. When they are used they are ground upon a marble with such liquids as are best suited to the purpose for which they are intended. This wood, mentioned Cantic. iv, 14, in conjunction with several other odoriferous plants there referred to, was in high esteem among the Hebrews for its exquisite exhalations.

The scented aloe, and each shrub that showers

Gum from its veins, and odours from its flowers.

Thus the son of Sirach, Ecclesiasticus xxiv, 15: "I gave a sweet smell like the cinnamon and aspalathus. I yielded a pleasant odour like the best myrrh; like galbanum and onyx, and fragrant storax, and like the fume of frankincense in the tabernacle." It may not be amiss to observe that the Persian translator renders AHALIM, sandal wood; and the same was the opinion of a certain Jew in Arabia who was consulted by Neibuhr.

ALPHA, the first letter of the Greek alphabet; Omega being the last letter. Hence Alpha and Omega is a title which Christ appropriates to himself, Rev. i, 8; xxi, 6; xxii, 13; as signifying the beginning and the end, the first and the last, and thus properly denoting his perfection and eternity.

ALPHEUS, father of James the less, Matt. x, 3; Luke vi, 15. Alpheus was the husband of Mary, believed to have been sister to the mother of Christ; for which reason, James is called the Lord's brother; but the term brother is too general in its application to fix their relation, though the fact is probable. Many are of opinion that Cleopas, mentioned Luke xxiv, 18, is the same as Alpheus; Alpheus being his Greek name, and Cleopas his Hebrew, or Syriac name, according to the custom of this province, (or of the time,) where men often had two names; by one of which they were known to their friends and countrymen, by the other to the Romans or strangers.

2. Alpheus, father of Levi, or Matthew, whom Jesus took to be an Apostle and Evangelist, Mark ii, 14.

ALTAR. Sacrifices are nearly as ancient as worship, and altars are of almost equal antiquity. Scripture speaks of altars, erected by the patriarchs, without describing their form, or the materials of which they were composed. The altar which Jacob set up at Bethel, was the stone which had served him for a pillow; Gideon sacrificed on the rock before his house. The first altars which God commanded Moses to raise, were of earth or rough stones; and it was declared that if iron were used in constructing them they would become impure, Exod. xx, 24, 25. The altar which Moses enjoined Joshua to build on Mount Ebal, was to be of unpolished stones, Deut. xxvii, 5; Josh. viii, 31; and it is very probable that such were those built by Samuel, Saul, and David. The altar which Solomon erected in the temple was of brass, but filled, it is believed, with rough stones, 2 Chron. iv, 1–3. It was twenty cubits long, twenty wide, and ten high. That built at Jerusalem, by Zerubbabel, after the return from Babylon, was of rough stones; as was that of Maccabees. Josephus says that the altar which in his time was in the temple was of rough stones, fifteen cubits high, forty long, and forty wide.

Among the Romans altars were of two kinds, the higher and the lower; the higher were intended for the celestial gods, and were called ALTARIA, from ALTUS; the lower were for the terrestrial and infernal gods, and were called ARÆ. Those dedicated to the heavenly gods were raised a great height above the surface of the earth; those of the terrestrial gods were almost even with the surface; and those for the infernal deities were only holes dug in the ground called SCROBICULI.

Before temples were in use the altars were placed in the groves, highways, or on tops of mountains, inscribed with the names, ensigns, or characters of the respective gods to whom they belonged. The great temples at Rome generally contained three altars; the first in the sanctuary, at the foot of the statue, for incense and libations; the second before the gate of the temple, for the sacrifices of victims; and the third was a portable one for the offerings and sacred vestments or vessels to lie upon. The ancients used to swear upon the altars upon solemn occasions, such as confirming alliances, treaties of peace, &c. They were also places of refuge, and served as an asylum and sanctuary to all who fled to them, whatever their crimes were.

The principal altars among the Jews were those of incense, of burnt-offering, and the altar or table for the shew bread. The altar of incense was a small table of shittim wood covered with plates of gold. It was a cubit long, a cubit broad, and two cubits high. At the four corners were four horns. The priest, whose turn it was to officiate, burnt incense on this altar, at the time of the morning sacrifice between the sprinkling of the blood and the laying of the pieces of the victim on the altar of burnt-offering. He did the same also in the evening, between the laying of the pieces on the altar and the drink-offering. At the same time the people prayed in silence, and their prayers were offered up by the priests. The altar of burnt-offering was of shittim wood also, and carried upon the shoulders of the priests, by staves of the same wood overlaid with brass. In Moses's days it was five cubits square, and three high: but it was greatly enlarged in the days of Solomon, being twenty cubits square, and ten in height. It was covered with brass, and had a horn at each corner to which the sacrifice was tied. This altar was placed in the open air, that the smoke might not sully the inside of the tabernacle or temple. On this altar the holy fire was renewed from time to time, and kept constantly burning. Hereon, likewise, the sacrifices of lambs and bullocks were burnt, especially a lamb every morning at the third hour, or nine of the clock, and a lamb every afternoon at three, Exod. xx, 24, 25; xxvii, 1, 2, 4; xxxviii, 1. The altar of burnt-offering had the privilege of being a sanctuary or place of refuge. The wilful murderer, indeed, sought protection there in vain; for by the express command of God he might be dragged to justice, even from the altar. The altar or table of shew bread was of shittim wood also, covered with plates of gold, and had a border round it adorned with sculpture. It was two cubits long, one wide, and one and a half in height. This table stood in the SANCTUM SANCTORUM, [holy of holies,] and upon it were placed the loaves of shew bread. After the return of the Jews from their captivity, and the building of the second temple, the form and size of the altars were somewhat changed.

Sacrifices according to the laws of Moses, could not be offered except by the priests; and at any other place than on the altar of the tabernacle or the temple. Furthermore, they were not to be offered to idols, nor with any superstitious rites. See Lev. xvii, 1–7; Deut. xii, 15, 16. Without these precautionary measures, the true religion would hardly have been secure. If a different arrangement had been adopted, if the priests had been scattered about to various altars, without being subjected to the salutary restraint which would result from a mutual observation of each other, they would no doubt some of them have willingly consented to the worship of idols; and others, in their separate situation, would not have been in a condition to resist the wishes of the multitude, had those wishes been wrong. The necessity of sacrificing at one altar, (that of the tabernacle or temple,) is frequently and emphatically insisted on, Deut. xii, 13, 14; and all other altars are disapproved, Lev. xxvi, 30, compare Joshua xxii, 9–34. Notwithstanding this, it appears that, subsequently to the time of Moses, especially in the days of the kings, altars were multiplied; but they fell under suspicions, although some of them were perhaps sacred to the worship of the true God. It is, nevertheless, true, that prophets, whose characters were above all suspicion, sacrificed, in some instances, in other places than the one designated by the laws, 1 Sam. xiii, 3–14; xvi, 1–5; 1 Kings xviii, 21–40.

AMALEKITES, a people whose country adjoined the southern border of the land of Canaan, in the north-western part of Arabia Petræa. They are generally supposed to have been the descendants of Amalek, the son of Eliphaz, and grandson of Esau. But Moses speaks of the Amalekites long before this Amalek was born; namely in the days of Abraham, when Chedorlaomer, king of Elam, devastated their country, Gen. xiv, 7; from which it may be inferred that there was some other and more ancient Amalek, from whom this people sprang. The Arabians have a tradition that this Amalek was a son of Ham; and when we consider that so early as the march from Egypt the Amalekites were a people powerful enough to attack the Israelites, it is far more probable that they should derive their ancestry from Ham, than from the then recent stock of the grandson of Esau. It may also be said, that the character and fate of this people were more consonant with the dealings of Providence toward the families of the former. This more early origin of the Amalekites will likewise explain why Balaam called them the "first of the nations."

They are supposed by some to have been a party or tribe of the shepherds who invaded Egypt, and kept it in subjection for two hundred years. This will agree with the Arabian tradition as to their descent. It also agrees with their pastoral and martial habits, as well as with their geographical position; which was perhaps made choice of on their retiring from Egypt, adjoining that of their countrymen the Philistines, whose history is very similar. It also furnishes a motive for their hostility to the Jews, and their treacherous attempt to destroy them in the desert. The ground of this hostility has been very generally supposed to have been founded in the remembrance of Jacob's depriving their progenitor of his birthright. But we do not find that the Edomites, who had this ground for a hatred to the Jews, made any attempt to molest them, nor that Moses ever reproaches the Amalekites for attacking the Israelites as their brethren; nor do we ever find in Scripture that the Amalekites joined with the Edomites, but always with the Canaanites and the Philistines. These considerations would be sufficient, had we no other reasons for believing them not to be of the stock of Esau. They may, however, be deduced from a higher origin; and viewing them as Cuthite shepherds and warriors, we have an adequate explanation both of their imperious and warlike character, and of the motive of their hostility to the Jews in particular. If expelled with the rest of their race from Egypt, they could not but recollect the fatal overthrow at the Red Sea; and if not participators in that catastrophe, still, as members of the same family, they must bear this event in remembrance with bitter feelings of revenge. But an additional motive is not wanting for this hostility, especially for its first act. The Amalekites probably knew that the Israelites were advancing to take possession of the land of Canaan, and resolved to frustrate the purposes of God in this respect. Hence they did not wait for their near approach to that country, but came down from their settlements, on its southern borders, to attack them unawares at Rephidim. Be this as it may, the Amalekites came on the Israelites, when encamped at that place, little expecting such an assault. Moses commanded Joshua, with a chosen band, to attack the Amalekites; while he, with Aaron and Hur, went up the mountain Horeb. During the engagement, Moses held up his hands to heaven; and so long as they were maintained in this attitude, the Israelites prevailed, but when through weariness they fell, the Amalekites prevailed. Aaron and Hur, seeing this, held up his hands till the latter were entirely defeated with great slaughter, Exod. xvii.

The Amalekites were indeed the earliest and the most bitter enemies the Jews had to encounter. They attacked them in the desert; and sought every opportunity afterward of molesting them. Under the judges, the Amalekites, in conjunction with the Midianites, invaded the land of Israel; when they were defeated by Gideon, Judges vi, vii. But God, for their first act of treachery, had declared that he would "utterly put out the remembrance of Amalek from under heaven;" a denunciation which was not long after accomplished. Saul destroyed their entire army, with the exception of Agag their king; for sparing whom, and permitting the Israelites to take the spoil of their foes, he incurred the displeasure of the Lord, who took the sceptre from him. Agag was immediately afterward hewn in pieces by Samuel, 1 Sam. xv. It is remarkable, that most authors make Saul's pursuit of the Amalekites to commence from the lower Euphrates, instead of from the southern border of the land of Canaan. (See HAVILAH.) David a few years after, defeated another of their armies; of whom only four hundred men escaped on camels, 1 Sam. xxx; after which event, the Amalekites appear to have been obliterated as a nation.

AMASA, the son of Ithra and Abigail, David's sister, whom Absalom, when he rebelled against his father, appointed general of his army, 2 Sam. xvii, 25. Amasa having thus received the command of Absalom's troops, engaged his cousin Joab, general of David's army, and was worsted. But, after the defeat of Absalom's party, David, being angry at Joab for killing Absalom, pardoned Amasa, and gave him the command of his own army. Upon the revolt of Sheba, the son of Bichri, David gave orders to Amasa to assemble all Judah and march against Sheba. Amasa not being able to form his army in the time prescribed, David directed Abishai to pursue Sheba with the guards. Joab, with his people, accompanied him; and these troops were scarcely got as far as the great stone in Gibeon, before Amasa came and joined them with his forces. Then said Joab to Amasa, "Art thou in health, my brother?" and took him by the beard with his right hand to kiss him; and treacherously smote him under the fifth rib, so that he expired.

AMAZIAH, one of the kings of Judah, 2 Chron. xxiv, 27, son of Joash, succeeded his father A. M. 3165, B. C. 839. He was twenty-five years of age when he began to reign, and reigned twenty-nine years at Jerusalem. "He did good in the sight of the Lord, but not with a perfect heart." When settled in his kingdom, he put to death the murderers of his father, but avoided a barbarous practice then too common, to destroy also their children; in which he had respect to the precept, "The fathers shall not be put to death for the children, neither shall the children be put to death for the fathers; every man shall be put to death for his own sin," Deut. xxiv, 16; 2 Chron. xxv, 1–3.

In the muster which Amaziah made of his people, he found three hundred thousand men able to bear arms. He hired, besides, one hundred thousand men of Israel; for which he paid the king of Israel a hundred talents, about thirty-four thousand pounds English. His design was to employ these troops against Edom, which had revolted from Judah, in the reign of Joram, about fifty-four years before, 2 Kings, viii, 20. But a prophet of the Lord came to him, and said, "O king, let not the army of Israel go with thee; for the Lord is not with Israel." Amaziah, hereupon, sent back those troops; and they returning, strongly irritated against Amaziah, dispersed themselves over the cities of Judah, from Bethoron to Samaria, killed three thousand men, and carried off a great booty, to make themselves amends for the loss of the plunder of Edom. Amaziah, with his own forces gave battle to the Edomites in the Valley of Salt, and defeated them; but having thus punished Edom, and taken their idols, he adored them as his own deities. This provoked the Lord, who permitted Amaziah to be so blinded as to believe himself invincible. He therefore sent to defy the king of Israel, saying, "Come, let us look one another in the face." The motive of this challenge was probably to oblige Joash, king of Israel, to repair the ravages which his troops had committed on their return homewards. Joash answered him by the fable of the cedar of Lebanon, and the thistle trodden down by a beast, 2 Kings xiv, 8, 9. But Amaziah, deaf to these reasonings, advanced to Bethshemesh, and was defeated and taken prisoner there, by Joash, who carried him to Jerusalem. Joash ordered the demolition of four hundred cubits of the city wall, carried to Samaria all the gold and silver, the rich vessels of the house of God, the treasuries of the royal palace, and the sons of those among his own people who had been hostages there. Amaziah reigned after this, fifteen or sixteen years at Jerusalem, but returned not to the Lord. He endeavoured to escape from a conspiracy to Lachish; but was assassinated. He was buried with his ancestors in the city of David, and Uzziah, or Azariah, his son, about sixteen years of age, succeeded him.

AMBASSADOR, a messenger sent by a sovereign, to transact affairs of great moment. Ministers of the Gospel are called ambassadors, because, in the name of Jesus Christ the King of kings, they declare his will to men, and propose the terms of their reconciliation to God, 2 Cor. v, 20; Eph. vi, 20. Eliakim, Shebna, and Joah, the servants of king Hezekiah, were called "ambassadors of peace." In their master's name they earnestly solicited a peace from the Assyrian monarch, but were made "to weep bitterly" with the disappointment and refusal, Isaiah xxxiii, 7.

AMBER, השמל, Ezek. i, 4, 27; viii, 2. The amber is a hard inflammable bitumen. When rubbed it is highly endowed with that remarkable property called electricity, a word which the moderns have formed from its Greek name ἠλέκτρον. But the ancients had also a mixed metal of fine copper and silver, resembling the amber in colour, and called by the same name. From the version of Ezekiel i, 4, by the **LXX**, Καὶ ἐν τῷ μέσω ἀυτου ὡς ὅρασις ἠλεκτρȣ ἐν μέσῳ τοῦ πυρὸς, "And in the midst of it as the appearance of electrum in the midst of the fire," it appears that those translators by ἠλέκτρον, could not mean amber, which grows dim as soon as it feels the fire, and quickly dissolves into a resinous or pitchy substance; but the mixed metal above mentioned, which is much celebrated by the ancients for its beautiful lustre, and which, when exposed to the fire like other metals, grows more bright and shining. St. Jerom, Theodoret, St. Gregory and Origen think, that, in the above cited passages from Ezekiel, a precious and highly polished metal is meant.

AMEN. אמן, in Hebrew, signifies TRUE, FAITHFUL, CERTAIN. It is used likewise in affirmation; and was often thus employed by our Saviour: "Amen, amen," that is, "Verily, verily." It is also understood as expressing a wish, "Amen! so be it!" or an affirmation, "Amen, yes, I believe it:" Num. v, 22. She shall answer, "Amen! Amen!" Deut. xxvii, 15, 16, 17, &c. "All the people shall answer, Amen! Amen!" 1 Cor. xiv, 16. "How shall he who occupieth the place of the unlearned, say, Amen! at thy giving of thanks? seeing he understandeth not what thou sayest." "The promises of God are Amen in Christ;" that is, certain, confirmed, granted, 2 Cor. i, 20. The Hebrews end the five books of Psalms, according to their distribution of them, with "Amen, amen;" which the Septuagint translate, Γένοιτο, γένοιτο, and the Latins, FIAT, FIAT. The Gospels, &c, are ended with AMEN. The Greek, Latin, and other churches, preserve this word in their prayers, as well as alleluia and hosanna. At the conclusion of the public prayers, the people anciently answered with a loud voice, "Amen!" and Jerom says, that, at Rome, when the people answered, "Amen!" the sound was like a clap of thunder, IN SIMILITUDINEM CŒLESTIS TONITRUI AMEN REBOAT. [Amen rings again like a peal of thunder.] The Jews assert that the gates of heaven are opened to him who answers, "Amen!" with all his might.

The Jewish doctors give three rules for pronouncing the word: 1. That it be not pronounced too hastily and rapidly, but with a grave and distinct voice. 2. That it be not louder than the tone of him that blesses. 3. That it be expressed in faith, with a certain persuasion that God would bless them, and hear their prayers.

Amen is a title of our Lord, "The Amen, the true and faithful witness," Rev. i, 14.

AMETHYST. אחלמה, Exod. xxviii, 19; and xxix, 12; and once in the New Testament, Rev. **XXI**, 20, ἀμέθυςος.

A transparent gem, of a colour which seems composed of a strong blue and deep red; and, according as either prevails, affords different tinges of purple, sometimes approaching to violet, and sometimes even fading to a rose colour. The stone called amethyst by the ancients was evidently the same with that now generally known by this name; which is far from being the case with regard to some other gems. The oriental is the hardest, scarcest, and most valuable. It was the ninth stone in the pectoral of the high priest, and is mentioned as the twelfth in the foundations of the New Jerusalem.

AMMINADAB, or **ABINADAB**, a Levite, and an inhabitant of Kirjath-jearim, with whom the ark was deposited after it was brought back from the land of the Philistines, 1 Sam. vii. This Amminadab dwelt in Gibeath, that is to say, in the highest part of the city of Kirjath-jearim.

2. The chariots of Amminadab are mentioned, Canticles vi, 12, as being extremely light. He is thought to have been some celebrated charioteer, whose horses were singularly swift.

AMMON, or **HAMMON**, or **JUPITER-AMMON**, an epithet given to Jupiter in Lybia, where was a celebrated temple of that deity under the denomination of Jupiter Ammon, which was visited by Alexander the Great.

The word AMOUN, which imports "shining," according to Jablonski, denoted the effects produced by the sun on attaining the equator, such as the increase of the days; a more splendid light; and, above all, the fortunate presage of the inundation of the Nile, and its consequent abundance.

Ammon is by others derived from Ham, the son of Noah, who first peopled Egypt and Lybia, after the flood; and, when idolatry began to gain ground soon after this period, became the chief deity of those two countries, in which his descendants continued. A temple, it is said, was built to his honour, in the midst of the sandy deserts of Lybia, upon a spot of good ground, about two leagues broad, which formed a kind of island or oasis in a sea of sand. He was esteemed the Zeus of Greece, and the Jupiter of Latium, as well as the Ammon of the Egyptians. In process of time, these two names were joined; and he was called Jupiter Ammon. For this reason the city of Ammon, No-ammon, or the city of Ham, was called by the Greeks Diospolis, or the city of Jupiter. Plutarch says, that of all the Egyptian deities which seemed to have any correspondence with the Zeus of Greece, Amon or Ammon was the most peculiar and appropriate. From Egypt his name and worship were brought into Greece; as indeed were almost all the names of all the deities that were there worshipped. Jupiter Ammon, or the Egyptian Jupiter, was usually represented under the figure of a ram; though in some medals he appears of a human shape, having only two ram's horns growing out beneath his ears. The Egyptians, says Proclus, in the Timæus of Plato, had a singular veneration for the ram, because the image of Ammon bore its head, and because this first sign of the zodiac was the presage of the fruits of the earth. Eusebius adds, that this symbol marked the conjunction of the sun and moon in the sign of the ram.

2. Ammon, or Ben-Ammi, the son of Lot, by his youngest daughter, Gen. xix, 38. He was the father of the Ammonites, and dwelt on the east side of the Dead Sea, in the mountains of Gilead.

AMMONIANS, the disciples of Ammonius Saccas, of the Alexandrian school. His character was so equivocal, that it is disputed whether he was a Heathen or a Christian. Mr. Milner calls him "a Pagan Christian," who imagined "that all religions, vulgar and philosophical, Grecian and barbarous, Jewish and Gentile, meant the same thing in substance. He undertook, by allegorizing and subtilizing various fables and systems, to make up a coalition of all sects and religions; and from his labours, continued by his disciples,--some of whose works still remain,--his followers were taught to look on Jew, philosopher, vulgar, Pagan, and Christian, as all of the same creed," and worshippers of the same God, whether denominated "Jehovah, Jove, or Lord."

AMMONITES, the descendants of Ammon, the son of Lot. They took possession of the country called by their name, after having driven out the Zamzummims, who were its ancient inhabitants. The precise period at which this expulsion took place is not ascertained. The Ammonites had kings, and were uncircumcised, Jer. ix, 25, 26, and seem to have been principally addicted to husbandry. They, as well as the Moabites, were among the nations whose peace or prosperity the Israelites were forbidden to disturb, Deut. ii, 19, &c. However, neither the one nor the other were to be admitted into the congregation to the tenth generation, because they did not come out to relieve them in the wilderness, and were implicated in hiring Balaam to curse them. Their chief and peculiar deity is, in Scripture, called Moloch. Chemosh was also a god of the Ammonites. Before the Israelites entered Canaan, the Amorites conquered a great part of the country belonging to the Ammonites and Moabites; but it was retaken by Moses, and divided between the tribes of Gad and Reuben. Previous to the time of Jephthah, B. C. 1188, the Ammonites engaged as principals in a war, under a king whose name is not given, against the Israelites. This prince, determining to recover the ancient country of the Ammonites, made a sudden irruption into it, reduced the land, and kept the inhabitants in subjection for eighteen years. He afterward crossed Jordan with a design of falling upon the tribes of Judah, Benjamin, and Ephraim. The Israelites resisted the invader; and, assembling at Mizpeh, chose Jephthah for their general, and sent an expostulatory message to the king of the Ammonites, Judges x, xi. The king replied, that those lands belonged to the Ammonites, who had been unjustly dispossessed of them by the Israelites, when they came out of Egypt, and exhorted Jephthah to restore them peaceably to the lawful owners. Jephthah remonstrated on the injustice of his claim; but finding a war inevitable, he fell upon the Ammonites near Aroer, and defeated them with great slaughter. On this occasion the Ammonites lost twenty cities; and thus an end was put, after eighteen years' bondage, to the tyranny of Ammon over the Israelites beyond Jordan. In the days of Saul, 1 Sam. xi, B. C. 1095, the old claim of the Ammonites was revived by Nahash their king, and they laid siege to the city of Jabesh. The inhabitants were inclined to acknowledge Nahash as their sovereign; but he would accept their submission only on condition that every one of them should consent to lose his right eye, and that thus he might fix a lasting reproach upon Israel: but from this humiliating and severe requisition they were delivered by Saul, who vanquished and dispersed the army of Nahash. Upon the death of Nahash, David sent ambassadors to his son and successor Hanun, to congratulate him on his accession; but these ambassadors were treated as spies, and dismissed in a very reproachful manner, 2 Sam. x. This indignity was punished by David with rigour. Rabbah, the capital of Hanun, and the other cities of Ammon, which resisted the progress of the conqueror, were destroyed and razed to the ground; and the inhabitants were put to death or reduced to servitude. In the reign of Jehoshaphat the Ammonites united with their brethren, the Moabites, and the inhabitants of Mount Seir, against the king of Judah; but they were completely routed. They were afterward overthrown by Uzziah, king of Judah, and made tributary, 2 Chron. xxvi, 8; and rebelling in the reign of his son Jotham, they were reduced to the necessity of purchasing peace at a very dear rate. After the tribes of Reuben, Gad, and the half tribe of Manasseh, were carried into captivity by Tiglath Pileser, B. C. 740, the Ammonites and Moabites took possession of the cities belonging to these tribes, and were reproached for it by Jeremiah, xlix, 1. Their ambassadors were exhorted to submit to Nebuchadnezzar, and threatened, on their refusal, with captivity and slavery, Jer. xxvii, 2, 3, 4. The Prophet Ezekiel, xxv, 4–10, denounces their entire destruction, and informs them, that God would deliver them up to the people of the east; and that the Ammonites should no more be mentioned among the nations: and this punishment they were to suffer for insulting the Israelites on account of their calamities, and the destruction of their temple by the Chaldeans. This malediction began to be inflicted upon them in the fifth year after the taking of Jerusalem, when Nebuchadnezzar made war against all the people around Judea, A. M. 3420 or 3421, B. C. 583. It is probable that Cyrus granted to the Ammonites and Moabites liberty to return into their own country, whence they had been removed by Nebuchadnezzar; for they were exposed to the revolutions that were common to the people of Syria and Palestine, and were subject sometimes to the kings of Egypt, and sometimes to the kings of Syria. Polybius informs us, that Antiochus the Great took Rabboth, or Philadelphia, the capital of the Ammonites, demolished the walls, and put a garrison into it, A. M. 3806, B. C. 198. During the persecutions of Antiochus Epiphanes, the Ammonites manifested their hatred to the Jews, and exercised great cruelties against such of them as lived in their parts. At length their city Jaser, and the neighbouring town, fell a prey to the Jews, who smote the men, carried their wives and children into captivity, and plundered and burned the city. Thus ended their last conflict with the descendants of Israel. Ammon was, however, a highly productive and populous country when the Romans became masters of all the provinces of Syria; and several of the ten allied cities, which gave name to the celebrated Decapolis, were included within its boundaries. Even when first invaded by the Saracens, this country, including Moab, was enriched by the various benefits of trade, covered with a line of forts, and possessed some strong and populous cities. Volney bears witness, "that in the immense plains of the Hauran, ruins are continually to be met with, and that what is said of its actual fertility perfectly corresponds with the idea given of it in the Hebrew writings." The fact of its natural fertility is corroborated by every traveller who has visited it. And "it is evident," says Burckhardt, "that the whole country must have been extremely well cultivated in order to have afforded subsistence to the inhabitants of so many towns," as are now visible only in their ruins. While the fruitfulness of the land of Ammon, and the high degree of prosperity and power in which it subsisted long prior and long subsequent to the date of the predictions, are thus indisputably established by historical evidence and by existing proofs, the researches of recent travellers (who were actuated by the mere desire of exploring these regions and obtaining geographical information) have made known its present aspect; and testimony the most clear, unexceptionable, and conclusive, has been borne to the state of dire desolation to which it is and has long been reduced.

It was prophesied concerning Ammon, "Son of man, set thy face against the Ammonites, and prophesy against them. I will make Rabbah of the Ammonites a stable for camels and a couching place for flocks. Behold, I will stretch out my hand upon thee, and deliver thee for a spoil to the Heathen; I will cut thee off from the people, and cause thee to perish out of the countries; I will destroy thee. The Ammonites shall not be remembered among the nations. Rabbah" (the chief city) "of the Ammonites shall be a desolate heap. Ammon shall be a perpetual desolation," Ezek. xxv, 2, 5, 7, 10; xxi, 32; Jer. xlix, 2; Zeph. ii, 9.

Ammon was to be delivered to be a spoil to the Heathen-- to be destroyed, and to be a perpetual desolation. "All this country, formerly so populous and flourishing, is now changed into a vast desert." (*Seetzen's Travels.*) Ruins are seen in every direction. The country is divided between the Turks and the Arabs, but chiefly possessed by the latter. The extortions of the one, and the depredations of the other, keep it in "perpetual desolation," and make it "a spoil to the Heathen." "The far greater part of the country is uninhabited, being abandoned to the wandering Arabs, and the towns and villages are in a state of total ruin." (*Ibid.*) "At every step are to be found the vestiges of ancient cities, the remains of many temples, public edifices, and Greek churches." (*Burckhardt's Travels.*) The cities are left desolate. "Many of the ruins present no objects of any interest. They consist of a few walls of dwelling houses, heaps of stones, the foundations of some public edifices, and a few cisterns filled up; there is nothing entire, though it appears that the mode of building was very solid, all the remains being formed of large stones. In the vicinity of Ammon there is a fertile plain interspersed with low hills, which for the greater part are covered with ruins." (*Burckhardt's Travels in*

Syria.) While the country is thus despoiled and desolate, there are valleys and tracts throughout it which "are covered with a fine coat of verdant pasture, and are places of resort to the Bedouins, where they pasture their camels and their sheep." (*Buckingham's Travels in Palestine.*) "The whole way we traversed," says Seetzen, "we saw villages in ruins, and met numbers of Arabs with their camels," &c. Mr. Buckingham describes a building among the ruins of Ammon, "the masonry of which was evidently constructed of materials gathered from the ruins of other and older buildings on the spot. On entering it at the south end," he adds, "we came to an open square court, with arched recesses on each side, the sides nearly facing the cardinal points. The recesses in the northern and southern wall were originally open passages, and had arched door ways facing each other; but the first of these was found wholly closed up, and the last was partially filled up, leaving only a narrow passage, just sufficient for the entrance of one man and of the goats, which the Arab keepers drive in here occasionally for shelter during the night." He relates that he lay down among "flocks of sheep and goats," close beside the ruins of Ammon; and particularly remarks that, during the night, he "was almost entirely prevented from sleeping by the bleating of flocks." So literally true is it, although Seetzen, and Burckhardt, and Buckingham, who relate the facts, make no reference or allusion whatever to any of the prophecies, and travelled for a different object than the elucidation of the Scriptures,--that "the chief city of the Ammonites is a stable for camels, and a couching place for flocks."

"The Ammonites shall not be remembered among the nations." While the Jews, who were long their hereditary enemies, continue as distinct a people as ever, though dispersed among all nations, no trace of the Ammonites remains; none are now designated by their name, nor do any claim descent from them. They did exist, however, long after the time when the eventual annihilation of their race was foretold; for they retained their name, and continued a great multitude until the second century of the Christian æra. (*Justin Martyr.*) "Yet they are cut off from the people. Ammon has perished out of the countries; it is destroyed." No people is attached to its soil; none regard it as their country and adopt its name: "And the Ammonites are not remembered among the nations."

"Rabbah" (Rabbah Ammon, the chief city of Ammon) "shall be a desolate heap." Situated, as it was, on each side of the borders of a plentiful stream, encircled by a fruitful region, strong by nature and fortified by art, nothing could have justified the suspicion, or warranted the conjecture in the mind of an uninspired mortal, that the royal city of Ammon, whatever disasters might possibly befal it in the fate of war or change of masters, would ever undergo so total a transmutation as to become a desolate heap. But although, in addition to such tokens of its continuance as a city, more than a thousand years had given uninterrupted experience of its stability, ere the prophets of Israel denounced its fate; yet a period of equal length has now marked it out, as it exists to this day, a desolate heap, a perpetual or permanent desolation. Its ancient name is still preserved by the Arabs, and its site is now "covered with the ruins of private buildings--nothing of them remaining except the foundations and some of the door posts. The buildings, exposed to the atmosphere, are all in decay," (*Burckhardt's Travels in Syria,*) so that they may be said literally to form a desolate heap. The public edifices, which once strengthened or adorned the city, after a long resistance to decay, are now also desolate; and the remains of the most entire among them, subjected as they are to the abuse and spoliation of the wild Arabs, can be adapted to no better object than "a stable for camels." Yet these broken walls and ruined palaces, says Mr. Keith, which attest the ancient splendour of Ammon, can now be made subservient, by means of a single act of reflection, to a far nobler purpose than the most magnificent edifices on earth can be, when they are contemplated as monuments on which the historic and prophetic truth of Scripture is blended in one bright inscription.

AMORITES, the descendants of Amori, or Hæmorri, or Amorrhæus, Gen. x, 16, the fourth son of Canaan, whose first possessions were in the mountains of Judea, among the other families of Canaan: but, growing strong above their fellows, and impatient of confinement within the narrow boundaries of their native district, they passed the Jordan, and extended their conquests over the finest provinces of Moab and Ammon; seizing and maintaining possession of that extensive and almost insulated portion of country included between the rivers Jordan, Jabbok, and Arnon. This was the kingdom, and Heshbon the capital, of the Amorites, under Sihon their king, when the Israelites, in their way from Egypt, requested a passage through their country. This request, however, Sihon refused; and came out against them with all his force, when he was slain, his people extirpated, and his kingdom taken possession of by the Israelites. It was subsequently divided between the tribes of Reuben and Gad, Num. xiii, 29; xxi, 13, 25; Joshua v, 1; xi, 3; Judges xi, 19, 22.

AMOS, the fourth of the minor prophets, who in his youth had been a herdsman in Tekoa, a small town about four leagues southward of Jerusalem. He was sent to the people of Samaria, to bring them back to God by repentance, and reformation of manners. Hence it is natural to suppose that he must have been born within the territories of Israel, and that he only retired to Tekoa, on being expelled from Bethel by Amaziah, the priest of the calves at Bethel. He frequently complains of the violence offered him by those who endeavoured to impose silence on him. He boldly inveighs against the crying sins of the Israelites, such as idolatry, oppression, wantonness, and obstinacy. Nor does he spare the sins of Judah, such as their carnal security, sensuality, and injustice. He utters frequent threatenings against them both, and predicts their ruin. It is observable in this prophecy, that, as it begins with denunciations of judgment and destruction against the Syrians, Philistines, Tyrians, and other enemies of the Jews, so it concludes with comfortable promises of the restoration of the tabernacle of David, and the establishment of the kingdom of Christ. Amos was called to the prophetic office in the time of Uzziah, king of Judah, and Jeroboam, the son of Joash, king of Israel.

Some writers, in adverting to the condition of Amos, have, with a minute affectation of criticism, pretended to discover a certain rudeness and vulgarity in his style; and even Jerom is of opinion that he is deficient in magnificence and sublimity. He applies to him the words which St. Paul speaks of himself, that he was rude in speech, though not in knowledge; and his authority, says Bishop Lowth, "has influenced many commentators to represent him as entirely rude, and void of elegance; whereas it requires but little attention to be convinced that he is not a whit behind the very chiefest of the prophets;" equal to the greatest in loftiness of sentiment, and scarcely inferior to any in the splendour of his diction, and in the elegance of his composition. Mr. Locke has observed, that his comparisons are chiefly drawn from lions, and other animals, because he lived among, and was conversant with, such objects. But, indeed, the finest images and allusions, which adorn the poetical parts of Scripture, in general are drawn from scenes of nature, and from the grand objects that range in her walks; and true genius ever delights in considering these as the real sources of beauty and magnificence. The whole book of Amos is animated with a fine and masculine eloquence.

AMULET, a charm or supposed preservative against diseases, witchcraft, or any other mischief. They were very frequent among the Jews, the Greeks, and the Romans, and were made of stone, metal, animal substances, or, in short, any thing which a weak imagination suggested. The Jews were very superstitious in the use of amulets, but the Mishna forbids them, unless received from some person of whose cures, at least, three instances could be produced. The phylacteries worn by the Pharisees and others of the Jewish nation were a sort of amulets.

Amulets among the Greeks were called, φυλακτήρια, περιάπτα, ἀποτέλεσματα, περιάμματα, βρήβια, and εξκόλπια. The Latins called them AMULETA, APPENSA, PENTACULA, &C. Remains of this superstition continue among ignorant people even in this country, which ought to be strongly discountenanced as weak or wicked. The word amulet is probably derived from AMULA, a small vessel with lustral water in it, anciently carried in the pocket for the sake of purification and expiation.

AMYRALDISM, a name given by some writers to the doctrine of universal grace, as explained and asserted by Amyraldus, or Moses Amyraut, and his followers, among the reformed in France, toward the middle of the seventeenth century. This doctrine principally consisted of the following particulars, viz. that God desires the happiness of all men, from which none are excluded by a divine decree; that none can obtain salvation without faith in Christ; that God refuses to none the power of believing, though he does not grant to all his assistance, that they may improve this power to saving purposes; and that many perish through their own fault. Those who embraced this doctrine were called Universalists, although, it is evident that they rendered grace universal in words, but partial in reality, and are chargeable with greater inconsistencies than the Supralapsarians. Amyraldus is said to have formed his system with a view of producing a reconciliation between the Lutherans and Calvinists. This theory was supported in England by Baxter. See Baxterianism.

ANABAPTISTS, a name given to those Christians who maintain that baptism ought always to be performed by immersion; that it ought not to be administered to children before the age of discretion; and that at this age it ought to be readministered to those who have been baptized in their infancy. They affirm that the administration of this sacrament is neither valid nor useful, if it be done by sprinkling only, and not by immersion; or if the persons who receive it be not in a condition to give the reasons of their belief. The Anabaptists of Germany brought the name into great odium by their turbulent conduct; but by the people of this persuasion generally, the conduct of these fanatics was at all times condemned. In England they form a most respectable, though not a very numerous body.

The word Anabaptist is compounded of ἀνὰ, new, and βαπτιςὴς, a baptist; and has been indiscriminately applied to people of very different principles. Many of them object to the name, because the baptism of infants by sprinkling is, in their opinion, no baptism; and others hold nothing in common excepting some one or other of the above mentioned opinions concerning baptism. See Baptism.

ANAGOGICAL. This is one of the four senses in which Scripture may be interpreted, viz. the literal, allegorical, anagogical, and tropological. The anagogical sense is given when the text is explained with regard to the end which Christians should have in view, that is, eternal life: for example, the rest of the Sabbath, in the anagogical sense, corresponds to the repose of everlasting blessedness.

ANAK, ANAKIM, famous giants in Palestine. Anak, father of the Anakim, was son of Arba, who gave his name to Kirjath-Arba, or Hebron. Anak had three sons, Sheshai, Ahiman, and Talmai, whose descendants were terrible for their fierceness and stature. The Hebrew spies reported that in comparison of those monstrous men, they themselves were but grasshoppers. Some have thought that the name PHŒNICIAN, given to the Canaanites, and particularly to the Sidonians, was originally from BENE-ANAK, sons of Anak. Caleb, assisted by the tribe of Judah, took Kirjath-Arba, and destroyed the Anakim, A. M. 2559. Josh. xv, 14; Judg. i, 20.

ANALOGY OF FAITH. This has been often and largely descanted upon as an important rule for interpreting Scripture, founded, as it is said, upon Rom. xii, 6, "Let us prophesy according to the proportion" (ANALOGY) "of faith."

The principle of this rule has been thus stated: It is evident the Almighty doth not act without a design in the system of Christianity, any more than in the works of nature. Now this design must be uniform; for as in the system of the universe every part is proportioned to the whole, and made subservient to it,--so, in the system of the Gospel, all the various truths, doctrines, declarations, precepts, and promises must correspond with, and tend to, the end designed. For instance, supposing the glory of God in the salvation of sinners by free grace be the grand design,--then, whatever doctrine, assertion, or hypothesis agrees not with this, it is to be considered as false. The effect however of this view of the case appears to be often delusive. If nothing more be meant than that, what is obscure in a revelation should be interpreted by that which is plain, the same rule applies to all sober interpretations of any book whatever; but if we call our opinions, perhaps hastily taken up, or admitted on some authority without examination by the light of Scripture, "the analogy of faith," we shall greatly err. On this subject Dr. Campbell remarks:--

"In vain do we search the Scriptures for their testimony concerning Christ, if, independently of these Scriptures, we have received a testimony from another quarter, and are determined to admit nothing as the testimony of Scripture which will not perfectly quadrate with that formerly received. This was the very source of the blindness of the Jews in our Saviour's time. They searched the Scriptures as much as we do; but, in the disposition they were in, they would never have discovered what that sacred volume testifies of Christ. Why? because their great rule of interpretation was THE ANALOGY OF THE FAITH; or, in other words, the system of the Pharisean scribes, the doctrine then in vogue, and in the profound veneration of which they had been educated. This is that veil by which the understandings of that people were darkened, even in reading the law, and of which the Apostle observed, that it remained unremoved in his day, and of which we ourselves have occasion to observe, that it remains unremoved in ours. And is it not precisely in the same way that the phrase is used by every sect of Christians, for the particular system or digest of tenets for which they themselves have the greatest reverence? The Latin church, and even the Greek, are explicit in their declarations on this article. With each, THE ANALOGY OF THE FAITH is their own system alone. And that different parties of Protestants, though more reserved in their manner of speaking, aim at the same thing, is undeniable; the same, I mean, considered relatively to the speakers; for, absolutely considered, every party means a different thing. 'But,' say some, 'is not this mode of interpretation warranted by Apostolical authority? Does not Paul, Rom. xii, 6, in speaking of the exercise of the spiritual gifts, enjoin the prophets to prophesy κατὰ τὴν ἀναλογίαν τῆς ϖίςεως, ACCORDING TO THE PROPORTION OF FAITH, as our translators render it, but as some critics explain it, ACCORDING TO THE ANALOGY OF THE FAITH?' Though this exposition has been admitted into some versions, and adopted by Hammond and other commentators, and may be called literal, it is suited neither to the ordinary meaning of the words, nor to the tenor of the context. The word ἀναλογία strictly denotes proportion, measure, rate, but by no means that complex notion conveyed in the aforesaid phrase by the term ANALOGY, which has been well observed by Whitby to be particularly unsuitable in this place, where the Apostle treats of those who speak by inspiration, not of those who explain what has been thus spoken by others. The context manifestly leads us to understand ἀναλογία ϖίςεως, verse 6, as equivalent to μέτϱον ϖίστεως, verse 3. And for the better understanding of this phrase, THE MEASURE OF FAITH, it may be proper to observe, 1. That a strong conviction of any tenet, from whatever cause it arises, is in Scripture sometimes termed FAITH. Thus in the same epistle, Rom. xiv, 22, the Apostle says, 'Hast thou faith? have it to thyself before God.' The scope of his reasoning shows that nothing is there meant by faith, but a conviction of the truth in regard to the article of which he had been treating, namely, the equality of days and meats, in point of sanctity, under the Gospel dispensation. The same is evidently the meaning of the word, verse 23, 'Whatsoever is not of faith, is sin;' where, without regard to the morality of an action abstractly considered, that is concluded to be sin which is done by one who doubts of its lawfulness. 2. As to spiritual gifts, prophecy and inspiration in particular, they appear to have been accompanied with such a faith or conviction that they came from the Spirit, as left no room for hesitation. And indeed it is easy to perceive that something of this kind was absolutely necessary to enable the inspired person to distinguish what proceeded from the Spirit of God, from what was the creature of his own imagination. The prophets of God were not acted upon like machines in delivering their predictions, as the diviners were supposed to be among the Heathen, but had then, as at other times, the free use of their faculties, both of body and mind." This caution is therefore with great propriety given them by the Apostle, to induce them to be attentive in prophesying, not to exceed the precise measure allowed them, (for different measures of the same gift were committed to different persons,) and not to mingle aught of their own with the things of God's Spirit. Let him prophesy according to the proportion in which he has received this gift, which is in proportion to his faith. Though a sense somewhat different has been given to the words by some ancient Greek expositors, none of them seems to have formed a conception of that sense, which, as was observed above, has been given by some moderns. This has, nevertheless, a sound and sober principle included in it, although capable of great abuse. Undoubtedly there is a class of great and leading truths in the Scriptures so clearly revealed as to afford principles of interpretation in doubtful passages, and these are so obvious that persons of sound minds and hearts will not need those formal rules for the application of the analogy of faith to interpretation, which have been drawn up by several writers, and which when not misleading, are generally superfluous.

ANANIAS was the son of Nebedæus, high priest of the Jews. According to Josephus, he succeeded Joseph, the son of Camith, in the forty-seventh year of the Christian æra; and was himself succeeded by Ishmael, the son of Tabæus, in the year 63. Quadratus, governor of Syria, coming into Judæa, on the rumours which prevailed among the Samaritans and Jews, sent the high priest Ananias to Rome, to vindicate his conduct to the emperor. The high priest justified himself, was acquitted, and returned. St. Paul being apprehended at Jerusalem by the tribune of the Roman troops that guarded the temple, declared to him that he was a citizen of Rome. This obliged the officer to treat him with some regard. As he was ignorant of what the Jews accused him, the next day he convened the priests, and placed St. Paul in the midst of them, that he might justify himself. St. Paul began as follows: "Men and brethren, I have lived in all good conscience before God until this day." He had scarcely spoken this, when the high priest, Ananias, commanded those who were near him to smite him on the face. The Apostle immediately replied, "God shall judge thee, thou whited wall; for, sittest thou to judge me after the law, and commandest me to be smitten contrary to the law?" They that stood by said, "Revilest thou God's high priest?" And Paul answered, "I wist not, brethren, that he was the high priest; for it is written, Thou shalt not speak evil of the ruler of thy people," Acts xxii, 23, 24; xxiii, 1–5; by which words many suppose that the Apostle spake in bitter irony; or at least that he considered Ananias as a usurper of the office of the priesthood.

After this, the assembly being divided in opinion, St. Paul was sent by the tribune to Cæsarea, that Felix, governor of the province, might take cognizance of the affair. When it was known that the Apostle had arrived at Cæsarea, Ananias the high priest, and other Jews, went thither to accuse him; but the affair was adjourned, and St. Paul continued two years in prison in that city, Acts xxiv.

The Apostle's prediction that God would smite Ananias, was thus accomplished: Albinus, governor of Judæa, being come into that country, Ananias found means to gain him by presents; and Ananias, by reason of this patronage, was considered as the first man of his nation. However, there were in his party some violent persons, who plundered the country, and seized the tithes of the priests; and this they did with impunity, on account of the great credit of Ananias. At the same time, several companies of assassins infested Judæa, and committed great ravages. When any of their companions fell into the hands of the governors of the province, and were about to be executed, they failed not to seize some domestic or relation of the high priest Ananias, that he might procure the liberty of their associates, in exchange for those whom they detained. Having taken Eleazer, one of Ananias's sons, they did not release him till ten of their companions were liberated. By this means their number considerably increased, and the country was exposed to their ravages. At length, Eleazer, the son of Ananias, heading a party of mutineers, seized the temple, and forbade any sacrifices for the emperor. Being joined by the assassins, he pulled down the house of his father Ananias, with his brother, hid himself in the aqueducts belonging to the royal palace, but was soon discovered, and both of them were killed. Thus God smote this whited wall, in the very beginning of the Jewish wars.

2. Ananias, one of the first Christians of Jerusalem, who being converted, with his wife Sapphira, sold his estate; (as did the other Christians at Jerusalem, under a temporary regulation that they were to have all things in common;) but privately reserved a part of the purchase money to himself. Having brought the remainder to St. Peter, as the whole price of the inheritance sold, the Apostle, to whom the Holy Ghost had revealed this falsehood, rebuked him severely, as having lied not unto men but unto God, Acts v. At that instant, Ananias, being struck dead, fell down at the Apostle's feet; and in the course of three hours after, his wife suffered a similar punishment. This happened, A. D. 33, or 34. It is evident, that in this and similar events, the spectators and civil magistrates must have been convinced that some extraordinary power was exerted; for if Peter had himself slain Ananias, he would have been amenable to the laws as a murderer. But, if by forewarning him that he should immediately die, and the prediction came to pass, it is evident that the power which attended this word of Peter was not from Peter, but from God. This was made the more certain by the death of two persons, in the same manner, and under the same circumstances, which could not be attributed to accident.

3. ANANIAS, a disciple of Christ, at Damascus, whom the Lord directed to visit Paul, then lately converted. Ananias answered, "Lord, I have heard by many of this man, how much evil he hath done to thy saints at Jerusalem; and how he hath authority from the chief priests to bind all that call upon thy name." But the Lord said unto him, "Go thy way, for he is a chosen vessel unto me." Ananias, therefore, went to the house in which God had revealed unto him that Paul was, and putting his hands on him, said, "Brother Saul, the Lord Jesus who appeared unto thee in the way, hath sent me that thou mightest receive thy sight, and be filled with the Holy Ghost," Acts ix, 10–12, &c. We are not informed of any other circumstance of the life of Ananias.

ANATHEMA, from ἀνατίθημι, signifies something set apart, separated, or devoted, Mic. iv, 13, or the FORMULA by which this is effected. To anathematize is generally understood to denote the cutting off or separating any one from the communion of the faithful, the number of the living, or the privileges of society; or the devoting of an animal, city, or other thing, to destruction. See Accursed.

ANATHEMA MARANATHA. "If any man love not the Lord Jesus Christ, let him be Anathema Maranatha," 1 Cor. xvi, 22. Why these two words, one Greek and the other Syriac, were not translated, is not obvious. They are the words with which the Jews began their greater excommunication, whereby they not only excluded sinners from their society, but delivered them up to the divine CHEREM, or anathema, that is, to misery in this life, and perdition in the life to come. "Let him be Anathema" is, "Let him be accursed." Maranatha signifies, "The Lord cometh," or, "will come;" that is, to take vengeance. See See Accursed.

ANDREW, an Apostle of Jesus Christ, a native of Bethsaida, and the brother of Peter. He was at first a disciple of John the Baptist, whom he left to follow our Saviour, after the testimony of John, "Behold the Lamb of God which taketh away the sin of the world," John i, 29, and was the first disciple received by our Saviour. Andrew then introduced his brother Simon, and they went with him to the marriage in Cana, but afterward returned to their ordinary occupation, not expecting, perhaps, to be farther employed in his service. However, some months after, Jesus meeting them, while fishing together, called them to a regular attendance upon him, and promised to make them fishers of men, Matt. iv, 19.

After our Saviour's ascension, tradition states that Andrew was appointed to preach in Scythia and the neighbouring countries. According to Eusebius, after this Apostle had planted the Gospel in several places, he came to Patræ, in Achaia, where, endeavouring to convert the pro-consul Ægeas, he was, by that governor's orders, first scourged, and then crucified. The time of his suffering martyrdom is not known; but all the ancient and modern martyrologies of the Greeks and Latins agree in celebrating his festival on the 30th of November. His body was embalmed, and decently interred at Patræ, by Maximilla, a lady of great quality and estate. It was afterward removed to Constantinople, by Constantine the Great, who buried it in the great church which he had built to the honour of the Apostles. It is not known for what reason painters represent St. Andrew's cross like an X. Peter Chrysologus says that he was crucified upon a tree; and the spurious Hippolytus assures us that it was an olive tree. Nevertheless, the tradition which describes him to have been nailed to a cross is very ancient.

ANGEL, a spiritual, intelligent substance, the first in rank and dignity among created beings. The word angel, ἀγγέλος, is not properly a denomination of nature but of office; denoting as much as NUNCIUS, messenger, a person employed to carry one's orders, or declare his will. Thus it is St. Paul represents angels, Heb. i, 14, where he calls them "ministering spirits;" and yet custom has prevailed so much, that angel is now commonly taken for the denomination of a particular order of spiritual beings, of great understanding and power, superior to the souls or spirits of men. Some of these are spoken of in Scripture in such a manner as plainly to signify that they are real beings, of a spiritual nature, of high power, perfection, dignity, and happiness. Others of them are distinguished as not having kept their first station, Jude 6. These are represented as evil spirits, enemies of God, and intent on mischief. The devil as the head of them, and they as his angels, are represented as the rulers of the darkness of this world, or spiritual wickednesses, or wicked spirits, τὰ ϖνευματικὰ τῆς ϖονηρίας ἐν τοῖς ἐπϐρανίοις, Eph. vi, 12; which may not be unfitly rendered, "the spiritual managers of opposition to the kingdom of God."

The existence of angels is supposed in all religions, though it is incapable of being proved A PRIORI. Indeed, the ancient Sadducees are represented as denying all spirits; and yet the Samaritans, and Caraites, who are reputed Sadducees, openly allowed them: witness Abusaid, the author of an Arabic version of the Pentateuch; and Aaron, a Caraite Jew, in his comment on the Pentateuch; both extant in manuscript in the king of France's library. In the Alcoran we find frequent mention of angels. The Mussulmen believe them of different orders or degrees, and to be destined for different employments both in heaven and on earth. They attribute exceedingly great power to the angel Gabriel, as that he is able to descend in the space of an hour from heaven to earth; to overturn a mountain with a single feather of his wing, &c. The angel Asrael, they suppose, is appointed to take the souls of such as die; and another angel, named Esraphil, they tell us, stands with a trumpet ready in his mouth to proclaim the day of judgment.

The Heathen philosophers and poets were also agreed as to the existence of intelligent beings, superior to man; as is shown by St. Cyprian in his treatise of the vanity of idols; from the testimonies of Plato, Socrates, Trismegistus, &c. They were acknowledged under different appellations; the Greeks calling them dæmons, and the Romans genii, or lares. Epicurus seems to have been the only one among the old philosophers who absolutely rejected them.

Authors are not so unanimous about the nature as about the existence of angels. Clemens Alexandrinus believed they had bodies; which was also the opinion of Origen, Cæsarius, Tertullian, and several others. Athanasius, St. Basil, St. Gregory Nicene, St. Cyril, St. Chrysostom, &c, held them to be mere spirits. It has been the more current opinion, especially in later times, that they are substances entirely spiritual, who can, at any time, assume bodies, and appear in human or other shapes. Ecclesiastical writers make a hierarchy of nine orders of angels. Others have distributed angels into nine orders, according to the names by which they are called in Scripture, and reduced these orders into three hierarchies; to the first of which belong seraphim, cherubim, and thrones; to the second, dominions, virtues, and powers; and to the third, principalities, archangels, and angels. The Jews reckon four orders or companies of angels, each headed by an archangel; the first order being that of Michael; the second, of Gabriel; the third, of Uriel; and the fourth, of Raphael. Following the Scripture account, we shall find mention made of different orders of these superior beings; for such a distinction of orders seems intimated in the names given to different classes. Thus we have THRONES, DOMINIONS, PRINCIPALITIES, or princedoms, POWERS, AUTHORITIES, LIVING ONES, CHERUBIM, and SERAPHIM. That some of these titles may indicate the same class of angels is probable; but that they all should be but different appellations of one common and equal order is improbable. We learn also from Scripture, that they dwell in the immediate presence of God; that they "excel in strength;" that they are immortal; and that they are the agents through which God very often accomplishes his special purposes of judgment and mercy. Nothing is more frequent in Scripture than the missions and appearances of good and bad angels, whom God employed to declare his will; to correct, teach, reprove, and comfort. God gave the law to Moses, and appeared to the old patriarchs, by the mediation of angels, who represented him, and spoke in his name, Acts vii, 30, 35; Gal. iii, 19; Heb. xiii, 2.

Though the Jews, in general, believed the existence of angels, there was a sect among them, namely, the Sadducees, who denied the existence of all spirits whatever, God only excepted, Acts xxiii, 8. Before the Babylonish captivity, the Hebrews seem not to have known the names of any angel. The Talmudists say they brought the names of angels from Babylon. Tobit, who is thought to have resided in Nineveh some time before the captivity, mentions the angel Raphael, Tob. iii, 17; xi, 2, 7; and Daniel, who lived at Babylon some time after Tobit, has taught us the names of Michael and Gabriel, Dan. viii, 16; ix, 21; x, 21. In the New Testament, we find only the two latter mentioned by name.

There are various opinions as to the time when the angels were created. Some think this took place when our heavens and the earth were made. For this opinion, however, there is no just foundation in the Mosaic account. Others think that angels existed long before the formation of our solar system; and Scripture seems to favour this opinion, Job xxxviii, 4, 7, where God says, "Where wast thou when I laid the foundations of the earth?--and all the sons of God shouted for joy." Though it be a universal opinion that angels are of a spiritual and incorporeal nature, yet some of the fathers, misled by a passage in Gen. vi, 2, where it is said, "The sons of God saw the daughters of men, that they were fair, and they took them wives of all which they chose," imagined them to be corporeal, and capable of sensual pleasures. But, without noticing all the wild reveries which have been propagated by bold or ignorant persons, let it suffice to observe, that by "the sons of God" we are evidently to understand the descendants of Seth, who, for the great piety wherein they continued for some time, were so called; and that "the daughters of men" were the progeny of wicked Cain.

As to the doctrine of tutelary or guarding angels, presiding over the affairs of empires, nations, provinces, and particular persons, though received by the later Jews, it appears to be wholly Pagan in its origin, and to have no countenance in the Scriptures. The passages in Daniel brought to favour this notion are capable of a much better explanation; and when our Lord declares that the "ANGELS" of little children "do always behold the face of God," he either speaks of children as being the objects of the general ministry of angels, or, still more probably, by ANGELS he there means the disembodied spirits of children; for that the Jews called disembodied spirits by the name of angels, appears from Acts xii, 15.

On this question of guardian angels, Bishop Horsley observes: "That the holy angels are often employed by God in his government of this sublunary world, is indeed to be clearly proved by holy writ. That they have power over the matter of the universe, analogous to the powers over it which men possess, greater in extent, but still limited, is a thing which might reasonably be supposed, if it were not declared. But it seems to be confirmed by many passages of holy writ; from which it seems also evident that they are occasionally, for certain specific purposes, commissioned to exercise those powers to a prescribed extent. That the evil angels possessed before their fall the like powers, which they are still occasionally permitted to exercise for the punishment of wicked nations, seems also evident. That they have a power over the human sensory, which they are occasionally permitted to exercise, and by means of which they may inflict diseases, suggest evil thoughts, and be the instruments of temptation, must also be admitted. But all this amounts not to any thing of a discretional authority placed in the hands of tutelar angels, or to an authority to advise the Lord God with respect to the measures of his government. Confidently I deny that a single text is to be found in holy writ, which, rightly understood, gives the least countenance to the abominable doctrine of such a participation of the holy angels in God's government of the world. In what manner then, it may be asked, are the holy angels made at all subservient to the purposes of God's government? This question is answered by St. Paul in his Epistle to the Hebrews, in the last verse of the first chapter; and this is the only passage in the whole Bible in which we have any thing explicit upon the office and employment of angels: 'Are they not all,' saith he, 'ministering spirits, sent forth to minister for them that shall be heirs of salvation?' They are all, however high in rank and order, nothing more than 'ministering spirits,' or, literally, 'serving spirits;' not invested with authority of their own, but 'sent forth,' occasionally sent forth, to do such service as may be required of them, 'for them that shall be heirs of salvation.'"

The exact number of angels is no where mentioned in Scripture; but it is always represented as very great. Daniel, vii, 10, says of the Ancient of Days, "A fiery stream came from before him; thousand thousands ministered unto him, and ten thousand times ten thousand stood before him." Jesus Christ says, that his heavenly Father could have given him more than twelve legions of angels, that is, more than seventy-two thousand, Matt. xxvi, 53; and the Psalmist declares, that the chariots of God are twenty thousand, even thousands of angels, lxviii, 17, These are all intended not to express any exact number, but indefinitely a very large one.

Though all the angels were created alike good, yet Jude informs us, verse 6, that some of them "kept not their first estate, but left their own habitation," and these God hath "reserved in everlasting chains under darkness, unto the judgment of the great day." Speculations on the cause and occasion of their fall are all vain and trifling. Milton is to be read on this subject, as on others, not as a divine, but as a poet. All we know, is, that they are not in their first "estate," or in their original place; that this was their own fault, for "they left their own habitation;" that they are in chains, yet with liberty to tempt; and that they are reserved to the general judgment.

Dr. Prideaux observes, that the minister of the synagogue, who officiated in offering the public prayers, being the mouth of the congregation, delegated by them, as their representative, messenger, or angel, to address God in prayer for them, was in Hebrew called SHELIACK-ZIBBOR, that is, the ANGEL OF THE CHURCH; and that from hence the chief ministers of the seven churches of Asia are in the Revelation, by a name borrowed from the synagogue, called angels of those churches.

THE ANGEL OF THE LORD, or THE ANGEL JEHOVAH, a title given to Christ in his different appearances to the patriarchs and others in the Old Testament.

When the Angel of the Lord found Hagar in the wilderness, "she called the name of Jehovah that spake to her, Thou God seest me."--Jehovah appeared unto Abraham in the plains of Mamre. Abraham lifted up his eyes, and three MEN, three persons in human form, "stood by him." One of the three is called Jehovah. And Jehovah said, "Shall I hide from Abraham the thing that I do?" Appearances of the same personage occur to Isaac and to Jacob under the name of "the God of Abraham, and of Isaac." After one of these manifestations, Jacob says, "I have seen God face to face;" and at another, "Surely the Lord (Jehovah) is in this place." The same Jehovah was made visible to Moses, and gave him his commission; and God said, "I am that I am; thou shalt say to the children of Israel, I am hath sent me unto you." The same Jehovah went before the Israelites by day in a pillar of cloud, and by night in a pillar of fire; and by Him the law was given amidst terrible displays of power and majesty from Mount Sinai. "I am the Lord (Jehovah) thy God, which have brought thee out of the land of Egypt, out of the house of bondage: Thou shalt have no other gods before me," &c. The collation of a few passages, or of the different parts of the same passages, of Scripture, will show that Jehovah, and "the Angel of the Lord," when used in this eminent sense, are the same person. Jacob says of Bethel, where he had exclaimed, "Surely JEHOVAH is in this place;" "The ANGEL of God appeared to me in a dream, saying, I am the God of Bethel." Upon his death bed he gives the names of GOD and ANGEL to this same person: "The GOD which fed me all my life long unto this day, the ANGEL which redeemed me from all evil, bless the lads." So in Hosea xii, 2, 5, it is said, "By his strength he had power with GOD; yea, he had power over the ANGEL, and prevailed." "We found him in Bethel, and there he spake with us, even the LORD GOD OF HOSTS; the Lord is his memorial." Here the same person has the names, GOD, ANGEL, and LORD GOD OF HOSTS. "The ANGEL OF THE LORD called to Abraham a second time from heaven, and said, By MYSELF have I sworn, saith the Lord, (Jehovah,) that, since thou hast done this thing, in blessing will I bless thee." The ANGEL OF THE LORD appeared to Moses in a flame of fire; but this same Angel "called to him out of the bush, and said, I am the God of thy fathers, the God of Abraham, the God of Isaac, and the God of Jacob; and Moses hid his face, for he was afraid to look upon God." To omit many other passages, St. Stephen, in alluding to this part of the history of Moses, in his speech before the council, says, "There appeared to Moses in the wilderness of Mount Sinai, AN ANGEL OF THE LORD in a flame of fire," showing that that phraseology was in use among the Jews in his day, and that this Angel and Jehovah were regarded as the same being; for he adds, "Moses was in the church in the wilderness with the ANGEL which spoke unto him in Mount Sinai." There is one part of the history of the Jews in the wilderness, which so fully shows that they distinguished this Angel of Jehovah from all created angels, as to deserve particular attention. In Exodus xxiii, 20, God makes this promise to Moses and the Israelites: "Behold, I send an Angel before thee to keep thee in the way, and to bring thee into the place which I have prepared. Beware of him, and obey his voice; provoke him not; for he will not pardon your transgressions, for my name is in him." Of this Angel let it be observed, that he is here represented as the guide and protector of the Israelites; to him they were to owe their conquests and their settlement in the promised land, which are in other places often attributed to the IMMEDIATE agency of God; that they are cautioned to "beware of him," to reverence and stand in dread of him; that the pardoning of transgressions belongs to him; finally, "that the NAME of God was in him." This NAME must be understood of God's own peculiar name, Jehovah, I am, which he assumed as his distinctive appellation at his first appearing to Moses; and as the names of God are indicative of his nature, he who had a right to bear the peculiar name of God, must also have his essence. This view is put beyond all doubt by the fact, that Moses and the Jews so understood the matter; for afterward when their sins had provoked God to threaten not to go up with them HIMSELF, but to commit them to "an angel who should drive out the Canaanite," &c, the people mourned over this as a great calamity, and Moses betook himself to special intercession, and rested not until he obtained the repeal of the threat, and the renewed promise, "My PRESENCE shall go with thee, and I will give thee rest." Nothing, therefore, can be more clear than that Moses and the Israelites considered the promise of the Angel, in whom was "the name of God," as a promise that God HIMSELF would go with them. With this uncreated Angel, this PRESENCE of the Lord, they were satisfied, but not with "an angel" indefinitely, who was by NATURE of that order of beings usually so called, and therefore a created being; for at the news of God's determination not to go up with them, Moses hastens to the tabernacle to make his intercessions, and refuses an inferior conductor:--"If thy presence go not with me, carry us not up hence."

The Jews held this Word, or Angel of the Lord, to be the future Messiah, as appears from the writings of their older rabbins. So that he appears as the Jehovah of all the three dispensations, and yet is invariably described as a separate person from the unseen Jehovah who sends him. He was then the Word to be made flesh, and to dwell for a time among us, to open the way to God by his sacrifice, and to rescue the race, whose nature he should assume, from sin and death. This he has now actually effected; and the Patriarchal, Mosaic, and Christian religions are thus founded upon the same great principles,--the fall and misery of mankind, and their deliverance by a DIVINE REDEEMER.

ANGELICS, worshippers of angels. Those who consider this as a sect of the Apostolic age, think St. Paul, Coloss. ii, 18, cautions Christians against a superstitious reverence of these celestial agents of the Deity, which they conceive to have been borrowed from the idolatrous reverence paid by the Heathen to genii and demons. The Jews of that time are also accused of worshipping angels, and probably this superstition might through them influence the Judaizing members of some of the Apostolic churches. This idolatry may now be too justly charged upon the Romish and some other corrupt churches.

ANGER, a resentful emotion of the mind, arising upon the receipt, or supposed receipt, of an affront or injury; and also simple feeling of strong displacency at that which is in itself evil, or base, or injurious to others. In the latter sense it is not only innocent but commendable. Strong displeasure against evil doers, provided it be free from hatred and malice, and interferes not with a just placableness, is also blameless, Eph. iv, 26. When it is vindictive against the person of our neighbour, or against the innocent creatures of God, it is wicked, Matt. v, 22. When anger, hatred, wrath, and fury, are ascribed to God, they denote no tumultuous passion, but merely his holy and just displeasure with sin and sinners; and the evidence of it in his terrible threatenings, or righteous judgments, Psalm vi, 1, and vii, 11. We must, however, take care that we refine not too much. These are Scriptural terms, and are often used of God; and though they express not a tumultuous, much less an unjust, passion, there is something in God which answers to them. In him they are PRINCIPLES arising out of his holy and just nature; and for this reason they are more steady and uniform, and more terrible, than if they were emotions, or as we say passions. Nor can we rightly regard the severity of the judgments which God has so often executed upon sin without standing in awe of him, "as a consuming fire" to the ungodly.

ANIMAL, is an organized and living body, endowed with sensation. Minerals are said to grow or increase, plants to grow and live, and animals alone to have sensation. The Hebrews distinguished animals into pure and impure, clean and unclean; or those which might be eaten and offered, and those whose use was prohibited. The sacrifices which they offered, were, 1. Of the beeve kind; a cow, bull, or calf. The ox could not be offered, because it was mutilated; and when it is said oxen were sacrificed, we are to understand bulls, Lev. xxii, 18, 19. Calmet thinks, that the mutilation of animals was neither permitted, nor used, among the Israelites. 2. Of the goat kind; a he-goat, a she-goat, or kid, Lev. xxii, 24. 3. Of the sheep kind; a ewe, ram, or lamb. When it is said sheep are offered, rams are chiefly meant, especially in burnt-offerings and sacrifices for sin; for as to peace-offerings, or sacrifices of pure devotion, a female might be sometimes offered, provided it was pure, and without blemish, Lev. iii, 1.

Besides these three sorts of animals, used in sacrifices, many others might be eaten, wild or tame; as the stag, the roe-buck, and in general all that have cloven feet, or that chew the cud, Lev. ix, 2, 3, &c. All that have not cloven hoofs, and do not chew the cud, were esteemed impure, and could neither be offered nor eaten. The fat of all sorts of animals sacrificed was forbidden to be eaten. The blood of all kinds of animals generally, and in all cases, was prohibited on pain of death, Lev. iii, 17; vii, 23–27. Neither did the Israelites eat animals which had been taken and touched by a devouring or impure beast, as a dog, a wolf, a boar, &c, Exodus xxii, 3; nor of any animal that died of itself. Whoever touched its carcass was impure until the evening; and till that time, and before he had washed his clothes, he did not return to the company of other Jews, Lev. xi, 39, 40; xvii, 15; xxii, 8. Fish that had neither fins nor scales were unclean, Lev. xi, 20. Birds which walk on the ground with four feet, as bats, and flies that have many feet, were impure. The law, however, excepts locusts, which have their hind feet higher than those before, and rather leap than walk. These were clean, and might be eaten, Lev. xi, 21, 22, as they still are in Palestine. The distinction between clean and unclean animals has been variously accounted for. Some have thought it SYMBOLICAL, intended to teach the avoidance of those evil qualities for which the unclean animals were remarkable; others, that, in order that the Hebrews might be preserved from IDOLATRY, they were commanded to kill and eat many animals which were sacred among the Egyptians, and were taught to look with abhorrence upon others which they reverenced. Others have found a reason in the unwholesomeness of the flesh of the creatures pronounced by the law to be unclean, so that they resolve the whole into a SANATIVE regulation. But it is not to be forgotten that this division of animals into clean and unclean existed both before the law of Moses, and even prior to the flood. The foundation of it was therefore clearly SACRIFICIAL; for before the deluge it could not have reference to health, since animal food was not allowed to man prior to the deluge; and as no other ground for the distinction appears, except that of sacrifice, it must therefore have had reference to the selection of victims to be solemnly offered to God, as a part of worship, and as the means of drawing near to him by expiatory rites for the forgiveness of sins. Some it is true, have regarded this distinction of clean and unclean beasts as used by Moses by way of PROLEPSIS, or anticipation,--a notion which, if it could not be refuted by the context, would be perfectly arbitrary. Not only are the beasts, which Noah was to receive, spoken of as clean and unclean; but it will be noticed, that, in the command to take them into the ark, a difference is made in the NUMBER to be preserved--the CLEAN being to be received by SEVENS, and the UNCLEAN by TWO of a kind. This shows that this distinction among beasts had been established in the time of Noah; and thus the assumption of a prolepsis is refuted. The critical attempts which have been made to show that animals were allowed to man for food, previous to the flood, have wholly failed.

A second argument is furnished by the prohibition of blood for food, after animals had been granted to man for his sustenance along with the "herb of the field." This prohibition is repeated by Moses to the Israelites, with this explanation:--"I have given it upon the altar to make AN ATONEMENT for your souls." From this it has indeed been argued, that the doctrine of the atoning power of blood was new, and was then, for the first time, announced by Moses, or the same reason for the prohibition would have been given to Noah. To this we may reply, 1. That unless the same be supposed as the ground of the prohibition of blood to Noah, as that given by Moses to the Jews, no reason at all can be conceived for this restraint being put upon the appetite of mankind from Noah to Moses. 2. That it is a mistake to suppose, that the declaration of Moses to the Jews, that God had "given them the blood for an atonement," is an ADDITIONAL REASON for the interdict, not to be found in the original prohibition to Noah. The whole passage in Lev. xvii, is, "And thou shalt say to them, Whatsoever man there be of the house of Israel, or of the strangers that sojourn among you, that eateth any manner of blood, I will even set my face against that soul that eateth blood, and I will cut him off from among his people: FOR THE LIFE of the flesh is in the blood; and I have given it upon the altar, to make atonement for your souls: FOR IT IS THE BLOOD (or LIFE) that maketh atonement for the soul." The great reason, then, of the prohibition of blood is, that it is the LIFE; and what follows respecting atonement is EXEGETICAL of this reason; the life is in the blood, and the blood or life is given as an atonement. Now, by turning to the original prohibition in Genesis, we find that precisely the same reason is given: "But the flesh with the blood, which is THE LIFE thereof, shall ye not eat." The reason, then, being the same, the question is, whether the exegesis added by Moses must not necessarily be understood in the general reason given for the restraint to Noah. Blood is prohibited for this cause, that it is the LIFE; and Moses adds, that it is "the blood," OR LIFE, "which makes atonement." Let any one attempt to discover any cause for the prohibition of blood to Noah, in the mere circumstance that it is "the life," and he will find it impossible. It is no reason at all, moral or instituted, except that as it was LIFE substituted for LIFE, the life of the animal in sacrifice for the life of man, and that it had a sacred appropriation. The manner, too, in which Moses introduces the subject is indicative that, although he was renewing a prohibition, he was not publishing a "new doctrine;" he does not teach his people that God had then given, or appointed, blood to make atonement; but he prohibits them from eating it, because he had made this appointment, without reference to time, and as a subject with which they were familiar. Because the blood was the life, it was sprinkled upon, and poured out at, the altar: and we have in the sacrifice of the paschal lamb, and the sprinkling of its blood, a sufficient proof, that, before the giving of the law, not only was blood not eaten, but was appropriated to a sacred sacrificial purpose. Nor was this confined to the Jews; it was customary with the Romans and Greeks, who, in like manner, poured out and sprinkled the blood of victims at their altars, a rite derived, probably, from the Egyptians, as they derived it, not from Moses, but from the sons of Noah. The notion, indeed, that the blood of the victims was peculiarly sacred to the gods, is impressed upon all ancient Pagan mythology.

If, therefore, the distinction of animals into clean and unclean existed before the flood, and was founded upon the practice of animal sacrifice, we have not only a proof of the antiquity of that practice, but that it was of divine institution and appointment, since almighty God gave laws for its right and acceptable performance. Still farther, if animal sacrifice was of divine appointment, it must be concluded to be typical only, and designed to teach the great doctrine of moral atonement, and to direct faith to the only true sacrifice which could take away the sins of men;--"the Lamb slain from the foundation of the world,"--the victim "without spot," who suffered the just for the unjust, that he might bring us to God. See Sacrifices.

ANISE, an annual umbeliferous plant, the seeds of which have an aromatic smell, a pleasant warm taste, and a carminative quality. But by ἄνηθον, Matt. xxiii, 23, the DILL is meant. Our translators seem to have been first misled by a resemblance of the sound. No other versions have fallen into the mistake. The Greek of ANISE is ἄνισον; but of DILL, ἄνηθον.

ANNA, the daughter of Phanuel, a prophetess and widow, of the tribe of Asher, Luke ii, 36, 37. She was married early, and had lived only seven years with her husband. Being then disengaged from the ties of marriage, she thought only of pleasing the Lord; and continued without ceasing in the temple, serving God night and day, with fasting and prayer, as the Evangelist expresses it. However, her serving God at the temple night and day, says Dr. Prideaux, is to be understood no otherwise than that she constantly attended the morning and evening sacrifice at the temple; and then with great devotion offered up her prayers to God; the time of morning and evening sacrifice being the most solemn time of prayer among the Jews, and the temple the most solemn place for this devotion. Anna was fourscore years of age when the holy virgin came to present Jesus in the temple; and entering accidentally, while Simeon was pronouncing his thanksgiving, she likewise began to praise God, and to speak of the Messiah to all those who waited for redemption in Jerusalem. We know nothing more either of the life or death of this holy woman.

ANNAS, or **ANANUS**, as Josephus calls him, was the son of Seth, and high priest of the Jews. He succeeded Joazar, the son of Simon, enjoyed the high priesthood eleven years, and was succeeded by Ishmael, the son of Phabi. After he was deposed, he still preserved the title of high priest, and had a great share in the management of public affairs. He is called high priest in conjunction with Caiaphas, when John the Baptist entered upon the exercise of his mission; though Calmet thinks that at that time he did not, strictly speaking, possess or officiate in that character, Luke iii, 2. On the contrary, Macknight and some others are of opinion, that at this time Caiaphas was only the deputy of Annas. He was father-in-law to Caiaphas; and Jesus Christ was carried before him, directly after his seizure in the garden of Olives, John xviii, 13. Josephus remarks, that Annas was considered as one of the happiest men of his nation, for five of his sons were high priests, and he himself possessed that great dignity many years. This was an instance of good fortune which, till that time, had happened to no person.

ANOINT, to pour oil upon, Gen. xxviii, 18; xxxi, 13. The setting up of a stone and anointing it by Jacob, as here recorded, in grateful memory of his celestial vision, probably became the occasion of idolatry in succeeding ages, and gave rise to the erection of temples composed of shapeless masses of unhewn stone, of which so many astonishing remains are scattered up and down the Asiatic and the European world.

Under the law persons and things set apart for sacred purposes were anointed with the holy oil; which appears to have been a typical representation of the communication of the Holy Ghost to Christ and to his church. See Exod. xxviii, xxix. Hence the Holy Spirit is called an UNCTION or ANOINTING, 1 John ii, 20, 27; and our Lord is called the "Messiah," or "Anointed One," to denote his being called to the offices of mediator, prophet, priest, and king, to all of which he was consecrated by the anointing of the Holy Ghost, Matt. iii, 16, 17.

When we hear of the anointing of the Jewish kings, we are to understand by it the same as their inauguration; inasmuch as anointing was the principal ceremony on such an occasion, 2 Sam. ii, 4; v, 3. As far as we are informed, however, unction, as a sign of investiture with the royal authority, was bestowed only upon Saul and David, and subsequently upon Solomon and Joash, who ascended the throne under such circumstances, that there was danger of their right to the succession being forcibly disputed, 1 Sam. x, 24; 2 Sam. ii, 4; v, 1–3; 1 Chron. xi, 1, 2; 2 Kings xi, 12–20; 2 Chron. xxiii, 1–21. The ceremony of regal anointing needed not to be repeated in every instance of succession to the throne, because the unction which the first one who held the sceptre in any particular line of princes had received was supposed to suffice for the succeeding incumbents in the same descent.

In the kingdom of Israel, those who were inducted into the royal office appear to have been inaugurated with some additional ceremonies, 2 Kings ix, 13. The private anointings which we learn to have been performed by the prophets, 2 Kings ix, 3, comp. 1 Sam. x, 1; xvi, 1–13, were only prophetic symbols or intimations that the persons who were thus anointed should eventually receive the kingdom.

The holy anointing oil which was made by Moses, Exod. xxx, 22–33, for the maintaining and consecrating of the king, the high priest, and all the sacred vessels made use of in the house of God, was one of those things, as Dr. Prideaux observes, which was wanting in the second temple. The oil made and consecrated for this use was commanded to be kept by the children of Israel, throughout their generations, and therefore it was laid up in the most holy place of the tabernacle and the first temple.

ANOMŒANS, the name by which the pure Arians were called in the fourth century, in contradistinction to the Semi-Arians. The word is formed from the Greek ἀνόμοιος, DIFFERENT. For the pure Arians asserted, that the Son was of a nature different from, and in nothing like, that of the Father; whereas the Semi-Arians acknowledged a likeness of nature in the Son, at the same time that they denied, with the pure Arians, the consubstantiality of the Word. The Semi-Arians condemned the Anomœans in the council of Seleucia; and the Anomœans, in their turn, condemned the Semi-Arians in the councils of Constantinople and Antioch, erasing the word LIKE out of the formula of Rimini and Constantinople.

ANSWER. Beside the common usage of this word, in the sense of a reply, it has other significations. Moses, having composed a thanksgiving, after the passage of the Red Sea, Miriam, it is said, ANSWERED, "Sing ye to the Lord" &c,--meaning, that Moses, with the men on one side, and Miriam, with the women on the other side, sung the same song, as it were, in two choruses, or divisions; of which one ANSWERED the other. Num. xxi, 17, "Then Israel sung this song, Spring up, O well, ANSWER unto it;" that is, sing responsively, one side (or choir) singing first, and then the other. 1 Sam. xxix, 5, "Is not this David of whom they sung one to another in dances, saying, Saul hath slain his thousands, and David his ten thousands?" They sung this song to his honour in distinct choruses.

This word is taken likewise for, TO ACCUSE or to DEFEND any one, JUDICIALLY. Gen. xxx, 33, "My righteousness shall ANSWER for me;" it shall be my advocate before thee. Deut. xxxi, 21, "The song which thou shalt compose and teach them shall TESTIFY (answer) against them as a witness." Isaiah says, "The show of their countenance will TESTIFY (answer) against them;" their impudence will be like a witness and an accuser. Hosea, v, 5, "The pride of Israel doth TESTIFY (answer) to his face."

TO ANSWER, is likewise taken in a bad sense; as when it is said that a son ANSWERS his father insolently, or a servant his master. Rom. ix, 20, "Who art thou that REPLIEST against God?" that is, to contest or debate with him. John xviii, 22, "Answerest thou the high priest so?" St. Paul declares that he "had in himself the ANSWER (or sentence) of death;" 2 Cor. i, 9; like a man who has had notice of condemnation, he had a certain assurance of dying.

TO ANSWER is also used in Scripture for the commencement of a discourse, when no reply to any question or objection is intended. This mode of speaking is often used by the evangelists, "And Jesus ANSWERED and said." It is a Hebrew idiom.

ANT, נמלה, in the Turkish and Arabic, NEML, Prov. vi, 6; xxx, 25. It is a little insect, famous from all antiquity for its social habits, its economy, unwearied industry, and prudent foresight. It has afforded a pattern of commendable frugality to the profuse, and of unceasing diligence to the slothful. Solomon calls the ants "exceeding wise; for though a race not strong, yet they prepare their meat in the summer." He therefore sends the sluggard to these little creatures, to learn wisdom, foresight, care, and diligence.

"Go to the ant; learn of its ways, be wise;

It early heaps its stores, lest want surprise.

Skill'd in the various year, the prescient sage

Beholds the summer chill'd in winter's rage.

Survey its arts; in each partition'd cell

Economy and plenty deign to dwell."

That the ant hoarded up grains of corn against winter for its sustenance, was very generally believed by the ancients, though modern naturalists seem to question the fact. Thus Horace says,

"------SICUT

PARVULA (NAM EXEMPLO EST) MAGNI FORMICA LABORIS

ORE TRAHIT QUODCUNQUE POTEST, ATQUE ADDIT ACERVO

QUEM STRUIT, HAUD IGNARA AC NON INCAUTA FUTURI;

QUÆ, SIMUL INVERSUM CONTRISTAT AQUARIUS ANNUM,

NON USQUAM PROREPIT, ET ILLIS UTITUR ANTE

QUÆSITIS SAPIENS."

Sat. i, l. i, v. 33.

"For thus the little ant (to human lore

No mean example) forms her frugal store,

Gather'd with mighty toil on every side,

Nor ignorant nor careless to provide

For future want; yet, when the stars appear

That darkly sadden the declining year,

No more she comes abroad, but wisely lives

On the fair stores industrious summer gives."

The learned Bochart, in his *Hierozoicon*, has displayed his vast reading on this subject, and has cited passages from Pliny, Lucian, Ælian, Zoroaster, Origen, Basil, and Epiphanius, the Jewish rabbins and Arabian naturalists, all concurring in opinion that ants cut off the heads of grain, to prevent their germinating; and it is observable that the Hebrew name of the insect is derived from the verb נמל, which signifies TO CUT OFF, and is used for cutting off ears of corn, Job xxiv, 24.

The following remarks are from "the Introduction to Entomology," by Kirby and Spence:

"Till the manners of exotic ants are more accurately explored, it would be rash to affirm that no ants have magazines of provisions; for, although, during the cold of our winters in this country, they remain in a state of torpidity, and have no need of food, yet in warmer regions, during the rainy seasons, when they are probably confined to their nests, a store of provisions may be necessary for them. Even in northern climates, against wet seasons, they may provide in this way for their sustenance and that of the young brood, which, as Mr. Smeatham observes, are very voracious, and cannot bear to be long deprived of their food; else why do ants carry worms, living insects, and many other such things, into their nests? Solomon's lesson to the sluggard has been generally adduced as a strong confirmation of the ancient opinion: it can, however, only relate to the species of a warm climate, the habits of which are probably different from those of a cold one; so that his words, as commonly interpreted, may be perfectly correct and consistent with nature, and yet be not at all applicable to the species that are indigenous to Europe."

The ant, according to the royal preacher, is one of those things which are little upon the earth, but exceeding WISE. The superior wisdom of the ant has been recognised by many writers. Horace in the passage from which the preceding quotation is taken, praises its sagacity; Virgil celebrates its foresight, in providing for the wants and infirmities of old age, while it is young and vigorous:--

----ATQUE INOPI METUENS FORMICA SENECTÆ.

[And the ant dreading a destitute old age.]

And we learn from Hesiod, that among the earliest Greeks it was called Idris, that is, wise, because it foresaw the coming storm, and the inauspicious day, and collected her store. Cicero believed that the ant is not only furnished with senses, but also with mind, reason and memory:--IN FORMICA NON MODO SENSUS SED ETIAM MENS, RATIO, MEMORIA. [The ant possesses not only senses, but also mind, reason, memory.] The union of so many noble qualities in so small a corpuscle, is indeed one of the most remarkable phenomena in the works of nature.

ANTHROPOMORPHITES, a sect of ancient heretics, who were so denominated from two Greek words ἄνθρωπος, MAN, and μόρφη, SHAPE. They understood every thing spoken in Scripture in a literal sense, and particularly that passage of Genesis in which it is said, "God made man after his own image." Hence they maintained, that God had a human shape.

ANTHROPOPATHY, a metaphor by which things belonging to creatures and especially to man are ascribed to God. Instances of this abound in the Scriptures, by which they adapt themselves to human modes of speaking, and to the limited capacities of men. These anthropopathies we must however interpret in a manner suitable to the majesty of the divine nature. Thus, when the members of a human body are ascribed to God, we must understand by them those perfections of which such members in us are the instruments. The EYE, for instance, represents God's knowledge and watchful care; the ARM, his power and strength; the EARS, the regard he pays to prayer and to the cry of oppression and misery, &c. Farther, when human affections are attributed to God, we must so interpret them as to imply no imperfection, such as perturbed feeling in him. When God is said to repent, the antecedent, by a frequent figure of speech, is put for the consequent; and in this case we are to understand an altered mode of proceeding on the part of God, which in man is the effect of repenting.

ANTICHRIST, compounded of ἀντὶ, CONTRA, AGAINST, and Χριϛὸς, CHRIST, in a general sense, denotes an adversary of Christ, or one who denies that the Messiah is come. In this sense, Jews, infidels, &c, may be said to be ANTICHRISTS. The epithet, in the GENERAL sense of it, is also applicable to any power or person acting in direct opposition to Christ or his doctrine. Its PARTICULAR meaning is to be collected from those passages of Scripture in which it occurs. Accordingly, it may either signify one who assumes the place and office of Christ, or one who maintains a direct enmity and opposition to him. The Fathers all speak of antichrist as a single man; though they also assure us, that he is to have divers precursors, or forerunners. Yet many Protestant writers apply to the Romish church, and the pope who is at the head of it, the several marks and signatures of antichrist enumerated in the Apocalypse, which would imply antichrist to be, not a single person, but a corrupt society, or a long series of persecuting pontiffs, or rather, a certain power and government, that may be held for many generations, by a number of individuals succeeding one another. The antichrist mentioned by the Apostle John, first Epistle ii, 18, and more particularly described in the book of Revelation, seems evidently to be the same with the MAN OF SIN, &c, characterized by St. Paul in his Second Epistle to the Thessalonians, chap. ii; and the whole description literally applies to the Papal power. A late writer, after collecting the principal prophecies relating to antichrist, infers from them that a power, sometimes represented as the little horn, the man of sin, the antichrist, the beast, the harlot, the star falling from heaven, the false prophet, the dragon, or as the operation of false teachers, was to be expected to arise in the Christian world to persecute and oppress, and delude the disciples of Christ, corrupt the doctrine of the primitive church, enact new laws, and establish its dominion over the minds of mankind. He then proceeds to show, from the application of prophecy to history, and to the remarkable train of events that are now passing in the world, how exactly Popery, Mohammedanism, and Infidelity, correspond with the character given in Scripture of the power of antichrist, which was to prevail a certain time for the especial trial and punishment of the corrupted church of Christ. Upon this system, the different opinions of the Protestants and Papists, concerning the power of antichrist, derived from partial views of the subject, are not wholly incompatible with each other. With respect to the commonly received opinion, that the church of Rome is antichrist, Mede and Newton, Daubuz and Clarke, Lowman and Hurd, Jurieu, Vitringa, and many other members of the Protestant churches who have written upon the subject, concur in maintaining, that the prophecies of Daniel, St. Paul, and St. John, point directly to this church. This was likewise the opinion of the first reformers; and it was the prevalent opinion of Christians, in the earliest ages, that antichrist would appear soon after the fall of the Roman empire. Gregory the Great, in the sixth century, applied the prophecies concerning the beast in the Revelation, the man of sin, and the apostasy from the faith mentioned by St. Paul, to him who should presume to claim the title of universal priest, or universal bishop, in the Christian church; and yet his immediate successor, Boniface **III**, received from the tyrant Phocas the precise title which Gregory had thus censured. At the synod of Rheims, held in the tenth century, Arnulphus, bishop of Orleans, appealed to the whole council, whether the bishop of Rome was not the antichrist of St. Paul, "sitting in the temple of God," and perfectly corresponding with the description of him given by St. Paul. In the eleventh century, all the characters of antichrist seemed to be so united in the person of Pope Hildebrand, who took the name of Gregory **VII**, that Johannes Aventinus, a Romish historian, speaks of it as a subject in which the generality of fair, candid, and ingenuous writers agreed, that at that time began the reign of antichrist. And the Albigenses and Waldenses, who may be called the Protestants of the twelfth and thirteenth centuries, expressly asserted in their declarations of faith, that the church of Rome was the whore of Babylon. The Papists imagine they view in the prophetical picture of antichrist, imperial Rome, elated by her victories, exulting in her sensuality and her spoils, polluted by idolatry, persecuting the people of God, and finally falling like the first Babylon; whilst a new and holy city, represented by their own communion, filled with the spotless votaries of the Christian faith, rises out of its ruins, and the victory of the cross is completed over the temples of Paganism. This scheme has had its able advocates, at the head of whom may be placed Bossuet, bishop of Meaux, Grotius, and Hammond. Some writers have maintained, that Caligula was antichrist; and others have asserted the same of Nero. But in order to establish the resemblance, they violate the order of time, disregard the opinions of the primitive Christians, and overlook the appropriate descriptions of the Apostles. After the point had been maturely debated at the council of Gap, held in 1603, a resolution was taken thereupon to insert an article in the confession of faith, whereby the Pope is formally declared to be antichrist. Pope Clement **VIII** was stung with this decision; and even king Henry **IV**, of France was not a little mortified, to be thus declared, as he said, an imp of antichrist.

In the book of Daniel it is foretold, that this power should exercise dominion until a time and times, and the dividing of time, Dan. vii, 25. This expression is generally admitted to denote 1260 years. The Papal power was completely established in the year 755, when it obtained the exarchate of Ravenna. Some, however, date the rise of antichrist in the year of Christ 606; and Mede places it in 456. If the rise of antichrist be not reckoned till he was possessed of secular authority, his fall will happen when this power shall be taken away. If his rise began, according to Mede in 456, he must have fallen in 1716; if in 606, it must be in 1866; if in 755, in 2015. If, however, we use prophetical years, consisting of three hundred and sixty days, and date the rise of antichrist in the year 755, his fall will happen in the year of Christ 2000. Every thing however in the state of the world betokens a speedy overthrow of the Papal and Mohammedan powers, both of which have indeed been already greatly weakened.

ANTI-LIBANUS. The Greeks give this name to that chain of mountains east of Libanus, which, properly speaking, forms, together with Libanus, but one ridge of mountains, extending from north to south, and afterward from south to north, in the shape almost of a horse shoe, for the space of about fourscore leagues. The western part of these mountains was called Libanus; the eastern was called Antilibanus; the former reached along the Mediterranean, from Sidon, almost to Arada, or Symira. The Hebrew text never mentions Antilibanus; but uses the general name Libanus: and the coins struck at Laodicea and Hierapolis, have the inscription, "cities of Libanus," though they belong rather to Antilibanus. The Septuagint, on the contrary, puts Antilibanus often instead of Libanus. The valley which separates Libanus from Antilibanus is very fruitful: it was formerly, on the side of Syria, inclosed with a wall, whereof there are now no traces. Strabo says, that the name of Cœlo-Syria, or "the hollow Syria," belongs principally to the valley between Libanus and Antilibanus.

ANTINOMIANS are those who maintain that the law is of no use or obligation under the Gospel dispensation, or who hold doctrines that clearly supersede the necessity of good works and a virtuous life. The Antinomians took their origin from John Agricola, about the year 1538, who taught that the law was in no wise necessary under the Gospel; that good works do not promote our salvation, nor ill ones hinder it; that repentance is not to be preached from the decalogue, but only from the Gospel. This sect sprung up in England during the protectorate of Oliver Cromwell; and extended their system of libertinism much farther than Agricola, the disciple of Luther. Some of their teachers expressly maintained, that as the elect cannot fall from grace nor forfeit the divine favour, the wicked actions they commit are not really sinful, nor are to be considered as instances of their violation of the divine law; and that consequently they have no occasion either to confess their sins, or to break them off by repentance. According to them, it is one of the essential and distinctive characters of the elect, that they cannot do any thing which is displeasing to God. Luther, Rutherford, Schlusselburgh, Sedgwick, Gataker, Witsius, Bull, Williams, &c, have written refutations; Crisp, Richardson, Saltmarsh, &c, defences, of the Antinomians; Wigandus, a comparison between ancient and modern Antinomians.

The doctrine of Agricola was in itself obscure, and is thought to have been represented worse than it really was by Luther, who wrote against him with acrimony, and first styled him and his followers Antinomians. Agricola, in defending himself, complained that opinions were imputed to him which he did not hold. The writings of Dr. Crisp in the seventeenth century are considered as highly favourable to Antinomianism, though he acknowledges that, "in respect of the rules of righteousness, or the matter of obedience, we are under the law still, or else," as he adds, "we are lawless, to live every man as seems good in his own eyes, which no true Christian dares so much as think of." The following sentiments, however, among others, are taught in his sermons: "The law is cruel and tyrannical, requiring what is naturally impossible." "The sins of the elect were so imputed to Christ, as that though he did not commit them, yet they became actually his transgressions, and ceased to be theirs." "The feelings of conscience, which tell them that sin is theirs, arise from a want of knowing the truth." "It is but the voice of a lying spirit in the hearts of believers, that saith they have yet sin wasting their consciences, and lying as a burden too heavy for them to bear." "Christ's righteousness is so imputed to the elect, that they, ceasing to be sinners, are as righteous as he was, and all that he was." "An elect person is not in a condemned state while an unbeliever; and should he happen to die before God call him to believe, he would not be lost." "Repentance and confession of sin are not necessary to forgiveness. A believer may certainly conclude before confession, yea, as soon as he hath committed sin, the interest he hath in Christ, and the love of Christ embracing him." These dangerous sentiments, and others of a similar bearing, have been fully answered by many writers; but by none more ably than by the Rev. John Fletcher, in his "Checks to Antinomianism."

ANTIOCH, a city of Upper Syria, on the river Orontes, about twenty miles from the place where it discharges itself into the Mediterranean. It was built by Seleucus Nicanor, about three hundred years before Christ; and became the seat of empire of the Syrian kings of the Macedonian race, and afterward of the Roman governors of the eastern provinces; being very centrally and commodiously situated midway between Constantinople and Alexandria, about seven hundred miles from each, in 37° 17′ north latitude, and 36° 45′ east longitude. No city perhaps, Jerusalem excepted, has experienced more frequent revolutions, or suffered more numerous and dire calamities, than Antioch; as, besides the common plagues of eastern cities, pestilence, famine, fire, and sword, it has several times been entirely overthrown by earthquakes.

In 362, the emperor Julian spent some months at Antioch; which were chiefly occupied in his favourite object of reviving the mythology of Paganism. The grove at Daphne, planted by Seleucus, which, with its temple and oracle, presented, during the reigns of the Macedonian kings of Syria, the most splendid and fashionable place of resort for Pagan worship in the east, had sunk into neglect since the establishment of Christianity. The altar of the god was deserted, the oracle was silenced, and the sacred grove itself defiled by the interment of Christians. Julian undertook to restore the ancient honours and usages of the place; but it was first necessary to take away the pollution occasioned by the dead bodies of the Christians, which were disinterred and removed! Among these was that of Babylas, a bishop of Antioch, who died in prison in the persecution of Decius, and after resting near a century in his grave within the walls of Antioch, had been removed by order of Gallus into the midst of the grove of Daphne, where a church was built over him; the remains of the Christian saint effectually supplanting the former divinity of the place, whose temple and statue, however, though neglected, remained uninjured. The Christians of Antioch, undaunted by the conspiracy against their religion, or the presence of the emperor himself, conveyed the relics of their former bishop in triumph back to their ancient repository within the city. The immense multitude who joined in the procession, chanted forth their execrations against idols and idolaters; and on the same night the image and the temple of the Heathen god were consumed by the flames. A dreadful vengeance might be expected to have followed these scenes; but the real or affected clemency of Julian contented itself with shutting up the cathedral, and confiscating its wealth. Many Christians, indeed, suffered from the zeal of the Pagans; but, as it would appear, without the sanction of the emperor.

In 1268, Antioch was taken by Bibars, or Bondocdar, sultan of Egypt. The slaughter of seventeen thousand, and the captivity of one hundred thousand of its inhabitants, mark the final siege and fall of Antioch; which, while they close the long catalogue of its public woes, attest its extent and population. From this time it remained in a ruinous and nearly deserted condition, till, with the rest of Syria, it passed into the hands of the Ottoman Turks, with whose empire it has ever since been incorporated.

To distinguish it from other cities of the same name, the capital of Syria was called ANTIOCHIA APUD DAPHNEM, or Antioch near Daphne, a village in the neighbourhood, where was a temple dedicated to the goddess of that name; though, in truth, the chief deity of the place was Apollo, under the fable of his amorous pursuit of the nymph Daphne; and the worship was worthy of its object. The temple stood in the midst of a grove of laurels and cypresses, where every thing was assembled which could minister to the senses; and in whose recesses the juvenile devotee wanted not the countenance of a libertine god to abandon himself to voluptuousness. Even those of riper years and graver morals could not with safety breathe the atmosphere of a place where pleasure, assuming the character of religion, roused the dormant passions, and subdued the firmness of virtuous resolution. Such being the source, the stream could scarcely be expected to be more pure; in fact, the citizens of Antioch were distinguished only for their luxury in life and licentiousness in manners. This was an unpromising soil for Christianity to take root in. But here, nevertheless, it was planted at an early period, and flourished vigorously. It should be observed, that the inhabitants of Antioch were partly Syrians, and partly Greeks; chiefly, perhaps, the latter, who were invited to the new city by Seleucus. To these Greeks, in particular, certain Cypriot and Cyrenian converts, who had fled from the persecution which followed the death of Stephen, addressed themselves; "and a great number believed, and turned unto the Lord." When the heads of the church at Jerusalem were informed of this success, they sent Barnabas to Antioch, who encouraged the new disciples, and added many to their number; and finding how great were both the field and the harvest, went to Tarsus to solicit the assistance of Paul. Both this Apostle and Barnabas then taught conjointly at Antioch; and great numbers were, by their labours during a whole year, added to the rising church, Acts xi, 19–26; xv, 22–35. Here they were also joined by Peter, who was reproved by Paul for his dissimulation, and his concession to the Jews respecting the observance of the law, Gal. ii, 11–14.

Antioch was the birthplace of St. Luke and Theophilus, and the see of the martyr Ignatius. In this city the followers of Christ had first the name of Christians given them. We have the testimony of Chrysostom, both of the vast increase of this illustrious church in the fourth century, and of the spirit of charity which continued to actuate it. It consisted at this time of not less than a hundred thousand persons, three thousand of whom were supported out of the public donations. It is painful to trace the progress of declension in such a church as this. But the period now referred to, namely, the age of Chrysostom, toward the close of the fourth century, may be considered as the brightest of its history subsequent to the Apostolic age, and that from which the church at Antioch may date its fall. It continued, indeed, outwardly prosperous; but superstition, secular ambition, the pride of life; pomp and formality in the service of God, in place of humility and sincere devotion; the growth of faction, and the decay of charity; showed that real religion was fast disappearing, and that the foundations were laid of that great apostasy which, in two centuries from this time, overspread the whole Christian world, led to the entire extinction of the church in the east, and still holds dominion over the fairest portions of the west.

Antioch, under its modern name of Antakia, is now but little known to the western nations. It occupies, or rather did till lately occupy, a remote corner of the ancient enclosure of its walls. Its splendid buildings were reduced to hovels; and its population of half a million, to ten thousand wretched beings, living in the usual debasement and insecurity of Turkish subjects. Such was nearly its condition when visited by Pocock about the year 1738, and again by Kinneir in 1813. But its ancient subterranean enemy, which, since its destruction in 587, never long together withheld its assaults, has again triumphed over it: the earthquake of the 13th of August, 1822, laid it once more in ruins; and every thing relating to Antioch is past.

ANTIOCH, of Pisidia. Beside the Syrian capital, there was another Antioch visited by St. Paul when in Asia, and called, for the sake of distinction, ANTIOCHIA AD PISIDIAM, as belonging to that province, of which it was the capital. Here Paul and Barnabas preached; but the Jews, jealous, as usual, of the reception of the Gospel by the Gentiles, raised a sedition against them, and obliged them to leave the city, Acts xiii, 14, to the end. There were several other cities of the same name, sixteen in number, in Syria and Asia Minor, built by the Seleucidæ, the successors of Alexander in these countries; but the above two are the only ones which it is necessary to describe as occurring in Scripture.

ANTIOCHUS. There were many kings of this name in Syria, much celebrated in the Greek, Roman, and Jewish histories, after the time of Seleucus Nicanor, the father of Antiochus Soter, and reckoned the first king of Syria, after Alexander the Great.

1. Antiochus Soter was the son of Seleucus Nicanor, and obtained the surname of Soter, or Saviour, from having hindered the invasion of Asia by the Gauls. Some think that it was on the following occasion: The Galatians having marched to attack the Jews in Babylon, whose army consisted only of eight thousand men, reinforced with four thousand Macedonians, the Jews defended themselves with so much bravery, that they killed one hundred and twenty thousand men, 2 Mac. viii, 20. It was perhaps, too, on this occasion, that Antiochus Soter made the Jews of Asia free of the cities belonging to the Gentiles, and permitted them to live according to their own laws.

2. Antiochus Theos, or, the God, was the son and successor of Antiochus Soter. He married Berenice, daughter of Ptolemy Philadelphus, king of Egypt. Laodice, his first wife, seeing herself despised, poisoned Antiochus, Berenice, and their son, who was intended to succeed in the kingdom. After this, Laodice procured Seleucus Callinicus, her son by Antiochus, to be acknowledged king of Syria. These events were foretold by Daniel: "And in the end of years," the king of Egypt, or of the south, and the king of Syria, or of the north, "shall join themselves together; for the king's daughter of the south shall come to the king of the north to make an agreement: but she shall not retain the power of the arm; neither shall he stand, nor his arm: but she shall be given up, and they that brought her, and he that begat her, and he that strengthened her in these times," Dan. xi, 6.

3. Antiochus the Great was the son of Seleucus Callinicus, and brother to Seleucus Ceraunus, whom he succeeded in the year of the world 3781, and before Jesus Christ 223. He made war against Ptolemy Philopator, king of Egypt, but was defeated near Raphia, 3 Mac. i. Thirteen years after, Ptolemy Philopator being dead, Antiochus resolved to become master of Egypt. He immediately seized Cœlo-Syria, Phenicia, and Judea; but Scopas, general of the Egyptian army, entered Judea while Antiochus was occupied by the war against Attalus, and retook those places. However, he soon lost them again to Antiochus. On this occasion happened what Josephus relates of this prince's journey to Jerusalem. After a victory which he had obtained over Scopas, near the springs of Jordan, he became master of the strong places in Cœlo-Syria and Samaria; and the Jews submitted freely to him, received him into their city and furnished his army plentifully with provisions. In reward for their affection, Antiochus granted them, according to Josephus, twenty thousand pieces of silver, to purchase beasts for sacrifice, one thousand four hundred and sixty measures of meal, and three hundred and seventy-five measures of salt to be offered with the sacrifices, and timber to rebuild the porches of the Lord's house. He exempted the senators, scribes, and singing men of the temple, from the capitation tax; and he permitted the Jews to live according to their own laws in every part of his dominions. He also remitted the third part of their tribute, to indemnify them for their losses in the war; he forbade the Heathens to enter the temple without being purified, and to bring into the city the flesh of mules, asses, and horses to sell, under a severe penalty.

In the year of the world 3815, Antiochus was overcome by the Romans, and obliged to cede all his possessions beyond Mount Taurus, to give twenty hostages, among whom was his own son Antiochus, afterward surnamed Epiphanes, and to pay a tribute of twelve thousand Euboic talents, each fourteen Roman pounds in weight. To defray these charges, he resolved to seize the treasures of the temple of Belus, at Elymais; but the people of that country, informed of his design, surprised and destroyed him, with all his army, in the year of the world 3817, and before Jesus Christ 187. He left two sons, Seleucus Philopator, and Antiochus Epiphanes, who succeeded him.

4. Antiochus Epiphanes, the son of Antiochus the Great, having continued a hostage at Rome fourteen years, his brother Seleucus resolved to procure his return to Syria, and sent his own son Demetrius to Rome in the place of Antiochus. Whilst Antiochus was on his journey to Syria, Seleucus died, in the year of the world 3829. When, therefore, Antiochus landed, the people received him as some propitious deity come to assume the government, and to oppose the enterprises of Ptolemy, king of Egypt, who threatened to invade Syria. For this reason Antiochus obtained the surname of Epiphanes, the illustrious, or of one appearing like a god.

Antiochus quickly turned his attention to the possession of Egypt, which was then enjoyed by Ptolemy Philometor, his nephew, son to his sister Cleopatra, whom Antiochus the Great had married to Ptolemy Epiphanes, king of Egypt. He sent Apollonius, one of his officers, into Egypt, apparently to honour Ptolemy's coronation, but in reality to obtain intelligence whether the great men of the kingdom were inclined to place the government of Egypt in his hands during the minority of the king his nephew, 2 Mac. iv, 21, &c. Apollonius, however, found them not disposed to favour his master; and this obliged Antiochus to make war against Philometor. He came to Jerusalem in 3831, and was received there by Jason, to whom he had sold the high priesthood. He designed to attack Egypt, but returned without effecting any thing. The ambition of those Jews who sought the high priesthood, and bought it of Antiochus, was the beginning of those calamities which overwhelmed their nation under this prince. Jason procured himself to be constituted in this dignity in the stead of Onias **III**; but Menelaus offering a greater price, Jason was deprived, and Menelaus appointed in his place. These usurpers of the high priesthood, to gratify the Syrians, assumed the manners of the Greeks, their games and exercises, and neglected the worship of the Lord, and the temple service.

War broke out between Antiochus Epiphanes and Ptolemy Philometor. Antiochus entered Egypt in the year of the world 3833, and reduced almost the whole of it to his obedience, 2 Mac. v, 3–5. The next year he returned; and whilst he was engaged in the siege of Alexandria, a false report was spread of his death. The inhabitants of Jerusalem testifying their joy at this news, Antiochus, when returning from Egypt, entered this city by force, treated the Jews as rebels, and commanded his troops to slay all they met. Eighty thousand were killed, made captives, or sold on this occasion. Antiochus, conducted by the corrupt high priest Menelaus, entered into the holy of holies, whence he took and carried off the most precious vessels of that holy place, to the value of one thousand eight hundred talents. In the year 3835, Antiochus made a third expedition against Egypt, which he entirely subdued. The year following, he sent Apollonius into Judea, with an army of twenty-two thousand men, and commanded him to kill all the Jews who were of full age, and to sell the women and young men, 2 Mac. v, 24, 25. These orders were too punctually executed. It was on this occasion that Judas Maccabæus retired into the wilderness with his father and his brethren, 2 Mac. v, 29. These misfortunes were only preludes of what they were to suffer; for Antiochus, apprehending that the Jews would never be constant in their obedience to him, unless he obliged them to change their religion, and to embrace that of the Greeks, issued an edict, enjoining them to conform to the laws of other nations, and forbidding their usual sacrifices in the temple, their festivals, and their Sabbath. The statue of Jupiter Olympus was placed upon the altar of the temple, and thus the abomination of desolation was seen in the temple of God. Many corrupt Jews complied with these orders; but others resisted them. Mattathias and his sons retired to the mountains. Old Eleazar, and the seven brethren, suffered death with great courage at Antioch, 2 Mac. vii. Mattathias being dead, Judas Maccabæus headed those Jews who continued faithful, and opposed with success the generals whom king Antiochus sent into Judea. The king, informed of the valour and resistance of Judas, sent new forces; and, finding his treasures exhausted, he resolved to go into Persia to levy tributes, and to collect large sums which he had agreed to pay to the Romans, 1 Mac. iii, 5–31; 2 Mac. ix, 1, &c; 1 Mac. vi, 1, &c. Knowing that very great riches were lodged in the temple of Elymaïs, he determined to carry it off; but the inhabitants of the country made so vigorous a resistance, that he was forced to retreat toward Babylonia. When he was come to Ecbatana, he was informed of the defeat of Nicanor and Timotheus, and that Judas Maccabæus had retaken the temple of Jerusalem, and restored the worship of the Lord, and the usual sacrifices. On receiving this intelligence, the king was transported with indignation; and, threatening to make Jerusalem a grave for the Jews, commanded the driver of his chariot to urge the horses forward, and to hasten his journey. However, divine vengeance soon overtook him: he fell from his chariot, and bruised all his limbs. He was also tormented with such pains in his bowels, as allowed him no rest; and his disease was aggravated by grief and vexation. In this condition he wrote to the Jews very humbly, promised them many things, and engaged even to turn Jew, if God would restore him to health. He earnestly recommended to them his son Antiochus, who was to succeed him, and entreated them to favour the young prince, and to continue faithful to him. He died, overwhelmed with pain and grief, in the mountains of Paratacene, in the little town of Tabes, in the year of the world 3840, and before Jesus Christ 164.

5. Antiochus Eupator, son of Antiochus Epiphanes, was only nine years old when his father died and left him the kingdom of Syria. Lysias, who governed the kingdom in the name of the young prince, led against Judea an army of one hundred thousand foot, twenty thousand horse, and thirty elephants, 1 Mac. vi; 2 Mac. xiii. He besieged and took the

fortress of Bethsura, and thence marched against Jerusalem. The city was ready to fall into his hands when Lysias received the news that Philip, whom Antiochus Epiphanes had entrusted with the regency of the kingdom, had come to Antioch to take the government, according to the disposition of the late king. He therefore proposed an accommodation with the Jews, that he might return speedily to Antioch and oppose Philip. After concluding a peace, he immediately returned into Syria, with the young king and his army.

In the meantime, Demetrius Soter, son of Seleucus Philopator, and nephew to Antiochus Epiphanes, to whom by right the kingdom belonged, having escaped from Rome, came into Syria. Finding the people disposed for revolt, Demetrius headed an army, and marched directly to Antioch, against Antiochus and Lysias. However, the inhabitants did not wait till he besieged the city; but opened the gates, and delivered to him Lysias and the young king Antiochus Eupator, whom Demetrius caused to be put to death, without suffering them to appear in his presence. Antiochus Eupator reigned only two years, and died in the year of the world 3842, and before Jesus Christ 162.

6. Antiochus Theos, or the DIVINE, the son of Alexander Balas, king of Syria, was brought up by the Arabian prince Elmachuel, or, as he is called in the Greek, Simalcue, 1 Mac. xi, 39, 40, &c. Demetrius Nicanor, king of Syria, having rendered himself odious to his troops, one Diodotus, otherwise called Tryphon, came to Zabdiel, a king in Arabia, and desired him to entrust him with young Antiochus, whom he promised to place on the throne of Syria, which was then possessed by Demetrius Nicanor. After some hesitation, Zabdiel complied with the request; and Tryphon carried Antiochus into Syria, and put the crown on his head. The troops dismissed by Demetrius, came and joined Tryphon, who, having formed a powerful army, defeated Demetrius, and forced him to retreat to Seleucia. Tryphon seized his elephants, and rendered himself master of Antioch, in the year of the world 3859, and before Jesus Christ 145. Antiochus Theos, to strengthen himself in his new acquisition, sent letters to Jonathan Maccabæus, high priest and prince of the Jews, confirming him in the high priesthood, and granting him four toparchies, or four considerable places, in Judea. He also received Jonathan into the number of his friends, sent him vessels of gold, permitted him to use a gold cup, to wear purple, and a golden buckle; and he gave his brother, Simon Maccabæus, the command of all his troops on the coast of the Mediterranean, from Tyre to Egypt. Jonathan, engaged by so many favours, declared resolutely for Antiochus, or rather for Tryphon, who reigned under the name of this young prince; and on several occasions, he attacked the generals of Demetrius, who still possessed many places beyond Jordan and in Galilee, 1 Macc. xi, 63, &c; xii, 24, 34. Tryphon, seeing young Antiochus in peaceable possession of the kingdom of Syria, resolved to usurp his crown. He thought it necessary, in the first place, to secure Jonathan Maccabæus who was one of the most powerful supporters of Antiochus's throne. He came, therefore, with troops into Judea, invited Jonathan to Ptolemais, and there, on frivolous pretences, made him prisoner. However, Simon, Jonathan's brother, headed the troops of Judea, and opposed Tryphon, who intended to take Jerusalem. Tryphon, being disappointed, put Jonathan to death at Bassa or Bascama, and returned into Syria, where, without delay, he executed his design of killing Antiochus. He corrupted the royal physicians, who, having published that Antiochus was tormented with the stone, murdered him, by cutting him without any necessity. Thus Tryphon was left master of Syria, in the year of the world 3861, and before Jesus Christ 143.

7. Antiochus Sidetes, or SOTER the Saviour, or EUSEBES the pious, was the son of Demetrius Soter, and brother to Demetrius Nicanor. Tryphon, the usurper of the kingdom of Syria, having rendered himself odious to his troops, they deserted him, and offered their services to Cleopatra, the wife of Demetrius Nicanor. She lived in the city of Seleucia, shut up with her children, while her husband Demetrius was a prisoner in Persia, where he had married Rodeguna, the daughter of Arsaces king of Persia. Cleopatra, therefore sent to Antiochus Sidetes, her brother-in-law, and offered him the crown of Syria, if he would marry her; to which Antiochus consented. This prince was then at Cnidus, where his father, Demetrius Soter had placed him with one of his friends. He came into Syria, and wrote to Simon Maccabæus, to engage him against Tryphon, 1 Macc. xv, 1, 2, 3, &c. He confirmed the privileges which the kings of Syria had granted to Simon, permitted him to coin money with his own stamp, declared Jerusalem and the temple exempt from royal jurisdiction, and promised other favours as soon as he should obtain peaceable possession of the kingdom which had belonged to his ancestors. Antiochus Sidetes having married his sister-in-law, Cleopatra, in the year of the world 3865, the troops of Tryphon resorted to him in crowds. Tryphon, thus abandoned, retired to Dora, in Phœnicia, whither Antiochus pursued him with an army of 120,000 foot, 800 horse, and a powerful fleet. Simon Maccabæus sent Antiochus two thousand chosen men, but the latter refused them and revoked all his promises. He also sent Athenobius to Jerusalem to oblige Simon to restore to him Gazara and Joppa, with the citadel of Jerusalem; and to demand of him five hundred talents more, as reparation for injuries the king had suffered, and as tribute for his own cities. At the same time he threatened to make war upon him, if he did not comply. Simon showed Athenobius all the lustre of his wealth and power, told him he had in his possession no place which belonged to Antiochus, and said that the cities of Gazara and Joppa had greatly injured his people, and he would give the king for the property of them one hundred talents. Athenobius returned with great indignation to Antiochus, who was extremely offended at Simon's answer. In the meantime, Tryphon having escaped privately from Dora, embarked in a vessel and fled. Antiochus pursued him, and sent Cendebeus with troops into the maritime parts of Palestine, and commanded him to rebuild Cedron, and fight the Jews. John Hircanus, son of Simon Maccabæus, was then at Gaza, and gave notice to his father

of the coming of Cendebeus. Simon furnished his sons, John Hircanus and Judas with troops, and sent them against Cendebeus, whom they routed in the plain and pursued to Azotus.

Antiochus followed Tryphon, till he forced him to kill himself in the year of the world 3869. After this, Antiochus thought only of reducing to his obedience those cities which, in the beginning of his father's reign, had shaken off their subjection. Simon Maccabæus, prince and high priest of the Jews, being treacherously murdered by Ptolemy, his son-in-law, in the castle of Docus, near Jericho, the murderer immediately sent to Antiochus Sidetes to demand troops, that he might recover for him the country and cities of the Jews. Antiochus came in person with an army, and besieged Jerusalem, which was bravely defended by John Hircanus. The siege was long protracted; and the king divided his army into seven parts, and guarded all the avenues of the city. It being the time for celebrating the feast of tabernacles, the Jews desired of Antiochus a truce for seven days. The king not only granted this request, but sent them bulls with gilded horns, and vessels of gold and silver filled with incense, to be offered in the temple. He also ordered such provisions as they wanted, to be given to the Jewish soldiers. This courtesy of the king so won the hearts of the Jews, that they sent ambassadors to treat of peace, and to desire that they might live according to their own laws. Antiochus required that they should surrender their arms, demolish the city walls, pay tribute for Joppa and the other cities they possessed out of Judea, and receive a garrison into Jerusalem. To these conditions, except the last, the Jews consented; for they could not be induced to see an army of strangers in their capital, and chose rather to give hostages and five hundred talents of silver. The king entered the city, beat down the breast work above the walls, and returned to Syria, in the year of the world 3870, and before Jesus Christ 134. Three years after, Antiochus marched against the Persians, or Parthians, and demanded the liberty of his brother Demetrius Nicanor, who had been made prisoner long before by Arsaces, and was detained for the purpose of being employed in exciting a war against Antiochus. This war, therefore, Antiochus thought proper to prevent. With an army of eighty thousand, or, as Orosius says, of one hundred thousand men, he marched toward Persia, and no sooner appeared on the frontiers of that country, than several eastern princes, detesting the pride and avarice of the Persians, came and surrendered. Antiochus defeated his enemies in three engagements, and took Babylon. He was accompanied in these expeditions by John Hircanus, high priest of the Jews, who, it is supposed, obtained the surname of Hircanus from some gallant action which he performed.

As the army of Antiochus was too numerous to continue assembled in any one place, he was obliged to divide it, to put it into winter quarters. These troops behaved with so much insolence, that they alienated the minds of all men. The cities in which they were, privately surrendered to the Persians; and all resolved to attack, in one day, the garrisons they contained, that the troops being separated might not assist each other. Antiochus at Babylon obtained intelligence of this design, and, with the few soldiers about him, endeavoured to succour his people. He was attacked in the way by Phraates, king of Persia, whom he fought with great bravery; but being at length deserted by his own forces, according to the generality of historians, he was overpowered and killed by the Persians or Parthians. Appian, however, says that he killed himself, and Ælian, that he threw himself headlong from a precipice. This event took place in the year of the world 3874, and before Jesus Christ 130. After the death of Sidetes, Demetrius Nicanor, or Nicetor, reascended the throne of Syria.

ANTIPÆDOBAPTISTS, a denomination given to those who object to the baptism of infants. The word is derived from ἀντὶ, AGAINST, ϖᾶις, ϖαιδὸς, A CHILD, βαπτίζω, I BAPTIZE. See Baptism.

ANTIPAS, Antipas-Herod, or Herod-Antipas, was the son of Herod the Great, and Cleopatra of Jerusalem. Herod the Great, in his first will, declared him his successor in the kingdom; but he afterward named his son Archelaus king of Judea, and gave to Antipas only the title of tetrarch of Galilee and Peræa. Archelaus going to Rome, to persuade the emperor to confirm his father's will, Antipas also went thither. The emperor bestowed on Archelaus one moity of what had been assigned him by Herod, with the quality of ethnarch, and promised to grant him the title of king when he had shown himself deserving of it by his virtues. To Antipas, Augustus gave Galilee and Peræa; and to Philip, Herod's other son, the Batanæa, Trachonitis, and Auranitis, with some other places.

Antipas, returning to Judea, took great pains in adorning and fortifying the principal places of his dominions. He married the daughter of Aretas, king of Arabia, whom he divorced about A. D. 33, that he might marry his sister-in-law, Herodias, the wife of his brother Philip, who was still living. John the Baptist, exclaiming against this incest, was seized by order of Antipas, and imprisoned in the castle of Machærus. Josephus says, that Antipas caused John to be taken, because he drew too great a concourse after him; and Antipas was afraid he should use his influence over the people to induce them to revolt. But Josephus has reported the pretence for the true cause. The evangelists, who were better informed than Josephus, as being eye witnesses of what passed, and particularly acquainted with John and his disciples, assure us, that the true reason of imprisoning John was the aversion of Herod and Herodias against him, on account of his liberty in censuring their scandalous marriage, Matt. xiv, 3, 4; Mark vi, 14, 17, 18; Luke iii, 19, 20. When the king was celebrating his birth day, with the principal persons of his court, the daughter of Herodias danced before them, and pleased him so well that he swore to give her whatever she should ask. She consulted her mother, who advised her to ask the head of John the Baptist. Returning, therefore, to the hall, she addressed herself to the king, and said, "Give me here John Baptist's head in a charger." The king was afflicted at this request; but in consideration of his oath, and of the persons at table with him, he sent one of his guards, who beheaded John in prison. The head was brought in, and given to the young woman, who delivered it to her mother, Matt. xiv, 5, 6, &c. Aretas, king of Arabia, to revenge the affront which Herod had offered to his daughter, declared war against him, and vanquished him in a very obstinate contest. Josephus tells us, that the Jews attributed the defeat of Herod to the death of John the Baptist. In the year of the Christian æra 39, Herodias being jealous of the prosperity of her brother Agrippa, who from a private person had become king of Judea, persuaded her husband, Herod-Antipas, to visit Rome, and desire the same dignity of the emperor Caius. She resolved to accompany him; and hoped that her presents and appearance would contribute to procure the emperor's favour. However, Agrippa obtaining intelligence of this design, wrote to the emperor and accused Antipas. The messenger of Agrippa arrived at Baiæ, where the emperor was, at the very time when Herod received his first audience. Caius, on the delivery of Agrippa's letters, read them with great earnestness. In these letters, Agrippa accused Antipas of having been a party in Sejanus's conspiracy against Tiberius, and said that he still carried on a correspondence with Artabanus, king of Partha, against the Romans. As a proof of this, he affirmed that Antipas had in his arsenals arms for seventy thousand men. Caius being angry, demanded hastily of Antipas, if it were true that he had such a quantity of arms? The king not daring to deny it, was instantly banished to Lyons in Gaul. The emperor offered to forgive Herodias, in consideration of her brother Agrippa; but she chose rather to follow her husband, and to share his fortune in banishment. This is that Antipas, who, being at Jerusalem at the time of our Saviour's passion, ridiculed Jesus whom Pilate had sent to him, dressed him in worn-out royalty, and sent him back to Pilate as a mock king, whose ambition gave him no umbrage, Luke xxiii, 7, 11. The year of the death of Antipas is unknown; but it is certain that he, as well as Herodias, died in exile. Josephus says, that he died in Spain, whither Caius, on his coming into Gaul the first year of his banishment, might order him to be sent.

2. Antipas, the faithful martyr or witness mentioned in the book of Revelation, ii, 13. He is said to have been one of our Saviour's first disciples, and to have suffered martyrdom at Pergamus, of which he was bishop. His Acts relate that he was burnt in a brazen bull. Though ancient ecclesiastical history furnishes no account of this Antipas, yet it is certain that, according to all the rules of language, what is said concerning him by St. John must be understood literally, and not mystically, as some interpreters have done.

ANTIPATRIS, Acts xxiii, 31, a town in Palestine, anciently called Caphar-Saba, according to Josephus; but named Antipatris by Herod the Great, in honour of his father Antipater. It was situated in a pleasant valley, near the mountains, in the way from Jerusalem to Cæsarea. Josephus places it at about the distance of seventeen miles from Joppa. To this place St. Paul was brought in his way to the governor of Judea at Cæsarea, Acts xxiii, 31.

ANTITYPE, that which answers to a type or figure. A type is a model, mould, or pattern; that which is formed according to it is an antitype. See Type.

ANTONIA, one of the towers of Jerusalem, called by Herod after M. Antony. The Romans generally kept a garrison in this tower; and from thence it was that the tribune ran with his soldiers to rescue St. Paul out of the hands of the Jews, who had seized him in the temple, and designed to have murdered him, Acts xxi, 31, 32.

APE, קוֹף, κῆφος and κῆπος, CEPHUS, 1 Kings x, 22; 2 Chron. ix, 21. This animal seems to be the same with the CEPH of the Ethiopians, of which Pliny speaks, l. viii, c. 19: "At the games given by Pompey the Great," says he, "were shown CEPHS brought from Ethiopia, which had their fore feet like a human hand, their hind legs and feet also resembled those of a man." The Scripture says that the fleet of Solomon brought apes, or rather monkeys, &c, from Ophir. The learned are not agreed respecting the situation of that country; but Major Wilford says that the ancient name of the River Landi sindh in India was COPHES. May it not have been so called from the קפים inhabiting its banks?

We now distinguish this tribe of creatures into 1. MONKEYS, those with long tails; 2. APES, those with short tails; 3. BABOONS, those without tails. The ancient Egyptians are said to have worshipped apes; it is certain that they are still adored in many places in India. Maffeus describes a magnificent temple dedicated to the ape, with a portico for receiving the victims sacrificed, supported by seven hundred columns.

"With glittering gold and sparkling gems they shine,

But apes and monkeys are the gods within."

Figures of apes are also made and reverenced as idols, of which we have several in Moore's "Hindoo Pantheon;" also in the avatars, given in Maurice's "History of India," &c. In some parts of the country the apes are held sacred, though not resident in temples; and incautious English gentlemen, by attempting to shoot these apes, (rather, perhaps, monkeys,) have been exposed, not only to all manner of insults and vexations from the inhabitants of the villages, &c, adjacent, but have even been in danger of their lives.

APHARSACHITES, a people sent by the kings of Assyria to inhabit the country of Samaria, in the room of those Israelites who had been removed beyond the Euphrates, Ezra v, 6. They, with the other Samaritans, opposed the rebuilding of the walls of Jerusalem, Ezra iv, 9.

APIS, a symbolical deity worshipped by the Egyptians. It was an ox, having certain exterior marks, in which animal the soul of the great Osiris was supposed to subsist. The ox was probably made the symbol of Osiris because he presided over agriculture.

APOCALYPSE, Ἀποκάλυψις, signifies REVELATION. It is, however, particularly applied to the Revelations which St. John had in the isle of Patmos, whither he had been banished. The testimonies in favour of the book of the Revelation being a genuine work of St. John the Evangelist are very full and satisfactory. Andrew, bishop of Cæsarea in Capadocia, in the fifth century, assures us that Papias acknowledged the Revelation to be inspired. But the earliest author now extant who mentions this book is Justin Martyr, who lived about sixty years after it was written, and he ascribes it to St. John. So does Iræneus, whose evidence is alone sufficient upon this point; for he was the disciple of Polycarp, who was the disciple of John himself; and he expressly tells us that he had the explanation of a certain passage in this book from those who had conversed with St. John the author. These two fathers are followed by Clement of Alexandria, Theophilus of Antioch, Tertullian, Origen, Cyprian, Lactantius, Jerome, Athanasius, and many other ecclesiastical writers, all of whom concur in considering the Apostle John as the author of the Revelation. Some few persons, however, doubted the genuineness of this book in the third and fourth centuries; but since that time it has been very generally acknowledged to be canonical; and, indeed, as Mr. Lowman observes, "hardly any one book has received more early, more authentic, and more satisfactory attestations." The omission of this book in some of the early catalogues of the Scriptures, was probably not owing to any suspicion concerning its authenticity or genuineness, but because its obscurity and mysteriousness were thought to render it less fit to be read publicly and generally. It is called the Revelation of John the Divine; and this appellation was first given to St. John by Eusebius, not to distinguish him from any other person of the same name, but as an honourable title, intimating that to him was more fully revealed the system of divine counsels than to any other prophet of the Christian dispensation.

St. John was banished to Patmos in the latter part of the reign of Domitian, and he returned to Ephesus immediately after the death of that emperor, which happened in the year 96; and as the Apostle states, that these visions appeared to him while he was in that island, we may consider this book as written in the year 95 or 96.

In the first chapter, St. John asserts the divine authority of the predictions which he is about to deliver; addresses himself to the churches of the Proconsular Asia; and describes the first vision, in which he is commanded to write the things then revealed to him. The second and third chapters contain seven epistles to the seven churches in Asia; namely, of Ephesus, Smyrna, Pergamus, Thyatira, Sardis, Philadelphia, and Laodicea, which relate chiefly to their then respective circumstances and situation. At the fourth chapter the prophetic visions begin, and reach to the end of the book. They contain a prediction of all the most remarkable revolutions and events in the Christian church from the time of the Apostle to the final consummation of all things. An attempt to explain these prophecies does not fall within the design of this work; and therefore those who are disposed to study this sublime and mysterious book are referred to Mede, Daubuz, Sir Isaac Newton, Lowman, Bishop Newton, Bishop Hurd, and many other excellent commentators. These learned men agree in their general principles concerning the interpretation of this book, although they differ in some particular points; and it is not to be expected that there should be a perfect coincidence of opinion in the explanation of those predictions which relate to still future times; for, as the incomparable Sir Isaac Newton observes, "God gave these and the prophecies of the Old Testament, not to gratify men's curiosity, by enabling them to foreknow things, but that after they were fulfilled they might be interpreted by the event, and his own prescience, not that of the interpreters, be then manifested thereby to the world." "To explain this book perfectly," says Bishop Newton, "is not the work of one man, or of one age; but probably it never will be clearly understood, till it is all fulfilled." It is graciously designed, that the gradual accomplishment of these predictions should afford, in every succeeding period of time, additional testimony to the divine origin of our holy religion.

APOCRYPHA, books not admitted into the sacred canon, being either spurious, or at least not acknowledged to be divine. The word Apocrypha is of Greek origin, and is either derived from the words ἀπὸ τῆς κρύπτης, because the books in question were removed FROM THE CRYPT, chest, ark, or other receptacle in which the sacred books were deposited whose authority was never doubted, or more probably from the verb ἀποκρύπτω, TO HIDE or CONCEAL, because they were concealed from the generality of readers, their authority not being recognised by the church, and because they are books which are destitute of proper testimonials, their original being obscure, their authors unknown, and their character either heretical or suspected. The advocates of the church of Rome, indeed, affirm that some of these books are divinely inspired; but it is easy to account for this: the apocryphal writings serve to countenance some of the corrupt practices of that church. The Protestant churches not only account those books to be apocryphal and merely human compositions which are esteemed such by the church of Rome, as the Prayer of Manasseh, the third and fourth books of Esdras, the addition at the end of Job, and the hundred and fifty-first Psalm; but also the books of Tobit, Judith, the additions to the book of Esther, Wisdom, Ecclesiasticus, Baruch the Prophet, with the Epistle of Jeremiah, the Song of the Three Children, the Story of Susanna, the Story of Bel and the Dragon, and the first and second books of Maccabees. The books here enumerated are unanimously rejected by Protestants for the following reasons:--

1. They possess no authority whatever, either external or internal, to procure their admission into the sacred canon. None of them are extant in Hebrew; all of them are in the Greek language, except the fourth book of Esdras, which is

only extant in Latin. They were written for the most part by Alexandrian Jews, subsequently to the cessation of the prophetic spirit, though before the promulgation of the Gospel. Not one of the writers in direct terms advances a claim to inspiration; nor were they ever received into the sacred canon by the Jewish church, and therefore they were not sanctioned by our Saviour. No part of the apocrypha is quoted, or even alluded to, by him or by any of his Apostles; and both Philo and Josephus, who flourished in the first century of the Christian æra, are totally silent concerning them.

2. The apocryphal books were not admitted into the canon of Scripture during the first four centuries of the Christian church. They are not mentioned in the catalogue of inspired writings made by Melito bishop of Sardis, who flourished in the second century, nor in those of Origen in the third century, of Athanasius, Hilary, Cyril of Jerusalem, Epiphanius, Gregory Nazianzen, Amphilochius, Jerom, Rufinus, and others of the fourth century; nor in the catalogue of canonical books recognised by the council of Laodicea, held in the same century, whose canons were received by the catholic church; so that as Bishop Burnet well observes, we have the concurring sense of the whole church of God in this matter. To this decisive evidence against the canonical authority of the apocryphal books, we may add that they were never read in the Christian church until the fourth century; when, as Jerom informs us, they were read "for example of life, and instruction of planners; but were not applied to establish any doctrine." And contemporary writers state, that although they were not approved as canonical or inspired writings, yet some of them, particularly Judith, Wisdom, and Ecclesiasticus, were allowed to be perused by catechumens. As a proof that they were not regarded as canonical in the fifth century, Augustine relates, that when the book of Wisdom and other writings of the same class were publicly read in the church, they were given to the readers or inferior ecclesiastical officers, who read them in a lower place than those which were universally acknowledged to be canonical, which were read by the bishops and presbyters in a more eminent and conspicuous manner. To conclude: notwithstanding the veneration in which these books were held by the western church, it is evident that the same authority was never ascribed to them as to the Old and New Testament until the last council of Trent, at its fourth session, presumed to place them all (except the Prayer of Manasseh and the third and fourth books of Esdras) in the same rank with the inspired writings of Moses and the Prophets.

APOLLINARIANS, or Apollinarists, or, as they are called by Epiphanius, Dimaritæ, a sect who derive their principal name from Apollinaris, bishop of Laodicea, in the fourth century. Apollinaris strenuously defended the divinity of Christ against the Arians; but by indulging too freely in philosophical distinctions and subtleties, he denied in some measure his humanity. He maintained that the body which Christ assumed was endowed with a sensitive, and not a rational, soul; and that the divine nature performed the functions of reason, and supplied the place of the intellectual principle in man. Hence it seemed to follow, that the divine nature in Christ was blended with the human and suffered with it the pains of crucifixion and death. Apollinaris and his followers have been charged with other errors by certain ancient waiters; but it is not easy to determine how far their charge is worthy of credit. The doctrine of Apollinaris was first condemned by a council at Alexandria in 362, and afterward in a more formal manner by a council at Rome in 375, and by another council in 378, which deposed Apollinaris from his bishopric. In short, it was attacked at the same time by the laws of the emperors, the decrees of councils, and the writings of the learned; and sunk by degrees under their united force.

APOLLOS was a Jew of Alexandria, who came to Ephesus in the year of our Lord 54, during the absence of St. Paul, who had gone to Jerusalem, Acts xviii, 24. He was an eloquent man, and mighty in the Scriptures; but he knew only the baptism of John, and was not fully informed of the higher branches of Gospel doctrine. However, he acknowledged that Jesus Christ was the Messiah, and declared himself openly as his disciple. At Ephesus, therefore, he began to speak boldly in the synagogue, and demonstrated by the Scriptures that Jesus was the Christ. Aquila and Priscilla, having heard him there, took him with them, and instructed him more fully in the ways of God. Some time after, he was inclined to go into Achaia, and the brethren wrote to the disciples there, desiring them to receive him. He was very useful at Corinth, where he watered what St. Paul had planted, 1 Cor. iii, 6. It has been supposed, that the great admiration of his disciples for him tended to produce a schism. Some said, "I am of Paul;" some, "I am of Apollos;" and others, "I am of Cephas." But this division, which St. Paul mentions and reproves in his First Epistle to the Corinthians, did not prevent Paul and Apollos, personally, from being closely united in the bonds of Christian charity and affection. Apollos, hearing that the Apostle was at Ephesus, went to meet him, and was there when St. Paul wrote the First Epistle to the Corinthians; in which he observes, that he had earnestly entreated Apollos to return to Corinth: but though he had not prevailed with him, Apollos gave him room to hope that he would visit that city at a favourable opportunity. Some have supposed, that the Apostle names Apollos and Cephas, not as the real persons in whose name parties had been formed in Corinth, but that, in order to avoid provoking a temper which he wished to subside, he transfers "by a figure" to Apollos and himself what was really meant of other parties, whom from prudence he declines to mention. However this might be, the reluctance of Apollos to return to Corinth seems to countenance the general opinion. St. Jerom says that Apollos was so dissatisfied with the division which had happened on his account at Corinth, that he retired into Crete with Zeno, a doctor of the law; but that the evil having been corrected by the letter of St. Paul to the Corinthians, Apollos returned to that city, of which he afterward became bishop. The Greeks say that he was bishop of Duras; some, that he was bishop of Iconium, in Phrygia; and others of Cæsarea.

APOLLYON. See Abaddon.

APOLOGIES, in ecclesiastical history, were defences (so the Greek word means) of Christianity, presented to Heathen emperors, by the Christian fathers, who were therefore called Apologists. The first was presented to the emperor Adrian, by Quadratus, A. D. 126, a fragment of which is preserved by Eusebius; but another, presented soon after to the same, by Aristides, a converted Athenian philosopher, is totally lost. Justin Martyr wrote two apologies; the latter (to the Roman senate) is imperfect at the beginning; but the former, addressed to Antoninus Pius, is preserved entire, and was published in English, in 1709, by the Rev. W. Reeves, together with one by Tertullian, the Octavius (a dialogue) of Minucius Felix, and the Commentary of Vincentius Lirinensis, with notes and preliminary dissertations to each, in 2 vols. 8vo. The Apologies are curious and valuable remains of antiquity, as showing what were the objections of the Heathens, and the manner in which they were rebutted by the early Christians.

APOSTASY, a deserting or abandoning of the true religion. The word is borrowed from the Latin APOSTATARE, or APOSTARE, TO DESPISE or VIOLATE any thing. Hence APOSTATARE LEGES anciently signified TO TRANSGRESS THE LAWS. The Latin APOSTATARE, again, comes from ἀπὸ, FROM, and ἵϛημι, I STAND. Among the Romanists, apostasy also signifies the forsaking of a religious order, whereof a man had made profession, without a lawful dispensation. The ancients distinguished three kinds of apostasy: the first, A SUPEREROGATIONE, is committed by a priest, or religious, who abandons his profession, and returns to his lay state; the second, A MANDATIS DEI, by a person of any condition, who abandons the commands of God, though he retains his faith; the third, A FIDE, by him who not only abandons his works, but also the faith. There is this difference between an apostate and a heretic; that the latter only abandons a part of the faith, whereas the former renounces the whole. The primitive Christian church distinguished several kinds of apostasy. The first was that of those who relapsed from Christianity into Judaism; the second, that of those who blended Judaism and Christianity together; and the third was that of those who, after having been Christians, voluntarily relapsed into Paganism.

APOSTLE, ἀπόϛολος, one of the twelve disciples of Jesus Christ, commissioned by him to preach his Gospel, and propagate it to all parts of the earth. The word originally signifies a person DELEGATED or SENT; from ἀποϛέλλω, MITTO; in which sense it occurs in Herodotus, and other profane authors. Hence, in the New Testament, the term is applied to divers sorts of delegates; and to the twelve disciples by way of eminence. They were limited to the number twelve, in allusion to the twelve tribes of Israel. See Matt. xix, 28; Luke xxii, 30; Rev. xxi, 12–14; and compare Exod. xxiv, 4; Deut. i, 23; and Josh. iv, 2, 3. Accordingly care was taken, on the death of Judas, to choose another, to make up the number, Acts i, 21, 22, 26. Of the first selection and commission of the twelve Apostles, we have an account, Luke vi, 13, &c; Matt. x, 1, &c. Having chosen and constituted twelve persons, under the name of Apostles, our blessed Lord determined that for some time they should be continually with him, not only to attend upon his public ministry, but to enjoy the benefit of his private conversation, that he might furnish them the better for the great work in which they were to be employed; and that, at length, after suitable preparation, he might, with greater advantage, send them abroad to preach his Gospel, and thus make way for his own visits to some more distant parts, where he had not yet been; and to enable them more effectually to do this, he endowed them with the power of working miracles, of curing diseases, and casting out demons. About the commencement of the third year of his ministry, according to the common account of its duration, he sent them out two by two, that they might be assistants to each other in their work; and commanded them to restrict their teaching and services to the people of Israel, and to avoid going to the Gentiles or to the Samaritans; to declare the approach of the kingdom of heaven, and the establishment of the Gospel dispensation; to exercise the miraculous powers with which they had been endowed gratuitously; and to depend for their subsistence on the providence of God, and on the donations of those to whom they ministered. Their names were, Simon Peter; Andrew, his brother; James the greater, the son of Zebedee; and John his brother, who was the beloved disciple; Philip of Bethsaida; Bartholomew; Thomas, called Didymus, as having a twin brother; Matthew or Levi, who had been a publican; James, the son of Alpheus, called James the less; Lebbeus, surnamed Thaddeus, and who was also called Judas or Jude, the brother of James; Simon, the Canaanite, so called, as some have thought, because he was a native of Cana, or, as Dr. Hammond thinks, from the Hebrew קנא, signifying the same with Zelotes, or the Zelot, a name given to him on account of his having before professed a distinguishing zeal for the law; and Judas Iscariot, or a man of Carioth, Josh. xv, 25, who afterward betrayed him, and then laid violent hands on himself. Of these, Simon, Andrew, James the greater, and John, were fishermen; Matthew, and James the son of Alpheus, were publicans; and the other six were probably fishermen, though their occupation is not distinctly specified.

After the resurrection of our Saviour, and not long before his ascension, the place of Judas the traitor was supplied by Matthias, supposed by some to have been Nathanael of Galilee, to whom our Lord had given the distinguishing character of an "Israelite indeed, in whom there was no guile;" and the twelve Apostles, whose number was now completed, received a new commission, of a more extensive nature than the first, to preach the Gospel to all nations, and to be witnesses of Christ, not only in Jerusalem, in all Judea, and in Samaria, but unto the uttermost parts of the earth; and they were qualified for the execution of their office by a plenteous effusion of miraculous powers and spiritual gifts, and particularly the gift of tongues. In consequence of this commission, they preached first to the

Jews, then to the Samaritans, and afterward to the idolatrous Gentiles. Their signal success at Jerusalem, where they opened their commission, alarmed the Jewish sanhedrim, before which Peter and John were summoned, and from which they received a strict charge never more to teach, publicly or privately, in the name of Jesus of Nazareth. The noble reply and subsequent conduct of the Apostles are well known. This court of the Jews was so awed and incensed, as to plot the death of the twelve Apostles, as the only effectual measure for preventing the farther spread of Christianity. Gamaliel interposed, by his prudent and moderate counsel; and his speech had so good an effect upon the sanhedrim, that, instead of putting Peter and John to death, they scourged them, renewed their charge and threats, and then dismissed them. The Apostles, however, were not discouraged nor restrained; they counted it an honour to suffer such indignities, in token of their affection to their Master, and zeal in his cause; and they persisted in preaching daily in the courts of the temple, and in other places, that Jesus of Nazareth was the promised and long expected Messiah. Their doctrine spread, and the number of converts in Jerusalem still increased. During the violent persecution that raged at Jerusalem, soon after the martyrdom of St. Stephen, several of the leading men among the Christians were dispersed; some of them travelled through the regions of Judea and Samaria, and others to Damascus, Phœnicia, the Island of Cyprus, and various parts of Syria; but the twelve Apostles remained, with undaunted firmness, at Jerusalem, avowing their attachment to the persecuted interest of Christ, and consulting how they might best provide for the emergencies of the church, in its infant and oppressed state.

When the Apostles, during their abode at Jerusalem, heard that many of the Samaritans had embraced the Gospel, Peter and John were deputed to confer upon them the gift of the Holy Spirit; for to the Apostles belonged the prerogative of conferring upon others spiritual gifts and miraculous powers. In their return to Jerusalem, from the city of Samaria, they preached the Gospel in many Samaritan villages. The manner of its being sent to Ethiopia, by the conversion of the eunuch who was chief treasurer to Candace, queen of the country, is related in Acts viii, 26, &c. After the Christian religion had been planted in Jerusalem, Judea, and Samaria, and sent into Ethiopia, one of the uttermost parts of the earth, Acts i, 8; and after it had been preached about eight years to the Jews only, God, in his wise and merciful providence, disposed things for the preaching of it among the Gentiles. Cæsarea was the scene in which the Apostle Peter was to open his commission for this purpose; and Cornelius, one of the devout Gentiles, and a man distinguished by his piety and charity, was the first proselyte to Christianity. After Peter had laid the foundation of a Christian church among the devout Gentiles, others imitated his example, and a great number of persons of this description embraced the Christian faith, more especially at Antioch, where the disciples, whom their enemies had hitherto called Galileans, Nazarenes, and other names of reproach, and who, among themselves, had been called "disciples," "believers," "the church," "the saints," and "brethren," were denominated, probably not without a divine direction, Christians.

When Christianity had been preached for about eight years among the Jews only, and for about three years more among the Jews and devout Gentiles, the next stage of its progress was to the idolatrous Gentiles, in the year of Christ 44, and the fourth year of the emperor Claudius. Barnabas and Saul were selected for this purpose, and constituted in an extraordinary manner Apostles of the Gentiles, or uncircumcision. Barnabas was probably an elder of the first rank; he had seen Christ in the flesh, had been an eye witness of his being alive again after his crucifixion, and had received the Holy Spirit on the day of Pentecost, as being one of the hundred and twenty. Saul also, since his conversion had preached as a superior prophet, about seven years to the Jews only, and about two years more to the Jews and devout Gentiles. They had both been born in Gentile countries; and therefore may be supposed to have had more respect and affection for the Gentiles than most of the Jews, who were natives of Judea. Saul had been converted, and had hitherto preached chiefly on Gentile ground; and he had joined with Barnabas in teaching devout Gentiles for a whole year, at Antioch in Syria; by all which previous steps they were regularly conducted to the last gradation, or the conversion of the idolatrous Gentiles. But it was necessary, in order to the being an Apostle, to have seen our Lord Jesus Christ alive after his crucifixion, for the Apostles were in a peculiar manner the witnesses of his resurrection. Some have supposed that Saul saw the person of Jesus, when he was converted, near the city of Damascus; but others, who conceive from the history of this event, that this could not have been the case, as he was instantly struck blind, are of opinion that the season, when his Apostolic qualification and commission were completed, was that mentioned by himself, Acts xxii, 17, when he returned to Jerusalem the second time after his conversion, saw the Lord Jesus Christ in person, and received the command to go quickly out of Jerusalem, that he might be sent unto the Gentiles. See also Acts xxvi, 16–20, where he gives an account of the object of his commission. He also received a variety of gifts and powers, which, superadded to his own genius and learning, as well as fortitude and patience, eminently qualified him for the office of an Apostle, and for that particular exercise of it which was assigned to him. St. Paul is frequently called the APOSTLE, by way of eminence; and the APOSTLE OF THE GENTILES, because his ministry was chiefly employed for the conversion of the Gentiles, as that of St. Peter was for Jews, who is therefore styled the APOSTLE OF THE CIRCUMCISION.

The Apostles having continued at Jerusalem twelve years after the ascension of Christ, as tradition reports, according to his command, determined to disperse themselves in different parts of the world. But what were the particular provinces assigned to each, does not certainly appear from any authentic history. Socrates says, that Thomas took Parthia for his lot; Matthew, Ethiopia, and Bartholomew, India. Eusebius gives the following account: "Thomas, as we learn by tradition, had Parthia for his lot; Andrew, Scythia; John, Asia, who having lived there a long time, died at Ephesus. Peter, as it seems, preached to the dispersed Jews in Pontus and Galatia, Bithynia, Cappadocia, and Asia; at length, coming to Rome, he was crucified with his head downward, as he had desired. What need I to speak of St. Paul, who fully preached the Gospel of Christ, from Jerusalem to Illyricum, and at last died a martyr at Rome, in the time of Nero?" From this passage we may conclude, that at the beginning of the fourth century, there were not any certain and well attested accounts of the places out of Judea, in which several of the Apostles of Christ preached; for if there had, Eusebius must have been acquainted with them.

The stories that are told concerning their arrival and exploits among the Gauls, the English, the Spaniards, the Germans, the Americans, the Chinese, the Indians, and the Russians, are too romantic in their nature, and of too recent a date, to be received by an impartial inquirer after truth. These fables were for the most part forged after the time of Charlemagne, when most of the Christian churches contended about the antiquity of their origin, with as much vehemence as the Arcadians, Egyptians, and Greeks disputed formerly about their seniority and precedence.

It appears, however, that all of the Apostles did not die by martyrdom. Heraclion, cited by Clemens Alexandrinus, reckons among the Apostles who did not suffer martyrdom, Matthew, Thomas, Philip, and Levi, probably meaning Lebbeus.

To the Apostles belonged the peculiar and exclusive prerogative of writing doctrinal and preceptive books of authority in the Christian church; and it sufficiently appears that no epistles or other doctrinal writings of any person who was of a rank below that of an Apostle, were received by Christians as a part of their rule of faith. With respect to the writings of Mark and Luke, they are reckoned historical, not doctrinal or dogmatical; and Augustine says, that Mark and Luke wrote at a time when their writings might be approved not only by the church, but by Apostles still living.

The appellation of Apostles was also given to the ordinary travelling ministers of the church. Thus St. Paul, in the Epistle to the Romans, xvi, 7, says, "Salute Andronicus and Junia, my kinsmen and fellow prisoners, who are of note among the Apostles." In this inferior sense the appellation is applied, by Clement of Alexandria, to Barnabas; who was not an Apostle in the highest sense of the word, so as the twelve and Paul were Apostles. Tertullian calls all the seventy disciples Apostles; and Clement calls Barnabas Apostolical merely in another place, and says that he was one of the seventy, and fellow labourer of Paul. These, says Dr. Lardner, are the highest characters which he really intends to give to Barnabas, and what he means when he styles him Apostle; therefore he need not be supposed to ascribe to Barnabas that large measure of inspiration and high authority, which was peculiar to the Apostles, strictly and properly so called. In a similar subordinate form, St. Clement of Rome is called Apostle. Timothy also is called by Salvian, Apostle, meaning merely Apostolical, or a companion and disciple of Apostles.

Apostle was likewise a title given to those sent by the churches, to carry their alms to the poor of other churches. This usage they borrowed from the synagogues, who called those whom they sent on this message, by the same name; and the function or office itself ἀποϛολὴ, that is, MISSION. Thus St. Paul, writing to the Philippians, tells them, that Epaphroditus, their APOSTLE, had ministered to his wants, chap. ii, 25. It is applied in like manner to those persons who first planted the Christian faith in any place.

Apostle is also used among the Jews, for a kind of officer anciently sent into the several parts and provinces in their jurisdiction, by way of visiter, or commissary; to see that the laws were duly observed, and to receive the moneys collected for the reparation of the temple, and the tribute payable to the Romans. These apostles were a degree below the officers of the synagogues, called PATRIARCHS, and received their commissions from them. Some authors observe, that St. Paul had borne this office; and that it is this he alludes to in the beginning of the Epistle to the Galatians: as if he had said, Paul, no longer an apostle of the synagogue, nor sent by men to maintain the law of Moses, but now an Apostle and envoy of Jesus Christ, &c. St. Jerom, though he does not believe that St. Paul had been an apostle of this kind, yet imagines that he alludes to it in the passage just cited.

APOSTLES' **CREED**. See Creed.

APPELLATIO, an appeal. The Sempronian law secured this privilege to the Roman citizens, that they could not be capitally convicted, but by the suffrage of the people; and in whatever provinces they happened to reside, if the governor showed a disposition to condemn them to death, to scourge, or deprive them of their property, they had liberty to appeal from his jurisdiction to the judgment of the people. This law, which was enacted under the republican form of government, continued in force under the emperors; so that if any freeman of Rome thought himself ill used and aggrieved by the presidents in any of the provinces, he could, by appeal, remove his cause to Rome, to the determination of the emperor. A number of persons, we are told, were delegated by Augustus, all of consular rank, to receive the appeals of the people in the provinces. These observations will explain the nature of St. Paul's appeal in the Acts of the Apostles.

APPII FORUM, a place about fifty miles from Rome, near the modern town of Piperno on the road to Naples. It probably had its name from the statue of Appius Claudius, a Roman consul, who paved the famous way from Rome to Capua, and whose statue was set up here. To this place some Christians from Rome came to meet St. Paul, Acts xxviii, 15.

APPLE TREE, תפוח, Prov. xxv, 11; Cant. ii, 3, 5; vii, 8; viii, 5; Joel i, 12. As the best apples of Egypt, though ordinary, are brought thither by sea from Rhodes, and by land from Damascus, we may believe that Judea, an intermediate country between Egypt and Damascus, has none that are of any value. Can it be imagined, then, that the apple trees of which the Prophet Joel speaks, i, 12, and which he mentions among the things that gave joy to the inhabitants of Judea, were those that we call by that name? Our translators must surely have been mistaken here, since the apples which the inhabitants of Judea eat at this day are of foreign growth, and at the same time but very indifferent.

There are five places, beside this in Joel, in which the word occurs; and from them we learn that it was thought the noblest of the trees of the wood, and that its fruit was very sweet or pleasant, Cant. ii, 3; of the colour of gold, Prov. xxv, 11; extremely fragrant, Cant. vii, 8; and proper for those to smell that were ready to faint, Cant. ii, 5. We may be sure that the TAPHUACH was very early known in the holy land, as it is mentioned in the book of Joshua as having given name to a city of Manasseh and one of Judah. Several interpreters and critics render הדר עץ פר, Lev. xxiii, 40, BRANCHES, or fruit, OF THE BEAUTIFUL TREE; and understand it of the citron; and it is known that the Jews still make use of the fruit of this tree at their yearly feast of tabernacles.

Citron trees are very noble, being large, their leaves beautiful, ever continuing on the trees, of an exquisite smell, and affording a most delightful shade. It might well, therefore, be said, "As the citron tree is among the trees of the wood, so is my beloved among the sons." This is a delicate compliment, comparing the fine appearance of the prince, amid his escort, to the superior beauty with which the citron tree appears among the ordinary trees of the forest; and the compliment is heightened by an allusion to the refreshing shade and the exhilarating fruit.

The exhilarating effects of the fruit are mentioned Cant. ii, 5, "Comfort me with citrons." Egmont and Heyman tell us of an Arabian who was in a great measure brought to himself, when overcome with wine, by the help of citrons and coffee.

To the manner of serving up these citrons in his court, Solomon seems to refer, when he says, "A word fitly spoken is like golden citrons in silver baskets;" whether, as Maimonides supposes, in baskets wrought with open work, or in salvers curiously chased, it nothing concerns us to determine; the meaning is, that an excellent saying, suitably expressed, is as the most acceptable gift in the fairest conveyance. So the rabbins say, that the tribute of the first ripe fruits was carried to the temple in silver baskets.

APRIES, a king of Egypt, called in the sacred writings Pharaoh Hophrah, Jer. xliv, 30. Apries was the son of Psammis, and grandson of Necho, or Nechao, who waged war against Josiah, king of the Jews. He reigned twenty-five years, and was long considered as one of the happiest princes in the world; but having equipped a fleet for the reduction of the Cyrenians, he lost in this expedition almost the whole of his army. The Egyptians resolved to make him responsible for this ill success, rebelled, and pretended that he undertook the war only to get rid of his subjects, and that he might govern the remainder more absolutely. Apries deputed Amasis, one of his officers, to suppress the rebellion, and induce the people to return to their allegiance. But, while Amasis was haranguing them, one of the multitude placed a diadem about his helmet, and proclaimed him king. The rest applauded him; and Amasis having accepted their offer, continued with them, and confirmed them in their rebellion. Amasis put himself at the head of the rebels, and marched against Apries, whom he defeated and took prisoner. Amasis treated him with kindness; but the people were not satisfied till they had taken him from Amasis and strangled him. Such was the end of Apries, according to Herodotus. Jeremiah threatened this prince with being delivered into the hands of his enemies, as he had delivered Zedekiah, king of Judah, into the hands of Nebuchadnezzar, king of Babylon.

Apries had made a league with Zedekiah, and promised him assistance, Ezek. xvii, 15. Zedekiah, therefore, relying on his forces, revolted from Nebuchadnezzar, in the year of the world 3414, and before Jesus Christ 590. Early in the year following, Nebuchadnezzar marched against Hezekiah; but as other nations of Syria had shaken off their obedience, he first reduced them to their duty, and toward the end of the year besieged Jerusalem, 2 Kings xxv, 5; 2 Chron. xxxvi, 17; Jer. xxxix, 1; lii, 4. Zedekiah defended himself in Jerusalem, long and obstinately, that he might give time to Pharaoh Hophrah, or Apries, to come to his assistance. Apries advanced with a powerful army; and the king of Babylon raised the siege, and marched to meet him. But Apries not daring to hazard a battle against the Chaldeans, retreated into Egypt, and abandoned Zedekiah. Ezekiel reproaches Egypt severely with this baseness, and says that it had been a staff of reed to the house of Israel, and an occasion of falling; for when they took hold of it by the hand, it broke and rent all their shoulder. He therefore prophesies that Egypt should be reduced to a solitude, and that God would send against it the sword, which would destroy in it man and beast, Ezek. xxix. This was afterward accomplished, first, in the time of Apries; and secondly, in the conquest of Egypt by the Persians.

AQUILA. This person was a native of Pontus in Asia Minor, and was converted by St. Paul, together with his wife Priscilla, to the Christian religion. As Aquila was by trade a tentmaker, Acts xviii, 2, 3, as St. Paul was, the Apostle lodged and wrought with him at Corinth. Aquila came thither, not long before, from Italy, being obliged to leave Rome upon the edict which the emperor Claudius had published, banishing the Jews from that city. St. Paul afterward quitted Aquila's house, and abode with Justus, near the Jewish synagogue at Corinth; probably, as Calmet thinks, because Aquila was a converted Jew, and Justus was a convert from Paganism, that in this case the Gentiles might come and hear him with more liberty. When the Apostle left Corinth, Aquila and Priscilla accompanied him as far as Ephesus, where he left them with that church while he pursued his journey to Jerusalem. They rendered him great service in that city, so far as to expose their own lives to preserve his. They had returned to Rome when St. Paul wrote his Epistle to the Romans, xvi, 4, wherein he salutes them with great kindness. Lastly, they were come back to Ephesus again, when St. Paul wrote his Second Epistle to Timothy, iv, 19, wherein he desires him to salute them in his name. What became of them after this time is not known.

AR, the capital city of the Moabites, situated in the hills on the south of the river Arnon. This city was likewise called Rabbah or Rabbath Moab, to distinguish it from the Ammonite Rabbah. It was afterward called by the Greeks Areopolis; and is at present termed El-Rabba. See Moab.

ARABIA. A vast country of Asia, extending one thousand five hundred miles from north to south, and one thousand two hundred from east to west; containing a surface equal to four times that of France. The near approach of the Euphrates to the Mediterranean constitutes it a peninsula, the largest in the world. It is called Jezirat-el-Arab by the Arabs; and by the Persians and Turks, Arebistan. This is one of the most interesting countries on the face of the earth. It has, in agreement with prophecy, never been subdued; and its inhabitants, at once pastoral, commercial, and warlike, are the same wild, wandering people as the immediate descendants of their great ancestor Ishmael are represented to have been.

Arabia, or at least the eastern and northern parts of it, were first peopled by some of the numerous families of Cush, who appear to have extended themselves, or to have given their name as the land of Cush, or Asiatic Ethiopia, to all the country from the Indus on the east, to the borders of Egypt on the west, and from Armenia on the north to Arabia Deserta on the south. By these Cushites, whose first plantations were on both sides of the Euphrates and Gulf of Persia, and who were the first that traversed the desert of Arabia, the earliest commercial communications were established between the east and the west. But of their Arabian territory, and of the occupation dependent on it, they were deprived by the sons of Abraham, Ishmael, and Midian; by whom they were obliterated in this country as a distinct race, either by superiority of numbers after mingling with them, or by obliging them to recede altogether to their more eastern possessions, or over the Gulf of Arabia into Africa. From this time, that is, about five hundred and fifty years after the flood, we read only of Ishmaelites and Midianites as the shepherds and carriers of the deserts; who also appear to have been intermingled, and to have shared both the territory and the traffic, as the traders who bought Joseph are called by both names, and the same are probably referred to by Jeremiah, xxv, as "the mingled people that dwell in the desert." But Ishmael maintained the superiority, and succeeded in giving his name to the whole people.

Arabia, it is well known, is divided by geographers into three separate regions, called Arabia Petræa, Arabia Deserta, and Arabia Felix.

The first, or Arabia Petræa, is the north-western division, and is bounded on the north by Palestine and the Dead Sea, on the east by Arabia Deserta, on the south by Arabia Felix, and on the west by the Heroopolitan branch of the Red Sea and the Isthmus of Suez. The greater part of this division was more exclusively the possession of the Midianites, or land of Midian; where Moses, having fled from Egypt, married the daughter of Jethro, and spent forty years keeping the flocks of his father-in-law: no humiliating occupation in those days, and particularly in Midian, which was a land of shepherds; the whole people having no other way of life than that of rearing and tending their flocks, or in carrying the goods they received from the east and south into Phenicia and Egypt. The word flock, used here, must not convey the idea naturally entertained in our own country of sheep only, but, together with these or goats, horned cattle and camels, the most indispensable of animals to the Midianite. It was a mixed flock of this kind which was the sole care of Moses, during a third part of his long life; in which he must have had abundance of leisure, by night and by day, to reflect on the unhappy condition of his own people, still enduring all the rigours of slavery in Egypt. It was a similar flock also which the daughters of Jethro were watering when first encountered by Moses; a trifling event in itself, but important in the history of the future leader of the Jews; and showing, at the same time, the simple life of the people among whom he was newly come, as well as the scanty supply of water in their country, and the strifes frequently occasioned in obtaining a share of it. Through a considerable part of this region, the Israelites wandered after they had escaped from Egypt; and in it were situated the mountains Horeb and Sinai. Beside the tribes of Midian, which gradually became blended with those of Ishmael, this was the country of the Edomites, the Amalekites, and the Nabathæi, the only tribe of pure Ishmaelites within its precincts. But all those families have long since been confounded under the general name of Arabs. The greater part of this district consists of naked rocks and sandy and flinty plains; but it contained also some fertile spots, particularly in the peninsula of Mount Sinai, and through the long range of Mount Seir.

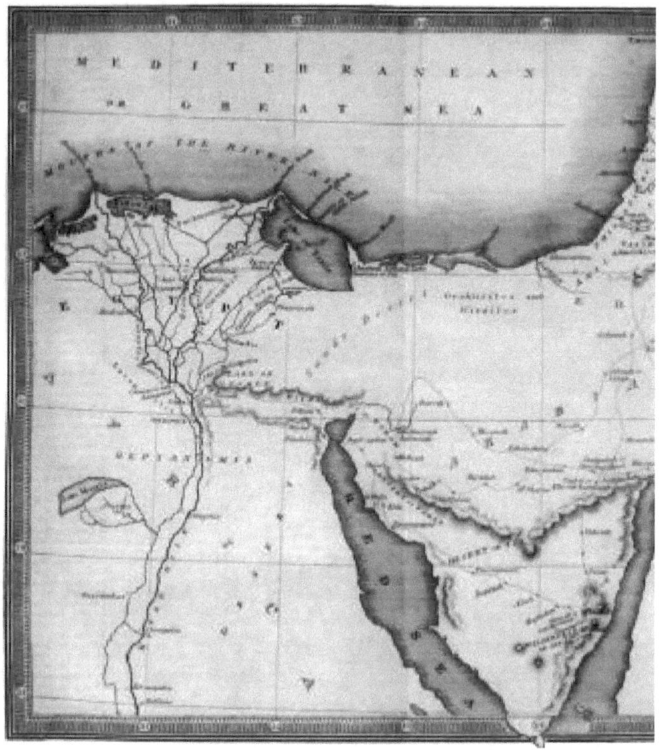

Map of the
JOURNEYINGS & ENCAMPMENTS
OF THE ISRAELITES FROM
EGYPT to CANAAN
Through the Desert of
ARABIA PETRÆA

The second region, or Arabia Deserta, is bounded on the north and north-east by the Euphrates, on the east by a ridge of mountains which separates it from Chaldea, on the south by Arabia Felix, and on the west by Syria, Judea, and Arabia Petræa. This was more particularly the country first of the Cushites, and afterward of the Ishmaelites; as it is still of their descendants, the modern Bedouins, who maintain the same predatory and wandering habits. It consists almost entirely of one vast and lonesome wilderness, a boundless level of sand, whose dry and burning surface denies existence to all but the Arab and his camel. Yet, widely scattered over this dreary waste, some spots of comparative fertility are to be found, where, spread around a feeble spring of brackish water, a stunted verdure, or a few palm trees, fix the principal settlement of a tribe, and afford stages of refreshment in these otherwise impassable deserts. Here, with a few dates, the milk of his faithful camel, and perhaps a little corn, brought by painful journeys from distant regions, or plundered from a passing caravan, the Arab supports a hard existence, until the failure of his resources impels him to seek another OASIS, or the scanty herbage furnished on a patch of soil by transient rains; or else, which is frequently the case, to resort, by more distant migration, to the banks of the Euphrates; or, by hostile inroads on the neighbouring countries, to supply those wants which the recesses of the desert have denied. The numbers leading this wandering and precarious mode of life are incredible. From these deserts Zerah drew his army of a million of men; and the same deserts, fifteen hundred years after, poured forth the countless swarms, which, under Mohammed and his successors, devastated half of the then known world.

The third region, or Arabia Felix, so denominated from the happier condition of its soil and climate, occupies the southern part of the Arabian peninsula. It is bounded on the north by the two other divisions of the country; on the south and south-east by the Indian Ocean; on the east by part of the same ocean and the Persian Gulf; and on the west by the Red Sea. This division is subdivided into the kingdoms or provinces of Yemen, at the southern extremity of the peninsula; Hejaz, on the north of the former, and toward the Red Sea; Nejed, in the central region; and Hadramant and Oman, on the shores of the Indian Ocean. The four latter subdivisions partake of much of the character of the other greater divisions of the country, though of a more varied surface, and with a larger portion capable of cultivation. But Yemen seems to belong to another country and climate. It is very mountainous, is well watered with rains and springs, and is blessed with an abundant produce in corn and fruits, and especially in coffee, of which vast quantities are exported. In this division were the ancient cities of Nysa, Musa or Moosa, and Aden. This is also supposed to have been the country of the queen of Sheba. In Hejaz are the celebrated cities of Mecca and Medina.

Arabia Felix is inhabited by a people who claim Jotkan for their father, and so trace their descent direct from Shem, instead of Abraham and Ham. They are indeed a totally different people from those inhabiting the other quarters, and pride themselves on being the only pure and unmixed Arabs. Instead of being shepherds and robbers, they are fixed in towns and cities; and live by agriculture and commerce, chiefly maritime. Here were the people who were found by the Greeks of Egypt enjoying an entire monopoly of the trade with the east, and possessing a high degree of wealth and consequent refinement. It was here, in the ports of Sabæa, that the spices, muslins, and precious stones of India, were for many ages obtained by the Greek traders of Egypt, before they had acquired skill or courage sufficient to pass the straits of the Red Sea; which were long considered by the nations of Europe to be the produce of Arabia itself. These articles, before the invention of shipping, or the establishment of a maritime intercourse, were conveyed across the deserts by the Cushite, Ishmaelite, and Midianite carriers. It was the produce partly of India, and partly of Arabia, which the travelling merchants, to whom Joseph was sold, were carrying into Egypt. The balm and myrrh were probably Arabian, as they are still the produce of the same country; but the spicery was undoubtedly brought farther from the east. These circumstances are adverted to, to show how extensive was the communication, in which the Arabians formed the principal link: and that in the earliest ages of which we have any account, in those of Joseph, of Moses, of Isaiah, and of Ezekiel, "the mingled people" inhabiting the vast Arabian deserts, the Cushites, Ishmaelites, and Midianites, were the chief agents in that commercial intercourse which has, from the most remote period of antiquity, subsisted between the extreme east and west. And although the current of trade is now turned, caravans of merchants, the descendants of these people, may still be found traversing the same deserts, conveying the same articles, and in the same manner as described by Moses!

The singular and important fact that Arabia has never been conquered, has already been cursorily adverted to. But Mr. Gibbon, unwilling to pass by an opportunity of cavilling at revelation, says, "The perpetual independence of the Arabs has been the theme of praise among strangers and natives; and the arts of controversy transform this singular event into a prophecy and a miracle in favour of the posterity of Ishmael. Some exceptions, that can neither be dissembled nor eluded, render this mode of reasoning as indiscreet as it is superfluous. The kingdom of Yemen has been successively subdued by the Abyssinians, the Persians, the Sultans of Egypt, and the Turks; the holy cities of Mecca and Medina have repeatedly bowed under a Scythian tyrant; and the Roman province of Arabia embraced the peculiar wilderness in which Ishmael and his sons must have pitched their tents in the face of their brethren." But this learned writer has, with a peculiar infelicity, annulled his own argument; and we have only to follow on the above passage, to obtain a complete refutation of the unworthy position with which it begins: "Yet these exceptions," says Mr. Gibbon, "are temporary or local; the body of the nation has escaped the yoke of the most powerful monarchies: the arms of Sesostris and Cyrus, of Pompey, and Trajan, could never achieve the conquest of Arabia; the present sovereign of the Turks may exercise a shadow of jurisdiction, but his pride is reduced to solicit the friendship of a people whom it is dangerous to provoke, and fruitless to attack. The obvious causes of their freedom are inscribed on the character and country of the Arabs. Many ages before Mohammed, their intrepid valour had been severely felt by their neighbours, in offensive and defensive war. The patient and active virtues of a soldier are insensibly nursed in the habits and discipline of a pastoral life. The care of the sheep and camels is abandoned to the women of the tribe; but the martial youth, under the banner of the emir, is ever on horseback and in the field, to practise the exercise of the bow, the javelin, and the scimitar. The long memory of their independence is the firmest pledge of its perpetuity; and succeeding generations are animated to prove their descent, and to maintain their inheritance. Their domestic feuds are suspended on the approach of a common enemy; and in their last hostilities against the Turks, the caravan of Mecca was attacked and pillaged by four score thousand of the confederates. When they advance to battle, the hope of victory is in the front, in the rear the assurance of a retreat. Their horses and camels, who in eight or ten days can perform a march of four or five hundred miles, disappear before the conqueror; the secret waters of the desert elude his search; and his victorious troops are consumed with thirst, hunger, and fatigue, in the pursuit of an invisible foe, who scorns his efforts, and safely reposes in the heart of the burning solitude. The arms and deserts of the Bedouins are not only the safeguards of their own freedom, but the barriers also of the happy Arabia, whose inhabitants, remote from war, are enervated by the luxury of the soil and climate. The legions of Augustus melted away in disease and lassitude; and it is only by a naval power that the reduction of Yemen has been successfully attempted. When Mohammed erected his holy standard, that kingdom was a province of the Persian empire; yet seven princes of the Homerites still reigned in the mountains; and the vicegerent of Chosroes was tempted to forget his distant country and his unfortunate master."

Yemen was the only Arabian province which had the appearance of submitting to a foreign yoke; but even here, as Mr. Gibbon himself acknowledges, seven of the native princes remained unsubdued: and even admitting its subjugation to have been complete, the perpetual independence of the Ishmaelites remains unimpeached. For this is not their country. Petra, the capital of the Stony Arabia, and the principal settlement of the Nabathæi, it is true, was long in the hands of the Persians and Romans; but this never made them masters of the country. Hovering troops of Arabs confined the intruders within their walls, and cut off their supplies; and the possession of this fortress gave as little reason to the Romans to exult as the conquerors of Arabia Petræa, as that of Gibraltar does to us to boast of the conquest of Spain.

The Arabian tribes were confounded by the Greeks and Romans under the indiscriminate appellation of Saracens; a name whose etymology has been variously, but never satisfactorily, explained. This was their general name when Mohammed appeared in the beginning of the seventh century. Their religion at this time was Sabianism, or the worship of the sun, moon, &c; variously transformed by the different tribes, and intermingled with some Jewish and Christian maxims and traditions. The tribes themselves were generally at variance, from some hereditary and implacable animosities; and their only warfare consisted in desultory skirmishes arising out of these feuds, and in their predatory excursions, where superiority of numbers rendered courage of less value than activity and vigilance. Yet of such materials Mohammed constructed a mighty empire; converted the relapsed Ishmaelites into good Musselmen; united the jarring tribes under one banner; supplied what was wanting in personal courage by the ardour of religious zeal; and out of a banditti, little known and little feared beyond their own deserts, raised an armed multitude, which proved the scourge of the world.

Mohammed was born in the year 569, of the noble tribe of the Koreish, and descended, according to eastern historians, in a direct line from Ishmael. His person is represented as beautiful, his manners engaging, and his eloquence powerful; but he was illiterate, like the rest of his countrymen, and indebted to a Jewish or Christian scribe for penning his Koran. Whatever the views of Mohammed might have been in the earlier part of his life, it was not till the fortieth year of his age that he avowed his mission as the Apostle of God: when so little credit did he gain for his pretensions, that in the first three years he could only number fourteen converts; and even at the end of ten years his labours and his friends were alike confined within the walls of Mecca, when the designs of his enemies compelled him to fly to Medina, where he was favourably received by a party of the most considerable inhabitants, who had recently imbibed his doctrines at Mecca. This flight, or HEGIRA, was made the Mohammedan æra, from which time is computed, and corresponds with the 16th of July, 622, of the Christian æra. Mohammed now found himself sufficiently powerful to throw aside all reserve; declared that he was commanded to compel unbelievers by the sword to receive the faith of one God, and his prophet Mohammed; and confirming his credulous followers by the threats of eternal pain on the one hand, and the allurements of a sensual paradise on the other, he had, before his death, which happened in the year 632, gained over the whole of Arabia to his imposture. His death threw a temporary gloom over his cause, and the disunion of his followers threatened its extinction. Any other empire placed in the same circumstances would have crumbled to pieces; but the Arabs felt their power; they revered their founder as the chosen prophet of God; and their ardent temperament, animated by a religious enthusiasm, gave an earnest of future success, and encouraged the zeal or the ambition of their leaders. The succession, after some bloodshed, was settled, and unnumbered hordes of barbarians were ready to carry into execution the sanguinary dictates of their prophet; and, with "the Koran, tribute, or death," as their motto, to invade the countries of the infidels. During the whole of the succeeding century, their rapid career was unchecked; the disciplined armies of the Greeks and Romans were unable to stand against them; the Christian churches of Asia and Africa were annihilated; and from India to the Atlantic, through Persia, Arabia, Syria, Palestine, Asia Minor, Egypt, with the whole of northern Africa, Spain, and part of France, the impostor was acknowledged. Constantinople was besieged; Rome itself was plundered; and nothing less than the subjection of the whole Christian world was meditated on the one hand and tremblingly expected on the other.

All this was wonderful; but the avenging justice of an incensed Deity, and the sure word of prophecy, relieve our astonishment. It was to punish an apostate race, that the Saracen locusts were let loose upon the earth; and the countries which they were permitted to ravage were those in which the pure light of revelation had been most abused. The eastern church was sunk in gross idolatry; vice and wickedness prevailed in their worst forms; and those who still called themselves Christians trusted more to images, relics, altars, austerities, and pilgrimages, than to a crucified Saviour.

About a hundred and eighty years from the foundation of Bagdad, during which period the power of the Saracens had gradually declined, a dreadful reaction took place in the conquered countries. The Persians on the east, and the Greeks on the west, were simultaneously roused from their long thraldom, and, assisted by the Turks, who, issuing from the plains of Tartary, now for the first time made their appearance in the east, extinguished the power of the caliphate, and virtually put an end to the Arabian monarchy in the year 936. A succession of nominal caliphs continued to the year 1258: but the provinces were lost; their power was confined to the walls of their capital; and they were in real subjection to the Turks and the Persians until the above year, when Mostacem, the last of the Abbassides, was dethroned and murdered by Holagou, or Hulaku, the Tartar, the grandson of Zingis. This event, although it terminated the foreign dominion of the Arabians, left their native independence untouched. They were no longer, indeed, the masters of the finest parts of the three great divisions of the ancient world: their work was finished; and returning to the state in which Mohammed found them three centuries before, with the exception of the change in their religion, they remained, and still remain, the unconquered rovers of the desert.

It is not the least singular circumstance in the history of this extraordinary people, that those who, in the enthusiasm of their first successes, were the sworn foes of literature, should become for several ages its exclusive patrons. Almansor, the founder of Bagdad, has the merit of first exciting this spirit, which was encouraged in a still greater degree by his grandson Almamon. This caliph employed his agents in Armenia, Syria, Egypt, and at Constantinople, in collecting the most celebrated works on Grecian science, and had them translated into the Arabic language. Philosophy, astronomy, geometry, and medicine, were thus introduced and taught; public schools were established; and learning, which had altogether fled from Europe, found an asylum on the banks of the Tigris. Nor was this spirit confined to the capital: native works began to appear; and by the hands of copyists were multiplied out of number, for the information of the studious, or the pride of the wealthy. The rage for literature extended to Egypt and to Spain. In the former country, the Fatimites collected a library of a hundred thousand manuscripts, beautifully transcribed, and very elegantly bound; and in the latter, the Ommiades formed another of six hundred thousand volumes; forty-four of which were employed in the catalogue. Their capital, Cordova, with the towns of Malaga, Almeria, and Murcia, produced three hundred writers; and seventy public libraries were established in the cities of Andalusia. What a change since the days of Omar, when the splendid library of the Ptolemies was wantonly destroyed by the same people! A retribution, though a slight one, was thus made for their former devastations; and many Grecian works, lost in the original, have been recovered in their Arabic dress. Neither was this learning confined to mere parade, though much of it must undoubtedly have been so. Their proficiency in astronomy and geometry is attested by their astronomical tables, and by the accuracy with which, in the plain of Chaldea, a degree of the great circle of the earth was measured. But it was in medicine that, in this dark age, the Arabians shone most: the works of Hippocrates and

Galen had been translated and commented on; their physicians were sought after by the princes of Asia and Europe; and the names of Rhazis, Albucasis, and Avicenna are still revered by the members of the healing art. So little, indeed, did the physicians of Europe in that age know of the history of their own science, that they were astonished, on the revival of learning, to find in the ancient Greek authors those systems for which they thought themselves indebted to the Arabians!

The last remnant of Arabian science was found in Spain; from whence it was expelled in the beginning of the seventeenth century, by the intemperate bigots of that country, who have never had any thing of their own with which to supply its place. The Arabians are the only people who have preserved their descent, their independence, their language, and their manners and customs, from the earliest ages to the present times; and it is among them that we are to look for examples of patriarchal life and manners. A very lively sketch of this mode of life is given by Sir R. K. Porter, in the person and tribe of an Arab sheik, whom he encountered in the neighbourhood of the Euphrates. "I had met this warrior," says Sir R. K. P., "at the house of the British resident at Bagdad; and came, according to his repeated wish, to see him in a place more consonant with his habits, the tented field; and, as he expressed it, 'at the head of his children.' As soon as we arrived in sight of his camp, we were met by crowds of its inhabitants, who, with a wild and hurrying delight, led us toward the tent of their chief. The venerable old man came forth to the door, attended by his subjects of all sizes and descriptions, and greeted us with a countenance beaming kindness; while his words, which our interpreter explained, were demonstrative of patriarchal welcome. One of my Hindoo troopers spoke Arabic; hence the substance of our succeeding discourse was not lost on each other. Having entered, I sat down by my host; and the whole of the persons present, to far beyond the boundaries of the tent, (the sides of which were open,) seated themselves also, without any regard to those more civilized ceremonies of subjection, the crouching of slaves, or the standing of vassalage. These persons, in rows beyond rows, appeared just as he had described, the offspring of his house, the descendants of his fathers, from age to age; and like brethren, whether holding the highest or the lowest rank, they seemed to gather round their common parent. But perhaps their sense of perfect equality in the mind of their chief could not be more forcibly shown, than in the share they took in the objects which appeared to interest his feelings; and as I looked from the elders or leaders of the people, seated immediately around him, to the circles beyond circles of brilliant faces, bending eagerly toward him and his guest, (all, from the most respectably clad to those with hardly a garment covering their active limbs, earnest to evince some attention to the stranger he bade welcome,) I thought I had never before seen so complete an assemblage of fine and animated countenances, both old and young: nor could I suppose a better specimen of the still existing state of the true Arab; nor a more lively picture of the scene which must have presented itself, ages ago, in the fields of Haran, when Terah sat in his tent door, surrounded by his sons, and his sons' sons, and the people born in his house. The venerable Arabian sheik was also seated on the ground with a piece of carpet spread under him; and, like his ancient Chaldean ancestor, turned to the one side and the other, graciously answering or questioning the groups around him, with an interest in them all which clearly showed the abiding simplicity of his government, and their obedience. On the smallest computation, such must have been the manners of these people for more than three thousand years; thus, in all things, verifying the prediction given of Ishmael at his birth, that he, in his posterity, should 'be a wild man,' and always continue to be so, though 'he shall dwell for ever in the presence of his brethren.' And that an acute and active people, surrounded for ages by polished and luxurious nations, should from their earliest to their latest times, be still found A WILD PEOPLE, DWELLING IN THE PRESENCE OF ALL THEIR BRETHREN, (as we may call these nations,) unsubdued and unchangeable, is, indeed, a standing miracle: one of those mysterious facts which establish the truth of prophecy." But although the manners of the Arabians have remained unaltered through so many ages, and will probably so continue, their religion, as we have seen, has sustained an important change; and must again, in the fulness of time, give place to a faith more worthy of the people.

St. Paul first preached the Gospel in Arabia, Gal. i, 17. Christian churches were subsequently founded, and many of their tribes embraced Christianity prior to the fifth century; most of which appear to have been tinctured with the Nestorian heresy. At this time, however, it does not appear that the Arabians had any version of the Scriptures in their own language, to which some writers attribute the ease with which they were drawn into the Mohammedan delusion; while the "Greeks, Syrians, Armenians, Abyssinians, Copts, and others," who enjoyed that privilege, were able to resist it.

ARAM, the fifth son of Shem, Gen. x, 22. He was the father of the Syrians, who from him were called Aramæans, or Aramites.

ARARAT, a mountain of Asia, in Armenia, on which the ark of Noah rested after the cessation of the deluge. Concerning the etymology of the name, Dr. Bryant observes, that it is a compound of AR-ARAT, and signifies "the mountain of descent," being equivalent to הר־ירר, of the Hebrews. Of the precise situation of this mountain, different accounts have been given. Some have supposed that it was one of the mountains which divide Armenia on the south from Mesopotamia, and that part of Assyria inhabited by the Curds, from whom those mountains took the name of Curdue, or Cardu; by the Greeks denominated GORDYÆI. It is called by the Arabs AL-JUDI, and also THAMANIN. In confirmation of this opinion, it is alleged that the remains of the ark were to be seen on these mountains; and it is said, that Berosus and Abydenus both declare, that such a report existed in their time. Epiphanius pretends, if we may credit his assertion, that the relics of the ark were to be seen in his day; and we are farther told, that the emperor Heraclius went from the town of Thamanin, up the mountain Al-Judi, and saw the place of the ark. Others maintain, that mount Ararat was situated toward the middle of Armenia, near the river Araxes, or Aras, about twelve miles from it, according to Tournefort, above two hundred and eighty miles distant from Al-Judi, to the north-east. Ararat seems to be a part of that vast chain of mountains called Caucasus and Taurus; and upon these mountains, and in the adjacent country, were preserved more authentic accounts of the ark than in almost any other part of the world. The region about Ararat, called Araratia, was esteemed among the ancients as nearly a central part of the earth; and it is certainly as well calculated as any other for the accommodation of its first inhabitants, and for the migration of colonies, upon the increase of mankind. The soil of the country was very fruitful, and especially of that part where the patriarch made his first descent. The country also was very high, though it had fine plains and valleys between the mountains. Such a country, therefore, must, after the flood, have been the soonest exsiccated, and, consequently, the soonest habitable.

The mountain which has still the name of Ararat, has retained it through all ages. Tournefort has particularly described it, and from his account it seems to consist chiefly of freestone, or calcareous sandstone. It is a detached mountain in form of a sugar loaf, in the midst of a very extensive plain, consisting of two summits; the lesser, more sharp and pointed; the higher, which is that of the ark, lies north-west of it, and raises its head far above the neighbouring mountains, and is covered with perpetual snow. When the air is clear, it does not appear to be above two leagues from Erivan, and may be seen at the distance of four or five days' journey. Its being visible at such a distance, however, is ascribed not so much to its height, as to its lonely situation, in a large plain, and upon the most elevated part of the country. The ascent is difficult and fatiguing. Tournefort attempted it; and, after a whole day's toil, he was obliged, by the snow and intense cold, to return without accomplishing his design, though in the middle of summer. On the side of the mountain that looks toward Erivan, is a prodigious precipice, very deep, with perpendicular sides, and of a rough, black appearance, as if tinged with smoke.

The summit of Ararat has never been reached, though several attempts have been made; and if the ark rested on the summit, it is certain that those who have spoken of its fragments being seen there in different ages, must have been imposed upon. It is, however, not necessary to suppose that the ark rested upon either of its tops; and that spot would certainly be chosen which would afford the greatest facility of descent. Sir Robert Ker Porter is among the modern travellers who have given us an account of this celebrated mountain:--"As the vale opened beneath us in our descent, my whole attention became absorbed in the view before me. A vast plain, peopled with countless villages; the towers and spires of the churches of Eitch-mai-adzen, arising from amidst them; the glittering waters of the Araxes, flowing through the fresh green of the vale; and the subordinate range of mountains, skirting the base of the awful monument of the antediluvian world. It seemed to stand a stupendous link in the history of man, uniting the two races of men before and after the flood. But it was not until we had arrived upon the flat plain, that I beheld Ararat in all its amplitude of grandeur. From the spot on which I stood, it appeared as if the hugest mountains of the world had been piled upon each other, to form this one sublime immensity of earth, and rock, and snow. The icy peaks of its double heads rose majestically into the clear and cloudless heavens; the sun blazed bright upon them; and the reflection sent forth a dazzling radiance, equal to other suns. This point of the view united the utmost grandeur of plain and height. But the feelings I experienced while looking on the mountain, are hardly to be described. My eye, not able to rest for any length of time upon the blinding glory of its summits, wandered down the apparently interminable sides, till I could no longer trace their vast lines in the mists of the horizon; when an inexpressible impulse, immediately carrying my eye upward again, refixed my gaze upon the awful glare of Ararat; and this bewildered sensibility of sight being answered by a similar feeling in the mind, for some moments I was lost in a strange suspension of the powers of thought."

The separate peaks are called Great and Little Ararat, and the space between them is about seven miles. "These inaccessible summits," continues Sir R. K. Porter, "have never been trodden by the foot of man since the days of Noah, if even then; for my idea is, that the ark rested in the space between these heads, and not on the top of either. Various attempts have been made in different ages to ascend these tremendous mountain-pyramids, but in vain: their form, snows, and glaciers, are insurmountable obstacles: the distance being so great from the commencement of the icy region to the highest points, cold alone would be the destruction of any person who should have the hardihood to persevere. On viewing mount Ararat from the northern side of the plain, its two heads are separated by a wide cleft, or rather glen, in the body of the mountain. The rocky side of the greater head runs almost perpendicularly down to the north-east, while the lesser head rises from the sloping bottom of the cleft, in a perfectly conical shape. Both heads are covered with snow. The form of the greater is similar to the less, only broader and rounder at the top; and shows to the north-west a broken and abrupt front, opening, about half way down, into a stupendous chasm, deep, rocky, and peculiarly black. At that part of the mountain, the hollow of the chasm receives an interruption from the projection of minor mountains, which start from the sides of Ararat like branches from the root of a tree, and run along, in undulating progression, till lost in the distant vapours of the plain." Dr. Shuckford argues that the true Ararat lies among the mountains of the north of India; but Mr. Faber has answered his reasoning, and proved by a comparison of geographical notices incidentally mentioned in the Old Testament, that the Ararat of Armenia is the true Ararat.

ARCHANGEL, according to some, means an angel occupying the eighth rank in the celestial order or hierarchy; but others reckon it a title only applicable to our Saviour; Jude 9; Dan. xii, 1; 1 Thess. iv, 16. On this point Bishop Horsley has the following observations:--"It has been for a long time a fashion in the church to speak very frequently and familiarly of archangels as beings of an order with which we are perfectly well acquainted. Some say there are seven of them. Upon what solid ground that assertion stands, I know not; but this I know, the word 'archangel' is not to be found in any one passage of the Old Testament: in the New Testament it occurs twice, and only twice. One of the two passages is in the First Epistle to the Thessalonians; where the Apostle, among the circumstances of the pomp of our Lord's descent from heaven to the final judgment, mentions 'the voice of the archangel;' the other passage is in the Epistle of St. Jude, where the title of archangel is coupled with the name of 'Michael the archangel.' This passage is so remarkably obscure that I shall not attempt to draw any conclusion from it but this, which manifestly follows, be the particular sense of the passage what it may: since this is one of the two texts in which alone the word 'archangel' is found in the whole Bible; since in this one text only the title of archangel is coupled with any name; and since the name with which it is here coupled is Michael; it follows undeniably that the archangel Michael is the only archangel of whom we know any thing from holy writ. It cannot be proved from holy writ, and, if not from holy writ, it cannot be proved at all, that any archangel exists but the one archangel Michael, and this one archangel Michael is unquestionably the Michael of the book of Daniel.

"I must observe by the way, with respect to the import of the title of archangel, that the word, by etymology, clearly implies a superiority of rank and authority in the person to whom it is applied. It implies a command over angels; and this is all that the word of necessity implies. But it follows not, by any sound rule of argument, that, because no other superiority than that of rank and authority is implied in the title, no other belongs to the person distinguished by the title, and that he is in all other respects a mere angel. Since we admit various orders of intelligent beings, it is evident that a being highly above the angelic order may command angels.

"To ascertain, if we can, to what order of beings the archangel Michael may belong, let us see how he is described by the Prophet Daniel, who never mentions him by that title; and what action is attributed to him in the book of Daniel and in another book, in which he bears a principal part.

"Now Daniel calls him 'one of the chief princes,' or 'one of the capital princes,' or 'one of the princes that are at the head of all:' for this I maintain to be the full and not more than the full import of the Hebrew words. Now we are clearly got above the earth, into the order of celestials, who are the princes that are FIRST, or AT THE HEAD OF ALL? Are they any other than the three persons in the Godhead? Michael, therefore, is one of them; but which of them? This is not left in doubt. Gabriel, speaking of him to Daniel, calls him 'Michael YOUR prince,' and 'the great prince which standeth for the children of thy people;' that is, not for the nation of the Jews in particular, but for the children, the spiritual children, of that holy seed the elect people of God; a description which applies particularly to the Son of God, and to no one else; and in perfect consistence with this description of Michael in the book of Daniel, is the action assigned to him in the Apocalypse, in which we find him fighting with the old serpent, the deceiver of the world, and victorious in the combat. That combat who was to maintain? in that combat who was to be victorious, but the seed of the woman? From all this it is evident, that Michael is a name for our Lord himself, in his particular character of the champion of his faithful people, against the violence of the apostate faction and the wiles of the devil." To this opinion there is nothing irreconcilable in the "voice of the archangel" mentioned in 1 Thess. iv, 16: since the "shout," the "voice," the "trump of God," may all be the majestic summons of the Judge himself. At the same time we must feel that the reasoning of Bishop Horsley, though ingenious, is for from being conclusive against the existence of one or more archangels.

ARCHBISHOP, a bishop of the first class, who superintends the conduct of other bishops. Archbishops were not known in the east till about the year 320; and though there were some soon after this, who had the title, yet it was only a personal honour, by which the bishops of considerable cities were distinguished. It was not till of late that archbishops became metropolitans, and had suffragans under them. Athanasius appears to have been the first who used the title archbishop, which he gave occasionally to his predecessor. Gregory Nazianzen, in like manner, gave it to Athanasius; not that either of them was entitled to any jurisdiction, or even any precedency, in virtue of this title. Among the Latins, Isidore Hispalensis is the first who speaks of archbishops.

ARCHELAUS, son of Herod the Great, and Maltace, his fifth wife. Herod having put to death his sons Alexander, Aristobulus, and Antipater, and expunged out of his will Herod Antipas, whom he had declared king, he substituted Archelaus, and gave Antipas the title of tetrarch only. After the death of Herod, Archelaus ordered that king's will to be read, wherein he, Archelaus, was declared king, on condition that Augustus consented. Hereupon the assembly cried, "Long live king Archelaus!" and the soldiers promised the same fidelity to him as they had shown to his father. Archelaus buried his father magnificently, came to Jerusalem, and there mourned seven days, according to custom. He then gave a splendid entertainment to the people, went to the temple, harangued the multitude, promised them good treatment, and declared he would not assume the title of king till the emperor had confirmed it, A. M. 4001; B. C. 3. The people, notwithstanding, tumultuously demanded the execution of those who advised Herod to slay certain zealots, who had pulled down a golden eagle from one of the temple gates. They also required Archelaus to divest Joazar of the high priesthood; and they vehemently reproached the memory of the late king. Archelaus sent troops to suppress the mutineers, and killed near three thousand of them about the temple. After this he embarked at Cæsarea for Rome, to procure from Augustus the confirmation of Herod's will. Antipas, his brother, went to Rome likewise, to dispute his title, pretending that Herod's first will should be preferred to his last, which he alleged to have been made by him when his understanding was not sound.

The two brothers, Archelaus and Antipas, procured able orators to display their pretensions before the emperor; and when they had done speaking, Archelaus threw himself at Augustus's feet. Augustus gently raised him, said he would do nothing contrary to Herod's intention or his interest, but refused to decide the affair at that time. Some time afterward, the Jews sent a solemn embassy to Rome, to desire Augustus would permit them to live according to their own laws, and on the footing of a Roman province, without being subject to kings of Herod's family, but only to the governors of Syria. Augustus heard them, and likewise heard Archelaus in reply; then broke up the assembly without declaring himself. After some days, he sent for Archelaus, gave him the title, not of king, but of ethnarch, with one moiety of the territories which his father Herod had enjoyed; promising him the crown likewise, if his good conduct deserved it. Archelaus returned to Judea, and, under pretence that he had countenanced the seditious against him, he deprived Joazar of the high priesthood, and gave that dignity to his brother Eleazar. He governed Judea with so much violence, that, after seven years, the chiefs of the Samaritans and Jews accused him before Augustus. The emperor immediately sent for his agent at Rome, and without condescending to write to Archelaus he commanded the agent to depart instantly for Judea, and order Archelaus to Rome, to give an account of his conduct. On his arrival at Rome, the emperor called for his accusers, and permitted him to defend himself; which he did so insufficiently, that Augustus banished him to Vienne, in Gaul, where he continued in exile to the end of his life. See Antipas.

ARCHI-SYNAGOGUS, THE RULER OF A SYNAGOGUE. See Synagogue.

ARCHITRICLINUS, ἀρχιτρίκλινος, generally translated steward, signifies rather the MASTER or SUPERINTENDENT OF THE FEAST; "one," says Gaudentius, "who is the husband's friend, and commissioned to conduct the order and economy of the feast." He gave directions to the servants, superintended every thing, commanded the tables to be covered, or to be cleared of the dishes, as he thought proper: whence his name, as regulator of the triclinium, or festive board. He also tasted the wine, and distributed it to the guests. The author of Ecclesiasticus thus describes this office, xxxii, 1, 2: "If thou be made the master of a feast, lift not thyself up, but be among them as one of the rest: take diligent care of them, and so sit down. And when thou hast done all thy office, take thy place, that thou mayest be merry with them, and receive a crown for the well ordering of the feast." This office is mentioned, John ii, 8, 9, upon which Theophylact remarks: "That no one might suspect that their taste was vitiated by having drunk to excess, so as not to know water from wine, our Saviour orders it to be first carried to the governor of the feast, who CERTAINLY was sober; for those who on such occasions are intrusted with this office, observe the strictest sobriety, that they may be able properly to regulate the whole."

AREOPAGUS, the high court at Athens, famed for the justice of its decisions; and so called, because it sat on a hill of the same name, or in the suburbs of the city, dedicated to Mars, the god of war, as the city was to Minerva, his sister. St. Paul, Acts xvii, 19, &c, having preached at Athens, was carried before the Areopagites, as "a setter forth of strange gods." On this occasion he delivered that fine sermon which is in substance recorded in Acts xvii. Dionysius, one of the judges, was converted; and the Apostle was dismissed without any farther trouble.

ARGOB, a canton lying beyond Jordan, in the half tribe of Manasseh, and in the country of Bashan, one of the most fruitful on the other side of Jordan. In the region of Argob there were sixty cities, called Bashan-havoth-Jair, which had very high walls and strong gates, without reckoning many villages and hamlets, which were not inclosed, Deut. iii, 4–14; 1 Kings iv, 13. But Argob was more peculiarly the name of the capital city of the region of Argob, which Eusebius says was fifteen miles west of Gerara.

ARIANS, this ancient sect, was unquestionably so called from Arius, a presbyter of Alexandria, in the early part of the fourth century. It is said that he aspired to episcopal honours; and after the death of Achilles, in A. D. 313, felt not a little chagrined that Alexander should be preferred before him. Whether this circumstance had any influence on his opinions, it is impossible to say; but one day, when his rival (Alexander) had been addressing the clergy in favour of the orthodox doctrine, and maintaining, in strong and pointed language, "that the Son of God was co-eternal, co-essential, and co-equal with the Father," Arius considered this as a species of Sabellianism, and ventured to say, that it was inconsistent and impossible, since the Father, who begat, must be before the Son, who was begotten: the latter, therefore, could not be absolutely eternal. Alexander at first admonished Arius, and endeavoured to convince him of his error; but without effect, except that he became the more bold in contradiction. Some of the clergy thought their bishop too forbearing, and it is possible he felt his inferiority of talent; for Arius was a man of accomplished learning, and commanding eloquence; venerable in person, and fascinating in address. At length Alexander was roused, and attempted to silence Arius by his authority; but this not succeeding, as the latter was bold and pertinacious, Alexander, about the year 320, called a council of his clergy, by whom the reputed heretic was deposed and excommunicated. Arius now retired into Palestine, where his talents and address soon made a number of converts; and among the rest, the celebrated Eusebius, bishop of Nicomedia, and other bishops and clergy of those parts, who assembled in council, and received the excommunicated presbyter into their communion. Eusebius also, having great interest with Constantia, the sister of Constantine, and wife of Licinius, recommended Arius to her protection and patronage; through which, and by his own eloquent letters to the clergy in various parts, his system spread with great rapidity, and to a vast extent. The emperor Constantine, who had no great skill in these matters, was grieved to see the Christian church (but just escaped from the red dragon of persecution) thus torn by intestine animosity and dissensions; he therefore determined to summon a general council of the clergy, which met at Nice, A. D. 325, and contained more than 300 bishops. Constantine attended in person, and strongly recommended peace and unanimity. Athanasius was the chief opponent of the Arians. Both parties were willing to subscribe to the language of the Scriptures, but each insisted on interpreting for themselves. "Did the Trinitarians," says Mr. Milner, "assert that Christ was God? The Arians allowed it, but in the same sense as holy men and angels are styled gods in Scripture. Did they affirm that he was truly God? The others allowed that he was made so by God. Did they affirm that the Son was naturally of God? It was granted: Even we, said they, are of God, 'of whom are all things.'" At length the Athanasians collected a number of texts, which they conceived amounted to full proof of the Son being of one and THE SAME substance with the Father; the Arians admitted he was of LIKE substance, the difference in the Greek phrases being only in a single letter,-- ὁμοούσιος, HOMOOUSIOS and ὁμοιούσιος, HOMOIOUSIOS. At length the former was decreed to be the orthodox faith, and the Nicene creed was framed as it remains at this day so far as concerns the person of the Son of God, who is said to be "begotten of his Father before all worlds; God of God, Light of Light, very God of very God, begotten, not made, of one substance with the Father, by whom all things were made," &c.

Arius was now excommunicated. The sentence of the council pronounced against him and his associates was followed by another of the emperor, whereby the excommunicated persons were condemned to banishment, that they might be debarred the society of their countrymen whom the church had judged unworthy to remain in her communion. Soon after which, Eusebius of Nicomedia, and Theognis of Nice, being found to continue their countenance and protection to the Arian cause, to communicate with those whom they had anathematized, and to concur in those sentiments which they had condemned by their subscriptions; they were both subjected to the same penalty of exile by the emperor, and were actually deposed, (as we learn from Athanasius,) and had successors ordained to their sees, though history is silent as to the council by which this was done. But such was the good nature and credulity of Constantine, that these men, by their usual artifices, easily imposed upon him, and brought him to such a full persuasion of their agreement with the Nicene faith, that in about three years' time they were not only recalled from banishment, but restored to their sees, and to a considerable degree of interest at court. Their thorough attachment to the cause of Arius, and their hatred of Athanasius, who had so vigorously withstood them in the council, and was now advanced to the see of Alexandria, made them watchful of every opportunity to defeat the decisions of the council.

In the meantime one who wished well to their designs, and whom Constantia had upon her death bed recommended to the emperor, did so far prevail upon the easy credulity of Constantine, by complaining that Arius had been misrepresented, and differed nothing in his sentiments from the Nicene fathers, that the indulgent emperor recalled him from his banishment, and required him to exhibit in writing, a confession of his faith. He did this in such terms as, though they admitted of a latent reservation, yet bore the appearance of being entirely catholic; and therefore not only gave satisfaction to the emperor, but even offended some of his own followers, who from that time forth separated from him. The discerning Athanasius was not so easily imposed upon as Constantine; but, well assured of the heretic's prevarication, was resolute in refusing to admit him to communion, whom the Nicene council had so openly condemned. Upon this the emperor sent for Arius to Constantinople, and insisted upon his being received into communion, by Alexander, bishop of that city. However, on the day before this was to have taken place, Arius died suddenly from a complaint in his bowels. Some attributed this to poison; others to the judgment of God. The emperor did not long survive; and Constantius, his successor, became warmly attached to the Arian cause, as were all the court party. Successive emperors took different sides, and thus was the peace of the church agitated for many years, and practical religion sacrificed alternately to the dogmas or the interests of one party or the other; and each was in turn excommunicated, fined, imprisoned, or banished. Constantius supported Arianism triumphantly, Julian laughed at both parties, but persecuted neither, Jovian supported the Nicene doctrine. Valentinian, and his brother Valens, took contrary sides; the former supporting Athanasianism in the west, and the latter Arianism in the east; so that what was orthodoxy at Rome was heresy at Constantinople, and VICE VERSA. The Arians themselves were not unanimous, but divided into various shades of sentiment, under their respective leaders; as Eusebians, Eudoxians, Acasians, Aëtians, &c; but the more general distinction was into Arians and Semi-Arians; the former sinking the character of the Son of God into that of a mere creature, while the latter admitted every thing but the HOMOOUSIAN doctrine, or his absolute equality with the Father. After this period we hear little of Arianism, till it was revived in England in the beginning of the last century by the eccentric Mr. Whiston, by Mr. Emlyn, and Dr. Samuel Clarke. The latter was what may be called a HIGH or Semi-Arian, who came within a shade of orthodoxy; the two FORMER were low Arians, reducing the rank of our Saviour to the scale of angelic beings--a creature "made out of nothing." Since this time, however, both Arians and Socinians are sunk into the common appellation of UNITARIANS, or rather HUMANITARIANS, who believe our Saviour (as Dr. Priestley expresses it) to be "a MAN like themselves." The last advocates of the pure Arian doctrine, of any celebrity, were Mr. Henry Taylor, (under the signature of Ben Mordecai,) and Dr. Richard Price, in his "Sermons on the Christian Doctrine." It may be proper to observe, that the Arians, though they denied the absolute ETERNITY of the Son, strongly contended for his preëxistence, as the LOGOS, or the Word of God, "by whom the worlds were made;" and admitted, more or less explicitly, the sacrifice which he offered for sin upon the cross.

ARIEL, the capital city of Moab, frequently mentioned in Scripture, Ezra viii, 16. See Moab.

ARIMATHEA, or **RAMAH**, now called Ramlè, or Ramla, a pleasant town, beautifully situated on the borders of a fertile and extensive plain, abounding in gardens, vineyards, olive and date trees. It stands about thirty miles north-west of Jerusalem, on the high road to Jaffa. At this Rama, which was likewise called Ramathaim Zophim, as lying in the district of Zuph, or Zoph, Samuel was born, 1 Sam. i. This was likewise the native place of Joseph, called Joseph of Arimathea, who begged and obtained the body of Jesus from Pilate, Matt. xxvi, 57. There was another Ramah, about six miles north of Jerusalem, in a pass which separated the kingdoms of Israel and Judah, which Baasha, king of Israel, took and began to fortify; but he was obliged to relinquish it, in consequence of the alliance formed between Asa, king of Judah, and Benhadad, king of Syria, 1 Kings xv. This is the Ramah, supposed to be alluded to in the lamentation of Rachel for her children.

ARISTARCHUS, spoken of by St. Paul in his Epistle to the Colossians, iv, 10, and often mentioned in the Acts of the Apostles. He was a Macedonian, and a native of Thessalonica. He accompanied St. Paul to Ephesus, and there continued with him during the two years of his abode in that place, sharing with him in all the dangers and labours of the ministry, Acts xix, 29; xx, 4; xxvii, 2. He was near losing his life in a tumult raised by the Ephesian silversmiths. He left Ephesus with the Apostle, and went with him into Greece. From thence he attended him into Asia; from Asia into Judea, and from Judea to Rome.

ARK, ARCA, denotes a kind of floating vessel built by Noah, for the preservation of himself and family, with several species of animals during the deluge. The Hebrew word by which the ark is expressed, is תבה or תיבה, the constructive form of תבה, which is evidently the Greek θίβη; and so the **LXX** render the word in Exod. ii, 3, where only it again occurs. They also render it κιβωτὸν; Josephus, λαρνάκα; and the Vulgate, ARCAM; signifying an ark, coffer, or chest. Although the ark of Noah answered, in some respects, the purpose of a ship, it is not so certain that it was of the same form and shape. It has been inconclusively argued by Michaelis and some others, that if its form had not been like that of a ship, it could not have resisted the force of the waves; because it was not intended to be conducted, like a ship, from one place to another, but merely "to float on the surface of the waters," Gen. vii, 17. It appears to have had neither helm, nor mast, nor oars; but was merely a bulky capacious vessel, light enough to be raised aloft with all its contents, by the gradual rise of the deluge. Its shape, therefore, was of little importance; more especially as it seems to have been the purpose of Providence, in this whole transaction, to signify to those who were saved, as well as to their latest posterity, that their preservation was not in any degree effected by human contrivance. The ark in which Moses was exposed bears the same name; and some have thought that both were of the same materials. With respect to the etymology of the Hebrew word, the most rational seems to be that of Clodius, who derives it from the Arabic word תאה, "he collected," from which is formed תבה, or תיבה, denoting a place in which things are collected. Foster deduces it from two Egyptian words, THOI, "a ship," and BAI, "a palm tree branch"; and such ships are still to be seen not only in Egypt, but in India and other countries; particularly in some isles of the Pacific Ocean.

To the insufficiency of the ark to contain all the creatures said to have been brought into it, objections have, at different times, been made. Bishop Wilkins and others have learnedly discussed this subject, and afforded the most satisfactory answers. Dr. Hales proves the ark to have been of the burden of forty-two thousand four hundred and thirteen tons; and asks, "Can we doubt of its being sufficient to contain eight persons, and about two hundred or two hundred and fifty pair of four-footed animals, (a number to which, according to M. Buffon, all the various distinct species may be reduced,) together with all the subsistence necessary for a twelvemonth, with the fowls of the air, and such reptiles and insects as cannot live under water?" All these various animals were controlled by the power of God, whose special agency is supposed in the whole transaction, and "the lion was made to lie down with the kid."

Whether Noah was commanded to bring with him, into the ark, a pair of ALL living creatures, zoologically and numerically considered, has been doubted. During the long period between the creation and the flood, animals must have spread themselves over a great part of the antediluvian earth, and certain animals would, as now, probably become indigenous to certain climates. The pairs saved must therefore, if all the kinds were included, have travelled from immense distances. But of such marches no intimation is given in the history; and this seems to render it probable that the animals which Noah was "TO BRING WITH HIM" into the ark, were the animals clean and unclean of the country in which he dwelt, and which, from the capacity of the ark, must have been in great variety and number. The terms used, it is true, are universal; and it is satisfactory to know, that if taken in the largest sense there was ample accommodation in the ark. Nevertheless, universal terms in Scripture are not always to be taken mathematically, and in the vision of Peter, the phrase ϖάντα τὰ τετράποδα τῆς γῆς,--ALL THE FOUR-FOOTED BEASTS OF THE EARTH, must be understood of VARII GENERIS QUADRUPEDES, as Schleusner paraphrases it. Thus we may easily account for the exuviæ of animals, whose species no longer exist, which have been discovered in various places. The number of such extinct species probably has been greatly over-rated by Cuvier; but of the fact, to a considerable extent, there can be no doubt. It is also to be observed that the presumptive evidence of the truth of the fact of the preparation of such a vessel, and of the supernatural circumstances which attended it, is exceedingly strong. It is, in truth, the only solution of a difficulty which has no other explanation; for as a universal deluge is confirmed by the general history of the world, and by a variety of existing facts and monuments, such a structure as the ark, for the preservation and sustenance of various animals, seems to have been absolutely necessary; for as we can trace up the first imperfect rudiments of the art of ship building among the Greeks, there could be no ships before the flood; and, consequently, no animals could have been saved. Nay, it is highly improbable that even men and domestic animals could be saved, not to mention wild beasts, serpents, &c, though we should admit that the antediluvians had shipping, unless we should suppose, also, that they had a divine intimation respecting the flood, such as Moses relates; but this would be to give up the cause of infidelity. Mr. Bryant has collected a variety of ancient historical relations, which show that some records concerning the ark had been preserved among most nations of the world, and in the general system of Gentile mythology. Abydenus, with whom all the eastern writers concur, informs us that the place of descent from the ark was Armenia; and that its remains had been preserved for a long time. Plutarch mentions the Noachic dove, and its being sent out of the ark. Lucian speaks of Deucalion's going forth from the ark, and raising an altar to God. The priests of Ammonia had a custom, at particular seasons, of carrying in procession a boat, in which was an oracular shrine, held in great veneration: and this custom of carrying the deity in an ark or boat was in use also among the Egyptians. Bishop Pococke has preserved three specimens of ancient sculpture, in which this ceremony is displayed. They were very ancient, and found by him in Upper Egypt. The ship of Isis referred to the ark, and its name, "Baris," was that of the mountain corresponding to Ararat in Armenia. Bryant finds reference to the ark in the temples of the serpent worship, called DRACONTIA; and also in that of Sesostris, fashioned after the model of the ark, in commemoration of which it was built, and consecrated to Osiris at Theba; and he conjectures that the city, said to be one of the most ancient in Egypt, as well as the province, was denominated from it, Theba being the appellation of the ark. In other countries, as well as in Egypt, an ark, or ship, was introduced in their mysteries, and often carried about in the seasons of their festivals. He finds, also, in the story of the Argonauts several particulars, that are thought to refer to the ark of Noah. As many cities, not in Egypt only and Bœotia, but in Cilicia, Ionia, Attica, Phthiotis, Cataonia, Syria, and Italy, were called Theba; so likewise the city Apamea was denominated CIBOTUS, from κιϐωτος, in memory of the ark, and of the history connected with it. The ark, according to the traditions of the Gentile world, was prophetic; and was regarded as a kind of temple or residence of the deity. It comprehended all mankind, within the circle of eight persons, who were thought to be so highly favoured of Heaven that they at last were reputed to be deities. Hence in the ancient mythology of Egypt, there were precisely eight gods; and the ark was esteemed an emblem of the system of the heavens. The principal terms by which the ancients distinguished the ark were Theba, Baris, Arguz, Aren, Arene, Arni, Laris, Boutas, Bœotus, and Cibotus; and out of these they formed different personages. See Deluge.

ARK OF THE COVENANT, a small chest or coffer, three feet nine inches in length, two feet three inches in breadth, and two feet three inches in height; in which were contained the golden pot that had manna, Aaron's rod, and the tables of the covenant, Num. xvii, 10; Heb. ix, 4. This coffer was made of shittim wood, and was covered with a lid, called the MERCY SEAT, Exod. xxv, 17–22, &c, which was of solid gold, at the two ends whereof were two figures, called CHERUBIM, looking toward each other, with expanded wings, which, embracing the whole circumference of the mercy seat, met in the middle. The whole, according to the rabbins, was made out of the same mass, without any of the parts being joined by solder. Over this it was that the Shechinah, or visible display of the divine presence in a luminous cloud rested, both in the tabernacle and in the temple, Lev. xvi, 2; and from hence the divine oracles were given forth by an audible voice, as often as God was consulted in behalf of his people. Hence it is that God is said in Scripture to dwell between the cherubim, on the mercy seat, because there was the seat or throne of the visible appearance of his glory among them, 2 Kings xix, 15; 2 Chron, xiii, 6; Psalm lxxx, 1, &c; and for this reason the high priest appeared before the mercy seat once every year, on the great day of expiation, at which time he was to make his nearest approach to the divine presence, to mediate and make atonement for the whole people of Israel. On the two sides of the ark there were four rings of gold, two on each side, through which staves, overlaid with gold, were put, by means whereof they carried it as they marched through the wilderness, &c, on the shoulders of the Levites, Exod. xxv, 13, 14; xxvii, 5. After the passage of the Jordan, the ark continued for some time at Gilgal, from whence it was removed to Shiloh. From this place the Israelites carried it to their camp, where, in an engagement with the Philistines, it fell into their hands. The Philistines, having gotten possession of the ark, carried it in triumph to one of their principal cities, named Ashdod, and placed it in the temple of Dagon, whose image fell to the ground and was broken. The Philistines also were so afflicted with emerods, that they afterward returned the ark with various presents; and it was lodged at Kirjath-Jearim, and afterward at Nob. David conveyed it to the house of Obededom, and from thence to his palace at Zion; and lastly, Solomon brought it into the temple which he had built at Jerusalem. It remained in the temple till the times of the last kings of Judah, who gave themselves up to idolatry, and even dared to place their idols in the holy temple itself. The priests, being unable to bear this profanation, took the ark and carried it from place to place, to preserve it from the hands of those impious princes. Josiah commanded them to bring it back to the sanctuary, and it was accordingly replaced, 2 Chron. xxxv, 3. What became of the ark at the destruction of the temple by Nebuchadnezzar, is a dispute among the rabbins. Had it been carried to Babylon with the other vessels of the temple, it would, in all probability, have been brought back with them at the close of the captivity. But that this was not the case, is agreed on all hands; whence it is probable that it was destroyed with the temple.

The ark of the covenant was, as it were, the centre of worship to all those of the Hebrew nation who served God according to the Levitical law; and not only in the temple, when they came thither to worship, but every where else in their dispersions through the whole world; whenever they prayed, they turned their faces toward the place where the ark stood, and directed all their devotions that way, Dan. vi, 10. Whence the author of the book of Cosri, justly says, that the ark, with the mercy seat and cherubim, were the foundation, root, heart, and marrow of the whole temple, and all the Levitical worship performed therein; and, therefore, had there been nothing else wanting in the second temple but the ark only, this alone would have been a sufficient reason for the old men to have wept when they remembered the first temple in which it stood; and for the saying of Haggai, ii, 3, that the second temple was as nothing compared with the first; so great a share had the ark of the covenant in the glory of Solomon's temple. However, the defect was supplied as to the outward form, for in the second temple there was also an ark of the same dimensions with the first, and put in the same place; but it wanted the tables of the law, Aaron's rod, and the pot of manna; nor was there any appearance of the divine glory over it; nor any oracles delivered from it. The only use that was made of it was to be a representation of the former on the great day of expiation, and to be a repository of the Holy Scriptures, that is, of the original copy of that collection of them made by Ezra after the captivity; in imitation of which the Jews, in all their synagogues, have a like ark or coffer in which they keep their Scriptures.

For the temple of Solomon a new ark was not made; but he constructed cherubim in the most holy place, which were designed to give additional state to this most sacred symbol of God's grace and mercy. These cherubim were fifteen feet high, and were placed at equal distance from the centre of the ark and from each side of the wall, so that their wings being expanded, the two wings which were extended behind touched the wall, and the other two met over the ark and so overshadowed it. When these magnificent cherubim were finished, the ark was brought in and placed under their wings, 2 Chron. v, 7–10.

The ark was called the ARK OF THE COVENANT, because it was a symbol of the covenant between God and his people. It was also named the ARK OF THE TESTIMONY, because the two tables which were deposited in it were witnesses against every transgression.

ARM. As it is by this member of the body that we chiefly exert our strength, it is therefore used in Scripture for an emblem of power. Thus God is said to have delivered his people from Egyptian bondage "with a stretched-out arm," Deut. v, 15; and he thus threatens Eli the high priest, "I will cut off thine arm, and the arm of thy father's house," 1 Sam. ii, 31; that is, I will deprive thee and thy family of power and authority.

ARMAGEDDON, a place spoken of, Rev. xvi, 16, which literally signifies "the mountain of Mageddon," or "Megiddo," a city situated in the great plain at the foot of Mount Carmel, where the good prince Josiah received his mortal wound, in the battle against Necho, king of Egypt. At Armageddon, the three unclean spirits coming out of the dragon's mouth shall gather together the kings of the earth, to the battle of the great day of God Almighty, Rev. xvi, 13, 14; where the word Armageddon, according to Mr. Pool, does not signify any particular place, but is used in allusion to Megiddo, mentioned Judges v, 19, where Barak overcame Sisera with his great army, and where Josiah was slain, 2 Kings xxiii, 30. If so, the term must have been a proverbial one for a place of destruction and mourning.

ARMENIA, a considerable country of Asia, having Colchis and Iberia on the north, Media on the east, Mesopotamia on the south, Pontus and Cappadocia on the west, and the Euphrates and Syria on the south-west. Armenia is often confounded with Aramæa, the land of Aram or Syria; but they are totally different. Armenia, which is separated from Aram by Mount Taurus, was so denominated from Ar-Men, the mountainous country of Meni or Minni, the people of which country are mentioned under this name by Jeremiah, when summoning the nations against Babylon.

The people of this country have in all ages maintained a great similarity of character, partly commercial and partly pastoral. They have, in fact, in the northern parts of the Asiatic continent, been what the Cushites and Ishmaelites were in the south, tenders of cattle, living on the produce of their flocks and herds, and carriers of merchandize between the neighbouring nations; a part living at home with their flocks, and a part travelling as merchants and dealers into distant countries. In the flourishing times of Tyre, the Armenians, according to Ezekiel, xxvii, 14, brought horses and mules to the markets of that city; and, according to Herodotus, they had a considerable trade in wine, which they sent down the Euphrates to Babylon, &c. At the present day, the Armenians are the principal traders of the east; and are to be found in the capacity of merchants or commercial agents all over Asia, a patient, frugal, industrious, and honest people, whose known character for these virtues has withstood the tyranny and extortions of the wretched governments under which they chiefly live.

The religion of the Armenians is a corrupt Christianity of the sect of Eutyches; that is, they own but one nature in Jesus Christ. Their rites partake of those of the Greek and Latin churches, but they reject the idolatries of both. It is indeed a remarkable instance of the firmness of this people, that while the surrounding nations submitted to the religion as well as the arms of the Turks, they have preserved the purity of their ancient faith, such as it is, to the present day. It cannot be supposed but that the Turks used every effort to impose on the conquered Armenians the doctrines of the Koran. More tolerant, indeed, than the Saracens, liberty of conscience was still not to be purchased of them but by great sacrifices, which for three centuries the Armenians have patiently endured, and exhibit to the world an honourable and solitary instance of a successful national opposition of Christianity to Mohammedanism.

ARMENIAN CHURCH, a branch, originally, of the Greek church, residing in Armenia. They probably received Christianity in the fourth century. Mr. Yeates gives the most recent account of them:--

"Their whole ecclesiastical establishment is under the government of four patriarchs; the first has his residence in Echmiadzin, or Egmiathin, near Irivan; the second, at Sis, in the lesser Armenia; the third, in Georgia; and the fourth, in Achtamar, or Altamar, on the Lake of Van; but the power of the two last is bounded within their own diocesses, while the others have more extensive authority, and the patriarch of Egmiathan has, or had, under him eighteen bishops, beside those who are priors of monasteries. The Armenians every where perform divine service in their own tongue, in which their liturgy and offices are written, in the dialect of the fourth or fifth centuries. They have the whole Bible translated from the Septuagint, as they say, so early as the time of Chrysostom. The Armenian confession is similar to that of the Jacobite Christians, both being Monophysites, acknowledging but one nature in the person of Christ; but this, according to Mr. Simon, is little more than a dispute about terms; few of them being able to enter into the subtilties of polemics.

"In the year 1664, an Armenian bishop, named Uscan, visited Europe for the purpose of getting printed the Armenian Bible, and communicated the above particulars to Mr. Simon. In 1667, a certain patriarch of the lesser Armenia visited Rome, and made a profession of faith which was considered orthodox, and procured him a cordial reception, with the hope of reconciling the Armenian Christians to the Roman church; but, before he got out of Italy, it was found he had prevaricated, and still persisted in the errors of his church. About this time, Clement **IX**, wrote to the king of Persia, in favour of some Catholic converts in Armenia, and received a favourable answer; but the Armenian church could never be persuaded to acknowledge the authority of Rome.

"They have among them a number of monasteries and convents, in which is maintained a severe discipline; marriage is discountenanced, though not absolutely prohibited; a married priest cannot obtain promotion, and the higher clergy are not allowed to marry. They worship in the eastern manner, by prostration: they are very superstitious, and their ceremonies much resemble those of the Greek church. Once in their lives they generally perform a pilgrimage to Jerusalem; and in 1819, the number of Armenian pilgrims was thirteen hundred, nearly as many as the Greeks. Dr. Buchanan, however, says, 'Of all the Christians in central Asia, they have preserved themselves most free from Mohammedan and Papal corruptions.'"

ARMIES. In the reign of David, the Hebrews acquired such skill in the military art, together with such strength, as gave them a decided superiority over their competitors on the field of battle. David increased the standing army, which Saul had introduced. Solomon introduced cavalry into the military force of the nation, also chariots. Both cavalry and chariots were retained in the subsequent age; an age, in which military arms were improved in their construction, the science of fortification made advances, and large armies were mustered. From this period, till the time when the Hebrews became subject to the Assyrians and Chaldeans, but little improvement was made in the arts of war. The Maccabees, after the return of the Hebrews from the captivity, gave a new existence to the military art among them. But their descendants were under the necessity of submitting to the superior power of the Romans.

Whenever there was an immediate prospect of war, a levy was made by the genealogists, Deut. xx, 5–9. In the time of the kings, there was a head or ruler of the persons, that made the levy, denominated השוטר, who kept an account of the number of the soldiers, but who is, nevertheless, to be distinguished from the generalissimo, הסופר, 2 Chron. xxvi, 11. Compare 2 Sam. viii, 17; xx, 25; 1 Chron. xviii, 16. After the levy was fully made out, the genealogists gave public notice, that the following persons might be excused, from military service, Deut. xx, 5–8: 1. Those who had built a house, and had not yet inhabited it. 2. Those who had planted a כרם, that is, AN OLIVE or VINE GARDEN, and had not as yet tasted the fruit of it; an exemption, consequently, which extended through the first five years after such planting. 3. Those who had bargained for a spouse, but had not celebrated the nuptials; also those who had not as yet lived with their wife, for a year. 4. The faint-hearted, who would be likely to discourage others, and who, if they had gone into battle, where, in those early times, every thing depended on personal prowess, would only have fallen victims.

At the head of each rank or file of fifty, was the captain of fifty. The other divisions consisted of a hundred, a thousand, and ten thousand men, each one of which was headed by its appropriate commander. These divisions ranked in respect to each other according to their families, and were subject to the authority of the heads of those families, 2 Chron. xxv, 5; xxvi, 12, 13. The centurions, and CHILIARCHS or captains of thousands, were admitted into the councils of war, 1 Chron. xiii, 1–3; 1 Sam. xviii, 13. The leader of the whole army was denominated אל־שרהצבא, THE CAPTAIN OF THE HOST. The genealogists, (in the English version, OFFICERS,) according to a law in Deut. xx, 9, had the right of appointing the persons who were to act as officers in the army; and they, undoubtedly, made it a point, in their selections, to choose those who are called heads of families. The practice of thus selecting military officers ceased under the kings. Some of them were then chosen by the king, and in other instances the office became permanent and hereditary in the heads of families. Both kings and generals had armour bearers, כלים נשא. They were chosen from the bravest of the soldiery, and not only bore the arms of their masters, but were employed to give his commands to the subordinate captains, and were present at his side in the hour of peril, 1 Sam. xiv, 6; xvii, 7. The infantry, the cavalry, and the chariots of war were so arranged, as to make separate divisions of an army, Exod. xiv, 6, 7. The infantry were divided likewise into light-armed troops, גדודים, and into spearmen, Genesis xlix, 19; 1 Samuel xxx, 8, 15, 23; 2 Sam. iii, 22; iv, 2; xxii, 30; Psalm xviii, 30; 2 Kings v, 2; Hosea vii, 1. The light-armed infantry were furnished with a sling and javelin, with a bow, arrows, and quiver, and also, at least in latter times, with a buckler. They fought the enemy at a distance. The spearmen, on the contrary, who were armed with spears, swords, and shields, fought hand to hand, 1 Chron. xii, 24, 34; 2 Chron. xiv, 8; xvii, 17. The light-armed troops were commonly taken from the tribes of Ephraim and Benjamin, 2 Chron. xiv, 8; xvii, 17. Compare Gen. xlix, 27; Psalm lxxviii, 9.

The art of laying out an encampment appears to have been well understood in Egypt, long before the departure of the Hebrews from that country. It was there that Moses became acquainted with that mode of encamping, which, in the second chapter of Numbers, is prescribed to the Hebrews. In the encampment of the Israelites, it appears that the holy tabernacle occupied the centre. In reference to this circumstance, it may be remarked, that it is the common practice in the east, for the prince or leader of a tribe to have his tent pitched in the centre of the others; and it ought not to be forgotten, that God, whose tent or palace was the holy tabernacle, was the prince, the leader of the Hebrews. The tents nearest to the tabernacle were those of the Levites, whose business it was to watch it, in the manner of a Pretorian guard. The family of Gershom pitched to the west, that of Kehath to the south, that of Merari to the north. The priests occupied a position to the east, opposite to the entrance of the tabernacle, Num. i, 53; iii, 21–38. At some distance to the east, were the tribes of Judah, Issachar, and Zebulon; on the south were those of Reuben, Simeon, and Gad; to the west were Ephraim, Manasseh, and Benjamin; to the north, Dan, Asher, and Napthali. The people were thus divided into four bodies, three tribes to a division; each of which divisions had its separate standard, דגל. Each of the large family associations likewise, of which the different tribes were composed, had a separate standard, termed, in contradistinction from the other, אות; and every Hebrew was obliged to number himself with his particular division, and follow his appropriate standard. Of military standards, there were,--1. The standard, denominated דגל; one of which pertained to each of the four general divisions. The four standards of this name were large, and ornamented with colours in white, purple, crimson, and dark blue. The Jewish Rabbins assert, (founding their statement on Genesis xlix, 3, 9, 17, 22, which in this case is very doubtful authority,) that the first of these standards, namely, that, of Judah, bore a lion; the second, or that of Reuben, bore a man; that of Ephraim, which was the third, displayed the figure of a bull; while that of Dan, which was the fourth, exhibited the representation of cherubim. They were wrought into the standards with embroidered work. 2. The standard, called אות. The ensign of this name belonged to the separate classes of families. 3. The standard, called נס. This standard was not, like the others, borne from place to place. It appears from Num. xxi, 8, 9, that it was a long pole, fixed into the earth. A flag was fastened to its top, which was agitated by the wind, and seen at a great distance, Jer. iv, 6, 21; li, 2, 12, 27; Ezek. xxvii, 7. In order to render it visible, as far as possible, it was erected on lofty mountains, and was in this way used as a signal, to assemble soldiers. It no sooner made its appearance on such an elevated position, than the war-cry was uttered, and the trumpets were blown, Isaiah v, 26; xiii, 2; xviii, 3; xxx, 17; xlix, 22; lxii, 10–13.

Before battle the various kinds of arms were put into the best order; the shields were anointed, and the soldiers refreshed themselves by taking food, lest they should become weary and faint under the pressure of their labours, Jer. xlvi, 3, 4; Isaiah xxi, 5. The soldiers, more especially the generals and kings, except when they wished to remain unknown, 1 Kings xxii, 30–34, were clothed in splendid habiliments, which are denominated, קדש-בהדרי, THE SACRED DRESS, Psalm cx, 3. It was the duty of the priests, before the commencement of the battle, to exhort the Hebrews to exhibit that courage which was required by the exigency of the occasion. The words which they used were as follows:--"Hear, O Israel; ye approach this day unto battle against your enemies; let not your hearts faint; fear not, and do not tremble; neither be ye terrified, because of them. For the Lord your God is he that goeth with you, to fight for you against your enemies, to save you," Deut. xx, 2, &c. The last ceremony, previous to an engagement, was the sounding of the sacred trumpets by the priests, Num. x, 9, 10; 2 Chron. xiii, 12–14; 1 Macc. iii, 54.

ARMINIANISM, strictly speaking, is that system of religious doctrine which was taught by Arminius, professor of divinity in the university of Leyden. If therefore we would learn precisely what Arminianism is, we must have recourse to those writings in which that divine himself has stated and expounded his peculiar tenets. This, however, will by no means give us an accurate idea of that which, since his time, has been usually denominated Arminianism.

On examination, it will be found, that in many important particulars, those who have called themselves Arminians, or have been accounted such by others, differ as widely from the nominal head and founder of their sect, as he himself did from Calvin, and other doctors of Geneva. There are, indeed, certain points, with regard to which he has been strictly and uniformly followed by almost all his pretended adherents; but there are others of equal or of greater importance, dogmatically insisted on by them, to which he unquestionably never gave his sanction, and even appears to have been decidedly hostile. Such a distinction, obvious as it must be to every attentive reader, has yet been generally so far overlooked, that the memory of Arminius is frequently loaded with imputations the most unreasonable and unjust. He is accused, by the ignorant and the prejudiced, of introducing corruptions into the Christian church, which he probably never thought of, and which certainly have no place in his works. And all the odium which his followers have from time to time incurred by their varied and increasing heterodoxy, has been absurdly reflected upon him, as if he could be responsible for every error that may be sent abroad under the sanction of his name. Whatever be the number or the species of these errors, and in whatever way they may be associated with his principles, it is fair to the character of Arminius, and useful to the interests of religious truth, to revert to his own writings as the only source from which we ought to derive information concerning the Arminian scheme; and by doing so, it may be discovered, that genuine unadulterated Arminianism is not that great and dangerous heresy which among a certain class of Christians it is too often represented to be.

Arminianism, in its proper sense, is to be considered as a separation from Calvinism, with regard to the doctrines of unconditional election, particular redemption, and other points necessarily resulting from these. The Calvinists held that God had elected a certain portion of the human race to eternal life, passing by the rest, or rather dooming them to everlasting destruction; that God's election proceeded upon no prescience of the moral principles and character of those whom he had thus predestinated, but originated solely in the motions of his free and sovereign mercy; that Christ died for the elect only, and therefore that the merits of his death can avail for the salvation of none but them; and that they are constrained by the irresistible power of divine grace to accept of him as their Saviour. To this doctrine, that of Arminius and his legitimate followers stands opposed. They do not deny an election; but they deny that it is absolute and unconditional. They argue, that an election of this kind is inconsistent with the character of God, that it destroys the liberty of the human will, that it contradicts the language of Scripture, and that it tends to encourage a careless and licentious practice in those by whom it is believed. They maintain that God has elected those only who, according, not to his decree, but to his foreknowledge, and in the exercise of their natural powers of self-determination, acting under the influence of his grace, would possess that faith and holiness to which salvation is annexed in the Gospel scheme. And those who are NOT elected are allowed to perish, not because they were not elected, but merely and solely in consequence of their infidelity and disobedience; on account, indeed, of which infidelity and disobedience being foreseen by God, their election did not take place. They hold, that Christ died for ALL men in the literal and unrestricted sense of that phrase; that his atonement is able, both from its own merit, and from the intention of him who appointed it, to expiate the guilt of every individual; that every individual is invited to partake of the benefits which it has procured; that the grace of God is offered to make the will comply with this invitation, but that this grace may be resisted and rendered ineffectual by the sinner's perversity. Whether true believers necessarily persevered, or whether they might fall from their faith, and forfeit their state of grace, was a question which Arminius left in a great measure unresolved, but which was soon determined by his followers in this additional proposition, that saints may fall from the state of grace, in which they are placed by the operation of the Holy Spirit. This, indeed, seems to follow as a corollary, from what Arminius maintained respecting the natural freedom and corruption of the will, and the resistibility of divine grace.

It may now be proper to mention some tenets with regard to which Arminianism has been much misrepresented. If a man hold that good works are necessary to justification; if he maintain that faith includes good works in its own nature; if he reject the doctrine of original sin; if he deny that divine grace is requisite for the whole work of sanctification; if he speak of human virtue as meritorious in the sight of God; it is very generally concluded, that he is an Arminian. But the truth is, that a man of such sentiments is properly a disciple of the Pelagian and Socinian schools. To such sentiments pure Arminianism is as diametrically opposite as Calvinism itself. The genuine Arminians admit the corruption of human nature in its full extent. They admit, that we are justified by faith only. They admit, that our justification originates solely in the grace of God. They admit, that the procuring and meritorious cause of our justification is the righteousness of Christ. PROPTER QUAM, says Arminius, DEUS CREDENTIBUS PECCATUM CONDONAT, EOSQUE PRO JUSTIS REPUTAT NON ALITER ATQUE SI LEGEM PERFECTÈ IMPLEVISSENT. [For the sake of which God pardons believers, and accounts them as righteous precisely as if they had perfectly obeyed the law.] They admit in this way, that justification implies not merely forgiveness of sin, but acceptance to everlasting happiness. JUNCTAM HABET ADOPTIONEM IN FILIOS, ET COLLATIONEM JURIS IN HEREDITATEM VITÆ ETERNÆ. [It has connected with it adoption to sonship, and the grant of a right to the inheritance of eternal life.] They admit, in fine, that the work of sanctification, from its very commencement to its perfection in glory, is carried on by the operation of the Holy Spirit, which is the gift of God by Jesus Christ. So sound, indeed, are the Arminians with respect to the doctrine of justification, a doctrine so important and essential in the opinion of Luther, that he scrupled not to call it, ARTICULUS ECCLESIÆ STANTIS VEL CADENTIS; [the article with which the church stands or falls;] that those who look into the writings of Arminius may be disposed to suspect him of having even exceeded Calvin in orthodoxy. It is certain, at least, that he declares his willingness to subscribe to every thing that Calvin has written on that leading subject of Christianity, in the third book of his Institutes; and with this declaration the tenor of his writings invariably corresponds.

The system of Arminius, then, appears to have been the same with that which was generally maintained in the reformed churches at that time; except in so far as the doctrine of the divine decrees was concerned. But the most eminent of those who became Arminians, or ranked among his professed followers, by embracing and avowing his peculiar tenets with respect to election and redemption, soon began to depart widely from the other tenets of his theological creed. They adopted views of the corruption of man, of justification, of the righteousness of Christ, of the nature of faith, of the province of good works, of the necessity and operations of grace, that are quite contrary to those which he had entertained and published. Many of them, in process of time, differed more or less from one another, on some or all of these points. And so diversified are the forms which Arminianism, as it is called, has assumed in the course of its progress, that to describe precisely what it has been since the synod of Dort, or what it is at the present day, would be a most difficult, if not an impossible, task. Even the confession of faith, which was drawn out for the Arminians by Episcopius, and is to be found in the second volume of his works, cannot be referred to as a standard. It was composed merely to counteract the reproach of their being a society without any common principles. It is expressed chiefly in the words and phrases of Scripture, to which, of course, every one would annex his own meaning. Beside, no person, not even a pastor, was obliged, by any form, to adhere strictly to it; but every one was left entirely at liberty to interpret its language in the manner that was most agreeable to his own private sentiments. Accordingly, so various and inconsistent are their opinions, that could Arminius peruse the unnumbered volumes which have been written as expositions and illustrations of Arminian doctrine, he would be at a loss to discover his own simple system, amidst that heterogeneous mass of error with which it has been rudely mixed; and would be astonished to find, that the controversy which he had conscientiously introduced, had wandered far from the point to which he had confined it, and that with his name dogmas were associated, the unscriptural and dangerous nature of which he had pointed out and condemned.

The same temper of mind which led him to renounce the peculiarities of Calvinism, induced him also to adopt more enlarged and liberal views of church communion than those which had hitherto prevailed. While he maintained that the mercy of God is not confined to a chosen few, he conceived it to be quite inconsistent with the genius of Christianity, that men of that religion should keep at a distance from each other, and constitute separate churches, merely because they differed in their opinions as to some of its doctrinal articles. He thought that Christians of all denominations should form one great community, united and upheld by the bonds of charity and brotherly love; with the exception, however, of Roman Catholics, who, on account of their idolatrous worship and persecuting spirit, must be unfit members of such a society. That this was not only agreeable to the wishes of Arminius, but one chief object of his labours, is evident from a passage in his last will, which he made a little before his death:--EA PROPOSUI ET DOCUI QUÆ AD PROPAGATIONEM AMPLIFICATIONEMQUE VERITATIS RELIGIONIS CHRISTIANÆ, VERI DEI CULTUS, COMMUNIS PIETATIS, ET SANCTÆ INTER HOMINES CONVERS[AT]IONIS, DENIQUE AD CONVENIENTEM CHRISTIANO NOMINI TRANQUILLITATEM ET PACEM JUXTA VERBUM DEI POSSENT CONFERRE, EXCLUDENS EX IIS PAPATUM, CUM QUO NULLA UNITAS FIDEI, NULLUM PIETATIS AUT CHRISTIANÆ PACIS VINCULUM SERVARI POTEST. [I have advanced and taught those things which might contribute to the propagation and spread of the truth of Christianity, the worship of the true God, general piety, and a holy fellowship among men;--in fine, to a tranquillity and peace according to God's word and becoming the Christian name, excluding the Papacy, with which no unity of faith, no bond of piety, or of Christian peace can be maintained.]

Mosheim has stated this circumstance in a note to his history of the Arminian church; but his statement, or rather the conclusion which he deduces from it, is evidently unfair and incorrect. He alleges, that Arminius had actually laid the plan of that theological system which was afterward embraced by his followers; that he had inculcated the main and leading principles of it on the minds of his disciples; and that Episcopius and others, who rejected Calvinism in more points than in that which related to the divine decrees, only propagated, with greater courage and perspicuity, the doctrines which Arminianism, as taught by its founder, already contained. These allegations, it is clear, have no sort of connection with the passage from which they are drawn as inferences; and they are wholly inconsistent with the assertions, and reasonings, and declarations of Arminius, when he is discussing the merits of the question that was agitated between him and the Geneva school. Arminius, in addition to the scheme of doctrine which he taught, was anxious to establish this maxim, and to reduce it to practice, that, with the exception above mentioned, no difference of opinions should prevent Christians from remaining in one church or religious body. He did not mean to insinuate, that a difference of opinion was of no consequence at all; that they who thought one way were just as right as they who thought a contrary way; or that men have no occasion to be solicitous about the religious tenets which they hold. He did not mean to give up his own system as equally true, or equally false, with that of Calvin; and as little could he be supposed to sanction those sentiments of his followers which were in direct opposition to the sentiments which he himself had maintained. But he endeavoured, in the first place, to assert liberty of conscience, and of worship; and then, upon that fundamental principle, to persuade all Christians, however divided in opinion, to lay aside the distinctions of sect and party, and in one united body to consult that tranquillity and peace which is so agreeable to the Christian name. This we conceive to have been the object of Arminius; an object so indicative of an enlightened mind, so congenial to that charity which hopeth all things, and thinketh no evil, and so conducive to the interests of religion and the peace of the world, as to reflect the highest honour on him by whom it was first pursued, and to constitute the true glory of Arminianism.

The controversy to which Arminianism had given rise, was carried on after the death of its founder, with the greatest eagerness, and produced the most bitter and deplorable dissensions. The Arminians requested nothing more than a bare toleration. This moderate demand, at all times reasonable and just, was particularly so in Holland, which had thrown off the yoke of civil and spiritual despotism, and where the received confession of faith had not determined the questions under debate. It was strongly urged by Grotius, Hoogerbeets, Olden Barnevelt, and other persons of respectability and influence. And Maurice, prince of Orange, and his mother the princess dowager, giving countenance to the claim, there was some prospect of the Calvinists being persuaded to enter into pacific measures, and to treat their dissenting brethren with forbearance. Accordingly, in the year 1611, a conference between the contending parties was held at the Hague, on which occasion, it is commonly asserted, the toleration required was offered to the Arminians, provided they would renounce the errors of Socinianism,--though the papers which passed between the parties at that conference, as authenticated by each of them, contain no proviso of that description. Another conference was held at Delft, in 1613. And in 1614, the States of Holland promulgated an edict, exhorting the disputants to the exercise of mutual charity. But these and other expedients employed for the same purpose, had not the desired effect. The Calvinists expressed great indignation at the magistrates, for endeavouring, by their authority, to promote a union with such adversaries. The conduct of the States was ably and eloquently defended by Grotius, in two treatises, entitled, "*De Jure Summarum Potestatum circa sacra*," and "*Ordinum Hollandiæ, ac West-Frisiæ Pietas a multorum calumniis vindicata*."

The hopes of success which the Arminians entertained from the indulgent manner in which they were treated by the civil authorities, were soon blasted by a misunderstanding which had secretly subsisted for some time between the stadtholder and the principal magistrates, and at last broke forth into an open rupture. Maurice, being suspected of aiming at sovereign power, was firmly opposed by the leading persons in the government, who had been the friends and patrons of the Arminians, and to whom, therefore, these adhered at this difficult crisis. On the other hand, the Gomarists, or Calvinists, attached themselves to Maurice, and inflamed the resentment which he had already, for various reasons, conceived against the Arminians. The prince was resolved, at once to ruin the ministers who had ventured to oppose his schemes of usurpation, and to crush the Arminians, by whom those statesmen had been warmly supported. For this purpose he got the leading men cast into prison. Barnevelt, whose long and faithful services deserved a better fate, died on the scaffold: and Grotius and Hoogerbeets, under pretexts more plausible than solid, were unjustly condemned to perpetual imprisonment, from which, however, the former afterward escaped, and fled into France. The alleged crime of the Arminians being of an ecclesiastical nature, it was thought proper to bring their cause before a national assembly of divines by which their religious opinions might be regularly and finally condemned.

Under the auspices of Maurice, therefore, and by the authority of the states general, a synod was convoked at Dort, in the year 1618. Before this meeting, which consisted of deputies from the United Provinces, from England, Scotland, Switzerland, and other places, the Arminians appeared, with Episcopius at their head, to answer to the accusations brought against them, of departing from the established religion. For a full account of the proceedings of this synod, the reader may consult the second and third volumes of Brandt's History of the Reformation, and the Remains of Mr. John Hales of Eaton, who was present at the meeting, and gives a simple narrative of what he saw and heard. The conduct of the synod has been applauded by some, and condemned by others. On the one hand, it has been placed above every other synod since the Apostolic age, for its temper, moderation, and sanctity; on the other, it has been charged with injustice and cruelty, and burlesqued in such lines as these:--

DORDRECHTI SYNODUS NODUS; CHORUS INTEGER, ÆGER; CONVENTUS, VENTUS; SESSIO, STRAMEN, AMEN.

[The point of this doggrel, which consists chiefly in the gingle of the Latin words, is lost in a translation. The following is a literal version:--

The synod of Dort, a knot; the whole assembly, sick;

The convention, wind; the session, straw, Amen.]

Neal remarks, that it behaved as well as most assemblies of a similar kind have done, "who have pretended to establish articles for other men's faith, with penal sanctions." This says very little for the synod of Dort; though, perhaps, it is even more than can be said with truth. Martinius of Bremen seems to have spoken much more correctly, when he told his friends, "I believe now what Gregory Nazianzen says, that he had never seen any council attended with good effects, but that it always increased the evil rather than removed it. I declare as well as that father, that I will never set my foot in any synod again. O Dort! Dort! would to God that I had never seen thee!" The Arminians, it is contended, asked more indulgence than they had reason to expect; however it is certain that the treatment which they received from the synod, was arbitrary, faithless, and oppressive. They were at length found guilty of heresy, and of hostility to their country and its religion. And the measures adopted against them, in consequence of this sentence, were of the most severe and rigorous kind. They were excommunicated; they were driven from all their offices, civil and ecclesiastical; their ministers were prohibited from preaching; and their congregations were suppressed. Refusing to submit to the two last of these hard decrees, they were subjected to fines, imprisonments, and various other punishments. To avoid this tyrannical treatment, many of them retired to Antwerp, others to France, and a considerable number into Holstein, where they were kindly received by Frederick the duke, and where, in the form of a colony, they built for themselves a handsome town, naming it Frederickstadt, in compliment to their friend and protector. The history of this colony may be found in a work entitled *Epistolæ Præstantium et Eruditorum Virorum Ecclesiasticæ et Theologicæ*, and published by Limborch and Hartsoeker.

The tenets of the Arminians may be comprised in the following five articles relating to predestination, universal redemption, the corruption of men, conversion, and perseverance, viz. 1. That God, from all eternity, determined to bestow salvation on those whom he foresaw would persevere unto the end in their faith in Christ Jesus; and to inflict everlasting punishment on those who should continue in their unbelief, and resist unto the end his divine succours; so that election was conditional, and reprobation in like manner the result of foreseen infidelity and persevering wickedness. 2. That Jesus Christ, by his sufferings and death, made an atonement for the sins of all mankind in general, and of every individual in particular; that, however, none but those who believe in him can be partakers of the divine benefits. 3. That true faith cannot proceed from the exercise of our natural faculties and powers, nor from the force and operation of free will; since man, in consequence of his natural corruption, is incapable either of thinking or doing any good thing; and that, therefore, it is necessary, in order to his salvation, that he be regenerated and renewed by the operation of the Holy Ghost, which is the gift of God through Jesus Christ. 4. That this divine grace or energy of the Holy Ghost begins and perfects every thing that can be called good in man, and consequently all good works are to be attributed to God alone; that, nevertheless, this grace is offered to all, and does not force men to act against their inclinations, but may be resisted and rendered ineffectual by the perverse wills of impenitent sinners. 5. That God gives to the truly faithful, who are regenerated by his grace, the means of preserving themselves in this state; and though the first Arminians made some doubt with respect to the closing part of this article, their followers uniformly maintain, that the regenerate may lose true justifying faith, forfeit their state of grace, and die in their sins. The Arminians are also called REMONSTRANTS, from an humble petition entitled their REMONSTRANCE, which, in the year 1610, they addressed to the States of Holland. Their principal writers are, ARMINIUS, EPISCOPIUS, UITENBOGART, GROTIUS, CURCELLÆUS, LIMBORCH, LE CLERC, WETSTEIN, GOODWIN, WHITBY, WESLEY, FLETCHER, TOMLINE, *&c.* The works of Arminius, with a copious account of his life and times, have been recently translated into English, by Mr. James Nichols; and have not only served to dissipate many misconceptions respecting the sentiments of this celebrated divine, which had prevailed in England, where the Pelagianism of some eminent divines, generally called Arminian, had been unjustly charged upon him; but have added a most valuable collection of treatises to our theological literature.

ARMS. The Hebrews do not appear to have had any peculiar military habit. As the flowing dress which they ordinarily wore would have impeded their movements, they girt it closely around them when preparing for battle, and loosened it on their return, 2 Sam. xx, 8; 1 Kings xx, 11. They used the same arms as the neighbouring nations, both defensive and offensive; and these were made either of iron or of brass, principally of the latter metal. Of the defensive arms of the Hebrews, the following were the most remarkable; namely,

1. The helmet, כובע, for covering and defending the head. This was a part of the military provision made by Uzziah for his vast army, 2 Chron. xxvi, 14; and long before the time of that king, the helmets of Saul and of the Philistine champion were of the same metal, 1 Sam. xvii, 38. This military cap was also worn by the Persians, Ethiopians, and Libyans, Ezek. xxxviii, 5, and by the troops which Antiochus sent against Judas Maccabeus, 1 Mac. vi, 35.

2. The breastplate or corslet, שדיון, was another piece of defensive armour. Goliath, and the soldiers of Antiochus, 1 Sam. xvii, 5; 1 Mac. vi, 35, were accoutred with this defence; which, in our authorized translation, is variously rendered HABERGEON, COAT OF MAIL, and BRIGANDINE, 1 Sam. xvii, 38; 2 Chron. xxvi, 14; Isa. lix, 17; Jer. xlvi, 4. Between the joints of this HARNESS, as it is termed in 1 Kings xxii, 4, the profligate Ahab was mortally wounded by an arrow, shot at a venture. From these various renderings of the original word, it should seem that this piece of armour covered both the back and breast, but principally the latter. The corslets were made of various materials: sometimes they were made of flax or cotton, woven very thick, or of a kind of woollen felt: others again were made of iron or brazen scales, or laminæ, laid one over another, like the scales of a fish; others were properly what we call coats of mail; and others were composed of two pieces of iron or brass, which protected the back and breast. All these kinds of corslets are mentioned in the Scriptures. Goliath's coat of mail, 1 Sam. xvii, 5, was literally a corslet of scales, that is, composed of numerous laminæ of brass, crossing each other. It was called by Virgil, and other Latin writers, SQUAMA LORICA. Similar corslets were worn by the Persians and other nations. The breastplate worn by the unhappy Saul, when he perished in battle, is supposed to have been of flax,

or cotton, woven very close and thick, 2 Sam. i, 9, marginal rendering.

3. The shield defended the whole body during the battle. It was of various forms, and made of wood covered with tough hides, or of brass, and sometimes was overlaid with gold, 1 Kings x, 16, 17; xiv, 26, 27. Two sorts are mentioned in the Scriptures; namely, the צנה, GREAT SHIELD or BUCKLER, and the מלן, or SMALLER SHIELD. It was much used by the Jews, Babylonians, Chaldeans, Assyrians, and Egyptians. David, who was a great warrior, often mentions a shield and buckler in his divine poems, to signify that defence and protection of Heaven which he expected and experienced, and in which he reposed all his trust, Psalm v, 12; and when he says, "God will with favour compass the righteous as with a shield," he seems to allude to the use of the great shield TSINNAH, (which is the word he uses,) with which they covered and defended their whole bodies. King Solomon caused two different sorts of shields to be made; namely, the TSINNAH, (which answers to CLYPEUS among the Latins,) such a large shield as the infantry wore, and the MAGINNIM, or SCUTA, which were used by the horsemen, and were of a much less size, 2 Chron. ix, 15, 16. The former of these are translated TARGETS, and are double in weight to the other. The Philistines came into the field with this weapon: so we find their formidable champion was appointed, 1 Sam. xvii, 7. One bearing a shield went before him, whose proper duty it was to carry this and some other weapons, with which to furnish his master upon occasion.

The loss of the shield in fight was excessively resented by the Jewish warriors, as well as lamented by them; for it was a signal aggravation of the public mourning, that "the shield of the mighty was vilely cast away," 2 Sam. i, 21. David, a man of arms, who composed this beautiful elegy on the death of Saul, felt how disgraceful a thing it was for soldiers to quit their shields in the field.

These honourable sentiments were not confined to the Jews. We find them prevailing among most other ancient nations, who considered it infamous to cast away or lose their shield. With the Greeks it was a capital crime, and punished with death. The Lacedemonian women, it is well known, in order to excite the courage of their sons, used to deliver to them their fathers' shields, with this short address: "This shield thy father always preserved: do thou preserve it also, or perish." Alluding perhaps to these sentiments, St. Paul, when exhorting the Hebrew Christians to steadfastness in the faith of the Gospel, urges them not to cast away their confidence, which "hath great recompense of reward," Heb. x, 35.

4. Another defensive provision in war was the military girdle, which was for a double purpose: first, in order to hold the sword, which hung, as it to this day, at the soldier's girdle or belt, 1 Sam. xvii, 39: secondly, it was necessary to gird the clothes and the armour together. TO GIRD and TO ARM are synonymous words in Scripture; for those who are said to be able to put on armour are, according to the Hebrew and the Septuagint, girt with a girdle; and hence comes the expression of "girding to the battle," 1 Kings xx, 11; Isa. viii, 9; 2 Sam. xxii, 40; 1 Sam. xviii, 4. There is express mention of this military girdle, where it is recorded that Jonathan, to assure David of his entire love and friendship by some visible pledges, stripped himself not only of his usual garments, but of his military habiliments, his sword, bow, and girdle, and gave them to David.

5. Boots or greaves were part of the ancient defensive harness, because it was the custom to cast certain εμποδια, IMPEDIMENTS, (so called, because they entangled the feet,) in the way before the enemy. The military boot or shoe was therefore necessary to guard the legs and feet from the iron stakes placed in the way to gall and wound them; and thus we are enabled to account for Goliath's greaves of brass which were upon his legs.

The offensive weapons were of two sorts; namely, such as were employed when they came to a close engagement, and those with which they annoyed the enemy at a distance. Of the former description were the sword and the battle-axe.

1. The sword is the most ancient weapon of offence mentioned in the Bible. With it Jacob's sons treacherously assassinated the Shechemites, Gen. xxxiv, 2. It was worn on the thigh, Psalm xlv, 4; Exod. xxxii, 27; and, it should seem on the left thigh; for it is particularly mentioned that Ehud put a dagger or short sword under his garments on his right thigh, Judges iii, 16. There appear to have been two kinds of swords in use, a larger one with one edge, which is called in Hebrew the MOUTH of the sword, Joshua vi, 21; and a shorter one with two edges, like that of Ehud. The modern Arabs, it is well known, wear a sabre on one side, and a CANGIAR or dagger in their girdles.

2. Of the battle-axe we have no description in the sacred volume: it seems to have been a most powerful weapon in the hands of cavalry, from the allusion made to it by Jeremiah: "Thou art my battle-axe and weapons of war; for with thee will I break in pieces the nations, and with thee will I destroy kingdoms: and with thee will I break in pieces the horse and his rider, and with thee will I break in pieces the chariot and his rider," Jer. li, 20, 21.

3. The spear and javelin (as the words רמח and חנית are variously rendered in Num. xxv, 7; 1 Sam. xiii, 19, and Jer. xlvi, 4) were of different kinds, according to their length or make. Some of them might be thrown or darted, 1 Sam. xviii, 11; others were a kind of long swords, Num. xxv, 8; and it appears from 2 Sam. ii, 23, that some of them were pointed at both ends. When armies were encamped, the spear of the general or commander-in-chief was stuck into the ground at his head.

4. Slings are enumerated among the military stores collected by Uzziah, 2 Chron. xxvi, 14. In the use of the sling David eminently excelled, and he slew Goliath with a stone from

one. The Benjaminites were celebrated in battle because they had attained to great skill and accuracy in handling this weapon; "they could sling stones to a hair's breadth, and not miss," Judges xx, 16; and where it is said that they were left-handed, it should rather be rendered AMBIDEXTERS; for we are told they could use "both the right hand and the left," 1 Chron. xii, 2; that is, they did not constantly use the right hand as others did, when they shot arrows or slung stones; but they were so expert in their military exercises, that they could perform them with their left hand as well as with their right.

5. Bows and arrows are of great antiquity; indeed, no weapon is mentioned so early. Thus Isaac said to Esau, "Take thy weapons, thy quiver and thy bow," Gen. xxvii, 3; though, it is true, these are not spoken of as used in war, but in hunting; and so they are supposed and implied before this, where it is said of Ishmael, that he became an archer, he used bows and arrows in shooting of wild beasts, Gen. xxi, 20. This afterward became so useful a weapon, that care was taken to train up the Hebrew youth to it betimes. When David had, in a solemn manner, lamented the death of King Saul, he gave orders for teaching the young men the use of the bow, 1 Sam. i, 18, that they might be as expert as the Philistines, by whose bows and arrows Saul and his army were slain. These were part of the military ammunition; for in those times bows were used instead of guns, and arrows supplied the place of powder and ball. From the book of Job, xx, 24, it may be collected, that the military bow was made of steel, and consequently was very stiff and hard to bend, on which account they used their foot in bending their bows; and therefore when the prophets speak of TREADING THE BOW and of BOWS TRODDEN, they are to be understood of BOWS BENT, as our translators rightly render it, Jer. 1, 14; Isa. v, 28; xxi, 15; but the Hebrew word which is used in these places, signifies TO TREAD UPON. This weapon was thought so necessary in war, that it is there called, "the bow of war," or the "battle-bow," Zech. ix, 10; x, 14.

ARNON, a river or brook, mentioned Num. xxi, 24, and elsewhere. Its spring head is in the mountains of Gilead, or of the Moabites, and it discharges itself into the Dead Sea.

ARROW. See Arms. Divination with arrows was a method of presaging future events, practised by the ancients. Ezekiel, xxi, 21, informs us, that Nebuchadnezzar, putting himself at the head of his armies, to march against Zedekiah, king of the Jews, and against the king of the Ammonites, stood at the parting of two ways, to mingle his arrows together in a quiver, in order to divine from thence which way he should march. Jerom, Theodoret, and the modern commentators after them, believe that this prince took several arrows, and upon each of them wrote the name of the king, town, or province, which he was to attack: for example, upon one, Jerusalem; upon another, Rabbah, the capital of the Ammonites; and upon another, Egypt, &c. After having put these into a quiver, he shook them together, and then drew them out; and the arrow which was drawn was thought to declare the will of the gods to attack first that city, province, or kingdom, with whose name it was inscribed.

ARTAXERXES, or Ahasuerus, a king of Persia, the husband of Esther, who, in the opinion of the learned Usher and Calmet, was the Darius of profane authors. See Ahasuerus.

2. Artaxerxes Longimanus is supposed by Dr. Prideaux to be the Ahasuerus of Esther. He was the son of Xerxes, and grandson of Darius Hystaspes, and reigned in Persia from the year of the world 3531 to 3579. He permitted Ezra, with all those inclined to follow him, to return into Judea, in the year of the world 3537, Ezra vii, viii. Afterward, Nehemiah also obtained leave to return, and to build the walls and gates of Jerusalem, in the year of the world 3550, Nehem. i, 11. From this year, chronologers reckon the beginning of Daniel's seventy weeks, Daniel xi, 29. These are weeks of years, and make four hundred and ninety years. Dr. Prideaux, who discourses very copiously, and with great learning, on this prophecy, maintains that the decree mentioned in it for the restoring and rebuilding of Jerusalem, cannot be understood of that granted to Nehemiah, in the twentieth year of Artaxerxes; but of that granted to Ezra, by the same Artaxerxes, in the seventh year of his reign. From that time to the death of Christ, are exactly four hundred and ninety years, to a month: for in the month Nisan the decree was granted to Ezra; and in the middle of the same month Nisan, Christ suffered, just four hundred and ninety years afterward.

The easterns think that the surname of Longimanus was given to Artaxerxes by reason of the extent of his dominions; as it is commonly said that princes have long hands: but the Greeks maintain that this prince had really longer hands or arms than usual; and that, when he stood upright, he could touch his knees. He is said to have been the handsomest man of his time. The eastern people call him Bahaman, and give him the surname of Ardschir-diraz-dest, or the long-handed. He was the son of Asfendiar, sixth king of the second dynasty of the Persians. After having extinguished the family of Rostam, which was formidable to him on account of the great men who composed it, he carried his arms into the western provinces, Mesopotamia and Syria, which formed part of his empire. He took Babylon from Belshazzar, son of Nebuchadnezzar; and he put in his place Kiresch, who by us is called Cyrus. Some Persian historians assert that the mother of Artaxerxes was a Jewess, of the tribe of Benjamin, and family of Saul; and that the most beloved of his wives was of the tribe of Judah, and race of Solomon, by Rehoboam, king of Judah. If this be true, we need not wonder that he should recommend to Cyrus to favour the Jewish nation. This Cyrus performed, by sending back the people into their own country, and permitting them to rebuild their temple. But the truth of this story is doubtful; and were it true, the interference of the special providence of God must still be acknowledged. Artaxerxes reigned forty-seven years, and died in the year of the world 3579, and before Jesus Christ 425.

ARTEMAS, St. Paul's disciple, who was sent by that Apostle into Crete, in the room of Titus, chap. iii, 12, while he continued with St. Paul at Nicopolis, where he passed the winter. We know nothing particular of the life or death of Artemas; but the employment to which he was appointed by the Apostle is a proof of his great merit.

ASA, the son and successor of Abijam, king of Judah, began to reign in the year of the world 3049, and before Christ 955. He reigned forty-one years at Jerusalem, and did right in the sight of the Lord. He purged Jerusalem from the infamous practices attending the worship of idols; and he deprived his mother of her office and dignity of queen, because she erected an idol to Astarte, which he burnt in the valley of Hinnom, 1 Kings xv, 8, &c.

The Scripture reproaches Asa with not destroying the high places, which, perhaps, he thought it politic to tolerate, to avoid the greater evil of idolatry. He carried into the house of the Lord the gold and silver vessels which his father Abijam had vowed to consecrate. He fortified several cities, and repaired others, encouraging his people to this labour while the kingdom was at peace; and the Lord favoured them with his protection. After this he levied three hundred thousand men in Judah, armed with shields and pikes; and two hundred and eighty thousand men in Benjamin, armed with shields and bows, all men of courage and valour. About this time, Zerah, king of Ethiopia, or rather of Cush, which is part of Arabia, marched against Asa with a million of foot, and three hundred chariots of war, and advanced as far as Mareshah. This probably happened in the fifteenth year of Asa's reign, and in the year of the world 3064, 2 Chron. xv, 10. Asa advanced to meet Zerah, and encamped in the plain of Zephathah, or rather Zephatah, near Mareshah, and having prayed to the Lord, God struck the forces of Zerah with such a panic that they began to flee. Asa and his army pursued them to Geran, and slew of them a great number. After this, Asa's army returned to Jerusalem, laden with booty. The prophet Azariah met them, and said, "Hear ye me, Asa, and all Judah and Benjamin, The Lord is with you while ye be with him, and if ye seek him he will be found of you; but if ye forsake him, he will forsake you.--Be ye strong, therefore, and let not your hands be weak: for your work shall be rewarded," 2 Chron. xv, 2, 7. After this exhortation, Asa, being animated with new courage, destroyed the idols of Judah, Benjamin, and Mount Ephraim; repaired the altar of burnt-offerings; and assembled Judah and Benjamin, with many from the tribes of Simeon, Ephraim, and Manasseh, and on the third day, in the fifteenth year of his reign, celebrated a solemn festival. Of the cattle taken from Zerah, they sacrificed seven hundred oxen, and seven thousand sheep; they renewed the covenant with the Lord; and, with cymbals and trumpets sounding, they swore to the covenant, and declared that whoever should forsake the true worship of God, should be put to death. The Lord gave them peace; and, according to the Chronicles, the kingdom of Judah had rest till the thirty-fifth year of Asa. Concerning this year, however, there are difficulties; and some think that we should read the twenty-fifth, instead of the thirty-fifth; since Baasha, who made war on Asa, lived no longer than the twenty-sixth year of Asa, 1 Kings xvi, 8.

In this year Baasha, king of Israel, began to fortify Ramah, on the frontiers of the two kingdoms of Judah and Israel, that he might prevent the Israelites from resorting to the kingdom of Judah, and the temple of the Lord at Jerusalem. When Asa was informed of this, he sent to Benhadad, king of Damascus, all the gold and silver of his palace, and of the temple, to induce him to break his alliance with Baasha, and to assist him against the king of Israel. Benhadad accepted Asa's presents, and invaded Baasha's country, where he took several cities belonging to the tribe of Naphtali. This obliged Baasha to retire from Ramah, that he might defend his dominions nearer home. Asa immediately ordered his people to Ramah, carried off all the materials prepared by Baasha, and employed them in building Geba and Mizpah. This application to Benhadad for assistance was inexcusable. It implied, that Asa distrusted God's power and goodness, which he had so lately experienced. Therefore the Prophet Hanani was sent to reprove him for his conduct. Asa, however, was so exasperated at his rebukes that he put the Prophet in chains, and at the same time ordered the execution of several persons in Judah. Toward the latter part of his life, he was incommoded with swellings in his feet, which, gradually rising upwards, killed him. The Scripture reproaches him with having had recourse to physicians, rather than to the Lord. He was buried in the sepulchre which he had provided for himself in the city of David; and after his death they placed on the bed great quantities of perfumes and spices, with which his body was burned. His bones and ashes were then collected, and put into his grave.

ASAHEL, the son of Zeruiah, and brother of Joab. He was killed by Abner, in the battle of Gibeon, 2 Sam. ii, 18, 19, while he obstinately persisted in the pursuit of that general. To revenge his death, his brother Joab, some years after, treacherously killed Abner, who had come to wait on David at Hebron, in order to procure him to be acknowledged king by all Israel, 2 Sam. iii, 26, 27. See Abner.

ASAPH, a celebrated musician in the time of David, was the son of Barachias of the tribe of Levi. Asaph, and also his descendants, presided over the musical band in the service of the temple. Several of the psalms, as the fiftieth, the seventy-third to the eighty-third, have the name of Asaph prefixed; but it is not certain whether the words or the music were composed by him. With regard to some of them, which were written during the Babylonish captivity, they cannot in any respect be ascribed to him. Perhaps they were written or set to music by his descendants, who bore his name, or by some of that class of musicians of which the family of Asaph was the head, 1 Chron. vi, 39; 2 Chron. xxix, 30; xxxv, 15; Neh. xii, 46. The psalms which bear the name of Asaph are doctrinal or preceptive: their style, though less sweet than that of David, is more vehement, and little inferior to the grandeur of Isaiah.

ASCENSION OF CHRIST, his visible elevation to heaven. Our Saviour, having repeatedly conversed with his Apostles after his resurrection, and afforded them many infallible proofs of its reality, led them from Jerusalem to Bethany, and was raised up to heaven in their sight; there to continue till he shall descend at the last day to judge the quick and the dead. The evidences of this fact were numerous. The disciples saw him ascend, Acts i, 9, 10. Two angels testified that he did ascend, Acts i, 11. Stephen, Paul, and John saw him in his ascended state, Acts vii, 55, 56; ix; Rev. i. The ascension was demonstrated by the descent of the Holy Ghost, John xvi, 7, 14; Acts ii, 33; and the terrible overthrow and dispersion of the Jewish nation is still a standing proof of it, John viii, 21; Matt. xxvi, 64. The time of Christ's ascension was forty days after his resurrection. He continued so many days upon earth that he might give repeated proofs of his resurrection, Acts i, 3; instruct his Apostles in every thing of importance respecting their office and ministry, Acts i, 3; and might open to them the Scriptures concerning himself, and renew their commission to preach the Gospel, Acts i, 5, 6; Mark xvi, 15. As to the manner of his ascension, it was from mount Olivet to heaven, not in appearance only, but in reality, and that visibly and locally. It was a real motion of his human nature; sudden, swift, glorious, and in a triumphant manner. He was parted from his disciples while he was solemnly blessing them; and multitudes of angels attended him with shouts of praise, Psalm lxviii, 17; xlvii, 5, 6.

The effects or ends of his ascension were, 1. To fulfil the types and prophecies concerning it; 2. To "appear" as a priest "in the presence of God for us;" 3. To take upon him more openly the exercise of his kingly office; 4. To receive gifts for men, both ordinary and extraordinary, Psalm lxviii, 18; 5. To open the way to heaven for his people, Heb. x, 19, 20; 6. To assure the saints of their ascension to heaven after their resurrection from the dead, John xiv, 1, 2.

ASHDOD, Azoth, according to the Vulgate, or Azotus, according to the Greek, a city which was assigned by Joshua to the tribe of Judah, but was possessed a long time by the Philistines, and rendered famous for the temple of their god Dagon, Joshua xv, 47. It lies upon the Mediterranean Sea, about nine or ten miles north of Gaza; and in the times when Christianity flourished in these parts was made an episcopal see, and continued a fair village till the days of St. Jerom. Here the ark of Jehovah triumphed over the Philistine idol Dagon, 1 Sam. v, 2.

ASHER, tribe of. The province allotted to this tribe was a maritime one, stretching along the coast from Sidon on the north to Mount Carmel on the south; including the cities Abdon, Achshaph, Accho, Achzib, Sarepta, Sidon, and Tyre. But of the northern half of this territory, that is, from Tyre northward, this tribe never became possessed, not having expelled the Phœnician inhabitants, who are supposed not to have been pure Canaanites, but a mixture of this people with a Cuthite colony from Egypt. Asher was the most northerly of the tribes; and had that of Naphtali on the west, and Zebulun on the south.

ASHES. Several religious ceremonies, and some symbolical ones, anciently depended upon the use of ashes. To repent in sackcloth and ashes, or, as an external sign of self-affliction for sin, or of suffering under some misfortune, to sit in ashes, are expressions common in Scripture. "I am but dust and ashes," exclaims Abraham before the Lord, Gen. xviii, 27; indicating a deep sense of his own meanness in comparison with God. God threatens to shower down dust and ashes on the lands instead of rain, Deut. xxviii, 24; thereby to make them barren instead of blessing them, to dry them up instead of watering them. Tamar, after the injury she had received from Amnon, covered her head with ashes, 2 Sam. xiii, 19. The Psalmist, in great sorrow, says poetically, he had "eaten ashes as it were bread," Psalm cii, 9; that is, he sat on ashes, he threw ashes on his head; and his food, his bread, was sprinkled with the ashes wherewith he was himself covered. So Jeremiah introduces Jerusalem saying, "The Lord hath covered me with ashes," Lamentations iii, 16. Sitting on ashes, or lying down among ashes, was a token of extreme grief. We find it adopted by Job, ii, 8; by many Jews when in great fear, Esther iv, 3; and by the king of Nineveh, Jonah iii, 6. He arose from his throne, laid aside his robe, covered himself with sackcloth, and sat in ashes. This token of affliction is illustrated by Homer's description of old Laertes grieving for the absence of his son, "Sleeping in the apartment where the slaves slept, in the ashes, near the fire." Compare Jer. vi, 26, "Daughter of my people, wallow thyself in ashes." There was a sort of ley and lustral water, made with the ashes of the heifer sacrificed on the great day of expiation; these ashes were distributed to the people, and used in purifications, by sprinkling, to such as had touched a dead body, or had been present at funerals, Num. xix, 17.

ASHKENAZ, one of the sons of Gomer, and grandson of Japheth, who gave his name to the country first peopled by him in the north and north-western part of Asia Minor, answering to Bithynia; where were traces long after of his name, particularly in that of Ascanius, applied to a bay and city, as well as to some islands lying along the coast. It was also from this country, most probably, that the king Ascanius, mentioned by Homer, came to the aid of Priamus at the siege of Troy. From the same source, likewise, the Pontus Euxinus, or Black Sea, derived its name. It may farther be remarked on the identity of these countries, that the Prophet Jeremiah, predicting the capture of Babylon, and calling by name the countries which were to rise against it, exclaims, "Call together against her the kingdoms of Ararat, (or Armenia,) Minni, and Ashkenaz:" which was literally fulfilled; as Xenophen informs us that Cyrus, after taking Sardis, became master of Phrygia on the Hellespont, and took along with him many soldiers of that country.

ASHTAROTH, or Astarte, a goddess of the Zidonians. The word Ashtaroth properly signifies flocks of sheep, or goats; and sometimes the grove, or woods, because she was goddess of woods, and groves were her temples. In groves consecrated to her, such lasciviousness was committed as rendered her worship infamous. She was also called the queen of heaven; and sometimes her worship is said to be that of "the host of heaven." She was certainly represented in the same manner as Isis, with cows' horns on her head, to denote the increase and decrease of the moon. Cicero calls her the fourth Venus of the Syrians. She is almost always joined with Baal, and is called a god, the Scriptures having no particular word to express a goddess. It is believed that the moon was adored in this idol. Her temples generally accompanied those of the sun; and while bloody sacrifices or human victims were offered to Baal, bread, liquors, and perfumes were presented to Astarte. For her, tables were prepared upon the flat terrace roofs of houses, near gates, in porches, and at crossways, on the first day of every month; and this was called by the Greeks, Hecate's supper.

Solomon, seduced by his foreign wives, introduced the worship of Ashtaroth into Israel; but Jezebel, daughter of the king of Tyre, and wife to Ahab, principally established her worship. She caused altars to be erected to this idol in every part of Israel; and at one time four hundred priests attended the worship of Ashtaroth, 1 Kings xviii, 7.

ASHUR, the son of Shem, who gave his name to Assyria. It is believed that Ashur originally dwelt in the land of Shinar and about Babylonia, but that he was compelled by the usurper Nimrod to depart from thence, and settle higher toward the springs of the Tigris, in the province of Assyria, so called from him, where some think he built the famous city of Nineveh, and those of Rehoboth, Calah, and Resen, Gen. x, 11, 12.

ASIA, one of the four grand divisions of the earth. It is also used in a more restricted sense for Asia Minor, or Anatolia. In the New Testament it always signifies the Roman Proconsular Asia, in which the seven Apocalyptic churches were situated.

ASKELON, a city in the land of the Philistines, situated between Azoth and Gaza, upon the coast of the Mediterranean Sea, about 520 furlongs from Jerusalem. The tribe of Judah, after the death of Joshua, took the city of Askelon, Judges i, 18, being one of the five governments belonging to the Philistines. The place at present is in ruins.

ASMONÆANS, a name given to the Maccabees, the descendants of Mattathias. After the death of Ezra and Nehemiah, the Jews were governed by their high priest, in subjection, however, to the Persian kings, to whom they paid tribute; but with full enjoyment of their liberties, civil and religious. Nearly three centuries of prosperity ensued, until they were cruelly oppressed by Antiochus Epiphanes, king of Syria, when they were compelled to take up arms in their own defence. Under the able conduct of Judas, surnamed Maccabeus, and his valiant brothers, the Jews maintained a religious war for twenty-six years with five successive kings of Syria; and after destroying upwards of two hundred thousand of their best troops, the Maccabees finally established the independence of their own country, and the aggrandisement of their family. This illustrious house, whose princes united the regal and pontifical dignity in their own persons, administered the affairs of the Jews during a period of a hundred and twenty-six years; until, disputes arising between Hyrcanus **II**, and his brother Aristobulus, the latter was defeated by the Romans, who captured Jerusalem, and reduced Judea to a military province, B. C. 59.

ASNAPPER, the king of Assyria, who sent the Cutheans into the country belonging to the ten tribes, Ezra iv, 10. Many take this prince to be Shalmaneser; but others, with more probability, think him to be Esar-haddon.

ASP, פתן. Deut. xxxii, 33; Job xx, 14, 16; Psalm lviii, 4; xci, 13; Isaiah xi, 8. A very venomous serpent, whose poison is so subtle as to kill within a few hours with a universal gangrene. This may well refer to the BÆTEN of the Arabians, which M. Forskal describes as spotted with black and white, about one foot in length, and nearly half an inch in thickness, oviparous, and whose bite is death. It is the ASPIC of the ancients, and is so called now by the literati of Cyprus, though the common people call it KUFI, (κȣ́φη,) DEAF. With the PETHEN we may connect the PYTHON of the Greeks, which was, according to fable, a huge serpent that had an oracle at mount Parnassus, famous for predicting future events. Apollo is said to have slain this serpent, and hence he was called "Pythius." Those possessed with a spirit of divination were also styled Πυθωνες. The word occurs in Acts, xvi, 16, as the characteristic of a young woman who had A PYTHONIC SPIRIT. It is well known that the SERPENT was particularly employed by the Heathens in their enchantments and divinations. See Serpent].

Pethen, פתן, is variously translated in our version; but interpreters generally consider it as referring to the asp. Zophar alludes to it more than once in his description of a wicked man: "Yet his meat in his bowels is turned, it is the gall of asps within him. He shall suck the poison of asps: the viper's tongue shall slay him." The venom of asps is the most subtle of all; it is incurable; and, if the wounded part be not instantly amputated, it speedily terminates the existence of the sufferer. To these circumstances, Moses evidently alludes in his character of the Heathen: "Their wine is the poison of dragons, and the cruel venom of asps." To tread upon the asp is attended with extreme danger; therefore, to express in the strongest manner the safety which the godly man enjoys under the protection of his heavenly Father, it is promised, that he shall tread with impunity upon these venomous creatures. No person of his own accord approaches the hole of these deadly reptiles; for he who gives them the smallest disturbance is in extreme danger of paying the forfeit of his rashness with his life. Hence, the Prophet Isaiah, predicting the conversion of the Gentiles to the faith of Christ, and the glorious reign of peace and truth in those regions which, prior to that period, were full of horrid cruelty, marvellously heightens the force of the whole description by declaring, "The sucking child shall play on the hole of the asp, and the weaned child shall put his hand on the cockatrice' den. They shall not hurt nor destroy in all my holy mountain; for the earth shall be full of the knowledge of the Lord, as the waters cover the sea."

ASS, המור, Arabic, CHAMARA and HAMAR. There are three words referred by translators to the ass: 1. המור, which is the usual appellation, and denotes the ordinary kind; such as is employed in labour, carriage, and domestic services. 2. פררא, rendered ONAGER, or "wild ass." 3. אתון, rendered SHE ASS. To these we must add, ערדיא, rendered WILD ASSES, Dan. v, 21. The prevailing colour of this animal in the east is reddish; and the Arabic word, CHAMARA, signifies TO BE RED.

In his natural state he is fleet, fierce, formidable, and intractable; but when domesticated, the most gentle of all animals, and assumes a patience and submission even more humble than his situation. Le Clerc observes, that the Israelites not being allowed to keep horses, the ass was not only made a beast of burden, but used on journeys; and that even the most honourable of the nation were wont to be mounted on asses, which in the eastern countries were much larger and more beautiful than they are with us. Jair of Gilead had thirty sons who rode on as many asses, and commanded in thirty cities, Judges x, 4. Abdon's sons and grandsons rode also upon asses, Judges xii, 4. And Christ makes his solemn entry into Jerusalem riding upon an ass, Matt. xxi, 4; John xii, 14. To draw with an ox and ass together was prohibited in the Mosaic law, Deut. xxii, 10. This law is thought to have respect to some idolatrous custom of the Gentiles, who were taught to believe that their fields would be more fruitful if thus ploughed; for it is not likely that men would have yoked together two creatures so different in their tempers and motions, had they not been led to it by some superstition. There might be, however, a physical reason for this injunction. Two beasts of a different species cannot well associate together; and on this account never pull pleasantly either in the cart or plough, and are not therefore "true yoke fellows." Le Clerc considers this law as merely symbolical, importing that we are not to form improper alliances in civil and religious life; and he thinks his opinion confirmed by these words of St. Paul, 2 Cor. vi, 14: "Be ye not unequally yoked with unbelievers;" which are simply to be understood as prohibiting all intercourse between Christians and idolaters, in social, matrimonial, and religious life. To teach the Jews the propriety of this, a variety of precepts relative to improper and heterogeneous mixtures were interspersed through their law; so that in civil and domestic life they might have them ever before their eyes.

The WILD ASS, called PARA, is probably the ONAGER of the ancients. It is taller and a much more dignified animal than the common or domestic ass; its legs are more elegantly shaped; and it bears its head higher. It is peculiarly distinguished by a dusky woolly mane, long erect ears, and a forehead highly arched. The colour of the hair, in general, is of a silvery white. These animals associate in herds, under a leader, and are very shy. They inhabit the mountainous regions and desert parts of Tartary, Persia, &c. Anciently they were likewise found in Lycaonia, Phrygia, Mesopotamia, and Arabia Deserta. They are remarkably wild; and Job, xxxix, 5–8, describes the liberty they enjoy, the place of their retreat, their manners, and wild, impetuous, and untamable spirit. "Vain man would be wise, though he be born a wild ass's colt," Job xi, 12; עיר פרא, "ass colt," not "ass's colt;" יר being in apposition with פרא, and not in government. The whole is a proverbial expression, denoting extreme perversity and ferocity, and repeatedly alluded to in the Old Testament. Thus, Gen. xvi, 12, it is prophesied of Ishmael that he should be אדם פרא, a wild ass man; rough, untaught, and libertine as a wild ass. So Hosea, xiii, 15; "He (Ephraim) hath RUN WILD (literally ASSIFIED himself) amidst the braying monsters." So again, Hosea viii, 9, the very same character is given of Ephraim, who is called "a solitary wild ass by himself," or perhaps a solitary wild ass of the DESERT; for the original will bear to be so rendered. This proverbial expression has descended among the Arabians to the present day, who still employ, as Schultens has remarked, the expressions, "the ass of the desert," or "the wild ass," to describe an obstinate, indocile, and contumacious person. The Prophet Isaiah, xxxii, 14, describes great desolation by saying that "the wild asses shall rejoice where a city stood." There is another kind of ass called, אתון. Abraham had ATONOTH, Gen. xii, 16; Balaam rode on an ATON, Num. xxii, 23. We find from 1 Chron. xxvii, 30, that David had an officer expressly appointed to superintend his ATONOTH; not his ordinary asses, but those of a nobler race; which implies at least equal dignity in this officer to his colleagues mentioned with him. This notion of the ATON gives also a spirit to the history of Saul, who, when his father's ATONOTH were lost, was at no little pains to seek them; moreover, as beside being valuable, they were UNCOMMON, he might the more readily hear of them if they had been noticed or taken up by any one; and this leads to the true interpretation of the servant's proposed application to Samuel, verse 6, as though he said, "In his office of magistracy this honourable man may have heard of these strayed rarities, and secured them; peradventure he can direct us."

Thus we find that these ATONOTH are mentioned in Scripture, only in the possession of judges, patriarchs, and other great men; insomuch that where these are there is dignity, either expressed or implied. They were also a present for a prince; for Jacob presented Esau with twenty, Gen. xxxii, 15. What then shall we say of the wealth of Job, who possessed a thousand? Another word which is rendered "WILD ASS" by our translators, Job xxxix, 5, is ORUD; which seems to be the same, that in the Chaldee of Daniel, v, 21, is called OREDIA. Mr. Parkhurst supposes that this word denotes THE BRAYER, and that PARA and ORUD are only two names for the same animal. But these names MAY perhaps refer to different races, though of the same species; so that a description of the properties of one may apply to both, though not without some variation.

Who sent out the PARA free?

Or who hath loosed the bands of the ORUD?

Whose dwelling I have made the wilderness,

And the barren land (salt deserts) his resort:

The range of open mountains are his pasture,

And he searcheth after every green thing.

Gmelin observes that the ONAGER is very fond of salt. Whether the "deserts" of the above text were salt marshes, or salt deserts, is of very little consequence; the circumstance shows the correctness of the Hebrew poet. In Daniel we read that Nebuchadnezzar dwelt with the OREDIA. We need not suppose that he was banished to the deserts, but was at most kept safely in an enclosure of his own park, where curious animals were kept for state and pleasure. If this be correct, then the ORUD was somewhat, at least, of a rarity at Babylon; and it might be of a kind different from the PARA, as it is denoted by another name. May it not be the GICQUETEI of Professor Pallas, the wild mule of Mongalia which surpasses the ONAGER in size, beauty, and perhaps in swiftness.

ASSIDEANS, by some named Chasideans, from CHASIDIM, "merciful, pious." They were a kind of religious society among the Jews, whose chief and distinguishing character was, to maintain the honour of the temple, and observe punctually the traditions of the elders. They were therefore not only content to pay the usual tribute for the maintenance of the house of God, but charged themselves with farther expense upon that account; for every day, except that of the great expiation, they sacrificed a lamb, in addition to the daily oblation, which was called the sin offering of the Assideans. They practised greater hardships and mortifications than others; and their common oath was, "By the temple;" for which our Saviour reproves the Pharisees, who had learned that oath of them, Matt. xxiii, 16. From this sect the Pharisees sprung. The Assideans are represented as a numerous sect, distinguished by its valour, as well as by its zeal for the law, 1 Mac. ii, 42. A company of them resorted to Mattathias, to fight for the law of God, and the liberties of their country. This sect arose either during the captivity, or soon after the restoration, of the Jews; and were probably in the commencement, and long afterward, a truly pious part of the nation; but they at length became superstitious.

ASSURANCE. The sense in which this term is used theologically is that of a firm persuasion of our being in a state of salvation. The doctrine itself has been matter of dispute among divines, and when considered as implying not only that we are now accepted of God through Christ, but that we shall be finally saved, or when it is so taken as to deny a state of salvation to those who are not so assured as to be free from all doubt, it is in many views questionable. Assurance of final salvation must stand or fall with the doctrine of personal unconditional election, and is chiefly held by divines of the Calvinistic school; and that nothing is an evidence of a state of present salvation but so entire a persuasion as amounts to assurance in the strongest sense, might be denied upon the ground that degrees of grace, of real saving grace, are undoubtedly mentioned in Scripture. Assurance, however, is spoken of in the New Testament, and stands prominent as one of the leading doctrines of religious experience. We have "full assurance of understanding;" that is a perfect knowledge and entire persuasion of the truth of the doctrine of Christ. The "assurance of faith," in Hebrews ix, 22, is an entire trust in the sacrifice and priestly office of Christ. The "assurance of hope," mentioned in Hebrews vi, 11, relates to the heavenly inheritance, and must necessarily imply a full persuasion that we are "the children of God," and therefore "heirs of his glory;" and from this passage it must certainly be concluded that such an assurance is what every Christian ought to aim at, and that it is attainable. This, however, does not exclude occasional doubt and weakness of faith, from the earlier stages of his experience.

A comforting and abiding persuasion of present acceptance by God, through Christ, we may therefore affirm, must in various degrees follow true faith. In support of this view, the following remarks may be offered:--

If it is the doctrine of the inspired records, that man is by nature prone to evil, and that in practice he violates that law under which as a creature he is placed, and is thereby exposed to punishment;--if also it is there stated, that an act of grace and pardon is promised on the conditions of repentance toward God, and faith in our Lord Jesus Christ;--if that repentance implies consideration of our ways, a sense of the displeasure of Almighty God, contrition of heart, and consequently trouble and grief of mind, mixed, however, with a hope inspired by the promise of forgiveness, and which leads to earnest supplication for the actual pardon of sin so promised, it will follow from these premises--either, 1. That forgiveness is not to be expected till after the termination of our course of probation, that is, in another life; and that, therefore, this trouble and apprehension of mind can only be assuaged by the hope we may have of a favourable final decision on our case;--or, 2. That sin is, in the present life, forgiven as often as it is thus repented of, and as often as we exercise the required and specific acts of trust in the merits of our Saviour; but that this forgiveness of our sins is not in any way made known unto us: so that we are left, as to our feelings, in precisely the same state as if sin were not forgiven till after death, namely, in grief and trouble of mind, relieved only by hope;--or, 3. The Scriptural view is, that when sin is forgiven by the mercy of God through Christ, we are, by some means, assured of it, and peace and satisfaction of mind take the place of anxiety and fear.

The first of these conclusions is sufficiently disproved by the authority of Scripture, which exhibits justification as a blessing attainable in this life, and represents it as actually experienced by true believers. "Therefore being justified by faith." "There is NOW no condemnation to them who are in Christ Jesus." "Whosoever believeth is justified from all things," &c. The quotations might be multiplied, but these are decisive. The notion that though an act of forgiveness may take place, we are unable to ascertain a fact so important to us, is also irreconcilable with many scriptures in which the writers of the New Testament speak of an experience, not confined personally to themselves, or to those Christians who were endowed with spiritual gifts, but common to all Christians. "Being justified by faith we have PEACE with God." "We joy in God, by whom we have received the RECONCILIATION." "Being reconciled unto God by the death of his Son." "We have not received the spirit of bondage again unto fear, but the spirit of adoption, by which we cry, Abba, Father." To these may be added innumerable passages which express the comfort, the confidence, and the joy of Christians; their "friendship" with God; their "access" to him; their entire union and delightful intercourse with him; and their absolute confidence in the success of their prayers. All such passages are perfectly consistent with deep humility, and self-diffidence; but they are irreconcilable with a state of hostility between the parties, and with an unascertained and only hoped-for restoration of friendship and favour.

An assurance, therefore, that the sins which are felt to "be a burden intolerable" are forgiven, and that the ground of that apprehension of future punishment which causes the penitent to "BEWAIL his manifold sins," is taken away by restoration to the favour of the offended God, must be allowed, or nothing would be more incongruous and impossible than the comfort, the peace, the rejoicing of spirit, which in the Scriptures are attributed to believers.

Few Christians of evangelical views have, therefore, denied the possibility of our becoming assured of the favour of God in a sufficient degree to give substantial comfort to the mind. Their differences have rather respected the means by which the contrite become assured of that change in their relation to Almighty God, whom they have offended, which in Scripture is expressed by the term justification. The question has been, (where the notion of an assurance of eternal salvation has not been under discussion,) by what means the assurance of the divine favour is conveyed to the mind. Some have concluded that we obtain it by INFERENCE, others by the DIRECT TESTIMONY of the Holy Spirit to the mind. See Holy Spirit.

ASSYRIA, a kingdom of Asia, of the extent, origin, and duration of which very different accounts have been given by ancient writers. Ctesias and Diodorus Siculus affirm, that the Assyrian monarchy, under Ninus and Semiramis, comprehended the greater part of the known world: but, if this had been the case, it is not likely that Homer and Herodotus would have omitted a fact so remarkable. The sacred records intimate that none of the ancient states or kingdoms were of considerable extent; for neither Chederlaomer, nor any of the neighbouring princes, were tributary or subject to Assyria; and "we find nothing," says Playfair, "of the greatness or power of this kingdom in the history of the judges and succeeding kings of Israel, though the latter kingdom was oppressed and enslaved by many different powers in that period." It is therefore highly probable that Assyria was originally of small extent. According to Ptolemy, this country was bounded on the north by part of Armenia and Mount Niphates; on the west by the Tigris; on the south by Susiana; and on the east by part of Media and the mountains Choatra and Zagros. Of the origin, revolutions, and termination of Assyria, properly so called, and distinguished from the grand monarchy which afterward bore this appellation, the following account is given by Mr. Playfair, as the most probable:-- "The founder of it was Ashur, the second son of Shem, who departed from Shinar, upon the usurpation of Nimrod, at the head of a large body of adventurers, and laid the foundations of Nineveh, where he resided, and erected a new kingdom, called Assyria, after his name, Gen. x, 11. These events happened not long after Nimrod had established the Chaldean monarchy, and fixed his residence at Babylon; but it does not appear that Nimrod reigned in Assyria. The kingdoms of Assyria and Babylon were originally distinct and separate, Micah v, 6; and in this state they remained until Ninus conquered Babylon, and made it tributary to the Assyrian empire. Ninus, the successor of Ashur, Gen. x, 11, seized on Chaldea after the death of Nimrod, and united the kingdoms of Assyria and Babylon. This great prince is said to have subdued Asia, Persia, Media, Egypt, &c. If he did so, the effects of his conquests were of no long duration; for, in the days of Abraham, we do not find that any of the neighbouring kingdoms were subject to Assyria. Ninus was succeeded by Semiramis, a princess bold, enterprising, and fortunate; of whose adventures and exploits many fabulous relations have been recorded. Playfair is of opinion that there were two princesses of this name, who flourished at different periods: one, the consort of Ninus; and another, who lived five generations before Nitocris, queen of Nebuchadnezzar. Of the successors of Ninus and Semiramis nothing certain is recorded. The last of the ancient Assyrian kings was Sardanapalus, who was besieged in his capital by Arbaces, governor of Media, in concurrence with the Babylonians. These united forces defeated the Assyrian army, demolished the capital, and became masters of the empire, B. C. 821.

"After the death of Sardanapalus," says Mr. Playfair, "the Assyrian empire was divided into three kingdoms; namely, the Median, Assyrian, and Babylonian. Arbaces retained the supreme authority, and nominated governors in Assyria and Babylon, who were honoured with the title of kings, while they remained subject and tributary to the Persian monarchs Belesis," he says, "a Chaldean priest, who assisted Arbaces in the conquest of Sardanapalus, received the government of Babylon as the reward of his services;

and Phul was intrusted with that of Assyria. The Assyrian governor gradually enlarged the boundaries of his kingdom, and was succeeded by Tiglath-pileser, Salmanasar, and Sennacherib, who asserted and maintained their independence. After the death of Assar-haddon, the brother and successor of Sennacherib, the kingdom of Assyria was split, and annexed to the kingdoms of Media and Babylon. Several tributary princes afterward reigned in Nineveh; but we hear no more of the kings of Assyria, but of those of Babylon. Cyaxares, king of Media, assisted Nebuchadnezzar, king of Babylon, in the siege of Nineveh, which they took and destroyed, B. C. 606."

The history of Assyria, deduced from Scripture, and acknowledged as the only authentic one by Sir Isaac Newton and many others, ascribes the foundation of the monarchy to Pul, or Phul, about the second year of Menahem, king of Israel, twenty-four years before the æra of Nabonassar, 1579 years after the flood, and, according to Blair, 769, or, according to Newton, 790, years before Christ. Menahem, having taken forcible possession of the throne of Israel by the murder of Shallum, 2 Kings xv, 10, was attacked by Pul, but prevented the hostilities meditated against him by presenting the invader with a thousand talents of silver. Pul, thus gratified, took the kingdom of Israel under his protection, returned to his own country, after having received voluntary homage from several nations in his march, as he had done from Israel, and became the founder of a great empire. As it was in the days of Pul that the Assyrians began to afflict the inhabitants of Palestine, 2 Kings xi, 9; 1 Chron. v, 26, this was the time, according to Sir Isaac Newton, when the Assyrian empire arose. Thus he interprets the words, "since the time of the kings of Assyria," Nehem. ix, 32; that is, since the time of the kingdom of Assyria, or since the rise of that empire. But though this was the period in which the Assyrians afflicted Israel, it is not so evident that the time of the kings of Assyria must necessarily be understood of the rise of the Assyrian empire. However, Newton thus reasons; and observes, that "Pul and his successors afflicted Israel, and conquered the nations round about them; and upon the ruin of many small and ancient kingdoms erected their empire; conquering the Medes, as well as other nations." It is farther argued, that God, by the Prophet Amos, in the reign of Jeroboam, about ten or twenty years before the reign of Pul, (see Amos vi, 13, 14,) threatened to raise up a nation against Israel; and that, as Pul reigned presently after the prophecy of Amos, and was the first upon record who began to fulfil it, he may be justly reckoned the first conqueror and founder of this empire. See 1 Chron. v, 26. Pul was succeeded on the throne of Assyria by his elder son Tiglath-pileser; and at the same time he left Babylon to his younger son Nabonassar, B. C. 747. Of the conquests of this second king of Assyria against the kings of Israel and Syria, when he took Damascus, and subdued the Syrians, we have an account in 2 Kings xv, 29, 37; xvi, 5,9; 1 Chron. v, 26; by which the prophecy of Amos was fulfilled, and from which it appears that the empire of the Assyrians was now become great and powerful. The next king of Assyria was Shalmaneser, or Salmanassar, who succeeded Tiglath-pileser, B. C. 729, and invaded Phœnicia, took the city of Samaria, and, B. C. 721, carried the ten tribes into captivity, placing them in Chalach and Chabor, by the river Gazon, and in the cities of the Medes, 2 Kings xvii, 6. Shalmaneser was succeeded by Sennacherib, B. C. 719; and in the year B. C. 714, he was put to flight with great slaughter by the Ethiopians and Egyptians. In the year B. C. 711 the Medes revolted from the Assyrians; Sennacherib was slain; and he was succeeded by his son Esar-Haddon, Asserhaddon, Asordan, Assaradin, or Sarchedon, by which names he is called by different writers. He began his reign at Nineveh, in the year of Nabonassar 42; and in the year 68 extended it over Babylon. He then carried the remainder of the Samaritans into captivity, and peopled Samaria with captives brought from several parts of his kingdom; and in the year of Nabonassar 77 or 78 he seems to have put an end to the reign of the Ethiopians over Egypt. "In the reign of Sennacherib and Asser-Hadon," says Sir I. Newton, "the Assyrian empire seems arrived at its greatness; being united under one monarch, and containing Assyria, Media, Apolloniatis, Susiana, Chaldea, Mesopotamia, Cilicia, Syria, Phœnicia, Egypt, Ethiopia, and part of Arabia; and reaching eastward into Elymais, and Parætæcene, a province of the Medes; and if Chalach and Chabor be Colchis and Iberia, as some think, and as may seem probable from the circumcision used by those nations till the days of Herodotus, we are also to add these two provinces, with the two Armenias, Pontus, and Cappadocia, as far as to the river Halys: for Herodotus tells us that the people of Cappadocia, as far as to that river, were called Syrians by the Greeks, both before and after the days of Cyrus; and that the Assyrians were also called Syrians by the Greeks." Asser-Hadon was succeeded in the year B. C. 668 by Saosduchinus. At this time Manasseh was allowed to return home, and fortify Jerusalem; and the Egyptians also, after the Assyrians had harassed Egypt and Ethiopia three years, Isa. xx, 3, 4, were set at liberty. Saosduchinus, after a reign of twenty years, was succeeded at Babylon, and probably at Nineveh also, by Chyniladon, in the year B. C. 647. This Chyniladon is supposed by Newton to be the Nebuchadonosor mentioned in the book of Judith, i, 1–15, who made war upon Arphaxad, king of the Medes; and, though deserted by his auxiliaries of Cilicia, Damascus, Syria, Phœnicia, Moab, Ammon, and Egypt, routed the army of the Medes, and slew Arphaxad. This Arphaxad is supposed to be either Dejoces or his son Phraortes, mentioned by Herodotus. Soon after the death of Phraortes, in the year B. C. 635, the Scythians invaded the Medes and Persians; and in 625, Nabopolassar, the commander of the forces of Chyniladon in Chaldea, revolted from him, and became king of Babylon. Chyniladon was either then or soon after succeeded at Nineveh by the last king of Assyria, called Sarac by Polyhistor. The authors of the Universal History suppose Saosduchinus to have been the Nebuchadonosor of Scripture, and Chyniladon or Chynaladan to have been the Sarac of Polyhistor. At length Nebuchadnezzar, the son of Nabopolassar, married Amyit, the daughter of Astyages, king of the Medes, and sister of Cyaxares; and by this marriage the two families having contracted affinity, they conspired against the Assyrians. Nabopolassar being old, and Astyages dead, their sons Nebuchadnezzar and Cyaxares led the armies of the two nations against Nineveh, slew Sarac, destroyed the city, and shared the kingdom of the Assyrians. This victory the Jews refer to the Chaldeans; the Greeks, to the Medes; Tobit, xiv, 15, Polyhistor, and Ctesias, to both. With this victory commenced the great successes of Nebuchadnezzar and Cyaxares, and it laid the foundation of the two collateral empires of the Babylonians and Medes, which were branches of the Assyrian empire; and hence the time of the fall of the Assyrian empire is determined, the conquerors being then in their youth. In the reign of Josiah, when Zephaniah prophesied, Nineveh and the kingdom of Assyria were standing; and their fall was predicted by that Prophet, Zeph. i, 3; ii, 13. And in the end of his reign, Pharaoh-Necho, king of Egypt, the successor of Psammitichus, went up against the king of Assyria to the river Euphrates, to fight against Carchemish, or Circutium; and in his way thither slew Josiah, 2 Kings xxiii, 29; 2 Chron. xxxv, 20; and therefore the last king of Assyria was not yet slain. But in the third and fourth years of Jehoiakim, the successor of Josiah, the two conquerors having taken Nineveh, and finished their war in Assyria, prosecuted their conquests westward; and, leading their forces against the king of Egypt, as an invader of their right of conquest, they beat him at Carchemish, and took from him whatever he had recently taken from the Assyrians, 2 Kings xxiv, 7; Jer. xlvi, 2; "and therefore we cannot err," says Sir Isaac Newton, "above a year or two, if we refer the destruction of Nineveh, and fall of the Assyrian empire, to the third year, of Jehoiakim," or the hundred and fortieth, or, according to Blair, the hundred and forty-first year of Nabonassar; that is, the year B. C. 607.

Of the government, laws, religion, learning, customs, &c, of the ancient Assyrians, nothing absolutely certain is recorded. Their kingdom was at first small, and subsisted for several ages under hereditary chiefs; and their government was simple. Afterward, when they rose to the sublimity of empire, their government seems to have been despotic, and the empire hereditary. Their laws were probably few, and depended upon the mere will of the prince. To Ninus we may ascribe the division of the Assyrian empire into provinces and governments; for we find that this institution was fully established in the reigns of Semiramis and her successors. The people were distributed into a certain number of tribes; and their occupations or professions were hereditary. The Assyrians had several distinct councils, and several tribunals for the regulation of public affairs. Of councils there were three, which were created by the body of the people, and who governed the state in conjunction with the sovereign. The first consisted of officers who had retired from military employments; the second, of the nobility; and the third, of the old men. The sovereigns also had three tribunals, whose province it was to watch over the conduct of the people. The Assyrians have been competitors with the Egyptians for the honour of having invented alphabetic writing. It appears, from the few remains now extant of the writing of these ancient nations, that their letters had a great affinity with each other. They much resembled one another in shape; and they ranged them in the same manner, from right to left.

ASTROLOGY, the art of foretelling future events, from the aspects, positions, and influences of the heavenly bodies. The word is compounded of ἀςὴϱ star, and λόγος, discourse; whence, in the literal sense of the term, astrology should signify no more than the doctrine or science of the stars. Astrology judiciary, or judicial, is what we commonly call simple astrology, or that which pretends to foretel mortal events, even those which have a dependence on the free will and agency of man; as if they were directed by the stars. This art, which owed its origin to the practice of knavery on credulity, is now universally exploded by the intelligent part of mankind. Judicial astrology is commonly said to have been invented in Chaldea, and thence transmitted to the Egyptians, Greeks, and Romans; though some will have it of Egyptian origin, and ascribe the invention to Cham. But we derive it from the Arabians. The Chaldeans, and the Egyptians, and indeed almost all the nations of antiquity, were infatuated with the chimæras of astrology. It originated in the notion, that the stars have an influence, either beneficial or malignant, upon the affairs of men, which may be discovered, and made the ground of certain prediction, in particular cases; and the whole art consisted in applying astronomical observations to this fanciful purpose. Diodorus Siculus relates, that the Chaldeans learned these arts from the Egyptians; and he would not have made this assertion, if there had not been at least a general tradition that they were practised from the earliest times in Egypt. The system was, in those remote ages, intimately connected with Sabaism, or the worship of the stars as divinities; but whether it emanates from idolatry or fatality, it denies God and his providence, and is therefore condemned in the Scriptures, and ranked with practices the most offensive and provoking to the Divine Majesty.

ASTYAGES, otherwise, Cyaxares, king of the Medes, and successor to Phraortes. He reigned forty years, and died A. M. 3409. He was father to Astyages, otherwise called Darius the Mede. He had two daughters, Mandane and Amyit: Mandane married Cambyses, the Persian, and was the mother of Cyrus; Amyit married Nebuchadnezzar, the son of Nabopolassar, and was the mother of Evilmerodach.

Astyages, otherwise called Ahasuerus in the Greek, Dan. ix, 1, or Cyaxares in Xenophon, or Apandus in Ctesias, was appointed by his father Cyaxares governor of Media, and sent with Nabopolassar, king of Babylon, against Saracus, otherwise called Chynaladanus, king of Assyria. These two princes besieged Saracus in Nineveh, took the city, and dismembered the Assyrian empire. Astyages was with Cyrus at the conquest of Babylon, and succeeded Belshazzar, king of the Chaldeans, as is expressly mentioned in Daniel, v, 30, 31, A. M. 3447. After his death Cyrus succeeded him, A. M. 3456.

ASUPPIM, a word which signifies gatherings, and the name of the treasury of the temple of Jerusalem, 1 Chron. xxvi, 15.

ATHALIAH, the daughter of Omri, king of Samaria, and wife to Jehoram, king of Judah. This princess, being informed that Jehu had slain her son Ahaziah, resolved to take the government upon herself, 2 Kings xi; which that she might effect without opposition, she destroyed all the children that Jehoram had by other wives, and all their offspring. But Jehosheba, the sister of Ahaziah, by the father's side only, was at this time married to Jehoiada, the high priest; and while Athaliah's executioners were murdering the rest, she conveyed Joash the son of Ahaziah away, and kept him and his nurse concealed in an apartment of the temple, during six years. In the seventh year, his uncle Jehoiada being determined to place him on the throne of his ancestors, and procure the destruction of Athaliah, he engaged the priests and Levites, and the leading men in all the parts of the kingdom in his interest, and in a public assembly produced him, and made them take an oath of secrecy and fidelity to him. He then distributed arms among the people, whom he divided into three bodies, one to guard the person of the king, and the other two to secure the gates of the temple. After this, he brought out the young prince, set the crown on his head, put the book of the law into his hand, and with sound of trumpet proclaimed him; which was seconded with the joyful shouts and acclamations of the people. Athaliah, hearing the noise, made all haste to the temple; but when, to her astonishment, she saw the young king seated on a throne, she rent her clothes and cried out, "Treason!" But, at the command of Jehoiada, the guards seized and carried her out of the temple, putting all to the sword who offered to rescue or assist her; and then taking her to the stable gate belonging to the palace, there put her to death, A. M. 3126.

ATHANASIANS, the orthodox followers of St. Athanasius, the great and able antagonist of Arius. The Athanasian Creed, though generally admitted not to be drawn up by this father, (but probably, as Doctor Waterland says, by Hilary, bishop of Arles, in the fifth century,) is universally allowed to contain a fair expression of his sentiments. This creed says, "The Catholic faith is this: that we worship One God in Trinity, and Trinity in Unity: neither confounding the persons, nor dividing the substance. For there is one person of the Father, another of the Son, and another of the Holy Ghost. But the Godhead of the Father, of the Son, and of the Holy Ghost, is all one; the glory equal, the majesty co-eternal. Such as the Father is, such is the Son, and such is the Holy Ghost;" namely, "uncreate, incomprehensible, eternal," &c. The true key to the Athanasian Creed lies in the knowledge of the errors to which it was opposed. The Sabellians considered the Father, Son, and Holy Spirit as one in person;--this was "confounding the persons:" the Arians considered them as differing in essence--three beings;--this was "dividing the substance:" and against these two hypotheses was the creed originally framed. And since every sect was willing to adopt the language of Scripture, it was thought necessary to adopt scholastic terms, in order to fix the sense of Scripture language. Many, however, hold the doctrine of the Athanasian Creed, and approve its terms, who object to its damnatory clauses. See Arians.

ATHANASIUS, the celebrated patriarch of Alexandria, resisted Arius and his erroneous doctrines; and his sentiments as to the Trinity are embodied in the creed which bears his name, though not composed by him. At the Council of Nice, though then but a deacon of Alexandria, his reputation for skill in controversy gained him an honourable place in the council, and with great dexterity he exposed the sophistry of those who pleaded on the side of Arius. Notwithstanding the influence of the emperor, who had recalled Arius from banishment, and upon a plausible confession of his faith, in which he affected to be orthodox in his sentiments, directed that he should be received by the Alexandrian church, Athanasius refused to admit him to communion, and exposed his prevarication. The Arians upon this exerted themselves to raise tumults at Alexandria, and to injure the character of Athanasius with the emperor, who was prevailed upon to pronounce against him a sentence of banishment. In the beginning of the reign of Constantius he was recalled; but was again disturbed and deposed through the influence of the Arians. Accusations were also sent against him and other bishops from the east to the west, but they were acquitted by Pope Julius in full council. Athanasius was restored to his see upon the death of the Arian bishop, who had been placed in it. Arianism, however, being in favour at court, he was condemned by a council convened at Arles, and by another at Milan, and was obliged to fly into the deserts. He returned with the other bishops whom Julian the apostate recalled from banishment, and in A. D. 362, held a council at Alexandria, where the belief of a consubstantial Trinity was openly professed. Many now were recovered from Arianism, and brought to subscribe the Nicene Creed. During the reign of Jovian also Athanasius held another council, which declared its adherence to the Nicene faith; and with the exception of a short retirement under Valens he was permitted to sit down in quiet and govern his affectionate church of Alexandria. Athanasius was an eminent instrument of maintaining the truth in an age when errors affecting the great foundation of our faith were urged with great subtlety. He was by his acuteness able to trace the enemy through his most insidious modes of attack; and thus to preserve the simple and unwary from being misled by terms and distinctions, which, whilst they sounded in unison with the true faith of the Gospel, did in fact imply, or at least open the door to, the most deadly errors. The Scripture doctrine of the Trinity, as explained by him, at length triumphed over the heresies which at one time met with so much support and sanction; and the views of Athanasius have been received, in substance, by all orthodox churches to the present time.

ATHEIST, in the strict and proper sense of the word, is one who does not believe in the existence of a God, or who owns no being superior to nature. It is compounded of the two terms, α negative, and Θεὸς, God, signifying WITHOUT GOD. Atheists have been also known by the name infidels; but the word infidel is now commonly used to distinguish a more numerous party, and is become almost synonymous with Deist. He who disbelieves the existence of a God, as an infinite, intelligent, and a moral agent, is a direct or speculative Atheist; he who confesses a Deity and providence in words, but denies them in his life and actions, is a practical Atheist. That Atheism existed in some sense before the flood, may be suspected from what we read in Scripture, as well as from Heathen tradition; and it is not very unreasonable to suppose, that the deluge was partly intended to evince to the world a heavenly power, as Lord of the universe, and superior to the visible system of nature. This was at least a happy consequence of that fatal catastrophe; for, as it is observed by Dean Sherlock, "The universal deluge, and the confusion of languages, had so abundantly convinced mankind of a divine power and providence, that there was no such creature as an Atheist, till their ridiculous idolatries had tempted some men of wit and thought, rather to own no God than such as the Heathens worshipped."

Atheistical principles were long nourished and cherished in Greece, and especially among the atomical, peripatetic, and skeptical philosophers; and hence some have ascribed the origin of Atheism to the philosophy of Greece. This is true, if they mean that species of refined Atheism, which contrives any impious scheme of principles to account for the origin of the world, without a divine being. For though there may have been in former ages, and in other countries, some persons irreligious in principle as well as in practice, yet we know of none who, forming a philosophical scheme of impiety, became a sect, and erected colleges of Atheistical learning, till the arrogant and enterprising genius of Greece undertook that detestable work. Carrying their presumptuous and ungoverned speculations into the very essence of the divinity, at first they doubted, and at length denied, the existence of a first cause independent of nature and of a providence that superintends its laws, and governs the concerns of mankind. These principles, with the other improvements of Greece, were transferred to Rome; and, excepting in Italy, we hear little of Atheism, for many ages after the Christian æra. "For some ages before the Reformation," says Archbishop Tillotson, "Atheism was confined to Italy, and had its chief residence at Rome. But, in this last age, Atheism has travelled over the Alps and infected France, and now of late it hath crossed the seas, and invaded our nation, and hath prevailed to amazement." However, to Tillotson, and other able writers, we owe its suppression in this country; for they pressed it down with a weight of sound argument, from which it has never been able to raise itself. For although in our time, in France and Germany a subtle Atheism was revived, and spread its unhallowed and destructive influence for many years throughout the Continent, it made but little progress in this better-instructed nation.

Atheism, in its primary sense, comprehends, or at least goes beyond, every heresy in the world; for it professes to acknowledge no religion, true or false. The two leading hypotheses which have prevailed, among Atheists, respecting this world and its origin, are, that of Ocellus Lucanus, adopted and improved by Aristotle, that it was eternal; and that of Epicurus, that it was formed by a fortuitous concourse of atoms. "That the soul is material and mortal, Christianity an imposture, the Scripture a forgery, the worship of God superstition, hell a fable, and heaven a dream, our life without providence, and our death without hope, like that of asses and dogs, are part of the glorious gospel of our modern Atheists."

The being of a God may be proved from the marks of design, and from the order and beauty visible in the world; from universal consent; from the relation of cause and effect; from internal consciousness; and from the necessity of a final as well as an efficient cause.

Of all the false doctrines and foolish opinions that ever infested the mind of man, nothing can possibly equal that of Atheism, which is such a monstrous contradiction of all evidence, to all the powers of understanding, and the dictates of common sense, that it may be well questioned whether any man can really fall into it by a deliberate use of his judgment. All nature so clearly points out, and so loudly proclaims, a Creator of infinite power, wisdom, and goodness, that whoever hears not its voice, and sees not its proofs, may well be thought wilfully deaf, and obstinately blind. If it be evident, self-evident to every man of thought, that there can be no effect without a cause, what shall we say of that manifold combination of effects, that series of operations, that system of wonders, which fill the universe, which present themselves to all our perceptions, and strike our minds and our senses on every side? Every faculty, every object of every faculty, demonstrates a Deity. The meanest insect we can see, the minutest and most contemptible weed we can tread upon, is really sufficient to confound Atheism, and baffle all its pretensions. How much more that astonishing variety and multiplicity of God's works with which we are continually surrounded! Let any man survey the face of the earth, or lift up his eyes to the firmament; let him consider the nature and instincts of brute animals, and afterward look into the operations of his own mind, and will he presume to say or suppose that all the objects he meets with are nothing more than the result of unaccountable accidents and blind chance? Can he possibly conceive that such wonderful order should spring out of confusion? or that such perfect beauty should be ever formed by the fortuitous operations of unconscious, unactive particles of matter? As well, nay better, and more easily, might he suppose that an earthquake might happen to build towns and cities; or the materials carried down by a flood fit themselves up without hands into a regular fleet. For what are towns, cities, or fleets, in comparison of the vast and amazing fabric of the universe! In short, Atheism offers such violence to all our faculties, that it seems scarce credible it should ever really find any place in the human understanding. Atheism is unreasonable, because it gives no tolerable account of the existence of the world. This is one of the greatest difficulties with which the Atheist has to contend. For he must suppose either that the world is eternal, or that it was formed by chance and a fortuitous concourse of the parts of matter. That the world had a beginning, is evident from universal tradition, and the most ancient history that exists; from there being no memorials of any actions performed previously to the time assigned in that history as the æra of the creation; from the origin of learning and arts, and the liability of the parts of matter to decay. That the world was not produced by chance, is also evident. Nothing can be more unreasonable than to ascribe to chance an effect which appears with all the characters of a wise design and contrivance. Will chance fit means to ends, even in ten thousand instances, and not fail in a single one? How often might a man, after shaking a set of letters in a bag, throw them on the ground, before they would become an exact poem, or form a good discourse in prose? In short, the arguments in proof of Deity are so numerous, and at the same time so obvious to a thinking mind, that to waste time in disputing with an Atheist, is approaching too much toward that irrationality, which may be considered as one of the most striking characteristics of the sect.

The more noted Atheist, since the Reformation, are Machiavel, Spinoza, Hobbes, Blount, and Vanini. To these may be added Hume, and Voltaire the corypheus of the sect, and the great nursing father of that swarm of them which has appeared in these last days.

Dr. Samuel Clarke, in his "Demonstration of the Being of a God," says, that Atheism arises either from stupid ignorance, or from corruption of principles and manners, or from the reasonings of false philosophy; and he adds, that the latter, who are the only Atheistical persons capable of being reasoned with at all, must of necessity own that, supposing it cannot be proved to be true, yet it is a thing very desirable, and which any wise man would wish to be true, for the great benefit and happiness of man, that there was a God, an intelligent and wise, a just and good Being, to govern the world. Whatever hypothesis these men can possibly frame, whatever argument they can invent, by which they would exclude God and providence out of the world; that very argument or hypothesis, will of necessity lead them to this concession. If they argue, that our notion of God arises not from nature and reason, but from the art and contrivance of politicians; that argument itself forces them to confess, that it is manifestly for the interest of human society, that it should be believed there is a God. If they suppose that the world was made by chance, and is every moment subject to be destroyed by chance again; no man can be so absurd as to contend, that it is as comfortable and desirable to live in such an uncertain state of things, and so continually liable to ruin, without any hope of renovation, as in a world that is under the preservation and conduct of a powerful, wise, and good God. If they argue against the being of God, from the faults and defects which they imagine they can find in the frame and constitution of the visible and material world; this supposition obliges them to acknowledge that it would have been better the world had been made by an intelligent and wise Being, who might have prevented all faults and imperfections. If they argue against providence, from the faultiness and inequality which they think they discover in the management of the moral world; this is a plain confession, that it is a thing more fit and desirable in itself, that the world should be governed by a just and good Being, than by mere chance or unintelligent necessity. Lastly, if they suppose the world to be eternally and necessarily self-existent, and consequently that every thing in it is established by a blind and eternal fatality; no rational man can at the same time deny, but that liberty and choice, or a free power of acting, is a more eligible state, than to be determined thus in all our actions, as a stone is to move, downward, by an absolute and inevitable fate. In a word, which way soever they turn themselves, and whatever hypothesis they make, concerning the original and frame of things, nothing is so certain and undeniable, as that man, considered without the protection and conduct of a superior Being, is in a far worse case than upon supposition of the being and government of God, and of men's being under his peculiar conduct, protection, and favour.

ATHENS, a celebrated city of Greece, too well known to be here described. St. Paul's celebrated sermon, Acts xvii, was preached on the Areopagus, or Hill of Mars, where a celebrated court was held which took cognizance of matters of religion, blasphemies against the gods, the building of temples, &c. (See AREOPAGUS.) The inscription on the altar, "to the unknown God," which St. Paul so appropriately made the text of his discourse, was adopted on the occasion of the city having been relieved from a pestilence; and they erected altars to "the God unknown," either as not knowing to which of their divinities they were indebted for the favour, or, which is more probable, because there was something in the circumstances of this deliverance, which led them to refer it to a higher power than their own gods, even to the supreme God, who was not unfrequently styled, the "unknown," by the wiser Heathens. The existence of such altars is expressly mentioned by Lucian. On the place where the great Apostle bore his noble testimony against idols, and declared to them the God whom they ignorantly worshipped, Dr. E. D. Clarke, the traveller, remarks, "It is not possible to conceive a situation of greater peril, or one more calculated to prove the sincerity of a preacher, than that in which the Apostle was here placed; and the truth of this, perhaps, will never be better felt than by a spectator, who from this eminence actually beholds the monuments of Pagan pomp and superstition by which he, whom the Athenians considered as the SETTER FORTH OF STRANGE GODS, was then surrounded: representing to the imagination the disciples of Socrates and of Plato, the dogmatist of the porch, and the skeptic of the academy, addressed by a poor and lowly man, who, 'rude in speech,' without the 'enticing words of man's wisdom,' enjoined precepts contrary to their taste, and very hostile to their prejudices. One of the peculiar privileges of the Areopagitæ seems to have been set at defiance by the zeal of St. Paul on this occasion; namely, that of inflicting extreme and exemplary punishment upon any person who should slight the celebration of the holy mysteries, or blaspheme the gods of Greece. We ascended to the summit by means of steps cut in the natural stone. The sublime scene here exhibited is so striking, that a brief description of it may prove how truly it offers to us a commentary upon the Apostle's words, as they were delivered upon the spot. He stood upon the top of the rock, and beneath the canopy of heaven. Before him there was spread a glorious prospect of mountains, islands, seas, and skies; behind him towered the lofty Acropolis, crowned with all its marble temples. Thus every object, whether in the face of nature, or among the works of art, conspired to elevate the mind, and to fill it with reverence toward that Being who made and governs the world, Acts xvii, 24, 28; who sitteth in that light which no mortal eye can approach, and yet is nigh unto the meanest of his creatures; in whom we live, and move, and have our being."

ATONEMENT, the satisfaction offered to divine justice by the death of Christ for the sins of mankind, by virtue of which all true penitents who believe in Christ are personally reconciled to God, are freed from the penalty of their sins, and entitled to eternal life. The atonement for sin made by the death of Christ, is represented in the Christian system as the means by which mankind may be delivered from the awful catastrophe of eternal death; from judicial inflictions of the displeasure of a Governor, whose authority has been contemned, and whose will has been resisted, which shall know no mitigation in their degree, nor bound to their duration. This end it professes to accomplish by means which, with respect to the Supreme Governor himself, preserve his character from mistake, and maintain the authority of his government; and with respect to man, give him the strongest possible reason for hope, and render more favourable the condition of his earthly probation. These are considerations which so manifestly show, from its own internal constitution, the superlative importance and excellence of Christianity, that it would be exceedingly criminal to overlook them.

How sin may be forgiven without leading to such misconceptions of the divine character as would encourage disobedience, and thereby weaken the influence of the divine government, must be considered as a problem of very difficult solution. A government which admitted no forgiveness, would sink the guilty to despair; a government which never punishes offence, is a contradiction,--it cannot exist. Not to punish the guilty, is to dissolve authority; to punish without mercy, is to destroy, and where all are guilty, to make the destruction universal. That we cannot sin with impunity, is a matter determined. The Ruler of the world is not careless of the conduct of his creatures; for that penal consequences are attached to the offence, is not a subject of argument, but is matter of fact evident by daily observation of the events and circumstances of the present life. It is a principle therefore already laid down, that the authority of God must be preserved; but it ought to be remarked, that in that kind of administration which restrains evil by penalty, and encourages obedience by favour and hope, we and all moral creatures are the interested parties, and not the divine Governor himself, whom, because of his independent and all-sufficient nature, our transgressions cannot injure. The reasons, therefore, which compel him to maintain his authority do not terminate in himself. If he treats offenders with severity, it is for our sake, and for the sake of the moral order of the universe, to which sin, if encouraged by a negligent administration, or by entire or frequent impunity, would be the source of endless disorder and misery; and if the granting of pardon to offence be strongly and even severely guarded, so that no less a satisfaction could be accepted than the death of God's own Son, we are to refer this to the moral necessity of the case as arising out of the general welfare of accountable creatures, liable to the deep evil of sin, and not to any reluctance on the part of our Maker to forgive, much less to any thing vindictive in his nature,--charges which have been most inconsiderately and unfairly said to be implied in the doctrine of Christ's vicarious sufferings. If it then be true, that the release of offending man from future punishment, and his restoration to the divine favour, ought, for the interests of mankind themselves, and for the instruction and caution of other beings, to be so bestowed, that no license shall be given to offence;--that God himself, whilst he manifests his compassion, should not appear less just, less holy, than he really is;--that his authority should be felt to be as compelling, and that disobedience should as truly, though not unconditionally, subject us to the deserved penalty, as though no hope of forgiveness had been exhibited;--we ask, On what scheme, save that which is developed in the New Testament, are these necessary conditions provided for? Necessary they are, unless we contend for a license and an impunity which shall annul all good government in the universe, a point for which no reasonable man will contend; and if so, then we must allow that there is strong internal evidence of the truth of the doctrine of Scripture, when it makes the offer of pardon consequent only upon the securities we have before mentioned. If it be said, that sin may be pardoned in the exercise of the divine prerogative, the reply is, that if this prerogative were exercised toward a part of mankind only, the passing by of the rest would be with difficulty reconciled to the divine character; and if the benefit were extended to all, government would be at an end. This scheme of bringing men within the exercise of a merciful prerogative, does not therefore meet the obvious difficulty of the case; nor is it improved by confining the act of grace only to repentant criminals. For in the immediate view of danger, what offender, surrounded with the wreck of former enjoyments, feeling the vanity of guilty pleasures, now past for ever, and beholding the approach of the delayed penal visitation, but would repent? Were the principle of granting pardon to repentance to regulate human governments, every criminal would escape, and judicial forms would become a subject for ridicule. Nor is it recognised by the divine Being in his conduct to men in the present state, although in this world punishments are not final and absolute. Repentance does not restore health injured by intemperance; property, wasted by profusion; or character, once stained by dishonourable practices. If repentance alone could secure pardon, then all must be pardoned, and government dissolved, as in the case of forgiveness by the exercise of mere prerogative; but if an arbitrary selection be made, then different and discordant principles of government are introduced into the divine administration, which is a derogatory supposition.

The question proposed abstractedly, How may mercy be extended to offending creatures, the subjects of the divine government, without encouraging vice, by lowering the righteous and holy character of God, and the authority of his government, in the maintenance of which the whole universe of beings are interested? is, therefore, at once one of the most important and one of the most difficult that can employ the human mind. None of the theories which have been opposed to Christianity affords a satisfactory solution of the problem. They assume principles either destructive of moral government, or which cannot, in the circumstances of man, be acted upon. The only answer is found in the Holy Scriptures. They alone show, and, indeed, they alone profess to show, how God may be "just," and yet the "justifier" of the ungodly. Other schemes show how he may be merciful; but the difficulty does not lie there. The Gospel meets it, by declaring "the righteousness of God," at the same time that it proclaims his mercy. The voluntary sufferings of the Divine Son of God "for us," that is, in our room and stead, magnify the justice of God; display his hatred to sin; proclaim "the exceeding sinfulness" of transgression, by the deep and painful manner in which they were inflicted upon the Substitute; warn the persevering offender of the terribleness, as well as the certainty, of his punishment; and open the gates of salvation to every penitent. It is a part of the same divine plan also to engage the influence of the Holy Spirit, to awaken penitence in man, and to lead the wanderer back to himself; to renew our fallen nature in righteousness, at the moment we are justified through faith, and to place us in circumstances in which we may henceforth "walk not after the flesh, but after the Spirit." All the ends of government are here answered--no license is given to offence,--the moral law is unrepealed,--a day of judgment is still appointed,--future and eternal punishments still display their awful sanctions,--a new and singular display of the awful purity of the divine character is afforded,--yet pardon is offered to all who seek it; and the whole world may be saved.

With such evidence of suitableness to the case of mankind, under such lofty views of connection with the principles and ends of moral government, does the doctrine of the atonement present itself. But other important considerations are not wanting to mark the united wisdom and goodness of that method of extending mercy to the guilty, which Christianity teaches us to have been actually and exclusively adopted. It is rendered, indeed, "worthy of all acceptation," by the circumstance of its meeting the difficulties we have just dwelt upon,--difficulties which could not otherwise have failed to make a gloomy impression upon every offender awakened to a sense of his spiritual danger; but it must be very inattentively considered, if it does not farther commend itself to us, by not only removing the apprehensions we might feel as to the severity of the divine Lawgiver, but as exalting him in our esteem as "the righteous Lord, who loveth righteousness," who surrendered his beloved Son to suffering and death, that the influence of moral goodness might not be weakened in the hearts of his creatures; and as a God of love, affording in this instance a view of the tenderness and benignity of his nature infinitely more impressive and affecting than any abstract description could convey, or than any act of creating and providential power and grace could exhibit, and, therefore, most suitable to subdue that enmity which had unnaturally grown up in the hearts of his creatures, and which, when corrupt, they so easily transfer from a law which restrains their inclination to the Lawgiver himself. If it be important to us to know the extent and reality of our danger, by the death of Christ it is displayed, not in description, but in the most impressive action; if it be important that we should have an assurance of the divine placability toward us, it here receives a demonstration incapable of being heightened; if gratitude be the most powerful motive of future obedience, and one which renders command on the one part, and active service on the other, "not grievous but joyous," the recollection of such obligations as those which the "love of Christ" has laid us under, is a perpetual spring to this energetic affection, and will be the means of raising it to higher and more delightful activity for ever. All that can most powerfully illustrate the united tenderness and awful majesty of God, and the odiousness of sin; all that can win back the heart of man to his Maker and Lord, and render future obedience a matter of affection and delight as well as duty; all that can extinguish the angry and malignant passions of man to man; all that can inspire a mutual benevolence, and dispose to a self-denying charity for the benefit of others; all that can arouse by hope, or tranquillize by faith; is to be found in the vicarious death of Christ, and the principles and purposes for which it was endured.

The first declaration, on this subject, after the appearance of Christ, is that of John the Baptist, when he saw Jesus coming unto him, "Behold the Lamb of God, which taketh away the sin of the world;" where it is obvious, that when John called our Lord, "the Lamb of God," he spoke of him under a sacrificial character, and of the effect of that sacrifice as an atonement for the sins of mankind. This was said of our Lord, even before he entered on his public office; but if any doubt should exist respecting the meaning of the Baptist's expression, it is removed by other passages, in which a similar allusion is adopted, and in which it is specifically applied to the death of Christ, as an atonement for sin. In the Acts of the Apostles, the following words of Isaiah are, by Philip the evangelist, distinctly applied to Christ, and to his death: "He was led as a sheep to the slaughter; and like a lamb dumb before his shearer, so opened he not his mouth. in his humiliation his judgment was taken away: and who shall declare his generation? for his life is taken from the earth." This particular part of the prophecy being applied to our Lord's death, the whole must relate to the same subject; for it is undoubtedly one entire prophecy, and the other expressions in it are still stronger: "He was wounded for our transgressions; he was bruised for our iniquities; the chastisement of our peace was upon him; and with his stripes we are healed: the Lord hath laid on him the iniquity of us all." In the First Epistle of Peter, is also a strong and very apposite text, in which the application of the term "lamb" to our Lord, and the sense in which it is applied, can admit of no doubt: "Forasmuch as ye know that ye were not redeemed with corruptible things, but with the precious blood of Christ, as of a lamb without blemish and without spot," 1 Peter i, 18, 19. It is therefore evident that the Prophet Isaiah, six hundred years before the birth of Jesus; that John the Baptist, on the commencement of his ministry; and that St. Peter, his friend, companion and Apostle, subsequent to the transaction; speak of Christ's death as an atonement for sin, under the figure of a lamb sacrificed.

The passages that follow, plainly and distinctly declare the atoning efficacy of Christ's death: "Now once in the end of the world hath he appeared to put away sin by the sacrifice of himself." "Christ was once offered to bear the sins of many; and unto them that look for him shall he appear the second time without sin unto salvation," Heb. ix, 26, 28. "This man, after he had offered one sacrifice for sin, for ever sat down on the right hand of God; for by one offering he hath perfected for ever them that are sanctified," Heb. x, 12. It is observable, that nothing similar is said of the death of any other person, and that no such efficacy is imputed to any other martyrdom. "While we were yet sinners Christ died for us; much more then, being now justified by his blood, we shall be saved from wrath through him: for if, when we were enemies, we were reconciled to God by the death of his Son, much more, being reconciled, we shall be saved by his life," Rom. v, 8–10. The words, "reconciled to God by the death of his Son," show that his death had an efficacy in our reconciliation; but reconciliation is only preparatory to salvation. "He has reconciled us to his Father in his cross, and in the body of his flesh through death," Col. i, 20, 22. What is said of reconciliation in these texts, is in some others spoken of sanctification, which is also preparatory to salvation. "We are sanctified,"--how? "by the offering of the body of Christ once for all," Heb. x, 10. In the same epistle, the blood of Jesus is called "the blood of the covenant by which we are sanctified." In these and many other passages that occur in different parts of the New Testament, it is therefore asserted that the death of Christ had an efficacy in the procuring of human salvation. Such expressions are used concerning no other person, and the death of no other person; and it is therefore evident, that Christ's death included something more than a confirmation of his preaching; something more than a pattern of a holy and patient martyrdom; something more than a necessary antecedent to his resurrection, by which he gave a grand and clear proof of our resurrection from the dead. Christ's death was all these, but it was something more. It was an atonement for the sins of mankind; and in this way only it became the accomplishment of our eternal redemption. See Day of Expiation.

AUGSBURGH, or **AUGUSTAN CONFESSION**. In 1530, a diet of the German princes was convened by the emperor Charles V, to meet at Augsburgh, for the express purpose of composing the religious troubles which then distracted Germany. On this occasion Melancthon was employed to draw up this famous confession of faith which may be considered as the creed of the German reformers, especially of the more temperate among them. It consisted of twenty-one articles, including the following points:--The Trinity, original sin, the incarnation, justification by faith, the word and sacraments, necessity of good works, the perpetuity of the church, infant baptism, the Lord's Supper, repentance and confession, the proper use of the sacraments, church order, rites and ceremonies, the magistracy, a future judgment, free will, the worship of saints, &c. It then proceeds to state the abuses of which the reformers chiefly complained, as the denial of the sacramental cup to the laity, the celibacy of the clergy, the mass, auricular confession, forced abstinence from meats, monastic vows, and the enormous power of the church of Rome. The confession was read at a full meeting of the diet, and signed by the elector of Saxony, and three other princes of the German empire.

John Faber, afterward archbishop of Vienna, and two other Catholic divines, were employed to draw up an answer to this confession, which was replied to by Melancthon in his "Apology for the Augsburgh Confession" in 1531. This confession and defence; the articles of Smalcald, drawn up by Luther; his catechisms, &c, form the symbolical books of the Lutheran church; and it must be owned that they contain concessions in favour of some parts of popery, particularly the real presence, that few Protestants in this country would admit.

AUGUSTINE, or, as he is sometimes called in the court style of the middle ages, St. Austin, one of the ancient fathers of the church, whose writings for many centuries had almost as potent an influence on the religious opinions of Christendom as those of Aristotle exercised over philosophy. Indeed, it has often been mentioned as a fact, with expressions of regret, that the writings of no man, those of the Stagirite excepted, contributed more than those of St. Augustine to encourage that spirit of subtle disquisition which subsequently distinguished the era of the Schoolmen. He was born, November 13th, A. D. 354, at Tagasta, an episcopal city of Numidia in Africa. His parents, Patricius and Monica, were Christians of respectable rank in life, who afforded their son all the means of instruction which his excellent genius and wonderful aptitude for learning seemed to require. He studied grammar and rhetoric at Madura, until he was sixteen years old; and afterward removed to Carthage, to complete his studies. In both these cities, in all the fervour of unregenerate youth, he entered eagerly into the seducing scenes of dissipation and folly with which he was surrounded, and became not only depraved but infamous in his conduct. In this respect he was not improved by his subsequent connection with the Manichees, whose unhallowed principles afforded an excuse for his immorality, and threw a veil over the vilest of his actions. The simplicity and minuteness with which he has narrated the numerous incidents of his childhood, youth, and mature age, in his celebrated book of "Confessions," have afforded abundant matter of ridicule to the profane and infidel wits of this and the last age. The reflections, however, which accompany his narrative, are generally important and judicious, and furnish to the moral philosopher copious materials for a history of the varieties of the human heart, and are of superior value to the humble Christian for the investigation and better knowledge of his own. With a strange though not uncommon inconsistency, few books have been more frequently quoted as authority on matters relating to general literature and philosophy by infidels themselves, than St. Augustine's otherwise despised "Confessions," and his "City of God." But, whatever else is taught in this remarkable piece of autobiography, every pious reader will be delighted with the additional proofs which it contains of the ultimate prevalence of faithful prayer, especially on the part of Christian parents. Monica's importunate prayers to heaven followed the aberrations of her graceless son,--when he settled at Carthage as a teacher of rhetoric; when he removed to Rome, and lodged with a Manichee;--and when he finally settled at Milan as professor of rhetoric. St. Ambrose was at that time, A. D. 384, bishop of Milan, and to his public discourses Augustine began to pay much attention. His heart became gradually prepared for the reception of divine truth, and for that important change of heart and principles which constitutes "conversion." The circumstances attending this change, though often related, are not unworthy of being repeated, if only to show that the mode of the Holy Spirit's operations was in substance the same in those early days as they are now; and time was when some of the soundest divines and most worthy dignitaries of the church of England were in the habit of referring with approbation to this well attested instance of change of heart. One of his Christian countrymen, Pontinius, who held a high situation at court, having perceived a copy of St. Paul's Epistles lying on the table, entered one day into conversation with him and his friend Alipius about the nature of faith and the happiness of those who lived in the enjoyment of religion. Augustine was deeply affected at the close of this visit; and when Pontinius had retired, giving vent to his feelings he addressed Alipius in a most animated strain: "How is this? What shall we do? Ignorant people come, and seize upon heaven; and we, with our learning, (senseless wretches that we are!) behold we are immersed in flesh and blood! Are we ashamed to follow them? Yet is it not a still greater shame, not even to be able to follow them?" Full of remorse and contrition Augustine left the house and retired to a secret part of the garden, followed by his friend, who seemed on this occasion to be a partaker of his grief only because he saw him grieved in spirit. Unwilling to unman himself, as he accounted it, before Alipius, he left him; and throwing himself down under the branches of a large fig tree he poured out a torrent of tears which he was unable any longer to restrain, and exclaimed in bitterness of soul, "When, O Lord, when will thy anger cease? Why tomorrow? Why not at this time?" He instantly heard what he considered to be the voice of a child, saying TOLLE, LEGE, "Take and read." These two Latin words were repeated several times; Augustine reflected upon them, checked his tears, received them as the voice of God, and running into the house, opened, according to the divine direction, the Epistles of St. Paul which he had left on the table, and attentively read the first passage which he found. It was Romans xiii, 13, 14; a passage peculiarly applicable to him, in reference to his former habits and present state of mind: "Not in rioting and drunkenness, not in chambering and wantonness, not in strife and envying: but put ye on the Lord Jesus Christ, and make not provision for the flesh to fulfil the lusts thereof." He shut up the book, and was amazed that all his doubts and fears had vanished. Alipius was speedily informed of this wonderful change in his feelings and views; and after having desired to see the two verses, in the spirit of a true seeker he pointed out to Augustine the passage which immediately follows, and which he considered as peculiarly adapted to his own case: "Him that is weak in the faith receive ye," &c, Rom. xiv, 1. The two friends then ran to acquaint Monica with these circumstances, the knowledge of which transported her with joy.

In a frame of mind not unfamiliar to those who have themselves had "much forgiven," Augustine wished to retire at once from so wicked a world as that in which he had passed the first thirty-two years of his dissolute life. His secession, however, was only a temporary one; for he and Alipius were, a few months afterward, received by baptism into the Christian church. After having composed several religious treatises in his retreat near Tagasta, especially against the errors of the Manichees, from which he had been so recently reclaimed, he was, in the year 392, ordained priest by Valerius, bishop of Hippo, now a part of the Barbary States on the coast of Africa. He there held a public disputation with Fortunatus, a celebrated priest among the Manichees, and acquitted himself with great spirit and success, he also wrote and preached largely and to great effect against the Donatists and Manichees. His reputation as a divine increased; and he was, at the close of the year 395, ordained bishop of Hippo, in which high station he continued with great advantage to wage war against various orders of heretics.

Augustine had hitherto directed his theological artillery principally against the predestinarian errors of the Manichees; but he was soon called upon to change his weapons and his mode of warfare, in attacking a new and not less dangerous class of heretics. In the year 412 he began to write against the injurious doctrines of Pelagias, a native of Britain, who had resided for a considerable time at Rome, and acquired universal esteem by the purity of his manners, his piety, and his erudition. Alarmed at the consequences which seemed to him obviously to result from allowing that Adam's sin is transmitted to all his posterity, and fortified in his sentiments on this subject by those of Origen and Ruffinus, with the latter of whom he had associated, he boldly denied tenets which he did not believe. In the defence of his opinions, Pelagius, was seconded by Celestius, a man equally eminent for his talents and his virtues. Their principles were propagated at first rather by hints and intimations, than by open avowal and plain declarations; but this reserve was laid aside when they perceived the ready reception which their doctrines obtained; and Celestius began zealously to disseminate them in Africa, while Pelagius sowed the same tares in Palestine, whence they were speedily transplanted to almost every corner of Christendom. If the brief notices, which have come down to us respecting their tenets, in the writings of their adversaries, be correct, they affirmed, "It is not FREE will if it requires the aid of God; because every one has it within the power of his own will to do any thing, or not to do it. Our victory over sin and Satan proceeds not from the help which God affords, but is owing to our own free will. The prayers which the church offers up either for the conversion of unbelievers and other sinners, or for the perseverance of believers, are poured forth in vain. The unrestricted capability of men's own free will is amply sufficient for all these things, and therefore no necessity exists for asking of God those things which we are able of ourselves to obtain; the gifts of grace being only necessary to enable men to do that more easily and completely which yet they could do themselves though more slowly and with greater difficulty; and that they are perfectly free creatures," in opposition to all the current notions of predestination and reprobation. These novel opinions were refuted by St. Augustine and St. Jerom, as well as by Orosius a Spanish presbyter, and they were condemned as heresies in the council of Carthage and in that of Milevum. The discussions which then arose have been warmly agitated in various subsequent periods of the Christian church, though little new light has been thrown upon them from that age to the present. In his eagerness to confute these opponents St. Augustine employed language so strong as made it susceptible of an interpretation wholly at variance with the accountability of man. This led to farther explanations and modifications of his sentiments, which were multiplied when the Semi-Pelagians arose, who thought that the truth lay between his doctrines and those of the Pelagians. Concerning original sin, he maintained that it was derived from our first parents; and he believed he had ascertained in what the original sin conveyed by Adam to his posterity consisted. In his sentiments, however, upon the latter point he was rather inconsistent, at one time asserting that the essence of original sin was concupiscence, and at another expressing doubts respecting his own position. This subject was bequeathed as a legacy to the schoolmen of a subsequent age, who exercised their subtle wits upon all its ramifications down to the period of the council of Trent. On the consequences of the fall of our first parents, St. Augustine taught that by it human nature was totally corrupted, and deprived of all inclination and ability to do good. Before the age in which he lived, the early fathers held what, in the language of systematic theology, is termed the synergestic system, or the needfulness of human coöperation in the works of holiness; but though the freedom of the will was not considered by them as excluding or rendering unnecessary the grace of God, yet much vagueness is perceptible in the manner in which they express themselves, because they had not examined the subject with the same attention as the theologians by whom they were succeeded. Those early divines generally used the language of Scripture, the fertile invention of controversial writers, not having as yet displayed itself, except on the divine nature of Jesus Christ, and subsidiary terms and learned distinctions not being then required by any great differences of opinion. But as soon as Pelagius broached his errors, the attention of Christians was naturally turned to the investigation of the doctrine of grace. The opinions of St. Augustine on this subject, which soon became those of the great body of the Christian church, admitted the necessity of divine grace, or the influence of the Holy Spirit, for our obedience to the law of God. He ascribed the renovation of our moral constitution wholly to this grace, denied all coöperation of man with it for answering the end to be accomplished, and represented it as irresistible. He farther affirmed that it was given only to a certain portion of the human race, to those who showed the fruits of it in their sanctification, and that it secured the perseverance of all upon whom it was bestowed. Plaifere in his "*Appello Evangelium*" has given the following as the substance of that opinion of the order of predestination of which "many do say that St. Austin was the first author: 1. That God from all eternity decreed to create mankind holy and good. 2. That he foresaw man, being tempted by Satan, would fall into sin, if God did not hinder it; he decreed not to hinder. 3. That out of mankind, seen fallen into sin and misery, he chose a certain number to raise to righteousness and to eternal life, and rejected the rest, leaving them in their sins. 4. That for these his chosen he decreed to send his Son to redeem them, and his Spirit to call them and sanctify them; the rest he decreed to forsake, leaving them to Satan and themselves, and to punish them for their sins."

After St. Augustine had thus in a great degree new moulded the science of theology, and had combined with it as an essential part of divine truth, that the fate of mankind was determined by the divine decree independently of their own efforts and conduct, and that they were thus divided into the elect and reprobate, it became necessary, in order to preserve consistency, to introduce into his system a limitation with respect to baptism, and to prevent the opinions concerning it from interfering with those which flowed from the doctrine of predestination. He accordingly taught, that baptism brings with it the forgiveness of sins; that it is so essential, that the omission of it will expose us to condemnation; and that it is attended with regeneration. He also affirmed that the virtue of baptism is not in the water; that the ministers of Christ perform the external ceremony, but that Christ accompanies it with invisible grace; that baptism is common to all, whilst, grace is not so; and that the same external rite may be death to some, and life to others. By this distinction he rids himself of the difficulty which would have pressed upon his scheme of theology, had pardon, regeneration, and salvation been NECESSARILY connected with the outward ordinance of baptism; and limits its proper efficacy to those who are comprehended, as the heirs of eternal life, in the decree of the Almighty. Many, however, of those who strictly adhere to him in other parts of his doctrinal system, desert him at this point. Bishop Bedell speaks thus in disparagement of his baptismal views, in a letter to Dr.

Ward: "This I do yield to my Lord of Sarum most willingly, that the justification, sanctification, and adoption which children have in baptism, is not UNIVOCÈ [univocally] the same with that which ADULTI [adults] have. I think the emphatical speeches of Augustine against the Pelagians, and of Prosper, are not so much to be regarded (who say the like of the eucharist also) touching the necessity and efficacy in the case of infants; and they are very like the speeches of Lanfranc and Guitmund of Christ's presence in the sacrament, opposing VERACITÉR, [truly] and VERÉ [truly] to SACRAMENTALITÉR; [sacramentally;] which is a false and absurd contraposition. The opinion of the Franciscans out of Scotus and Bernard, mentioned in the council of Trent, seems to be the true opinion; for they make the sacraments to be effectual, 'because God gives them EFFECTUS REGULARITÉR CONCOMITANTES,' [regularly accompanying effects,] and to contain grace no otherwise than as an effectual sign; and that grace is received by them as an investiture by a ring or staff, which is OBSIGNANDO, [by signation.] Consider that if you will aver, that baptism washes away otherwise than sacramentally, that is, obsignatorily, original sin; yet you must allow that manner of washing for future actual sins; and you must make two sorts of justification, one for children, another for ADULTI; [adults;] and (which passes all the rest) you must find some promise in God's covenant wherein he binds himself to wash away sin without faith or repentance. By this doctrine, you must also maintain that children do spiritually eat the flesh of Christ and drink his blood, if they receive the eucharist, as for ages they did, and by the analogy of the passover they may; and sith [if] the use of this sacrament TOTIES QUOTIES [as often as it is used] must needs confer grace, it seems it were necessary to let them communicate, and the oftener the better, to the intent they might be stronger in grace: which opinion, though St. Austin and many more of the ancients do maintain, I believe you will not easily condescend unto, or that children dying without baptism are damned." These remarks are important, as proceeding from the pen of the personal friend of Father Paul, who wrote the History of the council of Trent.

In the various discussions which have arisen concerning predestination and the doctrines with which it is connected, some modern divines have quoted the arguments of St. Augustine against the Manichees, and others those which he employed against the Pelagians, according to the discordant views which the combatants severally entertain on these controverted points. One of them has thus expressed himself, in his endeavour to reconcile St Augustine with himself:--"The heresy of Pelagius being suppressed, the catholic doctrine in that point became more settled and confirmed by the opposition; such freedom being left to the will of man, as was subservient unto grace, coöperating in some measure with those heavenly influences. And so much is confessed by St. Augustine himself, where he asks this question, 'Doth any man affirm that free will is perished utterly from man by the fall of Adam?' And thereunto he makes this answer: 'Freedom is perished by sin; but it is that freedom only which we had in paradise, of having perfect righteousness with immortality.' For, otherwise, it appears to be his opinion, that man was not merely passive in all the acts of grace which conduced to glory, according to the memorable saying of his, so common in the mouths of all men, 'He who first made us without our help will not vouchsafe to save us at last without our concurrence.' If any harsher expressions have escaped his pen, (as commonly it happeneth in the heats of a disputation,) they are to be qualified by this last rule, and by that before, in which it was affirmed, that 'God could not with justice judge and condemn the world, if all men's sins proceeded not from their own free will, but from some overruling providence which inforced them to it.'" Another admirer of this father offers the following as an attempt at reconciliation: "St. Augustine denied that the coöperation of man is at all exerted to produce the renewal of our nature; but, when the renewal had been produced, he admitted that there was an exercise of the will combined with the workings of grace. In the tenth chapter of his work against the Manichæans, the bishop of Hippo thus expresses himself: 'Who is it that will not exclaim, HOW FOOLISH IT IS TO DELIVER PRECEPTS TO THAT MAN WHO IS NOT AT LIBERTY TO PERFORM WHAT IS COMMANDED! AND HOW UNJUST IT IS TO CONDEMN HIM WHO HAD NOT POWER TO FULFIL THE COMMANDS! Yet these unhappy persons [the Manichees] do not perceive that they are ascribing such injustice and want of equity to God. But what greater truth is there than this, that God has delivered precepts, and that human spirits have freedom of will?' Elsewhere he says, 'Nothing is more within our power than our own will. The will is that by which we commit sin, and by which we live righteously.' Nothing can be plainer than that the writer of these passages admitted the liberty of the human will, and the necessity of our own exertions in conjunction with divine grace. How this is to be reconciled with his general doctrine, is perhaps indicated in the following passage from his book DE GRATIÂ ET LIB. ARBITRIO, C. 17. Speaking of grace he says, 'That we may WILL God WORKS without us; but when we WILL, and so WILL as to DO, he CO-WORKS with us; yet unless he either WORKS that we may will, or CO-WORKS when we do will, we are utterly incapable of doing any thing in the good works of piety.'" These are but very slight specimens of the mode in which learned and ingenious men have tried to give a kind of symmetrical proportion to this father's doctrinal system. Several large treatises have been published with the same praiseworthy intention; the pious authors of them either entirely forgetting, or having never read, the rather latitudinarian indulgence of opinion which St. Augustine claims for himself in his "Retractations," in which he has qualified the harshness of his previous assertions on many subjects. If, however, an estimate may be formed of what this father intended in his various pacificatory doctrinal explanations from what he has actually admitted and expressed, it may be safely affirmed that no systematic writer of theology seems so completely to have entered into the last and best views of the bishop of Hippo, or so nearly reconciled the apparent discordances in them, as Arminius has done; and few other authors have rendered more ample justice to his sentiments, talents, and character, than the famous Dutch Professor.

Many were the theological labours to which he was invited by the most eminent of his contemporaries; and hastily as some of his lucubrations were executed, it is not surprising that among two hundred and seventy-two treatises on different subjects, some are of inferior value and unworthy of the fame which he had acquired in the church. After a life of various changes, and of a mixed character, he died A. D. 430, in the seventy-sixth year of his age; having been harassed at the close of life by seeing his country invaded by the Vandals, and the city of which he was the bishop besieged. Though those barbarians took Hippo and burned it, they saved his library, which contained his voluminous writings.

St. Augustine was a diligent man in the sacred calling; and that the office of a bishop even in that age of the church was no sinecure, is evident from several notices in his letters. At the close of one addressed to Marcellinus he gives the subjoined account: "If I were able to give you a narrative of the manner in which I spend my time, you would be both surprised and distressed on account of the great number of affairs which oppress me without my being able to suspend them. For when some little leisure is allowed me by those who daily attend upon me about business, and who are so urgent with me that I can neither shun them nor ought to despise them, I have always some other writings to compose, which indeed ought to be preferred, [to those which Marcellinus requested,] because the present juncture will not permit them to be postponed. For the rule of charity is, not to consider the greatness of the friendship, but the necessity of the affair. Thus I have continually something or other to compose which diverts me from writing what would be more agreeable to my inclinations, daring the little intervals in that multiplicity of business with which I am burdened either through the wants or the passions of others." He frequently complains of this oppressive weight of occupation in which his love of his flock had engaged him, by obeying the Apostolical precept, which forbids Christians from going to law before Pagan tribunals. In reference to this employment his biographer, Posidonius, says: "At the desire of Christians, or of men belonging to any sect whatever, he would hear causes with patience and attention, sometimes till the usual hour of eating, and sometimes the whole day without eating at all, observing the dispositions of the parties, and how much they advanced or decreased in faith and good works; and when he had opportunity he instructed them in the law of God, and gave them suitable advice, requiring nothing of them except Christian obedience. He sometimes wrote letters, when desired, on temporal subjects; but looked upon all this as unprofitable occupation, which drew him aside from that which was better and more agreeable to himself."

The character of this eminent father has been much misrepresented both as a man and as a writer. Whoever looks into his writings for accurate and enlarged views of Christian doctrine, looks for that which could not be expected in the very infancy of Biblical criticism. He was a rhetorician by profession, and the degenerate taste of that age must be blamed, rather than the individual who wrote in the style which then prevailed. The learning of St. Augustine, and particularly his knowledge of Greek, have been disputed; and hence the importance of his Biblical criticisms has been depreciated. In the account of the early part of his life he confesses his great aversion to the study of that language; and as he tells us, in his maturer age, that he read the Platonists in a Latin version, it has perhaps been too hastily concluded that he never made any great proficiency in it. But though it be allowed that his comments on Scripture consist chiefly of popular reflections, spiritual and moral, or allegorical and mystical perversions of the literal meaning; yet the works of this father are not wholly destitute of remarks and critical interpretations, that are pertinent and judicious: to such, after a series of extracts from his writings, Dr. Lardner has referred his readers. With regard to his knowledge of Greek, this impartial and candid author is of opinion, that he understood that language better than some have supposed; and he has cited several passages from which it may be perceived, that St. Augustine frequently compared his copies of the Latin version with those of the Greek original. Le Clerc himself allows that he sometimes explains Greek words and phrases in a very felicitous manner. Indeed, the commencement of his correspondence with St. Jerom proves him to have been no contemptible critic. In this he besought him, in the name of all the African churches, to apply himself to the translation into Latin of the Greek interpreters of Scripture, rather than to enter upon a new translation from the original Hebrew; and to point out those passages in which the Hebrew differed from the Septuagint, as he had previously done in the book of Job. Voltaire and other profane wits have, in the exercise of their buffoonery, impeached his moral conduct; but their charges, when impartially examined, will be seen to be founded in ignorance or in malice. They resemble those which the same parties prefer against Prophets, Apostles, and against Christ himself. Mosheim observes that Augustine's high reputation filled the Christian world; and "not without reason, as a variety of great and shining qualities were united in the character of that illustrious man. A sublime genius, an uninterrupted and zealous pursuit of truth, an indefatigable application, an invincible patience, a sincere piety, and a subtle and lively wit, conspired to establish his fame upon the most lasting foundations." Such a testimony as this far outweighs the vituperative remarks and petty sneers of a thousand infidels. See Pelagians and Synods.

AUGUSTUS, emperor of Rome, and successor of Julius Cæsar. The battle of Actium, which he fought with Mark Antony, and which made him master of the empire, happened fifteen years before the birth of Christ. This is the emperor who appointed the enrolment mentioned Luke ii, 1, which obliged Joseph and the Virgin Mary to go to Bethlehem, the place where Jesus Christ was born. Augustus procured the crown of Judea for Herod, from the

Roman senate. After the defeat of Mark Antony, Herod adhered to Augustus, and was always faithful to him; so that Augustus loaded him with honours and riches.

AVEN, a city of Egypt, afterward called Heliopolis, and On, Ezek. xxx, 17. Herodotus informs us that in this city there was an annual assembly in honour of the sun, and a temple dedicated to him. It appears, however, highly probable, by the behaviour of Pharaoh to Joseph and Jacob, and especially by Joseph's care to preserve the land to the priests, Gen. xlvii, 22, 26, that the true religion prevailed in Egypt in his time; and it is incredible that Joseph should have married the daughter of the priest of On, had that name among the Egyptians denoted only the material light; which, however, no doubt they, like all the rest of the world, idolized in after times, and to which we find a temple dedicated among the Canaanites, under this name, Joshua vii, 2.

AVENGER OF BLOOD. He who prosecuted the man-slayer under the law was called the avenger of blood, and had a right to slay the person, if he found him without a city of refuge. See Goel.

AVIMS, a people descended from Hevus, the son of Canaan. They dwelt at first in the country which was afterward possessed by the Caphtorims, or Philistines. The Scripture says expressly, that the Caphtorims drove out the Avims, who dwelt in Hazerim, even unto Azzah, Deut. ii, 23. There were also Avims, or Hivites, at Shechem, or Gibeon, Joshua xi, 19; for the inhabitants of Shechem were Hivites. Lastly, there were some of them beyond Jordan, at the foot of Mount Hermon. Bochart thinks, that Cadmus, who conducted a colony of the Phœnicians into Greece, was a Hivite. His name, Cadmus, comes from the Hebrew KEDEM, "the east," because he came from the eastern parts of the land of Canaan. The name of his wife Hermione was taken from Mount Hermon, at the foot whereof the Hivites dwelt. The metamorphoses of the companions of Cadmus into serpents is founded upon the signification of the name of Hivites, which, in the Phœnician language, signifies SERPENTS.

AZARIAH, or **UZZIAH**, king of Judah, son of Amaziah. He began to reign at the age of sixteen years, and reigned fifty-two years in Jerusalem; his mother's name being Jecholiah, 2 Kings xv. Azariah did that which was right in the sight of the Lord; nevertheless he did not destroy the high places; and, against the express prohibition of God, the people continued to sacrifice there. Having taken upon him to offer incense in the temple, which office belonged entirely to the priests, he was struck with a leprosy, and continued without the city, separated from other men until the day of his death, 2 Chron. xxvi. Josephus says, that upon this occasion a great earthquake happened; and that the temple opening at the top, a ray of light darted upon the king's forehead, the very moment he took the censer into his hand, and he instantly became a leper; nay, that the earthquake was so very violent, that it tore in sunder a mountain west of Jerusalem, and rolled one half of it over and over to the distance of four furlongs, till at length it was stopped by another mountain which stood over against it; but choked up the highway, and covered the king's gardens with dust. This is what Josephus adds to the history related in the Chronicles; but the truth of it may be justly suspected. We know, indeed, that there was a very great earthquake in the reign of Uzziah; for Amos, chap. i, 1, and Zechariah, chap. xiv, 5, make mention of it: however, it is not certain that it happened at the very time that Uzziah took upon him to offer incense.

During the time that Uzziah was a leper, his son Jotham, as his father's viceroy, took the public administration upon himself, and succeeded him after his death, which happened in the fifty-second year of his reign, A. M. 3246. He was not buried in the royal sepulchre; but in the same field, at some distance, on account of his leprosy.

The first part of Uzziah's reign was very successful: he obtained great advantages over the Philistines, Ammonites, and Arabians. He made additions to the fortifications at Jerusalem, and always kept an army on foot of three hundred and seven thousand men, and upwards, 2 Chron. xxvi; and he had great magazines, well stored with all sorts of arms, as well offensive as defensive; and he was a great lover of agriculture.

BAAL, **BEL**, or **BELUS**, denoting LORD, a divinity among several ancient nations; as the Canaanites, Phœnicians, Sidonians, Carthaginians, Babylonians, Chaldeans, and Assyrians. The term BAAL, which is itself an appellative, served at first to denote the true God, among those who adhered to the true religion. Accordingly, the Phœnicians, being originally Canaanites, having once had, as well as the rest of their kindred, the knowledge of the true God, probably called him BAAL, or LORD. But they, as well as other nations, gradually degenerating into idolatry, applied this appellation to their respective idols; and thus were introduced a variety of divinities, called BAALIM, or BAAL, with some epithet annexed to it, as BAAL BERITH, BAAL GAD, BAAL MOLOCH, BAAL PEOR, BAAL ZEBUB, &c. Some have supposed that the descendants of Ham first worshipped the sun under the title of Baal, 2 Kings xxiii, 5, 11; and that they afterward ascribed it to the patriarch who was the head of their line; making the sun only an emblem of his influence or power. It is certain, however, that when the custom prevailed of deifying and worshipping those who were in any respect distinguished among mankind, the appellation of Baal was not restricted to the sun, but extended to those eminent persons who were deified, and who became objects of worship in different nations. The Phœnicians had several divinities of this kind, who were not intended to represent the sun. It is probable that Baal, Belus, or Bel, the great god of the Carthaginians, and also of the Sidonians, Babylonians, and Assyrians, who, from the testimony of Scripture, appears to have been delighted with human sacrifices, was the Moloch of the Ammonites; the Chronus of the Greeks, who was the chief object of adoration in Italy, Crete, Cyprus, and Rhodes, and all other countries where divine honours were paid him; and the Saturn of the Latins. In process of time, many other deities, beside the principal ones just mentioned, were distinguished by the title of Baal among the Phœnicians, particularly those of Tyre, and of course among the Carthaginians, and other nations. Such were Jupiter, Mars, Bacchus, and Apollo, or the sun.

The temples and altars of Baal were generally placed on eminences: they were places inclosed by walls, within which was maintained a perpetual fire; and some of them bad statues or images, called in Scripture "Chamanim." Maundrell, in his journey from Aleppo to Jerusalem, observed, some remains of these enclosures in Syria. Baal had his prophets and his priests in great numbers; accordingly, we read of four hundred and fifty of them that were fed at the table of Jezebel only; and they conducted the worship of this deity, by offering sacrifices, by dancing round his altar with violent gesticulations and exclamations, by cutting their bodies with knives and lancets, and by raving and pretending to prophesy, as if they were possessed by some invisible power.

It is remarkable that we do not find the name Baal so much in popular use east of Babylonia; but it was general west of Babylonia, and to the very extremity of western Europe, including the British isles. The worship of Bel, Belus, Belenus, or Belinus, was general throughout the British islands; and certain of its rites and observances are still maintained among us, notwithstanding the establishment of Christianity during so many ages. A town in Perthshire, on the borders of the Highlands, is called TILLIEBELTANE or TULLIEBELTANE; that is, the EMINENCE, or RISING GROUND, OF THE FIRE OF BAAL. In the neighbourhood is a Druidical temple of eight upright stones, where it is supposed the fire was kindled. At some distance from this is another temple of the same kind, but smaller; and near it a well still held in great veneration. On Beltane morning, superstitious people go to this well, and drink of it; then they make a procession round it nine times. After this they in like manner go round the temple. So deep-rooted is this Heathenish superstition in the minds of many who reckon themselves good Protestants, that they will not neglect these rites, even when Beltane falls on the Sabbath.

In Ireland, Bel-tein is celebrated on the twenty-first of June, at the time of the solstice. There, as they make fires on the tops of hills, every member of the family is made to pass through the fire; as they reckon this ceremony necessary to ensure good fortune through the succeeding year. This resembles the rites used by the Romans in the Palilia. Bel-tein is also observed in Lancashire.

In Wales, this annual fire is kindled in autumn, on the first day of November; which being neither at the solstice nor equinox, deserves attention. It may be accounted for by supposing that the lapse of ages has removed it from its ancient station, and that the observance is kept on the same day, nominally, though that be now removed some weeks backward from its true station. However that may be, in North Wales especially, this fire is attended by many ceremonies; such as running through the fire and smoke, each participator casting a stone into the fire.

The Hebrews often imitated the idolatry of the Canaanites in adoring Baal. They offered human sacrifices to him in groves, upon high places, and upon the terraces of houses. Baal had priests and prophets consecrated to his service. All sorts of infamous and immodest actions were committed in the festivals of Baal and Astarte. See Jer. xxxii, 35; 2 Kings xvii, 16; xxiii, 4, 5, 12; 1 Kings xviii, 22; 2 Kings x, 19; 1 Kings xiv, 24; xv, 12; 2 Kings xxiii, 7; Hosea iv, 14. This false deity is frequently mentioned in Scripture in the plural number, BAALIM, which may intimate that the name BAAL was given to several different deities.

There were many cities in Palestine, whose names were compounded of BAAL and some other word: whether it was that the god Baal was adored in them, or that these places were looked upon as the capital cities,--LORDS of their respective provinces,--is uncertain.

BAAL BERITH, the god of the Shechemites, Judges viii, 33; ix, 4, 46.

BAAL PEOR. Peor is supposed to have been a part of Mount Abarim; and Baal was the great idol or chief god of the Phœnicians, and was known and worshipped under a similar name, with tumultuous and obscene rites, all over Asia. He is the same as the Bel of the Babylonians. Baal, by itself, signifies LORD, and was a name of the solar or principal god. But it was also variously compounded, in allusion to the different characters and attributes of the particular or local deities who were known by it, as Baal Peor, Baal Zebub, Baal Zephon, &c. Baal Peor, then, was probably the temple of an idol belonging to the Moabites, on Mount Abarim, which the Israelites worshipped when encamped at Shittim; this brought a plague upon them, of which twenty-four thousand died, Num. xxxv. Chemosh, the abomination of Moab, to whom Solomon erected an altar, 1 Kings xi, 7, is supposed to have been the same deity. Baal Peor has been farther supposed by some to have been Priapus; by others, Saturn; by others, Pluto; and by others again, Adonis. Mr. Faber agrees with Calmet in making Baal Peor the same with Adonis; a part of whose worship consisted in bewailing him with funeral rites, as one lost or dead, and afterward welcoming, with extravagant joy, his fictitious return to life. He was in an eminent degree the god of impurity. Hosea, speaking of the worship of this idol, emphatically calls it "that shame," Hos. ix, 10. Yet in the rites of this deity the Moabite and Midianite women seduced the Israelites to join.

BAAL ZEBUB, **BEELZEBUB**, or **BEL-ZEBUB**, signifies the GOD OF FLIES, and was an idol of the

Ekronites. It is not easy to discover how this false deity obtained its name. Some commentators think that he was called Baal Samin, or the lord of heaven; but that the Jews, from contempt, gave him the name of Baal-zebub. Others with greater reason believe that he was denominated "the god of flies" by his votaries, because he defended them from flies, which are extremely troublesome in hot countries; in the same manner as the Eleans worshipped Hercules under the appellation of Ἀπόμυιος, THE FLY CHASER. Pliny is of opinion, that the name of Achor, the god invoked at Cyrene against flies, is derived from Accaron, or Ekron, where Baal-zebub was worshipped, and where he had a famous temple and oracle. Winkelman has given the figures of two heads, "both of them images of Jupiter, called by the Greeks Ἀπόμυιος, and by the Romans MUSCARIUS; that is to say, FLY DRIVER; for to this Jupiter was attributed the function of driving away flies."

It is evident that Beelzebub was considered as the patron deity of medicine; for this is plainly implied in the conduct of Ahaziah, 2 Kings i. The Greek mythology considered Apollo as the god of medicine, and attributed also to him those possessions by a pythonic spirit which occasionally perplexed spectators, and of which we have an instance in Acts xvi, 19. Apollo, too, was the sun. Hence we probably see the reason why Ahaziah sent to Beelzebub to inquire the issue of his accident; since Beelzebub was Apollo, and Apollo was the god of physic. The Jews, who changed BEELZEBUB into BEELZEBUL, "god of a dunghill," perhaps had a reference to the Greek of PYTHO, which signifies PUTREFIED. In Scripture Beelzebub is called "the prince of devils," Matt. xii, 24; Luke xi, 15; merely, it would seem, through the application of the name of the chief idol of the Heathen world to the prince of evil spirits. This was natural, since the Jews were taught in their own Scriptures to consider all the idols of the Heathens "devils." Those commentators who think that the idol of Ekron himself is intended, have indulged in an improbable fancy. See Hornet.

BAAL ZEPHON, or THE GOD OF THE WATCH TOWER, was probably the temple of some idol, which served at the same time for a place of observation for the neighbouring sea and country, and a beacon to the travellers by either. It was situated on a cape or promontory on the eastern side of the western or Heroopolitan branch of the Red Sea, near its northern extremity, over against Pihahiroth, or the opening in the mountains which led from the desert, on the side of Egypt, to the Red Sea.

BAASHA, the son of Ahijah, commander-in-chief of the armies belonging to Nadab, the son of Jeroboam, king of Israel. Baasha killed his master treacherously at the siege of Gibbethon, a city of the Philistines, A. M. 3051, and usurped the crown, which he possessed twenty-four years, 1 Kings xv, 27, &c. And, to secure himself in his usurpation, he massacred all the relatives of his predecessor; which barbarous action proved the accomplishment of the prophecy denounced against the house of Jeroboam by Ahijah, the prophet, 1 Kings xiv, 1, &c.

BABEL, the tower and city founded by the descendants of Noah in the plain of Shinar. The different tribes descended from Noah were here collected, and from this point were dispersed, through the confusion of their language. The time when this tower was built is differently stated in the Hebrew and Samaritan chronologies. The former fixes it in the year 101 after the flood, which Mr. Faber thinks encumbered with insuperable difficulties. This writer then goes on to show, that the chronology of the Samaritan Pentateuch reconciles every date, and surmounts every difficulty. It represents Shem as dying nearly a century and a half before the death of Peleg, instead of more than that number of years afterward, and almost four centuries and a half before the death of Abraham; whom, in accordance with the history, it makes to survive his father Terah precisely a hundred years. It removes the difficulties with which the Hebrew chronology invests the whole history, by giving time, while it allows the dispersion to have taken place in the latter part of Peleg's life, for the thirteen sons of his younger brother Joktan to have become heads of families; for Noah and his sons to have died, as it is proved they must have done, prior to the emigration from Armenia; for Nimrod, instead of being a boy, to have been of an age suitable to his exploits, and to have acquired the sovereign command, not, in the face of all probability, while the four great patriarchs were living, but after their decease; and for the families of mankind to have multiplied sufficiently to undertake the stupendous work of the tower. It explains also the silence respecting Shem in the history of Abraham, by making the former die in Armenia four hundred and forty years before the latter was born, instead of surviving him thirty-five years; and, lastly, it makes sacred history accord with profane; the Babylonic history of Berosus, and the old records consulted by Epiphanius, both placing the death of Noah and his sons before the emigration from Armenia.

The sum of the whole is as follows: All the descendants of Noah remained in Armenia in peaceable subjection to the patriarchal religion and government during the lifetime of the four royal patriarchs, or till about the beginning of the sixth century after the flood; when, gradually falling off from the pure worship of God, and from their allegiance to the respective heads of families, and seduced by the schemes of the ambitious Nimrod, and farther actuated by a restless disposition, or a desire for a more fertile country, they migrated in a body southwards, till they reached the plains of Shinar, probably about sixty years after the death of Shem. Here, under the command of their new leader, and his dominant military and sacerdotal Cuthites, by whom the original scheme of idolatry, the groundwork of which was probably laid in Armenia, was now perfected; and, with the express view to counteract the designs of the Almighty in their dispersion into different countries, they began to build the city and tower, and set up a banner which should serve as a mark of national union, and concentrate them in one unbroken empire; when they were defeated and dispersed by the miraculous confusion of tongues. All this probably occupied the farther space of twenty or twenty-one years; making eighty-one from the death of Shem, and five hundred and eighty-three after the flood. All of which also will come within the life of Peleg, who, according to the Samaritan Pentateuch, died in the year 640. The tower of Belus in Babylon, mentioned by Herodotus, was probably either the original tower of Babel repaired, or it was constructed upon its massive foundations. The remains of this tower are still to be seen, and are thus described by Captain Mignan, in his Travels in Chaldea:--

"At day light I departed for the ruins, with a mind absorbed by the objects which I had seen yesterday. An hour's walk, indulged in intense reflection, brought me to the grandest and most gigantic northern mass, on the eastern bank of the Euphrates, and distant about four miles and a half from the eastern suburb of Hillah. It is called by the natives, EL MUJELLIBAH, 'the overturned;' also HAROOT and MAROOT, from a tradition handed down, with little deviation, from time immemorial, that near the foot of the ruin there is a well, invisible to mortals, in which those rebellious angels were condemned by God to be hung with their heels upward, until the day of judgment, as a punishment for their wickedness. This solid mound, which I consider, from its situation and magnitude, to be the remains of the Tower of Babel, (an opinion likewise adopted by that venerable and highly distinguished geographer, Major Rennell,) is a vast oblong square, composed of kiln-burnt and sun-dried bricks, rising irregularly to the height of one hundred and thirty-nine feet, at the south-west; whence it slopes toward the north-east to a depth of one hundred and ten feet. Its sides face the four cardinal points. I measured them carefully, and the following is the full extent of each face: that to the north, along the visible face, is two hundred and seventy-four yards; to the south, two hundred and fifty-six yards; to the east, two hundred and twenty-six yards; and to the west, two hundred and forty yards. The summit is an uneven flat, strewed with broken and unbroken bricks, the perfect ones measuring thirteen inches square, by three thick. Many exhibited the arrow-headed character, which appeared remarkably fresh. Pottery, bitumen, vitrified and petrified brick, shells, and glass, were all equally abundant. The principal materials composing this ruin are, doubtless, mud bricks baked in the sun, and mixed up with straw. It is not difficult to trace brick work along each front, particularly at the south-west angle, which is faced by a wall, composed partly of kiln-burnt brick, that in shape exactly resembles a watch tower or small turret. On its summit there are still considerable traces of erect building; at the western end is a circular mass of sold brick work, sloping toward the top, and rising from a confused heap of rubbish. The chief material forming this fabric appeared similar to that composing the ruin called Akercouff, a mixture of chopped straw, with slime used as cement; and regular layers of unbroken reeds between the horizontal courses of the bricks. The base is greatly injured by time and the elements; particularly to the south-east, where it is cloven into a deep furrow from top to bottom. The sides of the ruin exhibit hollows worn partly by the weather, but more generally formed by the Arabs, who are incessantly digging for bricks, and hunting for antiquities."

BABYLON, 2 Kings xxiv, 1. The capital of Chaldea, built by Nimrod, Gen. x, 10. It was under Nebuchadnezzar that Babylon, then become the seat of universal empire, is supposed to have acquired that extent and magnificence, and that those stupendous works were completed which rendered it the wonder of the world and of posterity: and accordingly, this prince, then the most potent on the earth, arrogated to himself the whole glory of its erection; and in the pride of his heart exclaimed, "Is not this great Babylon that I have built?" The city at this period stood on both sides of the river, which intersected it in the middle. It was, according to the least computation, that of Diodorus Siculus, 45 miles in circumference; and according to Herodotus, the older author of the two, 60 miles. Its shape was that of a square, traversed each way by 25 principal streets; which of course intersected each other, dividing the city into 626 squares. These streets were terminated at each end by gates of brass, of prodigious size and strength, with a smaller one opening toward the river. The walls, from the most moderate accounts, were 75 feet in height and 32 in breadth; while Herodotus makes them 300 in height and 75 in breadth: which last measurement, incredible as it may seem, is worthy of credit, as Herodotus is much the oldest author who describes them, and who gives their original height; whereas, those who follow him in their accounts of these stupendous walls, describe them as they were after they had been taken down to the less elevation by Darius Hystaspes. They were built of brick, cemented with bitumen instead of mortar; and were encompassed by a broad and deep ditch, lined with the same materials, as were also the banks of the river in its course through the city: the inhabitants descending to the water by steps through the smaller brazen gates before mentioned. The houses were three or four stories high, separated from each other by small courts or gardens, with open spaces and even fields interspersed over the immense area enclosed within the walls. Over the river was a bridge, connecting the two halves of the city, which stood, the one on its eastern, and the other on its western, bank; the river running nearly north and south. The bridge was 5 furlongs in length, and 30 feet in breadth, and had a palace at each end, with, it is said, a subterraneous passage beneath the river, from one to the other: the work of Semiramis. Within the city was the temple of Belus, or Jupiter, which Herodotus describes as a square of two stadia, or a quarter of a mile: in the midst of which arose the celebrated tower, to which both the same writer, and Strabo, give an elevation of one stadium, or 660 feet; and the same measure at its base; the whole being divided into eight separate towers, one above another, of decreasing dimensions to the summit; where stood a chapel, containing a couch, table, and other things of gold. Here the principal devotions were performed; and over this, on the highest platform of all, was the observatory, by the help of which the Babylonians arrived to such perfection in astronomy, that Calisthenes the philosopher, who accompanied Alexander to Babylon, found astronomical observations for 1903 years backwards from that time; which reach as high as the 115th year after the flood. On either side of the river, according to Diodorus, adjoining to the bridge, was a palace; that on the western bank being by much the larger. This palace was eight miles in circumference, and strongly fortified with three walls one within another. Within it were the celebrated pensile or hanging gardens, enclosed in a square of 400 feet. These gardens were raised on terraces, supported by arches, or rather by piers, laid over with broad flat stones; the arch appearing to be unknown to the Babylonians: which courses of piers rose above one another, till they reached the level of the top of the city walls. On each terrace or platform, a deep layer of mould was laid, in which flowers, shrubs and trees were planted; some of which are said to have reached the height of 50 feet. On the highest level was a reservoir, with an engine to draw water up from the river by which the whole was watered. This novel and astonishing structure, the work of a monarch who knew not how to create food for his own pampered fancy, or labour for his debased subjects or unhappy captives, was undertaken to please his wife Amyitis; that she might see an imitation of the hills and woods of her native country, Media.

Yet, while in the plenitude of its power, and, according to the most accurate chronologers, 160 years before the foot of an enemy had entered it, the voice of an enemy had entered it, the voice of prophecy pronounced the doom of the mighty and unconquered Babylon. A succession of ages brought it gradually to the dust; and the gradation of its fall is marked till it sinks at last into utter desolation. At a time when nothing but magnificence was around this city, emphatically called the great, fallen Babylon was delineated by the pencil of inspiration exactly as every traveller now describes its ruins.

The immense fertility of Chaldea, which retained also the name of Babylonia till after the Christian æra, corresponded with the greatness of Babylon. It was the most fertile region of the whole east. Babylonia was one vast plain, adorned and enriched by the Euphrates and the Tigris, from which, and from the numerous canals that intersected the country from the one river to the other, water was distributed over the fields by manual labour and by hydraulic machines, giving rise, in that warm climate and rich exhaustless soil, to an exuberance of produce without a known parallel, over so extensive a region, either in ancient or modern times. Herodotus states, that he knew not how to speak of its wonderful fertility, which none but eye witnesses would credit; and, though writing in the language of Greece, itself a fertile country, he expresses his own consciousness that his description of what he actually saw would appear to be improbable, and to exceed belief. Such was the "Chaldees' excellency," that it departed not on the first conquest, nor on the final extinction of its capital, but one metropolis of Assyria arose after another in the land of Chaldea, when Babylon had ceased to be "the glory of kingdoms."

2. Manifold are the prophecies respecting Babylon and the land of the Chaldeans; and the long lapse of ages has served to confirm their fulfilment in every particular, and to render it at last complete. The judgments of Heaven are not casual, but sure; they are not arbitrary, but righteous. And they were denounced against the Babylonians, and the inhabitants of Chaldea, expressly because of their idolatry, tyranny, oppression, pride, covetousness, drunkenness, falsehood, and other wickedness. The burden of Babylon, which Isaiah the son of Amos did see: "The noise of a multitude in the mountains, like as of a great people: a tumultuous noise of the kingdoms of nations gathered together: the Lord of Hosts mustereth the host of the battle. They come from a far country, from the end of heaven, even the Lord and the weapons of his indignation, to destroy the whole land. Behold, the day of the Lord cometh, cruel both with wrath and fierce anger, to lay the land desolate: and he shall destroy the sinners thereof out of it. Babylon, the glory of kingdoms, the beauty of the Chaldees' excellency, shall be as when God overthrew Sodom and Gomorrah. It shall never be inhabited, neither shall it be dwelt in from generation to generation: neither shall the Arabian pitch tent there: neither shall the shepherds make their fold there. But wild beasts of the desert shall lie there: and their houses shall be full of doleful creatures; and owls shall dwell there, and satyrs shall dance there. And the wild beasts of the islands shall cry in their desolate houses, and dragons in their pleasant palaces." "Thou shalt take up this proverb against the king of Babylon, and say, How hath the oppressor ceased! the golden city ceased! Thy pomp is brought down to the grave, and the noise of thy viols: the worm is spread under thee, and the worms cover thee. Thou shalt be brought down to hell, to the sides of the pit. Thou art cast out of the grave like an abominable branch.--I will cut off from Babylon the name, and remnant, the son, and nephew, saith the Lord. I will also make it a possession for the bittern, and pools of water: and I will sweep it with the besom of destruction, saith the Lord of Hosts." "Babylon is fallen, is fallen; and all the graven images of her gods he hath broken unto the ground." "Thus saith the Lord, that saith unto the deep, Be dry; and I will dry up thy rivers: that saith of Cyrus, He is my shepherd, and shall perform all my pleasure,--and I will loose the loins of kings, to open before him the two-leaved gates; and the gates shall not be shut." "Bel boweth down," &c. "Come down, and sit in the dust, O virgin daughter of Babylon: sit on the ground, there is no throne, O daughter of the Chaldeans. Sit thou silent, and get thee into darkness, O daughter of the Chaldeans; for thou shalt no more be called the lady of kingdoms."

Many other prophecies against Babylon, and the whole land of Chaldea, are found in the Old Testament; and though the limits of this article will only allow a reference to be made to the exact fulfilment of a few, there is not one of the great number of predictions on record, the accomplishment of which has not been remarked by numerous writers, and more especially by those who have visited the spot. For, though for many centuries the site of Babylon was unknown, or the ruins of other Chaldean cities mistaken for its remains, its true situation and present condition have been, within a few years, satisfactorily ascertained, and accurately described, by several most intelligent and enterprising travellers.

When in the plenitude of its greatness, splendour and strength, Babylon first yielded to the arms of Cyrus, whose name, and the manœuvre by which the city was taken, were mentioned by Isaiah nearly two hundred years before the event; which was also predicted by Jeremiah: "Go up, O Elam, (or Persia,) besiege, O Media. The Lord hath raised up the spirit of the kings of the Medes, for his device is against Babylon, to destroy it." The kings of Persia and Media, prompted by a common interest, freely entered into a league against Babylon, and with one accord entrusted the command of their united armies to Cyrus, the relative and eventually the successor of them both.--But the taking of Babylon was not reserved for these kingdoms alone: other nations had to be "prepared against her." "Set up a standard in the land; blow the trumpet among the nations, prepare the nations against her, call together against her the kingdoms of Ararat, Minni, and Aschenaz: Lo, I will raise and cause to come up against Babylon an assembly of great nations from the north country," &c. Cyrus subdued the Armenians, who had revolted against Media, spared their king, bound them over anew to their allegiance, by kindness rather than by force, and incorporated their army with his own.--"The mighty men of Babylon have foreborne to fight. They have remained in their holds; their might hath failed, they became as women." So dispirited became its people, that Babylon, which had made the world to tremble, was long besieged, without making any effort to drive off the enemy. But, possessed of provisions for twenty years, which in their timid caution they had plentifully stored, they derided Cyrus from their impregnable walls, within which they remained. Their profligacy, their wickedness and false confidence were unabated; they continued to live carelessly in pleasures: and Babylon the great, unlike to many a small fortress and unwalled town, made not one struggle to regain its freedom or to be rid of the foe.--Much time having been lost, and no progress being made in the siege, the anxiety of Cyrus was strongly excited, and he was reduced to great perplexity, when at last it was suggested and immediately determined to divert the course of the Euphrates. And while the unconscious and reckless citizens were engaged in dancing and merriment, the river was suddenly turned into the lake, the trench, and the canals; and the Persians, both foot and horse, so soon as the subsiding of the water permitted, entered by its channel, and were followed by the allies in array, along the dry part of the river. "I will dry up thy sea, and make thy springs dry. That saith to the deep, Be dry, I will dry up thy rivers."--One detachment was placed where the river first enters the city, and another where it leaves it. And "one post did run to meet another, and one messenger to meet another, to show the king of Babylon that his city is taken at the end, and that the passages are shut." "They were taken," says Herodotus, "by SURPRISE; and such is the extent of the city, that, as the inhabitants themselves affirm, they who lived in the extremities were made prisoners before any alarm was communicated to the centre of the place," where the palace stood. Thus a "snare was laid for Babylon, it was taken, and it was not aware; it was found and also caught; for it had sinned against the Lord. How is the praise of the whole earth surprised!"--"In their heat I will make their feasts, and I will make them drunken, that they may rejoice and sleep a perpetual sleep, and not wake, saith the Lord. I will bring them down like lambs to the slaughter," &c. "I will make drunken her princes and her wise men, her captains and her rulers, and her mighty men, and they shall sleep a perpetual sleep," &c. Cyrus, as the night drew on, stimulated his assembled troops to enter the city, because in that night of general revel within the walls, many of them were asleep, many drunk, and confusion universally prevailed. On passing, without obstruction or hinderance, into the city, the Persians, slaying some, putting others to flight, and joining with the revellers, as if slaughter had been merriment, hastened by the shortest way to the palace, and reached it ere yet a messenger had told the king that his city was taken. The gates of the palace, which was strongly fortified, were shut. The guards stationed before them, were DRINKING beside a blazing light, when the Persians rushed impetuously upon them. A louder and altered clamour, no longer joyous, caught the ear of the inmates of the palace, and the bright light showed them the work of destruction, without revealing its cause. And not aware of the presence of an enemy in the midst of Babylon, the king himself, (who had been roused from his revelry by the hand writing on the wall,) excited by the warlike tumult at the gates, commanded those within to examine from whence it arose; and according to the same word, by which "the gates" (leading from the river to the city) "were not shut, the loins of kings were loosed to open before Cyrus the two-leaved gates" of the palace. The eager Persians sprang in. "The king of Babylon heard the report of them; anguish took hold of him;" he and all who were about him perished; God had "numbered" his kingdom and finished it; it was "divided," and given to the Medes and Persians; the lives of the Babylonian princes, and lords, and rulers, and captains, closed with that night's festival; the drunken slept "a perpetual sleep, and did not wake."--"I will fill thee with men as with caterpillars." Not only did the Persian army enter with ease as caterpillars, together with all the nations that had come up against Babylon, but they seemed also as numerous. Cyrus, after the capture of the city, made a great display of his cavalry in the presence of the Babylonians, and in the midst of Babylon. Four thousand guards stood before the palace gates, and two thousand on each side. These advanced as Cyrus approached; two thousand spearmen followed them. These were succeeded by four square masses of Persian cavalry, each consisting of ten thousand men: and to these again were added, in their order, the Median, Armenian, Hyrcanian, Caducian, and Sacian horsemen,--all, as before, "riding upon horses, every man in array,"--with lines of chariots, four abreast, concluding the train of the numerous hosts. Cyrus afterward reviewed, at Babylon, the whole of his army, consisting of one hundred and twenty thousand horse, two thousand chariots, and six hundred thousand foot. Babylon, which was taken when not aware, and within whose walls no enemy, except a captive, had been ever seen, was thus "filled with men as with caterpillars," as if there had not been a wall around it. The Scriptures do not relate the manner in which Babylon was taken, nor do they ever allude to the exact fulfilment of the prophecies. But there is, in every particular, a strict coincidence between the predictions of the prophets and the historical narratives, both of Herodotus and Xenophon.

3. Every step in the progress of the decline of Babylon was the accomplishment of a prophecy. Conquered, for the first time, by Cyrus, it was afterward reduced from an imperial to a tributary city. "Come down and sit in the dust, O daughter of Babylon: sit on the ground, there is no throne, O daughter of the Chaldeans." After the Babylonians rebelled against Darius, the walls were reduced in height, and all the gates destroyed. "The wall of Babylon shall fall, her walls are thrown down."--Xerxes, after his ignominious retreat from Greece, rifled the temples of Babylon, the golden images alone of which were estimated at 20,000,000*l*, beside treasures of vast amount. "I will punish Bel in Babylon, and I will bring forth out of his mouth that which he has swallowed up; I will do judgment upon the graven images of Babylon."--Alexander the Great attempted to restore it to its former glory, and designed to make it the metropolis of a universal empire. But while the building of the temple of Belus, and the reparation of the embankments of the Euphrates, were actually carrying on, the conqueror of the world died, at the commencement of this his last undertaking, in the height of his power, and in the flower of his age. "Take balm for her pain, if so be that she may be healed. We would have healed Babylon, but she is not healed." The building of the neighbouring city of Seleucia was the chief cause of the decline of Babylon, and drained it of a great part of its population. And at a later period, or about 130 years before the birth of Christ, Humerus, a Parthian governor, who was noted as excelling all tyrants in cruelty, exercised great severities on the Babylonians; and having burned the forum and some of the temples, and destroyed the fairest parts of the city, reduced many of the inhabitants to slavery on the slightest pretexts, and caused them, together with all their households, to be sent into Media. "They shall remove, they shall depart, both man and beast." The "golden city" thus gradually verged, for centuries, toward poverty and desolation. Notwithstanding that Cyrus resided chiefly at Babylon, and sought to reform the government, and remodel the manners of the Babylonians, the succeeding kings of Persia preferred, as the seat of empire, Susa, Persepolis, or Ecbatana, situated in their own country: and in like manner the successors of Alexander did not attempt to complete his purpose of restoring Babylon to its preeminence and glory; but, after the subdivision of his mighty empire, the very kings of Assyria, during their temporary residence even in Chaldea, deserted Babylon, and dwelt in Seleucia. And thus the foreign inhabitants, first Persians and afterward Greeks, imitating their sovereigns by deserting Babylon, acted as if they verily had said, "Forsake her, and let us go every man unto his own country; for her judgment is reached unto heaven, and is lifted up even to the skies."

4. But kindred judgments, the issue of common crimes, rested on the land of Chaldea, as well as on its doomed metropolis. "They come from a far country, from the end of the earth, to destroy the whole land. Many nations and great kings shall serve themselves of thee also," &c. The Persians, the Macedonians, the Parthians, the Romans, the Saracens, and the Turks, are the chief of the many nations who have unscrupulously and unsparingly "served themselves" of the land of the Chaldeans: and Cyrus and Darius, kings of Persia; Alexander the Great; and Seleucus, king of Assyria; Demetrius and Antiochus the Great; Tragan, Severus, Julian, and Heraclius, emperors of Rome; the victorious Omar, the successor of Mohammed; Holagou, and Tamerlane,--are "great kings" who successively subdued or desolated Chaldea, or exacted from it tribute to such an extent, as scarcely any other country ever paid to a single conqueror. And though the names of some of these nations were unknown to the Babylonians, and unheard of in the world at the time of the prophecy, most of these "many nations and great kings" need now but to be named, to show that, in local relation to Chaldea, "they came from the utmost border, from the coasts of the earth."--"I will punish the land of the Chaldeans, and will make it perpetual desolations; cut off the sower from Babylon, and him that handleth the sickle in the time of harvest. A drought is on her waters, and they shall be dried up. Behold the hinder-most of the nations, a dry land and a desert." The land of the Chaldeans was indeed made--perpetual, or long continued, desolation. Ravaged and spoiled for ages, the Chaldees' excellency finally disappeared, and the land became desolate, as still it remains. Rauwolff, who passed through it in 1574, describes the country as bare, and "so dry and barren that it cannot be tilled." And the most recent travellers all concur in describing it in similar terms. On the one side, near to the site of Opis, "the country all around," says Mr. Buckingham, "appears to be one wide desert, of sandy and barren soil, thinly scattered over with brushwood and tufts of reedy grass." On the other, between Bussorah and Bagdad, "immediately on either bank of the Tigris," observes Mignan, "is the UNTRODDEN DESERT. The absence of all cultivation, the sterile, arid, and wild character of the whole scene, formed a contrast to the rich and delightful accounts delineated in Scripture. The natives, in travelling over these pathless deserts, are compelled to explore their way by the stars." "The whole country between Bagdad and Hillah is a perfectly flat and (with the exception of a few spots as you approach the latter place) UNCULTIVATED WASTE. That it was at some former period in a far different state, is evident from the number of canals by which it is traversed, now DRY and neglected; and the quantity of heaps of earth covered with fragments of brick and broken tiles, which are seen in every direction, the indisputable traces of former population. At present the only inhabitants of the tract are the Sobeide Arabs. Around, as far as the eye can reach is a TRACKLESS DESERT."--"Her cities are desolations." The course of the Tigris through Babylonia, instead of being adorned with cities, is marked with the sites of

"ancient ruins." Sitace, Sabata, Narisa, Fuchera, Sendia, "no longer exist." A succession of longitudinal mounds, crossed at right angles by others, mark the supposed site of Artemita, or Destagered. Its once luxuriant gardens are covered with grass; and a higher mound distinguishes "the royal residence" from the ancient streets. "Extensive ridges and mountains, (near to Houmania,) varying in height and extent, are seen branching in every direction." A wall, with sixteen bastions, is the only memorial of Apollonia. The once magnificent Seleucia is now a scene of desolation. There is not a single entire edifice, but the country is strewed for miles with fragments of decayed buildings. "As far," says Major Keppel, "as the eye could reach, the horizon presented a broken line of mounds; the whole of this place was a desert flat." On the opposite bank of the Tigris, where Ctesiphon its rival stood, beside fragments of walls and broken masses of brick work, and remains of vast structures encumbered with heaps of earth, there is one magnificent monument of antiquity "in a remarkably perfect state of preservation," "a large and noble pile of building, the front of which presents to view a wall three hundred feet in length, adorned with four rows of arched recesses, with a central arch, in span eighty-six feet, and above a hundred feet high, supported by walls sixteen feet thick, and leading to a hall which extends to the depth of a hundred and fifty-six feet," the width of the building. A great part of the back wall, and of the roof, is broken down; but that which remains "still appears much larger than Westminster Abbey." It is supposed to have been the lofty palace of Chosroes; but there desolation now reigns. "On the site of Ctesiphon," says Mignan, "the smallest insect under heaven would not find a single blade of grass wherein to hide itself, nor one drop of water to allay its thirst." In the rear of the palace, and attached to it, are mounds two miles in circumference, indicating the utter desolation of buildings, formed to minister to luxury.

5. But let us come to the fulfilment of these wonderful prophecies in the present condition of Babylon itself, as described by those who have most recently visited it.

"Babylon shall become heaps." Babylon the glory of kingdoms is now the greatest of ruins. "Immense tumuli of temples, palaces, and habitations of every description," are every where seen, and form "long and varied lines of ruins," which, in some places, says Sir R. K. Porter, "rather resemble natural hills than MOUNDS which cover the remains of great and splendid edifices." These buildings, which were once the labour of slaves and the pride of kings, are now misshapen heaps of rubbish. "The whole face of the country," observes Rich, "is covered with vestiges of building, in some places consisting of brick walls surprisingly fresh, in others, merely a VAST SUCCESSION OF MOUNDS of rubbish, of such indeterminate figures, variety, and extent, as to involve the person who should have formed any theory in inextricable confusion."--"Let nothing of her be left." "Vast heaps constitute ALL THAT NOW REMAINS of ancient Babylon," says Rich. All its grandeur is departed; all its treasures have been spoiled; all its excellence has utterly vanished; the very heaps are searched for bricks, when nothing else can be found; even these are NOT LEFT, wherever they can be taken away; and Babylon has for ages been "a quarry above ground," ready to the hand of every successive despoiler. Without the most remote allusion to this prophecy, Captain Mignan describes a mound attached to the palace, ninety yards in breadth by half that height, the whole of which is deeply furrowed, in the same manner as the generality of the mounds. "The ground is extremely soft, and tiresome to walk over, and appears COMPLETELY EXHAUSTED of all its building materials; NOTHING NOW IS LEFT, save one towering hill, the earth of which is mixed with FRAGMENTS of broken brick, red varnished pottery, tile, bitumen, mortar, glass, shells, and pieces of mother of pearl,"--worthless fragments, of no value to the poorest. "From thence shall she be taken, let nothing of her be left." While the workmen "cast her up as heaps" while excavating for bricks, that they may "take" them "from thence," and that "nothing may be left;" they labour more than trebly in the fulfilment of prophecy: for the numerous and deep excavations form pools of water, on the over-flowing of the Euphrates, and, annually filled, they are not dried up throughout the year. "Deep cavities are also formed by the Arabs, when digging for hidden treasure." Thus "the ground," says Buckingham, "is sometimes covered with pools of water in the hollows."

"Sit in the dust, sit on the ground, O daughter of the Chaldeans." The surface of the mounds which form all that remains of Babylon, consists of decomposed buildings, reduced to dust; and over all the ancient streets and habitations, there is literally nothing but the dust of the ground on which to sit.--"Thy nakedness shall be uncovered." "Our path," says Captain Mignan, "lay through the great mass of ruined heaps on the site of 'shrunken Babylon;' and I am perfectly incapable of conveying an adequate idea of the dreary, lonely nakedness that appeared before me."--"Sit thou silent, and get thee into darkness." "There reigns throughout the ruins," says Sir R. K. Porter, "a silence profound as the grave." "Babylon is now a silent scene, a sublime solitude."--"It shall never be inhabited, nor dwelt in from generation to generation." From Rauwolff's testimony it appears that, in the sixteenth century, "there was not a house to be seen." And now "the eye wanders over a barren desert, in which the ruins are nearly the only indication that it had ever been inhabited." "It is impossible," adds Major Keppel, "to behold this scene and not to be reminded how exactly the predictions of Isaiah and Jeremiah have been fulfilled, even in the appearance Babylon was doomed to present, that 'she should never be inhabited;' that 'the Arabian should not pitch his tent there;' that she should 'become heaps;' that her cities should be 'a desolation, a dry land, and a wilderness.'" "Babylon is spurned alike by the heel of the Ottomans, the Israelites, and the sons of Ishmael." It is "a tenantless and desolate metropolis," remarks Mignan. "It shall not be inhabited, but be wholly desolate. Neither shall the Arabian pitch tent there, neither shall the shepherds make their folds there." It was prophesied of Ammon that it should be a stable for camels and a couching place for flocks; and of Philistia, that it should be cottages for shepherds, and a pasture of flocks. But Babylon was to be visited with a far greater desolation, and to become unfit or unsuited even for such a purpose; and that neither a tent would be pitched there, even by an Arab, nor a fold made by a shepherd, implies the last degree of solitude and desolation. "It is common in these parts for shepherds to make use of ruined edifices to shelter their flocks in." But Babylon is an exception. Instead of taking the bricks from thence, the shepherd might very readily erect a defence from wild beasts, and make a fold for his flock amidst the heaps of Babylon; and the Arab who fearlessly traverses it by day, might pitch his tent by night. But neither the one nor the other could now be persuaded to remain a single night among the ruins. The superstitious dread of evil spirits, far more than the natural terror of the wild beasts, effectually prevents them. Captain Mignan was accompanied by six Arabs, completely armed; but he "could not induce them to remain toward night, from the apprehension of evil spirits. It is impossible to eradicate this idea from the minds of this people, who are very deeply imbued with superstition."

"Wild beasts of the deserts shall lie there, and their houses shall be full of doleful creatures; and owls shall dwell there, and satyrs (goats) shall dance there," &c. "There are many dens of wild beasts in various parts. And while the lower excavations are often pools of water, in most of the cavities are numbers of bats and owls." The king of the forest now ranges over the site of that Babylon which Nebuchadnezzar built for his own glory. And the temple of Belus, the greatest work of man, is now like unto a natural den of lions. Two or three majestic lions were seen upon its heights by Sir Robert Ker Porter, as he was approaching it; and "the broad prints of their feet were left plain in the clayey soil." Major Keppel saw there a similar foot-print of a lion. It is also the unmolested retreat of jackalls, hyenas, and other noxious animals. Wild beasts are numerous at the Mujelibé, as well as on Birs Nimrood. "The mound," says Kinneir, "was full of large holes: we entered some of them, and found them strewed with the carcasses and skeletons of animals recently killed. The ordure of wild beasts was so strong, that prudence got the better of curiosity; for we had no doubt as to the savage nature of the inhabitants. Our guides, indeed, told us, that all the ruins abounded in lions, and other wild beasts: so literally has the divine prediction been fulfilled, that wild beasts of the deserts should lie there, and their houses be full of doleful creatures; that the wild beasts of the islands should cry in their desolate houses."

"The sea is come upon Babylon. She is covered with the multitude of the waves thereof." The traces of the western bank of the Euphrates are now no longer discernible. The river overflows unrestrained; and the very ruins, with "every appearance of the embankment," have been swept away. "The ground there is low and marshy, and presents not the slightest vestige of former buildings, of any description whatever." "Morasses and ponds," says Porter, "tracked the ground in various parts. For a long time after the general subsiding of the Euphrates, great part of this plain is little better than a swamp," &c. "The ruins of Babylon are then inundated, so as to render many parts of them inaccessible, by converting the valleys among them into morasses." But while Babylon is thus "covered with the multitude of waves, and the waters come upon it;" yet, in striking contrast and seeming contradiction to such a feature of desolation, (like the formation of "pools of water," from the "casting up of heaps,") are the elevated sunburnt ruins, which the waters do not overflow, and the "dry waste" and "parched and burning plain," on which the heaps of Babylon lie, equally prove that it is "a desert, a dry land, and a wilderness." One part, even on the western side of the river, is "low and marshy, and another," says Mignan, "an arid desert."

Many other striking particulars might be collected; and we may conclude in the words of Mr. Keith, from whose work on the prophecies several of the above particulars have been extracted:--"Is it possible that there can be any attestation of the truth of prophecy, if it be not witnessed here? Is there any spot on earth which has undergone a more complete transformation? 'The records of the human race,' it has been said with truth, 'do not present a contrast more striking than that between the primeval magnificence of Babylon and its long desolation.' Its ruins have of late been carefully and scrupulously examined by different natives of Britain, of unimpeached veracity; and the result of every research is a more striking demonstration of the literal accomplishment of every prediction. How few spots are there on earth of which we have so clear and faithful a picture as prophecy gave to fallen Babylon at a time when no spot on earth resembled it less than its present desolate solitary site! or could any prophecies respecting any single place have been more precise, or wonderful, or numerous, or true, or more gradually accomplished throughout many generations? And when they look at what Babylon was, and what it is, and perceive the minute realization of them all, may not nations learn wisdom, may not tyrants tremble, and may not skeptics think?"

The reasons why prophecies so numerous and particular were recorded concerning Babylon, appear to have been, 1. That Babylon was the great oppressor of the Jews. 2. That it was the type of all the powerful persecuting enemies of the church of God, especially of Rome; and in its fate they may read their own. 3. That the accomplishment of prophecy in the destruction of so eminent an empire might give a solemn testimony to the truth of the Scriptures to the whole earth, and to all ages.

BACKSLIDING, a falling off, or defection in matters of religion; an apostasy, Acts xxi, 21; 2 Thess. ii, 3; 1 Tim. iv, 1. This may be either partial or complete: partial, when it is in the heart, as Prov. xiv, 14; complete, as that described in Heb. vi, 4, &c; x, 6, &c. On the latter passage Chrysostom observes, "When a house has a strong foundation, suppose an arch fall, some of the beams break, or a wall decline, while the foundation is good, these breaches may be repaired; so in religion, whilst a person maintains the true doctrines, and remains on the firm rock, though he fall, true repentance may restore him to the favour and image of God: but as in a house, when the foundation is bad, nothing can save the building from ruin; so when heretical doctrines are admitted for a foundation, nothing can save the professor from destruction." It is important in interpreting these passages to keep it steadfastly in mind, that the apostasy they speak of is not only MORAL but DOCTRINAL.

BADGER, תחש. This word in a plural form occurs, Exod. xxv, 5; xxvi, 14; xxxv, 7, 23; xxxvi, 19; xxxix, 34; Num. iv, 6, 8, 10–12, 14, 25; Ezek. xvi, 10; and is joined with ערת, skins used for the covering of the tabernacle in the wilderness. The Jewish interpreters are agreed as to its being some animal. Jarchi says it was a beast of many colours, which no more exists. Kimchi holds the same opinion. Aben Ezra thinks it some animal of the bovine kind, of whose skins shoes are made; alluding to Ezek. xvi, 10. Most modern interpreters have taken it to be the badger, and among these our English translators; but, in the first place, the badger is not an inhabitant of Arabia; and there is nothing in its skin peculiarly proper either for covering a tabernacle or making shoes. Hasæus, Michaelis, and others, have laboured to prove that it is the mermaid, or HOMO MARINUS, the TRICHEKUS of Linnæus. Faber, Dathe, and Rosenmuller, think that it is the seal, or sea calf, VITULUS MARINUS, the skin of which is both strong and pliable, and was accounted by the ancients as a most proper outer covering for tents, and was also made into shoes, as Rau has clearly shown. Niebuhr says, "A merchant of Abushahr called DAHASH that fish which the captains in English vessels call porpoise, and the Germans, sea hog. In my voyage from Maskat to Abushahr, I saw a prodigious quantity together near Ras Mussendom, that were all going the same way, and seemed to swim with great vehemence." Bochart thinks that not an ANIMAL, but a COLOUR, was intended, Exodus xxv, 5; so that the covering of the tabernacle was to be azure, or sky blue.

BAG, a purse or pouch, Deut. xxv, 13; 1 Sam. xvii, 40; Luke xii, 33; Job xiv, 17. The money collected in the treasuries of eastern princes was reckoned up in certain equal sums, put into bags and sealed. These are, in some parts of the Levant, called PURSES, where they estimate great expenses by so many purses. The money collected in the temple in the time of Joash, for its reparation, seems, in like manner, to have been told up in bags of equal value; and these were probably delivered sealed to those who paid the workmen, 2 Kings xii, 10. In the east, in the present day, a bag of money passes, for some time at least, currently from hand to hand, under the authority of a banker's seal, without any examination of its contents. See Tobit ix, 5; xi, 16.

BAKING BREAD. Abraham directed Sarah to bake cakes upon the hearth, for the use of the strangers who had visited him, Genesis xviii, 6. Elijah requests the same of the widow of Zarephath, 1 Kings xvii, 13. Amnon the son of David requests Tamar his sister to come and make cakes in his sight, that he might eat at her hand, 2 Sam. xiii, 6. These and other allusions to the preparation of bread will be explained by referring to eastern customs. Rauwolff observes that travellers frequently bake bread in the deserts of Arabia, on the ground heated for that purpose by fire, covering their cakes of bread with ashes and coals, and turning them several times till they are enough. The eastern bread is made in small thin cakes, and is generally eaten new. Sometimes it was however made to keep several days, as the shew bread; and a sort of rusks, or bread for travelling, Joshua ix, 12. The eastern ladies of rank often prepare cakes, pastry, &c, in their own apartments.

BALAAM, a prophet of the city of Pethor, or Bosor, upon the Euphrates, whose intercourse with Balak, king of the Moabites, who sent for him to curse the Israelites, is recorded at large by Moses, Num. xxii-xxiv. It has been a subject of controversy, whether Balaam was a true prophet or a mere diviner, magician, or fortune teller. Origen says that his whole power consisted in magic and cursing. Theodoret is of opinion that Balaam did not consult the Lord, but that he was supernaturally inspired, and constrained to speak against his own inclination. Cyril says that he was a magician, an idolater, and a false prophet, who spoke truth against his will; and St. Ambrose compares him to Caiaphas, who prophesied without being aware of the import of what he said. Jerom seems to have adopted the opinion of the Hebrews; which was, that Balaam knew the true God, erected altars to him, and that he was a true prophet, though corrupted by avarice, Num. xxii, 18. St. Austin and other commentators have inclined to this opinion. Dr. Jortin supposes that Balaam was a worshipper of the true God, and a priest and prophet of great reputation; and that he was sent for by Balak from a notion which generally prevailed, that priests and prophets could sometimes, by prayers and sacrifices duly and skilfully applied, obtain favours from God, and that their imprecations were efficacious. He conceives that the prophet had been accustomed to revelations, and that he used to receive them in visions, or in dreams of the night. It cannot be denied that the Scripture expressly calls him a prophet, 2 Pet. ii, 15, and therefore those are probably right who think that he had once been a good man and a true prophet, till, loving the wages of unrighteousness, and prostituting the honour of his office to covetousness, he apostatized from God, and, betaking himself to idolatrous practices, fell under the delusion of the devil, of whom he learned all his magical enchantments; though at this juncture, when the preservation of his people was concerned, it might be consistent with God's wisdom to appear to him and overrule his mind by the impulse of real revelations. As to what passed between him and his ass, when that animal was miraculously enabled to speak to its master, commentators are divided in their opinions; whether it really and literally happened as Moses relates it, or whether it be an allegory only, or was the mere imagination or vision of Balaam. But St. Peter evidently mentions it as a fact literally and certainly occurring: "the dumb ass, speaking with man's voice, when she forbade the madness of the prophet," 2 Pet. ii, 16. This, it is true, has frequently been made the subject of profane banter by those whose skepticism leads them to scoff at all prodigies.

But how absurd is it to subject a miraculous event to the ordinary rules of reasoning! "Say what you will of the formation of the tongue and jaws being unfit for speaking," says Bishop Newton, "yet an adequate cause is assigned for this wonderful event; for it is expressly said that 'the Lord opened the mouth of the ass;' and who that believes a God, can doubt his power to do this and much more? The miracle was by no means needless or superfluous; it was well adapted to convince Balaam that the mouth and tongue were under God's direction, and that the same divine power which caused the dumb ass to speak contrary to its nature, could, in like manner, make him utter blessings contrary to his inclination. And, accordingly, he was overruled to bless the people, though he came prepared and disposed to curse them; which was the greater miracle of the two; for the ass was merely passive, but Balaam resisted the good motions of God." The prophecy which Balaam delivered concerning Israel on this remarkable occasion, and which is contained in Numbers xxiv, 5–9, has been greatly admired by critics. Bishop Lowth, in particular, remarks that he knows nothing in the whole scope of the Hebrew poetry more exquisite or perfect. "It abounds," says he, "in splendid imagery, copied immediately from the tablet of nature; and is chiefly conspicuous for the glowing elegance of the style, and the form and diversity of the figures."

After his predictions, Balaam returned into his own country; but before he left the land of Moab, as if vexed with his own disappointment in missing the promised reward, and with a purpose of revenging himself on the Israelites, as the cause of it, he instructed the Moabites and Midianites in a wicked scheme, which was to send their daughters into the camp of the Israelites, in order to draw them first into lewdness, and then into idolatry, the certain means of depriving them of the help of that God who protected them. This artifice succeeded; for as the Israelites lay encamped at Shittim, many of them were deluded by these strange women, not only to commit whoredom with them, but to assist at their sacrifices, and worship their god Baal-Peor, Num. xxv, 1–3; xxxi, 16; Mic. vi, 5; 2 Pet. ii, 15; Jude 11; Rev. ii, 14; Deut. xxiii, 4, 5; Joshua xxiv, 9, 10; Neh. xiii, 2. God commanded Moses to avenge this crime. He therefore declared war against the Midianites, killed five of their princes, and a great number of other persons without distinction of age or sex, among whom was Balaam himself.

Moses says that Balaam consulted the Lord, and calls the Lord his God: "I cannot go beyond the commandment of the Lord MY God," Num. xxii, 18. The reason why Balaam calls Jehovah, "MY God" may be, because he was of the posterity of Shem, who maintained the worship of Jehovah, not only in his own person, but among his descendants; so that while the posterity of Ham fell into idolatry, and the posterity of Japhet were settled at a distance in Europe, the Shemites generally, though not universally, retained the worship of God.

BALDNESS is a natural effect of old age, in which period of life the hair of the head, wanting nourishment, falls off, and leaves the head naked. Artificial baldness was used as a token of mourning; it is threatened to the voluptuous daughters of Israel, instead of well set hair, Isaiah iii, 24. See Mic. i, 16; and instances of it occur, Isaiah xv, 2; Jer. xlvii, 5. See Ezek, vii, 18; Amos viii, 10.

The insult offered to Elisha by the young people of Bethel, improperly rendered "little children," who cried out after him, "Go up, thou bald head," may here be noticed. The town of Bethel was one of the principal nurseries of Ahab's idolatry, and the contempt was offered to Elisha in his public character as a prophet of the Lord. If in the expression, "Go up," there was also a reference to the translation of Elijah, as turning it into jest, this was another aggravation of the sin, to which these young people were probably instigated by their parents. The malediction laid upon them by the prophet was not an act of private resentment, but evidently proceeded from prophetic impulse.

BALM, צרי, Gen. xxxvii, 25; xliii, 11; Jer. viii, 22; xlvi, 11; li, 8; Ezek. xxvii, 17. Balm, or balsam, is used with us as a common name for many of those oily resinous substances, which flow spontaneously or by incision, from certain trees or plants, and are of considerable use in medicine and surgery. It serves therefore very properly to express the Hebrew word צרי, which the **LXX** have rendered ῥητίνη, and the ancients have interpreted RESIN indiscriminately.

BALSAM TREE, בעל־שמין; in Arabic, ABUSCHÂM, that is, "father of scent," sweet-scented. According to Mr. Bruce, the BALESSAN, BALSAM, or BALM, is an evergreen shrub, or tree, which grows to about fourteen feet high, spontaneously and without culture in its native country, Azab, and all along the coast to Babelmandel. There were three kinds of balsam extracted from this tree. The first was called OPOBALSAMUM, and was most highly esteemed. It was that which flowed spontaneously, or by means of incision, from the trunk or branches of the tree in summer time. The second was CARPOBALSAMUM, made by expressing the fruit when in maturity. The third, and least esteemed of all, was HYLOBALSAMUM, made by a decoction of the buds and small young twigs. The great value set upon this drug in the east is traced to the earliest ages. The Ishmaelites, or Arabian carriers and merchants, trafficking with the Arabian commodities into Egypt, brought with them צרי as a part of their cargo, Gen. xxxvii, 25; xliii, 11. Josephus, in the history of the antiquities of his country, says that a tree of this balsam was brought to Jerusalem by the queen of Saba, and given among other presents to Solomon, who, as we know from Scripture, was very studious of all sorts of plants, and skilful in the description and distinction of them. And here, indeed, it seems to have been cultivated and to have thriven; so that the place of its origin, through length of time, combined with other reasons, came to be forgotten. Notwithstanding the positive authority of Josephus, and the great probability that attends it, we cannot put it in competition with what we have been told in Scripture, as we have just now seen that the place where it grew, and was sold to merchants, was Gilead in Judea, more than 1730 years before Christ, or 1000 before the queen of Saba; so that in reading the verse, nothing can be plainer than that it had been transplanted into Judea, flourished, and had become an article of commerce in Gilead, long before the period he mentions. "A company of Ishmaelites came from Gilead with their camels, bearing spicery and balm, and myrrh, going to carry it down to Egypt," Gen. xxxvii, 25. Theophrastus, Dioscorides, Pliny, Strabo, Diodorus Siculus, Tacitus, Justin, Solinus, and Serapion, speaking of its costliness and medicinal virtues, all say that this balsam came from Judea. The words of Pliny are, "But to all other odours whatever, the balsam is preferred, produced in no other part but the land of Judea, and even there in two gardens only; both of them belonging to the king, one no more than twenty acres, the other still smaller." The whole valley of Jericho was once esteemed the most fruitful in Judea; and the obstinacy with which the Jews fought here to prevent the balsam trees from falling into the possession of the Romans, attests the importance which was attached to them. This tree Pliny describes as peculiar to the vale of Jericho, and as "more like a vine than a myrtle." It was esteemed so precious a rarity, that both Pompey and Titus carried a specimen to Rome in triumph; and the balsam, owing to its scarcity, sold for double its weight in silver, till its high price led to the practice of adulteration. Justin makes it the chief source of the national wealth. He describes the country in which it grew, as a valley like a garden, environed with continual hills, and, as it were, enclosed with a wall. "The space of the valley contains 200,000 acres, and is called Jericho. In that valley, there is wood as admirable for its fruitfulness as for its delight, for it is intermingled with palm trees and opobalsamum. The trees of the opobalsamum have a resemblance to fir trees; but they are lower, and are planted and husbanded after the manner of vines. On a set season of the year they sweat balsam. The darkness of the place is beside as wonderful as the fruitfulness of it; for although the sun shines no where hotter in the world, there is naturally a moderate and perpetual gloominess of the air." According to Mr. Buckingham, this description is most accurate. "Both the heat and the gloominess," he says, "were observed by us, though darkness would be an improper term to apply to this gloom."

BANGORIAN CONTROVERSY, a controversy that arose with Dr. Hoadly, bishop of Bangor. That prelate, in a sermon preached before George I, asserted that Christ was supreme in his own kingdom; that he had not delegated his power, like temporal lawgivers during their absence, to any persons as his vicegerents or deputies; and that the church of England, as all other national churches, was merely a civil or human institution, established for the purpose of diffusing and perpetuating the knowledge and belief of Christianity. On the meeting of the convocation, a committee was appointed to examine this publication. A heavy censure was passed against it, as tending to subvert all government and discipline in the church of Christ, to reduce his kingdom to a state of anarchy and confusion, and to impugn and impeach the royal supremacy in matters ecclesiastical, and the authority of the legislature to enforce obedience in matters of religion, by severe sanction. To these proceedings a sudden stop was put by proroguing the convocation; but the controversy which had been commenced was continued for several years.

BANNER, an ensign, or standard, used by armies or caravans on their journeys in the eastern countries. The original דגל, is rendered by lexicographers and translators under this word, as a noun, in which form it often occurs, A STANDARD, BANNER; as a verb, once, TO SET UP A BANNER; Psalm xx, 5; as a participle pahul, VEXILLATUS, one distinguished by a banner, the chief; as a participle niphal, bannered, or with banners. The meaning of the root is illustrated by the very ingenious and sensible author of "Observations on Divers Passages of Scripture," who shows, from Pitts and Pococke, that, "as in Arabia and the neighbouring countries, on account of the intense heat of the sun by day, people generally choose to travel in the night; so, to prevent confusion in their large caravans, particularly in the annual one to Mecca, each company, of which the caravan consists, has its distinct portable beacon, which is carried on the top of a pole, and consists of several lights, which are somewhat like iron stoves, into which they put short dry wood, with which some of the camels are loaded. Every company has one of these poles belonging to it; some of which have ten, some twelve, of these lights on their tops, more or less; and they are likewise of different figures, as well as numbers; one, perhaps, in an oval shape; another, triangular, or in the form of an M, or N, &c, so that by these every one knows his respective company. They are carried in the front, and set up in the place where the caravan is to pitch, before that comes up, at some distance from one another. As travelling then in the night must be, generally speaking, more agreeable to a great multitude in that desert, we may believe a compassionate God, for the most part, directed Israel to move in the night. And in consequence, must we not rather suppose the standards of the tribes were movable beacons, like those of the Mecca pilgrims, than flags or any thing of that kind?" This ingenious author seems, however, to forget, 1. That the pillar of fire was with the Israelites to direct their marches. 2. That the Israelites were not a mere caravan, but an army; and, as such, for order, required standards as well by day as by night. See Armies.

BANQUET. The hospitality of the present day in the east exactly resembles that of the remotest antiquity. The parable of the "great supper" is in those countries literally realized. And such was the hospitality of ancient Greece and Rome. When a person provided an entertainment for his friends or neighbours, he sent round a number of servants to invite the guests; these were called VOCATORES by the Romans, and κλητῶρες by the Greeks. The day when the entertainment is to be given is fixed some considerable time before; and in the evening of the day appointed, a messenger comes to bid the guests to the feast. The custom is thus introduced in Luke: "A certain man made a great supper, and bade many; and sent his servant at supper time to say to them that were bidden, Come, for all things are now ready." They were not now asked for the first time; but had already accepted the invitation, when the day was appointed, and were therefore already pledged to attend at the hour when they might be summoned. They were not taken unprepared, and could not in consistency and decency plead any prior engagement. They could not now refuse, without violating their word, and insulting the master of the feast, and, therefore, justly subjected themselves to punishment. The terms of the parable exactly accord with established custom. The Jews did not always follow the same method; sometimes they sent a number of servants different ways among the friends they meant to invite; and at other times, a single male domestic.

The Persians send a deputation to meet their guests: this deputation are called openers of the way; and the more distinguished the persons sent, and the greater the distance to which they go, so much greater is the honour. So it is proclaimed, "Go forth and behold king Solomon, with the crown wherewith his mother crowned him." "The bridegroom cometh, go ye forth to meet him." The names of the persons to be invited were inscribed upon tablets, and the gate was set open to receive those who had obtained them; but to prevent any getting in that had no ticket, only one leaf of the door was left open; and that was strictly guarded by the servants of the family. Those who were admitted had to go along a narrow passage to the room; and after all who had received tickets of admission were assembled, the master of the house rose and shut to the door; and then the entertainment began. The first ceremony, after the guests arrived at the house of entertainment, was the salutation performed by the master of the house, or one appointed in his place. Among the Greeks, this was sometimes done by embracing with arms around; but the most common salutation was by the conjunction of their right hands, the right hand being reckoned a pledge of fidelity and friendship. Sometimes they kissed the lips, hands, knees, or feet, as the person deserved more or less respect. The Jews welcomed a stranger to their house in the same way; for our Lord complains to Simon, that he had given him no kiss, had welcomed him to his table with none of the accustomed tokens of respect.

The custom of reclining was introduced from the nations of the east, and particularly from Persia, where it seems to have been adopted at a very remote period. The Old Testament Scriptures allude to both customs; but they furnish undeniable proofs of the antiquity of sitting. As this is undoubtedly the most natural and dignified posture, so it seems to have been universally adopted by the first generations of men; and it was not till after the lapse of many ages, and when degenerate man had lost much of the firmness of his primitive character, that he began to recline.

The tables were constructed of three different parts or separate tables, making but one in the whole. One was placed at the upper end crossways, and the two others joined to its ends, one on each side, so as to leave an open space between, by which the attendants could readily wait at all the three. Round these tables were placed beds or couches, one to each table; each of these beds was called CLINIUM; and three of these being united, to surround the three tables, made the TRICLINIUM. At the end of each CLINIUM was a footstool, for the convenience of mounting up to it. These beds were formed of mattresses, and supported on frames of wood, often highly ornamented; the mattresses were covered with cloth or tapestry, according to the quality of the entertainer. At the splendid feast which Ahasuerus made for the nobles of his kingdom, beds of silver and gold were placed round the tables; according to a custom in the east of naming a thing from its principal ornament, these must have been couches profusely ornamented with the precious metals. Each guest inclined the superior part of his body upon his left arm, the lower part being stretched out at length, or a little bent; his head was raised up, and his back sometimes supported with pillows. In conversation, those who spoke raised themselves almost upright, supported by cushions. When they ate, they raised themselves on their elbow, and made use of the right hand; which is the reason our Lord mentions the hand of Judas in the singular number: "He that dippeth his hand with me in the dish, the same shall betray me," Matt. xxvi, 23. See Accubation.

When a Persian comes into an assembly, and has saluted the house, he then measures with his eye the place to which his degree of rank entitles him; he straightway wedges himself into the line of guests, without offering any apology for the general disturbance which he produces. It often happens that persons take a higher seat than that to which they are entitled. The Persian scribes are remarkable for their arrogance in this respect, in which they seem to bear a striking resemblance to the Jews of the same profession in the days of our Lord. The master of the entertainment has, however, the privilege of placing any one as high in the rank of the assembly as he may choose. And Mr. Morier saw an instance of it at a public entertainment to which he was invited. When the assembly was nearly full, the governor of Kashan, a man of humble mien, although of considerable rank, came in and seated himself at the lowest place; when the master of the house, after numerous expressions of welcome, pointed with his hand to an upper seat in the assembly, to which he desired him to move, and which he accordingly did. These circumstances furnish a beautiful and striking illustration of the parable which our Lord uttered, when he saw how those that were invited chose the highest places.

Before the Greeks went to an entertainment, they washed and anointed themselves; for it was thought very indecent to appear on such an occasion, defiled with sweat and dust; but they who came off a journey were washed, and clothed with suitable apparel, in the house of the entertainer, before they were admitted to the feast. When Telemachus and Pisistratus arrived at the palace of Menelaus, in the course of their wanderings, they were immediately supplied with water to wash, and with oil to anoint, themselves, before they took their seats by the side of the king. The oil used on such occasions, in the palaces of nobles and princes, was perfumed with roses and other odoriferous herbs. They also washed their hands before they sat down to meat. To these customary marks of respect, to which a traveller, or one who had no house of his own, was entitled, our Lord alludes in his defence of Mary: "And he turned to the woman, and said unto Simon, Seest thou this woman? I entered into thine house; thou gavest me no water for my feet, but she hath washed my feet with her tears, and wiped them with the hairs of her head. Thou gavest me no kiss; but this woman, since the time I came in, hath not ceased to kiss my feet. My head with oil thou didst not anoint; but this woman hath anointed my feet with ointment," Luke vii, 44. Homer mentions it as a custom quite common in those days, for daughters to wash and afterward to anoint the feet of their parents. Our Saviour was in the circumstances of a traveller; he had no home to wash and anoint himself in, before he went to Simon's house; and, therefore, had a right to complain that his entertainer had failed in the respect that was due to him as a stranger, at a distance from the usual place of his residence. The Jews regularly washed their hands and their feet before dinner; they considered this ceremony as essential, which discovers the reason of their astonishment, when they observed the disciples of Christ sit down at table without having observed this ceremony: "Why do thy disciples transgress the tradition of the elders? for they wash not their hands when they eat bread," Matt. xv, 2. After meals they wash them again; for, says the evangelist, "the Pharisees and all the Jews, except they wash their hands oft, eat not, holding the tradition of the elders," Mark vii, 3, 4. When they washed their hands themselves, they plunged them into the water up to the wrists; but when others performed this office for them, it was done by pouring it upon their hands. The same custom prevailed in Greece, for Homer says, the attendants poured water on the hands of their chiefs. This was a part of the service which Elisha performed for his master Elijah; and in every instance under the law where water was applied to the body by another, it was done, not by plunging, but by pouring or sprinkling. To wash the feet was a mean and servile office, and, therefore, generally performed by the female servants of the family. It was occasionally performed, however, by females of the highest rank; for the daughter of Cleobulus, one of the Grecian sages, and king of Lindus, a city on the south-east part of Rhodes, was not ashamed to wash the feet of her father's guests. And it was customary for them to kiss the feet of those to whom they thought a more than common respect was due; for the daughter of Philocleon, in Aristophanes, washed her father, anointed his feet, and, stooping down, kissed them. The towel which was used to wipe the feet after washing, was considered through all the east as a badge of servitude. Suetonius mentions it as a sure mark of the intolerable pride of Caligula, the Roman emperor, that when at supper he suffered senators of the highest rank, sometimes to stand by his couch, sometimes at his feet, girt with a towel. Hence it appears that this honour was a token of humiliation, which was not, however, absolutely degrading and inconsistent with all regard to rank. Yet our blessed Redeemer did not refuse to give his disciples, and Judas Iscariot himself, that proof of his love and humility.

The entertainment was conducted by a SYMPOSIARCH, or governor of the feast. He was, says Plutarch, one chosen among the guests, the most pleasant and diverting in the company, that would not get drunk, and yet would drink freely; he was to rule over the rest, to forbid any disorder, but to encourage their mirth. He observed the temper of the guests, and how the wine worked upon them; how every one could bear his wine, and to endeavour accordingly to keep them all in harmony, and in an even composure, that there might be no disquiet nor disturbance. To do this effectually, he first proclaimed liberty to every one to drink what he thought proper, and then observing who among them was most ready to be disordered, mixed more water with his wine, to keep him equally sober with the rest of the company; so that this officer took care that none should be forced to drink, and that none, though left to their own choice, should get intoxicated. Such, we have reason to believe, was the governor of the feast at the marriage in Cana of Galilee, which our Lord honoured with his presence. The term ἀρχιτρίκλινος literally signifies the governor of a place furnished with three beds; and he acted as one having authority; for he tasted the wine before he distributed it to the company, which, it is universally admitted, was one of the duties of a symposiarch. Neither the name nor the act accords with the character and situation of a guest; he must, therefore, have been the symposiarch, or governor of the feast. The existence of such an officer among the Jews is placed beyond a doubt, by a passage in the apocryphal book of Ecclesiasticus, where his office is thus described: "If thou be made the master of a feast, lift not thyself up, but be among them as one of the rest; take diligent care of them, and so sit down. And when thou hast done all thine office, take thy place, that thou mayest be merry with them, and receive a crown for the well-ordering of the feast," Ecclesiasticus xxxii, 1. See Architriclinus.

BAPTISM, from the Greek word βαπτίζω, is a rite or ceremony by which persons are initiated into the profession of the Christian religion; or, it is the appointed mode by which a person assumes the profession of Christianity, or is admitted to a participation of the privileges belonging to the disciples of Christ. It was by this mode that those who believed the Gospel were to be separated from unbelievers, and joined to the visible Christian church; and the rite accompanying it, or washing with water, was probably intended to represent the washing away, or renouncing, the impurities of some former state, viz. the sins that had been committed, and the vicious habits that had been contracted; and to this purpose it may be observed, that the profession of repentance always accompanied, or was understood to accompany, the profession of faith in Christ. That our Lord instituted such an ordinance as baptism, is plain from the commission given to the Apostles after his resurrection, and recorded in Matt. xxviii, 19, 20. To this rite there is also an allusion in Mark xvi, 16; John iii, 5; Acts ii, 41; viii, 12, 36–38; xxii, 16. The design of this institution, which was to express faith in Christ on the part of those who were baptized, and to declare their resolution of openly professing his religion, and cultivating real and universal holiness, appears from Rom. vi, 3, 4; 1 Peter iii, 21; Ephes. v, 26; and Titus iii, 5. We find no account of baptism as a distinct religious rite, before the mission of John, the forerunner of Christ, who was called the "Baptist," on account of his being commanded by God to baptize with water all who should hearken to his invitation to repent. Washing, however, accompanied many of the Jewish rites, and, indeed, was required after contracting any kind of uncleanness. Also, soon after the time of our Saviour, we find it to have been the custom of the Jews solemnly to baptize, as well as to circumcise, all their proselytes. As their writers treat largely of the reasons for this rite, and give no hint of its being a novel institution, it is probable that this had always been the custom antecedent to the time of Moses, whose account of the rite of circumcision, and of the manner of performing it, is by no means circumstantial. Or, baptism, after circumcision, might have come into use gradually from the natural propriety of the thing, and its easy conformity to other Jewish customs. For if no Jew could approach the tabernacle, or temple, after the most trifling uncleanness, without washing, much less would it be thought proper to admit a proselyte from a state so impure and unclean as Heathenism was conceived to be, without the same mode of purification. The antiquity of this practice of proselyte baptism among the Jews, has been a subject of considerable debate among divines. It is strenuously maintained by Lightfoot. Dr. John Owen considers the opinion, that Christian baptism came from the Jews, as destitute of all probability. On the other hand, Mr. Wall has made it highly probable, to say the least, from many testimonies of the Jewish writers, who without one dissenting voice allow the fact, that the practice of Jewish baptism obtained before and at, as well as after, our Saviour's time. There is also a strong intimation, even in the Gospel itself, of such a known practice among the Jews in the time of John the Baptist, John i, 25. The testimonies of the Jewish writers are of the greater weight, because the practice, reported by them to have been of so ancient a date, did still remain among them; for if it had not been of that antiquity to which it pretends, viz. before the time of Christ, it is not likely that it would ever have become a custom among the Jews afterward. Would they begin to proselyte persons to their religion by baptism in imitation of the disciples of Jesus of Nazareth, whom they held accursed? And yet if this proselyte baptism were adopted by the Jews since the time of Christ, it must have been a mere innovation in imitation of Christians, which is not very likely. This ceremony is performed by immersion in the oriental churches. The practice of the western churches is, to sprinkle the water on the head or face of the person to be baptized, except in the church of Milan, in whose ritual it is ordered, that the head of the infant be plunged three times into the water; the minister at the same time pronouncing the words, "I BAPTIZE THEE IN THE NAME OF THE FATHER, THE SON, AND THE HOLY GHOST;" importing that by this ceremony the person baptized is received among the professors of that religion which God, the Father of all, revealed to mankind by the ministry of his Son, and confirmed by the miracles of his Spirit.

2. It is observable that the baptismal form, above cited from St. Matthew, never occurs in the same words, either in the book of the Acts, or in any of the Epistles. But though the form in St. Matthew never appears elsewhere, the thing intended thereby is always implied. There are many ceremonies delivered by ecclesiastical writers, as used in baptism, which were introduced after the age of Justin Martyr, but which are now disused; as the giving milk and honey to the baptized, in the east; wine and milk, in the west, &c. They also added unction and the imposition of hands. Tertullian is the first who mentions the signing with the sign of the cross, but only as used in private, and not in public worship; and he particularly describes the custom of baptizing without it. Indeed, it does not appear to have been used in baptism till the latter end of the fourth or fifth century; at which time great virtue was ascribed to it. Lactantius, who lived in the beginning of the fourth century, says the devil cannot approach those who have the heavenly mark of the cross upon them as an impregnable fortress to defend them; but he does not say it was used in baptism. After the council of Nice, Christians added to baptism the ceremonies of exorcism and adjuration, to make evil spirits depart from the persons to be baptized. They made several signings with the cross, they used lighted candles, they gave salt to the baptized person to taste, and the priest touched his mouth and ears with spittle, and also blew and spat upon his face. At that time also baptized persons wore white garments till the Sunday following. They had also various other ceremonies; some of which are now abolished, though others of them remain in the church of Rome to this day.

3. The Quakers assert, that water baptism was never intended to continue in the church of Christ any longer than while Jewish prejudices made such an external ceremony necessary. They argue from Eph. iv, 5, in which ONE baptism is spoken of as necessary to Christians, that this must be a baptism of the Spirit. But from comparing the texts that relate to this institution, it will plainly appear that water baptism was instituted by Christ in more general terms than will agree with this explication. That it was administered to all the Gentile converts, and not confined to the Jews, appears from Matt. xxviii, 19, 20, compared with Acts x, 47; and that the baptism of the Spirit did not supersede water baptism appears to have been the judgment of Peter and of those that were with him; so that the one baptism spoken of seems to have been that of water; the communication of the Holy Spirit being only called baptism in a figurative sense. As for any objection which may be drawn from 1 Cor. i, 17, it is sufficiently answered by the preceding verses, and all the numerous texts, in which, in epistles written long after this, the Apostle speaks of ALL Christians as baptized; and argues from the obligation of baptism, in such a manner as we can never imagine he would have done, if he had apprehended it to have been the will of God that it

should be discontinued in the church. Compare Rom. vi, 3, &c; Col. ii, 12; Gal. iii, 27.

4. Baptism, in early times, was only administered at Easter and Whitsuntide, except in cases of necessity. Adult persons were prepared for baptism by abstinence, prayer, and other pious exercises. It was to answer for them, says Mosheim, that sponsors, or godfathers, were first instituted in the second century, though they were afterward admitted also in the baptism of infants. This, according to M. Daillé, was not done till the fourth century. Wall refers the origin of sponsors, or godfathers, on the authority of Tertullian, to the commencement of the second century; who were used in the baptism of infants that could not answer for themselves. The catechumens were not forward in coming to baptism. St. Ambrose was not baptized before he was elected bishop of Milan; and some of the fathers not till the time of their death. Some deferred it out of a tender conscience; and others out of too much attachment to the world; it being the prevailing opinion of the primitive times, that baptism, whenever conferred, washed away all antecedent stains and sins. Accordingly they deferred this sanctifying rite as long as possible, even till they apprehended they were at the point of death. Cases of this kind occur at the beginning of the third century. Constantine the Great was not baptized till he was at the last gasp, and in this he was followed by his son Constantius; and two of his other sons, Constantine and Constans, were killed before they were baptized. As to the necessity of baptism, we may observe, however, that, though some seem to have laid too great stress upon it, as if it were indispensably necessary in order to salvation; it must be allowed, that for any person to omit baptism, when he acknowledges it to be an institution of Christ, and that it is the will of Christ that he should submit to it, is an act of disobedience to his authority, which is inconsistent with true faith.

5. The word BAPTISM is frequently taken for SUFFERINGS, Mark x, 38; Luke xii, 50; Matt. xx, 22, 23. Of expressions like these we find some traces in the Old Testament also, where waters often denote tribulations, Psalm lxix, 1, 15; cxxiv, 4, 5; and where to be swallowed up by the waters, and to pass through the great waters, signify to be overwhelmed with miseries and calamities.

6. St. Paul, endeavouring to prove the resurrection of the dead, among several other reasons in support of the doctrine, says, "If the dead rise not at all, what shall they do who are baptized for the dead?" 1 Cor. xv, 29. Of this phrase various interpretations have been given; three of which only shall be here mentioned. "It means," say some, "'baptized in the room of the dead just fallen in the cause of Christ, and who are thus supported by a sucession of new converts, immediately offering themselves to fill up their places, as ranks of soldiers who advance to combat in the room of their companions, who have just been slain in their sight.'" Others think it signifies, "In hope of blessings to be received after they are numbered with the dead." Dr. Macknight supplies the words, τῆς ἀναςάσεως, and reads the clause, "Who are baptized for the resurrection of the dead;" or in consequence of their believing in the doctrine of the resurrection of the dead; on account of which faith, and their profession of it, they are exposed to great sufferings, for which they can have no recompense, if there be no resurrection of the dead, nor any future life at all.

7. As to the subjects of baptism, the anti-pædobaptists hold that believing adults only are proper subjects, because the commission of Christ to baptize appears to them to restrict this ordinance to such only as are taught, or made disciples; and that, consequently, infants, who cannot be thus taught, ought to be excluded. "It does not appear," say they, "that the Apostles, in executing the commission of Christ, ever baptized any but those who were first instructed in the Christian faith, and professed their belief of it." They contend that infants can receive no benefit from baptism, and are not capable of faith and repentance, which are to be considered as prerequisites.

8. As to the mode, they observe that the meaning of the word βαπτίζω signifies to IMMERSE or DIP, and that only; that John baptized in Jordan; that he chose a place where there was much water; that Jesus came up out of the water; that Philip and the eunuch went down both into the water; that the terms, WASHING, PURIFYING, BURYING IN BAPTISM, so often mentioned in the Scriptures, allude to this mode; that immersion only was the practice of the Apostles and the first Christians; and that it was only laid aside from the love of novelty, and the coldness of climate. These positions, they think, are so clear from Scripture, and the history of the church, that they stand in need of but little argument for their support. Farther, they also insist that all positive institutions depend entirely upon the will and declaration of the institutor; and that, therefore, reasoning by analogy from previously abrogated rites is to be rejected, and the express command of Christ respecting baptism ought to be our rule.

9. The Pædobaptists, however, are of a different opinion. As to the subjects of baptism, they believe that qualified adults, who have not been baptized before, are certainly proper subjects; but then they think, also, that infants ought not to be excluded. They believe that, as the Abrahamic and Christian covenants are the same, Gen. xvii, 7; Heb. viii, 12; that as children were admitted under the former; and that as baptism is now a sign, seal, or confirmation of this covenant, infants have as great a right to it as the children of the Israelites had to the seal of circumcision under the law, Acts ii, 39; Rom. iv, 11. Farther, if children are not to be baptized because there is no positive command for it, for the same reason they say that women should not come to the Lord's Supper; nor ought we to keep holy the first day of the week; neither of these being expressly commanded. If baptizing infants had been a human invention, they also ask, how such a practice could have been so universal in the first three hundred years of the church, and yet no record have remained when it was introduced, nor any dispute or controversy about it have taken place? Some reduce the matter to a narrower

compass; urging, (1.) That God constituted in his church the membership of infants, and admitted them to that privilege by a religious ordinance, Gen. xvii; Gal. iii, 14, 17. (2.) That this right of infants to church membership was never taken away: and this being the case, they argue, that infants must be received, because God has appointed it; and, since they must be received, it must be either with baptism or without it; but none must be received without baptism; therefore, infants must of necessity be baptized. Hence it is clear that, under the Gospel, infants are still continued exactly in the same relation to God and his church in which they were originally placed under former dispensations. That infants are to be received into the church, and as such baptized, is also inferred from the following passages of Scripture: Gen. xvii; Isa. xliv, 3; Matt. xix, 13; Luke ix, 47, 48; Acts ii, 38, 39; Rom. xi, 17, 21; 1 Cor. vii, 14.

10. Though there are no express examples in the New Testament of Christ and his Apostles baptizing infants, yet there is no proof that they were excluded. Jesus Christ actually blessed little children; and it is difficult to believe that such received his blessing, and yet were not to be members of the Gospel church. If Christ received them, and would have us "receive" them, how can we keep them out of the visible church? Beside, if children were not to be baptized, it is reasonable to expect that they would have been expressly forbidden. As whole households were baptized, it is also probable there were children among them. From the year 400 to 1150, no society of men, in all that period of seven hundred and fifty years, ever pretended to say it was unlawful to baptize infants: and still nearer the time of our Saviour there appears to have been scarcely any one who advised the delay of infant baptism. Irenæus, who lived in the second century, and was well acquainted with Polycarp, who was John's disciple, declares expressly, that the church learned from the Apostles to baptize children. Origen, in the third century, affirms, that the custom of baptizing infants was received from Christ and his Apostles. Cyprian, and a council of ministers, held about the year 254, no less than sixty-six in number, unanimously agreed that children might be baptized as soon as they were born. Ambrose, who wrote about 274 years from the Apostles, declares that the baptism of infants had been practised by the Apostles themselves, and by the church down to that time. "The catholic church every where declares," says Chrysostom, in the fifth century, "that infants should be baptized;" and Augustine affirmed, that he never heard or read of any Christian, catholic or sectarian, but who always held that infants were to be baptized. They farther believe that there needed no mention in the New Testament of receiving infants into the church, as it had been once appointed and never repealed. So far from confining baptism to adults, it must be remembered that there is not a single instance recorded in the New Testament, in which the descendants of Christian parents were baptized in adult years. The objection that infants are not proper subjects for baptism, because they cannot profess faith and repentance, falls with as much weight upon the institution of circumcision as infant baptism; since they are as capable or are as fit subjects for the one as the other. Finally, it is generally acknowledged, that if infants die, (and a great part of the human race die in their infancy,) they are saved: if this be the case then why refuse them the sign of union with Christ, if they be capable of enjoying the thing signified?

11. As to the mode, the Pædobaptists deny that the term βαπτίζω, which is a derivative of βάπτω, and, consequently, must be something less in its signification, is invariably used in the New Testament to express plunging. It is denied, therefore, that dipping is its only meaning; that Christ absolutely enjoined immersion; and that it is his positive will that no other mode should be used. As the word βαπτίζω is used to express the various ablutions among the Jews, such as sprinkling, pouring, &c, Heb. ix, 10, for the custom of washing before meals, and the washing of household furniture, pots, &c, it is evident from hence that it does not express the manner of doing a thing, whether by immersion or effusion, but only the thing done; that is, washing; or the application of water in some form or other. It no where signifies TO DIP, but in denoting a mode of, and in order to, washing or cleansing; and the mode or use is only the ceremonial part of a positive institute; just as in the Lord's Supper, the time of day, the number and posture of the communicants, the quantity and quality of bread and wine, are circumstances not accounted essential by any part of Christians. If in baptism there be an expressive emblem of the descending influence of the Spirit, pouring must be the mode of administration; for that is the Scriptural term most commonly and properly used for the communication of divine influences, Matt. iii, 11; Mark i, 8, 10; Luke iii, 16–22; John i, 33; Acts i, 5; ii, 38, 39; viii, 12, 17; xi, 15, 16. The term SPRINKLING, also, is made use of in reference to the act of purification, Isa. lii, 15; Ezek. xxxvi, 25; Heb. ix, 13, 14; and therefore cannot be inapplicable to baptismal purification. But, it is observed, that John baptized "IN Jordan:" to this it is replied, To infer always a plunging of the whole body in water from this particle, would, in many instances, be false and absurd. The same Greek preposition, ἐν, is used when it is said they should be "baptized with fire;" but few will assert that they should be plunged into it. The Apostle, speaking of Christ, says, he came not, ἐν, "by water only;" but, ἐν, "by water and blood." There the same word, ἐν, is translated BY; and with justice and propriety; for we know no good sense in which we could say he came IN water. It has been remarked that ἐν is, more than a hundred times, in the New Testament, rendered AT; and in a hundred and fifty others it is translated WITH. If it be rendered so here, John baptized at Jordan, or with the water of Jordan, there is no proof that he plunged his disciples in it.

Jesus, it is said, came up OUT OF the water; but this is no proof that he was immersed, as the Greek term, ἀπὸ, often signifies FROM: for instance, "Who hath warned you to flee FROM," not OUT OF, "the wrath to come?" with many others that might be mentioned. Again: it is urged that Philip and the eunuch went down both into the water. To this it is answered, that here also is no proof of immersion: for, if the expression of their going down INTO the water necessarily includes dipping, then Philip was dipped, as well as the eunuch. The preposition εἰς, translated INTO, often signifies no more than TO, or UNTO: see Matt. xv, 24; Rom. x, 10; Acts xxviii, 14; Matt. iii, 11; xvii, 27: so that from none of these circumstances can it be proved that there was one person of all the baptized, who went into the water ankle deep. As to the Apostle's expression, "buried with him in baptism," that has no force in the argument for immersion, since it does not allude to a custom of dipping, any more than our baptismal crucifixion and death has any such reference. It is not the sign, but the thing signified, that is here alluded to. As Christ was buried, and rose again to a heavenly life, so we by baptism signify that we are separated from sin, that we may live a new life of faith and love.

To conclude: it is urged, against the mode of immersion, that, as it carries with it too much of the appearance of a burdensome rite for the Gospel dispensation; as it is too indecent for so solemn an ordinance; as it has a tendency to agitate the spirits, often rendering the subject unfit for the exercise of proper thoughts and affections, and indeed utterly incapable of them; as in many cases the immersion of the body would, in all probability, be instant death; as in other situations it would be impracticable, for want of water; it cannot be considered as necessary to the ordinance of baptism, and there is the strongest improbability that it was ever practised in the times of the New Testament, or in the earliest periods of the Christian church.

BAPTISTS, or **ANTIPÆDOBAPTISTS**, so called from their rejecting the baptism of infants. The Baptists in England form one of "the three denominations of Protestant Dissenters." The constitution of their churches, and their modes of worship, are congregational, or independent. They bore a considerable share in the sufferings of the seventeenth and preceding centuries: for there were many among the Lollards and Wickliffites who disapproved of infant baptism. There were also many of this faith among the Protestants and Reformers abroad. In Holland, Germany, and the north, they went by the names of Anabaptists and Mennonites; and in Piedmont and the south, they were found among the Albigenses and Waldenses. The Baptists subsist chiefly under two denominations,--the Particular or Calvinistical, and the General or Arminian. The former is by far the most numerous. Some of both denominations, General and Particular, allow of free or mixed communion; admitting to the Lord's table pious persons who have not been immersed, while others consider that as an essential requisite to communion. These are sometimes called Strict Baptists. Other societies of this denomination observe the seventh day of the week as their Sabbath, apprehending the original law of the Sabbath to remain in force, unaltered and unrepealed. These are called Seventh-day Baptists. A considerable number of the General Baptists have gone into Unitarianism; in consequence of which, those who maintained the doctrines of the Trinity and atonement, in the latter part of the eighteenth century, formed themselves into what is called "The New Connection," or Association. These preserve a friendly correspondence with their other brethren in things which concern the general interests of the denomination, but hold no religious communion with them. Some congregations of General Baptists admit three distinct orders of church officers: messengers or ministers, elders, and deacons. The Baptists in America, and in the East and West Indies, are chiefly Calvinists; but most of them admit of free communion. The Scottish Baptists form a distinct denomination, and are distinguished by several peculiarities of church government. "No trace can be found of a Baptist church in Scotland," says Mr. Jones, "excepting one which appears to have been formed out of Cromwell's army, previous to 1765, when a church was settled at Edinburgh, under the pastoral care of Mr. Carmichael and Mr. Archibald M'Lean. Others have since been formed at Dundee, Glasgow, and in most of the principal towns of Scotland:" also at London, and in various parts of England. They think that the order of public worship, which uniformly obtained in the Apostolic churches, is clearly set forth in Acts ii, 42–47; and therefore they endeavour to follow it out to the utmost of their power. They require a plurality of elders in every church, administer the Lord's Supper, and make contributions for the poor every first day of the week. The prayers and exhortations of the brethren form a part of their church order, under the direction and control of the elders, to whom it exclusively belongs to preside in conducting the worship, to rule in cases of discipline, and to labour in the word and doctrine, in distinction from the brethren exhorting one another. The elders are all laymen, generally chosen from among the brethren; but, when circumstances require, are supported by their contributions. They approve also of persons who are properly qualified for it, being appointed by the church to preach the Gospel and baptize, though not vested with any pastoral charge. The discipline and government of the Scottish Baptists are strictly congregational.

BARACHIAS, the father of Zacharias, mentioned Matt. xxiii, 35, as slain between the temple and the altar. There is a great diversity of opinions concerning the person of this Zacharias, the son of Barachias. Some think him to be Zacharias, the son of Jehoiada, who was killed by the orders of Joash, between the temple and the altar, 2 Chron. xxiv, 21. Campbell thinks, with Father Simon, that Jehoiada had two names, Barachias and Jehoiada. See Zacharias.

BARAK, son of Abinoam, chosen by God to deliver the Hebrews from that bondage under which they were held by Jabin, king of the Canaanites, Judges iv, 4, 5, &c. He refused to obey the Lord's commands, signified to him by Deborah, the prophetess, unless she consented to go with him. Deborah accompanied Barak toward Kedesh of Naphtali; and, having assembled ten thousand men, they advanced to mount Tabor. Sisera, being informed of this movement, marched with nine hundred chariots of war, and encamped near the river Kishon. Barak rapidly descended from mount Tabor, and the Lord having spread terror through Sisera's army Barak easily obtained a complete victory. Sisera was killed by Jael. Barak and Deborah composed a hymn of thanksgiving; and the land had peace forty years from A. M. 2719 to 2759, B. C. 1245.

BARBARIAN. The word לעז (rendered BARBARIAN; **LXX**, βάρβαρος,) in the Hebrew sense of it, signifies A STRANGER; one who knows neither the holy language nor the law. According to the notions of the Greeks, all nations who were not Greeks, or not governed by laws like the Greeks, were barbarians. The Persians, Egyptians, Hebrews, Arabians, Gauls, Germans, and even the Romans, were, in their phraseology, barbarians, however learned or polite they might be in themselves. St. Paul comprehends all mankind under the names of Greeks and barbarians: "I am a debtor both to the Greeks and to the barbarians; to the wise and to the unwise," Rom. i, 14. St. Luke calls the inhabitants of the island of Malta barbarians, Acts xxviii, 2, 4. St. Paul, writing to the Colossians, uses the terms BARBARIAN and SCYTHIAN almost in the same signification. In 1 Cor. xiv, 11, he says, that if he who speaks a foreign language in an assembly be not understood by those to whom he discourses, with respect to them he is a barbarian; and, reciprocally, if he understand not those who speak to him, they are to him barbarians. Barbarian, therefore, is used for every stranger or foreigner who does not speak our native language, and includes no implication whatever of savage nature or manners in those respecting whom it is used. It is most probably derived from BERBIR, "a shepherd;" whence BARBARY, the country of wandering shepherds; BEDOUINS, SCENI, SCYTHEI, as if, wanderers in tents; therefore barbarians.

BAR-JESUS, or, according to some copies, **BAR-JEU**, was a Jewish magician in the island of Crete, Acts xiii, 6. St. Luke calls him Elymas. He was with the pro-consul Sergius Paulus, who, sending for Paul and Barnabas, desired to hear the word of God. Bar-Jesus endeavouring to hinder the pro-consul from embracing Christianity, Paul, filled with the Holy Ghost, "set his eyes upon him, and said, O full of all subtilty and mischief, thou child of the devil, thou enemy of all righteousness, wilt thou not cease to pervert the right ways of the Lord? Behold, the hand of the Lord is upon thee, and thou shalt be blind, not seeing the sun for a season;" which took place immediately. The pro-consul, who saw this miracle, was converted. Origen and Chrysostom think that Elymas, or Bar-Jesus, was converted likewise; and that St. Paul speedily restored his sight.

BARLEY, שערה, Exod. ix, 31; Lev. xxvii, 16, &c;; a well-known kind of grain. It derives its Hebrew name from the long hairy beard which grows upon the ear. Pliny, on the testimony of Menander, says that barley was the most ancient aliment of mankind. In Palestine the barley was sown about October, and reaped in the end of March, just after the passover. In Egypt the barley harvest was later; for when the hail fell there, Exodus ix, 31, a few days before the passover, the flax and barley were bruised and destroyed: for the flax was at its full growth, and the barley began to form its green ears; but the wheat, and more backward grain, were not damaged, because they were only in the blade, and the hail bruised the young shoots which produce the ears.

The rabbins sometimes called barley the food of beasts, because in reality they fed their cattle with it, 1 Kings iv, 28; and from Homer and other ancient writers we learn, that barley was given to horses. The Hebrews, however, frequently used barley bread, as we find by several passages of Scripture: for example, David's friends brought to him in his flight wheat, barley, flour, &c, 2 Sam. xvii, 28. Solomon sent wheat, barley, oil, and wine, to the labourers King Hiram had furnished him, 2 Chron. ii, 15. Elijah had a present made him, of twenty barley loaves, and corn in the husk, 2 Kings iv, 22. And, by miraculously increasing the five barley loaves, Christ fed a multitude of about five thousand, John vi, 8–10. The jealousy-offering, in the Levitical institution, was to be barley meal, Num. v, 15. The common mincha, or offering, was of fine wheat flour, Lev. ii, 1; but this was of barley, a meaner grain, probably to denote the vile condition of the person in whose behalf it was offered. For which reason, also, there was no oil or frankincense permitted to be offered with it. Sometimes barley is put for a low, contemptible reward or price. So the false prophets are charged with seducing the people for handfuls of barley, and morsels of bread, Ezek. xiii, 19. Hosea bought his emblematic bride for fifteen pieces of silver, and a homer and a half of barley, Hosea iii, 2.

BARNABAS, a disciple of Jesus Christ, and companion of St. Paul in his labours. He was a Levite, born in the isle of Cyprus. His proper name was Joses, to which the Apostles added Barnabas, signifying THE SON OF CONSOLATION. He is generally considered one of the seventy disciples, chosen by our Saviour. He was brought up with Paul at the feet of Gamaliel. When that Apostle came to Jerusalem, three years after his conversion, Barnabas introduced him to the other Apostles, Acts ix, 26, 27, about A. D. 37. Five years afterward, the church at Jerusalem, being informed of the progress of the Gospel at Antioch, sent Barnabas thither, who beheld with great joy the wonders of the grace of God, Acts xi, 22, 24. He exhorted the faithful to perseverance. Some time afterward, he went to Tarsus, to seek Paul, and bring him to Antioch, where they jointly laboured two years, and converted great numbers; and here the disciples were first called Christians. They left Antioch A. D. 44, to convey alms from this church to that at Jerusalem. At their return they brought John Mark, the cousin of Barnabas. While they were at Antioch, the Holy Ghost directed that they should be separated for those labours among the Gentiles to which he had appointed them. They departed into Cyprus, where they converted Sergius Paulus, the pro-consul. They preached at Perga in Pamphylia without much success, by reason of the obstinacy and malice of the Jews; but being come to Iconium, they made many converts. Here the Jews stirred up a sedition, and obliged them to retire to Derbe and Lystra, in Lycaonia, where St. Paul curing one Æneas, who had been lame from his birth, the people of Lystra regarded them as gods; calling Barnabas, Jupiter; and Paul, Mercury; and would have sacrificed to them, which the two

Apostles with great difficulty hindered: nevertheless, soon afterward, they were persecuted in this very city. Having revisited the cities through which they had passed, and where they had preached the Gospel, they returned to Antioch in Syria.

In A. D. 51, Barnabas was sent with Paul from Antioch to Jerusalem, on occasion of disputes concerning the observance of legal rites, to which the Jews wished to subject the Gentiles. Paul and Barnabas were present in the council at Jerusalem, and returned immediately to Antioch. Peter, arriving there soon afterward, was led to countenance, in some degree, by his conduct, the observance of the Mosaic distinctions. Barnabas, too, (who, being by descent a Levite, might retain some former notions,) used the like dissimulation: but Paul reproved Peter and Barnabas with great freedom. Paul afterward determining to visit the churches in the isle of Cyprus, and in Asia Minor, Barnabas desired that John Mark might accompany them: but Paul objected, because Mark had left them on the first journey. Hereupon the two Apostles separated: Paul went toward Asia; and Barnabas, with Mark, to Cyprus. This is all we know certainly concerning Barnabas.

There is extant among the writings of the fathers an epistle which is attributed to Barnabas; though, being without an inscription, it is not known to whom it professes to have been addressed. It was first published by Archbishop Usher, in Greek and Latin, and translated by Archbishop Wake, in his "Genuine Epistles of the Apostolical Fathers," and has often been reprinted. That it is not the production of Barnabas, the companion of Paul, may be safely concluded from internal evidence; though it may have been written by some other person of the same name. There is also a tract which goes by the name of, "The Gospel of Barnabas," still extant; from which Dr. White, at the end of his Bampton Lectures, has given extracts sufficiently copious to satisfy any impartial mind that it is spurious.

BARRENNESS. This was looked upon as reproachful among the Greeks and Romans, but more particularly so among the Jews; which may be accounted for by the constant expectation of Messiah, and the hope that every woman had, that she might be the mother of the promised seed. This constant hope of the speedy coming of the great "Seed of the woman" serves also to account for many circumstances in the Old Testament history. "Couple it," says the Rev. J. J. Blunt, "with this consideration, and I see the scheme of revelation, like the physical scheme, proceeding with beautiful uniformity: a unity of plan 'connecting,' as it has been well said by Paley, 'the chicken roosting upon its perch with the spheres revolving in the firmament;' and a unity of plan connecting in like manner the meanest accidents of a household with the most illustrious visions of a prophet. Abstracted from this consideration, I see in the history of Moses details of actions, some trifling, some even offensive, pursued at a length (when compared with the whole) singularly disproportionate; while things which the angels would desire to look into are passed over and forgotten. But this principle once admitted, all is consecrated; all assumes a new aspect; trifles, that seem at first not bigger than a man's hand, occupy the heavens; and wherefore Sarah laughed, for instance, at the prospect of a son, and wherefore that laugh was rendered immortal in his name; and wherefore the sacred historian dwells on a matter so trivial, whilst the world and its vast concerns were lying at his feet, I can fully understand. For then I see the hand of God shaping every thing to his own ends, and in an event thus casual, thus easy, thus unimportant, telling forth his mighty design of salvation to the world, and working it up into the web of his noble prospective counsels, Gen. xxi, 6. I see that nothing is great or little before Him who can bend to his purposes whatever he willeth, and convert the light-hearted and thoughtless mockery of an aged woman into an instrument of his glory, effectual as the tongue of the seer which he touched with living coals from the altar. Bearing this master-key in my hand, I can interpret the scenes of domestic mirth, of domestic stratagem, or of domestic wickedness, with which the history of Moses abounds. The Seed of the woman, that was to bruise the serpent's head, Gen. iii, 15, however indistinctly understood, (and probably it was understood very indistinctly,) was the one thing longed for in the families of old; was 'the desire of all nations,' as the Prophet Haggai expressly calls it, Hag. ii, 7; and, provided they could accomplish this desire, they (like others, when urged by an overpowering motive) were often reckless of the means, and rushed upon deeds which they could not defend. Then did the wife forget her jealousy, and provoke, instead of resenting, the faithlessness of her husband, Gen. xvi, 2; xxx, 3, 9; then did the mother forget a parent's part, and teach her own child treachery and deceit, Gen. xxv, 23; xxvii, 13; then did daughters turn the instincts of nature backward, and deliberately work their own and their father's shame, Gen. xix, 31; then did the daughter-in-law veil her face, and court the incestuous bed, Gen. xxxviii, 14; and to be childless, was to be a by-word, Gen. xvi, 5; xxx, 1; and to refuse to raise up seed to a brother, was to be spit upon, Gen. xxxviii, 26; Deut. xxv, 9; and the prospect of the promise, like the fulfilment of it, did not send peace into families, but a sword; and three were set against two, and two against three, Gen. xxvii, 41; and the elder, who would be promoted unto honour, was set against the younger, whom God would promote, Gen. iv, 5; xxvii, 41; and national differences were engendered by it, as individuals grew into nations, Gen. xix, 37; xxvi, 35; and even the foulest of idolatries may be traced, perhaps, to this hallowed source; for the corruption of the best is the worst corruption of all, Num. xxv, 1, 2, 3. It is upon this principle of interpretation, and I know not upon what other so well, that we may put to silence the ignorance of foolish men, who have made those parts of the Mosaic history a stumbling-block to many, which, if rightly understood, are the very testimony of the covenant; and a principle which is thus extensive in its application and successful in its results; which explains so much that is difficult, and answers so much that is objected against, has, from this circumstance alone, strong presumption in its favour, strong claims upon our sober regard."

BARSABAS. Joseph Barsabas, surnamed Justus, was one of the first disciples of Jesus Christ, and probably one of the seventy. When St. Peter proposed to the disciples to fill up the place of Judas the traitor, by choosing another Apostle, Acts i, 21, Barsabas was nominated along with Matthias; but the lot fell on Matthias, who was therefore numbered with the eleven Apostles. We know nothing farther of the life of this Barsabas.

2. Barsabas was also the surname of Judas, one of the principal disciples mentioned, Acts xv, 22, &c. Barsabas and some others were sent by the Apostles, with Paul and Barnabas, to Antioch, and carried a letter with them from the Apostles, signifying what the council at Jerusalem had decreed. After the reading of the letter to the brethren, which was received with joy, Barsabas and Silas continued here some time longer, instructing and confirming the brethren; after which Silas and Barsabas returned to Jerusalem. This is all we know of Barsabas Judas.

BARTHOLOMEW, one of the twelve Apostles, Matt. x, 3, is supposed to be the same person who is called Nathanael, one of the first of Christ's disciples. This opinion is founded on the circumstance, that as the evangelist John never mentions Bartholomew in the number of the Apostles, so the other evangelists never mention Nathanael. And as in John i, 45, Philip and Nathanael are mentioned together as coming to Jesus, so in the other evangelists Philip and Bartholomew are constantly associated together. The supposition also acquires additional probability from considering, that Nathanael is particularly mentioned among the Apostles to whom Christ appeared at the sea of Tiberias, after his resurrection; Simon Peter, Thomas, and Nathanael, of Cana in Galilee; the sons of Zebedee, namely, James and John; with two other of his disciples, probably Andrew and Philip, John xxi, 2. It is an early tradition, that Bartholomew propagated the faith as far as India, and also in the more northern and western parts of Asia, and that he finally suffered martyrdom. But all the particulars respecting the life and labours of the Apostles, not mentioned in the New Testament, are exceedingly uncertain.

BARUCH, the son of Neriah, and grandson of Maaseiah, was of illustrious birth, and of the tribe of Judah. He had a brother of the name of Seraiah, who occupied an important station in the court of King Zedekiah; but he himself adhered to the person of the Prophet Jeremiah, and was his most steady friend, though his attachment to him drew on himself several persecutions and much ill treatment. He appears to have acted as his secretary during a great part of his life, and never left him till they were parted by death. In the reign of Jehoiakim, king of Judah, A. M. 3398, Jeremiah having been thrown into prison, the Lord commanded him to commit to writing all the prophecies that he had delivered until that time. He accordingly sent for Baruch, and dictated them to him by word of mouth. Some time afterward he instructed the latter to go and read them to the people, who were then assembled in the temple; on which Michaiah, who happened to be present, and heard them, instantly gave notice of them to the king's counsellors. The latter immediately sent for Baruch, and commanded him to repeat to them what he had been reading to the people in the temple; which he accordingly did, to their great astonishment: and, finding that they contained some very unwelcome tidings respecting the fate of the kingdom, they inquired how he came into possession of them; intimating that their duty to the king required that they should make him acquainted therewith. Baruch was at the same time advised to consult his own safety, and to let no man know where he was to be found; after which they took from him the roll of his prophecies, and deposited it in the chamber of Elishama, the scribe. They next waited on the king, and told him what had passed. The latter sent Jehudi to fetch the book; which being brought, Jehoiakim commanded it to be read in his presence, and in the presence of his nobles who surrounded him. But Jehudi had not proceeded far before the king took the book, cut it with his secretary's penknife, and threw it into the fire, where it was consumed before their faces. He at the same time gave orders to have both Baruch and Jeremiah seized; but the hand of Providence concealed them from his fury.

Jeremiah was instructed a second time to commit his prophecies to writing; and Baruch wrote them as before, with the addition of several others which were not contained in the former book. In the fourth year of the reign of Zedekiah, Baruch went to Babylon, carrying with him a long letter from Jeremiah, in which the Prophet foretold the judgments that should come upon Babylon, and promised the Jews, who were then captives in that country, that they should again be restored to their own land. The latter were exceedingly affected at hearing Jeremiah's letter read to them, and returned an answer to their brethren at Jerusalem. After his return to Jerusalem, Baruch continued his constant attendance on Jeremiah; and when Jerusalem was besieged by Nebuchadnezzar, and Jeremiah thrown into prison, Baruch also was confined with him: but when the city had surrendered, Nebuzaraddan showed him much kindness, granted him his liberty, and permitted him to go with Jeremiah wherever he chose.

The remnant of the people who had been left in Judea under the care of Gedaliah, having adopted the resolution of going into Egypt, and finding that Jeremiah opposed their taking that journey, threw the blame upon Baruch; insinuating that the latter had influenced the Prophet to declare against it. They were, however, both of them at last compelled to follow the people into Egypt, where Jeremiah soon afterward died; on which Baruch retired to Babylon, where the rabbins say he also died in the twelfth year of the captivity, Jer. xxxvi; xliii. The book of Baruch is justly placed among the apocryphal writings. Grotius thinks it a fiction written by some Hellenistic Jew; and St. Jerome gives as the reason why he did not write a commentary upon it, that the Jews themselves did not deem it canonical.

BASHAN, or **BASAN**, one of the most fertile cantons of Canaan, which was bounded on the west by the river Jordan, on the east by the mountains of Gilead, on the south by the brook of Jabbok, and on the north by the land of Geshur. The whole kingdom took its name from the hill of Bashan, which is situated in the middle of it, and by the Greeks is called Batanæa. It had no less than sixty walled towns in it, beside villages. It afforded an excellent breed of cattle, and stately oaks, and was, in short, a plentiful and populous country. Og, king of the Amorites, possessed this country when Moses made the conquest thereof. In the division of the Holy Land, it was assigned to the half tribe of Manasseh. Of the present state of this portion of the ancient possessions of the Israelites, Mr. Buckingham, in his Travels, gives the following account: "We ascended the steep on the north side of the Zerkah, or Jabbok; and, on reaching the summit, came again on a beautiful plain, of an elevated level, and still covered with a very rich soil. We had now quitted the land of Sihon, king of the Amorites, and entered into that of Og, the king of Bashan, both of them well known to all the readers of the early Scriptures. We had quitted too, the districts apportioned to the tribes of Reuben and of Gad, and entered that part which was allotted to the half tribe of Manasseh, beyond Jordan eastward, leaving the land of the children of Ammon on our right, or to the east of the Jabbok, which, according to the authority before quoted, divided Ammon, or Philadelphia, from Gerasa. The mountains here are called the land of Gilead in the Scriptures, and in Josephus; and, according to the Roman division, this was the country of the Decapolis, so often spoken of in the New Testament, or the province of Gaulonitis, from the city of Gaulon, its early capital. We continued our way over this elevated tract, continuing to behold, with surprise and admiration, a beautiful country on all sides of us: its plains covered with a fertile soil, its hills clothed with forests; at every new turn presenting the most magnificent landscapes that could be imagined. Among the trees, the oak was frequently seen; and we know that this territory produced them of old. In enumerating the sources from which the supplies of Tyre were drawn in the time of her great wealth and naval splendour, the Prophet says, 'Of the oaks of Bashan have they made thine oars,' Ezek. xxvii, 6. Some learned commentators indeed, believing that no oaks grew in these supposed desert regions, have translated the word by 'alders,' to prevent the appearance of inaccuracy in the inspired writer. The expression of 'the fat bulls of Bashan,' which occurs more than once in the Scriptures, seemed to us equally inconsistent, as applied to the beasts of a country generally thought to be a desert, in common with the whole tract which is laid down in our modern maps as such between the Jordan and the Euphrates; but we could now fully comprehend, not only that the bulls of this luxuriant country might be proverbially fat, but that its possessors, too, might be a race renowned for strength and comeliness of person. The general face of this region improved as we advanced farther in it; and every new direction of our path opened upon us views which surprised and charmed us by their grandeur and their beauty. Lofty mountains gave an outline of the most magnificent character; flowing beds of secondary hills softened the romantic wildness of the picture; gentle slopes, clothed with wood, gave a rich variety of tints, hardly to be imitated by the pencil; deep valleys, filled with murmuring streams and verdant meadows, offered all the luxuriance of cultivation; and herds and flocks gave life and animation to scenes as grand, as beautiful, and as highly picturesque as the genius or taste of a Claude could either invent or desire."

BASILIDEANS, the followers of Basilides of Alexandria, a gnostic leader of the early part of the second century. See Gnostics.

BASTARD, one born out of wedlock. A bastard among the Greeks was despised, and exposed to public scorn, on account of his spurious origin. In Persia the son of a concubine is never placed on a footing with the legitimate offspring; any attempt made by parental fondness to do so would be resented by the relations of the legitimate wife, and outrage the feelings of a whole tribe. The Jewish father bestowed as little attention on the education of his natural children as the Greek: he seems to have resigned them, in a great measure, to their own inclinations; he neither checked their passions, nor corrected their faults, nor stored their minds with useful knowledge. This is evidently implied in these words of the Apostle: "If ye endure chastening, God dealeth with you as with sons; for what son is he whom the father chasteneth not? But if ye be without chastisement, whereof all are partakers, then are ye bastards and not sons," Heb. xii, 7, 8. To restrain the licentious desires of the heart, Jehovah by an express law fixed a stigma upon the bastard, which was not to be removed till the tenth generation; and to show that the precept was on no account to be violated, or suffered to fall into disuse, it is emphatically repeated, "A bastard shall not enter into the congregation of the Lord; even to his tenth generation shall he not enter into the congregation of the Lord," Deut. xxiii, 2.

BASTINADO, the punishment of beating with sticks. It is also called TYMPANUM, [a drum,] because the patient was beaten like a drum. Upwards of a hundred blows were often inflicted, and sometimes the beating was unto death. St. Paul, Heb. xi, 35, says that some of the saints were TORTURED, τυμπανίζω, suffered the tympanum, that is, were stretched on an instrument of torture, and beaten to death.

BAT, עטלף, Lev. xi, 19; Deut. xiv, 18; Isaiah ii, 20; Baruch vi, 22. The Jewish legislator, having enumerated the animals legally unclean, as well beasts as birds, closes his catalogue with a creature whose equivocal properties seem to exclude it from both those classes: it is too much a bird to be properly a mouse, and too much a mouse to be properly a bird. The bat is therefore well described in Deut. xiv, 18, 19, as the passage should be read, "Moreover the OTHELAPH, and EVERY CREEPING THING THAT FLIETH, is unclean to you: they shall not be eaten." This character is very descriptive, and places this creature at the head of a class of which he is a clear and well-known instance. It has feet or claws growing out of its pinions, and contradicts the general order of nature, by creeping with the instruments of its flight. The Hebrew name of the bat is from עטל DARKNESS, and עט TO FLY, as if it described "the flier in darkness." So the Greeks called the creature νυκτερὶς, from νὺξ, NIGHT; and the Latins, VESPERTILIO, from VESPER, "evening." It is prophesied, Isaiah ii, 20, "In that day shall they cast away their idols to the moles and to the bats;" that is, they shall carry them into the dark caverns, old ruins, or desolate places, to which they shall fly for refuge, and so shall give them up, and relinquish them to the filthy animals that frequent such places, and have taken possession of them as their proper habitation.

BATH, a measure of capacity for things liquid, being the same with the ephah, Ezek. xlv, 11, and containing ten homers, or seven gallons and four pints.

BATH-KOL, בת־קול, DAUGHTER OF THE VOICE. By this name the Jewish writers distinguish what they called a revelation from God, after verbal prophecy had ceased in Israel; that is, after the prophets Haggai, Zechariah, and Malachi. The generality of their traditions and customs are founded on this Bath-Kol. They pretend that God revealed them to their elders, not by prophecy, but by the DAUGHTER OF THE VOICE. The Bath-Kol, as Dr. Prideaux shows, was a fantastical way of divination, invented by the Jews, like the SORTES VIRGILIANÆ [divination by the works of Virgil] among the Heathen. For, as with them, the words first opened upon in the works of that poet, was the oracle whereby they prognosticated those future events which they desired to be informed of; so with the Jews when they appealed to Bath-Kol, the next words which they should hear drop from any one's mouth were taken as the desired oracle. With some it is probable that Bath-Kol, THE DAUGHTER OF THE VOICE, was only an elegant personification of TRADITION. Others, however, more bold, said that it was a voice from heaven, sometimes attended by a clap of thunder.

BATTLE. See Armies.

BAXTERIANISM, a modification of the Calvinistic doctrine of election advocated by the celebrated Baxter in his treatise of "Universal Redemption," and in his "*Methodus Theologiæ*." The real author of the scheme, at least in a systematized form, was Camero, who taught divinity at Saumur, and it was unfolded and defended by his disciple Amyraldus, whom Curcellæus refuted. Baxter says, in his preface to his "Saint's Rest," "The middle way which Camero, Crocius, Martinius, Amyraldus, Davenant, with all the divines of Britain and Bremen in the synod of Dort, go, I think is nearest the truth of any that I know who have written on these points." Baxter first differs from the majority of Calvinists, though not from all, in his statement of the doctrine of satisfaction:--

"Christ's sufferings were not a FULFILLING of the LAW'S THREATENING; (though he bore its CURSE MATERIALLY;) but a satisfaction for our NOT FULFILLING the PRECEPT, and to prevent GOD'S FULFILLING the THREATENING on us. Christ paid not, therefore, the IDEM, but the TANTUNDEM, or ÆQUIVALENS; not the VERY DEBT which we owed and the law required, but the VALUE: (else it were not STRICTLY SATISFACTION, which is REDDITIO ÆQUIVALENTIS: [the rendering of an equivalent:]) and (it being improperly called the PAYING OF A DEBT, but properly A SUFFERING FOR THE GUILTY) the IDEM is nothing but SUPPLICIUM DELINQUENTIS. [The punishment of the guilty individual.] In CRIMINALS, DUM ALIUS SOLVET SIMUL ALIUD SOLVITUR. [When another suffers, it is another thing also that is suffered.] The law knoweth no VICARIUS PŒNÆ; [substitute in punishment;] though the LAW MAKER may admit it, as he is ABOVE LAW; else there were no place for PARDON, if the PROPER DEBT be paid and the LAW NOT RELAXED, but FULFILLED. Christ did neither OBEY nor SUFFER in any man's STEAD, by a STRICT, PROPER REPRESENTATION of his PERSON in point of law; so as that the LAW should take it, as done or suffered by the PARTY HIMSELF. But only as a THIRD PERSON, as a MEDIATOR, he voluntarily bore what else the sinner should have borne. To assert the contrary (especially as to particular persons considered in actual sin) is to overthrow all Scripture theology, and to introduce all Antinomianism; to overthrow all possibility of pardon, and assert justification before we sinned or were born, and to make OURSELVES to have satisfied God. Therefore, we must not say that CHRIST DIED NOSTRO LOCO, [in our stead,] so as to PERSONATE US, or REPRESENT OUR PERSONS in LAW SENSE; but only to bear what else we must have borne."

This system explicitly asserts, that Christ made a satisfaction by his death equally for the sins of every man; and thus Baxter essentially differs both from the higher Calvinists, and, also, from the Sublapsarians, who, though they may allow that the reprobate derive some benefits from Christ's death, so that there is a vague sense in which he may be said to have died for all men, yet they, of course, deny to such the benefit of Christ's satisfaction or atonement which Baxter contends for:--

"Neither the law, whose curse Christ bore, nor God, as the legislator to be satisfied, did distinguish between men as elect and reprobate, or as believers and unbelievers, DE PRESENTI VEL DE FUTURO; [with regard to the present or the future;] and to impose upon Christ, or require from him satisfaction for the sins of one sort more than of another, but for mankind in general. God the Father, and Christ the Mediator, now dealeth with no man upon the mere rigorous terms of the first law; (OBEY PERFECTLY AND LIVE, ELSE THOU SHALT DIE;) but giveth to all much mercy, which, according to the tenor of that violated law, they could not receive, and calleth them to repentance, in order to their receiving farther mercy offered them. And accordingly he will not judge any at last according to the mere law of works, but as they have obeyed or not obeyed his conditions or terms of grace. It was not the SINS of the ELECT ONLY, but of all MANKIND FALLEN, which lay upon Christ satisfying. And to assert the contrary, injuriously diminisheth the honour of his sufferings; and hath other desperate ill consequences."

The benefits derived to all men EQUALLY, from the satisfaction of Christ, he thus states:--

"All mankind, IMMEDIATELY upon Christ's satisfaction, are redeemed and delivered from that legal necessity of perishing which they were under, (not by remitting sin or punishment directly to them, but by giving up God's JUS PUNIENDI [right of punishing] into the hands of the Redeemer; nor by giving any right directly to them, but PER MERAM RESULTANTIAM [by mere consequence] this happy change is made for them in their relation, upon the said remitting of God's right and advantage of justice against them,) and they are given up to the Redeemer as their owner and ruler, to be dealt with upon terms of mercy which have a tendency to their recovery. God the Father and Christ the Mediator hath freely, without any prerequisite condition on man's part, enacted a law of grace of universal extent, in regard of its tenor, by which he giveth, as a deed or gift, Christ himself, with all his following benefits which he bestoweth; (as benefactor and legislator;) and this to all alike, without excluding any; upon condition they believe and accept the offer. By this law, testament, or covenant, ALL MEN ARE CONDITIONALLY pardoned, justified, and reconciled to God already, and no man absolutely; nor doth it make a difference, nor take notice of any, till men's performance or non-performance of the condition makes a difference. In the new law Christ hath truly GIVEN HIMSELF with a CONDITIONAL PARDON, JUSTIFICATION, and CONDITIONAL RIGHT TO SALVATION, to all men in the WORLD, WITHOUT EXCEPTION."

But the peculiarity of Baxter's scheme will be seen from the following farther extracts:--

"Though Christ DIED EQUALLY FOR ALL MEN, in the aforesaid LAW SENSE, as he satisfied the offended legislator, and as giving himself to ALL ALIKE in the CONDITIONAL COVENANT; yet he NEVER PROPERLY INTENDED OR PURPOSED THE ACTUAL JUSTIFYING AND SAVING OF ALL, nor of any but those that come to be justified and saved; he did not, therefore, die for all, nor for any that perish, with a decree or resolution to save them, MUCH LESS DID HE DIE FOR ALL ALIKE, AS TO THIS INTENT. Christ hath given FAITH to none by his law or testament, though he hath revealed, that to some he will, as benefactor and DOMINUS ABSOLUTUS, [absolute Lord,] give that grace which shall infallibly produce it; and God hath given some to Christ that he might prevail with them accordingly; yet this is no giving IT TO THE PERSON, nor hath he in himself ever the more title to it, nor can any lay claim to it as their due. It belongeth not to Christ as SATISFIER, nor yet as LEGISLATOR, to make wicked refusers to become willing, and receive him and the benefits which he offers; therefore he may do all for them that is fore-expressed, though he cure not their unbelief. Faith is a fruit of the death of Christ, (and so is all the good which we do enjoy,) but not DIRECTLY, as it is SATISFACTION to JUSTICE; but only REMOTELY, as it proceedeth from that JUS DOMINII [right of dominion] which Christ has received to send the Spirit in what measure and TO WHOM HE WILL, and to succeed it accordingly; and as it is necessary to the attainment of the farther ends of his death in the certain gathering and saving of THE ELECT."

Thus the whole theory amounts to this, that, although a CONDITIONAL SALVATION has been purchased by Christ for all men, and is offered to them, and all legal difficulties are removed out of the way of their pardon as sinners by the atonement, yet Christ hath not purchased for any man the gift of FAITH, OR THE POWER OF PERFORMING THE CONDITION OF SALVATION REQUIRED; but gives this to some, and does not give it to others, by virtue of that ABSOLUTE DOMINION over men which he has purchased for himself, so that, as the Calvinists refer the decree of election to the sovereignty of the FATHER, Baxter refers it to the sovereignty of the SON; one makes the decree of reprobation to issue from the Creator and Judge, the other, from the Redeemer himself.

If, however, any one expects to find something in the form of system in Baxter's opinions on the five disputed points, he will be much disappointed. The parties to whom he refers as the authors of this supposed "middle way," differ as much among themselves as Baxter occasionally does from himself. Bishop Davenant and Dr. S. Ward differed from Amyraut, Martinius, and others of that school, on the topic of BAPTISMAL REGENERATION; and, as the subjects of baptism, according to the sentiments of the two former, are invested with invisible grace, and are regenerated in virtue of the ordinance when canonically performed, such divines far more easily disposed of their baptized converts in the ranks of strict predestination, than the others could who did not hold those sentiments. But they exhibited much ingenuity in not suffering it to "intrench upon the question of perseverance." Their friend Bishop Bedell, however, maintained, that "reprobates coming to years of discretion, after baptism, shall be condemned for original sin; for their absolution and washing in baptism was but conditional and expectative; which doth truly interest them in all the promises of God, but under the condition of repenting, believing and obeying, which they never perform, and therefore never attain the promise." Bishop Overal has also been claimed as a patron of this diversified "middle system;" but it will be evident to every one who peruses his productions, that his chief endeavour was to display the doctrines of the English church as identical with those of St. Augustine, yet basing them upon THE ANTECEDENT WILL OF GOD and CONDITIONAL DECREES. After all the refined distinctions which Baxter employed to render the theory of COMMON and SPECIAL grace plausible and popular, the real meaning of the inventors was frequently elicited when such a question as this was asked, "Have any men in the world grace sufficient to repent and believe savingly who do not?" After asserting that he knows nothing about the matter, the reply of Baxter is, "If we may conjecture upon probabilities, it seemeth most likely that there is such a sufficient grace, or power, to repent and believe savingly, in some that use it not, but perish." "This," says one of Baxter's apologists, "seems to me very inexplicable!" and in the same light it will be viewed by all who recollect that this "sufficient grace or power" is that "portion of special grace which never fails to accomplish its design,--the salvation of the individual on whom it is bestowed!" Baxter's celebrated "Aphorisms of Justification," published in 1649, afforded employment to himself and his theological critics till near the close of his life; and in the many modifications, concessions, and alterations which were extorted from him by men of different religious tenets, he sometimes incautiously proved himself to be more Calvinistic than Calvin, and at others more Arminian than Arminius. The following observations, from "Orme's *Life of Baxter*," are on the whole just and instructive:--

"Thus did Baxter, at a very early period of his life, launch into the ocean of controversy, on some of the most interesting subjects that can engage the human mind. The manner in which he began to treat them was little favourable to arriving at correct and satisfactory conclusions. Possessed of a mind uncommonly penetrating, he yet seems not to have had the faculty of compressing within narrow limits his own views, or the accounts he was disposed to give of the views of others. All this arose, not from any indisposition to be explicit, but from the peculiar character of his mind. He is perpetually distinguishing things into physical and moral, real and nominal, material and formal. However important these distinctions are, they often render his writings tiresome to the reader, and his reasonings more frequently perplexing than satisfactory. Baxter is generally understood to have pursued a middle course between Calvinism and Arminianism. That he tried to hold and adjust the balance between the two parties, and that he was most anxious to reconcile them, are very certain. But it seems scarcely less evident, that he was much more a Calvinist than he was an Arminian. While this seems to me very apparent, it must be acknowledged, that if certain views which have often been given of Calvinism are necessary to constitute a Calvinist, Richard Baxter was no believer in that creed.

"While satisfied that among Baxter's sentiments, no important or vital error will be found, yet in the style and method in which he too generally advocated or defended them, there is much to censure. The wrangling and disputatious manner in which he presented many of his views, was calculated to gender an unsanctified state of mind in persons who either abetted or opposed his sentiments. His scholastic and metaphysical style of arguing is unbefitting the simplicity of the Gospel, and cannot fail to injure it wherever such is employed. It not only savours too much of the spirit of the schools, and the philosophy of this world; but places the truths of revelation on a level with the rudiments of human science. I am not sure whether certain effects which began early in the last century to appear among the Presbyterian part of the Nonconformists, may not be traced, in some degree, to the speculative and argumentative writings of Baxter. His influence over this class of his brethren was evidently very great. He contributed more than any other man to mitigate the harsh and forbidding aspect which the Presbyterians presented during the civil wars and the commonwealth. This was well, but he did not stop here. He was inimical to all the existing systems of doctrine and discipline then contended for, or ever before known in the world; while he did not present any precisely defined system as his own. He opposed Calvinism; he opposed Arminianism; he would not allow himself to be considered an Episcopalian, in the ordinary acceptation of the word; he denied that he was a Presbyterian, and scorned to be thought an Independent. He held something in common with them all, and yet he was somewhat different from all. He contended for a system more general, and more liberal, than was then approved; and, as we have stated, wished to place a variety of theological truths on grounds belonging rather to philosophy or metaphysics, than to revelation.

"On himself, this species of latitudinarianism produced little injurious effect, but I fear it had a baneful influence on others. The rejection of all human authority and influence in religion, requires to be balanced by a very strong sense of the divine authority, to prevent its generating a state of mind more characterized by pride of intellect, and independence of spirit, than by the humility and diffidence which are essential features in the Christian character. It is a singular fact, that the Presbyterians, though at first more rigid in their doctrinal views, and more exclusive in their spirit and system of church government, than the Independents, became before the death of Baxter the more liberal party. High views began to be ascribed by them to their now moderate brethren; and, to avoid the charge of Antinomianism, which Baxter was too ready to prefer against such as differed from some of his views, the Presbyterians seem gradually to have sunk into a state of low, moderate orthodoxy, in which there was little of the warmth or vitality of evangelical religion.

"In farther illustration of the influence now adverted to, it must be remarked, that the first stage in that process of deterioration which took place among the Presbyterian Dissenters, was generally characterized by the term Baxterianism; a word to which it is difficult to attach a definite meaning. It denotes no separate sect or party, but rather a system of opinions on doctrinal points, verging toward Arminianism, and which ultimately passed to

Arianism and Socinianism. Even during Baxter's own life, while the Presbyterians taxed the Independents with Antinomianism, the latter retorted the charge of Socinianism, or at least of a tendency toward it, in some of the opinions maintained both by Baxter and others of that party. To whatever cause it is to be attributed, it is a melancholy fact, that the declension which began even at this early period in the Presbyterian body, went on slowly, but surely, till, from the most fervid orthodoxy, it finally arrived at the frigid zone of Unitarianism.

"I wish not to be understood as stating that Baxter either held any opinions of this description, or was conscious of a tendency in his sentiments toward such a fearful consummation; but, that there was an injurious tendency in his manner of discussing certain important subjects. It was subtle, and full of logomachy; it tended to unsettle, rather than to fix and determine; it gendered strife, rather than godly edifying. It is not possible to study such books as his '*Methodus*,' and his 'Catholic Theology,' without experiencing that we are brought into a different region from Apostolic Christianity; a region of fierce debate and altercation about words, and names, and opinions; in which all that can be said for error is largely dwelt upon, as well as what can be said for truth. The ambiguities of language, the diversities of sects, the uncertainties of human perception and argument are urged, till the force of revealed truth is considerably weakened, and confidence in our own judgment of its meaning greatly impaired. Erroneous language is maintained to be capable of sound meaning, and the most Scriptural phrases to be susceptible of unscriptural interpretation, till truth and error almost change places, and the mind is bewildered, confounded, and paralyzed. Into this mode of discussing such subjects, was this most excellent man led, partly by the natural constitution of his mind, which has often been adverted to; partly by his ardent desire of putting an end to the divisions of the Christian world, and producing universal concord and harmony. He failed where success was impossible, however plausible might have been the means which he employed. He understood the causes of difference and contention better than their remedies; hence the measures which he used frequently aggravated instead of curing the disease. While a portion of evil, however, probably resulted from Baxter's mode of conducting controversy, and no great light was thrown by him on some of the dark and difficult subjects which he so keenly discussed, I have no doubt he contributed considerably to produce a more moderate spirit toward each other, between Calvinists and Arminians, than had long prevailed. Though he satisfied neither party, he must have convinced both, that great difficulties exist on the subjects in debate, if pursued beyond a certain length; that allowance ought to be made by each, for the weakness or prejudices of the other; and that genuine religion is compatible with some diversity of opinion respecting one or all of the five points." A similar effect as that which Mr. Orme ascribes to Baxter's writings on the English Presbyterians, followed also, on the continent among the reformed churches. It was the same middle system with its philosophical subtleties, which Camero and Amyraut taught abroad, and which produced in them those effects that have been falsely ascribed, both in England and abroad, to Arminianism. See Amyraut and Cameron.

BAY-TREE. אזרח. It is mentioned only in Psalm xxxvii, 35, 36: "I have seen the ungodly in great power, and flourishing like a green bay-tree. Yet he passed away, and lo, he was not. Yea, I sought him, but he could not be found." Aben Ezra, Jarchi, Kimchi, Jerom, and some others say that the original may mean only A NATIVE TREE; a tree growing in its native soil, not having suffered by transplantation. Such a tree spreads itself luxuriantly. The Septuagint and Vulgate render it CEDARS; but the high Dutch of Luther's Bible, the old Saxon, the French, the Spanish, the Italian of Diodati, and the version of Ainsworth, make it the laurel.

BDELLIUM, בדלח, occurs Gen. ii, 12, and Num. xi, 7. Interpreters seem at a loss to know what to do with this word, and have rendered it variously. Many suppose it a mineral production. The Septuagint translates in the first place, ἀνθϱάκα, A CARBUNCLE, and in the second, κϱύςαλλον, A CRYSTAL. The rabbins are followed by Reland in calling it a crystal; but some, instead of BEDOLAH, read BEROLAH, changing the ב into ר, which are not always easily distinguished, and are often mistaken by transcribers; and so render it the BERYL, which, say they, is the prime kind of crystal. The BEDOLEH, in Genesis, is undoubtedly some precious stone; and its colour, mentioned in Numbers, where the manna is spoken of as of the colour of BDELLIUM, is explained by a reference to Exod. xvi, 14, 31, where it is likened to hoar frost, which being like little fragments of ice, may confirm the opinion that the bdellium is the beryl, perhaps that pellucid kind, called by Dr. Hill the ELLIPOMOCROSTYLA, or beryl crystal.

BEAN, פול, occurs 2 Sam. xvii, 28, and Ezek. iv, 9. A common legume. Those most usually cultivated in Syria are the white horse-bean, FABA ROTUNDA OBLONGA, and the kidney-bean, PHASEOLIS MINIMUS, FRUCTU VIRIDI OVATO, called by the natives MASCH. The Arabic BAN, the name of the coffee berry, corresponds with our bean, and is probably its etymon.

BEAR. That bears were common in Palestine appears from several passages of the Old Testament. Their strength, rapacity, and fierceness, furnish many expressive metaphors to the Hebrew poets. The Hebrew name of this animal is taken from his GROWLING; so Varro deduces his Latin name URSUS by an onomatopæia from the noise which he makes: "URSI LUCANA ORIGO, VEL UNDE ILLI, NOSTRI AB IPSIUS VOCE:" [the origin of the term URSUS (bear) is Lucanian, (whence also the bears themselves,) from the noise made by the animal.] David had to defend his flock against bears as well as lions, 1 Sam. xvii, 34. And Dr. Shaw gives us to understand that these rugged animals are not peculiar to the bleak regions of the north, being found in Barbary; and Thevenot informs us that they inhabit the wilderness adjoining the Holy Land, and that he saw one near the northern extremities of the Red Sea. The ferocity of the bear, especially when hungry or robbed of its whelps, has been mentioned by many authors. The Scripture alludes in three places to this furious disposition. The first is, 2 Sam. xvii, 8, "They be mighty men, and they be chafed in their minds as a bear robbed of her whelps in the field." The second, Prov. xvii, 12, "Let a bear robbed of her whelps meet a man rather than a fool in his folly." And the third, Hosea xiii, 8, "I will meet them as a bear that is bereaved of her whelps, and will rend the caul of their heart."

BEARD. The Hebrews wore their beards, but had, doubtless, in common with other Asiatic nations, several fashions in this, as in all other parts of dress. Moses forbids them, Lev. xix, 27, "to cut off entirely the angle, or extremity of their beard;" that is, to avoid the manner of the Egyptians, who left only a little tuft of beard at the extremity of their chins. The Jews, in some places, at this day suffer a little fillet of hair to grow from below the ears to the chin: where, as well as upon their lower lips, their beards are long. When they mourned, they entirely shaved the hair of their heads and beards, and neglected to trim their beards, to regulate them into neat order, or to remove what grew on their upper lips and cheeks, Jer. xli, 5; xlviii, 37. In times of grief and affliction, they plucked away the hair of their heads and beards, a mode of expression common to other nations under great calamities. The king of the Ammonites, designing to insult David in the person of his ambassadors, cut away half of their beards, and half of their clothes; that is, he cut off all their beard on one side of their faces, 2 Sam. x, 4, 5; 1 Chron. xix, 5. To avoid ridicule, David did not wish them to appear at his court till their beards were grown again. When a leper was cured of his leprosy, he washed himself in a bath, and shaved off all the hair of his body; after which, he returned into the camp, or city; seven days afterward, he washed himself and his clothes again, shaved off all his hair, and offered the sacrifices appointed for his purification, Lev. xiv, 9. The Levites, at their consecration, were purified by bathing, and washing their bodies and clothes; after which, they shaved off all the hair of their bodies, and then offered the sacrifices appointed for their consecration, Num. viii, 7.

Nothing has been more fluctuating in the different ages of the world and countries than the fashion of wearing the beard. Some have cultivated one part and some another; some have endeavoured to extirpate it entirely, while others have almost idolized it; the revolutions of countries have scarcely been more famous than the revolutions of beards. It is a great mark of infamy among the Arabs to cut off the beard. Many people would prefer death to this kind of treatment. As they would think it a grievous punishment to lose it, they carry things so far as to beg for the sake of it: "By your beard, by the life of your beard, God preserve your blessed beard." When they would express their value for any thing, they say, "It is worth more than a man's beard." And hence we may easily learn the magnitude of the offence of the Ammonites in their treatment of David's ambassadors, as above mentioned; and also the force of the emblem used Ezek. v, 1–5, where the inhabitants of Jerusalem are compared to the hair of his head and beard. Though they had been dear to God as the hair of an eastern beard to its owner, they should be taken away and consumed, one part by pestilence and famine, another by the sword, another by the calamities incident on exile.

BEASTS. When this word is used in opposition to man, as Psalm xxxvi, 5, any brute creature is signified; when to creeping things, as Lev. xi, 2, 7; xxix, 30, four-footed animals, from the size of the hare and upward, are intended; and when to wild creatures, as Gen. i, 25, cattle, or tame animals, are spoken of. In Isaiah xiii, 21, several wild animals are mentioned as dwelling among the ruins of Babylon: "Wild beasts of the desert," ציים, those of the dry wilderness, as the root of the word implies, "shall dwell there. Their houses shall be full of doleful creatures," אחים, MARSH ANIMALS. "Owls shall dwell there," ostriches, "and satyrs," שעירים, SHAGGY ONES, "shall dance there. And the wild beasts of the islands," איים, OASES OF THE DESERT, "shall cry in their desolate houses, and dragons," תנים, CROCODILES, or amphibious animals, "shall be in their desolate places." St. Paul, 1 Cor. xv, 32, speaks of fighting with beasts, &c: by which he does not mean his having been exposed in the amphitheatre to fight as a gladiator, as some have conjectured, but that he had to contend at Ephesus with the fierce uproar of Demetrius and his associates. Ignatius uses the same figure in his Epistle to the Romans: "From Syria even unto Rome I fight with wild beasts, both by sea and land, both night and day, being bound to ten leopards;" that is, to a band of soldiers. So Lucian, in like manner, says, "For I am not to fight with ordinary wild beasts, but with men, insolent and hard to be convinced." In Rev. iv, v, vi, mention is made of four beasts, or rather, as the word ζῶα signifies, LIVING CREATURES, as in Ezek. i; and so the word might have been less harshly translated. Wild beasts are used in Scripture as emblems of tyrannical and persecuting powers. The most illustrious conquerors of antiquity also have not a more honourable emblem.

BED. Mattresses, or thick cotton quilts folded, were used for sleeping upon. These were laid upon the duan, or divan, a part of the room elevated above the level of the rest, covered with a carpet in winter, and a fine mat in summer. (See ACCUBATION and BANQUETS.) A divan cushion serves for a pillow and bolster. They do not keep their beds made; the mattresses are rolled up, carried away, and placed in a cupboard till they are wanted at night. And hence the propriety of our Lord's address to the paralytic, "Arise, take up thy bed," or mattress, "and walk," Matt. ix, 6. The duan on which these mattresses are placed, is at the end of the chamber, and has an ascent of several steps. Hence Hezekiah is said to turn his face to the wall when he prayed, that is, from his attendants. In the day the duan was used as a seat, and the place of honour was the corner, Amos iii, 12.

BEELZEBUB, Matt. x, 25. See Baalzebub.

BEERSHEBA, or the well of the oath; so named from a well which Abraham dug in this place, and the covenant which he here made with Abimelech, king of Gerar, Gen. xx, 31. Here also he planted a grove, as it would appear, for the purpose of retirement for religious worship. In process of time, a considerable town was built on the same spot, which retained the same name. Beersheba was given by Joshua to the tribe of Judah, and afterward transferred to Simeon, Joshua xv, 28. It was situated twenty miles south of Hebron, in the extreme south of the land of Israel, as Dan was on the north. The two places are frequently thus mentioned in Scripture, as "from Dan to Beersheba," to denote the whole length of the country.

דבורה **BEE**, דבורה, occurs Deut. i, 44; Judges xiv, 8; Psalm cviii, 12; Isa. vii, 18. A well known, small, industrious insect; whose form, propagation, economy, and singular instinct and ingenuity, have attracted the attention of the most inquisitive and laborious inquirers into nature. Bees were very numerous in the east. SERID, OR SERIAD, means "the land of the hive;" and Canaan was celebrated as "a land flowing with milk and honey." The wild bees formed their comb in the crevices of the rocks, and in the hollows of decayed trees. The passage in Isa. vii, 8, which mentions the "hissing for the bee," is supposed to involve an allusion to the practice of calling out the bees from their hives, by a hissing or whistling sound, to their labour in the fields, and summoning them again to return when the heavens begin to lower, or the shadows of evening to fall. In this manner Jehovah threatens to rouse the enemies of Judah, and lead them to the prey. However widely scattered, or far remote from the scene of action, they should hear his voice, and with as much promptitude as the bee that has been taught to recognise the signal of its owner and obey his call, they should assemble their forces; and although weak and insignificant as a swarm of bees, in the estimation of a proud and infatuated people, they should come, with irresistible might, and take possession of the rich and beautiful region which had been abandoned by its terrified inhabitants.

The bee is represented by the ancients as a vexatious and even a formidable enemy; and the experience of every person who turns his attention to the temper and habits of this insect attests the truth of their assertion. The allusion, therefore, of Moses to their fierce hostility, Deut. i, 44, is both just and beautiful: "The Amorites, which dwelt in that mountain, came out against you, and chased you as bees do, and destroyed you in Seir even unto Hormah." The Amorites, it appears, were the most bitter adversaries to Israel of all the nations of Canaan. Like bees that are easily irritated, that attack with great fury and increasing numbers the person that dares to molest their hive, and persecute him in his flight to a considerable distance, the incensed Amorites had collected their hostile bands, and chased the Israelites from their territory. The Psalmist also complains that his enemies compassed him about like bees; fiercely attacking him on every side. From these allusions it would however appear, that the bees of the east were of a more quarrelsome temper than ours, which exist chiefly in a domesticated state.

BEETLE. חרגל. It occurs only Lev. xi, 22. A species of locust is thought to be there spoken of. The word still remains in the Arabic, and is derived from an original, alluding to the vast number of their swarms. Golius explains it of the locust without wings. The Egyptians paid a superstitious worship to the beetle. Mr. Molyneaux, in the "Philosophical Transactions," says, "It is more than probable that this destructive beetle we are speaking of was that very kind of scarabæus, which the idolatrous Egyptians of old had in such high veneration as to pay divine worship unto it, and so frequently engrave its image upon their obelisks, &c, as we see at this day. For nothing can be supposed more natural than to imagine a nation, addicted to polytheism, as the Egyptians were, in a country frequently suffering great mischief and scarcity from swarms of devouring insects, should, from a strange sense and fear of evil to come, (the common principle of superstition and idolatry,) give sacred worship to the visible authors of these their sufferings, in hopes to render them more propitious for the future. See Fly and Locust.

BEHEMOTH. בהמות. This term has greatly tried the ingenuity of the critics. By some, among whom are Bythner and Reiske, it is regarded in Job xl, 16, as a plural noun for beasts in general: the peculiar name of the animal immediately described not being mentioned, as unnecessary, on account of the description itself being so easily applied at the time. In this sense it is translated in various passages in the Psalms. Thus, l, 10, in which it is usually rendered cattle, as the plural of בהמת it means unquestionably a BEAST or BRUTE, in the general signification of these words: "For every beast of the field is mine, and the cattle," BEHEMOTH, "upon a thousand hills." So again, Isa. lxxiii, 22: "So foolish was I, and ignorant; I was as a beast," BEHEMOTH, "before thee." It is also used in the same sense in chap. xxxv, 11, of the book of Job: "Who teacheth us more than the beasts," BEHEMOTH, "of the earth." The greater number of critics, however, have understood the word behemoth, in the singular number, as the peculiar name of the quadruped described, Job xl, of whatever kind or nature it may be; although they have materially differed upon this last point, some regarding it as the hippopotamus, or river horse, and others as the elephant. The evidence in favour of the hippopotamus appears, however, to predominate. The hippopotamus is nearly as large as the rhinoceros. The male has been found seventeen feet in length, fifteen in circumference, and seven in height. The head is enormously large, and the jaws extend upwards two feet, and are armed with four cutting teeth, each of which is twelve inches in length. The body is of a lightish colour, thinly covered with hair. The legs are three feet long. Though amphibious, the hoofs, which are quadrifid, are not connected by membranes. The hide is so thick and tough as to resist the edge of a sword or sabre. Although an inhabitant of the waters, the hippopotamus is well known to breathe air like land animals. On land, indeed, he finds the chief part of his food. It has been pretended that he devours vast quantities of fish; but it appears with the fullest evidence, both from the relations of many travellers, and from the structure of the stomach, in specimens that have been dissected, that he is nourished solely, or almost solely, on vegetable food. Though he feeds upon aquatic plants, yet he very often leaves the waters, and commits wide devastations through all the cultivated fields adjacent to the river. Unless when accidentally provoked, or wounded, he is never offensive; but when he is assaulted or hurt, his fury against the assailants is terrible. He will attack a boat, break it in pieces with his teeth; or, where the river is not too deep, he will raise it on his back and overset it. If he be irritated when on shore, he will immediately betake himself to the water; and there, in his native element, shows all his strength and resolution.

BEHMENISTS, a name given to those mystics who adopted the explication of the mysteries of nature and grace, as given by Jacob Behmen. This writer was born in the year 1575, at Old Siedenburg, near Gorlitz, in Upper Lusatia. He was a shoemaker by trade, and is described as having been thoughtful and religious from his youth up, taking peculiar pleasure in frequenting the public worship. At length, seriously considering within himself that speech of our Saviour, "Your heavenly Father will give the Holy Spirit to them that ask him," he was thereby awakened to desire that promised Comforter; and, continuing in that earnestness, he was at last, to use his own expression, "surrounded with a divine light for seven days, and stood in the highest contemplation and kingdom of joys!" After this, about the year 1600, he was again surrounded with a divine light and replenished with the heavenly knowledge; insomuch as, going abroad into the fields, and viewing the herbs and grass, by his inward light, he saw into their essences, uses, and properties, which were discovered to him by their lineaments, figures, and signatures. In the year 1610, he had a third special illumination, wherein still farther mysteries were revealed to him; but it was not till the year 1612 that Behmen committed these revelations to writing. His first treatise is entitled, "Aurora," which was seized by the senate of Gorlitz before it was completed. His next production is called, "The Three Principles," by which he means the dark world, or hell; the light world, or heaven; and the external, or visible world, which we inhabit. In this work he more fully illustrates the subjects treated of in the former, and supplies what is wanting in that work, showing, 1. How all things came from a working will of the holy, triune, incomprehensible God, manifesting himself as Father, Son, and Holy Spirit, through an outward, perceptible, working, triune power of fire, light, and spirit, in the kingdom of heaven. 2. How and what angels and men were in their creation; that they are in and from God, his real offspring; that their life begun in and from this divine fire, which is the Father of Light, generating a birth of light in their souls; from both which proceeds the Holy Spirit, or breath of divine love, in the triune creature, as it does in the triune Creator. 3. How some angels, and all men, are fallen from God, and their first state of a divine triune life in him; what they are in their fallen state, and the difference between the fall of angels and that of man. 4. How the earth, stars, and elements were created in consequence of the fall of angels. 5. Whence there is good and evil in all this temporal world; and what is meant by the curse that dwells in it. 6. Of the kingdom of Christ, how it is set in opposition to the kingdom of hell. 7. How man, through faith in Christ, is able to overcome the kingdom of hell, and thereby obtain eternal salvation. 8. How and why sin and misery shall only reign for a time, until God shall, in a supernatural way, make fallen man rise to the glory of angels, and this material system shake off its curse, and enter into an everlasting union with that heaven from whence it fell.

The next year, Behmen produced his "Three-fold Life of Man," according to the three principles above mentioned. In this work he treats more largely of the state of man in this world: that he has, 1. That immortal spark of life, which is common to angels and devils. 2. That divine life of the light and Spirit of God, which makes the essential difference between an angel and a devil; and, 3. The life of this external and visible world. The first and last are common to all men; but the second only to a true Christian, or child of God. Behmen wrote several other treatises; but these are the basis of all his other writings. His conceptions are often clothed under allegorical symbols; and, in his later works, he frequently adopted chemical and Latin phrases, which he borrowed from conversation with learned men. But as to the matter contained in his writings, he disclaims having borrowed it either from men or books. He died in the year 1624; and his last words were, "Now I go hence into paradise!" Behmen's principles were adopted by Mr. Law, who clothed them in a more modern dress, and in a style less obscure. The essential obscurity of the subjects indeed he could not remedy. If they were understood by the author himself, he is probably the only one who ever made that attainment.

BEL, or Belus, a name by which many Heathens, and particularly the Babylonians, called their chief idol. But whether under this appellation they worshipped Nimrod, their first Baal, or lord, or Pul, king of Assyria, or some other monarch, or the sun, or all in one, is uncertain. It is, however, probable, that Bel is the same as the Phenician Baal, and that the worship of the same deity passed over to the Carthagenians, who were a colony of Phenicians. Hence the names Hannibal, Asdrubal, &c, compounded with Bel or Baal, according to the custom of the east, where great men added the names of the gods to their own. Bel had a temple erected to him in the city of Babylon, on the very uppermost range of the famous tower of Babel, wherein were many statues of this pretended deity; and one, among the rest, of massy gold, forty feet high. The whole furniture of this magnificent temple was of the same metal, and valued at eight hundred talents of gold. This temple, with its riches, was in being till the time of Xerxes, who, returning from his unfortunate expedition into Greece, demolished it, and carried off the immense wealth which it contained. It was, probably, the statue of this god which Nebuchadnezzar, being returned to Babylon after the end of the Jewish war, set up and dedicated in the plain of Dura; the story of which is related at large, Dan. iii. See Babel.

Bel and the Dragon, an apocryphal and uncanonical book. It was always rejected by the Jewish church, and is extant neither in the Hebrew, nor in the Chaldee languages; nor is there any proof that it ever was so, although the council of Trent allowed it to be part of the canonical book of Daniel, in which it stands in the Latin Vulgate. There are two Greek texts of this fragment, that of the Septuagint, and that found in Theodotion's Greek version of Daniel. The Latin and Arabic versions are from the text of Theodotion. Daniel probably, by detecting the mercenary contrivances of the idolatrous priests of Babylon, and by opening the eyes of the people to the follies of superstition, might furnish some foundation for the story; but the whole is evidently charged with fiction, though introduced with a pious intent. St. Jerom gives it no better title than, "The fable of Bel and the Dragon." Selden thinks that this history ought rather to be considered as a poem or fiction, than a true account: as to the dragon, he observes, that serpents, DRACONES, made a part of the hidden mysteries of the Pagan religion, as appears from Clemens Alexandrinus, Julius Firmicus, Justin Martyr, and others. See Serpent.

BELIAL. The phrase, "sons of Belial," signifies WICKED, WORTHLESS MEN. It was given to the inhabitants of Gibeah, who abused the Levite's wife, Judges xix, 22; and to Hophni and Phineas, the wicked and profane sons of Eli, 1 Samuel ii, 12. In later times the name Belial denoted the devil: "What concord hath Christ with Belial?" 2 Cor. vi, 15; for as the word literally imports "one who will do no one good," the positive sense of a doer of evil was applied to Satan, who is the author of evil, and, eminently, "the Evil One."

BELLS. Moses ordered that the lower part of the blue robe, which the high priest wore in religious ceremonies, should be adorned with pomegranates and bells, intermixed alternately, at equal distances. The pomegranates were of wool, and in colour, blue purple, and crimson; the bells were of gold. Moses adds, "And it shall be upon Aaron to minister; and his sound shall be heard when he goeth in unto the holy place before the Lord, and when he cometh out; that he die not." Some of the Hebrews believe that these little bells are round; others, that they were such as were commonly in use. The ancient kings of Persia are said to have had the hem of their robes adorned like that of the Jewish high priest, with pomegranates and golden bells. The Arabian ladies, who are about the king's person, have little gold bells fastened to their legs, their neck, and elbows, which, when they dance, make a very agreeable harmony. The Arabian women of rank, generally, wear on their legs large hollow gold rings, containing small flints, that sound like little bells when they walk; or they are large circles, with little rings hung all round, which produce the same effect. These, when they walk, give notice that the mistress of the house is passing, that so the servants of the family may behave themselves respectfully, and strangers may retire, to avoid seeing the person who advances. It was, in all probability, with some such design of giving notice that the high priest was passing, that he also wore little bells at the hem of his robe. Their sound intimated also when he was about to enter the sanctuary, and served to keep up the attention of the people. A reverential respect for the Divine Inhabitant was also indicated. The palace of kings was not to be entered without due notice, by striking some sonorous body, much less the sanctuary of God; and the high priest did, by the sound of his bells at the bottom of his robe, ask leave to enter. "And his sound shall be heard when he goeth into the holy place before the Lord, and when he cometh out; that he die not."

Bells were a part of the martial furniture of horses employed in war. The Jewish warrior adorned his charger with these ornaments; and the prophet foretels that these in future times should be consecrated to the service of God: "In that day shall there be upon the bells of the horses, Holiness unto the Lord." Chardin observes that something like this is seen in several places of the east; in Persia, and in Turkey, the reins of their bridles are of silk, of the thickness of a finger, on which are wrought the name of God, or other inscriptions. A horse which had not been trained was by the Greeks called, "one that had never heard the noise of bells."

BELLY is used in Scripture for gluttony, Titus i, 12; Philip iii, 16; Rom. xvi, 18. For the heart, or the secrets of the mind, Prov. xx, 27, 30; xxii, 18. The "belly of hell" signifies the grave, or some imminent danger, or deep distress, Jonah ii, 2; Ecclus. ii, 5.

BELSHAZZAR, the last king of Babylon, and, according to Hales and others, the grandson of Nebuchadnezzar, Dan. v, 18. During the period that the Jews were in captivity at Babylon, a variety of singular events concurred to prove that the sins which brought desolation on their country, and subjected them for a period of seventy years to the Babylonish yoke, had not dissolved that covenant relation which, as the God of Abraham, Jehovah had entered into with them; and that any act of indignity perpetrated against an afflicted people, or any insult cast upon the service of their temple, would be regarded as an affront to the Majesty of heaven, and not suffered to pass with impunity, though the perpetrators were the princes and potentates of the earth. Belshazzar was a remarkable instance of this. He had an opportunity of seeing, in the case of his ancestor, how hateful pride is, even in royalty itself; how instantly God can blast the dignity of the brightest crown, and reduce him that wears it to a level with the beasts of the field; and consequently how much the prosperity of kings and the stability of their thrones depend upon acknowledging that "the Most High ruleth in the kingdom of men, and giveth it to whomsoever he will." But all these awful lessons were lost upon Belshazzar.

The only circumstances of his reign, recorded, are the visions of the Prophet Daniel, in the first and third years, Dan. vii, 1; viii, 1; and his sacrilegious feast and violent death, Dan. v, 1–30. Isaiah, who represents the Babylonian dynasty as "the scourge of Palestine," styles Nebuchadnezzar "a serpent," Evil Merodach "a cockatrice," and Belshazzar "a fiery flying serpent," the worst of all, Isaiah xiv, 4–29. And Xenophon confirms this prophetic character by two atrocious instances of cruelty and barbarity, exercised by Belshazzar upon some of his chief and most deserving nobles. He slew the only son of Gobryas, in a transport of rage, because at a hunting match he hit with his spear a bear, and afterward a lion, when the king had missed both; and in a fit of jealousy, he brutally castrated Gadatus, because one of his concubines had commended him as a handsome man. His last and most heinous offence was the profanation of the sacred vessels belonging to the temple of Jerusalem, which his wise grandfather, and even his foolish father Evil Merodach, had respected. Having made a great feast for a thousand of his lords, he ordered those vessels to be brought during the banquet, that he, his princes, his wives, and his concubines, might drink out of them, which they did; and to aggravate sacrilege by apostasy and rebellion, and ingratitude against the Supreme Author of all their enjoyments, "they praised the gods of gold, silver, brass, iron, and stone, but the God in whose hand was their breath, and whose were all their ways, they praised or glorified not." For these complicated crimes his doom was denounced in the midst of the entertainment; a divine hand appeared, which wrote on the plaister of the wall, opposite to the king, and full in his view, a mysterious inscription. This tremendous apparition struck Belshazzar with the greatest terror and agony: "his countenance was changed, and his thoughts troubled him, so that the joints of his loins were loosed, and his knees smote against each other." This is one of the liveliest and finest amplifications of dismay to be found throughout the sacred classics, and infinitely exceeds, both in accuracy and force, the most admired of the Heathen; such as "ET CORDE ET GENIBUS TREMIT," of Horace, and "TARDA TREMENTI GENUA LABANT," of Virgil.

Unable himself to decypher the writing, Belshazzar cried aloud to bring in the astrologers, the Chaldeans, and the soothsayers, promising that whosoever should read the writing, and explain to him its meaning, should be clothed with scarlet, have a chain of gold about his neck, and be the third ruler in his kingdom. But the writing was too difficult for the Magi; at which the king was still more greatly troubled. In this crisis, and at the instance of the queen mother, the Prophet Daniel was sent for, to whom honours were promised, on condition of his explaining the writing. Daniel refused the honours held out to him; but having with great faithfulness pointedly reproved the monarch for his ingratitude to God who had conferred on him such dignity, and particularly for his profanation of the vessels which were consecrated to his service, he proceeded to the interpretation of the words which had been written, and still stood visible on the wall. They were, MENE, TEKEL, UPHARSIN. "This is the interpretation of the thing, MENE, 'God hath numbered thy kingdom and finished it;' TEKEL, 'thou art weighed in the balances and art found wanting;' PERES, 'thy kingdom is divided, and given to the Medes and Persians.'" In that very night, in the midst of their mirth and revelling, the city was taken by surprise, Belshazzar himself put to death, and the kingdom transferred to Darius the Mede. If the character of the hand-writing was known to the Magi of Babylon, the meaning could not be conjectured. Perhaps, however, the character was that of the ancient Hebrew, or what we now call the Samaritan; and in that case it would be familiar to Daniel, though rude and unintelligible to the Chaldeans. But even if Daniel could read the words, the import of this solemn graphic message to the proud and impious monarch could only have been made known to the prophet by God. All the ideas the three words convey, are NUMBERING, WEIGHING, and DIVIDING. It was only for the power which sent the omen to unfold, not in equivocal terms, like the responses of Heathen oracles, but in explicit language, the decision of the righteous Judge, the termination of his long suffering, and the instant visitation of judgment. See Babylon.

BELUS, a river of Palestine. On leaving Acre, and turning toward the south-east, the traveller crosses the river Belus, near its mouth, where the stream is shallow enough to be easily forded on horseback. This river rises out of a lake, computed to be about six miles distant, toward the south-east, called by the ancients PALUS CENDOVIA. Of the sand of this river, according to Pliny, glass was first made; and ships from Italy continued to convey it to the glass houses of Venice and Genoa, so late as the middle of the seventeenth century.

BENEDICTION, in a general sense, the act of blessing in the name of God, or of giving praise to God, or returning thanks for his favours. Hence benediction is the act of saying grace before or after meals. Neither the ancient Jews, nor Christians, ever ate without a short prayer. The Jews are obliged to rehearse a hundred benedictions every day; of which, eighty are to be spoken in the morning. Rabbi Nehemiah Baruch, in 1688, published a discourse on the manner wherein the sacerdotal benediction is to be pronounced. In the synagogue of Ferrara, it is rather sung than spoken. Among the ancient Jews, as well as Christians, benedictions were attended with the imposition of hands; and Christians, in process of time, added the sign of the cross, which was made with the same hand, elevated or extended. Hence, in the Romish church, benediction was used to denote the sign of the cross, made by a bishop or prelate, from an idea that it conferred some grace on the people. The custom of receiving benediction by bowing the head before the bishops, is very ancient; and was so universal, that emperors themselves did not decline this mark of submission. Under the name benediction the Hebrews also frequently understood the presents which friends made to one another; in all probability because they were generally attended with blessings and prayers, both from those who gave and those who received them. The solemn blessing pronounced by the Jewish high priest upon the people, is recorded Num. vi, 22, &c: "The Lord bless thee, and keep thee: the Lord make his face to shine upon thee, and be gracious unto thee: the Lord lift up his countenance upon thee, and give thee peace." The great

Christian benediction is, "The grace of our Lord Jesus Christ, the love of God the Father, and the fellowship of the Holy Ghost, be with you always." See Blessing.

BENHADAD, the son of Tibrimon, king of Syria, came to the assistance of Asa, king of Judah, against Baasha, king of Israel, obliging the latter to return home and succour his own country, and to abandon Ramah, which he had undertaken to fortify, 1 Kings xv, 18. This Benhadad is thought by some to have been the same person with Hadad the Edomite, who rebelled against Solomon toward the end of that prince's reign, 1 Kings xi, 25.

2. Benhadad, king of Syria, son of the preceding, made war upon Ahab, king of Israel, but was defeated. In the following year, however, he came with a most powerful army to Aphek, where Ahab again engaged him, killed a hundred thousand of his men, and the remainder endeavouring to take refuge in Aphek, the walls of the city fell upon them, and killed twenty-seven thousand more. Thus completely defeated, Benhadad submitted to beg his life of the king of Israel, who not only granted his request, but gave him his liberty, and restored him to his crown upon certain conditions, 1 Kings xx. Twelve years afterward, A. M. 3115, Benhadad declared war against Jehoram, the son and successor of Ahab, 2 Kings vi, 8; but his designs were made known to Jehoram by the Prophet Elisha, and they were accordingly frustrated. Suspecting some treachery in this affair, Benhadad was informed that all his projects were revealed to his enemy by Elisha, and getting intelligence that the latter was at Dothan, he sent a detachment of his best troops to invest the city and apprehend the prophet; but they were struck with blindness at Elisha's prayer, so that they were unable to distinguish him, when he was in the midst of them and held a conversation with them. He then led them into the city of Samaria, and having conducted them safely there, he prayed to God again to open their eyes, and induced Jehoram to dismiss them without violence. Generous as this conduct was, it produced no salutary effect on the infatuated Benhadad; for about four years afterward, he laid close siege to Samaria, and reduced the city to such distress that the head of an ass, which the Israelites considered to be an unclean animal, was sold for fourscore pieces of silver, about 2*l.* 9*s.* sterling; and the fourth part of a cab of dove's dung, or rather three quarters of a pint of chick pease, as Bochart understands the word, for five pieces of silver. In fact, such was the pressure of the famine at this time in Samaria, that mothers were constrained to eat their own children. Jehoram, hearing of these calamities, attributed them to Elisha, and sent orders to have him put to death; but before his messengers could reach the prophet's house, he came thither himself. Elisha predicted that the next day, about the same hour, a measure of fine flour would be sold at the gate of Samaria for a shekel, which, however incredible at the moment, proved to be the case; for in the night, a general panic, supernaturally induced, pervaded the Syrian camp; they imagined that Jehoram had procured an army of Egyptians to come to his assistance, and, abandoning their horses, tents, and provisions, they all took to flight. Four lepers, whose disease did not permit them to live within the city, and being ready to perish with hunger, ventured into the Syrian camp; and finding it deserted, and at the same time abounding with all sorts of provisions, communicated the information to Jehoram. The king immediately rose, though in the middle of the night; but reflecting that probably it was only a stratagem of Benhadad to draw his people out of the town, he first sent parties to reconnoitre. They, however, speedily returned, and informed him that the enemy was fled, and that the roads were every where strewed with arms and garments, which the Syrians had abandoned to facilitate their flight. As soon as the news was confirmed, the Samaritans went out, pillaged the Syrian camp, and brought in such quantities of provisions, that a measure of fine flour was, at the time specified by Elisha, sold at the gate of Samaria for a shekel, 2 Kings vii.

The following year, A. M. 3120, Benhadad fell sick, and sent Hazael, one of his officers, with forty camels, loaded with valuable presents, to the Prophet Elisha, to interrogate him, whether or not he should recover of his indisposition. Elisha fixed his eyes steadfastly on Hazael, and then burst into tears: "Go," said he, "and tell Benhadad, Thou mayest certainly recover; though the Lord hath showed me that he shall assuredly die." He at the same time apprised Hazael that he himself would reign in Syria, and do infinite mischief to Israel. Hazael on this returned and told Benhadad that his health should be restored. But on the next day he took a thick cloth, which, having dipped in water, he spread over the king's face and stifled him. He then took possession of the kingdom of Syria, according to the prediction of Elisha, 2 Kings viii.

3. Benhadad, the son of Hazael, mentioned in the preceding article, succeeded his father as king of Syria, 2 Kings xiii, 24. During his reign, Jehoash, king of Israel, recovered from him all that his father Hazael had taken from Jehoahaz his predecessor. He defeated him in three several engagements, and compelled him to surrender all the country beyond Jordan, 2 Kings xiii, 25.

BENI KHAIBIR, sons of Keber, the descendants of the Rechabites, to whom it was promised, Jer. xxxv, 19, "Thus saith the Lord, Jonadab, the son of Rechab, shall not want a man to stand before me for ever." They were first brought into notice in modern times by Mr. Samuel Brett, who wrote a narrative of the proceedings of the great council of the Jews in Hungary, A. D. 1650. He says of the sect of the Rechabites, "that they observe their old rules and customs, and neither sow, nor plant, nor build houses; but live in tents, and often remove from one place to another with their whole property and families." They are also mentioned in Neibuhr's travels. Mr. Wolff, a converted Jew, gives the following account in a late journal. He inquired of the rabbins at Jerusalem, relative to these wandering Jews, and received the following information: "Rabbi Mose Secot is quite certain that the Beni Khaibir are descendants of the Rechabites; at this present moment they drink no wine, and have neither vineyard, nor field, nor seed; but dwell, like Arabs, in tents, and are wandering nomades. They receive and observe the law of Moses by tradition, for they are not in possession of the written law." Mr. Wolff afterward himself visited this people, who have remained, amidst all the changes of nations, a most remarkable monument of the exact fulfilment of a minute, and apparently at first sight an unimportant, prophecy. So true is it, that not one jot or tittle of the word of God shall pass away! See Rechabites.

BENJAMIN, the youngest son of Jacob and Rachel, who was born, A. M. 2272. Jacob, being on his journey from Mesopotamia, as he was proceeding southward with Rachel in the company, Gen. xxxv, 16, 17, &c, the pains of child-bearing came upon her, about a quarter of a league from Bethlehem, and she died after the delivery of a son, whom, with her last breath, she named Benoni, that is, "the son of my sorrow;" but soon afterward Jacob changed his name, and called him Benjamin, that is, "the son of my right hand." See Joseph.

BEREA, a city of Macedonia, where St. Paul preached the Gospel with great success, and where his hearers were careful to compare what they heard with the scriptures of the Old Testament, Acts, xvii, 10; for which they are commended, and held out to us as an example of subjecting every doctrine to the sole test of the word of God.

BERNICE, the daughter of Agrippa, surnamed the Great, king of the Jews, and sister to young Agrippa, also king of the Jews. This lady was first betrothed to Mark, the son of Alexander Lysimachus, albarach of Alexandria; afterward she married Herod, king of Chalcis, her own uncle by the father's side. After the death of Herod, which happened A. D. 48, she was married to Polemon, king of Pontus, but did not long continue with him. She returned to her brother Agrippa, and with him heard the discourse which Paul delivered before Festus, Acts xxv.

BERYL, תרשיש, a pellucid gem of a bluish green colour, whence it is called by the lapidaries, AQUA MARINA. Its Hebrew name is a word also for the same reason given to the sea, Psalm xlviii, 7. It is found in the East Indies, Peru, Siberia, and Tartary. It has a brilliant appearance, and is generally transparent. It was the tenth stone belonging to the high priest's pectoral, Exod. xxviii, 10, 20; Rev. xxi, 20.

BETHABARA, or **BETHBARAH**, signifies in the Hebrew a place of passage, because of its ford over the river Jordan, on the east bank of which river it stood over against Jericho, Joshua ii, 7; iii, 15, 16. To this place Gideon sent a party to secure the passage of the river, previous to his attack on the Midianites, Judges vii, 24. Here John commenced his baptizing, and here Christ himself was baptized, John i, 28. To this place, also, Jesus retired, when the Jews sought to take him at the feast of dedication; and many who resorted there to him believed on him, John x, 39–42.

BETHANY, a considerable place, situated on the ascent of the mount of Olives, about two miles from Jerusalem, John xi, 18; Matt. xxi, 17; xxvi, 6, &c. Here it was that Martha and Mary lived, with their brother Lazarus, whom Jesus raised from the dead; and it was here that Mary poured the perfume on our Saviour's head. Bethany at present is but a very small village. One of our modern travellers tells us, that, at the entrance into it, there is an old ruin, called the castle of Lazarus, supposed to have been the mansion house where he and his sisters resided. At the bottom of a descent, not far from the castle, you see his sepulchre, which the Turks hold in great veneration, and use it for an oratory, or place for prayer. Here going down by twenty-five steps, you come at first into a small square room, and from thence creep into another that is smaller, about a yard and a half deep, in which the body is said to have been laid. About a bow-shot from hence you pass by the place which they say was Mary Magdalene's house; and thence descending a steep hill, you come to the fountain of the Apostles, which is so called because, as the tradition goes, these holy persons were wont to refresh themselves there between Jerusalem and Jericho,--as it is very probable they might, because the fountain is close to the road side, and is inviting to the thirsty traveller. Bethany is now a poor village, but pleasantly situated, says Dr. Richardson, on the shady side of the mount of Olives, and abounds in trees and long grass.

BETHAVEN, the same with Bethel. This city, upon the revolt of the ten tribes, belonged to the kingdom of Israel, and was therefore one of the cities in which Jeroboam set up his golden calves. Whence the prophet in derision calls it, "Bethaven," THE HOUSE OF VANITY or IDOLS, Hosea iv, 15, instead of "Bethel," THE HOUSE OF GOD, the name which Jacob formerly gave it, when he had the vision of the mysterious ladder, reaching from earth to heaven, Gen. xxviii, 19.

BETHEL, a city which lay to the west of Ai, about eight miles to the north of Jerusalem, in the confines of the tribe of Ephraim and Benjamin. Here Jacob slept and had his vision. The name of this city had formerly been Luz, which signifies AN ALMOND, and was probably so called from the number of almond trees which grew in those parts. See Jacob.

BETHESDA. This word signifies THE HOUSE OF MERCY, and was the name of a pool, or public bath, at Jerusalem, which had five porticos, piazzas, or covered walks around it. This bath was called Bethesda, because, as some observe, the erecting of baths was an act of great kindness to the common people, whose infirmities in hot countries required frequent bathing; but the generality of expositors think it had this name rather from the great goodness of God manifested to his people, in bestowing healing virtues upon its waters. The account of the evangelist is, "Now there was at Jerusalem, by the sheep market, a pool, which is called in the Hebrew tongue, Bethesda, having five porches. In these lay a multitude of impotent folk, of blind, halt, withered, waiting for the moving of the water; for an angel went down at a certain season into the pool: whosoever then first after the troubling of the water stepped in was made whole of whatsoever disease he had," John v, 2–4. The genuineness of the fourth verse has been disputed, because it is wanting in some ancient **MSS**, and is written in the margin of another as a scholion; but even were the spuriousness of this verse allowed, for which, however, the evidence is by no means satisfactory, the supernatural character of the account, as it is indicated by the other parts of the narrative, remains unaffected. The AGITATION of the water; its SUDDENLY healing virtue as to all diseases; and the LIMITATION to the first that should go in, are all miraculous circumstances. Commentators have however resorted to various hypotheses to account for the whole without divine agency. Dr. Hammond says, "The sacrifices were exceedingly numerous at the passover, κατὰ καιρὸν, (once a year, Chrysostom,) when the pool being warm from the immediate washing of the blood and entrails, and thus adapted to the cure of the blind, the withered, the lame, and perhaps the paralytic, was yet farther troubled, and the congelations and grosser parts stirred up by an officer or messenger, ἄγγελος, to give it the full effect." To this hypothesis Whitby acutely replies, 1. How could this natural virtue be adapted to, and cure, all kinds of diseases? 2. How could the virtue only extend to the cure of one man, several probably entering at the same instant? 3. How unlikely is it, if natural, to take place only at one certain time, at the passover? for there was a multitude of sacrifices slain at other of the feasts. 4. Lastly, and decisively, Lightfoot shows that there was a laver in the temple for washing the entrails; therefore they were not washed in this pool at all.

Others, however, suppose that the blood of the victims was conveyed from the temple to this pool by pipes; and Kuinoel thinks that it cannot be denied that the blood of animals recently slaughtered may impart a medicinal property to water; and he refers to Richter's "*Dissertat. de Balneo Animali*," and Michaelis IN LOC. But he admits that it cannot be proved whether the pool was situated out of the city at the sheep gate, or in the city, and in the vicinity of the temple; nor that the blood of the victims was ever conveyed thither by canals. Kuinoel justly observes, that though in Josephus no mention is made of the baths here described, yet this silence ought not to induce us to question the truth of this transaction; since the historian omits to record many other circumstances which cannot be doubted; as, for instance, the census of Augustus, and the murder of the infants. This critic also supposes that St. John only acts the part of an historian, and gives the account as it was current among the Jews, without vouching for its truth, or interposing his own judgment. Mede follows in the track of absurdly attempting to account for the phenomenon on natural principles:--"I think the water of this pool acquired a medicinal property from the mud at its bottom, which was heavy with metallic salts,--sulphur perhaps, or alum, or nitre. Now this would, from the water being perturbed from the bottom by some natural cause, perhaps subterranean heat, or storms, rise upward and be mingled with it, and so impart a sanative property to those who bathed in it before the metallic particles had subsided to the bottom. That it should have done so, κατὰ καιρὸν, is not strange, since Bartholin has, by many examples, shown, that it is usual with many medicinal baths, to exert a singular force and sanative power at stated times, and at periodical, but uncertain, intervals." Doddridge combines the common hypothesis with that of Mede; namely, that the water had at all times more or less of a medicinal property; but at some period, not far distant from that in which the transaction here recorded took place, it was endued with a miraculous power; an extraordinary commotion being probably observed in the water, and Providence so ordering it, that the next person who accidentally bathed here, being under some great disorder, found an immediate and unexpected cure: the like phenomenon in some other desperate case, was probably observed on a second commotion: and these commotions and cures might happen periodically.

All those hypotheses which exclude miracle in this case are very unsatisfactory, nor is there any reason whatever to resort to them; for, when rightly viewed, there appears a mercy and a wisdom in this miracle which must strike every one who attentively considers the account, unless he be a determined unbeliever in miraculous interposition. For, 1. The miracle occurred κατὰ καιρὸν, from time to time, that is, occasionally, perhaps frequently. 2. Though but one at a time was healed, yet, as this might often occur, a singularly gracious provision was made for the relief of the sick inhabitants of Jerusalem in desperate cases. 3. The angel probably acted invisibly, but the commotion in the waters was so strong and peculiar as to mark a supernatural agent. 4. There is great probability in what Doddridge, following Tertullian, supposes, that the waters obtained their healing property not long before the ministry of Christ, and lost it after his rejection and crucifixion by the Jews. In this case a connection was established between the healing virtue of the pool and the presence of Christ on earth, indicating HIM to be the source of this benefit, and the true agent in conferring it; and thus it became, afterward at least, a confirmation of his mission. 5. The whole might also be emblematical, "intended," says Macknight, "to show that Ezekiel's vision of waters issuing out of the sanctuary was about to be fulfilled, of which waters it is said, They shall be healed, and every thing shall live where the river cometh." It cannot be objected that this was not an age of miracles; and if miracles be allowed, we see in this particular supernatural visitation obvious reasons of fitness, as well as a divine compassion. If however the ends to be accomplished by so public and notable a miraculous interposition were less obvious, still we must admit the fact, or either force absurd interpretations upon the text, or make the evangelist carelessly give his sanction to an instance of vulgar credulity and superstition.

Maundrell and Chateaubriand both describe a bason or reservoir, near St. Stephen's gate, and bounding the temple on the north, as the identical pool of Bethesda; which, if it really be what it is represented to be, is all that now remains of the primitive architecture of the Jews at Jerusalem. The latter says, "It is a reservoir, a hundred and fifty feet long and forty wide. The sides are walled, and these walls are composed of a bed of large stones joined together by iron cramps; a wall of mixed materials runs up on these large stones; a layer of flints is stuck upon the surface of this wall; and a coating is laid over these flints. The four beds are perpendicular with the bottom, and not horizontal: the coating was on the side next to the water; and the large stones rested, as they still do, against the ground. This pool is now dry, and half filled up. Here grow some pomegranate trees, and a species of wild tamarind of a bluish colour: the western angle is quite full of nopals. On the west side may also be seen two arches, which probably led to an aqueduct that carried the water into the interior of the temple."

BETH-HORON. About twelve miles from Jerusalem, lies the Arab village of Bethoor, where Dr. E. D. Clarke was by accident compelled to pass a night. It is noticed by no other traveller; and yet, there is the highest probability that this is the Beth-horon of the Scriptures. St. Jerom associates it with Rama, in the remark that they were in his time, together with other noble cities built by Solomon, only poor villages. Beth-horon stood on the confines of Ephraim and Benjamin; which, according to the learned traveller, exactly answers to the situation of Bethoor. He supposes it, from its situation on a hill, to be Beth-horon the upper, the Beth-horon superior of Eusebius, of which frequent notice occurs in the apocryphal writings. Josephus mentions that Cestius, the Roman general, marched upon Jerusalem by way of Lydda and Beth-horon.

BETHLEHEM, a city in the tribe of Judah, Judges xvii, 7; and likewise called Ephrath, Gen. xlviii, 7; or Ephratah, Micah v, 2; and the inhabitants of it, Ephrathites, Ruth i, 2; 1 Sam. xvii, 12. Here David was born, and spent his early years as a shepherd. And here also the scene of the beautiful narrative of Ruth is supposed to be laid. But its highest honour is, that here our divine Lord condescended to be born of woman:--"And thou, Bethlehem Ephratah, though thou be little among the thousands of Judah, yet out of thee shall he come forth unto me, that is to be ruler in Israel, whose goings forth have been of old, from everlasting." Travellers describe the first view of Bethlehem as imposing. The town appears covering the ridge of a hill on the southern side of a deep and extensive valley, and reaching from east to west. The most conspicuous object is the monastery erected over the supposed "Cave of the Nativity;" its walls and battlements have the air of a large fortress. From this same point, the Dead Sea is seen below on the left, seemingly very near, "but," says Sandys, "not so found by the traveller; for these high, declining mountains are not to be directly descended." The road winds round the top of a valley which tradition has fixed on as the scene of the angelic vision which announced the birth of our Lord to the shepherds; but different spots have been selected, the Romish authorities not being agreed on this head. Bethlehem (called in the New Testament Bethlehem Ephrata and Bethlehem of Judea, to distinguish it from Bethlehem of Zabulon) is situated on a rising ground, about two hours' distance, or not quite six miles from Jerusalem. Here the traveller meets with a repetition of the same puerilities and disgusting mummery which he has witnessed at the church of the sepulchre. "The stable," to use the words of Pococke, "in which our Lord was born, is a GROTTO cut out of the rock, according to the eastern custom." It is astonishing to find so intelligent a writer as Dr. E. D. Clarke gravely citing St. Jerom, who wrote in the fifth century, as an authority for the truth of the absurd legend by which the cave of the nativity is supposed to be identified. The ancient tombs and excavations are occasionally used by the Arabs as places of shelter; but the Gospel narrative affords no countenance to the notion that the Virgin took refuge in any cave of this description. On the contrary, it was evidently a manger belonging to the inn or khan: in other words, the upper rooms being wholly occupied, the holy family were compelled to take up their abode in the court allotted to the mules and horses, or other animals. But the New Testament was not the guide which was followed by the mother of Constantine, to whom the original church owed its foundation. The present edifice is represented by Chateaubriand as of undoubtedly high antiquity; yet Doubdan, an old traveller, says that the monastery was destroyed in the year 1263 by the Moslems; and in its present state, at all events, it cannot lay claim to a higher date. The convent is divided among the Greek, Roman, and Armenian Christians, to each of whom separate parts are assigned as places of worship and habitations for the monks; but, on certain days, all may perform their devotions at the altars erected over the consecrated spots. The church is built in the form of a cross; the nave being adorned with forty-eight Corinthian columns in four rows, each column being two feet six inches in diameter, and eighteen feet high, including the base and the capital. The nave, which is in possession of the Armenians, is separated from the three other branches of the cross by a wall, so that the unity of the edifice is destroyed. The top of the cross is occupied by the choir, which belongs to the Greeks. Here is an altar dedicated to the wise men of the east, at the foot of which is a marble star, corresponding, as the monks say, to the point of the heavens where the miraculous meteor became stationary, and directly over the spot where the Saviour was born in the subterranean church below! A flight of fifteen steps, and a long narrow passage, conduct to the sacred crypt or grotto of the nativity, which is thirty-seven feet six inches long, by eleven feet three inches in breadth, and nine feet high. It is lined and floored with marble, and provided on each side with five oratories, "answering precisely to the ten cribs or stalls for horses that the stable in which our Saviour was born contained!" The precise spot of the birth is marked by a glory in the floor, composed of marble and jasper encircled with silver, around which are inscribed the words, HÌC DE VIRGINE MARIÂ JESUS CHRISTUS NATUS EST. [Here Jesus Christ was born of the Virgin Mary.] Over it is a marble table or altar, which rests against the side of the rock, here cut into an arcade. The MANGER is at the distance of seven paces from the altar; it is in a low recess hewn out of the rock, to which you descend by two steps, and consists of a block of marble, raised about a foot and a half above the floor, and hollowed out in the form of a manger. Before it is the altar of the Magi. The chapel is illuminated by thirty-two lamps, presented by different princes of Christendom. Chateaubriand has described the scene in his usual florid and imaginative style: "Nothing can be more pleasing, or better calculated to excite devotional sentiments, than this subterraneous church. It is adorned with pictures of the Italian and Spanish schools, which represent the mysteries of the place. The usual ornaments of the manger are of blue satin, embroidered with silver. Incense is continually burning before the cradle of our Saviour. I have heard an organ, touched by no ordinary hand, play, during mass, the sweetest and most tender tunes of the best Italian composers. These concerts charm the Christian Arab, who, leaving his camels to feed, repairs, like the shepherds of old, to Bethlehem, to adore the King of kings in the manger. I have seen this inhabitant of the desert communicate at the altar of the Magi, with a fervour, a piety, a devotion, unknown among the Christians of the west. The continual arrival of caravans from all the nations of Christendom; the public prayers; the prostrations; nay, even the richness of the presents sent here by the Christian princes, altogether produce feelings in the soul, which it is much easier to conceive than to describe."

Such are the illusions which the Roman superstition casts over this extraordinary scene! In another subterraneous chapel, tradition places the sepulchre of the Innocents. From this, the pilgrim is conducted to the grotto of St. Jerom, where they show the tomb of that father, who passed great part of his life in this place; and who, in the grotto shown as his oratory, is said to have translated that version of the Bible which has been adopted by the church of Rome, and is called the Vulgate. He died at the advanced age of ninety-one, A. D. 422. The village of Bethlehem contains about three hundred inhabitants, the greater part of whom gain their livelihood by making beads, carving mother-of-pearl shells with sacred subjects, and manufacturing small tables and crucifixes, all which are eagerly purchased by the pilgrims.

Bethlehem has been visited by many modern travellers. The following notice of it by Dr. E. D. Clarke will be read with interest: "After travelling for about an hour from the time of our leaving Jerusalem, we came in view of Bethlehem, and halted to enjoy the interesting sight. The town appeared covering the ridge of a hill on the southern side of a deep and extensive valley, and reaching from east to west; the most conspicuous object being the monastery, erected over the cave of the nativity, in the suburbs, and upon the eastern side. The battlements and walls of this building seemed like those of a vast fortress. The Dead Sea below, upon our left, appeared so near to us that we thought we could have rode thither in a very short space of time. Still nearer stood a mountain upon its western shore, resembling in its form the cone of Vesuvius near Naples, and having also a crater upon its top which was plainly discernible. The distance, however, is much greater than it appears to be; the magnitude of the objects beheld in this fine prospect causing them to appear less remote than they really are. The atmosphere was remarkably clear and serene; but we saw none of those clouds of smoke, which, by some writers, are said to exhale from the surface of the lake, nor from any neighbouring mountain. Every thing about it was in the highest degree grand and awful. Bethlehem is six miles from Jerusalem. Josephus describes the interval between the two cities as equal only to twenty stadia; and in the passage referred to, he makes an allusion to a celebrated well, which, both from the account given by him of its situation, and more especially from the text of the sacred Scriptures, 2 Sam. xxiii, 15, seems to have contained the identical fountain, of whose pure and delicious water we were now drinking. Considered merely in point of interest, the narrative is not likely to be surpassed by any circumstance of Pagan history. David, being a native of Bethlehem, calls to mind, during the sultry days of harvest, verse 13, a well near the gate of the town, the delicious waters of which he had often tasted; and expresses an earnest desire to assuage his thirst by drinking of that limpid spring. 'And David longed, and said, O that one would give me to drink of the water of the well of Bethlehem, which is by the gate!' The exclamation is overheard by 'three of the mighty men whom David had,' namely, Adino, Eleazar, and Shamnah, verses 8, 9, 11. These men sallied forth, and having fought their way through the garrison of the Philistines at Bethlehem, verse 14, 'drew water from the well that was by the gate,' on the other side of the town, and brought it to David. Coming into his presence, they present to him the surprising testimony of their valour and affection. The aged monarch receives from their hands a pledge they had so dearly earned, but refuses to drink of water every drop of which had been purchased with blood, 2 Sam. xxiii, 17. He returns thanks to the Almighty, who had vouchsafed the deliverance of his warriors from the jeopardy they had encountered; and pouring out the water as a libation on the ground, makes an offering of it to the Lord. The well still retains its pristine renown; and many an expatriated Bethlehemite has made it the theme of his longing and regret."

BETHPHAGE, so called from its producing figs, a small village situated in Mount Olivet, and, as it seems, somewhat nearer Jerusalem than Bethany. Jesus being come from Bethany to Bethphage, commanded his disciples to seek out an ass for him that he might ride, in his triumphant entrance into Jerusalem, Matt. xxi, 1, &c. The distance between Bethphage and Jerusalem is about fifteen furlongs.

BETHSAIDA, a city whose name in Hebrew imports a place of fishing or of hunting, and for both of these exercises it was well situated. As it belonged to the tribe of Naphtali, it was in a country remarkable for plenty of deer; and as it lay on the north end of the lake Gennesareth, just where the river Jordan runs into it, it became the residence of fishermen. Three of the Apostles, Philip, Andrew, and Peter, were born in this city. It is not mentioned in the Old Testament, though it frequently occurs in the New: the reason is, that it was but a village, as Josephus tells us, till Philip the tetrarch enlarged it, making it a magnificent city, and gave it the name of Julias, out of respect to Julia, the daughter of Augustus Cæsar.

The evangelists speak of Bethsaida; and yet it then possessed that name no longer: it was enlarged and beautified nearly at the same time as Cæsarea, and called Julias. Thus was it called in the days of our Lord, and so would the sacred historians have been accustomed to call it. But if they knew nothing of this, what shall we say of their age? In other respects they evince the most accurate knowledge of the circumstances of the time. The solution is, that, though Philip had exalted it to the rank of a city, to which he gave the name of Julias, yet, not long afterward, this Julia, in whose honour the city received its name, was banished from the country by her own father. The deeply wounded honour of Augustus was even anxious that the world might forget that she was his daughter. Tiberius, whose wife she had been, consigned the unfortunate princess, after the death of Augustus, to the most abject poverty, under which she sank without assistance. Thus adulation must under two reigns have suppressed a name, from which otherwise the city might have wished to derive benefit to itself; and for some time it was called by its ancient name Bethsaida instead of Julias. At a later period this name again came into circulation, and appears in the catalogue of Jewish cities by Pliny. By such incidents, which are so easily overlooked, and the knowledge of which is afterward lost, do those who are really acquainted with an age disclose their authenticity. "But it is strange," some one will say, "that John reckons this Bethsaida, or Julias, where he was born, in Galilee, John xii, 21. Should he not know to what province his birthplace belonged?" Philip only governed the eastern districts by the sea of Tiberias; but Galilee was the portion of his brother Antipas. Bethsaida or Julias could therefore not have been built by Philip, as the case is; or it did not belong to Galilee, as John alleges. In fact, such an error were sufficient to prove that this Gospel was not written by John. Julias, however, was situated in Gaulonitis, which district was, for deep political reasons, divided from Galilee; but the ordinary language of the time asserted its own opinion, and still reckoned the Gaulonitish province in Galilee. When, therefore, John does the same, he proves, that the peculiarity of those days was not unknown to him; for he expresses himself after the ordinary manner of the period. Thus Josephus informs us of Judas the Gaulonite from Gamala, and also calls him in the following chapters, the Galilean; and then in another work he applies the same expression to him; from whence we may be convinced that the custom of those days paid respect to a more ancient division of the country, and bade defiance, in the present case, to the then existing political geography. Is it possible that historians who, as it is evident from such examples, discover throughout so nice a knowledge of geographical arrangements and local and even temporary circumstances, should have written at a time when the theatre of events was unknown to them, when not only their native country was destroyed, but their nation scattered, and the national existence of the Jews extinguished and extirpated? On the contrary, all this is in proof that they wrote at the very period which they profess, and it also proves the usual antiquity assigned to the Gospels.

BETHSHAN, a city belonging to the half tribe of Manasseh, on the west of Jordan, and not far from the river. It was a considerable city in the time of Eusebius and St. Jerom, and was then, as it had been for several ages before, called Scythopolis, or the city of the Scythians, from some remarkable occurrence when the Scythians made an irruption into Syria. It is said to be six hundred furlongs from Jerusalem, 2 Macc. xii, 29. After the battle of Mount Gilboa, the Philistines took the body of Saul, and hung it against the wall of Bethshan, 1 Sam. xxxi, 10. Bethshan is now called Bysan, and is described by Burckhardt as situated on rising ground on the west of the Ghor, or valley of Jordan.

BETHSHEMESH, a city of the tribe of Judah, belonging to the priests, Joshua xxi, 16. The Philistines having sent back the ark of the Lord, it was brought to Bethshemesh, 1 Sam. vi, 12, where some of the people out of curiosity having looked into it, the Lord destroyed seventy of the principal men belonging to the city, and fifty thousand of the common people, verse 19. It is here to be observed that it was solemnly enjoined, Num. iv, 20, that not only the common people but that even the Levites themselves should not dare to look into the ark, upon pain of death. "It is a fearful thing," says Bishop Hall, "to use the holy ordinances of God with an irreverent boldness; fear and trembling become us in our access to the majesty of the Almighty."

BETHUEL, the son of Nahor and Milcah. He was Abraham's nephew, and father to Laban and Rebekah, the wife of Isaac, Genesis xxii, 20, 23.

BETROTHMENT, a mutual promise or compact between two parties for a future marriage. The word imports as much as giving one's troth; that is, true faith, or promise. Among the ancient Jews, the betrothing was performed either by a writing, or by a piece of silver given to the bride. After the marriage was contracted, the young people had the liberty of seeing each other, which was not allowed them before. If, after the betrothment, the bride should trespass against that fidelity she owed to her bridegroom she was treated as an adulteress. See Marriage.

BEZER, or Bozra, or Bostra, a city beyond Jordan, given by Moses to Reuben: this town was designed by Joshua to be a city of refuge; it was given to the Levites of Gershom's family, Deut. iv, 43. When Scripture mentions Bezer, it adds, "in the wilderness," because it lay in Arabia Deserta, and the eastern part of Edom, encompassed with deserts. Eusebius places Bozra twenty-four miles from Adraa, or Edrai. This city is sometimes said to belong to Reuben, sometimes to Moab, and sometimes again to Edom; because, as it was a frontier town to these three provinces, it was occasionally in the hands of one party, and then was taken by another. The bishops of Bostra subscribed the decrees of several councils.

BIBLE, THE BOOK, by way of eminence so called, as containing the sacred Scriptures, that is, the inspired writings of the Old and New Testament; or the whole collection of those which are received among Christians as of divine authority. The word Bible comes from the Greek Βίβλος, or Βιβλίον, and is used to denote any book; but is emphatically applied to the book of inspired Scripture, which is "the book" as being superior in excellence to all other books. Βιβλίον again comes from Βίβλος, the Egyptian reed, from which the ancient paper was procured. The word Bible seems to be used in the particular sense just given by Chrysostom: "I therefore exhort all of you to procure to yourselves Bibles, Βιβλια. If you have nothing else, take care to have the New Testament, particularly the Acts of the Apostles and the Gospels, for your constant instructers." And Jerome says, "that the Scriptures being all written by one Spirit, are ONE BOOK." Augustine also informs us, "that some called all the canonical Scriptures ONE BOOK, on account of their wonderful harmony and unity of design throughout." It is not improbable that this mode of speaking gradually introduced the general use of the word Bible for the whole collection of the Scriptures, or the books of the Old and New Testament. By the Jews the Bible, that is, the Old Testament, is called MIKRA, that is, "lecture, or reading." By Christians the Bible, comprehending the Old and New Testament, is usually denominated "Scripture;" sometimes also the "Sacred Canon," which signifies the rule of faith and practice. These, and similar appellations, are derived from the divine original and authority of the Bible. As it contains an authentic and connected history of the divine dispensations with regard to mankind; as it was given by divine inspiration; as its chief subject is religion; and as the doctrines it teaches, and the duties it inculcates, pertain to the conduct of men, as rational, moral, and accountable beings, and conduce by a divine constitution and promise, to their present and future happiness; the Bible deserves to be held in the highest estimation, and amply justifies the sentiments of veneration with which it has been regarded, and the peculiar and honourable appellations by which it has been denominated.

2. The list of the books contained in the Bible constitutes what is called the canon of Scripture. Those books that are contained in the catalogue to which the name of canon has been appropriated, are called canonical, by way of contradistinction from others called deutero-canonical, apocryphal, pseudo-apocryphal, &c, which either are not acknowledged as divine books, or are rejected as heretical and spurious. (See APOCRYPHA.) The first canon or catalogue of the sacred books was made by the Jews; but the original author of it is not satisfactorily ascertained. It is certain, however, that the five books of Moses, called the Pentateuch, were collected into one body within a short time after his death; since Deuteronomy, which is, as it were, the abridgment and recapitulation of the other four, was laid in the tabernacle near the ark, according to the order which he gave to the Levites, Deut. xxxi, 24. Hence the first canon of the sacred writings consisted of the five books of Moses: for a farther account of which see PENTATEUCH. It does not appear that any other books were added to these, till the division of the ten tribes, as the Samaritans acknowledged no others. However, after the time of Moses, several prophets, and other writers divinely inspired, composed either the history of their own times, or prophetical books and divine writings, or psalms appropriated to the praise of God. But these books do not seem to have been collected into one body, or comprised under one and the same canon, before the Babylonish captivity. This was not done till after their return from the captivity, about which time the Jews had a certain number of books digested into a canon, which comprehended none of those books that were written since the time of Nehemiah. The book of Ecclesiasticus affords sufficient evidence that the canon of the sacred books was completed when that tract was composed; for that author, in chapter xlix, having mentioned among the famous men and sacred writers, Isaiah, Jeremiah, Ezekiel, adds the twelve minor prophets who follow those three in the Jewish canon; and from this circumstance we may infer that the prophecies of these twelve were already collected and digested into one body. It is farther evident, that in the time of our Saviour the canon of the Holy Scriptures was drawn up, since he cites the law of Moses, the Prophets, and the Psalms, which are the three kinds of books of which that canon is composed, and which he often styles, "the Scriptures," or, "the Holy Scripture," Matt. xxi, 42; xxii, 29; xxvi, 54; John v, 39; and by him therefore the Jewish canon, as it existed in his day, was fully authenticated, by whomsoever or at what time it had been formed.

3. The person who compiled this canon is generally allowed to be Ezra. According to the invariable tradition of Jews and Christians, the honour is ascribed to him of having collected together and perfected a complete edition of the Holy Scriptures. The original of the Pentateuch had been carefully preserved in the side of the ark, and had been probably introduced with the ark into the temple at Jerusalem. After having been concealed in the dangerous days of the idolatrous kings of Judah, and particularly in the impious reigns of Manasseh and Amon, it was found in the days of Josiah, the succeeding prince, by Hilkiah the priest, in the temple. Prideaux thinks, that during the preceding reigns the book of the law was so destroyed and lost, that, beside this copy of it, there was then no other to be obtained. To this purpose he adds, that the surprise manifested by Hilkiah, on the discovery of it, and the grief expressed by Josiah when he heard it read, plainly show that neither of them had seen it before. On the other hand, Dr. Kennicott, with better reason, supposes, that long before this time there were several copies of the law in Israel, during the separation of the ten tribes, and that there were some copies of it also among the tribes of Judah and Benjamin, particularly in the hands of the prophets, priests, and Levites; and that by the instruction and authority of these **MSS**, the various services in the temple were regulated, during the reigns of the good kings of Judah. He adds, that the surprise expressed by Josiah and the people,

at his reading the copy found by Hilkiah, may be accounted for by adverting to the history of the preceding reigns, and by recollecting how idolatrous a king Manasseh had been for fifty-five years, and that he wanted neither power nor inclination to destroy the copies of the law, if they had not been secreted by the servants of God. The law, after being so long concealed, would be unknown almost to all the Jews; and thus the solemn reading of it by Josiah would awaken his own and the people's earnest attention; more especially, as the copy produced was probably the original written by Moses. From this time copies of the law were extensively multiplied among the people; and though, within a few years, the autograph, or original copy of the law, was burnt with the city and temple by the Babylonians, yet many copies of the law and the prophets, and of all the other sacred writings, were circulated in the hands of private persons, who carried them with them into their captivity. It is certain that Daniel had a copy of the Holy Scriptures with him at Babylon; for he quotes the law, and mentions the prophecies of Jeremiah, Dan. ix, 2, 11, 13. It appears also, from the sixth chap. of Ezra, and from the ninth chap. of Nehemiah, that copies of the law were dispersed among the people. The whole which Ezra did may be comprised in the following particulars: He collected as many copies of the sacred writings as he could find, and compared them together, and, out of them all, formed one complete copy, adjusted the various readings, and corrected the errors of transcribers. He likewise made additions in several parts of the different books, which appeared to be necessary for the illustration, correction, and completion of them. To this class of additions we may refer the last chapter of Deuteronomy, which, as it gives an account of the death and burial of Moses, and of the succession of Joshua after him, could not have been written by Moses himself. Under the same head have also been included some other interpolations in the Bible, which create difficulties that can only be solved by allowing them; as in Gen. xii, 6; xxii, 14; xxxvi, 3; Exodus xvi, 35; Deut. ii, 12; iii, 11, 14; Prov. xxv, 1. The interpolations in these passages are ascribed by Prideaux to Ezra; and others which were afterward added, he attributes to Simon the Just. Ezra also changed the old names of several places that were become obsolete, putting instead of them the new names by which they were at that time called; instances of which occur in Genesis xiv, 4, where Dan is substituted for Laish, and in several places in Genesis, and also in Numbers, where Hebron is put for Kirjath Arba, &c. He likewise wrote out the whole in the Chaldee character, changing for it the old Hebrew character, which has since that time been retained only by the Samaritans, and among whom it is preserved even to this day. The canon of the whole Hebrew Bible seems, says Kennicott, to have been closed by Malachi, the latest of the Jewish prophets, about fifty years after Ezra had collected together all the sacred books which had been composed before and during his time. Prideaux supposes the canon was completed by Simon the Just, about one hundred and fifty years after Malachi: but, as his opinion is founded merely on a few proper names at the end of the two genealogies, 1 Chron. iii, 19; Nehem. xii, 22, which few names might very easily be added by a transcriber afterward, it is more probable, as Kennicott thinks, that the canon was finished by the last of the prophets, about four hundred years before Christ.

4. It is an inquiry of considerable importance, in its relation to the subject of this article, what books were contained in the canon of the Jews. The Old Testament, according to our Bibles, comprises thirty-nine books, viz. the Pentateuch or five books of Moses, called Genesis, Exodus, Leviticus, Numbers, and Deuteronomy, the books of Joshua, Judges, Ruth, 1 & 2 Samuel, 1 & 2 Kings, 1 & 2 Chronicles, Ezra, Nehemiah, Esther, Job, Psalms, Proverbs, Ecclesiastes, the Song of Solomon, the prophecies of Isaiah, Jeremiah with his Lamentations, Ezekiel, Daniel, Hosea, Joel, Amos, Obadiah, Jonah, Micah, Nahum, Habakkuk, Zephaniah, Haggai, Zechariah, and Malachi. But, among the ancient Jews, they formed only twenty-two books, according to the letters of their alphabet, which were twenty-two in number; reckoning Judges and Ruth, Ezra and Nehemiah, Jeremiah and his Lamentations, and the twelve minor prophets, (so called from the comparative brevity of their compositions,) respectively as one book. Josephus says, "We have not thousands of books, discordant, and contradicting each other: but we have only TWENTY-TWO, which comprehend the history of all former ages, and are justly regarded as divine. FIVE of them proceed from Moses; they include as well the LAWS, as an account of the creation of man, extending to the time of his (Moses) death. This period comprehends nearly three thousand years. From the death of Moses to that of Artaxerxes, who was king of Persia after Xerxes, the PROPHETS, who succeeded Moses, committed to writing, in thirteen books, what was done in their days. The remaining four books contain HYMNS to God, (the Psalms,) and instructions of life for man." The threefold division of the Old Testament into the Law, the Prophets, and the Psalms, mentioned by Josephus, was expressly recognised before his time by Jesus Christ, as well as by the subsequent writers of the New Testament. We have therefore sufficient evidence that the Old Testament existed at that time; and if it be only allowed that Jesus Christ was a teacher of a fearless and irreproachable character, it must be acknowledged that we draw a fair conclusion, when we assert that the Scriptures were not corrupted in his time: for, when he accused the Pharisees of making the law of no effect by their traditions, and, when he enjoined his hearers to search the Scriptures, he could not have failed to mention the corruptions or forgeries of Scripture, if any had existed in that age. About fifty years before the time of Christ were written the Targums of Onkelos on the Pentateuch, and of Jonathan Ben-Uzziel on the Prophets; (according to the Jewish classification of the books of the Old Testament;) which are evidence of the genuineness of those books at that time. We have, however, unquestionable testimony of the genuineness of the Old Testament, in the FACT that its canon was fixed some centuries before the birth of Jesus Christ. Jesus the son of Sirach, author of the book of Ecclesiasticus, makes evident references to the prophecies of Isaiah, Jeremiah, and Ezekiel, and mentions these prophets by name: he speaks also of the twelve minor

prophets. It likewise appears from the prologue to that book, that the law and the prophets, and other ancient books, were extant at the same period. The book of Ecclesiasticus, according to the best chronologers, was written in the Syro-Chaldaic dialect A. M. 3772, that is, two hundred and thirty-two years before the Christian æra, and was translated by the grandson of Jesus into Greek, for the use of the Alexandrian Jews. The prologue was added by the translator; but this circumstance does not diminish the evidence for the antiquity of the Old Testament: for he informs us, that the law and the prophets, and the other books of their fathers, were studied by his grandfather; a sufficient proof that they were extant in his time. Fifty years, indeed, before the age of the author of Ecclesiasticus, or two hundred and eighty-two years before the Christian æra, the Greek version of the Old Testament, usually called the Septuagint, was executed at Alexandria, the books of which are the same as in our Bibles; whence it is evident that we still have those identical books, which the most ancient Jews attested to be genuine. The Christian fathers too, Origen, Athanasius, Hilary, Gregory, Nazianzen, Epiphanius, and Jerom, speaking of the books that are allowed by the Jews as sacred and canonical, agree in saying that they are the same in number with the letters in the Hebrew alphabet, that is, twenty-two, and reckon particularly those books which we have already mentioned. Nothing can be more satisfactory and conclusive than all the parts of the evidence for the authenticity and integrity of the canon of the Old Testament scriptures. The Jews, to whom they were first committed, never varied respecting them; while they were fully recognised by our Lord and his Apostles; and, consequently, their authenticity is established by express revelation. And that we now possess them as thus delivered and authenticated, we have the concurrent testimony of the whole succession of the most distinguished early Christian writers, as well as of the Jews to this day, who, in every age, and in all countries, the most remote from one another, have constantly been in the habit of reading them in their synagogues.

5. The five books of the law are divided into fifty-four sections, which division is attributed to Ezra, and was intended for the use of their synagogues, and for the better instruction of the people in the law of God. For, one of these sections was read every Sabbath in their synagogues. They ended the last section with the last words of Deuteronomy on the Sabbath of the feast of the tabernacles, and then began anew with the first section from the beginning of Genesis the next Sabbath after, and so went round in this circle every year. The number of these sections was fifty-four, because in their intercalated years (a month being then added) there were fifty-four Sabbaths. On other years they reduced them to the number of the Sabbaths which were in those years, by joining two short ones several times into one. For they held themselves obliged to have the whole law thus read over in their synagogues every year. Till the time of the persecution of Antiochus Epiphanes, they read only the law; but being then prohibited from reading it any more, they substituted in the room of the fifty-four sections of the law, fifty-four sections out of the prophets, the reading of which they ever after continued. Thus, when the reading of the law was restored by the Maccabees, the section which was read every Sabbath out of the law served for their first lesson, and the section out of the prophets for their second lesson; and this practice was continued to the times of the Apostles, Acts xiii, 15, 27. These sections were divided into verses, called by the Jews PESUKIM, and they are marked out in the Hebrew Bible by two great points at the end of them, called from hence, SOPH-PASUK, that is, the end of the verse. This division, if not made by Ezra, is very ancient; for when the Chaldee came into use in the room of the Hebrew language, after the return of the Jews from their captivity in Babylon, the law was read to the people first in the Hebrew language, and then rendered by an interpreter into the Chaldee language; and this was done period by period. The division of the Holy Scriptures into chapters is of a much later date. The Psalms, indeed, appear to have been always divided as they are at present, Acts xiii, 33; but as to the rest of the Bible, the present division into chapters was unknown to the ancients.

6. From the time when the Old Testament was completed by Malachi, the last of the prophets, till the publication of the New Testament, about four hundred and sixty years elapsed. During the life of Jesus Christ, and for some time after his ascension, nothing on the subject of his mission was committed to writing. The period of his remaining upon earth may be regarded as an intermediate state between the old and new dispensations. His personal ministry was confined to the land of Judea; and, by means of his miracles and discourses, together with those of his disciples, the attention of men, in that country, was sufficiently directed to his doctrine. They were also in possession of the Old Testament scriptures; which, at that season, it was of the greatest importance they should consult, in order to compare the ancient predictions with what was then taking place. Immediately after the resurrection of Jesus Christ, his disciples, in the most public manner, and in the place where he had been crucified, proclaimed that event, and the whole of the doctrine which he had commanded them to preach. In this service they continued personally to labour for a considerable time, first among their countrymen the Jews, and then among the other nations. During the period between the resurrection and the publication of the New Testament, the churches possessed miraculous gifts, and the prophets were enabled to explain the predictions of the Old Testament, and to show their fulfilment. After their doctrine had every where attracted attention, and, in spite of the most violent opposition, had forced its way through the civilized world; and when churches or societies of Christians were collected, not only in Judea, but in the most celebrated cities of Italy, Greece, and Asia Minor, the scriptures of the New Testament were written by the Apostles, and other inspired men, and intrusted to the keeping of these churches.

The whole of the New Testament was not written at once, but in different parts, and on various occasions. Six of the Apostles, and two inspired disciples who accompanied them in their journeys, were employed in this work. The histories which it contains of the life of Christ, known by the name of the Gospels, were composed by four of his contemporaries, two of whom had been constant attendants on his public ministry. The first of these was published within a few years after his death, in that very country where he had lived, and among the people who had seen him and observed his conduct. The history called the Acts of the Apostles, which contains an account of their proceedings, and of the progress of the Gospel, from Jerusalem, among the Gentile nations, was published about the year 64, being thirty years after our Lord's crucifixion, by one who, though not an Apostle, declares that he had "perfect understanding of all things, from the very first," and who had written one of the Gospels. This book, commencing with a detail of proceedings, from the resurrection of Jesus Christ, carries down the evangelical history till the arrival of Paul as a prisoner at Rome. The Epistles, addressed to churches in particular places, to believers scattered up and down in different countries, or to individuals, in all twenty-one in number, were separately written, by five of the Apostles, from seventeen, to twenty, thirty, and thirty-five years after the death of Christ. Four of these writers had accompanied the Lord Jesus during his life, and had been "eye witnesses of his majesty." The fifth was the Apostle Paul, who, as he expresses it, was "one born out of due time," but who had likewise seen Jesus Christ, and had been empowered by him to work miracles, which were "the signs of an Apostle." One of these five also wrote the book of Revelation, about the year A. D. 96, addressed to seven churches in Asia, containing Epistles to these churches from Jesus Christ himself, with various instructions for the immediate use of all Christians, together with a prophetical view of the kingdom of God till the end of time. These several pieces, which compose the scriptures of the New Testament, were received by the churches with the highest veneration; and, as the instructions they contain, though partially addressed, were equally intended for all, they were immediately copied, and handed about from one church to another, till each was in possession of the whole. The volume of the New Testament was thus completed before the death of the last of the Apostles, most of whom had sealed their testimony with their blood. From the manner in which these scriptures were at first circulated, some of their parts were necessarily longer in reaching certain places than others. These, of course, could not be so soon received into the canon as the rest. Owing to this circumstance, and to that of a few of the books being addressed to individual believers, or to their not having the names of their writers affixed, or the designation of Apostle added, a doubt for a time existed among some respecting the genuineness of the Epistle to the Hebrews, the Epistle of James, the second Epistle of Peter, the second and third Epistles of John, the Epistle of Jude, and the book of Revelation. These, however, though not universally, were generally acknowledged; while all the other books of the New Testament were without dispute received from the beginning. This discrimination proves the scrupulous care of the first churches on this highly important subject. At length these books, which had not at first been admitted, were, like the rest, universally received, not by the votes of a council, as is sometimes asserted, but after deliberate and free inquiry by many separate churches, under the superintending providence of God, in different parts of the world. It is at the same time a certain fact, that no other books beside those which at present compose the volume of the New Testament, were admitted by the churches. Several apocryphal writings were published under the name of Jesus Christ and his Apostles, which are mentioned by the writers of the first four centuries, most of which have perished, though some are still extant. Few or none of them were composed before the second century, and several of them were forged as late as the third century. But they were not acknowledged as authentic by the first Christians; and were rejected by those who have noticed them, as spurious and heretical. Histories, too, as might have been expected, were written of the life of Christ; and one forgery was attempted, of a letter said to have been written by Jesus himself to Abgarus, king of Edessa; but of the first, none were received as of any authority, and the last was universally rejected. "Beside our Gospels, and the Acts of the Apostles," says Paley, "no Christian history claiming to be written by an Apostle, or Apostolical man, is quoted within three hundred years after the birth of Christ, by any writer now extant or known, or, if quoted, is quoted with marks of censure and rejection." This agreement of Christians respecting the Scriptures, when we consider their many differences in other respects, is the more remarkable, since it took place without any public authority being interposed. "We have no knowledge" says the above author, "of any interference of authority in the question before the council of Laodicea, in the year 363. Probably the decree of this council rather declared than regulated the public judgment, or, more properly speaking, the judgment of some neighbouring churches, the council itself consisting of no more than thirty or forty bishops of Lydia and the adjoining countries. Nor does its authority seem to have extended farther." But the fact, that no public authority was interposed, does not require to be supported by the above reasoning. The churches at the beginning, being widely separated from each other, necessarily judged for themselves in this matter, and the decree of the council was founded on the coincidence of their judgment. In delivering this part of his written revelation, God proceeded as he had done in the publication of the Old Testament scriptures. For a considerable time, his will was declared to mankind through the medium of oral tradition. At length he saw meet, in his wisdom, to give it a more permanent form. But this did not take place till a nation, separated from all others, was provided for its reception. In the same manner, when Jesus Christ set up his kingdom in the world, of which the nation of Israel was a type, he first made known his will by means of verbal communication, through his servants whom he commissioned and sent out for that purpose; and when, through their means, he had prepared his subjects and collected them into churches, to be the depositaries of his word, he caused it to be delivered to them in writing. His kingdom was not to consist of any particular nation, like that of Israel, but of all those individuals, in every part of the world, who should believe in his name. It was to be ruled, not by means of human authority, or compulsion of any kind, but solely by his authority. These sacred writings were thus intrusted to a people prepared for their reception,--a nation among the nations, but singularly distinct from all the rest, who guarded and preserved them with the same inviolable attachment as the Old Testament scriptures had experienced from the Jews.

7. Respecting the lateness of the time when the scriptures of the New Testament were written, no objection can be offered, since they were published before that generation passed away which had witnessed the transactions they record. The dates of these writings fall within the period of the lives of many who were in full manhood when the Lord Jesus was upon earth; and the facts detailed in the histories, and referred to in the Epistles, being of the most public nature, were still open to full investigation. It must also be recollected, that the Apostles and disciples, during the whole intermediate period, were publicly proclaiming to the world the same things which were afterward recorded in their writings. Thus were the Scriptures, as we now possess them, delivered to the first churches. By the concurrent testimony of all antiquity, both of friends and foes, they were received by Christians of different sects, and were constantly appealed to on all hands, in the controversies that arose among them. Commentaries upon them were written at a very early period, and translations made into different languages. Formal catalogues of them were published, and they were attacked by the adversaries of Christianity, who not only did not question, but expressly admitted, the facts they contained, and that they were the genuine productions of the persons whose names they bore. In this manner the Scriptures were also secured from the danger of being in any respect altered or vitiated. "The books of Scripture," says Augustine, "could not have been corrupted. If such an attempt had been made by any one, his design would have been prevented and defeated. His alterations would have been immediately detected by many and more ancient copies." The difficulty of succeeding in such an attempt is apparent hence, that the Scriptures were early translated into divers languages, and copies of them were numerous. The alterations which any one attempted to make would have been soon perceived; just even as now, in fact, lesser faults in some copies are amended by comparing ancient copies or those of the original. "If any one," continues Augustine, "should charge you with having interpolated some texts alleged by you as favourable to your cause, what would you say? Would you not immediately answer that it is impossible for you to do such a thing in books read by all Christians; and that if any such attempt had been made--by you, it would have been presently discerned and defeated by comparing the ancient copies? Well, then, for the same reason that the Scriptures cannot be corrupted by you, neither could they be corrupted by any other people." Accordingly, the uniformity of the manuscripts of the Holy Scriptures that are extant, which are incomparably more numerous than those of any ancient author, and which are dispersed through so many countries, and in so great a variety of languages, is truly astonishing. It demonstrates both the veneration in which the Scriptures have been always held, and the singular care that has been taken in transcribing them. The number of various readings, that by the most minute and laborious investigation and collations of manuscripts have been discovered in them, are said to amount to one hundred and fifty thousand; though at first sight they may seem calculated to diminish confidence in the sacred text, yet in no degree whatever do they affect its credit and integrity. They consist almost wholly in palpable errors in transcription, grammatical and verbal differences, such as the insertion or omission of a letter or article, the substitution of a word for its equivalent, or the transposition of a word or two in a sentence. Taken altogether, they neither change nor affect a single doctrine or duty announced or enjoined in the word of God. When, therefore, we consider the great antiquity of the sacred books, the almost infinite number of copies, of versions, and of editions, which have been made of them in all languages, in languages which have not any analogy one with another, among nations differing so much in their customs and their religious opinions,--when we consider these things, it is truly astonishing, and can only be ascribed to the watchful providence of God over his own word, that, among the various readings, nothing truly essential can be discerned, which relates to either precept or doctrine, or which breaks that connection, that unity which subsists in all the various parts of divine revelation, and which demonstrates the whole to be the work of one and the same Spirit.

8. Having considered the appellations by which the Bible is distinguished, the books of which it consists, the time and manner in which they were collected, it may not be improper to subjoin a few observations on the genuineness and authenticity of the Scriptures, on their high original and divine authority, and on their great importance and utility.

It should here be considered, that the genuineness of the Scriptures proves the truth of the principal facts contained in them; to which purpose we may observe that it is very rare to meet with any genuine writings of the historical kind, in which the principal facts are not true, unless it be in instances where both the motives which engaged the author to falsify, and the circumstances which gave some plausibility to the fiction, are apparent; neither of which can be alleged in the present case with any colour of reason. As this is rare in general, it is more rare when the writer treats of things that happened in his own time, and under his own cognizance and direction, and communicates his history to persons under the same circumstances; all which may be said of the writers of the Scripture history. Beside, the great importance of the facts mentioned in the Scriptures makes it more improbable, that the several authors should either have attempted to falsify, or have succeeded in such an attempt. The same observation may be applied to the great number of particular circumstances of time, place, persons, &c, mentioned in the Scriptures, and to the harmony of the books with themselves, and with each other. These are arguments both for the genuineness of the books, and truth of the facts distinctly considered, and also arguments for deducing the truth from the genuineness. Moreover, if the books of the Old and New Testaments were written by the persons to whom they have been ascribed, that is, if they be genuine, the moral characters of these writers afford the strongest assurance, that the facts asserted by them are true. The sufferings which several of the writers underwent both in life and in death, in attestation of the facts delivered by them, furnish a particular argument in favour of these facts. Again, the arguments here alleged for proving the truth of the Scripture history from the genuineness of the books, are as conclusive in respect of the miraculous facts, as of the common ones. It may also be observed, that if we allow the genuineness of the books to be a sufficient evidence of the common facts which they record, the miraculous facts must also be allowed from their close connection with the others. It is necessary to admit both or neither. We cannot conceive that Moses should have delivered the Israelites from their slavery in Egypt, or conducted them through the wilderness for forty years, at all in such manner as the common history represents, unless we suppose the miraculous facts intermixed with it to be true also. In like manner, the fame of Christ's miracles, the multitudes which followed him, the adherence of his disciples, the jealousy and hatred of the chief priests, scribes, and Pharisees, with many other facts of a common nature, are impossible to be accounted for, unless we allow that he did really work miracles. And the same observations hold, in general, of the other parts of the Scripture history. We might urge that a particular argument in favour of the miraculous part of the Scripture history, may be deduced from the reluctance of mankind to receive miraculous facts; which would put the writers and readers very much upon their guard, and would operate as a strong check upon the publication of a miraculous history at or near the time when the miracles were said to be performed; and thus it would serve as a strong confirmation of such a history, if its genuineness be previously granted.

9. In connection with the preceding proposition we may observe, that the genuineness of the Scriptures proves their divine authority. Porphyry in effect acknowledges the truth of this proposition, in its reference to the book of Daniel, by being unable to devise a method of invalidating its divine authority implied in the accomplishment of the prophecies which it contains, without asserting that they were written after the event, or that they were forgeries. Many of the other books of the Old and New Testaments have unquestionable evidences of the divine foreknowledge, if they be allowed genuine; such are those supplied by Moses's prophecy concerning the captivity of the Israelites, or of a state not yet erected; Isaiah's concerning Cyrus; Jeremiah's concerning the duration of the Babylonish captivity; Christ's concerning the destruction of Jerusalem, and the captivity that was to follow; St. John's concerning the great corruption of the Christian church; and Daniel's concerning the fourth empire in its declension; which last was extant in the time of Porphyry, at least; that is, before the events which it represents. The truth of the proposition might also be argued from the sublimity and excellence of the doctrines contained in the Scriptures; in no respect suiting the supposed authors, or the ages in which they lived, their education or occupation; so that, if they were the real authors, we are under the necessity of admitting the divine assistance. The converse of this proposition, namely, that the divine authority of the Scriptures infers their genuineness, will be readily and universally acknowledged. Moreover, the truth of the principal facts contained in the Scriptures proves their divine authority. Such is the frame of the human mind, that the Scripture history, allowed to be true, must convince us that Christ, the Prophets, and the Apostles, were endued with a power greater than human, and acted by the authority of a Being of the highest wisdom and goodness. By such mode of reasoning it is shown that the genuineness of the Scriptures, the truth of the principal facts contained in them, and their divine authority, appear to be so connected with each other, that, any one being established upon independent principles, the other two may be inferred from it. On the subject of the inspiration of the Scriptures, see Inspiration.

10. Another argument in favour of the genuineness of the books of the Old and New Testaments, and of the truth of the principal facts contained in them, may be deduced from the manner in which they have been transmitted down from one age to another; resembling that in which all other genuine books and true histories have been conveyed down to posterity. As the works of the Greek and Roman writers were considered by these nations as having been transmitted to them by their ancestors in a continued succession from the times when the respective authors lived, so have the books of the Old Testament been accounted by the Jews, and those of the New by the Christians; and it is an additional evidence in the last case, that the primitive Christians were not a distinct nation, but a great multitude of people dispersed through all the nations of the Roman empire, and even extending itself beyond the bounds of that empire. As the Greeks and Romans always believed the principal facts of their historical books, so the Jews and Christians did more, and never seem to have doubted of the truth of any part of theirs. In short--whatever can be said of the traditional authority due to the Greek and Roman writers--something analogous to this, and for the most part of greater weight, may be urged for the Jewish and Christian. Now, as all sober minded persons admit the books usually ascribed to the Greek and Roman historians, philosophers, &c, to be genuine, and the principal facts related or alluded to in them to be true, and that one chief evidence for this is the general traditionary one here recited, they ought, therefore, to pay the same regard to the books of the Old and New Testaments, since there are the same, or even greater, reasons for it. Beside, these traditionary evidences are sufficient; and we thus obtain a real argument, as well as one AD HOMINEM, for receiving books thus handed down to us. For it is not conceivable, that whole nations should either be imposed upon themselves, or concur to deceive others by forgeries of books or of facts. These books and facts must therefore, in general, be genuine and true; and it is a strong additional evidence of this, that all

nations must be jealous of forgeries for the same reasons as we are.

11. We may proceed to state farther, that the great importance of the histories, precepts, promises, threatenings, and prophecies contained in the Scriptures, is in evidence both of their genuineness, and of the truth of the principal facts mentioned in them. The history of the creation, fall, deluge, longevity of the patriarchs, dispersion of mankind, calling of Abraham, descent of Jacob with his family into Egypt, and the precepts of abstaining from blood, and of circumcision, were of such concern, either to mankind in general, or to the Israelites in particular, and some of them of so extraordinary a nature, as that it could not be a matter of indifference to the people among whom the account given of them in Genesis was first published, whether they received them or not. On the supposition that this account was first published among the Israelites by Moses, and then confirmed by clear, universal, uninterrupted tradition, it will be easy to conceive how it should be handed down from age to age among the Jews, and received by them as indubitable. But, supposing the account to be false, or that there were no such vestiges and evidences of these histories and precepts, it will be difficult to conceive how this could have happened, let the time of publication be what it may. If early, the people would reject at once the account, for want of a clear tradition; if late, it would be natural to inquire how the author was informed of things never known before to others. As to other cosmogonies and theogonies current among Pagans, which are evident fictions, they furnish no just objection against the Mosaic history, because they were generally regarded merely as amusing fictions; and yet they concealed in figures, or expressed in plain words, some truths which agree with the book of Genesis, and afford a strong presumptive evidence in favour of this book. With respect to the law of Moses, this was extremely burdensome, expensive, and severe, particularly in its reference to the crime of idolatry, to which mankind were then extravagantly prone; and it was absurd, according to human judgment, in the instances of prohibiting their furnishing themselves with horses for war, and of commanding all the males of the whole nation to appear at Jerusalem three times a year. Nevertheless, it claims a divine authority, and appeals to facts of the most notorious kind, and to customs and ceremonies of the most peculiar nature, as the memorials of these facts. Can we then conceive that any nation, with such motives to reject, and such opportunities of detecting, the forgery of the books of Exodus, Leviticus, Numbers, and Deuteronomy, should yet receive them, and submit to this heavy yoke? That the Jews did submit to the law of Moses in these circumstances, is evident from the books of the Old and New Testaments, if we allow them the least truth and genuineness, or even from profane writers, and from the present observance of it by the Jews scattered through all the kingdoms of the world. Should it be said that other nations have ascribed divine authority to their lawgivers, and submitted to very severe laws, it may be alleged in reply to this, that the pretences of lawgivers among the Pagans to inspiration, and the submission of the people, may be accounted for from their peculiar circumstances at the time, without recurring to real inspiration; and more especially if we admit the patriarchal revelations related by Moses, and his own divine legation, as Heathen lawgivers copied after these, and hence we derive a strong argument in their favour. Beside, no instance occurs among the Pagans of a body of laws framed at once and remaining invariable; whereas the body politic of the Israelites assumed a complete form at once, and has preserved it, with little variation, to the present time, and under many external disadvantages; thus supplying us with an instance altogether without parallel, and showing the high opinion which they entertained of the great importance of their law. In short, of all the fictions or forgeries that can happen among any people, the most improbable is that of the Jewish body of civil laws, and seems to be utterly impossible.

12. If we farther examine the history contained in the books of Joshua, Judges, Ruth, Samuel, Kings, Chronicles, Ezra, and Nehemiah, and extending from the death of Moses to the reëstablishment of the Jews after the Babylonish captivity by Ezra and Nehemiah, we shall find a variety of important facts, most of which must be supposed to leave such vestiges of themselves, either external and visible, or internal in the minds and memories of the people, as would verify them if true, or cause them to be rejected if false. The conquest of the land of Canaan, the division of it, and the appointment of cities for the priests and Levites by Joshua; the frequent slaveries of the Israelites to the neighbouring kings, and their deliverance by the judges; the creation of a kingdom by Samuel; the translation of this kingdom from Saul's family to David, with his conquests; the glory of Solomon's kingdom; the building of the temple; the division of the kingdom; the idolatrous worship set up at Dan and Bethel; the captivity of the Israelites by the kings of Assyria; the captivity of the Jews by Nebuchadnezzar; the destruction of their temple; their return under Cyrus, rebuilding the temple under Darius Hystaspes, and reëstablishment under Artaxerxes Longimanus, by Ezra and Nehemiah:--these events are some of them the most glorious, and some of them the most reproachful, that can happen to any people. How can we reconcile forgeries of such opposite kinds, and especially as they are interwoven together by various complicated and necessary connections, which do not admit of separation? The facts, indeed, are of such importance, notoriety, and permanency in their effects, that no particular persons among the Israelites could first project the design of feigning them, that their own people would not concur with such a design, and that neighbouring nations would not permit the fiction to pass. Nothing but the invincible evidence of the facts here alleged, could induce a jealous multitude among the Israelites or neighbouring nations to acquiesce. This must be acknowledged upon the supposition that the several books were published in or near the times when the facts that are recorded in them happened. But suppose all these historical books forged by Ezra; the hypothesis is evidently impossible. Things so important and notorious, so honourable and so reproachful to the people for whose

sake they were forged, would have been rejected with the utmost indignation, unless there were the strongest and most genuine traces of these things already among the people. They must therefore, in part at least, be true. If it be said that additions were made by Ezra, these additions must have been either of important or trivial matters. On the first supposition, the difficulty already stated recurs; and if the important facts are true, what possible motive could have induced Ezra to make additions of no importance? Beside, if any ancient writings were extant, Ezra must either copy after them, which destroys the present supposition, or differ from and oppose them, which would betray him. If there were no such ancient writings, the people would be led to inquire with regard to matters of importance, for what reason Ezra was so particular in things of which there was neither any memory, nor account in writing. Should it be said that the people did not regard what Ezra had thus forged, this reduces the subject in question to matters of small or of no importance. Beside, why should Ezra write if no one would read or regard? Farther: Ezra must have had, like other men, friends, enemies, and rivals; and some, or all of these, would have been a check upon him, and a security against him, in matters of importance. If we suppose these books, instead of having been forged at once, to have been forged successively, at the interval of one, two, or three centuries after the facts related, we shall involve ourselves in the same or similar difficulties. Upon the whole, then, we may conclude, that the forgery of the annals of the Israelites appears to be impossible, as well as that of the body of their civil laws. It is needless to examine the books of Esther, Job, the Psalms, Proverbs, Ecclesiastes, and Canticles; and we might proceed to the Prophecies; but this will be resumed under the article PROPHECY. For the subjects comprehended in the books of the New Testament. See Gospel:**GOSPEL**, and #Christianity.

13. We shall here subjoin some general evidences in attestation of the truth of the books of Scripture. That Jews and Christians have thought their sacred books very highly important, most genuine, and true, appears from the persecutions and sufferings which they have undergone on account of their attachment to them, and because they would not be prevailed upon to surrender them. The preservation of the law of Moses, probably the first book written in any language, whilst many others of a later date have been lost, shows the great regard that has been paid to it; and from this circumstance we may infer that this and the other books of the Old Testament have been preserved on account of their importance, or from some other cause, equally evincing their genuineness and truth. The great value set upon these books appears also from the many early translations and paraphrases of them; and these translations and paraphrases serve to correct errors that are unavoidable in the lapse of time, and to secure their integrity and purity. The hesitation and difficulty with which some few books of the New Testament were received into the canon, show the great care and concern of the primitive Christians about the canon, and the high importance of the books admitted into it; and afford a strong evidence of their genuineness and truth. The same observation is in a degree applicable to the Jewish canon. Moreover, the religious hatred and animosity which subsisted between the Jews and Samaritans, and between several of the ancient sects among the Christians, convince us of what importance they all thought their sacred books, and disposed them to watch over one another with a jealous eye. Farther: the genuineness of the books of the Old and New Testaments may be evinced from the language, style, and manner of writing used in them. The Hebrew language, in which the Old Testament was written, being the language of an ancient people, who had little intercourse with their neighbours, would not change so fast as modern languages have done, since different nations have been variously blended with one another by the extension of trade, arts, and sciences; and yet some changes must have occurred in the interval that elapsed between the time of Moses and that of Malachi. The biblical Hebrew corresponds so exactly to this criterion, as to afford a considerable argument in favour of the genuineness of the books of the Old Testament. Beside, these books have too great a diversity of style to be the work of either one Jew, or of any set of contemporary Jews. If they be forgeries, there must have been a succession of impostors in different ages, who concurred in the same iniquitous design. Again: the Hebrew language ceased to be spoken, as a living language, soon after the time of the Babylonish captivity; and it would be difficult or impossible to forge any thing in it after it became a dead language. Hence it appears, that all the books of the Old Testament must at least be nearly as ancient as the Babylonish captivity; and as they could not all be written in the same age, some must be much more ancient, and this would reduce us to the necessity of supposing a succession of conspiring impostors. Moreover, there is, as we have already observed, a simplicity of style, and an unaffected manner of writing, in all the books of the Old Testament, which is a strong evidence of their genuineness. The style of the New Testament, in particular, is not only simple and unaffected, but is Greek influenced by the Hebrew idiom, and exactly answers to the circumstances of time, places, and persons. To which we may add, that the narrations and precepts of both the Old and New Testament are delivered without hesitation; the writers teaching as having authority: and this circumstance is peculiar to those who unite, with a clear knowledge of what they deliver, a perfect integrity of heart. But a farther argument for the genuineness and truth of the Scriptures is supplied by the very great number of particular circumstances of time, place, persons, &c, mentioned in them. It is needless to recount these; but they are incompatible with forged and false accounts, that do not abound in such particularities, and the want of which furnishes a suspicion to their discredit. Compare, in this respect, Manetho's account of the dynasties of Egypt, Ctesias's of the Assyrian kings, and those which the technical chronologers have given of the ancient kingdoms of Greece, which are defective in such particulars, with the history by Thucydides of the Peloponnesian war, and with Cæsar's of the war in Gaul, and the difference will be sufficiently apparent. Dr. Paley's admirable treatise, entitled, "*Horæ Paulinæ*," affords very valuable illustrations of this argument as it respects the genuineness of the books

of the New Testament. The agreement of the Scriptures with history, natural and civil, is a farther proof of their genuineness and truth. The history of the fall agrees in an eminent manner both with the obvious facts of labour, sorrow, pain, and death, with what we see and feel every day, and with all our philosophical inquiries into the frame of the human mind, the nature of social life, and the origin of evil. Natural history bears a strong testimony to Moses's account of the deluge. Civil history affords many evidences which corroborate the same account. (See DELUGE.) The Mosaic account of the confusion of languages, of the dispersion of Noah's sons, and of the state of religion in the ancient postdiluvian world, is not only rendered probable, but is in a very high degree established, by many collateral arguments. See Confusion of Languages, and Division of the Earth.

14. The agreement of the books of the Old and New Testaments with themselves and with each other, affords another argument both of their genuineness and truth. The laws of the Israelites are contained in the Pentateuch, and referred to, in a great variety of ways, direct and indirect, in the historical books, in the Psalms, and in the Prophecies. The historical facts also in the preceding books are often referred to in those that succeed, and in the Psalms and Prophecies. In like manner, the Gospels have the greatest harmony with each other, and the Epistles of St. Paul with the Acts of the Apostles; and, indeed, there is scarcely any book of either the Old or New Testament, which may not be shown to refer to many of the rest, in one way or other. For the illustration of this argument, let us suppose that no more remained of the Roman writers than Livy, Tully, and Horace; would they not, by their references to the same facts and customs, by the sameness of style in the same writer, and difference in the different ones, and numberless other such like circumstances of critical consideration, prove themselves, and one another to be genuine, and the principal facts related, or alluded to, to be true? Whoever will apply this reasoning to the present case will perceive, that the numberless minute, direct, and indirect agreements and coincidences, that present themselves to all diligent readers of the Scriptures, prove their truth and genuineness beyond all contradiction.

The harmony and agreement of the several writers of the Old and New Testament appear the more remarkable, when it is considered that their various parts were penned by several hands in very different conditions of life, from the throne and sceptre down to the lowest degree, and in very distant ages, through a long interval of time; which would naturally have led a spirit of imposture to have varied its schemes, and to have adapted them to different stations in the world, and to the different vicissitudes of every age. David wrote about four hundred years after Moses, and Isaiah about two hundred and fifty after David, and Matthew more than seven hundred years after Isaiah; and yet these authors, with all the other Prophets and Apostles, write in perfect harmony, confirming the authority of their predecessors, labouring to reduce the people to the observance of their instructions, and loudly exclaiming against the neglect and contempt of them, and denouncing the severest judgments against such as continued disobedient. Consequently, as the writers of the Holy Scriptures, though they all claim a divine authority, yet write in perfect connection and harmony, mutually confirming the doctrine and testimony of each other, and concurring to establish the very same religious truths and principles, it is a strong proof that they all derived their instructions from the same fountain, the wisdom of God, and were indeed under the direction and illumination of the same Spirit. This leads us to add, that the unity of design, which appears in the dispensations recorded in the Scriptures, is an argument not only of their truth and genuineness, but also of their divine authority. In order to perceive the force of this argument, it is only necessary to inquire what this design is, and how it is pursued by the series of events and divine interpositions recorded in the Scriptures. (See DISPENSATION.) It should also be considered, that the historical evidences in favour of the genuineness, truth, and divine authority of the Scriptures, do not become less from age to age; but, on the contrary, it may rather be presumed that they increase. Since the three great concurring events of printing, the reformation of religion in these western parts, and the restoration of letters, so many more evidences and coincidences have been discovered in favour of the Jewish and Christian histories, as may serve, in some measure, to supply the want of those that have been lost in the preceding times; and as this accumulation of evidences is likely to continue, there is great reason to hope that it will at length become irresistible to all and silence even every gainsayer.

15. The moral characters of the Prophets, and the Apostles, prove the truth and divine authority of the Scriptures. The characters of the persons who are said in the Scriptures to have had divine communications, and a divine mission, are so much superior to the characters that occur in common life, that we can scarcely account for the more eminent individuals, and much less so for so large a succession of them, continued through so many ages, without allowing the divine communications and assistance which they allege. Notwithstanding considerable imperfections that pertained to many of these eminent persons, and the occasional offences chargeable upon one or two of them, yet the impartial reader should consider whether the Prophets, Apostles, &c, were not so much superior, not only to mankind at an average, but even to the best men among the Greeks and Romans, as is not fairly to be accounted for by the mere powers of human nature. If this statement should not be conceded, their characters, however, are too good to allow the supposition of an impious fraud and imposture, which must have been the case if they had not divine authority. Beside, it should be recollected, that the undisguised and impartial manner in which the imperfections and faults of the eminent persons mentioned in Scripture are related, furnishes a remarkable additional evidence for the truth of those parts of the Scripture history in which such relations occur, beside such evidences as extend to the whole.

16. The excellence of the doctrine contained in the Scriptures is an additional evidence of their authority. This argument has great force independently of all other considerations. Suppose, for instance, that the author of the Gospel, which goes under the name of St. Matthew, was not known, and that it was unsupported by the writers of the primitive times; yet such are the unaffected simplicity of the narrations, the purity of the doctrine, and the sincere piety and goodness of the sentiments, that it carries its own authority with it. The same observation is applicable in general to all the books of the Old and New Testaments; so that if there was no other book in the world beside the Bible, a man could not reasonably doubt of the truth of revealed religion. If all other arguments were set aside, we may conclude from this single consideration, that the authors of the books of the Old and New Testaments, whoever they were, cannot have made a false claim to divine authority. The Scriptures contain doctrines concerning God, providence, a future state, the duty of man, &c, far more pure and sublime than can in any way be accounted for from the natural powers of men, so circumstanced as the sacred writers were. Let the reader consider whether it can be reasonably supposed, that Jewish shepherds, fishermen, &c, should, both before and after the rise of the Heathen philosophy, so far exceed men of the greatest abilities and accomplishments in other nations, by any other means than divine communications. Indeed, no writers, from the invention of letters to the present times, are equal to the penmen of the books of the Old and New Testaments in true excellence, utility and dignity; and this is surely such an internal criterion of their divine authority, as ought not to be resisted.

17. The many and great advantages which have accrued to the world from the patriarchal, Judaical, and Christian revelations, confirm the whole. These advantages relate partly to the knowledge, and partly to the practice, of religion. The internal worth and excellence of the Scriptures, as containing the best principles of knowledge, holiness, consolation, and hope, and their consequent utility and importance in a moral and practical view, fully and directly demonstrate their divine original. For an enlarged view of this branch of evidence see Christianity.

BIBLISTS, or **BIBLICI**, a term applied to certain doctors in the twelfth and thirteenth centuries, who expounded the sacred writings in their public schools, and endeavoured to establish their doctrines by the authority of Scripture, in opposition to uncertain traditions, or the speculations of the schools. Upon the same principle, the Pietists of the seventeenth century formed what they called Biblical colleges, for expounding the Scriptures.

BIER. See Burial.

BILDAD, the Shuhite, one of Job's friends, thought by some to have descended from Shuah, the son of Abraham, by Keturah, Job ii, 11; viii, xviii, xxv.

BILHAH, Rachel's handmaid, given by her to Jacob her husband, as a concubinary wife, that, through her she might have a son, Gen. xxx, 3, 4, &c. See Barrenness.

BIND. To bind and loose are taken for condemning and absolving: "And I will give unto thee the keys of the kingdom of heaven: and whatsoever thou shalt bind on earth shall be bound in heaven: and whatsoever thou shalt loose on earth shall be loosed in heaven," Matt. xvi, 19. By binding and loosing, in the language of the Jews, is understood, likewise, permitting and forbidding; or declaring any thing in a judicial manner to be permitted or forbidden; and on the promotion of their doctors, they put the keys into their hands with these words, "Receive the power of binding and loosing." So our Lord says, "I am not come to destroy," to unloose or dissolve, "the law, but to fulfil," that is, to confirm and establish it, Matt. v, 17. See Keys.

BIRD, צפור, a common name for all birds, but is sometimes used for the sparrow in particular.

Birds are distinguished by the Jewish legislator into clean and unclean. Such as fed upon grain and seeds were allowed for food, and such as devoured flesh and carrion were prohibited.

Moses, to inspire the Israelites with sentiments of tenderness toward the brute creation, commands them, if they find a bird's nest, not to take the dam with the young, but to suffer the old one to fly away, and to take the young only, Deut. xxii, 6. This is one of those merciful constitutions in the law of Moses which respect the animal creation, and tended to humanize the heart of that people, to excite in them a sense of the divine providence extending itself to all creatures, and to teach them to exercise their dominion over them with gentleness. Beside, the young never knew the sweets of liberty; the dam did: they might be taken and used for any lawful purpose; but the dam must not be brought into a state of captivity. The poet Phocylides has a maxim, in his admonitory poem, very similar to that in the sacred texts:--

Μηδέ τις ὄρνιθας καλιῆς ἅμα ϖάντας ἑλέσθω,

Μητερα δ' ἐκπρολίπης, ἵν' ἔχῃς ϖάλι τῆσδε νεοττούς.

Nor from a nest take all the birds away,

The mother spare, she'll breed a future day.

It appears that the ancients hunted birds. Baruch, iii, 17, speaking of the kings of Babylon, says, "They had their pastime with the fowls of the air;" and Daniel, iii, 38, tells Nebuchadnezzar that God had made the fowls of the air subject to him.

Birds were offered in sacrifice on many occasions. In the sacrifices for sin, he who had not a lamb, or a kid, "might offer two turtles, or two young pigeons; one for a sin-offering, the other for a burnt-offering. These he presented to the priest, who offered that first which was for the sin-offering, and wrung off the head from the neck, but did not divide it asunder: the other he was to offer for a burnt-offering," Lev. v, 7, 8. When a man who had been smitten with a leprosy was healed, he came to the entrance of the camp of Israel, and the priest went out to inspect him, whether he were entirely cured, Lev. xiv, 5, 6. After this inspection, the leprous person came to the door of the tabernacle, and offered two living sparrows, or two birds; (pure birds, those of which it was lawful to eat;) he made a wisp with branches of cedar and hyssop, tied together with a thread, or scarlet ribbon; he filled an earthen pot with running water, that the blood of the bird might be mingled with it; then the priest, dipping the bunch of hyssop and cedar into the water, sprinkled with it the leper who was healed; after which he let loose the living bird, to fly where it would. In Palestine dead bodies were sometimes left exposed to birds of prey, as appears from Scripture; but, generally, they were buried in the evening: even criminals were taken down from the gallows.

BIRTHRIGHT, or **PRIMOGENITURE**, the right of the first-born or eldest son. The birthright, or right of primogeniture, had many privileges annexed to it. The first-born was consecrated to the Lord, Exod. xxii, 29; had a double portion of the estate allotted him, Deut. xxi, 17; had a dignity and authority over his brethren, Gen. xlix, 3; succeeded in the government of the family or kingdom, 2 Chron. xxi, 3; and, as some with good reason suppose, in ancient times to the priesthood or chief government in matters ecclesiastical. Jacob, having bought Esau's birthright, acquired a title to the particular blessing of his dying father; and, accordingly, he had consigned to him the privilege of the covenant which God made with Abraham, that from his loins the Messiah should spring: a prerogative which descended to his posterity. Reuben forfeited the blessings of his birthright, as we see by the express declaration of his father Jacob, in his benediction of his children, Gen. xlix, 1, &c, for the crime of incest with his father's concubine, on account of which his tribe continued all along in obscurity; while the priesthood was conferred on Levi, the government on Judah, and the double portion on Joseph, to descend to their respective tribes. And this preëminence of the first-born took place from the beginning, and as much belonged to Cain, before his forfeiture of it, as it did to Reuben before his. See Genesis iv, 7; xlix, 3. Thus the patriarchs, Abraham, Isaac, and Jacob, offered sacrifices, and were priests as well as kings in their respective families, Gen. xii, 7, 8; xiii, 18; xvii, 7; xxvi, 25; xxxi, 54; xxxv, 7. Job, in Arabia, acted in the same capacity, Job, i, 5; and it is highly probable that, among the ancient Heathen nations in general, the first-born were entitled not only to the civil authority, but also to the priesthood. This seems to have been the case in Egypt, in the time of Moses: and hence Jehovah's destroying their first-born, as it was the last miracle wrought in that country before the Exodus, so was it the most dreadful, and most effectual in prevailing on Pharaoh and the Egyptians to dismiss the Israelites.

BISHOP, פקיד, ἐπίσκοπος, signifies AN OVERSEER, or one who has the inspection and direction of any thing. Nehemiah speaks of the overseer of the Levites at Jerusalem, Neh. xi, 22. The most common acceptation of the word BISHOP is that in Acts xx, 28, and in St. Paul's Epistles, Philip, i, 1, where it signifies the pastor of a church. St. Peter calls Jesus Christ "the Shepherd and Bishop of our souls," 1 Peter ii, 25; and St. Paul describes the qualities requisite in a bishop, 1 Tim. iii, 2; Titus 1, 2, &c. It is not improbable that the overseers of Christ's church are in the New Testament called ἐπισκόποι, from the following passage in Isaiah: "I will also make thy officers peace, and thine OVERSEERS" (ἐπισκόπȣς,) "righteousness," Isa. lx, 17. The word, as used by the Apostolic writers, when referring to the pastors of Christian churches, is evidently of the same import as PRESBYTER or ELDER; for the terms, as they occur in the New Testament, appear to be synonymous, and are used indifferently. Thus the same persons that are called ἐπισκόποι, BISHOPS are also called πρεσβύτεροι, ELDERS. Hence, when St. Paul came to Miletus, he sent to Ephesus for the presbyters of the church, and thus addressed them: "Take heed unto yourselves, and to all the flock over which the Holy Ghost hath made you" (the presbyters) "ἐπισκόπȣς, bishops," or overseers, Acts xx, 17. "Here," says Dr. Campbell, "there can be no question that the same persons are denominated presbyters and bishops." Nor is this the only passage in which we find the terms used convertibly. In Titus i, 5, it is said, "For this cause left I thee in Crete, that thou shouldest set in order the things that are wanting, and ordain elders" (Greek, πρεσβυτέρȣς) "in every city;" and then it follows in verse 7, "For a bishop" (ἐπίσκοπον) "must be blameless." In like manner, the Apostle Peter, 1 Peter v, 1: "The elders" (πρεσβυτέρȣς) "which are among you I exhort; feed the flock of God which is among you, TAKING THE OVERSIGHT THEREOF; ἐπισκοποῦντες, that is, discharging the office of bishops." See Episcopacy.

BITHYNIA, a country of Asia Minor, stretching along the shore of the Pontus Euxinus, or Black Sea, from Mysia to Paphlagonia; having Phrygia and Galatia on the south. In it are the two cities of Nicæa, or Nice, and Chalcedon: both celebrated in ecclesiastical history, on account of the general councils held in them, and called after their names. The former city is at present called Is-Nick, and the latter Kadi-Keni. Within this country, also, are the celebrated mountains of Olympus. St. Peter addressed his first Epistle to the Hebrew Christians who were scattered through this and the neighbouring countries.

BITTER HERBS. מרורים. Exod. xii, 8, and Num. ix, 11. The Jews were commanded to eat their passover with a salad of bitter herbs; but whether one particular plant was intended, or any kind of bitter herbs, has been made a question. By the Septuagint it is rendered επι πικριδων; by Jerom, "CUM LACTUCIS AGRESTIBUS;" and by the Gr.

Venet., επι ϖικρισιν. Dr. Geddes remarks, that "it is highly probable that the succory or wild lettuce is meant." The Mischna in PESACHIM, cap. 2, reckons five species of these bitter herbs: 1. Chazareth, taken for lettuce: 2. Ulsin, supposed to be endive or succory: 3. Tamca, probably tansy: 4. Charubbinim, which Bochart thought might be the nettle, but Scheuchzer shows to be the camomile: 5. Meror, the sow-thistle, or dent-de-lion, or wild lettuce. Mr. Forskal says, "the Jews in Sana and in Egypt eat the lettuce with the paschal lamb." He also remarks, that MORU is centaury, of which the young stems are eaten in February and March.

BITTERN. קפוד. Isa. xiv, 23; xxxiv, 11; and Zephaniah ii, 14. Interpreters have rendered this word variously: an OWL, an OSPREY, a TORTOISE, a PORCUPINE, and even an OTTER. "How unhappy," says Mr. Harmer, "that a word which occurs but three times in the Hebrew Bible should be translated by three different words, and that one of them should be OTTER!" Isaiah, prophesying the destruction of Babylon, says that "the Lord will make it a possession for the bittern, and pools of water;" and Zephaniah, ii, 14, prophesying against Nineveh, says that "the cormorant and bittern shall lodge in the upper lintels of it: their voice shall sing in the windows." The Arabic version reads "AL-HOUBARA." According to Dr. Shaw, the HOUBARA is "of the bigness of a capon, but of a longer body. It feeds on little shrubs and insects, like the GRAAB EL SAHARA; frequenting, in like manner, the confines of the desert." Golius interprets it THE BUSTARD; and Dr. Russel says that the Arabic name of the bustard is "houbry."

BITTERNESS, WATERS OF. See Adultery.

BLASPHEMY, βλασφημία, properly denotes CALUMNY, DETRACTION, REPROACHFUL or ABUSIVE LANGUAGE, against whomsoever it be vented. That βλασφημία and its conjugates are very often applied, says Dr. Campbell, to reproaches not aimed against God, is evident from the following passages: Matt. xii, 31, 32; xxvii, 39; Mark xv, 29; Luke xxii, 65; xxiii, 39; Rom. iii, 8; xiv, 16; 1 Cor. iv, 13; x, 30; Eph. iv, 31; 1 Tim. vi, 4; Titus iii, 2; 1 Pet. iv, 14; Jude 9, 10; Acts vi, 11, 13; 2 Pet. ii, 10, 11; in the much greater part of which the English translators, sensible that they could admit no such application, have not used the words BLASPHEME or BLASPHEMY, but RAIL, REVILE, SPEAK EVIL, &c. In one of the passages quoted, a reproachful charge brought even against the devil is called κρισις βλασφημίας, Jude 9; and rendered by them, "railing accusation." The import of the word βλασφημία is MALEDICENTIA, in the largest acceptation; comprehending all sorts of verbal abuse, imprecation, reviling, and calumny. And let it be observed, that when such abuse is mentioned as uttered against God, there is properly no change made in the signification of the word: the change is only in the application; that is, in the reference to a different object. The idea conveyed in the explanation now given is always included, against whomsoever the crime be committed. In this manner every term is understood that is applicable to both God and man. Thus the meaning of the word DISOBEY is the same, whether we speak of disobeying God or of disobeying man. The same may be said of BELIEVE, HONOUR, FEAR, &c. As, therefore, the sense of the term is the same, though differently applied, what is essential to constitute the crime of detraction in the one case, is essential also in the other. But it is essential to this crime, as commonly understood, when committed by one man against another, that there be in the injurious person the will or disposition to detract from the person abused. Mere mistake in regard to character, especially when the mistake is not conceived by him who entertains it to lessen the character, nay, is supposed, however erroneously, to exalt it, is never construed by any into the crime of defamation. Now, as blasphemy is in its essence the same crime, but immensely aggravated by being committed against an object infinitely superior to man, what is fundamental to the very existence of the crime will be found in this, as in every other species which comes under the general name. There can be no blasphemy, therefore, where there is not an impious purpose to derogate from the Divine Majesty, and to alienate the minds of others from the love and reverence of God. The blasphemer is no other than the calumniator of Almighty God. To constitute the crime, it is as necessary that this species of calumny be intentional. He must be one, therefore, who by his impious talk endeavours to inspire others with the same irreverence toward the Deity, or perhaps, abhorrence of him, which he indulges in himself. And though, for the honour of human nature, it is to be hoped that very few arrive at this enormous guilt, it ought not to be dissembled, that the habitual profanation of the name and attributes of God by common swearing, is but too manifest an approach toward it. There is not an entire coincidence: the latter of these vices may be considered as resulting solely from the defect of what is good in principle and disposition; the former from the acquisition of what is evil in the extreme: but there is a close connection between them, and an insensible gradation from the one to the other. To accustom one's self to treat the Sovereign of the universe with irreverent familiarity, is the first step; malignly to arraign his attributes, and revile his providence, is the last. The first divine law published against it, "He that blasphemeth the name of the Lord" (or JEHOVAH, as it is in the Hebrew) "shall be put to death," Lev. xxiv, 16, when considered along with the incident that occasioned it, suggests a very atrocious offence in words, no less than abuse or imprecations vented against the Deity. For, in what way soever the crime of the man there mentioned be interpreted,--whether as committed against the true God, the God of Israel, or against any of the false gods whom his Egyptian father worshipped,--the law in the words now quoted is sufficiently explicit; and the circumstances of the story plainly show, that the words which he had used were derogatory from the Godhead, and shocking to the hearers. And if we add to this the only other memorable instance in sacred history, namely, that of Rabshakeh, it will lead us to conclude that it is solely a malignant attempt, in words, to lessen men's reverence of the true God, and, by vilifying his perfections, to prevent their placing confidence in him, which is called in Scripture BLASPHEMY, when the word is employed to denote a sin committed directly against God. This was manifestly the attempt of Rabshakeh, when he said, "Neither let Hezekiah make you trust in the Lord," (the word is JEHOVAH,) "saying, Jehovah will surely deliver us. Hath any of the gods of the nations delivered his land out of the hand of the king of Assyria? Where are the gods of Hamath and of Arpad? Where are the gods of Sepharvaim, Hena, and Iva? Have they delivered Samaria out of my hand? Who are they, among all the gods of the countries, that have delivered their country out of mine hand, that Jehovah should deliver Jerusalem out of mine hand?" 2 Kings xviii, 30, 33–35.

2. It will naturally occur to inquire, what that is, in particular, which our Lord denominates "blasphemy against the Holy Spirit," Matt. xii, 31, 32; Mark iii, 28, 29; Luke xii, 10. But without entering minutely into the discussion of this question, it may suffice here to observe, that this blasphemy is certainly not of the constructive kind, but direct, manifest, and malignant. First, it is mentioned as comprehended under the same genus with abuse against men, and contradistinguished only by the object. Secondly, it is farther explained by being called SPEAKING AGAINST in both cases: ὂς ἂν ἐίπη λόγον κατὰ τοῦ ὑιοῦ τοῦ ἀνθρωπ8,--ὂς δ' ἂν ἐίπη κατὰ τοῦ ϖνεύματος τοῦ ἀγίς. "Whosoever speaketh a word against the Son of Man."--"Whosoever speaketh against the Holy Ghost." The expressions are the same, in effect, in all the Evangelists who mention it, and imply such an opposition as is both intentional and malevolent. This cannot have been the case of all who disbelieved the mission of Jesus, and even decried his miracles; many of whom, we have reason to think, were afterward converted by the Apostles. But it was the wretched case of some who, instigated by worldly ambition and avarice, slandered what they knew to be the cause of God; and, against conviction, reviled his work as the operation of evil spirits. This view of the sin against the Holy Ghost is confirmed by the circumstances under which our Lord spoke.

If we consider the Scripture account of this sin, nothing can be plainer than that it is to be understood of the Pharisees' imputing the miracles wrought by the power of the Holy Ghost to the power of the devil; for our Lord had just healed one possessed of a devil, and upon this the Pharisees gave this malicious turn to the miracle. This led our Saviour to discourse on the sin of blasphemy. The Pharisees were the persons charged with the crime: the sin itself manifestly consisted in ascribing what was done by the finger of God to the agency of the devil; and the reason, therefore, why our Lord pronounced it unpardonable, is plain; because, by withstanding the evidence of miracles, they resisted the strongest means of conviction, and that wilfully and malignantly; and, giving way to their passions, opprobriously treated that Holy Spirit whom they ought to have adored. From all which it will probably follow, that no person can now be guilty of the blasphemy against the Holy Ghost, in the sense in which our Saviour originally intended it; but there may be sins which bear a very near resemblance to it. This appears from the case of the apostates mentioned in the Epistle to the Hebrews, to whom "no more sacrifice for sins" is said to remain; whose defection, however, is not represented so much as a direct sin against the Holy Ghost as against Christ, whom the apostate Jews blasphemed in the synagogues. It implied, however, a high offence against the Holy Spirit also, with whose gifts they had, probably, been endowed, and their conduct must be considered, if not the same sin as that committed by the Pharisees, yet as a CONSENTING with it, and thus as placing them in nearly, if not altogether, the same desperate condition. Even apostasy in the present day, although a most aggravated and perilous offence, cannot be committed with circumstances of equal aggravation to those which were found in the case of the persons mentioned by St. Paul; and it may be laid down as certain, for the relief of those who may be tempted to think that they have committed the unpardonable sin, that their horror of it, and the trouble which the very apprehension causes them, are the sure proofs that they are mistaken. But although there may be now fearful approaches to the unpardonable offence, it is to be remembered that there may be many dangerous and fatal sins against the Holy Ghost, which are not THE sin against him, which has no forgiveness.

BLEMISH, whatever renders a person or thing imperfect or uncomely. The Jewish law required the priests to be free from blemishes of person, Lev. xxi, 17–23; xxii, 20–24. Scandalous professors are blemishes to the church of God, 2 Peter ii, 13; Jude 12, and therefore ought to be put away from it, in the exercise of a godly discipline.

BLESS, BLESSING. There are three points of view in which the acts of blessing may be considered. The first is, when men are said to bless God, as in Psalm ciii, 1, 2. We are then not to suppose that the divine Being, who is over all, and, in himself, blessed for evermore, is capable of receiving any augmentation of his happiness, from all the creatures which he has made: such a supposition, as it would imply something of imperfection in the divine nature, must ever be rejected with abhorrence; and, therefore, when the creatures bless the adorable Creator, they only ascribe to him that praise and dominion, and honour, and glory, and blessing, which it is equally the duty and joy of his creatures to render. But when God is said to bless his people, Gen. i, 22; Eph. i, 3; the meaning is, that he confers benefits upon them, either temporal or spiritual, and so communicates to them some portion of that blessedness which, in infinite fulness, dwells in himself, James i, 17; Psalm civ, 24, 28; Luke xi, 9–13. In the third place men are said to bless their fellow creatures. From the time that God entered into covenant with Abraham, and promised extraordinary blessings to his posterity, it appears to have been customary for the father of each family, in the direct line, or line of promise, previous to his death, to call his children around him, and to inform them, according to the knowledge which it pleased God then to give him, how, and in what manner, the divine blessing conferred upon

Abraham was to descend among them. Upon these occasions, the patriarchs enjoyed a divine illumination; and under its influence, their benediction was deemed a prophetic oracle, foretelling events with the utmost certainty, and extending to the remotest period of time. Thus Jacob blessed his sons, Gen. xlix; and Moses, the children of Israel, Deut. xxxiii. When Melchizedeck blessed Abraham, the act of benediction included in it not merely the pronouncing solemn good wishes, but also a petitionary address to God that he would be pleased to ratify the benediction by his concurrence with what was prayed for. Thus Moses instructed Aaron, and his descendants, to bless the congregation, "In this wise shall ye bless the children of Israel, saying unto them, The Lord bless thee, and keep thee; the Lord make his face to shine upon thee; the Lord lift up his countenance upon thee, and give thee peace," Num. iv, 23. David says, "I will take the cup of salvation, and call upon the name of the Lord," Psalm cxvi, 13. This phrase appears to be taken from the practice of the Jews in their thank-offerings, in which a feast was made of the remainder of their sacrifices, and the offerers, together with the priests, did eat and drink before the Lord; when, among other rites, the master of the feast took a cup of wine in his hand and solemnly blessed God for it, and for the mercies which were then acknowledged, and gave it to all the guests, every one of whom drank in his turn. To this custom it is supposed our blessed Lord alludes in the institution of the cup, which also is called, 1 Cor. x, 16, "the cup of blessing." At the family feasts also, and especially that of the passover, both wine and bread were in this solemn and religious manner distributed, and God was blessed, and his mercies acknowledged. They blessed God for their present refreshment, for their deliverance out of Egypt, for the covenant of circumcision, and for the law given by Moses; and prayed that God would be merciful to his people Israel, that he would send the Prophet Elijah, and that he would render them worthy of the kingdom of the Messiah. See also 1 Chron. xvi, 2, 3. In the Mosaic law, the manner of blessing is appointed by the lifting up of hands. Our Lord lifted up his hands, and blessed his disciples. It is probable that this action was constantly used on such occasions. The palm of the hand held up was precatory; and the palm turned outward or downward was benedictory. See Benediction and Lord's Supper.

BLINDFOLDING. This is the treatment which Christ received from his enemies. It refers to a sport which was common among children, called μυῖνδα, in which it was the manner first to blindfold, then to strike, and to ask who gave the blow, and not to let the person go till he had named the right man who had struck him. It was used in reproach of our blessed Lord as a Prophet, or divine instructer, and to expose him to ridicule, Luke xxii, 63, 64.

BLINDNESS is often used in Scripture to express ignorance or want of discernment in divine things, as well as the being destitute of natural sight. See Isa. xlii, 18, 19; vi, 10; Matt. xv, 14. "Blindness of heart" is the want of understanding arising from the influence of vicious passions. "Hardness of heart" is stubbornness of will, and destitution of moral feeling. Moses says, "Thou shalt not put a stumbling block before the blind," Lev. xix, 14, which may be understood literally; or figuratively, as if Moses recommended that charity and instruction should be shown to them who want light and counsel, or to those who are in danger of going wrong through their ignorance. Moses says also, "Cursed be he who maketh the blind to wander out of his way," Deut. xxvii, 18, which may also be taken in the same manner. An ignorant or erring teacher is compared by our Lord to a blind man leading a blind man;--a strong representation of the presumption of him that professes to teach the way of salvation without due qualifications, and of the danger of that implicit faith which is often placed by the people in the authority of man, to the neglect of the Holy Scriptures.

BLOOD. Beside its proper sense, the fluid of the veins of men and animals, the term in Scripture is used, 1. For life. "God will require the blood of a man," he will punish murder in what manner soever committed. "His blood be upon us," let the guilt of his death be imputed to us. "The voice of thy brother's blood crieth;" the murder committed on him crieth for vengeance. "The avenger of blood;" he who is to avenge the death of his relative, Num. xxxv, 24, 27. 2. Blood means relationship, or consanguinity. 3. Flesh and blood are placed in opposition to a superior nature: "Flesh and blood hath not revealed it unto thee, but my Father who is in heaven," Matt. xvi, 17. 4. They are also opposed to the glorified body: "Flesh and blood cannot inherit the kingdom of God," 1 Cor. xv, 50. 5. They are opposed also to evil spirits: "We wrestle not against flesh and blood," against visible enemies composed of flesh and blood, "but against principalities and powers," &c, Eph. vi, 12. 6. Wine is called the pure blood of the grape: "Judah shall wash his garments in the blood of the grape," Gen. xlix, 11; Deut. xxxii. 14. 7. The priests were established by God to judge between blood and blood; that is, in criminal matters, and where the life of man is at stake;--to determine whether the murder be casual, or voluntary; whether a crime deserve death, or admit of remission, &c. 8. In its most eminent sense blood is used for the sacrificial death of Christ; whose blood or death is the price of our salvation. His blood has "purchased the church," Acts xx, 28. "We are justified by his blood," Rom. v, 9. "We have redemption through his blood," Eph. i, 7, &c. See Atonement.

That singular and emphatic prohibition of blood for food from the earliest times, which we find in the Holy Scriptures, deserves particular attention. God expressly forbade the eating of blood alone, or of blood mixed with the flesh of animals, as when any creature was suffocated, or strangled, or killed without drawing its blood from the carcass. For when the grant of animal food was made to Noah, in those comprehensive words, "Even as the green herb have I given you all things," it was added, "but flesh with the life thereof, namely, its blood, ye shall not eat," Gen. ix, 4. And when the law was given to the children of Israel, we find the prohibition against the eating of blood still more explicitly enforced, both upon Jews and Gentiles, in the following words, "Whatsoever man there be of the house of Israel, or of the strangers that sojourn among you, that eateth any manner of blood; I will even set my face against that soul that eateth blood, and will cut him off from among his people: for the life of the flesh is in the blood; and I have given it to you upon the altar to make atonement for your souls: for it is the blood that maketh an atonement for the soul," Lev. xvii, 10, 11. And to cut off all possibility of mistake upon this particular point, it is added: "Therefore I said unto the children of Israel, No soul of you shall eat blood, neither shall any stranger that sojourneth among you eat blood; and whatsoever man there be of the children of Israel, or of the strangers that sojourn among you, which hunteth and catcheth any beast or fowl that may be eaten; he shall even pour out the blood thereof and cover it with dust, for it is the life of all flesh; the blood of it is for the life thereof; therefore I said unto the children of Israel, Ye shall eat the blood of no manner of flesh: for the life of all flesh is the blood thereof; whosoever eateth it shall be cut off," verses 12–14. This restraint, than which nothing can be more express, was also, under the new covenant, enjoined upon believing Gentiles, as "a burden" which "it seemed necessary to the Holy Spirit to impose upon them," Acts xv, 28, 29. For this prohibition no MORAL reason seems capable of being offered; nor does it clearly appear that blood is an unwholesome aliment, which some think was the physical reason of its being inhibited; and if, in fact, blood is deleterious as food, there seems no greater reason why this should be pointed out by special revelation to man, to guard him against injury, than many other unwholesome aliments. There is little force in the remark, that the eating of blood produces a ferocious disposition; for those nations that eat strangled things, or blood cooked with other aliments, do not exhibit more ferocity than others. The true reason was, no doubt, a SACRIFICIAL one. When animals were granted to Noah for food, the blood was reserved; and when the same law was reënacted among the Israelites, the original prohibition is repeated with an explanation which at once shows the original ground upon which it rested: "I have given it upon the altar to make an atonement for your souls." From this "additional reason," as it has been called, it has been argued, that the doctrine of the atoning power of blood was new, and was, then, for the first time, announced by Moses, or the same cause for the prohibition would have been assigned to Noah. To this we may reply, 1. That unless the same reason be supposed as the ground of the prohibition of blood to Noah, as that given by Moses to the Jews, no reason at all can be conceived for this restraint being put upon the appetite of mankind from Noah to Moses; and yet we have a prohibition of a most solemn kind, which in itself could have no reason, enjoined without any external reason being either given or conceivable. 2. That it is a mistake to suppose that the declaration of Moses to the Jews, that God had "given them the blood for an atonement," is an "ADDITIONAL REASON" for the interdict, not to be found in the original prohibition to Noah. The whole passage occurs in Lev. xvii; and the great reason there given of the prohibition of blood is, that it is "the LIFE;" and what follows respecting "atonement," is exegetical of this reason;--the life is in the blood, and the blood or life is given as an atonement. Now, by turning to the original prohibition in Genesis we find that precisely the same reason is given: "But the flesh with the blood, which is THE LIFE thereof, shall ye not eat." The reason, then, being the same, the question is, whether the exegesis added by Moses must not necessarily be understood in the general reason given for the restraint to Noah. Blood is prohibited because it is the LIFE; and Moses adds, that it is "the blood," or LIFE, "which makes atonement." Let any one attempt to discover any reason for the prohibition of blood to Noah, in the mere circumstance that it is "the life," and he will find it impossible. It is no reason at all, moral or instituted, except that as it was LIFE SUBSTITUTED FOR LIFE, the life of the animal in sacrifice for the life of man, and that, therefore, blood had a sacred appropriation. The manner, too, in which Moses introduces the subject, is indicative that, though he was renewing a prohibition, he was not publishing a new doctrine; he does not teach his people that God had then given, or appointed, blood to make atonement; but he prohibits them from eating it, because he had already made this appointment, without reference to time, and as a subject with which they were familiar. Because the blood was the life, it was sprinkled upon, and poured out at, the altar: and we have in the sacrifice of the paschal lamb, and the sprinkling of its blood, a sufficient proof that, before the giving of the law, not only was blood not eaten, but was appropriated to a sacred sacrificial purpose. Nor was this confined to the Jews; it was customary with the Romans and Greeks, who, in like manner, poured out and sprinkled the blood of victims at their altars; a rite derived, probably, from the Egyptians, who deduced it, not from Moses, but from the sons of Noah. The notion, indeed, that the blood of the victims was peculiarly sacred to the gods, is impressed upon all ancient Pagan mythology.

BOANERGES. This word is neither Hebrew nor Syriac, and some have thought that the transcribers have not exactly copied it, and that the word was BENEREEN, βενερεὲν, which expresses the sound of the Hebrew of the phrase, "sons of thunder." Parkhurst judges the word to be the Galilean pronunciation of the Hebrew בנירעש expressed in Greek letters. Now, רעש properly signifies a violent trembling or commotion, and may therefore be well rendered by βροντὴ, THUNDER, which is a violent commotion in the air; so, VICE VERSÂ, any violent commotion is figuratively, and not unusually, in all languages, called thunder. When our Saviour named the sons of Zebedee, Boanerges, he perhaps had an eye to that prophecy of Haggai, "Yet once, and I will shake the heavens and the earth," ii, 6; which is by the Apostle to the Hebrews, xii, 26, applied to the great alteration made in the economy of the Jews by the publication of the Gospel. The name Boanerges, therefore, given to James and John, imports that they should be eminent instruments in accomplishing the wondrous change, and should, like an earthquake or thunder, mightily bear down all opposition, by their inspired preaching and miraculous powers. That it does not relate to their MODE of preaching is certain; for that clearly appears to have been calmly argumentative, and sweetly persuasive--the very reverse of what is usually called a thundering ministry.

BOAR, חזיר. The wild boar is considered as the parent stock of our domestic hog. He is smaller, but at the same time stronger and more undaunted, than the hog. In his own defence, he will turn on men or dogs; and scarcely shuns any denizen of the forests, in the haunts where he ranges. His colour is always an iron grey, inclining to black. His snout is longer than that of the common breed, and his ears are comparatively short. His tusks are very formidable, and all his habits are fierce and savage. It should seem, from the accounts of ancient authors, that the ravages of the wild boar were considered as more formidable than those of other savage animals. The conquest of the Erymanthian boar was one of the fated labours of Hercules; and the story of the Calydonian boar is one of the most beautiful in Ovid. The destructive ravages of these animals are mentioned in Psalm lxxx, 14. Dr. Pococke observed very large herds of wild boars on the side of Jordan, where it flows out of the sea of Tiberias; and saw several of them on the other side lying among the reeds by the sea. The wild boars of other countries delight in the like moist retreats. These shady marshes then, it should seem, are called in the Scripture, "woods;" for it calls these animals, "the wild boars of the woods."

BOHEMIAN BRETHREN, a sect of heretics, according to the church of Rome; but, in truth, a race of early reformers, who preceded Luther. At first they were charged with so many heresies, that the great reformer was shy of them; but, upon receiving from themselves an account of their tenets, in 1522, he readily acknowledged them as brethren, and received them into communion. Some time after this, they were driven by persecution from their native country, and entered into communion with the Swiss church, as reformed by Zuinglius; and from thence sprang the church of the United Brethren.

BONDS were of two kinds, public and private; the former were employed to secure a prisoner in the public jail, after confession or conviction; the latter when he was delivered to a magistrate, or even to private persons, to be kept at their houses till he should be tried. The Apostle Paul was subjected to private bonds by Felix, the Roman governor, who "commanded a centurion to keep him, and to let him have liberty, and that he should forbid none of his acquaintance to minister, or come unto him," Acts xxiv, 23. And after he was carried prisoner to Rome, he "dwelt two whole years in his own hired house, and received all that came in unto him," xxviii, 30.

BONNET was a covering for the head, worn by the Jewish priests. Josephus says, that the bonnet worn by the private priests was composed of several rounds of linen cloth, turned in and sewed together, so as to appear like a thick linen crown. The whole was entirely covered with another piece of linen, which came down as low as their forehead, and concealed the deformity of the seams. See Exodus xxviii, 40. The high priest's bonnet was not much different from that which has been described.

BOOK, a writing composed on some point of knowledge by a person intelligent therein, for the instruction or amusement of the reader. The word is formed from the Gothic BOKA, or Saxon BOC, which comes from the Northern BUECH, of BUECHAUS, a beech or service tree, on the bark of which our ancestors used to write. Book is distinguished from pamphlet, or single paper, by its greater length; and from tome or volume, by its containing the whole writing on the subject. Isidore makes this distinction between LIBER and CODEX; that the former denotes a single book, the latter a collection of several; though, according to Scipio Maffei, CODEX signifies a book in the square form; LIBER, a book in the roll form. The primary distinction between LIBER and CODEX seems to have been derived, as Dr. Heylin has observed, from the different materials used for writing, among the ancients: from the innerside of the bark of a tree, used for this purpose, and called in Latin LIBER, the name of LIBER applied to a book was deduced; and from that tablet, formed from the main body of a tree, called CAUDEX, was derived the appellation of CODEX.

2. Several sorts of materials were formerly used in making books: stone and wood were the first materials employed to engrave such things upon as men were desirous of having transmitted to posterity. Porphyry makes mention of some pillars preserved in Crete, on which the ceremonies observed by the Corybantes in their sacrifices were recorded. The works of Hesiod were originally written on tables of lead, and deposited in the temple of the Muses in Bœotia. The laws of Jehovah were written on tables of stone, and those of Solon on wooden planks. Tables of wood and ivory were common among the ancients: those of wood, were very frequently covered with wax, that persons might write on them with more ease, or blot out what they had written. And the instrument used to write with was a piece of iron, called a STYLE; and hence the word "style" came to be taken for the composition of the writing. The leaves of the palm-tree were afterward used instead of wooden planks, and the finest and thinnest part of the bark of such trees as the lime, ash, maple, and elm; and especially the TILIO, or PHILLYREA, and Egyptian PAPYRUS. Hence came the word LIBER, (a book,) which signifies the inner bark of the trees. And as these barks were rolled up in order to be removed with greater ease, each roll was called VOLUMEN, a volume; a name afterward given to the like rolls of paper or parchment. From the Egyptian papyrus the word PAPER is derived. After this, leather was introduced, especially the skins of goats and sheep. For the king of Pergamus, in collecting his library, was led to the invention of parchment made of those skins. The ancients likewise wrote upon linen. Pliny says, the Parthians, even in his time, wrote upon their clothes; and Livy speaks of certain books made of linen, LINTEI LIBRI, upon which the names of magistrates, and the history of the Roman commonwealth,

were written, and preserved in the temple of the goddess Moneta.

3. The materials generally used by the ancients for their books, were liable to be easily destroyed by the damp, when hidden in the earth; and in times of war, devastation, and rapacity, it was necessary to bury in the earth whatever they wished to preserve from the attacks of fraud and violence. With this view, Jeremiah ordered the writings, which he delivered to Baruch, to be put in an earthen vessel, Jer. xxxii. In the same manner the ancient Egyptians made use of earthen urns, or pots of a proper shape, for containing whatever they wanted to inter in the earth, and which, without such care, would have been soon destroyed. We need not wonder then, that the Prophet Jeremiah should think it necessary to inclose those writings in an earthen pot, which were to be buried in Judea, in some place where they might be found without much difficulty on the return of the Jews from captivity. Accordingly two different writings, or small rolls of writing, called books in the original Hebrew, were designed to be inclosed in such an earthen vessel; but commentators have been much embarrassed in giving any probable account of the necessity of two writings, one sealed, the other open; or, as the passage has been commonly understood, the one SEALED UP, the other left OPEN for any one to read; more especially, as both were to be alike buried in the earth and concealed from every eye, and both were to be examined at the return from the captivity. But the word translated OPEN, in reference to the evidence, or book which was open, (1 Sam. iii, 7, 21; Dan. ii, 19, 30; x, 1,) signifies the revealing of future events to the minds of men by a divine agency; and it is particularly used in the book of Esther, viii, 13, to express a book's making known the decree of an earthly king. Consequently the OPEN BOOK of Jeremiah seems to signify, not its being then lying open or unrolled before them, while the other was sealed up; but the book that had revealed the will of God, to bring back Israel into their own country, and to cause buying and selling of houses and lands again to take place among them. This was a BOOK OF PROPHECY, opening and revealing the future return of Israel, and the other little book, which was ordered to be buried along with it, was the purchase deed.

4. By adverting to the different modes of writing in eastern countries, we obtain a satisfactory interpretation of a passage in the book of Job, xix, 23, 24, and a distinct view of the beautiful gradation which is lost in our translation: "O that my words were now written! O that they were printed (written) in a book! that they were graven with an iron pen and lead in the rock for ever!" In the east there is a mode of writing, which is designed to fix words in the memory, but the writing is not intended for duration. Accordingly we are informed by Dr. Shaw, that children learn to write in Barbary by means of a smooth thin board, slightly covered with whiting, which may be wiped off or renewed at pleasure. Job expresses his wish not only that his words were written, but also written in a book, from which they should not be blotted out, nay, still farther, graven in a rock, the most permanent mode of recording them, and especially if the engraved letters were filled with lead; or the rock was made to receive leaden tablets, the use of which was known among the ancients. So Pliny, "At first men wrote on the leaves of palm, and the bark of certain trees, but afterward public documents were preserved on leaden plates, and those of a private nature on wax, or linen."

5. The first books were in the form of blocks and tables, of which we find frequent mention in Scripture, under the appellation SEPHER, which the Septuagint render ἀξίνες, that is, SQUARE TABLES: of which form the book of the covenant, book of the law, book, or bill of divorce, book of curses, &c, appear to have been. As flexible matters came to be written on, they found it more convenient to make their books in form of rolls, called by the Greeks κοντάκια, by the Latins VOLUMINA, which appear to have been in use among the ancient Jews as well as the Grecians, Romans, Persians, and even Indians; and of such did the libraries chiefly consist, till some centuries after Christ. The form which obtains among us is the square, composed of separate leaves; which was also known, though little used, among the ancients; having been invented by Attalus, king of Pergamus, the same who also invented parchment: but it has now been so long in possession, that the oldest manuscripts are found in it. Montfaucon assures us, that of all the ancient Greek manuscripts he has seen, there are but two in the roll form; the rest being made up much after the manner of the modern books. The rolls, or volumes, were composed of several sheets, fastened to each other, and rolled upon a stick, or UMBILICUS; the whole making a kind of column, or cylinder, which was to be managed by the UMBILICUS, as a handle; it being reputed a kind of crime to take hold of the roll itself. The outside of the volume was called FRONS; the ends of the UMBILICUS were called CORNUA, "horns;" which were usually carved and adorned likewise with silver, ivory, or even gold and precious stones. Whilst the Egyptian papyrus was in common use, its brittle nature made it proper to roll up what they wrote; and as this had been a customary practice, many continued it when they used other materials, which might very safely have been treated in a different manner. To the form of books belongs the ECONOMY OF THE INSIDE, or the order and arrangement of points and letters into lines and pages, with margins and other appurtenances. This has undergone many varieties: at first, the letters were only divided into lines, then into separate words; which, by degrees, were noted with accents, and distributed by points and stops into periods, paragraphs, chapters, and other divisions. In some countries, as among the orientals, the lines began from the right, and ran to the left; in others, as in northern and western nations, from the left to the right; others, as the Grecians, followed both directions alternately, going in the one and returning in the other, called BOUSTROPHEDON, because it was after the manner of oxen turning when at plough. In the Chinese books, the lines ran from top to bottom. Again: the page in some is entire, and uniform; in others, divided into

columns; in others distinguished into texts and notes, either marginal, or at the bottom: usually it is furnished with signatures and catch words; also with a register to discover whether the book be complete. To these are occasionally added the apparatus of summaries, or side notes; the embellishments of red, gold, or figured initial letters, head pieces, tail pieces, effigies, schemes, maps, and the like. The end of the book now denoted by FINIS, was anciently marked with a <, called CORONIS, and the whole frequently washed with an oil drawn from cedar, or citron chips, strewed between the leaves to preserve it from rotting. There also occur certain FORMULÆ at the beginning and end of books; as among the Jews, the word חוק, ESTO FORTIS, which we find at the end of the books of Exodus, Leviticus, Numbers, Ezekiel, &c, to exhort the reader to be courageous, and proceed on to the following book. The conclusions were also often guarded with imprecations against such as should falsify them; of which we have an instance in the Apocalypse. The Mohammedans, for the like reason, place the name of God at the beginning of all their books, which cannot fail to procure them protection, on account of the infinite regard which they pay to that name, wherever found. For the like reason it is, that divers of the laws of the ancient emperors begin with the formula, IN NOMINE DEI. [In the name of God.] At the end of each book the Jews also added the number of verses contained in it, and at the end of the Pentateuch the number of sections; that, it might be transmitted to posterity entire. The Masorites and Mohammedan doctors have gone farther; so as to number the several words and letters in each book, chapter, verse, &c, of the Old Testament and the Alcoran. The scarcity and high price of books in former ages, ought to render us the more grateful for the discovery of the great art of printing, as especially by that means the Holy Bible, "the word of truth and Gospel of our salvation," is made familiar to all classes.

The universal ignorance that prevailed in Europe, from the seventh to the eleventh century, may be ascribed to the scarcity of books during that period, and the difficulty of rendering them more common, concurring with other causes arising from the state of government and manners. The Romans wrote their books either on parchment, or on paper made of the Egyptian papyrus. The latter, being the cheapest, was of course the most commonly used. But after the Saracens conquered Egypt, in the seventh century, the communication between that country and the people settled in Italy, or in other parts of Europe, was almost entirely broken off, and the papyrus was no longer in use among them. They were obliged on that account to write all their books upon parchment; and as the price of that was high, books became extremely rare and of great value. We may judge of the scarcity of materials for writing them from one circumstance. There still remain several manuscripts of the eighth, ninth, and following centuries, written on parchment, from which some former writing had been erased, in order to substitute a new composition in its place. Thus, it is probable, several of the works of the ancients perished. A book of Livy or of Tacitus might be erased, to make room for the legendary tale of a saint, or the superstitious prayers of a missal. Nay, worse instances are recorded, of obliterating copies of the Holy Scriptures to make room for the lucubrations of some of the more modern fathers of the church. Manuscripts thus defaced, the vellum or parchment of which is occupied with some other writings, are called "palimpsests," CODICES RESCRIPTI or PALIMPSESTI, from ϖαλίμψηϛος, "that which has been twice scraped." As this want of materials for writing will serve to account for the loss of many of the works of the ancients, and for the small number of **MSS**. previous to the eleventh century, many facts prove the scarcity of books at this period. Private persons seldom possessed any books whatever; and even monasteries of note had only one missal. In 1299, John de Pontissara, bishop of Winchester, borrows of his cathedral convent of St. Swithin, at Winchester, "BIBLIAM BENE GLOSSATAM," that is, the Bible, with marginal annotations, in two folio volumes; but gives a bond for the return of it, drawn up with great solemnity. For the bequest of this Bible to the convent, and one hundred marks, the monks founded a daily mass for the soul of the donor. If any person gave a book to a religious house, he believed that so valuable a donation merited eternal salvation, and he offered it on the altar with great ceremony. The prior and convent of Rochester declare, that they will every year pronounce the irrevocable sentence of damnation on him who shall purloin or conceal a Latin translation of Aristotle's Poetics, or even obliterate the title. Sometimes a book was given to a monastery, on condition that the donor should have the use of it for his life; and sometimes to a private person, with the reservation that he who receives it should pray for the soul of his benefactor. In the year 1225, Roger de Insula, dean of York, gave several Latin Bibles to the university of Oxford, on condition that the students who perused them should deposit a cautionary pledge. The library of that university, before the year 1300, consisted only of a few tracts, chained or kept in chests, in the choir of St. Mary's church. The price of books became so high, that persons of a moderate could not afford to purchase them. In the year 1174, Walter, prior of St. Swithin's at Winchester, purchased of the monks of Dorchester, in Oxfordshire, Bede's homilies, and St. Austin's psalter for twelve measures of barley and a pall, on which was embroidered in silver the history of St. Birinus converting a Saxon king. About the year 1400, a copy of John of Meun's "Roman de la Rose" was sold before the palace gate at Paris for forty crowns, or 33*l.* 6*s.* 6*d.* The countess of Anjou paid, for a copy of the homilies of Haimon, bishop of Halberstadt, two hundred sheep, five quarters of wheat, and the same quantity of rye and millet. Even so late as the year 1471, when Louis **XI**. of France borrowed the works of Rhasis, the Arabian physician, from the faculty of medicine at Paris, he not only deposited by way of pledge a considerable quantity of plate, but he was obliged to procure a nobleman to join with him as surety in a deed, binding himself under a great forfeiture to restore it. But when, in the eleventh century, the art of making paper was invented, and more especially after the manufacture became general, the number of **MSS**. increased, and the study of the sciences was wonderfully facilitated. Indeed, the invention of the art of making paper, and the invention of the art of printing, are two very memorable events in the history of literature and of human civilization. It is remarkable, that the former preceded the first dawning of letters and improvement in knowledge, toward the close of the eleventh century; and the latter ushered in the light which spread over Europe at the æra of the reformation.

6. If the ancient books were large, they were formed of a number of skins, of a number of pieces of linen and cotton cloth, or of papyrus, or parchment, connected together. The leaves were rarely written over on both sides, Ezek. ii, 9; Zech. v, 1. Books, when written upon very flexible materials, were, as stated above, rolled round a stick; and, if they were very long, round two, from the two extremities. The reader unrolled the book to the place which he wanted, ἀναπτύζας τὸ βιλβλίον, and rolled it up again, when he had read it, πτύζας τὸ βιβλίον, Luke iv, 17–20; whence the name מגלה, A VOLUME, or thing rolled up, Psalm xl, 7; Isaiah xxxiv, 4; Ezek. ii, 9; 2 Kings xix, 14; Ezra vi, 2. The leaves thus rolled round the stick, which has been mentioned, and bound with a string, could be easily sealed, Isaiah xxix, 11; Dan. xii, 4; Rev. v, 1; vi, 7. Those books, which were inscribed on tablets of wood, lead, brass, or ivory, were connected together by rings at the back, through which a rod was passed to carry them by. The orientals appear to have taken pleasure in giving tropical or enigmatical titles to their books. The titles, prefixed to the fifty-sixth, sixtieth, and eightieth psalms appear to be of this description. And there can be no doubt, that David's elegy upon Saul and Jonathan, 2 Sam. i, 18, is called קשת or THE BOW, in conformity with this peculiarity of taste.

The book, or flying roll, spoken of in Zech. v, 1, 2, twenty cubits long and ten wide, was one of the ancient rolls, composed of many skins, or parchments, glued or sewed together at the end. Though some of these rolls or volumes were very long, yet none, probably, was ever made of such a size as this. This contained the curses and calamities which should befal the Jews. The extreme length and breadth of it shows the excessive number and enormity of their sins, and the extent of their punishment.

Isaiah, describing the effects of God's wrath, says, "The heavens shall be folded up like a book," (scroll,) Isaiah xxxiv, 4. He alludes to the way among the ancients, of rolling up books, when they purposed to close them. A volume of several feet in length was suddenly rolled up into a very small compass. Thus the heavens should shrink into themselves, and disappear, as it were, from the eyes of God, when his wrath should be kindled. These ways of speaking are figurative, and very energetic.

7. Book is sometimes used for letters, memoirs, an edict, or contract. In short, the word BOOK, in Hebrew, SEPHER, is much more extensive than the Latin LIBER. The letters which Rabshakeh delivered from Sennacherib to Hezekiah are called a book. The English translation, indeed, reads LETTER; but the Septuagint has βιβλίον, and the Hebrew text, הספרים. The contract, confirmed by Jeremiah for the purchase of a field, is called by the same name, Jer. xxxii, 10; and also the edict of Ahasuerus in favour of the Jews, Esther ix, 20, though our translators have called it LETTERS. The writing which a man gave to his wife when he divorced her, was denominated, in Hebrew, "a book of divorce," Deut. xxiv.

Books, WRITERS OF. The ancients seldom wrote their treatises with their own hand, but dictated them to their freedmen and slaves. These were either ταχυγράφοι, AMANUENSES, NOTARII, "hasty writers," or καλλιγράφοι, LIBRARII, "fair writers," or βιβλιογράφοι, LIBRARII, "copyists." The office of these last was to transcribe fairly that which the former had written hastily and from dictation; they were those who were obliged to write books and other documents which were intended to be durable. The correctness of the copies was under the care of the EMENDATOR, CORRECTOR, ὁ δοκιμάζων τὰ γεγραμμένα. A great part of the books of the New Testament was dictated after this custom. St. Paul noted it as a particular circumstance in the Epistle to the Galatians, that he had written it with his own hand, Gal. vi, 11. But he affixed the salutation with his own hand, 2 Thess. iii, 17; 1 Cor. xvi, 21; Col. iv, 18. The amanuensis who wrote the Epistle to the Romans, has mentioned himself near the conclusion, Rom. xvi, 22.

Books, MODES OF PUBLICATION. Works could only be multiplied by means of transcripts. Whenever in this way they passed over to others, they were beyond the control of the author, and published. The edition, or publication, by means of the booksellers, was, only at a later period, advantageous to the Christians. The RECITATIO [reading aloud] preceded the publication, which took place often merely among some few friends, and often with great preparations before many persons, who were invited for that purpose. From hence the author became known as the writer, and the world became previously informed of all which they might expect from the work. If the composition pleased them, he was requested to permit its transcription; and thus the work left the hands of the author, and belonged to the PUBLICUM: [public.] Frequently an individual sent his literary labours to some illustrious man, as a present, STRENA, [a new-year's gift,] MUNUSCULUM; [a small present;] or he prefixed his name to it, for the sake of giving him a proof of friendship or regard, by means of this express and particular direction of his work. When it was only thus presented or sent to him, and he accepted it, he was considered as the person bound to introduce it to the world, or as the PATRONUS LIBRI, [patron of the book,] who had pledged himself, as the PATRONUS PERSONÆ [patron of the person] to this duty. It now became his office to provide for its publication by means of transcripts, to facilitate its approach AD LIMINA POTENTIORUM to the gates of men of great influence, and to be its DEFENSOR.

Thus the works of the first founders of the Christian church made their appearance before their community. Their Epistles were read in those congregations to which they were directed; and whoever wished to possess them either took a transcript of them, or caused one to be procured for him. The historical works were made known by the authors in the congregations of the Christians, PER RECITATIONEM: [by reading aloud:] the object and general interest in them procured for them readers and transcribers. St. Luke dedicated his writings to an illustrious man of the name of Theophilus.

Book of Life, or Book of the Living, or Book of the Lord, Psalm lxix, 28. Some have thought it very probable that these descriptive phrases, which are frequent in Scripture, are taken from the custom, observed generally in the courts of princes, of keeping a list of persons who are in their service, of the provinces which they govern, of the officers of their armies, of the number of their troops, and sometimes even of the names of their soldiers. Thus, when it is said that any one is written in the book of life, it means that he particularly belongs to God, and is enrolled among the number of his friends and servants: and to be "blotted out of the book of life," is to be erased from the list of God's friends and servants, as those who are guilty of treachery are struck off the roll of officers belonging to a prince. The most satisfactory explanation of these phrases is, however, that which refers them to the genealogical lists of the Jews, or to the registers kept of the living, from which the names of all the dead were blotted out.

Book of Judgment. Daniel, speaking of God's judgment, says, "The judgment was set, and the books were opened," Dan. vii, 10. This is an allusion to what was practised when a prince called his servants to account. The accounts are produced and examined. It is possible he might allude, also, to a custom of the Persians, among whom it was a constant practice every day to write down the services rendered to the king, and the rewards given to those who had performed them. Of this we see an instance in the history of Ahasuerus and Mordecai, Esther iv, 12, 34. When, therefore, the king sits in judgment, the books are opened: he obliges all his servants to reckon with him; he punishes those who have failed in their duty; he compels those to pay who are indebted to him; and he rewards those who have done him services. A similar proceeding will take place at the day of God's final judgment.

Sealed Book, mentioned Isa. xxix, 11, and the book sealed with seven seals, in the Revelation v, 1–3, are the prophecies of Isaiah and of John, which were written in a book, or roll, after the manner of the ancients, and were sealed, which figure truly signifies that they were mysterious: they had respect to times remote, and to future events; so that a complete knowledge of their meaning could not be obtained till after what was foretold should happen, and the seals, as it were taken off. In old times, letters, and other writings that were to be sealed, were first wrapped round with thread or flax, and then wax and the seal were applied to them. To read them, it was necessary to cut the thread or flax, and to break the seals.

BOOTY, spoils taken in war, Num. xxxi, 27–32. According to the law of Moses, the booty was to be divided equally between those who were in the battle and those who were in the camp, whatever disparity there might be in the number of each party. The law farther required that, out of that part of the spoils which was assigned to the fighting men, the Lord's share should be separated; and for every five hundred men, oxen, asses, sheep, &c, they were to take one for the high priest, as being the Lord's first fruits. And out of the other moiety, belonging to the children of Israel, they were to give for every fifty men, oxen, asses, sheep, &c, one to the Levites.

BOOZ, or **BOAZ**, the son of Salmon and Rahab, Ruth iv, 21, &c; Matt., i, 5. Rahab, we know, was a Canaanite of Jericho, Joshua ii, 1. Salmon, who was of the tribe of Judah, married her, and she bore him Booz, one of our Saviour's ancestors according to the flesh. Some say there were three of this name, the son, the grandson, and the great grandson, of Salmon: the last Booz was Ruth's husband, and the father of Obed.

2. Booz, or Boaz, was the name of one of the two brazen pillars which Solomon erected in the porch of the temple, the other column being called Jachin. This last pillar was on the right hand of the entrance into the temple, and Booz on the left, 1 Kings vii, 21. The word signifies STRENGTH or FIRMNESS. Mr. Hutchinson has an express treatise upon these two columns, attempting to show that they represented the true system of the universe, which he insists was given by God to David, and by him to Solomon, and was wrought by Hiram upon these pillars.

BOSOM. See Accubation.

BOSSES, the thickest and strongest parts of a buckler, Job xv, 20.

BOTTLE. The eastern bottle is made of a goat or kid skin, stripped off without opening the belly; the apertures made by cutting off the tail and legs are sewed up, and, when filled, it is tied about the neck. The Arabs and Persians never go a journey without a small leathern bottle of water hanging by their side like a scrip. These skin bottles preserve their water, milk, and other liquids, in a fresher state than any other vessels they can use. The people of the east, indeed, put into them every thing they mean to carry to a distance, whether dry or liquid, and very rarely make use of boxes and pots, unless to preserve such things as are liable to be broken. They enclose these leathern bottles in woollen sacks, because their beasts of carriage often fall down under their load, or cast it down on the sandy desert. These skin bottles were not confined to the countries of Asia; the roving tribes, which passed the Hellespont soon after the deluge, and settled in Greece and Italy, probably introduced them into those countries. We learn from Homer, that they were in common use among the Greeks at the siege of Troy; for, with a view to an accommodation between the hostile armies, the heralds carried through the city the things which were necessary to ratify the compact, two lambs, and exhilarating wine, the fruit of the earth, in a bottle of goat skin:

Ἄρνε δύω, καὶ οἶνον εὔφρονα, καρπὸν ἀρούρης,

Ἀσκῷ ἐν αἰγείῳ. *Il.* lib. iii, l. 246.

The bottle of wine which Samuel's mother brought to Eli, 1 Sam. i, 24, is called נבל, and was an earthen jug. Another word is used to signify the vessel out of which Jael gave milk to Sisera: she opened a bottle of milk, and gave him drink, Judges iv, 19. This is called נאוד, which refers to something supple, moist, oozing, or, perhaps, imports MOISTENED INTO PLIANCY, as that skin must be which is kept constantly filled with milk. This kind was usually made of goat skins. This word is also used to denote the bottle in which Jesse sent wine by David to Saul, 1 Sam. xvi, 20. It is likewise employed to express the bottle into which the Psalmist desires his tears may be collected, Psalm lvi, 8; and that to which he resembles himself, and which he calls a bottle in the smoke, Psalm cxix, 83, that is, a skin bottle, blackened and shrivelled. Beside the words already considered, another אבות, in the plural, is used, Job xxxii, 19. This signifies, in general, to swell or distend. On receiving the liquor poured into it, a skin bottle must be greatly swelled and distended; and it must be swelled still farther by the fermentation of the liquor within it, as that advances to ripeness. In this state, if no vent be given to the liquor, it may overpower the strength of the bottle, or it may penetrate by some secret crevice or weaker part. Hence arises the propriety of putting new wine into new bottles, which, being strong, may resist the expansion, the internal pressure of their contents, and preserve the wine to due maturity; while old bottles may, without danger, contain old wine, whose fermentation is already past, Matt. ix, 17; Luke v, 38.

BOUDDHISTS, or **BUDHISTS**, one of the three great sects of India, distinct both from the Brahminical sect, and the Jainas. The Bouddhists do not believe in a First Cause: they consider matter as eternal; that every portion of animated existence has in itself its own rise, tendency, and destiny; that the condition of creatures on earth is regulated by works of merit and demerit; that works of merit not only raise individuals to happiness, but, as they prevail, exalt the world itself to prosperity; while, on the other hand, when vice is predominant, the world degenerates till the universe itself is dissolved. They suppose, however, that there is always some superior deity, who has attained to this elevation by religious merit; but they do not regard him as the governor of the world. To the present grand period, comprehending all the time included in a "kulpu," they assign five deities, four of whom have already appeared, including Goutumu, or Bouddhu, whose exaltation continues five thousand years, two thousand three hundred and fifty-six of which had expired, A. D. 1814. After the expiration of the five thousand years, another saint will obtain the ascendancy, and be deified. Six hundred millions of saints are said to be canonized with each deity, though it is admitted that Bouddhu took only twenty-four thousand devotees to heaven with him. The lowest state of existence is in hell; the next is that in the forms of brutes: both these are states of punishment. The next ascent is to that of man, which is probationary. The next includes many degrees of honour and happiness up to demigods, &c, which are states of reward for works of merit. The ascent to superior deity is from the state of man. The Bouddhists are taught that there are four superior heavens which are not destroyed at the end of "kulpu;" that below these there are twelve other heavens, followed by six inferior heavens; after which follows the earth; then the world of snakes; and then thirty-two chief hells: to which are to be added, one hundred and twenty hells of milder torments. The highest state of glory is absorption. The person who is unchangeable in his resolution; who has obtained the knowledge of things past, present, and to come, through one "kulpu;" who can make himself invisible; go where he pleases; and who has attained to complete abstraction; will enjoy absorption. Those who perform works of merit are admitted to the heavens of the different gods, or are made kings or great men on earth; and those who are wicked are born in the forms of different animals, or consigned to different hells. The happiness of these heavens is described as entirely sensual. The Bouddhists believe that at the end of a "kulpu" the universe is destroyed. To convey some idea of the extent of this period, the illiterate Cingalese use this comparison: "If a man were to ascend a mountain nine miles high, and to renew these journeys once in every hundred years, till the mountain were worn down by his feet to an atom, the time required to do this would be nothing to the fourth part of a 'kulpu.'" Bouddhu, before his exaltation, taught his followers that, after his death, the remains of his body, his doctrine, or an assembly of his disciples, were to be held in equal reverence with himself. When a Cingalese, therefore, approaches an image of Bouddhu, he says, "I take refuge in Bouddhu; I take refuge in his doctrine; I take refuge in his followers." There are five commands given to the common Bouddhists; the first forbids the destruction of animal life; the second forbids theft; the third, adultery; the fourth, falsehood; the fifth, the use of spirituous liquors. There are other commands for superior classes, or devotees, which forbid dancing, songs, music, festivals, perfumes, elegant dresses, elevated seats, &c. Among works of the highest merit, one is the feeding of a hungry infirm tiger with a person's own flesh.

BOURIGNONISTS, the followers of the celebrated Mad. Antoinette Bourignon de la Ponte, a native of Flanders, born at Lisle, in 1616. She was so much deformed at her birth, that it was even debated whether she should not be stifled as a monster. As she grew up, however, this deformity greatly decreased, and she discovered a superior mind, a strong imagination, and very early indications of a devotional spirit, strongly tinctured with mysticism. She conceived herself to be divinely called, and set apart to revive the true spirit of Christianity that had been extinguished by theological animosities and debates. In her confession of faith, she professes her belief in the Scriptures, and in the divinity and atonement of Christ. The leading principles which pervade her productions are these: that man is perfectly free to resist or receive divine grace; that God is ever unchangeable in love toward all his creatures, and does not inflict any arbitrary punishment, but that the evils they suffer are the natural consequences of sin; that true religion consists not in any outward forms of worship, nor systems of faith, but in immediate communion with the Deity, by internal feelings and impulses, and by a perfect acquiescence in his will.

This lady was educated in the Roman Catholic religion; but she declaimed equally against the corruptions of the church of Rome and those of the Reformed churches: hence she was opposed and persecuted by both Catholics and Protestants, and after being driven about from place to place, she died at Franeker, in 1680. She maintained that there ought to be a general toleration of all religions. Her notion on God's foreknowledge was, that God was capable of foreknowing all events, but, his power being equal to his knowledge, he purposely withheld from himself that knowledge in certain cases, that he might not interfere with the free agency and responsibility of his creatures. Her works are very numerous, making eighteen volumes in octavo: of which the principal are, "The Light of the World;" "The Testimony of Truth;" and "The Renovation of the Gospel Spirit;" which are much in esteem among the admirers of mystical theology.

BOW. The expression, "to break the bow," so frequent in Scripture, signifies to destroy the power of a people, because the principal offensive weapon of armies was anciently the bow. "A deceitful bow" is one that, from some defect, either in bending or the string, carries the arrow wide of the mark, however well aimed. See Arms.

BOWELS. The bowels are the seat of mercy, tenderness, and compassion. Joseph's bowels were moved at the sight of his brother Benjamin; that is, he felt himself softened and affected. The true mother of the child whom Solomon commanded to be divided, felt her bowels move, and consented that it should be given to the woman who was not its real mother, 1 Kings, iii, 26. The Hebrews also sometimes place wisdom and understanding in the bowels, "Who hath put wisdom in the inner parts?" or bowels, Job xxxviii, 36. The Psalmist says, "Thy law is within my heart," literally, in the midst of my bowels,--it is by me strongly and affectionately regarded, Psalm xl, 8.

BOX TREE, תאשור, Isa. xli, 9; lx, 13; Ezek. xxvii, 6; 2 Esdras xiv, 24, where the word appears to be used for TABLETS. Most of the ancient, and several of the modern, translators render this word the BUXUS, or "box tree;" but from its being mentioned along with trees of the forest, some more stately tree must be intended, probably the cedar.

BRACELET. A bracelet is commonly worn by the oriental princes, as a badge of power and authority. When the calif Cayem Bemrillah granted the investiture of certain dominions to an eastern prince, he sent him letters patent, a crown, a chain, and bracelets. This was probably the reason that the Amalekite brought the bracelet which he found on Saul's arm, along with his crown, to David, 2 Sam. i, 10. It was a royal ornament, and belonged to the regalia of the kingdom. The bracelet, it must be acknowledged, was worn both by men and women of different ranks; but the original word, in the second book of Samuel, occurs only in two other places, and is quite different from the term which is employed to express the more common ornament known by that name. And beside, this ornament was worn by kings and princes in a different manner from their subjects. It was fastened above the elbow; and was commonly of great value.

BRAHMINS, or **BRACHMINS**, the highest caste of Hindoos, to whom is confined the priesthood, and, in general, all their ancient learning, which is locked up in their sacred language, called the Sanscrit. The Brahmins derive that name from Brahma, the Creator; for they maintain the doctrine of three embodied energies, the creative, the preserving, and the destroying; personified under the names of Brahma, Vishnu, and Shiva, all sprung from Brimh; and to each of them is assigned a kind of celestial consort, a female deity, which they describe as a passive energy.

Like the philosophers of Greece, they seem to have had an open and a secret doctrine: the latter, a species of Spinozism, considering the great Supreme as "the soul of the world;" endowed with no other quality than ubiquity; requiring no worship, and exerting no power, but in the production of the three great energies above mentioned. These are so ingeniously diversified as to produce three hundred and thirty millions of gods, or objects of idolatry; so various in character as to suit every man's taste or humour, and to furnish examples of every vice and folly to which humanity is subject.

As it respects a future state, two of the principal doctrines of Brachminism are transmigration and absorption. After death, the person is conveyed, by the messengers of Yumu, through the air to the place of judgment. After receiving his sentence, he wanders about the earth for twelve months, as an aërial being or ghost; and then takes a body suited to his future condition, whether he ascend to the gods, or suffer in a new body, or be hurled into some hell. This is the doctrine of several "pooranus;" others maintain, that immediately after death and judgment, the person suffers the pains of hell, and removes his sin by suffering; and then returns to the earth in some bodily form. The descriptions which the "pooranus" give of the heavens of the gods are truly in the eastern style; all things, even the beds of the gods, are made of gold and precious stones. All the pleasures of these heavens are exactly what we should expect in a system formed by uninspired and unrenewed men: like the paradise of Mohammed, they are brothels, rather than places of rewards for "the pure in heart." Here all the vicious passions are personified, or rather, deified: the quarrels and licentious intrigues of the gods fill these places with perpetual uproar, while their impurities are described with the same literality and gross detail, as similar things are talked of among these idolaters on earth.

But the highest degree of happiness is absorption. God, as separated from matter, the Hindoos contemplate as a being reposing in his own happiness, destitute of ideas; as infinite placidity; as an unruffled sea of bliss; as being perfectly abstracted, and void of consciousness. They therefore deem it the height of perfection to be like this being. Hence Krishnu, in his discourse to Urjoonu, praises the man "who forsaketh every desire that entereth into his heart; who is happy of himself; who is without affection; who rejoiceth not either in good or evil; who, like the tortoise, can restrain his members from their wonted purpose; to whom pleasure and pain, gold, iron, and stones are the same." "The learned," adds Krushnu, "behold Brumhu alike in the reverend 'branhun,' perfected in knowledge; in the ox, and in the elephant; in the dog, and in him who eateth of the flesh of dogs." The person whose very nature, say they, is absorbed in divine meditation; whose life is like a sweet sleep, unconscious and undisturbed; who does not even desire God, and who is thus changed into the image of the ever blessed; obtains absorption into Brumhu. The ceremonies leading to absorption are called by the name of "tupushya" and the persons performing them, a "tupushwee." Forsaking the world; retiring to a forest; fasting, living on roots, fruits, &c;--remaining in certain postures; exposure to all the inclemencies of the weather, &c; these, and many other austere practices are prescribed, to subdue the passions, to fix the mind, habituate it to meditation, and fill it with that serenity and indifference to the world which is to prepare it for absorption, and place it beyond the reach of future birth.

BRAMBLE, אטד, a prickly shrub, Judges ix, 14, 15; Psalm lviii, 9. In the latter place it is translated "thorn." Hiller supposes ATAD to be the CYNOBASTUS, or sweetbrier. The author of "Scripture Illustrated" says, that the bramble seems to be well chosen as the representative of the original; which should be a plant bearing fruit of some kind, being associated, Judges ix, 14, though by opposition, with the vine. The apologue or fable of Jotham has always been admired for its spirit and application. It has also been considered as the oldest fable extant.

BRANCH, a title of Messiah: "And there shall come forth a rod out of the stem of Jesse, and a Branch shall grow out of his roots," Isaiah xi, 1. See also Zech. iii, 8; vi, 12; Jer. xxiii, 5; xxxiii, 15. When Christ is represented as a slender twig, shooting out from the trunk of an old tree lopped to the very root and decayed, and becoming itself a mighty tree, reference is made, 1. To the kingly dignity of Christ, springing up from the decayed house of David; 2. To the exaltation which was to succeed his humbled condition on earth, and to the glory and vigour of his mediatorial reign.

BRASS, נחשת. The word BRASS occurs very often in our translation of the Bible; but that is a mixed metal, for the making of which we are indebted to the German metallurgists of the thirteenth century. That the ancients knew not the art of making it, is almost certain. None of their writings even hint at the process. There can be no doubt that copper is the original metal intended. This is spoken of as known prior to the flood; and to have been discovered, or at least wrought, as was also iron, in the seventh generation from Adam, by Tubal-cain: whence the name VULCAN. The knowledge of these two metals must have been carried over the world afterward with the spreading colonies of the Noachidæ. Agreeably to this, the ancient histories of the Greeks and Romans speak of Cadmus as the inventor of the metal which by the former is called χαλκὸς, and by the latter ÆS; and from him had the denomination CADMEA. According to others, Cadmus discovered a mine, of which he taught the use. The name of the person here spoken of was undoubtedly the same with Ham, or Cam, the son of Noah, who probably learned the art of assaying metals from the family of Tubal-cain, and communicated that knowledge to the people of the colony which he settled.

BRASEN SERPENT, the, was an image of polished brass, in the form of one of those fiery serpents which were sent to chastise the murmuring Israelites in the wilderness, and whose bite caused violent heat, thirst, and inflammation. By divine command "Moses made a serpent of brass," or copper, and "put it upon a pole; and it came to pass, that if a serpent had bitten any man, when he beheld the serpent of brass, he lived," Num. xxi, 6–9. This brasen serpent was preserved as a monument of the divine mercy, but in process of time became an instrument of idolatry. When this superstition began, it is difficult to determine; but the best account is given by the Jewish rabbi, David Kimchi, in the following manner: From the time that the kings of Israel did evil, and the children of Israel followed idolatry, till the reign of Hezekiah, they offered incense to it; for it being written in the law of Moses, "Whoever looketh upon it shall live," they fancied they might obtain blessings by its mediation, and therefore thought it worthy to be worshipped. It had been kept from the days of Moses, in memory of a miracle, in the same manner as the pot of manna was: and Asa and Jehoshaphat did not extirpate it when they rooted out idolatry, because in their reign they did not observe that the people worshipped this serpent, or burnt incense to it; and therefore they left it as a memorial. But Hezekiah thought fit to take it quite away, when he abolished other idolatry, because in the time of his father they adored it as an idol; and though pious people among them accounted it only as a memorial of a wonderful work, yet he judged it better to abolish it, though the memory of the miracle should happen to be lost, than suffer it to remain, and leave the Israelites in danger to commit idolatry hereafter with it. On the subject of the serpent-bitten Israelites being healed by looking at the brasen serpent, there is a good comment in the book of Wisdom, chap. xvi, 4–12, in which are these remarkable words:--"They were admonished, having a sign of salvation," that is, the brasen serpent, "to put them in remembrance of the commandments of thy law. For he that turned himself toward it, was not saved by the THING that he saw, but by THEE, that art the Saviour of all," verses 6, 7. To the circumstance of looking at the brasen serpent in order to be healed, our Lord refers, John iii, 14, 15: "As Moses lifted up the (brasen) serpent in the wilderness, even so must the Son of man be lifted up, that whosoever believeth in him should not perish, but have eternal life."

BREAD, a term which in Scripture is used, as by us, frequently for food in general; but is also often found in its proper sense. Sparing in the use of flesh, like all the nations of the east, the chosen people usually satisfied their hunger with bread, and quenched their thirst in the running stream. Their bread was generally made of wheat or barley, or lentiles and beans. Bread of wheat flour, as being the most excellent, was preferred: barley bread was used only in times of scarcity and distress. So mean and contemptible, in the estimation of the numerous and well-appointed armies of Midian, was Gideon, with his handful of undisciplined militia, that he seems to have been compared to bread of this inferior quality, which may account for the ready interpretation of the dream of the Midianite respecting him: "And when Gideon was come, behold, there was a man that told a dream unto his fellow, and said, Behold, I dreamed a dream, and lo, a cake of barley bread tumbled into the host of Midian, and came unto a tent and smote it that it fell, and overturned it, that the tent lay along. And his fellow answered and said, This is nothing else save the sword of Gideon, the son of Joash, a man of Israel; for into his hand hath God delivered Midian, and all the host." In the cities and villages of Barbary, where public ovens are established, the bread is usually leavened; but among the Bedoweens and Kabyles, as soon as the dough is kneaded, it is made into thin cakes, either to be baked immediately upon the coals, or else in a shallow earthen vessel like a frying-pan, called Tajen. Such were the unleavened cakes which we so frequently read of in Scripture; and those also which Sarah made quickly upon the hearth. These last are about an inch thick; and, being commonly prepared in woody countries, are used all along the shores of the Black Sea, from the Palus Mæotis to the Caspian, in Chaldea and Mesopotamia, except in towns. A fire is made in the middle of the room: and when the bread is ready for baking, a corner of the hearth is swept, the bread is laid upon it, and covered with ashes and embers; in a quarter of an hour, they turn it. Sometimes they use small convex plates of iron, which are most common in Persia, and among the nomadic tribes, as being the easiest way of baking, and done with the least expense; for the bread is extremely thin, and soon prepared. The oven is also used in every part of Asia: it is made in the ground, four or five feet deep, and three in diameter, well plastered with mortar. When it is hot, they place the bread (which is commonly long, and not thicker than a finger) against the sides: it is baked in a moment. Ovens, Chardin apprehends, were not used in Canaan in the patriarchal age: all the bread of that time was baked upon a plate, or under the ashes; and he supposes, what is nearly self-evident, that the cakes which Sarah baked on the hearth were of the last sort, and that the shew bread was of the same kind. The Arabs about Mount Carmel use a great strong pitcher, in which they kindle a fire; and when it is heated, they mix meal and water, which they apply with the hollow of their hands to the outside of the pitcher; and this extremely soft paste, spreading itself, is baked in an instant. The heat of the pitcher having dried up all the moisture, the bread comes off as thin as our wafers; and the operation is so speedily performed, that in a very little time a sufficient quantity is made. But their best sort of bread they bake, either by heating an oven, or a large pitcher full of little smooth shining flints, upon which they lay the dough, spread out in the form of a thin broad cake. Sometimes they use a shallow earthen vessel, resembling a frying pan, which seems to be the pan mentioned by Moses, in which the meat-offering was baked. This vessel, Dr. Shaw informs us, serves both for baking and frying; for the bagreah of the people of Barbary differs not much from our pancakes; only, instead of rubbing the pan in which they fry them with butter, they rub it with soap, to make them like a honey-comb. If these accounts of the Arab stone pitcher, the pan, and the iron hearth or copper plate, be attended to, it will not be difficult to understand the laws of Moses in the second chapter of Leviticus: they will be found to answer perfectly well to the description which he gives us of the different ways of preparing the meat-offerings. As the Hebrews made their bread thin, in the form of little flat cakes, they did not cut it with a knife, but broke it; which gave rise to the expression, BREAKING BREAD, so frequent in Scripture.

The Arabians and other eastern people, among whom wood is scarce, often bake their bread between two fires made of cow dung, which burns slowly, and bakes the bread very leisurely. The crumb of it is very good, if it be eaten the same day; but the crust is black and burnt, and retains a smell of the materials that were used in baking it. This may serve to explain a passage in Ezekiel, iv, 9–13. The straits of a siege and the scarcity of fuel were thus intimated to the Prophet. During the whole octave of the passover, the Hebrews use only unleavened bread, as a memorial that at the time of their departure out of Egypt they wanted leisure to bake leavened bread; and, having left the country with precipitation, they were content to bake bread which was not leavened, Exod. xii, 8. The practice of the Jews at this day, with relation to the use of unleavened bread, is as follows: They forbid to eat, or have in their houses, or in any place belonging to them, either leavened bread or any thing else that is leavened. That they may the better observe this rule, they search into all the corners of the house with scrupulous exactness for all bread or paste, or any thing that is leavened. After they have thus well cleansed their houses, they whiten them, and furnish them with kitchen and table utensils, all new, and with others which are to be used only on that day. If they are movables, which have served only for something else, and are made of metal, they have them polished, and put into the fire, to take away all the impurity which they may have contracted by touching any thing leavened. All this is done on the thirteenth day of Nisan, or on the vigil of the feast of the passover, which begins with the fifteenth of the same month, or the fourteenth day in the evening; for the Hebrews reckon their days from one evening to another. On the fourteenth of Nisan, at eleven o'clock, they burn the common bread, to show that the prohibition of eating leavened bread is then commenced; and this action is attended with words, whereby the master of the house declares that he has no longer any thing leavened in his keeping; that, at least, he believes so. In allusion to this practice, we are commanded to "purge out the old leaven;" by which "malice and wickedness" are intended; and to feed only on the "unleavened bread of sincerity and truth."

2. Shew Bread, or, according to the Hebrews, THE BREAD OF FACES, was bread offered every Sabbath day upon the golden table in the holy place, Exod. xxv, 30. The Hebrews affirm that these loaves were square, and had four sides, and were covered with leaves of gold. They were twelve in number, according to the number of the twelve tribes, in whose names they were offered. Every loaf was composed of two assarons of flour, which make about five pints and one-tenth. These loaves were unleavened. They were presented hot every Sabbath day, the old ones being taken away and eaten by the priests only. This offering was accompanied with salt and frankincense, and even with wine, according to some commentators. The Scripture mentions only salt and incense; but it is presumed that wine was added, because it was not wanting in other sacrifices and offerings. It is believed that these loaves were placed one upon another, in two piles of six each; and that between every loaf were two thin plates of gold, folded back in a semicircle the whole length of them, to admit air, and to prevent the loaves from growing mouldy. These golden plates, thus turned in, were supported at their extremities by two golden forks, which rested on the ground. The twelve loaves, because they stood before the Lord, were called לחם הפנים, ἄρτοι ϖροθέσεως, or ἐνωπίοι, the bread of faces, or of the presence; and are therefore denominated in our English translation THE SHEW BREAD.

Since part of the frankincense put upon the bread was to be burnt on the altar for a memorial, even an offering made by fire unto the Lord; and since Aaron and his sons were to eat it in the holy place, Lev. xxiv, 5–9, it is probable that this bread typified Christ, first presented as a sacrifice to Jehovah, and then becoming spiritual food to such as in and through him are spiritual priests to God, even his Father, Rev. i, 6; v, 10; xx, 6; 1 Peter ii, 5. It appears, from some places in Scripture, (see Exodus xxix, 32, and Numbers vi, 15,) that there was always near the altar a basket full of bread, in order to be offered together with the ordinary sacrifices.

BREASTPLATE, or **PECTORAL**, one part of the priestly vestments, belonging to the Jewish high priests. It was about ten inches square, Exod. xxviii, 13–31; and consisted of a folded piece of the same rich embroidered stuff of which the ephod was made. It was worn on the breast of the high priest, and was set with twelve precious stones, on each of which was engraven the name of one of the tribes. They were set in four rows, three in each row, and were divided from each other by the little golden squares or partitions in which they were set. The names of these stones, and that of the tribe engraven on them, as also their disposition on the breastplate, are usually given as follows; but what stones really answer to the Hebrew name, is for the most part very uncertain:--

SARDINE,

Reuben.

EMERALD,

Judah.

LIGURE,

Gad.

BERYL,

Zebulun.

This breastplate was fastened at the four corners, those on the top to each shoulder, by a golden hook or ring, at the end of a wreathen chain; and those below to the girdle of the ephod, by two strings or ribbons, which had likewise two rings or hooks. This ornament was never to be separated from the priestly garment; and it was called the MEMORIAL, because it was a sign whereby the children of Israel might know that they were presented to God, and that they were had in remembrance by him. It was also called the BREASTPLATE OF JUDGMENT, because it had the divine oracle of Urim and Thummim annexed to it. These words signify LIGHTS and PERFECTIONS, and are mentioned as in the high priest's breastplate; but what they were, we cannot determine. Some think they were two precious stones added to the other twelve, by the extraordinary lustre of which, God marked his approbation of a design, and, by their becoming dim, his disallowance of it; others, that these two words were written on a precious stone, or plate of gold, fixed in the breastplate; others, that the letters of the names of the tribes, were the Urim and Thummim; and that the letters by standing out, or by an extraordinary illumination, marked such words as contained the answer of God to him who consulted this oracle. Le Clerc will have them to be the names of two precious stones, set in a golden collar of the high priest, and coming down to his breast, as the magistrates of Egypt wore a golden chain, at the end of which hung the figure of truth, engraven on a precious stone. Prideaux thinks the words chiefly denote the clearness of the oracles dictated to the high priest, though perhaps the lustre of the stones in his breastplate might represent this clearness. Jahn says the most probable opinion is, that Urim and Thummim (אורים, ותמים, LIGHT and JUST ICE, Septuagint, δήλωσις καὶ ἀλήθεια) [manifestation and truth] was a sacred lot, 1 Samuel xiv, 41, 42. There were employed, perhaps, in determining this lot, three precious stones, on one of which was engraven כן, YES; on the other, לא, NO; the third being destitute of any inscription. The question proposed, therefore, was always to be put in such a way, that the answer might be direct, either YES or NO, provided any answer was given at all.

These stones were carried in the purse or bag, formed by the lining or interior of the pectoral; and when the question was proposed, if the high priest drew out the stone which exhibited YES, the answer was affirmative; if the one on which NO was written, the answer was negative; if the third, no answer was to be given, Joshua vii, 13–21; 1 Sam. xiv, 40–43; xxviii, 6. In the midst of all this conjecture, only two things are certain: 1. That one of the appointed methods of consulting God, on extraordinary emergencies, was by Urim and Thummim: 2. That the oracles of God rejected all equivocal and enigmatical replies, which was the character of the Heathen pretended oracles. "The words of the Lord are pure words." His own oracle bears, therefore, an inscription which signifies LIGHTS and PERFECTIONS, or, THE SHINING and THE PERFECT; or, according to the **LXX**, MANIFESTATION and TRUTH. In this respect it might be a type of the Christian revelation made to the true Israel, the Christian church, by the Gospel. St. Paul seems especially to allude to this translation of Urim and Thummim by the Septuagint, when he speaks of himself and his fellow labourers, "commending themselves to every man's conscience BY MANIFESTATION OF THE TRUTH;" in opposition to those who by their errors and compliances with the Jewish prejudices, or with the philosophical taste of the Greeks, obscured the truth, and rendered ambiguous the guidance of Christian doctrine. His preaching is thus tacitly compared to the oracles of God; theirs, to the misleading and perplexed oracles of the Heathen.

BRIDE and **BRIDEGROOM**. Under this head an account of the marriage customs of ancient times, the knowledge of which is so necessary to explain many allusions in the Holy Scriptures, may be properly introduced. Among the Jews, the state of marriage was, from the remotest periods of their history, reckoned so honourable, that the person who neglected or declined to enter into it without a good reason, was thought to be guilty of a great crime. Such a mode of thinking was not confined to them; in several of the Grecian states, marriage was held in equal respect. The Jews did not allow marriageable persons to enter into that honourable state without restriction; the high priest was forbidden by law to marry a widow; and the priests of every rank, to take a harlot to wife, a profane woman, or one put away from her husband. To prevent the alienation of inheritances, an heiress could not marry but into her own tribe. The whole people of Israel, being a holy nation, separated from all the earth to the service of the true God, and to be the depositaries of his law, were forbidden to contract matrimonial alliances with the idolatrous nations in their vicinity. The marriage engagement of a minor, without the knowledge and consent of the parents, was of no force; so sacred was the parental authority held among that people. These customs appear to have been derived from a very remote antiquity; for when Eliezer of Damascus went to Mesopotamia to take a wife from thence unto his master's son, he disclosed the motives of his journey to the father and brother of Rebecca; and Hamor applied to Jacob and his sons, for their consent to the union of Dinah with his son Shechem. Samson also consulted his parents about his marriage; and entreated them to get for him the object of his choice. Marriage contracts seem to have been made in the primitive ages with little ceremony. The suitor himself, or his father, sent a messenger to the father of the woman, to ask her in marriage. In the remote ages of antiquity, women were literally purchased by their husbands; and the presents made to their parents or other relations were called their dowry. Thus, we find Shechem bargaining with Jacob and his sons for Dinah: "Let me find grace in your eyes, and what ye shall say unto me, I will give: ask me never so much dowry and gift, and I will give according as ye shall say unto me; but give me the damsel to wife," Gen. xxxiv, 2. The practice still continues in the country of Shechem; for when a young Arab wishes to marry, he must purchase his wife; and for this reason, fathers, among the Arabs, are never more happy than when they have many daughters. They are reckoned the principal riches of a house. An Arabian suitor will offer fifty sheep, six camels, or a dozen of cows: if he be not rich enough to make such offers, he proposes to give a mare or a colt, considering in the offer the merit of the young woman, the rank of her family, and his own circumstances. In the primitive times of Greece, a well-educated lady was valued at four oxen. When they are agreed on both sides, the contract is drawn up by him that acts as cadi or judge among these Arabs. In some parts of the east, a measure of corn is formally mentioned in contracts for their concubines, or temporary wives, beside the sum of money which is stipulated by way of dowry. This custom is probably as ancient as concubinage, with which it is connected; and if so, it will perhaps account for the Prophet Hosea's purchasing a wife of this kind, for fifteen pieces of silver, and for a homer of barley, and a half homer of barley. When the intended husband was not able to give a dowry, he offered an equivalent. The patriarch Jacob, who came to Laban with only his staff, offered to serve him seven years for Rachel: a proposal which Laban accepted. This custom has descended to modern times; for in Cabul the young men who are unable to advance the required dowry "live with their future father-in-law, and earn their bride by their services, without ever seeing the object of their wishes." The contract of marriage was made in the house of the woman's father, before the elders and governors of the city or district. The espousals by money, or a written instrument, were performed by the man and woman under a tent or canopy erected for that purpose. Into this chamber the bridegroom was accustomed to go with his bride, that he might talk with her more familiarly; which was considered as a ceremony of confirmation to the wedlock. While he was there, no person was allowed to enter: his friends and attendants waited for him at the door, with torches and lamps in their hands; and when he came out, he was received by all that were present with great joy and acclamation. To this ancient custom, the Psalmist alludes in his magnificent description of the heavens: "In them he set a tabernacle for the sun; which, as a bridegroom coming out of his chamber, rejoices as a strong man to run a race," Psalm xix, 4. A Jewish virgin legally betrothed was considered as a lawful wife; and, by consequence, could not be put away without a bill of divorce. And if she proved unfaithful to her betrothed husband, she was punished as an adulteress; and her seducer incurred the same punishment as if he had polluted the wife of his neighbour. This is the reason that the angel addressed Joseph, the betrothed husband of Mary, in these terms: "Joseph, thou son of David, fear not to take unto thee Mary thy wife; for that which is conceived in her is of the Holy Ghost." The Evangelist Luke gives her the same title: "And Joseph also went up from Galilee unto Bethlehem, to be taxed, with Mary his espoused wife," Luke ii, 4, 5.

2. Ten or twelve months commonly intervened between the ceremony of espousals and the marriage: during this interval, the espoused wife continued with her parents, that she might provide herself with nuptial ornaments suitable to her station. This custom serves to explain a circumstance in Samson's marriage, which is involved in some obscurity. "He went down," says the historian, "and talked with the woman," (whom he had seen at Timnath,) "and she pleased him well," Judges xiv, 7, &c. These words seem to refer to the ceremony of espousals; the following, to the subsequent marriage: "And after a time he returned to take her," Judges xiv, 8. Hence a considerable time intervened between the espousals and their actual union. From the time of the espousals, the bridegroom was at liberty to visit his espoused wife in the house of her father; yet neither of the parties left their own abode during eight days before the marriage; but persons of the same age visited the bridegroom, and made merry with him. These circumstances are distinctly marked in the account which the sacred historian has given us of Samson's marriage: "So his father went down unto the woman, and made there a feast; for so used the young men to do. And it came to pass when they saw him, that they brought thirty companions to be with him," Judges xiv, 10. These companions were the children of the bride chamber, of whom our Lord speaks: "Can the children of the bride chamber mourn as long as the bridegroom is with them?" Matt. xix, 15. The marriage ceremony was commonly performed in a garden, or in the open air; the bride was placed under a canopy, supported by four youths, and adorned with jewels according to the rank of the married persons; all the company crying out with joyful acclamations, "Blessed be he that cometh!" It was anciently the custom, at the conclusion of the ceremony, for the father and mother and kindred of the woman, to pray for a blessing upon the parties. Bethuel and Laban, and the other members of their family, pronounced a solemn benediction upon Rebecca before her departure: "And they blessed Rebecca, and said unto her, Thou art our sister, be thou the mother of thousands of millions; and let thy seed possess the gate of those that hate them," Gen. xxiv, 60. And in times long posterior to the age of Isaac, when Ruth, the Moabitess, was espoused to Boaz, "all the people that were in the gate, and the elders, said, We are witnesses: the Lord make the woman that is come into thine house like Rachel, and like Leah, which two did build the house of Israel; and do thou worthily in Ephratah, and be famous in Bethlehem," Ruth iv, 11, 12. After the benedictions, the bride is conducted with great pomp to the house of her husband: this is usually done in the evening; and as the procession moved along, money, sweetmeats, flowers, and other articles, were thrown among the populace, which they caught in cloths made for such occasions, stretched in a particular manner upon frames. The use of perfumes at eastern marriages is common; and upon great occasions very profuse.

3. It was the custom among the ancient Greeks, and the nations around them, to conduct the new-married couple with torches and lamps to their dwelling; as appears from the messenger in Euripides, who says he called to mind the time when he bore torches before Menelaus and Helena. These torches were usually carried by servants; and the procession was sometimes attended by singers and dancers. Thus Homer, in his description of the shield of Achilles:--

--ἐν τῇ μέν ῥα γάμοι τ' ἔσαν εἰλαπίναι τε,

Νύμφας δ' ἐκ θαλάμων, δαΐδων ὑπο λαμπομενάων,

Ἠγίνεον ἀνὰ ἄστυ. κ. τ. λ.   *Il.* lib. xviii, l. 490.

"In one of the sculptured cities, nuptials were celebrating, and solemn feasts; through the city they conducted the new-married pair from their chambers, with flaming torches, while frequent shouts of Hymen burst from the attending throng, and young men danced in skilful measures to the sound of the pipe and the harp."

A similar custom is observed among the Hindoos. The husband and wife, on the day of their marriage, being both in the same palanquin, go about seven and eight o'clock at night, accompanied with all their kindred and friends; the trumpets and drums go before them; and they are lighted by a number of flambeaux; immediately before the palanquin walk many women, whose business it is to sing verses, in which they wish them all manner of prosperity. They march in this equipage through the streets for the space of some hours, after which they return to their own house, where the domestics are in waiting. The whole house is illumined with small lamps; and many of those flambeaux already mentioned are kept ready for their arrival, beside those which accompany them, and are carried before the palanquin. These flambeaux are composed of many pieces of old linen, squeezed hard against one another in a round figure, and thrust down into a mould of copper. The persons that hold them in one hand have in the other a bottle of the same metal with the copper mould, which is full of oil, which they take care to pour out from time to time upon the linen, which otherwise gives no light. The Roman ladies also were led home to their husbands in the evening by the light of torches. A Jewish marriage seems to have been conducted in much the same way; for in that beautiful psalm, where David describes the majesty of Christ's kingdom, we meet with this passage: "And the daughter of Tyre shall be there with a gift; even the rich among the people shall entreat thy favour. The king's daughter is all-glorious within; her clothing is of wrought gold. She shall be brought unto the king in raiment of needle work; the virgins, her companions that follow her, shall be brought unto thee. With gladness and rejoicing shall they be brought: they shall enter into the king's palace," Psalm xlv, 12, &c. In the parable of the ten virgins, the same circumstances are introduced: "They that were foolish took their lamps, and took no oil with them: but the wise took oil in their vessels with their lamps. While the bridegroom tarried," leading the procession through the streets of the city, the women and domestics that were appointed to wait his arrival at home, "all slumbered and slept. And at midnight there was a cry made, Behold, the bridegroom cometh! Go ye out to meet him. Then all those virgins arose and trimmed their lamps. And the foolish said unto the wise, Give us of your oil; for our lamps are gone out," Matt. xxv, 6.

The following extract from Ward's "View of the Hindoos" very strikingly illustrates this parable: "At a marriage, the procession of which I saw some years ago, the bridegroom came from a distance, and the bride lived at Serampore, to which place the bridegroom was to come by water. After waiting two or three hours, at length, near midnight, it was announced, as if in the very words of Scripture, 'Behold, the bridegroom cometh! Go ye out to meet him.' All the persons employed now lighted their lamps, and ran with them in their hands to fill up their stations in the procession; some of them had lost their lights, and were unprepared; but it was then too late to seek them, and the cavalcade moved forward to the house of the bride, at which place the company entered a large and splendidly illuminated area, before the house covered with an awning, where a great multitude of friends dressed in their best apparel were seated upon mats. The bridegroom was carried in the arms of a friend, and placed on a superb seat in the midst of the company, where he sat a short time, and then went into the house, the door of which was immediately shut, and guarded by Sepoys. I and others expostulated with the door keepers, but in vain."

4. But among the Jews, the bridegroom was not always permitted to accompany his bride from her father's house; an intimate friend was often sent to conduct her, while he remained at home to receive her in his apartment. Her female attendants had the honour to introduce her; and whenever they changed the bride's dress, which is often done, they presented her to the bridegroom. It is the custom, and belongs to their ideas of magnificence, frequently to dress and undress the bride, and to cause her to wear on that same day all the clothes made up for her nuptials. These circumstances discover the force of St. John's language, in his magnificent description of the Christian church in her millennial state: "And I, John, saw the holy city, New Jerusalem, coming down from God out of heaven, prepared as a bride adorned for her husband," Rev. xxi, 2.

5. Those that were invited to the marriage were expected to appear in their best and gayest attire. If the bridegroom was in circumstances to afford it, wedding garments were prepared for all the guests, which were hung up in the antechamber for them to put on over the rest of their clothes, as they entered the apartments where the marriage feast was prepared. To refuse, or even to neglect, putting on the wedding garment, was reckoned an insult to the bridegroom; aggravated by the circumstance that it was provided by himself for the very purpose of being worn on that occasion, and was hung up in the way to the inner apartment, that the guests must have seen it, and recollected the design of its suspension. This accounts for the severity of the sentence pronounced by the king, who came in to see the guests, and found among them one who had neglected to put it on: "And he saith unto him, Friend, how camest thou in hither, not having a wedding garment? And he was speechless," Matt. xxii, 11, because it was provided at the expense of the entertainer, and placed full in his view. "Then said the king to the servants, Bind him hand and foot, and take him away, and cast him into outer darkness: there shall be weeping and gnashing of teeth."

The following extract will show the importance of having a suitable garment for a marriage feast, and the offence taken against those who refuse it when presented as a gift. "The next day, Dec. 3d, the king sent to invite the ambassadors to dine with him once more. The Mehemander told them, it was the custom that they should wear over their own clothes the best of those garments which the king had sent them. The ambassadors at first made some scruple of that compliance; but when they were told that it was a custom observed by all ambassadors, and that no doubt the king would take it very ill at their hands if they presented themselves before him without the marks of his liberality, they at last resolved to do it; and, after their example, all the rest of the retinue."

BRIER. This word occurs several times in our translation of the Bible, but with various authorities from the original. 1. הברקנים, Judges viii, 7, 16, is a particular kind of thorn. 2. חדק, Prov. xv, 19; Micah vii, 4. It seems hardly possible to determine what kind of plant this is. Some kind of tangling prickly shrub is undoubtedly meant. In the former passage there is a beautiful opposition, which is lost in our rendering: "The NARROW WAY of the slothful is like a perplexed path among briers; whereas the BROAD ROAD" (elsewhere rendered CAUSEWAY) "of the righteous is a high bank;" that is, free from obstructions, direct, conspicuous, and open. The common course of life of these two characters answers to this comparison. Their manner of going about business, or of transacting it, answers to this. An idle man always takes the most intricate, the most oblique, and eventually the most thorny, measures to accomplish his purpose; the honest and diligent man prefers the most open and direct. In Micah, the unjust judge, taking bribes, is a brier, holding every thing that comes within his reach, hooking all that he can catch. 3. סרבים, Ezek. ii, 6. This word is translated by the Septuagint, παϱοιςϱήσουσιν, STUNG BY THE ŒSTRUS, or GADFLY; and they use the like word in Hosea iv, 16, where, what in our version is "a backsliding heifer," they render "a heifer stung by the œstrus." These coincident renderings lead to the belief that both places may be understood of some venomous insect. The word סרר may lead us to SARRAN, by which the Arabs thus describe "a great bluish fly, having greenish eyes, its tail armed with a piercer, by which it pesters almost all horned cattle, settling on their heads, &c. Often it creeps up the noses of asses. It is a species of gadfly; but carrying its sting in its tail." 4. סלון, Ezek. xxviii, 24, and סלונים, Ezek. ii, 6, must be classed among thorns. The second word Parkhurst supposes to be a kind of thorn, overspreading a large surface of ground, as the dewbrier. It is used in connection with קוצ, which, in Gen. iii, 18, is rendered THORNS. The author of "Scripture Illustrated" queries, however, whether, as it is associated with "scorpions" in Ezek. ii, 6, both this word and SEREBIM may not mean some species of venomous insects. 5. סרפד, mentioned only in Isaiah lv, 13, probably means a prickly plant; but what particular kind it is impossible to determine. 6. שמיר. This word is used only by the Prophet Isaiah, and in the following places: Isa. v, 6; vii, 23–25; ix, 17; x, 17; xxvii, 4; and xxxii, 13. It is probably a brier of a low kind; such as overruns uncultivated lands.

BRIMSTONE, גפרית, Gen. xix, 24; Deut. xxix, 23; Job xviii, 15; Psalm xi, 6; Isaiah xxx, 33; xxxiv, 9; Ezek. xxxviii, 22. It is rendered θεῖον by the Septuagint, and is so called in Luke xvii, 29. Fire and brimstone are represented in many passages of Scripture as the elements by which God punishes the wicked; both in this life, and another. There is in this a manifest allusion to the overthrow of the cities of the plain of the Jordan, by showers of ignited sulphur, to which the physical appearances of the country bear witness to this day. The soil is bituminous, and might be raised by eruptions into the air, and then inflamed and return in horrid showers of overwhelming fire. This awful catastrophe, therefore, stands as a type of the final and eternal punishment of the wicked in another world. In Job. xviii, 15, Bildad, describing the calamities which overtake the wicked person, says, "Brimstone shall be scattered upon his habitation." This may be a general expression, to designate any great destruction: as that in Psalm xi, 6, "Upon the wicked he shall rain fire and brimstone." Moses, among other calamities which he sets forth in case of the people's disobedience, threatens them with the fall of brimstone, salt, and burning like the overthrow of Sodom, &c, Deut. xxix, 23. The Prophet Isaiah, xxxiv, 9, writes that the anger of the Lord shall be shown by the streams of the land being turned into pitch, and the dust thereof into brimstone. See Dead Sea.

BROOK is distinguished from a river by its flowing only at particular times; for example, after great rains, or the melting of the snow; whereas a river flows constantly at all seasons. However, this distinction is not always observed in the Scripture; and one is not unfrequently taken for the other,--the great rivers, such as the Euphrates, the Nile, the Jordan, and others being called brooks. Thus the Euphrates, Isaiah xv, 7, is called the brook of willows. It is observed that the Hebrew word, נחל, which signifies A BROOK, is also the term for a valley, whence the one is often placed for the other, in different translations of the Scriptures. To deal deceitfully "as a brook," and to "pass away as the stream thereof," is to deceive our friend when he most needs and expects our help and comfort, Job vi, 15; because brooks, being temporary streams, are dried up in the heats of summer, when the traveller most needs a supply of water on his journey.

BROTHER. 1. A brother by the same mother, a uterine brother, Matt. iv, 21; xx, 20. 2. A brother, though not by the same mother, Matt. i, 2. 3. A near kinsman, a cousin, Matt. xiii, 55; Mark vi, 3. Observe, that in Matt. xiii, 55, James, and Joses, and Judas, are called the ἀδελφοὶ, BRETHREN, of Christ, but were most probably only his cousins by his mother's side; for James and Joses were the sons of Mary, Matt. xxvii, 56; and James and Judas, the sons of Alpheus, Luke vi, 15, 16; which Alpheus is therefore probably the same with Cleopas, the husband of Mary, sister to our Lord's mother, John xix, 25.

BUCKLER. See Arms.

BUILD. Beside the proper and literal signification of this word, it is used with reference to children and a numerous posterity. Sarah desires Abraham to take Hagar to wife, that by her she may be builded up, that is, have children to uphold her family, Gen. xvi, 2. The midwives who refused obedience to Pharaoh's orders, when he commanded them to put to death all the male children of the Hebrews, were rewarded for it; God built them houses, that is, he gave them a numerous posterity. The Prophet Nathan tells David that God would build his house; that is, give him children and successors, 2 Sam. vii, 27. Moses, speaking of the formation of the first woman, says, God built her with the rib of Adam, Gen. ii, 22.

BUL, the eighth month of the ecclesiastical year of the Jews, and the second month of the civil year. It answers to October, and consists of twenty-nine days. On the sixth day of this month the Jews fasted, because on that day Nebuchadnezzar put to death the children of Zedekiah in the presence of their unhappy father, whose eyes, after they had been witnesses of this sad spectacle, he ordered to be put out, 2 Kings xxv, 7. We find the name of this month mentioned in Scripture but once, 1 Kings vi, 38.

BULL, the male of the beeve kind; and it is to be recollected that the Hebrews never castrated animals. There are several words translated "bull" in Scripture, of which the following is a list, with the meaning of each: שור, a bove, or cow, of any age. תאו, the wild bull, oryx, or buffalo, occurs only Deut. xiv, 5; and in Isaiah li, 20, תוא, with the interchange of the two last letters. אבירי, a word implying STRENGTH, translated "bulls," Psalm xxii, 12; l, 13; lxviii, 30; Isaiah xxxiv, 7; Jer. xlvi, 15. בקר, herds, horned cattle of full age. פר, a full grown bull, or cow, fit for propagating. עגל, a full grown, plump young bull; and in the feminine, a heifer. תור, Chaldee TAUR, and

Latin TAURUS; the ox accustomed to the yoke: occurs only in Ezra vi, 9, 17; vii, 17; Dan. iv, 25, 32, 33; xxii, 29, 30.

This animal was reputed by the Hebrews to be clean, and was generally made use of by them for sacrifices. The Egyptians had a particular veneration for it, and paid divine honours to it; and the Jews imitated them in the worship of the golden calves or bulls, in the wilderness, and in the kingdom of Israel. The wild bull is found in the Syrian and Arabian deserts. It is frequently mentioned by the Arabian poets, who are copious in their descriptions of hunting it, and borrow many images from its beauty, strength, swiftness, and the loftiness of its horns. They represent it as fierce and untamable; as being white on the back, and having large shining eyes. Bulls, in a figurative and allegorical sense, are taken for powerful, fierce, and insolent enemies, Psalm xxii, 12; lxviii, 30.

BULRUSH, גמא, Exodus ii, 3; Job viii, 11; Isaiah xviii, 2; xxxv, 7. A plant growing on the banks of the Nile, and in marshy grounds. The stalk rises to the height of six or seven cubits, beside two under water. This stalk is triangular, and terminates in a crown of small filaments resembling hair, which the ancients used to compare to a THYRSUS. This reed, the CYPERUS PAPYRUS of Linnæus, commonly called "the Egyptian reed," was of the greatest use to the inhabitants of the country where it grew; the pith contained in the stock served them for food, and the woody part for building vessels, figures of which are to be seen on the engraven stones and other monuments of Egyptian antiquity. For this purpose they made it up, like rushes, into bundles; and, by tying these bundles together, gave their vessels the necessary shape and solidity. "The vessels of bulrushes," or papyrus, "that are mentioned in sacred and profane history," says Dr. Shaw, "were no other than large fabrics of the same kind with that of Moses, Exodus ii, 3; which, from the late introduction of plank and stronger materials, are now laid aside." Thus Pliny takes notice of the "NAVES PAPYRACEAS ARMAMENTAQUE NILI," "ships made of papyrus, and the equipments of the Nile;" and he observes, "EX IPSÂ QUIDEM PAPYRO NAVIGIA TEXUNT," "of the papyrus itself they construct sailing vessels." Herodotus and Diodorus have recorded the same fact; and among the poets, Lucan, "CONSERITUR BIBULÂ MEMPHITIS CYMBA PAPYRO," "the Memphian" or Egyptian boat is made of the thirsty papyrus; where the epithet BIBULÂ, "drinking," "soaking," "thirsty," is particularly remarkable, as corresponding with great exactness to the nature of the plant, and to its Hebrew name, which signifies TO SOAK or DRINK UP. These vegetables require much water for their growth; when, therefore, the river on whose banks they grew was reduced, they perished sooner than other plants. This explains Job viii, 11, where the circumstance is referred to as an image of transient prosperity: "Can the flag grow without water? Whilst it is yet in its greenness, and not cut down, it withereth before any other herb."

BURIAL, the interment of a deceased person; an office held so sacred, that they who neglected it have in all nations been held in abhorrence. As soon as the last breath had fled, the nearest relation, or the dearest friend, gave the lifeless body the parting kiss, the last farewell and sign of affection to the departed relative. This was a custom of immemorial antiquity; for the patriarch Jacob had no sooner yielded up his spirit, than his beloved Joseph, claiming for once the right of the first-born, "fell upon his face and kissed him." It is probable he first closed his eyes, as God had promised he should do: "Joseph shall put his hands upon thine eyes." The parting kiss being given, the company rent their clothes, which was a custom of great antiquity, and the highest expression of grief in the primitive ages. This ceremony was never omitted by the Hebrews when any mournful event happened, and was performed in the following manner: they took a knife, and holding the blade downward, gave the upper garment a cut in the right side, and rent it a hand's breadth. For very near relations, all the garments are rent on the right side. After closing the eyes, the next care was to bind up the face, which it was no more lawful to behold. The next care of surviving friends was to wash the body, probably, that the ointments and perfumes with which it was to be wrapped up, might enter more easily into the pores, when opened by warm water. This ablution, which was always esteemed an act of great charity and devotion, was performed by women. Thus the body of Dorcas was washed, and laid in an upper room, till the arrival of the Apostle Peter, in the hope that his prayers might restore her to life. After the body was washed, it was shrouded, and swathed with a linen cloth, although in most places, they only put on a pair of drawers and a white tunic; and the head was bound about with a napkin. Such were the napkin and grave clothes in which the Saviour was buried.

2. The body was sometimes embalmed, which was performed by the Egyptians after the following method: the brain was removed with a bent iron, and the vacuity filled up with medicaments; the bowels were also drawn out, and the trunk being stuffed with myrrh, cassia, and other spices, except frankincense, which were proper to exsiccate the humours, it was pickled in nitre, in which it lay for seventy days. After this period, it was wrapped in bandages of fine linen and gums, to make it adhere; and was then delivered to the relations of the deceased entire; all its features, and the very hairs of the eyelids, being preserved. In this manner were the kings of Judah embalmed for many ages. But when the funeral obsequies were not long delayed, they used another kind of embalming. They wrapped up the body with sweet spices and odours, without extracting the brain, or removing the bowels. This is the way in which it was proposed to embalm the lifeless body of our Saviour; which was prevented by his resurrection. The meaner sort of people seem to have been interred in their grave clothes, without a coffin. In this manner was the sacred body of our Lord committed to the tomb. The body was sometimes placed upon a bier, which bore some resemblance to a coffin or bed, in order to be carried out to burial. Upon one of these was carried forth the widow's son of Nain, whom

our compassionate Lord raised to life, and restored to his mother. We are informed in the history of the kings of Judah, that, Asa being dead, they laid him in the bed, or bier, which was filled with sweet odours. Josephus, the Jewish historian, describing the funeral of Herod the Great, says, His bed was adorned with precious stones; his body rested under a purple covering; he had a diadem and a crown of gold upon his head, a sceptre in his hand; and all his house followed the bed. The bier used by the Turks at Aleppo is a kind of coffin, much in the form of ours, only the lid rises with a ledge in the middle.

3. The Israelites committed the dead to their native dust; and from the Egyptians, probably, borrowed the practice of burning many spices at their funerals. "They buried Asa in his own sepulchres, which he made for himself in the city of David, and laid him in the bed which was filled with sweet odours, and divers kinds of spices, prepared by the apothecaries' art; and they made a very great burning for him," 2 Chron. xvi, 14. Thus the Old Testament historian entirely justifies the account which the Evangelist gives, of the quantity of spices with which the sacred body of Christ was swathed. The Jews object to the quantity used on that occasion, as unnecessarily profuse, and even incredible; but it appears from their own writings, that spices were used at such times in great abundance. In the Talmud it is said, that no less than eighty pounds of spices were consumed at the funeral of rabbi Gamaliel the elder. And at the funeral of Herod, if we may believe the account of their most celebrated historian, the procession was followed by five hundred of his domestics carrying spices. Why then should it be reckoned incredible, that Nicodemus brought of myrrh and aloes about a hundred pounds' weight, to embalm the body of Jesus?

4. The funeral procession was attended by professional mourners, eminently skilled in the art of lamentation, whom the friends and relations of the deceased hired, to assist them in expressing their sorrow. They began the ceremony with the stridulous voices of old women, who strove, by their doleful modulations, to extort grief from those that were present. The children in the streets through which they passed, often suspended their sports, to imitate the sounds, and joined with equal sincerity in the lamentations. "But whereunto shall I liken this generation? It is like unto children sitting in the markets, and calling unto their fellows, and saying, We have mourned unto you, and ye have not lamented," Matt. ix, 17. Music was afterward introduced to aid the voices of the mourners: the trumpet was used at the funerals of the great, and the small pipe or flute for those of meaner condition. Hired mourners were in use among the Greeks as early as the Trojan war, and probably in ages long before; for in Homer, a choir of mourners were planted around the couch on which the body of Hector was laid out, who sung his funeral dirge with many sighs and tears:--

Όι δ' ἐπεὶ εἰσάγαγον κλυτὰ δώματα, τὸν μὲν ἔπειτα

Τρητοῖς ἐν λεχέεσσι θέσαν, ϖαρὰ δ' εἷσαν ἀοιδοὺς,

Θρήνων ἐξάρχȣς. κ. τ. λ. *Il.* lib. xxiv, l. 720.

"A melancholy choir attend around,

With plaintive sighs and music's solemn sound;

Alternately they sing, alternate flow

The obedient tears, melodious in their wo." Pope.

In Egypt, the lower class of people call in women who play on the tabor; and whose business it is, like the hired mourners in other countries, to sing elegiac airs to the sound of that instrument, which they accompany with the most frightful distortions of their limbs. These women attend the corpse to the grave, intermixed with the female relations and friends of the deceased, who commonly have their hair in the utmost disorder; their heads covered with dust; their faces daubed with indigo, or at least rubbed with mud; and howling like maniacs. Such were the minstrels whom our Lord found in the house of Jairus, making so great a noise round the bed on which the dead body of his daughter lay. The noise and tumult of these retained mourners, and the other attendants, appear to have begun immediately after the person expired. It is evident that this sort of mourning and lamentation was a kind of art among the Jews: "Wailing shall be in the streets; and they shall call such as are skilful of lamentation to wail," Amos v, 16. Mourners are still hired at the obsequies of Hindoos and Mohammedans, as in former times. To the dreadful noise and tumult of the hired mourners, the following passage of Jeremiah indisputably refers; and shows the custom to be derived from a very remote antiquity: "Call for the mourning women that they may come; and send for cunning women, that they may come, and let them make haste, and take up a wailing for us, that our eyes may run down with tears, and our eyelids gush out with waters," Jer. ix, 17. The funeral processions of the Jews in Barbary are conducted nearly in the same manner as those in Syria. The corpse is borne by four to the place of burial: in the first rank march the priests, next to them the kindred of the deceased; after whom come those that are invited to the funeral; and all singing in a sort of plain song, the forty-ninth Psalm. Hence the Prophet, Amos viii, 3, warns his people that public calamities were approaching, so numerous and severe, as should make them forget the usual rites of burial, and even to sing one of the songs of Zion over the dust of a departed relative. This appears to be confirmed by a prediction in the eighth chapter: "And the songs of the temple shall be howlings in that day, saith the Lord God; there shall be many dead bodies in every place; they shall cast them forth with SILENCE;" they shall have none to lament and bewail; none to blow the funeral trump or touch the pipe and tabor; none to sing the plaintive dirge, or express their hope of a blessed resurrection, in the strains of inspiration. All shall be silent despair. See Sepulchres.

BUSH. סנה. This word occurs in Exod. iii, 2, 4, and Deut. xxxiii, 16, as the name of the bush in which God appeared to Moses. If it be the χιονὸς mentioned by Dioscorides, it is the white thorn. Celsius calls it the RUBUS FRUCTICOSUS. The number of these bushes in this region seems to have given the name to the mountain Sinai. The word נהללים, found only in Isa. vii, 19, and there rendered "bushes," means FRUITFUL PASTURES.

BUTTER is taken in Scripture, as it has been almost perpetually in the east, for cream or liquid butter, Prov. xxx, 33; 2 Sam. xvii, 29. The ancient way of making butter in Arabia and Palestine was probably nearly the same as is still practised by the Bedoween Arabs, and Moors in Barbary, and which is thus described by Dr. Shaw: "Their method of making butter is by putting the milk or cream into a goat's skin turned inside out, which they suspend from one side of the tent to the other; and then pressing it to and fro in one uniform direction, they quickly separate the unctious and wheyey parts. In the Levant they tread upon the skin with their feet, which produces the same effect." The last method of separating the butter from the milk, perhaps may throw light upon a passage in Job of some difficulty: "When I washed my steps with butter, and the rock poured me out rivers of oil," Job xxxi, 6. The method of making butter in the east illustrates the conduct of Jael, the wife of Heber, described in the book of Judges: "And Sisera said unto her, Give me, I pray thee, a little water to drink, for I am thirsty: and she opened a bottle of milk, and gave him drink and covered him." In the Song of Deborah, the statement is repeated: "He asked water, and she gave him milk; she brought forth butter in a lordly dish," Judges iv, 19; v, 25. The word חמאה, which our translators rendered BUTTER, properly signifies CREAM; which is undoubtedly the meaning of it in this passage: for Sisera complained of thirst, and asked a little water to quench it;--a purpose to which butter is but little adapted. Mr. Harmer, indeed, urges the same objection to cream, which, he contends, few people would think a very proper beverage for one that was extremely thirsty; and concludes that it must have been butter-milk which Jael, who had just been churning, gave to Sisera. But the opinion of Dr. Russel is preferable,--that the HEMAH of the Scriptures is probably the same as the HAYMAK of the Arabs, which is not, as Harmer supposed, simple cream, but cream produced by simmering fresh sheep's milk for some hours over a slow fire. It could not be butter newly churned, which Jael presented to Sisera, because the Arab butter is apt to be foul, and is commonly passed through a strainer before it is used: and Russel declares, he never saw butter offered to a stranger, but always HAYMAK; nor did he ever observe the orientals drink butter-milk, but always LEBAN, which is coagulated sour milk, diluted with water. It was LEBAN, therefore, which Pococke mistook for butter-milk, with which the Arabs treated him in the Holy Land. A similar conclusion may be drawn concerning the butter and milk which the wife of Heber presented to Sisera: they were forced cream or HAYMAK, and LEBAN, or coagulated sour milk, diluted with water, which is a common and refreshing beverage in those sultry regions. In Isaiah vii, 15, butter and honey are mentioned as food which, in Egypt and other places in the east, is in use to this day. The butter and honey are mixed, and the bread is then dipped in it.

BYSSUS. By this word we generally understand that fine Egyptian linen of which the priests' tunics were made. But we must distinguish three kinds of commodities, which are generally comprehended under the name of LINEN: 1. The Hebrew בד, which signifies LINEN: 2. שש, which signifies COTTON: 3. בוץ, which is commonly called BUSSUS, and is the silk growing from a certain shell fish, called PINNA. We do not find the name BUTZ in the text of Moses, though the Greek and Latin use the word BYSSUS, to signify the fine linen of certain habits belonging to the priests. The word BUTZ occurs only in 1 Chron. xv, 27; Ezek. xxvii, 16; Esther i, 6. In the Chronicles we see David dressed in a mantle of BUTZ, with the singers and Levites. Solomon used BUTZ in the veils of the temple and sanctuary. Ahasuerus's tents were upheld by cords of BUTZ; and Mordecai was clothed with a mantle of purple and BUTZ, when king Ahasuerus honoured him with the first employment in his kingdom. Lastly, it is observed that there was a manufacture of BUTZ in the city of Beersheba, in Palestine. This BUTZ must have been different from common linen, since in the same place where it is said, David wore a mantle of byssus, we read likewise that he had on a linen ephod.

CAB, or **KAB**, a Hebrew measure, containing three pints one-third of our wine measure, or two pints five-sixths of our corn measure.

CABBALA, a mysterious kind of science, delivered to the ancient Jews, as they pretend, by revelation, and transmitted by oral tradition to those of our times; serving for the interpretation of the books both of nature and Scripture. The word is variously written, as CABALA, CABALLA, KABBALA, KABALA, CABA LISTICA, ARS CABALA, and GABALLA. It is originally Hebrew, קבלה, and properly signifies RECEPTION; formed from the verb קבל, TO RECEIVE BY TRADITION, or FROM FATHER TO SON; especially in the Chaldee and Rabbinical Hebrew. Cabbala, then, primarily denotes any sentiment, opinion, usage, or explication of Scripture, transmitted from father to son. In this sense the word CABBALA is not only applied to the whole art, but also to each operation performed according to the rules of that art. Thus it is, rabbi Jacob Ben Ascher, surnamed Baal-Hatturim, is said to have compiled most of the cabbalas invented on the books of Moses before his time. As to the origin of the cabbala, the Jews relate many marvellous tales. They derive the mysteries contained in it from Adam; and assert, that whilst the first man was in paradise, the angel Raphael brought him a book from heaven, which contained the doctrines of heavenly wisdom; and that when Adam received this book, angels came down from heaven to learn its contents; but that he refused to admit them to the knowledge of sacred things, intrusted to himself alone: that, after the fall, this book was taken back into heaven; that, after many prayers and tears, God restored it to Adam; and that it passed from Adam to Seth. The Jewish fables farther relate, that the book being lost, and the mysteries contained in it almost forgotten, in the degenerate age preceding the flood, they were restored by special revelation to Abraham, who transmitted them to writing in the book "Jezirah;" and that the revelation was renewed to Moses, who received a traditionary and mystical, as well as a written and preceptive, law from God. Accordingly, the Jews believe that God gave to Moses on Mount Sinai, not only the law, but also the explication of that law; and that Moses, after his coming down, retiring to his tent, rehearsed to Aaron both the one and the other. When he had done, the sons of Aaron, Eleazar and Ithamar, were introduced to a second rehearsal. This being over, the seventy elders that composed the sanhedrim were admitted; and, lastly, the people, as many as pleased; to all of whom Moses again repeated both the law and explanation, as he received them from God: so that Aaron heard it four times, his sons thrice, the elders twice, and the people once. Now, of the two things which Moses taught them, the laws and the explanation, only the first were committed to writing; which is what we have in Exodus, Leviticus, and Numbers. As to the second, or the explication of those laws, they were contented to impress it well in their memory, to teach it their children; they to theirs, &c. Hence the first part they call simply the law, or the written law; the second, the oral law, or cabbala. Such is the original notion of the cabbala.

2. The cabbala being again lost amidst the calamities of the Babylonish captivity, was once more revealed to Esdras; and it is said to have been preserved in Egypt, and transmitted to posterity through the hands of Simeon Ben Setach, Elkanah, Akibha, Simeon Ben Jochai, and others. The only warrantable inference from these accounts, which bear the obvious marks of fiction, is, that the cabbalistic doctrine obtained early credit among the Jews as a part of their sacred tradition, and was transmitted, under this notion, by the Jews in Egypt to their brethren in Palestine. Under the sanction of ancient names, many fictitious writings were produced, which greatly contributed to the spreading of this mystical system. Among these were "Sepher Happeliah," or the book of wonders; "Sepher Hakkaneh," or the book of the pen; and "Sepher Habbahir," or the book of light. The first unfolds many doctrines said to have been delivered by Elias to the rabbi Elkanah; the second contains mystical commentaries on the divine commands; and the third illustrates the most sublime mysteries. Among the profound doctors who, beside the study of tradition, cultivated with great industry the cabbalistic philosophy, the most celebrated persons are the rabbis Akibba, who lived soon after the destruction of Jerusalem, and Simeon Ben Jochai, who flourished in the second century. To the former is ascribed the book entitled "Jezirah," concerning the creation; and to the latter, the book "Sohar," or brightness; and these are the principal sources from which we derive our knowledge of the cabbala.

3. That this system of the cabbalistic philosophy, which we may consider as the acroamatic, esoteric, or concealed doctrine of the Jews, by way of contradistinction from the exoretic or popular doctrine, was not of Hebrew origin, we may conclude with a very great degree of probability, from the total dissimilarity of its abstruse and mysterious doctrines to the simple principles of religion taught in the Mosaic law; and that it was borrowed from the Egyptian schools will sufficiently appear from a comparison of its tenets with those of the oriental and Alexandrian philosophy. Many writers have, indeed, imagined that they have found in the cabbalistic dogmas a near resemblance of the doctrines of Christianity; and they have thought that the fundamental principles of this mystical system were derived from divine revelation. This opinion, however, may be traced up to a prejudice which originated with the Jews, and passed from them to the Christian fathers, by which they were led to ascribe all Pagan wisdom to a Hebrew origin: a notion which very probably took its rise in Egypt, when Pagan tenets first crept in among the Jews. Philo, Josephus, and other learned Jews, in order to flatter their own vanity, and that of their countrymen, industriously propagated this opinion; and the more learned fathers of the Christian church, who entertained a high opinion of the Platonic philosophy, hastily adopted it, from an imagination that if they could trace back the most valuable doctrines of Paganism to a Hebrew origin, this could not fail to recommend the Jewish and Christian religions to the attention of the Gentile philosophers. Many learned moderns, relying implicitly upon these authorities, have maintained the same opinion; and have thence been inclined to credit the report of the divine original of the Jewish cabbala. But the opinion is unfounded; and the cabbalistic system is essentially inconsistent with the pure doctrine of divine revelation. The true state of the case seems to be, that during the prophetic ages, the traditions of the Jews consisted in a simple explanation of those divine truths which the prophets delivered, or their law exhibited, under the veil of emblems. After this period, when the sects of the Essenes and Therapeutæ were formed in Egypt, foreign tenets and institutions were borrowed from the Egyptians and Greeks; and, in the form of allegorical interpretations of the law, were admitted into what might then be called the Jewish mysteries, or secret doctrines. These innovations chiefly consisted in certain dogmas concerning God and divine things, at this time received in the Egyptian schools; particularly at Alexandria, where the Platonic and Pythagorean doctrines on these subjects had been blended with the oriental philosophy. The Jewish mysteries, thus enlarged by the accession of Pagan dogmas, were conveyed from Egypt to Palestine, at the time when the Pharisees, who had been driven into Egypt under Hyrcanus, returned with many other Jews into their own country. From this time the cabbalistic mysteries continued to be taught in the Jewish schools; but at length they were

adulterated by a mixture of Peripatetic doctrines, and other tenets. These mysteries were not, probably, reduced to any systematic forms in writing, till after the dispersion of the Jews; when in consequence of their national calamities, they became apprehensive that those sacred treasures would be corrupted or lost. In preceding periods, the cabbalistic doctrines underwent various corruptions, particularly from the prevalence of the Aristotelian philosophy. The similarity, or rather the coincidence, of the cabbalistic, Alexandrian, and oriental philosophy, will be sufficiently evinced by briefly stating the common tenets in which these different systems agreed. They are as follow:--"All things are derived by emanation from one principle; and this principle is God. From him a substantial power immediately proceeds, which is the image of God, and the source of all subsequent emanations. This second principle sends forth, by the energy of emanation, other natures, which are more or less perfect, according to their different degrees of distance, in the scale of emanation, from the first source of existence, and which constitute different worlds or orders of being, all united to the eternal power from which they proceed. Matter is nothing more than the most remote effect of the emanative energy of the Deity. The material world receives its form from the immediate agency of powers far beneath the first source of being. Evil is the necessary effect of the imperfection of matter. Human souls are distant emanations from Deity; and, after they are liberated from their material vehicles, will return, through various stages of purification, to the fountain whence they first proceeded." From this brief view it appears, that the cabbalistic system, which is the offspring of the other two, is a fanatical kind of philosophy, originating in defect of judgment and eccentricity of imagination, and tending to produce a wild and pernicious enthusiasm.

4. Among the explications of the law which are furnished by the cabbala, and which, in reality, are little else but the several interpretations and decisions of the rabbins on the laws of Moses, some are mystical; consisting of odd abstruse significations given to a word, or even to the letters whereof it is composed: whence, by different combinations, they draw meanings from Scripture very different from those it seems naturally to import. The art of interpreting Scripture after this manner is called more particularly CABBALA; and it is in this last sense the word is more ordinarily used among us. This cabbala, called also artificial cabbala, to distinguish it from the first kind, or simple tradition, is divided into three sorts. The first, called GEMATRIA, consists in taking letters as figures, or arithmetical numbers, and explaining each word by the arithmetical value of the letters whereof it is composed; which is done various ways: the second is called NOTARICON, and consists either in taking each letter of a word for an entire diction, or in making one entire diction out of the initial letters of many: the third kind, called THEMURAH, that is, CHANGING, consists in changing and transposing the letters of a word; which is done various ways. The generality of the Jews prefer the cabbala to the literal Scripture; comparing the former to the sparkling lustre of a precious stone, and the latter to the fainter glimmering of a candle. The cabbala only differs from masorah, as the latter denotes the science of reading the Scripture; the former, of interpreting it. Both are supposed to have been handed down from generation to generation by oral tradition only, till at length the readings were fixed by the vowels and accents, as the interpretations were by the gemara.

5. Cabbala is also applied to the use, or rather abuse, which visionaries and enthusiasts make of Scripture, for discovering futurity by the study and consideration of the combination of certain words, letters, and numbers, in the sacred writings. All the words, terms, magic figures, numbers, letters, charms, &c, used in the Jewish magic, as also in the hermetical science, are comprised under this species of cabbala; which professes to teach the art of curing diseases, and performing other wonders, by means of certain arrangements of sacred letters and words. But it is only the Christians that call it by this name, on account of the resemblance this art bears to the explications of the Jewish cabbala: for the Jews never used the word CABBALA in any such sense; but ever with the utmost respect and veneration. It is not, however, the magic of the Jews alone which we call cabbala; but the word is also used for any kind of magic.

CABUL, the name which Hiram, king of Tyre, gave to the twenty cities in the land of Galilee, of which Solomon made him a present, in acknowledgment for the great services in building the temple, 1 Kings ix, 31. These cities not being agreeable to Hiram, on viewing them, he called them the land of Cabul, which in the Hebrew tongue denotes DISPLEASING; others take it to signify BINDING or ADHESIVE, from the clayey nature of the soil.

CÆSAR, a title borne by all the Roman emperors till the destruction of the empire. It took its rise from the surname of the first emperor, Caius Julius Cæsar; and this title, by a decree of the senate, all the succeeding emperors were to bear. In Scripture, the reigning emperor is generally mentioned by the name of Cæsar, without expressing any other distinction: so in Matt. xxii, 21, "Render unto Cæsar," &c, Tiberias is meant; and in Acts xxv, 10, "I appeal unto Cæsar," Nero is intended.

CÆSAREA, a city and port of Palestine, built by Herod the Great, and thus called in honour of Augustus Cæsar. It was on the site of the tower of Strato. This city, which was six hundred furlongs from Jerusalem, is often mentioned in the New Testament. Here it was that Herod Agrippa was smitten of the Lord for not giving God the glory, when the people were so extravagant in his praise. Cornelius the centurion, who was baptized by St. Peter, resided here, Acts x, 1, &c; and also Philip the deacon, with his four maiden daughters. At Cæsarea the Prophet Agabus foretold that Paul would be bound and persecuted at Jerusalem. Lastly, the Apostle himself continued two years a prisoner at Cæsarea, till he was conducted to Rome. When Judea was reduced to the state of a Roman province, Cæsarea became the stated residence of the proconsul, which accounts for the circumstance of Paul being carried thither from Jerusalem, to defend himself.

Dr. E. D. Clarke's remarks upon this once celebrated city will be read with interest: "On the 15th of July, 1801, we embarked, after sunset, for Acre, to avail ourselves of the land wind, which blows during the night, at this season of the year. By day break, the next morning, we were off the coast of Cæsarea; and so near with the land that we could very distinctly perceive the appearance of its numerous and extensive ruins. The remains of this city, although still considerable, have long been resorted to as a quarry, whenever building materials are required at Acre. Djezzar Pacha brought from hence the columns of rare and beautiful marble, as well as the other ornaments of his palace, bath, fountain, and mosque at Acre. The place at present is inhabited only by jackals and beasts of prey. As we were becalmed during the night, we heard the cries of these animals until day break. Pococke mentions the curious fact of the former existence of crocodiles in the river of Cæsarea. Perhaps there has not been in the history of the world an example of any city, that in so short a space of time rose to such an extraordinary height of splendour as did this of Cæsarea; or that exhibits a more awful contrast to its former magnificence, by the present desolate appearance of its ruins. Not a single inhabitant remains. Its theatres, once resounding with the shouts of multitudes, echo no other sound than the nightly cries of animals roaming for their prey. Of its gorgeous palaces and temples, enriched with the choicest works of art, and decorated with the most precious marbles, scarcely a trace can be discerned. Within the space of ten years after laying the foundation, from an obscure fortress, it became the most celebrated and flourishing city of all Syria. It was named Cæsarea by Herod, in honour of Augustus, and dedicated by him to that emperor, in the twenty-eighth year of his reign. Upon this occasion, that the ceremony might be rendered illustrious, by a degree of profusion unknown in any former instance, Herod assembled the most skilful musicians, wrestlers, and gladiators from all parts of the world. This solemnity was to be renewed every fifth year. But, as we viewed the ruins of this memorable city, every other circumstance respecting its history was absorbed in the consideration that we were actually beholding the very spot where the scholar of Tarsus, after two years' imprisonment, made that eloquent appeal, in the audience of the king of Judea, which must ever be remembered with piety and delight. In the history of the actions of the holy Apostles, whether we regard the internal evidence of the narrative, or the interest excited by a story so wonderfully appalling to our passions and affections, there is nothing that we call to mind with fuller emotions of sublimity and satisfaction. 'In the demonstration of the Spirit and of power,' the mighty advocate for the Christian faith had before 'reasoned of righteousness, temperance, and judgment to come,' till the Roman governor, Felix, trembled as he spoke. Not all the oratory of Tertullus; not the clamour of his numerous adversaries; not even the countenance of the most profligate of tyrants availed against the firmness and intrepidity of the oracle of God. The judge had trembled before his prisoner; and now a second occasion offered, in which, for the admiration and the triumph of the Christian world, one of the bitterest persecutors of the name of Christ, and a Jew, appeals, in the public tribunal of a large and populous city, to all its chiefs and its rulers, its governor and its king, for the truth of his conversion founded on the highest evidence."

CÆSAREA PHILIPPI was first called Laish or Leshem, Judg. xviii, 7. After it was subdued by the Danites, Judg. v, 29, it received the name of Dan; and is by Heathen writers called Paneas. Philip, the youngest son of Herod the Great, made it the capital of his tetrarchy, enlarged and embellished it, and gave it the name of Cæsarea Philippi. It was situated at the foot of Mount Hermon, near the head of the Jordan; and was about fifty miles from Damascus, and thirty from Tyre. Our Saviour visited and taught in this place, and healed one who was possessed of an evil spirit: here also he gave the memorable rebuke to Peter, Mark viii.

CAIAPHAS, high priest of the Jews, succeeded Simon, son of Camith; and after possessing this dignity nine years, from A. M. 4029 to 4038, he was succeeded by Jonathan, son of Ananas, or Annas. Caiaphas was high priest, A. M. 4037, which was the year of Jesus Christ's death. He married a daughter of Annas, who also is called high priest in the Gospel, because he had long enjoyed that dignity. When the priests deliberated on the seizure and death of Jesus Christ, Caiaphas declared, that there was no room for debate on that matter, "because it was expedient that one man should die for the people, that the whole nation should not perish," John xi, 49, 50. This sentiment was a prophecy, which God suffered to proceed from the mouth of the high priest on this occasion, importing, that the death of Jesus would be for the salvation of the world. When Judas had betrayed Jesus, he was first taken before Annas, who sent him to his son-in-law, Caiaphas, who possibly lived in the same house, John xviii, 24. The priests and doctors of the law there assembled to judge our Saviour, and to condemn him. The depositions of certain false witnesses being insufficient to justify a sentence of death against him, and Jesus continuing silent, Caiaphas, as high priest, said to him, "I adjure thee by the living God, that thou tell us whether thou art the Christ, the Son of God!" To this adjuration, so solemnly made by the superior judge, Jesus answered, "Thou hast said; nevertheless I say unto you, Hereafter shall ye see the Son of man sitting on the right hand of power, and coming in the clouds of heaven." On hearing these words, Caiaphas rent his clothes, saying, "What farther need have we of witnesses? Behold, now you have heard his blasphemy. What think ye?" They answered, "He is worthy of death." And as the power of life and death was not at this time in their hands, but was reserved by the Romans, they conducted him to Pilate, that he might confirm their sentence, and order his execution.

Two years after this, Vitellus, governor of Syria, coming to Jerusalem at the passover, was received very magnificently by the people. As an acknowledgment for this honour, he restored the custody of the high priest's ornaments to the priests, he remitted certain duties raised on the fruits of the earth, and deposed the high priest Caiaphas. From this it appears that Caiaphas had fallen under popular odium, for his deposition was to gratify the people.

CAIN, the eldest son of Adam and Eve. He was the first man who had been a child, and the first man born of woman. For his history, as connected with that of Abel, see ABEL. The curse pronounced upon Cain, on account of his fratricide, is thus expressed: "And the Lord said unto Cain, Where is thy brother Abel? And he said, I know not: am I my brother's keeper? And God said, What hast thou done? The voice of thy brother's blood crieth unto me from the ground. And now art thou cursed from the earth, which hath opened her mouth to receive thy brother's blood from thy hand. When thou tillest it, it shall not henceforth yield unto thee its strength; a fugitive and a vagabond shalt thou be in the earth. And Cain said unto the Lord, My punishment is greater than I can bear. Behold, thou hast driven me out this day from THE FACE OF THE EARTH," meaning, probably, from his own native district, and from the presence of his kindred, "and from THY FACE shall I be hid;" by which he probably intended the divine glory, or Shekinah, whose appearance sanctified the place of primitive worship, and was the pledge of acceptance and protection. The mark set upon Cain "lest any one finding him should kill him," has been variously interpreted. Some have supposed it a change in the colour of his skin, others a certain horror of countenance. The **LXX**. understood the passage to mean, that the Lord gave him a sign, to assure him that his life should be preserved. Whatever it was, its object was not to aggravate, but to mitigate, his punishment, which may intimate that Cain had manifested repentance. Cain, being thus banished from the presence of the Lord, retired into the land of Nod, lying east from the province of Eden. While he dwelt in this country, which is generally understood to be Susiana, or Chusistan, he had a son, whom he named Enoch, in memory of whom he built a city of the same name. This is all we learn from Scripture concerning Cain.

CAKE. See Bread.

CALAH, a city of Assyria, built by Ashur, Gen. x, 12. From it the adjacent country, on the north-east of the Tigris, and south of the Gordian mountains of Armenia, was called Callachene, or Callacine.

CALAMUS, קנה. Exod. xxx, 23; Cantic. iv, 14; Isa. xliii, 24; Jer. vi, 20; Ezek. xxvii, 19. An aromatic reed, growing in moist places in Egypt, in Judea near lake Genezareth, and in several parts of Syria. It grows to about two feet in height; bearing from the root a knotted stalk, quite round, containing in its cavity a soft white pith. The whole is of an agreeable aromatic smell; and the plant is said to scent the air with a fragrance even while growing. When cut down, dried, and powdered, it makes an ingredient in the richest perfumes. It was used for this purpose by the Jews.

Calamus Scriptorius, a reed answering the purpose of a pen to write with. The ancients used styles, to write on tablets covered with wax; but reeds, to write on parchment or papyrus. The Psalmist says, "My tongue is the pen of a ready writer," xlv, 1. The Hebrew signifies rather a style. The third book of Maccabees states, that the writers employed in making a list of the Jews in Egypt, produced their reeds quite worn out. Baruch wrote his prophecies WITH INK, Jer. xxxvi, 4; and, consequently, used reeds; for it does not appear that quills were then used to write with. In third John 13, the Apostle says, he did not design to write with pen (reed) and ink. The Arabians, Persians, Turks, Greeks, and Armenians, to this day, write with reeds or rushes.

CALEB, the son of Jephunneh, of the tribe of Judah, was one of those who accompanied Joshua, when he was deputed by Moses to view the land of Canaan, which the Lord had promised them for an inheritance, Num. xiii. The deputies sent on this occasion were twelve in number, selected one out of each of the tribes, and they performed their commission with great promptitude and skill; they traversed the country in every direction, bringing with them, on their return, some of its finest fruits for the inspection of their brethren. Some of them, however, after making the report of the beauty and goodness of the country, which they described to be a land flowing with milk and honey, added, that the inhabitants of it were remarkable for their strength, while its cities were large and enclosed with walls. These later particulars having excited a spirit of murmuring among the Israelites, Caleb endeavoured to animate their courage by dwelling upon the fertility of the country, and exhorting them to go boldly and take possession of it. Others, however, dissuaded the people from making the attempt, assuring them that they would never make themselves masters of it. We have seen giants there, said they, in comparison of whom we were as grasshoppers; on which the people declared against the project, and intimated their wish to return again into Egypt. Moses and Aaron no sooner heard this than they fell upon their faces before the whole congregation, and Joshua and Caleb rent their clothes, imploring them to take courage and march boldly on; since, if God were with them, they might easily make a conquest of the whole land. So exasperated, however, were the multitude, that they were proceeding to stone Caleb and Joshua, when the glory of the Lord appeared upon the tabernacle, and threatened their extermination. Moses, having fervently interceded for them, the Lord graciously heard his prayer; but though he was pleased not to destroy them immediately, he protested with an oath, that none of those who had murmured against him should see the land of Canaan, but that they should all die in the wilderness. "As for my servant Caleb," it was added, "who hath faithfully followed me, him will I bring into the land, and he shall possess it, he and his children after him," Num. xiv, 1–24. Joshua also obtained a similar exception, verses 30, 38. When Joshua had entered the promised land, and conquered a considerable part of it, Caleb, with the people of his tribe, came to meet him at Gilgal, and finding that he was about to divide the land among the twelve tribes, Caleb petitioned to have the country which was inhabited by the giants allotted to him, on which Joshua blessed him and granted his request. Assisted by a portion of his tribe, he marched against Hebron, and slew the children of Anak: thence he proceeded to Debir, and finding the place almost impregnable, he offered his daughter Achsah in marriage to the hero that should take it. This was done by his nephew Othniel, who in consequence obtained Achsah with a considerable portion also of territory. We are not informed of the particular time or manner of the death of Caleb; but by his three sons, Iru, Elah, and Naam, he had a numerous posterity, who maintained an honourable rank among their brethren. See Num. xiii, xiv, Josh. xiv, 6–15; xv, 13–19; Judges i, 9–15; 1 Chron. iv, 15–20. עגל

CALF, עגל. The young of the ox kind. There is frequent mention in Scripture of calves, because they were made use of commonly in sacrifices. The "fatted calf," mentioned in several places, as in 1 Sam. xxviii, 24, and Luke xv, 23, was stall fed, with special reference to a particular festival or extraordinary sacrifice. The "calves of the lips," mentioned by Hosea, xiv, 2, signify the sacrifices of praise which the captives of Babylon addressed to God, being no longer in a condition to offer sacrifices in his temple. The Septuagint render it the "fruit of the lips;" and their reading is followed by the Syriac, and by the Apostle to the Hebrews, xiii, 15. The "golden calf" was an idol set up and worshipped by the Israelites at the foot of mount Sinai in their passage through the wilderness to the land of Canaan. Having been conducted through the wilderness by a pillar of cloud and fire, which preceded them in their marches, while Moses was receiving the divine commands that cloud covered the mountain, and they probably imagined that it would no longer be their guide; and, therefore, applied to Aaron to make for them a sacred sign or symbol, as other nations had, which might visibly represent God. With this request, preferred tumultuously, and in a menacing manner, Aaron in a moment of weakness complied. The image thus formed is supposed to have been like the Egyptian deity, Apis, which was an ox, an animal used in agriculture, and so a symbol of the god who presided over their fields, or of the productive power of the Deity. The means by which Moses reduced the golden calf to powder, so that when mixed with water he made the people drink it, in contempt, has puzzled commentators. Some understand that he did this by a chymical process, then well known, but now a secret; others, that he beat it into gold leaf, and then separated this into parts so fine, as to be easily potable; others, that he reduced it by filing. The account says, that he took the calf, burned it to powder, and mixed the powder with water; from which it is probable, as several Jewish writers have thought, that the calf was not wholly made of gold, but of wood, covered with a profusion of gold ornaments cast and fashioned for the occasion. For this reason it obtained the epithet golden, as afterward some ornaments of the temple were called, which we know were only overlaid with gold. It would in that case be enough to reduce the wood to powder in the fire, which would also blacken and deface the golden ornaments; but there is no need to suppose they were also reduced to powder. It is plain from Aaron's proclaiming a fast to Jehovah, Exod. xxxii, 4, and from the worship of Jeroboam's calves being so expressly distinguished from that of Baal, 2 Kings x, 28–31, that both Aaron and Jeroboam meant the calves they formed and set up for worship to be emblems of Jehovah. Nevertheless, the inspired Psalmist speaks of Aaron's calf with the utmost abhorrence, and declares that, by worshipping it, they forgat God their Saviour, (see 1 Cor. x, 9,) who had wrought so many miracles for them, and that for this crime God threatened to destroy them, Psalm cvi, 19–24; Exod. xxxii, 10; and St. Stephen calls it plainly εἴδωλον, AN IDOL, Acts vii, 41. As for Jeroboam, after he had, for political reasons, 1 Kings xii, 27, &c, made a schism in the Jewish church, and set up two calves in Dan and Bethel, as objects of worship, he is scarcely ever mentioned in Scripture but with a particular stigma set upon him: "Jeroboam, the son of Nebat, who made Israel to sin."

CALL, to name a person or thing, Acts xi, 26; Rom. vii, 3. 2. To cry to another for help; and hence, to pray. The first passage in the Old Testament in which we meet with this phrase, is Gen. iv, 26, where we read, "Then began men to call on the name of the Lord," or Jehovah; the meaning of which seems to be, that they then first began to worship him in public assemblies. In both the Old and New Testament, to call upon the name of the Lord, imports invoking the true God in prayer, with a confession that he is Jehovah, that is, with an acknowledgment of his essential and incommunicable attributes. In this view the phrase is applied to the worship of Christ.

CALLING, a term in theology, which is taken in a different sense by the advocates and the impugners of the Calvinistic doctrine of grace. By the former it is thus stated: In the golden chain of spiritual blessings which the Apostle enumerates in Rom. viii, 30, originating in the divine predestination, and terminating in the bestowment of eternal glory on the heirs of salvation, that of calling forms an important link. "Moreover, whom he did predestinate, them he also called; and whom he called, them he also glorified." Hence we read of "the called according to his purpose," Rom. viii, 28. There is indeed a universal call of the Gospel to all men; for wherever it comes it is the voice of God to those who hear it, calling them to repent and believe the divine testimony unto the salvation of their souls; and it leaves them inexcusable in rejecting it, John iii, 14–19; but this universal call is not inseparably connected with salvation; for it is in reference to it that Christ says, "Many are called, but few are chosen," Matt. xxii, 14. But the Scripture also speaks of a calling which is effectual, and which consequently is more than the outward ministry of the word; yea, more than some of its partial and temporary effects upon many who hear it, for it is always ascribed to God's making his word effectual through the enlightening and sanctifying influences of his Holy Spirit. Thus it is said, "Paul may plant, and Apollos water, but God giveth the increase," 1 Cor. iii, 6, 7. Again, he is said to have "opened the heart of Lydia, that she attended to the doctrine of Paul," Acts xvi, 14. "No man can come unto Christ, except the Father draw him," John vi, 44. Hence faith is said to be the gift of God, Eph. ii, 8; Phil. i, 29. The Spirit takes of the things of Christ and shows them to men, John xvi, 14; and thus opens their eyes, turning them from darkness to light, and from the power of Satan unto God, Acts xxvi, 18. And so God saves his people, not by works of righteousness which they have done, but according to his mercy, by the washing of regeneration and renewing of the Holy Spirit, Titus iii, 5. Thus they are saved, and called with a holy calling, not according to their works, but according to the divine purpose and grace which was given them in Christ Jesus before the world began, 2 Tim. i, 9.

2. To this it is replied, that this whole statement respecting a believer's calling is without any support from the Scriptures, and is either a misunderstanding, or a misapplication of their sense. "To call" signifies to invite to the blessings of the Gospel, to offer salvation through Christ, either by God himself, or, under his appointment, by his servants; and in the parable of the marriage of the king's son, Matt. xxii, 1–14, which appears to have given rise, in many instances, to the use of this term in the Epistles, we have three descriptions of "called" or invited persons. First, the disobedient, who would not come in at the call, but made light of it. Second, the class of persons represented by the man who, when the king came in to see his guests, had not on the wedding garment; and with respect to whom our Lord makes the general remark, "For many are called, but few are chosen;" so that the persons thus represented by this individual culprit were not only "called," but actually came into the company. Third, the approved guests; those who were both called and chosen. As far as the simple calling or invitation is concerned, all these three classes stood upon equal ground--all were invited; and it depended upon their choice and conduct whether they embraced the invitation, and were admitted as guests. We have nothing here to countenance the notion of what is termed "effectual calling." This implies an irresistible influence exerted upon all the approved guests, but withheld from the disobedient, who could not, therefore, be otherwise than disobedient; or at most could only come in without that wedding garment, which it was never put into their power to take out of the king's wardrobe; and the want of which would necessarily exclude them, if not from the church on earth, yet from the church in heaven. The doctrine of Christ's parables is in entire contradiction to this notion of irresistible influence; for they who refused, and they who complied but partially with the calling, are represented, not merely as being left without the benefit of the feast, but as incurring additional guilt and condemnation for refusing the invitation. It is to this offer of salvation by the Gospel, this invitation to spiritual and eternal benefits, that St. Peter appears to refer, when he says, "For the PROMISE is unto you and to your children, and to all that are afar off, even as many as the Lord our God shall CALL," Acts ii, 39; a passage which declares "the promise" to be as extensive as the "calling;" in other words, as the offer or invitation. To this also St. Paul refers, Rom. i, 5, 6: "By whom we have received grace and Apostleship, for obedience to the faith among all nations, for his name;" that is, to publish his Gospel, in order to bring all nations to the obedience of faith; "among whom are ye also the CALLED of Jesus Christ;" you at Rome have heard the Gospel, and have been invited to salvation in consequence of this design. This promulgation of the Gospel, by the personal ministry of the Apostle, under the name of CALLING, is also referred to in Gal. i, 6: "I marvel that ye are so soon removed from him that CALLED YOU into the grace of Christ," obviously meaning, that it was he himself who had called them, by his preaching, to embrace the grace of Christ. So also in chap. v, 13: "For, brethren, ye have been CALLED unto liberty." Again: 1 Thess. ii, 12: "That ye would walk worthy of God, who hath CALLED you," invited you, "to his kingdom and glory."

3. In our Lord's parable it will also be observed, that the persons called are not invited as separate individuals to partake of solitary blessings; but they are called to "a feast," into a company or society, before whom the banquet is spread. The full revelation of the transfer of the visible church of Christ from Jews by birth, to believers of all nations, was not, however, then made. When this branch of the evangelic system was fully revealed to the Apostles, and taught by them to others, that part of the meaning of our Lord's parable which was not at first developed was more particularly discovered to his inspired followers. The calling of guests to the evangelical feast, we then more fully learn, was not the mere calling of men to partake of spiritual benefits; but calling them also to form a spiritual society composed of Jews and Gentiles, the believing men of all nations; to have a common fellowship in these blessings, and to be formed into this fellowship for the purpose of increasing their number, and diffusing the benefits of salvation among the people or nation to which they respectively belonged. The invitation, "the calling," of the first preachers was to all who heard them in Rome, in Ephesus, in Corinth, and other places; and those who embraced it, and joined themselves to the church by faith, baptism, and continued public profession, were named, especially and eminently, "the called," because of their obedience to the invitation. They not only put in their claim to the blessings of Christianity individually, but became members of the new church, that spiritual society of believers which God now visibly owned as his people. As they were thus called into a common fellowship by the Gospel, this is sometimes termed their "vocation;" as the object of this church state was to promote "holiness," it is termed a "holy vocation;" as sanctity was required of the members, they are said to have been "called to be saints;" as the final result was, through the mercy of God, to be eternal life, we hear of "the hope of their calling," and of their being "called to his eternal glory by Christ Jesus."

4. These views will abundantly explain the various passages in which the term CALLING occurs in the Epistles: "Even us whom he hath CALLED, not of the Jews only, but also of the Gentiles," Rom. ix, 24; that is, whom he hath made members of his church through faith. "But unto them which are CALLED, both Jews and Greeks, Christ the power of God, and the wisdom of God;" the wisdom and

efficacy of the Gospel being, of course, acknowledged in their very profession of Christ, in opposition to those to whom the preaching of "Christ crucified" was "a stumbling block," and "foolishness," 1 Cor. i, 24. "Is any man CALLED," (brought to acknowledge Christ, and to become a member of his church,) "being circumcised? let him not become uncircumcised. Is any CALLED in uncircumcision? let him not be circumcised," 1 Cor. vii, 18. "That ye walk worthy of the VOCATION, wherewith ye are called. There is one body, and one Spirit, even as ye are CALLED in one hope of your calling," Eph. iv, 1, 4. "That ye would walk worthy of God, who hath CALLED you to his kingdom and glory," 1 Thess. ii, 12. "Through sanctification of the Spirit, and belief of the truth, whereunto he CALLED you by our Gospel, to the obtaining of the glory of our Lord Jesus Christ," 2 Thess. ii, 13, 14. "Who hath saved us and CALLED us with a holy calling; not according to our works, but according to his own purpose and grace, which was given us in Christ Jesus before the world began; but is now made manifest by the appearing of our Saviour Jesus Christ," 2 Tim. i, 9, 10. On this passage we may remark, that the "calling," and the "purpose" mentioned in it, must of necessity be interpreted to refer to the establishment of the church on the principle of faith, so that it might include men of all nations; and not, as formerly, be restricted to natural descent. For PERSONAL ELECTION, and a purpose of EFFECTUAL PERSONAL CALLING, could not have been hidden till manifested by the "appearing of Christ;" since every instance of true conversion to God in any age prior to the appearing of Christ, would be as much a manifestation of eternal election, and an instance of personal effectual calling, according to the Calvinistic scheme, as it was after the appearance of Christ. The Apostle is speaking of a purpose of God, which was kept SECRET till revealed by the Christian system; and, from various other parallel passages, we learn that this secret, this "mystery," as he often calls it, was the union of the Jews and Gentiles in "one body," or church, by faith.

5. In none of these passages is the doctrine of the exclusive calling of a set number of men contained; and the synod of Dort, as though they felt this, only attempt to INFER the doctrine from a text already quoted; but which we will now more fully notice: "Whom he did predestinate, them he also CALLED; and whom he CALLED, them he also justified; and whom he justified, them he also glorified," Rom. viii, 30. This is the text on which the Calvinists chiefly rest their doctrine of effectual calling; and tracing it, as they say, through its steps and links, they conclude, that a set and determinate number of persons having been predestinated unto salvation, this set number only are CALLED EFFECTUALLY, then justified, and finally glorified. But this passage was evidently nothing to the purpose, unless it had spoken of a set and determinate number of men as predestinated and called, independent of any consideration of their faith and obedience; which number as being determinate, would, by consequence exclude the rest. The context declares that those who are foreknown, and predestinated to eternal glory, are true believers, those who "love God," as stated in a subsequent verse; for of such only the Apostle speaks; and when he adds, "Moreover, whom he did predestinate, them he also called; and whom he called, them he also justified; and whom he justified, them he also glorified;" he shows in particular how the divine purpose to glorify believers is carried into effect, through all its stages. The great instrument of bringing men to "love God" is the Gospel; they are, therefore, CALLED, invited by it, to this state and benefit; the calling being obeyed, they are JUSTIFIED; and being justified, and continuing in that state of grace, they are GLORIFIED. Nothing, however, is here said to favour the conclusion, that many others who were CALLED by the Gospel, but refused, might not have been justified and glorified as well as they; nothing to distinguish this calling into common and effectual: and the very guilt which those are every where represented as contracting who despised the Gospel calling, shows that they reject a grace which is sufficient, and sincerely intended, to save them.

CALNEH, a city in the land of Shinar, built by Nimrod, and one of the cities mentioned Genesis x, 10, as belonging to his kingdom. It is believed to be the same with Calno, mentioned in Isa. x, 9. It is said by the Chaldee interpreters, as also by Eusebius and Jerom, to be the same with Ctesiphon, standing upon the Tigris, about three miles distant from Seleucia, and that for some time it was the capital city of the Parthians. Bochart, Wells, and Michaëlis, agree in this opinion.

CALVARY, or, as it is called in Hebrew, GOLGOTHA, "a skull," or "place of skulls," supposed to be thus denominated from the similitude it bore to the figure of a skull or man's head, or from its being a place of burial. It was a small eminence or hill to the north of Mount Sion, and to the west of old Jerusalem, upon which our Lord was crucified. The ancient summit of Calvary has been much altered, by reducing its level in some parts, and raising it in others, in order to bring it within the area of a large and irregular building, called "The Church of the Holy Sepulchre," which now occupies its site. But in doing this, care has been taken that none of the parts connected with the crucifixion should suffer any alteration. The same building also encloses within its spacious walls several other places reputed sacred. The places which claim the chief attraction of the Christian visitant of this church, and those only perhaps which can be relied on, are, the spot on which the crucifixion took place, and the sepulchre in which our Lord was afterward laid. The first has been preserved without mutilation: being a piece of ground about ten yards square, in its original position; and so high above the common floor of the church, that there are, according to Chateaubriand, twenty-one steps to ascend up to it. Mr. Buckingham describes the present mount as a rock, the summit of which is ascended by a steep flight of eighteen or twenty steps from the common level of the church, which is equal with that of the street without; and beside this, there is a descent of thirty steps, from the level of the church, into the chapel of St. Helena, and by eleven more to the place where the cross was said to be found. On this little mount is shown the hole in which the cross was fixed; and near it the position of the crosses of the two thieves: one, the penitent, on the north; and the other on the south. Here, also, is shown a cleft in the rock, said to have been caused by the earthquake which happened at the crucifixion. The sepulchre, distant, according to Mr. Jolliffe, forty-three yards from the cross, presents rather a singular and unexpected appearance to a stranger; who, for such a place, would naturally expect to find an excavation in the ground, instead of which, he perceives it altogether raised, as if artificially, above its level. The truth is, that in the alterations which were made on Calvary, to bring all the principal places within the projected church, the earth around the sepulchre was dug away; so that, what was originally a cave in the earth has now the appearance of a closet or grotto above ground. The sepulchre itself is about six feet square and eight high. There is a solid block of the stone left in excavating the rock, about two feet and a half from the floor, and running along the whole of the inner side; on which the body of our Lord is said to have been laid. This, as well as the rest of the sepulchre, is now faced with marble: partly from the false taste which prevailed in the early ages of Christianity, in disguising with profuse and ill-suited embellishments the spots rendered memorable in the history of its Founder; and partly, perhaps, to preserve it from the depredations of the visitants. This description of the holy sepulchre will but ill accord with the notions entertained by some English readers of a grave; but a cave or grotto, thus excavated in rocky ground, on the side of a hill, was the common receptacle for the dead among the eastern nations. Such was the tomb of Christ; such that of Lazarus; and such are the sepulchres still found in Judea and the east. It may be useful farther to observe, that it was customary with Jews of property to provide a sepulchre of this kind on their own ground, as the place of their interment after death; and it appears that Calvary itself, or the ground immediately around it, was occupied with gardens; one of which belonged to Joseph of Arimathea, who had then recently caused a new sepulchre to be made for himself. It was this sepulchre, so close at hand, and so appropriate, which he resigned for the use of our Lord; little thinking perhaps, at the time, how soon it would again be left vacant for its original purpose by his glorious resurrection.

CALVINISM, that scheme of doctrine on predestination and grace, which was taught by Calvin, the celebrated reformer, in the early part of the sixteenth century. His opinions are largely opened in the third book of his "Institutes:" "Predestination we call the eternal decree of God; by which he hath determined in himself what he would have to become of every individual of mankind. For they are not all created with similar destiny; but eternal life is foreordained for some, and eternal damnation for others. Every man, therefore, being CREATED FOR ONE OR OTHER OF THESE ENDS, we say, he is predestinated, either to life, or to death." After having spoken of the election of the race of Abraham, and then of particular branches of that race, he proceeds: "Though it is sufficiently clear, that God, in his secret counsel, freely chooses whom he will, and rejects others, his gratuitous election is but half displayed till we come to particular individuals, to whom God not only offers salvation, but ASSIGNS it in such a manner that the certainty of the effect is liable to no suspense or doubt." He sums up the chapter, in which he thus generally states the doctrine, in these words: "In conformity, therefore, to the clear doctrine of the Scripture, we assert, that, by an eternal and immutable counsel, God hath once for all determined both whom he would admit to salvation, and whom he would condemn to destruction. We affirm that this counsel, as far as concerns the elect, is founded on his gratuitous mercy, totally irrespective of human merit; but that to those whom he devotes to condemnation, the gate of life is closed by a just and irreprehensible, but INCOMPREHENSIBLE, judgment. In the elect, we consider calling as an evidence of election; and justification as another token of its manifestation, till they arrive in glory, which constitutes its completion. As God seals his elect by vocation and justification, so by EXCLUDING the reprobate from the knowledge of his name, and sanctification of his Spirit, he affords another indication of the judgment that awaits them," chap. 21, book iii.

2. In the commencement of the following chapter he thus rejects the notion that predestination is to be understood as resulting from God's foreknowledge of what would be the conduct of either the elect or the reprobate: "It is a notion commonly entertained, that God, foreseeing what would be the respective merits of every individual, makes a correspondent distinction between different persons; that he adopts as his children such as he foreknows will be deserving of his grace; and devotes to the damnation of death others, whose dispositions he sees will be inclined to wickedness and impiety. Thus they not only obscure election by covering it with the veil of foreknowledge, but pretend that it originates in another cause," book iii, chap. 22. Consistently with this, he a little farther on asserts, that election does not flow from holiness, but holiness from election: "For when it is said, that the faithful are elected that they should be holy, it is fully implied, that the holiness they were in future to possess had its origin in election." He proceeds to quote the example of Jacob and Esau, as loved and hated before they had done good or evil, to show that the only reason of election and reprobation is to be placed in God's "secret counsel." He will not allow the future wickedness of the reprobate to have been considered in the decree of their rejection, any more than the righteousness of the elect, as influencing their better fate: "'God hath mercy on whom he will have mercy, and whom he will he hardeneth.' You see how he (the Apostle) attributes BOTH to the MERE WILL of God. If, therefore, we can assign no reason why he grants mercy to his people but because such is his pleasure, neither shall we find any other cause but HIS WILL for the reprobation of others. For when God is said to harden, or show mercy to whom he pleases, men are taught, by this declaration, to seek NO CAUSE BESIDE HIS WILL." (*Ibid.*) "Many, indeed, as if they wished to avert odium from God, admit election in such a way as to deny that any one is reprobated.

But this is puerile and absurd; because election itself could not exist, without being opposed to reprobation;--whom God PASSES BY HE THEREFORE REPROBATES; and FROM NO OTHER CAUSE than his determination to exclude them from the inheritance which he predestines for his children," book iii, chap. xxiii.

3. This is the scheme of predestination as exhibited by Calvin; and to the objection taken from justice, he replies, "They" (the objectors) "inquire by what right the Lord is angry with his creatures who had not provoked him by any previous offence; for that to devote to destruction whom he pleases, is more like the caprice of a tyrant, than the lawful sentence of a judge. If such thoughts ever enter into the minds of pious men, they will be sufficiently enabled to break their violence by this one consideration, how exceedingly presumptuous it is, only to inquire into the causes of the divine WILL; which is, in fact, and is justly entitled to be, the CAUSE of every thing that exists. For if it has any cause, then there must be something antecedent on which it depends, which it is impious to suppose. For the will of God is the highest rule of justice; so that what he wills must be considered just, for this very reason, because he wills it." Thus he assumes the very thing in dispute, that God has willed the destruction of any part of the human race, "for no other cause than because he WILLS IT;" of which assumption there is not only not a word of proof in Scripture; but, on the contrary, it ascribes the death of him that dieth to his own will, and not to the will of God. 2. He pretends that to assign any CAUSE to the divine will is to suppose something antecedent to, something above God, and therefore "impious;" as if we might not suppose something IN God to be the rule of his will, not only without any impiety, but with truth and piety; as, for instance, his perfect wisdom, holiness, justice, and goodness; or, in other words, to believe the exercise of his will to flow from the perfection of his whole nature; a much more honourable and Scriptural view of the will of God than that which subjects it to no rule, even though it should arise from the nature of God himself. 3. When he calls the will of God, "the highest rule of justice," beyond which we cannot push our inquiries, he confounds the will of God, as a rule of justice TO US, and as a rule to himself. This will is our rule; yet even then, because we know that it is the will of a perfect being: but when Calvin represents MERE WILL as constituting God's own rule of justice, he shuts out knowledge, discrimination of the nature of things, and holiness; which is saying something very different from that great truth, that God cannot will any thing but what is perfectly just. It is to say that blind will, will which has no respect to any thing but itself, is God's highest rule of justice; a position which, if presented abstractedly, many Calvinists themselves would spurn. 4. He determines the question by the authority of his own metaphysics, and totally forgets that one DICTUM of inspiration overturns his whole theory,--God "WILLETH all men to be saved;" a declaration, which in no part of the sacred volume is opposed or limited by any contrary declaration.

4. Calvin was not, however, content thus to leave the matter; but resorts to an argument, in which he has been generally followed by those who have adopted his system with some mitigations: "As we are all corrupted by sin, we must necessarily be odious to God, and that not from tyrannical cruelty, but in the most EQUITABLE ESTIMATION of justice. If all whom the Lord predestinates to death are, in their natural condition, liable to the sentence of death, what injustice do they complain of receiving from him?" To this Calvin very fairly states the obvious rejoinder made in his day; and which the common sense of mankind will always make,--"They object, Were they not by the decree of God antecedently predestinated to that corruption which is now stated as the CAUSE of their condemnation? When they perish in their corruption, therefore, they only suffer the punishment of that misery into which, in consequence of his predestination, Adam fell, and precipitated his posterity with him." The manner in which Calvin attempts to meet this objection, shows how truly unanswerable it is upon his system. "I confess," says he, "indeed, that all the descendants of Adam fell, BY THE DIVINE WILL, into that miserable condition in which they are now involved; and this is what I asserted from the beginning, that we must always return at last TO THE SOVEREIGN DETERMINATION OF GOD'S WILL; the cause of which is hidden in himself. But it follows not, therefore, that God is liable to this reproach; for we will answer them in the language of Paul, 'O man, who art thou that repliest against God? Shall the thing formed say to him that formed it, Why hast thou made me thus'" That is, in order to escape the pinch of the objection, he assumes that St. Paul affirms that God has "formed" a part of the human race for eternal misery; and that, by imposing silence upon them, he intended to declare that this proceeding in God was just. Now the passage may be proved from its context to have no respect to the eternal state of men at all; but, if that were less obvious, it gives no answer to the objection; and we are brought round again, as indeed he confesses, to his former, and indeed only, argument, that the whole matter as he states it, is to be referred back to the divine will; which will, though perfectly arbitrary, is, as he contends, the highest rule of justice: "I say, with Augustine, that the Lord created those whom he certainly foreknew would fall into destruction; and that this was actually so, because HE WILLED IT; but of his will, it belongs not to us to demand the reason, which we are incapable of comprehending; nor is it reasonable, that the divine will should be made the subject of controversy with us, which is only another name for the highest rule of justice." Thus he shuts us out from pursuing the argument. But the evasion proves the objection unanswerable. For if all is to be resolved into the mere will of God as to the destruction of the reprobate; if they were created for this purpose, as Calvin expressly affirms; if they fell into their corruption in pursuance of God's determination; if, as he had said before, "God passes them by, and reprobates them, FROM NO OTHER cause than his determination to exclude them from the inheritance of his children," why refer to their natural corruption at all, and their being odious to God in that state, since the same reason is given for their

corruption as for their reprobation?--not any fault of theirs; but the mere will of God, "the reprobation hidden in his secret counsel," and that not grounded on the visible and tangible fact of their demerit. Thus the election taught by Calvin is not the choice of some persons to peculiar grace from the whole mass, equally deserving of punishment; (though this is a sophism;) since, in that case, the decree of reprobation would rest upon God's foreknowledge of those passed by as corrupt and guilty, which notion he rejects: "For since God foresees future events only in consequence of HIS DECREE THAT THEY SHALL HAPPEN, it is useless to contend about foreknowledge, while it is evident that all things come to pass rather by ORDINATION AND DECREE." "It is a HORRIBLE DECREE, I confess; but no one can deny that God foreknew the future fate of man before he created him; and that he did foreknow it, because it was APPOINTED by his own decree." Agreeably to this, he repudiates the distinction between will and permission: "For what reason shall we assign for his permitting it, but because it is his will? It is NOT PROBABLE, however, that man procured his own destruction by the mere PERMISSION, and without any APPOINTMENT, of God."

5. With this doctrine he again attempts to reconcile the demerit of men: "Their perdition depends on the divine predestination in such a manner, that the CAUSE and MATTER of it are found IN THEMSELVES. For the first man fell because the Lord had determined it should so happen. The reason of this determination is unknown to us.--Man, therefore, falls according to the APPOINTMENT of divine providence; but he falls by HIS OWN FAULT. The Lord had a little before pronounced every thing that he had made to be 'very good.' Whence, then, comes the depravity of man to revolt from his God? Lest it should be thought to come from creation, God approved and commended what had proceeded from himself. By his own wickedness, therefore, man corrupted the nature he had received pure from the Lord, and by his fall he drew all his posterity with him to destruction." It is in this way that Calvin attempts to avoid the charge of making God the author of sin. But how God should not merely PERMIT the defection of the first man, but APPOINT it, and WILL it, and that his will should be the "necessity of things," (all which he had before asserted,) and yet that Deity should not be the author of that which he APPOINTED, WILLED, and IMPOSED A NECESSITY UPON, would be rather a delicate inquiry. It is enough that Calvin rejects the impious doctrine; and even though his principles directly lead to it, since he has put in his disclaimer, he is entitled to be exempted from the charge;--but the logical conclusion is inevitable.

6. In much the same manner he contends that the necessity of sinning is laid upon the reprobate by the ordination of God, and yet denies God to be the author of their sinful acts, since the corruption of men was derived from Adam, by his own fault, and not from God. He exhorts us "rather to contemplate the evident cause of condemnation, which is nearer to us, in the corrupt nature of mankind, than search after a hidden and altogether incomprehensible one, in the predestination of God." "For though, by the eternal providence of God, man was CREATED to that misery to which he is subject, yet the GROUND of it he has derived from himself, not God; since he is thus ruined, solely in consequence of his having degenerated from the pure creation of God to vicious and impure depravity." Thus, almost in the same breath, he affirms that men became reprobate from no other cause than "the will of God," and his "sovereign determination;" that men have no reason "to expostulate with God, if they are predestinated to eternal death, without ANY DEMERIT of their own, merely by his sovereign will;"--and then, that the corrupt nature of mankind is the EVIDENT and NEARER cause of condemnation; (which cause, however, was still a matter of "appointment," and "ordination," not "permission;") and that man is "ruined solely in consequence of his having degenerated from the pure state in which God created him." These propositions manifestly fight with each other; for if the reason of reprobation be laid in man's corruption, it cannot be laid in the mere will and sovereign determination of God, unless we suppose him to be the author of sin. It is this offensive doctrine only, which can reconcile them. For if God so wills, and appoints, and necessitates the depravity of man, as to be the author of it, then there is no inconsistency in saying that the ruin of the reprobate is both from the mere will of God, and from the corruption of their nature, which is but the result of that will. The one is then, as Calvin states, the "evident and nearer cause," the other the more remote and hidden one; yet they have the same source, and are substantially acts of the same will. But if it be denied that God is, in any sense, the author of evil, and if sin is from man alone, then is the "corruption of nature" the effect of an independent will; and if this corruption be the "real source," as he says, of men's condemnation, then the decree of reprobation rests not upon the sovereign will of God, as its sole cause, which he affirms; but upon a cause dependent on the will of the first man: but as this is denied, then the other must follow. Calvin himself, indeed, contends for the perfect concurrence of these proximate and remote causes, although in point of fact, to have been perfectly consistent with himself, he ought rather to have called the MERE WILL OF GOD THE CAUSE of the decree of reprobation, and the corruption of man THE MEANS by which it is carried into effect:--language which he sanctions, and which many of his followers have not scrupled to adopt.

7. So certainly does this opinion involve in it the consequences, that in sin man is the instrument, and God the actor, that it cannot be maintained, as stated by Calvin, without this conclusion. For as two causes of reprobation are expressly laid down, they must be either opposed to each other, or be consenting. If they are opposed, the scheme is given up; if consenting, then are both reprobation and human corruption the results of the same will, the same decree, and necessity. It would be trifling to say that the decree does not influence; for if so, it is no decree in Calvin's sense, who understands the decree of God, as the foregoing extracts and the whole third book of his

"Institutes" plainly show, as APPOINTING what shall be, and by that appointment making it NECESSARY. Otherwise, he could not reject the distinction between will and permission, and avow the sentiment of St. Augustine, "that the will of God is the necessity of things; and that what he has willed will necessarily come to pass," book iii, chap. 23, sec. 8. So, in writing to Castellio, he makes the sin of Adam the result of an act of God: "You say Adam fell by his free will. I except against it. That he might not fall, he stood in need of that strength and constancy with which God armeth all the elect, as long as he will keep them blameless. Whom God has elected, he props up with an invincible power unto perseverance. Why did he not afford this to Adam, if he would have had him stand in his integrity?" And with this view of necessity, as resulting from the decree of God, the immediate followers of Calvin coincided; the end and the means, as to the elect, and as to the reprobate, are equally fixed by the decree, and are both to be traced to the APPOINTING and ORDAINING will of God. On such a scheme it is therefore worse than trifling to attempt to make out a case of justice in favour of this assumed divine procedure, by alleging the corruption and guilt of man: a point which, indeed, Calvin himself, in fact, gives up when he says, "That the reprobate obey not the word of God, when made known to them, is justly imputed to the wickedness and depravity of their hearts, PROVIDED IT BE AT THE SAME TIME STATED, that they are abandoned to this depravity, because they have been raised up by a just but INSCRUTABLE judgment of God, to display his glory in their condemnation."

8. It was by availing themselves of the ineffectual struggles of Calvin to give some colour of justice to his reprobating decree by fixing upon the corruption of man as a cause of reprobation, that some of his followers endeavoured, in the very teeth of his own express words, to reduce his system to sublapsarianism. This was attempted by Amyraldus; who was answered by Curcellæus, in his tract "*De Jure Dei in Creaturas.*" This last writer, partly by several of the same passages we have given above from Calvin's Institutes, and by extracts from his other writings, proves that Calvin did by no means consider man, as fallen, to be the object of reprobation; but man not yet created; man as to be created, and so reprobated, under no consideration in the divine mind of his fall or actual guilt, except as CONSEQUENCES of an eternal preterition of the PERSONS of the reprobate, resolvable only into the sovereign pleasure of God. The references he makes to men as corrupt, and to their corrupt state as the proximate cause of their rejection, are all manifestly used to parry off rather than to answer objections, and somewhat to moderate and soften, as Curcellæus observes, the harsher parts of his system. And, indeed, for what reason are we so often brought back to that unfailing refuge of Calvin, "the presumption and wickedness of replying against God?" For if reprobation be a matter of human DESERT, it cannot be a mystery; if it be adequate punishment for an adequate fault, there is no need to urge it upon us to bow with submission to an unexplained sovereignty. We may add, there is no need to speak of a remote or first cause of reprobation, if the PROXIMATE cause will explain the whole case; and that Calvin's continual reference to God's SECRET COUNSEL, and WILL, and INSCRUTABLE JUDGMENT, could have no aptness to his argument. Among English divines, Dr. Twisse has sufficiently defended Calvin from the CHARGE, as he esteems it, of sublapsarianism; and, whatever merit Twisse's own supralapsarian creed may have, his argument on this point is unanswerable.

9. As it is not intended here to enter into this controversy, on which multitudes of books have been written, and the leading authors are known almost to every one, the above may be sufficient to convey a just notion of Calvin's own opinions. After these subjects had long agitated the reformed churches, and given rise to several modifications of Calvin's original scheme, and to numerous writings in refutation of it, the synod of Dort digested the whole into five articles from which arose the celebrated controversy on the FIVE POINTS. These articles, as being the standard of what is generally called strict Calvinism, are, in substance, as follows:--

(1.) "OF PREDESTINATION. As all men have sinned in Adam, and have become exposed to the curse and eternal death, God would have done no injustice to any one, if he had determined to leave the whole human race under sin and the curse, and to condemn them on account of sin; according to those words of the Apostle, 'All the world is become guilty before God,' Rom. iii, 19, 23; vi, 23. That some, IN TIME, have faith given them by God, and others have it not given, proceeds from his eternal decree; for 'known unto God are all his works from the beginning,' &c, Acts xv, 18; Eph. i, 11. According to which decree, he graciously softens the hearts of the elect, however hard, and he bends them to believe; but the non-elect he leaves, in his judgment, to their own perversity and hardness. And here, especially, a deep discrimination, at the same time both merciful and just; a discrimination of men equally lost, opens itself to us; or that decree of election and reprobation which is revealed in the word of God; which, as perverse, impure, and unstable persons do wrest to their own destruction, so it affords ineffable consolation to holy and pious souls. But election is the immutable purpose of God; by which, before the foundations of the world were laid, he chose, out of the whole human race, fallen by their own fault from their primeval integrity into sin and destruction, according to the most free GOOD PLEASURE of his own will, and of MERE GRACE, a certain number of men, neither better nor worthier than others, but lying in the same misery with the rest, to salvation in Christ; whom he had, even from eternity, constituted Mediator and head of all the elect, and the foundation of salvation; and therefore he decreed to give them unto him to be saved, and effectually to call and draw them into communion with him, by his word and Spirit; or he decreed himself to give unto them true faith, to justify, to sanctify, and at length powerfully to glorify them, &c, Eph. i, 4–6; Rom. viii, 30. This same election is not made from any FORESEEN faith, obedience of faith, holiness, or any other good quality and disposition, as a PRE-REQUISITE cause or condition in the man who should be elected, &c. 'He hath chosen us,' not because we WERE, but 'that we MIGHT be, holy,' &c, Eph. i, 4; Rom. ix, 11–13; Acts xiii, 48. Moreover, Holy Scripture doth illustrate and commend to us this eternal and free grace of our election, in this more especially, that it doth testify all men not to be elected; but that some are non-elect, or PASSED BY, in the eternal election of God, whom truly God, from most free, just, irreprehensible, and immutable good pleasure, decreed to leave in the COMMON MISERY into which they had, by THEIR OWN FAULT, cast themselves; and not to bestow on them living faith, and the grace of conversion; but having been left in their own ways, and under just judgment, at length, not only on account of their unbelief, but also of all their other sins, to condemn and eternally punish them, to the manifestation of his own justice. And this is the decree of REPROBATION, which determines that God is, in no wise, the author of sin, (which, to be thought of, is blasphemy,) but a tremendous, incomprehensible, just judge, and avenger."

(2.) "OF THE DEATH OF CHRIST." Passing over, for brevity's sake, what is said of the necessity of atonement, in order to pardon, and of Christ having offered that atonement and satisfaction, it is added, "This death of the Son of God is a single and most perfect sacrifice and satisfaction for sins; of infinite value and price, abundantly sufficient to expiate the sins of the whole world; but because many who are called by the Gospel do not repent, nor believe in Christ, but perish in unbelief; this doth not arise from defect or insufficiency of the sacrifice offered by Christ upon the cross, but from their own fault. God willed that Christ, through the blood of the cross, should, out of every people, tribe, nation, and language, EFFICACIOUSLY redeem all those, and those ONLY, who were from eternity chosen to salvation, and given to him by the Father; that he should confer on them the gift of faith," &c.

(3.) "OF MAN'S CORRUPTION, &C. All men are conceived in sin, and born the children of wrath, indisposed (INEPTI) to all saving good, propense to evil, dead in sin, and the slaves of sin; and without the regenerating grace of the Holy Spirit, they neither are willing nor able to return to God, to correct their depraved nature, or to dispose themselves to the correction of it."

(4.) "OF GRACE AND FREE WILL. But in like manner as, by the fall, man does not cease to be man, endowed with intellect and will; neither hath sin, which hath pervaded the whole human race, taken away the nature of the human species, but it hath depraved and spiritually stained it; so that even this divine grace of regeneration does not act upon men like stocks and trees, nor take away the properties of his will; or violently compel it, while unwilling; but it spiritually quickens, heals, corrects, and sweetly, and at the same time powerfully, inclines it; so that whereas before it was wholly governed by the rebellion and resistance of the FLESH, now prompt and sincere obedience of the Spirit may begin to reign; in which the renewal of our spiritual will, and our liberty, truly consist; in which manner, (or for which reason,) unless the admirable Author of all good should work in us, there could be no hope to man of rising from the fall by that FREE WILL, by which, when standing, he fell into ruin."

(5.) "ON PERSEVERANCE. God, who is rich in mercy, from his immutable purpose of election, does not wholly take away his Holy Spirit from his own, even in lamentable falls; nor does he so permit them to glide down, (PROLABI,) that they should fall from the grace of adoption, and the state of justification; or commit the 'sin unto death,' or against the Holy Spirit; that, being deserted by him, they should cast themselves headlong into eternal destruction. So that not by their own merits or strength, but by the gratuitous mercy of God, they obtain it, that they neither TOTALLY FALL from faith and grace, nor FINALLY CONTINUE in their falls and perish."

10. The controversy on these difficult subjects was not decided by the decrees of the synod of Dort, which, it will be seen under that article, were purposely drawn up in a politic and wary manner, so as to quadrate with the opinions, and not to outrage the feelings, of any grade of Calvinists. Prior to the convention of that celebrated assembly, the doctrines of Calvin had been refined upon and incautiously carried out to some of their legitimate consequences, in a manner almost without precedent, except that of the Mohammedan doctors on the absolute fate which holds a distinguished place in the Koran. Several of the brightest and most acute wits in Europe occupied themselves in sublimating to the height of extravagance the two kindred branches of predestination,--the eternal and absolute election of certain men to everlasting glory, and the reprobation of the rest of mankind to endless punishment, without regard in the divine mind to the foreseen faith of one class or to the foreseen unbelief of the other. This course was commenced by Beza, the contemporary and successor of Calvin, who possessed neither his genius nor his caution; and his writings contain several rash assertions on these points, which, it is probable, would never have obtained the approbation of his departed friend and instructer. Zanchius, with true Italian astuteness, carried on this process of refinement in high style; and his predestinarian IMPROVEMENTS were only equalled by those of Piscator, Pareus, Keckerman, Hommius, Kimedontius, Polanus, Sturmius, Danæus, Thysius, Donteklock, Bogerman, Gomar, Smoutius, Triglandius, down to the minor tribe of Contra-Remonstrants, Damman, Maccovius, and Sibrandus Lubbertus. Nor were the clever divines of our own country a whit behind the foreigners in accomplishing this grand object; and the theological reader, on seeing the names of Perkins, Whitaker, Abbot, and Twisse, will instantly recognise men whose doctrinal vagaries were familiar to all the Calvinists in Europe. No one can form an adequate conception of the injury thus inflicted on the divine attributes of wisdom, goodness, and mercy, as they have been revealed in the

Scriptures, unless he has read the immense mass of quotations from the writings of these and other divines, which were presented to the notice of the synod of Dort by the Remonstrants, especially in their REJECTION OF ERRORS under each of the five points in dispute; the proofs of which were quoted from their respective authors, and the accuracy and faithfulness of which were never called in question. Not only would the minds of all sober Christians in these days be shocked when perusing the monstrous sentiments propounded in those extracts, but even the tolerably stiff Calvinists of Oliver Cromwell's time felt themselves scandalized by any allusion to them, and would not admit that their opinions had the least affinity to such desecrating dogmas. Little more than twenty years after the synod of Dort, that distinguished polemical divine and accurate scholar, Dr. Thomas Pierce, published his able and very interesting pamphlet, entitled, "A Correct Copy of Some Notes concerning God's Decrees;" in which, without naming the authors, he gave ten extracts from celebrated Calvinistic treatises, to prove, that "there are men of no small name who have told the world, that all the evil of sin which is in man proceedeth from God only as the author, and from man only as the instrument." Four of these extracts will furnish sufficient matter to every judicious mind for mournful reflections on the strange obliquities to which the human understanding is liable:--(1.) "A wicked man, by the just impulse of God, doeth that which is not lawful for him to do." (2.) "When God makes an angel or a man a transgressor, he himself doth not transgress, because he doth not break a law. The very same sin, namely, adultery or murder, inasmuch as it is the work of God, the author, mover, and compeller, is not a crime; but inasmuch as it is of man, it is a wickedness." (3.) "God can will that man shall not fall, by his will which is called VOLUNTAS SIGNI; and in the mean while he can ordain that the same man shall infallibly and efficaciously fall, by his will which is called VOLUNTAS BENEPLACITI. The former will of God is improperly called his will, for it only signifieth what man ought to do by right; but the latter will is properly called a will, because by that he decreed what should inevitably come to pass." (4.) "God's will doth pass, not only into the permission of the sin, but into the sin itself which is permitted. The Dominicans," the high predestinarian order in the church of Rome, "do imperfectly and obscurely relate the truth whilst, beside God's concurrence to the making way for sin, they require nothing but the negation of efficacious grace, when it is manifest that there is a farther prostitution of sin required." Of these four passages the first is from Calvin himself, the second from Zuinglius, and the third and fourth from Dr. Twisse. This pamphlet was the first in a smart controversy, in which Doctor (afterward Bishop) Reynolds, Baxter, Hickman, and Barlee, took part against Dr. Pierce, but in which those eminent men virtually disclaimed all community of sentiment between themselves and such high predestinarians. In their warmth, however, they accused the Doctor of having "rifled the well-furnished cabinet of the Batavian Remonstrant writings," and of not having hesitated "to be beholden to very thieves, namely, such roguish pamphlets as *Fur Predestinatus* and others are, rather than want materials for invectives against Calvin, Beza, Twisse," &c. In his reply, the Doctor says, "When I published my papers on God's decrees, I had never so much as seen that well-furnished cabinet, the '*Acta Synodalia Remonstrantium*;'" and he proves that he has copied none of his extracts from *Fur Predestinatus*. As his opponents were "so unthankful for the lenity" which he had displayed in giving "so SHORT a catalogue," he added other affirmations of a still more revolting import, if that were possible. The four extracts which follow, will serve as a correct specimen of the gross and unguarded assertions of some of those good men who were thus exposed; the first two are from Zanchius, the other two from Piscator, both of them men of renown in that age:--(1.) "Reprobates are compelled with a necessity of sinning, and so of perishing, by this ordination of God; and so compelled that they cannot choose but sin and perish." (2.) "God works all things in all men, not only in the godly, but also in the ungodly." (3.) "Judas could not but betray Christ, seeing that God's decrees are immutable; and whether a man bless or curse, he always doth it necessarily in respect of God's providence, and in so doing he doeth always according to the will of God." (4.) "It doth or at least may appear from the word of God, that we neither can do more good than we do, nor omit more evil than we omit; because God from eternity hath precisely decreed that both [the good and the evil] should so be done. It is fatally constituted when, and how, and how much, every one of us ought to study and love piety, or not to love it." In that newly emancipated age, the ample discussion of these topics could not fail to produce much good; and the result in the course of a few years was, that a vast number of those who had implicitly followed the guidance of Calvin, deserted his standard, and either went completely over to the ranks of Arminius, or halted midway under the command of Baxter. From that time to the middle of the eighteenth century, those dogmas which are usually designated as ultra-Calvinian or Antinomian, received no support except from such shallow divines as Dr. Crisp and his immediate admirers. But when the Rev. John Wesley and his brother, as Arminians, propounded the doctrines of the Gospel in as evangelical a manner, and with as marked success, as any Calvinist, a number of those excellent men, both in the church and among the Dissenters, who had been early benefited by the ministry of the two brothers, thought, as many now do, that it was impossible for any thing to be evangelical that was not Calvinistic; and, apparently with the design of being at as great a remove as possible from a reputed heresy, they became in principle real Antinomians. In forming this conclusion, and in running to a supposed opposite extreme, such persons seem to have forgotten that those truly evangelical principles,--which in Germany and the neighbouring states effected the reformation from Popery, which transformed sinners into Christians and martyrs, and which, in the perverted state of society that then obtained, but too painfully reminded the sainted sufferers of the domestic, municipal, and national grievances and persecutions to which the earliest confessors of the name of Christ were subjected,--had been in beneficial operation long before Calvin's doctrinal system was brought to maturity, and when he was known only as the humble and diligent pastor of the church of Geneva. And even after the publication of his "Institutes," which contained the peculiarities of his creed, he had to wait many years, to labour hard, not always in the most sanctified spirit, both from the pulpit and the press, and to endure many personal mortifications, before he was able to obtrude his novel dogmas on his own immediate connections, or to make any sensible impression on the generally received theology of his learned contemporaries. Such persons ought also to recollect, that, as Dr. Watts justly observes, "some of the most rigid and narrow limitations of grace to men are found chiefly in Calvin's *Institutions*, which were written in his youth. But his comments on Scripture were the labours of his riper years and maturer judgment."

11. His first tract on predestination was published in 1552; and the first complete edition of his "Institutes" did not see the light till the year 1558; but the change in Melancthon's opinions, from the fatality of Stoicism, to the universality of the Gospel, occurred at least six years prior to 1535, when the second edition of his "Common Places" was published, that contained his amended creed, and strong cautions against the contrary doctrines. One of the most eloquent and best informed writers of the present age has, in reference to this subject, justly observed: "Both Luther and Melancthon, after their creed became permanently settled at the diet of Augsburg, (A. D. 1530,) kept one object constantly in view,--to inculcate only what was plain and practical, and never to attempt philosophizing. They perceived, that before the reformation the doctrine of divine foreknowledge had been grossly misconceived and abused, although guarded by all the logic of the schools; and they felt, that, after it, they had themselves at first contributed to increase the evil, by grounding upon the same high argument, although for a very different purpose, the position of an infallible necessity. Thenceforward, therefore, they only taught a predestination which the Christian religion explains, and the Christian life exemplifies. Thus, while their adversaries philosophized upon a predestination of individuals, preferred one before another by divine regard because worthy of such a preference, they taught only that which has been revealed with certainty,--the predestination of a peculiar description of persons, of A PEOPLE ZEALOUS OF GOOD WORKS, of the Christian church contemplated as an aggregate, not on account of its own dignity, but on account of Christ its supreme Head, and THE AUTHOR OF ETERNAL SALVATION TO ALL WHO OBEY HIM. While restoring Scriptural simplicity to the doctrine of predestination, perplexed and disfigured by the vanity of the schools, they studiously and anxiously preserved every trace of that universal benevolence by which Christianity is particularly distinguished. 'Let us,' they said, 'with both our hands, or rather with all our heart, hold fast the true and pious maxim, that God is not the author of sin, that he sits not in heaven writing Stoical laws in the volumes of fate; but, endowed with a perfect freedom himself, he communicates a liberty of action to his creatures; firmly opposing the position of necessity as false, and pernicious to morals and religion. God, we may be assured, is no cruel and merciless tyrant; he does not hate and reject men, but loves them as a parent loves his children.' Universal grace, indeed, was at all times a favourite topic with the Lutherans; nor would they admit of any predestination except that of a beneficent Deity, who was IN CHRIST RECONCILING THE WORLD TO HIMSELF; except a predestination conformable with that order of things which he has established, and with the use or abuse of the means which he has ordained. 'The Almighty,' they said, 'has seriously willed and decreed, from eternity, all men to be saved and to enjoy everlasting felicity; let us not therefore indulge in evil suggestions, and separate ourselves from his grace, which is as expanded as the space between heaven and earth; let us not restrain the general promise, in which he offers his favour to all without discrimination, nor confine it to those who, affecting a peculiar garb, wish to be alone esteemed pious and sanctified. If many perish, the fault is not to be imputed to the divine will, but to human obstinacy, which despises that will, and disregards a salvation destined for all men.' 'And because MANY ARE CALLED, BUT FEW ARE CHOSEN, let us not,' they added, 'entertain an opinion highly impious,--that God tenders his grace to many, but communicates it only to a few; for should we not in the greatest degree detest a Deity by whose arbitrary will we believed ourselves to be excluded from salvation?' Upon the important point likewise of the conditional acceptance of the individual, their ideas were not more distinct than their language was explicit. 'If God chose,' they argued, 'certain persons only in order to unite them to himself, and rejected the remainder in all respects alike, would not such AN ELECTION WITHOUT CAUSES seem tyrannical? Let us therefore be persuaded, that some cause exists in us, as some difference is to be found between those who are, and those who are not, accepted.' Thus they conceived that, predestinating his elect in Christ, or the Christian church, to eternal salvation, he excludes none from that number by a partial adoption of favourites, but calls all equally, and accepts of all who obey his calling, or, in other words, who become true Christians by possessing the qualifications which Christianity requires.--'He,' they stated, who 'falls from grace, cannot but perish, completely losing remission of sin, with the other benefits which Christ has purchased for him, and acquiring in their stead divine wrath and death eternal.' Melancthon, who in his private correspondence expressly termed Calvin the Zeno of his day, says, 'Let us execrate the Stoical disputations which some introduce, who imagine that the elect always retain the Holy Spirit, even when they commit atrocious crimes,--a manifest and highly reprehensible error; and let us not confirm in fools security and blindness.'"

These quotations might be augmented by others from the earliest Lutheran authors, more Arminian in their import than any which Arminius ever wrote: but the preceding are sufficient to show, that, during upward of thirty years, the Protestant church in Germany was nourished by doctrines most manifestly at variance with the refinements afterward promulgated by Calvin. Real conversions of sinners were never more abundant than in that golden age; yet these were produced by the blessing of God upon an evangelical agency that had scarcely any thing in common with the Genevan dogmas. With these and similar facts before him, therefore, no Calvinist can in common honesty claim for the peculiarities of his creed, for those doctrines which distinguish it from the Melancthonism of the Protestant churches of England and Germany, the exclusive title of Evangelical. Equally fallacious is the ground on which he can prefer any such claim on account of the alleged counsel and advice given by Calvin to our reformers while they were engaged in the formation of our Articles and Liturgy. On no fact in the ecclesiastical history of this country are our annalists more completely at agreement than on this,--that Calvin's name and writings were scarcely known in England till the time when the persecution under Queen Mary forced many of our best divines into banishment; and that, to the great future disquietude of the church, several of these exiles on their return imported a personal bias either in favour of his discipline or of his dogmas. Anterior to that period he had received no such pressing invitations from our reformers, and from the king himself, as Melancthon had done, for his friendly theological aid in drawing up the doctrinal and disciplinary formulæ of our national church. The man who asserts the contrary to this, and who has the hardihood to deny the Melancthonian origin of the Articles and Liturgy, discovers at once his want of correct information on these subjects, and has never read the convincing documents appended to the Archbishop of Cashel's (Dr. Laurence's) "Eight Sermons," being the Bampton Lectures for 1804, and entitled, "AN ATTEMPT TO ILLUSTRATE THOSE ARTICLES OF THE CHURCH OF ENGLAND WHICH THE CALVINISTS IMPROPERLY CONSIDER AS CALVINISTICAL;" Todd's treatise "*On Original Sin, Free Will, &c, as maintained by certain Declarations of our Reformers*;" Plaifere's "*Appello Evangelium*;" nor even the portable yet convincing pamphlets of Kipling and Winchester, the former entitled "*The Articles not Calvinistic*;" the latter, "*A Dissertation on the Seventeenth Article of the Church.*"

12. There is one fact connected with these assumed yet unfounded claims, which has never yet been placed in its proper light, but which it may be well briefly to notice in this place. Calvin himself, in 1535, wrote the following truly Melancthonian paragraphs as part of his preface to the New Testament in French: "This Mediator, our Lord Jesus Christ, was the only, true, and eternal Son of God, whom the Father was about to send into the world, that he might collect all men together from this horrid dispersion and devastation. When, at length, that fulness of time arrived, that day preordained by the Lord, he openly showed himself as that Messiah who had for so many ages been the desire of all nations, and hath most abundantly performed all those things which were necessary for the redemption of all men. But this great blessing was not confined solely within the boundaries of the land of Israel, since, on the contrary, it was intended [PORRIGENDUM] to be held out for the acceptance of the whole human race; because through Christ alone the entire family of man was to be reconciled to God, as will be seen, and most amply demonstrated, in these pages of the New Testament." "To this inheritance of our heavenly Father's kingdom we are all called without respect of persons,--whether we be men or women, high or low, masters or servants, teachers or disciples, [DOCTORES] divines or laics, Jews or Greeks, Frenchmen or [ROMANI] Italians. From this inheritance no one is excluded, if he only so receive Christ as he is offered by the Father for the salvation of all men, and embrace him when received." Great research has been displayed by the Calvinists at different periods, in endeavouring to discover, in the public formularies of the church, or in the private productions of our reformers, some trace of affinity between them and the writings of Calvin. Only two cases of such affinity have yet been found; and, unfortunately for the validity of all pretensions of this kind, neither of them contains a single peculiarity of Calvinism, but, on the contrary, both are of the moderate and EVANGELICAL class of the Melancthonian school. One of the passages thus discovered is here subjoined from Cranmer's "*Defence of the True and Catholic Doctrine of the Sacrament*," &c; and bears all the marks of verisimilitude to the second of the preceding paragraphs from Calvin, though written fifteen years after it:--"Almighty God, without respect of person, accepteth the oblation and sacrifice of priest and lay person, of king and subject, of master and servant, of man and woman, of young and old, yea, of English, French, Scot, Greek, Latin, Jew, and Gentile; of every man according to his faithful and obedient heart unto him, and that through the sacrifice propitiatory of Jesus Christ." Had either this or the other passage contained the least tinge of what is now considered as belonging exclusively to the system of Calvin, the English admirers of that great man would have had some grounds for the assertions which have been too confidently made, because so easily refuted.

13. Having given this summary of the sentiments of Calvin himself, and of the ancient or strict Calvinists, it is proper to observe, that there are, and always have been, many who generally embrace the Calvinistic system, but object to some particular PARTS, and to the strong language in which some of the propositions are expressed. These are called MODERATE or MODERN Calvinists, who differ from Calvin, and the synod of Dort, chiefly on two points,--the doctrine of reprobation, and the extent of the death of Christ. The theory of Baxter has already been noticed. This and all other mitigated schemes rest on two principles, the sufficiency of the atonement for all mankind, and the sufficiency of grace for those who do not believe. Still something more is held to be necessary than this sufficiency of grace in order to actual salvation; namely, an acceptance by man, which can only be made under that degree of effectual supernatural aid which is dispensed only to a certain number of persons, who are thus distinguished as the "elect of God." The main characteristic of all these theories, from the first to the last, from the highest to the lowest, is, that a part of mankind are shut out from the mercies of God, on some ground irrespective of their refusal of a sincere offer to them of salvation through Christ, made with a communicated power of embracing it.

Some power they allow to the reprobate, as natural power, and degrees of superadded moral power; but in no case the power to believe unto salvation; and thus, as one well observes, "When they have cut some fair trenches, as if they would bring the water of life unto the dwellings of the reprobate, on a sudden they open a sluice which carries it off again." The whole labour of these theories is to find out some plausible reason for the infliction of punishment on them that perish, independent of the only cause assigned by the word of God--their rejection of a mercy free for all, and made attainable by all. See Baxterianism.

14. After all, however, it is pleasant to find these indications of a growing consciousness, on the part of modern predestinarians, that the common notions and common language of mankind on these deep subjects are not far from the truth. And though some too fastidious Arminians may complain, that, in this desire to enlist the views and words of common sense on the side of Calvinism, many of those by whom they are employed attach to them a meaning very different from that which ordinary usage warrants; yet even this tendency to approximate to right views should be regarded as favourable to the progress of truth, and the evidently improved feeling which has suggested such approximation ought to be met in a conciliating spirit. But this is a fault which must always be an appendage to such a system, however it may be modified; and does not exclusively apply to its modern supporters. The following remarks by Archbishop Laurence on the ambiguity of language not unfrequently discernible in the writings of Calvin himself, are worthy of consideration:--"In whatsoever sense he wished these words to be understood, it must be admitted that he sometimes adapted the style of others, who had a very different object in view, to his own peculiar opinions. And hence, from the want of a due discrimination, the sentiments of his contemporaries, opposite in their natural tendency, are often improperly forced into the vortex of Calvinism. Systematizing was his darling propensity, and the ambition of being distinguished as a leader in reform his predominant passion: in the arrangements of the former, he never felt a doubt, or found a difficulty; and in the pursuits of the latter he displayed an equal degree of perseverance and ardour. Thus, in the doctrine of the eucharist, it is well known that he laboured to acquire celebrity, and conciliate followers, by maintaining a kind of middle sacramental presence between the corporeal of the Lutherans, and the mere spiritual of the Zuinglians; expressing himself in language which, partly derived from one, and partly from the other, verged toward neither extreme; but which, by his singular talent at perspicuous combination, he applied, and not without success, to his own particular purpose. Nor was he less solicitous to press into his service a foreign phraseology upon the subject more immediately before me; a subject on his theory of which he not a little prided himself, and seemed contented to stake his reputation. He perceived that the Lutherans, strongly reprobating every discussion upon the decrees of a Deity unrevealed to us, founded predestination solely on a Scriptural basis; contending for a divine will which is seriously, not fictitiously, disposed to save all men, and predetermined to save all who become and continue sincere Christians. Zuingle, indeed, had reasoned from a different principle; and, although persuaded that God's mercies in Christ were liberally bestowed on all without distinction, on infants who commit not actual crime, and on the Heathen as well as the Christian world, he nevertheless was a necessitarian in the strictest sense of the expression; referring events of every kind to an uncontrollable and absolute predetermination. Zuingle, however, died in 1531, before the youth of Calvin permitted him to assume the character of a reformer; who found Bullinger then at the head of the Zuinglian church, not only applauding, but adopting, the moderation of the Lutherans; and, to use the phrase of Turretin, plainly MELANCTHONIZING. But the doctrine alluded to, it may be imagined, was of a species too limited and unphilosophical for one of his enterprising turn of mind, who never met with an obstacle which he attempted not instantly to surmount. Disregarding, therefore, the sober restrictions of the times, he gave loose to the most unbounded speculation: yet, anxious by all means to win over all to his opinion, he studiously laboured to preserve, on some popular points, a verbal conformity with the Lutherans. With them, in words, he taught the universality of God's good will; but it was a universality which he extended only to the OFFER of salvation; conceiving the reprobate to be precluded from the reception of that offer by the secret decree of an immutable Deity. The striking feature of THEIR system was an election in Christ, by which they meant an election as Christians. This also, in words, he inculcated: his idea, however, of an election in Christ was totally different from theirs; for he held it to be the previous election of certain favourites by an irrespective will of God, whom, and whom alone, Christ was subsequently appointed to save. But his ingenuity was such, in adapting the terms borrowed from another source to his own theory, that some erroneously conceive them to have been thus originally used by the Lutherans themselves. Hence, therefore, much confusion has arisen in the attempt of properly discriminating between the various sentiments of Protestants upon this question, at the period under consideration: all have been regarded as formed upon the model which Calvin exhibited; at least by writers who have contemplated him as the greatest reformer of his age, but who have forgotten that, although they chose to esteem him the greatest, they could not represent him as the first in point of time; and that his title to preëminence, in the common estimation of his contemporaries, was then far from being acknowledged."

15. On one topic, however, Calvin and the older divines of that school were very explicit. They tell us plainly, that they found all the Christian fathers, both of the Greek and the Latin church down to the age of St. Augustine, quite unmanageable for their purpose; and therefore occasionally bestow upon them and their productions epithets not the most courteous. Yet some modern writers, not possessing half the splendid qualifications of those veterans in learning, make a gorgeous display of the little that they know concerning antiquity; and wish to lead their readers

to suppose, that the whole stream of early Christianity has flowed down only in their channel. Every one must have remarked how much like Calvin all those fathers speak whose works are quoted by Toplady in his "Historic Defence." Nor can the two Milners, in their "History of the Church," entirely escape censure on this account,--though both were excellent men, and better scholars than Toplady. But from the manner in which they "show up" only those ancient Christian authors, some of whose sentiments SEEM to be nearly in unison with their own, they induce the unlearned or half informed to draw the erroneous conclusion,--that the peculiarities of Calvinism are not the inventions of a comparatively recent æra, and that they have always formed a prominent part of the profession of faith of every Christian community since the days of the Apostles.

All men must admire the candid and liberal spirit which breathes in the subjoined high but just eulogium on Calvin, from the pen of the same amiable Archbishop: "Calvin himself was both a wise and a good man; inferior to none of his contemporaries in general ability, and superior to almost all in the art, as well as elegance, of composition, in the perspicuity and arrangement of his ideas, the structure of his periods, and the Latinity of his diction. Although attached to a theory, which he found it difficult in the extreme to free from the suspicion of blasphemy against God, as the author of sin, he certainly was no blasphemer; but, on the contrary, adopted that very theory from an anxiety not to commit, but, as he conceived, to avoid blasphemy,--that of ascribing to human, what he deemed alone imputable to divine, agency."

CAMBYSES, the son of Cyrus, king of Persia. He succeeded his father, A. M. 3475, and is the Ahasuerus mentioned in Ezra iv, 6, to whom, as soon as he came to the crown, the Samaritans applied by petition, desiring that the rebuilding of Jerusalem might be stopped. What the motives were which they made use of to prevail upon this prince, we are ignorant; but it is certain, that though he was not persuaded to revoke his father's decree, yet he put a stop to the works, so that for the remaining seven years and five months which he reigned, the building of the city and temple was suspended. See Ahasuerus.

CAMEL, גמל. This animal is called in ancient Arabic, GIMEL; and in modern, DIAMMEL; in Greek, κάμηλος. With very little variation, the name is retained in modern languages. The camel is very common in Arabia, Judea, and the neighbouring countries; and is often mentioned in Scripture, and reckoned among the most valuable property, 1 Chron. v, 21; Job i, 3, &c. "No creature," says Volney, "seems so peculiarly fitted to the climate in which he exists as the camel. Designing this animal to dwell in a country where he can find little nourishment, nature has been sparing of her materials in the whole of his formation. She has not bestowed upon him the fleshiness of the ox, horse, or elephant; but limiting herself to what is strictly necessary, has given him a long head, without ears, at the end of a long neck without flesh; has taken from his legs and thighs every muscle not immediately requisite for motion; and, in short, bestowed upon his withered body only the vessels and tendons necessary to connect its frame together. She has furnished him with a strong jaw, that he may grind the hardest aliments; but, lest he should consume too much, has straitened his stomach, and obliged him to chew the cud; has lined his foot with a lump of flesh, which sliding in the mud, and being no way adapted to climbing, fits him only for a dry, level, and sandy soil, like that of Arabia. So great, in short, is the importance of the camel to the desert, that, were it deprived of that useful animal, it must infallibly lose every inhabitant." The chief use of the camel has always been as a beast of burden, and for performing journeys across the deserts. They have sometimes been used in war, to carry the baggage of an oriented army, and mingle in the tumult of the battle. Many of the Amalekite warriors, who burnt Ziklag in the time of David, were mounted on camels; for the sacred historian remarks, that of the whole army not a man escaped the furious onset of that heroic and exasperated leader, "save four hundred young men, which rode upon camels, and fled," 1 Sam. xxx, 17.

The passage of Scripture in which our Lord says, "It is easier for a camel to go through the eye of a needle, than for a rich man to enter into the kingdom of heaven," Matt. xix, 24, has been the occasion of much criticism. Some assert that near Jerusalem was a low gate called "the needle's eye," through which a camel could not pass unless his load was taken off. Others conjecture that κάμιλος should be read κάβιλος, A CABLE. But there are no ancient manuscripts to support the reading. In the Jewish Talmud, there is, however, a similar proverb respecting an elephant: "Rabbi Shesheth answered Rabbi Amram, who had advanced an absurdity, 'Perhaps thou art one of the Pambidithians, who can make an elephant pass through the eye of a needle;'" that is, says the Aruch, "who speak things impossible." There is also a saying of the same kind in the Koran: "The impious, who in his arrogancy shall accuse our doctrine of falsity, shall find the gates of heaven shut; nor shall he enter there, till a camel shall pass through the eye of a needle. It is thus that we shall recompense the wicked," Surat. vii, 37. Indeed, Grotius, Lightfoot, Wetstein, and Michaëlis join in opinion, that the comparison is so much in the figurative style of the oriental nations and of the rabbins, that the text is sufficiently authentic.

CAMEL's **HAIR**, mentioned Matt. iii, 4; Mark i, 6. John the Baptist, we are told, was habited in a raiment of camel's hair; and Chardin assures us, that the modern dervises wear such garments; as they do also great leathern girdles. Camel's hair is also made into those beautiful stuffs, called shawls; but certainly the coarser manufacture of this material was adopted by John, and we may receive a good idea of its texture, from what Braithwaite says of the Arabian tents: "They are made of camel's hair, somewhat like our coarse hair cloths to lay over goods." By this coarse vesture the Baptist was not merely distinguished, but contrasted with those in royal palaces, who wore "soft raiment," such as shawls or other superfine manufactures, whether of the same material or not.

CAMERONIANS, a sect in Scotland, who separated from the Presbyterians in 1666, and continued to hold their religious assemblies in the fields. The Cameronians took their denomination from Richard Cameron, a famous field preacher, who, refusing to accept the indulgence to tender consciences granted by King Charles **II**, as such an acceptance seemed an acknowledgment of the king's supremacy, and that he had before a right to silence them, separated from his brethren, and even headed a rebellion in which he was killed. His followers were never entirely reduced till the Revolution, when they voluntarily submitted to King William. The Cameronians adhered rigidly to the form of government established in 1648.

CAMERONISTS, or **CAMERONITES**, is the denomination of a party of Calvinists in France, who asserted, that the cause of men's doing good or evil proceeds from the knowledge which God infuses into them; and that God does not move the will physically, but only morally, in virtue of its dependence on the judgment of the mind. They had this name from John Cameron, one of the most famous divines among the Protestants of France, in the seventeenth century, who was born at Glasgow, in Scotland, about the year 1580, and taught Greek there till he removed to Bourdeaux in 1600. Here he acquired such celebrity by the fluency with which he spoke Greek, that he was appointed to teach the learned languages at Bergerac. He afterward became professor of philosophy at Sedan; but returning to Bourdeaux in 1604, he devoted himself to the study of divinity. Upon being appointed tutor to the sons of the chancellor of Navarre, he accompanied them to Paris, Geneva, and Heidelberg. After having discharged the office of a minister at Bourdeaux, which he assumed in 1608, for ten years, he accepted the professorship of divinity at Saumur. Upon the dispersion of that academy by the public commotions in 1621, he removed to England, and taught divinity at his own house in London. King James inclined to favour him on account of his supposed attachment to the hierarchy, made him master of the college, and professor of divinity, at Glasgow; but after holding this office, which he found to be unpleasant to him, for a year, he returned to Saumur, where he read private lectures. From thence he removed, in 1624, to Montauban; where the disturbances excited by the emissaries of the duke de Rohan led him to remonstrate against the principles which produced them, with more zeal than prudence. This occasioned his being insulted by a private person in the streets, and severely beaten: and this treatment so much affected him, that he soon after died, in 1625, at the early age of forty-six years. Bayle represents him as "a man of great parts and judgment, of an excellent memory, very learned, a good philosopher, good humoured, liberal not only of his knowledge but his purse, a great talker, a long-winded preacher, little versed in the fathers, inflexible in his opinions, and inclined to turbulence." He was one of those who attempted to reconcile the doctrine of predestination, as it had been taught at Geneva, and confirmed at Dort, with the sentiments of those who believe that God offers salvation to all mankind. His opinion was maintained and propagated by Moses Amyraut, and several others of the most learned among the reformed ministers, who thought Calvin's doctrine too harsh. They were called HYPOTHETICAL UNIVERSALISTS. Cameron likewise maintained the possibility of salvation in the church of Rome. See Amyraut and Baxterianism.

CAMP, or **ENCAMPMENT**, of the Israelites. The whole body of the people, consisting of six hundred thousand fighting men, beside women and children, was disposed under four battalions, so placed as to enclose the tabernacle, in the form of a square, and each under one general standard. (See ARMIES.) There were forty-one encampments, from their first in the month of March, at Rameses, in the land of Goshen, in Egypt, and in the wilderness, until they reached the land of Canaan. They are thus enumerated in Numbers xxxiii:--

- 1. Rameses
- 2. Succoth
- 3. Etham, on the edge of the wilderness
- 4. Pihahiroth
- 5. Marah
- 6. Elim
- 7. By the Red Sea
- 8. Wilderness of Sin
- 9. Dophkah
- 10. Alush
- 11. Rephidim
- 12. Wilderness of Sinai
- 13. Kibroth-hattaavah
- 14. Hazeroth
- 15. Rithmah
- 16. Rimmon-parez
- 17. Libnah
- 18. Rissah
- 19. Kehelatha

- 20. Shapher
- 21. Haradah
- 22. Makheloth
- 23. Tahath
- 24. Tarah
- 25. Mithcah
- 26. Hashmonah
- 27. Moseroth
- 28. Bene-jaakan
- 29. Hor-hagidgad
- 30. Jotbathah
- 31. Ebronah
- 32. Ebion-gaber
- 33. Kadesh
- 34. Mount Hor
- 35. Zalmonah
- 36. Punon
- 37. Oboth
- 38. Ije-abarim
- 39. Dibon-gad
- 40. Almon-diblathaim
- 41. Mountains of Abarim

In the second year after their exodus from Egypt they were numbered; and upon an exact poll, the number of their males amounted to six hundred and three thousand, five hundred and fifty, from twenty years old and upward, Num. i, ii. This vast mass of people, encamped in beautiful order, must have presented a most impressive spectacle. That it failed not to produce effect upon the richly endowed and poetic mind of Balaam, appears from Num. xxiv, 2; "And Balaam lifted up his eyes and he saw Israel abiding in his tents according to their tribes; and the Spirit of God came upon him, and he took up his parable and said, How goodly are thy tents, O Jacob, and thy tabernacles, O Israel! As the valleys are they spread forth, as gardens by the river side, as the trees of lign aloes which the Lord hath planted, and as cedar trees beside waters." Grandeur, order, beauty, and freshness, were the ideas at once suggested to the mind of this unfaithful prophet, and called forth his unwilling admiration. Perhaps we may consider this spectacle as a type of the order, beauty, and glory of the true "church in the wilderness," in those happy days when God "shall not behold iniquity in Jacob, nor perverseness in Israel;" when it shall be said, "The Lord his God is with him, and the shout of a king is among them."

CAMPHIRE. כפר. Greek, κύπρος. Latin CYPRUS. Canticles i, 14; iv, 13. Sir T. Browne supposes that the plant mentioned in the Canticles, rendered κύπρος in the Septuagint, and CYPRUS in the Vulgate, is that described by Dioscorides and Pliny, which grows in Egypt, and near to Ascalon, producing an odorate bush of flowers, and yielding the celebrated OLEUM CYPRINUM. [A sweet oil made of the flowers of the privet tree.] This is one of the plants which is most grateful to the eye and the smell. The deep colour of its bark, the light green of its foliage, the softened mixture of white and yellow with which the flowers, collected into long clusters like the lilac, are coloured; the red tint of the ramifications which support them, form an agreeable combination. The flowers, whose shades are so delicate, diffuse around the sweetest odours, and embalm the gardens and apartments which they embellish. The women take pleasure in decking themselves with them. With the powder of the dried leaves they give an orange tincture to their nails, to the inside of their hands, and to the soles of their feet. The expression, את־ עשתה צפרניה, rendered "pare their nails," Deut. xxi, 12, may perhaps rather mean, "ADORN their nails;" and imply the antiquity of this practice. This is a universal custom in Egypt, and not to conform to it would be considered indecent. It seems to have been practised by the ancient Egyptians, for the nails of the mummies are most commonly of a reddish hue.

In the Song of Solomon, the bride is described as saying, "My beloved is unto me as a cluster of camphire in the vineyards of Engedi," chap. i, 24; and again, "Thy plants are an orchard of pomegranates, with pleasant fruits, camphire with spikenard," chap. iv, 13.

CANA, a town of Galilee, where Jesus performed his first miracle, John ii, 1, 2, &c. It lay in the tribe of Zebulun, not far from Nazareth. Cana was visited by Dr. E. D. Clarke, who says, "It is worthy of note, that, walking among the ruins of a church, we saw large massy stone pots, answering the description given of the ancient vessels of the country; these were not preserved nor exhibited as reliques, but lying about, disregarded by the present inhabitants, as antiquities with whose original use they were unacquainted. From their appearance, and the number of them, it was quite evident that a practice of keeping water in large stone pots, each holding from eighteen to twenty-seven gallons, was once common in the country."

CANAAN, the son of Ham. The Hebrews believe that Canaan, having first discovered Noah's nakedness, told his father Ham; and that Noah, when he awoke, having understood what had passed, cursed Canaan, the first author of the offence. Others are of opinion that Ham was punished in his son Canaan, Gen. ix, 25. For though Canaan is mentioned, Ham is not exempted from the malediction; on the contrary, he suffers more from it, since parents are more affected with their children's misfortunes than with their own; especially if the evils have been inflicted through some fault or folly of theirs. Some have thought that CANAAN may be put elliptically for THE FATHER OF CANAAN, that is, Ham, as it is rendered in the Arabic and Septuagint translations.

The posterity of Canaan was numerous. His eldest son, Sidon, founded the city of Sidon, and was father of the Sidonians and Phenicians. Canaan had ten other sons, who were fathers of as many tribes, dwelling in Palestine and Syria; namely, the Hittites, the Jebusites, the Amorites, the Girgasites, the Hivites, the Arkites, the Sinites, the Arvadites, the Zemarites, and the Hemathites. It is believed that Canaan lived and died in Palestine, which from him was called the land of Canaan. Notwithstanding the curse is directed against Canaan the son, and not against Ham the father, it is often supposed that all the posterity of Ham were placed under the malediction, "Cursed be Canaan; a servant of servants shall he be unto his brethren." But the true reason why Canaan only was mentioned probably is, that the curse was in fact restricted to the posterity of Canaan. It is true that many Africans, descendants of other branches of Ham's family, have been largely and cruelly enslaved; but so have other tribes in different parts of the world. There is certainly no proof that the negro race were ever placed under this malediction. Had they been included in it, this would neither have justified their oppressors, nor proved that Christianity is not designed to remove the evil of slavery. But Canaan alone in his descendants, is cursed, and Ham only in that branch of his posterity. It follows that the subjugation of the Canaanitish races to Israel fulfils the prophecy. To them it was limited, and with them it expired. Part of the seven nations of the Canaanites were made slaves to the Israelites, when they took possession of their land; and the remainder by Solomon.

Canaan, Land of. In the map it presents the appearance of a narrow slip of country, extending along the eastern coast of the Mediterranean; from which, to the river Jordan, the utmost width does not exceed fifty miles. This river was the eastern boundary of the land of Canaan, or Palestine, properly so called, which derived its name from the Philistines or Palestines originally inhabiting the coast. To three of the twelve tribes, however, Reuben, Gad, and Manasseh, portions of territory were assigned on the eastern side of the river, which were afterward extended by the subjugation of the neighbouring nations. The territory of Tyre and Sidon was its ancient border on the north-west; the range of the Libanus and Antilibanus forms a natural boundary on the north and north-east; while in the south it is pressed upon by the Syrian and Arabian deserts. Within this circumscribed district, such were the physical advantages of the soil and climate, there existed, in the happiest periods of the Jewish nation, an immense population. The kingdom of David and Solomon, however, extended far beyond these narrow limits. In a north-eastern direction, it was bounded only by the river Euphrates, and included a considerable part of Syria. It is stated that Solomon had dominion over all the region on the western side of the Euphrates, from Thiphsah, or Thapsacus, on that river, in latitude 25° 20´, to Azzah, or Gaza. "Tadmore in the wilderness," (Palmyra,) which the Jewish monarch is stated to have built, (that is, either founded or fortified,) is considerably to the north-east of Damascus, being only a day's journey from the Euphrates; and Hamath, the Epiphania of the Greeks, (still called Hamah,) in the territory belonging to which city Solomon had several "store cities," is seated on the Orontes, in latitude 34° 45´ N. On the east and south-east, the kingdom of Solomon was extended by the conquest of the country of Moab, that of the Ammonites, and Edom; and tracts which were either inhabited or pastured by the Israelites, lay still farther eastward. Maon, which belonged to the tribe of Judah, and was situated in or near the desert of Paran, is described by Abulfeda as the farthest city of Syria toward Arabia, being two days' journey beyond Zoar. In the time of David, the people of Israel, women and children included, amounted, on the lowest computation, to five millions; beside the tributary Canaanites, and other conquered nations.

The vast resources of the country, and the power of the Jewish monarch, may be estimated not only by the consideration in which he was held by the contemporary sovereigns of Egypt, Tyre, and Assyria, but by the strength of the several kingdoms into which the dominions of David were subsequently divided. Damascus revolted during the reign of Solomon, and shook off the Jewish yoke. At his death, ten of the tribes revolted under Jeroboam, and the country became divided into the two rival kingdoms of Judah and Israel, having for their capitals Jerusalem and Samaria. The kingdom of Israel fell before the Assyrian conqueror, in the year B. C. 721, after it had subsisted about two hundred and fifty years. That of Judah survived about one hundred and thirty years, Judea being finally subdued and laid waste by Nebuchadnezzar, and the temple burned B. C. 588. Idumea was conquered a few years after. From this period till the æra of Alexander the Great, Palestine remained subject to the Chaldean, Median, and Persian dynasties. At his death, Judea fell under the dominion of the kings of Syria, and, with some short and troubled intervals, remained subject either to the kings of Syria or of Egypt, till John Hyrcanus shook off the Syrian yoke, and assumed the diadem, B. C. 130. The Asmonean dynasty, which united, in the person of the monarch, the functions of king and pontiff, though tributary to Roman conquerors, lasted one hundred and twenty-six years, till the kingdom was given by Anthony to Herod the Great, of an Idumean family, B. C. 39.

2. At the time of the Christian æra, Palestine was divided into five provinces; Judea, Samaria, Galilee, Perea, and Idumea. On the death of Herod, Archelaus, his eldest son, succeeded to the government of Judea, Samaria, and Idumea, with the title of tetrarch; Galilee being assigned to Herod Antipas; and Perea, or the country beyond Jordan, to the third brother, Philip. But in less than ten years the dominions of Archelaus became annexed, on his disgrace, to the Roman province of Syria; and Judea was thenceforth governed by Roman procurators. Jerusalem, after its final destruction by Titus, A. D. 71, remained desolate and almost uninhabited, till the emperor Hadrian colonized it, and erected temples to Jupiter and Venus on its site. The empress Helena, in the fourth century, set the example of repairing in pilgrimage to the Holy Land, to visit the scenes consecrated by the Gospel narrative; and the country became enriched by the crowds of devotees who flocked there. In the beginning of the seventh century, it was overrun by the Saracens, who held it till Jerusalem was taken by the crusaders in the twelfth. The Latin kingdom of Jerusalem continued for about eighty years, during which the Holy Land streamed continually with Christian and Saracen blood. In 1187, Judea was conquered by the illustrious Saladin, on the decline of whose kingdom it passed through various revolutions, and at length, in 1317, was finally swallowed up in the Turkish empire.

Palestine is now distributed into pashalics. That of Acre or Akka extends from Djebail nearly to Jaffa; that of Gaza comprehends Jaffa and the adjacent plains; and these two being now united, all the coast is under the jurisdiction of the pasha of Acre. Jerusalem, Hebron, Nablous, Tiberias, and in fact, the greater part of Palestine, are included in the pashalic of Damascus, now held in conjunction with that of Aleppo; which renders the present pasha, in effect, the viceroy of Syria. Though both pashas continue to be dutiful subjects to the Grand Seignior in appearance, and annually transmit considerable sums to Constantinople to insure the yearly renewal of their office, they are to be considered as tributaries, rather than subjects of the Porte; and it is supposed to be the religious supremacy of the Sultan, as caliph and vicar of Mohammed, more than any apprehension of his power, which prevents them from declaring themselves independent. The reverence shown for the firmauns of the Porte throughout Syria attests the strong hold which the Sultan maintains, in this character, on the Turkish population. The pashas of Egypt and Bagdad are attached to the Turkish sovereign by the same ecclesiastical tie, which alone has kept the ill-compacted and feeble empire from crumbling to ruin.

3. A few additional remarks upon the topography and climate will tend to elucidate the force of many of those parts of Scripture which contain allusions to these topics. Dr. E. D. Clarke, after stating his resolve to make the Scriptures his only guide throughout this interesting territory, says, "The delight afforded by the internal evidences of truth, in every instance where their fidelity of description was proved by a comparison of existing documents, surpassed even all we had anticipated. Such extraordinary instances of coincidence even with the customs of the country as they are now exhibited, and so many wonderful examples of illustration afforded by contrasting the simple narrative with the appearances presented, made us only regret the shortness of our time, and the limited sphere of our abilities for the comparison." Judea is beautifully diversified with hills and plains--hills now barren and gloomy, but once cultivated to their summits, and smiling in the variety of their produce, chiefly the olive and the vine; and plains, over which the Bedouin now roves to collect a scanty herbage for his cattle, but once yielding an abundance of which the inhabitants of a northern climate can form no idea. Rich in its soil; glowing in the sunshine of an almost perpetual summer; and abounding in scenery of the grandest, as well as of the most beautiful kind; this happy country was indeed a land which the Lord had blessed: but Mohammedan sloth and despotism, as the instruments employed to execute the curse of Heaven, have converted it into a waste of rock and desert, with the exception of some few spots, which remain to attest the veracity of the accounts formerly given of it. The hills of Judea frequently rise into mountains; the most considerable of which are those of Lebanon and Hermon, on the north; those which surround the sea of Galilee, and the Dead Sea, also attain a respectable elevation. The other mountains of note are, Carmel, Tabor, Ebal, and Gerizim, and the mountains of Gilboa, Gilead, and Abarim; with the summits of the latter, Nebo and Pisgah: a description of which will be found under their respective heads. Many of the hills and rocks abound in caverns, the refuge of the distressed, or the resorts of robbers.

4. From the paucity of rain which falls in Judea, and the heat and dryness of the atmosphere for the greater part of the year, it possesses but few rivers; and as these, have all their rise within its boundaries, their course is short, and their size inconsiderable: the principal is the Jordan, which runs about a hundred miles. The other remarkable streams are, the Arnon, the Jabbok, the Kishon, the Kedron, the Besor, the Sorek, and the stream called the river of Egypt. These, also, will be found described under their respective heads. This country was once adorned with woods and forests: as we read of the forest of cedars in Lebanon, the forest of oaks in Bashan, the forest or wood of Ephraim, and the forest of Hareth in the tribe of Judah. Of these, the woods of Bashan alone remain; the rest have been swept away by the ravages of time and of armies, and by the gradual consumption of the inhabitants, whose indolence and ignorance have prevented their planting others.

5. There are no volcanoes now existing in Judea or its vicinity: nor is mention made of any in history, although volcanic traces are found in many parts on its eastern side, as they are also in the mountains of Edom on the south, the Djebel Shera and Hesma, as noticed by Burckhardt. There can be no doubt that many of the sacred writers were familiarly acquainted with the phenomena of volcanoes;

whence it may be inferred that they were presented to their observation at no great distance, and from which they drew some of their sublimest imagery. Mr. Horne has adduced the following instances: "The mountains quake at him, and the hills MELT, and the earth is BURNED at his presence. His fury is POURED OUT LIKE FIRE, and the rocks are thrown down by him," Nahum i, 5, 6. "Behold, the Lord cometh forth out of his place, and will come down and tread upon the high places of the earth. And THE MOUNTAINS SHALL BE MOLTEN under him, and the valleys shall be CLEFT AS WAX BEFORE THE FIRE, and as the waters that are poured down a steep place," Micah i, 3, 4. "O that thou wouldest rend the heavens, that thou wouldest come down, that the MOUNTAINS MIGHT FLOW DOWN at thy presence. As when THE MELTING FIRE BURNETH, THE FIRE CAUSETH THE WATERS TO BOIL, to make thy name known to thine adversaries, that the nations may tremble at thy presence. When thou didst terrible things which we looked not for, thou camest down, the mountains flowed down at thy presence," Isa. lxiv, 1–3.

6. The climate of Judea, from the southern latitude of the country, is necessarily warm. The cold of winter is, indeed, sometimes greater than in European climates situated some degrees farther to the north; but it is of short duration, and the general character of the climate is that of heat. Both heat and cold are, however, tempered by the nature of the surface; the winter being scarcely felt in the valleys, while in the summer the heat is almost insupportable; and, on the contrary, in the more elevated parts, during the winter months, or rather weeks, frosts frequently occur, and snow sometimes falls, while the air in summer is comparatively cool and refreshing. Many winters pass without either snow or frost; and in the coldest weather which ever occurs, the sun in the middle of the day is generally warm, and often hot; so that the pain of cold is in reality but little felt, and the poor who cannot afford fires may enjoy, during several hours of the day, the more genial and invigorating influence of the sun. This is the ordinary character of the winters; though in some years, as will be seen presently, the cold is more severely felt during the short time that it prevails, which is never more than two months, and more frequently not so much as one. Toward the end of November, or beginning of December, domestic fires become agreeable. It was at this time that Jehoiakim, king of Judah, is represented by Jeremiah as sitting in his winter house, with a fire burning on the hearth before him, Jer. xxxvi, 22. The same luxury, though frequently by no means necessary, is used by the wealthy till the end of March.

7. Rain only falls during the autumn, winter, and spring, when it sometimes descends with great violence: the greatest quantity, and that which properly constitutes the rainy season, happening between the autumnal equinox, or somewhat later, and the beginning of December; during which period, heavy clouds often obscure the sky, and several days of violent rain sometimes succeed each other with winds. This is what in Scripture is termed the early or the former rain. Showers continue to fall at uncertain intervals, with some cloudy but more fair weather, till toward the vernal equinox, when they become again more frequent and copious till the middle of April. These are the latter rains, Joel ii, 23. From this time to the end of May, showers come on at irregular intervals, gradually decreasing as the season advances; the sky being for the most part serene, and the temperature of the air agreeable, though sometimes acquiring a high degree of heat. From the end of May, or beginning of June, to the end of September, or middle of October, scarce a drop of rain falls, the sky being constantly unclouded, and the heat generally oppressive. During this period, the inhabitants commonly sleep on the tops of their houses. The storms, especially in the autumn, are preceded by short but violent gusts of wind, which, from the surface of a parched soil, raise great clouds of dust; which explains what is meant by, "Ye shall not SEE wind," 2 Kings iii, 7. The continuation of the same passage likewise implies, that such circumscribed whirlwinds were generally considered as the precursors of rain: a circumstance likewise alluded to by Solomon, who says, "Whoso boasteth himself of a false gift, is like clouds and wind without rain," Prov. xxv, 14. Another prognostic of an approaching storm is a small cloud rising in the west, and increasing until it overspreads the whole heavens. Such was the cloud, "like a man's hand," which appeared to Elijah, on mount Carmel; which spread "till the heaven was black with clouds and wind, and there was a great rain," 1 Kings xviii, 44. To this phenomenon, and the certainty of the prognostic, our Saviour alludes: "When ye see a cloud" (or THE cloud, *την νεφελην*) "rise out of the west, straightway ye say, There cometh a shower; and so it is," Luke xii, 54. The same appearance is noticed by Homer:--

Ὡς δ' ὅτ' ἀπὸ σκοπιῆς εἶδεν νεφος αιπολος ανηρ

Ἐρχόμενον κατὰ πόντον ὑπὸ Ζεφύροιο ἰωῆς,

Τῷ δε τ', ἄνευθεν ἐόντι, μελάντερον, ἠΰτι πὶσσα,

Φαίνετ' ἰὸν κατὰ πόντον, ἄγεί δέ τέ λαίλαπα πολλην.

Ῥίγησεν τε ἰδὼν. κ. τ. λ. *Il.* lib. iv, 275.

"Slow from the main the heavy vapours rise,

Spread in dim streams, and sail along the skies,

Till black as night the swelling tempest shows,

The cloud condensing as the west wind blows.

He dreads the impending storm," &c. Pope.

Hail frequently falls in the winter and spring in very heavy storms, and with hailstones of an enormous size. Dr. Russel says that he has seen some at Aleppo which measured two inches in diameter; but sometimes they are found to consist of irregularly shaped pieces, weighing near three ounces. The copious dew forms another peculiarity of this climate, frequently alluded to in Scripture: so copious, indeed, is it sometimes, as to resemble small rain, and to supply the wants of superficial vegetation. Mr. Maundrell, when travelling near mount Hermon, says, "We were instructed by experience what the Psalmist means by 'the dew of Hermon,' Psalm cxxxiii, 3; our tents being as wet with it, as if it had rained all night."

8. The seasons are often adverted to in Scripture, under the terms "seed time and harvest." The former, for wheat, is about the middle of October to the middle or end of November: barley is put into the ground two and sometimes three months later. The wheat harvest commences about the twentieth of May, and early in June the whole is off the ground. The barley harvest, it is to be observed, is generally a fortnight earlier. A survey of the astonishing produce of this country, and of the manner in which its most rocky and, to appearance, insuperably sterile parts, are made to yield to the wants of man, will be sufficient to refute the objections raised by skeptical writers against the possibility of its furnishing subsistence to the multitude of its former inhabitants recorded in Scripture. Dr. Clarke, when travelling from Napolose to Jerusalem, relates, "The road was mountainous, rocky, and full of loose stones; yet the cultivation was every where marvellous: it afforded one of the most striking pictures of human industry which it is possible to behold. The limestone rocks and stony valleys of Judea were entirely covered with plantations of figs, vines, and olive trees: not a single spot seemed to be neglected. The hills, from their bases to their upmost summits, were entirely covered with gardens: all of these were free from weeds, and in the highest state of agricultural perfection. Even the sides of the most barren mountains had been rendered fertile, by being divided into terraces, like steps rising one above another, whereon soil had been accumulated with astonishing labour. Among the standing crops, we noticed millet, cotton, linseed, and tobacco; and occasionally small fields of barley. A sight of this territory can alone convey any adequate idea of its surprising produce: it is truly the Eden of the east, rejoicing in the abundance of its wealth. Under a wise and a beneficent government, the produce of the Holy Land would exceed all calculation. Its perennial harvest; the salubrity of its air; its limpid springs; its rivers, lakes, and matchless plains; its hills and dales;--all these, added to the serenity of its climate, prove this land to be indeed 'a field which the Lord hath blessed: God hath given it of the dew of heaven, and the fatness of the earth, and plenty of corn and wine.'" An oriental's ideas of fertility differ, however, from ours; for to him, plantations of figs, vines, and olives, with which the limestone rocks of Judea were once covered, would suggest the same associations of plenty and opulence that are called up in the mind of an Englishman by rich tracts of corn land. The land of Canaan is characterized as flowing with milk and honey; and it still answers to this description; for it contains extensive pasture lands of the richest quality, and the rocky country is covered with aromatic plants, yielding to the wild bees, who hive in the hollow of the rocks, such abundance of honey as to supply the poorer classes with an article of food. Honey from the rocks is repeatedly referred to in the Scriptures, as a delicious food, and an emblem of plenty, 1 Sam. xiv, 25; Psa. lxxxi, 16. Dates are another important article of consumption; and the neighbourhood of Judea was famous for its numerous palm trees, which are found springing up from chance-sown kernels in the midst of the most arid districts. When to these wild productions we add the oil extracted from the olive, so essential an article to an oriental, we shall be at no loss to account for the ancient fertility of the most barren districts of Judea, or for the adequacy of the soil to the support of so numerous a population, notwithstanding the comparatively small proportion of arable land. There is no reason to doubt, however, that corn and rice would be imported by the Tyrian merchants; which the Israelites would have no difficulty in exchanging for the produce of the olive ground and the vineyard, or for their flocks and herds. Delicious wine is still produced in some districts, and the valleys bear plentiful crops of tobacco, wheat, barley, and millet. Tacitus compares both the climate and the soil, indeed, to those of Italy; and he particularly specifies the palm tree and balsam tree as productions which gave the country an advantage over his own. Among other indigenous productions may be enumerated the cedar and other varieties of the pine, the cypress, the oak, the sycamore, the mulberry tree, the fig tree, the willow, the turpentine tree, the acacia, the aspen, the arbutus, the myrtle, the almond tree, the tamarisk, the oleander, the peach tree, the chaste tree, the carob or locust tree, the oskar, the doom, the mustard plant, the aloe, the citron, the apple, the pomegranate, and many flowering shrubs. The country about Jericho was celebrated for its balsam, as well as for its palm trees; and two plantations of it existed during the last war between the Jews and the Romans, for which both parties fought desperately. But Gilead appears to have been the country in which it chiefly abounded: hence the name, "balm of Gilead." Since the country has fallen under the Turkish dominion, it has ceased to be cultivated in Palestine, but is still found in Arabia. Other indigenous productions have either disappeared or are now confined to circumscribed districts. Iron is found in the mountain range of Libanus, and silk is produced in abundance in the plains of Samaria.

9. The grand distinction of Canaan, however, is, that it was the only part of the earth made, by divine institution, a type of heaven. So it was exhibited to Abraham, and also to the Jews. It pointed to the eternal rest which the spiritual seed of the father of the faithful were to enjoy after the pilgrimage of life; its holy city was the figure of the "Jerusalem above;" and Zion, with its solemn and joyful services represented that "hill of the Lord" to which the redeemed shall come with songs, and everlasting joy upon their heads; where they shall obtain joy and gladness, and sorrow and sighing shall fly away.

CANAANITES, the posterity of Canaan by his eleven sons, who are supposed to have settled in the land of Canaan, soon after the dispersion of Babel. Five of these are known to have dwelt in the land of Canaan; viz. Heth, Jebus, Hemor or Amor, Girgashi, and Hevi or Hivi; and these, together with their father Canaan, became the heads of so many nations. Sina or Sini was another son of Canaan, whose settlement is not so precisely ascertained; but some authors infer, from the affinity of the names, that the Desert of Sin, and Mount Sinai, were the places of his abode, and that they were so called from him. The Hittites inhabited the country about Hebron, as far as Beersheba, and the brook Besor, reckoned by Moses the southern limits of Canaan. The Jebusites dwelt near them on the north, as far as the city of Jebus, since called Jerusalem. The Amorites possessed the country on the east side of Jordan, between the river Arnon on the south-east, and Mount Gilead on the north, afterward the lot of Reuben and Gad. The Girgashites lay next above the Amorites, on the east side of the Sea of Tiberias, and their land was afterward possessed by the half tribe of Manasseh. The Hivites dwelt northward, under Mount Libanus. The Perizzites, who make one of the seven nations of the Canaanites, are supposed, by Heylin and others, to be the descendants of Sina or Sini; and it is probable, since we do not read of their abode in cities, that they lived dispersed, and in tents, like the Scythians, roving on both sides of the Jordan, on the hills and plains; and that they were called by that name from the Hebrew PHARATZ, which signifies "to disperse." The Canaanites dwelt in the midst of all, and were surrounded by the rest. This appears from the sacred writings to have been the respective situation of those seven nations, which are said to have been doomed to destruction for their idolatry and wickedness, when the Israelites first invaded their country. The learned have not absolutely determined whether the nations proceeding from Canaan's other six sons should be reckoned among the inhabitants of the land of Canaan. The prevalent opinion is, that they were not included. As to the customs, manners, arts, sciences, and language of the seven nations that inhabited the land of Canaan, they must, from the situation they severally occupied, have been very different. Those who inhabited the sea coast were merchants, and by reason of their commerce and wealth scattered colonies over almost all the islands and maritime provinces of the Mediterranean. (See PHENICIA) The colonies which Cadmus carried to Thebes in Bæotia, and his brother Cilix into Cilicia, are said to have proceeded from the stock of Canaan. Sicily, Sardinia, Malta, Cyprus, Corfu, Majorca, Minorca, Gades, and Ebutris, are supposed to have been peopled by the Canaanites. The other Canaanites, whose situation was inland, were employed partly in pasturage, and partly in tillage, and they were also well skilled in the exercise of arms. Those who dwelt in the walled cities, and who had fixed abodes, cultivated the land; and those who wandered about, as the Perizzites seem to have done, grazed cattle: so that among the Canaanites, we discover the various classes of merchants, and, consequently, mariners; of artificers, soldiers, shepherds, and husbandmen. We learn, also, from their history, that they were all ready, however diversified by their occupations or local interests, to join in a common cause; that they were well appointed for war, both offensive and defensive; that their towns were well fortified; that they were sufficiently furnished with military weapons and warlike chariots; that they were daring, obstinate, and almost invincible; and that they were not destitute of craft and policy. Their language, we find, was well understood by Abraham, who was a Hebrew, for he conversed readily with them on all occasions; but as to their mode of writing, whether it was originally their own or borrowed from the Israelites, it is not so easy to determine. Their religion, at least in part, seems to have been preserved pure till the days of Abraham, who acknowledged Melchisedek to be priest of the most high God; and Melchisedek was, without doubt, a Canaanite, or, at least, dwelt at that time in Canaan in high esteem and veneration.

2. But we learn from the Scripture history, that the Hittites in particular were become degenerate in the time of Isaac and Rebekah; for they could not endure the thoughts of Jacob's marrying one of the daughters of Heth, as Esau had done. From this time, then, we may date the prevalence of those abominations which subjected them to the divine displeasure, and made them unworthy of the land which they possessed. In the days of Moses, they were become incorrigible idolaters; for he commands his people to destroy their altars, and break down their images, (statues or pillars,) and cut down their groves, and burn their graven images with fire. And lest they should pervert the Israelites, the latter were strictly enjoined not to intermarry with them; but "to smite them, and utterly destroy them, nor show mercy upon them," Deut. vii, 1–5. They are accused of the cruel custom of sacrificing men, and are said to have made their seed pass through the fire to Moloch, Lev. xviii, 21. Their morals were as corrupt as their doctrine: adultery, bestiality of all sorts, profanation, incest, and all manner of uncleanness, are the sins laid to their charge. "The Canaanites," says Mr. Bryant, "as they were a sister tribe of the Mizraim, resembled them in their rites and religion. They held a heifer, or cow, in high veneration, agreeably to the customs of Egypt. Their chief deity was the sun, whom they worshipped, together with the Baalim, under the titles of Ourchol, Adonis, or Thamuz."

3. When the measure of the idolatries and abominations of the Canaanites was filled up, God delivered their country into the hands of the Israelites, who conquered it under Joshua. However, they resisted with obstinate valour, and kept Joshua employed six years from the time of his passing the river Jordan, and entering Canaan, in the year B. C. 1451, to the year B. C. 1445, the sabbatical year beginning from the autumnal equinox; when he made a division of the land among the tribes of Israel, and rested from his conquests. As God had commanded this people, long before, to be treated with rigour, see Deut. vii, 2, Joshua extirpated great numbers, and obliged the rest to fly, some of them into Africa, and others into Greece. Procopius says, they first retreated into Egypt, but advanced into Africa, where they built many cities, and spread themselves over those vast regions which reach to the straits, preserving their old language with little alteration. In the time of Athanasius, the Africans still said they were descended from the Canaanites; and when asked their origin, they answered,

"Canani." It is agreed, that the Punic tongue was nearly the same as the Canaanitish or Hebrew.

4. On the rigorous treatment of the nations of Canaan by the Israelites, to which infidels have taken so many exceptions, the following remarks of Paley are a sufficient reply: The first thing to be observed is, that the nations of Canaan were destroyed for their wickedness. This is plain from Lev. xviii, 24, &c. Now the facts disclosed in this passage sufficiently testify, that the Canaanites were a wicked people; that detestable practices were general among them, and even habitual; that it was for these enormities the nations of Canaan were destroyed. It was not, as some have imagined, to make way for the Israelites; nor was it simply to make away with their idolatry; but it was because of the abominable crimes which usually accompanied the latter. And we may farther learn from the passage, that God's abhorrence of these crimes and his indignation against them are regulated by the rules of strict impartiality, since Moses solemnly warns the Israelites against falling into the like wicked courses, "that the land," says he, "cast not you out also, when you defile it, as it cast out the nations that were before you; for whosoever shall commit any of these abominations, even the souls that commit them shall be cut off from among their people," Lev. xviii, 28, 29. Now, when God, for the wickedness of a people, sends an earthquake, or a fire, or a plague among them, there is no complaint of injustice, especially when the calamity is known, or expressly declared beforehand, to be inflicted for the wickedness of such people. It is rather regarded as an act of exemplary penal justice, and, as such, consistent with the character of the moral Governor of the universe. The objection, therefore, is not to the Canaanitish nations being destroyed; (for when their national wickedness is considered, and when that is expressly stated as the cause of their destruction, the dispensation, however severe, will not be questioned;) but the objection is solely to the manner of destroying them. I mean there is nothing but the manner left to be objected to: their wickedness accounts for the thing itself. To which objection it may be replied, that if the thing itself be just, the manner is of little signification, of little signification even to the sufferers themselves. For where is the great difference, even to them, whether they were destroyed by an earthquake, a pestilence, a famine, or by the hands of an enemy? Where is the difference, even to our imperfect apprehensions of divine justice, provided it be, and is known to be, for their wickedness that they are destroyed? But this destruction, you say, confounded the innocent with the guilty. The sword of Joshua, and of the Jews spared neither women nor children. Is it not the same with all other national visitations? Would not an earthquake, or a fire, or a plague, or a famine among them have done the same? Even in an ordinary and natural death the same thing happens; God takes away the life he lends, without regard, that we can perceive, to age, or sex, or character. "But, after all, promiscuous massacres, the burning of cities, the laying waste of countries, are things dreadful to reflect upon." Who doubts it? so are all the judgments of Almighty God. The effect, in whatever way it shows itself, must necessarily be tremendous, when the Lord, as the Psalmist expresses it, "moveth out of his place to punish the wicked." But it ought to satisfy us; at least this is the point upon which we ought to rest and fix our attention; that it was for excessive, wilful, and forewarned wickedness, that all this befel them, and that it is all along so declared in the history which recites it.

But, farther, if punishing them by the hands of the Israelites rather than by a pestilence, an earthquake, a fire, or any such calamity, be still an objection, we may perceive, I think, some reasons for this method of punishment in preference to any other whatever; always bearing in our mind, that the question is not concerning the justice of the punishment, but the mode of it. It is well known, that the people of those ages were affected by no proof of the power of the gods which they worshipped, so deeply as by their giving them victory in war. It was by this species of evidence that the superiority of their own gods above the gods of the nations which they conquered, was, in their opinion, evinced. This being the actual persuasion which then prevailed in the world, no matter whether well or ill founded, how were the neighbouring nations, for whose admonition this dreadful example was intended, how were they to be convinced of the supreme power of the God of Israel above the pretended gods of other nations; and of the righteous character of Jehovah, that is, of his abhorrence of the vices which prevailed in the land of Canaan? How, I say, were they to be convinced so well, or at all indeed, as by enabling the Israelites, whose God he was known and acknowledged to be, to conquer under his banner, and drive out before them, those who resisted the execution of that commission with which the Israelites declared themselves to be invested, namely, the expulsion and extermination of the Canaanitish nations? This convinced surrounding countries, and all who were observers or spectators of what passed, first, that the God of Israel was a real God; secondly, that the gods which other nations worshipped, were either no gods, or had no power against the God of Israel; and thirdly, that it was he, and he alone, who possessed both the power and the will, to punish, to destroy, and to exterminate from before his face, both nations and individuals, who gave themselves up to the crimes and wickedness for which the Canaanites were notorious. Nothing of this sort would have appeared, or with the same evidence, from an earthquake, or a plague, or any natural calamity. These might not have been attributed to divine agency at all, or not to the interposition of the God of Israel.

Another reason which made this destruction both more necessary, and more general, than it would have otherwise been, was the consideration, that if any of the old inhabitants were left, they would prove a snare to those who succeeded them in the country; would draw and seduce them by degrees into the vices and corruptions which prevailed among themselves. Vices of all kinds, but vices most particularly of the licentious kind, are astonishingly infectious. A little leaven leaveneth the whole lump. A small number of persons addicted to them, and allowed to practise them with impunity or encouragement, will spread them through the whole mass. This reason is formally and expressly assigned, not simply for the punishment, but for the extent to which it was carried; namely, extermination: "Thou shalt utterly destroy them, that they teach you not to do after all their abominations, which they have done unto their gods."

In reading the Old Testament account, therefore, of the Jewish wars and conquests in Canaan, and the terrible destruction brought upon the inhabitants thereof, we are always to remember that we are reading the execution of a dreadful but just sentence, pronounced by Jehovah against the intolerable and incorrigible crimes of these nations; that they were intended to be made an example to the whole world of God's avenging wrath against sins, which, if they had been suffered to continue, might have polluted the whole ancient world, and which could only be checked by the signal and public overthrow of nations notoriously addicted to them, and so addicted as even to have incorporated them into their religion and their public institutions; and that the Israelites were mere instruments in the hands of a righteous Providence for effecting the extirpation of a people, of whom it was necessary to make a public example to the rest of mankind; that this extermination, which might have been accomplished by a pestilence, by fire, by earthquakes, was appointed to be done by the hands of the Israelites, as being the clearest and most intelligible method of displaying the power and the righteousness of the God of Israel; his power over the pretended gods of other nations; and his righteous indignation against the crimes into which they were fallen.

CANDACE, the name of an Ethiopian queen, whose eunuch coming to Jerusalem to worship the Lord, was baptized by Philip the deacon, near Bethsura, in the way to Gaza, as he was returning to his own country, Acts viii, 27. The Ethiopia here mentioned was the isle or peninsula of Meroë to the south of Egypt, which, as Mr. Bruce shows, is now called Atbara, up the Nile. Candace was the common name of the queens of that country. Strabo and Pliny mention queens of that name as reigning in their times. That the queen mentioned in the Acts was converted by the instrumentality of her servant, and that the country thus received Christianity at that early period, are statements not supported by any good testimony. See Abyssinian Church.

CANDLESTICK. The instrument so rendered by our translators was more properly a stand for lamps. One of beaten gold was made by Moses, Exod. xxv, 31, 32, and put into the tabernacle in the holy place, over against the table of shew bread. The basis of this candlestick was also of pure gold; it had seven branches, three on each side, and one in the middle. When Solomon had built the temple, he was not satisfied with placing one golden candlestick there, but had ten put up, of the same form and metal with that described by Moses, five on the north, and five on the south side of the holy place, 1 Kings vii, 49. After the Jews returned from their captivity, the golden candlestick was again placed in the temple, as it had been before in the tabernacle by Moses. The lamps were kept burning perpetually; and were supplied morning and evening with pure olive oil. Josephus says, that after the Romans had destroyed the temple, the several things which were found within it, were carried in triumph to Rome, namely, the golden table, and the golden candlestick with seven branches. These were lodged in the temple built by Vespasian, and consecrated to Peace; and at the foot of Mount Palatine, there is a triumphal arch still visible, upon which Vespasian's triumph is represented, and the several monuments which were carried publicly in the procession are engraved, and among the rest the candlestick with the seven branches, which are still discernible upon it. In Rev. i, 12, 20, mention is made of seven golden candlesticks, which are said to be emblems of the seven Christian churches.

CANKER-WORM, ילק, Psalm cv, 34; Jer. li, 27, where it is rendered CATERPILLAR; Joel i, 4; ii, 25; Nahum iii, 15, CANKER-WORM. As it is frequently mentioned with the locust, it is thought by some to be a species of that insect. It certainly cannot be the canker-worm, as our version renders it; for in Nahum, it is expressly said to have wings and fly, to camp in the hedges by day, and commit its depredations in the night. But it may be, as the Septuagint renders it in five passages out of eight where it occurs, the BRUCHUS, or "hedge-chaffer." Nevertheless, the passage, Jer. li, 27, where the IALEK is described as "rough," that is, with hair standing on end on it, leads us very naturally to the rendering of our translators in that place, "the rough caterpillar," which, like other caterpillars, at a proper time, casts its exterior covering and flies away in a winged state. Scheuchzer observes that we should not, perhaps, be far from the truth, if with the ancient interpreters, we understood this IALEK, after all, as a kind of locust; as some species of them have hair principally on the head, and others have prickly points standing out.

CANON, a word used to denote the authorized catalogue of the sacred writings. The word is originally Greek, κανὼν, and signifies a RULE or STANDARD, by which other things are to be examined and judged. Accordingly the same word has been applied to the tongue of a balance, or that small part which, by its perpendicular position, determines the even poise or weight, or, by its inclination either way, the uneven poise of the things which are weighed. Hence it appears, that as the writings of the Prophets, Apostles, and Evangelists contain an authentic account of the revealed will of God, they are the rule of the belief and practice of those who receive them. Canon is also equivalent to a list or catalogue, in which are inserted those books which contain the rule of faith.

For an account of the settling of the canon of Scripture, see BIBLE. The following observations of Dr. Alexander, in his work on the canon, proving that no canonical book of the Old or New Testament has been lost, may here be properly introduced.--No canonical book of the Old Testament has been lost. On this subject, there has existed some diversity of opinion. Chrysostom is cited by

Bellarmine as saying, "that many of the writings of the prophets had perished, which may readily be proved from the history in Chronicles. For the Jews were negligent, and not only negligent, but impious; so that some books were lost through carelessness, and others were burned, or otherwise destroyed." In confirmation of this opinion, an appeal is made to 1 Kings iv, 32, 33, where it is said of Solomon, "that he spake three thousand proverbs, and his songs were a thousand and five. And he spake of trees, from the cedar in Lebanon even unto the hyssop that springeth out of the wall: he spake also of beasts, and of fowl, and of creeping things, and of fishes." All these productions, it is acknowledged, have perished. Again it is said in 1 Chron. xxix, 29, 30: "Now, the acts of David the king, first and last, behold they are written in the book of Samuel the seer, and in the book of Nathan the prophet, and in the book of Gad the seer; with all his reign, and his might, and the times that went over him, and over Israel, and over all the kingdoms of the countries." The book of Jasher, also, is twice mentioned in Scripture. In Joshua x, 13: "And the sun stood still, and the moon stayed, until the people had avenged themselves on their enemies. Is not this written in the book of Jasher?" And in 2 Sam. i, 18: "And he bade them teach the children of Israel the use of the bow: behold, it is written in the book of Jasher."

The book of the wars of the Lord is referred to in Numbers xxi, 14. But we have in the canon no books under the name of Nathan and Gad, nor any book of Jasher, nor of the wars of the Lord. Moreover, we frequently are referred, in the sacred history, to other chronicles or annals, for a fuller account of the matters spoken of, which chronicles are not now extant. And in 2 Chron. ix, 29, it is said, "Now, the rest of the acts of Solomon, first and last, are they not written in the book of Nathan the prophet, and in the prophecy of Ahijah the Shilonite, and in the visions of Iddo the seer, against Jeroboam, the son of Nebat?" Now, it is well known that none of these writings of the prophets are in the canon; at least, none of them under their names. It is said, also, in 2 Chron. xii, 15, "Now, the acts of Rehoboam, first and last, are they not written in the book of Shemaiah the prophet, and of Iddo the seer, concerning genealogies?" Of which works nothing remains under the names of these prophets.

1. The first observation which may be made on this subject is, that every book referred to or quoted in the sacred writings is not necessarily an inspired or canonical book. Because St. Paul cites passages from the Greek poets, it does not follow that we must receive their poems as inspired.

2. A book may be written by an inspired man, and yet be neither inspired nor canonical. Inspiration was not constantly afforded to the prophets; but was occasional, and for particular important purposes. In common matters, and especially in things no way connected with religion, it is reasonable to suppose that the Prophets and Apostles were left to the same guidance of reason and common sense as other men. A man, therefore, inspired to deliver some prophecy, or even to write a canonical book, might write other books with no greater assistance than other good men receive. Because Solomon was inspired to write some canonical books, it does not follow that what he wrote on natural history was also inspired, any more than Solomon's private letters to his friends, if ever he wrote any. Let it be remembered that the Prophets and Apostles were only inspired on special occasions, and on particular subjects, and all difficulties respecting such works as these will vanish. How many of the books referred to in the Bible, and mentioned above, may have been of this description, it is now impossible to tell; but probably several of them belong to this class. No doubt there were many books of annals much more minute and particular in the narration of facts than those which we have. It was often enough merely to refer to these STATE PAPERS, or public documents, as being sufficiently correct, in regard to the facts on account of which the reference was made. The book of the wars of the Lord might, for aught that appears, have been merely a muster roll of the army. The word translated BOOK has so extensive a meaning in Hebrew, that it is not even necessary to suppose that it was a writing at all. The book of Jasher (or of RECTITUDE, if we translate the word) might have been some useful compend taken from Scripture, or composed by the wise, for the regulation of justice and equity between man and man. Augustine, in his "City of God," has distinguished accurately on this subject. "I think," says he, "that those books which should have authority in religion were revealed by the Holy Spirit, and that men composed others by historical diligence, as the prophets did these by inspiration. And these two classes of books are so distinct, that it is only by those written by inspiration that we are to suppose that God, through them, is speaking unto us. The one class is useful for fulness of knowledge; the other, for authority in religion; in which authority the canon is preserved."

3. But again: it may be maintained, without any prejudice to the completeness of the canon, that there may have been inspired writings which were not intended for the instruction of the church in all ages, but composed by the prophets for some special occasion. These writings, though inspired, were not canonical. They were temporary in their design; and when that was accomplished, they were no longer needed. We know that the prophets delivered, by inspiration, many discourses to the people, of which we have not a trace on record. Many true prophets are mentioned, who wrote nothing that we know of; and several are mentioned, whose names are not even given. The same is true of the Apostles. Very few of them had any concern in writing the canonical Scriptures, and yet they all possessed plenary inspiration. And if they wrote letters on special occasions, to the churches planted by them; yet these were not designed for the perpetual instruction of the universal church. Therefore, Shemaiah, and Iddo, and Nathan, and Gad, might have written some things by inspiration which were never intended to form a part of the sacred volume. It is not asserted that there certainly existed such temporary inspired writings: all that is necessary to be maintained is, that, supposing such to have existed, which

is not improbable, it does not follow that the canon is incomplete by reason of their loss.

4. The last remark in relation to the books of the Old Testament supposed to be lost is, that it is highly probable that we have several of them now in the canon, under another name. The books of Samuel, Kings, and Chronicles, were, probably, not written by one, but by a succession of prophets. There is reason to believe that, until the canon of sacred Scripture was closed, the succession of prophets was never interrupted. Whatever was necessary to be added, by way of explanation, to any book already received into the canon, they were competent to annex; or, whatever annals or histories it was the purpose of God to have transmitted to posterity, they would be directed and inspired to prepare. Thus, different parts of these books might have been penned by Gad, Nathan, Iddo, Shemaiah, &c. That some parts of these histories were prepared by prophets, we have clear proof in one instance; for Isaiah has inserted in his prophecy several chapters which are contained in 2 Kings, and which, I think, there can be no doubt were originally written by himself. The Jewish doctors are of opinion that the book of Jasher is one of the books of the Pentateuch, or the whole law. The book of the wars of the Lord has by many been supposed to be no other than the book of Numbers.

Thus, it sufficiently appears from an examination of particulars, that there exists no evidence that any canonical book of the Old Testament has been lost. To which we may add, that there are many general considerations of great weight which go to prove that no part of the Scriptures of the Old Testament has been lost. The translation of these books into Greek is sufficient to show that the same books existed nearly two hundred years before the advent of Christ. And, above all, the unqualified testimony to the Scriptures of the Old Testament, by Christ and his Apostles, ought to satisfy us that we have lost none of the inspired books of the canon. The Scriptures are constantly referred to, and quoted as infallible authority by them, as we have before shown. These oracles were committed to the Jews as a sacred deposit, and they are never charged with unfaithfulness in this trust. The Scriptures are declared to have been written "for our learning;" and no intimation is given that they had ever been mutilated, or in any degree corrupted.

As to the New Testament, the same author proceeds: With respect to the New Testament, I am ready to concede, as was before done, that there may have been books written by inspired men that have been lost; for inspiration was occasional, not constant; and confined to matters of faith, and not afforded on the affairs of this life, or in matters of mere science. And if such writings have been lost, the canon of Scripture has suffered no more by this means, than by the loss of any other uninspired books. But again: I am willing to go farther, and say that it is possible (although I know no evidence of the fact) that some things, written under the influence of inspiration, for a particular occasion, and to rectify some disorder in a particular church, may have been lost, without injury to the canon. For, since much that the Apostles preached by inspiration is undoubtedly lost, so there is no reason why every word which they wrote must necessarily be preserved, and form a part of the canonical volume. For example: suppose that when St. Paul said, "I wrote to you in an epistle not to company with fornicators," 1 Cor. v, 9, he referred to an epistle which he had written to the Corinthians, before the one now called the First; it might never have been intended that this letter should form a constituent part of the canon; for although it treated of subjects connected with Christian faith or practice, yet, an occasion having arisen, in a short time, of treating these subjects more at large, every thing in that epistle (supposing it ever to have been written) may have been included in the two Epistles to the Corinthians which are now in the canon.

1. The first argument to prove that no canonical book has been lost, is derived from the watchful care of providence over the sacred Scriptures. Now, to suppose that a book written by the inspiration of the Holy Spirit, and intended to form a part of the canon, which is the rule of faith to the church, should be utterly and irrecoverably lost, is surely not very honourable to the wisdom of God, and in no way consonant with the ordinary method of his dispensations, in regard to his precious truth. There is good reason to think that, if God saw it needful, and for the edification of the church, that such books should be written under the inspiration of the Holy Spirit, by his providence he would have taken care to preserve them from destruction. We do know that this treasure of divine truth has been, in all ages, and in the worst times, the special care of God, or not one of the sacred books would now be in existence. And if one canonical book might be lost through the negligence or unfaithfulness of men, why not all? And thus the end of God, in making a revelation of his will, might have been defeated. But whatever other corruptions have crept into the Jewish or Christian churches, it does not appear that either of them, as a body, ever incurred the censure of having been careless in preserving the oracles of God. Our Saviour never charges the Jews, who perverted the sacred Scriptures to their own ruin, with having lost any portion of the sacred deposit intrusted to them. History informs us of the fierce and malignant design of Antiochus Epiphanes, to abolish every vestige of the sacred volume; but the same history assures us that the Jewish people manifested a heroic fortitude and invincible patience in resisting and defeating his impious purpose. They chose rather to sacrifice their lives, and suffer a cruel death, than to deliver up the copies of the sacred volume in their possession. And the same spirit was manifested, and with the same result, in the Dioclesian persecution of the Christians. Every effort was made to obliterate the sacred writings of Christians; and multitudes suffered death for refusing to deliver up the New Testament. Some, indeed, overcome by the terrors of a cruel persecution, did, in the hour of temptation, consent to surrender the holy book; but they were ever afterward called traitors; and it was with the utmost difficulty that any of them could be received again into the communion of the church, after a long repentance, and the most humbling

confessions of their fault. Now, if any canonical book was ever lost, it must have been in these early times, when the word of God was valued far above life, and when every Christian stood ready to seal the truth with his blood.

2. Another argument which appears to me to be convincing is, that in a little time, all the sacred books were dispersed over the whole world. If a book had, by some accident or violence, been destroyed in one region, the loss could soon have been repaired, by sending for copies to other countries. The considerations just mentioned would, I presume, be satisfactory to all candid minds, were it not that it is supposed that there is evidence that some things were written by the Apostles which are not now in the canon. We have already referred to an epistle to the Corinthians, which St. Paul is supposed to have written to them, previously to the writing of those which we now possess. But it is by no means certain, or even probable, that St. Paul ever did write such an epistle; for not one ancient writer makes the least mention of any such letter, nor is there any where to be found any citation from it, or any reference to it. It is a matter of testimony, in which all the fathers concur, as with one voice, that St. Paul wrote no more than fourteen epistles, all of which we now have. But still, St. Paul's own declaration stands in the way of our opinion: "I wrote to you in an epistle," 1 Cor. v, 9, 11. The words in the original are, Ἔγραψα ὑμῖν ἐν τῇ ἐπιϛολῇ; the literal version of which is, "I have written to you in the epistle," or "in this epistle;" that is, in the former part of it; where, in fact, we find the very thing which he says that he had written. See 1 Cor. v, 2, 5, 6. But it is thought by learned and judicious commentators, that the words following, Νυνὶ δὲ ἔγραψα ὑμῖν, "But now I have written unto you," require that we should understand the former clause, as relating to some former time; but a careful attention to the context will convince us that this reference is by no means necessary. The Apostle had told them in the beginning of the chapter, to avoid the company of fornicators, &c; but it is manifest, from the tenth verse, that he apprehended that his meaning might be misunderstood, by extending the prohibition too far, so as to decline all intercourse with the world; therefore, he repeats what he had said, and informs them that it had relation only to the professors of Christianity, who should be guilty of such vices. The whole may be thus paraphrased: "I wrote to you above in my letter, that you should separate from those who were fornicators, and that you should purge them out as old leaven; but, fearing lest you should misapprehend my meaning, by inferring that I have directed you to avoid all intercourse with the Heathen around you, who are addicted to these shameful vices, which would make it necessary that you should go out of the world, I now inform you that my meaning is, that you do not associate familiarly with any who make a profession of Christianity, and yet continue in these evil practices." In confirmation of this interpretation, we can adduce the old Syriac version, which, having been made soon after the days of the Apostles, is good testimony in relation to this matter of fact. In this venerable version, the meaning of the eleventh verse is thus given: "This is what I have written unto you," or, "the meaning of what I have written unto you."

The only other passage in the New Testament which has been thought to refer to an epistle of St. Paul not now extant, is that in Colossians iv, 16: "And when this epistle is read among you, cause also that it be read in the church of the Laodiceans, and that ye likewise read the epistle from Laodicea." But what evidence is there that St. Paul ever wrote an epistle to the Laodiceans? The text on which this opinion has been founded, in ancient and modern times, correctly interpreted, has no such import. The words in the original are, καὶ τὴν ἐκ Λαοδικείας ἵνα καὶ ὑμεῖς ἀναγνῶτε, "and that ye likewise read the epistle from Laodicea," Col. iv, 16. These words have been differently taken; for, by them some understand that an epistle had been written by St. Paul to the Laodiceans, which he desired might be read in the church at Colosse. Chrysostom seems to have understood them thus; and the Romish writers almost universally have adopted this opinion. "Therefore," says Bellarmine, "it is certain that St. Paul's epistle to the Laodiceans is now lost." And their opinion is favoured by the Latin Vulgate, where we read, EAMQUE LAODICENSIUM, "that which is of the Laodiceans;" but even these words admit of another construction. Many learned Protestants, also, have embraced the same interpretation; while others suppose that St. Paul here refers to the epistle to the Ephesians, which they think he sent to the Laodiceans, and that the present inscription is spurious. But that neither of these opinions is correct, may be rendered very probable. That St. Paul could not intend, by the language used in the passage under consideration, an epistle written by himself, will appear by the following arguments: (1.) St. Paul could not, with any propriety of speech, have called an epistle written by himself, and sent to the Laodiceans, an epistle FROM Laodicea. He certainly would have said, πρὸς Λαοδικείαν, [to Laodicea,] or some such thing. Who ever heard of an epistle addressed to any individual, or to any society, denominated an epistle from them? (2.) If the epistle referred to in this passage had been one written by St. Paul, it would have been most natural for him to call it his epistle; and this would have rendered his meaning incapable of misconstruction. (3.) All those best qualified to judge of the fact, and who were well acquainted with St. Paul's history and writings, never mention any such epistle: neither Clement, Hermas, nor the Syriac interpreter, knew any thing of such an epistle of St. Paul. But it may be asked, To what epistle, then, does St. Paul refer? It seems safest in such a case, where testimony is deficient, to follow the literal sense of the words, and to believe that it was an epistle written by the Laodiceans, probably to himself, which he had sent to the Colossians, together with his own epistle, for their perusal.

CANTICLES, THE BOOK OF, in Hebrew, שיר השירים, THE SONG OF SONGS. The church, as well as the synagogue, received this book generally as canonical. The royal author appears, in the typical spirit of his times, to have designed to render a ceremonial appointment descriptive of a spiritual relation; and this song is accordingly considered, by judicious writers, to be a mystical allegory of that sort which induces a more sublime sense on historical truths, and which, by the description of human events, shadows out divine circumstances. The sacred writers were, by God's condescension, authorized to illustrate his strict and intimate relation to the church by the figure of a marriage; and the emblem must have been strikingly becoming and expressive to the conceptions of the Jews, since they annexed ideas of peculiar mystery to this appointment, and imagined the marriage union to be a counterpart representation of some original pattern in heaven. Hence it was performed among them with very peculiar ceremonies and solemnity, with every thing that could give dignity and importance to its rites. Solomon, therefore, in celebrating the circumstances of his marriage, was naturally led, by a train of correspondent reflections, to consider that spiritual connection which it was often employed to symbolize; and the idea must have been the more forcibly suggested to him, as he was at this period preparing to build a temple to God, and thereby to furnish a visible representation of the Hebrew church. The spiritual allegory thus worked up by Solomon to its highest perfection, was very consistent with the prophetic style, which was accustomed to predict evangelical blessings by such parabolical figures; and Solomon was more immediately furnished with a pattern for this representation by the author of the forty-fifth Psalm, who describes, in a compendious allegory, the same future connection between Christ and his church.

2. But though the work be certainly an allegorical representation, many learned men, in an unrestrained eagerness to explain the song, even in its minutest and most obscure particulars, have too far indulged their imaginations; and, by endeavouring too nicely to reconcile the literal with the spiritual sense, have been led beyond the boundaries which a reverence for the sacred Scriptures should ever prescribe. The ideas which the sacred writers furnish concerning the mystical relation between Christ and his church, though well accommodated to our apprehensions by the allusion of a marriage union, are too general to illustrate every particular contained in this poem, which may be supposed to have been intentionally decorated with some ornaments appropriate to the literal construction. When the general analogy is obvious, we are not always to expect minute resemblance, and should not be too curious in seeking for obscure and recondite allusions. Solomon, in the glow of an inspired fancy, and unsuspicious of misconception or deliberate perversion, describes God and his church, with their respective attributes and graces, under colourings familiar and agreeable to mankind, and exhibits their ardent affection under the authorized figures of earthly love. No similitude, indeed, could be chosen so elegant and apposite for the illustration of this intimate and spiritual alliance, as a marriage union, if considered in the chaste simplicity of its first institution, or under the interesting circumstances with which it was established among the Jews.

3. This poem may be considered, as to its form, as a dramatic poem of the pastoral kind. There is a succession of time, and a change of place, to different parts of the palace and royal gardens. The persons introduced as speakers, are the bridegroom and bride, and their respective attendants. The interchange of dialogue is carried on in a wild and digressive manner; but the speeches are adapted to the persons with appropriate elegance. The companions of the bride compose a kind of chorus, which seems to bear some resemblance to that afterward adopted in the Grecian tragedy. Solomon and his queen assume the pastoral simplicity of style, which is favourable to the communication of their sentiments. The poem abounds throughout with beauties, and presents every where a delightful and romantic display of nature, painted at its most interesting season, and described with every ornament that an inventive fancy could furnish. It is justly entitled Song of Songs, or most excellent song, as being superior to any that an uninspired writer could have produced, and tending, if properly understood, to purify the mind, and to elevate the affections from earthly to heavenly things.

CAPERNAUM, a city celebrated in the Gospels, being the place where Jesus usually resided during the time of his ministry. It stood on the sea coast, that is, on the coast of the sea of Galilee, in the borders of Zebulun and Naphtalim, Matt. iv, 15, and consequently toward the upper part of it. As it was a convenient port from Galilee to any place on the other side of the sea, this might be our Lord's inducement to make it the place of his most constant residence. Upon this account Capernaum was highly honoured; and though "exalted unto heaven," as its inhabitants boasted, because it made no proper use of this signal favour it drew from him the severe denunciation, that it should "be brought down to hell," Matt. xi, 23. This sentence of destruction has been fully realized; the ancient city is reduced to a state of utter desolation. Burckhardt supposes the ruins called Tal Houm, near the rivulet called El Eshe, to be those of Capernaum. Mr. Buckingham, who gives this place the name of Talhhewn, describes considerable and extensive ruins; the only remains of those edifices which exalted Capernaum above its fellows.

CAPPADOCIA, is called in Hebrew CAPHTOR. Cappadocia joined Galatia on the east, and is mentioned in Acts ii, 9, and by St. Peter, who addresses his First Epistle to the dispersed throughout Pontus, Galatia, Cappadocia, Bithynia, and Asia. The people of this country were formerly infamous for their vices; but after the promulgation of Christianity, it produced many great and worthy men: among these may be reckoned Gregory Nazianzen, Gregory Nyssen, and St. Basil, commonly styled the Great.

CAPTIVES. The treatment of persons taken in war among ancient nations throws great light upon many passages of Scripture. The eastern conqueror often stripped his unhappy captives naked, shaved their heads, and made them travel in that condition, exposed to the burning heat of a vertical sun by day, and the chilling cold of the night.

Such barbarous treatment was to modest women the height of cruelty and indignity; especially to those who had been educated in softness and elegance, who had figured in all the superfluities of ornamental dress, and whose faces had hardly ever been exposed to the sight of man. The Prophet Isaiah mentions this as the hardest part of the sufferings in which female captives are involved: "The Lord will expose their nakedness." The daughter of Zion had indulged in all the softness of oriental luxury; but the offended Jehovah should cause her unrelenting enemies to drag her forth from her secret chambers into the view of an insolent soldiery; strip her of her ornaments, in which she so greatly delighted; take away her splendid and costly garments, discover her nakedness, and compel her to travel in that miserable plight to a far distant country, a helpless captive, the property of a cruel lord. Arrived in the land of their captivity, captives were often purchased at a very low price. The Prophet Joel complains of the contemptuous cheapness in which the people of Israel were held by those who made them captives: "And they have cast lots for my people; and have given a boy for a harlot, and sold a girl for wine, that they might drink." The custom of casting lots for the captives taken in war appears to have prevailed both among the Jews and the Greeks. The same allusion occurs in the prophecy of Obadiah: "Strangers carried away captive his forces, and foreigners entered into his gates, and cast lots upon Jerusalem," Obadiah 11. With respect to the Greeks, we have an instance in Tryphiodorus:--

"Shared out by lot the female captives stand,

The spoils divided with an equal hand;

Each to his ship conveys his rightful share,

Price of their toil, and trophies of the war."

2. By an inhuman custom which is still retained in the east, the eyes of captives taken in war were not seldom put out, sometimes literally scooped or dug out of their sockets. This dreadful calamity Samson had to endure from the unrelenting vengeance of his enemies. In a posterior age, Zedekiah, the last king of Judah and Benjamin, after being compelled to behold the violent death of his sons and nobility, had his eyes put out, and was carried in chains to Babylon. The barbarous custom long survived the decline and fall of the Babylonian empire; for by the testimony of Mr. Maurice, in his history of Hindostan, the captive princes of that country were often treated in this manner by their more fortunate rivals; a red hot iron was passed over their eyes, which effectually deprived them of sight, and at the same time of their title and ability to reign. To the wretched state of such prisoners, the Prophet Isaiah alludes in a noble prediction, where he describes in very glowing colours the character and work of the promised Messiah: "He hath sent me to heal the broken hearted, to preach deliverance to the captives, and recovering of sight to the blind, to set at liberty them that are bruised," as captives too frequently were by the weight of their fetters.

3. It seems to have been the practice of eastern kings, to command their captives taken in war, especially those that had, by the atrociousness of their crimes, or the stoutness of their resistance, greatly provoked their indignation, to lie down on the ground, and then put to death a certain part of them, which they measured with a line, or determined by lot. This custom was not, perhaps, commonly practised by the people of God, in their wars with the nations around them; but one instance is recorded in the life of David, who inflicted this punishment on the Moabites: "And he smote Moab, and measured them with a line, casting them down to the ground; even with two lines measured he to put to death, and with one full line to keep alive: and so the Moabites became David's servants, and brought gifts," 2 Sam. viii, 2. But the most shocking punishment which the ingenious cruelty of a haughty and unfeeling conqueror ever inflicted on the miserable captive, is described by Virgil in the eighth book of the Æneid; and which even a Roman, inured to blood, could not mention without horror:--

"QUID MEMOREM INFANDAS CÆDES? QUID FACTA TYRANNI," &c.

Line 483.

"What words can paint those execrable times,

The subjects' sufferings, and the tyrant's crimes!

That blood, those murders, O ye gods! replace

On his own head, and on his impious race:

The living and the dead at his command

Were coupled face to face, and hand to hand,

Till, choked with stench, in loathed embraces tied,

The lingering wretches pined away, and died."

Dryden.

It is to this deplorable condition of a captive that the Apostle refers, in that pathetic exclamation, "O wretched man that I am! who shall deliver me from the body of this death?" Who shall rescue me, miserable captive as I am, from this continual burden of sin which I carry about with me; and which is cumbersome and odious, as a dead carcass bound to a living body, to be dragged along with it where-ever it goes?

CAPTIVITY. God generally punished the sins and infidelities of the Jews by different captivities or servitudes. The first captivity is that of Egypt, from which they were delivered by Moses, and which should be considered rather as a permission of providence, than as a punishment for sin. Six captivities are reckoned during the government by judges: the first, under Chushanrishathaim, king of Mesopotamia, which continued about eight years; the second, under Eglon, king of Moab, from which the Jews were delivered by Ehud; the third, under the Philistines, from which they were rescued by Shamgar; the fourth, under Jabin, king of Hazor, from which they were delivered by Deborah and Barak; the fifth, under the Midianites, from which Gideon freed them; and the sixth, under the Ammonites and Philistines, during the judicatures of Jephthah, Ibzan, Elon, Abdon, Eli, Samson, and Samuel. But the greatest and most remarkable captivities were those of Israel and Judah, under their regal government.

Captivities of Israel. In the year of the world 3264, Tiglath-pileser took several cities, and carried away captives, principally from the tribes of Reuben, Gad, and the half tribe of Manasseh, 2 Kings xv, 29. In the year of the world 3283, Shalmaneser took and destroyed Samaria, after a siege of three years, and transplanted the tribes that had been spared by Tiglath-pileser, to provinces beyond the Euphrates, 2 Kings xviii, 10, 11. It is generally believed, there was no return of the ten tribes from this second captivity. But when we examine carefully the writings of the Prophets, we find a return of at least a great part of Israel from the captivity clearly pointed out. Hosea says, "They shall tremble as a bird out of Egypt, and as a dove out of the land of Assyria; and I will place them in their houses, saith the Lord," Hosea xi, 11. Amos says, "And I will bring again my people Israel from their captivity: they shall build their ruined cities and inhabit them," &c, Amos ix, 14. Obadiah observes, "The captivity of this host of the children of Israel shall possess that of the Canaanites," &c, Obadiah 18, 19. To the same purpose speak the other Prophets. "The Lord shall assemble the outcast of Israel, and gather together the dispersed of Judah," Isa. xi, 12, 13. Ezekiel received an order from God to take two pieces of wood, and write on one, "For Judah and for the children of Israel;" and on the other, "For Joseph and for all the house of Israel;" and to join these two pieces of wood, that they might become one, and designate the reunion of Judah and Israel, Ezek. xxxvii, 16. Jeremiah is equally express: "The house of Judah shall walk with the house of Israel; and they shall come together out of the north, to the land which I have given for an inheritance to their fathers," Jer. iii, 18. See also Jer. xxxi, 7–9, 16, 17, 20; xvi, 15; xlix, 2, &c; Zech. ix, 13; x, 6, 10; Micah ii, 12. In the historical books of Scripture, we find that Israelites of the ten tribes, as well as of Judah and Benjamin, returned from the captivity. Among those that returned with Zerubbabel are reckoned some of Ephraim and Manasseh, who settled at Jerusalem with the tribe of Judah. When Ezra numbered those who returned from the captivity, he only inquired whether they were of the race of Israel; and at the first passover which was then celebrated in the temple, was a sacrifice of twelve he-goats for the whole house of Israel, according to the number of the tribes, Ezra vi, 16, 17; viii, 35. Under the Maccabees, and in our Saviour's time, we see Palestine peopled by Israelites of all the tribes indifferently. The Samaritan Chronicle asserts that in the thirty-fifth year of the pontificate of Abdelus, three thousand Israelites, by permission of King Sauredius, returned from captivity, under the conduct of Adus, son of Simon.

Captivities of Judah. The captivities of Judah are generally reckoned four: the first, in the year of the world 3398, under King Jehoiakim, when Daniel and others were carried to Babylon; the second, in the year of the world 3401, and in the seventh year of the reign of Jehoiakim, when Nebuchadnezzar carried three thousand and twenty-three Jews to Babylon; the third, in the year of the world 3406, and in the fourth of Jehoiachin, when this prince, with part of his people, was sent to Babylon; and the fourth in the year 3416, under Zedekiah, from which period begins the captivity of seventy years, foretold by the Prophet Jeremiah. Dr. Hales computes that the first of these captivities, which he thinks formed the commencement of the Babylonish captivity, took place in the year before Christ 605. The Jews were removed to Babylon by Nebuchadnezzar, who, designing to render that city the capital of the east, transplanted thither very great numbers of people, subdued by him in different countries. In Babylon the Jews had judges and elders, who governed them, and who decided matters in dispute juridically, according to their laws. Of this we see a proof in the story of Susanna, who was condemned by elders of her own nation. Cyrus, in the year of the world 3457, and in the first year of his reign at Babylon, permitted the Jews to return to their own country, Ezra i, 1. However, they did not obtain leave to rebuild the temple; and the completion of those prophecies which foretold the termination of their captivity after seventy years, was not till the year of the world 3486. In that year, Darius Hystaspes, by an edict, allowed them to rebuild the temple. In the year of the world 3537, Artaxerxes Longimanus sent Nehemiah to Jerusalem. The Jews assert that only the refuse of their nation returned from the captivity, and that the principal of them continued in and near Babylon, where they had been settled, and where they became very numerous. It may, however, be doubted whether the refuse of Judah was really carried to Babylon. It appears from incidental observations in Scripture that some remained; and Major Rennell has offered several reasons for believing that only certain classes of the Jews were deported to Babylon, as well as into Assyria. Nebuchadnezzar carried away only the principal inhabitants, the warriors, and artisans of every kind; and he left the husbandmen, the labourers, and in general, the poorer classes, that constitute the great body of the people.

CARAITES, or **KARÆITES**, an ancient Jewish sect. The name signifies TEXTUALISTS, or SCRIPTURISTS, and was originally given to the school of Shammai, (about thirty years or more before Christ,) because they rejected the traditions of the elders, as embraced by the school of Hillel and the Pharisees, and all the fanciful interpretations of the Cabbala. They claim, however, a much higher antiquity, and produce a catalogue of doctors up to the time of Ezra. The rabbinists have been accustomed to call them Sadducees;

but they believed in the inspiration of the Scriptures, the resurrection of the dead, and the final judgment. They believe that Messiah is not yet come, and reject all calculations of the time of his appearance: yet they say, it is proper that even every day they should receive their salvation by Messiah, the Son of David. As to the practice of religion, they differ from the rabbinists in the observance of the festivals, and keep the Sabbath with more strictness. They extend their prohibition of marriage to more degrees of affinity, and admit not of divorce on any slight or trivial grounds. The sect of Caraites still exists, but their number is inconsiderable. They are found chiefly in the Crimea, Lithuania, and Persia; at Damascus, Constantinople, and Cairo. Their honesty in the Crimea is said to be proverbial.

CARBUNCLE, ברקת, Exod. xxviii, 17; xxxix, 10; Ezek. xxviii, 13; and ἄνθραξ, Eccles. xxxii, 5; Tobit xiii, 17; a very elegant and rare gem, known to the ancients by the name ἄνθραξ, or COAL, because, when held up before the sun, it appears like a piece of bright burning charcoal: the name CARBUNCULUS has the same meaning. It was the third stone in the first row of the pectoral; and is mentioned among the glorious stones of which the new Jerusalem is figuratively said to be built. Bishop Lowth observes that the precious stones, mentioned Isa. liv, 11, 12, and Rev. xxi, 18, seem to be general images to express beauty, magnificence, purity, strength, and solidity, agreeably to the ideas of the eastern nations; and to have never been intended to be strictly scrutinized, and minutely and particularly explained, as if they had some precise moral or spiritual meaning. Tobit, in his prophecy of the final restoration of Israel, Tobit xii, 16,17, describes the new Jerusalem in the same oriental manner.

CARMEL, in the southern part of Palestine, where Nabal the Carmelite, Abigail's husband, dwelt, Joshua xv, 55; 1 Sam. xxv.

2. Carmel was also the name of a celebrated mountain in Palestine. Though spoken of in general as a single mountain, it ought rather to be considered as a mountainous region, the whole of which was known by the name of Carmel, while to one of the hills, more elevated than the rest, that name was usually applied by way of eminence. It had the plain of Sharon on the south; overlooked the port of Ptolemais on the north; and was bounded on the west by the Mediterranean sea; forming one of the most remarkable promontories that present themselves on the shores of that great sea. According to Volney, it is about two thousand feet in height, and has the shape of a flattened cone. Its sides are steep and rugged; the soil neither deep nor rich; and among the naked rocks stinted with plants, and wild forests which it presents to the eye, there are at present but few traces of that fertility which we are accustomed to associate with the idea of Mount Carmel. Yet even Volney himself acknowledges that he found among the brambles, wild vines and olive trees, which proved that the hand of industry had once been employed on a not ungrateful soil. Of its ancient productiveness there can be no doubt; the etymology and ordinary application of its name being sufficient evidence of the fact. Carmel is not only expressly mentioned in Scripture as excelling other districts in that respect; but, every place possessed of the same kind of excellence obtained from it the same appellation in the language both of the prophets and the people. Mount Carmel is celebrated in the Old Testament, as the usual place of residence of the Prophets Elijah and Elisha. It was here that Elijah so successfully opposed the false prophets of Baal, 1 Kings xviii; and there is a certain part of the mountain facing the west, and about eight miles from the point of the promontory, which the Arabs call Mansur, and the Europeans the place of sacrifice, in commemoration of that miraculous event. Near the same place is also still shown a cave, in which it is said the Prophet had his residence. The brook Kishon, which issues from Mount Tabor, waters the bottom of Carmel, and falls into the sea toward the northern side of the mountain, and not the southern, as some writers have erroneously stated. Its greatest elevation is about one thousand five hundred feet; hence, when the sea coast on one side, and the plain on the other, are oppressed with sultry heat, this hill is refreshed by cooling breezes, and enjoys a delightful temperature. The fastnesses of this rugged mountain are so difficult of access, that the Prophet Amos classes them with the deeps of hell, the height of heaven, and the bottom of the sea: "Though they dig into hell," (or the dark and silent chambers of the grave,) "thence shall mine hand take them; though they climb up to heaven, thence will I bring them down; and though they hide themselves in the top of Carmel, I will search and take them out thence; and though they be hid from my sight in the bottom of the sea, thence will I command the serpent, and he shall bite them," Amos ix, 2, 3. Lebanon raises to heaven a summit of naked and barren rocks, covered for the greater part of the year with snow; but the top of Carmel, how naked and sterile soever its present condition, was clothed with verdure which seldom was known to fade. Even the lofty genius of Isaiah, stimulated and guided by the Spirit of inspiration, could not find a more appropriate figure to express the flourishing state of the Redeemer's kingdom, than "the excellency of Carmel and Sharon."

CART, a machine used in Palestine to force the corn out of the ear, and bruise the straw, Isaiah xxviii, 27, 28. The wheels of these carts were low, broad, and shod with iron, and were drawn over the sheaves spread on the floor by means, of oxen.

CASTOR and **POLLUX**. It is said that the vessel which carried Paul to Rome had the sign of Castor and Pollux, Acts xxviii, 11. Castor and Pollux were sea-gods, and invoked by sailors; and even the light balls or meteors which are sometimes seen on ships, were called Castor and Pollux. An inscription in Gruter proves that seamen implored Castor and Pollux in dangers at sea. It is to be observed, that St. Luke does not mention the name, but the sign, of the ship. By the word sign, the sacred writer meant a protecting image of the deity, to whom the vessel was in some sort consecrated; as at present in Catholic countries, most of their vessels are named after some saint, St. Xavier, St. Andero, St. Dominique, &c. It appears to be certain, that the figure which gave name to the ship was at the head, and the tutelary deity was placed on the poop.

CASUIST, one who studies and decides upon cases of conscience. Escobar has made a collection of the opinions of all the casuists before his time. M. Le Feore, preceptor to Louis **XIII**, said that the books of the casuists taught "the art of quibbling with God;" which does not seem far from truth, by reason of the multitude of distinctions and subtleties with which they abound. Mayer has published a bibliotheca of casuists, containing an account of all the writers on cases of conscience, ranged under three heads; the first comprehending the Lutheran; the second, the Calvinistic; and the third, the Roman casuists.

CASUISTRY, the doctrine and science of conscience and its cases, with the rules and principles of resolving the same; drawn partly from natural reason, or equity, and partly from the authority of Scripture, the canon law, councils, fathers, &c. To casuistry belongs the decision of all difficulties arising about what a man may lawfully do or not do; what is sin or not sin; what things a man is obliged to do in order to discharge his duty, and what he may let alone without breach of it. Although the morality of the Gospel is distinguished by its purity and by its elevation, it is necessarily exhibited in a general form; certain leading principles are laid down; but the application of these to the innumerable cases which occur in the actual intercourse of life, is left to the understanding and the conscience of individuals. Had it been otherwise, the Christian code would have swelled to an extent which would have rendered it in a great degree useless; it would have been difficult or impossible to recollect all its provisions; and, minute as these would have been, they would still have been defective,--new situations or combinations of circumstances modifying duty continually arising, which it would have been impracticable or hurtful to anticipate. When the principles of duty are rightly unfolded, and when they are placed on a sound foundation, there is, to a fair mind, no difficulty in accommodating them to its own particular exigencies. A few cases, it is true, may occur, where it is a matter of doubt in what way men should act; but these are exceedingly rare, and the lives of vast numbers may come to an end without any of them happening to occasion perplexity. Every man may be, and perhaps is, sensible, that his errors are to be ascribed, not to his having been at a loss to know what he should have done, but to his deliberately or hastily violating what he saw to be right, or to his having allowed himself to confound, by vain and subtile distinctions, what, in the case of any one else, would have left in his mind no room for hesitation. The manner, however, in which the Gospel inculcates the law of God, combined with other causes in leading to a species of moral discussion, which, pretending to ascertain in every case what ought to be practised, and thus to afford plain and safe directions to the conscience, terminated in what has been denominated casuistry. The schoolmen delighted in this species of intellectual labour. They transferred their zeal for the most fanciful and frivolous distinctions in what respected the doctrines of religion to its precepts; they anatomized the different virtues; nicely examined all the circumstances by which our estimate of them should be influenced; and they thus rendered the study of morality inextricable, confounded the natural notions of right and wrong, and so accustomed themselves and others to weigh their actions, that they could easily find some excuse for what was most culpable, while they continued under the impression that they were not deviating from what, as moral beings, was incumbent upon them. The corruption of manners which was introduced into the church during the dark ages rendered casuistry very popular; and, accordingly, many who affected to be the most enlightened writers of their age, and perhaps really were so, tortured their understanding or their fancy in solving cases of conscience, and often in polluting their own imaginations and those of others, by employing them on possible crimes, upon which, however unlikely was their occurrence in life, they were eager to pronounce a decision. The happy change which the Reformation produced upon the views of men respecting the sacred Scriptures, tended to erect that pure standard of duty which for ages had been laid in the dust. Yet for a considerable time Protestant divines occupied themselves with the intricacies of casuistry, thus in some degree shutting out the light which they had fortunately poured upon the world. The Lutheran theologians walked very much in the tract which the schoolmen had opened, although their decisions were much more consonant with Christianity; and it was not uncommon in some countries for ecclesiastical assemblies to devote part of their time to the resolution of questions which might have been safely left unnoticed, which now are almost universally regarded as frivolous, and about which almost the most ignorant would be ashamed to ask an opinion. Even after much of the sophistry, and much of the moral perversion connected with casuistry, were exploded, the form of that science was preserved, and many valuable moral principles in conformity to it delivered. The venerable Bishop Hall published a celebrated work, to which he gave the appellation of "Cases of Conscience Practically resolved;" and he introduces it with the following observations addressed to the reader: "Of all divinity, that part is most useful which determines cases of conscience; and of all cases of conscience, the practical are most necessary, as action is of more concernment than speculation; and of all practical cases, those which are of most common use are of so much greater necessity and benefit to be resolved, as the errors thereof are more universal, and therefore more prejudicial to the society of mankind. These I have selected out of many; and having turned over divers casuists, have pitched upon those decisions which I hold most conformable to enlightened reason and religion; sometimes I follow them, and sometimes I leave them for a better guide." He divides his work into four parts,--Cases of profit and traffic, Cases of life and liberty, Cases of piety and religion, and Cases matrimonial; under each of these solving a number of questions, or rather giving a number of moral dissertations.

Casuistry, as a systematic perversion of Christian morality, is now, in the Protestant world, very much unknown; though there still is, and perhaps always will be, that softening down of the strict rules of duty, to which mankind are led either by self-deceit, or by the natural desire of reconciling, with the hope of the divine favour, considerable obliquity from that path of rectitude and virtue which alone is acceptable to God. But the most striking specimen of the length to which casuistry was carried, and of the dangerous consequences which resulted from it, is furnished by the history of the maxims and sentiments of the Jesuits, that celebrated order, which combined with profound literature, and the most zealous support of Popery, an ambition that perverted their understandings, or rather induced them to employ their rational powers in the melancholy work of poisoning the sources of morality, and of casting the name and the appearance of virtue over a dissoluteness of principle and a profligacy of licentiousness, which, had they not been checked by sounder views, and by feelings and habits favourable to morality, would have spread through the world the most degrading misery. See Jesuits.

CATERPILLAR. חסיל. The word occurs Deut. xxviii, 38; Psa. lxviii, 46; Isa. xxxiii, 4; 1 Kings viii, 37; 2 Chron. vi, 28; Joel i, 4; ii, 25. In the four last cited texts, it is distinguished from the locust, properly so called; and in Joel i, 4, is mentioned as "eating up" what the other species had left, and therefore might be called THE CONSUMER, by way of eminence. But the ancient interpreters are far from being agreed what particular species it signifies. The Septuagint in Chronicles, and Aquila in Psalms, render it βροῦχος: so the Vulgate in Chronicles and Isaiah, and Jerom in Psalms, BRUCHUS, the chafer, which is a great devourer of leaves. From the Syriac version, however, Michaëlis is disposed to understand it the TAUPE GRILLON, "mole cricket," which, in its grub state, is very destructive to corn and other vegetables, by feeding on their roots. See Locust.

CATHOLIC denotes what is general or universal. The rise of heresies induced the primitive Christian church to assume to itself the appellation of CATHOLIC, as being a characteristic to distinguish itself from them. The Romish church now proudly assumes the title CATHOLIC, in opposition to all who have separated from her communion, and whom she considers as heretics and schismatics, while she herself remains the only true and Christian church. The church of Christ is called catholic, because it extends throughout the world, and endures through all time.

2. Catholic, GENERAL, Epistles. They are seven in number; namely, one of James, two of Peter, three of John, and one of Jude. They are called catholic, because directed to Christian converts generally, and not to any particular church. Hug, in his "Introduction to the New Testament," takes another view of the import of this term, which was certainly used at an early period, as by Origen and others:--"When the Gospels and Acts of the Apostles constituted one peculiar division, the works of Paul also another, there still remained writings of different authors, which might likewise form a collection of themselves, to which a name must be given. It might most aptly be called THE COMMON COLLECTION, καθολικὸν σύνταγμα, of the Apostles, and the treatises contained in it, κοιναὶ and καθολικαὶ, which are commonly used by the Greeks as synonyms. For this we find a proof even in the most ancient ecclesiastical language. Clemens Alexandrinus calls the epistle which was despatched by the assembly of the Apostles, Acts xv, 23, the 'catholic epistle,' as that in which all the Apostles had a share, την ἐπιστολὴν καθολικὴν τῶν Ἀποστόλων ἅπαντων. Hence our seven epistles are catholic, or epistles of ALL the Apostles who are authors."

CAVES, or **CAVERNS**. The country of Judea, being mountainous and rocky, is in many parts full of caverns, to which allusions frequently occur in the Old Testament. At Engedi, in particular, there was a cave so large, that David, with six hundred men, hid themselves in the sides of it, and Saul entered the mouth of the cave without perceiving that any one was there, 1 Sam. xxiv. Josephus tells us of a numerous gang of banditti, who, having infested the country, and being pursued by Herod with his army, retired into certain caverns, almost inaccessible, near Arbela in Galilee, where they were with great difficulty subdued. "Beyond Damascus," says Strabo, "are two mountains, called Trachones, from which the country has the name of Trachonitis; and from hence, toward Arabia and Iturea, are certain rugged mountains, in which there are deep caverns; one of which will hold four thousand men." Tavernier, in his "Travels in Persia," speaks of a grotto between Aleppo and Bir, that would hold near three thousand horse. And Maundrel assures us, that "three hours distant from Sidon, about a mile from the sea, there runs along a high rocky mountain, in the sides of which are hewn a multitude of grottoes, all very little differing from each other. They have entrances about two foot square. There are of these subterraneous caverns two hundred in number. It may, with probability, at least, be concluded that these places were contrived for the use of the living, and not of the dead." These extracts may be useful in explaining such passages of Scripture as the following: "Because of the Midianites, the children of Israel made them dens which are in the mountains, and caves, and strong holds," Judges vi, 2. To these they betook themselves for refuge in times of distress and hostile invasion:--"When the men of Israel saw that they were in a strait, for the people were distressed, then the people did hide themselves in caves, and in thickets, and in rocks, and in high places, and in pits," 1 Sam. xiii, 6. See also Jer. xli, 9: "To enter into the holes of the rocks and into the caves of the earth," became with the prophets a very proper and familiar image to express a state of terror and consternation. Thus Isa. ii, 19: "They shall go into the holes of the rocks, and into the caves of the earth, for fear of the Lord, and for the glory of his majesty, when he ariseth to shake terribly the earth."

CEDAR, ארז. The cedar is a large and noble evergreen tree. Its lofty height, and its far extended branches, afford spacious shelter and shade, Ezek. xxxi, 3, 6, 8. The wood is very valuable; is of a reddish colour, of an aromatic smell, and reputed incorruptible. This is owing to its bitter taste, which the worms cannot endure, and to its resin, which preserves it from the injuries of the weather. The ark of the covenant, and much of the temple of Solomon, and that of Diana at Ephesus, were built of cedar. The tree is much celebrated in Scripture. It is called, "the glory of Lebanon," Isa. lx, 13. On that mountain it must in former times have flourished in great abundance. There are some cedars still growing there which are prodigiously large. But the travellers who have visited the place within these two or three centuries, and who describe trees of vast size, inform us that their number is diminished greatly; so that, as Isaiah says, "a child may number them," Isa. x, 19. Maundrell measured one of the largest size, and found it to be twelve yards and six inches in girt, and yet sound; and thirty-seven yards in the spread of its boughs. Gabriel Sionita, a very learned Syrian Maronite, who assisted in editing the Paris Polyglott, a man worthy of all credit, thus describes the cedars of mount Lebanon, which he had examined on the spot: "The cedar grows on the most elevated part of the mountain, is taller than the pine, and so thick, that five men together could scarcely encompass one. It shoots out its branches at ten or twelve feet from the ground: they are large and distant from each other, and are perpetually green. The wood is of a brown colour, very solid and incorruptible, if preserved from wet. The tree bears a small cone like that of the pine."

CELSUS. A Pagan philosopher of the second century, who composed a work against Christianity, in which he so expressly refers to the facts of the Gospels, and to the books of the New Testament, as to have furnished important undesigned testimony to their antiquity and truth.

CEMETERY. See Sepulchre.

CENSER, a sacred instrument made use of in the religious rites of the Hebrews. It was a vase which contained incense to be used in sacrifice. When Aaron made an atonement for himself and his house, he was to take a censer full of burning coals of fire from off the altar of the Lord, Lev. xvi, 12. And Solomon, when he provided furniture for the temple of the Lord, made, among other things, censers of pure gold, 1 Kings vii, 50.

CENTURION, an officer in the Roman army, who, as the term indicates, had the command of a hundred men, Matt. viii, 5, &c.

CEPHAS, Κηφᾶς, from כיפא, a ROCK. The Greek Πέτρος, and the Latin PETRUS, have the same signification. See Peter.

CEREMONY, an assemblage of several actions, forms, and circumstances, serving to render a thing magnificent and solemn. Applied to religious services, it signifies the external rites and manner in which the ministers of religion perform their sacred functions, and direct or lead the worship of the people. In 1646, M. Ponce, published a history of ancient ceremonies, showing the rise, growth, and introduction of each rite into the church, and its gradual advancement to superstition. Many of them were borrowed from Judaism, but more from Paganism. In all religions adapted to the nature of man there must be some positive institutions for fixing the mind upon spiritual objects, and counteracting that influence of material things upon habits and pursuits which is, and must be, constantly exerted. Without such institutions, religion might be preserved, indeed, by a few of superior understanding and of strong powers of reflection; but among mankind in general all trace of it would soon be lost. When the end for which they are appointed is kept in view, and the simple examples of the New Testament are observed, they are of vast importance to the production both of pious feelings and of virtuous conduct; but there has constantly been a propensity in the human race to mistake the means for the end, and to consider themselves as moral and religious, when they scrupulously observe what was intended to produce morality and religion. The reason is obvious: ceremonial observances can be performed without any great sacrifice of propensities and vices; they are palpable; when they are observed by men who, in the tenor of public life, do not act immorally, they are regarded by others as indicating high attainments in virtue; and through that self-deceit which so wonderfully misleads the reason, and inclines it to minister to the passions which it should restrain, men have themselves become persuaded that their acknowledgment of divine authority, implied in their respect to the ritual which that authority is conceived to have sanctioned, may be taken as a proof that they have nothing to apprehend from the violation of the law under which they are placed. But, whatever be the causes of this, the fact itself is established by the most extensive and the most incontrovertible evidence. We find it, indeed, wherever mankind have had notions of superior power, and of their obligation to yield obedience to the will of the supreme Being.

Under the system of polytheism which prevailed in the most enlightened nations previous to the publication of Christianity, this was carried so far, that the connection between religion and morality was in a great degree dissolved, rites and ceremonies, sacrifices and oblations, were all that it was thought requisite to observe; when these were carefully performed, there was no hesitation in ascribing piety to the persons who did perform them, however deficient they might be in virtuous and pious dispositions. Even under the Mosaical dispensation, proceeding as it did, immediately from heaven, and adapted, as in infinite wisdom it was, to the situation of those to whom it was given, the same evil early began to be experienced; and although it was lamented and exposed by the prophets, and the most enlightened men among the Jews, it was so far from being eradicated, that it continued to acquire strength, till it was exhibited in all its magnitude in the character prevalent among the Pharisees at the period of Christ's manifestation. With this highly popular and revered class of men, religion was either merely a matter of ceremony, or was employed, for base and interested purposes, to cast a veil of sanctity over their actions. They said long prayers, but it was for a show; they gave alms, but it was after they had sounded a trumpet, that the eye of man might be fixed upon their beneficence; and, as to the point now under review, they were most strikingly described by our Saviour, when he said of them, "They pay tithe of mint, and anise, and cummin, but they neglect the weightier matters of the law, justice, and mercy, and truth." The Christian religion not only expressly guards against an evil which had become so prevalent, but its whole spirit is at variance with it, its own ceremonial observances being few, and obviously emblematical of whatever is excellent and holy. But still the Gospel finds human nature as other religions found it; and ecclesiastical history, even from the earliest periods, shows with what astonishing perverseness, and with what wonderful ingenuity, men departed from the simplicity of Christianity, and substituted in its room the most childish, and often the most pernicious, practices and observances. The POWER of godliness was lost in FORMS; and the innovations of a profane WILL-WORSHIP became almost innumerable. The effect was, that men regarded God as less concerned with the moral conduct of his creatures, than with the QUANTUM of SERVICE they performed in his temples; and religion and morals were so disjoined, that one became the substitute for the other, to the universal corruption of the Christian world.

CERINTHIANS. Of Cerinthus, the founder of this sect, Dr. Burton gives the following account: Cerinthus is said to have been one of those Jews who, when St. Peter returned to Jerusalem, expostulated with him for having baptized Cornelius, Acts xi, 2. He is also stated to have been one of those who went down from Judea to Antioch, and said, "Except ye be circumcised after the manner of Moses, ye cannot be saved," Acts xv, 1. According to the same account, he was one of the false teachers who seduced the Galatians to Judaism; and he is also charged with joining in the attack which was made upon St. Paul, for polluting the temple by the introduction of Greeks, Acts xxi, 27, 28. I cannot find any older authority for these statements than that of Epiphanius, who wrote late in the fourth century, and is by no means worthy of implicit credit. He asserts, also, that Cerinthus was one of the persons alluded to by St. Luke, as having already undertaken to write the life of Jesus. But all these stories I take to be entirely inventions; and there is no evidence that Cerinthus made himself conspicuous at so early a period. Irenæus speaks of the heresy of the Nicolaitans, as being considerably prior to that of the Cerinthians. According to the same writer, Carpocrates also preceded Cerinthus; and if it be true, as so many of the fathers assert, that St. John wrote his Gospel expressly to confute this heresy, we can hardly come to any other conclusion, than that it was late in the first century when Cerinthus rose into notice. He appears undoubtedly to have been a Jew; and there is evidence that, after having studied philosophy in Egypt, he spread his doctrines in Asia Minor. This will account for his embracing the Gnostic opinions, and for his exciting the notice of St. John, who resided at Ephesus. He was certainly a Gnostic in his notion of the creation of the world, which he conceived to have been formed by angels; and his attachment to that philosophy may explain what otherwise seems inconsistent, that he retained some of the Mosaic ceremonies, such as the observance of Sabbaths and circumcision; though, like other Gnostics, he ascribed the law and the prophets to the angel who created the world. This adoption or rejection of different parts of the same system was a peculiar feature of the Gnostic philosophy; and the name of Cerinthus probably became eminent, because he introduced a fresh change in the notion concerning Christ. The Gnostics, like their leader, Simon Magus, had all of them been Docetæ, and denied the real humanity; but Cerinthus is said to have maintained that Jesus had a real body, and was the son of human parents, Joseph and Mary. In the other points he agreed with the Gnostics, and believed that Christ was one of the æons who descended on Jesus at his baptism. It is difficult to ascertain who was the first Gnostic that introduced this opinion. Some writers give the merit of it to Ebion; and yet it is generally said that Cerinthus and Ebion agreed in their opinions concerning Christ, and that Cerinthus preceded Ebion. Again Carpocrates is said to have held the same sentiments; and he is placed by Irenæus before Cerinthus: so that it is difficult, if not impossible, to decide the chronological precedence of these heretics. Perhaps the safest inference to draw from so many conflicting testimonies is this: that Carpocrates was the first Gnostic of eminence who was not a Docetist; but that the notion of Jesus being born of human parents was taught more explicitly and with more success by Cerinthus. Carpocrates is reported to have been distinguished by the gross immorality of his life; and whatever we may think of the imputations cast upon the Gnostics in general, it seems impossible to deny that this person, at least, professed and practised a perfect liberty of action. There is also strong evidence that in this instance Cerinthus followed his example.

There is a peculiar doctrine ascribed to this heretic, which, if it originated with him, may well account for the celebrity of his name. Cerinthus has been handed down as the first person who held the notion of a millennium; and though the fathers undoubtedly believed that, previous to the general resurrection, the earth would undergo a renovation, and the just would rise to enjoy a long period of terrestrial happiness, yet there was a marked and palpable difference between the millennium of the fathers and that of Cerinthus. The fathers conceived this terrestrial happiness to be perfectly pure and freed from the imperfections of our nature; but Cerinthus is said to have promised his followers a millennium of the grossest pleasures and the most sensual gratifications. It is singular that all the three sources, to which we may trace the Gnostic doctrines, might furnish some foundation for this notion of a millennium. Thus Plato has left some speculations concerning the "great year," when, after the expiration of thirty-six thousand years, the world was to be renewed, and the golden age to return. It was the belief of the Persian magi, according to Plutarch, that the time would come, when Ahreman, or the evil principle, would be destroyed; when the earth would lose its impediments and inequalities, and all mankind would be of one language, and enjoy uninterrupted happiness. It was taught, in the Cabbala, that the world was to last six thousand years, which would be followed by a period of rest for a thousand years more. There appears in this an evident allusion, though on a much grander scale, to the sabbatical years of rest. The institution of the jubilee, and the glowing descriptions given by the prophets of the restoration of the Jews, and the reign of the Messiah, may have led the later Jews to some of their mystical fancies; and when all these systems were blended together by the Gnostics, it is not strange, if a millennium formed part of their creed long before the time of Cerinthus. It seems probable, however, that he went much farther than his predecessors in teaching that the millennium would consist in a course of sensual indulgence; and it may have been his notions upon this subject, added to those concerning the human nature of Christ, which led him to maintain, contrary to the generality of Gnostics, that Christ had not yet risen, but that he would rise hereafter. The Gnostics, as we have seen, denied the resurrection altogether. Believing Jesus to be a phantom, they did not believe that he was crucified; and they could not therefore believe that he had risen. But Cerinthus, who held that Jesus was born, like other human beings, found no difficulty in believing literally that he was crucified; and he is said also to have taught that he would rise from the dead at some future period. It is most probable that this period was that of the millennium; and the words of St. John in the Revelation would easily be perverted, where it is said of the souls of the martyrs, that "they lived and reigned with Christ a thousand years," Rev. xx, 4.

CHALCEDONY, χαλκηδών, Rev. xxi, 19; a precious stone. Arethas, who has written an account of Bithynia, says that it was so called from Chalcedon, a city of that country, opposite to Byzantium; and it was in colour like a carbuncle. Some have supposed this also to be the stone called נפך, translated "emerald," Exodus xxviii, 18.

CHALDEA, or Babylonia, the country lying on both sides of the Euphrates, of which Babylon was the capital; and extending southward to the Persian Gulf, and northward into Mesopotamia, at least as far as Ur, which is called Ur of the Chaldees. This country had also the name of Shinar. See Babylon.

CHALDEAN PHILOSOPHY claims attention on account of its very high antiquity. The most ancient people, next to the Hebrews, among the eastern nations, who appear to have been acquainted with philosophy, in its more general sense, were the Chaldeans; for though the Egyptians have pretended that the Chaldeans were an Egyptian colony, and that they derived their learning from Egypt, there is reason to believe that the kingdom of Babylon, of which Chaldea was a part, flourished before the Egyptian monarchy; and that the Egyptians were rather indebted to the Chaldeans, than the Chaldeans to the Egyptians. Nevertheless, the accounts that have been transmitted to us by the Chaldeans themselves, of the antiquity of their learning, are blended with fable, and involved in considerable uncertainty. There are other circumstances, independently of the antiquity of the Chaldean philosophy, which render our knowledge of it imperfect and uncertain. We derive our acquaintance with it from other nations, and principally from the Greeks, whose vanity led them to despise and misrepresent the pretended learning of barbarous nations. The Chaldeans also adopted a symbolical mode of instruction, and transmitted their doctrines to posterity under a veil of obscurity, which it is not easy to remove. To all which, we may add that, about the commencement of the Christian æra, a race of philosophers sprung up, who, with a view of gaining credit to their own wild and extravagant doctrines, passed them upon the world as the ancient wisdom of the Chaldeans and Persians, in spurious books, which they ascribed to Zoroaster, or some other eastern philosopher. Thus, the fictions of these impostors were confounded with the genuine dogmas of the ancient eastern nations. Notwithstanding these causes of uncertainty, which perplex the researches of modern inquirers into the distinguishing doctrines and character of the Chaldean philosophy, it appears probable that the philosophers of Chaldea were the priests of the Babylonian nation, who instructed the people in the principles of religion, interpreted its laws, and conducted its ceremonies. Their character was similar to that of the Persian magi, and they are often confounded with them by the Greek historians. Like the priests in most other nations, they employed religion in subserviency to the ruling powers, and made use of imposture to serve the purposes of civil policy. Accordingly, Diodorus Siculus relates, that they pretended to predict future events by divination, to explain prodigies, and interpret dreams, and to avert evils, or confer benefits, by means of augury and incantations. For many ages, they retained a principal place among diviners. In the reign of Marcus Antonius, when the emperor and his army, who were perishing with thirst, were suddenly relieved by a shower, the prodigy was ascribed to the power and skill of the Chaldean soothsayers. Thus accredited for their miraculous powers, they maintained their consequence in the courts of princes. The principal instrument which they employed in support of their superstition, was astrology. The Chaldeans were probably the first people who made regular observations upon the heavenly bodies, and hence the appellation of Chaldean became afterward synonymous with that of astronomer. Nevertheless all their observations were applied to the sole purpose of establishing the credit of judicial astrology; and they employed their pretended skill in this art, in calculating nativities, foretelling the weather, predicting good and bad fortune, and other practices usual with impostors of this class. While they taught the vulgar that all human affairs are influenced by the stars, and professed to be acquainted with the nature and laws of their influence, and consequently to possess a power of prying into futurity, they encouraged much idle superstition, and many fraudulent practices. Hence other professors of these mischievous arts were afterward called Chaldeans, and the arts themselves were called Babylonian arts. Among the Romans these impostors were so troublesome, that, during the time of the republic, it became necessary to issue an edict requiring the Chaldeans, or mathematicians, (by which latter appellation they were commonly known,) to depart from Rome and Italy within ten days; and, afterward, under the emperors, these soothsayers were put under the most severe interdiction.

The Chaldean philosophy, notwithstanding the obscurity that has rendered it difficult of research, has been highly extolled, not only by the orientals and Greeks, but by Jewish and Christian writers: but upon recurring to authorities that are unquestionable, there seems to be little or nothing in this branch of the barbaric philosophy which deserves notice. The following brief detail will include the most interesting particulars. From the testimony of Diodorus, and also from other ancient authorities, collected by Eusebius, it appears, that the Chaldeans believed in God, the Lord and Parent of all, by whose providence the world is governed. From this principle sprung their religious rites, the immediate object of which was a supposed race of spiritual beings or demons, whose existence could not have been imagined, without first conceiving the idea of a supreme Being, the source of all intelligence. The belief of a supreme Deity, the fountain of all the divinities which were supposed to preside over the several parts of the material world, was the true origin of all religious worship, however idolatrous, not excepting even that which consisted in paying divine honours to the memory of dead men. Beside the supreme Being, the Chaldeans supposed spiritual beings to exist, of several orders; gods, demons, heroes: these they probably distributed into subordinate classes, agreeably to their practice of theurgy or magic. The Chaldeans, in common with the eastern nations in general, admitted the existence of certain evil spirits, clothed in a vehicle of grosser matter; and in subduing or counteracting these, they placed a great part of the efficacy of their religious incantations. These doctrines were the mysteries of the Chaldean religion, imparted only to the initiated. Their popular religion consisted in the worship of the sun, moon, planets, and stars, as divinities, after the general practice of the east, Job xxxi, 27. From the religious system of the Chaldeans were derived two arts, for which they were long celebrated; namely, magic and astrology. Their magic, which should not be confounded with witchcraft, or a supposed intercourse with evil spirits, consisted in the performance of certain religious ceremonies or incantations, which were supposed, by the interposition of good demons, to produce supernatural effects. Their astrology was founded upon the chimerical principle, that the stars have an influence, either beneficial or malignant, upon the affairs of men, which may be discovered, and made the certain ground of prediction, in particular cases; and the whole art consisted in applying astronomical observations to this fanciful purpose, and thus imposing upon the credulity of the vulgar.

CHAMBER. See Upper Room.

CHAPTERS. The New Testament was early portioned out into certain divisions, which appear under various names. The custom of reading it publicly in the Christian assemblies after the law and the prophets, would soon cause such divisions to be applied to it. The law and the prophets were for this end already divided into PARASHIM and HAPTAROTH, and the New Testament could not long remain without being treated in the same way. The distribution into church lessons was indeed the oldest that took place in it. The Christian teachers gave the name of PERICOPES, to the sections read as lessons by the Jews. Justin Martyr avails himself of this expression, when he quotes prophetical passages. Such is the case also in Clemens of Alexandria; but this writer also gives the name of ϖερικόπαι to larger sections of the Gospels and St. Paul's Epistles. PERICOPES therefore were nothing else but ἀναγνώσματα, church lessons, or sections of the New Testament, which were read in the assemblies after Moses and the Prophets. In the third century another division also into κεφαλαία occurs. Dionysius of Alexandria speaks of them in reference to the Apocalypse, and the controversies respecting it. Some, says he, went through the whole book, from chapter to chapter, to show that it bore no sense. In the fifth century Euthalius produced again a division into chapters, which was accounted his invention. He himself however lays claim to nothing more than having composed τὴν τῶν κεφαλαίων ἐκθεσίν, the summaries of the contents of the chapters in the Acts of the Apostles and the Catholic Epistles. In the Epistles of St. Paul, not even these are his property; but they are derived "from one of the wisest of the fathers, and worshippers of Christ," as he himself says, and he only incorporated them into his stichometrical edition of the New Testament. The chapters must, therefore, have been in existence before Euthalius, if the father whom he mentions composed notices of their contents. But how old they are cannot easily be known. The Euthalian κεφαλαία are distinguished from the PERICOPES, or reading portions, by their extent. The Jews had divided the law into fifty-three PARASHIM, according to the number of the Sabbaths, taking into account the leap year. Nearly so distributed were the Acts of the Apostles, St. Paul's and the Catholic Epistles, according to the Alexandrine ritual, which Euthalius follows in his stichometrical edition, namely, into fifty-six PERICOPES; three more than the number of κουριάκαι ἡμέραι, Sundays, probably for three festivals, which might be observed at Christmas, Easter, and Whitsuntide. The Gospels too had naturally in the same way many PERICOPES. Such in older times was the practice in Asia also; for Justin says, that the believers there assemble themselves for prayer and reading on Sunday only, ἐν τῇ τοῦ ἡλίου ἡμερᾷ. Since then the whole New Testament was distributed into so few sections, these must necessarily have been great, and a PERICOPE in Euthalius sometimes includes in it four, five, and even six chapters. We have spoken hitherto only of the chapters of the Acts of the Apostles and the Epistles. In the Gospels there occur to us κεφαλαία of two sorts, the greater and the lesser. The lesser are the Ammonian which Eusebius rejected, after which he composed his ten canons in order to point out in the Monotessaron of Ammonius the respective contents of every Evangelist. He has explained himself in the Epistle to Carpianus on their use, and on the formation of his ten canons, where he names his sections sometimes κεφαλαία, sometimes ϖερικόπαι. Matthew has three hundred and fifty-five of these, Mark two hundred and thirty-six, Luke three hundred and forty-two, and John two hundred and thirty-two. The other chapters are independent of these, which from their extent are also named the greater. Of these, Matthew contains sixty-eight, Mark forty-nine, Luke eighty-three, and John only eighteen. There are but very few manuscripts which have not both of them together. As to the church lessons, to come back to them once more, various alterations took place in them. As the festival days multiplied, the old division could no longer subsist, and in many churches the PERICOPES were shortened. At last as the ritual of ceremonies was enlarged, only certain portions were extracted from the Gospels, the Acts of the Apostles, and the Epistles, which sometimes were very short. A codex of this sort was termed ἐκλογάδιον; in reference to the Gospels alone, εὐαγγελιςάριον; and in respect to the other books, ϖραξαπόςολος. This seems to have taken place among the Latins much earlier than among the Greeks. There are perfectly credible testimonies, which establish such an arrangement among the former at the middle of the fifth century, at which date nothing of the kind is perceptible among the latter. The expression, ϖραξαπόςολος, appears indeed frequently in the Typicum of St. Sabas, who died in the beginning of the fifth century. But the Greeks do not disavow, that this Typicum or monastic ritual was not by himself, that it perished in the invasions of the barbarians, and was composed anew by John of Damascus, with references MEMORITER, [from memory,] to that of Sabas. He lived toward the middle of the eighth century, and with an earlier notice of lectionaries among the Greeks we are not acquainted. Finally, our present chapters come, as it is well known, from Cardinal Hugo de St. Cher, who in the twelfth century composed a concordance, and to this end distributed the Bible according to his own discretion into smaller portions. They are now moreover generally admitted in the editions of the Hebrew and Greek texts. The verses, however, are from Robert Stephens, who first introduced them in his edition of the New Testament, A. D. 1551. His son, Henry Stephens, was the first to record this for the information of posterity, in the preface to his Greek Concordance to the New Testament; in which he says, that two facts connected with it equally demand our admiration: "The first is, that my father, while travelling from Paris to Lyons, finished this division of each chapter into verses, and indeed the greater part of it [INTER EQUITANDUM] when riding on his horse. The second fact is, that, a short time prior to this journey, while he had the matter still in contemplation, almost all those to whom he mentioned it told him plainly that he was an indiscreet man, as though he had a wish to spend his time and labour on an affair which would prove utterly useless, and which would not obtain for him any commendation, but, on the contrary, would expose him to much ridicule. But behold the result: in opposition to the opinion which condemned and discountenanced my father's undertaking, as soon as his invention was published, every edition of the New Testament, whether in the Greek, Latin, French, German, or in any other language, which did not adopt it, was immediately discarded." It perhaps will not be unedifying to add, that this passage has yielded mankind another proof that LEARNING is not always synonymous with WISDOM: for the phrase respecting riding, which occurs in it, has furnished matter of warm dispute to literary men; some of them contending that INTER EQUITANDUM means, that Robert Stephens performed the greater part of his task while actually on horseback; but others, giving a more extended construction to the expression, assert that he was engaged in this occupation only when stopping for refreshment at inns on the road. Though the first interpretation would probably obtain the greatest number of suffrages from really learned and impartial men; yet it is quite sufficient for mankind to know, in either way, that this division into verses was completed in the course of that journey.

CHARIOTS OF WAR. The Scripture speaks of two sorts of these chariots, one for princes and generals to ride in, the other used to break the enemies battalions, by letting them loose armed with iron, which made dreadful havoc among the troops. The most ancient chariots of which we have any notice are Pharaoh's, which were overwhelmed in the Red Sea, Exodus xiv, 7. The Canaanites, whom Joshua engaged at the waters of Merom, had cavalry and a multitude of chariots, Joshua xi, 4. Sisera, the general of Jabin, king of Hazor, had nine hundred chariots of iron in his army, Judges iv, 3. The tribe of Judah could not get possession of all the lands of their lot, because the ancient inhabitants of the country were strong in chariots of iron. The Philistines, in the war carried on by them against Saul, had thirty thousand chariots and six thousand horsemen, 1 Sam. xiii, 5. David, having taken one thousand chariots of war from Hadadezer, king of Syria, hamstrung the horses, and burned nine hundred chariots, reserving only one hundred to himself, 2 Sam. viii, 4. Solomon had a considerable number of chariots, but we know of no military expedition in which they were employed, 1 Kings x, 26. As Judea was a very mountainous country, chariots could be of no great use there, except in the plains; and the Hebrews often evaded them by fighting on the mountains. The kings of the Hebrews, when they went to war, were themselves generally mounted in chariots from which they fought, and issued their orders; and there was always a second chariot empty, which followed each of them, that if the first was broken he might ascend the other, 2 Chron. xxxv, 24. Chariots were sometimes consecrated to the sun; and the Scripture observes, that Josiah burned those which had been dedicated to the sun by his predecessors, 2 Kings xxiii, 11. This superstitious custom was borrowed from the Heathens, and principally from the Persians.

CHARITY, considered as a Christian grace, ought in our translation, in order to avoid mistake, to have been translated LOVE. It is the love of God, and the love of our neighbour flowing from the love of God; and is described with wonderful copiousness, felicity, and even grandeur, by St. Paul, 1 Cor. xiii; a portion of Scripture which, as it shows the habitual temper of a true Christian, cannot be too frequently referred to for self-examination, and ought to be constantly present to us as our rule. 2. In the popular sense, charity is almsgiving; a duty of practical Christianity which is solemnly enjoined, and to which special promises are annexed.

CHARM. See Divination.

CHEBAR, a river of Chaldea, Ezek. i, 1. It is thought to have risen near the head of the Tigris, and to have run through Mesopotamia, to the south-west, and emptied itself into the Euphrates.

CHEDORLAOMER, a king of the Elamites, who were either Persians, or people bordering upon the Persians. This was one of the four confederated kings, who made war upon the five kings of the pentapolis of Sodom; and who, after having defeated them, and made themselves masters of a great booty, were pursued and dispersed by Abraham, Gen. xiv.

CHEMARIM. This word occurs only once in our version of the Bible: "I will cut off the remnant of Baal, and the name of the Chemarims (Chemarim) with the priests," Zeph. i, 4; but it frequently occurs in the Hebrew, and is generally translated "priests of the idols," or "priests clothed in black," because CHAMAR signifies BLACKNESS. By this word the best commentators understand the priests of false gods, and in particular the worshippers of fire, because they were, it is said, dressed in black. Le Clerc, however, declares against this last opinion. Our translators of the Bible would seem sometimes to understand by this word the idols or objects of worship, rather than their priests. This is also the opinion of Le Clerc. Calmet observes that CAMAR in Arabic signifies THE MOON, and that Isis is the same deity. "Among the priests of Isis," says Calmet, "were those called MELANEPHORI, that is, wearers of black; but it is uncertain whether this name was given them by reason of their dressing wholly in black, or because they wore a black shining veil in the processions of this goddess."

CHEMOSH, כמוש, an idol of the Moabites, Numbers xxi, 29. The name is derived from a root which in Arabic signifies TO HASTEN. For this reason, many believe Chemosh to be the sun, whose precipitate course might well procure it the name of swift. Some identify Chemosh with Ammon; and Macrobius shows that Ammon was the sun, whose rays were denoted by his horns. Calmet is of opinion that the god Hamanus and Apollo Chomeus, mentioned by Strabo and Ammianus Marcellinus, was Chamos, or the sun. These deities were worshipped in many parts of the east. Some, from the resemblance of the Hebrew Chamos with the Greek Comos, have thought Chamos to signify Bacchus. Jerom and most interpreters consider Chamosh and Peor as the same deity; but some think that Baal-Peor was Tammuz, or Adonis. To Chemosh Solomon erected an altar upon the Mount of Olives, 1 Kings xi, 7. As to the form of the idol Chemosh, the Scripture is silent; but if, according to Jerom, it were like Baal-Peor, it must have been of the beeve kind; as were, probably, all the Baals, though accompanied with various insignia. There can be little doubt that part of the religious services performed to Chemosh, as to Baal-Peor, consisted in revelling and drunkenness, obscenities and impurities of the grossest kinds. From Chemosh the Greeks seem to have derived their Κῶμος, called by the Romans COMUS, the god of feasting and revelling.

CHERETHIM. כרתים. Cherethim, or Cherethites, are denominations for the Philistines: "I will stretch out mine hand upon the Philistines, and will cut off the Cherethim, and destroy the remnant of the sea coast," Ezek. xxv, 16. Zephaniah, exclaiming against the Philistines, says, "Wo unto the inhabitants of the sea coasts, the nation of the Cherethites," Zeph. ii, 5. It is said, 1 Sam. xxx, 14, that the Amalekites invaded the south of the Cherethites; that is, of the Philistines. David, and some of the kings, his successors, had guards called Cherethites and Pelethites, 2 Sam. xv, 18; xx, 7. Calmet thinks that they were of the country of the Philistines; but several expositors of our own country are of a different opinion. "We can hardly suppose," say the latter, "that David would employ any of these uncircumcised people as his body-guard, or that the Israelitish soldiers would have patiently seen foreigners of that nation advanced to such places of honour and trust." It may, therefore, be inferred that guards were called Cherethites, because they went with David into Philistia, where they continued with him all the time he was under the protection of Achish. These were the persons who accompanied David from the first, and who remained with him in his greatest distresses; and it is no wonder, if men of such approved fidelity should be chosen for his body-guard. Beside, it is not uncommon for soldiers to derive their names, not from the place of their nativity, but of their residence.

CHERUB. כרב, plural כרבים. It appears, from Gen. iii, 29, that this is a name given to angels; but whether it is the name of a distinct class of celestials, or designates the same order as the seraphim, we have no means of determining. But the term CHERUBIM generally signifies those figures which Moses was commanded to make and place at each end of the mercy seat, or propitiatory, and which covered the ark with expanded wings in the most holy place of the Jewish tabernacle and temple. See Exodus xxv, 18, 19. The original meaning of the term, and the shape or form of these, any farther than that they were ALATA ANIMATA, "winged creatures," is not certainly known. The word in Hebrew is sometimes taken for a calf or ox; and Ezekiel, x, 14, sets down the face of a cherub as synonymous to the face of an ox. The word CHERUB, in Syriac and Chaldee, signifies to till or plough, which is the proper work of oxen. CHERUB also signifies strong and powerful. Grotius says they were figures much like that of a calf; and Bochart, likewise, thinks that they were more like the figure of an ox than any thing beside; and Spencer is of the same mind. But Josephus says they were extraordinary creatures of a figure unknown to mankind. The opinion of most critics, taken, it seems, from Ezek. i, 9, 10, is, that they were figures composed of parts of various creatures; as a man, a lion, an ox, an eagle. But certainly we have no decided proof that the figures placed in the holy of holies, in the tabernacle, were of the same form with those described by Ezekiel. The contrary, indeed, seems rather indicated, because they looked DOWN upon the mercy seat, which is an attribute not well adapted to a four-faced creature, like the emblematical cherubim seen by Ezekiel.

The cherubim of the sanctuary were two in number; one at each end of the mercy seat; which, with the ark, was placed exactly in the middle, between the north and south sides of the tabernacle. It was here that atonement was made, and that God was rendered propitious by the high priest sprinkling the blood upon and before the mercy seat, Lev. xvi, 14, 15. Here the glory of God appeared, and here he met his high priest, and by him his people, and from hence he gave forth his oracles; whence the whole holy place was called דביר, THE ORACLE. These cherubim, it must be observed, had feet whereon they stood, 2 Chron. iii, 13; and their feet were joined, in one continued beaten work, to the ends of the mercy seat which covered the ark: so that they were wholly over or above it. Those in the tabernacle were of beaten gold, being but of small dimensions, Exod. xxv, 18; but those in the temple of Solomon were made of the wood of the olive tree overlaid with gold; for they were very large, extending their wings to the whole breadth of the oracle, which was twenty cubits, 1 Kings vi, 23–28; 2 Chron. iii, 10–13. They are called "cherubim of glory," not merely or chiefly on account of the matter or formation of them, but because they had the glory of God, or the glorious symbol of his presence, "the Shekinah," resting between them. As this glory abode in the inward tabernacle, and as the figures of the cherubim represented the angels who surround the manifestation of the divine presence in the world above, that tabernacle was rendered a fit image of the court of heaven, in which light it is considered every where in the Epistle to the Hebrews. See chapters iv, 14; viii, 1; ix, 8, 9, 23, 24; xii, 22, 23.

The cherubim, it is true, have been considered by the disciples of Mr. Hutchinson as designed emblems of Jehovah himself, or rather of the Trinity of Persons in the Godhead, with man taken into the divine essence. But that God, who is a pure Spirit, without parts or passions, perfectly separate and remote from all matter, should command Moses to make material and visible images or emblematical representations of himself, is utterly improbable: especially, considering that he had repeatedly, expressly, and solemnly forbidden every thing of this kind in the second commandment of the moral law, delivered from Mount Sinai, amidst thunder and lightning, "blackness, darkness, and tempest," pronouncing with an audible and awful voice, while "the whole mount quaked greatly, and the sound of the trumpet waxed louder and louder, Thou shalt not make unto thee any graven image, nor the likeness of any thing that is in heaven above, or in the earth beneath, or in the water under the earth." Hence the solemn caution of Moses, Deut. iv, 15, &c: "Take ye good heed unto yourselves, (for ye saw no manner of similitude on the day the Lord spake unto you in Horeb out of the midst of the fire,) lest ye corrupt yourselves, and make you a graven image, the similitude of any figure, the likeness of male or female, of any beast that is on the earth, of any winged fowl that flieth in the air, of any thing that creepeth on the ground, of any fish that is in the waters." Hence God's demand by his prophet: "To what will ye liken me, or shall I be equal, saith the Holy One?" And hence the censure of the inspired penman, Psalm cvi, 20: "They changed their glory into the similitude of an ox that eateth grass." Add to this, that in most or all of the places where the cherubim are mentioned in the Scriptures, God is expressly distinguished from them. Thus, "He," the Lord, "placed at the east of the garden cherubim, and a flaming sword," Gen. iii, 24. "He rode on a cherub and did fly," Psalm xviii, 10. "He sitteth between the cherubim," Psalm xcix, 1. "He dwelleth between the cherubim," Psalm lxxx, 1. We also read of "the glory of the God of Israel going up, from the cherub whereupon he was, to the threshold of the house," Ezek. ix, 3. And again, "The glory of the Lord went up from the cherub, and the court was full of the brightness of the Lord's glory," Ezek. x, 4. And again, "The glory of the Lord departed from off the threshold, and stood over the cherubim," Ezek. x, 18. In all these passages the glory of the Lord, that is, the Shekinah, the glorious symbol of his presence, is distinguished from the cherubim; and not the least intimation is given in these passages, or any others, of the Scripture, that the cherubim were images or emblematical representations of him. Mr. Parkhurst's laborious effort to establish Mr. Hutchinson's opinion on the subject of the cherubim, in his Hebrew Lexicon, SUB VOCE, is so obviously fanciful and contradictory, that few will be converted to this strange opinion. It seems much more probable that, as most eminent divines have supposed, the cherubim represented the angels who surround the divine presence in heaven. Accordingly, they had their faces turned toward the mercy seat, where God was supposed to dwell, whose glory the angels in heaven always behold, and upon which their eyes are continually fixed; as they are also upon Christ, the true propitiatory, which mystery of redemption they "desire," St. Peter tells us, "to look into," 1 Peter i, 12: a circumstance evidently signified by the faces of the cherubim being turned inward, and their eyes fixed on the mercy seat. We may here also observe that, allowing St. Peter in this passage to allude to the cherubic figures, which, from his mode of expression, can scarcely be doubted, this amounts to a strong presumption that the cherubim represented, not so much one order, as "the angels" in general, all of whom are said to "desire to look into" the subjects of human redemption, and to all whose orders, "the principalities and powers in heavenly places, the manifold wisdom of God is made known by the church." In Ezekiel, the cherubic figures are evidently connected with the dispensations of providence; and they have therefore appropriate forms, emblematical of the strength, wisdom, swiftness, and constancy, with which the holy angels minister in carrying on God's designs: but in the sanctuary they are connected with the administration of grace; and they are rather adoring beholders, than actors, and probably appeared under forms more simple. As to the living creatures, improperly rendered "beasts" in our translation, Rev. iv, 7, some think them a hieroglyphical representation, not of the qualities of angels, but of those of real Christians; especially of those in the suffering and active periods of the church. The first a lion, signifying their undaunted courage, manifested in meeting with confidence the greatest sufferings; the second a calf or ox, emblematical of unwearied patience; the third with the face of a man representing prudence and compassion; the fourth a flying eagle, signifying activity and vigour. The four qualities thus emblematically set forth in these four living creatures, namely, undaunted courage, unwearied patience under sufferings, prudence united with kindness, and vigorous activity, are found, more or less, in the true members of Christ's church in every age and nation. But others have imagined that this representation might be intended to intimate also that these qualities would especially prevail in succeeding ages of the church, in the order in which they are here placed: that is, that in the first age true Christians would be eminent for the courage, fortitude, and success, wherewith they should spread the Gospel; that in the next age they would manifest remarkable patience in bearing persecution, when they should be "killed all the day," like calves or oxen appointed for the slaughter; that in the subsequent age or ages, when the storms of persecution were blown over, and Christianity was generally spread through the whole Roman empire, knowledge and wisdom, piety and virtue, should increase, and the church should wear the face of a man, and excel in prudence, humanity, love, and good works; and that in ages still later, being reformed from various corruptions in doctrine and practice, and full of vigour and activity, it should carry the Gospel, as upon the wings of a flying eagle, to the remotest nations under heaven, "to every kindred, and tongue, and people." This is a thought which deserves some consideration. The four great monarchies of the earth had their prophetic emblems, taken both from metals and from beasts and birds; and it is not unreasonable to look for prophetic emblems of the one kingdom of Christ, in its varied and successive states. Perhaps, however, the most reasonable conclusion is, that, like the "living creatures" in the vision of Ezekiel, they are emblematical of the ministrations of angels in what pertains to those providential events which more particularly concern the church.

CHESNUT TREE, ערמון. This tree, which is mentioned only in Gen. xxx, 37, and Ezek. xxxi, 8, is by the Septuagint and Jerom rendered PLANE TREE; and Drusius, Hiller, and most of the modern interpreters render it the same. The name is derived from a root which signifies NAKEDNESS; and it is often observed of the plane tree that the bark peels off from the trunk, leaving it naked, which peculiarity may have been the occasion of its Hebrew name. The son of Sirach says, "I grew up as a plane tree by the water," Ecclesiasticus xxiv, 14.

CHILD. Mothers, in the earliest times, suckled their offspring themselves, and that from thirty to thirty-six months. The day when the child was weaned was made a festival, Gen. xxi, 8; Exod. ii, 7, 9; 1 Sam. i, 22–24; 2 Chron. xxxi, 16; 2 Mac. vii, 27, 28; Matt, xxi, 16. Nurses were employed, in case the mother died before the child was old enough to be weaned, and when from any circumstances she was unable to afford a sufficient supply of milk for its nourishment. In later ages, when matrons had become more delicate, and thought themselves too infirm to fulfil the duties which naturally devolved upon them, nurses were employed to take their place, and were reckoned among the principal members of the family. They are, accordingly, in consequence of the respectable station which they sustained, frequently mentioned in sacred history, Gen. xxxv, 8; 2 Kings xi, 2; 2 Chron. xxii, 11. The sons remained till the fifth year in the care of the women; they then came into the father's hands, and were taught not only the arts and duties of life, but were instructed in the Mosaic law, and in all parts of their country's religion, Deut, vi, 20–25; vii, 19; xi, 19. Those who wished to have them farther instructed, provided they did not deem it preferable to employ private teachers, sent them away to some priest or Levite, who sometimes had a number of other children to instruct. It appears from 1 Sam. i, 24–28, that there was a school near the holy tabernacle, dedicated to the instruction of youth. There had been many other schools of this kind, which had fallen into decay, but were restored again by the Prophet Samuel; after whose time, the members of the seminaries in question, who were denominated by way of distinction "the sons of the prophets," acquired no little notoriety. Daughters rarely departed from the apartments appropriated to the females, except when they went out with an urn to draw water. They spent their time in learning those domestic and other arts, which are befitting a woman's situation and character, till they arrived at that period in life when they were to be sold, or, by a better fortune, given away in marriage, Prov. xxxi, 13; 2 Sam. xiii, 7.

2. In Scripture, disciples are often called children or sons, Solomon, in his Proverbs, says,to his disciple, "Hear, my son." The descendants of a man, how remote soever, are denominated his sons or children; as "the children of Edom," "the children of Moab," "the children of Israel." Such expressions as "the children of light," "the children of darkness," "the children of the kingdom," signify those who follow truth, those who remain in error, and those who belong to the church. Persons arrived at almost the age of maturity are sometimes called "children." Thus, Joseph is termed "the child," though he was at least sixteen years old, Gen. xxxvii, 30; and Benjamin, even when above thirty, was so denominated, xliv, 20. By the Jewish law, children were reckoned the property of their parents, who could sell them for seven years to pay their debts. Their creditors had also the power of compelling them to resort to this measure. The poor woman, whose oil Elisha increased so much as enabled her to pay her husband's debts, complained to the prophet, that, her husband being dead, the creditor was come to take away her two sons to be bondmen, 2 Kings iv, 1. "Children, or sons of God," is a name by which the angels are sometimes described: "There was a day when the sons of God came to present themselves before the Lord," Job i, 6; ii, 1. Good men, in opposition to the wicked, are also thus denominated; the children of Seth's family, in opposition to those of Cain: "The sons of God saw the daughters of men," Gen. vi, 2. Judges, magistrates, priests, are also termed children of God: "I have said, Ye are gods, and all of you are the children of the Most High," Psa. lxxxii, 6. The Israelites are called "sons of God," in opposition to the Gentiles, Hosea i, 10; John xi, 52. In the New Testament, believers are commonly called "children of God" by virtue of their adoption. St. Paul, in several places, extols the advantages of being adopted sons of God, Rom. viii, 14; Gal. iii, 26. "Children, or sons of men," is a name given to Cain's family before the deluge, and, in particular, to the giants who were violent men, and had corrupted their ways. Afterward, the impious Israelites were thus called: "O ye sons of men, how long will ye love vanity?" Psa. iv, 2. "The sons of men, whose teeth are spears and arrows," lvii, 4.

CHILD BIRTH. In oriental countries child birth is not an event of much difficulty; and mothers at such a season were originally the only assistants of their daughters, as any farther aid was deemed unnecessary, Exod. i, 19. In cases of more than ordinary difficulty, those matrons who had acquired some celebrity for skill and expertness on occasions of this kind, were invited in; and in this way there eventually rose into notice that class of women denominated midwives. The child was no sooner born, than it was washed in a bath, rubbed with salt, and wrapped in swaddling clothes, החתל, Ezek. xvi, 4. It was the custom at a very ancient period, for the father, while music in the mean while was heard to sound, to clasp the new born child to his bosom, and by this ceremony was understood to declare it to be his own, Gen. l, 23; Job iii, 12; Psa. xxii, 11. This practice was imitated by those wives who adopted the children of their maids, Gen. xvi, 2; xxx, 3–5. The birth day of a son, especially, was made a festival, and on each successive year was celebrated with renewed demonstrations of festivity and joy, Gen. xl, 20; Job i, 4; Matt. xiv, 6. The messenger, who brought the news of the birth of a son, was received with joy, and rewarded with presents, Job iii, 3; Jer. xx, 15. This is the case at the present day in Persia.

CHISLEU, the third month of the Jewish civil year, and the ninth of their sacred, answering to our November and December, Nehem. i, 1. It contains thirty days.

CHITTIM, the country, or countries, implied by this name in Scripture, are variously interpreted by historians and commentators. Chittim has been taken, by Hales and Lowth, for all the coasts and islands of the Mediterranean; which appears most consonant with the general use of the word by the different inspired writers.

CHRIST, an appellation synonymous with Messiah. The word Χϱιϛὸς, signifies ANOINTED, from χϱίω, I ANOINT. Sometimes the word Christ is used singly, by way of AUTONOMASIS, to denote a person sent from God, as an anointed prophet, king, or priest. "Christ," says Lactantius, "is no proper name, but one denoting power; for the Jews used to give this appellation to their kings, calling them Christ, or anointed, by reason of their sacred unction." But he adds, "The Heathens, by mistake, call Jesus Christ, Chrestus." Accordingly, Suetonius, speaking of Claudius, and of his expelling the Jews from Rome, says that "he banished them because they were continually promoting tumults, under the influence of one Chrestus:" "JUDÆOS, IMPULSORE CHRESTO, ASSIDUÈ TUMULTUANTES, ROMÂ EXPULIT," taking Christ to be a proper name. The names of Messiah and Christ were originally derived from the ceremony of anointing, by which the kings and the high priests of God's people, and sometimes the prophets, 1 Kings xix, 16, were consecrated and admitted to the exercise of their functions; for all these functions were accounted holy among the Israelites. But the most eminent application of the word is to that illustrious personage, typified and predicted from the beginning, who is described by the prophets, under the character of God's Anointed, the Messiah, or the Christ. As to the use of the term in the New Testament, were we to judge by the common version, or even by most versions into modern tongues, we should receive it rather as a proper name, than an appellative, or name of office, and should think of it only as our Lord's surname. To this mistake our translators have contributed, by too seldom prefixing the article before Christ. The word Christ was at first as much an appellative as the word Baptist, and the one was as regularly accompanied with the article as the other. Yet our translators, who would always say "the Baptist," have, it should seem, studiously avoided saying "the Christ." The article, in such expressions as occur in Acts xvii, 3; xviii, 5, 28, adds considerable light to them, and yet no more than what the words of the historian manifestly convey to every reader who understands his language. It should therefore be, "Paul testified to the Jews that Jesus was the Christ," or the

Messiah, &c. Many other similar instances occur. Should it be asked, Is the word Christ never to be understood in the New Testament as a proper name, but always as having a direct reference to the office or dignity? it may be replied, that this word came at length, from the frequency of application to one individual, and only to one, to supply the place of a proper name. It would also very much accelerate this effect, that the name Jesus was common among the Jews at that time, and this rendered an addition necessary for distinguishing the person. To this purpose, Grotius remarks, that in process of time the name Jesus was very much dropped, and Christ, which had never been used before as the proper name of any person, and was, for that reason, a better distinction, was substituted for it; insomuch that, among the Heathens, our Lord came to be more known by the latter than by the former. This use seems to have begun soon after his ascension. During his life, it does not appear that the word was ever used in this manner; nay, the contrary is evident from several passages of the Gospels. The evangelists wrote some years after the period above mentioned; and therefore they adopted the practice common among Christians at that time, which was to employ the word as a surname for the sake of distinction. See Matt. i, 1, 18; Mark i, 1.

CHRISTIAN, a follower of the religion of Christ. It is probable that the name Christian, like that of Nazarenes and Galileans, was given to the disciples of our Lord in reproach or contempt. What confirms this opinion is, that the people of Antioch in Syria, Acts xi, 26, where they were first called Christians, are observed by Zosimus, Procopius, and Zonaras, to have been remarkable for their scurrilous jesting. Some have indeed thought that this name was given by the disciples to themselves; others, that it was imposed on them by divine authority; in either of which cases surely we should have met with it in the subsequent history of the Acts, and in the Apostolic Epistles, all of which were written some years after; whereas it is found but in two more places in the New Testament, Acts xxvi, 28, where a Jew is the speaker, and in 1 Pet. iv, 16, where reference appears to be made to the name as imposed upon them by their enemies. The word used, Acts xi, 26, signifies simply to be called or named, and when Doddridge and a few others take it to IMPLY a divine appointment, they disregard the USUS LOQUENDI [established acceptation of the term] which gives no support to that opinion. The words of Tacitus, when speaking of the Christians persecuted by Nero, are remarkable, "VULGUS CHRISTIANOS APPELLABAT," "the vulgar called them Christians." Epiphanius says, that they were called Jesseans, either from Jesse, the father of David, or, which is much more probable, from the name of Jesus, whose disciples they were. They were denominated Christians, A. D. 42 or 43; and though the name was first given reproachfully, they gloried in it, as expressing their adherence to Christ, and they soon generally assumed it.

CHRISTIANITY, the religion of Christians. By Christianity is here meant, not that religious system as it may be understood and set forth in any particular society calling itself Christian; but as it is contained in the sacred books acknowledged by all these societies, or churches, and which contained the only authorized rule of faith and practice.

2. The lofty profession which Christianity makes as a religion, and the promises it holds forth to mankind, entitle it to the most serious consideration of all. For it may in truth be said, that no other religion presents itself under aspects so sublime, or such as are calculated to awaken desires and hopes so enlarged and magnificent. It not only professes to be from God, but to have been taught to men by the Son of God incarnate in our nature, the Second Person in the adorable trinity of divine Persons, "the same in substance, equal in power and glory." It declares that this divine personage is the appointed Redeemer of mankind from sin, death, and misery; that he was announced as such to our first parents upon their lapse from the innocence and blessedness of their primeval state; that he was exhibited to the faith and hope of the patriarchs in express promises; and, by the institution of sacrifices, as a propitiatory sacrifice for the sins of the whole world, so that man might be reconciled to God through Him, and restored to his forfeited inheritance of eternal life. It represents all former dispensations of true religion, all revelations of God's will, and all promises of grace from God to man, as emanating from the anticipated sacrifice and sacerdotal intercession of its Author, and as all preparatory to the introduction of his perfect religion; and that as to the great political movements among the nations of antiquity, the rise and fall of empires were all either remotely or proximately connected with the designs of his advent among men. It professes to have completed the former revelations of God's will and purposes; to have accomplished ancient prophecies; fulfilled ancient types; and taken up the glory of the Mosaic religion into its own "glory that excelleth;" and to contain within itself a perfect system of faith, morals, and acceptable worship. It not only exhibits so effectual a sacrifice for sin, that remission of all offences against God flows from its merits to all who heartily confide in it; but it proclaims itself to be a remedy for all the moral disorders of our fallen nature; it casts out every vice, implants every virtue, and restores man to "the image of God in which he was created," even to "righteousness and true holiness."

3. Its promises both to individuals and to society are of the largest kind. It represents its Founder as now exercising the office of the High Priest of the human race before God, and as having sat down at his right hand, a mediatorial and reconciling government being committed to him, until he shall come to judge all nations, and distribute the rewards of eternity to his followers, and inflict its never-terminating punishments upon those who reject him. By virtue of this constitution of things, it promises pardon to the guilty, of every age and country, who seek it in penitence and prayer, comfort to the afflicted and troubled, victory over the fear of death, a happy intermediate state to the disembodied spirit, and finally the resurrection of the body from the dead, and honour and immortality to be conferred upon the whole man glorified in the immediate presence of God. It holds out the loftiest hopes also as to the world at large. It promises to

introduce harmony among families and nations, to terminate all wars and all oppressions, and ultimately to fill the world with truth, order, and purity. It represents the present and past state of society, as in contest with its own principles of justice, mercy, and truth; but teaches the final triumph of the latter over every thing contrary to itself. It exhibits the ambition, the policy, and the restlessness of statesmen and warriors, as but the overruled instruments by which it is working out its own purposes of wisdom and benevolence; and it not only defies the proudest array of human power, but professes to subordinate it by a secret and irresistible working to its own designs. Finally, it exhibits itself as enlarging its plans, and completing its designs, by moral suasion, the evidence of its truth, and the secret divine influence which accompanies it. Such are the professions and promises of Christianity, a religion which enters into no compromise with other systems; which represents itself as the only religion now in the world having God for its author; and in his name; and by the hope of his mercy, and the terrors of his frown, it commands the obedience of faith to all people to whom it is published upon the solemn sanction, "He that believeth shall be saved, and he that believeth not shall be damned."

4. Corresponding with these professions, which throw every other religion that pretends to offer hope to man into utter insignificance, it is allowed that the evidences of its truth ought to be adequate to sustain the weight of so vast a fabric, and that men have a right to know that they are not deluded with a grand and impressive theory, but are receiving from this professed system of truth and salvation "the true sayings of God." Such evidence it has afforded in its splendid train of miracles; in its numerous appeals to the fulfilment of ancient PROPHECIES; in its own powerful INTERNAL EVIDENCE; in the INFLUENCE which it has always exercised, and continues to exert, upon the happiness of mankind; and in various collateral circumstances. Under the heads of MIRACLES and PROPHECY, those important branches of evidence will be discussed, and to them the reader is referred. It is only necessary here to say, that the miracles to which Christianity appeals as proofs of its divine authority, are not only those which were wrought by Christ and his Apostles, but also those which took place among the patriarchs, under the law of Moses, and by the ministry of the Prophets; for the religion of those ancient times was but Christianity in its antecedent revelations. All these miracles, therefore, must be taken collectively, and present attestations of the loftiest kind, as being manifestly the work of the "finger of God," wrought under circumstances which precluded mistake, and exhibiting an immense variety, from the staying of the very wheels of the planetary system,--as when the sun and moon paused in their course, and the shadow on the dial of Ahaz went backward,--to the supernatural changes wrought upon the elements of matter, the healing of incurable diseases, the expulsion of tormenting demons, and the raising of the dead. Magnificent as this array of miracles is, it is equalled by the prophetic evidence, founded upon the acknowledged principle, that future and distant contingencies can only be known to that Being, one of whose attributes is an absolute prescience. And here, too, the variety and the grandeur presented by the prophetic scheme exhibit attestations to the truth of Christianity suited to its great claims and its elevated character. Within the range of prophetic vision all time is included, to the final consummation of all things; and the greatest as well as the smallest events are seen with equal distinctness, from the subversion of mighty empires and gigantic cities, to the parting of the raiment of our Lord, and the casting of the lot for his robe by the Roman guard stationed at his cross.

5. These subjects are discussed under the articles assigned to them; as also the INTERNAL EVIDENCE of the truth of Christianity, which arises from the excellence and beneficial tendency of its doctrines. Of its just and sublime conceptions and exhibitions of the divine character; of the truth of that view of the moral state of man upon which its disciplinary treatment is founded; of the correspondence that there is between its views of man's mixed relation to God as a sinful creature, and yet pitied and cared for, and that actual mixture of good and evil, penalty and forbearance, which the condition of the world presents; of the connection of its doctrine of atonement with hope; of the adaptation of its doctrine of divine influence to the moral condition of mankind when rightly understood, and the affecting benevolence and condescension which it implies; and of its noble and sanctifying revelations of the blessedness of a future life, much might be said:--they are subjects indeed on which volumes have been written, and they can never be exhausted. But we confine ourselves to the MORAL TENDENCY, and the consequent BENEFICIAL INFLUENCE, of Christianity. No where except in the Scriptures have we a perfect system of morals; and the deficiencies of Pagan morality only exalt the purity, the comprehensiveness, the practicability of ours. The character of the Being acknowledged as supreme must always impress itself upon moral feeling and practice; the obligation of which rests upon his will. The God of the Bible is "holy," without spot; "just," without partiality; "good," boundlessly benevolent and beneficent; and his law is the image of himself, "holy, just, and good." These great moral qualities are not made known to us merely in the abstract, so as to be comparatively feeble in their influence: but in the person of Christ, our God, incarnate, they are seen exemplified in action, displaying themselves amidst human relations, and the actual circumstances of human life. With Pagans the authority of moral rules was either the opinion of the wise, or the tradition of the ancient, confirmed, it is true, in some degree, by observation and experience; but to us, they are given as commands immediately issuing from the supreme Governor, and ratified as his by the most solemn and explicit attestations. With them many great moral principles, being indistinctly apprehended, were matters of doubt and debate; to us, the explicit manner in which they are given excludes both: for it cannot be questioned, whether we are commanded to love our neighbour as ourselves; to do to others as we would that they should do to us, a precept which comprehends almost all relative morality in one plain

principle; to forgive our enemies; to love all mankind; to live righteously and soberly, as well as godly; that magistrates must be a terror only to evil doers, and a praise to them that do well; that subjects are to render honour to whom honour, and tribute to whom tribute, is due; that masters are to be just and merciful, and servants faithful and obedient. These, and many other familiar precepts, are too explicit to be mistaken, and too authoritative to be disputed; two of the most powerful means of rendering law effectual. Those who never enjoyed the benefit of revelation, never conceived justly and comprehensively of that moral state of the heart from which right and beneficent conduct alone can flow; and therefore when they speak of the same virtues as those enjoined by Christianity, they are to be understood as attaching to them a lower idea. In this the infinite superiority of Christianity displays itself. The principle of obedience is not only a sense of duty to God, and the fear of his displeasure; but a tender love, excited by his infinite compassions to us in the gift of his Son, which shrinks from offending. To this influential motive as a REASON of obedience, is added another, drawn from its END: one not less influential, but which Heathen moralists never knew,--the testimony that we please God, manifested in the acceptance of our prayers, and in spiritual and felicitous communion with him. By Christianity, impurity of thought and desire is restrained in an equal degree as are their overt acts in the lips and conduct. Humanity, meekness, gentleness, placability, disinterestedness, and charity are all as clearly and solemnly enjoined as the grosser vices are prohibited; and on the unruly tongue itself is impressed "the law of kindness." Nor are the injunctions feeble; they are strictly LAW, and not mere advice and recommendations: "Without holiness no man shall see the Lord;" and thus our entrance into heaven, and our escape from perdition, are made to depend upon this preparation of mind. To all this is added possibility, nay certainty, of attainment, if we use the appointed means. A Pagan could draw, though not with lines so perfect, a BEAU IDEAL of virtue, which he never thought attainable; but the "full assurance of hope" is given by the religion of Christ to all who are seeking the moral renovation of their nature; because "it is God that worketh in us to will and to do of his good pleasure."

6. When such is the moral nature of Christianity, how obvious is it that its tendency both as to individuals and to society must be in the highest sense beneficial! From every passion which wastes, and burns, and frets, and enfeebles the spirit, the individual is set free, and his inward peace renders his obedience cheerful and voluntary: and we might appeal to infidels themselves, whether, if the moral principles of the Gospel were wrought into the hearts, and embodied in the conduct, of all men, the world would not be happy; whether if governments ruled, and subjects obeyed, by the laws of Christ; whether if the rules of strict justice which are enjoined upon us regulated all the transactions of men, and all that mercy to the distressed which we are taught to feel and to practise came into operation; and whether, if the precepts which delineate and enforce the duties of husbands, wives, masters, servants, parents, children, did, in fact, fully and generally govern all these relations,--whether a better age than that called GOLDEN by the poets, would not then be realized, and Virgil's

JAM REDIT ET VIRGO, REDEUNT SATURNIA REGNA,

[Now Astraea returns, and the Saturnian reign,]

be far too weak to express the mighty change? [It was in the reign of Saturn that the Heathen poets fixed the golden age. At that period, according to them, Astraea, (the goddess of justice,) and many other deities lived on earth; but being offended with the wickedness of men, they successively fled to heaven. Astraea staid longest, but at last retired to her native seat, and was translated into the sign Virgo, next to Libra, who holds her balance.] Such is the tendency of Christianity. On immense numbers of individuals it has superinduced these moral changes; all nations, where it has been fully and faithfully exhibited, bear, amidst their remaining vices, the impress of its hallowing and benevolent influence: it is now in active exertion in many of the darkest and worst parts of the earth, to convey the same blessings; and he who would arrest its progress, were he able, would quench the only hope which remains to our world, and prove himself an enemy, not only to himself, but to all mankind. What then, we ask, does all this prove, but that the Scriptures are worthy of God, and propose the very ends which rendered a revelation necessary? Of the whole system of practical religion which it contains we may say, as of that which is embodied in our Lord's sermon on the mount, in the words of one, who, in a course of sermons on that divine composition, has entered most deeply into its spirit, and presented a most instructive delineation of the character which it was intended to form: "Behold Christianity in its native form, as delivered by its great Author. See a picture of God, as far as he is imitable by man, drawn by God's own hand. What beauty appears in the whole! How just a symmetry! What exact proportion in every part! How desirable is the happiness here described! How venerable, how lovely is the holiness!" "If," says Bishop Taylor, "wisdom, and mercy, and justice, and simplicity, and holiness, and purity, and meekness, and contentedness, and charity, be images of God, and rays of divinity, then that doctrine, in which all these shine so gloriously, and in which nothing else is ingredient, must needs be from God. If the holy Jesus had come into the world with less splendour of power and mighty demonstrations, yet the excellency of what he taught makes him alone fit to be the Master of the world;" and agreeable to all this, has been its actual influence upon mankind. Although, says Bishop Porteus, Christianity has not always been so well understood, or so honestly practised, as it ought to have been; although its spirit has been often mistaken, and its precepts misapplied, yet, under all these disadvantages, it has gradually produced a visible change in those points which most materially concern the peace and quiet of the world. Its beneficent spirit has spread itself through all the different relations and modifications of life, and communicated its kindly influence to almost every public and private concern of mankind. It has insensibly worked itself into the inmost frame and constitution of civil states. It has given a tinge to the complexion of their governments, to the temper and administration of their laws. It has restrained the spirit of the prince, and the madness of the people. It has softened the rigours of despotism, and tamed the insolence of conquest. It has, in some degree, taken away the edge of the sword, and thrown even over the horrors of war a veil of mercy. It has descended into families; has diminished the pressure of private tyranny; improved every domestic endearment; given tenderness to the parent, humanity to the master, respect to superiors, to inferiors ease; so that mankind are, upon the whole, even in a temporal view, under infinite obligations to the mild and pacific temper of the Gospel, and have reaped from it more substantial worldly benefits than from any other institution upon earth. As one proof of this, among many others, consider only the shocking carnage made in the human species by the exposure of infants, the gladiatorial shows, which sometimes cost Rome twenty or thirty lives in a month; and the exceedingly cruel usage of slaves allowed and practised by the ancient Pagans. These were not the accidental and temporary excesses of a sudden fury, but were legal and established, and constant methods of murdering and tormenting mankind. Had Christianity done nothing more than brought into disuse, as it confessedly has done, the two former of these inhuman customs entirely, and the latter to a very great degree, it has justly merited the title of the benevolent religion. But this is far from being all. Throughout the more enlightened parts of Christendom there prevails a gentleness of manners widely different from the ferocity of the most civilized nations of antiquity; and that liberality with which every species of distress is relieved, is a virtue peculiar to the Christian name. But we may ask farther, What success has it had on the mind of man, as it respects his eternal welfare? How many thousands have felt its power, rejoiced in its benign influence, and under its dictates been constrained to devote themselves to the glory and praise of God! Burdened with guilt, incapable of finding relief from human resources, the mind has here found peace unspeakable in beholding that sacrifice which alone could atone for transgression. Here the hard and impenitent heart has been softened, the impetuous passions restrained, the ferocious temper subdued, powerful prejudices conquered, ignorance dispelled, and the obstacles to real happiness removed. Here the Christian, looking round on the glories and blandishments of this world, has been enabled, with a noble contempt, to despise all. Here death itself, the king of terrors, has lost his sting; and the soul, with a holy magnanimity, has borne up in the agonies of a dying hour, and sweetly sung itself away to everlasting bliss. In respect to its future spread, we have reason to believe that all nations shall feel its happy effects. The prophecies are pregnant with matter as to this belief. It seems that not only a nation, or a country, but the whole habitable globe, shall become the kingdom of our God, and of his Christ. And who is there that has ever known the excellency of this system; who is there that has ever experienced its happy efficacy; who is there that has ever been convinced of its divine origin, its delightful nature and peaceful tendency, but must join the benevolent and royal poet in saying, "Let the whole earth be filled with its glory? Amen and amen!"

7. Among the collateral proofs of the truth and divine origin of Christianity, its rapid and wonderful success justly holds an important place. Of its early triumphs, the history of the Acts of the Apostles is a splendid record; and in process of time it made a wonderful progress through Europe, Asia, and Africa. In the third century there were Christians in the camp, in the senate, and in the palace; in short, every where, as we are informed, except in the temples and the theatres: they filled the towns, the country, and the islands. Men and women of all ages and ranks, and even those of the first dignity, embraced the Christian faith; insomuch that the Pagans complained that the revenues of their temples were ruined. They were in such great numbers in the empire, that, as Tertullian expresses it, if they had retired into another country, they would have left the Romans only a frightful solitude. (See the next article.) For the illustration of this argument, we may observe, that the Christian religion was introduced every where in opposition to the sword of the magistrate, the craft and interest of the priests, the pride of the philosophers, the passions and prejudices of the people, all closely combined in support of the national worship, and to crush the Christian faith, which aimed at the subversion of Heathenism and idolatry. Moreover, this religion was not propagated in the dark, by persons who tacitly endeavoured to deceive the credulous; nor delivered out by little and little, so that one doctrine might prepare the way for the reception of another; but it was fully and without disguise laid before men all at once, that they might judge of the whole under one view. Consequently mankind were not deluded into the belief of it, but received it upon proper examination and conviction. Beside, the Gospel was first preached and first believed by multitudes in Judea, where Jesus exercised his ministry, and where every individual had the means of knowing whether the things that were told him were matters of fact; and in this country, the scene of the principal transactions on which its credibility depended, the history of Christ could never have been received, unless it had been true, and known to all as truth. Again: the doctrine and history of Jesus were preached and believed in the most noted countries and cities of the world, in the very age when he is said to have lived. On the fiftieth day after our Lord's crucifixion, three thousand persons were converted in Jerusalem by a single sermon of the Apostles; and a few weeks after this, five thousand who believed were present at another sermon preached also in Jerusalem, Acts ii, 41; iv, 4; vi, 7; viii, 1; ix, 1, 20. About eight or ten years after our Lord's death, the disciples were become so numerous at Jerusalem and in the adjacent country, that they were objects of jealousy and alarm to Herod himself, Acts xii, 1. In the twenty-second year after the crucifixion, the disciples in Judea are said to have been many myriads, Acts xxi, 20. The age in which Christianity was introduced and received, was famous for men whose faculties were improved by the most

perfect state of social life, but who were good judges of the evidence offered in support of the facts recorded in the Gospel history. For it should be recollected, that the success of the Gospel was not restricted to Judea; but it was preached in all the different provinces of the Roman empire. The first triumphs of Christianity were in the heart of Greece itself, the nursery of learning and the polite arts; for churches were planted at a very early period at Corinth, Ephesus, Beræa, Thessalonica, and Philippi. Even Rome herself, the seat of wealth and empire, was not able to resist the force of truth at a time when the facts related were recent, and when they might, if they had been false, have easily been disproved. From Greece and Rome, at a period of cultivation and refinement, of general peace, and extensive intercourse, when one great empire united different nations and distant people, the confutation of these facts would very soon have passed from one country to another, to the utter confusion of the persons who endeavoured to propagate the belief of them. Nor ought it to be forgotten that the religion to which such numbers were proselyted, was an exclusive one. It denied, without reserve, the truth of every article of Heathen mythology, and the existence of every object of their worship. It accepted no compromise; it admitted of no comprehension. If it prevailed at all, it must prevail by the overthrow of every statue, altar, and temple in the world. It pronounced all other gods to be false, and all other worship vain. These are considerations which must have strengthened the opposition to it; augmented the hostility which it must encounter; and enhanced the difficulty of gaining proselytes: and more especially when we recollect, that among the converts to Christianity in the earliest age, a number of persons remarkable for their station, office, genius, education, and fortune, and who were personally interested by their emoluments and honours in either Judaism or Heathenism, appeared among the Christian proselytes. Its evidences approved themselves, not only to the multitude, but to men of the most refined sense and most distinguished abilities; and it dissolved the attachments which all powerful interest and authority created and upheld. Among the proselytes to Christianity we find Nicodemus, and Joseph of Arimathea, members of the senate of Israel; Jairus, a ruler of the synagogue; Zaccheus, the chief of the publicans at Jericho; Apollos, distinguished for eloquence; Paul, learned in the Jewish law; Sergius Paulus, governor of the island of Cyprus; Cornelius, a Roman captain; Dionysius, a judge and senator of the Athenian areopagus; Erastus, treasurer of Corinth; Tyrannus, a teacher of grammar and rhetoric at Corinth; Publius, governor of Malta; Philemon, a person of considerable rank at Colosse; Simon, a noted sophist in Samaria; Zenas, a lawyer; and even the domestics of the emperor himself. These are noticed in the sacred writings; and the Heathen historians also mention some persons of great note who were converted at an early period. To all the preceding circumstances we may add a consideration of peculiar moment, which is, that the profession of Christianity led all, without exception, to renounce the pleasures and honours of the world, and to expose themselves to the most ignominious sufferings. And now, without adding any more to this argument, we may ask, How could the Christian religion have thus prevailed had it not been introduced by the power of God and of truth? And it has been supported in the world by the same power through a course of many ages, amidst the treachery of its friends, the opposition of its enemies, the dangers of prosperous periods, and the persecutions and violence of adverse circumstances; all which must have destroyed it, if it had not been founded in truth, and guarded by the protection of an almighty Providence.

CHRISTIANITY: SKETCH OF ITS HISTORY. The Christian religion was published by its great Author in Judea, a short time before the death of Herod the Great, and toward the conclusion of the long reign of Augustus. While other religions had been accommodated to the peculiar countries in which they had taken their origin, and had indeed generally grown out of incidents connected with the history of those to whom they were addressed, Christianity was so framed as to be adapted to the whole human race; and although, for the wisest reasons, it was first announced to the Jews, who had peculiar advantages for forming an accurate judgment with regard to it, it was early declared that, in conformity to predictions which had long been known, and long interpreted, as referring to a new communication of the divine will, it was to be a light to lighten the Gentiles, and was to carry salvation to the ends of the earth. Although Christianity originated in Judea, it was not long confined within the narrow limits of the Holy Land. The open manner in which it was announced, the length of time during which its Author publicly addressed his countrymen, the innumerable miracles which he performed, and, above all, the report of the resurrection under circumstances which must have been communicated to the imperial government at Rome, excited the deep attention of the numerous Jews and proselytes who, from surrounding nations, regularly went up to Jerusalem, and of whom vast numbers were actually in that city when the resurrection must have been the subject of universal discussion. They very naturally carried to the different countries in which they usually resided, the astonishing intelligence with which they had been furnished; and provision was soon made for fulfilling the prediction which Jesus had uttered, that his Gospel would, before the destruction of Jerusalem, be circulated and embraced by many through the wide extent of the Roman empire. The Apostle Peter, in consequence of what he knew to be a solemn injunction from Heaven, communicated to a Gentile the truths of Christianity. St. Paul, who had distinguished himself by his enmity to the Christians, and by the cruelty with which he had persecuted them, having been converted, devoted himself to lay the foundations of the Gospel through a large portion of the most enlightened part of the world; and the miraculous gift of tongues, by which humble and illiterate men found themselves at once able to speak the languages of different nations, left no doubt that they were bound to preach their faith as extensively as had been marked out to them by the last instructions which they had received from their Master. They had to struggle with the most formidable difficulties in prosecuting this undertaking; for which, had they trusted merely to their own strength, and their own natural endowments, they were wholly unqualified.

2. The Roman empire at the period of their commencing the attempt, comprehended almost the whole of the civilized world, and thus included within it nations whose habits, customs, and sentiments essentially differed, and whom it required the most dexterous policy to unite in one community, or to subject to one government. The most effectual method by which, during the commonwealth, and at the rise of the empire, this had been accomplished, was a politic respect to the religious opinions which all these nations entertained. Not only were their modes of worship treated with scrupulous reverence, but their gods, in conformity with the genius of Paganism, were incorporated or associated with the deities of Rome, and they were thus joined to their conquerors by the strongest ties by which the affections can be secured. At all times religion had been an object of prominent interest with the Romans: at the foundation of the city, Romulus had professed to be directed by Heaven: during the whole period of the republic, the most sacred attention had been paid to the rites and ceremonies sanctioned by the prevailing superstition, the prosperity of the state was invariably ascribed to the protection of the gods, and the most impressive solemnities, combined with the richest splendour and magnificence, cast around polytheism a mysterious sanctity, which even the philosophers affected to revere. Precautions accordingly had been early taken to prevent innovations upon the established ritual; foreign rites were prohibited till they had obtained the sanction of the senate; and when the solicitation of this sanction was neglected, the persons guilty of the neglect were frequently punished. From the nature of Paganism, it was perfectly consistent with its spirit to conjoin, with any particular mode of it, the forms which elsewhere prevailed. These additions left all which had been previously honoured in unimpaired vigour and influence, and, in fact, only increased the appearance of profound regard for religion, which the Romans so long assumed. But this part of the political constitution, lightly as it affected other religions, at once struck at the root of Christianity, which, unlike the prevailing modifications of idolatry, prohibited the worship of all the deities before whose altars mankind had for ages bent, and required, as essential for obtaining the divine favour, that they who believed in it should pay undivided homage to the one God, whose existence it revealed. The extension of the Gospel thus necessarily carried with it opposition to the most ancient and most revered law of the empire, and it was impossible for those who judged of it merely from this circumstance, without investigating its nature and tendency, to hesitate in directing against it the statutes which the zeal of their fathers had provided, to prevent such a revolution as would be produced by so thorough and so alarming a change in their religious principles. No sooner, however, had the message of salvation been addressed indiscriminately to all men, and, from the evidence by which it was accompanied, had brought numbers to acknowledge the heavenly source from which it is derived, than the detestation of it previously entertained burst forth in all its violence; and it is apparent that this had been widely and openly expressed before any imperial edicts were directed against the Christians. Tacitus, in the celebrated passage in which he mentions the disciples of Jesus, and which refers to a period not more than thirty years distant from the ascension, represents it as notorious in Rome, that Christ, during the reign of Tiberius, had been put to death as a criminal; he asserts that his adherents had long been odious on account of their enormities; he laments that their destructive superstition had found its way to the capital of the empire; and he attributes the melancholy fate to which they were condemned to the general persuasion, that they were actuated by hatred to the whole human race. It is necessary to keep this fact steadily in view, to form an accurate idea of that opposition which Christianity had to encounter. This opposition is not to be estimated merely by reference to particular statutes, or even to be considered as fully exhibited when we have gathered together the public proceedings which have been recorded in history, or deplored in the writings of those who sought to avert them. It is to be remembered that even when the laws which the frantic zeal of some of the emperors had enacted were repealed, the general law of the empire was still in force; that it was competent for every one who had the cruelty to do so, to turn it against the Christians; and that the firm, though mistaken, conviction that the Christian profession involved in it the most revolting impiety, the most tremendous guilt, and the most dangerous hostility to the best interests of the state, would lead numbers to indulge their antipathy, when little notice was taken of the sufferers, and would keep the disciples of the hated faith in a state of unceasing alarm. (See PERSECUTION.) What was the effect of this depressing situation? Did it check the dissemination of the Gospel, or confine it to the men by whom it was preached? So far was this from being the case, that from the period of the death, and, as it must here he termed, the alleged resurrection of Jesus, it was embraced by immense numbers in all the countries to which it was conveyed; and even while they were contemplating the sacrifices and the trials to which, by attaching themselves to it, they would be exposed, they did not hesitate to relinquish the religion in which they had been educated, and to exchange for misery and death all the comforts which the strongest feelings and propensities of our nature lead men to value and to pursue. Finally, imperial Rome bowed to the religion it had persecuted, and the emperor Constantine became a Christian.

3. The propagation of Christianity assumes a new aspect after it became the religion of the empire, and was guarded by the protection and surrounded by the munificence of imperial power. The causes which, in the first stage of its existence, had most powerfully acted against it, were now turned to its support; and all the motives by which men are usually guided led them to enter with, at least, apparent conviction into its sanctuaries. Not only was persecution, after the reign of Constantine, at an end, but with the exception of the short reign of Julian, who, having apostatized from Christianity, and become intoxicated with the fascinating speculations of the Platonic philosophy, was

eager to raise the temples which his predecessor had laid in ruins, promotion and wealth and honour could be most effectually secured by transferring to the Gospel the zeal which had been in vain exhausted to preserve the sinking fabric of Paganism and idolatry. The emperors, who had displayed their zeal and their attachment to the religion of Jesus, by forcing their own subjects to profess it, conceived it to be their duty to communicate so great a blessing to all the nations which they could influence; and when they found it necessary to declare war against the savage tribes which pressed upon the frontiers, or forced themselves within the precincts of the empire, they carried on hostilities with the view of rendering these instrumental no less to the diffusion of their religious tenets, than to the vindication of their authority, and the security of their dominions. The vanquished invaders felt little reluctance to purchase the forbearance or the clemency of their conquerors, by submitting to receive their religion; and this species of conversion, so little connected with the great objects which revelation was designed to accomplish, leaving, in fact, all the gross superstitious practices and all the immoral abominations which had previously existed, was boastfully held forth as a decisive proof of the triumph of the Gospel.

4. The foundation of the empire, not long after the days of Constantine, began to be shaken: and it experienced numberless assaults and convulsions, till it was finally divided into the eastern and western empires. The luxury and wealth which had enervated their possessors, and destroyed the heroism and intrepidity by which their ancestors had been distinguished, presented the most powerful temptations to the lawless bands which, driven from the sterile regions of the north of Europe, had pressed forward to seek for new and more favoured habitations. The feeble attempts to turn aside, by bribery, these ferocious barbarians increased the danger which they were intended to remove; and the history of Europe presents, for several ages, the disgusting spectacle of war, conducted with an atrocity eclipsing the stern virtues which sometimes were strikingly displayed. But although the insubordination of this turbulent and sanguinary period was little favourable to the mild influence of genuine Christianity, it did not prove so fatal to it as might have been apprehended; and it was even instrumental in extending its nominal dominion. Mankind, when scarcely emerged from barbarism, and attached to no particular country, but seeking wherever it can be found the food necessary for themselves and the flocks upon which they in a great measure depend, although they entertain those sentiments with regard to religion which seem almost interwoven with our nature, feel little attachment to any one system of superstition, and are open to the reception of new doctrines, which an association with what they value may have led them to venerate. When, accordingly, the tribes which finally overran the Roman empire had ceased from the destructive contests by which they got possession of the regions that had long been blessed with civilization and enlightened by science, they surveyed with amazement and with admiration the people whom they had conquered; they were delighted with the luxuries which abounded among them; they were charmed with their manners and customs; and they eagerly conformed to institutions from which they hoped that they should reap what the original inhabitants of their settlement had enjoyed. The religion of the vanquished they contemplated with reverence; they connected it with the wealth, the refinement, and the power which they saw spread around them; and they easily exchanged the rude and careless worship of their native deities, for the polished and splendid devotional rites, which, with the most imposing solemnity, were celebrated by the Christians. Hence, they soon embraced the religion by which it was believed that these rites were prescribed; and they communicated it to the nations with whom they still maintained an alliance. There is no doubt that motives very little connected with the conviction of the understanding led to the progress of Christianity now described; and, in fact, that progress was occasioned by causes so different from those which should have produced it, that, had circumstances been changed, and had the religion of Jesus been continued to be persecuted by the most powerful states, multitudes who affected to revere it would, upon the same ground on which their veneration rested, have exerted themselves to deride its tenets, and to exterminate its professors.

5. But it was not the secular arm alone that was stretched forth to lead men to the reception of Christianity. The church, after it had been firmly established, and had, amidst the riches and honours with which it was endowed, forgotten that it should not have been of this world, conceived it incumbent, as an evidence of its zeal, or, as was too often the case, for extending its power and its influence, to make attempts to substitute the cross of Christ for the emblems of Paganism. In accomplishing this object, it employed different means. But although the conversions which took place, from the establishment of Christianity till the restoration of learning, or the reformation, which forms a new æra in the dissemination of the Gospel, were often unfortunately very far from planting the word of life in the hearts of those to whom it was conveyed, they were very extensive. They reached to almost every country in Europe; to Arabia, China, Judea, and many other parts of Asia; and the obscure tribes, to whom no missionaries were despatched, gradually conformed to the religion of those more powerful states upon which they depended, or to which they looked with respect or veneration.

6. Mohammedanism, however, arrested the progress of Christianity in some of these countries, and humbled it and oppressed it in others; but since the reformation, and especially within the last century, it has been extended, not so much by conquest, as by the legitimate means of colonization, and by missions and education, to the most distant and important parts of the world, to China, India, Africa, the American Islands, and those of the Pacific Ocean. The zeal, self-denial, and successes, of those missionaries, who have been sent forth within a few years by various Protestant societies, and their great successes form, indeed, a splendid section in the modern history of the church. They

have sown the seed in almost every land, and the fruit has spread itself throughout the world.

CHRONICLES, BOOKS OF. This name is given to two historical books of Scripture, which the Hebrews call DIBRI-JAMIM, "Words of Days," that is, "Diaries," or "Journals." They are called in the **LXX**, PARALIPOMENA, which signifies, "things omitted;" as if these books were a supplement of what had been omitted, or too much abridged, in the books of Kings, and other historical books of Scripture. And, indeed, we find in them many particulars which are not extant elsewhere: but it must not be thought that these are the records, or books of the acts, of the kings of Judah and Israel, so often referred to. Those ancient registers were much more extensive than these are; and the books of Chronicles themselves refer to those original memoirs, and make long extracts from them. They were compiled, and probably by Ezra, from the ancient chronicles of the kings of Judah and Israel just now mentioned, and they may be considered as a kind of supplement to the preceding books of Scripture. The former part of the first book of Chronicles contains a great variety of genealogical tables, beginning with Adam; and in particular gives a circumstantial account of the twelve tribes, which must have been very valuable to the Jews after their return from captivity. The descendants of Abraham, Isaac, Jacob, and David, from all of whom it was predicted that the Saviour of the world should be born, are here marked with precision. These genealogies occupy the first nine chapters, and in the tenth is recorded the death of Saul From the eleventh chapter to the end of the book, we have a history of the reign of David, with a detailed statement of his preparation for the building of the temple, of his regulations respecting the priests and Levites, and his appointment of musicians for the public service of religion. The second book of Chronicles contains a brief sketch of the Jewish history, from the accession of Solomon to the return from the Babylonian captivity, being a period of four hundred and eighty years; and in both these books we find many particulars not noticed in the other historical books of Scripture.

CHRYSOLITE, Rev. xxi, 20, a precious stone of a golden colour. Schroder says it is the gem now called the Indian topaz, which is of a yellowish green colour, and very beautiful.

CHRYSOPRASUS, Rev. xxi, 20, a precious stone, which Pliny classes among the beryls; the best of which, he says, are of a sea-green colour; after these he mentions the chrysoberyls, which are a little paler, inclining to golden colour; and next, a sort still paler, and by some reckoned a distinct species, and called chrysoprasus.

CHURCH. The Greek word ἐκκλησία, so rendered, denotes an assembly met about business, whether spiritual or temporal, Acts xix, 32, 39. It is understood also of the collective body of Christians, or all those over the face of the earth who profess to believe in Christ, and acknowledge him to be the Saviour of mankind; this is called the visible church. But by the word CHURCH, we are more strictly to understand the whole body of God's true people, in every period of time: this is the invisible or spiritual church. The people of God on earth are called the church militant, and those in heaven the church triumphant. It has been remarked by Dr. John Owen, that sin having entered into the world, God was pleased to found his church (the catholic or universal church) in the promise of the Messiah given to Adam; that this promise contained in it something of the nature of a covenant, including the grace which God designed to show to sinners in the Messiah, and the obedience which he required from them; and that consequently, from its first promulgation, that promise became the sole foundation of the church and of the whole worship of God therein. Prior to the days of Abraham, this church, though scattered up and down the world, and subject to many changes in its worship through the addition of new revelations, was still but one and the same, because founded in the same covenant, and interested thereby in all the benefits or privileges that God had granted, or would at any time grant. In process of time, God was pleased to restrict his church, as far as visible acknowledgment went, in a great measure, to the seed of Abraham. With the latter he renewed his covenant, requiring that he should walk before him and be upright. He also constituted him the father of the faithful, or of all them that believe, and the "heir of the world." So that since the days of Abraham, the church has, in every age, been founded upon the covenant made with that patriarch, and on the work of redemption which was to be performed according to that covenant. Now wheresoever this covenant made with Abraham is, and with whomsoever it is established, with them is the church of God, and to them all the promises and privileges of the church really belong. Hence we may learn that at the coming of the Messiah, there was not one church taken away and another set up in its room; but the church continued the same, in those that were the children of Abraham, according to the faith. It is common with divines to speak of the Jewish and the Christian churches, as though they were two distinct and totally different things; but that is not a correct view of the matter. The Christian church is not another church, but the very same that was before the coming of Christ, having the same faith with it, and interested in the same covenant. Great alterations indeed were made in the outward state and condition of the church, by the coming of the Messiah. The carnal privilege of the Jews, in their separation from other nations to give birth to the Messiah, then failed, and with that also their claim on that account to be the children of Abraham. The ordinances of worship suited to that state of things then expired, and came to an end. New ordinances of worship were appointed, suitable to the new light and grace which were then bestowed upon the church. The Gentiles came into the faith of Abraham along with the Jews, being made joint partakers with them in his blessing. But none of these things, nor the whole collectively, did make such an alteration in the church, but that it was still one and the same. The olive tree was still the same, only some branches were broken off, and others grafted into it. The Jews fell, and the

Gentiles came in their room. And this may enable us to determine the difference between the Jews and Christians relative to the Old Testament promises. They are all made to the church. No individual has any interest in them except by virtue of his membership with the church. The church is, and always was, one and the same. The Jewish plea, is, that the church is with them, because they are the children of Abraham according to the flesh. Christians reply, that their privilege on that ground was of another nature, and ended with the coming of the Messiah: that the church of God, unto whom all the promises belong, are only those who are heirs of the faith of Abraham, believing as he did, and are consequently interested in his covenant. These are Zion, Jerusalem, Israel, Jacob, the temple, or church of God.

2. By a particular church we understand an assembly of Christians united together, and meeting in one place, for the solemn worship of God. To this agrees the definition given by the compilers of the Thirty-nine Articles of the Church of England: "A congregation of faithful men, in which the true word of God is preached, and the sacraments duly administered according to Christ's ordinances, in all those things that of necessity are requisite to the same," Acts ix, 31; xx, 17; Gal. i, 2, 22; 1 Cor. xiv, 34; Col. iv, 15. The word is now also used to denote any particular denomination of Christians, distinguished by particular doctrines, ceremonies, &c, as the Romish church, the Greek church, the English church, &c.

3. On the subject of the church, opinions as opposite or varying as possible have been held, from that of the Papists, who contend for its visible unity throughout the world under a visible head, down to that of the Independents, who consider the universal church as composed of congregational churches, each perfect in itself, and entirely independent of every other. The first opinion is manifestly contradicted by the language of the Apostles, who, while they teach that there is but one church, composed of believers throughout the world, think it not at all inconsistent with this to speak of "the churches of Judea," "of Achaia," "the seven churches of Asia," "the church at Ephesus," &c. Among themselves the Apostles had no common head; but planted churches and gave directions for their government, in most cases without any apparent correspondence with each other. The Popish doctrine is certainly not found in their writings; and so far were they from making provision for the government of this one supposed church, by the appointment of one visible and exclusive head, that they provide for the future government of the respective churches raised up by them in a totally different manner, that is, by the ordination of ministers for each church, who are indifferently called bishops, and presbyters, and pastors. The only unity of which they speak is the unity of the whole church in Christ, the invisible head, by faith; and the unity produced by "fervent love toward each other." Nor has the Popish doctrine of the visible unity of the church any countenance from early antiquity. The best ecclesiastical historians have showed, that, through the greater part of the second century, the Christian churches were independent of each other. "Each Christian assembly," says Mosheim, "was a little state governed by its own laws, which were either enacted, or at least approved, by the society. But in process of time, all the churches of a province were formed into one large ecclesiastical body, which, like confederate states, assembled at certain times in order to deliberate about the common interests of the whole." So far indeed this union of churches appears to have been a wise and useful arrangement, although afterward it was carried to an injurious extreme, until finally it gave birth to the assumptions of the bishop of Rome, as universal bishop; a claim, however, which, when most successful, was but partially submitted to, the eastern churches having, for the most part, always maintained their independence. No very large association of churches of any kind existed till toward the close of the second century, which sufficiently refutes the papal argument from antiquity. The independence of the early Christian churches does not, however, appear to have resembled that of the churches which, in modern times, are called Independent. During the lives of the Apostles and Evangelists they were certainly subject to their counsel and control, which proves that the independency of separate societies was not the first form of the church. It may, indeed, be allowed, that some of the smaller and more insulated churches might, after the death of the Apostles and Evangelists, retain this form for some considerable time; but the larger churches, in the chief cities, and those planted in populous neighbourhoods, had many presbyters, and, as the members multiplied, they had several separate assemblies or congregations, yet all under the same common government. And when churches were raised up in the neighbourhood of cities, the appointment of CHOREPISCOPI, or country bishops, and of visiting presbyters, both acting under the presbytery of the city, with the bishop at its head, is sufficiently in proof, that the ancient churches, especially the larger and more prosperous of them, existed in that form which, in modern times, we should call a religious connection, subject to a common government. This appears to have arisen out of the very circumstance of the increase of the church, through the zeal of the first Christians; and it was doubtless much more in the spirit of the very first discipline exercised by the Apostles and Evangelists, (when none of the churches were independent, but remained under the government of those who had been chiefly instrumental in raising them up,) to place themselves under a common inspection, and to unite the weak with the strong, and the newly converted with those who were "in Christ before them." There was also in this, greater security afforded both for the continuance of wholesome doctrine, and of godly discipline.

4. Church members are those who compose or belong to the visible church. As to the real church, the true members of it are such as come out from the world, 2 Cor. vi, 17; who are born again, 1 Peter i, 23; or made new creatures, 2 Cor. v, 17; whose faith works by love to God and all mankind, Gal. v, 6; James ii, 14, 26; who walk in all the ordinances of the Lord blameless. None but such are members of the true church; nor should any be admitted into any particular church

without some evidence of their earnestly seeking this state of salvation.

5. Church fellowship is the communion that the members enjoy one with another. The ends of church fellowship are, the maintenance and exhibition of a system of sound doctrine; the support of the ordinances of evangelical worship in their purity and simplicity; the impartial exercise of church government and discipline; the promotion of holiness in all manner of conversation. The more particular duties are, earnest study to keep peace and unity; bearing of one another's burdens, Gal. vi, 1, 2; earnest endeavours to prevent each other's stumbling, 1 Cor. x, 23–33; Heb. x, 24–27; Rom. xiv, 13; steadfast continuance in the faith and worship of the Gospel, Acts ii, 42; praying for and sympathizing with each other, 1 Sam. xii, 23; Eph. vi, 18. The advantages are, peculiar incitement to holiness; the right to some promises applicable to none but those who attend the ordinances of God, and hold communion with the saints, Psalm xcii, 13; cxxxii, 13, 16; xxxvi, 8; Jer. xxxi, 12; the being placed under the watchful eye of pastors, Heb. xiii, 7; that they may restore each other if they fall, Gal. vi, 1; and the more effectually promote the cause of true religion.

6. As to church order and discipline, without entering into the discussion of the many questions which have been raised on this subject, and argued in so many distinct treatises, it may be sufficient generally to observe, that the church of Christ being a visible and permanent society, bound to observe certain rites, and to obey certain rules, the existence of government in it is necessarily supposed. All religious rites suppose order, all order direction and control, and these a directive and controlling power. Again: all laws are nugatory without enforcement, in the present mixed and imperfect state of society; and all enforcement supposes an executive. If baptism be the door of admission into the church, some must judge of the fitness of candidates, and administrators of the rite must be appointed; if the Lord's Supper must be partaken of, the times and the mode are to be determined, the qualifications of communicants judged of, and the administration placed in suitable hands; if worship must be social and public, here again there must be an appointment of times, an order, and an administration; if the word of God is to be read and preached, then readers and preachers are necessary; if the continuance of any one in the fellowship of Christians be conditional upon good conduct, so that the purity and credit of the church may be guarded, then the power of enforcing discipline must be lodged some where. Thus government flows necessarily from the very nature of the institution of the Christian church; and since this institution has the authority of Christ and his Apostles, it is not to be supposed, that its government was left unprovided for; and if they have in fact made such a provision, it is no more a matter of mere option with Christians whether they will be subject to government in the church, than it is optional with them to confess Christ by becoming its members. The nature of this government, and the persons to whom it is committed, are both points which we must briefly examine by the light of the Holy Scriptures. As to the first, it is wholly spiritual:--"My kingdom," says our Lord, "is not of this world." The church is a society founded upon faith, and united by mutual love, for the personal edification of its members in holiness, and for the religious benefit of the world. The nature of its government is thus determined; it is concerned only with spiritual objects. It cannot employ force to compel men into its pale; for the only door of the church is faith; to which there can be no compulsion;--"he that believeth and is baptized" becomes a member. It cannot inflict pains and penalties upon the disobedient and refractory, like civil governments; for the only punitive discipline authorized in the New Testament, is comprised in "admonition," "reproof," "sharp rebukes," and, finally, "excision from the society." The last will be better understood, if we consider the special relations in which true Christians stand to each other, and the duties resulting from them. They are members of one body, and are therefore bound to tenderness and sympathy; they are the conjoint instructers of others, and are therefore to strive to be of "one judgment;" they are brethren, and they are to love one another as such, that is, with an affection more special than that general good will which they are commanded to bear to all mankind; they are therefore to seek the intimacy of friendly society among themselves, and, except in the ordinary and courteous intercourse of life, they are bound to keep themselves separate from the world; they are enjoined to do good unto all men, but "especially to them that are of the household of faith;" and they are forbidden "to eat" at the Lord's table with immoral persons, that is, with those who, although they continue their Christian profession, dishonour it by their practice. With these relations of Christians to each other and to the world, and their correspondent duties, before our minds, we may easily interpret the nature of that extreme discipline which is vested in the church. "Persons who will not hear the church" are to be held "as Heathen men and publicans," as those who are not members of it; that is, they are to be separated from it, and regarded as of "the world," quite out of the range of the above mentioned relations of Christians to each other, and their correspondent duties; but still, like "Heathen men and publicans" they are to be the objects of pity, and general benevolence. Nor is this extreme discipline to be hastily inflicted before "a first and second admonition," nor before those who are "spiritual" have attempted "to restore a brother overtaken by a fault;" and when the "wicked person" is "put away," still the door is to be kept open for his reception again upon repentance. The true excommunication of the Christian church is therefore a merciful and considerate separation of an incorrigible offender from the body of Christians, without any infliction of civil pains or penalties. "Now we command you, brethren, in the name of our Lord Jesus Christ, that ye withdraw yourselves from every brother that walketh disorderly, and not after the tradition which ye have received from us," 2 Thess. iii, 6. "Purge out therefore the old leaven, that ye may be a new lump," 1 Cor. v, 7. "But now I have written to you not to keep company, if any man that is called a brother be a fornicator, or covetous, or an idolater, or a railer, or a drunkard, or an extortioner, with such a one, no not to eat,"

1 Cor. v, 11. This then is the moral discipline which is imperative upon the church of Christ, and its government is criminally defective whenever it is not enforced. On the other hand, the disabilities and penalties which established churches in different places have connected with these sentences of excommunication, have no countenance at all in Scripture, and are wholly inconsistent with the spiritual character and ends of the Christian association.

7. As to the PERSONS to whom the government of the church is committed, it is necessary to consider the composition, so to speak, of the primitive church, as stated in the New Testament. A full enunciation of these offices we find in Ephesians iv, 11: "And he gave some, Apostles; and some, Prophets; and some, Evangelists; and some, pastors and teachers; for the perfecting of the saints, for the work of the ministry, for the edifying of the body of Christ." Of these, the office of Apostle is allowed by all to have been confined to those immediately commissioned by Christ to witness the fact of his miracles, and of his resurrection from the dead, and to reveal the complete system of Christian doctrine and duty; confirming their extraordinary mission by miracles wrought by themselves. If by "prophets" we are to understand persons who foretold future events, then the office was from its very nature extraordinary, and the gift of prophecy has passed away with the other miraculous endowments of the first age of Christianity. If, with others, we understand that these prophets were extraordinary teachers raised up until the churches were settled under permanent qualified instructors; still the office was temporary. The "Evangelists" are generally understood to be assistants of the Apostles, who acted under their especial authority and direction. Of this number were Timothy and Titus; and as the Apostle Paul directed them to ordain bishops or presbyters in the several churches, but gave them no authority to ordain successors to themselves in their particular office as Evangelists, it is clear that the Evangelists must also be reckoned among the number of extraordinary and temporary ministers suited to the first age of Christianity. Whether by "pastors and teachers" two offices be meant, or one, has been disputed. The change in the mode of expression seems to favour the latter view, and so the text is interpreted by St. Jerom, and St. Augustine; but the point is of little consequence. A pastor was a teacher, although every teacher might not be a pastor; but in many cases his office might be one of subordinate instruction, whether as an expounder of doctrine, a catechist, or even a more private instructer of those who as yet were unacquainted with the first principles of the Gospel of Christ. The term PASTOR implies the duties both of instruction and of government, of feeding and of ruling the flock of Christ; and, as the presbyters or bishops were ordained in the several churches, both by the Apostles and Evangelists, and rules are left by St. Paul as to their appointment, there can be no doubt but that these are the "pastors" spoken of in the Epistle to the Ephesians, and that they were designed to be the permanent ministers of the church; and that with them both the government of the church and the performance of its leading religious services were deposited. Deacons had the charge of the gifts and offerings for charitable purposes, although, it appears from Justin Martyr, not in every instance; for he speaks of the weekly oblations as being deposited with the chief minister, and distributed by him. These pastors appear to have been indifferently called Bishops and Presbyters, and with them the regulation of the churches was, doubtless, deposited; not without checks and guards, the principal of which, however, was, in the primitive church, and continues to be in all modern churches which have no support from the magistracy, or are made independent of the people by endowments, the voluntariness of the association. A perfect religious liberty is always supposed by the Apostles to exist among Christians; no compulsion of the civil power is any where assumed by them as the basis of their advices or directions; no binding of the members to one church, without liberty to join another, by any ties but those involved in moral considerations, of sufficient weight, however, to prevent the evils of faction and schism. It was this which created a natural and competent check upon the ministers of the church; for being only sustained by the opinion of the churches, they could not but have respect to it; and it was this which gave to the sound part of a fallen church the advantage of renouncing, upon sufficient and well-weighed grounds, their communion with it, and of kindling up the light of a pure ministry and a holy discipline, by forming a separate association, bearing its testimony against errors in doctrine, and failures in practice. Nor is it to be conceived, that, had this simple principle of perfect religious liberty been left unviolated through subsequent ages, the church could ever have become so corrupt, or with such difficulty and slowness have been recovered from its fall. This ancient Christian liberty has happily been restored in a few parts of Christendom. See Episcopacy and Presbyterianism.

CHURCH OF ENGLAND and **IRELAND** is that established by law in England and Ireland, where it forms a part of the common law of the land, or constitution of the country.

1. When and by whom Christianity was first introduced into Britain, cannot at this distance of time be exactly ascertained. Eusebius, indeed, positively declares that it was by the Apostles and their disciples; Bishops Jewel and Stillingfleet, Dr. Cave, and others, insist that it was by St. Paul; and Baronius affirms, on the authority of an ancient manuscript in the Vatican Library, that the Gospel was planted in Britain by Simon Zelotes, the Apostle, and Joseph of Arimathea; and that the latter came over A. D. 35, or about the twenty-first year of Tiberius, and died in this country. According to Archbishop Usher, the British churches had a school of learning in the year 182, to provide them with proper teachers; and it would appear that they flourished, without dependence on any foreign church, till the arrival of Austin the monk, in the latter part of the sixth century.

2. Episcopacy was early established in this country; and it ought to be remembered, to the honour of the British bishops and clergy, that during several centuries they

withstood the encroachments of the see of Rome. Popery, however, was at length introduced into England, and, as some say, by Austin, the monk; and we find its errors every where prevalent during several ages preceding the reformation, till they were refuted by Wickliffe. The seed which Wickliffe had sown ripened after his death, and produced a glorious harvest. However, it was not till the reign of Henry **VIII**, that the reformation in England in reality commenced. When Luther declared war against the pope, Henry wrote his treatise on the seven sacraments against Luther's book, "Of the Captivity of Babylon," and was repaid by the pontiff with the title of "Defender of the Faith." This title, in a sense diametrically opposite, and by a claim of higher desert, was transmitted by Henry with his crown, and now belongs to his successors. Henry's affections being estranged from his queen Catharine, and fixed on Anne Boleyn, he requested a divorce from his wife; but the pope hesitating, the archbishop of Canterbury annulled his former marriage. The sentence of the archbishop was condemned by the pope, whose authority Henry therefore shook off, and was declared by parliament "supreme head of the church." In the year 1800, when the kingdoms of Britain and Ireland were united, the churches of England and Ireland, which had always been the same in government, faith, and worship, became one united church.

3. The acknowledged standards of the faith and doctrines of the united church are, after the Scriptures, the Book of Homilies and the Thirty-nine Articles. Her liturgy is also doctrinal, as well as devotional. The homilies were composed by Cranmer, Latimer, and Ridley, men of unexceptionable learning and orthodoxy; or, according to others, the first book was written principally by Cranmer, and the second by Jewel. They were appointed to be read in churches at the beginning of the reformation, when, by reason of the scarcity of learned divines, few ministers were found who could safely be trusted to preach their own compositions. The first draught of the Articles was composed by Archbishop Cranmer, assisted by Bishop Ridley, in the year 1551; and after being corrected by the other bishops, and approved by the convocation, they were published in Latin and English in 1553, and amounted to forty-two in number. In 1562 they were revised and corrected. Being then reduced to thirty-nine, they were drawn up in Latin only; but in 1571 they were subscribed by the members of the two houses of convocation, both in Latin and English; and therefore the Latin and English copies are to be considered as equally authentic. The original manuscripts, subscribed by the houses of convocation, were burned in the fire of London; but Dr. Bennet has collated the oldest copies now extant, in which it appears that there are no variations of any importance. During the last century, disputes arose among the clergy respecting the propriety of subscribing to any human formulary of religious sentiments. Parliament, in 1772, was applied to for the abolition of the subscription, by certain clergymen and others, whose petition received the most ample discussion, but was rejected by a large majority. It has been generally held by most, if not all, Calvinists, both in and out of the church, that the doctrinal parts of our Articles are Calvinistic. This opinion, however, has been warmly controverted. It is no doubt nearer the truth to conclude that the Articles are framed with comprehensive latitude; and that neither Calvinism nor Arminianism was intended to be exclusively established. In this view such liberal sentiments as the following, from the *Apology of the Church of England*, in 1732, are not of uncommon occurrence: "This, I know, I am myself an Anti-Calvinian; and yet, were I to compile articles for the church, I would abhor the thoughts of forming them so fully according to my own scheme of thinking, or of descending so minutely into all the particular branches of it, that none but Arminians should be able to subscribe, or that the church should lose the credit and service of such valuable men as the Abbots, Davenant, Usher, and other Calvinists undoubtedly were. And since our reformers were men of temper and moderation, it seems but justice, I am sure it is but reasonable, to think they intended such a latitude as I contend for, so that both parties, the followers of Arminius as well as of Calvin, might subscribe." In a subsequent page, however, the same author says, "But what, if there was not so entire a harmony among the compilers or imposers, as was before supposed? What if several of them were Anti-Calvinian? This will incline the balance still more in our favour, and enlarge the probability of THE ARTICLES BEING DRAWN UP IN A MODERATE, INDEFINITE WAY. The divines who fled for refuge, in Queen Mary's reign, to Geneva, Zurich, and other places beyond sea, (where, by conceiving a great veneration for Calvin, they were mightily changed in their sentiments and ways of thinking,) began to propagate his notions soon after their return in the next reign: and this seems to have been the prime occasion of Calvinism taking any considerable root in this kingdom. In King Edward's time it doth not appear to have prevailed, except among a few 'gospelers,' and how they were reflected on by Bishop Latimer and Hooper has been already observed. When the articles were formed in 1552, I do not find that any deference was paid to Calvin's judgment or authority: instead of that, the assistance he offered was, to his no little grief and dissatisfaction, refused. Next to the Scriptures and the doctrine of the primitive church, the compilers had an eye to the Augustan Confession, as appears from the identity of many of the articles; to the writings of Melancthon, whose assistance they desired, and whom King Edward invited over hither; the works of Erasmus; and the *Necessary Doctrine and Erudition for any Christian Man*. This last book was published by King Henry's authority in 1543; and because it then had the approbation of most of those who compiled the Articles nine years afterward, it will be of consequence to see how it stands affected toward Calvinism. It teaches the cardinal point of universal redemption in several places; which strikes directly at the root of the Calvinian system, and, as Dr. Whitby expresses it, 'draws all the rest after it, on which side soever the truth lies.'" This judicious amplitude has received much elucidation in Dr. Puller's *Moderation of the Church of England considered*, 1679; and in other works of more recent date.

4. In this church, divine service is conducted by a liturgy, which was composed in 1547, and has undergone several alterations, the last of which took place in 1661, in the reign of Charles **II**. Many applications have been since made for a review; and particular alterations were proposed in 1689, by several learned and excellent divines, in the number of whom were Archbishops Tillotson and Tenison, and Bishops Patrick, Burnet, Stillingfleet, Kidder, &c. This subject has been recently revived; and it is believed that some changes are under consideration. To this liturgy every clergyman promises at his ordination to conform in his public ministrations.

5. Ever since the reign of Henry **VIII**, the sovereigns of England have been styled "supreme heads of the church," as well as "defenders of the faith;" but this title is said to convey no spiritual meaning; or, in other words, it only substitutes the king in place of the pope, with respect to temporalities, and the external economy of the church. The church of England is governed by two archbishops and twenty-four bishops, beside the bishop of Sodor and Man. The benefices of the bishops were converted by William the Conqueror into temporal baronies; and, therefore, all of them, except the bishop of Man, are barons or lords of parliament, and sit and vote in the house of lords, where they represent the clergy. The bishops' representatives and assistants are the archdeacons, of whom there are sixty in England. The other dignitaries of the church are the deans, prebendaries, canons, &c; and the inferior clergy are the rectors, vicars, and curates. The united church knows only three orders of ministers; bishops, priests, and deacons: but in these orders are comprehended archbishops, bishops, deans, archdeacons, rectors, vicars, and curates. The church of Ireland is governed by four archbishops and eighteen bishops. Since the union of Britain and Ireland, one archbishop and three bishops sit alternately in the house of peers, by rotation of sessions.

CILICIA, a country in the south-east of Asia Minor, and lying on the northern coast, at the east end of the Mediterranean Sea: the capital city thereof was Tarsus, the native city of St. Paul, Acts xxi, 39.

CINNAMON, קינמון, an agreeable aromatic; the inward bark of the CANELLA, a small tree of the height of the willow. It is mentioned, Exodus xxx, 23, among the materials in the composition of the holy anointing oil; and in Proverbs vii, 17; Canticles iv, 14; Ecclesiasticus xxiv, 15; and Revelation xviii, 13, among the richest perfumes. This spice is now brought from the east Indies; but as there was no traffic with India in the days of Moses, it was then brought, probably, from Arabia, or some neighbouring country. We learn, however, from Pliny, that a species of it grew in Syria.

CINNEROTH, or **CINNERETH**, a city on the north-western side of the sea of Galilee; which, from it, is frequently called in the Old Testament the sea of Cinneroth: from which word, that of Genesaret, in the New Testament, is conjectured by Dr. Wells to have been framed.

CIRCUMCISION is from the Latin, CIRCUMCIDERE, "to cut all round," because the Jews, in circumcising their children, cut off after this manner the skin which covers the prepuce. God enjoined Abraham to use circumcision, as a sign of his covenant. In obedience to this order, Abraham, at ninety-nine years of age, was circumcised: also his son Ishmael, and all the males of his property, Gen. xvii, 10. God repeated the precept of circumcision to Moses: he ordered that all who were to partake of the paschal sacrifice should receive circumcision; and that this rite should be performed on children, on the eighth day after their birth. The Jews have always been very exact in observing this ceremony, and it appears that they did not neglect it when in Egypt. But Moses, while in Midian with Jethro his father-in-law, did not circumcise his two sons born in that country; and during the journey of the Israelites in the wilderness, their children were not circumcised. Circumcision was practised among the Arabians, Saracens, and Ishmaelites. These people, as well as the Israelites, sprung from Abraham. Circumcision was introduced with the law of Moses among the Samaritans and Cutheans. The Idumeans, though descended from Abraham and Isaac, were not circumcised till subdued by John Hircanus. Those who assert that the Phenicians were circumcised, mean, probably, the Samaritans; for we know, from other authority, that the Phenicians did not observe this ceremony. As to the Egyptians, circumcision never was of general and indispensable obligation on the whole nation; certain priests only, and particular professions, were obliged to it. Circumcision is likewise the ceremony of initiation into the Mohammedan religion. There is, indeed, no law in the Koran which enjoins it, and they have the precept only in tradition. They say that Mohammed commanded it out of respect to Abraham, the head of his race. They have no fixed day for the performance of this rite, and generally wait till the child is five or six years of age.

Circumcision, COVENANT OF. That the covenant with Abraham, of which circumcision was made the sign and seal, Genesis xvii, 7–14, was the general covenant of grace, and not wholly, or even chiefly, a political and national covenant, may be satisfactorily established. The first engagement in it was, that God would "greatly bless" Abraham; which promise, although it comprehended temporal blessings, referred, as we learn from St. Paul, more fully to the blessing of his justification by the imputation of his faith for righteousness, with all the spiritual advantages consequent upon the relation which was thus established between him and God, in time and eternity. The second promise in the covenant was, that he should be "the father of many nations;" which we are also taught by St. Paul to interpret more with reference to his spiritual seed, the followers of that faith whereof cometh justification, than to his natural descendants. "That the promise might be sure to all the seed, not only to that which is by the law, but to that also which is by THE FAITH of Abraham, who is the father of US ALL,"--of all believing Gentiles as well as Jews. The third stipulation in God's covenant with the patriarch, was the gift to Abraham and to his seed of "the land of Canaan," in which the temporal promise was manifestly but the type of the higher promise of a heavenly inheritance. Hence St. Paul says, "By FAITH he sojourned in the land of promise, dwelling in tabernacles with Isaac and Jacob, the heirs with him of the same promise;" but this "faith" did not respect the fulfilment of the temporal promise; for St. Paul adds, "they looked for a city which had foundations, whose builder and maker is God," Heb. xi, 19. The next promise was, that God would always be "a God to Abraham and to his seed after him," a promise which is connected with the highest spiritual blessings, such as the remission of sins, and the sanctification of our nature, as well as with a visible church state. It is even used to express the felicitous state of the church in heaven, Rev. xxi, 3. The final engagement in the Abrahamic covenant was, that in Abraham's "seed, all nations of the earth should be blessed;" and this blessing, we are expressly taught by St. Paul, was nothing less than the justification of all nations, that is, of all believers in all nations, by faith in Christ: "And the Scripture, foreseeing that God would justify the Heathen by faith, preached before the Gospel to Abraham, saying, In thee shall all nations be blessed. So then they who are of faith are blessed with believing Abraham;" they receive the same blessing, justification, by the same means, faith, Gal. iii, 8, 9. This covenant with Abraham, therefore, although it respected a natural seed, Isaac, from whom a numerous progeny was to spring; and an earthly inheritance provided for this issue, the land of Canaan; and a special covenant relation with the descendants of Isaac, through the line of Jacob, to whom Jehovah was to be "a God," visibly and specially, and they a visible and "peculiar people;" yet was, under all these temporal, earthly, and external advantages, but a higher and spiritual grace embodying itself under these circumstances, as types of a dispensation of salvation and eternal life, to all who should follow the faith of Abraham, whose justification before God was the pattern of the justification of every man, whether Jew or Gentile, in all ages. Now, of this covenant, in its spiritual as well as in its temporal provisions, circumcision was most certainly the sacrament, that is the "sign" and the "seal;" for St. Paul thus explains the case: "And he received the SIGN of circumcision, a SEAL of the righteousness of the faith which he had yet being uncircumcised." And as this rite was enjoined upon Abraham's posterity, so that every "uncircumcised man-child whose flesh of his foreskin was not circumcised on the eighth day," was to be "cut off from his people," by the special judgment of God, and that because "he had broken God's COVENANT," Gen. xvii, 14; it therefore follows that this rite was a constant publication of God's covenant of grace among the descendants of Abraham, and its repetition a continual confirmation of that covenant, on the part of God, to all practising it in that faith of which it was the ostensible expression.

2. As the covenant of grace made with Abraham was bound up with temporal promises and privileges, so circumcision was a sign and seal of the covenant in both its parts,--its spiritual and its temporal, its superior and inferior provisions. The spiritual promises of the covenant continued unrestricted to all the descendants of Abraham, whether by Isaac or by Ishmael; and still lower down, to the descendants of Esau as well as to those of Jacob. Circumcision was practised among them all by virtue of its divine institution at first; and was extended to their foreign servants, and to proselytes, as well as to their children; and where-ever the sign of the covenant of grace was by divine appointment, there it was as a SEAL of that covenant, to all who believingly used it; for we read of no restriction of its spiritual blessings, that is, its saving engagements, to one line of descent from Abraham only. But over the TEMPORAL branch of the covenant, and the EXTERNAL religious privileges arising out of it, God exercised a rightful sovereignty, and expressly restricted them first to the line of Isaac, and then to that of Jacob, with whose descendants he entered into special covenant by the ministry of Moses. The temporal blessings and external privileges comprised under general expressions in the covenant with Abraham, were explained and enlarged under that of Moses, while the spiritual blessings remained unrestricted as before. This was probably the reason why circumcision was reënacted under the law of Moses. It was a confirmation of the temporal blessings of the Abrahamic covenant, now, by a covenant of peculiarity, made over to them, while it was still recognized as a consuetudinary rite which had descended to them from their fathers, and as the sign and seal of the covenant of grace, made with Abraham and with all his descendants without exception. This double reference of circumcision, both to the authority of Moses and to that of the patriarchs, is found in the words of our Lord, John vii, 22: "Moses therefore gave unto you circumcision, not because it is of Moses, but of the fathers;" or, as it is better translated by Campbell, "Moses instituted circumcision among you, (not that it is from Moses, but from the patriarchs,) and ye circumcise on the Sabbath. If on the Sabbath a child receive circumcision, that the LAW OF MOSES may not be violated," &c.

3. From these observations, the controversy in the Apostolic churches respecting circumcision will derive much elucidation. The covenant with Abraham prescribed circumcision as an act of faith in its promises, and as a pledge to perform its conditions on the part of his descendants. But the object on which this faith rested, was "the Seed of Abraham," in whom the nations of the earth were to be blessed: which Seed, says St. Paul, "is Christ,"--Christ as promised, not yet come. When the Christ had come, so as fully to enter upon his redeeming offices, he could no longer be the object of faith, as still to come; and this leading promise of the covenant being accomplished, the sign and seal of it vanished away. Nor could circumcision be continued in THIS VIEW by any, without an implied denial that Jesus was the Christ, the expected Seed of Abraham. Circumcision also as an institution of Moses, who continued it as the sign and seal of the Abrahamic covenant both in its spiritual and temporal provisions, but with respect to the latter made it also a sign and seal of the restriction of its temporal blessings and peculiar religious privileges to the descendants of Israel, was terminated by the entrance of our

Lord upon his office of Mediator, in which office all nations were to be blessed in him. The Mosaic edition of the covenant not only guaranteed the land of Canaan, but the peculiarity of the Israelites, as the people and visible church of God to the exclusion of others, except by proselytism. But when our Lord commanded the Gospel to be preached to "all nations," and opened the gates of the "common salvation" to all, whether Gentiles or Jews, circumcision, as the sign of a covenant of peculiarity and religious distinction, was also done away. It had not only no reason remaining, but the continuance of the rite involved the recognition of exclusive privileges which had been terminated by Christ. This will explain the views of the Apostle Paul on this great question. He declares that in Christ there is neither circumcision nor uncircumcision; that neither circumcision availeth any thing, nor uncircumcision, but "faith that worketh by love;" faith in the Seed of Abraham already come and already engaged in his mediatorial and redeeming work; faith, by virtue of which the Gentiles came into the church of Christ on the same terms as the Jews themselves, and were justified and saved. The doctrine of the non-necessity of circumcision, he applies to the Jews as well as to the Gentiles, although he specially resists the attempts of the Judaizers to impose this rite upon the Gentile converts; in which he was supported by the decision of the Holy Spirit when the appeal upon this question was made to "the Apostles and elders at Jerusalem," from the church at Antioch. At the same time it is clear that he takes two different views of the practice of circumcision, as it was continued among many of the first Christians. The first is that strong one which is expressed in Gal. v, 2–4, "Behold, I Paul say unto you, that if ye be circumcised, Christ shall profit you nothing; for I testify again to every man that is circumcised, that he is a debtor to do the whole law. Christ is made of no effect unto you, whosoever of you are justified by the law, ye are fallen from grace." The second is that milder view which he himself must have had when he circumcised Timothy to render him more acceptable to the Jews; and which also appears to have led him to abstain from all allusion to this practice when writing his epistle to the believing Hebrews, although many, perhaps most of them, continue to circumcise their children, as did the Jewish Christians for a long time afterward. These different views of circumcision, held by the same person, may be explained by considering the different principles on which circumcision might be practised after it had become an obsolete ordinance.

(1.) It might be taken in the simple view of its first institution, as the sign and seal of the Abrahamic covenant; and then it was to be condemned as involving a denial that Abraham's Seed, the Christ, had already come, since, upon his coming, every old covenant gave place to the new covenant introduced by him.

(2.) It might be practised and enjoined as the sign and seal of the Mosaic covenant, which was still the Abrahamic covenant with its spiritual blessings, but with restriction of its temporal promises and special ecclesiastical privileges to the line of Jacob, with a law of observances which was obligatory upon all entering that covenant by circumcision. In that case it involved, in like manner, the notion of the continuance of an old covenant, after the establishment of the new; for thus St. Paul states the case in Galatians iii, 19: "Wherefore then serveth the law? It was added because of transgressions until the Seed should come." After that therefore it had no effect:--it had waxed old, and had vanished away.

(3.) Again: circumcision might imply an obligation to observe all the ceremonial usages and the moral precepts of the Mosaic law, along with a general belief in the mission of Christ, as necessary to justification before God. This appears to have been the view of those among the Galatian Christians who submitted to circumcision, and of the Jewish teachers who enjoined it upon them; for St. Paul in that epistle constantly joins circumcision with legal observances, and as involving an obligation to do "the whole law," in order to justification.--"I testify again to every man that is circumcised, that he is a debtor to do the whole law; whosoever of you are justified by the law, ye are fallen from grace." "Knowing that a man is not justified by the works of the law, but by the faith of our Lord Jesus Christ," Gal. ii, 16. To all persons therefore practising circumcision in this view it was obvious, that "Christ was become of none effect," the very principle of justification by faith alone in him was renounced even while his divine mission was still admitted.

(4.) But there are two grounds on which circumcision maybe conceived to have been innocently, though not wisely, practised, among the Christian Jews. The first was that of preserving an ancient national distinction on which they valued themselves; and were a converted Jew in the present day disposed to perform that rite upon his children for this purpose only, renouncing in the act all consideration of it as a sign and seal of the old covenants, or as obliging to ceremonial acts in order to justification, no one would censure him with severity. It appears clear that it was under some such view that St. Paul circumcised Timothy, whose mother was a Jewess; he did it because of "the Jews which were in those quarters," that is, because of their national prejudices, "for they knew that his father was a Greek." The second was a lingering notion, that, even in the Christian church, the Jews who believed would still retain some degree of eminence, some superior relation to God; a notion which, however unfounded, was not one which demanded direct rebuke, when it did not proudly refuse spiritual communion with the converted Gentiles, but was held by men who "rejoiced that God had granted to the Gentiles repentance unto life." These considerations may account for the silence of St. Paul on the subject of circumcision in his Epistle to the Hebrews. Some of them continued to practise that rite, but they were probably believers of the class just mentioned; for had he thought that the rite was continued among them on any principle which affected the fundamental doctrines of Christianity, he would no doubt have been equally prompt and fearless in pointing out that apostasy from Christ which was implied in it, as when he wrote to the Galatians.

Not only might circumcision be practised with views so opposite that one might be wholly innocent, although an infirmity of prejudice; the other such as would involve a rejection of the doctrine of justification by faith in Christ; but some other Jewish observances also stood in the same circumstances. St. Paul in his Epistle to the Galatians, a part of his writings from which we obtain the most information on these questions, grounds his "doubts" whether the members of that church were not seeking to be "justified by the law" upon their observing "days, and months, and times, and years." Had he done more than "doubt," he would have expressed himself more positively. He saw their danger on this point; he saw that they were taking steps to this fatal result, by such an observance of these "days," &c, as had a strong leaning and dangerous approach to that dependence upon them for justification, which would destroy their faith in Christ's solely sufficient sacrifice; but his very doubting, not of the fact of their being addicted to these observances, but of the ANIMUS with which they regarded them, supposes it possible, however dangerous this Jewish conformity might be, that they might be observed for reasons which would still consist with their entire reliance upon the merits of Christ for salvation. Even he himself, strongly as he resisted the imposition of this conformity to Jewish customs upon the converts to Christianity as a matter of necessity, yet in practice must have conformed to many of them, when no sacrifice of principle was understood; for, in order to gain the Jews, he became "as a Jew." See Abraham, and Baptism.

CISLEU, the ninth month of the ecclesiastical, and the third of the civil, year among the Hebrews. It answers nearly to our November.

CISTERN, a reservoir chiefly for rain water. Numbers of these are still to be seen in Palestine, some of which are a hundred and fifty paces long, and sixty broad. The reason of their being so large was, that their cities were many of them built in elevated situations; and the rain falling only twice in the year, namely, spring and autumn, it became necessary for them to collect a quantity of water, as well for the cattle as for the people. A broken cistern would of course be a great calamity to a family, or in some cases even to a town; and with reference to this we may see the force of the reproof, Jer. ii, 13.

CITIES. By referring to some peculiarities in the building, fortifying, &c, of eastern cities we shall the better understand several allusions and expressions of the Old Testament. It is evident that the walls of fortified cities were sometimes partly constructed of combustible materials; for the Prophet, denouncing the judgments of God upon Syria and other countries, declares, "I will send a fire on the wall of Gaza, which shall devour the palaces thereof," Amos i, 7. The walls of Tyre and Rabbah seem to have been of the same perishable materials; for the Prophet adds, "I will send a fire upon the wall of Tyrus, which shall devour the palaces thereof;" and again, "I will kindle a fire in the walls of Rabbah, and it shall devour the palaces thereof with shouting in the day of battle," verses 10, 14. One method of securing the gates of fortified places, among the ancients, was to cover them with thick plates of iron; a custom which is still used in the east, and seems to be of great antiquity. We learn from Pitts, that Algiers has five gates, and some of these have two, some three, other gates within them; and some of them are plated all over with thick iron. The place where the Apostle was imprisoned seems to have been secured in the same manner; for, says the inspired historian, "When they were past the first and second ward, they came unto the iron gate that leadeth unto the city; which opened to them of its own accord," Acts xii, 10. Pococke, speaking of a bridge not far from Antioch, called the iron bridge, says, there are two towers belonging to it, the gates of which are covered with iron plates; which he supposes is the reason of the name it bears. Some of their gates are plated over with brass; such are the enormous gates of the principal mosque at Damascus, formerly the church of John the Baptist. To gates like these, the Psalmist probably refers in these words: "He hath broken the gates of brass," Psalm cvii, 16; and the Prophet, in that remarkable passage, where God promises to go before Cyrus his anointed, and "break in pieces the gates of brass, and cut in sunder the bars of iron," Isa. xlv, 2. But, conscious that all these precautions were insufficient for their security, the orientals employed watchmen to patrol the city during the night, to suppress any disorders in the streets, or to guard the walls against the attempts of a foreign enemy. To this custom Solomon refers in these words: "The watchmen that went about the city found me, they smote me, they wounded me; the keepers of the wall took away my veil from me," Song v, 7. This custom may be traced to a very remote antiquity; so early as the departure of Israel from the land of Egypt, the morning watch is mentioned, certainly indicating the time when the watchmen were commonly relieved. In Persia, the watchmen were obliged to indemnify those who were robbed in the streets; which accounts for the vigilance and severity which they display in the discharge of their office, and illustrates the character of watchman given to Ezekiel, and the duties he was required to perform. If the wicked perished in his iniquities without warning, the Prophet was to be accountable for his blood; but if he duly pointed out his danger, he delivered his own soul, Ezek. xxxiii, 2. They were also charged, as with us, to announce the progress of the night to the slumbering city: "The burden of Dumah; he calls to me out of Seir, Watchman, what of the night? watchman, what of the night? The watchman said, The morning cometh, and also the night," Isa. xxi, 11. This is confirmed by an observation of Chardin upon these words of Moses: "For a thousand years in thy sight are but as yesterday when it is past, and as a watch in the night:" that "as the people of the east have no clocks, the several parts of the day and of the night, which are eight in all, are announced. In the Indies, the parts of the night are made known, as well by instruments of music, in great cities, as by the rounds of the watchmen, who, with cries and small drums, give them notice that a fourth part of the night is past. Now, as these cries awaked those who had slept all that quarter part of the night, it appeared to them but as a moment." It is evident the ancient Jews knew, by some public notice, how the night watches passed away; but, whether they simply announced the termination of the watch, or made use of trumpets, or other sonorous instruments, in making the proclamation, it may not be easy to determine; and still less what kind of chronometers the watchmen used. The probability is, that the watches were announced with the sound of a trumpet; for the Prophet Ezekiel makes it a part of the watchman's duty, at least in time of war, to blow the trumpet, and warn the people. The watchman, in a time of danger, seems to have taken his station in a tower, which was built over the gate of the city.

The fortified cities in Canaan, as in some other countries, were commonly strengthened with a citadel, to which the inhabitants fled when they found it impossible to defend the place. The whole inhabitants of Thebez, unable to resist the repeated and furious assaults of Abimelech, retired into one of these towers, and bid defiance to his rage: "But there was a strong tower within the city, and thither fled all the men and women, and all they of the city, and shut it to them, and gat them up to the top of the tower." The extraordinary strength of this tower, and the various means of defence which were accumulated within its narrow walls, may be inferred from the violence of Abimelech's attack, and its fatal issue: "And Abimelech came unto the tower, and fought against it, and went hard unto the door of the tower, to burn it with fire. And a certain woman cast a piece of a millstone upon Abimelech's head, and all to break his skull," Judges ix, 52. The city of Shechem had a tower of the same kind, into which the people retired, when the same usurper took it and sowed it with salt, Judges ix, 46. These strong towers which were built within a fortified city, were commonly placed on an eminence, to which they ascended by a flight of steps. Such was the situation of the city of David, a strong tower upon a high eminence at Jerusalem; and the manner of entrance, as described by the sacred writer: "But the gate of the fountain repaired Shallum, unto the stairs that go down from the city of David," Nehemiah iii, 15.

Cities of Refuge. See Refuge.

CLAUDIUS, a Roman emperor; he succeeded Caius Caligula, A. D. 41, and reigned thirteen years, eight months, and nineteen days, dying A. D. 54. King Agrippa was the principal means of persuading Claudius to accept the empire, which was tendered him by the soldiers. As an acknowledgment for this service, he gave Agrippa all Judea, and the kingdom of Chalcis to his brother Herod. He put an end to the dispute which had for some time existed between the Jews of Alexandria and the other freemen of that city, and confirmed the Jews in the possession of their right of freedom, which they had enjoyed from the beginning, and every where maintained them in the free exercise of their religion. But he would not permit them to hold any assemblies at Rome. King Agrippa dying A. D. 44, the emperor again reduced Judea into a province, and sent Cuspius Fadus to be governor. About the same time the famine happened which is mentioned Acts xi, 28–30, and was foretold by the Prophet Agabus. Claudius, in the ninth year of his reign, published an edict for expelling all Jews out of Rome, Acts xviii, 2. It is very probable that the Christians, who were at that time confounded with the Jews, were banished likewise.

2. Claudius Felix, successor of Cumanus in the government of Judea. Felix found means to solicit and engage Drusilla, sister of Agrippa the Younger, to leave her husband Azizus, king of the Emessenians, and to marry him, A. D. 53. Felix sent to Rome Eleazar, son of Dinæus, captain of a band of robbers, who had committed great ravages in Palestine; he procured the death of Jonathan, the high priest, who sometimes freely represented to him his duty; he defeated a body of three thousand men, whom an Egyptian, a false prophet, had assembled upon the Mount of Olives. St. Paul being brought to Cesarea, where Felix usually resided, was well treated by this governor, who permitted his friends to see him, and render him services, hoping the Apostle would procure his redemption by a sum of money. He however neither condemned Paul, nor set him at liberty, when the Jews accused him; but adjourned the determination of this affair till the arrival of Lysias, who commanded the troops at Jerusalem, where he had taken Paul into custody, and who was expected at Cesarea, Acts xxiii, 26, 27, &c; xxiv, 1–3, &c.

While the Apostle was thus detained, Felix, with his wife Drusilla, who was a Jewess, sent for him, and desired him to explain the religion of Jesus Christ. The Apostle spoke with his usual boldness, and discoursed to them on justice, temperance, and the last judgment. Felix trembled before this powerful exhibition of truths so arousing to his conscience; but he remanded St. Paul to his confinement. He farther detained him two years at Cesarea, in compliance with the wishes of the Jews, and in order to do something to propitiate them, because they were extremely dissatisfied with his government. Being recalled to Rome, A. D. 60; and many Jews going thither to complain of the extortions and violence committed by him in Judea, he would have been put to death, if his brother Pallas, who had been Claudius's slave, and was now his freedman, had not preserved him. Felix was succeeded in the government of Judea by Porcius Festus.

CLAY, חמר, is often mentioned in Scripture, nor is it necessary to explain the various references to what is so well known. It may be remarked, however, that clay was used for sealing doors. Norden and Pococke observe, that the inspectors of the granaries in Egypt, after closing the door, put their seal upon a handful of clay, with which they cover the lock. This may help to explain Job xxxviii, 14, in which the earth is represented as assuming form and imagery from the brightness of the rising sun, as rude clay receives a figure from the impression of a seal or signet.

CLEOPAS, according to Eusebius and Epiphanius, was brother of Joseph, both being sons of Jacob. He was the father of Simeon, of James the Less, of Jude, and Joseph or Joses. Cleopas married Mary, sister to the blessed virgin. He was therefore uncle to Jesus Christ, and his sons were first cousins to him. Cleopas, his wife, and sons, were disciples of Christ. Having beheld our Saviour expire upon the cross, he, like the other disciples, appears to have lost all hopes of seeing the kingdom of God established by him on earth. The third day after our Saviour's death, on the day of his resurrection, Cleopas, with another disciple, departed from Jerusalem to Emmaus; and in the way discoursed on what had lately happened. Our Saviour joined them, appearing as a traveller; and, taking up their discourse, he reasoned with them, convincing them out of the Scriptures, that it was necessary the Messiah should suffer death, previously to his being glorified. At Emmaus, Jesus seemed as if inclined to go farther; but Cleopas and his companion detained him, and made him sup with them. While they were at table, Jesus took bread, blessed it, brake, and gave it to them, and by this action their eyes were opened, and they knew him. Upon his disappearing they instantly returned to Jerusalem, to announce the fact to the Apostles, who in their turn declared that "the Lord was risen indeed and had appeared to Peter." In our translation of Luke xxiv, 31, it is said that Jesus "vanished out of their sight;" but the original is more properly rendered, "He suddenly went away from them," the word being often applied by the Greek writers to those who in any way, but especially suddenly and abruptly, withdraw from any one's company. No other actions of Cleopas are known. It is the opinion of Jerom, that his residence was at Emmaus, and that he invited our Saviour into his own house. Supposing Cleopas to have been the brother of Joseph, and father of James, &c, Calmet thinks it more probable that as he was a Galilean, he dwelt in some city of Galilee.

CLOUD, a collection of vapours suspended in the atmosphere. When the Israelites had left Egypt, God gave them a pillar of cloud to direct their march, Exod. xiii, 21, 22. According to Jerom, in his Epistle to Fabiola, this cloud attended them from Succoth; or, according to others, from Rameses; or, as the Hebrews say, only from Ethan, till the death of Aaron; or, as the generality of commentators are of opinion, to the passage of Jordan. This pillar was commonly in front of the Israelites; but at Pihahiroth, when the Egyptian army approached behind them, it placed itself between Israel and the Egyptians, so that the Egyptians could not come near the Israelites all night, Exod. xiv, 19, 20. In the morning, the cloud moving on over the sea, and following the Israelites who had passed through it, the Egyptians pressing after were drowned. From that time, this cloud attended the Israelites; it was clear and bright during night, in order to afford them light; but in the day it was thick and gloomy, to defend them from the excessive heats of the deserts. "The angel of God which went before the camp of Israel, removed and went behind them; and the pillar of the cloud went from before their face, and stood behind them," Exod. xiv, 19. Here we may observe, that the angel and the cloud made the same motion, as it would seem, in company. The cloud by its motions gave the signal to the Israelites to encamp or to decamp. Where, therefore, it stayed, the people stayed till it rose again; then they broke up their camp, and followed it till it stopped. It was called a pillar, by reason of its form, which was high and elevated. Some interpreters suppose that there were two clouds, one to enlighten, the other to shade, the camp.

The Lord appeared at Sinai in the midst of a cloud, Exod. xix, 9; xxiv, 5; and after Moses had built and consecrated the tabernacle, the cloud filled the court around it, so that neither Moses nor the priests could enter, Exodus xl, 34, 35. The same happened at the dedication of the temple of Jerusalem by Solomon, 2 Chronicles v, 13; 1 Kings viii, 10. When the cloud appeared upon the tent, in front of which were held the assemblies of the people in the desert, it was then indicated that God was present; for the tent was a sign of God's presence. The angel descended in the cloud, and thence spoke to Moses, without being seen by the people, Exod. xvi, 10; Num. xi, 25; xvi, 5. It is common in Scripture, when mentioning God's appearing, to represent him as encompassed with clouds, which serve as a chariot, and contribute to veil his dreadful majesty, Job xxii, 14; Isaiah xix, 1; Matt. xvii, 5; xxiv, 30, &c; Psalm xviii, 11, 12; xcvii, 2; civ, 3. Cloud is also used for morning mists: "Your goodness is as a morning cloud; and as the early dew it goeth away," Hosea vi, 4; xiii, 3. Job, speaking of the chaos, says, that God had confined the sea or the water, as it were with a cloud, and covered it with darkness, as a child is wrapped in its blankets. The author of Ecclesiasticus, xxiv, 6, used the same expression. The Son of God, at his second advent, is described as descending upon clouds, Matt. xxiv, 30; Luke xi, 27; Rev. xiv, 14–16.

COCCEIANS, the disciples of John Cocceius, a celebrated Dutch divine, born at Bremen, in 1608, where he was appointed professor of Hebrew, at the age of twenty-seven, and afterward filled the theological chair at Leyden, where he died in 1669. His works make ten volumes in folio. He was a man of good learning, and a vivid imagination. He considered the Old Testament as a mirror, which held forth figuratively the transactions and events that were to happen in the church under the dispensation of the New Testament, and unto the end of the world. He maintained, that by far the greater part of the ancient prophecies related to Christ's ministry and mediation, and the rise, progress, and revolutions of the church; not only under the figure of typical persons and transactions, but in a more direct manner; and that Christ was, indeed, as much the substance of the Old Testament as of the New. Cocceius also taught, that the covenant made between God and the Jews was of the same nature as the new covenant by Jesus Christ; that the law was promulgated by Moses, not merely as a rule of obedience, but also as a representation of the covenant of grace; that when the Jews had provoked the Deity by their various transgressions, particularly by the worship of the golden calf, the severe yoke of the ceremonial law was added as a punishment; that this yoke, which was painful in itself, became doubly so on account of its typical signification; since it admonished the Israelites from day to day of the imperfection of their state, filled them with anxiety, and was a perpetual proof that they had merited the righteous judgment of God, and could not expect, before the coming of the Messiah, the entire remission of their iniquities; that indeed good men, under the Mosaic dispensation, were, after death, made partakers of glory; but that, nevertheless, during the whole course of their lives they were far removed from that assurance of salvation, which rejoices the believer under the dispensation of the Gospel; and that their anxiety flowed from this consideration, that their sins, though they remained unpunished, were not yet pardoned; because Christ had not as yet offered himself up to make an atonement for them. Cocceius was also a millennarian, and expected a personal reign of Christ on earth in the last days. Many of his opinions were afterward adopted by the Hutchinsonians.

COCK, ἀλέκτωρ, a well known domestic fowl. Some derive the Greek name from α, and λέκτρον, A BED, because the crowing of cocks rouses men from their beds; but Mr. Parkhurst asks, "May not this name be as properly deduced from the Hebrew הלכת אור, THE COMING OF THE LIGHT, of which this 'bird of dawning,' as Shakspeare calls him, gives such remarkable notice, and for doing which he was, among the Heathen, sacred to the sun, who in Homer is himself called ἀλέκτωρ?" In Matt. xxvi, 34, our Lord is represented as saying, that before cock-crow Peter should deny him thrice; so Luke xxii, 34, and John xiii, 39. But according to Mark xiv, 30, he says, "Before the cock crow TWICE thou shalt deny me thrice." These texts may be very satisfactorily reconciled, by observing, that ancient authors, both Greek and Latin, mention two cock-crowings, the one of which was soon after midnight, the other about three o'clock in the morning; and this latter being most noticed by men as the signal of their approaching labours, was called by way of eminence, the cock-crowing; and to this alone, Matthew, giving the general sense of our Saviour's warning to Peter, refers; but Mark, recording his very words, mentions the two cock-crowings.

The rabbies tell us that cocks were not permitted to be kept in Jerusalem on account of the holiness of the place; and that for this reason some modern Jews cavil against this declaration of the Evangelists; but the cock is not among the birds prohibited in the law of Moses. If there was any restraint in the use and domestication of the animal, it must have been an arbitrary practice of the Jews, and could not have been binding on foreigners, of whom many resided at Jerusalem as officers or traders. Strangers would not be willing to forego an innocent kind of food in compliance with a conquered people; and the trafficking spirit of the Jews would induce them to supply aliens, if it did not expressly contradict the letter of their law. This is sufficient to account for fowl of this kind being there, even admitting a customary restraint. The celebrated Reland admits that it was not allowed to breed cocks in the city, but that the Jews were not prohibited from buying them to eat, and that therefore the cock mentioned in the Gospel might be in the house of a Jew who designed to kill it for his own table; or may have been kept in the precincts of Pilate, or of a Roman officer or soldier.

During the time of our Saviour, the night was divided into four watches, a fourth watch having been introduced among the Jews from the Romans, who derived it from the Greeks. The second and third watches are mentioned in Luke xii, 38; the fourth, in Matthew xiv, 25; and the four are all distinctly mentioned in Mark xiii, 35: "Watch, therefore; for ye know not when the master of the house cometh; at EVEN," ὀψὲ, or the late watch, "or at MIDNIGHT," μεσονυκτίου, "or at the COCK-CROWING," ἀλεκτοροφωνίας, "or in the MORNING," πρωῒ, the early watch. Here, the first watch was at even, and continued from six till nine; the second commenced at nine, and ended at twelve, or midnight; the third watch, called by the Romans GALLICINIUM, lasted from twelve to three; and the morning watch closed at six.

COCKATRICE, צפען, or צפעי, Proverbs xxiii, 32; Isaiah xi, 8; xiv, 29; lix, 5; Jer. viii, 17. A venomous serpent. The original Hebrew word has been variously rendered, the ASPIC, the REGULUS, the HYDRA, the HEMORHOOS, the VIPER, and the CERASTES. In Isaiah xi, 8, this serpent is evidently intended for a proportionate advance in malignity beyond the PETEN which precedes it; and in xiv, 29, it must mean a worse kind of serpent than the NAHASH. In lix, 5, it is referred to as oviparous. In Jer. viii, 17, Dr. Blayney, after Aquila, retains the rendering of basilisk. Bochart, who thinks it to be the regulus or basilisk, says that it may be so denominated by an onomatopœia from its hissing; and accordingly it is hence called in Latin SIBILUS, "the hisser." So the Arabic SAPHAA signifies "flatu adurere," [to scorch with a blast.] The Chaldee paraphrast, the Syriac, and the Arabic, render it the HURMAN or HORMAN; which rabbi Selomo on Gen. xlix, 17, declares to be the TZIPHONI of the Hebrews: "HURMAN VOCATUR SPECIES, CUJUS MORSUS EST INSANABILIS. IS EST HEBRÆIS tziphoni, ET CHALDAICÈ DICITUR hurman, QUIA OMNIA FACIT חרם VASTATIONEM; ID EST, QUIA OMNIA VASTAT, ET AD INTERNECIONEM DESTRUIT." [The species is called HURMAN, whose bite is incurable. It is the TZIPHONI of the Hebrews, and is called in Chaldee HURMAN, because it makes all things חרם--a waste; that is, because it lays waste and utterly destroys every thing.]

COCKLE, באשה. This word occurs only in Job xxxi, 40. By the Chaldee it is rendered NOXIOUS HERBS; by Symmachus, ἀτελεσφόρητα, PLANTS OF IMPERFECT FRUIT; by the Septuagint, βάτος, THE BLACKBERRY BUSH; by Castelio, EBULUS, "dwarf elder;" by Celsius, ACONITE; and by Bishop Stock and Dr. Good, THE NIGHT-SHADE. M. Michaëlis maintains, after Celsius, that both this word and באשים, Isaiah v, 2, 4, denote the ACONITE, a poisonous plant, growing spontaneously and luxuriantly on sunny hills, such as are used for vineyards. He says that this interpretation is certain, because, as Celsius had observed, ביש, in Arabic, denotes the ACONITE; and he intimates that it best suits Job xxxi, 40, where it is mentioned as growing instead of barley. The word appears to import a weed not only noxious, but of a fetid smell.

CŒLO-SYRIA, HOLLOW or DEPRESSED Syria, Syria in the vale, 1 Macc. xiii, 10. This name imports the hollow land, or region, situated between two long ridges of mountains; and those mountains have been always understood to be Libanus and Anti-libanus. As these ridges run parallel for many leagues, they contain between them a long, extensive, and extremely fruitful valley.

COLOSSE, a city of Phrygia Minor, which stood on the river Lyceus, at an equal distance between Laodicea and Hierapolis. These three cities, says Eusebius, were destroyed by an earthquake, in the tenth of Nero, or about two years after the date of St. Paul's Epistle to the Colossians. Laodicea, Hierapolis, and Colosse were at no great distance from each other; which accounts for the Apostle Paul, when writing to his Christian brethren in the latter of these places, mentioning them all in connection with each other, Col. iv, 13. Of these cities, however, Laodicea was the greatest, for it was the metropolis of Phrygia, though Colosse is said to have been a great and wealthy place. The inhabitants of Phrygia, says Dr. Macknight, were famous for the worship of Bacchus, and of Cybele the mother of the gods; whence the latter was called Phrygia mater, by way of eminence. In her worship, as well as in that of Bacchus, both sexes practised every species of debauchery in speech and action, with a frantic rage which they pretended was occasioned by the inspiration of the deities whom they worshipped. These were the orgies, from ὀϱγὴ, RAGE, of Bacchus and Cybele, so famed in antiquity, the lascivious rites of which being perfectly adapted to the corruptions of the human heart, were performed by both sexes without shame or remorse. Hence as the Son of God came into the world to destroy the works of the devil, it appeared, in the eye of his Apostle, a matter of great importance to carry the light of the Gospel into countries where these abominable impurities were not only practised, but even dignified with the honourable appellation of religious worship; especially as nothing but the heaven-descended light of the Gospel could dispel such a pernicious infatuation. That this salutary purpose might be effectually accomplished, Paul, accompanied by Silas and Timothy, went at different times into Phrygia, and preached the Gospel in many cities of that country with great success; but it is thought by many persons, that the Epistle to the Colossians contains internal marks of his never having been at Colosse when he wrote it. This opinion rests principally upon the following passage: "For I would that ye knew what great conflict I have for you, and for them at Laodicea, and for as many as have NOT SEEN MY FACE in the flesh," Col. ii, 1: but these words, if they prove any thing upon this question, prove that St. Paul had never been either at Laodicea or Colosse; but surely it is very improbable that he should have travelled twice into Phrygia for the purpose of preaching the Gospel, and not have gone either to Laodicea or Colosse, which were the two principal cities of that country; especially as in the second journey into those parts it is said, that he "went over all the country of Galatia and Phrygia, strengthening all the disciples;" and moreover, we know that it was the Apostle's practice to preach at the most considerable places of every district into which he went. Dr. Lardner, after arguing this point, says, "From all these considerations, it appears to me very probable that the church at Colosse had been planted by the Apostle Paul, and that the Christians there were his friends, disciples, and converts."

The Epistle greatly resembles that to the Ephesians, both in sentiment and expression. After saluting the Colossian Christians in his own name, and that of Timothy, St. Paul assures them, that since he had heard of their faith in Christ Jesus, and of their love to all Christians, he had not ceased to return thanks to God for them, and to pray that they might increase in spiritual knowledge, and abound in every good work; he describes the dignity of Christ, and declares the universality of the Gospel dispensation, which was a mystery formerly hidden, but now made manifest; and he mentions his own appointment, through the grace of God, to be the Apostle of the Gentiles; he expresses a tender concern for the Colossians and other Christians of Phrygia, and cautions them against being seduced from the simplicity of the Gospel, by the subtlety of Pagan philosophers, or the superstition of Judaizing Christians; he directs them to set their affections on things above, and forbids every species of licentiousness; he exhorts to a variety of Christian virtues, to meekness, veracity, humility, charity, and devotion; he enforces the duties of wives, husbands, children, fathers, servants, and masters; he inculcates the duty of prayer, and of prudent behaviour toward unbelievers; and after adding the salutations of several persons then at Rome, and desiring that this epistle might be read in the church of their neighbours the Laodiceans, he concludes with a salutation from himself, written, as usual, with his own hand.

COMFORTER, one of the titles by which the Holy Spirit is designated in the New Testament, John xiv, 16, 26; xv, 26. The name has no doubt a reference to his peculiar office in the economy of redemption; namely, that of imparting consolation to the hearts of Christ's disciples, which he effects by "taking of the things that are Christ's," and explaining them; or, in other words, by illuminating their minds as to the meaning of the Scriptures, assuring them of the Saviour's love, bringing to their recollection his consolatory sayings, and filling their souls with peace and joy in believing them.--The word has also been rendered ADVOCATE, HELPER, MONITOR, TEACH ER, &c. The first does not apply to the office of the Spirit; and the others are not so well supported by the connection of our Lord's discourse, which favours the translation, COMFORTER; because whatever gracious offices the Holy Spirit was to perform for the disciples, the great end of all was to remove that sorrow which the approach of the departure of Christ had produced, and to render their joy full and complete.

COMMERCE. Merchandise, in its various branches, was carried on in the east at the earliest period of which we have any account; and it was not long before the traffic between nations, both by sea and land, was very considerable. Accordingly, frequent mention is made of public roads, fords, bridges, and beasts of burden; also of ships for the transportation of property, of weights, measures, and coin, both in the oldest books of the Bible, and in the most ancient profane histories. The Phenicians anciently held the first rank as a commercial nation. They were in the habit of purchasing goods of various kinds throughout all the east. They then carried them in ships down the Mediterranean, as far as the shores of Africa and Europe, brought back in return merchandise and silver, and disposed of these again in the more eastern countries. The first metropolis of the Phenicians was Sidon: afterward Tyre became the principal city. Tyre was built two hundred and forty years before the temple of Solomon, or twelve hundred and fifty-one before Christ. The Phenicians had ports of their own in almost every country; the most distinguished of which were Carthage and Tarshish, or Tartessus, in Spain. The ships from the latter place undertook very distant voyages: hence, any vessels that performed distant voyages were called "ships of Tarshish," תרשיש אנות. Something is said of the commerce of the Phenicians in the twenty-seventh and twenty-eighth chapters of Ezekiel, and the twenty-third chapter of Isaiah. The inhabitants of Arabia Felix carried on a commerce with India. They carried some of the articles which they brought from India through the straits of Babelmandel into Abyssinia and Egypt; some they transported to Babylon through the Persian Gulf and the Euphrates; and some by the way of the Red Sea to the port of Eziongeber. They thus became rich; though it is possible their wealth may have been too much magnified by the ancients. The eminence of the Egyptians, as a commercial nation, commences with the reign of Necho. Their commerce, nevertheless, was not great, till Alexander had destroyed Tyre and built Alexandria.

2. The Phenicians sometimes received the goods of India by way of the Persian Gulf, where they had colonies in the islands of Dedan, Arad, and Tyre. Sometimes they received them from the Arabians, who either brought them by land through Arabia, or up the Red Sea to Eziongeber. In the latter case, having landed them at the port mentioned, they transported them through the country by the way of Gaza to Phenicia. The Phenicians increased the amount of their foreign goods by the addition of those which they themselves fabricated; and were thus enabled to supply all parts of the Mediterranean. The Egyptians at first received their goods from the Phenicians, Arabians, Africans, and Abyssinians; in all of which countries there are still the remains of large trading towns; but in a subsequent age, they imported goods from India in their own vessels; and eventually carried on an export trade with various ports on the Mediterranean. Oriental commerce, however, was chiefly carried on by land: accordingly, vessels are hardly mentioned in the Bible, except in Psalm cvii, 23–30, and in passages where the discourse turns upon the Phenicians, or upon the naval affairs of Solomon and Jehoshaphat. The two principal routes from Palestine into Egypt were, the one along the shores of the Mediterranean from Gaza to Pelusium, and the other from Gaza by the way of Mount Sinai and the Elanitic branch of the Red Sea.

3. The merchants transported their goods upon camels; animals which are patient of thirst, and are easily supported in the deserts. For the common purpose of security against depredations, the oriental merchants travelled in company, as is common in the east at the present day. A large travelling company of this kind is called a CARAVAN or CARVAN, a smaller one was called KAFILE or KAFLE, Job vi, 18–20; Gen. xxxvii, 25; Isa. xxi, 13; Jer. ix, 2; Judges v, 6; Luke ii, 44. The furniture carried by the individuals of a caravan consisted of a mattress, a coverlet, a carpet for sitting upon, a round piece of leather, which answered the purpose of a table, a few pots and kettles of copper covered with tin; also a tin-plated cup, which was suspended before the breast under the outer garment, and was used for drinking, 1 Sam. xxvi, 11, 12, 16: leathern bags for holding water, tents, lights, and provisions in quality and abundance as each one could afford. Every caravan had a leader to conduct it through the desert, who was acquainted with the direction of its route, and with the cisterns and fountains. These he was able to ascertain, sometimes from heaps of stones, sometimes by the character of the soil, and, when other helps failed him, by the stars, Num. x, 29–32; Jer. xxxi, 21; Isa. xxi, 14. When all things are in readiness, the individuals who compose the caravan assemble at a distance from the city. The commander of the caravan, who is a different person from the conductor or leader, and is chosen from the wealthiest of its members, appoints the day of their departure. A similar arrangement was adopted among the Jews, whenever they travelled in large numbers to the city of Jerusalem. The caravans start very early, sometimes before day. They endeavour to find a stopping place or station to remain at during the night, which shall afford them a supply of water, Job vi, 15–20. They arrive at their stopping place before the close of the day; and, while it is yet light, prepare every thing that is necessary for the recommencement of their journey. In order to prevent any one from wandering away from the caravan, and getting lost during the night, lamps or torches are elevated upon poles and carried before it. The pillar of fire answered this purpose for the Israelites, when wandering in the wilderness. Sometimes the caravans lodge in cities; but when they do not, they pitch their tents so as to form an encampment; and during the night keep watch alternately for the sake of security. In the cities there are public inns, called CHAN and CARVANSERAI, in which the caravans are lodged without expense. They are large square buildings, in the centre of which is an area, or open court. Carvanserais are denominated in the Greek of the New Testament, ϖανδοχεῖον, *κατάλυσις* and *κατάλυμα*, Luke ii, 7; x, 34. The first mention of one in the Old Testament is in Jer. xli, 17, כמהם גרות. It was situated near the city of Bethlehem.

4. Moses enacted no laws in favour of commerce, although there is no question that he saw the situation of Palestine to be very favourable for it. The reason of this was, that the

Hebrews, who were designedly set apart to preserve the true religion, could not mingle with foreign idolatrous nations without injury. He therefore merely inculcated good faith and honesty in buying and selling, Lev. xix, 36, 37; Deut. xxv, 13–16; and left all the other interests of commerce to a future age. By the establishment, however, of the three great festivals, he gave occasion for some mercantile intercourse. At these festivals all the adult males of the nation were yearly assembled at one place. The consequence was, that those who had any thing to sell brought it; while those who wished to buy articles came with the expectation of having an opportunity. As Moses, though he did not encourage, did not interdict foreign commerce, Solomon, at a later period, not only carried on a traffic in horses, as already stated, but sent ships from the port of Eziongeber through the Red Sea to Ophir, probably the coast of Africa, 1 Kings ix, 26; 2 Chron. ix, 21. This traffic, although a source of emolument, appears to have been neglected after the death of Solomon. The attempt made by Jehoshaphat to restore it was frustrated, by his ships being dashed upon the rocks and destroyed, 1 Kings xxii, 48, 49; 2 Chron. xx, 36. Joppa, though not a very convenient one, was properly the port of Jerusalem; and some of the large vessels which went to Spain sailed from it, Jonah i, 3. In the age of Ezekiel, the commerce of Jerusalem was so great, that it gave an occasion of envy even to the Tyrians themselves, Ezek. xxvi, 2. After the captivity, a great number of Jews became merchants, and travelled for the purpose of traffic into all countries. About the year 150 B. C. prince Simon rendered the port at Joppa more convenient than it had hitherto been. In the time of Pompey the Great, there were so many Jews abroad on the ocean, even in the character of pirates, that King Antigonus was accused before him of having sent them out on purpose. A new port was built by Herod at Cesarea.

COMMUNION, in a religious sense, refers chiefly to the admission of persons to the Lord's Supper. This is said to be open, when all are admitted who apply, as in the Church of England; to be strict, when confined to the members of a single society, or, at least, to members of the same denomination; and it is mixed, when persons are admitted from societies of different denominations, on the profession of their faith, and evidence of their piety. The principal difficulty on this point arises between the strict Baptists and Pædo-Baptists.

CONCUBINE, פילגש. This term, in western authors, commonly signifies, a woman, who, without being married to a man, yet lives with him as his wife; but, in the sacred writers, the word concubine is understood in another sense; meaning a lawful wife, but one not wedded with all the ceremonies and solemnities of matrimony; a wife of the second rank, inferior to the first wife, or mistress of the house. Children of concubines did not inherit their father's fortune; but he might provide for, and make presents to, them. Thus Abraham, by Sarah his wife, had Isaac, his heir; but, by his two concubines, Hagar and Keturah, he had other children, whom he did not make equal to Isaac. As polygamy was tolerated in the east, it was common to see in every family, beside lawful wives, several concubines. Since the abrogation of polygamy by Jesus Christ, and the restoration of marriage to its primitive institution, concubinage is ranked with adultery or fornication.

CONEY, שפן, Levit. xi, 5; Deut. xiv, 7; Psalm civ, 8; and Prov. xxx, 26. Bochart and others have supposed the SHAPHAN of the Scriptures to be the jerboa; but Mr. Bruce proves that the ashkoko is intended. This curious animal is found in Ethiopia, and in great numbers on Mount Lebanon, &c. Instead of holes, they seem to delight in more airy places, in the mouths of caves, or clefts in the rock. They are gregarious, and frequently several dozens of them sit upon the great stones at the mouths of caves, and warm themselves in the sun, or come out and enjoy the freshness of the summer evening. They do not stand upright upon their feet, but seem to steal along as in fear, their belly being nearly close to the ground; advancing a few steps at a time, and then pausing. They have something very mild, feeble-like, and timid, in their deportment; are gentle and easily tamed, though, when roughly handled at the first, they bite very severely. Many are the reasons to believe this to be the animal called SAPHAN in Hebrew, and erroneously by our translators, "the coney," or rabbit. The latter are gregarious indeed, and so far resemble the other, as also in size; but they seek not the same place of retreat; for the rabbit burrows most generally in the sand. Nor is there any thing in the character of rabbits that denotes excellent wisdom, or that they supply the want of strength by any remarkable sagacity. The SAPHAN, then, is not the rabbit; which last, unless it was brought to him by his ships from Europe, Solomon never saw.

Let us now apply the characters of the ashkoko to the SAPHAN. "He is above all other animals so much attached to the rocks, that I never once," says Mr. Bruce, "saw him on the ground, or from among large stones in the mouth of caves, where is his constant residence. He lives in families or flocks. He is in Judea, Palestine, and Arabia, and consequently must have been familiar to Solomon. David describes him very pertinently, and joins him to other animals perfectly known: 'The hills are a refuge for the wild goats, and the rocks for the SAPHAN:' and Solomon says that 'they are exceeding wise,' that they are 'but a feeble folk, yet make their houses in the rocks.' Now this, I think, very obviously fixes the ashkoko to be the SAPHAN; for his weakness seems to allude to his feet, and how inadequate these are to dig holes in the rock, where yet, however, he lodges. From their tenderness these are very liable to be excoriated or hurt; notwithstanding which, they build houses in the rocks more inaccessible than those of the rabbit, and in which they abide in greater safety, not by exertion of strength, for they have it not, but are truly, as Solomon says, 'a feeble folk,' but by their own sagacity and judgment; and are therefore justly described as wise. Lastly, what leaves the thing without doubt is, that some of the Arabs, particularly Damir, say that the SAPHAN has no tail, that it is less than a cat, that it lives in houses or nests, which it builds of straw, in contradistinction to the rabbit and the rat, and those animals that burrow in the ground."

CONFESSION signifies a public acknowledgment of any thing as our own: thus Christ will confess the faithful in the day of judgment, Luke xii, 8. 2. To own and profess the truths of Christ, and to obey his commandments, in spite of opposition and danger from enemies, Matt. x, 32. 3. To utter or speak the praises of God, or to give him thanks. 4. To acknowledge our sins and offences to God, either by private or public confession; or to our neighbour whom we have wronged; or to some pious persons from whom we expect to receive comfort and spiritual instruction; or to the whole congregation when our fault is published, Psalm xxxii, 5; Matt. iii, 6; James v, 16; 1 John i, 9. 5. To acknowledge a crime before a judge, Josh. vii, 19.

2. In the Jewish ceremony of annual expiation, the high priest confessed in general his own sins, the sins of other ministers of the temple, and those of all the people. When an Israelite offered a sacrifice for sin, he put his hand on the head of the victim, and confessed his faults, Lev. iv. On the day of atonement, the Jews still make a private confession of their sins, which is called by them CIPPUR, and which is said to be done in the following manner: Two Jews retire into a corner of the synagogue. One of them bows very low before the other, with his face turned toward the north. He who performs the office of confessor gives the penitent nine-and-thirty blows on the back with a leathern strap, repeating these words, "God, being full of compassion, forgave their iniquity, and destroyed them not; yea, many a time turned he his anger away, and did not stir up all his wrath." As there are only thirteen words in this verse recited in the Hebrew, he repeats it three times, and at every word strikes one blow; which makes nine-and-thirty words, and as many lashes. In the meantime, the penitent declares his sins, and at the confession of every one beats himself on his breast. This being finished, he who has performed the office of confessor prostrates himself on the ground, and receives in turn from his penitent nine-and-thirty lashes.

3. The Romish church not only requires confession as a duty, but has advanced it to the dignity of a sacrament. These confessions are made in private to the priest, who is not to reveal them under pain of the highest punishment. The council of Trent requires "secret confession to the priest alone, of all and every mortal sin, which, upon the most diligent search and examination of our consciences, we can remember ourselves to be guilty of since our baptism; together with all the circumstances of those sins, which may change the nature of them; because, without the perfect knowledge of these, the priest cannot make a judgment of the nature and quality of men's sins, nor impose fitting penance for them." This is the confession of sins which the same council confidently affirms "to have been instituted by our Lord, and by the law of God, to be necessary to salvation, and to have been always practised in the catholic church." It is, however, evident, that such confession is unscriptural. St. James, indeed, says, "Confess your faults one to another," James v, 16; but priests are not here mentioned, and the word FAULTS seems to confine the precept to a mutual confession among Christians, of those offences by which they may have injured each other. Certain it is, that from this passage the necessity of auricular confession, and the power of priestly absolution, cannot be inferred. Though many of the early ecclesiastical writers earnestly recommend confession to the clergy, yet they never recommend it as essential to the pardon of sin, or as having connection with a sacrament. They only urge it as entitling a person to the prayers of the congregation; and as useful for supporting the authority of wholesome discipline, and for maintaining the purity of the Christian church. Chrysostom condemns all secret confession to men, as being obviously liable to great abuses; and Basil, Hilary, and Augustine, all advise confession of sins to God only. It has been proved by M. Daillé, that private, auricular, sacramental confession of sins was unknown in the primitive church. But, though private auricular confession is not of divine authority, yet, as Archbishop Tillotson properly observes, there are many cases in which men, under the guilt and trouble of their sins, can neither appease their own minds, nor sufficiently direct themselves, without recourse to some pious and prudent guide. In these cases, men certainly do very well, and many times prevent a great deal of trouble and perplexity to themselves, by a timely discovery of their condition to some faithful minister, in order to their direction and satisfaction. To this purpose a general confession is for the most part sufficient; and where there is occasion for a more particular discovery, there is no need of raking into the minute and foul circumstances of men's sins to give that advice which is necessary for the cure and ease of the penitent. Auricular confession is unquestionably one of the greatest corruptions of the Romish church. It goes upon the ground that the priest has power to forgive sins; it establishes the tyrannical influence of the priesthood; it turns the penitent from God who only can forgive sins, to man who is himself a sinner; and it tends to corrupt both the confessors and the confessed by a foul and particular disclosure of sinful thoughts and actions of every kind without exception.

Confessions of Faith, simply considered, is the same with CREED, and signifies a summary of the principal articles of belief adopted by any individual or society. In its more common acceptation, it is restricted to the summaries of doctrine published by particular Christian churches, with the view of preventing their religious sentiments from being misunderstood or misrepresented, or, by requiring subscription to them, of securing uniformity of opinion among those who join their communion. Except a single sentence in one of the Ignatian Epistles, (A. D. 180,) which relates exclusively to the reality of Christ's personality and sufferings in opposition to the *Docetæ*, the earliest document of this kind is to be found in the writings of Irenæus, who flourished toward the end of the second century of the Christian æra. In his treatise against heresies, this father affirms that "the faith of the church planted throughout the whole world," consisted in the belief of "one God, the Father Almighty, Maker of heaven and earth and sea, and all that are in them; and one Christ Jesus, the Son of God, who became incarnate for our salvation; and one Holy Spirit, who foretold, through the Prophets, the dispensations and advents, and the generation by the virgin, and the passion, and the resurrection from the dead, and the ascension in the flesh into heaven, of Jesus Christ our beloved Lord, and his appearing from heaven in the glory of the Father, to unite together all things under one head, and to raise every individual of the human race; that unto Christ Jesus, our Lord and God, and Saviour and King, every knee may bow, and every tongue confess; that he may pronounce just sentence upon all." In various parts of Tertullian's writings similar statements occur, (A. D. 200,) which it is unnecessary particularly to quote. We shall only remark, that in one of them, the miraculous conception of Christ by the power of the Holy Ghost is distinctly mentioned; that in another, he declares it to have been the uniform doctrine from the beginning of the Gospel, that Christ was born of the virgin, both man and God, EX EÂ NATUM HOMINEM ET DEUM; and that in each of these, faith in the Father, Son, and Spirit, is recognised as essential to Christianity. The following passage we cite, for the purpose of marking its coincidence with the Apostles' Creed, to which we shall have occasion soon to advert: "This," says he, "is the sole, immovable, irreformable rule of faith; namely, to believe in the only God Almighty, maker of the world; and his Son Jesus Christ, born of the virgin Mary, crucified under Pontius Pilate, the third day raised from the dead, received into heaven, now sitting at the right hand of the Father, about to come and judge the quick and the dead, by the resurrection also of the flesh." The summaries contained in the works of Origen (A. D. 520) nearly resemble the preceding; any difference between them being easily accounted for, from the tenets of the particular heresies against which they were directed. In his "Commentary on St. John's Gospel," he thus writes: "We believe that there is one God, who created all things, and framed and made all things to exist out of nothing. We must also believe in the Lord Jesus Christ, and in all the truth concerning his Deity and humanity; and we must likewise believe in the Holy Spirit; and that, being free agents, we shall be punished for the things in which we sin, and rewarded for those in which we do well." According to Cyprian, the formula, to which assent was required from adults at their baptism, was in these terms: "Dost thou believe in God the Father, Christ the Son, the Holy Spirit, the remission of sins, and eternal life, through the holy church?" This was called by him SYMBOLI LEX, "the law of the creed;" and by Novatian, REGULA VERITATIS, "the rule of truth."

2. From these and similar sources, the different clauses of what is commonly called the Apostles' Creed appear to have sprung. For, though it was long believed to be the composition of the Apostles, its claims to such an inspired origin are now universally rejected. Of its great antiquity, however, there can be no doubt; the whole of it, as it stands in the English liturgy, having been generally received as an authoritative confession in the fourth century. Toward the end of that century, Rufinus wrote a commentary on it, which is still extant, in which he acknowledges that the clause respecting Christ's descent into hell was not admitted into the creeds either of the western or the eastern churches. We learn also that the epithet CATHOLIC was not at that time applied in it to the church. Its great simplicity and conciseness, beside, prove it to have been considerably earlier than the council of Nice, when the heretical speculations of various sects led the defenders of the orthodox faith to fence the interests of religion with more complicated and cumbrous barriers.

This confession of faith was then preëminently named SYMBOLUM; which might be understood in the general acceptation of SIGN, as the characteristic, representative sign of the Christian faith; or, in a more restricted sense, in reference to the σύμβολον ϛρατιωτικὸν, or TESSERA MILITARIS, the watch word of the Christian soldier, communicated to each man at his first entrance into the service of Christ. Perhaps this word, at first, only denoted the formula of baptism, and was afterward transferred to the confession of faith.

3. In the celebrated council of Nice, (A. D. 325,) in which Arianism was not only condemned, but proscribed, the confession established as the universal standard of truth and orthodoxy runs thus: "I believe in one God, the Father Almighty, maker of heaven and earth, and of all things visible and invisible; and in one Lord Jesus, the only begotten Son of God, begotten of the Father, before all worlds, God of God, Light of Light, very God of very God, begotten not made, being of one substance with the Father; by whom all things were made; who for us men, and for our salvation, descended from heaven, and became incarnate by the Holy Ghost, of the virgin Mary; and was made man, was crucified for us under Pontius Pilate. He suffered and was buried; and the third day he rose again according to the Scriptures, and ascended into heaven, and sitteth on the right hand of the Father; and he shall come again with glory to judge both the quick and the dead, of whose kingdom there will be no end. And I believe in the Holy Ghost who spake by the Prophets; and one catholic, and Apostolical church. I acknowledge one baptism for the remission of sins, and I look for the resurrection of the dead, and the life of the world to come."

It were endless to specify the particular shades of difference by which the Arian confessions (the number of which amounted nearly to twenty in the space of a very few years) were distinguished from each other: suffice it to say, that while they agreed generally in substance, especially in rejecting the Nicene term, ὁμοούσιος, as applied to the Son, their variations of expression concerning the nature of his subordination to the Father were so astonishingly minute, as almost to bid defiance to any attempt which might be made, at this distance of time, to determine in what their real and essential differences consisted.

4. "The Book of Armagh," a very ancient collection of interesting national documents, which have recently been published by Sir William Betham in the second part of his

curious "Irish Antiquarian Researches," contains the Confession of St. Patrick; who has been supposed, from several collateral circumstances, to have flourished some years prior to the time of St. Jerom, or about the commencement of the fourth century. The subjoined are the first two paragraphs in it, and will be admired for the orthodoxy, artlessness, and Christian experience which they exhibit:--"I, Patrick, a sinner, the rudest, the least, and the most insignificant of the faithful, had Calphurnius, a deacon, for my father, who was the son of Potitus, heretofore a priest, the son of Odissus, who lived in the village of Banavem Taberniæ. For he had a little farm adjacent, where I was captured. I was then almost sixteen years of age; but I knew not God, and was led into captivity by the Irish, with many thousand men, as we deserved, because we estranged ourselves from God, and did not keep his laws, and were disobedient to our pastors, who admonished us with respect to our salvation: and the Lord brought down upon us the anger of his Spirit, and dispersed us among many nations, even to the extremity of the earth, where my meanness was conspicuous among foreigners, and where the Lord discovered to me a sense of my unbelief; that late I should remember my transgressions, and that I should be converted with my whole heart to the Lord my God, who had respect to my humiliation, and pitied my youth and ignorance, even before I knew him, and before I was wise, or could distinguish between right and wrong, and strengthened me, and cherished me, as a father would a son. From which time I could not remain silent; nor, indeed, did he cease to bless me with many acts of kindness; and so great was the favour of which he thought me worthy in the land of my captivity. For this is my retribution, that, after my rebuking, punishment, and acknowledgment of God, I should exalt him, and confess his wonderful acts before every nation which is under the whole heaven; because there is no other God, nor ever was before, nor will be after him, except God, the unbegotten Father, without beginning, possessing all things, as we have said, and his Son Jesus Christ, who, we bear witness, was always with the Father, before the formation of the world, in spirit (or spiritually) with the Father, inexpressibly begotten before all beginning, through whom visible things were made: he became man, having overcome death, and was received into heaven. And God has given to him all power 'above every name, as well of the inhabitants of heaven as of the earth and of the powers below, that every tongue should confess that Jesus Christ is Lord and God;' whom we believe, and whose coming we expect, as presently about to be Judge of the living and dead, who will render unto every man according to his actions, and has poured upon us abundantly the gift of his Holy Spirit, and the pledge of immortality; who makes us that believe and are obedient to be the sons of God and joint heirs of Christ; whom we believe and adore, one God in the Trinity of the sacred name. For he spoke by the Prophet, 'Call upon me in the day of tribulation, and I will deliver thee, and thou shalt glorify me.' And again he says, 'It is an honourable thing to reveal and confess the works of God.'"

5. Macedonius having denied not only the divinity but the personality of the Holy Spirit, maintaining that he is only a divine energy diffused throughout the universe, a general council was called at Constantinople, A. D. 381, in order to crush this rising heresy. The confession promulgated on this occasion, and which "gave the finishing touch to what the council of Nice had left imperfect, and fixed, in a full and determinate manner, the doctrine of the Trinity, as it is still received among the generality of Christians," exactly coincides with the Nicene confession, except in the article respecting the Spirit, which it thus extends: "And I believe in the Holy Ghost, the Lord, and Giver of life, who proceedeth from the Father and the Son, who, together with the Father and the Son, is worshipped and glorified."

6. Subsequent to this, and probably toward the middle of the fifth century, the creed which bears the name of Athanasius appears to have been composed. That it was not the work of this distinguished opposer of Arianism is established by the most satisfactory evidence. No traces of it are to be found in any of his writings, though they relate chiefly to the very subject of which it is an exposition; and so far from its being ascribed to him, not the least notice is taken of it by any of his contemporaries. Its language, beside, concerning the Spirit is so similar to that of the council of Constantinople, but still more precise and explicit, that there can be no doubt of its having been written posterior to the time of that assembly. Yet Athanasius died in the year 373. Accordingly, it has been, with great probability of truth, attributed, particularly by Dr. Waterland, to Hilary, bishop of Arles, who is said by one of his biographers to have composed an Exposition of the Creed: a title which certainly is more appropriate and characteristic of it than that of Creed simply, by which it is now so universally known. The damnatory clauses in this creed have frequently been made subjects of reprehension; and some clergymen of the church of England have scrupled to read them as directed by the Rubric. The following is an apology for those clauses, by the late venerable Archdeacon Dodwell, who seems to have felt none of those misgivings which troubled his doubting brethren:--"The form, as well as the substance, of this creed, and the very introduction to the main article, has been objected to: 'Whosoever will be saved, before all things it is necessary that he hold the catholic faith;' to which is added, 'Which faith, except every one do keep whole and undefiled, without doubt he shall perish everlastingly.' This, with a like condemnatory sentence in the conclusion of the creed, wherein a possibility of salvation is denied to him who does not cordially embrace this doctrine, is pronounced UNREASONABLE, UNCHARITABLE, UN CHRISTIAN, with every other aggravating appellation that can be used. But the ground of this charge, and the whole of the difficulty suggested in it, from the variety of the circumstances of different persons, depends upon the interpretation of the phrase of 'being saved.' The meaning of this term in its primary signification, and as it is applied to common subjects in common discourse, means a preservation from threatening perils, or from threatened punishment. But, in an evangelical sense, and as it occurs in

the New Testament, it includes much more: it means the whole Christian scheme of redemption and justification by the Son of God, with all the glorious privileges and promises contained in that scheme. It means not merely a hope of deliverance from danger or from vengeance, but a federal title to positive happiness, purchased by the merits, and declared to mankind by the Gospel of Christ Jesus our Lord. St. Paul calls it 'THE OBTAINING THE SALVATION WHICH IS IN CHRIST JESUS WITH ETERNAL GLORY,' 2 Tim. ii, 10. 'Whosoever,' then, says the creed, 'will' thus 'be saved,' will be desirous to secure the glorious promises of the Gospel, must pursue it upon the terms which that Gospel proposes, and particularly must embrace the doctrines which it reveals. The creed speaks of those only to whom the evidence of the Gospel has been fully set forth, and the importance of it fully explained. We are to justify it only to professed believers, and of them only. The state and lot of the Heathen world are quite out of the question. Neither common sense nor Scripture will permit us to interpret it of those who still 'SIT IN DARKNESS AND THE SHADOW OF DEATH,' and never had the means of grace and the hope of glory proposed to them. Even with respect to those to whom the Gospel is preached, there is no necessity of interpreting the words here used in the harshest and strictest sense. There are many distinctions and limitations, which are always understood and supposed in such cases, though they are not expressly mentioned. General rules are laid down as such, are true as such; while excepted cases are referred to the judgment of those who are qualified to judge of them, and are not particularly pointed out; as for other reasons, so lest they should be extended too far, and defeat the general rule. Sufficient capacity in the persons to whom it is applied, and sufficient means of information and conviction, are always presupposed, where faith is spoken of as necessary. Where either of these is wanting, the case is (where it should be) in the hands of God. The creed is laid down as a rule of judgment to men, not to their Maker. We may learn from thence on what terms alone we can claim a title to the promises of the Gospel; but we do not learn from thence how far uncovenanted favour may be extended to particular persons. It is not intended to exclude the mercy of God to Heathens or heretics; it being his prerogative, and his alone, to judge how far the error or ignorance of any one is his wilful fault, or his unavoidable infirmity. But it is intended to establish the terms on which WE may now claim acceptance, and, in consequence of his gracious promise, may say, that 'GOD IS FAITHFUL AND JUST TO FORGIVE US OUR SINS.' The creed relates only to the covenant of salvation; and any expression which, used separately without this view and connection, might be thought to bear a stronger and more absolute sense, yet is limited by this relative coherence, and is to be interpreted by it. 'Perishing everlastingly,' in other discourses, may sometimes be understood of everlasting damnation; but here it means the being for ever excluded from the only stated claim of promised mercy. And 'without doubt,' he who does not embrace the truths proposed by revelation, has no title to those hopes which that revelation, and that only, offers to mankind. And even when such expressions of terror are used in the strongest sense, and threatened to unbelief or disobedience, they universally imply such exceptions as these,--'Unless personal disabilities lessen the guilt, or repentance intervene to prevent the punishment.' In short, no objection can be made against this assertion in the creed, but what would hold as strongly against that declaration of our blessed Lord, 'HE THAT BELIEVETH, AND IS BAPTIZED, SHALL BE SAVED; BUT HE THAT BELIEVETH NOT SHALL BE DAMNED,' Mark xvi, 15. Indeed, this condemnatory sentence in this form by human authority is plainly founded on and borrowed from that divine authority in the Gospel; and whatever distinctions and limitations are allowed in that case are equally applicable to this, and will fully justify both. The necessity of a true belief in all whom Providence has blessed with the means and opportunities of learning it, in order to entitle them federally to eternal salvation, being thus established upon Scripture proof, the creed goes on very regularly to declare what is that true belief so indispensably necessary." This is, perhaps, all that can be said in favour of these comminations; but few will think it quite satisfactory. The effect of them has doubtless been, to induce many to fly to the opposite extreme of laxity on the subject of fundamental doctrines.

Before leaving the ancient formulas of Christian doctrine, it may be stated, that both in the council of Ephesus against the Nestorians, held A. D. 431; and in that of Chalcedon, against the Eutychians, in 451; it was solemnly declared and decreed, that "Christ was one divine person, in whom two natures, the human and the divine, were most closely united, but without being mixed or confounded together."

7. Amid the variance and opposition of council to council, and pope to pope, (A. D. 1553,) which prevailed for centuries in the Romish church, it would be no easy task to ascertain the real articles of its confession. The decrees of the council of Trent, however, together with the creed of Pope Pius **IV**, are now commonly understood to be the authoritative standards of its faith and worship. These, beside recognising the authority of the Apostles' and the Nicene Creeds, embrace a multitude of dogmas which it is unnecessary particularly to specify, relating to traditions, the sacraments of baptism, confirmation, eucharist, penance, extreme unction, order, and matrimony, transubstantiation, the sacrifice of the mass, worshipping of images, purgatory, indulgences, &c, &c.

8. The Greek church has no public or established confession; but its creed, so far as can be gathered from its authorized catechisms, admits the doctrines of the Nicene and Athanasian Creeds, with the exception of the article in each concerning the procession of the Holy Spirit, which it affirms to be "from the Father only, and not from the Father and the Son." It disowns the supremacy and infallibility of the pope, purgatory by fire, graven images, and the restriction of the sacrament to one kind; but acknowledges the seven sacraments of the catholics, the religious use of

pictures, invocation of saints, transubstantiation, and masses and prayers for the dead.

9. Though the Romish church early appropriated to itself the exclusive title of catholic, or universal; and though, for many centuries, its unscriptural tenets pervaded the far greater part of Europe; not only were there always some individuals who adhered to the doctrines of genuine Christianity, but, long before the Protestant reformation, there appear to have been whole congregations who maintained, in considerable purity, the substance of the faith contained in Scripture. Such were the churches of the Waldenses in the valleys of Piedmont, whose confession, of so early a date as the beginning of the twelfth century, is still preserved. It consists of fourteen articles, of which the following is a copy, taken from the Cambridge **MSS**, and bearing date A. D. 1120:--"(1.) We believe and firmly hold all that which is contained in the twelve articles of the symbol, which is called the Apostles' Creed, accounting for heresy whatsoever is disagreeing, and not consonant to the said twelve articles. (2.) We do believe that there is one God, Father, Son, and Holy Spirit. (3.) We acknowledge for the holy canonical Scriptures the books of the Holy Bible. [Here follows a list of the books of the Old and New Testament, exactly the same as those we have in our English authorized version. Then follows a list of "the books apocryphal, which," with admirable simplicity they say, "are not received of the Hebrews. But we read them, as saith St. Jerom in his Prologue to the Proverbs, 'for the instruction of the people, not to confirm the authority of the doctrine of the church.'"] (4.) The books above-said teach this, that there is one God, almighty, all-wise, and all-good, who has made all things by his goodness; for he formed Adam in his own image and likeness, but that by the envy of the devil, and the disobedience of the said Adam, sin has entered into the world, and that we are sinners in Adam and by Adam. (5.) That Christ was promised to our fathers who received the law, that so knowing by the law their sin, unrighteousness, and insufficiency, they might desire the coming of Christ, to satisfy for their sins, and accomplish the law by himself. (6.) That Christ was born in the time appointed by God the Father; that is to say, in the time when all iniquity abounded, and not for the cause of good works, for all were sinners; but that he might show us grace and mercy, as being faithful. (7.) That Christ is our life, truth, peace, and righteousness; also our pastor, advocate, sacrifice, and priest; who died for the salvation of all those that believe, and is risen for our justification. (8.) In like manner, we firmly hold that there is no other Mediator and Advocate with God the Father, save only Jesus Christ. And as for the virgin Mary, that she was holy, humble, and full of grace. And in like manner do we believe concerning all the other saints; namely, that, being in heaven, they wait for the resurrection of their bodies at the day of judgment. (9.) ITEM, We believe that, after this life, there are only two places, the one for the saved, and the other for the damned; the which two places we call paradise and hell, absolutely denying that purgatory invented by antichrist, and forged contrary to the truth. (10.) ITEM, We have always accounted as an unspeakable abomination before God all those inventions of men; namely, the feasts and the vigils of saints, the water which they call holy: as likewise to abstain from flesh upon certain days, and the like; but especially their masses. (11.) We esteem for an abomination, and as antichristian, all those human inventions which are a trouble or prejudice to the liberty of the spirit. (12.) We do believe that the sacraments are signs of the holy thing, or visible forms of the invisible grace; accounting it good that the faithful sometimes use the said signs or visible forms, if it may be done. However, we believe and hold, that the above-said faithful may be saved without receiving the signs aforesaid, in case they have no place nor any means to use them. (13.) We acknowledge no other sacrament than baptism and the Lord's Supper. (14.) We ought to honour the secular powers by submission, ready obedience, and paying of tributes." These churches had, in modern times, another confession imposed upon them, after they began to receive pastors from Geneva, which is strongly tinged with Calvinism. It bears date A. D. 1655.

10. The first Protestant confession was that presented in 1530, to the diet of Augsburg, by the suggestion and under the direction of John, elector of Saxony. This wise and prudent prince, with the view of having the principal grounds on which the Protestants had separated from the Romish communion, distinctly submitted to that assembly, entrusted the duty of preparing a summary of them to the divines of Wittemberg. Nor was that task a difficult one; for the reformed doctrines had already been digested into seventeen articles, which had been proposed at the conferences both at Sultzbach and Smalcald, as the confession of faith to be adopted by the Protestant confederates. These, accordingly, were delivered to the elector by Luther, and served as the basis of the celebrated Augsburg confession, written "by the elegant and accurate pen of Melancthon:" a work which has been admired by many even of its enemies, for its perspicuity, piety, and erudition. It contains twenty-eight chapters, the leading topics of which are, the true and essential divinity of Christ; his substitution and vicarious sacrifice; original sin; human inability; the necessity, freedom, and efficacy of divine grace; consubstantiation; and particularly justification by faith, to establish the truth and importance of which was one of its chief objects. The last seven articles condemn and confute the Popish tenets of communion in one kind, clerical celibacy, private masses, auricular confession, legendary traditions, monastic vows, and the exorbitant power of the church. This confession is silent on the doctrine of predestination. This is the universal standard of orthodox doctrine among those who profess to be Lutherans, in which no authoritative alteration has ever been made.

11. The confession of Basle, originally presented, like the preceding, to the diet of Augsburg, but not published till 1534, consists of only twelve articles, which, in every essential point, agree with those of the Augsburg confession, except that it rejects the doctrine of consubstantiation; affirming that Christ is only spiritually present in the Lord's Supper, SACRAMENTALITER NIMIRUM, ET PER

MEMORATIONEM FIDEI; [that is to say sacramentally, and by faith;] and that it asserts the doctrine of predestination and infant baptism. But the more detailed creed of the whole Swiss Protestant churches is contained in the former and latter Helvetic confessions. The first was drawn up in 1536, by Bullinger, Myconius, and Grynæus, in behalf of the churches of Helvetia, and presented to an assembly of divines at Wittemberg, by whom it was cordially approved. But being deemed too concise, a second was prepared in 1556, by the pastors of Zurich; which was subscribed not only by all the Swiss Protestants, but by the churches of Geneva and Savoy, and by many of those in Hungary and Poland. They fully harmonize with each other, with only this difference, that the doctrine of predestination, and an approbation of the observance of such religious festivals, as the nativity, &c, are to be found in the latter confession only.

12. The Bohemic confession was compiled from various ancient confessions of the Waldenses who had settled in Bohemia, and approved of by Luther and Melancthon in 1532; but it was not published till 1535; when it was presented by the barons and other nobles to King Ferdinand. It extends to twenty articles, similar to those of the Waldensian confession, with the addition of others on the divinity of Christ, justification by faith in him, "without any human help or merit," predestination, and the absolute necessity of sanctification and good works.

13. The confession of the Saxon churches was composed in 1551 by Melancthon, at the desire of the pastors of Saxony and Misnia met in assembly at Wittemberg, in order to be presented to the council of Trent. It is contained in twenty-two articles; and while, like that of Augsburg, it is silent on the subject of predestination, it lays equal stress on the doctrine of justification by faith; and has a separate article entitled "Rewards," in which the doctrine of human merit, particularly as connected with future blessedness, is condemned and refuted.

14. Some account of the framing of the English Confession of Faith has been already given under the article *Church of England and Ireland.* The "Articles of Religion" are there said to have been amended and completed in the year 1571; and the Rev. Henry J. Todd, in his very able work on this subject, has shown their Melancthonian origin and character by extracts from the "*Articles of Religion*," "set out by the Convocation, and published by the king's authority," in 1536;--from those of 1540;--from Cranmer's "*Necessary Erudition of any Christian Man*," published in 1543;--from the *Homilies on Salvation, Faith, and Good Works*, in 1547, which three were, according to Bishop Woolton's unimpeached testimony (in 1576) composed by Archbishop Cranmer;--from the "*Reformatio Legum Ecclesiasticarum*," "composed under the superintendence of the same watchful primate, in 1551;"--from the "*Articles of Religion*" formed in 1552, almost wholly by Cranmer;"--from "*Catechismus Brevis, Christianæ Disciplinæ Summam continens*," in 1553, which was published in English, as well as Latin, and commonly called "Edward the Sixth's Catechism;" and from Bishop Jewel's celebrated "*Apologia Ecclesiæ Anglicanæ*," "published in 1562 by the queen's authority, thus recognised as a national Confession of Faith, and as such has been printed in the *Corpus Confessionum Fidei*." "Such," says Mr. Todd, "are the several public documents or declarations, produced or made before the establishment of the *Thirty-nine Articles of Religion*, from which I have given extracts, to which the framers of these Articles directed their attention, with the spirit of which they concur, and the words of which they almost literally adopt. There will also be found, as chronologically preceding these, considerable extracts from the *Confession of Augsburg*, the whole article from the Saxon Confession, *De Remissione Peccatorum, et Justificatione*, [respecting the forgiveness of sins, and justification,] and such passages in our *Liturgy* as concern the points which the Articles and Homilies exhibit." No one who has perused these documents will require any additional argument to convince him, that, in its very foundations, the English Confession of Faith was most explicitly in favour of general redemption. We cannot therefore be surprised at all the old orthodox divines of the church of England, from 1610 to 1660, refusing to be called Arminians; for they repeatedly declared that their own church openly professed similar doctrines to those promulgated by the Dutch professor, long before his name was known in the world. In this assertion they were perfectly correct; and by every important fact in our ecclesiastical history, as connected with doctrinal matters, their views are confirmed. If the Articles were actually of a Calvinistic complexion, as they are now often represented to be, what could have induced Whitaker and other learned Calvinists to waste so much valuable time and labour in fabricating the Lambeth Articles in 1595? Those worthies avowed, that the original Thirty-nine Articles were not doctrinal enough for their purpose.--When four choice divines, two of them professors of divinity at Cambridge, were sent to the synod of Dort as deputies from the English church, and one from the church of Scotland, though their political instructions went the full length of assisting in the condemnation and oppression of the Arminians, personally considered as a troublesome party in the republic, yet they had different instructions respecting their doctrines. On the second article, discussed in that synod, "the extent of Christ's redemption," Balcanqual, the deputy from the church of Scotland, informs the English ambassador at the Hague, that a difference had arisen among the British deputies: "The question among us is, whether the words of Scripture, which are likewise the words of our confession, be to be understood of all particular men, or only of the elect who consist of all sorts of men? Dr. Davenant and Dr. Ward are of Martinius of Breme his mind, THAT IT IS TO BE UNDERSTOOD OF ALL PARTICULAR MEN: the other three [Bishop Carleton, Dr. Goad, and Dr. Balcanqual] take the other exposition, which is that of the writers of the reformed churches." The ambassador wrote home for instructions, and received orders for the British deputies "to have those conclusions concerning Christ's death, and the application of it to us, couched in manner and terms as near as possibly may be to those which were used in the primitive church, by the fathers of that time, against

the Pelagians and Semi-Pelagians, and not in any new phrase of the modern age; and that the same may be as agreeable to the confessions of the church of England and other reformed churches, and with as little distaste and umbrage to the Lutheran churches, as may be." Archbishop Abbott expressed his approbation of their "cautelous moderation" in withholding their "hand from pressing in public any rigorous exclusive propositions in the doctrine of the extent of our Saviour Christ's oblation." The history of this affair, which cannot be here detailed, shows, that, however willing the three deputies were to condemn the remonstrants, the resistance of the two more moderate divines was approved by the authorities at home, and their opinions on this subject were recorded in such theses as no true Calvinist could consistently subscribe. During our civil troubles in 1643, the Assembly of Divines at Westminster revised the first fifteen of the Thirty-nine Articles "with a design," as Neal in his "*History of the Puritans*" candidly declares, "to render their sense more express and determinate in favour of Calvinism." This they found to be a hopeless task, as the ancient creed was too incorrigible to be bent to their views; and they found it much easier to frame one after their own hearts, some account of which the reader will find in a subsequent paragraph.--All these facts go to prove, that the best informed Calvinists have always viewed the English articles as not sufficiently high in doctrine, unless, as in the case of the seventeenth, they be allowed to interpret them by interpolations or qualifying epithets.

15. The confession of the reformed Gallican churches was prepared by order of a synod at Paris in 1559; and presented to Charles **IX**. in 1561, by the celebrated Beza, in a conference with that monarch at Poissy. It was published for the first time in 1566, with a preface by the French clergy to the pastors of all Protestant churches; and afterward, in 1571, it was solemnly ratified and subscribed in the national synod of Rochelle. It is extended to forty articles; but they are in general concise, and embrace the usual topics of the other Protestant confessions, including the doctrines of election, and justification by faith only.

16. The Protestants in Scotland having presented a petition to parliament in 1560, requesting the public condemnation of Popery, and the legal acknowledgment of the reformed doctrine and worship, they were required to draw up a summary of the doctrines which they could prove to be consonant with Scripture, and which they were anxious to have established. The ministers on whom this duty was devolved, being well acquainted with the subject, prepared the required summary in the course of four days, and laid it before parliament, when, after having been read first before the Lords of the Articles, and afterward twice (the second time article by article) before the whole parliament, it received their sanction as the established system of belief and worship. It consists of twenty-five articles, and coincides with all the other Protestant confessions which affirm the doctrine of election, and reject that of consubstantiation; for although it is not so explicit as some of them respecting the unconditional nature of election, yet a distinct recognition of this doctrine pervades the whole of it; and though it has no separate article on justification, it no less plainly recognises this fundamental principle of the Protestant faith.

17. The tenets of Arminius having obtained considerable prevalence in Holland toward the beginning of the seventeenth century, the Calvinists, or Gomarists, as they were then called, appealed to a national synod, which was convened at Dort in 1618, by order of the states-general; and attended by ecclesiastical deputies from England, Switzerland, Bremen, Hesse, and the Palatinate, beside the clerical and lay representatives of the reformed churches in the United Provinces. The canons of this synod, contained in five chapters, relate to what are commonly called the FIVE POINTS; namely, particular and unconditional election; particular redemption, or the limitation of the saving effects of Christ's death to the elect only; the total corruption of human nature, and the total moral inability of man in his fallen state; the irresistibility of divine grace; and the final perseverance of the saints; all of which are declared to be the true and the only doctrines of Scripture.

18. The Remonstrants, as the Dutch Arminians are generally called, did not present a confession of faith to the synod of Dort, but only their sentiments on the five points enumerated in the preceding paragraph, with corresponding REJECTIONS OF ERRORS under each of those points. However, in the first year of their exile, they applied themselves diligently to this task, and soon produced an ample confession, principally composed by the celebrated Episcopius. In the preface they give copious reasons for such a record of their opinions; which Courcelles has thus expressed in a more summary manner:--"They did not publish it for the purpose of making it a standard of schism, by which they might separate themselves from men who held other opinions; nor for the purpose of having it esteemed by those under their pastoral care as a secondary rule of faith;--which is in these days with many persons a most pernicious abuse of this kind of confessions. But it was published solely with the intention to stop the mouths of those who calumniously assert, that the Remonstrants cherish within their bosoms portentous dogmas which they dare not divulge. For there is no cause for doubting, whether under such circumstances and for this purpose, it is not lawful for men to publish a confession of their faith, especially as St. Peter admonishes us 'always to be ready to give an answer to every man that asketh us a reason of the hope that is in us with meekness and fear.'" This confession is of a more practical character than any of the preceding: it inculcates, at great length, all the most important duties of Christianity, and, in the words of the preface, "directs all things to the practice of Christian piety. For we believe that true divinity is merely practical, and not either simply or for its greatest or chief part speculative; and therefore whatever things are delivered therein ought to be referred thither only,--that a man may be the more strongly and fitly inflamed and encouraged to a diligent performance of his duty, and keeping of the commandments of Jesus Christ." In the English translator's address to the reader in 1676, it is said,

"Touching the worth of this book, as a summary of Christian religion, if Doctor Jeremy Taylor's judgment be of credit with thee, I am credibly informed he should prefer it to be one of those two or three which, next the Holy Bible, he would have preserved from the supposed total destruction of books. A high encomium from the mouth of so learned and pious a divine!" But though its contents were chiefly practical, one expression in it, respecting the propriety of tolerating in a Christian community a man who denied the eternal generation of Jesus Christ, produced a controversy in Holland, as well as in this country, in which the famous Bishop Bull eminently distinguished himself. See Dort and Remonstrants.

19. The only other confession of which we shall take notice is that of the Westminster assembly, which met in 1643, and at which five ministers and three elders as commissioners from the general assembly of the church of Scotland attended, agreeably to engagements between the convention of estates there, and both houses of parliament in England. This confession is contained in thirty-three chapters, and in every point of doctrine, fully accords with the sentiments of the synod of Dort; and on some points going rather beyond it, as with respect to a supposed election of angels. It was approved and adopted by the general assembly in 1647; and two years after, ratified by act of parliament, as "the public and avowed confession of the church of Scotland." By act of parliament in 1690, it was again declared to be the national standard of faith in Scotland; and subscription to it as "the confession of his faith," specially required of every person who shall be admitted "a minister or preacher within this church." Subscription to it was also enjoined by the act of union in 1707, on all "professors, principals, regents, masters, and others bearing office," in any of the Scottish universities.

CONFLAGRATION, a general burning of a city, or other considerable place. But the word is more ordinarily restrained to that grand period, or catastrophe of our world, wherein the face of nature is expected to be changed by a deluge of fire, as it was anciently by that of water. The ancient Chaldeans, Pythagoreans, Platonists, Epicureans, Stoics, Celts, and Etrurians, appear to have had a notion of the conflagration; though whence they should derive it, unless from the sacred books, it is difficult to conceive; except, perhaps, from the Phenicians, who themselves had it from the Jews. The Celts, whose opinions resembled those of the eastern nations, held, that after the burning of the world, a new period of existence would commence. The ancient Etrurians, or Tuscans, also concurred with other western and northern nations of Celtic origin, as well as with the Stoics, in asserting the entire renovation of nature after a long period, or great year, when a similar succession of events would again take place. The cosmogony of an ancient Etrurian, preserved by Suidas, limits the duration of the universe to a period of twelve thousand years; six thousand of which passed in the production of the visible world, before the formation of man. The Stoics also maintained that the world is liable to destruction from the prevalence of moisture or of drought; the former producing a universal inundation, and the latter, a universal conflagration. "These," they say, "succeed each other in nature, as regularly as winter and summer." The doctrine of conflagration is a natural consequence of the general system of Stoicism; for, since, according to this system, the whole process of nature is carried on in a necessary series of causes and effects, when that operative fire, which at first, bursting from chaos, gave form to all things, and which has since pervaded and animated all nature, shall have consumed its nutriment; that is, when the vapours, which are the food of the celestial fires, shall be exhausted, a deficiency of moisture must produce a universal conflagration. This grand revolution in nature is, after the doctrine of the Stoics, thus elegantly described by Ovid:--

"ESSE QUOQUE IN FATIS REMINISCITUR, AFFORE TEMPUS

QUO MARE, QUO TELLUS, CORREPTAQUE REGIA CŒLI

ARDEAT; ET MUNDI MOLES OPEROSA LABORET."

Metamor. lib. i, 256.

or, as Dryden has translated the passage,--

"Rememb'ring in the fates a time when fire

Should to the battlements of heaven aspire;

When all his blazing worlds above should burn,

And all the inferior globe to cinders turn."

Seneca, speaking of the same event, says expressly, "TEMPUS ADVENERIT QUO SIDERA SIDERIBUS INCURRENT, ET OMNI FLAGRANTE MATERIA UNO IGNE, QUICQUID NUNC EX DEPOSITO LUCET, ARDEBIT;" that is, "the time will come when the world will be consumed, that it may be again renewed; when the powers of nature will be turned against herself, when stars will rush upon stars, and the whole material world, which now appears resplendent with beauty and harmony, will be destroyed in one general conflagration." In this grand catastrophe of nature, all animated beings, (excepting the Universal Intelligence,) men, heroes, demons, and gods, shall perish together. Seneca, the tragedian, who was of the same school with the philosopher, writes to the same purpose:--

"CŒLI REGIA CONCIDENS

CERTOS ATQUE OBITUS TRAHET:

ATQUE OMNES PARITER DEOS

PERDET MORS ALIQUA, ET CHAOS."

"The mighty palace of the sky

In ruin fall'n is doomed to lie;

And all the gods, its wreck beneath,

Shall sink in chaos and in death."

The Pythagoreans also maintained the dogma of conflagration. To this purpose Hippasus, of Metapontum, taught that the universe is finite, is always changing, and undergoes a periodical conflagration. Philolaus, who flourished in the time of Plato, maintained that the world is liable to destruction both by fire and water. Mention of the conflagration is also several times made in the books of the Sibyls, Sophocles, Lucan, &c. Dr. Burnet, after F. Tachard and others, relates that the Siamese believe that the earth will at last be parched up with heat, the mountains melted down, and the earth's whole surface reduced to a level, and then consumed with fire. And the Bramins of Siam do not only hold that the world shall be destroyed by fire, but also that a new earth shall be made out of the cinders of the old. The sacred Scriptures announce this general destruction of the world by fire in a variety of passages.

2. Various are the sentiments of authors on the subject of the conflagration; the cause whence it is to arise, and the effects it is to produce. Divines ordinarily account for it metaphysically; and will have it take its rise from a miracle, as a fire from heaven. Philosophers contend for its being produced from natural causes; and will have it effected according to the laws of mechanics: some think an eruption of a central fire sufficient for the purpose; and add, that this may be occasioned several ways; namely, either by having its intensity increased, (which, again, may be effected either by being driven into less space by the encroachments of the superficial cold, or by an increase of the inflammability of the fuel whereon it is fed,) or by having the resistance of imprisoning earth weakened; which may happen either from the diminution of its matter, by the consumption of its central parts, or by weakening the cohesion of the constituent parts of the mass, by the excess or the defect of moisture. Others look for the cause of the conflagration in the atmosphere; and suppose that some of the meteors there engendered in unusual quantities, and exploded with unusual vehemence, from the concurrency of various circumstances, may be made to effect it, without seeking any farther. The astrologers account for it from a conjunction of all the planets in the sign Cancer; "as the deluge," say they, "was occasioned by their conjunction in Capricorn." This was an opinion adopted by the ancient Chaldeans. Lastly: others have recourse to a still more effectual and flaming machine; and conclude the world is to undergo its conflagration from the near approach of a comet, in its return from the sun. It is most natural to conclude, that, as the Scriptures represent the catastrophe as the work of a moment, no gradually operating natural cause will be employed to effect it, but that He who spake and the world was created, will again destroy it by the same word of his power; setting loose at once the all-devouring element of fire to absorb all others. Beyond this, all is conjecture.

CONFUSION OF TONGUES is a memorable event, which happened in the one hundred and first year, according to the Hebrew chronology, after the flood, B. C. 2247, at the overthrow of Babel; and which was providentially brought about, in order to facilitate the dispersion of mankind, and the population of the earth. Until this period, there had been one common language, which formed a bond of union, that prevented the separation of mankind into distinct nations.

2. There has been a considerable difference of opinion as to the nature of this confusion, and the manner in which it was effected. Some learned men, prepossessed with the notion that all the different idioms now in the world did at first arise from one original language, to which they may be reduced, and that the variety among them is no more than must naturally have happened in a long course of time by the mere separation of the builders of Babel, have maintained, that there were no new languages formed at the confusion; but that this event was accomplished by creating a misunderstanding and variance among the builders, without any immediate influence on their language. But this opinion, advanced by Le Clerc, &c, seems to be directly contrary to the obvious meaning of the word שפה, LIP, used by the sacred historian; which, in other parts of Scripture signifies SPEECH, Psalm lxxxi, 5; Isaiah xxviii, 11; xxxiii, 19; Ezekiel iii, 5. It has been justly remarked, that unanimity of sentiment, and identity of language, are particularly distinguished from each other, in the history: "The people is one, and they have all one language," Gen. xi, 6. It has been also suggested, that if disagreement in opinion and counsel were the whole that was intended, it would have had a contrary effect; they would not have desisted from their project, but strenuously have maintained their respective opinions, till the greater number of them had compelled the minority either to fly or to submit. Others have imagined, that this was brought about by a temporary confusion of their speech, or rather of their apprehensions, causing them, while they continued together and spoke the same language, to understand the words differently: Scaliger is of this opinion. Others again account for this event, by the privation of all language, and by supposing that mankind were under a necessity of associating together, and of imposing new names on things by common consent. Another opinion ascribes the confusion to such an indistinct remembrance of the original language which they spoke before, as made them speak it very differently; so that by the various inflections, terminations, and pronunciations of divers dialects, they could no more understand one another, than they who understand Latin can understand those who speak French, Italian, or Spanish, though all these languages arise out of it. This opinion is adopted by Casaubon, and by

Bishop Patrick in his Commentary, and is certainly much more probable than either of the former: and Mr. Shuckford maintains, that the confusion arose from small beginnings, by the invention of new words in either of the three families of Shem, Ham, and Japhet, which might contribute to separate them from one another; and that in each family new differences of speech might gradually arise, so that each of these families went on to divide and subdivide among themselves. Others, again, as Mr. Joseph Mede and Dr. Wotton, &c, not satisfied with either of the foregoing methods of accounting for the diversity of languages among mankind, have recourse to an extraordinary interposition of divine power, by which new languages were framed and communicated to different families by a supernatural infusion or inspiration; which languages have been the roots and originals from which the several dialects that are, or have been, or will be, spoken, as long as this earth shall last, have arisen, and to which they may with ease be reduced.

3. It is, however, unnecessary to suppose, that the primitive language was completely obliterated, and entire new modes of speech at once introduced. It was quite sufficient, if such changes only were effected, as to render the speech of different companies or different tribes unintelligible to one another, that their mutual coöperation in the mad attempt in which they had all engaged might be no longer practicable. The radical stem of the first language might therefore remain in all, though new dialects were formed, bearing among themselves a similar relation with what we find in the languages of modern Europe, derived from the same parent stem, whether Gothic, Latin, or Sclavonian. In the midst of these changes, it is reasonable to suppose that the primitive language itself, unaltered, would still be preserved in some one at least of the tribes or families of the human race. Now in none of these was the transmission so likely to have taken place, as among that branch of the descendants of Shem, from which the patriarch Abraham proceeded. Upon these grounds, therefore, we may probably conclude, that the language spoken by Abraham, and by him transmitted to his posterity, was in fact the primitive language, modified indeed and extended in the course of time, but still retaining its essential parts far more completely than any other of the languages of men. If these conclusions are well founded, they warrant the inference, that, in the ancient Hebrew, there are still to be found the traces of the original speech. Whether this ancient Hebrew more nearly resembled the Chaldean, the Syrian, or what is now termed the Hebrew, it is unnecessary here to inquire; these languages, it has never been denied, were originally and radically the same, though, from subsequent modifications, they appear to have assumed somewhat different aspects.

CONGREGATIONALISTS, a denomination of Protestants who reject all church government, except that of a single congregation under the direction of one pastor, with their elders, assistants, or managers. In one particular, the Congregationalists differ from the Independents: the former invite councils, which, however, only tender their advice; but the latter are accustomed to decide all difficulties within themselves. See Independents.

CONSCIENCE is that principle, power, or faculty within us, which decides on the merit or demerit of our own actions, feelings, or affections, with reference to the rule of God's law. It has been called the MORAL SENSE by Lord Shaftesbury and Dr. Hutcheson. This appellation has been objected to by some, but has been adopted and defended by Dr. Reid, who says, "The testimony of our moral faculty, like that of the external senses, is the testimony of nature, and we have the same reason to rely upon it." He therefore considers conscience as an original faculty of our nature, which decides clearly, authoritatively, and instantaneously, on every object that falls within its province. "As we rely," says he, "upon the clear and distinct testimony of our eyes, concerning the colours and figures of the bodies about us, we have the same reason to rely, with security, upon the clear and unbiassed testimony of our conscience, with regard to what we ought and ought not to do." But Dr. Reid is surely unfortunate in illustrating the power of conscience by the analogy of the external senses. With regard to the intimations received through the organs of sense, there can be no difference of opinion, and there can be no room for argument. They give us at once correct information, which reasoning can neither invalidate nor confirm. But it is surely impossible to say as much for the power of conscience, which sometimes gives the most opposite intimations with regard to the simplest moral facts, and which requires to be corrected by an accurate attention to the established order of nature, or to the known will of God, before we can rely with confidence on its decisions. It does not appear, that conscience can with propriety be considered as a principle distinct from that which enables us to pronounce on the general merit or demerit of moral actions. This principle, or faculty, is attended with peculiar feelings, when we ourselves are the agents; we are then too deeply interested to view the matter as a mere subject of reasoning; and pleasure or pain are excited, with a degree of intensity proportioned to the importance which we always assign to our own interests and feelings. In the case of others, our approbation or disapprobation is generally qualified, sometimes suspended, by our ignorance of the motives by which they have been influenced; but, in our own case, the motives and the actions are both before us, and when they do not correspond, we feel the same disgust with ourselves that we should feel toward another, whose motives we knew to be vicious, while his actions are specious and plausible. But in our own case, the uneasy feeling is heightened in a tenfold degree, because self-contempt and disgust are brought into competition with the warmest self-love, and the strongest desire of self-approbation. We have then something of the feelings of a parent, who knows the worthlessness of the child he loves, and contemplates with horror the shame and infamy which might arise from exposure to the world.

2. Conscience, then, cannot be considered as any thing else than the general principle of moral approbation or disapprobation applied to our own feelings or conduct,

acting with increased energy from the knowledge which we have of our motives and actions, and from the deep interest which we take in whatever concerns ourselves; nor can we think that they have deserved well of morals or philosophy, who have attempted to deduce our notions of right and wrong from any one principle. Various powers both of the understanding and of the will are concerned in every moral conclusion; and conscience derives its chief and most salutary influence from the consideration of our being continually in the presence of God, and accountable to him for all our thoughts, words, and actions. A conscience well informed, and possessed of sensibility, is the best security for virtue, and the most awful avenger of wicked deeds; an ill-informed conscience is the most powerful instrument of mischief; a squeamish and ticklish conscience generally renders those who are under its influence ridiculous.

HIC MURUS AHENEUS ESTO,

NIL CONSCIRE SIBI, NULLA PALLESCERE CULPA.

[Let a consciousness of innocence, and a fearlessness of any accusation, be thy brazen bulwark.]

3. The rule of conscience is the will of God, so far as it is made known to us, either by the light of nature, or by that of revelation. With respect to the knowledge of this rule, conscience is said to be rightly informed, or mistaken; firm, or wavering, or scrupulous, &c. With respect to the conformity of our actions to this rule when known, conscience is said to be good or evil. In a moral view, it is of the greatest importance that the understanding be well informed, in order to render the judgment or verdict of conscience a safe directory of conduct, and a proper source of satisfaction. Otherwise, the judgment of conscience may be pleaded, and it has actually been pleaded, as an apology for very unwarrantable conduct. Many atrocious acts of persecution have been perpetrated, and afterward justified, under the sanction of an erroneous conscience. It is also of no small importance, that the sensibility of conscience be duly maintained and cherished; for want of which men have often been betrayed into criminal conduct without self-reproach, and have deluded themselves with false notions of their character and state. See Moral Obligation.

CONSECRATION, a devoting or setting apart any thing to the worship or service of God. The Mosaical law ordained that all the first-born, both of man and beast, should be sanctified or consecrated to God. The whole race of Abraham was in a peculiar manner consecrated to his worship; and the tribe of Levi and family of Aaron were more immediately consecrated to the service of God, Exod. xiii, 2, 12, 15; Num. iii, 12; 1 Peter ii, 9. Beside the consecrations ordained by the sovereign authority of God, there were others which depended on the will of men, and were either to continue for ever or for a time only. David and Solomon devoted the Nethinims to the service of the temple for ever, Ezra viii, 20; ii, 58. Hannah, the mother of Samuel, offered her son to the Lord, to serve all his life-time in the tabernacle, 1 Sam. i, 11; Luke i, 15. The Hebrews sometimes devoted their fields and cattle to the Lord, and the spoils taken in war, Leviticus xxvii, 28, 29; 1 Chron. xviii, 11. The New Testament furnishes us with instances of consecration. Christians in general are consecrated to the Lord, and are a holy race, a chosen people, 1 Peter ii, 9. Ministers of the Gospel are in a peculiar manner set apart for his service; and so are places of worship; the forms of dedication varying according to the views of different bodies of Christians; and by some a series of ceremonies has been introduced, savouring of superstition, or at best of Judaism.

CONSUBSTANTIALISTS. This term was applied to the orthodox, or Athanasians, who believed the Son to be of the same substance with the Father; whereas the Arians would only admit the Son to be of like substance with the Father.

CONSUBSTANTIATION, a tenet of the Lutheran church respecting the presence of Christ in the Lord's Supper. Luther denied that the elements were changed after consecration, and therefore taught that the bread and wine indeed remain; but that together with them, there is present the substance of the body of Christ, which is literally received by communicants. As in red-hot iron it may be said two distinct substances, iron and fire, are united, so is the body of Christ joined with the bread. Some of his followers, who acknowledged that similes prove nothing, contented themselves with saying that the body and blood of Christ are really present in the sacrament in an inexplicable manner. See Lord's Supper.

CONVERSATIONS. These were held by the orientals in the gate of the city. Accordingly, there was an open space near the gate, which was fitted up with seats for the accommodation of the people, Gen. xix, 1; Psalm lxix, 12. Those who were at leisure occupied a position on these seats, and either amused themselves with witnessing those who came in and went out, and with any trifling occurrences that might offer themselves to their notice, or attended to the judicial trials, which were commonly investigated at public places of this kind, namely, the gate of the city, Gen. xix, 1; xxxiv, 20; Psalm xxvi, 4, 5; lxix, 12; cxxvii, 5; Ruth iv, 11; Isaiah xiv, 31; or held intercourse by conversation. Promenading, so fashionable and so agreeable in colder latitudes, was wearisome and unpleasant in the warm climates of the east, and this is probably one reason why the inhabitants of those climates preferred holding intercourse with one another, while sitting near the gate of the city, or beneath the shade of the fig tree and the vine, 1 Samuel xxii, 6; Micah iv, 4. The formula of assent in conversation was Σὺ εἶπας, דברתכן, THOU HAST SAID, or THOU HAST RIGHTLY SAID. We are informed by the traveller Aryda, that this is the prevailing mode of a person's expressing his assent or affirmation to this day, in the vicinity of Mount Lebanon, especially where he does not wish to assert any thing in express terms. This explains the answer of the Saviour to the high priest Caiaphas in Matt. xxvi, 64, when he was asked whether he was the Christ, the Son of God, and replied, Σὺ εἶπας, THOU HAST SAID.

The English word conversation has now a more restricted sense than formerly; and it is to be noted that in several passages of our translation of the Bible it is used to comprehend our whole conduct.

CONVERSION, a change from one state or character to another. Conversion, considered theologically, consists in a renovation of the heart and life, or a being turned from sin and the power of Satan unto God, Acts xxvi, 18; and is produced by the influence of divine grace upon the soul. This is conversion considered as a state of mind; and is opposed both to a careless and unawakened state, and to that state of conscious guilt and slavish dread, accompanied with struggles after a moral deliverance not yet attained, which precedes our justification and regeneration; both of which are usually understood to be comprised in conversion. But this is not the only Scriptural import of the term; for the first TURNING of the whole heart to God in penitence and prayer is generally termed conversion. In its stricter sense, as given above, it is, however, now generally used by divines.

CONVICTION, in general, is the assurance of the truth of any proposition. In a religious sense, it is the first degree of repentance, and implies an affecting sense of our guilt before God; and that we deserve and are exposed to his wrath.

COPPER. נחשת. Anciently, copper was employed for all the purposes for which we now use iron. Arms, and tools for husbandry and the mechanic arts, were all of this metal for many ages. Job speaks of bows of copper, Job xx, 24; and when the Philistines had Samson in their power, they bound him with fetters of copper. Our translators indeed say "brass;" but under that article their mistake is pointed out. In Ezra viii, 27, are mentioned "two vessels of copper, precious as gold." The Septuagint renders it σκεύη χαλκοῦ ςίλβοντος; the Vulgate and Castellio, following the Arabic, "VASA ÆRIS FULGENTIS;" and the Syriac, "vases of Corinthian brass." It is more probable, however, that this brass was not from Corinth, but a metal from Persia or India, which Aristotle describes in these terms: "It is said that there is in India a brass so shining, so pure, so free from tarnish, that its colour differs nothing from that of gold. It is even said that among the vessels of Darius there were some respecting which the sense of smelling might determine whether they were gold or brass." Bochart is of opinion that this is the CHASMAL of Ezekiel i, 27, the χαλκολίβανον of Rev. i, 15, and the ELECTRUM of the ancients.

Mr. Harmer quotes from the manuscript notes of Sir John Chardin a reference to a mixed metal in the east, and highly esteemed there; and suggests that this composition might have been as old as the time of Ezra, and be brought from those more remote countries into Persia, where these two basins were given to be conveyed to Jerusalem. Ezekiel, xxvii, 13, speaks of the merchants of Javan, Jubal, and Meshech, as bringing vessels of NEHESH (copper) to the markets of Tyre. According to Bochart and Michaëlis, these were people situated toward Mount Caucasus, where copper mines are worked at this day. See Brass.

COPTS, a name given to the Christians of Egypt who do not belong to the Greek church, but are Monophysites, and in most respects Jacobites. Scaliger and Father Simon derive the name from Coptos, once a celebrated town of Egypt, and the metropolis of the Thebaid; but Volney and others are of opinion, that the name COPTS is only an abbreviation of the Greek word AIGOUPTIOS, "an Egyptian." The Copts have a patriarch, whose jurisdiction extends over both Egypts, Nubia, and Abyssinia; who resides at Cairo, but who takes his title from Alexandria. He has under him eleven or twelve bishops, beside the abuna, or bishop of the Abyssinians, whom he appoints and consecrates. The rest of the clergy, whether secular or regular, are composed of the orders of St. Anthony, St. Paul, and St. Macarius, who have each their monasteries. Their arch-priests, who are next in degree to bishops, and their deacons, are said to be numerous; and they often confer the order of deacon even on children. Next to the patriarch is the bishop, or titular patriarch, of Jerusalem, who also resides at Cairo, because there are only few Copts at Jerusalem. He is, in reality, little more than bishop of Cairo; except that he goes to Jerusalem every Easter, and visits some other places in Palestine, which own his jurisdiction. To him belongs the government of the Coptic church, during the vacancy of the patriarchal see. The ecclesiastics are said to be, in general, of the lowest ranks of the people; and hence that great degree of ignorance which prevails among them. They have seven sacraments; baptism, the eucharist, confirmation, ordination, faith, fasting, and prayer. They admit only three œcumenical councils; those of Nice, Constantinople, and Ephesus. There are three Coptic liturgies; one attributed to St. Basil, another to St. Gregory, and the third to St. Cyril. At present, however, little more than the mere shadow of Christianity can be seen in Egypt; and, in point of numbers, not more than fifty thousand Christians in all can be found in this country. There are not more than three Christian churches at Cairo.

CORAL, ראמות, Job xxviii, 18; Ezek. xxvii, 16; a hard, cretaceous, marine production, resembling in figure the stem of a plant, divided into branches. It is of different colours,--black, white, and red. The latter is the sort emphatically called coral, as being the most valuable, and usually made into ornaments. This, though no gem, is ranked by the author of the book of Job, xxviii, 18, with the onyx and sapphire. Dr. Good observes, "It is by no means certain what the words here rendered 'corals and pearls,' and those immediately afterward rendered 'rubies and topaz,' really signified. Reiske has given up the inquiry as either hopeless or useless; and Schultens has generally introduced the Hebrew words themselves, and left the reader of the translation to determine as he may. Our common version is, in the main, concurrent with most of the oriental renderings: and I see no reason to deviate from it."

CORBAN, קרבן, Mark vii, 11; from the Hebrew קרב, TO OFFER, TO PRESENT. It denotes a gift, a present made to God, or to his temple. The Jews sometimes swore by corban, or by gifts offered to God, Matt. xxiii, 18. Theophrastus says that the Tyrians forbad the use of such oaths as were peculiar to foreigners, and particularly of corban, which, Josephus informs us, was used only by the Jews. Jesus Christ reproaches the Jews with cruelty toward their parents, in making a corban of what should have been appropriated to their use. For when a child was asked to relieve the wants of his father or mother, he would often say, "It is a gift," corban, "by whatsoever thou mightest be profited by me;" that is, I have devoted that to God which you ask of me; and it is no longer mine to give, Mark vii, 11. Thus they violated a precept of the moral law, through a superstitious devotion to Pharisaic observances, and the wretched casuistry by which they were made binding upon the conscience.

CORIANDER, גד, Exod. xvi, 31; Num. xi, 7; a strongly aromatic plant. It bears a small round seed, of a very agreeable smell and taste. The manna might be compared to the coriander seed in respect to its form or shape, as it was to bdellium in its colour. See Manna.

CORINTH, a celebrated city, the capital of Achaia, situated on the isthmus which separates the Peloponnesus from Attica. This city was one of the best peopled and most wealthy of Greece. Its situation between two seas drew thither the trade of both the east and west. Its riches produced pride, ostentation, effeminacy, and all vices, the consequences of abundance. For its insolence to the Roman legates, it was destroyed by L. Mummius. In the burning of it, so many statues of different metals were melted together, that they produced the famous Corinthian brass. It was afterward restored to its former splendour by Julius Cæsar.

Christianity was first planted at Corinth by St. Paul, who resided here eighteen months, between the years 51 and 53; during which time he enjoyed the friendship of Aquila and his wife Priscilla, two Jewish Christians, who had been expelled from Italy, with other Jews, by an edict of Claudius. The church consisted both of Jews and of Gentiles; but St. Paul began, as usual, by preaching in the synagogue, until the Jews violently opposed him, and blasphemed the name of Christ; when the Apostle, shaking his garment, and declaring their blood to be upon their own heads, left them, and made use afterward of a house adjoining the synagogue, belonging to a man named Justus. The rage of the Jews, however, did not stop here; but, raising a tumult, they arrested Paul, and hurrying him before the tribunal of the pro-consul Gallio, the brother of the famous Seneca, accused him of persuading men to worship God contrary to the law. But Gallio, who was equally indifferent both to Judaism and Christianity, and finding that Paul had committed no breach of morality, or of the public peace, refused to hear their complaint, and drove them all from the judgment seat. The Jews being thus disappointed in their malicious designs, St. Paul was at liberty to remain some time longer at Corinth; and after his departure, Apollos, a zealous and eloquent Jewish convert of Alexandria, was made a powerful instrument in confirming the church, and in silencing the opposition of the Jews, Acts xviii. How much it stood in need of such support, is evident from the Epistles of St. Paul; who cautions the Corinthians against divisions and party spirit; fornication, incest, partaking of meats offered to idols, thereby giving an occasion of scandal, and encouragement to idolatry; abusing the gifts of the Spirit, litigiousness, &c. The Corinthians, indeed, were in great danger: they lived at ease, free from every kind of persecution, and were exposed to much temptation. The manners of the citizens were particularly corrupt: they were, indeed, infamous to a proverb. In the centre of the city was a celebrated temple of Venus, a part of whose worship consisted in prostitution; for there a thousand priestesses of the goddess ministered to dissoluteness under the patronage of religion: an example which gave the Corinthians very lax ideas on the illicit intercourse of the sexes. Corinth also possessed numerous schools of philosophy and rhetoric; in which, as at Alexandria, the purity of the faith by an easy and natural process, became early corrupted.

There occurs a chronological difficulty in the visits of St. Paul to Corinth. In 2 Cor. xii, 14, and xiii, 1, 2, the Apostle expresses his design of visiting that city a third time; whereas only one visit before the date of the Second Epistle is noticed in the Acts, xviii, 1, about A. D. 51; and the next time that he visited Greece, Acts xx, 2, about A. D. 57, no mention is made of his going to Corinth. Mr. Horne observes on this subject, "It has been conjectured by Grotius, and Drs. Hammond and Paley, that his First Epistle virtually supplied the place of his presence; and that it is so represented by the Apostle in a corresponding passage, 1 Cor. v, 3. Admitting this solution to be probable, it is, however, far-fetched, and is not satisfactory as a matter of fact. Michaëlis has produced another, more simple and natural; namely, that Paul, on his return from Crete, visited Corinth a second time before he went to winter at Nicopolis. This second visit is unnoticed in the Acts, because the voyage itself is unnoticed. The third visit, promised in 2 Cor. xii, 14, and xiii, 1, 2, was actually paid on the Apostle's second return to Rome, when he took Corinth in his way, 2 Tim. iv, 20. 'Thus critically,' says Dr. Hales, 'does the book of the Acts harmonize, even in its omissions, with the epistles; and these with each other, in the minute incidental circumstances of the third visit.'"

About A. D. 268, the Heruli burned Corinth to ashes. In 525, it was again almost ruined by an earthquake. About 1180, Roger, king of Sicily, took and plundered it. Since 1458, it was till lately under the power of the Turks; and is so decayed, that its inhabitants amount to no more than about fifteen hundred, or two thousand; half Mohammedans, and half Christians. A late French writer, who visited this country, observes, "When the Cæsars rebuilt the walls of Corinth, and the temples of the gods rose from their ruins more magnificent than ever, an obscure architect was rearing in silence an edifice which still remains standing amidst the ruins of Greece. This man, unknown to the great, despised by the multitude, rejected as the offscouring of the world, at first associated himself with only two companions, Crispus and Gaius, and with the family of Stephanas. These were the humble architects of an indestructible temple, and the first believers at Corinth. The traveller surveys the site of this celebrated city; he discovers not a vestige of the altars of Paganism, but perceives some Christian chapels rising from among the cottages of the Greeks. The Apostle might still, from his celestial abode, give the salutation of peace to his children, and address them in the words, 'Paul to the church of God, which is at Corinth.'"

CORINTHIANS, EPISTLES TO. St. Paul left Corinth A. D. 53 or 54, and went to Jerusalem. From Ephesus he wrote his First Epistle to the Corinthians, in the beginning of A. D. 56. In this epistle he reproves some who disturbed the peace of the church, complains of some disorders in their assemblies, of law suits among them, and of a Christian who had committed incest with his mother-in-law, the wife of his father, and had not been separated from the church. This letter produced in the Corinthians great grief, vigilance against the vices reproved, and a very beneficial dread of God's anger. They repaired the scandal, and expressed abundant zeal against the crime committed, 2 Cor. vii, 9–11.

To form an idea of the condition of the Corinthian church, we must examine the epistles of the Apostle. The different factions into which they were divided, exalted above all others the chiefs, τοὺς ὑπὲρ λίαν ἀποςόλους, [the very chiefest Apostles,] 2 Cor. xi, 5; xii, 11, whose notions they adopted, and whose doctrines they professed to follow, and attempted to depreciate those of the opposite party. While, then, some called themselves disciples of Paul, Cephas, or Apollos, others assumed the splendid appellation of Christ's party. Probably they affected to be the followers of James, the brother of our Lord, and thought thus to enter into a nearer discipleship with Jesus than the other parties. The controversy, as we shall see from the whole, related to the obligation of Judaism. The advocates of it had appealed, even in Galatia, to Cephas and James, for the sake of opposing to Paul, who had banished Jewish ceremonies from Christianity, authorities which were not less admitted than his own. The question itself divided all these various parties into two principal factions: the partisans of Cephas and James were for the law; the friends of Paul adopted his opinion, as well as Apollos, who, with his adherents, was always in heart in favour of Paul, and never wished to take a part in a separation from him, 1 Cor. xvi, 12. The leaders of the party against Paul, these ψευδαπόςολοι, [false apostles,] as Paul calls them, and μετασχηματιζόμενοι εἰς ἀποςόλους Χριςοῦ, [transformers of themselves into the apostles of Christ,] who declared themselves the promulgators and defenders of the doctrines of Cephas, and James, were, as may be easily conceived, converted Jews, 2 Cor. xi, 22, who had come from different places,--to all appearance from Palestine, ἐρχομένοι, [the comers,] 2 Cor. xi, 4,--and could therefore boast of having had intercourse with the Apostles at Jerusalem, and of an acquaintance with their principles. They were not even of the orthodox Jews, but those who adhered to the doctrines of the Sadducees; and though they were even now converted to Christianity, while they spoke zealously in favour of the law, they were undermining the hopes of the pious, and exciting doubts against the resurrection, 1 Cor. xv, 35; so that Paul, from regard to the teachers, whose disciples they professed to be, was obliged to refute them from the testimony of James and Cephas, 1 Cor. xv, 5, 7. These, proud of their own opinions, 1 Cor. i, 17, not without private views, depreciated Paul's authority, and extolled their own knowledge, 1 Cor. ii, 12; 2 Cor. xi, 16, 17. Violently as the contest was carried on, they still did not withdraw from the same place of assembly for instruction and mutual edification; this, however, was even the cause of too many scandalous scenes and disorders. At the ἀγάπαι, LOVE FEASTS, love and benevolence were no where to be seen. Instead of eating together, and refreshing their poor brethren out of that which they had brought with them, each one, as he came, ate his own, without waiting for any one else, and feasted often to excess, while the needy was fasting, 1 Cor. xi, 17. When also some were preparing for prayers or singing, others raised their voices to instruct, and commenced exercises in SPIRITUAL GIFTS, tongues, prophesyings, and interpretations, 1 Cor. xii, xiii, xiv; moreover, the women, to bring confusion to its highest pitch, took their part in interlocutions and proposals of questions, 1 Cor. xiv, 34.

Such was the state of things as to the interior discipline of the assemblies and edification; but the exterior deportment, which the members of this society had maintained in civil life, soon disappeared also. Formerly, when differences arose among the believers, they were adjusted by the intervention of arbitrators from their own communion, and terminated quietly. Now, as their mutual confidence in each other more and more decreased, they brought, to the disgrace of Christianity, their complaints before the Pagan tribunals, 1 Cor. vi, 1. But as to what concerned the main object, namely, the obligation of Judaism, it was so little confined simply to words and reasons, that each party rather strove to display its opposite principles in its conduct. One party gave to the other, as much as possible, motives for ill will and reproach. The Jews required circumcision as an indispensable act of religion; while Paul's disciples attempted to lay the foundation of a new doctrine respecting it, and to extinguish all traces of circumcision, 1 Cor. vii, 18. As the Jewish party observed and maintained a distinction of meats, that of Paul ate without distinction any thing sold in the markets, and even meats from the Heathen sacrifices, 1 Cor. x, 25, 28; viii, 1. Nor was this enough; they often made no scruple to be present at the sacrificial feasts. Among other things, they also took part in many scandalous practices which were common there, and fell, by means of their imprudence, into still greater crimes, 1 Cor. x, 20, 21; viii, 10. According to the Jewish custom, the women were obliged to appear veiled in the synagogues and public assemblies. The anti-judaists abolished this custom of the synagogue, 1 Cor. xi, 5, 6, 10; and herein imitated the Heathen practices. From despite to Judaism, which considered matrimonial offspring as a particular blessing of God, some embraced celibacy, which they justified by St. Paul's example, 1 Cor. vii, 7, 8; and this they also recommended to others, 1 Cor. vii, 1–25. Some went even so far, that, although married, they resolved to practise a continual continency, 1 Corinthians, vii, 3–5. These were the evils, both in his own party and in that of his opponents, which St. Paul had to remedy.

Paul, having understood the good effects of his first letter among the Corinthians, wrote a second to them, A. D. 57, from Macedonia, and probably from Philippi. He expresses his satisfaction at their conduct, justifies himself, and comforts them. He glories in his suffering, and exhorts them to liberality. Near the end of the year 57, he came again to Corinth, where he staid about three months, and whence he went to Jerusalem. Just before his second departure from Corinth, he wrote his Epistle to the Romans, probably in the beginning of A. D. 58.

CORMORANT, שלך, Levit. xi, 17; Deut. xiv, 17; a large sea bird. It is about three feet four inches in length, and four feet two inches in breadth from the tips of the extended wings. The bill is about five inches long, and of a dusky colour; the base of the lower mandible is covered with a naked yellowish skin, which extends under the throat and forms a kind of pouch. It has a most voracious appetite, and lives chiefly upon fish, which it devours with unceasing gluttony. It darts down very rapidly upon its prey; and the Hebrew, and the Greek name, *καταρϱάκτης*, [a cataract,] are expressive of its impetuosity. The word קאת, which in our version of Isaiah xxxiv, 11, is rendered CORMORANT, is the pelican.

CORNER. Amos iii, 12. Sitting in the corner is a stately attitude. The place of honour is the corner of the room, and there the master of the house sits and receives his visitants.

COUNCIL sometimes denotes any kind of assembly; sometimes that of the sanhedrim; and, at other times, a convention of pastors met to regulate ecclesiastical affairs. It may be reasonably supposed that as Christianity spreads, circumstances would arise which would make consultation necessary among those who had embraced the Gospel, or at least among those who were employed in its propagation. A memorable instance of this kind occurred not long after the ascension of our Saviour. In consequence of a dispute which had arisen at Antioch concerning the necessity of circumcising Gentile converts, it was determined that "Paul and Barnabas, and certain others of them, should go up to Jerusalem unto the Apostles and elders about this question."--"And the Apostles and elders came together for to consider of this matter," Acts xv, 6. After a consultation, they decided the point in question; and they sent their decree, which they declared to be made under the direction of the Holy Ghost, to all the churches, and commanded that it should be the rule of their conduct. This is generally considered as the first council; but it differed from all others in this circumstance, that its members were under the ESPECIAL guidance of the Spirit of God. The Gospel was soon after conveyed into many parts of Europe, Asia, and Africa; but it does not appear that there was any public meeting of Christians for the purpose of discussing any contested point, till the middle of the second century. From that time councils became frequent; but as they consisted only of those who belonged to particular districts or countries, they were called provincial or national councils. The first general council was that of Nice, convened by the emperor Constantine, A. D. 325; the second general council was held at Constantinople, in the year 381, by order of Theodosius the Great; the third, at Ephesus, by order of Theodosius, Junior, A. D. 431; and the fourth at Chalcedon, by order of the emperor Marcian, A. D. 451. These, as they were the first four general councils, so they were by far the most eminent. They were caused respectively by the Arian, Apollinarian, Nestorian, and Eutychian controversies, and their decrees are in high esteem both among Papists and orthodox Protestants; but the deliberations of most councils were disgraced by violence, disorder, and intrigue, and their decisions were usually made under the influence of some ruling party. Authors are not agreed about the number of general councils; Papists usually reckon eighteen, but Protestant writers will not allow that nearly so many had a right to that name. The last general council was that held at Trent, for the purpose of checking the progress of the reformation. It first met by the command of Pope Paul **III**, A. D. 1545; it was suspended during the latter part of the pontificate of his successor, Julius **III**, and the whole of the pontificates of Marcellus **II**, and Paul **IV**, that is, from 1552 to 1562, in which year it met again by the authority of Pope Pius **IV**, and it ended, while he was pope, in the year 1563. Provincial councils were very numerous: Baxter enumerates four hundred and eighty-one, and Dufresnoy many more.

2. Of the eighteen councils denominated "general" by the Papists, four have already been enumerated; and they with the next four constitute the eight eastern councils, which alone, according to the "Body of Civil Law," each of the popes of Rome, on his elevation to the pontificate, solemnly professes to maintain. The fifth was convened at Constantinople, A. D. 556, by the emperor Justinian; the sixth, also at Constantinople, in 681, in which the emperor Constantine **IV**, himself presided; the seventh at Nice, in 787, by the empress Irene; and the eighth, at Constantinople, in 870, by the emperor Basilius. It is matter of historical record, and therefore cannot be denied, that the convening of all these councils appertained solely to the respective emperors; that they alone exercised authority on such occasions; that the bishop of Rome was never thought to possess any, although his power may be said to have been set up between the fifth and sixth general councils; nor did the bishop himself, PRO TEMPORE, think himself entitled to an authority of the kind. The other councils which the Romish church dignifies with the title of "general," are the ten western ones, which are here subjoined:--(9.) The first council of Lateran, held under Pope Calixtus, A. D. 1123; (10.) the second of Lateran, under Innocent **II**, in 1139; (11.) the third of Lateran, under Alexander **III**, in 1179, the decrees of which were intended to extirpate the Albigenses, as well as the Waldenses, who were variously called Leonists,

or poor men of Lyons; (12.) the fourth of Lateran, under Innocent **III**, in 1215, which incited Christian Europe to engage in a crusade for the recovery of the Holy Land, and whose canons obtruded on the church the monstrous doctrines of transubstantiation and auricular confession, the latter being ranked among the duties prescribed by the law of Christ; (13.) the first of Lyons, under Innocent **IV**, in 1245; (14.) the second of Lyons, under Gregory X, in 1274; (15.) that of Vienne, under Clement V, in 1311; (16.) that of Florence, under Eugenius **IV**, in 1439; (17.) the fifth of Lateran, under the infamous Julius **II**; and (18.) the council of Trent, of which an account is given in the preceding paragraph, and which grounds its fame on its opposition to the progress of the reformation under Luther. Though, according to Bellarmine, these eighteen alone are recognised by the Romish church œcumenical or universal councils, yet some of them did not deserve even the more restricted appellation of "general." For the council of Trent itself, in some of its sessions, could scarcely number more than forty or fifty ecclesiastics, and, of those, not one eminent for profound theological or classical knowledge. The lawyers who attended, says Father Paul, "knew little of religion, while the few divines were of less than ordinary sufficiency." Some of the other councils which are not acknowledged by the Papists to be "general" with respect to all their sessions, (as those of Basle and Constance,) are in part received by them, and in part rejected. Bellarmine and other celebrated writers of his church, are dubious about determining whether or not "the fifth of Lateran" was really a general council, and leave it as a thing discretionary with the faithful either to retain or reject it; if it be rejected, the only refuge which they have, is to receive in its place the council of Constance, held under John **XXIII**, in 1414, which is disclaimed by the Italian clergy but admitted by those of France, and which is rendered infamous in the annals of religion and humanity by its cruel and treacherous conduct toward those two early Protestant martyrs, John Huss and Jerome of Prague; "who went to the stake," says, Æneas Sylvius, "as if it had been to a banquet, without uttering a complaint that could betray the least weakness of mind. When they began to burn, they sung a hymn, which even the crackling of the flames could not interrupt. Never did any philosopher suffer death with so much courage, as they endured the fire." But this acknowledgment of Constance as one of the eighteen is resisted VI ET ARMIS, by the crafty Cisalpine ecclesiastics, because one of the earliest acts of that council declared the representatives of the church in general council assembled to be superior to the sovereign pontiff, not only when schism prevailed, but at all other times whatsoever.

3. A general council being composed of men every one of whom is fallible, they must also be liable to error when collected together; and that they actually have erred is sufficiently evident from this fact, that different general councils have made decrees directly opposite to each other, particularly in the Arian and Eutychian controversies, which were upon subjects immediately "pertaining unto God." Indeed, neither the first general councils themselves, nor those who defended their decisions, ever pretended to infallibility; this was a claim of a much more recent date, suited to the dark ages in which it was asserted and maintained, but now considered equally groundless and absurd in the case of general councils as in that of popes. If God had been pleased to exempt them from a possibility of error, he would have announced that important privilege in his written word; but no such promise or assurance is mentioned in the New Testament If infallibility belonged to the whole church collectively, or to any individual part of it, it must be so prominent and conspicuous that no mistake or doubt could exist upon the subject; and above all, it must have prevented those dissensions, contests, heresies, and schisms, which have abounded among Christians from the days of the Apostles to the present time; and of which that very church, which is the asserter and patron of this doctrine, has had its full share.

The Scriptures being the only source from which we can learn the terms of salvation, it follows that things ordained by general councils as necessary to salvation, have neither strength nor authority, as the church of England has well said, unless it may be declared that they he taken out of Holy Scripture. It is upon this ground we receive the decisions of the first four general councils, in which we find the truths revealed in the Scriptures, and therefore we believe them. We reverence the councils for the sake of the doctrines which they declared and maintained, but we do not believe the doctrines upon the authority of the councils.

COVENANT. The Greek word διαθήκη occurs often in the Septuagint, as the translation of a Hebrew word, which signifies COVENANT: it occurs also in the Gospels and the Epistles; and it is rendered in our English Bibles sometimes COVENANT, sometimes TESTAMENT. The Greek word, according to its etymology, and according to classical use, may denote a testament, a disposition, as well as a covenant; and the Gospel may be called a testament, because it is a signification of the will of our Saviour ratified by his death, and because it conveys blessings to be enjoyed after his death. These reasons for giving the dispensation of the Gospel the name of a testament appeared to our translators so striking, that they have rendered διαθήκη more frequently by the word TESTAMENT, than by the word COVENANT. Yet the train of argument, where διαθήκη occurs, generally appears to proceed upon its meaning a covenant; and therefore, although, when we delineate the nature of the Gospel, the beautiful idea of its being a testament, is not to be lost sight of, yet we are to remember that the word TESTAMENT, which we read in the Gospels and Epistles, is the translation of a word which the sense requires to be rendered COVENANT. A covenant implies two parties, and mutual stipulations. The new covenant must derive its name from something in the nature of the stipulations between the parties different from that which existed before; so that we cannot understand the propriety of the name, NEW, without looking back to what is called the OLD, or FIRST. On examining the passages in Gal. iii, in 2 Cor. iii, and in Heb. viii-x, where the old and the new covenant are contrasted, it will be found that the old covenant means the dispensation given by Moses to the children of Israel; and the new covenant the dispensation of the Gospel published by Jesus Christ; and that the object of the Apostle is to illustrate the superior excellence of the latter dispensation. But, in order to preserve the consistency of the Apostle's writings, it is necessary to remember that there are two different lights in which the former dispensation may be viewed. Christians appear to draw the line between the old and the new covenant, according to the light in which they view that dispensation. It may be considered merely as a method of publishing the moral law to a particular nation; and then with whatever solemnity it was delivered, and with whatever cordiality it was accepted, it is not a covenant that could give life. For, being nothing more than what divines call a covenant of works, a directory of conduct requiring by its nature entire personal obedience, promising life to those who yielded that obedience, but making no provision for transgressors, it left under a curse "every one that continued not in all things that were written in the book of the law to do them." This is the essential imperfection of what is called the covenant of works, the name given in theology to that transaction, in which it is conceived that the supreme Lord of the universe promised to his creature, man, that he would reward that obedience to his law, which, without any such promise, was due to him as the Creator.

No sooner had Adam broken the covenant of works, than a promise of a final deliverance from the evils incurred by the breach of it was given. This promise was the foundation of that transaction which Almighty God, in treating with Abraham, condescends to call "my covenant with thee," and which, upon this authority, has received in theology the name of the Abrahamic covenant. Upon the one part, Abraham, whose faith was counted to him for righteousness, received this charge from God, "Walk before me and be thou perfect;" upon the other part, the God whom he believed, and whose voice he obeyed, beside promising other blessings to him and his seed, uttered these significant words, "In thy seed shall all the families of the earth be blessed." In this transaction, then, there was the essence of a covenant; for there were mutual stipulations between two parties; and there was superadded, as a seal of the covenant, the rite of circumcision, which, being prescribed by God, was a confirmation of his promise to all who complied with it, and being submitted to by Abraham, was, on his part, an acceptance of the covenant.

The Abrahamic covenant appears, from the nature of the stipulations, to be more than a covenant of works; and, as it was not confined to Abraham, but extended to his seed, it could not be disannulled by any subsequent transactions, which fell short of a fulfilment of the blessing promised. The law of Moses, which was given to the seed of Abraham four hundred and thirty years after, did not come up to the terms of that covenant even with regard to them, for, in its form it was a covenant of works, and to other nations it did not directly convey any blessing. But although the Mosaic dispensation did not fulfil the Abrahamic covenant, it was so far from setting that covenant aside, that it cherished the expectation of its being fulfilled: for it continued the rite of circumcision, which was the seal of the covenant; and in those ceremonies which it enjoined, there was a shadow, a type, an obscure representation, of the promised blessing, Luke i, 72, 73.

Here, then, is another view of the Mosaic dispensation. "It was added, because of transgressions, till the seed should come to whom the promise was made," Gal. iii, 19. By delivering a moral law, which men felt themselves unable to obey; by denouncing judgments which it did not of itself provide any effectual method of escaping; and by holding forth, in various oblations, the promised and expected Saviour; "it was a schoolmaster to bring men unto Christ." The covenant made with Abraham retained its force during the dispensation of the law, and was the end of that dispensation.

The views which have been given furnish the ground upon which we defend that established language which is familiar to our ears, that there are only two covenants essentially different, and opposite to one another, the covenant of works, made with the first man, intimated by the constitution of human nature to every one of his posterity, and having for its terms, "Do this and live;"--and the covenant of grace, which was the substance of the Abrahamic covenant, and which entered into the constitution of the Sinaitic covenant, but which is more clearly revealed, and more extensively published in the Gospel. This last covenant, which the Scriptures call NEW in respect to the mode of its dispensation under the Gospel, although it is not new in respect of its essence, has received, in the language of theology, the name of the covenant of grace, for the two following obvious reasons: because, after man had broken the covenant of works, it was pure grace or favour in the Almighty to enter into a new covenant with him; and, because by the covenant there is conveyed that grace which enables man to comply with the terms of it. It could not be a covenant unless there were terms,--something required, as well as something promised or given,--duties to be performed, as well as blessings to be received. Accordingly, the tenor of the new covenant, founded upon the promise originally made to Abraham, is expressed by Jeremiah in words which the Apostle to the Hebrews has quoted as a description of it: "I will be to them a God, and they shall be to me a people," Heb. viii, 10:--words which intimate on one part not only entire reconciliation with God, but the continued exercise of all the perfections of the Godhead in promoting the happiness of his people, and the full communication of all the blessings which flow from his unchangeable love; on the other part, the surrender of the heart and affections of his people, the dedication of all the powers of their nature to his service, and the willing uniform obedience of their lives. But, although there are mutual stipulations, the covenant retains its character of a covenant of grace, and must be regarded as having its source purely in the grace of God. For the very circumstances which rendered the new covenant necessary, take away the possibility of there being any merit upon our part: the faith by which the covenant is accepted is the gift of God; and all the good works by which Christians continue to keep the covenant, originate in that change of character which is the fruit of the operation of his Spirit.

Covenants were anciently confirmed by eating and drinking together; and chiefly by feasting on a sacrifice. In this manner, Abimelech, the Philistine, confirmed the covenant with Isaac, and Jacob with his father Laban, Gen. xxvi, 26–31; xxxi, 44–46, 54. Sometimes they divided the parts of the victim, and passed between them, by which act the parties signified their resolution of fulfilling all the terms of the engagement, on pain of being divided or cut asunder as the sacrifice had been, if they should violate the covenant, Gen. xv, 9, 10, 17, 18; Jer. xxxiv, 18. Hence the Hebrew word CHARAT, which properly signifies to divide, is applied allusively in Scripture to the making of a covenant. When the law of Moses was established, the people feasted in their peace-offerings on a part of the sacrifice, in token of their reconciliation with God, Deut. xii, 6, 7. See Circumcision.

COURT, an entrance into a palace or house. (See HOUSE.) The great courts belonging to the temple of Jerusalem were three; the first called the court of the Gentiles, because the Gentiles were allowed to enter so far, and no farther; the second was the court of Israel, because all the Israelites, provided they were purified, had a right of admission into it; the third was that of the priests, where the altar of burnt-offerings stood, where the priests and Levites exercised their ministry. Common Israelites, who were desirous of offering sacrifices, were at liberty to bring their victims as far as the inner part of the court; but they could not pass a certain line of separation, which divided it into two; and they withdrew as soon as they had delivered their sacrifices and offerings to the priests, or had made their confession with the ceremony of laying their hands upon the head of the victim, if it were a sin-offering. Before the temple was built, there was a court belonging to the tabernacle, but not near so large as that of the temple, and encompassed only with pillars, and veils hung with cords.

CRANE. In Isaiah xxxviii, 14, and Jer. viii, 7, two birds are mentioned, the סיס and the עגור. The first in our version is translated CRANE, and the second SWALLOW; but Bochart exactly reverses them, and the reasons he adduces are incontrovertible. Aristophanes curiously observes, that "it is time to sow when the crane migrates clamouring into Africa; she also bids the mariner suspend his rudder and take his rest, and the mountaineer to provide himself with raiment;" and Hesiod, "When thou hearest the voice of the crane, clamouring annually from the clouds on high, recollect that this is the signal for ploughing, and indicates the approach of showery winter."

Where do the cranes or winding swallows go,

Fearful of gathering winds and falling snow?

Conscious of all the coming ills, they fly

To milder regions and a southern sky.

Prior.

The Prophet Jeremiah mentions this bird, thus intelligent of the seasons by an instinctive and invariable observation of their appointed times, as a circumstance of reproach to the chosen people of God, who, although taught by reason and religion, "knew not the judgment of the Lord."

CREATION, in its primary import, signifies the bringing into being something which did not exist before. The term is therefore most generally applied to the original production of the materials whereof the visible world is composed. It is also used in a secondary or subordinate sense, to denote those subsequent operations of the Deity upon the matter so produced, by which the whole system of nature, and all the primitive GENERA of things, received their forms, qualities, and laws. The accounts of the creation of the world which have existed among different nations, are called COSMOGONIES. Moses's is unquestionably the most ancient; and had it no other circumstance to recommend it, its superior antiquity alone would give it a just claim to our attention. It is evidently Moses's intention to give a history of man, and of religion, and an account of creation. In the way in which he has detailed it, it would have been foreign to his plan, had it not been necessary to obviate that most ancient and most natural species of idolatry, the worship of the heavenly bodies. His first care, therefore, is to affirm decidedly, that God created the heavens and the earth; and then he proceeds to mention the order in which the various objects of creation were called into existence. First of all, the materials, of which the future universe was to be composed, were created. These were jumbled together in one indigested mass, which the ancients called chaos, and which they conceived to be eternal; but which Moses affirms to have been created by the power of God. The materials of the chaos were either held in solution by the waters, or floated in them, or were sunk under them; and they were reduced into form by the Spirit of God moving upon the face of the waters. Light was the first distinct object of creation: fishes were the first living things; man was last in the order of creation.

2. The account given by Moses is distinguished by its simplicity. That it involves difficulties which our faculties cannot comprehend, is only what might be expected from a detail of the operations of the omnipotent mind, which can never be fully understood but by the Being who planned them. Most of the writers who come nearest to Moses in point of antiquity have favoured the world with cosmogonies; and there is a wonderful coincidence in some leading particulars between their accounts and his. They all have his chaos; and they all state water to have been the prevailing principle before the arrangement of the universe

began. The systems became gradually more complicated, as the writers receded farther from the age of primitive tradition; and they increased in absurdity in proportion to the degree of philosophy which was applied to the subject. The problem of creation has been said to be, "Matter and motion being given, to form a world;" and the presumption of man has often led him to attempt the solution of this intricate question. But the true problem was, "Neither matter nor motion being given, to form a world." At first, the cosmogonists contented themselves with reasoning on the traditional or historical accounts they had received; but it is irksome to be shackled by authority; and after they had acquired a smattering of knowledge, they began to think that they could point out a much better way of forming the world than that which had been transmitted to them by the consenting voice of antiquity. Epicurus was most distinguished in this hopeful work of invention; and produced a cosmogony on the principle of a fortuitous concourse of atoms, whose extravagant absurdity has hitherto preserved it from oblivion. From his day to ours, the world has been annoyed with systems; but these are now modified by the theories of chemists and geologists, whose speculations, in so far as they proceed on the principle of induction, have sometimes been attended with useful results; but, when applied to solve the problem of creation, will serve, like the systems of their forerunners, to demonstrate the ignorance and the presumption of man.

3. The early cosmogonies are chiefly interesting from their resemblance to that of Moses; which proves that they have either been derived from him, or from some ancient prevailing tradition respecting the true history of creation. The most ancient author next to Moses, of whose writings any fragments remain, is Sanchoniatho, the Phenician. His writings were translated by Philo Byblius; and portions of this version are preserved by Eusebius. These writings come to us rather in an apocryphal form; they contain, however, no internal evidence which can affect their authenticity; they pretty nearly resemble the traditions of the Greeks, and are, perhaps, the parent stock from which these traditions are derived. The notions detailed by Sanchoniatho are almost translated by Hesiod, who mentions the primeval chaos, and states ἔρος, or LOVE, to be its first offspring. Anaxagoras was the first among the Greeks who entertained tolerably accurate notions on the subject of creation: he assumed the agency of an intelligent mind in the arrangement of the chaotic materials. These sentiments gradually prevailed among the Greeks; from whom they passed to the Romans, and were generally adopted, notwithstanding the efforts which were made to establish the doctrines of Epicurus by the nervous poetry of Lucretius. Ovid has collected the orthodox doctrines which prevailed on the subject, both among Greeks and Romans; and has expressed them with uncommon elegance and perspicuity in the first chapter of his "Metamorphoses." There is so striking a coincidence between his account and that of Moses that one would almost think that he was translating from the first chapter of Genesis; and there can be no doubt that the Mosaic writings were well known at that time, both among the Greeks and Romans. Megasthenes, who lived in the time of Seleucus Nicanor, affirms, that all the doctrines of the Greeks respecting the creation, and the constitution of nature, were current among the Bramins in India, and the Jews in Syria. He must, of course, have been acquainted with the writings of the latter, before he could make the comparison. Juvenal talks of the writings of Moses as well known:--

TRADIDIT ARCANO QUODCUNQUE VOLUMINE MOSES.

[Whatever Moses has transmitted in his mystic volume.]

We are therefore inclined to think that Ovid actually copied from the Bible; for he adopts the very order detailed by Moses. Moses mentions the works of creation in the following order: the separation of the sea from the dry land; the creation of the heavenly bodies; of marine animals; of fowls and land animals; of man. Observe now the order of the Roman poet:--

ANTE MARE ET TERRAS, ET, QUOD TEGIT OMNIA, CŒLUM,

UNUS ERAT TOTO NATURÆ VULTUS IN ORBE,

QUEM DIXERE CHAOS, RUDIS, INDIGESTAQUE MOLES.

HANC DEUS, ET MELIOR LITEM NATURA DIREMIT.

NAM CŒLO TERRAS, ET TERRAS ABSCIDIT UNDIS;

ET LIQUIDUM SPISSO SECREVIT AB AËRE CŒLUM.

NEU REGIO FORET ULLA SUIS ANIMALIBUS ORBA;

ASTRA TENENT CŒLESTE SOLUM, FORMÆQUE DEORUM;

CESSERUNT NITIDIS HABITANDÆ PISCIBUS UNDÆ:

TERRA FERAS CEPIT, VOLUCRES AGITABILIS AËR.

SANCTIUS HIS ANIMAL, MENTISQUE CAPACIUS ALTÆ

DEERAT ADHUC, ET QUOD DOMINARI IN CÆTERA POSSET:

NATUS HOMO EST.

"Before the seas, and this terrestrial ball,
And heav'n's high canopy, that covers all,
One was the face of nature; if a face:
Rather, a rude and indigested mass:
A lifeless lump, unfashion'd, and unframed,
Of jarring seeds; and justly CHAOS named.
But God, or nature, while they thus contend,
To these intestine discords put an end;
Then earth from air, and seas from earth were driv'n,
And grosser air sunk from ethereal heav'n.
Thus when the God, whatever god was he,
Had form'd the whole, and made the parts agree,
That no unequal portions might be found,
He moulded earth into a spacious round.
Then, every void of nature to supply,
With forms of gods he fills the vacant sky:
New herds of beasts he sends, the plains to share:
New colonies of birds, to people air;
And to their oozy beds the finny fish repair.
A creature of a more exalted kind
Was wanting yet, and then was man design'd:
Conscious of thought, of more capacious breast,
For empire form'd, and fit to rule the rest:
Whether with particles of heav'nly fire
The God of nature did his soul inspire," &c.

Dryden.

Here we see all the principal objects of creation mentioned exactly in the same order which Moses had assigned to them in his writings; and when we consider what follows;--the war of the giants; the general corruption of the world; the universal deluge; the preservation of Deucalion and Pyrrha; their sacrifices to the gods on leaving the vessel in which they had been preserved;--there can scarcely remain a doubt that Ovid borrowed, either directly or at second hand, from Moses. What he says, too, is perfectly consistent with the received notions on the subject, though it is probable that they had never before been so regularly methodised. This train of reasoning would lead us to conclude that Ovid, and indeed the whole Heathen world, derived their notions respecting the creation, and the early history of mankind, from the sacred Scriptures: and it shows how deficient their own resources were, when the pride of philosophy was forced to borrow from those whom it affected to despise. With regard to the western mythologists, then, there can be little doubt that their cosmogonies, at least such of them as profess to be historical, and not theoretical, are derived from Moses; and the same may be affirmed with regard to the traditions of the east: as they were the same with those of Greece in the time of Megasthenes, whose testimony to this effect is quoted both by Clemens Alexandrinus and Strabo, we may naturally conclude that they had the same origin.

4. The Hindoo mythology has grown, in the natural uninterrupted progress of corruption, to such monstrous and complicated absurdity, that in many cases it stands unique in extravagance. In the more ancient Hindoo writings, however, many sublime sentiments occur; and in the "Institutes of Menu," many passages are found relating to the creation, which bear a strong resemblance to the account given by Moses. They are thus given in an advertisement, prefixed to the fifth volume of the "Asiatic Researches," and are intended as a supplement to a former treatise on the Hindoo religion:--

"This universe existed only in the first divine idea, yet unexpanded, as if involved in darkness, imperceptible, undefinable, undiscoverable by reason, and undiscovered by revelation, as if it were wholly immersed in sleep. When the sole self-existing Power, himself undiscerned, but making this world discernible, with five elements and other principles of nature, appeared with undiminished glory, expanding his idea, or dispelling the gloom. He, whom the mind alone can perceive, whose essence eludes the external organs, who has no visible parts, who exists from eternity, even he, the soul of all beings, whom no being can comprehend, shone forth in person. He, having willed to produce various beings from his own divine substance, first with a thought created the waters. The waters are called NARA, because they are the production of NARA, or the Spirit of God; and since they were his first AYANA, or place of motion, he thence is called NARAYANA, or moving on the waters. From that which is, the first cause, not the object of sense, existing every where in substance, not existing to our perception, without beginning or end, was produced the divine male. He framed the heaven above, and the earth beneath; in the midst he placed the subtile ether, the eight regions, and the permanent receptacle of waters. He framed all creatures. He, too, first assigned to all creatures distinct names, distinct acts, and distinct occupations. He gave being to time, and the divisions of time; to the stars also, and the planets; to rivers, oceans, and mountains; to level plains, and uneven valleys. For the sake of distinguishing actions, he made a total difference between right and wrong. Having divided his own substance, the mighty Power became half male, half female. He whose powers are incomprehensible, having created this universe, was again absorbed in the spirit, changing the time of energy for the time of repose."

In these passages we have evidently a philosophical comment on the account of creation given by Moses, or as transmitted from the same source of primitive tradition. We also see in these passages the rudiments of the Platonic philosophy, the eternal ideas in the divine mind, &c; and were any question to arise respecting the original author of these notions, we should have little hesitation in giving it against the Greeks. They were the greatest plagiaries both in literature and philosophy, and they have scarcely an article of literary property which they can call their own, except their poetry. Their sages penetrated into Egypt and India, and on their return stigmatized the natives of these countries as barbarians, lest they should be suspected of stealing their inventions.

5. The Chaldean cosmogony, according to Berosus, when divested of allegory, seems to resolve itself into this, that darkness and water existed from eternity; that Belus divided the humid mass, and gave birth to creation; that the human mind is an emanation from the divine nature. The cosmogony of the ancient Persians is very clumsy. They introduce two eternal principles, the one good, called OROMASDES, the other evil, called ARIMANIUS; and they make these two principles contend with each other in the creation and government of the world. Each has his province, which he strives to enlarge; and MITHRAS is the mediator to moderate their contentions. This is the most inartificial plan that has been devised to account for the existence of evil, and has the least pretensions to a philosophical basis. The Egyptian cosmogony, according to the account given of it by Plutarch, seems to bear a strong resemblance to the Phenician, as detailed by Sanchoniatho. According to the Egyptian account, there was an eternal chaos, and an eternal spirit united with it, whose agency at last arranged the discordant materials, and produced the visible system of the universe. The cosmogony of the northern nations, as may be collected from the Edda, supposes an eternal principle prior to the formation of the world. The Orphic Fragments state every thing to have existed in God, and to proceed from him. The notion implied in this maxim is suspected to be PANTHEISTIC, that is, to imply the universe to be God; which, however, might be a more modern perversion. Plato supposed the world to be produced by the Deity, uniting eternal, immutable ideas, or forms, to variable matter. Aristotle had no cosmogony, because he supposed the world to be without beginning and without end. According to the Stoical doctrine, the divine nature, acting on matter, first produced moisture, and then the other elements, which are reciprocally convertible.

CRETE, an island in the Mediterranean, now called Candia, Titus i, 5. Nature had endowed this island with all that renders man happy; the inhabitants, likewise, had formerly a constitution which was renowned and frequently compared with that of the Spartans; but at this time, and even long before, all, even laws and morals, had sunk very low. The character of this nation was mutable, prone to quarrelling, to civil disturbances and frays, to robberies and violences. Avaricious and base to a degree of sordid greediness, they considered nothing as ignoble which gratified this inclination. Thence arose their treachery, their false and deceitful disposition, which had passed into a common proverb. Even in the times of purer morals they were decidedly addicted to wine; and their propensity to incontinence was frequently censured and noticed by the ancients. Religion itself was one cause of the many excesses of this nation. Many deities were born among them; they also showed their tombs and catacombs, and celebrated the feasts and mysteries of all. They therefore had continually holydays, diversions, and idle times, and one of their native poets (Diodorus calls him Θεολόγος) gave them the testimony which Paul found to be so true, Titus i, 12. Jews also had established themselves among them, who according to all appearance could have improved here but very little in morality. The Apostle seems to have considered them a more dangerous people than the inhabitants themselves.

CRIMSON, כרמיל, 2 Chron. ii, 7, iii, 14, the name of a colour. Bochart supposes it to be the COCHLEA PURPURARIA, or purple from a kind of shell-fish taken near Mount Carmel. But as the name of the mount is said to mean a vineyard, one may rather suppose the colour to signify that of grapes; like the redness of the vesture of him who trod the wine-press, Isa. lxiii, 1, 2. What our version renders CRIMSON, Isa. i, 18; Jer. iv, 30, should be SCARLET.

CROSS, an ancient instrument of capital punishment. The cross was the punishment inflicted by the Romans, on servants who had perpetrated crimes, on robbers, assassins, and rebels; among which last Jesus was reckoned, on the ground of his making himself King or Messiah, Luke xxiii, 1–5, 13–15. The words in which the sentence was given were, "Thou shalt go to the cross." The person who was subjected to this punishment was then deprived of all his clothes excepting something around the loins. In this state of nudity he was beaten, sometimes with rods, but more generally with whips. Such was the severity of this flagellation, that numbers died under it. Jesus was crowned with thorns, and made the subject of mockery; but insults of this kind were not among the ordinary attendants of crucifixion. They were owing, in this case, merely to the petulant spirit of the Roman soldiers, Matt. xxvii, 29; Mark xv, 17; John xix, 2, 5. The criminal, having been beaten, was subjected to the farther suffering of being obliged to carry the cross himself to the place of punishment, which was commonly a hill, near the public way, and out of the city. The place of crucifixion at Jerusalem was a hill to the north-west of the city. The cross, ςαυρὸς, A POST, otherwise called the unpropitious or infamous tree, consisted of a piece of wood erected perpendicularly, and intersected by another at right angles near the top, so as to resemble the letter T. The crime for which the person suffered was inscribed on the transverse piece near the top of the perpendicular one.

There is no mention made in ancient writers of any thing on which the feet of the person crucified rested. Near the middle, however, of the perpendicular beam, there projected a piece of wood, on which he sat, and which answered as a support to the body, since the weight of the body might otherwise have torn away the hands from the nails driven through them. The cross, which was erected at the place of punishment, being there firmly fixed in the ground, rarely exceeded ten feet in height. The victim, perfectly naked, was elevated to the small projection in the middle: the hands were then bound by a rope round the transverse beam, and nailed through the palm.

The assertion that the persons who suffered crucifixion were not in some instances fastened to the cross by nails through the hands and feet, but were merely bound to it by ropes, cannot be proved by the testimony of any ancient writer whatever. That the feet, as well as the hands, were fastened to the cross by means of nails, is expressly asserted in the play of Plautus, entitled "Mostellaria," compared with Tertullian against the Jews, and against Marcion. In regard to the nailing of the feet, it may be farthermore observed, that Gregory Nazianzen has asserted, that one nail only was driven through both of them; but Cyprian, (DE PASSIONE,) who had been a personal witness to crucifixions, and is, consequently, in this case, the better authority, states, on the contrary, that two nails or spikes were driven, one through each foot. The crucified person remained suspended in this way till he died, and the corpse had become putrid. While he exhibited any signs of life, he was watched by a guard; but they left him when it appeared that he was dead. The corpse was not buried, except by express permission, which was sometimes granted by the emperor on his birth day, but only to a very few. An exception, however, to this general practice was made by the Romans in favour of the Jews, on account of Deut. xxi, 22, 23; and in Judea, accordingly, crucified persons were buried on the same day. When, therefore, there was not a prospect that they would die on the day of the crucifixion, the executioners hastened the extinction of life, by kindling a fire under the cross, so as to suffocate them with the smoke, or by letting loose wild beasts upon them, or by breaking their bones upon the cross with a mallet, as upon an anvil. The Jews, in the times of which we are speaking, namely, while they were under the jurisdiction of the Romans, were in the habit of giving the criminal, before the commencement of his sufferings, a medicated drink of wine and myrrh, Prov. xxxi, 6. The object of this was to produce intoxication, and thereby render the pains of the crucifixion less sensible to the sufferer. This beverage was refused by the Saviour for the obvious reason, that he chose to die with the faculties of his mind undisturbed and unclouded, Matt. xxvii, 34; Mark xv, 23. It should be remarked, that this sort of drink, which was probably offered out of kindness, was different from the vinegar which was subsequently offered to the Saviour by the Roman soldiers. The latter was a mixture of vinegar and water, denominated POSCA, and was a common drink for the soldiers in the Roman army, Luke xxiii, 36; John xix, 29.

2. Crucifixion was not only the most ignominious, it was likewise the most cruel, mode of punishment: so very much so, that Cicero is justified in saying, in respect to crucifixion, "AB OCULIS, AURIBUSQUE ET OMNI COGITATIONE HOMINUM, REMOVENDUM ESSE." [That it ought neither to be seen, heard of, nor even thought of by men.] The sufferings endured by a person on whom this punishment is inflicted are narrated by George Gottlieb Richter, a German physician, in a "Dissertation on the Saviour's Crucifixion." The position of the body is unnatural, the arms being extended back, and almost immovable. In case of the least motion, an extremely painful sensation is experienced in the hands and feet, which are pierced with nails, and in the back, which is lacerated with stripes. The nails, being driven through the parts of the hands and feet which abound in nerves and tendons, create the most exquisite anguish. The exposure of so many wounds to the open air brings on an inflammation, which every moment increases the poignancy of the suffering. In those parts of the body which are distended or pressed, more blood flows through the arteries than can be carried back in the veins. The consequence is, that a greater quantity of blood finds its way from the AORTA into the head and stomach, than would be carried there by a natural and undisturbed circulation. The blood vessels of the head become pressed and swollen, which of course causes pain, and a redness of the face. The circumstance of the blood being impelled in more than ordinary quantities into the stomach is an unfavourable one also, because it is that part of the system which not only admits of the blood being stationary, but is peculiarly exposed to mortification. The aorta, not being at liberty to empty, in the free and undisturbed way as formerly, the blood which it receives from the left ventricle of the heart, is unable to receive its usual quantity. The blood of the lungs, therefore, is unable to find a free circulation. This general obstruction extends its effects likewise to the right ventricle, and the consequence is, an internal excitement, and exertion, and anxiety, which are more intolerable than the anguish of death itself. All the large vessels about the heart, and all the veins and arteries in that part of the system, on account of the accumulation and

pressure of blood, are the source of inexpressible misery. The degree of anguish is gradual in its increase; and the person crucified is able to live under it commonly till the third, and sometimes till the seventh, day. Pilate, therefore, being surprised at the speedy termination of the Saviour's life, inquired in respect to the truth of it of the centurion himself, who commanded the soldiers, Mark xv, 44. In order to bring their life to a more speedy termination, so that they might be buried on the same day, the bones of the two thieves were broken with mallets, John xix, 31–37; and in order to ascertain this point in respect to Jesus, namely, whether he was really dead, or whether he had merely fallen into a swoon, a soldier thrust his lance into his side; but no signs of life appeared, John xix, 31–37.

3. Our Saviour says, that whosoever will be his disciple must take up his cross and follow him, Matt. xvi, 24: by which is meant, that his disciples must be willing to suffer for him, in any way in which God, in the course of his providence, may call them to suffer; even to endure martyrdom, if called to it. The cross is also often put for the whole of Christ's sufferings, Eph. ii, 16; Heb. xii, 2; and the doctrine of his perfect atonement, Gal. vi, 14.

CROWN is a term properly taken for a cap of state worn on the heads of sovereign princes, as a mark of regal dignity. In Scripture there is frequent mention made of crowns; and the use of them seems to have been very common among the Hebrews. The high priest wore a crown, which was girt about his mitre, or the lower part of his bonnet, and was tied about his head. On the forepart was a plate of gold, with these words engraven on it: "Holiness to the Lord," Exod. xxviii, 36; xxix, 6. New-married persons of both sexes wore crowns upon their wedding day, Cant., iii, 11; and, alluding to this custom, it is said that when God entered into covenant with the Jewish nation, he put a beautiful crown upon their head, Ezekiel xvi, 12. The first crowns were no more than a bandelet drawn round the head, and tied behind, as we see it still represented on medals, &c. Afterward, they consisted of two bandelets; by degrees they took branches of trees of divers kinds, &c; at length they added flowers; and Claudius Saturninus says there was not any plant of which crowns had not been made.

There was always a difference, either in matter or form, between the crowns of kings and great men, and those of private persons. The crown of a king was generally a white fillet bound about his forehead, the extremities whereof being tied behind the head, fell back on the neck. Sometimes they were made of gold tissue, adorned with jewels. That of the Jewish high priest, which is the most ancient of which we have any description, was a fillet of gold placed upon his forehead, and tied with a ribbon of a hyacinth colour, or azure blue. The crown, mitre, and diadem, royal fillet and tiara, are frequently confounded. Crowns were bestowed on kings and princes, as the principal marks of their dignity. David took the crown of the king of the Ammonites from off his head: the crown weighed a talent of gold, and was moreover enriched with jewels, 2 Sam. xii, 30; 1 Chron. xx, 2. The Amalekite who valued himself on killing Saul, brought this prince's crown unto David, 2 Sam. i, 10. The crown was placed upon the head of young King Josiah, when he was presented to the people, in order to be acknowledged by them, 2 Chron. xxiii, 11. Baruch says that the idols of the Babylonians wore golden crowns, Baruch vi, 9. Queens, too, wore diadems among the Persians. King Ahasuerus honoured Vashti with this mark of power; and, after her divorce, the same favour was granted to Esther, chap. ii, 17. The elders, in Rev. iv, 10, are said to "cast their crowns before the throne." The allusion is here to the tributary kings dependent upon the Roman emperors. Herod took off his diadem in the presence of Augustus, till ordered to replace it. Tiridates did homage to Nero by laying the ensigns of royalty at the foot of his statue.

Pilate's guard platted a crown of thorns, and placed it on the head of Jesus Christ, Matt. xxvii, 29, with an intention to insult him, under the character of the king of the Jews. See THORN. In a figurative sense, a crown signifies honour, splendour, or dignity, Lam. v, 16; Phil. iv, 1; and is also used for reward, because conquerors, in the Grecian games, were crowned, 1 Corinthians ix, 25.

CRYSTAL, קרח. This word is translated "crystal" in Ezek. i, 22; and "frost," Gen. xxxi, 40; Job xxxvii, 10; Jeremiah xxxvi, 30; and "ice," Job vi, 16; xxxviii, 29; Psalm cxlvii, 17; κρυϛαλλος, Rev. iv, 6; xxii, 1. Crystal is supposed to have its name from its resemblance to ice. The Greek word, κρύϛαλλος, is formed from κρύος, ICE, and ϛαλάσσομαι, TO CONCRETE. The word, זכוכית, is translated CRYSTAL, in Job xxviii, 17. Dr. Good observes, "We are not certain of the exact signification, farther than that it denotes some perfectly transparent and hyaline gem."

CUBIT, a measure used among the ancients. The Hebrews call it אמא, the mother of other measures: in Greek ϖῆχυς. A cubit originally was the distance from the elbow to the extremity of the middle finger: this is the fourth part of a well proportioned man's stature. The common cubit is eighteen inches. The Hebrew cubit, according to Bishop Cumberland and M. Pelletier, is twenty-one inches; but others fix it at eighteen inches. The Talmudists observe, that the Hebrew cubit was larger by one quarter than the Roman. Lewis Capellus and others have asserted that there were two sorts of cubits among the Hebrews; one sacred, the other common; the sacred containing three feet, the common containing a foot and a half. Moses assigns to the Levites a thousand sacred cubits of land round about their cities, Num. xxxv, 4; and in the next verse he gives them two thousand common ones. The opinion, however, is very probable, that the cubit varied in different districts and cities, and at different times, &c.

CUCUMBER, קשאים, σίκυος, CUCUMIS, Num. xi, 5, the fruit of a plant very common in our gardens. Tournefort mentions six kinds, of which the white and green are most esteemed. They are very plentiful in the east, especially in

Egypt, and much superior to ours. Maillet, in describing the vegetables which the modern Egyptians have for food, tells us, that melons, cucumbers, and onions are the most common; and Celsius and Alpinus describe the Egyptian cucumbers as more agreeable to the taste and of more easy digestion than the European.

CULDEES, a body of religious, who chiefly resided in Scotland, Ireland, and some of the adjacent isles. The name has been also written KELDEES and KYLDEES. Various etymons have been given of it. Two of these seem to have superior claims to attention. It may be deduced either from Irish CEILE, or, GILLE, a servant, and DE, DIA, God; or from CUIL, CEAL, in Welsh CEL, a sequestered corner, a retreat. The latter seems to derive support from the established sense of KIL, retained in the names of so many places, which, in an early age, have been consecrated to religion. It is more than probable that Christianity had found its way into Scotland before the close of the second century; and that it continued to be professed by a few scattered individuals even before the arrival of Ninian, in the beginning of the fifth. But we have no proof of the existence of any religious societies observing a particular institute, till the year 563, when Columba landed in Hii, or Iona; which, in honour of him, was afterward called I-COLUM-KILL; that is, the isle of Colum, or Columba, of the cells. He was born in Ireland, A. D. 521; and, after founding many seminaries of religion there, prompted by zeal for the propagation of Christianity, set sail for Scotland with twelve companions. According to Bede, having converted the northern Picts, he received from Brudi, their king, the island of Hii in possession, for the purpose of erecting a monastery. Here he almost constantly resided till the year 597, when he died. He made occasional visits to the mainland, proceeding even as far as to Inverness: also to Ireland, where he was held in high estimation. As he was himself much devoted to the study of the Holy Scriptures, he taught his disciples to confirm their doctrines by testimonies brought from this unpolluted fountain, and declared that only to be the divine counsel which he found there. His followers, faithful to his instructions, "would receive those things only which are contained in the writings of the Prophets, Evangelists, and Apostles, diligently observing the works of piety and purity." They lived, indeed, according to a certain institute, which, it is said, was composed by their venerable instructer. But there was this remarkable distinction between them and those societies properly called monastic, that they were not associated expressly for the purpose of observing this rule. While they seem to have reckoned something of this kind necessary for the preservation of order, and for the attainment of habits of diligence, their great design was, by the instruction of those committed to their charge, to train them up for the work of the ministry. Hence it has been justly observed, that the Culdean fraternities may more properly be viewed as colleges than as monasteries; as being in fact, the seminaries of the church both in North Britain and in Ireland. There were also Culdees in Wales; and, for many ages, the Christians of that country held the same doctrines, and observed the same rites, with their Scottish and Irish brethren. The presbyters not only acted as the ministers of religion to those in their vicinity, but were still instructing others, and sending forth missionaries whenever they had a call, or any prospect of success.

2. In each regular establishment of the Culdees, it would appear that there were twelve brethren, with one who presided over them. Their ecclesiastical government has been viewed as materially the same with the Presbyterian. Their president, or abbot, was not a bishop, but a presbyter; to whose authority, as we learn from Bede, even the bishops of the district were subject. In their meetings, all matters were settled by plurality of voices. The members of this council had the general designation of SENIORES, or elders. To them, collectively, belonged the trial of the gifts of those who had been educated in their seminaries, when they were to be employed in the public ministry; from them they received ordination and mission, and to them they were amenable in the discharge of their office. Those whom they thus employed are, by ancient writers, often denominated bishops. But that they attached to this designation no dignity superior to that of presbyter, appears incontrovertible from their being afterward called to account, and sometimes censured by the fraternity. It has been asserted by the friends of diocesan episcopacy, that a bishop MUST always have resided at Iona for the purpose of conferring ordination. But there is not the slightest evidence of this. The contrary appears from all the records of these early ages. We learn from the Saxon Chronicle, that "there was always an abbot at Hii, but no bishop." It is a singular fact, that those who were first acknowledged as bishops in the northern parts of England, and were indeed instrumental in the introduction of Christianity there, were not only trained up at Iona, but received all their authority from the council of seniors in that island. This was the case with respect to Corman, the bishop of the Northumbrians, as well as Aidan, Finan, and Colman, who succeeded each other in this mission. From the testimony of Bede, it is evident that by means of Scottish missionaries, or of those whom they had instructed and ordained, not only the Northumbrians, but the Middle-Angles, the Mercians and East-Saxons, all the way to the river Thames, that is, the inhabitants of by far the greatest part of the country now called England, were converted to Christianity; and for some time acknowledged subjection to the ecclesiastical government of the Scots. The latter lost their influence merely because their missionaries chose rather to give up their charges than to submit to the prevailing influence of the church of Rome, to which the Saxons of the west and of Kent had subjected themselves.

3. Their doctrines were not less unpalatable than their mode of government to the friends of the church of Rome. In England, in a very early period, the adherents of the Popish missionary Augustine were viewed by the delegates from Iona in the light of heretics. They accordingly refused to hold communion with them. Matters were carried so high in support of the Roman authority in the synod of Stroneschalch, now Whitby, in England, A. D. 662, that Colman, the Scottish bishop of Lindisfarne, left his

bishopric, and with his adherents returned to Scotland. Thus, as Bede informs us, "the Catholic institution daily increasing, all the Scots who resided among the Angles, either conformed to them or returned to their own country." It was decreed in the council of Cealhythe, A. D. 816, that no Scottish priest should be allowed to perform any duty of his function in England. But in Scotland the Culdean doctrine had taken deeper root; and, although equally offensive to the votaries of Rome, kept its ground for several centuries. The Popish writers themselves celebrate the piety, the purity, the humility, and even the learning, of the Culdees; but while they were displeased with the simplicity, or what they deemed the barbarism, of their worship, they charged them with various deviations from the faith of the Catholic church. It was not the least of these, that they did not observe Easter at the proper time. They did not acknowledge auricular confession; they rejected penance and authoritative absolution; they made no use of chrism in baptism; confirmation was unknown; they opposed the doctrine of the real presence; they withstood the idolatrous worship of saints and angels, dedicating all their churches to the Holy Trinity; they denied the doctrine of works of supererogation; they were enemies to the celibacy of the clergy, themselves living in the married state. One sweeping charge brought against them is, that they preferred their own opinions to "the statutes of the holy fathers."

4. The Scots, having received the Christian faith by the labours of the Culdees, long withstood the errors and usurpations of Rome. It was not till the twelfth century that their influence began to decline. The difference between the lower classes of society in England and those of the same description in Scotland, both with respect to religious knowledge and moral conduct, is generally considered to be very striking. Some writers, whose attention has been arrested by this singular circumstance, and who could not be influenced by local attachments, have ascribed the disparity to the relative influence, however remote it may seem, of the doctrine and example of the Culdees. Notwithstanding their great disinterestedness and diligence in propagating the Gospel in England, these good men, it has been remarked, within thirty years after the commencement of their mission, were obliged to give way to the adherents of Rome; whereas the Scots, it is certainly known, enjoyed the benefit of their labours for more than seven centuries, and seem to have still retained their predilection for the doctrines and modes which they so early received.

CUMMIN, כמון, Isaiah xxviii, 25, 27; κύμινον, Matt. xxiii, 23. This is an umbelliferous plant, in appeara resembling fennel, but smaller. Is seeds have a bitterish warm taste, accompanied with an aromatic flavour, not of the most agreeable kind. An essential oil is obtained from them by distillation. The Jews sowed it in their fields, and when ripe threshed out the seeds with a rod, Isaiah xxviii, 25, 27. The Maltese sow it, and collect the seeds in the same manner.

CUP. This word is taken in a twofold sense; proper, and figurative. In a proper sense, it signifies a vessel, such as people drink out of at meals, Gen. xl, 13. It was anciently the custom, at great entertainments, for the governor of the feast to appoint to each of his guests the kind and proportion of wine which they were to drink, and what he had thus appointed them it was deemed a breach of good manners either to refuse or not to drink up; hence a man's cup, both in sacred and profane authors, came to signify the portion, whether of good or evil, which happens to him in this world. Thus, to drink "the cup of trembling," or of "the fury of the Lord," is to be afflicted with sore and terrible judgments, Isaiah li, 17; Jeremiah xxv, 15–29; Psalm lxxv, 8. What Christ means by the expression, we cannot be at a loss to understand, since in two remarkable passages, Luke xxii, 42, and John xviii, 11, he has been his own interpreter. LETHALE POCULUM BIBERE, "to drink the deadly cup," or cup of death, was a common phrase among the Jews; and from them, we have reason to believe, our Lord borrowed it.

Cup of Blessing, 1 Corinth. x, 16, is that which was blessed in entertainments of ceremony, or solemn services; or, rather, a cup over which God was blessed for having furnished its contents; that is, for giving to men the fruit of the vine. Our Saviour, in the Last Supper, blessed the cup, and gave it to each of his Apostles to drink, Luke xxii, 20.

Cup of Salvation, Psalm cxvi, 13, a phrase of nearly the same import as the former, a cup of thanksgiving, of blessing the Lord for his saving mercies. We see, in 2 Macc. vi, 27, that the Jews of Egypt, in their festivals for deliverance, offered cups of salvation. The Jews have at this day cups of thanksgiving, which are blessed, in their marriage ceremonies, and in entertainments made at the circumcision of their children. Some commentators think that "the cup of salvation" was a libation of wine poured on the victim sacrificed on thanksgiving occasions, according to the law of Moses, Exod. xxix, 40.

CURSE. To curse, signifies to imprecate, to call for mischief upon, or wish evil to, any one. Noah cursed his grandson Canaan, Gen. ix, 25: Jacob cursed the fury of his two sons, Gen. xlix, 7: Moses enjoins the people of Israel to denounce curses against the violaters of the law, Deut. xxvii, 15, 16, &c. Joshua pronounced a curse upon him who should undertake to rebuild Jericho. These curses were such as were either ordained by God himself, and pronounced by men under the influence of his Spirit; or they were predictions of certain evils which would happen to individuals, or to a people, uttered in the form of imprecations. They were not the effects of passion, impatience, or revenge; and, therefore, were not things condemned by God in his law, like the cursing mentioned, Exodus xxi, 17, xxii, 28, Leviticus xix, 14.

CUSH, the eldest son of Ham, and father of Nimrod, Seba, Havilah, Sabtah, Raamah, and Sabtecha; and the grandfather of Sheba and Dedan. The posterity of Cush, spread over great part of Asia and Africa, were called Cushim, or Cushites; and by the Greeks and Romans, and in our Bible, Ethiopians.

Cush, Cutha, Cuthea, Cushan, Ethiopia, LAND OF CUSH, the country or countries peopled by the descendants of Cush; whose first plantations were on the gulf of Persia, in that part which still bears the name of Chuzestan, and from whence they spread over India and great part of Arabia; particularly its western part, on the coast of the Red Sea; invaded Egypt, under the name of Hyc-Sos, or shepherd-kings; and thence passed, as well probably as by the straits of Babelmandel, into Central Africa, and first peopled the countries to the south of Egypt, Nubia, Abyssinia, and parts farther to the south and west. The indiscriminate use of the term Ethiopia in our Bible, for all the countries peopled by the posterity of Cush, and the almost exclusive application of the same term by the Greek and Roman writers to the before mentioned countries of Africa, have involved some portions of both sacred and profane history in almost inextricable confusion. The first country which bore this name, and which was doubtless the original settlement, was that which is described by Moses as encompassed by the river Gihon, or Gyndes; which encircles a great part of the province of Chuzestan in Persia. In process of time, the increasing family spread over the vast territory of India and Arabia: the whole of which tract, from the Ganges to the borders of Egypt, then became the land of Cush, or Asiatic Ethiopia, the CUSHA DWEEPA WITHIN, of Hindoo geography. Until dispossessed of this country, or a great part of it, by the posterity of Abraham, the Ishmaelites and Midianites, they, by a farther dispersion, passed over into Africa; which, in its turn, became the land of Cush, or Ethiopia, the CUSHA DWEEPA WITHOUT, of the Hindoos: the only country so understood after the commencement of the Christian æra. Even from this last refuge, they were compelled, by the influx of fresh settlers from Arabia, Egypt, and Canaan, to extend their migrations still farther westward, into the heart of the African continent; where only in the woolly-headed negro, the genuine Cushite is to be found.

Herodotus relates that Xerxes had, in the army prepared for his Grecian expedition, both Oriental and African Ethiopians: and adds, that they resembled each other in every outward circumstance except their hair; that of the Asiatic Ethiopians being long and straight, while the hair of those of Africa was curled. This is a very remarkable fact; and leads to the question, How came this singular distinction between people of the same stock? Did it arise from change of climate and of habits? or from some original difference in a particular branch of the great family of Cush? The former appears by far the more probable. It is not likely that a people descended from a common parent should naturally be distinguished by such a peculiar difference; but that it might be acquired by change of soil and condition, we have every reason to believe. We have something exactly analogous to it, in the change which the hair of animals undergoes when removed from their native state. But a modern writer has furnished us with a fact which will go farther than either theory or analogy. Dr. Prichard, in his researches into the Physical History of Man, relates, on the authority of Dr. S. S. Smith, of the negroes settled in the southern districts of the United States of America, that the field-slaves, who live on the plantations, and retain pretty nearly the rude manners of their African progenitors, preserve in the third generation much of their original structure, though their features are not so strongly marked as those of imported slaves. But the domestic servants of the same race, who are treated with lenity, and whose condition is little different from that of the lower class of white people, in the third generation have the nose raised, the mouth and lips of moderate size, the eyes lively and sparkling, and often the whole composition of the features extremely agreeable. "The hair grows sensibly longer in each succeeding race, and extends to three, four, and sometimes to six or eight inches."

About four hundred years before Christ, Herodotus, in his second book which treats of Egypt, makes frequent mention of Ethiopia; meaning exclusively the Ethiopia above Egypt. In the time of our Saviour, (and indeed from that time forward,) by Ethiopia, was meant, in a general sense, the countries south of Egypt, then but imperfectly known: of one of which, that Candace was queen whose eunuch was baptized by Philip.

From a review of the history of this remarkable people, we may see that those writers must necessarily be wrong who would confine the Ethiopians to either Arabia or Africa. Many parts of Scripture history cannot possibly be understood, without supposing them to have settlements in both; which Herodotus expressly asserts was the case. In fine, we may conclude, that in the times of the prophets, and during the transactions recorded in the second books of Kings and Chronicles, the Cushites, still retaining a part of their ancient territories in Arabia, had crossed the Red Sea in great numbers, and obtained extensive possessions in Africa; where, being, in a farther course of time, altogether expelled from the east by the Ishmaelites, &c, their remains are now concentrated. It is to be observed, however, that the Cushites probably at the time of their expulsion from Egypt, migrated, or sent colonies into several other parts, particularly to Phenicia, Colchis, and Greece; where, in process of time, they became blended with the other inhabitants of those countries, the families of Javan, Meshek, and Tubal, and their distinctive character totally lost.

CYPRESS, תרזה, Isa. xliv, 14; and κυπάρισσος, Ecclus. xxiv, 13; l, 10; a large evergreen tree. The wood is fragrant, very compact, and heavy. It scarcely ever rots, decays, or is worm-eaten; for which reason the ancients used to make the statues of their gods with it. The unperishable chests which contain the Egyptian mummies were of cypress. The gates of St. Peter's church at Rome, which had lasted from the time of Constantine to that of Pope Eugene **IV**, that is to say eleven hundred years, were of cypress, and had in that time suffered no decay. But Celsius thinks that Isaiah speaks of the ilex, a kind of oak; and Bishop Lowth, that the pine is intended. The cypress, however, was more frequently used, and more fit for the purpose which the prophet mentions, than either of these trees.

CYPRUS, a large island in the Mediterranean, situated between Cilicia and Syria. Its inhabitants were plunged in all manner of luxury and debauchery. Their principal deity was Venus. The Apostles Paul and Barnabas landed in the isle of Cyprus, A. D. 44, Acts xiii, 4. While they continued at Salamis, they preached Jesus Christ in the Jewish synagogues; from thence they visited all the cities of the island, preaching the Gospel. At Paphos, they found Bar-Jesus, a false prophet, with Sergius Paulus, the governor: Paul struck Bar-Jesus with blindness; and the proconsul embraced Christianity. Some time after, Barnabas went again into this island with John, surnamed Mark, Acts xv, 39. Barnabas is considered as the principal Apostle, and first bishop, of Cyprus; where it is said he was martyred, being stoned to death by the Jews of Salamis.

CYRENE was a city of Lybia in Africa, which, as it was the principal city of that province, gave to it the name of Cyrenaica. This city was once so powerful as to contend with Carthage for preëminence. In profane writers, it is mentioned as the birthplace of Eratosthenes the mathematician, and Callimachus the poet; and in holy writ, of Simon, whom the Jews compelled to bear our Saviour's cross, Matt. xxvii, 32; Luke xxiii, 26. At Cyrene resided many Jews, a great part of whom embraced the Christian religion; but others opposed it with much obstinacy. Among the most inveterate enemies of Christianity, Luke reckons those of this province, who had a synagogue at Jerusalem, and excited the people against St. Stephen, Acts xi, 20.

CYRENIUS, governor of Syria, Luke ii, 1, 2. Great difficulties have been raised on the history of the taxing under Cyrenius, for the different solutions of which we must refer to the commentators.

It may be observed on the passage in Luke ii, 1, 2, That the word οἰϰ8μένη, rendered ALL THE WORLD, sometimes signifies the whole of a country, region, or district, as perhaps Acts xi, 28, and certainly Luke xxi, 26. The expression, "all the country," is peculiarly proper in this place, because Galilee, as well as Judea, was included, and perhaps all other parts in which were Jews. The word ἀπογϱαφὴ, which is rendered TAXING, should have been translated ENROLMENT; as a taxation did not always really follow such enrolment, though such enrolment generally preceded a taxation. The difficulty of the passage is in the word ϖϱώτη, FIRST, because, ten or eleven years after, there was actually a taxation, which, as a decisive mark of subjection to the Roman power, was very mortifying to the Jewish nation. To this taxation Gamaliel alludes, "Judas of Galilee rose up in the days of the taxing," Acts v, 37, when mobs and riots were frequent, under pretence of liberty.

The narrative of St. Luke may be combined in the following order, which is probably not far from its true import: "In those days Cæsar Augustus," who was displeased with the conduct of Herod, and wished him to feel his dependence on the Roman empire, "issued a decree that the whole land" of Judea "should be enrolled," as well persons as possessions, that the true state of the inhabitants, their families, and their property, might be known and recorded. Accordingly, "all were enrolled," but the taxation did not immediately follow this enrolment, because Augustus was reconciled to Herod; and this accounts for the silence of Josephus on an assessment not carried into effect. "And this was the first assessment (or enrolment) of Cyrenius, governor of Syria. And all went to be enrolled, each to his own city;" and, as the emperor's order was urgent, and Cyrenius was known to be active in the despatch of business, even Mary, though far advanced "in her pregnancy, went with Joseph, and while they waited" for their turn to be enrolled, "Mary was delivered of Jesus." It is not, however, improbable, that Mary had some small landed estate, for which her appearance was necessary. Jesus, therefore, was enrolled with Mary and Joseph, as Julian the Apostate expressly says.

An officer being sent from Rome to enrol and assess the subjects of a king, implied that such king was dependent on the Roman emperor, and demonstrates that the sceptre was departed from Judah. This occurrence, added to the alarm of Herod on the inquiry of the Magi respecting the birthplace of the Messiah, might sufficiently exasperate Herod, not merely to slay the infants of Bethlehem, but to every act of cruelty. Hence, after such an occurrence, all Jerusalem might well be alarmed with Herod, Matt. ii, 3; and the priests, &c, study caution in their answers to him. This occurrence would quicken the attention of all who expected temporal redemption in Israel, as it would extremely mortify every Jewish national feeling.

The overruling providence of God appointed, that, at the time of Christ's birth, there should be a public, authentic, and general production of titles, pedigrees, &c, which should prove that Jesus was descended from the house and direct family line of David; and that this should be proved judicially on such a scrutinizing occasion. This occurrence brought about the birth of the Messiah, at the very place appointed by prophecy long before, though the usual residence of Joseph and Mary was at Nazareth.

CYRUS, son of Cambyses the Persian, and of Mandane, daughter of Astyages, king of the Medes. At the age of thirty, Cyrus was made general of the Persian troops, and sent, at the head of thirty thousand men, to assist his uncle, Cyaxares, whom the Babylonians were preparing to attack. Cyaxares and Cyrus gave them battle, and dispersed them. After this, Cyrus carried the war into the countries beyond the river Halys; subdued Cappadocia; marched against Crœsus, king of Lydia, defeated him, and took Sardis, his capital. Having reduced almost all Asia, Cyrus repassed the Euphrates, and turned his arms against the Assyrians: having defeated them, he laid siege to Babylon, which he took on a festival day, after having diverted the course of the river which ran through it. On his return to Persia, he married his cousin, the daughter and heiress of Cyaxares; after which he engaged in several wars, and subdued all the nations between

Syria and the Red Sea. He died at the age of seventy, after a reign of thirty years. Authors differ much concerning the manner of his death.

2. We learn few particulars respecting Cyrus from Scripture; but they are more certain than those derived from other sources. Daniel, in the remarkable vision in which God showed him the ruin of several great empires which preceded the birth of the Messiah, represents Cyrus as "a ram which had two horns, both high, but one rose higher than the other, and the higher came up last. This ram pushed westward, and northward, and southward, so that no beasts might stand before him, neither was there any that could deliver out of his hand; but he did according to his will, and became great," Daniel viii, 3, 4, 20. The two horns signify the two empires which Cyrus united in his person, that of the Medes and that of the Persians. In another place, Daniel compares Cyrus to a bear, with three ribs in its mouth, to which it was said, "Arise, devour much flesh." Cyrus succeeded Cambyses in the kingdom of Persia, and Darius the Mede (by Xenophon called Cyaxares, and Astyages in the Greek of Dan. xiii, 65,) also in the kingdom of the Medes, and the empire of Babylon. He was monarch, as he speaks "of all the earth," Ezra i, 1, 2; 2 Chron. xxxvi, 22, 23, when he permitted the Jews to return into their own country, A. M. 3466, B. C. 538. He had always a particular regard for Daniel, and continued him in his great employments.

3. The prophets foretold the exploits of Cyrus. Isaiah, xliv, 28, particularly declares his name, above a century before he was born. Josephus says, that the Jews of Babylon showed this passage to Cyrus; and that, in the edict which he granted for their return, he acknowledged that he received the empire of the world from the God of Israel. The peculiar designation by name, which Cyrus received, must be regarded as one of the most remarkable circumstances in the prophetic writings. He was the heir of a monarch who ruled over one of the poorest and most inconsiderable kingdoms of Asia, but whose hardy inhabitants were at that time the bravest of the brave; and the providential circumstances in which he was placed precluded him from all knowledge of this oracular declaration in his favour. He did not become acquainted with the sacred books in which it was contained, nor with the singular people in whose possession it was found, till he had accomplished all the purposes for which he had been raised up, except that of saying to Jerusalem, as the "anointed" vicegerent of Heaven, "Thou shalt be inhabited;" and to the cities of Judah, "Ye shall be built, and I will raise up their ruins." The national pride of the Jews during the days of their unhallowed prosperity, would hinder them from divulging among other nations such prophecies as this, which contained the most severe yet deserved reflections upon their wicked practices and ungrateful conduct; and it was only when they were captives in Babylon that they submitted to the humiliating expedient of exhibiting, to the mighty monarch whose bondmen they had become, the prophetic record of their own apostasy and punishment, and of his still higher destination, as the rebuilder of Jerusalem. No temptation therefore could be laid before the conqueror in early life to excite his latent ambition to accomplish this very full and explicit prophecy; and the facts of his life, as recorded by historians of very opposite sentiments and feelings, all concur in developing a series of consecutive events, in which he acted no insignificant part; which, though astonishing in their results, differ greatly from those rapid strides perceptible in the hurried career of other mighty men of war in the east; and which, from the unbroken connection in which they are presented to us, appear like the common occurrences of life naturally following each other, and mutually dependent. Yet this consideration does not preclude the presence of a mighty Spirit working within him; which, according to Isaiah, said to him, "I will gird thee, though thou hast not known me." Concerning the genius, or guardian angel, of Socrates many learned controversies have arisen; but, though a few of the disputants have endeavoured to explain it away, the majority of them have left the Greek philosopher in possession of a greater portion of inspiration than, with marvellous inconsistency, some of them are willing to accord to the Jewish prophets. In this view it is highly interesting to recollect that the elegant historian who first informed his refined countrymen of this moral prodigy, is he who subsequently introduced them to an acquaintance with the noble and heroic Cyrus. The didactic discourses and the comparatively elevated morality which Xenophon embodied in his "Memoirs of Socrates," are generally admitted to have been purposely illustrated in his subsequent admirable production, the *Cyropædia*, or "Education of Cyrus;" the basis of which is true history adorned and refined by philosophy, and exhibiting for universal imitation the life and actions of a prince who was cradled in the ancient Persian school of the Pischdadians, the parent of the Socratic. Isaiah describes, in fine poetic imagery, the Almighty going before Cyrus to remove every obstruction out of his way:--

"I will go before thee, and level mountains,

I will burst asunder the folding-doors of brass,

And split in twain the bars of iron.

Even I will give thee the dark treasures,

And the hidden wealth of secret places:

That thou mayest know, that I the Lord,

Who call thee by thy name, am the God of ISRAEL."

According to Herodotus, Babylon was famous for its brazen gates and doors; a hundred were in the city walls, beside those which led to the river, and others which belonged to the temple of Belus. When Sardis and Babylon were taken by Cyrus, they were the wealthiest cities in the world. Crœsus gave an exact inventory of his immense treasures to Cyrus, and they were removed from Sardis in waggons. Pliny gives the following account of the wealth which Cyrus obtained by his conquests in Asia: "He found thirty-four thousand pounds' weight of gold, beside vessels of gold, and gold wrought into the leaves of a platanus and of a vine; five hundred thousand talents of silver, and the cup of Semiramis, which weighed fifteen talents. The Egyptian talent, according to Varro, was equal to eighty pounds." Mr. Brerewood estimates the value of the gold and silver in this enumeration at 126,224,000*l.* sterling. Other particulars relating to him, and the accomplishment of prophecy in his conquest of that large city, will be found under the article BABYLON. It is the God of Israel who, in these sublime prophecies, confounds the omens and prognostics of the Babylonian soothsayers or diviners, after they had predicted the stability of that empire; and who announces the restoration of Israel, and the rebuilding of the city and temple of Jerusalem, through Cyrus his "shepherd" and his "anointed" messenger. Chosen thus by God to execute his high behests, he subdued and reigned over many nations,--the Cilicians, Syrians, Paphlagonians, Cappadocians, Phrygians, Lydians, Carians, Phenicians, Arabians, Egyptians, Babylonians, Assyrians, Bactrians, &c.

"I am He who frustrateth the tokens of the impostors,

And maketh the diviners mad; &c.

Who saith to the abyss, [Babylon,]

'Be desolate, and I will dry up thy rivers:'

Who saith to Cyrus, 'He is my shepherd,

And shall perform all my pleasure.'

Thus saith the Lord to his anointed,

To Cyrus whom I hold by the right hand,

To subdue before him nations,

And ungird the loins of kings,

To open before him [palace] folding-doors;

Even [river] gates shall not be shut:

For Jacob my servant's sake, and Israel my chosen,

I have surnamed thee;" &c.

4. Herodotus has painted the portrait of Cyrus in dark colours, and has been followed in many particulars by Ctesias, Diodorus Siculus, Dionysius of Halicarnassus, Plato, Strabo, Justin, and others; in opposition to the contrary accounts of Æschylus, Xenophon, Josephus, the Persian historians, and, apparently, the Holy Scriptures. The motive for this conduct of Herodotus is probably to be found in his aversion to Cyrus, for having been the enslaver of his country. The Greek historian was a man of free and independent spirit, and could never brook the mention of the surrender of his native city, Halicarnassus, to the troops of Cyrus. But, allowing that heartlessness and cruelty are too often the accompaniments of mighty conquerors, and that very few escape their direful contagion; yet, when the worst is told about Cyrus, abundance of authentic facts remain to attest his worth, and to elevate his character above the standard of ordinary mortals. Xenophon informs us, that the seven last years of his full sovereignty this prince spent in peace and tranquillity at home, revered and beloved by all classes of his subjects. In his dying moments he was surrounded by his family, friends, and children; and delivered to them the noblest exhortations to the practice of piety, virtue, and concord. This testimony is in substance confirmed by the Persian historians, who relate, that, after a long and bloody war, Khosru, or Cyrus, subdued the empire of Turan, and made the city of Balk, in Chorasan, a royal residence, to keep in order his new subjects; that he repaid every family in Persia proper the amount of their war-taxes, out of the immense spoils which he had acquired by his conquests; that he endeavoured to promote peace and harmony between the Turanians and Iranians; that he regulated the pay of his soldiery, reformed civil and religious abuses throughout the provinces, and, at length, after a long and glorious reign, resigned the crown to his son Lohorasp, and retired to solitude, confessing that he had lived long enough for his own glory, and that it was then time for him to devote the remainder of his days to God. Saadi, in his Gulistan, copies the wise inscription which Cyrus ordered to be inscribed on his crown: "What avails a long life spent in the enjoyment of worldly grandeur, since others, mortal like ourselves, will one day trample under foot our pride! This crown, handed down to me from my predecessors, must soon pass in succession upon the head of many others." In the last book of the "Cyropædia" we find the following devout thanksgivings to the gods: "I am abundantly thankful for being truly sensible of your care, and for never being elated by prosperity above my condition. I beseech you to prosper my children, wife, friends, and country. And for myself, I ask, that such as is the life ye have vouchsafed to me, such may be my end." The reflections of Dr. Hales on this passage are very judicious: "Here, Xenophon, a polytheist himself, represents Cyrus praying to the gods in the plural number; but that he really prayed to one only, the patriarchal God, worshipped by his venerable ancestors, the Pischdadians, may appear from the watchword, or signal, which he gave to his soldiers before the great battle, in which Evil Merodach was slain:

ΖΕΥΣ ΣΩΤΗΡ ΚΑΙ ῾ΗΓΕΜΩΝ.

"JOVE, OUR SAVIOUR AND LEADER."

Who this god was, we learn from the preamble of his famous proclamation, permitting the Jews to return from the Babylonian captivity: 'The Lord, the God of heaven, hath given me all the kingdoms of the earth, and he hath charged me to build him a house at Jerusalem,' &c, Ezra i, 1, 2. But where did the Lord, (Iahoh, or Jove) so charge him?--In that signal prophecy of Isaiah, predicting his name and his actions, about B. C. 712, above a century before his birth; a prophecy which was undoubtedly communicated to him by the venerable Prophet Daniel, the Archimagus, who saw the beginning of the Babylonish captivity, and also its end, here foretold to be effected by the instrumentality of Cyrus."

5. Pliny notices the tomb of Cyrus at Passagardæ in Persia. Arrian and Strabo describe it; and they agree with Curtius, that Alexander the Great offered funeral honours to his shade there; that he opened the tomb, and found, not the treasures he expected, but a rotten shield, two Scythian bows, and a Persian scymetar. And Plutarch records the following inscription upon it, in his life of Alexander:--"O man, whoever thou art, and whenever thou comest, (for come, I know, thou wilt,) I am Cyrus, the founder of the Persian empire. Envy me not the little earth that covers my body." Alexander was much affected at this inscription, which set before him, in so striking a light, the uncertainty and vicissitude of worldly things. And he placed the crown of gold which he wore, upon the tomb in which the body lay, wondering that a prince so renowned, and possessed of such immense treasures, had not been buried more sumptuously than if he had been a private person. Cyrus, indeed, in his last instructions to his children, desired that "his body, when he died, might not be deposited in gold or silver, nor in any other sumptuous monument, but committed, as soon as possible, to the ground."

The observation which Dr. Hales here makes, is worthy of record:--"This is a most signal and extraordinary epitaph. It seems to have been designed as a useful MEMENTO MORI, [memento of death,] for Alexander the Great, in the full pride of conquest, "whose coming" it predicts with a prophetic spirit, "For come I know thou wilt." But how could Cyrus know of his coming?--Very easily. Daniel the Archimagus, his venerable friend, who warned the haughty Nebuchadnezzar, that "head of gold," or founder of the Babylonian empire, that it should be subverted by "the breast and arms of silver," Dan. ii, 37, 39, or "the Mede and the Persian," Darius and Cyrus, as he more plainly told the impious Belshazzar, Dan. v, 28, we may rest assured, communicated to Cyrus also, the founder of the Persian empire, the symbolical vision of the goat, with the notable horn in his forehead, Alexander of Macedon coming swiftly from the west, to overturn the Persian empire, Daniel viii, 5, 8, under the last king Codomannus, the fourth from Darius Nothus, as afterward more distinctly explained, Dan. xi, 1, 4. Cyrus, therefore, decidedly addresses the short-lived conqueror, O MAN, WHOEVER THOU ART, &C.

"Juvenal, in that noble satire, the tenth, verse 168, has a fine reflection on the vanity of Alexander's wild ambition to conquer worlds, soon destined himself to be confined in a narrow coffin; by a pointed allusion to the epitaph on the tomb of Cyrus:--

UNUS PELLÆO JUVENI NON SUFFICIT ORBIS;

ÆSTUAT, INFELIX ANGUSTO LIMITE MUNDI:

CUM TAMEN A FIGULIS MUNITAM INTRAVERIT URBEM,

SARCOPHAGO CONTENTUS ERIT.--MORS SOLA FATETUR

QUANTULA SINT HOMINUM CORPUSCULA!"

'A single globe suffices not the Pellæan youth;

Discontented, he scorns the scanty limits of the world;

As if within a prison's narrow bounds confined:

But when he shall enter the BRICK-WALLED city, [Babylon,]

A coffin will content him.--THE EPITAPH ALONE OWNS,

HOW SMALL ARE THE DIMINUTIVE BODIES OF MEN!'

"The emotion of Alexander, on visiting the tomb, and reading the inscription, is not less remarkable. He evidently applied to himself, as the destroyer, the awful rebuke of the founder of the Persian empire, for violating the sanctity of his tomb, from motives of profane curiosity, and perhaps of avarice. And we may justly consider the significant act of laying down his golden crown upon the tomb itself, as an AMENDE HONORABLE, a homage due to the offended shade of the pious and lowly-minded Cyrus the Great." These reflections must close our account of one of the most remarkable characters that ever appeared among the eastern conquerors.

DAGON, דגון, CORN, from דגן, or דג, A FISH, god of the Philistines. It is the opinion of some that Dagon was represented like a woman, with the lower parts of a fish, like a triton or syren. Scripture shows clearly that the statue of Dagon was human, at least, the upper part of it, 1 Sam. v, 4, 5. A temple of Dagon at Gaza was pulled down by Samson,

Judges xvi, 23, &c. In another, at Ashdod, the Philistines deposited the ark of God, 1 Sam. v, 1–3. A city in Judah was called Beth-Dagon; that is, the house, or temple, of Dagon, Joshua xv, 41; and another on the frontiers of Asher, Joshua xix, 27.

DALMANUTHA. St. Mark says that Jesus Christ embarked with his disciples on the lake of Tiberias, and came to Dalmanutha, Mark viii, 10, but St. Matthew calls it Magdala, Matt. xv, 39. It seems that Dalmanutha was near to Magdala, on the western side of the lake.

DALMATIA, a part of old Illyria, lying along the gulf of Venice. Titus preached here, 2 Tim. iv, 10.

DAMASCUS, a celebrated city of Asia, and anciently the capital of Syria, may be accounted one of the most venerable places in the world for its antiquity. It is supposed to have been founded by Ux, the son of Aram; and is, at least, known to have subsisted in the time of Abraham, Gen. xv, 2. It was the residence of the Syrian kings, during the space of three centuries; and experienced a number of vicissitudes in every period of its history. Its sovereign, Hadad, whom Josephus calls the first of its kings, was conquered by David, king of Israel. In the reign of Ahaz, it was taken by Tiglath Pileser, who slew its last king, Rezin, and added its provinces to the Assyrian empire. It was taken and plundered, also, by Sennacherib, Nebuchadnezzar, the generals of Alexander the Great, Judas Maccabeus, and at length by the Romans in the war conducted by Pompey against Tigranes, in the year before Christ, 65. During the time of the emperors, it was one of their principal arsenals in Asia, and is celebrated by the emperor Julian as, even in his day, "the eye of the whole east." About the year 634, it was taken by the Saracen princes, who made it the place of their residence, till Bagdad was prepared for their reception; and, after suffering a variety of revolutions, it was taken and destroyed by Tamerlane, A. D. 1400. It was repaired by the Mamelukes, when they gained possession of Syria; but was wrested from them by the Turks, in 1506; and since that period has formed the capital of one of their pachalics. The modern city is delightfully situated about fifty miles from the sea, in a fertile and extensive plain, watered by the river which the Greeks called Chrysorrhoras, or "Golden River," but which is known by the name of Barrady, and of which the ancient Abana and Pharpar are supposed to have been branches. The city is nearly two miles in length from its north-east to its north-west extremity; but of very inconsiderable breadth, especially near the middle of its extent, where its width is much contracted. It is surrounded by a circular wall, which is strong, though not lofty; but its suburbs are extensive and irregular. Its streets are narrow; and one of them, called Straight, mentioned in Acts ix, 11, still runs through the city about half a mile in length. The houses, and especially those which front the streets, are very indifferently built, chiefly of mud formed into the shape of bricks, and dried in the sun; but those toward the gardens, and in the squares, present a more handsome appearance. In these mud walls, however, the gates and doors are often adorned with marble portals, carved and inlaid with great beauty and variety; and the inside of the habitation, which is generally a large square court, is ornamented with fragrant trees and marble fountains, and surrounded with splendid apartments, furnished and painted in the highest style of luxury. The market places are well constructed, and adorned with a rich colonnade of variegated marble. The principal public buildings are, the castle, which is about three hundred and forty paces in length; the hospital, a charitable establishment for the reception of strangers, composing a large quadrangle lined with a colonnade, and roofed in small domes covered with lead; and the mosque, the entrance of which is supported by four large columns of red granite; the apartments in it are numerous and magnificent, and the top is covered with a cupola ornamented with two minarets.

Damascus is surrounded by a fruitful and delightful country, forming a plain nearly eighty miles in circumference; and the lands, most adjacent to the city, are formed into gardens of great extent, which are stored with fruit trees of every description. "No place in the world," says Mr. Maundrell "can promise to the beholder at a distance a greater voluptuousness;" and he mentions a tradition of the Turks, that their prophet, when approaching Damascus, took his station upon a certain precipice, in order to view the city; and, after considering its ravishing beauty and delightful aspect, was unwilling to tempt his frailty by going farther; but instantly took his departure with this remark, that there was but one paradise designed for man, and that, for his part, he was resolved not to take his in this world. The air or water of Damascus, or both, are supposed to have a powerful effect in curing the leprosy, or, at least, in arresting its progress, while the patient remains in the place.

The Rev. James Conner visited Damascus in 1820, as an agent of the Church Missionary Society. He had a letter from the archbishop of Cyprus to Seraphim, patriarch of Antioch, the head of the Christian church in the east, who resides at Damascus. This good man received Mr. Conner in the most friendly manner; and expressed himself delighted with the system and operations of the Bible Society. He undertook to encourage and promote, to the utmost of his power, the sale and distribution of the Scriptures throughout the patriarchate; and, as a proof of his earnestness in the cause, he ordered, the next day, a number of letters to be prepared, and sent to his archbishops and bishops, urging them to promote the objects of the Bible Society in their respective stations.

DAMN, and DAMNATION, are words synonymous with condemn and condemnation. Generally speaking, the words are taken to denote the final and eternal punishment of the ungodly. These terms, however, sometimes occur in the New Testament in what may be termed a less strict, or secondary sense. Thus, when the Apostle says to the Romans, "He that doubteth," namely, the lawfulness of what he is doing, "is DAMNED if he eat," Rom. xiv, 23; the meaning is, he stands condemned in his own mind. Again: when St. Paul tells the Corinthians, that "he that eateth and drinketh" of the Lord's Supper "unworthily, eateth and drinketh DAMNATION to himself," 1 Cor. xi, 29; the original word, κρίμα, there is thought by many to import no more than temporal judgments, and that the Apostle explains himself in the same sense when he says, "For this cause many among you are weak and sickly, and many sleep," or die. This is at least one mode of interpreting the "damnation" of which St. Paul here speaks; but probably the true sense is the bringing guilt upon the conscience, and thereby a liability, without remission, to future judgment.

DAN, the fifth son of Jacob, Gen. xxx, 1–6. Dan had but one son, whose name was Hushim, Gen. xlvi, 23; yet he had a numerous posterity; for, on leaving Egypt, this tribe consisted of sixty-two thousand seven hundred men able to bear arms, Num. i, 38. Of Jacob's blessing Dan, see Gen. xlix, 16, 17. They took Laish, Judges xviii, 1; Joshua xix, 47. They called the city Dan, after their progenitor. The city of Dan was situated at the northern extremity of the land of Israel: hence the phrase, "from Dan to Beersheba," denoting the whole length of the land of promise. Here Jeroboam, the son of Nebat, set up one of his golden calves, 1 Kings xii, 29; and the other at Bethel.

DANCING. It is still the custom in the east to testify their respect for persons of distinction by music and dancing. When Baron Du Tott, who was sent by the French government to inspect their factories in the Levant, approached an encampment of Turcomans, between Aleppo and Alexandretta, the musicians of the different hordes turned out, playing and dancing before him all the time he and his escort were passing by their camp. Thus, it will be recollected, "the women came out of all the cities of Israel, singing and dancing, to meet King Saul, with tabrets, with joy, and with instruments of music," when he returned in triumph from the slaughter of the Philistines. In the oriental dances, in which the women engage by themselves, the lady of highest rank in the company takes the lead, and is followed by her companions, who imitate her steps, and if she sings, make up the chorus. The tunes are extremely gay and lively, yet with something in them wonderfully soft. The steps are varied according to the pleasure of her who leads the dance, but always in exact time. This statement may enable us to form a correct idea of the dance, which the women of Israel performed under the direction of Miriam, on the banks of the Red Sea. The prophetess, we are told, "took a timbrel in her hand, and all the women went out after her, with timbrels and dances." She led the dance, while they imitated her steps, which were not conducted according to a set, well-known form, as in this country, but extemporaneous. The conjecture of Mr. Harmer is extremely probable, that David did not dance alone before the Lord, when he brought up the ark, but, as being the highest in rank, and more skilful than any of the people, he led the religious dance of the males.

DANIEL was a descendant of the kings of Judah, and is said to have been born at Upper Bethoron, in the territory of Ephraim. He was carried away captive to Babylon when he was about eighteen or twenty years of age, in the year 606 before the Christian æra. He was placed in the court of Nebuchadnezzar, and was afterward raised to situations of great rank and power, both in the empire of Babylon and of Persia. He lived to the end of the captivity, but being then nearly ninety years old, it is most probable that he did not return to Judea. It is generally believed that he died at Susa, soon after his last vision, which is dated in the third year of the reign of Cyrus. Daniel seems to have been the only prophet who enjoyed a great share of worldly prosperity; but amidst the corruptions of a licentious court he preserved his virtue and integrity inviolate, and no danger or temptation could divert him from the worship of the true God. The book of Daniel is a mixture of history and prophecy: in the first six chapters is recorded a variety of events which occurred in the reigns of Nebuchadnezzar, Belshazzar, and Darius; and, in particular, the second chapter contains Nebuchadnezzar's prophetic dream concerning the four great successive monarchies, and the everlasting kingdom of the Messiah, which dream God enabled Daniel to interpret. In the last six chapters we have a series of prophecies, revealed at different times, extending from the days of Daniel to the general resurrection. The Assyrian, the Persian, the Grecian, and the Roman empires, are all particularly described under appropriate characters; and it is expressly declared that the last of them was to be divided into ten lesser kingdoms; the time at which Christ was to appear is precisely fixed; the rise and fall of antichrist, and the duration of his power, are exactly determined; and the future restoration of the Jews, the victory of Christ over all his enemies, and the universal prevalence of true religion, are distinctly foretold, as being to precede the consummation of that stupendous plan of God, which "was laid before the foundation of the world," and reaches to its dissolution. Part of this book is written in the Chaldaic language, namely, from the fourth verse of the second chapter to the end of the seventh chapter; these chapters relate chiefly to the affairs of Babylon, and it is probable that some passages were taken from the public registers. This book abounds with the most exalted sentiments of piety and devout gratitude; its style is clear, simple, and concise; and many of its prophecies are delivered in terms so plain and circumstantial, that some unbelievers have asserted, in opposition to the strongest evidence, that they were written after the events which they describe had taken place. With respect to the genuineness and authenticity of the hook of Daniel, there is abundance both of external and internal evidence; indeed all that can well be had or desired in a case of this nature: not only the testimony of the whole Jewish church and nation, who have constantly received this book as canonical, but of Josephus particularly, who recommends him as the greatest of the prophets; of the Jewish Targums and Talmuds, which frequently cite and appeal to his authority; of St. Paul and St. John, who have copied many of his prophecies; and of our Saviour himself, who cites his words, and styles him, "Daniel the prophet." Nor is the internal less powerful and convincing than the external evidence; for the language, the style, the manner of writing, and all other internal marks and characters, are perfectly agreeable to that age; and finally he appears plainly and undeniably to have been a prophet by the exact accomplishment of his prophecies.

DARIUS was the name of several princes in history, some of whom are mentioned in Scripture.

1. Darius the Mede, spoken of in Daniel v, 31; ix, 1; xi, 1, &c, was the son of Astyages, king of the Medes, and brother to Mandane, the mother of Cyrus, and to Amyit, the mother of Evil-merodach, and grandmother of Belshazzar. Darius the Mede, therefore, was uncle by the mother's side to Evil-merodach and Cyrus. The Septuagint, in Daniel vii, give him the name of Artaxerxes; the thirteenth, or apocryphal chapter of Daniel, calls him Astyages; and Xenophon designates him by the name of Cyaxares. He succeeded Belshazzar, king of Babylon, his nephew's son, or his sister's grandson, in the year of the world, 3448, according to Calmet, or in 3468, according to Usher. Daniel does not inform us of any previous war between them; but the prophets Isaiah and Jeremiah supply this deficiency. Isa. xiii, xiv, xlv, xlvi, xlvii; Jer. l, li.

2. Darius, the son of Hystaspes, has been supposed by some, on the authority of Archbishop Usher and Calmet, to be the Ahasuerus of Scripture, and the husband of Esther. But Dr. Prideaux thinks, that Ahasuerus was Artaxerxes Longimanus. This prince recovered Babylon after a siege of twenty months. This city, which had been formerly the capital of the east, revolted from Persia, taking advantage of the revolutions that happened, first at the death of Cambyses, and afterward on the massacre of the Magi. The Babylonians employed four years in preparations, and when they thought that their city was furnished with provisions for a long time, they raised the standard of rebellion. Darius levied an army in great haste, and besieged Babylon. The Babylonians shut themselves up within their walls, whose height and thickness secured them from assault; and as they had nothing to fear but famine, they assembled all their women and children, and strangled them, each reserving only his most beloved wife, and one servant. Thus was fulfilled the prophecy of Isaiah, xlvii, 7–9. Some believe that the Jews were either expelled by the Babylonians, as being too much in the interest of Darius; or that, in obedience to the frequent admonitions of the prophets, they quitted that city when they saw the people determined to rebel, Isa. xlviii, 20; Jer. l, 8; li, 6–9; Zech. xi, 6, 7. Darius lay twenty months before Babylon, without making any considerable progress; but, at length, Zopyrus, one of his generals, obtained possession of the city by stratagem. Darius ordered the hundred gates of brass to be taken away, according to the prediction of Jeremiah, li, 58, "Thus saith the Lord, The broad walls of Babylon shall be utterly broken, and her high gates shall be burnt with fire, and the people shall labour in vain." This is related in Herodotus.

3. Darius Codomanus was of the royal family of Persia, but very remote from the crown. He was in a low condition, when Bagoas, the eunuch, who had procured the destruction of two kings, Ochus and Arses, placed him on the throne. His true name was Codoman, and he did not take that of Darius till he was king. He was descended from Darius Nothus, whose son, Ostanes, was father to Arsames, that begat Codomanus. He was at first only a courier to the emperor Ochus. But one day when he was at this prince's army, one of their enemies challenged the bravest of the Persians. Codomanus offered himself for the combat, and overcame the challenger, and was made governor of Armenia. From this situation, Bagoas placed him on the throne of Persia. Alexander the Great invaded the Persian empire, and defeated Darius in three successive battles. After the third battle, Darius fled toward Media, in hopes of raising another army. At Ecbatana, the capital of Media, he gathered the remains of his forces, and some new levies. Alexander having wintered at Babylon and Persepolis, took the field in search of Darius, who quitted Ecbatana, with an intention of retreating into Bactria; but, changing his resolution, Darius stopped short, and determined to hazard a battle, though his army at this time consisted only of forty thousand men. While he was preparing for this conflict, Bessus, governor of Bactria, and Narbazanes, a grandee of Persia, seized him, loaded him with chains, forced him into a covered chariot, and fled, carrying him with them toward Bactria. If Alexander pursued them, they intended to purchase their peace by delivering Darius into his hands; but if not, to kill him, seize the crown, and renew the war. Eight days after their departure, Alexander arrived at Ecbatana, and set out in pursuit of them, which he continued for eleven days: at length he stopped at Rages, in Media, despairing to overtake Darius. Thence he went into Parthia, where he learned what had happened to that unfortunate prince. After a precipitate march of many days, he overtook the traitors, who, seeing themselves pressed, endeavoured to compel Darius to get upon horseback, and save himself with them; but he refusing, they stabbed him in several places, and left him expiring in his chariot. He was dead when Alexander arrived, who could not forbear weeping at so sad a spectacle. Alexander covered Darius with his own cloak, and sent him to Sisygambis his wife, that she might bury him in the tombs of the kings of Persia. Thus were verified the prophecies of Daniel, viii, who had foretold the destruction of the Persian monarchy, under the symbol of a ram, which butted with its horns westward, northward, and southward, and which nothing could resist; but a goat which had a very large horn between his eyes, and which denoted Alexander the Great, came from the west, and overran the world without touching the earth; springing forward with impetuosity, the goat ran against the ram with all his force, attacked him with fury, struck him, broke his two horns, trampled him under foot, and no one could rescue the ram. Nothing can be clearer than these prophecies.

DARKNESS, the absence of light. "Darkness was upon the face of the deep," Gen. i, 2; that is, the chaos was immersed in thick darkness, because light was withheld from it. The most terrible darkness was that brought on Egypt as a plague; it was so thick as to be, as it were, palpable; so horrible, that no one durst stir out of his place; and so lasting, that it endured three days and three nights, Exod. x, 21, 22; Wisdom xvii, 2, 3. The darkness at our Saviour's death began at the sixth hour, or noon, and ended at the third hour, or three o'clock in the afternoon. Thus it lasted almost the whole time he was on the cross; compare Matt. xxvii, 45, with John xix, 14, and Mark xv, 25. Origen, Maldonatus, Erasmus, Vatablus, and others, were of opinion that this darkness covered Judea only; which is sometimes called the WHOLE EARTH; that is, the whole country. Chrysostom, Euthymius, Theophylact, and others, thought it extended over a hemisphere. Origen says it was caused by a thick mist, which precluded the sight of the sun. That it was preternatural is certain, for, the moon being at full, a natural eclipse of the sun was impossible. Darkness is sometimes used metaphorically for death. "The land of darkness" is the grave, Job x, 22; Psalm cvii, 10. It is also used to denote misfortunes and calamities: "A day of darkness" is a day of affliction, Esther xi, 8. "Let that day be darkness; let darkness stain it,"--let it be reckoned among the unfortunate days, Job iii, 4, 5. The expressions, "I will cover the heavens with darkness;" "The sun shall be turned into darkness, and the moon into blood," &c, signify very great political calamities, involving the overthrow of kings, princes, and nobles, represented by the luminaries of heaven. In a moral sense, darkness denotes ignorance and vice; hence "the children of light," in opposition to "the children of darkness," are the righteous distinguished from the wicked.

DAVID, the celebrated king of Israel, was the youngest son of Jesse, of the tribe of Judah, and was born 1085 years before Christ. The following is an abstract of his history: He was chosen of God to be king of Israel, and at his command was anointed to this dignity by the hands of Samuel, a venerable prophet, in the room of Saul; who had been rejected for his disobedience to the divine orders, in feloniously seizing, to his own use the prey of an enemy, which God, the supreme King of Israel, had devoted to destruction. He was introduced to court as a man expert in music, a singularly valiant man, a man of war, prudent in matters, of a comely person, and one favoured of the Lord. By his skill in music, he relieved Saul under a melancholy indisposition that had seized him, was highly beloved by his royal master, and made one of his guards. In a war with the Philistines he accepted the challenge of a gigantic champion, who defied the armies of Israel, and being skilful at the sling, he slew him with a stone, returned safely with his head, and thus secured to his prince an easy victory over his country's enemies. The reputation he gained, by this glorious action, raised an incurable jealousy and resentment against him, in the mind of the king his master; who made two unsuccessful attempts to murder him. In his exalted station, and amidst the dangers that encompassed him, he behaved with singular prudence, so that he was in high esteem both in the court and camp. The modesty and prudence of his behaviour, and his approved courage and resolution, gained him the confidence and friendship of Jonathan, the king's eldest son, "who loved him as his own soul," became his advocate with his father, and obtained from him a promise, confirmed by an oath, that he would no more attempt to destroy him. But Saul's jealousy returned by a fresh victory David gained over the Philistines; who, finding the king was determined to seek his life, retired from court, and was dismissed in peace by Jonathan, after a solemn renewal of their friendship, to provide for his own safety. In this state of banishment, there resorted to him companies of men, who were uneasy in their circumstances, oppressed by their creditors, or discontented with Saul's tyrannical government, to the number of six hundred men. These he kept in the most excellent order, and by their valour he gained signal advantages for his country; but never employed them in rebellion against the king, or in a single instance to distress or subvert his government. On the contrary such was the veneration he paid him, and such the generosity of his temper, that though it was thrice in his power to have him cut off, he spared him, and was determined never to destroy him, whom God had constituted the king of Israel. His friendship with Jonathan, the king's son, was a friendship of strict honour, for he never seduced him from his allegiance and filial duty. Being provoked by a churlish farmer, who evil treated and abused his messengers, he, in the warmth of his temper, swore he would destroy him and his family; but was immediately pacified by the address and prudence of a wife, of whom the wretch was unworthy: her he sent in peace and honour to her family, and blessed for her advice, and keeping him from avenging himself with his own hand. Being forced to banish himself into an enemy's country, he was faithful to the prince who protected him: and, at the same time, mindful of the interest of his own nation, he cut off many of those who had harassed and plundered his fellow subjects. When pressed by the king, into whose dominions he retired, to join in a war against his own country and father-in-law, he prudently gave him such an answer as his situation required; neither promising the aid demanded of him, nor tying up his hands from serving his own prince, and the army that fought under him; only assuring him in general, that he had never done any thing that could give him just reason to think he would refuse to assist him against his enemies. Upon the death of Saul, he cut off the Amalekite who came to make a merit of having slain him; and by the immediate direction of God, who had promised him the succession, went up to Hebron, where, on a free election, he was anointed king over the house of Judah; and after about a seven years' contest, he was unanimously chosen king by all the tribes of Israel, "according to the word of the Lord by Samuel." As king of Israel, he administered justice and judgment to all his people, was a prince of courage, and great military prudence and conduct; had frequent wars with the neighbouring nations, to which he was generally forced by their invading his dominions, and plundering his subjects. Against them he never lost a battle; he never besieged a city without taking it; nor, as for any thing that can be proved, used any severities against those he conquered, beyond what the law of arms allowed, his own safety required, or the cruelties of his enemies rendered just, by way of retaliation; enriching his people by the spoils he took, and providing large stores of every thing necessary for the magnificent temple he intended to erect, in honour of the God of Israel. Having rescued Jerusalem out of the hands of the Jebusites, he made it the capital of his kingdom, and the place of his residence; and being willing to honour it with the presence of the ark of God, he brought it to Jerusalem in triumph, and divesting himself of his royal robes, out of reverence to God, he clothed himself in the habit of his ministers, and with them expressed his joy by dancing and music; contemned only by one haughty woman; whom, as a just punishment of her insolence, he seems ever after to have separated from his bed. Though his crimes were henious, and highly aggravated, in the affair of Uriah and Bathsheba, he patiently endured reproof, humbly submitted to the punishment appointed him, deeply repented, and obtained mercy and forgiveness from God, though not without some severe marks of his displeasure, for the grievous offences of which he had been guilty. A rebellion was raised against him by his son Absalom. When forced by it to depart from Jerusalem, a circumstance most pathetically described by the sacred historian, he prevented the just punishment of Shimei, a wretch who cursed and stoned him. When restored to his throne, he spared him upon his submission, and would not permit a single man to be put to death in Israel upon account of this treason. He, with a noble confidence, made the commander of the rebel forces general of his own army, in the room of Joab, whom he intended to call to an account for murder and other crimes. After this, when obliged, by the command of God, to give up some of Saul's family to justice, for the murder of the Gibeonites, he spared Mephibosheth, Micah, and his family, the male descendants of Saul and Jonathan, who alone could have any pretence to dispute the crown with him, and surrendered only Saul's bastard children, and those of his daughter by Adriel, who had no right or possible claim to the throne, and could never give him any uneasiness in the possession of it; and thus showed his inviolable regard for his oaths, his tenderness to Saul, and the warmth of his gratitude and friendship to Jonathan. In the close of his life, and in the near prospect of death, to demonstrate his love of justice, he charged Solomon to punish with death Joab, for the base murder of two great men, whom he assassinated under the pretence of peace and friendship. To this catalogue of his noble actions must be added, that he gave the most shining and indisputable proofs of an undissembled reverence for, and sincere piety to, God; ever obeying the direction of his prophets, worshipping him alone, to the exclusion of all idols, throughout the whole of his life, and making the wisest settlement to perpetuate the worship of the same God, through all succeeding generations.

To this abstract a few miscellaneous remarks may be added.

1. When David is called "the man after God's own heart," a phrase which profane persons have often perverted, his general character, and not every particular of it, is to be understood as approved by God; and especially his faithful and undeviating adherence to the true religion, from which he never deviated into any act of idolatry.

2. He was chosen to accomplish to their full extent the promises made to Abraham to give to his seed, the whole country from the river of Egypt to the great river Euphrates. He had succeeded to a kingdom distracted with civil dissension, environed on every side by powerful and victorious enemies, without a capital, almost without an army, without any bond of union between the tribes. He left a compact and united state, stretching from the frontier of Egypt to the foot of Lebanon, from the Euphrates to the sea. He had crushed the power of the Philistines, subdued or curbed all the adjacent kingdoms: he had formed a lasting and important alliance with the great city of Tyre. He had organized an immense disposable force; for every month 24,000 men, furnished in rotation by the tribes, appeared in arms, and were trained as the standing militia of the country. At the head of his army were officers of consummate experience, and, what was more highly esteemed in the warfare of the time, extraordinary personal activity, strength, and valour. The Hebrew nation owed the long peace of Solomon the son's reign to the bravery and wisdom of the father.

3. As a conqueror he was a type of Christ, and the country "from the river to the ends of the earth," was also the prophetic type of Christ's dominion over the whole earth.

4. His inspired psalms not only place him among the most eminent prophets; but have rendered him the leader of the devotions of good men, in all ages. The hymns of David excel no less in sublimity and tenderness of expression than in loftiness and purity of religious sentiment. In comparison with them the sacred poetry of all other nations sinks into mediocrity. They have embodied so exquisitely the universal language of religious emotion, that they have entered with unquestioned propriety into the ritual of the higher and more perfect religion of Christ. The songs which cheered the solitude of the desert caves of Engedi, or resounded from the voice of the Hebrew people as they wound along the glens or the hill sides of Judea, have been repeated for ages in almost every part of the habitable world, in the remotest islands of the ocean, among the forests of America or the sands of Africa. How many human hearts have these inspired songs softened, purified, exalted! Of how many wretched beings have they been the secret consolation! On how many communities have they drawn down the blessings of Divine providence, by bringing the affections into unison with their deep devotional fervour, and leading to a constant and explicit recognition of the government, rights, and mercies of God!

DAY. The Hebrews, in conformity with the Mosaic law, reckoned the day from evening to evening. The natural day, that is, the portion of time from sunrise to sunset, was divided by the Hebrews, as it is now by the Arabians, into six unequal parts. These divisions were as follows:--1. The break of day. This portion of time was, at a recent period, divided into two parts, in imitation of the Persians; the first of which began when the eastern, the second, when the western, division of the horizon was illuminated. The authors of the Jerusalem Talmud divided it into four parts; the first of which was called in Hebrew השחר אילת, which occurs in Psalm xxii, 1, and corresponds to the phrase, λίαν πρωΐ, in the New Testament, Mark xvi, 2; John xx, 1. 2. The morning or sunrise. 3. The heat of the day. This began about nine o'clock, Gen. xviii, 1; 1 Sam. xi, 11. 4. Midday. 5. The cool of the day; literally, the wind of the day. This expression is grounded on the fact, that a wind commences blowing regularly a few hours before sunset, and continues till evening, Gen. iii, 8. 6. The evening. This was divided into two parts, ערבים; the first of which began, according to the Caraites and Samaritans, at sunset, the second, when it began to grow dark. But, according to the rabbins, the first commenced just before sunset, the second, precisely at sunset. The Arabians agree with the Caraites and Samaritans; and in this way the Hebrews appear to have computed, previous to the captivity.

The mention of שעה, HOURS, occurs first in Daniel iii, 6, 15; v, 5. They were first measured by GNOMONS, which merely indicated the meridian; afterward, by the HOUR-WATCH, σκιαθέρικον; and subsequently still, by the CLEPSYDRA, or instrument for measuring time by means of water. The hour-watch or dial, otherwise called the sun-dial, is mentioned in the reign of King Hezekiah, 2 Kings xx, 9, 10; Isaiah xxxviii, 8. Its being called "the sundial of Ahaz" renders it probable that Ahaz first introduced it from Babylon; whence, also, Anaximenes, the Milesian, brought the first SKIATHERICON into Greece. This instrument was of no use during the night, nor indeed during a cloudy day. In consequence of this defect, the CLEPSYDRA was invented, which was used in Persia as late as the seventeenth century in its simplest form. The CLEPSYDRA was a small circular vessel, constructed of thinly-beaten copper or brass, and having a small perforation through the bottom. It was placed in another vessel, filled with water. The diameter of the hole in the bottom of the CLEPSYDRA was such, that it filled with water in three hours, and sunk. It was necessary that there should be a servant to tend it, who should take it up when it had sunk, pour out the water, and place it again empty on the surface of the water in the vase.

The hours of principal note in the course of the day were the third, the sixth, and the ninth. These hours, it would seem, were consecrated by Daniel to prayer, Dan. vi, 10; Acts ii, 15; iii, 1; x, 9. The day was divided into twelve hours, which, of course, varied in length, being shorter in the winter and longer in the summer, John xi, 9. In the winter, therefore, the CLEPSYDRAS were so constructed that the water might sink them more rapidly. The hours were numbered from the rising of the sun, so that, at the season of the equinox, the third corresponded to the ninth of our reckoning; the sixth, to our twelfth; and the ninth, to three o'clock in the afternoon. At other seasons of the year, it is necessary to observe the time when the sun rises, and reduce the hours to our time accordingly. We observe, therefore, that the sun in Palestine, at the summer solstice, rises at five of our time, and sets about seven. At the winter solstice, it rises about seven, and sets about five.

Before the captivity, the night was divided into three watches. The first, which continued till midnight, was denominated the commencing or first watch, Lam. ii, 19. The second was denominated the middle watch, and continued from midnight till the crowing of the cock. The third, called the morning watch, extended from the second to the rising of the sun. These divisions and names appear to have owed their origin to the watches of the Levites in the tabernacle and temple, Exod. xiv, 24; 1 Sam. xi, 11. In the time of Christ, however, the night, in imitation of the Romans, was divided into four watches. According to the English mode of reckoning they were as follows: 1. The evening, from twilight to nine o'clock. 2. The midnight, from nine to twelve. 3. The cock crowing, from twelve to three. 4. From three o'clock till daybreak. A day is used in the prophetic Scripture for a year: "I have appointed thee each day for a year," Ezek. iv, 6. See Cock.

DEACON, from the Greek word διάκονος, in its proper and primitive sense, denotes a SERVANT who attends his master, waits on him at table, and is always near his person to obey his orders, which was accounted a more creditable kind of service than that which is imported by the word δοῦλος A SLAVE; but this distinction is not usually observed in the New Testament. Our Lord makes use of both terms in Matt. xx, 26, 27, though they are not distinctly marked in our translation: "Whosoever will be great among you, let him be your DEACON; and whosoever will be chief among you, let him be your SERVANT." The appointment of deacons in the first Christian church is distinctly recorded, Acts vi, 1–16. The number of disciples having greatly increased in Jerusalem, the Greeks, or Hellenistic Jews, began to murmur against the Hebrews, complaining that their widows were neglected in the daily distribution of the church's bounty. The twelve Apostles, who hitherto had discharged the different offices of Apostle, presbyter, and deacon, upon the principle that the greater office always includes the less, now convened the church, and said unto them, "It is not reasonable that we should leave the ministration of the word of God, and serve tables: look ye out, therefore, among yourselves, seven men of good report, full of the Holy Ghost, and wisdom, whom we may appoint over this business; but we will give ourselves continually to prayer, and to the ministry of the word." And the saying pleased the whole multitude; and they (the multitude) chose Stephen, and six others, whom they set before the Apostles, &c.

The qualifications of deacons are stated by the Apostle Paul, 1 Tim. iii, 8–12. There were also, in the primitive churches females invested with this office, who were termed deaconesses. Of this number was Phœbe, a member of the church of Cenchrea, mentioned by St. Paul, Rom. xvi, 1. "They served the church," says Calmet, "in those offices which the deacons could not themselves exercise, visiting those of their own sex in sickness, or when imprisoned for the faith. They were persons of advanced age, when chosen; and appointed to the office by imposition of hands." It is probably of these deaconesses that the Apostle speaks, where he describes the ministering widows, 1 Tim. v, 5–10.

DEAD. See Burial.

Dead, Mournings for the. The ancient Israelites, in imitation of the Heathen, from whom they borrowed the practice, frequently cut themselves with knives and lancets, scratched their faces, or pricked certain parts of their bodies with needles. These superstitious practices were expressly forbidden in their law: "Ye are the children of the Lord your God: ye shall not cut yourselves, nor make any baldness between your eyes for the dead." The bereaved Greeks tore, cut off, and sometimes shaved, their hair; they reckoned it a duty which they owed to the dead, to deprive their heads of the greatest part of their honours, or, in the language of Scripture, made a baldness between their eyes. The same custom prevailed among the ancient Persians, and the neighbouring states. When the patriarch Job was informed of the death of his children, and the destruction of his property, he arose and rent his mantle, and shaved his head, and fell down upon the ground and worshipped; and in the prophecies of Jeremiah, we read of eighty men who were going to lament the desolations of Jerusalem, having their beards shaven, and their clothes rent, and having cut themselves, in direct violation of the divine law, with offerings and incense in their hand, to bring them to the house of the Lord, Jer. xii, 5. Shaving, however, was, on some occasions, a sign of joy; and to let the hair grow long, the practice of mourners, or persons in affliction. Joseph shaved himself before he went into the palace, Gen. xli, 14; and Mephibosheth let his hair grow during the time David was banished from Jerusalem, but shaved himself on his return. In ordinary sorrows they only neglected their hair, or suffered it to hang down loose upon their shoulders; in more poignant grief they cut it off; but in a sudden and violent paroxysm, they plucked it off with their hands. Such a violent expression of sorrow is exemplified in the conduct of Ezra, which he thus describes: "And when I heard this thing I rent my garment and my mantle, and plucked off the hair of my head, and of my beard, and sat down astonied," Ezra ix, 3. The Greeks, and other nations around them, expressed the violence of their sorrow in the same way; for in Homer, Ulysses and his companions, bewailing the death of Elpenor, howled and plucked off their hair. Mourners withdrew as much as possible from the world; they abstained from banquets and entertainments; they banished from their houses as unsuitable to their circumstances, and even painful to their feelings, musical instruments of every kind, and whatever was calculated to excite pleasure, or that wore an air of mirth and gaiety. Thus did the king of Persia testify his sorrow for the decree, into which his wily courtiers had betrayed him, and which, without the miraculous interposition of Heaven, had proved fatal to his favourite minister: "Then the king went to his palace, and spent the night fasting; neither were instruments of music brought before him," Dan. vi, 18.

2. Oriental mourners divested themselves of all ornaments, and laid aside their jewels, gold, and every thing rich and splendid in their dress. This proof of humiliation and submission Jehovah required of his offending people in the wilderness: "Therefore, now put off thy ornaments from thee, that I may know what to do unto thee. And the children of Israel stripped themselves of their ornaments by the Mount Horeb," Exodus xxxiii, 5, 6. Long after the time of Moses, that rebellious nation again received a command of similar import: "Strip you, and make you bare, and gird sackcloth upon your loins," Isaiah xxxii, 11. The garments of the mourner were always black. Progne, having notice of Philomela's death, lays aside her robes, beaming with a profusion of gold, and appears in sable vestments; and Althæa, when her brethren were slain by Meleager, exchanged her glittering robes for black:--

"ET AURATAS MUTAVIT VESTIBUS ATRIS." Ovid.

These sable vestments differed from their ordinary dress, not only in colour, but also in value, being made of cheap and coarse stuff, as appears from these lines of Terence:--

"TEXENTEM TELAM STUDIOSE IPSAM OFFENDIMUS

MEDIOCRITER VESTITAM VESTE LUGUBRI

EJUS ANUS CAUSA, OPINOR, QUÆ ERAT MORTUA."

"We found her busy at the loom, in a cheap mourning habit, which she wore I suppose for the old woman's death." In Judea, the mourner was clothed in sackcloth of hair, and by consequence, in sable robes; and penitents, by assuming it, seemed to confess that their guilt exposed them to death. Some of the eastern nations, in modern times, bury in linen; but Chardin informs us, that others still retain the use of sackcloth for that purpose. To sit in sackcloth and ashes, was a frequent expression of mourning in the oriental regions; and persons overwhelmed with grief, and unable to sustain the weight of their calamities, often threw themselves upon the earth, and rolled in the dust; and the more dirty the ground was, the better it served to defile them, and to express their sorrow and dejection. In this way Tamar signified her distress, after being dishonoured by Amnon, "She put ashes on her head;" and when Mordecai understood that the doom of his nation was sealed, he "rent his clothes, and put on sackcloth with ashes." Our Lord alludes to the same custom, in that denunciation: "Wo unto thee, Chorazin! wo unto thee, Bethsaida! for if the mighty works which were done in you, had been done in Tyre and Sidon, they would have repented long ago, in sackcloth and ashes," Matt. xi, 21. Intimately connected with this, is the custom of putting dust upon the head. When the armies of Israel were defeated before Ai, "Joshua rent his clothes, and fell to the earth upon his face, he and the elders of Israel, and put dust upon their heads." The mourner sometimes laid his hands upon his head; for the prophet, expostulating with his people, predicts their humiliation in these words: "Yea, thou shalt go forth from him, and thine hands upon thine head; for the Lord hath rejected thy confidences, and thou shalt not prosper in them," Jer. ii, 37. In both these cases, the head of the mourner was uncovered; but they sometimes adopted the opposite custom, and covered their heads in great distress, or when they were loaded with disgrace and infamy.

3. To cover the lips was a very ancient sign of mourning; and it continues to be practised among the Jews of Barbary to this day. When they return from the grave to the house of the deceased, the chief mourner receives them with his jaws tied up with a linen cloth, in imitation of the manner in which the face of the dead is covered; and by this the mourner is said to testify that he was ready to die for his friend. Muffled in this way, the mourner goes for seven days, during which the rest of his friends come twice every twenty-four hours to pray with him. This allusion is perhaps involved in the charge which Ezekiel received when his wife died, to abstain from the customary forms of mourning: "Forbear to cry; make no mourning for the dead; bind the tire of thy head upon thee, and put on thy shoes upon thy feet, and cover not thy lips, and eat not the bread of men," Ezekiel xxiv, 17.

4. Sitting on the ground was a posture which denoted severe distress. Thus the prophet represents the elders of Israel, after the destruction of Jerusalem, and the captivity of those whom the sword had spared: "The elders of the daughter of Zion sit upon the ground, and keep silence; they have cast up dust upon their heads; they have girded themselves with sackcloth; the virgins of Jerusalem hang down their heads to the ground," Lam. ii, 10. Judea is represented on several coins of Vespasian and Titus, as a solitary female in this very posture of sorrow and captivity sitting upon the ground. It is remarkable, that we find Judea represented as a sorrowful woman sitting on the ground, in a passage of the prophet, where the same calamity which was recorded on the medals of these Roman emperors is foretold: "And she being desolate shall sit upon the ground," Isaiah iii, 26.

5. Chardin informs us that when the king of Persia dies, his physicians and astrologers lose their places, and are excluded from the court; the first, because they could not cure their sovereign, and the last, because they did not give previous notice of his death. This whimsical custom he supposes has descended to modern times from a very remote antiquity; and to have been the true reason that Daniel was absent when Belshazzar saw the hand writing his doom on the wall. If the conjecture of that intelligent traveller be well founded, the venerable prophet had been forced by the established etiquette of the court to retire from the management of public affairs at the death of Nebuchadnezzar; and had remained in a private station for twenty-three years, neglected or forgotten, till the awful occurrence of that memorable night rendered his assistance necessary, and brought him again into public notice. This accounts in a very satisfactory manner, as well for Belshazzar's ignorance of Daniel, as for the recollection of Nitocris, the queen-mother, who had long known his character and abilities during the reign of her husband. This solution of the difficulty is at least ingenious.

6. It was a custom among the Jews to visit the sepulchres of their deceased friends three days; for so long they supposed their spirits hovered about them; but when once they perceived their visage begin to change, as it would in that time in those warm countries, all hopes of a return to life were then at an end. But it appears from an incident in the narrative of the raising of Lazarus, that in Judea they were accustomed to visit the graves of their deceased relations after the third day, merely to lament their loss, and give vent to their grief. If this had not been a common practice, the people that came to comfort the sisters of Lazarus would not so readily have concluded, when Mary, on the fourth day, went hastily out to meet her Saviour, "She goeth to the grave to weep there." The Turkish women continue to follow this custom: they go before sunrising on Friday, the stated day of their worship, to the grave of the deceased, where, with many tears and lamentations, they sprinkle their monuments with water and flowers.

DEAD SEA. This was anciently called the SEA OF THE PLAIN, Deut. iii, 17; iv, 49, from its situation in the great hollow or plain of the Jordan; the SALT SEA, Deut. iii, 17; Joshua xv, 5, from the extreme saltness of its waters; and the EAST SEA, Ezek. xlvii, 18; Joel ii, 20, from its situation relative to Judea, and in contradistinction to the WEST SEA, or Mediterranean. It is likewise called by Josephus, and by the Greek and Latin writers generally, LACUS ASPHALTITES, from the bitumen found in it; and the DEAD SEA, its more frequent modern appellation, from a tradition, commonly though erroneously received, that no living creature could exist in its saline and sulphureous waters. It is at present known in Syria by the names of ALMOTANAH and BAHAR LOTH: and occupies what may be considered as the southern extremity of the vale of Jordan; forming, in that direction, the western boundary to the Holy Land. The Dead Sea is about seventy miles in length, and twenty in breadth at its broadest part; having, like the Caspian, no visible communication with the ocean. Its depth seems to be altogether unknown; nor does it appear that a boat has ever navigated its surface. Toward its southern extremity, however, in a contracted part of the lake, is a ford, about six miles over, made use of by the Arabs: in the middle of which they report the water to be warm; indicating the presence of warm springs beneath. In general, toward the shore, it is shallow; and rises and falls with the seasons, and the quantity of water carried into it by seven streams, which fall into this their common receptacle, the chief of which is the Jordan.

The water now covering these ruins occupies what was formerly the vale of Siddim; a rich and fruitful valley, in which stood the five cities, called the cities of the plain, namely, Sodom, Gomorrah, Admah, Zeboim, and Bela or

Zoar: the four first of which were destroyed, while the latter, being "a little city," was preserved at the intercession of Lot; to which he fled for refuge from the impending catastrophe, and where he remained in safety during its accomplishment.

The specific gravity of the waters of the Dead Sea is supposed to have been much exaggerated by the ancient writers, but their statements are now proved to be by no means very wide of the truth. Pliny says, that no living bodies would sink in it; and Strabo, that persons who went into it were borne up to their middle. Van Egmont and Heyman state, that, on swimming to some distance from the shore, they found themselves, to their great surprise, lifted up by the water. "When I had swam to some distance," says the latter, "I endeavoured to sink to the bottom, but could not; for the water kept me continually up, and would certainly have thrown me upon my face, had I not put forth all the strength I was master of, to keep myself in a perpendicular posture; so that I walked in the sea as if I had trod on firm ground, without having occasion to make any of the motions necessary in treading fresh water; and when I was swimming, I was obliged to keep my legs the greatest part of the time out of the water. My fellow traveller was agreeably surprised to find that he could swim here, having never learned. But this proceeded from the gravity of the water, as this certainly does from the extraordinary quantity of salt in it." Mr. Joliffe says, he found it very little more buoyant than other seas, but he did not go out of his depth. "The descent of the beach," he says, "is so gently gradual, that I must have waded above a hundred yards to get completely out of my depth, and the impatience of the Arabians would not allow of time sufficient for this." Captain Mangles says: "The water is as bitter and as buoyant as the people have reported. Those of our party who could not swim, floated on its surface like corks. On dipping the head in, the eyes smarted dreadfully." With regard to the agents employed in this catastrophe, there might seem reason to suppose that volcanic phenomena had some share in producing it; but Chateaubriand's remark is deserving of attention. "I cannot," he says, "coincide in opinion with those who suppose the Dead Sea to be the crater of a volcano. I have seen Vesuvius, Solfatara, Monte Nuovo in the lake of Fusino, the peak of the Azores, the Mamalif opposite to Carthage, the extinguished volcanoes of Auvergne; and remarked in all of them the same characters; that is to say, mountains excavated in the form of a tunnel, lava, and ashes, which exhibited incontestable proofs of the agency of fire." After noticing the very different shape and position of the Dead Sea, he adds: "Bitumen, warm springs, and phosphoric stones are found, it is true, in the mountains of Arabia; but then, the presence of hot springs, sulphur, and asphaltos is not sufficient to attest the anterior existence of a volcano." The learned Frenchman inclines to adopt the idea of Professors Michaëlis and Busching, that Sodom and Gomorrah were built upon a mine of bitumen; that lightning kindled the combustible mass, and that the cities sunk in the subterraneous conflagration. M. Malte Brun ingeniously suggests, that the cities might themselves have been built of bituminous stones, and thus have been set in flames by the fire of heaven. We learn from the Mosaic account, that the Vale of Siddim, which is now occupied by the Dead Sea, was full of "slime pits," or pits of bitumen. Pococke says: "It is observed, that the bitumen floats on the water, and comes ashore after windy weather; the Arabs gather it up, and it serves as pitch for all uses, goes into the composition of medicines, and is thought to have been a very great ingredient in the bitumen used in embalming the bodies in Egypt: it has been much used for cerecloths, and has an ill smell when burnt. It is probable that there are subterraneous fires, that throw up this bitumen at the bottom of the sea, where it may form itself into a mass, which may be broken by the motion of the water occasioned by high winds; and it is very remarkable, that the stone called the stone of Moses, found about two or three leagues from the sea, which burns like a coal, and turns only to a white stone, and not to ashes, has the same smell, when burnt, as this pitch; so that it is probable, a stratum of the stone under the Dead Sea is one part of the matter that feeds the subterraneous fires, and that this bitumen boils up out of it." To give force to this last conjecture, however, it would be requisite to ascertain, whether bitumen is capable of being detached from this stone, in a liquid state, by the action of fire. The stone in question is the black feited limestone, used at Jerusalem in the manufacture of rosaries and amulets, and worn as a charm against the plague. The effluvia which it emits on friction, is owing to a strong impregnation of sulphuretted hydrogen. If the buildings were constructed of materials of this description, with quarries of which the neighbouring mountains abound, they would be easily susceptible of ignition by lightning. The Scriptural account, however, is explicit, that "the Lord rained upon Sodom and Gomorrah brimstone and fire from heaven;" which we may safely interpret as implying a shower of inflamed sulphur, or nitre. At the same time it is evident, that the whole plain underwent a simultaneous convulsion, which seems referable to the consequences of a bituminous explosion. In perfect accordance with this view of the catastrophe, we find the very materials, as it were, of this awful visitation still at hand in the neighbouring hills; from which they might have been poured down by the agency of thunder storms, directed by the hand of offended Heaven. Captains Irby and Mangles collected, on the southern coast, lumps of nitre and fine sulphur, from the size of a nutmeg up to that of a small hen's egg, which, it was evident from their situation, had been brought down by the rain: "their great deposit must be sought for," they say, "in the cliff." These cliffs then were probably swept by the lightnings, and their flaming masses poured in a deluge of fire upon the plain.

DEBORAH, a prophetess, wife of Lapidoth, judged the Israelites, and dwelt under a palm tree between Ramah and Bethel, Judges iv, 4, 5. She sent for Barak, directed him to attack Sisera, and, in the name of God, promised him victory; but Barak refusing to go, unless she went with him, she told him, that the honour of this expedition would be given to a woman, and not to him. After the victory, Deborah and Barak sung a fine thanksgiving song, the composition probably of Deborah alone, which is preserved, Judges v.

DEBTS. In nothing, perhaps, do the Israelitish laws deviate so far from our own, as in regard to matters of debt. Imprisonment was unknown among the Hebrews, who were equally free from those long and expensive modes of procedure with which we are acquainted, for the recovery of debts. Their laws in this respect were simple, but efficient. Where pledges were lodged with a creditor for the payment of a debt, which was not discharged, the creditor was allowed to appropriate the pledge to his own benefit, without any interposition of a magistrate, and to keep it as rightfully as if it had been bought with the sum which had been lent for it. But, beside the pledge, every Israelite had various pieces of property, on which execution for debt might readily be made; as (1.) His hereditary land, the produce of which might be attached till the year of jubilee: (2.) His houses, which, with the sole exception of those of the Levites, might be sold in perpetuity, Lev. xxv, 29, 30: (3.) His cattle, household furniture, and ornaments, appear also liable to be taken in execution. See Job xxiv, 3; Proverbs xxii, 27. From Deut. xv, 1–11, we see that no debt could be exacted from a poor man in the seventh year; because the land lying fallow, he had no income whence to pay it: (4.) The person of the debtor, who might be sold, along with his wife and children, if he had any. See Lev. xxv, 39; Job xxiv, 9; 2 Kings iv, 1; Isaiah l, 1; Nehemiah v. We have no intimation, in the writings of Moses, that suretyship was practised among the Hebrews in cases of debt. In the Proverbs of Solomon, however, there are many admonitions respecting it. Where this warranty was given, the surety was treated with the same severity as if he had been the actual debtor; and if he could not pay, his very bed might be taken from under him, Prov. xxii, 27. There is a reference to the custom observed in contracting this obligation in Prov. xvii, 18: "A man void of understanding striketh hands," &c; and also in Prov. xxii, 26: "Be not thou one of them that strike hands," &c. It is to be observed that the hand was given, not to the creditor, but to the debtor, in the creditor's presence. By this act the surety intimated that he became in a legal sense one with the debtor, and rendered himself liable to pay the debt.

2. We have above noticed the practice of lending on pledge; but as this was liable to considerable abuse, the following judicial regulations were adopted: (1.) The creditor was not allowed to enter the house of the debtor to fetch the pledge, but was obliged to stand without the door, and wait till it was brought to him, Deut. xxiv, 10, 11. This law was wisely designed to restrain avaricious and unprincipled persons from taking advantage of their poor brethren in choosing their own pledges. (2.) The upper garment, which served by night for a blanket, Exod. xxii, 25, 26; Deut. xxiv, 12, 13, and mills and millstones, if taken in pledge, were to be restored to the owner before sunset. The reason of this law was, that these articles were indispensable to the comfortable subsistence of the poor; and for the same reason, it is likely that it extended to all necessary utensils. Such a restoration was no loss to the creditor; for he had it in his power at last, by the aid of summary justice, to lay hold of the whole property of the debtor; and if he had none, of his person: and, in the event of non-payment, as before stated, to take him for a bond slave.

DECALOGUE, the ten principal commandments, Exod. xx, 1, &c, from the Greek δεκὰ TEN, and λόγοι WORDS. The Jews call these precepts, THE TEN WORDS.

DECAPOLIS, a country in Palestine, so called, because it contained ten principal cities; some situated on the west, and some on the east side of Jordan, Matt. iv, 25; Mark v, 20.

DEDICATION, a religious ceremony, whereby any person or thing was set apart to the service of God, and the purposes of religion. Dedications of persons, temples, and houses, were frequent among the Jews. See Consecration.

DEFILEMENT. Under the law, many were those blemishes of person and conduct, which were considered as defilements: some were voluntary, others involuntary; some were inevitable, and the effect of nature itself, others arose from personal transgression. Under the Gospel, defilements are those of the heart, of the mind, the temper, and conduct. The ceremonial uncleannesses of the law are superseded as religious rites; though many of them claim attention as usages of health, decency, and civility.

DEGREES. PSALMS OF DEGREES is a name given to fifteen psalms, from the cxx, to the cxxxiv, inclusive. The Hebrew text calls them A SONG OF ASCENTS. Junius and Tremellius translate the Hebrew A SONG OF EXCELLENCES, OR AN EXCELLENT SONG, from the excellent matter they contain. Some call them PSALMS OF ELEVATION, because they were sung with an exalted voice, or because at every psalm the voice was raised; but the translation of PSALMS OF DEGREES has more generally obtained. Some think that they were called psalms of degrees, because they were sung upon the fifteen steps of the temple; but they are not agreed where these steps were. Others are of opinion, that they were so denominated, because sung in a gallery, which was in the court of Israel, where the Levites sometimes read the law. Calmet thinks, that they were called songs of degrees, or of ascent, because they were composed on occasion of the deliverance of the Jews from the captivity of Babylon, either to implore this deliverance from God, or to return thanks for it after it had been obtained; and that the Hebrews used the term TO GO UP, when they spoke of their journeying from Babylon to Jerusalem. Others are of opinion, that these psalms were sung during the time of service, while the flesh, &c, were consuming on the altar, and while the fume and smoke ASCENDED toward heaven; and that the title PSALMS OF ASCENT seems to favour this supposition. The point is involved in entire obscurity; and, after all, the title of these Psalms may be only a musical direction to the temple choir.

DEISTS. This term appears to have had an honourable origin, being of the same import as THEISTS, designating those who believe in the existence of a supreme intelligent cause, in opposition to the Epicureans, and other Atheistical philosophers. The name, in modern times, is said to have been first assumed about the middle of the sixteenth century, by some persons on the continent, in order to avoid the imputation of Atheism. Peter Viret, a divine of that century, mentions it as a new name assumed by those who rejected Christianity. Lord Edw. Herbert, baron of Cherbury, in the seventeenth century, has been regarded as the first Deistical writer in this country, or at least, the first who reduced Deism to a system; affirming the sufficiency of reason and natural religion, and rejecting divine revelation as unnecessary and superfluous. His system, however, embraced these five articles:--1. The being of God. 2. That he is to be worshipped. 3. That piety and moral virtue are the chief parts of worship. 4. That God will pardon our faults on repentance. And, 5. That there is a future state of rewards and punishment. Some have divided all Deists into two classes--those who admit a future state, and those who deny it. But Dr. S. Clarke, taking the term in the most extensive sense, arranges them under four classes:--1. Those who admit a Supreme Being, but deny that he concerns himself with the conduct or affairs of men; maintaining, with Lucretius, that God

"Ne'er smiles at good, nor frowns at wicked, deeds."

2. Those who admit not only the being but the providence of God, with respect to the natural world; but who allow no difference between moral good and evil, nor that God takes any notice of our moral conduct. 3. Such as believe in the natural attributes of God, and his all-governing providence; yet deny the immortality of the soul, or any future state. 4. Such as admit the existence of God, his providence, and the obligations of natural religion; but so far only as these things are discoverable by the light of nature, without any divine revelation. Some of the Deists have attempted to overthrow the Christian dispensation, by opposing to it what they call the absolute perfection of natural religion. Others, as Blount, Collins, and Morgan, have endeavoured to gain the same purpose, by attacking particular parts of the Christian scheme, by explaining away the literal sense and meaning of certain passages, or by placing one portion of the sacred canon in opposition to the other. A third class, wherein we meet with the names of Shaftesbury and Bolingbroke, advancing farther in their progress, expunge from their creed the doctrine of future existence, deny or controvert all the moral perfections of the Deity, and wholly reject the Scriptures.

The Deists of the present day are distinguished by their zealous efforts to diffuse the principles of infidelity among the common people. Hume, Bolingbroke, and Gibbon, addressed themselves solely to the more polished classes of the community; but of late the writings of Paine, Carlile, and others, have diffused infidelity among the lower orders of society, and clothed it in the dress of vulgar ridicule, the more effectually to destroy in the common people all reverence for sacred things. Among the disciples of this school, Deism has led to the most disgusting Atheism. Thus "evil men and seducers wax worse and worse."

DELUGE signifies, in general, any great inundation; but more particularly that universal flood by which the whole inhabitants of this globe were destroyed, except Noah and his family. According to the most approved systems of chronology, this remarkable event happened in the year 1656 after the creation, or about 2348 before the Christian æra. Of so general a calamity, from which only a single family of all who lived then on the face of the earth was preserved, we might naturally expect to find some memorials in the traditionary records of Pagan history, as well as in the sacred volume, where its peculiar cause, and the circumstances which attended it, are so distinctly and so fully related. Its magnitude and singularity could scarcely fail to make an indelible impression on the minds of the survivors, which would be communicated from them to their children, and would not be easily effaced from the traditions even of their latest posterity. A deficiency in such traces of this awful event, though perhaps it might not serve entirely to invalidate our belief of its reality, would certainly tend considerably to weaken its claim to credibility; it being scarcely probable that the knowledge of it should be utterly lost to the rest of the world, and confined to the documents of the Jewish nation alone. What we might reasonably expect has, accordingly, been actually and completely realized. The evidence which has been brought from almost every quarter of the world to bear upon the reality of this event, is of the most conclusive and irresistible kind; and every investigation, whether etymological or historical, which has been made concerning Heathen rites and traditions, has constantly added to its force, no less than to its extent.

And here, it were injustice to the memory of ingenuity and erudition almost unexampled in modern times, were we not to mention the labours of Bryant, the learned analysist of ancient mythology, whose patience and profoundness of research have thrown such new and convincing light on this subject. Nor must we forget his ardent and successful disciple, Mr. Faber, who, in his "Dissertation on the Mysteries of the Cabiri," has in travelling over similar ground with his illustrious master at once corrected some of his statements, and greatly strengthened his general conclusions. As the basis of their system, however, rests on a most extensive etymological examination of the names of the deities and other mythological personages worshipped and celebrated by the Heathen, compared with the varied traditions respecting their histories, and the nature of the rites and names of the places that were sacred to them, we cannot do more, in the present article, than shortly state the result of their investigations, referring for the particular details, to the highly original treatises already mentioned. According to them, the memory of the deluge was incorporated with almost every part of the Gentile mythology and worship; Noah, under a vast multitude of characters, being one of their first deities, to whom all the nations of the Heathen world looked up as their founder; and to some circumstance or other in whose history, and that of his sons and the first patriarchs, most, if not all, of their religious ceremonies may be considered as not indistinctly referring. Traces of these, neither vague nor obscure, they conceive to be found in the history and character, not only of Deucalion, but of Atlas, Cronus, or Saturn, Dionusos, Inachus, Janus, Minos, Zeus, and others among the Greeks; of Isis, Osiris, Sesostris, Oannes, Typhon, &c, among the Egyptians; of Dagon, Agruerus, Sydyk, &c, among the Phenicians; of Astarte, Derceto, &c, among the Assyrians; of Buddha, Menu, Vishnu, &c, among the Hindus; of Fohi, and a deity represented as sitting upon the lotos in the midst of waters, among the Chinese; of Budo and Iakusi among the Japanese, &c. They discover allusions to the ark, in many of the ancient mysteries, and traditions with respect to the dove and the rainbow, by which several of these allegorical personages were attended, which are not easily explicable, unless they be supposed to relate to the history of the deluge. By the celebrated Ogdoas of the Egyptians, consisting of eight persons sailing together in the sacred BARIS or ark, they imagine the family of Noah, which was precisely eight in number, to have been designated; and in the rites of Adonis or Thammuz, in particular, they point out many circumstances which seem to possess a distinct reference to the events recorded in the sixth and seventh chapters of Genesis. With regard to this system, we shall only farther observe, that, after every reasonable deduction is made from it, which the exuberant indulgence of fancy occasionally exhibited by its authors appears to render necessary, it contains so much that is relevant and conclusive, that it induces the conviction that it has a solid foundation in truth and fact; it being scarcely possible to conceive, that a mere hypothesis could be supported by evidence so varied, so extensive, and in many particulars so demonstrative, as that which its framers have produced.

Beside, however, the allusions to the deluge in the mythology and religious ceremonies of the Heathen, to which we have thus concisely adverted, there is a variety of traditions concerning it still more direct and circumstantial, the coincidence of which, with the narrative of Moses, it will require no common degree of skeptical hardihood to deny. We are informed by one of the circumnavigators of the world, who visited the remote island of Otaheite, that some of the inhabitants being asked concerning their origin, answered, that their supreme God having, a long time ago, been angry, dragged the earth through the sea, when their island was broken off and preserved. In the island of Cuba, the people are said to believe that the world was once destroyed by water by three persons, evidently alluding to the three sons of Noah. It is even related, that they have a tradition among them, that an old man, knowing that the deluge was approaching, built a large ship, and went into it with a great number of animals; and that he sent out from the ship a crow, which did not immediately come back, staying to feed on the carcasses of dead animals, but afterward returned with a green branch in its mouth. The author who gives the above account likewise affirms that it was reported by the inhabitants of Castella del Oro, in Terra Firma, that during a universal deluge, one man, and his children, were the only persons who escaped, by means of a canoe, and that from them the world was afterward peopled. According to the Peruvians, in consequence of a general inundation, occasioned by violent and continued rains, a universal destruction of the human species took place, a few persons only excepted, who escaped into caves on the tops of the mountains, into which they had previously conveyed a stock of provisions, and a number of live animals, lest when the waters abated, the whole race should have become extinct. Others of them affirm, that only six persons were saved, by means of a float or raft, and that from them all the inhabitants of the country are descended. They farther believe, that this event took place before there were any INCAS or kings among them, and when the country was extremely populous. The Brazilians not only preserve the tradition of a deluge, but believe that the whole race of mankind perished in it, except one man and his sister; or, according to others, two brothers with their wives, who were preserved by climbing the highest trees on their loftiest mountains; and who afterward became the heads of two different nations. The memory of this event they are even said to celebrate in some of their religious anthems or songs. Acosta, in his history of the Indies, says, that the Mexicans speak of a deluge in their country, by which all men were drowned; and that it was afterward peopled by VIRACOCHA, who came out of the lake Titicaca; and, according to Herrera, the Machoachans, a people comparatively in the neighbourhood of Mexico, had a tradition, that a single family was formerly preserved in an ark amid a deluge of waters; and that along with them, a sufficient number of animals were saved to stock the new world. During the time that they were shut up in the ark, several ravens were sent out, one of which brought back the branch of a tree. Among the Iroquois it is reported that a certain spirit, called by them Otkon, was the creator of the world; and that another being, called Messou, repaired it after a deluge, which happened in consequence of Otkon's dogs having one day while he was hunting with them lost themselves in a great lake, which, in consequence of this, overflowed its banks, and in a short time covered the whole earth.

Passing from the more remote western to the eastern continent, nearer to the region where Noah is generally supposed to have lived, we find the traditions respecting the deluge still more particular and minute. According to Josephus, there were a multitude of ancient authors who concurred in asserting that the world had once been destroyed by a flood: "This deluge," says he, "and the ark are mentioned by all who have written barbaric histories, one of whom is Berosus the Chaldean." Eusebius informs us, that Melo, a bitter enemy of the Jews, and whose testimony is on this account peculiarly valuable, takes notice of the person who was saved along with his sons from the flood, having been, after his preservation, driven away from Armenia, whence he retired to the mountainous parts of Syria. Abydenus, after giving an account of the deluge from which Xisuthrus, the Chaldean Noah, was saved, concludes with asserting, in exact concurrence with Berosus, that the ark first rested on the mountains of Armenia, and that its remains were used by the natives as a talisman; and Plutarch mentions the Noachic dove being sent out of the ark, and returning to it again, as an intimation to Deucalion that the storm had not yet ceased.

This, however, is by no means all: Sir W. Jones, speaking of one of the Chinese fables, says, "Although I cannot insist with confidence, that the rainbow mentioned in it alludes to the Mosaic narrative of the flood, nor build any solid argument on the divine person NIUVA, of whose character, and even of whose sex the historians of China speak very doubtfully; I may nevertheless assure you, after full inquiry and consideration, that the Chinese believe the earth to have been wholly covered with water, which, in works of undisputed authenticity, they describe as flowing abundantly, then subsiding, and separating the higher from the lower age of mankind." Still more coincident even than this with the Mosaic account, is the Grecian history of the deluge, as preserved by Lucian, a native of Samosata on the Euphrates; and its authority is the more incontrovertible, on account of his being an avowed derider of all religions. The antediluvians, according to him, had gradually become so hardened and profligate, as to be guilty of every species of injustice. They paid no regard to the obligation of oaths; were insolent, inhospitable, and unmerciful. For this reason they were visited with an awful calamity. Suddenly the earth poured forth a vast quantity of water, the rain descended in torrents, the rivers overflowed their banks, and the sea rose to a prodigious height, so that "all things became water," and all men were destroyed except Deucalion. He alone, for the sake of his prudence and piety, was reserved to a second generation. In obedience to a divine nomination, he entered, with his sons and their wives, into a large ark, which they had built for their preservation; and immediately swine, and horses, and lions, and serpents, and all other animals which live on earth, came to him by pairs, and were admitted by him into the ark. There they became perfectly mild and innoxious, their natures being changed by the gods, who created such a friendship between them, that they all sailed peaceably together, so long as the waters prevailed over the surface of the globe.

Scarcely less remarkable is the Hindoo tradition. It is contained in the ancient poem of the *Bhavagat*; and forms the subject of the first Purana, entitled *Matsya*, or "The Fish." The following is Sir William Jones's abridgment of it; and the identity of the event which it describes, with that of the Hebrew historian, is too obvious to require any particular illustration: "The demon Hayagriva, having purloined the Vedas from the custody of Brahma, while he was reposing at the close of the sixth Manwantara, the whole race of men became corrupt, except the seven Rishis, and Satyavrata, who then reigned in Dravira, a maritime region to the south of Carnata. This prince was performing his ablutions in the river Critimala, when Vishnu appeared to him in the shape of a small fish, and after several augmentations of bulk in different waters, was placed by Satyavrata in the ocean, where he thus addressed his amazed votary: 'In seven days all creatures who have offended me shall be destroyed by a deluge, but thou shalt be secured in a capacious vessel miraculously formed; take therefore all kinds of medicinal herbs, and esculent grain for food, and, together with the seven holy men, your respective wives, and pairs of all animals, enter the ark without fear: then shalt thou know God face to face, and all thy questions shall be answered.' Saying this, he disappeared; and after seven days the ocean began to overflow the coasts, and the earth to be flooded by constant showers, when Satyavrata, meditating on the deity, saw a large vessel moving on the waters. He entered it, having in all respects conformed to the instructions of Vishnu; who in the form of a vast fish, suffered the vessel to be tied with a great sea serpent, as with a cable, to his measureless horn. When the deluge had ceased, Vishnu slew the demon, and recovered the Vedas, instructed Satyavrata in divine knowledge, and appointed him the seventh Menu, by the name of Vaivaswata."

When we thus meet with some traditions of a deluge in almost every country, though the persons saved from it are said, in those various accounts to have resided in different districts widely separated from each other, we are constrained to allow that such a general concurrence of belief could never have originated merely from accident. While the mind is in this situation, Scripture comes forward, and, presenting a narrative more simple, better connected, and bearing an infinitely greater resemblance to authentic history, than any of those mythological accounts which occur in the traditions of Paganism, immediately flashes the conviction upon the understanding, that this must be the true history of those remarkable facts which other nations have handed down to us, only through the medium of allegory and fable. By the evidence adduced in this article, indeed, the moral certainty of the Mosaic history of the flood appears to be established on a basis sufficiently firm to bid defiance to the cavils of skepticism. "Let the ingenuity of unbelief first account satisfactorily for this universal agreement of the Pagan world; and she may then, with a greater degree of plausibility, impeach the truth of the Scriptural narrative of the deluge." The fact, however, is not only preserved in the traditions of all nations, as we have already seen; but after all the philosophical arguments which were formerly urged against it, philosophy has at length acknowledged that the present surface of the earth must have been submerged under water. "Not only," says Kirwan, "in every region of Europe, but also of both the old and new continents, immense quantities of marine shells, either dispersed or collected, have been discovered." This and several other facts seem to prove, that at least a great part of the present earth was, before the last general convulsion to which it has been subjected, the bed of an ocean which, at that time, was withdrawn from it. Other facts seem also to prove with sufficient evidence, that this was not a gradual retirement of the waters which once covered the parts now inhabited by men; but a violent one, such as may be supposed from the brief but emphatic relation of Moses. The violent action of water has left its traces in various undisputed phenomena. Stratified mountains of various heights exist in different parts of Europe, and of both continents; in and between whose strata, various substances of marine, and some vegetables of terrestrial, origin, repose either in their natural state, or petrified. To overspread the plains of the arctic circle with the shells of Indian seas, and with the bodies of elephants and rhinoceri, surrounded by masses of submarine vegetation; to accumulate on a single spot, as at La Bolca, in promiscuous confusion, the marine productions of the four quarters of the globe; what conceivable instrument would be efficacious but the rush of mighty waters? These facts, about which there is no dispute, and which are acknowledged by the advocates of each of the prevailing geological theories, give a sufficient attestation to the deluge of Noah, in which "the fountains of the great deep were broken up," and from which precisely such phenomena might be expected to follow. To this may be added, though less decisive in proof, yet certainly strong as presumptive evidence, that the very aspect of the earth's surface exhibits interesting marks both of the violent action, and the rapid subsidence, of waters; as well as affords a most interesting instance of the divine goodness in converting what was ruin itself into utility and beauty. The great frame-work of the varied surface of the habitable earth was probably laid by a more powerful agency than that of water; either when on the third day the waters under the heavens were gathered into one place, and the crust of the primitive earth was broken down to receive them, so that "the dry land might appear;" by those mighty convulsions which appear to have accompanied the general deluge; but the rounding, so to speak, of what was rugged, where the substance was yielding, and the graceful undulations of hill and dale which so frequently present themselves, were probably effected by the retiring waters. The flood has passed away; but the soils which it deposited remain; and the valleys through which its last streams were drawn off to the ocean, with many an eddy and sinuous course, still exist, exhibiting visible proofs of its agency, and impressed with forms so adapted to the benefit of man, and often so gratifying to the finest taste, that, when the flood "turned," it may be said to have "left a blessing behind it."

The objections once made to the FACT of a general deluge have, indeed, been greatly weakened by the progress of philosophical knowledge; and may be regarded as nearly given up, like the former notion of the high antiquity of the race of men, founded on the Chinese and Egyptian chronologies and pretended histories. Philosophy has even at last found out that there is sufficient water in the ocean, if called forth, to overflow the highest mountains to the height given by Moses,--a conclusion which it once stoutly denied. Keill formerly computed that twenty-eight oceans would be necessary for that purpose; but we are now informed "that a farther progress in mathematical and physical knowledge has shown the different seas and oceans to contain, at least, forty-eight times more water than they were then supposed to do; and that the mere raising of the temperature of the whole body of the ocean to a degree no greater than marine animals live in, in the shallow seas between the tropics, would so expand it as more than to produce the height above the mountains stated in the Mosaic account." As to the deluge of Noah, therefore, infidelity has almost entirely lost the aid of philosophy in framing objections to the Scriptures.

DEMONIAC, a human being possessed with and actuated by some spiritual malignant being of superior power. The word DEMON is used by Pagan writers often in a good sense, and is applied to their divinities; but the demons of holy writ are malignant spirits. We are not informed very particularly about their origin or destiny; but we find them represented as ϖνεύματα ἀκάθαρτα, and ϖνεύματα ϖονηρὰ, UNCLEAN and EVIL SPIRITS; and we must consider them as in league with the devil, as the subjects of his dominion, and the instruments of his will. They were the immediate agents in all possessions; and to expel or restrain them, or to cure the diseases which they were supposed to occasion, was one of the miraculous gifts of the early times.

2. On this subject an ardent controversy was agitated about the middle and toward the end of the last century, between Dr. Farmer and his opponents. In this controversy, of which we shall attempt to give a short view, it was contended, on the one hand, that the demoniacal cases recorded in the books of the New Testament, were instances of real possession; and, on the other, that they were merely diseases, set forth under the notion of possessions, in conformity with the belief which was prevalent at the time. By the one party, the language of holy writ was interpreted literally; and by the other it was considered as figurative, and used in the way of accommodation to the existing opinions. The leading asseveration of Dr. Farmer, upon the general question, is, that miracles, or works surpassing the power of men, are never performed without a divine interposition; and by a divine interposition he means, either the immediate agency of the Deity himself, or of beings empowered and commissioned by him. And the proof of this asseveration, he tells us, may very easily be found, if we consider that, on any other supposition, it is impossible to show that a religion supported by miracles is really from God. For the miracles in question, or works surpassing the power of human beings, may have been performed by evil spirits, acting independently of the Divinity, thwarting his purposes, and marring the operation of his goodness. Should it be said that, from the tendency of the miracle itself, and A FORTIORI, from the tendency of the miracle and religion when taken together, we may easily infer the character of the being from whom the whole scheme proceeds,--to this also Dr. Farmer is ready with his answer. "With regard to doctrines," says he "of a moral or useful tendency, it is not, in all cases, easy for the bulk of mankind, or even for the wise and learned, to form a certain judgment concerning them. What to men appeared to have a tendency to promote virtue and happiness, superior beings, who discerned its remotest effects, might know to be a curse rather than a blessing, and give it countenance from a motive of malevolence. On the other hand, a doctrine really subservient to the cause of piety and virtue, men might judge to be prejudicial to it. And were the sanctity of the doctrine ever so apparent, it would not (on the principles of those with whom we are here arguing)

were designed, not wantonly to fix the charge of being a leper upon an innocent person, and thus to impose upon him those restraints and inconveniences which the truth of such a charge naturally implies, but to ascertain, in the fairest and most satisfactory manner, and to separate those, and those only, who were truly and really leprous. As this was the prominent object of his laws that have come down to us on this subject, namely, to secure a fair and impartial decision on a question of this kind, he has not mentioned those signs of leprosy which admitted of no doubt, but those only which might be the subject of contention; and left it to the priests, who also fulfilled the office of physicians, to distinguish between the really leprous, and those who had only the appearance of being such. We find mention, in the rules laid down by Moses for the purpose of ascertaining the true tokens of leprosy, of a cutaneous disorder which is denominated by him BOHAK. The words of Moses, which may be found in Lev. xiii, 38, 39, are as follows: "If a man or woman have white spots on the skin, and the priest see that the colour of these spots is faint and pale, it is, in this case, the BOHAK that has broken out on the skin, and they are clean." A person, accordingly, who was attacked with this disease, the BOHAK, was not declared unclean; and the reason of it was, that it is not only harmless in itself, but is free from that infectious and hereditary character which belongs to the true leprosy. "The BOHAK" says Mr. Niebuhr, "is neither infectious nor dangerous. A black boy at Mocha, who was attacked with this sort of leprosy, had white spots here and there on his body. It was said that the use of sulphur had for some time been of service to this boy, but had not altogether removed the disease." He then adds the following extract from the papers of a Dr. Foster: "May 15th, 1763, I myself saw a case of the BOHAK in a Jew at Mocha. The spots in this disease are of unequal size. They have no shining appearance, nor are they perceptibly elevated above the skin; and they do not change the colour of the hair. Their colour is an obscure white or somewhat reddish. The rest of the skin of this patient was blacker than that of the people of the country was in general, but the spots were not so white as the skin of an European when not sunburnt. The spots, in this species of leprosy, do not appear on the hands, nor about the navel, but on the neck and face; not, however, on that part of the head where the hair grows very thick. They gradually spread, and continue sometimes only about two months; but in some cases, indeed, as long as two years, and then disappear, by degrees, of themselves. This disorder is neither infectious nor hereditary, nor does it occasion any inconvenience." "That all this," remarks Michaëlis, "should still be found exactly to hold at the distance of three thousand five hundred years from the time of Moses, ought certainly to gain some credit to his laws, even with those who will not allow them to be of divine authority." The pestilence, in its effects, is equally terrible with the leprosy, and is much more rapid in its progress; for it terminates the existence of those who are infected with it almost immediately, and at the farthest within three or four days. The Gentiles were in the habit of referring back the pestilence to the agency and interference of that being, whatever it might be, whether idol or spirit, whom they regarded as the divinity. The Hebrews, also, every where attribute it to the agency either of God himself, or of that legate or angel, whom they denominate מלאך.

3. The PALSY of the New Testament is a disease of very wide import. Many infirmities, as Richter has demonstrated, were comprehended under the word which is rendered PALSY in the New Testament. 1. The apoplexy, a paralytic shock, which affected the whole body. 2. The hemiplegy, which affects and paralyzes only one side of the body. 3. The paraplegy, which paralyzes all the parts of the system below the neck. 4. The catalepsy, which is caused by a contraction of the muscles in the whole or a part of the body, for example, in the hands, and is very dangerous. The effects upon the parts seized are very violent and deadly. For instance: when a person is struck with it, if his hand happens to be extended, he is unable to draw it back. If the hand is not extended when he is struck with the disease, he is unable to extend it: it appears diminished in size, and dried up in appearance. Hence the Hebrews were in the habit of calling it "a withered hand," 1 Kings xiii, 4–6; Zech. xi, 17; Matt. xii, 10–13; John v, 3. 5. The cramp, in oriental countries, is a fearful malady, and by no means unfrequent. It originates from the chills of the night. The limbs, when seized with it, remain immovable, sometimes turned in, and sometimes out, in the same position as when they were first seized. The person afflicted resembles those undergoing the torture βασανιζομένοι, and experiences nearly the same exquisite sufferings. Death follows the disease in a few days, Matt. viii, 6, 8; Luke vii, 2; 1 Macc. ix, 55–58.

DISPENSATIONS, Divine. These are otherwise called "the ways of God," and denote those schemes or methods which are devised and pursued by the wisdom and goodness of God, in order to manifest his perfections and will to mankind, for the purpose of their instruction, discipline, reformation, and advancement in rectitude of temper and conduct, in order to promote their happiness. These are the grand ends of the divine dispensations; and in their aptitude to promote these ends consist their excellence and glory. The works or constitutions of nature are, in a general sense, divine dispensations, by which God condescends to display to us his being and attributes, and thus to lead us to the acknowledgment, adoration, and love, of our Creator, Father, and Benefactor. The sacred Scriptures reveal and record other dispensations of divine providence, which have been directed to the promotion of the religious principles, moral conduct, and true happiness of mankind. These have varied in several ages of the world, and have been adapted by the wisdom and goodness of God to the circumstances of his intelligent and accountable creatures. In this sense the various revelations which God has communicated to mankind at different periods, and the means he has used, as occasion has required, for their discipline and improvement, have been justly denominated divine dispensations. Accordingly, we read in the works of theological writers of the various dispensations of religion; that of the patriarchs, that of Moses, and that of Christ, called the dispensation of grace, the perfection and ultimate object of every other. All these were adapted to the conditions of the human race at these several periods; all, in regular succession, were mutually connected and rendered preparatory one to the other; and all were subservient to the design of saving the world, and promoting the perfection and happiness of its rational and moral inhabitants. See Covenant.

DISPERSION OF MANKIND. See Division of the Earth.

DIVINATION, a conjecture or surmise, formed concerning future events, from things which are supposed to presage them. The eastern people were always fond of divination, magic, the curious arts of interpreting dreams, and of obtaining a knowledge of future events. When Moses published the law, this disposition had long been common in Egypt and the neighbouring countries. To prevent the Israelites from consulting diviners, fortune tellers, interpreters of dreams, &c, he forbade them, under very severe penalties, to consult persons of this description, and promised to them the true spirit of prophecy as infinitely superior. He commanded those to be stoned who pretended to have a familiar spirit, or the spirit of divination, Deut. xviii, 9, 10, 15. The writings of the prophets are full of invectives against the Israelites who consulted diviners, and against false prophets who by such means seduced the people.

2. Different kinds of divination have passed for sciences, as 1. Aëromancy, divining by the air. 2. Astrology, by the heavens. 3. Augury, by the flight and singing of birds, &c. 4. Cheiromancy, by inspecting the lines of the hand. 5. Geomancy, by observing cracks or clefts in the earth. 6. Haruspicy, by inspecting the bowels of animals. 7. Horoscopy, a branch of astrology, marking the position of the heavens when a person is born. 8. Hydromancy, by water. 9. Physiognomy, by the countenance. 10. Pyromancy, a divination made by fire.

3. The kinds of divination, to which superstition in modern times has given belief, are not less numerous, or less ridiculous, than those which were practised in the days of profound ignorance. The divining rod, which is mentioned in Scripture, is still in some repute in the north of England, though its application is now confined principally to the discovery of veins of lead ore, seams of coal, or springs. In order that it may possess the full virtue for this purpose, it should be made of hazel. Divination by Virgilian, Horatian, or Bible lots, was formerly very common; and the last kind is still practised. The works are opened by chance, and the words noticed which are covered by the thumb: if they can be interpreted in any respect relating to the person, they are reckoned prophetic. Charles I. is said to have used this kind of divination to ascertain his fate. The ancient Christians were so much addicted to the SORTES SANCTORUM, or divining by the Bible, that it was expressly forbidden by a council. Divination by the speal, or blade bone of a sheep, is used in Scotland. In the Highlands it is called SLEINA-REACHED, or reading the speal bone. It was very common in England in the time of Drayton, particularly among the colony of Flemings settled in Pembrokeshire. Camden relates of the Irish, that they looked through the bare blade bone of a sheep; and if they saw any spot in it darker than ordinary, they believed that somebody would be buried out of the house. The Persians used this mode of divination.

4. Of all attempts to look into futurity by such means, as well as resorting to charms and other methods of curing diseases, and discovering secrets, we may say, that they are relics of Paganism, and argue an ignorance, folly, or superstition, dishonourable to the Christian name; and are therefore to be reproved and discouraged.

DIVISION OF THE EARTH. The prophecy of Noah, says Dr. Hales, was uttered long after the deluge. It evidently alludes to a divine decree for the orderly division of the earth among the three primitive families of his sons, because it notices the "tents of Shem" and the "enlargement of Japheth," Genesis ix, 20–27. This decree was probably promulgated about the same time by the venerable patriarch. The prevailing tradition of such a decree for this threefold division of the earth, is intimated both in the Old and New Testament. Moses refers to it, as handed down to the Israelites, "from the days of old, and the years of many generations; as they might learn from their fathers and their elders," and farther, as conveying a special grant of the land of Palestine, to be the lot of the twelve tribes of Israel:--

"When the Most High divided to the nations their settlements,

When he separated the sons of Adam,

He assigned the boundaries of the peoples [of Israel]

According to the number of the sons of Israel:

For the portion of the Lord is his people,

Jacob is the lot of his inheritance," Deut. xxxii, 7–9.

And this furnishes an additional proof of the justice of the expulsion of the Canaanites, as usurpers, by the Israelites, the rightful possessors of the land of Palestine, under Moses, Joshua, and their successors, when the original grant was renewed to Abraham, Gen. xv, 13–21. And the knowledge of this divine decree may satisfactorily account for the panic terror with which the devoted nations of Canaan were struck at the miraculous passage of the Red Sea by the Israelites, and approach to their confines, so finely described by Moses:--

"The nations shall hear [this] and tremble,

Sorrow shall seize the inhabitants of Palestine.

Then shall the dukes of Edom be amazed,

Dismay shall possess the princes of Moab,

The inhabitants of Canaan shall melt away:

Fear and terror shall fall upon them,

By the greatness of thine arm they shall be petrified,

Till thy people pass over [Jordan] O Lord,

Till the people pass over, whom thou hast redeemed."

Exodus xv, 14–16.

St. Paul, also, addressing the Athenians, refers to the same decree, as a well-known tradition in the Heathen world: "God made of one blood every nation of men to dwell upon the whole face of the earth; having appointed the predetermined seasons and boundaries of their dwellings," Acts xvii, 26. Here he represents mankind as all of "one blood," race, or stock, "the sons of Adam" and of Noah in succession; and the seasons and the boundaries of their respective settlements, as previously regulated by the divine appointment. And this was conformable to their own geographical allegory; that Chronus, the god of time, or Saturn, divided the universe among his three sons, allotting the heaven to Jupiter, the sea to Neptune, and hell to Pluto. But Chronus represented Noah, who divided the world among his three sons, allotting the upper regions of the north to Japheth, the maritime or middle regions to Shem, and the lower regions of the south to Ham. According to the Armenian tradition recorded by Abulfaragi, Noah distributed the habitable earth from north to south between his sons, and gave to Ham the region of the blacks, to Shem the region of the tawny, FUSCORUM, and to Japheth the region of the ruddy, RUBRORUM: and he dates the actual division of the earth in the hundred and fortieth year of Peleg, B. C. 2614, or five hundred and forty-one years after the deluge, and one hundred and ninety-one years after the death of Noah, in the following order:--"To the sons of Shem was allotted the middle of the earth, namely, Palestine, Syria, Assyria, Samaria, Singar, [or Shinar,] Babel, [or Babylonia,] Persia, and Hegiaz; [Arabia;] to the sons of Ham, Teimen, [or Idumea, Jer. xlix, 7,] Africa, Nigritia, Egypt, Nubia, Ethiopia, Scindia, and India; [or India west and east of the river Indus;] to the sons of Japheth, also, Garbia, [the north,] Spain, France, the countries of the Greeks, Sclavonians, Bulgarians, Turks, and Armenians." In this curious and valuable geographical chart, Armenia, the cradle of the human race, was allotted to Japheth, by right of primogeniture; and Samaria and Babel to the sons of Shem; the usurpation of these regions, therefore, by Nimrod, and of Palestine by Canaan, was in violation of the divine decree. Though the migration of the primitive families began at this time, B. C. 2614, or about five hundred and forty-one years after the deluge, it was a length of time before they all reached their respective destinations. The "seasons," as well as the "boundaries" of their respective settlements were equally the appointment of God; the nearer countries to the original settlement being planted first, and the remoter in succession. These primitive settlements seem to have been scattered and detached from each other according to local convenience. Even so late as the tenth generation after the flood in Abraham's days, there were considerable tracts of land in Palestine unappropriated, on which he and his nephew, Lot, freely pastured their cattle without hinderance or molestation. That country was not fully peopled till the fourth generation after, at the exode of the Israelites from Egypt. And Herodotus represents Scythia as an uninhabited desert, until Targitorus planted the first colony there, about a thousand years, at most, before Darius Hystaspes invaded Scythia, or about B. C. 1508. The orderly settlements of the three primitive families are recorded in that most venerable and valuable geographical chart, the tenth chapter of Genesis, in which it is curious to observe how long the names of the first settlers have been preserved among their descendants, even down to the present day:--

1. Japheth, the eldest son of Noah, Gen. x, 21, and his family, are first noticed, Gen. x, 2–5. The name of the patriarch himself was preserved among his Grecian descendants, in the proverb, τοῦ Ἰάπετου ϖρεσβύτερος, OLDER THAN JAPETUS, denoting the remotest antiquity. The radical part of the word Ἰάπετ, evidently expresses JAPHETH. (1.) Gomer, his eldest son, was the father of the Gomerians. These, spreading from the regions north of Armenia and Bactriana, Ezek. xxxviii, 6, extended themselves westward over nearly the whole continent of Europe; still retaining their paternal denomination, with some slight variation, as Cimmerians, in Asia; Cimbri and Umbri, in Gaul and Italy; and Cymri, Cambri, and Cumbri, in Wales and Cumberland at the present day. They are also identified by ancient authors with the Galatæ of Asia Minor, the Gaels, Gauls, and Celtæ, of Europe, who likewise spread from the Euxine Sea, to the Western Ocean; and from the Baltic to Italy southward, and first planted the British Isles. Josephus remarks, that the Galatæ were called Γομαρείς, GOMARIANI, from their ancestor Gomar. See the numerous authorities adduced in support of the identity of the Gomerians and Celts, by that learned and ingenious antiquary, Faber, in his "Origin of Pagan Idolatry." Of Gomer's sons, Ashkenaz appears to have settled on the coasts of the Euxine Sea, which from him seems to have received its primary denomination of Ἄξενος, AXENUS, nearly resembling Ashkenaz; but forgetting its etymology in process of time, the Greeks considered it as a compound term in their own language, Α-ξένος, signifying INHOSPITABLE; and thence metamorphosed it into Εὔ-ξένος, EU-XENUS, "very hospitable." His precise settlement is represented in Scripture as contiguous to Armenia, westward; for the kingdoms of Ararat, Minni, and Ashkenaz, are noticed together, Jer. li, 27. Riphat, the second son of Gomer, seems to have given name to the Riphean mountains of the north of Asia; and Togarmah, the third son, may be traced in the

Trocmi of Strabo, the Trogmi of Cicero, and Trogmades of the council of Chalcedon, inhabiting the confines of Pontus and Cappadocia. (2.) Magog, Tubal, and Mesech, sons of Japhet, are noticed together by Ezekiel, as settled in the north, Ezek. xxxviii, 2, 14, 15. And as the ancestors of the numerous Sclavonic and Tartar tribes, the first may be traced in the Mongogians, Monguls, and Moguls; the second, in the Tobolski, of Siberia; and the third, Mesech, or Mosoc, in the Moschici, Moscow, and Muscovites. (3.) Madai was the father of the Medes, who are repeatedly so denominated in Scripture, 2 Kings xvii, 6; Isa. xiii, 17; Jer. li, 11; Dan. v, 28, &c. (4.) From Javan was descended the Javanians, or Ἰάονες of the Greeks, and the Yavanas of the Hindus. Greece itself is called Javan by Daniel, xi, 2; and the people Ἰάονες by Homer in his "Iliad." These aboriginal Ἰάονες of Greece are not to be confounded, as is usually the case, with the later Ἴωνες, who invaded and subdued the Javanian territories, and were of a different stock. The accurate Pausanias states, that the name of Ἴωνες, was comparatively modern, while that of Ἰάονες is acknowledged to have been the primitive title of the barbarians who were subdued by the Ἴωνες. Strabo remarks that Attica was formerly called both Ionia and Ias, or Ian; while Herodotus asserts, that the Athenians were not willing to be called Ἴωνες; and he derives the name from Ἴων, the son of Zuth, descended from Deucalion or Noah. And this Ion is said by Eusebius to have been the ringleader in the building of the tower of Babel, and the first introducer of idol worship, and Sabianism, or adoration of the sun, moon, and stars. This would identify Ion with Nimrod. And the Ionians appear to have been composed of the later colonists, the Palli, Pelasgi, or roving tribes from Asia, Phenicia, and Egypt, who, according to Herodotus, first corrupted the simplicity of the primitive religion of Greece, and who, by the Hindus, were called Yonigas, or worshippers of the yoni or dove. This critical distinction between the Iaones and the Iones, the Yavanas, and the Yonigas, we owe to the sagacity of Faber. Of Javan's sons, Elishah and Dodon, may be recognized in Elis and Dodona, the oldest settlements of Greece; Kittim, in the Citium of Macedonia, and Chittim, or maritime coasts of Greece and Italy, Num. xxiv, 24; and Tarshish, in the Tarsus of Cilicia, and Tartessus of Spain.

2. Ham and his family are next noticed, Gen. x, 6–20. The name of the patriarch is recorded in the title frequently given to Egypt, "The land of Ham," Psalm cv, 23, &c. (1.) Of his sons, the first and most celebrated appears to have been Cush, who gave name to the land of Cush, both in Asia and Africa; the former still called Chusistan by the Arabian geographers, and Susiana by the Greeks, and Cusha Dwipa Within, by the Hindus; the other, called Cusha Dwipa Without. And the enterprising Cushim or Cuthim, of Scripture, in Asia and Europe, assumed the title of Getæ, Guiths, and Goths; and of Scuths, Scuits, and Scots; and of Sacas, Sacasenas, and Saxons. The original family settlement of Abraham was "Ur of the Chasdim," or Chaldees, Gen. xi, 28, who are repeatedly mentioned in Scripture, Isa. xiii, 9; Dan. ix, 1, &c. According to Faber's ingenious remark, it may more properly be pronounced Chus-dim, signifying Godlike Cushites. It is highly improbable that they were so named from Chesed, Abraham's nephew, Gen. xxii, 22, who was a mere boy, if born at all, when Abraham left Ur, and was an obscure individual, never noticed afterward. Of Cush's sons, Seba, Havilah, Sabtah, Sabtacha, and Raamah; and the sons of Raamah, Sheba, and Dedan, seem to have settled in Idumea and Arabia, from the similar names of places there; and of his descendants, Nimrod, the mighty hunter, first founded the kingdom of Babylon, and afterward of Assyria, invading the settlements of the Shemites, contrary to the divine decree. His posterity were probably distinguished by the title of Chusdim, Isaiah xxiii, 13. (2.) The second son of Ham was Misr, or Mizraim. He settled in Egypt, whence the Egyptians were universally styled in Scripture, Mizraim, or Mizraites, in the plural form. But the country is denominated in the east, to this day, "the land of Misr;" which, therefore, seems to have been the name of the patriarch himself. The children of Misr, like their father, are denominated in Scripture by the plural number. Of these, the Ludim and Lehabim were probably the Copto-Libyans, Ezek. xxx, 5; the Naphtuhim occupied the sea coast, which by the Egyptians was called Nephthus; whence, probably, originated the name of the maritime god Neptune. The Pathrusim occupied a part of Lower Egypt, called from them Pathros, Isa. xi, 11. The Caphtorim and the Casluhim, whose descendants were the Philistim of Palestine, occupied the district which lies between the delta of the Nile and the southern extremity of Palestine, Deut. ii, 23; Amos ix, 7. (3.) Phut is merely noticed, without any mention of his family. But the tribes of Phut and Lud are mentioned together, with Cush, or Ethiopia, Jer. xlvi, 9; Ezek. xxx, 5; and Jerom notices a district in Libya, called Regio Phutensis, or the land of Phut. (4.) Canaan has been noticed already; and the original extent of the land of Canaan is carefully marked by Moses. Its western border, along the Mediterranean Sea, extended from Sidon, southward, to Gaza; its southern border from thence, eastward, to Sodom and Gomorrah, Admah and Zeboim, the cities of the plain, afterward covered by the Dead Sea, or Asphaltite Lake; its eastern border extending from thence northward, to Laish, Dan, or the springs of the Jordan; and its northern border, from thence to Sidon, westward. Of Canaan's sons, Sidon, the eldest, occupied the north-west corner, and built the town of that name, so early celebrated for her luxury and commerce in Scripture, Judges xviii, 7; 1 Kings v, 6; and by Homer, who calls the Sidonians, πολυδαίδαλοι, SKILLED IN MANY ARTS. And Tyre, so flourishing afterward, though boasting of her own antiquity, Isa. xxiii, 7, is styled, "a daughter of Sidon," or a colony from thence, Isa. v, 12. Heth, his second son, and the Hittites, his descendants appear to have settled in the south, near Hebron, Gen. xxiii, 3–7; and next to them, at Jerusalem, the Jebusites, or descendants of Jebus, both remaining in their original settlements till David's days; 2 Sam. xi, 3; v, 6–9. Beyond the Jebusites, were settled the Emorites, or Amorites, Num. xiii, 29, who extended themselves beyond Jordan, and were the most powerful of the Canaanite tribes, Gen. xv, 16; Num. xxi, 21, until they were destroyed by

Moses and Joshua, with the rest of the devoted nations of Canaan's family.

3. Shem and his family are noticed last, Gen. x, 21–30. His posterity were confined to middle Asia. (1.) His son Elam appears to have been settled in Elymais, or southern Persia, contiguous to the maritime tract of Chusistan, Dan. viii, 2. (2.) His son Ashur planted the land thence called Assyria, which soon became a province of the Cushite, or Cuthic empire, founded by Nimrod. (3.) Arphaxad, through his grandson, Eber, branched out into the two houses of Peleg and Joktan. Peleg probably remained in Chaldea, or southern Babylonia, at the time of the dispersion; for there we find his grandson, Terah, and his family, settled at "Ur of the Chaldees," Gen. xi, 31. Of the numerous children of Joktan, it is said by Moses, that "their dwelling was from Mesha, as thou goest unto Sephar, a mount of the east." Faber is inclined to believe that they were the ancestors of the great body of the Hindus, who still retain a lively tradition of the patriarch Shem, Shama, or Sharma; and that the land of Ophir, abounding in gold, so called from one of the sons of Joktan, lay beyond the Indus, eastward. (4.) Lud was probably the father of the Ludim or Lydians, of Asia Minor; for this people had a tradition that they were descended from Lud or Lydus, according to Josephus. (5.) The children of Aram planted the fertile country north of Babylonia, called Aram Naharaim, "Aram between the two rivers," the Euphrates and the Tigris, thence called by the Greeks, Mesopotamis, Gen. xxiv, 10, and Padan Aram, the level country of Aram, Gen. xxv, 20. This country of Aram is frequently rendered Syria in Scripture, Judges x, 6; Hosea xii, 12, &c; which is not to be confounded with Palestine Syria, into which they afterward spread themselves, still retaining their original name of Ἄριμοι, or Arameans, noticed by Homer in his "Iliad."

4. Upon this distribution of Noah's posterity we shall only observe, that the Deity presided over all their counsels and deliberations, and that he guided and settled all mankind according to the dictates of his all-comprehending wisdom and benevolence. To this purpose, the ancients themselves, according to Pindar, retained some idea that the dispersion of men was not the effect of chance, but that they had been settled in different countries by the appointment of Providence, Gen. xi, 8, 9; Deut. xxii, 8. This dispersion, and that confusion of languages with which it originated, was intended, by the counsel of an all-wise Providence, to counteract and defeat the scheme which had been projected by the descendants of Noah, for maintaining their union, implied in their proposing to make themselves a name, שם, which Schultens, in Job i, 1, derives from the Arabic verb שמה, or שמש, TO BE HIGH ELEVATED, or EMINENT. By this scheme, which seems to have been a project of state policy, for keeping all men together under the present chiefs and their successors, a great part of the earth must, for a long time, have been uninhabited, and overrun with wild beasts. The bad effects which this project would have had upon the minds, the morals, and religion of mankind, was, probably, the chief reason why God interposed to frustrate it as soon as it was formed. It had manifestly a direct tendency to tyranny, oppression, and slavery. Whereas in forming several independent governments by a small body of men, the ends of government, and the security of liberty and property, would be much better attended to, and more firmly established; which, in fact, was really the case; if we may judge of the rest by the constitution of one of the most eminent, the kingdom of Egypt, Gen. xlvii, 15–27. The Egyptians were masters of their persons and property, till they sold them to Pharaoh for bread; and then their servitude amounted to no more than the fifth part of the produce of the country, as an annual tax payable to the king. By this event, considered as a wise dispensation of Providence, bounds were set to the contagion of wickedness; evil example was confined, and could not extend its influence beyond the limits of one country; nor could wicked projects be carried on, with universal concurrence, by many small colonies, separated by the natural boundaries of mountains, rivers, barren deserts, and seas, and hindered from associating together by a variety of languages, unintelligible to each other. Moreover, in this dispersed state, they could, whenever God pleased, be made reciprocal checks upon each other, by invasions and wars, which would weaken the power, and humble the pride, of corrupt and vicious communities. This dispensation was, therefore, properly calculated to prevent a second universal degeneracy; God dealing in it with men as rational agents, and adapting his scheme to their state and circumstances.

DIVORCE. As the ancient Hebrews paid a stipulated price for the privilege of marrying, they seemed to consider it the natural consequence of making a payment of that kind, that they should be at liberty to exercise a very arbitrary power over their wives, and to renounce or divorce them whenever they chose. This state of things, as Moses himself very clearly saw, was not equitable as respected the woman, and was very often injurious to both parties. Finding himself, however, unable to overrule feelings and practices of very ancient standing, he merely annexed to the original institution of marriage a very serious admonition to this effect, viz. that it would be less criminal for a man to desert his father and mother, than without adequate cause to desert his wife, Gen. ii, 14, compared with Malachi ii, 11–16. He also laid a restriction upon the power of the husband as far as this, that he would not permit him to repudiate the wife without giving her a bill of divorce. He farther enacted in reference to this subject that the husband might receive the repudiated wife back, in case she had not in the meanwhile been married to another person; but if she had been thus married, she could never afterward become the wife of her first husband; a law, which the faith due to the second husband clearly required, Deut. xxiv, 1–4, compare Jer. iii, 1, and Matt. i, 19; xix, 8. The inquiry, "What should be considered an adequate cause of divorce," was left by Moses to be determined by the husband himself. He had liberty to divorce her, if he saw in her ANY THING NAKED, any thing displeasing or improper, any thing so much at war with propriety, and a source of so much dissatisfaction as to be, in the estimation of the husband, sufficient ground for separation. These expressions, however, were sharply contested as to their meaning in the later times of the Jewish nation. The school of Hillel contended, that the husband might lawfully put away the wife for any cause, even the smallest. The mistake committed by the school of Hillel in taking this ground was, that they confounded moral and civil law. It is true, as far as the Mosaic statute or the civil law was concerned, the husband had a right thus to do; but it is equally clear, that the ground of just separation must have been, not a TRIVIAL, but a prominent and important one, when it is considered, that he was bound to consult the rights of the woman, and was amenable to his conscience and his God. The school of Shammai explained the phrase, NAKEDNESS OF A THING, to mean ACTUAL ADULTERY. Our Lord agreed with the school of Shammai as far as this, that the ground of divorce should be one of a moral nature, and not less than adultery; but he does not appear to have agreed with them in their opinion in respect to the Mosaic statute. On the contrary, he denied the equity of that statute, and in justification of Moses maintained, that he permitted divorces for causes below adultery, only in consequence of the hardness of the people's hearts, Matt. v, 31, 32; xviii, 1–9; Mark x, 2–12; Luke xvi, 18. Wives, who were considered the property of their husbands, did not enjoy by the Mosaic statutes a reciprocal right, and were not at liberty to dissolve the matrimonial alliance by giving a bill of divorce to that effect. In the latter periods, however, of the Jewish state, the Jewish matrons, the more powerful of them at least, appear to have imbibed the spirit of the ladies of Rome, and to have exercised in their own behalf the same power that was granted by the Mosaic law only to their husbands, Mark vi, 17–29; x, 12.

DOCETÆ, the advocates of an early heresy, which taught that Christ acted and suffered, not in reality, but in appearance. They were so denominated from δοκεῖν, TO APPEAR. See Gnostics.

DOCTORS, or Teachers, of the law, a class of men in great repute among the Jews. They had studied the law of Moses in its various branches, and the numerous interpretations which had been grafted upon it in later times; and, on various occasions, they gave their opinion on cases referred to them for advice. Nicodemus, himself a doctor (διδάσκαλος, TEACHER) of the law, comes to consult Jesus, whom he compliments in the same terms as he was accustomed to receive from his scholars: "Rabbi, we know that thou art διδάσκαλος, a competent teacher from God." Doctors of the law were chiefly of the sect of the Pharisees; but they are sometimes distinguished from that sect, Luke v, 17.

DOG, כלב, an animal well known. By the law of Moses, the dog was declared unclean, and was held in great contempt among the Jews, 1 Sam. xvii, 43; xxiv, 14; 2 Sam. ix, 8; 2 Kings viii, 13. Yet they had them in considerable numbers in their cities. They were not, however, shut up in their houses or courts, but forced to seek their food where they could find it. The Psalmist compares violent men to dogs, who go about the city in the night, prowl about for their food, and growl, and become clamorous if they be not satisfied, Psalm lix, 6, 14, 15. Mr. Harmer has illustrated this by quotations from travellers into the east. The Turks also reckon the dog a filthy creature, and therefore drive him from their houses; so that with them dogs guard rather the streets and districts, than particular houses, and live on the offals that are thrown abroad. In 1 Sam. xxv, 3, Nabal is said to have been "churlish and evil in his manners; and he was of the house of Caleb;" but Caleb here is not a proper name. Literally, it is, "He was the son of a dog;" and so the Septuagint, Syriac, and Arabic render it,--he was irritable, snappish, and snarling as a dog. The irritable disposition of the dog is the foundation of that saying, "He that passeth by, and meddleth with strife belonging not to him, is like one that taketh a dog by the ears," Prov. xxvi, 17; that is, he wantonly exposes himself to danger.

In 1 Kings xxi, 23, it is said, "The dogs shall eat Jezebel." Mr. Bruce, when at Gondar, was witness to a scene in a great measure similar to the devouring of Jezebel by dogs. He says, "The bodies of those killed by the sword were hewn to pieces, and scattered about the streets, being denied burial. I was miserable, and almost driven to despair, at seeing my hunting dogs, twice let loose by the carelessness of my servants, bringing into the court yard the heads and arms of slaughtered men, and which I could no way prevent but by the destruction of the dogs themselves." He also adds, that upon being asked by the king the reason of his dejected and sickly appearance, among other reasons, he informed him, "it was occasioned by an execution of three men, which he had lately seen; because the hyænas, allured into the streets by the quantity of carrion, would not let him pass by night in safety from the palace; and because the dogs fled into his house, to eat pieces of human carcasses at their leisure." This account illustrates also the readiness of the dogs to lick the blood of Ahab, 1 Kings xxii, 38; in conformity to which is the expression of the Prophet Jeremiah, xv, 3, "I will appoint over them the sword to slay, and the dogs to tear."

2. The dog was held sacred by the Egyptians. This fact we learn from Juvenal, who complains, in his fifteenth satire,

OPPIDA TOTA CANEM VENCRANTUR, NEMO DIANAM.

"Thousands regard the hound with holy fear,

Not one, Diana."

Gifford.

The testimony of the Latin poet is confirmed by Diodorus, who, in his first book, assures us that the Egyptians highly venerate some animals, both during their life and after their death; and expressly mentions the dog as one object of this absurd adoration. To these witnesses may be added

Herodotus, who says, that when a dog expires, all the members of the family to which he belonged worship the carcass; and that, in every part of the kingdom, the carcasses of their dogs are embalmed, and deposited in consecrated ground. The idolatrous veneration of the dog by the Egyptians is shown in the worship of their dog-god Anubis, to whom temples and priests were consecrated, and whose image was borne in all religious ceremonies. Cynopolis, the present Minieh, situated in the lower Thebais, was built in honour of Anubis. The priests celebrated his festivals there with great pomp. "Anubis," says Strabo, "is the city of dogs, the capital of the Cynopolitan prefecture. These animals are fed there on sacred aliments, and religion has decreed them a worship." An event, however, related by Plutarch, brought them into considerable discredit with the people. Cambyses, having slain the god Apis, and thrown his body into the field, all animals respected it except the dogs, which alone ate of his flesh. This impiety diminished the popular veneration. Cynopolis was not the only city where incense was burned on the altars of Anubis. He had chapels in almost all the temples. On solemnities, his image always accompanied those of Isis and Osiris. Rome, having adopted the ceremonies of Egypt, the emperor Commodus, to celebrate the Isiac feasts, shaved his head, and himself carried the dog Anubis.

3. In Matt. vii, 6, we have this direction of our Saviour: "Give not that which is holy unto the dogs, neither cast ye your pearls before swine, lest they," the swine, "trample them under their feet, and," the dogs, "turn again and tear you." It was customary, not only with the writers of Greece and Rome, but also with the eastern sages, to denote certain classes of men by animals supposed to resemble them among the brutes. Our Saviour was naturally led to adopt the same concise and energetic method. By DOGS, which were held in great detestation by the Jews, he intends men of odious character and violent temper; by SWINE, the usual emblem of moral filth, he means the sensual and profligate; and the purport of his admonition is, that as it is a maxim with the priests not to give any part of the sacrifices to dogs, so it should be a maxim with you not to impart the holy instruction with which you are favoured, to those who are likely to blaspheme and to be only excited by it to rage and persecution. It is, however, a maxim of PRUDENCE not of COWARDICE; and is to be taken along with other precepts of our Lord, which enjoin the publication of truth, at the expense of ease and even life.

DORT, SYNOD OF. See Synods.

DOVE, יונה. This beautiful genus of birds is very numerous in the east. In the wild state they generally build their nests in the holes or clefts of rocks, or in excavated trees; but they are easily taught submission and familiarity with mankind; and, when domesticated, build in structures erected for their accommodation, called "dove-cotes." They are classed by Moses among the clean birds; and it appears from the sacred as well as other writers, that doves were always held in the highest estimation among the eastern nations. Rosenmuller, in a note upon Bochart, derives the name from the Arabic, where it signifies MILDNESS, GENTLENESS, &c. The dove is mentioned in Scripture as the symbol of simplicity, innocence, gentleness, and fidelity, Hosea vii, 11; Matt. x, 16.

The following extract from Morier's Persian Travels illustrates a passage in Isaiah: "In the environs of the city, to the westward, near the Zainderood, are many pigeon houses, erected at a distance from habitations, for the sole purpose of collecting pigeons' dung for manure. They are large round towers, rather broader at the bottom than the top, and crowned by conical spiracles, through which the pigeons descend. Their interior resembles a honey-comb, pierced with a thousand holes, each of which forms a snug retreat for a nest. More care appears to have been bestowed upon their outside than upon that of the generality of the dwelling houses; for they are painted and ornamented. The extraordinary flights of pigeons which I have seen alight upon one of these buildings afford, perhaps, a good illustration for the passage in Isaiah lx, 8: 'Who are these that fly as a cloud, and as the doves to their windows?' Their great numbers, and the compactness of their mass, literally look like a cloud at a distance, and obscure the sun in their passage."

The first mention of the dove in the Scripture is Genesis viii, 8, 10–12, where Noah sent one from the ark to ascertain if the waters of the deluge had assuaged. She was sent forth thrice. The first time she speedily returned; having, in all probability, gone but a little way from the ark, as she must naturally be terrified at the appearance of the waters. After seven days, being sent out a second time, she returned with an olive leaf plucked off, whereby it became evident that the flood was considerably abated, and had sank below the tops of the trees; and thus relieved the fears and cheered the heart of Noah and his family. And hence the olive branch has ever been among the forerunners of peace, and chief of those emblems by which a happy state of renovation and restoration to prosperity has been signified to mankind. At the end of other seven days, the dove, being sent out a third time, returned no more; from which Noah conjectured that the earth was so far drained as to afford sustenance for the birds and fowls; and he therefore removed the covering of the ark, which probably gave liberty to many of the fowls to fly off; and these circumstances afforded him the greater facility for making arrangements for disembarking the other animals. Doves might be offered in sacrifice, when those who were poor could not bring a more costly offering.

DOWRY. See Bride.

DRACHMA. The value of a common drachma was sevenpence, English. A didrachma, or double drachma, made very near half a shekel; and four drachmas made nearly a shekel.

DRAGON. This word is frequently to be met with in our English translation of the Bible. It answers generally to the Hebrew תן, תנין, תנים; and these words are variously rendered DRAGONS, SERPENTS, SEA-MONSTERS, and WHALES. The Rev. James Hurdis, in a dissertation relative to this subject, observes, that the word translated "whales," in Gen. i, 21, occurs twenty-seven times in Scripture; and he attempts, with much ingenuity, to prove that it every where signifies the crocodile. That it sometimes has this meaning, he thinks is clear from Ezekiel xxix, 3: "Behold, I am against thee, Pharaoh king of Egypt, the great dragon that lieth in the midst of his rivers." For, to what could a king of Egypt be more properly compared than the crocodile? The same argument he draws from Isaiah li, 9: "Art thou not he that hath cut Rahab, [Egypt,] and wounded the dragon?" Among the ancients the crocodile was the symbol of Egypt, and appears so on Roman coins. Some however have thought the hippopotamus intended; others, one of the larger species of serpents.

DRAUGHTS, stupifying potions. At the time of execution, they gave the malefactor a grain of frankincense in a cup of wine, in order to stupify and render him less sensible of pain. This custom is traced to the charge of the wise man: "Give strong drink to him that is ready to perish, and wine to those that be of heavy hearts," Prov. xxxiv, 6. The prophet makes an allusion to the powerful effects of this stupifying draught, in that prediction which announces the judgments of God upon the empire of Babylon: "Take the wine cup of this fury at my hand, and cause all the nations to whom I send thee to drink it. And they shall drink, and be moved, and be mad, because of the sword that I will send among them," Jer. xxv, 15, 16. The Jews, according to the custom of their country, gave our Lord wine mingled with myrrh at his crucifixion. See Cross.

DREAMS. The easterns, in particular the Jews, greatly regarded dreams, and applied for their interpretation to those who undertook to explain them. The ancient Greeks and Romans had the same opinion of them, as appears from their most eminent writers. We see the antiquity of this attention to dreams in the history of Pharaoh's butler and baker, Gen. xl. Pharaoh himself, and Nebuchadnezzar, are instances. God expressly condemned to death all who pretended to have prophetic dreams, and to foretel futurities, even though what they foretold came to pass, if they had any tendency to promote idolatry, Deut. xiii, 1–3. But the people were not forbidden, when they thought they had a significative dream, to address the prophets of the Lord, or the high priest in his ephod, to have it explained. Saul, before the battle of Gilboa, consulted a woman who had a familiar spirit, "because the Lord would not answer him by dreams, nor by prophets," 1 Sam. xxviii, 6, 7. The Lord himself sometimes discovered his will in dreams, and enabled persons to explain them. He informed Abimelech in a dream, that Sarah was the wife of Abraham, Gen. xx, 3, 6. He showed Jacob the mysterious ladder in a dream, Gen. xxviii, 12, 13; and in a dream an angel suggested to him a means of multiplying his flocks, Genesis xxxi, 11, 12, &c. Joseph was favoured very early with prophetic dreams, whose signification was easily discovered by Jacob, Gen. xxxvii, 5. God said, that he spake to other prophets in dreams, but to Moses face to face. The Midianites gave credit to dreams, as appears from that which a Midianite related to his companion; and from whose interpretation Gideon took a happy omen, Judges vii, 13, 15. The Prophet Jeremiah exclaims against impostors who pretended to have had dreams, and abused the credulity of the people: "They prophesy lies in my name, saying, I have dreamed, I have dreamed. The prophet that hath a dream, let him tell a dream; and he that hath my word, let him tell it faithfully, saith the Lord," Jer. xxiii, 25, 28, 29. The Prophet Joel promises from God, that in the reign of the Messiah, the effusion of the Holy Spirit should be so copious, that the old men should have prophetic dreams, and the young men should receive visions, Joel ii, 28.

DRESS. See Habits.

DROMEDARY. This name answers to two words in the original, בכר, and feminine בכרה, Isa. lx, 6; Jer. ii, 24; and אחשתרנים, Esther viii, 10, "young dromedaries;" probably the name in Persian. The dromedary is a race of camels chiefly remarkable for its prodigious swiftness. The most observable difference between it and the camel is, that it has but one protuberance on the back; and instead of the slow solemn walk to which that animal is accustomed, it will go as far in one day as the camel in three. For this reason it is used to carry messengers where haste is required. The animal is governed by a bridle, which, being usually fastened to a ring fixed in the nose, may very well illustrate the expression, 2 Kings xix, 28, of turning back Sennacherib by putting a hook into his nose; and may farther indicate his swift retreat.

DUST, or ashes, cast on the head was a sign of mourning, Josh. vii, 6: sitting in the dust, a sign of affliction, Lam. iii, 29; Isaiah xlvii, 1. The dust also denotes the grave, Gen. iii, 19; Job vii, 21; Psalm xxii, 15. It is put for a great multitude, Gen. xiii, 16; Numbers xxiii, 10. It signifies a low or mean condition, 1 Sam. ii, 8; Nahum iii, 18. To shake or wipe off the dust of a place from one's feet, marks the renouncing of all intercourse with it in future. God threatens the Jews with rain of dust, &c; Deut. xxviii, 24. An extract from Sir T. Roe's embassy may cast light on this: "Sometimes, in India, the wind blows very high in hot and dry seasons, raising up into the air a very great height, thick clouds of dust and sand. These dry showers most grievously annoy all those among whom they fall; enough to smite them all with present blindness; filling their eyes, ears, nostrils, and mouths too, if not well guarded; searching every place, as well within as without, so that there is not a little key-hole of any trunk or cabinet, if it be not covered, but receives this dust; add to this, that the fields, brooks, and gardens, suffer extremely from these terrible showers."

2. In almost every part of Asia, those who demand justice against a criminal throw dust upon him, signifying that he deserves to lose his life, and be cast into the grave; and that this is the true interpretation of the action, is evident from an imprecation in common use among the Turks and

Persians, "Be covered with earth!" "Earth be upon thy head." We have two remarkable instances of casting dust recorded in Scripture: the first is that of Shimei, who gave vent to his secret hostility to David, when he fled before his rebellious son, by throwing stones at him, and casting dust, 2 Sam. xvi, 13. It was an ancient custom, in those warm and arid countries, to lay the dust before a person of distinction, and particularly before kings and princes, by sprinkling the ground with water. To throw dust into the air while a person was passing, was therefore an act of great disrespect; to do so before a sovereign prince, an indecent outrage. But it is clear that Shimei meant more than disrespect and outrage to an afflicted king, whose subject he was: he intended to signify by that action, that David was unfit to live, and that the time was at last arrived to offer him a sacrifice to the ambition and vengeance of the house of Saul. This view of his conduct is confirmed by the behaviour of the Jews to the Apostle Paul, when they seized him in the temple, and had nearly succeeded in putting him to death: they cried out, "Away with such a fellow from the earth, for it is not fit that he should live; and as they cried out and cast off their clothes, and threw dust into the air, the chief captain commanded him to be brought into the castle," Acts xxii, 23. A great similarity appears between the conduct of the Jews on this occasion, and the behaviour of the peasants in Persia, when they go to court to complain of the governors, whose oppressions they can no longer endure. They carry their complaints against their governors by companies, consisting of several hundreds, and sometimes of a thousand; they repair to that gate of the palace nearest to which their prince is most likely to be, where they set themselves to make the most horrid cries, tearing their garments, and throwing dust into the air, and demanding justice. The king, upon hearing these cries, sends to know the occasion of them: the people deliver their complaints in writing, upon which he informs them that he will commit the cognizance of the affair to such a one as he names; and in consequence of this, justice is usually obtained.

EAGLE, נשר, Exod. xix, 4; Lev. xi, 13. The name is derived from a verb which signifies to LACERATE, or TEAR IN PIECES. The eagle has always been considered as the king of birds, on account of its great strength, rapidity and elevation of flight, natural ferocity, and the terror it inspires into its fellows of the air. Its voracity is so great that a large extent of territory is requisite for the supply of proper sustenance; and providence has therefore constituted it a solitary animal: two pair of eagles are never found in the same neighbourhood, though the genus is dispersed through every quarter of the world. Its sight is quick, strong, and piercing, to a proverb. In Job xxxix, 27, the natural history of the eagle is finely drawn up:--

Is it at thy voice that the eagle soars?

And therefore maketh his nest on high?

The rock is the place of his habitation.

He abides on the crag, the place of strength.

Thence he pounces upon his prey.

His eyes discern afar off.

Even his young ones drink down blood;

And wherever is slaughter, there is he.

Alluding to the popular opinion that the eagle assists its feeble young in their flight, by bearing them up on its own pinions, Moses represents Jehovah as saying, "Ye have seen what I did to the Egyptians, and how I bore you on eagles' wings, and brought you unto myself," Exod. xix, 4. Scheuchzer has quoted from an ancient poet, the following beautiful paraphrase on this passage:--

AC VELUT ALITUUM PRINCEPS, FULVUSQUE TONANTIS

ARMIGER, IMPLUMES, ET ADHUE SINE ROBORE NATOS

SOLLICITA REFOVET CURA, PINGUISQUE FERINÆ

INDULGET PASTUS: MOX UT CUM VIRIBUS ALÆ

VESTICIPES CREVERE, VOCAT SE BLANDIOR AURA,

EXPANSA INVITAT PLUMA, DORSOQUE MORANTES

EXCIPIT, ATTOLLITQUE HUMERIS, PLAUSUQUE SECUNDO

FERTUR IN ARVA, TIMENS ONERI, ET TAMEN IMPETE PRESSO

REMIGIUM TENTANS ALARUM, INCURVAQUE PINNIS

VELA LEGENS, HUMILES TRANAT SUB NUBIBUS ORAS.

HINC SENSIM SUPRA ALTA PETIT, JAM JAMQUE SUB ASTRA

ERIGITUR, CURSUSQUE LEVES CITUS URGET IN AURAS,

OMNIA PERVOLITANS LATE LOCA, ET AGMINE FŒTUS

FERTQUE REFERTQUE SUOS VARIO, MOREMQUE VOLANDI

ADDOCET: ILLI AUTEM, LONGA ASSUETUDINE DOCTI,

PAULATIM INCIPIUNT PENNIS SE CREDERE CÆLO

IMPAVIDI: TANTUM A TENERIS VALET ADDERE CURAM.

[And as the king of birds, and tawny armour-bearer of the Thunderer, cherishes with anxious care his unfledged, and as yet feeble young, and gratifies their appetite with rich prey: presently when their downy wings have increased in strength, a milder air calls them forth, with expanded plumage he invites them, and receives them hesitating on his back, and sustains them on his shoulders, and with easy flight is borne over the fields, fearing for his burden, and yet with a moderated effort trying the rowing of their wings, and furling with his pinions his curved sails, he glides through the low regions beneath the clouds. Hence by degrees he soars aloft, and now he mounts to the starry heaven, and swiftly urges his rapid flight through the air, sweeping widely over space, and in his gyrations bearing his offspring to and fro, teaches them the art of flying:--but they, taught by long practice, gradually begin to trust themselves fearlessly on their wings: So much does it avail to train the young with care.]

2. When Balaam delivered his predictions respecting the fate that awaited the nations which he then particularized, he said of the Kenites, "Strong is thy dwelling, and thou puttest thy nest in a rock," Num. xxiv, 21; alluding to that princely bird, the eagle, which not only delights in soaring to the loftiest heights, but chooses the highest rocks, and most elevated mountains, as desirable situations for erecting its nest, Hab. ii, 9; Obad. 4. What Job says concerning the eagle, which is to be understood in a literal sense, "Where the slain are, there is he," our Saviour turns into a fine parable: "Wheresoever the carcass is, there will the eagles be gathered together," Matt. xxiv, 28; that is, Wherever the Jews are, who have corruptly fallen from God, there will be the Romans, who bore the eagle as their standard, to execute vengeance upon them, Luke xvii, 37.

3. The swiftness of the flight of the eagle is alluded to in several passages of Scripture; as, "The Lord shall bring a nation against thee from afar, from the end of the earth, as swift as the eagle flieth," Deut. xxviii, 49. In the affecting lamentation of David over Saul and Jonathan, their impetuous and rapid career is described in forcible terms: "They were swifter than eagles; they were stronger than lions," 2 Sam. i, 23. Jeremiah when he beheld in vision the march of Nebuchadnezzar, cried, "Behold, he shall come up as clouds, and his chariots shall be as a whirlwind. His horses are swifter than eagles. Wo unto us, for we are spoiled," Jer. iv, 13. To the wide-expanded wings of the eagle, and the rapidity of his flight, the same prophet beautifully alludes in a subsequent chapter, where he describes the subversion of Moab by the same ruthless conqueror: "Behold, he shall fly as an eagle, and spread his wings over Moab," Jer. xlviii, 40. In the same manner he describes the sudden desolations of Ammon in the next chapter; but, when he turns his eye to the ruins of his own country, he exclaims, in still more energetic language, "Our persecutors are swifter than the eagles of the heavens," Lament. iv, 19. Under the same comparison the patriarch Job describes the rapid flight of time: "My days are passed away, as the eagle that hasteth to the prey," Job ix, 26. The surprising rapidity with which the blessings of common providence sometimes vanish from the grasp of the possessor is thus described by Solomon: "Riches certainly make themselves wings: they fly away as an eagle toward heaven," Prov. xxiii, 5. The flight of this bird is as sublime as it is rapid and impetuous. None of the feathered race soar so high. In his daring excursions he is said to leave the clouds of heaven, and regions of thunder, and lightning, and tempest, far beneath him, and to approach the very limits of ether. There is an allusion to this lofty soaring in the prophecy of Obadiah, concerning the pride of Moab: "Though thou exalt thyself as the eagle, and though thou set thy nest among the stars, thence will I bring thee down, saith the Lord," Obad. 4. The prophet Jeremiah pronounces the doom of Edom in similar terms: "O thou that dwellest in the clefts of the rock, that holdest the height of the hill; though thou shouldest make thy nest high as the eagle, I will bring thee down from thence, saith the Lord," Jer. xlix, 16. The eagle lives and retains its vigour to a great age; and, after moulting, renews its vigour so surprisingly, as to be said, hyperbolically, to become young again, Psalm ciii, 5, and Isaiah xl, 31. It is remarkable that Cyrus, compared, in Isaiah xlvi, 11, to an eagle, (so the word translated "ravenous bird" should be rendered,) had an eagle for his ensign according to Xenophon, who uses, without knowing it, the identical word of the prophet, with only a Greek termination to it: so exact is the correspondence between the prophet and the historian, the prediction and the event. Xenophon and other ancient historians inform us that the golden eagle with extended wings was the ensign of the Persian monarchs long before it was adopted by the Romans; and it is very probable that the Persians borrowed the symbol from the ancient Assyrians, in whose banners it waved, till imperial Babylon bowed her head to the yoke of Cyrus. If this conjecture be well founded, it discovers the reason why the sacred writers, in describing the victorious march of the Assyrian armies,

allude so frequently to the expanded eagle. Referring to the Babylonian monarch, the prophet Hosea proclaimed in the ears of all Israel, the measure of whose iniquities was nearly full, "He shall come as an eagle against the house of the Lord," Hosea viii, 1. Jeremiah predicted a similar calamity: "Thus saith the Lord, Behold, he shall fly as an eagle, and spread his wings over Moab," Jer. xlviii, 40; and the same figure was employed to denote the destruction that overtook the house of Esau: "Behold, he shall come up and fly as the eagle, and spread his wings over Bozrah," xlix, 22. The words of these prophets received a full accomplishment in the irresistible impetuosity and complete success with which the Babylonian monarchs, and particularly Nebuchadnezzar, pursued their plans of conquest. Ezekiel denominates him, with great propriety, "a great eagle with great wings," because he was the most powerful monarch of his time, and led into the field more numerous and better appointed armies, (which the prophet calls, by a beautiful figure, "his wings," the wings of his army,) than perhaps the world had ever seen. The Prophet Isaiah, referring to the same monarch, predicted the subjugation of Judea in these terms: "He shall pass through Judah. He shall overflow, and go over. He shall reach even to the neck; and the stretching out of his wings" (the array of his army) "shall fill the breadth of thy land, O Immanuel," Isaiah viii, 8. The king of Egypt is also styled by Ezekiel, "a great eagle, with great wings, and many feathers;" but he manifestly gives the preference to the king of Babylon, by adding, that he had "long wings, full of feathers, which had divers colours;" that is, greater wealth, and a more numerous army.

EAR, the organ of hearing. The Scripture uses the term figuratively. Uncircumcised ears are ears inattentive to the word of God. To signify God's regard to the prayers of his people, the Psalmist says, "His ears are open to their cry," Psalm xxxiv, 15. Among the Jews, the slave, who renounced the privilege of being made free from servitude in the sabbatical year, submitted to have his ear bored through with an awl; which was done in the presence of some judge, or magistrate, that it might appear a voluntary act. The ceremony took place at his master's door, and was the mark of servitude and bondage. The Psalmist says, in the person of the Messiah, "Sacrifice and offering thou didst not desire; mine ears hast thou opened." Heb. "Thou hast digged my ears." This either means, Thou hast opened them, removed impediments, and made them attentive; or, thou hast pierced them, as those of such servants were pierced, who chose to remain with their masters; and therefore imports the ABSOLUTE and VOLUNTARY submission of Messiah to the will of the Father. "Make the ears of this people heavy," Isaiah vi, 10; that is, render their minds inattentive and disobedient; the prophets being said often to do that of which they were the innocent occasion.

EAR-RINGS and nose-jewels were favourite ornaments among the eastern females. Both are frequently mentioned in Scripture. Thus the Prophet Ezekiel: "And I put a jewel on thy forehead," or, as it should have been rendered, on thy nose. This ornament was one of the presents which the servant of Abraham gave to Rebecca, in the name of his master: "I put," said he, "the ear-ring upon her face;" more literally, I put the ring on her nose. They wore ear-rings beside; for the household of Jacob, at his request, when they were preparing to go up to Bethel, gave him all the ear-rings which were in their ears, and he hid them under the oak which was by Shechem. Sir John Chardin says, "It is the custom in almost all the east for the women to wear rings in their noses, in the left nostril, which is bored low down in the middle. These rings are of gold, and have commonly two pearls and one ruby between them, placed in the ring; I never saw a girl, or young woman in Arabia, or in all Persia, who did not wear a ring after this manner in her nostril." Some writers contend, that by the nose-jewel, we are to understand rings, which women attached to their forehead, and let them fall down upon their nose; but Chardin, who certainly was a diligent observer of eastern customs, no where saw this frontal ring in the east, but every where the ring in the nose. His testimony is supported by Dr. Russel, who describes the women in some of the villages about Aleppo, and all the Arabs and Chinganas, (a sort of gipsies,) as wearing a large ring of silver or gold, through the external cartilage of their right nostril. It is worn, by the testimony of Egmont, in the same manner by the women of Egypt. Two words are used in the Scriptures to denote these ornamental rings, נזם and עגיל. Mr. Harmer seems to think they properly signified ear-rings; but this is a mistake; the sacred writers use them promiscuously for the rings both of the nose and of the ears. That writer, however, is probably right in supposing that NEZEM is the name of a much smaller ring than AGIL. Chardin observed two sorts of rings in the east; one so small and close to the ear, that there is no vacuity between them; the other so large, as to admit the fore finger between it and the ear; these last are adorned with a ruby and a pearl on each side, strung on the ring. Some of these ear-rings had figures upon them, and strange characters, which he believed were talismans or charms; but which were probably the names and symbols of their false gods. We know from the testimony of Pliny, that rings with the images of their gods were worn by the Romans. The Indians say, they are preservatives against enchantment; upon which Chardin hazards a very probable conjecture, that the ear-rings of Jacob's family were perhaps of this kind, which might be the reason of his demanding them, that he might bury them under the oak before they went up to Bethel.

EARTH is used for that gross element which sustains and nourishes us by producing plants and fruits; for the continent as distinguished from the sea, "God called the dry land earth," Gen. i, 10; for the terraqueous globe, and its contents, men, animals, plants, metals, waters, &c. "The earth is the Lord's, and the fulness thereof", Psalm xxiv, 1; for the inhabitants of the earth, or continent, "The whole earth was of one language," Genesis xi, 1; for Judea, or the whole empire of Chaldea and Assyria. Thus Cyrus says, Ezra i, 2, "The Lord God of heaven hath given me all the kingdoms of the earth." The restriction of the term "earth" to Judea is more common in Scripture than is usually supposed; and this acceptation of it has great effect on several passages, in which it ought to be so understood.

Earth in a moral sense is opposed to heaven, and to what is spiritual. "He that is of the earth is earthy, and speaketh of the earth; he that cometh from above is above all," John iii, 31. "If ye then be risen with Christ, set your affections on things above, not on things on the earth," Col. iii, 1, 2.

EARTHQUAKE. The Scripture speaks of several earthquakes. One happened in the twenty-seventh year of Uzziah, king of Judah, in the year of the world 3221. This is mentioned in Amos i, 1, and in Zechariah xiv, 5. Josephus says that its violence divided a mountain, which lay west of Jerusalem, and drove one part of it four furlongs. A very memorable earthquake is that which happened at our Saviour's death, Matt. xxvii, 51. Many have thought that this was perceived throughout the world. Others are of opinion that it was felt only in Judea, or even in the temple at Jerusalem. St. Cyril of Jerusalem says, that the rocks upon mount Calvary were shown in his time, which had been rent asunder by this earthquake. Maundrell and Sandys testify the same, and say that they examined the breaches in the rock, and were convinced that they were the effects of an earthquake. It must have been terrible, since the centurion and those with him were so affected by it, as to acknowledge the innocence of our Saviour, Luke xxiii, 47. Phlegon, Adrian's freedman, relates that, together with the eclipse, which happened at noon day, in the fourth year of the two hundred and second Olympiad, or A. D. 33, a very great earthquake was also felt, principally in Bythynia. The effects of God's power, wrath, and vengeance are compared to earthquakes, Psalm xviii, 7; xlvi, 2; cxiv, 4. An earthquake signifies also, in prophetic language, the dissolution of governments and the overthrow of states.

EAST, one of the four cardinal points of the world; namely, that particular point of the horizon in which the sun is seen to rise. The Hebrews express the east, west, north, and south by words which signify before, behind, left, and right, according to the situation of a man who has his face turned toward the east. By the east, they frequently describe, not only Arabia Deserta, and the lands of Moab and Ammon, which lay to the east of Palestine, but also Assyria, Mesopotamia, Babylonia, and Chaldea, though they are situated rather to the north than to the east of Judea. Balaam, Cyrus, and the wise men who visited Bethlehem at the time Christ was born, are said to come from the east, Num. xxiii, 7; Isaiah xlvi, 11; Matt. ii, 1.

EASTER, the day on which the Christian church commemorates our Saviour's resurrection. Easter is a word of Saxon origin, and imports a goddess of the east. This goddess was Astarte, in honour of whom sacrifices were annually offered about the passover time of the year, the spring; and hence the Saxon name "æaster" became attached by association of ideas to the Christian festival of the resurrection.

EATING. The ancient Hebrews did not eat indifferently with all persons: they would have esteemed themselves polluted and dishonoured by eating with people of another religion, or of an odious profession. In Joseph's day they neither ate with the Egyptians, nor the Egyptians with them, Gen. xliii, 32; nor, in our Saviour's time, with the Samaritans, John iv, 9. The Jews were scandalized at Christ's eating with publicans and sinners, Matt. ix, 11. As there were several sorts of meats, the use of which was prohibited, they could not conveniently eat with those who partook of them, fearing to receive pollution by touching such food, or if by accident any particles of it should fall on them. The ancient Hebrews, at their meals, had each his separate table. Joseph, entertaining his brethren in Egypt, seated them separately, each at his particular table; and he himself sat down separately from the Egyptians, who ate with him; but he sent to his brethren portions out of the provisions which were before him, Gen. xliii, 31, &c. Elkanah, Samuel's father, who had two wives, distributed their portions to them separately, 1 Sam. i, 4, 5. In Homer, each guest has his little table apart; and the master of the feast distributes meat to each. We are assured that this is still practised in China; and that many in India never eat out of the same dish, nor on the same table, with another person, believing that they cannot do so without sin; and this, not only in their own country, but when travelling, and in foreign lands.

The ancient manners which we see in Homer we see likewise in Scripture, with regard to eating, drinking, and entertainments: we find great plenty, but little delicacy; and great respect and honour paid to the guests by serving them plentifully. Joseph sent his brother Benjamin a portion five times larger than those of his other brethren. Samuel set a whole quarter of a calf before Saul. The women did not appear at table in entertainments with the men: this would have been an indecency; as it is at this day throughout the east. The present Jews, before they sit down to table, carefully wash their hands: they speak of this ceremony as essential and obligatory. After meals they wash them again. When they sit down to table, the master of the house, or the chief person in the company, taking bread, breaks it, but does not wholly separate it; then, putting his hand on it, he recites this blessing: "Blessed be thou, O Lord our God, the King of the world, who producest the bread of the earth." Those present answer, "Amen." Having distributed the bread among the guests, he takes the vessel of wine in his right hand, saying, "Blessed art thou, O Lord our God, King of the world, who hast produced the fruit of the vine." They then repeat the twenty-third Psalm. Buxtorf, and Leo of Modena, who have given particular accounts of the Jewish ceremonies, differ in some circumstances: the reason is, Buxtorf wrote principally the ceremonies of the German Jews, and Leo, those of the Italian Jews. They take care that, after meals, there shall be a piece of bread remaining on the table; the master of the house orders a glass to be washed, fills it with wine, and, elevating it, says, "Let us bless Him of whose benefits we have been partaking:" the rest answer, "Blessed be He who has heaped his favours on us, and by his goodness has now fed us." Then he recites a pretty long prayer, wherein he thanks God for his many benefits vouchsafed to Israel; beseeches him to pity Jerusalem and his temple, to restore the throne of David, to send Elias and the Messiah, to deliver them out of their long captivity, &c. All present answer, "Amen;" and then recite Psalm xxxiv, 9, 10. Then, giving the glass with the little wine in it to be drunk round, he drinks what is left, and the table is cleared. See Banquets.

Partaking of the benefits of Christ's passion by faith is also called eating, because this is the support of our spiritual life, John vi, 53, 56. Hosea reproaches the priests of his time with eating the sins of the people, Hosea iv, 8; that is, feasting on their sin offerings, rather than reforming their manners. John the Baptist is said to have come "neither eating nor drinking," Matt. xi, 18; that is, as other men did; for he lived in the wilderness, on locusts, wild honey, and water, Matt. iii, 4; Luke i, 15. This is expressed, in Luke vii, 33, by his neither eating "bread," nor drinking "wine." On the other hand, the Son of Man is said, in Matt. xi, 19, to have come "eating and drinking;" that is, as others did; and that too with all sorts of persons, Pharisees, publicans, and sinners.

EBAL, a celebrated mountain in the tribe of Ephraim, near Shechem, over against Mount Gerizim. These two mountains are within two hundred paces of each other, and separated by a deep valley, in which stood the town of Shechem. The two mountains are much alike in magnitude and form, being of a semi-circular figure, about half a league in length, and, on the sides nearest Shechem, nearly perpendicular. One of them is barren; the other, covered with a beautiful verdure. Moses commanded the Israelites, as soon as they should have passed the river Jordan, to go directly to Shechem, and divide the whole multitude into two bodies, each composed of six tribes; one company to be placed on Ebal, and the other on Gerizim. The six tribes that were on Gerizim were to pronounce blessings on those who should faithfully observe the law of the Lord, and the six others on Mount Ebal were to pronounce curses against those who should violate it, Deut. xi, 29, &c; xxvii, and xxviii; Joshua viii, 30, 31.

This consecration of the Hebrew commonwealth is thought to have been performed in the following manner: The heads of the first six tribes went up to the top of Mount Gerizim, and the heads of the other six tribes to the top of Mount Ebal. The priests, with the ark, and Joshua at the head of the elders of Israel, took their station in the middle of the valley which lies between the two mountains. The Levites ranged themselves in a circle about the ark; and the elders, with the people, placed themselves at the foot of the mountain, six tribes on a side. When they were thus disposed in order, the priests turned toward Mount Gerizim, on the top of which were the six heads of the six tribes who were at the foot of the same mountain, and pronounced, for example, these words:--"Blessed be the man that maketh not any graven images." The six princes who were upon the top of the mountain, and the six tribes who were below at its foot, answered, "Amen." Afterward, the priests, turning toward Mount Ebal, upon which were the princes of the other six tribes, cried, with a loud voice, "Cursed be the man that maketh any graven image;" and were answered by the princes opposite to them and their tribes, "Amen." The Scripture, at first view, seems to intimate that there were six tribes upon one mountain, and six on the other; but beside that it is by no means probable that the tribes of the Israelites, who were so numerous, should be able to stand on the summits of these two mountains, it would not have been possible for them to have seen the ceremony, nor to have heard the blessings and curses in order to answer them. Moreover, the Hebrew particle, in the original, signifies, NEAR, OVER AGAINST, as well as AT THE TOP, Joshua viii, 33. Accordingly, we may say, that neither Joshua, nor the priests or tribes, went up to the top of the mountains, but the heads only, who in their persons might represent all the tribes.

EBENEZER, the name of that field wherein the Israelites were defeated by the Philistines, when the ark of the Lord was taken, 1 Sam. iv, 1; also a memorial stone set up by Samuel to commemorate a victory over the Philistines. The word signifies THE STONE OF HELP; and it was erected by the prophet, saying, "Hitherto the Lord hath helped us."

EBIONITES, a sect of the first two or three centuries; but it is not certain whether they received their name from a leader of the name of Ebion, (whom Dr. Lardner considers as a disciple of Cerinthus,) or from the meaning of the Hebrew word EBION, which implies poverty; and if the latter, whether they assumed the name, as affecting to be poor, like the Founder of Christianity; or whether it was conferred on them by way of reproach, as being of the lower orders. The use of the term, also, according to Dr. Horsley, was various and indefinite. Sometimes it was the peculiar name of those sects that denied both the divinity of our Lord, and his miraculous conception. Then its meaning was extended, to take in another party; who admitted the miraculous conception of Jesus, but still denied his divinity, and questioned his previous existence. At last, it seems, the Nazarites, whose error was rather a superstitious severity in their practice, than any deficiency in their faith, were included by Origen in the infamy of the appellation. Dr. Priestley, claiming the Ebionites as Jewish Unitarians, considers the ancient Nazarenes, that is, the first Jewish converts, as the true Ebionites; these, he thinks, were called Nazarenes, from their attachment to Jesus of Nazareth; and Ebionites, from their poor and mean condition, just as some of the reformers were called Beghards, or beggars. The Doctor cites the authorities of Origen and Epiphanius, to prove that both these denominations related to the same people, differing only, like the Socinians, in receiving or rejecting the fact of the miraculous conception; and neither, as he assures us, were reckoned heretics by any writers of the two first centuries. To this Dr. Horsley replies, that both Jews and Heathens called the first Christians Nazarenes, in allusion to the mean and obscure birthplace of their Master, Jesus of Nazareth, Matthew ii, 23; Acts x, 38; but insists, and answers every pretended proof to the contrary, that the term

Nazarenes was never applied to any distinct sect of Christians before the final destruction of Jerusalem by Adrian. Dr. Semler, a German writer, gives the following opinion: "Those who more rigidly maintained the Mosaic observances, and who were numerous in Palestine, are usually called Ebionites and Nasaræans. Some believe that they ought not to be reckoned heretics; others think that they were united in doctrine, differing only in name; others place them in the second century. It is of little consequence whether we distinguish or not the Nazarenes, or Nazaræans from the Ebionites. It is certain that both these classes were tenacious of the Mosaic ceremonies, and more inclined to the Jews than to the Gentiles, though they admitted the Messiahship of Jesus in a very low and Judaizing manner. The Ebionites held in execration the doctrine of the Apostle Paul." Dr. J. Pye Smith, who quotes this passage from Dr. Semler, adds, "Such, it is apprehended, on grounds of reasonable probability, was the origin of Unitarianism; the child of Judaism misunderstood, and of Christianity imperfectly received."

2. On this controversy great light has, however, been since thrown by Dr. Burton. It is well known to those who have studied the Unitarian controversy, that it has been often asserted that the Cerinthians and Ebionites were the teachers of genuine Christianity, and that the doctrine of Christ's divinity, and of universal redemption through his blood, were the inventions of those who corrupted the preaching of the Apostles. If this were so, we must convict all the fathers, not merely of ignorance and mistake, but of deliberate and wilful falsehood. To suppose that the fathers of the second century were ignorant of what was genuine and what was false in Christianity, would be a bold hypothesis; but if Irenæus, the disciple of Polycarp, asserted, as a matter of fact, that St. John wrote his Gospel to refute the errors of Cerinthus, it is idle, or something worse, to say that Irenæus did not know for certain if the fact was really so. As far, then, as the testimony of the fathers is concerned, the Cerinthians and Ebionites were decidedly heretics. The Unitarians, on the other hand, maintain that the Ebionites were the true and genuine believers; and it is easy to see that the preference was given to these teachers, because they held that Jesus was born of human parents. Never, I conceive, was there a more unfortunate and fatal alliance formed than that between the Ebionites and modern Unitarians. We find the Ebionites referred to, as if they agreed in every point with the Socinian or Unitarian creed; and yet it may almost be asserted, that in not one single point do their sentiments exactly coincide. If a real Ebionite will declare himself, we are not afraid to meet him. Let him avow his faith; let him believe of Christ as Ebion or Cerinthus taught; let him adopt the ravings of the Gnostics; we shall then know with whom we have to combat; we may gird on the sword of Irenæus, and meet him in the field. But let him not select a few ingredients only from the poison; let him not take a part only of their infatuated system. If he will lean on that broken reed, let him talk no more of Ebion or Cerinthus only; but let him say boldly, either that the Gnostics agreed with the Apostles, or that the Gnostics preached the true Gospel, while the Apostles were in error.

3. We can hardly suppose the Unitarians to be ignorant that the Ebionites and Cerinthians were a branch of the Gnostics. If the fact be denied, the whole of this discussion might as well at once be closed. We know nothing of Cerinthus and Ebion, but from the writings of the fathers. If it had not been for them, we should never have known that these persons believed Jesus to be born of human parents: the same fathers unanimously add, that in this point they differed from the preceding Gnostics, though agreeing with them on other points. If we are to receive the testimony of the fathers in one particular, but to reject it in every other, I need not say that argument is useless. But the fact can never be denied nor evaded. The Cerinthians, to whom some Unitarians have appealed, did not ascribe the creation of the world to God, but to an inferior being. Like the rest of the Gnostics, who engrafted that philosophy on Judaism, the Cerinthians and Ebionites retained some of the Jewish ceremonies, though they rejected some of the Jewish Scriptures. Many of them taught that the restraints of morality were useless; and the Cerinthians, it is well known, promised to their followers a millennium of sensual indulgence. With respect to their notions concerning Christ, it is true that they believed Jesus to be born of human parents; and this fact is referred to, as if it proved the falsehood of what is called the miraculous conception of Jesus. But it is plain that this tenet is mentioned by the fathers, as being opposed to that of the other Gnostics, who held that the body of Jesus was an illusive phantom. Such had hitherto been the belief of all the Gnostics. But Cerinthus and Ebion, who were perhaps more rational in their speculations, and who lived after the publication of the three first Gospels, could not resist the evidence that Jesus was actually born, and that he had a real, substantial body. This is the meaning of the statement, that Cerinthus and Ebion believed Jesus to be born of human parents. It shows that they were not DOCETÆ. But because there were other Gnostics who were more irrational and visionary than themselves, we are not immediately to infer that their own notion concerning the birth of Christ was the true one. They believed, at least, many of them believed, that Jesus was born in the ordinary way; that Joseph was his parent as well as Mary. But they could hardly help believing so; for they agreed with all the Gnostics in thinking (though it might seem as if this point had been forgotten) that Jesus and Christ were separate persons: they believed, as I have already stated, that Christ descended upon Jesus at his baptism, and quitted him before his crucifixion. They were therefore almost compelled to believe that Jesus, who was wholly distinct from Christ, had nothing divine in his nature, and nothing miraculous in his birth; in the same manner that they believed that the death of Jesus, from whom Christ had then departed, was like the death of any ordinary mortal, and that no atonement was made by it. But are we on these grounds to reject the miraculous conception and the atonement of Christ? Or are the Unitarians to quote these Gnostics as holding the human nature of Jesus, and to forget

that by Jesus they meant a person wholly different from Christ?

4. We are told, indeed, that the first part of St. Matthew's Gospel is spurious, because the Ebionites rejected it. Undoubtedly they did. They read in it that Jesus Christ was born, not Jesus only; and that he was born of a virgin. They therefore rejected this part of St. Matthew's Gospel; or rather, by mutilating and altering the whole of it, they composed a new gospel of their own to suit their purpose; and yet this is the only authority which is quoted for rejecting the commencement of St. Matthew's Gospel. The fact, that some even of the Ebionites believed the miraculous conception, speaks infinitely more in favour of the genuineness of that part of the Gospel, and of the truth of the doctrine itself, than can be inferred on the contrary side from those who denied the doctrine, and mutilated the Gospel. Those other Ebionites appear in this respect to have agreed with the first Socinians, and to have held that Jesus was born of a virgin, though they did not believe in his preëxistence or divinity. But the miraculous conception was so entirely contrary to all preconceived opinions, and the more simple doctrine of the other Ebionites and Cerinthians was so much more suited to the Gnostic system, which separated Jesus from Christ, that the evidence must have been almost irresistible, which led one part of the Ebionites to embrace a doctrine contrary to all experience, contrary to the sentiments of their brethren, and hardly reconcilable with other parts of their own creed. The testimony, therefore, of these Ebionites, in favour of the miraculous conception, is stronger, perhaps, than even that of persons who received the whole of the Gospel, and departed in no points from the doctrine of the Apostles. If the Apostles had preached, according to the statement of the Unitarians, that Jesus Christ was a mere human being, born in the ordinary way, what could possibly have led the Gnostics to rank him immediately with their Æons, whom they believed to have been produced by God, and to have dwelt with him from endless ages in the pleroma? There literally was not one single heretic in the first century, who did not believe that Christ came down from heaven: they invented, it is true, various absurdities to account for his union with the man Jesus; but the fair and legitimate inference from this fact would be, that the Apostles preached that in some way or other the human nature was united to the divine. So far from the Socinian or Unitarian doctrine being supported by that of the Cerinthians and Ebionites, I have no hesitation in saying, that not one single person is recorded in the whole of the first century who ever imagined that Christ was a mere man. It has been observed, that one branch of the Ebionites resembled the first Socinians, that is, they believed in the miraculous conception of Jesus, though they denied his preëxistence; but this was because they held the common notion of the Gnostics, that Jesus and Christ were two separate persons; and they believed in the preëxistence and divine nature of Christ, which Socinus and his followers uniformly denied.

ECBATANA, a city of Media, which, according to Herodotus, was built by Dejoces, king of the Medes. It was situated on a gentle declivity, distant twelve stadia from Mount Orontes, and was in compass one hundred and fifty stadia, and, next to Nineveh and Babylon, was one of the strongest and most beautiful cities of the east. After the union of Media with Persia, it was the summer residence of the Persian kings. Sir R. K. Porter, in his Travels, says, "Having for a few moments gazed at the venerable mountain, (Orontes, at the foot of which Ecbatana was built,) and at the sad vacuum at its base; what had been Ecbatana, being now shrunk to comparative nothingness; I turned my eye on the still busy scene of life which occupied the adjacent country; the extensive plain of Hamadan, and its widely extending hills. On our right, the receding vale was varied, at short distances, with numberless castellated villages rising from amidst groves of the noblest trees; while the great plain itself stretched northward and eastward to such far remoteness, that its mountain boundaries appeared like clouds upon the horizon. This whole tract seemed one carpet of luxuriant verdure, studded with hamlets, and watered by beautiful rivulets. On the south-west, Orontes, or Elwund, (by whichever name we may designate this most towering division of the mountain,) presents itself, in all the stupendous grandeur of its fame and form. Near to its base, appear the dark coloured dwellings of Hamadan, crowded thickly on each other; while the gardens of the inhabitants with their connecting orchards and woods, fringe the entire slope of that part of the mountain." "The site of the modern town, like that of the ancient, is on a gradual ascent, terminating near the foot of the eastern side of the mountain; but there all trace of its past appearance would cease, were it not for two or three considerable elevations, and overgrown irregularities on and near them, which may have been the walls of the royal fortress, with those of the palaces, temples, and theatres, seen no more. I passed one of these heights, standing to the south-west, as I entered the city, and observed that it bore many vestiges of having been strongly fortified. The sides and summit are covered with large remnants of ruined walls of a great thickness, and also of towers, the materials of which were sun-dried bricks. It has the name of the Inner Fortress, and certainly holds the most commanding station near the plain." Of the interior of the city, the same author says, "The mud alleys, which now occupy the site of the ancient streets or squares, are narrow, interrupted by large holes or hollows in the way, and heaps of the fallen crumbled walls of deserted dwellings. A miserable bazaar or two are passed through in traversing the town; and large lonely spots are met with, marked by broken low mounds over older ruins; with here and there a few poplars, or willow trees, shadowing the border of a dirty stream, abandoned to the meanest uses; which, probably, flowed pellucid and admired, when these places were gardens, and the grass-grown heap some stately dwelling of Ecbatana. In one or two spots I observed square platforms, composed of large stones; the faces of many of which were chiselled all over into the finest arabesque fretwork, while others had, in addition, long inscriptions in the Arabic character. They had evidently been tomb-stones of the inhabitants, during the caliph rule in Persia. But when we compare relics of the seventh century, with the deep antiquity of the ruins on which they lie, these monumental remains seem but the register of yesterday." Here is shown the tomb of Mordecai and Esther; as well as that of Avicenna, the celebrated Arabian physician. The sepulchre of the former stands near the centre of the city of Hamadan: the tombs are covered by a dome, on which is the following inscription in Hebrew: "This day, 15th of the month Adar, in the year 4474 from the creation of the world, was finished the building of this temple over the graves of Mordecai and Esther, by the hands of the good-hearted brothers, Elias and Samuel, the sons of the deceased Ismael of Kashan." This inscription, the date of which proves the dome to have been built eleven hundred years, was sent by Sir Gore Ouseley to Sir John Malcolm, who has given it in his History of Persia; who also says that the tombs, which are of a black coloured wood, are evidently of very great antiquity, but in good preservation, as the wood has not perished, and the inscriptions are still very legible. Sir R. K. Porter has given a more particular description of this tomb. He says, "I accompanied the priest through the town, over much ruin and rubbish, to an enclosed piece of ground, rather more elevated than any in its immediate vicinity. In the centre was the Jewish tomb; a square building of brick, of a mosque-like form, with a rather elongated dome at the top. The whole seems in a very decaying state, falling fast to the mouldering condition of some wall fragments around, which, in former times, had been connected with, and extended the consequence of, the sacred enclosure. The door that admitted us into the tomb, is in the ancient sepulchral fashion of the country, very small; consisting of a small stone of great thickness, and turning on its own pivots from one side. Its key is always in possession of the head of the Jews resident at Hamadan." "On passing through the little portal, which we did in an almost doubled position, we entered a small arched chamber, in which are seen the graves of several rabbies: probably, one may cover the remains of the pious Ismael; and, not unlikely, the others may contain the bodies of the first rebuilders after the sacrilegious destruction by Timour. Having 'trod lightly by their graves,' a second door of such very confined dimensions presented itself at the end of this vestibule, we were constrained to enter it on our hands and knees, and then standing up, we found ourselves in a larger chamber, to which appertained the dome. Immediately under its concave, stand two sarcophagi, made of a very dark wood, carved with great intricacy of pattern, and richness of twisted ornament, with a line of inscription in Hebrew running round the upper ledge of each. Many other inscriptions, in the same language, are cut on the walls; while one of the oldest antiquity, engraved on a slab of white marble, is let into the wall itself." This inscription is as follows: "Mordecai, beloved and honoured by a king, was great and good. His garments were as those of a sovereign. Ahasuerus covered him with this rich dress, and also placed a golden chain around his neck. The city of Susa rejoiced at his honours, and his high fortune became the glory of the Jews." The inscription which encompasses the sarcophagus of Mordecai, is to this effect: "It is said by David, Preserve me, O God! I am now in thy presence. I have cried at the gate of heaven, that thou art my God; and what goodness I have received from thee, O Lord! Those whose bodies are now beneath in this earth, when animated by thy mercy were great; and whatever happiness was bestowed upon them in this world, came from thee, O God! Their grief and sufferings were many, at the first; but they became happy, because they always called upon thy holy name in their miseries. Thou liftedst me up, and I became powerful. Thine enemies sought to destroy me, in the early times of my life; but the shadow of thy hand was upon me, and covered me, as a tent, from their wicked purposes!--Mordecai." The following is the corresponding inscription on the sarcophagus of Esther: "I praise thee, O God, that thou hast created me! I know that my sins merit punishment, yet I hope for mercy at thy hands; for whenever I call upon thee, thou art with me; thy holy presence secures me from all evil. My heart is at ease, and my fear of thee increases. My life became, through thy goodness, at the last, full of peace. O God, do not shut my soul out from thy divine presence! Those whom thou lovest, never feel the torments of hell. Lead me, O merciful Father, to the life of life; that I may be filled with the heavenly fruits of paradise!--Esther." The Jews at Hamadan have no tradition of the cause of Esther and Mordecai having been interred at that place; but however that might be, there are sufficient reasons for believing the validity of their interment in this spot. The strongest evidence we can have of the truth of any historical fact, is, its commemoration by an annual festival. It is well known, that several important events in Jewish history are thus celebrated; and among the rest, the feast of Purim is kept on the 13th and 14th of the month Adar, to commemorate the deliverance obtained by the Jews, at the intercession of Esther, from the general massacre ordered by Ahasuerus, and the slaughter they were permitted to make of their enemies. Now on this same festival, in the same day and month, Jewish pilgrims resort from all quarters to the sepulchre of Mordecai and Esther; and have done so for centuries,--a strong presumptive proof that the tradition of their burial in this place rests on some authentic foundation.

ECCLESIASTES, a canonical book of the Old Testament, of which Solomon was the author, as appears from the first sentence. The design of this book is to show the vanity of all sublunary things; and from a review of the whole, the author draws this pertinent conclusion, "Fear God, and keep his commandments, for this is the whole of man;"--his whole wisdom, interest, and happiness, as well as his whole duty. Ecclesiastes, according to a modern author, is a dialogue, in which a man of piety disputes with a libertine who favoured the opinion of the Sadducees. His reason is, that there are passages in it which seem to contradict each other, and could not, he thinks, proceed from the same person. But this may be accounted for by supposing that it was Solomon's method to propose the objections of infidels and sensualists, and then to reply to them.

ECCLESIASTICAL POLITY, the rules by which churches are governed, as to their spiritual concerns. The reformers having renounced the pope as antichrist, and having laid it down as their fundamental principle, that Scripture is the only rule of faith, and that it is the privilege of every man to interpret it according to his own judgment, had to consider in what manner the churches which they had formed were to be regulated; and there soon arose among them upon this point diversity of sentiment. Melancthon and the earliest reformers viewed with veneration the hierarchy which had so long subsisted, as also many of the ceremonies which for ages had been observed; and they expressed their readiness to continue that distinction of pastors which their researches into the history of the church had enabled them to trace back to the early ages of Christianity. But while they declared in favour of this form of ecclesiastical polity, they did so, not upon the ground that it was of divine institution, or positively required by the author of Christianity as inseparable from a church; but on the ground, that taking into estimation every thing connected with it, it appeared to them eminently adapted to carry into effect that renovation of piety, and that religious influence, which they were so eager to promote. They thus made ecclesiastical polity a matter of expediency, or of prudential regulation; the one thing in their view, binding upon all Christians, being to strengthen the practical power of religion. That this is a just representation of the state of opinion among the first Protestants, will be placed beyond a doubt by a few quotations from the confession of Augsburg, and from the works of some of the most eminent divines who then flourished. Speaking of this subject, the compilers of the confession declare, "that they were most desirous to preserve the ecclesiastical polity, and those degrees in the church which had been introduced by human authority, knowing that, for wise and good purposes, the discipline, as described in the canons, had been introduced by the fathers." "We wish," they add, "to testify that we would willingly preserve the ecclesiastical and canonical polity, if the bishops would cease to act with cruelty against our churches." And once again they remark, that they had often declared that they venerated not only the ecclesiastical power which was instituted in the Gospel, but that they approved of the ecclesiastical polity which had subsisted, and wished, as much as was in their power, to preserve it. It is quite plain from these passages, that the framers of that confession, and those who adhered to it as the standard of their faith, viewed ecclesiastical polity as a matter of human appointment; and that, although they venerated that form of it which had long existed, they looked upon themselves as at liberty, under peculiar circumstances, to depart from it. The truth, accordingly, is, that a great part of the Lutheran churches, as we shall afterward find, did introduce many deviations from that model for which their founders had expressed respect and admiration; although episcopacy was in several places continued.

2. In consequence, however, of the exertions of Calvin, what were denominated the reformed churches deemed it expedient wholly to change this form of polity, and to introduce again the equality among pastors which had existed in the primitive times. That celebrated theologian, resting upon the undisputed fact, that in the Apostolic age no distinction subsisted between bishops and presbyters, thought himself at liberty to frame a system of polity upon this principle, persuaded that, by doing so, he would most effectually guard against those abuses that had given rise to the Papal tyranny which Protestants had abjured. He accordingly introduced his scheme where he had influence to do so; and he employed all the vigour of his talents in pressing upon distant churches the propriety of regulating, in conformity with his sentiments, their ecclesiastical government. But, while he was firmly persuaded that an equality among pastors was agreeable to the Apostolic practice, he has shown that he did not conceive this equality to be so absolutely required by Scripture, that there could in no case be a departure from it. He was, in fact, convinced that all the purposes of religion might be accomplished under a form of polity in which it was not recognised: "Wherever," he says, "the preaching of the Gospel is heard with reverence, and the sacraments are not neglected, there at that time there is a church." Speaking of faithful pastors, he describes them to be "those who by the doctrine of Christ lead men to true piety, who properly administer the sacred mysteries, and who preserve and exercise right discipline." In tracing the progress of the hierarchy, he observes, that "those to whom the office of teaching was assigned were denominated presbyters; that to avoid the dissensions often arising among equals, they chose one of their number to preside, to whom the title of bishop was exclusively given; and that the practice, as the ancients admitted, was introduced by human consent, from the necessity of the times." That this exaltation of the bishop, and, of course, this departure from parity, did not, in his estimation, render the church unchristian, is apparent from what he says of it after the change was introduced: "Such was the severity of these times, that all the ministers were led to discharge their duty as the Lord required of them." Even after archbishops and patriarchs had arisen, he merely says, in recording their introduction, "This arrangement was calculated to preserve discipline."

3. What Calvin thus taught in his "Institutes," he confirmed in many of the interesting letters which he wrote to various eminent persons. In these letters he speaks with the highest respect of the church of England, where the distinction of clerical orders was preserved. He corresponds with the highest dignitaries of that church in a style which he assuredly would not have adopted, had he considered them as upholding an antichristian polity; and he repeatedly avows the principle, that, in regulating the government of the church, attention must be paid to the circumstances in which its members were placed. Beza, who was warmly attached to presbytery, and who upon every occasion, strenuously defended it, still admits that the human order of episcopacy was useful, as long as the bishops were good; and he professes all reverence for those modern bishops who strive to imitate the primitive ones in the reformation of the church according to the word of God: adding that it was a calumny against him, and those who entertained his sentiments, to affirm, as some had done, that they wished to prescribe their

form of government to all other churches. In the excellent letter which he addressed to Grindal, bishop of London, and in which he pleads the cause of those ministers who scrupled to use the ceremonies which their brethren approved, he bears his testimony to the conformity of the church of England in doctrine with his church, expresses himself with the highest respect of the prelate to whom he was writing, and concludes by asking his prayers in his own behalf, and in that of the church of Geneva; all of which is quite inconsistent with the tenet, that presbytery is absolutely prescribed by divine authority.

4. The same general principle was avowed by the most eminent English divines. Cranmer explicitly declared, that bishops and priests were of the same order at the commencement of Christianity; and this was the opinion of several of his distinguished contemporaries. Holding this maxim, their support of episcopacy must have proceeded from views of expediency, or, in some instances, from a conviction which prevailed very generally at this early period, that it belonged to the supreme civil magistrate to regulate the spiritual no less than the political government; an idea involving in it that no one form of ecclesiastical polity is of divine institution. At a later period, during the reign of Queen Elizabeth, we find the same conviction, that it was no violation of Christianity to choose different modes of administering the church. Archbishop Whitgift, who distinguished himself by the zeal with which he supported the English hierarchy, frequently maintains, that the form of discipline is not particularly, and by name, set down in Scripture; and he also plainly asserts, "that no form of church government is, by the Scriptures, prescribed or commanded to the church of God." This principle is admirably illustrated and confirmed by the venerable Hooker, in the third book of his work on ecclesiastical polity; and another divine of the English church, who lived about the same period, has laid down what he conceives to be an unquestionable position, "that all churches have not the same form of discipline; neither is it necessary that they should, because it cannot be proved that any particular form of church government is enjoined by the word of God." We have, indeed, a succession of testimonies from the introduction of the reformation down through the reign of Elizabeth,--testimonies given by the primates, and bishops, and theologians, who have been venerated as the luminaries of the church of England, that the divine right or institution of episcopacy constituted no part of their faith; and this is confirmed by their correspondence with reformed divines, who did not live under the episcopal model, but who, notwithstanding, were often consulted as to the ecclesiastical arrangements which the convocation should adopt. The same general sentiment is to be traced in those churches which had reverted to the primitive equality among the ministers of Christ. In the second Helvetic confession, which was approved by many churches, it is taught, that bishops and presbyters in the beginning governed the church with equal power, none exalting himself above another; the inequality which soon was introduced originating from the desire of preserving order. Various passages from Cyprian and Jerom are quoted in confirmation of this; and the article thus concludes: "Wherefore no one can be lawfully hindered from returning to the ancient constitution of the church of God, and to adopt it in preference to what custom has introduced." Had the compilers believed that this ancient constitution was of divine obligation, they would have expressed themselves much more strongly with respect to it; and instead of representing the return to it as what ought not to be hindered, they would have enjoined it, as what it was a violation of the law of God to neglect.

5. The reformation in Scotland, conducted by Knox, who had spent a considerable part of his life at Geneva, and who had imbibed the opinions of Calvin, proceeded upon those views of polity which that reformer had adopted. Still, however, he authorized a modification of these opinions, accommodated to the state of his native country; for although the title of bishop was not used, superintendents, with powers little inferior to those committed to prelates in England, were sanctioned by the first Book of Discipline; and these superintendents were classed, in the acts of different general assemblies, among the necessary ministers of the church. The necessity must have arisen out of the circumstances of the period when the book was framed; for the polity which it prescribed was said to be only for a time; and the office of superintendent, as has been strenuously urged by some of the most zealous defenders of presbytery, was not intended to be permanent. The Lutheran church, with the exception of those branches of it established in Denmark and Sweden, has adopted a kind of intermediate constitution between episcopacy and presbytery. While it holds that there is no divine law creating a distinction among ministers, it yet contends that such a distinction is on many accounts expedient; and accordingly a diversity in point of rank and privileges has been universally introduced, approaching in different places, more or less, to the hierarchy which subsisted before the reformation. But, although it has thus regulated its own practice, it unambiguously admits, that as the Gospel is silent as to any particular form of polity, different forms may be chosen, without any breach of Christian union.

6. It appears from the statement which has now been given, that all Protestants immediately after the reformation, while they abjured the papal supremacy, were united in holding that the mode of administering the church might be varied, some of them being attached to episcopacy, others to presbytery; but all founding this attachment upon the judgment which they had formed as to the tendency or utility of either of these modes of government. An idea soon was avowed by some of the reformers, that the whole regulation of the church pertained to the magistrate; this branch of power being vested in him no less than that of administering the civil government; and to this opinion the name of Erastianism, from Erastus, who first defended it, was given. Cranmer, in an official reply which he made to certain questions that had been submitted for his consideration, declared, "that the civil ministers under the king's majesty be those that shall please his highness for the time to put in

authority under him; as, for example, the lord chancellor, lord great master, &c; the ministers of God's word under his majesty be the bishops, parsons, vicars, and such other priests as be appointed by his highness to that ministration; as, for example, the bishop of Canterbury, &c. All the said officers and ministers, as well of the one sort as the other, be appointed, assigned, and elected in every place by the laws and orders of kings and princes." By the great majority of Protestants, however, the tenets of Erastus were condemned; for they maintained that the Lord Jesus had conveyed to his church a spiritual power quite distinct from the temporal; and that it belonged to the ministers of religion to exercise it, for promoting the spiritual welfare of the Christian community. But, while they disputed as to this point, they agreed in admitting there was no model prescribed in the New Testament for a Christian church, as there had been in the Mosaical economy for the Jewish church; and that it was a branch of the liberty of the disciples of Christ, or one of their privileges, to choose the polity which seemed to them best adapted for extending the power and influence of religion.

ECLECTICS, a sect of ancient philosophers, who professed to select whatever was good and true from all the other philosophical sects. The Eclectic philosophy was in a flourishing state at Alexandria when our Saviour was upon earth. Its founders formed the design of selecting from the doctrines of all former philosophers such opinions as seemed to approach nearest the truth, and of combining them into one system. They held Plato in the highest esteem; but did not scruple to join with his doctrines whatever they thought conformable to reason in the tenets of other philosophers. Potamon, a Platonist, appears to have been the projector of this plan. The Eclectic system was brought to perfection by Ammonius Saccas, who blended Christianity with his philosophy, and founded the sect of the Ammonians, or New Platonists, in the second century. The moral doctrine of the Alexandrian school was as follows:-- The mind of man, originally a portion of the Divine Being, having fallen into a state of darkness and defilement, by its union with the body, is to be gradually emancipated from the chains of matter, and rise by contemplation to the knowledge and vision of God. The end of philosophy, therefore, is the liberation of the soul from its corporeal imprisonment. For this purpose, the Eclectic philosophy recommends abstinence, with other voluntary mortifications, and religious exercises. In the infancy of the Alexandrian school, not a few of the professors of Christianity were led, by the pretensions of the Eclectic sect, to imagine that a coalition might, with great advantage, be formed between its system and that of Christianity. This union appeared the more desirable, when several philosophers of this sect became converts to the Christian faith. The consequence was, that Pagan ideas and opinions were by degrees mixed with the pure and simple doctrines of the Gospel. See Platonism.

ECLIPSE. The word ECLIPSE, ἔκλειψις, signifies FAILURE, namely, of light. An eclipse of the sun is caused by the intervention of the moon, at new, or in conjunction with the sun, intercepting his light from the earth, either totally or partially. An eclipse of the moon is caused by the intervention of the earth, intercepting the sun's light from the moon, when full, or in opposition to the sun, either totally or partially. The reason why the sun is not eclipsed every new moon, nor the moon at every full, is owing to the inclination of the moon's orbit to the plane of the ecliptic, or earth's orbit, in an angle of about five degrees and a half; in consequence of which, the moon is generally too much elevated above the plane of the ecliptic, or too much depressed below it, for her disk to touch the earth's shadow at full, or for her shadow, or her penumbra, to touch the earth's disk at new. An eclipse, therefore, of either luminary can only take place when they are within their proper limits, or distances, from the nodes or intersections of both orbits. And because the limits of solar eclipses are wider than those of lunar, in general there will be more eclipses of the sun than of the moon. In any year, the number of eclipses of both luminaries cannot be less than two, and these will both be of the sun, nor more than seven: the usual number is four; and it is very rare to have more than six. But though solar eclipses happen oftener, lunar are more frequently observed in any particular place. For an eclipse of the moon is visible to the inhabitants of half the globe at the same instant; whereas, an eclipse of the sun is visible only within that part of the earth's surface, traversed by the moon's total shadow, and by her penumbra, or partial shadow. But her total shadow, when she is nearest to the earth, cannot cover a space of more than a hundred and fifty-eight geographical miles in diameter, nor at her mean distance more than seventy-nine, and at her greatest distance may not touch the earth at all. In the two former cases, the sun will be eclipsed in the places covered by the shadow totally, or by the penumbra partially: in the last it may be annular, but not total. Without the reach of the shadow, and within the limits of the penumbra, which cannot cover more than four thousand five hundred and fifty-two miles of the earth's surface, there will be a partial eclipse of the sun, and without these limits no eclipse at all. Hence lunar eclipses are more frequently noticed by historians than solar; and Diogenes Laertius may be credited when he relates, that, during the period in which the Egyptians had observed eight hundred and thirty-two eclipses of the moon, they had only observed three hundred and seventy-three of the sun. In the midst of a total lunar eclipse, the moon's disk is frequently visible, and of a deep red or copperish colour. This, in the poetic language of sacred prophecy, is expressed by "the moon's being turned into blood," Joel ii, 31. This remarkable phenomenon is caused by the sun's lateral rays in their passage through the dense atmosphere of the earth, being inflected into the shadow by refraction, and falling pretty copiously upon the moon's disk, are reflected from thence to the eye of the spectator. If the earth had no atmosphere, the moon's disk would then be as black as in a solar eclipse. A total eclipse of the moon may occasion a privation of her light for an hour and a half, during her total immersion in the shadow; whereas, a total eclipse of the sun can never last in any particular place above four minutes, when the moon is nearest to the earth, and her shadow thickest. Hence it appears, that the darkness which "overspread the whole land of Judea," at the time of our Lord's crucifixion, was preternatural, "from the sixth until the ninth hour," or from noon till three in the afternoon, in its duration, and also in its time, about full moon, when the moon could not possibly eclipse the sun. It was accompanied by an earthquake, which altogether struck the spectators, and among them the centurion and Roman guard, with great fear, and a conviction, that Jesus was the Son of God, Matt, xxvii, 51–54.

Eclipses, says Dr. Hales, are justly reckoned among the surest and most unerring characters of chronology; for they can be calculated with great exactness backward as well as forward; and there is such a variety of distinct circumstances of the time when, and the place where, they were seen; of the duration, or beginning, middle, or end of every eclipse, and of the quantity, or number of digits eclipsed; that there is no danger of confounding any two eclipses together, when the circumstances attending each are noticed with any tolerable degree of precision. Thus, to an eclipse of the moon incidentally noticed by the great Jewish chronologer, Josephus, shortly before the death of Herod the Great, we owe the determination of the true year of our Saviour's nativity. During Herod's last illness, and not many days before his death, there happened an eclipse of the moon on the very night that he burned alive Matthias, and the ringleaders of a sedition, in which the golden eagle, which he had consecrated and set up over the gate of the temple, was pulled down and broken to pieces by these zealots. This eclipse happened, by calculation, March 13, U. C. 750, B. C. 4. But it is certain from Scripture, that Christ was born during Herod's reign; and from the visit of the magi to Jerusalem "from the east," ἀπὸ ἀνατολῶν, from the Parthian empire, to inquire for the true "born King of the Jews," whose star they had seen "at its rising," ἐν τῇ ἀνατολῇ, and also from the age of the infants massacred at Bethlehem, "from two years old and under," Matt, ii, 1–16. It is no less certain, that Jesus could not have been born later than B. C. 5, which is the year assigned to the nativity by Chrysostom, Petavius and Prideaux.

EDEN, GARDEN OF, the residence of our first parents in their state of purity and blessedness. The word EDEN in the Hebrew denotes "pleasure" or "delight:" whence the name has been given to several places which, from their situation, were pleasant or delightful. Thus the Prophet Amos, i, 5, speaks of an Eden in Syria, which is generally considered to have been in the valley of Damascus, where a town called Eden is mentioned by Pliny and Ptolemy, and where the tomb of Abel is pretended to be shown. This has in consequence been selected by some as the site of the garden of Eden. By others, the garden has been placed on the eastern side of mount Libanus; and by others again, in Arabia Felix, where traces of the word EDEN are found. But the opinion which has been most generally received on this subject is that which places the garden on the Lower Euphrates; between the junction of that river with the Tigris and the gulf of Persia. This is Dr. Well's opinion; in which he is supported by Huetius, Grotius, Marinus, and Bochart. To this it is replied, that, according to this scheme, the garden was intersected by a great branch of the Euphrates, in the lower and broadest part of its course; which will give it an extent absolutely irreconcilable with the idea of Adam's "dressing" it by his own manual labour, or even of overlooking it: beside that all communication would be cut off between its different parts by a stream half a mile in width. Its local features, too, if in this situation, must have been of the most uninteresting kind; the whole of that region, as far as the sight can reach, being a dead, monotonous, sandy, or marshy flat, without a single undulation to relieve the eye, or give any of the beauties which the imagination involuntarily paints to itself as attendant on a spot finished by the hand of God as the residence of his creatures in a state of innocence; whose minds may be supposed to be tuned to the full enjoyment of the grand and beautiful in nature. How different will be the aspect and arrangement of this favoured spot, if it be placed where only, according to the words of Moses, it can be placed; namely, at the heads or fountains of the rivers described, instead of their mouths.

The country of Eden, therefore, according to others, was some where in Media, Armenia, or the north of Mesopotamia; all mountainous tracts, and affording, instead of the sickening plains of Babylonia, some of the grandest, as well as the richest scenery in the world. A river or stream rising in some part of this country, entered the garden; where it was parted into four others, in all probability, by first falling into a basin or lake, from which the other streams issued at different points, taking different directions, and growing into mighty rivers; although at their sources in the garden, they would be like all other rivers, mere brooks, and forming no barrier to a free communication between the parts of the garden. Dr. Wells, in order to support his hypothesis of the situation of Eden on the lower parts of the Euphrates and Tigris, after giving these rivers a distribution which has now no existence, makes the Pison and Gihon to be parts of the Tigris and Euphrates themselves: an arrangement at perfect disagreement with the particular description of Moses; beside, that the Gihon thus called, instead of compassing the whole land of Cush, can only be said to skirt an extreme corner of it. It appears, indeed, that in the time of Alexander, the Euphrates pursued a separate course to the sea; or, at least, that a navigable branch of it was carried in that direction: in the mouth of which, at Diridotis, Nearchus anchored with his fleet. But what reliance can be placed on the ever shifting channels of a river flowing through an alluvial soil, and over a perfect level divertible at the pleasure of the people inhabiting its banks? Or, what theory can be founded on their distribution, which will not be as unstable as the streams themselves? This very channel, so essential to the hypothesis which places Eden in this situation, was annihilated by the Orcheni, a neighbouring people; who directed the stream to water their own land, and thus gave it a shorter course into the Tigris, which it has ever since preserved. But it is only the lower parts of the Euphrates and Tigris, as they creep through the plains of Babylonia, which are thus inconstant: higher up in their courses, they flow over more solid strata, and in deeper valleys, unchanged by time. It is here that their conformity with the Mosaic account is to be sought; and it is here that they may be found, in the exact condition in which they were left by the deluge, and, indeed, according to Moses, in which they existed before that event. It is true, that the heads of the four rivers, above described, cannot now be found sufficiently near, to recognise thence the exact situation of paradise; but they all arise from the same mountainous region; and the springs of the Euphrates and Tigris, as already mentioned, are even now nearly interwoven. Mr. Faber supposes the lake Arsissa to cover the site of Eden; and that the change which carried the heads of the rivers to a greater distance from it, was occasioned by the deluge. But it is far more probable that this change, if we may infer from the account given by Moses that the courses of all the streams remained unaltered by the flood, may have taken place at man's expulsion from the garden: when God might choose to obliterate this fair portion of his works, unfitted for any thing but the residence of innocence; and to blot at once from the face of the earth, like the guilty cities of the plain, both the site and the memorial of man's transgression,--an awful event, which would add tenfold horrors to the punishment.

EDOM, a province of Arabia, which derives its name from Edom, or Esau, who there settled in the mountains of Seir, in the land of the Horites, south-east of the Dead Sea. His descendants afterward extended themselves throughout Arabia Petrea, and south of Palestine, between the Dead Sea and the Mediterranean. During the Babylonish captivity, and when Judea was almost deserted, they seized the south of Judah, and advanced to Hebron. Hence that tract of Judea, which they inhabited, retained the name of Idumea in the time of our Saviour, Mark iii, 8. Under Moses and Joshua, and even under the kings of Judah, the Idumeans were confined to the east and south of the Dead Sea, in the land of Seir; but afterward they extended their territories more to the south of Judah. The capital of east Edom was Bozrah; and that of south Edom, Petra, or Jectael. The Edomites, or Idumeans, the posterity of Esau, had kings long before the Jews. They were first governed by dukes or princes, and afterward by kings, Gen. xxxvi, 31. They continued independent till the time of David, who subdued them, in completion of Isaac's prophecy, that Jacob should rule Esau, Gen. xxvii, 29, 30. The Idumeans bore this subjection with great impatience; and at the end of Solomon's reign, Hadad, the Edomite, who had been carried into Egypt during his childhood, returned into his own country, where he procured himself to be acknowledged king, 1 Kings xi, 22. It is probable, however, that he reigned only in east Edom; for Edom south of Judea continued subject to the kings of Judah, till the reign of Jehoram, son of Jehoshaphat, against whom it rebelled, 2 Chron. xxi, 8. Jehoram attacked Edom, but did not subdue it. Amaziah king of Judah, took Petra, killed a thousand men, and compelled ten thousand more to leap from the rock, upon which stood the city of Petra, 2 Chron. xxv, 11, 12. But these conquests were not permanent. Uzziah took Elath on the Red Sea, 2 Kings xiv, 22; but Rezin, king of Syria, retook it. Some think that Esarhaddon, king of Syria, ravaged this country, Isaiah xxi, 11–17; xxxiv, 6. Holofernes subdued it, as well as other nations around Judea, Judith iii, 14. When Nebuchadnezzar besieged Jerusalem, the Idumeans joined him, and encouraged him to rase the very foundations of that city. This cruelty did not long continue unpunished. Five years after the taking of Jerusalem, Nebuchadnezzar humbled all the states around Judea, and in particular Idumea. John Hyrcanus entirely conquered the Idumeans, whom he obliged to receive circumcision and the law. They continued subject to the later kings of Judea till the destruction of Jerusalem by the Romans. They even came to assist that city when besieged, and entered it in order to defend it. However, they did not continue there till it was taken, but returned into Idumea loaded with booty. The prophecies respecting Edom are numerous and striking; and the present state of the country as described by modern travellers has given so remarkable an attestation to the accuracy of their fulfilment, that a few extracts from Mr. Keith's work, in which this is pointed out, may be fitly introduced:--

2. There are numerous prophecies respecting Idumea, that bear a literal interpretation, however hyperbolical they may appear. "My sword shall come down upon Idumea, and upon the people of my curse, to judgment. From generation to generation it shall lie waste, none shall pass through it for ever and ever. But the cormorant and the bittern shall possess it; the owl also and the raven shall dwell in it: and he shall stretch out upon it the line of confusion, and the stones of emptiness. They shall call the nobles thereof to the kingdom; but none shall be there, and all her princes shall be nothing. And thorns shall come up in her palaces, nettles and brambles in the fortresses thereof; and it shall be a habitation of dragons, and a court for owls. Seek ye out of the book of the Lord and read; no one of these shall fail, none shall want her mate; for my mouth it hath commanded, and his Spirit it hath gathered them. And he hath cast the lot for them, and his hand hath divided it unto them by line; they shall possess it for ever, from generation to generation shall they dwell therein," Isa. xxxiv, 5, 10–17. "I have sworn by myself, saith the Lord, that Bozrah" (the strong or fortified city) "shall become a desolation, a reproach, a waste, and a curse; and all the cities thereof shall be perpetual wastes. Lo, I will make thee small among the Heathen, and despised among men. Thy terribleness hath deceived thee, and the pride of thine heart, O thou that dwellest in the clefts of the rock, that holdest the height of the hill: though thou shouldest make thy nest as high as the eagle, I will bring thee down from thence, saith the Lord. Also Edom shall be a desolation; every one that goeth by shall be astonished, and shall hiss at all the plagues thereof. As in the overthrow of Sodom and Gomorrah, and the neighbour cities thereof, saith the Lord, no man shall abide there, neither shall a son of man dwell in it," Jer. xlix, 13–18. "Thus saith the Lord God, I will stretch out mine hand upon Edom, and will cut off man and beast from it, and I will make it desolate from Teman." "I laid the mountains of Esau and his heritage waste for the dragons of the wilderness. Whereas Edom saith, We are impoverished,

but we will return and build the desolate places; thus saith the Lord of hosts, They shall build, but I will throw down; and they shall call them, The border of wickedness," Malachi i, 3, 4.

Is there any country once inhabited and opulent, so utterly desolate? There is, and that land is Idumea. The territory of the descendants of Esau affords as miraculous a demonstration of the inspiration of the Scriptures as the fate of the children of Israel. A single extract from the Travels of Volney will be found to be equally illustrative of the prophecy and of the fact: "This country has not been visited by any traveller, but it well merits such an attention; for, from the report of the Arabs of Bakir, and the inhabitants of Gaza, who frequently go to Maan and Karak, on the road of the pilgrims, there are, to the south-east of the lake Asphaltites, (Dead Sea,) within three days' journey, upward of thirty ruined towns absolutely deserted. Several of them have large edifices, with columns that may have belonged to the ancient temples, or at least to Greek churches. The Arabs sometimes make use of them to fold their cattle in; but in general avoid them on account of the enormous scorpions with which they swarm. We cannot be surprised at these traces of ancient population, when we recollect that this was the country of the Nabatheans, the most powerful of the Arabs, and of the Idumeans, who, at the time of the destruction of Jerusalem, were almost as numerous as the Jews, as appears from Josephus, who informs us, that on the first rumour of the march of Titus against Jerusalem, thirty thousand Idumeans instantly assembled, and threw themselves into that city for its defence. It appears that, beside the advantages of being under a tolerably good government, these districts enjoyed a considerable share of the commerce of Arabia and India, which increased their industry and population. We know that as far back as the time of Solomon, the cities of Astioum Gaber (Ezion Geber) and Ailah (Eloth) were highly frequented marts. These towns were situated on the adjacent gulf of the Red Sea, where we still find the latter yet retaining its name, and perhaps the former in that of El Akaba, or 'the end of the sea.' These two places are in the hands of the Bedouins, who, being destitute of a navy and commerce, do not inhabit them. But the pilgrims report that there is at El Akaba a wretched fort. The Idumeans, from whom the Jews only took their ports at intervals, must have found in them a great source of wealth and population. It even appears that the Idumeans rivalled the Tyrians, who also possessed a town, the name of which is unknown, on the coast of Hedjaz, in the desert of Tih, and the city of Faran, and, without doubt, El-Tor, which served it by way of port. From this place the caravans might reach Palestine and Judea, (through Idumea,) in eight or ten days. This route, which is longer than that from Suez to Cairo, is infinitely shorter than that from Aleppo to Bassorah." Evidence, which must have been undesigned, which cannot be suspected of partiality, and which no illustration can strengthen, and no ingenuity pervert, is thus borne to the truth of the most wonderful prophecies. That the Idumeans were a populous and powerful nation long posterior to the delivery of the prophecies; that they possessed a tolerably good government, even in the estimation of Volney; that Idumea contained many cities; that these cities are now absolutely deserted; and that their ruins swarm with enormous scorpions; that it was a commercial nation, and possessed highly frequented marts; that it forms a shorter route than the ordinary one to India; and yet that it had not been visited by any traveller; are facts all recorded, and proved by this able but unconscious commentator.

3. A greater contrast cannot be imagined than the ancient and present state of Idumea. It was a kingdom previous to Israel, having been governed first by dukes or princes, afterward by eight successive kings, and again by dukes, before there reigned any king over the children of Israel, Gen. xxxvi, 31, &c. Its fertility and early cultivation are implied not only in the blessings of Esau, whose dwelling was to be the fatness of the earth, and of the dew of heaven from above; but also in the condition proposed by Moses to the Edomites, when he solicited a passage for the Israelites through their borders, that "they would not pass through the fields nor through the vineyards;" and also in the great wealth, especially in the multitudes of flocks and herds, recorded as possessed by an individual inhabitant of that country, at a period, in all probability even more remote, Gen. xxvii, 39; Num. xx, 17; Job xlii, 12. The Idumeans were, without doubt, both an opulent and a powerful people. They often contended with the Israelites, and entered into a league with their other enemies against them. In the reign of David they were indeed subdued and greatly oppressed, and many of them even dispersed throughout the neighbouring countries, particularly Phenicia and Egypt. But during the decline of the kingdom of Judah, and for many years previous to its extinction, they encroached upon the territories of the Jews, and extended their dominion over the south-western part of Judea.

4. There is a prediction which, being peculiarly remarkable as applicable to Idumea, and bearing reference to a circumstance explanatory of the difficulty of access to any knowledge respecting it, is entitled, in the first instance, to notice: "None shall pass through it for ever and ever. I will cut off from Mount Seir him that passeth out, and him that returneth," Isa. xxxiv, 10; Ezek. xxxv, 7. The ancient greatness of Idumea must, in no small degree, have resulted from its commerce. Bordering with Arabia on the east, and Egypt on the southwest, and forming from north to south the most direct and most commodious channel of communication between Jerusalem and her dependencies on the Red Sea, as well as between Syria and India, through the continuous valleys of El Ghor, and El Araba, which terminated on the one extremity at the borders of Judea, and on the other at Elath and Ezion Geber on the Elanitic gulf of the Red Sea, Idumea may be said to have formed the emporium of the commerce of the east. A Roman road passed directly through Idumea, from Jerusalem to Akaba, and another from Akaba to Moab; and when these roads were made, at a time long posterior to the date of the predictions, the conception could not have been formed, or held credible by man, that the period would ever arrive when

none would pass through it. Above seven hundred years after the date of the prophecy, Strabo relates that many Romans and other foreigners were found at Petra by his friend Athenodorus, the philosopher, who visited it. The prediction is yet more surprising when viewed in conjunction with another, which implies that travellers would "pass by" Idumea: "Every one that goeth by shall be astonished." And the Hadj routes (routes of the pilgrims) from Damascus and from Cairo to Mecca, the one on the east and the other toward the south of Idumea, along the whole of its extent, go by it, or touch partially on its borders, without passing through it. The truth of the prophecy, though hemmed in thus by apparent impossibilities and contradictions, and with extreme probability of its fallacy in every view that could have been visible to man, may yet be tried.

5. "Edom shall be a desolation. From generation to generation it shall lie waste," &c. Judea, Ammon, and Moab, exhibit so abundantly the remains and the means of an exuberant fertility, that the wonder arises in the reflecting mind, how the barbarity of man could have so effectually counteracted for so many generations the prodigality of nature. But such is Edom's desolation, that the first sentiment of astonishment on the contemplation of it is, how a wide extended region, now diversified by the strongest features of desert wildness, could ever have been adorned with cities, or tenanted for ages by a powerful and opulent people. Its present aspect would belie its ancient history, were not that history corroborated by "the many vestiges of former cultivation," by the remains of walls and paved roads, and by the ruins of cities still existing in this ruined country. The total cessation of its commerce; the artificial irrigation of its valleys wholly neglected; the destruction of all the cities, and the continued spoliation of the country by the Arabs, while aught remained that they could destroy; the permanent exposure, for ages, of the soil unsheltered by its ancient groves, and unprotected by any covering from the scorching rays of the sun; the unobstructed encroachments of the desert, and of the drifted sands from the borders of the Red Sea; the consequent absorption of the water of the springs and streamlets during summer,--are causes which have all combined their baneful operation in rendering Edom "most desolate, the desolation of desolations." Volney's account is sufficiently descriptive of the desolation which now reigns over Idumea; and the information which Seetzen derived at Jerusalem respecting it is of similar import. He was told, that at the distance of two days' journey and a half from Hebron, he would find considerable ruins of the ancient city of Abde, and that for all the rest of the journey he would see no place of habitation; he would meet only with a few tribes of wandering Arabs. From the borders of Edom, Captains Irby and Mangles beheld a boundless extent of desert view, which they had hardly ever seen equalled for singularity and grandeur. And the following extract, descriptive of what Burckhardt actually witnessed in the different parts of Edom, cannot be more graphically abbreviated than in the words of the prophet. Of its eastern boundary, and of the adjoining part of Arabia Petrea, strictly so called, Burckhardt writes: "It might, with truth, be called Petrea, not only on account of its rocky mountains, but also of the elevated plain already described, which is so much covered with stones, especially flints, that it may with great propriety be called a stony desert, although susceptible of culture; in many places it is overgrown with wild herbs, and must once have been thickly inhabited; for the traces of many towns and villages are met with on both sides of the Hadj road between Maan and Akaba, as well as between Maan and the plains of the Hauran, in which direction are also many springs. At present all this country is a desert, and Maan (Teman) is the only inhabited place in it: 'I will stretch out my hand against thee, O Mount Seir, and will make thee most desolate. I will stretch out my hand upon Edom, and will make it desolate from Teman.'" In the interior of Idumea, where the ruins of some of its ancient cities are still visible, and in the extensive valley which reaches from the Red to the Dead Sea, the appearance of which must now be totally and sadly changed from what it was, "the whole plain presented to the view an expanse of shifting sands, whose surface was broken by innumerable undulations and low hills. The sand appears to have been brought from the shores of the Red Sea, by the southern winds; and the Arabs told me that the valleys continue to present the same appearance beyond the latitude of Wady Mousa. In some parts of the valley the sand is very deep, and there is not the slightest appearance of a road, or of any work of human art. A few trees grow among the sand hills, but the depth of sand precludes all vegetation of herbage." "If grape gatherers come to thee, would not they leave some gleaning grapes? If thieves by night, they will destroy till they have enough; but I have made Esau bare. Edom shall be a desolate wilderness." "On ascending the western plain," continues Mr. Burckhardt, "on a higher level than that of Arabia, we had before us an immense expanse of dreary country, entirely covered with black flints, with here and there some hilly chain rising from the plain." "I will stretch out upon Idumea the line of confusion, and the stones of emptiness." Such is the present desolate aspect of one of the most fertile countries of ancient times! So visibly even now does the withering curse of an offended God rest upon it!

EGG, ביצים, Deut. xxii, 6; Job xxxix, 14; Isaiah x, 14; lix, 5; ὠὸν, Luke xi, 12. Eggs are considered as a very great delicacy in the east, and are served up with fish and honey at their entertainments. As a desirable article of food, the egg is mentioned, Luke xi, 12: "If a son ask for an egg, will his father offer him a scorpion?" It has been remarked that the body of the scorpion is very like an egg, as its head can scarcely be distinguished, especially if it be of the white kind, which is the first species mentioned by Ælian, Avicenna, and others. Bochart has produced testimonies to prove that the scorpions in Judea were about the bigness of an egg. So the similitude is preserved between the thing asked, and the thing given.

EGLON, a king of Moab, who oppressed the Israelites, and was slain by Ehud, Judges iii, 14, 21. It is thought to have been a common name of the kings of Moab, as Abimelech was of the Philistines.

EGYPT, a country of Africa, called also in the Hebrew Scriptures the land of Mizraim, and the land of Ham; by the Turks and Arabs, Masr and Misr; and by the native Egyptians, Chemi, or the land of Ham. Mr. Faber derives the name from Ai-Capht, or the land of the Caphtorim; from which, also, the modern Egyptians derive their name of Cophts. Egypt was first peopled after the deluge by Mizraim, or Mizr, the son of Ham, who is supposed to be the same with Menes, recorded in Egyptian history as the first king. Every thing relating to the subsequent history and condition of this country, for many ages, is involved in fable. Nor have we any clear information from Heathen writers, until the time of Cyrus, and his son Cambyses, when the line of Egyptian princes ceased in agreement with prophecies to that effect. Manetho, the Egyptian historian, has given a list of thirty dynasties, which, if successive, make a period of five thousand three hundred years to the time of Alexander, or three thousand two hundred and eighty-two years more than the real time, according to the Mosaic chronology. But this is a manifest forgery, which has, nevertheless, been appealed to by infidel writers, as authority against the veracity of the Mosaic history. The truth is, that this pretended succession of princes, if all of them can be supposed to have existed at all, constituted several distinct dynasties, ruling in different cities at the same time: thus these were the kingdoms of Thebes, Thin, Memphis, and Tanis. See Writing.

2. In the time of Moses we find Egypt renowned for learning; for he was instructed "in all its wisdom;" and it is one of the commendations of Solomon, at a later period, that he excelled in knowledge "all the wisdom of the children of the east country, and all the wisdom of Egypt." Astronomy, which probably, like that of the Chaldeans, comprehended also judicial astrology, physics, agriculture, jurisprudence, medicine, architecture, painting, and sculpture, were the principal sciences and arts; to which were added, and that by their wisest men, the study of divination, magic, and enchantments. They had also their consulters with familiar spirits, and necromancers, those who had, or pretended to have, intercourse with the infernal deities, and the spirits of the dead, and delivered responses to inquirers. Of all this knowledge, good and evil, and of a monstrous system of idolatry, Egypt was the polluted fountain to the surrounding nations; but in that country itself it appears to have degenerated into the most absurd and debased forms. Among nations who are not blessed by divine revelation, the luminaries of heaven are the first objects of worship. Diodorus Siculus, mentioning the Egyptians, informs us, that "the first men, looking up to the world above them, and, struck with admiration at the nature of the universe, supposed the sun and moon to be the principal and eternal gods." This, which may be called the natural superstition of mankind, we can trace in the annals of the west, as well as of the east; among the inhabitants of the new world, as well as of the old. The sun and moon, under the names of Isis and Osiris, were the chief objects of adoration among the Egyptians. But the earliest times had a purer faith. The following inscription, engraven in hieroglyphics in the temple of Neith, the Egyptian Minerva, conveys the most sublime idea of the Deity which unenlightened reason could form: "I am that which is, was, and shall be: no mortal hath lifted up my veil: the offspring of my power is the sun." A similar inscription still remains at Capua, on the temple of Isis: "Thou art one, and from thee all things proceed." Plutarch also informs us, that the inhabitants of Thebais worshipped only the immortal and supreme God, whom they called Eneph. According to the Egyptian cosmogony, all things sprung from ATHOR, or night, by which they denoted the darkness of chaos before the creation. Sanchoniathon relates, that, "from the breath of gods and the void were mortals created." This theology differs little from that of Moses, who says, "The earth was without form, and void; darkness was upon the face of the deep; and the Spirit of God moved upon the face of the waters."

3. A superstitious reverence for certain animals, as propitious or hurtful to the human race, was not peculiar to the Egyptians. The cow has been venerated in India from the most remote antiquity. The serpent has been the object of religious respect to one half of the nations of the known world. The Romans had sacred animals, which they kept in their temples, and distinguished with peculiar honours. We need not therefore be surprised that a nation so superstitious as the Egyptians should honour, with peculiar marks of respect, the ichneumon, the ibis, the dog, the falcon, the wolf, and the crocodile. These they entertained at great expense, and with much magnificence. Lands were set apart for their maintenance; persons of the highest rank were employed in feeding and attending them; rich carpets were spread in their apartments; and the pomp at their funerals corresponded to the profusion and luxury which attended them while alive. What chiefly tended to favour the progress of animal worship in Egypt, was the language of hieroglyphics. In the hieroglyphic inscriptions on their temples, and public edifices, animals, and even vegetables, were the symbols of the gods whom they worshipped. In the midst of innumerable superstitions, the theology of Egypt contained the two great principles of religion, the existence of a supreme Being, and the immortality of the soul. The first is proved by the inscription on the temple of Minerva; the second, by the care with which dead bodies were embalmed, and the prayer recited at the hour of death, by an Egyptian, expressing his desire to be received to the presence of the deities.

4. The opulence of Egypt was for ages increased by the large share it had in the commerce with the east; by its own favourable position, making it the connecting link of intercourse between the eastern and western nations; and especially by its own remarkable fertility, particularly in corn, so that it was, in times of scarcity, the granary of the world. Its extraordinary fertility was owing to the periodical inundation of the Nile; and sufficient proofs of the ancient accounts which we have of its productiveness are afforded

to this day. The Rev. Mr. Jowett has given a striking example of the extraordinary fertility of the soil of Egypt, which is alluded to in Genesis xli, 47: "The earth brought forth by handfuls." "I picked up at random," says Mr. Jowett, "a few stalks out of the thick corn fields. We counted the number of stalks which sprouted from single grains of seed; carefully pulling to pieces each root, in order to see that it was but one plant. The first had seven stalks, the next three, the next nine, then eighteen, then fourteen. Each stalk would have been an ear."

5. The architecture of the early Egyptians, at least that of their cities and dwellings, was rude and simple: they could indeed boast of little in either external elegance or internal comfort, since Herodotus informs us that men and beasts lived together. The materials of their structure were bricks of clay, bound together with chopped straw, and baked in the sun. Such were the bricks which the Israelites were employed in making, and of which the cities of Pithom and Rameses were built. Their composition was necessarily perishable, and explains why it is that no remains of the ancient cities of Egypt are to be found. They would indeed last longer in the dry climate of this country than in any other; but even here they must gradually decay and crumble to dust, and the cities so constructed become heaps. Of precisely the same materials are the villages of Egypt built at this day. "Village after village," says Mr. Jowett, speaking of Tentyra, "built of unburnt brick, crumbling into ruins, and giving place to new habitations, have raised the earth, in some parts, nearly to the level of the summit of the temple. In every part of Egypt, we find the towns built in this manner, upon the ruins, or rather the rubbish, of the former habitations. The expression in Jeremiah xxx, 18, literally applies to Egypt, in the meanest sense: 'The city shall be builded upon her own heap.' And the expression in Job xv, 28, might be illustrated by many of these deserted hovels: 'He dwelleth in desolate cities, and in houses which no man inhabiteth, which are ready to become heaps.' Still more touching is the allusion, in Job iv, 19, where the perishing generations of men are fitly compared to habitations of the frailest materials, built upon the heap of similar dwelling-places, now reduced to rubbish: 'How much less in them that dwell in houses of clay, whose foundation is in the dust!'"

6. The splendid temples of Egypt were not built, in all probability, till after the time of Solomon; for the recent progress made in the decyphering of hieroglyphics has disappointed the antiquaries as to the antiquity of these stupendous fabrics. It is well observed by Dr. Shuckford, that temples made no great figure in Homer's time. If they had, he would not have lost such an opportunity of exerting his genius on so grand a subject, as Virgil has done in his description of the temple built by Dido at Carthage. The first Heathen temples were probably nothing more than mean buildings, which served merely as a shelter from the weather: of which kind was, probably, the house of the Philistine god Dagon. But when the fame of Solomon's temple had reached other countries, it excited them to imitate its splendour; and nation vied with nation in the structures erected to their several deities. All were, however, outdone, at least in massiveness and durability, by the Egyptians; the architectural design of whose temples, as well as that of the Grecian edifices, was borrowed from the stems and branches of the grove temples.

7. It appears to be an unfounded notion, that the pyramids were built by the Israelites: they were, probably, Mr. Faber thinks, the work of the "Shepherds," or Cushite invaders, who, at an early period, held possession of Egypt for two hundred and sixty years, and reduced the Egyptians to bondage, so that "a shepherd was an abomination to the Egyptians" in Joseph's time. The Israelites laboured in making bricks, not in forming stones such as the pyramids are constructed with; and a passage in Mr. Jowett's "Researches," before referred to, will throw light upon this part of their history. Mr. Jowett saw at one place the people making bricks, with straw cut into small pieces, and mingled with the clay, to bind it. Hence it is, that when villages built of these bricks fall into rubbish, which is often the case, the roads are full of small particles of straws, extremely offensive to the eyes in a high wind. They were, in fact, engaged exactly as the Israelites used to be, making bricks with straw; and for a similar purpose, to build extensive granaries for the bashaw; "treasure-cities for Pharaoh." The same intelligent missionary also observes: "The mollems transact business between the bashaw and the peasants. He punishes them if the peasants prove that they oppress; and yet he requires from them that the work of those who are under them shall be fulfilled. They strikingly illustrate the case of the officers placed by the Egyptian task-masters over the children of Israel; and, like theirs, the mollems often find their case is evil, Exodus v."

8. It is not necessary to go over those parts of the Egyptian history which occur in the Old Testament. The prophecies respecting this haughty and idolatrous kingdom, uttered by Jeremiah and Ezekiel when it was in the height of its splendour and prosperity, were fulfilled in the terrible invasions of Nebuchadnezzar, Cambyses, and the Persian monarchs. It comes, however, again into an interesting connection with the Jewish history under Alexander the Great, who invaded it as a Persian dependence. So great, indeed, was the hatred of the Egyptians toward their oppressors, that they hailed the approach of the Macedonians, and threw open their cities to receive them. Alexander, merciless as he was to those who opposed his progress or authority, knew how to requite those who were devoted to his interests; and the Egyptians, for many centuries afterward, had reason to recollect with gratitude his protection and foresight. It was he who discerned the local advantages of the spot on which the city bearing his name afterward stood, who projected the plan of the town, superintended its erection, endowed it with many privileges, and peopled it with colonies drawn from other places for the purpose, chiefly Greeks. But, together with these, and the most favoured of all, were the Jews, who enjoyed the free exercise of their religion, and the same civil rights and liberties as the Macedonians themselves. Kindness shown to

the people of Israel has never, in the providence of God, brought evil on any country; and there can be no doubt but that the encouragement given to this enterprising and commercial people, assisted very much to promote the interests of the new city, which soon became the capital of the kingdom, the centre of commerce, of science, and the arts, and one of the most flourishing and considerable cities in the world. Egypt, indeed, was about to see better days; and, during the reigns of the Ptolemies, enjoyed again, for nearly three hundred years, something of its former renown for learning and power. It formed, during this period, and before the rapid extension of the Roman empire toward the termination of these years, one of the only two ancient kingdoms which had survived the Assyrian, Babylonian, Persian, and Macedonian empires: the other was the Syrian, where the Seleucidæ, another family of one of the successors of Alexander, reigned; who, having subdued Macedonia and Thrace, annexed them to the kingdom of Syria, and there remained out of the four kingdoms into which the empire of Alexander was divided these two only; distinguished, in the prophetic writings of Daniel, by the titles of the kings or kingdoms of the north and the south.

9. Under the reign of the three first Ptolemies, the state of the Jews was exceedingly prosperous. They were in high favour, and continued to enjoy all the advantages conferred upon them by Alexander. Judea was, in fact, at this time, a privileged province of Egypt; the Jews being governed by their own high priest, on paying a tribute to the kings of Egypt. But in the reign of Ptolemy Epiphanes, the fifth of the race, it was taken by Antiochus, king of Syria; which was the beginning of fresh sufferings and persecutions; for although this Antiochus, who was the one surnamed the Great, was a mild and generous prince, and behaved favourably toward them, their troubles began at his death; his successor, Seleucus, oppressing them with taxes; and the next was the monster, Antiochus Epiphanes, whose impieties and cruelties are recorded in the two books of Maccabees. But still, in Egypt, the Jews continued in the enjoyment of their privileges, so late as the reign of the sixth Ptolemy, called Philometor, who committed the charge of his affairs to two Jews, Onias and Dositheus; the former of whom obtained permission to build a temple at Heliopolis. The introduction of Christianity into Egypt is mentioned under the article Alexandria.

10. The prophecies respecting Egypt in the Old Testament have had a wonderful fulfilment. The knowledge of all its greatness and glory deterred not the Jewish prophets from declaring, that Egypt would become "a base kingdom, and never exalt itself any more among the nations." And the literal fulfilment of every prophecy affords as clear a demonstration as can possibly be given, that each and all of them are the dictates of inspiration. Egypt was the theme of many prophecies, which were fulfilled in ancient times; and it bears to the present day, as it has borne throughout many ages, every mark with which prophecy had stamped its destiny: "They shall be a base kingdom. It shall be the basest of kingdoms. Neither shall it exalt itself any more among the nations: for I will diminish them, that they shall no more rule over the nations. The pride of her power shall come down; and they shall be desolate in the midst of the countries that are desolate; and her cities shall be in the midst of the cities that are wasted. I will make the land of Egypt desolate, and the country shall be desolate of that whereof it was full. I will sell the land into the hand of the wicked. I will make the land waste and all that is therein, by the hand of strangers. I the Lord have spoken it. And there shall be no more a prince of the land of Egypt," Ezek. xxx, 5, 7, 12, 13. "The sceptre of Egypt shall depart away," Zech. x, 11.

11. Egypt became entirely subject to the Persians about three hundred and fifty years previous to the Christian æra. It was afterward subdued by the Macedonians, and was governed by the Ptolemies for the space of two hundred and ninety-four years; until, about B. C. 30, it became a province of the Roman empire. It continued long in subjection to the Romans,--tributary first to Rome, and afterward to Constantinople. It was transferred, A. D. 641, to the dominion of the Saracens. In 1250 the Mamelukes deposed their rulers, and usurped the command of Egypt. A mode of government, the most singular and surprising that ever existed on earth, was established and maintained. Each successive ruler was raised to supreme authority, from being a stranger and a slave. No son of the former ruler, no native of Egypt, succeeded to the sovereignty; but a chief was chosen from among a new race of imported slaves. When Egypt became tributary to the Turks in 1517, the Mamelukes retained much of their power; and every pasha was an oppressor and a stranger. During all these ages, every attempt to emancipate the country, or to create a prince of the land of Egypt, has proved abortive, and has often been fatal to the aspirant. Though the facts relative to Egypt form too prominent a feature in the history of the world to admit of contradiction or doubt, yet the description of the fate of that country, and of the form of its government, may be left, says Keith, to the testimony of those whose authority no infidel will question, and whom no man can accuse of adapting their descriptions to the predictions of the event. Volney and Gibbon are our witnesses of the facts: "Such is the state of Egypt. Deprived, twenty-three centuries ago, of her natural proprietors, she has seen her fertile fields successively a prey to the Persians, the Macedonians, the Romans, the Greeks, the Arabs, the Georgians, and, at length, the race of Tartars distinguished by the name of Ottoman Turks. The Mamelukes, purchased as slaves, and introduced as soldiers, soon usurped the power and elected a leader. If their first establishment was a singular event, their continuance is not less extraordinary. They are replaced by slaves brought from their original country. The system of oppression is methodical. Every thing the traveller sees or hears reminds him he is in the country of slavery and tyranny." "A more unjust and absurd constitution cannot be devised than that which condemns the natives of a country to perpetual servitude, under the arbitrary dominion of strangers and slaves. Yet such has been the state of Egypt above five hundred years. The most illustrious sultans of the Baharite and Borgite dynasties were themselves promoted

from the Tartar and Circassian bands; and the four-and-twenty beys, or military chiefs, have ever been succeeded, not by their sons, but by their servants." These are the words of Volney and of Gibbon; and what did the ancient prophets foretel?--"I will lay the land waste, and all that is therein, by the hands of STRANGERS. I the Lord have spoken it. And there shall be no more a prince of the land of Egypt. The sceptre of Egypt shall depart away." The prophecy adds: "They shall be a base kingdom: it shall be the basest of kingdoms." After the lapse of two thousand and four hundred years from the date of this prophecy, a scoffer at religion, but an eye witness of the facts, thus describes the self-same spot: "In Egypt," says Volney, "there is no middle class, neither nobility, clergy, merchants, landholders. A universal air of misery, manifest in all the traveller meets, points out to him the rapacity of oppression, and the distrust attendant upon slavery. The profound ignorance of the inhabitants equally prevents them from perceiving the causes of their evils, or applying the necessary remedies. Ignorance, diffused through every class, extends its effects to every species of moral and physical knowledge. Nothing is talked of but intestine troubles, the public misery, pecuniary extortions, bastinadoes, and murders. Justice herself puts to death without formality." Other travellers describe the most execrable vices as common, and represent the moral character of the people as corrupted to the core. As a token of the desolation of the country, mud-walled cottages are now the only habitations where the ruins of temples and palaces abound. Egypt is surrounded by the dominions of the Turks and of the Arabs; and the prophecy is literally true which marked it in the midst of desolation: "They shall be desolate in the midst of the countries that are desolate, and her cities shall be in the midst of the cities that are wasted." The systematic oppression, extortion, and plunder, which have so long prevailed, and the price paid for his authority and power by every Turkish pasha, have rendered the country "desolate of that whereof it was full," and still show both how it has been "wasted by the hands of strangers," and how it has been "sold into the hand of the wicked."

12. Egypt has, indeed, lately somewhat risen, under its present spirited but despotic pasha, to a degree of importance and commerce. But this pasha is still a STRANGER, and the dominion is foreign. Nor is there any thing like a general advancement of the people to order, intelligence and happiness. Yet this fact, instead of militating against the truth of prophecy, may, possibly at no distant period, serve to illustrate other predictions. "The Lord shall smite Egypt: he shall smite and heal it; and they shall return to the Lord, and he shall be entreated of them, and shall heal them. In that day shall Israel be the third with Egypt and with Assyria, even a blessing in the midst of the land," &c, Isaiah xix, 22–25.

ELAM, the eldest son of Shem, who settled in a country to which he gave his name, Gen. x, 22. It is frequently mentioned in Scripture, as lying to the south-east of Shinar. Susiana, in later times, seems to have been a part of this country, Daniel viii, 2; and before the captivity the Jews seem always to have intended Persia by the name of Elam. Stephanus takes it to be a part of Assyria, but Pliny and Josephus, more properly, of Persia, whose inhabitants, this latter tells us, sprung from the Elamites.

ELATH, or **ELOTH**, a part of Idumea, situate upon the Red Sea, the emporium of Syria in Asia. It was taken by David, 2 Sam. viii, 14, who there established an extensive trade. There Solomon built ships, 2 Chron. viii, 17, 18. The Israelites held possession of Elath one hundred and fifty years, when the Edomites, in the reign of Joram, recovered it, 2 Kings viii, 20. It was again taken from them by Azariah, and by him left to his son, 2 Kings xiv, 22. The king of Syria took it from his grandson, 2 Kings xvi, 6. In process of time it fell to the Ptolemies, and lastly to the Romans. The branch of the Red Sea on which this city stood, obtained among Heathen writers the name of SINUS ELANITICUS or Elanitic Gulf, from a town built on its site called Elana, and subsequently Ala; which, as we are informed by Eusebius and Jerom, was used as a port in their time. The modern Arabian town of Akaba stands upon or near the site either of Elath or Ezion-Geber; which of the two it is impossible to determine, as both ports, standing at the head of the gulf, were probably separated from each other by a creek or small bay only.

ELDAD and Medad were appointed by Moses among the seventy elders of Israel who were to assist in the government. Though not present in the general assembly, they were, notwithstanding, filled with the Spirit of God, equally with those who were in that assembly, and they began to prophesy in the camp. Joshua would have had Moses forbid them, but Moses replied, "Enviest thou for my sake? Would God that all the Lord's people were prophets, and that God would pour forth his Spirit upon them!" Numbers xi, 24–29.

ELDERS, a name given to certain laymen in the Presbyterian discipline, who are ecclesiastical officers, and in conjunction with the ministers and deacons compose the kirk sessions in Scotland. The number of elders is proportioned to the extent and population of the parish, and is seldom less than two or three, but sometimes exceeds fifty. They are laymen in this respect, that they have no right to teach, or to dispense the sacraments; and on this account they form an office in the Presbyterian church inferior in rank and power to that of pastors. They generally discharge the office which originally belonged to the deacons, of attending to the interests of the poor. But their peculiar business is expressed by the name ruling elders; for in every jurisdiction within the parish they are the spiritual court, of which the minister is officially moderator; and in the presbytery, of which the pastors of all the parishes within its bounds are officially members, lay elders sit as the representatives of the several sessions or consistories.

Elders of Israel. By this name we understand the heads of tribes, or rather of the great families in Israel, who, before the settlement of the Hebrew commonwealth, had a government and authority over their own families, and the people. When Moses was sent into Egypt to deliver Israel, he assembled the elders of Israel, and told them that the God of Abraham, Isaac, and Jacob, had appeared to him, Exod. iii, 15; iv, 29, &c. Moses and Aaron treat the elders of Israel as the representatives of the nation. When God gave the law to Moses, he said, "Take Aaron, Nadab, and Abihu, his sons, and the seventy elders of Israel, and worship ye afar off," Exod. xxiv, 1, 9, 10. They advanced only to the foot of the mountain. On all occasions afterward, we find this number of seventy elders. But it is credible, that as there were twelve tribes, there were seventy-two elders, six from each tribe, and that seventy is set down, instead of seventy-two; or rather, that Moses and Aaron should be added to the number seventy, and that, exclusive of them, there were but four elders from the tribe of Levi. After Jethro's arrival in the camp of Israel, Moses made a considerable change in the governors of the people. He established over Israel heads of thousands, hundreds, fifties, and tens, that justice might be readily administered to applicants; only difficult cases were referred to himself, Exod. xviii, 24, 25, &c. But this constitution did not continue long; for on the murmuring of the people at the encampment called the Graves of Lust, Num. xi, 24–35, Moses appointed seventy elders of Israel, to whom God communicated part of that legislator's spirit; they began to prophesy, and ceased not afterward. This, according to the generality of interpreters, was the beginning of the sanhedrim; but, to support this opinion, many things must be supposed, whereby to infer, that this court of justice was constantly in being during the Scripture history. It seems that the establishment of the seventy elders by Moses continued, not only during his life, but under Joshua likewise, and under the judges. The elders of the people and Joshua swore to the treaty with the Gibeonites, Josh, ix, 15. A little before his death, Joshua renewed the covenant with the Lord, in company with the elders, the princes, the heads, and officers of Israel, Joshua xxiii; xxiv, 1, 28. After the death of Joshua, and the elders who survived him, the people were several times brought into bondage, and were delivered by their judges. We do not see distinctly what authority the elders had during this time, and still less under the kings who succeeded the judges.

ELEAZAR, the third son of Aaron, and his successor in the dignity of high priest, Exod. vi, 23. He entered into the land of Canaan with Joshua, and is supposed to have lived there upward of twenty years. The high priesthood continued in his family till the time of Eli. He was buried in a hill that belonged to the son of Phineas, Joshua xxiv.

2. Eleazar, the son of Aminadab, to whose care the ark was committed when it was sent back by the Philistines, 1 Samuel vii. He is thought to have been a priest, or at least a Levite, though he is not mentioned in the catalogue of the sons of Levi.

ELECTION. Of a divine election, a choosing and separating from others, we have three kinds mentioned in the Scriptures. The first is the election of INDIVIDUALS to perform some particular and special service. Cyrus was "elected" to rebuild the temple; the twelve Apostles were "chosen," elected, to their office by Christ; St. Paul was a "chosen," or elected "vessel," to be the Apostle of the Gentiles. The second kind of election which we find in Scripture, is the election of NATIONS, OR BODIES OF PEOPLE, to eminent religious privileges, and in order to accomplish, by their superior illumination, the merciful purposes of God, in benefiting other nations or bodies of people. Thus the descendants of Abraham, the Jews, were CHOSEN to receive special revelations of truth; and to be "the people of God," that is, his visible church, publicly to observe and uphold his worship. "The Lord thy God hath CHOSEN thee to be a peculiar people unto himself, above all people that are upon the face of the earth." "The Lord had a delight in thy fathers to love them, and he CHOSE their seed after them, even you, above all people." It was especially on account of the application of the terms ELECT, CHOSEN, and PECULIAR, to the Jewish people, that they were so familiarly used by the Apostles in their epistles addressed to the believing Jews and Gentiles, then constituting the church of Christ in various places. For Christians were the subjects, also, of this second kind of election; the election of bodies of men to be the visible people and church of God in the world, and to be endowed with peculiar privileges. Thus they became, though in a more special and exalted sense, the chosen people, the elect of God. We say "in a more special sense," because as the entrance into the Jewish church was by natural birth, and the entrance into the Christian church, properly so called, is by faith and a spiritual birth, these terms, although many became Christians by mere profession, and enjoyed various privileges in consequence of their people or nation being chosen to receive the Gospel, have generally respect, in the New Testament, to bodies of true believers, or to the whole body of true believers as such. They are not, therefore, to be interpreted according to the scheme of Dr. Taylor of Norwich, by the constitution of the Jewish, but by the constitution of the Christian, church.

2. To understand the nature of this "election," as applied sometimes to particular bodies of Christians, as when St. Peter says, "The church which is at Babylon, ELECTED TOGETHER with you," and sometimes to the whole body of believers every where; and also the reason of the frequent use of the term ELECTION, and of the occurrence of allusions to the fact; it is to be remembered, that a great religious revolution, so to speak, had occurred in the age of the Apostles; with the full import of which we cannot, without calling in the aid of a little reflection, be adequately impressed. This change was no other than the abrogation of the CHURCH STATE of the Jews, which had continued for so many ages. They had been the only visibly acknowledged people of God in all the nations of the earth; for whatever pious people might have existed in other nations, they were not, in the sight of men, and collectively, acknowledged as "the people of Jehovah." They had no written revelations, no appointed ministry, no forms of authorized initiation into his church and covenant, no appointed holy days, or sanctioned ritual. All these were peculiar to the Jews, who

were, therefore, an elected and peculiar people. This distinguished honour they were about to lose. They might have retained it as Christians, had they been willing to admit the believing Gentiles of all nations to share it with them; but the great reason of their peculiarity and election, AS A NATION, was terminated by the coming of the Messiah, who was to be "a light to lighten the Gentiles," as well as "the glory of his people Israel." Their pride and consequent unbelief resented this, which will explain their enmity to the believing part of the Gentiles, who, when that which St. Paul calls "the fellowship of the mystery" was fully explained, chiefly by the glorious ministry of that Apostle himself, were called into that church relation and visible acknowledgment as the people of God, which the Jews had formerly enjoyed, and that with even a higher degree of glory, in proportion to the superior spirituality of the new dispensation. It was this doctrine which excited that strong irritation in the minds of the unbelieving Jews, and in some partially Christianized ones, to which so many references are made in the New Testament. They were "provoked," were made "jealous;" and were often roused to the madness of persecuting opposition by it. There was then a NEW ELECTION of a NEW PEOPLE of God, to be composed of Jews, not by virtue of their NATURAL DESCENT, but through their faith in Christ, and of Gentiles of all nations, also believing, and put as believers, on an equal ground with the believing Jews: and there was also a REJECTION, a reprobation, but not an absolute one; for THE ELECTION was offered to the Jews first, in every place, by offering them the Gospel. Some embraced it, and submitted to be the elect people of God, on the new ground of faith, instead of the old one of natural descent; and therefore the Apostle, Rom. xi, 7, calls the believing part of the Jews, "the ELECTION," in opposition to those who opposed this "election of grace," and still clung to their former and now repealed election as Jews and the descendants of Abraham: "But the election hath obtained it, and the rest were blinded." The offer had been made to the whole nation; all might have joined the one body of believing Jews and believing Gentiles; but the major part of them refused: they would not "come into the supper;" they made "light of it;" light of an election founded on faith, and which placed the relation of "the people of God" upon spiritual attainments, and offered to them only spiritual blessings. They were, therefore, deprived of election and church relationship of every kind: their temple was burned; their political state abolished; their genealogies confounded; their worship annihilated and all visible acknowledgment of them; by God as a church withdrawn, and transferred to a church henceforward to be composed chiefly of Gentiles: and thus, says St. Paul, "were fulfilled the words of Moses, I will provoke you to jealousy by them that are NO PEOPLE, and by a foolish," ignorant and idolatrous, "people I will anger you." It is easy, therefore, to see what is the import of the "calling" and "election" of the Christian church, as spoken of in the New Testament. It was not the calling and the electing of one nation in particular to succeed the Jews; but it was the calling and the electing of believers in all nations, wherever the Gospel should be preached, to be in reality what the Jews typically, and therefore in an inferior degree, had been,--the visible church of God, "his people," under Christ "the Head;" with an authenticated revelation; with an appointed ministry, never to be lost; with authorized worship; with holy days and festivals; with instituted forms of initiation; and with special protection and favour.

3. The THIRD kind of election is personal election; or the election of individuals to be the children of God, and the heirs of eternal life. This is not a choosing to particular offices and service, which is the first kind of election we have mentioned; nor is it that collective election to religious privileges and a visible church state, of which we have spoken. For although "the elect" have an individual interest in such an election as parts of the collective body, thus placed in possession of the ordinances of Christianity; yet many others have the same advantages, who still remain under the guilt and condemnation of sin and practical unbelief. The individuals properly called "the elect," are they who have been made partakers of the grace and saving efficacy of the Gospel. "Many," says our Lord, "are CALLED, but few CHOSEN." What true personal election is, we shall find explained in two clear passages of Scripture. It is explained by our Lord, where he says to his disciples, "I have chosen you out of the world:" and by St. Peter, when he addresses his First Epistle to the "elect according to the foreknowledge of God the Father, through sanctification of the Spirit, unto obedience and sprinkling of the blood of Jesus." To be elected, therefore, is to be separated from "the world," and to be sanctified by the Spirit, and by the blood of Christ. It follows, then, not only that election is an act of God done in TIME, but also that it is subsequent to the administration of the means of salvation. The "calling" goes before the "election;" the publication of the doctrine of "the Spirit," and the atonement, called by Peter "the sprinkling of the blood of Christ," before that "sanctification" through which they become "the elect" of God. In a word, "the elect" are the body of true believers; and personal election into the family of God is through personal faith. All who truly believe are elected; and all to whom the Gospel is sent have, through the grace that accompanies it, the power to believe placed within their reach; and all such might, therefore, attain to the grace of personal election.

ELEMENTS, ςοιχεῖα, the elements or first principles of any art, whence the subsequent parts proceed. The elements or first principles of the Christian doctrine, Heb, v, 12. St. Paul calls the ceremonial ordinances of the Mosaic law, "worldly elements," Gal. iv, 3; Col. ii, 8, 20; "weak and beggarly elements," Gal. iv, 9. Elements, as containing the rudiments of the knowledge of Christ, to which knowledge the law, as a pedagogue, Gal. iii, 24, was intended, by means of those ordinances, to bring the Jews; worldly, as consisting in outward worldly institutions, Heb. ix, 1; weak and beggarly, when considered in themselves, and set up in opposition to the great realities to which they were designed to lead. But, in Col. ii, 8, the elements or rudiments of the world are so closely connected with philosophy and vain deceit, or an empty and deceitful philosophy, that they must be understood there to include the dogmas of Pagan philosophy; to which, no doubt, many of the Colossians were in their unconverted state attached, and of which the Judaizing teachers, who also were probably themselves infected with them, took advantage to withdraw the Colossian converts from the purity of the Gospel, and from Christ their living head. And from the general tenor of this chapter, and particularly from verses 18–23, it appears, that these philosophical dogmas, against which the Apostle cautioned his converts, were partly Platonic, and partly Pythagorean; the former teaching the worship of angels, or demons, as mediators between God and man; the latter enjoining such abstinence from particular kinds of meats and drinks, and such severe mortifications of the body, as God had not commanded.

ELI, a high priest of the Hebrews, of the race of Ithamar, who succeeded Abdon, and governed the Hebrews, both as priest and judge, during forty years. How Eli came to the high priesthood, and how this dignity was transferred from Eleazar's family to that of Ithamar, who was Aaron's youngest son, we know not. This much, however, is certain, that it was not done without an express declaration of God's will, 1 Sam. ii, 27, &c. In the reign of Solomon, the predictions in relation to Eli's family were fulfilled; for the high priesthood was taken from Abiathar, a descendant of Eli, and given to Zadok, who was of the race of Eleazar, 1 Kings ii, 26. Eli appears to have been a pious, but indolent man, blinded by paternal affection, who suffered his sons to gain the ascendancy over him; and for want either of personal courage, or zeal for the glory of God sufficient to restrain their licentious conduct, he permitted them to go on to their own and his ruin. Thus he carried his indulgence to cruelty; while a more dignified and austere conduct on his part might have rendered them wise and virtuous, and thereby have preserved himself and family. A striking lesson for parents! God admonished him by Samuel, then a child; and Eli received those awful admonitions with a mind fully resigned to the divine will. "It is the Lord," said he, "let him do what seemeth him good." God deferred the execution of his vengeance many years. At length, however, Hophni and Phineas, the sons of Eli, were slain by the Philistines, the ark of the Lord was taken, and Eli himself, hearing this melancholy news, fell backward from his chair and broke his neck, in the ninety-eighth year of his age, 1 Sam. iv, 12, 18.

ELIEZER, a native of Damascus, and the steward of Abraham's house. It seems that Abraham, before the birth of Isaac, intended to make him his heir:--"One born in my house," a domestic slave, "is mine heir," Gen. xv, 1–3. He was afterward sent into Mesopotamia, to procure a wife for Isaac, Gen. xxiv, 2, 3, &c; which business he accomplished with fidelity and expedition. "It is still the custom in India," says Forbes, "especially among the Mohammedans, that in default of children, and sometimes where there are lineal descendants, the master of a family adopts a slave, frequently a Haffshee Abyssinian, of the darkest hue, for his heir. He educates him agreeably to his wishes, and marries him to one of his daughters. As the reward of superior merit, or to suit the caprice of an arbitrary despot, this honour is also conferred on a slave recently purchased, or already grown up in the family; and to him he bequeaths his wealth, in preference to his nephews, or any collateral branches. This is a custom of great antiquity in the east, and prevalent among the most refined and civilized nations. In the earliest period of the patriarchal history, we find Abraham complaining for want of children; and declaring that either Eliezer of Damascus, or probably one born from him in his house, was his heir, to the exclusion of Lot, his favourite nephew, and all the other collateral branches of his family."

ELIHU, one of Job's friends, a descendant of Nahor, Job xxxii, 2. See Job.

ELIJAH. Elijah or Elias, a prophet, was a native of Tishbe beyond Jordan in Gilead. Some think that he was a priest descended from Aaron, and say that one Sabaca was his father; but this has no authority. He was raised up by God, to be set like a wall of brass, in opposition to idolatry, and particularly to the worship of Baal, which Jezebel and Ahab supported in Israel. The Scripture introduces Elijah saying to Ahab, 1 Kings xvii, 1, 2, A. M. 3092, "As the Lord God of Israel liveth, before whom I stand, there shall not be dew nor rain these years, but according to my word." It is remarkable, that the number of years is not here specified; but in the New Testament we are informed that it was three years and six months. By the prohibition of dew as well as rain, the whole vegetable kingdom was deprived of that moisture, without which neither the more hardy, nor more delicate kinds of plants could shoot into herbage, or bring that herbage to maturity. The Lord commanded Elijah to conceal himself beyond Jordan, near the brook Cherith. He obeyed, and God sent ravens to him morning and evening, which brought him flesh and bread. Scheuzer observes, that he cannot think that the OREBIM of the Hebrew, rendered "ravens," means, as some have thought, the inhabitants of a town called OREB, nor a troop of Arabs called ORBHIM; and contends that the bird called the raven, or one of the same genus is intended. Suppose that Elijah was concealed from Ahab in some rocky or mountainous spot, where travellers never came; and that here a number of voracious birds had built their nests upon the trees which grew around it, or upon a projecting rock, &c. These flying every day to procure food for their young, the prophet availed himself of a part of what they brought; and while they, obeying the dictates of nature, designed only to provide for their offspring, Divine providence directed them to provide at the same time for the wants of Elijah. What, therefore, he collected, whether from their nests, from what they dropped, or under a supernatural influence, brought to him, or occasionally from all these means, was enough for his daily support. "And the OREBIM furnished him bread or flesh in the morning, and bread or flesh in the evening." But as there were probably several of them, some might furnish bread and others flesh, as it happened; so that a little from each formed his solitary but satisfactory meal. To such straits was the exiled prophet driven! perhaps these OREBIM were not strictly ravens, but rooks. The word rendered RAVEN, includes the whole genus, among which are some less impure than the raven, as the rook. Rooks living in numerous societies are supposed by some to be the kind of birds employed on this occasion rather than ravens, which fly only in pairs. But upon all these explanations we may observe, that when an event is evidently miraculous, it is quite superfluous, and often absurd, to invent hypotheses to make it appear more easy. After a time the brook dried up, and God sent Elijah to Zarephath, a city of the Sidonians. At the city gate he met with a widow woman gathering sticks, from whom he desired a little water, adding, "Bring me, I pray thee, also a morsel of bread." She answered, "As the Lord liveth, I have no bread, but only a handful of meal, and a little oil in a cruse; and I am gathering some sticks, that I may dress it for me and my son, that we may eat it, and die." Elijah said, "Make first a little cake, and bring it me, and afterward make for thee and thy son: for thus saith the Lord, the barrel of meal shall not waste, neither shall the cruse of oil fail, until the day the Lord sendeth rain upon the earth." His prediction was fully accomplished, and he dwelt at the house of this widow. Some time after, the son of this woman fell sick, and died. The mother, overwhelmed with grief, intreated the assistance and interposition of Elijah, who taking the child in his arms laid him on his own bed, and cried to the Lord for the restoration of the child's life. The Lord heard the prophet's petition, and restored the child.

2. After three years of drought the Lord commanded Elijah to show himself to Ahab. The famine being great in Samaria, Ahab sent the people throughout the country, to inquire after places where they might find forage for the cattle. Obadiah, an officer of the king's household, being thus employed, Elijah presented himself, and directed him to tell Ahab, "Behold, Elijah is here!" Ahab came to meet the prophet, and reproached him as the cause of the famine. Elijah retorted the charge upon the king, and his iniquities, and challenged Ahab to gather the people together, and the prophets of Baal, that it might be determined by a sign from heaven, the falling of fire upon the sacrifice, who was the true God. In this the prophet obeyed the impulse of the Spirit of God; and Ahab, either under an influence of which he was not conscious, or blindly confident in the cause of idolatry, followed Elijah's direction, and convened the people of Israel, and four hundred prophets of Baal. The prophets of Baal prepared their altar, sacrificed their bullock, placed it on the altar, and called upon their gods. They leaped upon the altar, and cut themselves after their manner, crying with all their might. Elijah ridiculed them, and said, "Cry aloud, for he is god; either he is talking, or he is pursuing, or he is on a journey, or peradventure he sleepeth, and must be awaked." When midday was past, Elijah repaired the altar of the Lord; and with twelve stones, in allusion to the twelve tribes of Israel, he built a new altar. He then laid his bullock upon the wood, poured a great quantity of water three times upon the sacrifice and the wood, so that the water filled the trench which was dug round the altar. After this he prayed, and, in answer to his prayer, the Lord sent fire from heaven, and consumed the wood, the burnt sacrifice, the stones, and dust of the place, and even dried up the water in the trench. Upon this, all the people fell on their faces, and exclaimed, "The Lord, he is the God." Elijah then, having excited the people to slay the false prophets of Baal, said to Ahab, "Go home, eat and drink, for I hear the sound of abundance of rain;" which long-expected blessing descended from heaven according to his prediction, and gave additional proof to the truth of his mission from the only living and true God.

3. Jezebel, the wife of Ahab, threatened Elijah for having slain her prophets. He therefore fled to Beersheba, in the south of Judah, and thence into Arabia Petrea. In the evening, being exhausted with fatigue, he laid himself down under a juniper tree, and prayed God to take him out of the world. An angel touched him, and he arose, and saw a cake baked on the coals, and a cruse of water; and he ate and drank, and slept again. The angel again awakened him, and said, "Rise and eat, for the journey is too great for thee;" and he ate and drank, and went in the strength of that meat forty days and forty nights, unto Horeb, the mount of God. Here he had visions of the glory and majesty of God, and conversed with him; and was commanded to return to the wilderness of Damascus, to anoint Hazael king over Syria, and Jehu king over Israel, and to appoint Elisha his successor in the prophetic office. Some years after, Ahab having seized Naboth's vineyard, the Lord commanded Elijah to reprove Ahab for the crime he had committed. Elijah met him going to Naboth's vineyard to take possession of it, and said, "In the place where dogs licked the blood of Naboth, shall they lick thy blood, even thine. And the dogs shall eat Jezebel by the wall of Jezreel." Both of which predictions were fulfilled in the presence of the people. Ahaziah, king of Israel, being hurt by a fall from the platform of his house, sent to consult Baalzebub, the god of Ekron, whether he should recover. Elijah met the messengers, and said to them, "Is it because there is no God in Israel that ye go to inquire of Baalzebub, the god of Ekron? Now, therefore, saith the Lord, Thou shalt surely die." The messengers of Ahaziah returned, and informed the king, that a stranger had told them he should certainly die; and Ahaziah knew that this was the Prophet Elijah. The king, therefore, sent a captain with his company of fifty men, to apprehend him; and when the officer was come to Elijah, who was sitting upon a hill, he said, "Thou man of God, the king commands thee to come down." Elijah answered, "If I be a man of God, let fire come down from heaven, and consume thee and thy fifty." The prophet's words were followed with the effect predicted. The king sent another captain, who was also consumed; but a third captain going to Elijah intreated him to save him and his people's lives, and Elijah accompanied him to the king. By these fearful miracles he was accredited to this successor of Ahab as a prophet of the true God, and the destruction of these companies of armed men was a demonstration of God's anger against the people at large. Elijah could not in this case act from any other impulse than that of the Spirit of God.

4. Elijah, understanding by revelation that God would soon translate him out of this world, was desirous of concealing this fact from Elisha, his inseparable companion. He

therefore said to Elisha, "Tarry thou here, for the Lord hath sent me to Bethel." But Elisha answered, "I will not leave thee." At Bethel, Elijah said, "Tarry thou here, the Lord hath sent me to Jericho;" but Elisha replied, he would not forsake him. At Jericho Elijah desired him to stay; but Elisha would not leave him. They went therefore together to Jordan, and fifty of the sons of the prophets followed them at a distance. When they were come to the Jordan, Elijah took his mantle, and with it struck the waters, which divided, and they went over on dry ground. Elijah then said to Elisha, "Ask what I shall do for thee before I be taken away from thee." "I pray thee," said Elisha, "let a double portion of thy spirit be upon me;" that is, obtain the gift of prophecy from God for me, in the same measure that thou possessest it. Double may signify like; or the gift of prophecy, and of miracles, in a degree double to what thou dost possess, or to what I now possess. Elijah answered, "Thou hast asked me a very hard thing; yet, if thou see me when I am taken from thee, it shall be so unto thee; but if not, it shall not be so." As they journeyed, a fiery chariot, with horses of fire, suddenly separated them, and Elijah was carried in a whirlwind to heaven; while Elisha exclaimed, "My father, my father, the chariots of Israel and the horsemen thereof!"

5. Elijah was one of the most eminent of that illustrious and singular race of men, the Jewish prophets. Every part of his character is marked by a moral grandeur, which is heightened by the obscurity thrown around his connections, and his private history. He often wears the air of a supernatural messenger suddenly issuing from another world, to declare the commands of heaven, and to awe the proudest mortals by the menace of fearful judgments. His boldness in reproof; his lofty zeal for the honour of God; his superiority to softness, ease, and suffering, are the characters of a man filled with the Holy Spirit; and he was admitted to great intimacy with God, and enabled to work miracles of a very extraordinary and unequivocal character. These were called for by the stupid idolatry of the age, and were in some instances equally calculated to demonstrate the being and power of Jehovah, and to punish those who had forsaken him for idols. The author of Ecclesiasticus has an encomium to his memory, and justly describes him as a prophet "who stood up as fire, and whose word burned as a lamp." In the sternness and power of his reproofs he was a striking type of John the Baptist, and the latter is therefore prophesied of, under his name. Malachi, iv, 5, 6, has this passage: "Behold, I will send you Elijah the prophet, before the coming of the great and dreadful day of the Lord." Our Saviour also declares that Elijah had already come in spirit, in the person of John the Baptist. At the transfiguration of our Saviour, Elijah and Moses both appeared and conversed with him respecting his future passion, Matt. xvii, 3, 4; Mark ix, 4; Luke ix, 30. Many of the Jews in our Lord's time believed him to be Elijah, or that the soul of Elijah had passed into his body, Matt. xvi, 14; Mark vi, 15; Luke ix, 8. In conclusion, we may observe, that to assure the world of the future existence of good men in a state of glory and felicity, and that in bodies changed from mortality to immortality, each of the three grand dispensations of religion had its instance of translation into heaven; the patriarchal in the person of Enoch, the Jewish in the person of Elijah, and the Christian in the person of Christ.

ELISHA, the son of Shaphat, Elijah's disciple and successor in the prophetic office, was of the city of Abelmeholah, 1 Kings xix, 16, &c. Elijah having received God's command to anoint Elisha as a prophet, came to Abelmeholah; and finding him ploughing with oxen, he threw his mantle over the shoulders of Elisha, who left the oxen, and accompanied him. Under the article ELIJAH, it has been observed that Elisha was following his master, when he was taken up to heaven; and that he inherited Elijah's mantle, with a double portion of his spirit. Elisha smote the waters of Jordan, and divided them; and he rendered wholesome the waters of a rivulet near Jericho. The kings of Israel, Judah, and Edom, having taken the field against the king of Moab, who had revolted from Israel, were in danger of perishing for want of water. Elisha was at that time in the camp; and seeing Jehoram, the king of Israel, he said, "What have I to do with thee? get thee to the prophets of thy father, and to the prophets of thy mother. As the Lord liveth, were it not out of respect to Jehoshaphat, the king of Judah, who is here present, I would not so much as look on thee. But now send for a minstrel; and while this man played, the Spirit of the Lord fell upon Elisha, and he said, Thus saith the Lord, Make several ditches along this valley; for ye shall see neither wind nor rain, yet this valley shall be filled with water, and you and your cattle shall drink of it." The widow of one of the prophets having told Elisha, that her husband's creditor was determined to take her two sons and sell them for slaves, Elisha multiplied the oil in the widow's house, in such quantity that she was enabled to sell it and to discharge the debt. Elisha went frequently to Shunem, a city of Manasseh, on this side Jordan, and was entertained by a certain matron at her house. As she had no children, Elisha promised her a son; and his prediction was accomplished. Some years after, the child died. Elisha, who was then at Mount Carmel, was solicited by the mother to come to her house. The prophet went, and restored the child. At Gilgal, during a great famine, one of the sons of the prophets gathered wild gourds, which he put into the pot, and they were served up to Elisha and the other prophets. It was soon found that they were mortal poison; but Elisha ordering meal to be thrown into the pot, corrected the quality of the pottage. Naaman, general of the king of Syria's forces, having a leprosy, was advised to visit Elisha in order to be cured. Elisha appointed him to wash himself seven times in the Jordan; and by this means Naaman was perfectly healed. He returned to Elisha, and offered him large presents, which the man of God resolutely refused. But Gehazi, Elisha's servant, did not imitate the disinterestedness of his master. He ran after Naaman, and in Elisha's name begged a talent of silver, and two changes of garments. Naaman gave him two talents. Elisha, to whom God had discovered Gehazi's action, reproached him with it, and declared, that the leprosy of Naaman should cleave to him and his family for ever. This is a striking instance of the disinterestedness of the Jewish prophets. Elisha, like his master Elijah, had learned to contemn the world. The king of Syria being at war with the king of Israel, could not imagine how all his designs were discovered by the enemy. He was told, that Elisha revealed them to the king of Israel. He therefore sent troops to seize the prophet at Dothan; but Elisha struck them with blindness, and led them in that condition into Samaria. When they were in the city, he prayed to God to open their eyes; and after he had made them eat and drink, he sent them back unhurt to their master. Some time after, Benhadad, king of Syria, having besieged Samaria, the famine became so extreme, that a certain woman ate her own child. Jehoram, king of Israel, imputing to Elisha these calamities, sent a messenger to cut off his head. Elisha, who was informed of this design against his life, ordered the door to be shut. The messenger was scarcely arrived, when the king himself followed, and made great complaints of the condition to which the town was reduced. Elisha answered, "To-morrow about this time shall a measure of fine flour be sold for a shekel, and two measures of barley for a shekel, in the gate of Samaria." Upon this, one of the king's officers said, "Were the Lord to open windows in heaven, might this thing be." This unbelief was punished; for the prophet answered, "Thou shalt see it with thine eyes, but shalt not eat thereof," which happened according to Elisha's prediction, for he was trodden to death by the crowd in the gate. At the end of the seven years' famine, which the prophet had foretold, he went to Damascus, to execute the command which God had given to Elijah many years before, of declaring Hazael king of Syria. Benhadad being at that time indisposed, and hearing that Elisha was come into his territories, sent Hazael, one of his principal officers, to the prophet to consult him, and inquire of him whether it were possible for him to recover. The prophet told Hazael, that he might recover, but that he was very well assured that he should not; and then looking steadfastly upon him, he broke out into tears upon the prospect, as he told him, of the many barbarous calamities which he would bring upon Israel, when once he was advanced to power, as he would soon be, because he was assured by divine revelation that he was to be king of Syria. Hazael, though offended at the time at being thought capable of such atrocities, did but too clearly verify these predictions; for at his return, having murdered Benhadad, and procured himself to be declared king, he inflicted the greatest miseries upon the Israelites.

2. Elisha sent one of the sons of the prophets to anoint Jehu, the son of Jehoshaphat, and grandson of Nimshi, to be king, in pursuance of an order given to Elijah some years before; and Jehu having received the royal unction, executed every thing that had been foretold by Elijah against Ahab's family, and against Jezebel. Elisha falling sick, Joash, king of Israel, came to visit him, and said, "O my father, my father, the chariot of Israel, and the horsemen thereof." Elisha desired the king to bring him a bow and arrows. Joash having brought them, Elisha requested him to put his hands on the bow, and at the same time the prophet put his own hand upon the king's, and said, Open the window which looks east, and let fly an arrow. The king having done this, Elisha said, This is the arrow of the Lord's deliverance: thou shalt be successful against Syria at Aphek. Elisha desired him again to shoot, which he did three times, and then stopped. But Elisha with vehemence said, "If thou hadst smitten five or six times, then thou hadst smitten Syria until thou hadst consumed it; whereas now thou shalt smite Syria only thrice." This is the last prediction of Elisha of which we read in Scripture, for soon after he died; but it was not his last miracle: for, some time after his interment, a company of Israelites, as they were going to bury a dead person, perceiving a band of Moabites making toward them, put the corpse for haste into Elisha's tomb, and, as soon as it had touched the prophet's body, it immediately revived; so that the man stood upon his feet: a striking emblem of the life-giving effect of the labours of the servants of God, after they themselves are gathered to their fathers.

ELUL, the sixth month of the Hebrew ecclesiastical year, and the twelfth of the civil year, answering to our August and part of September, containing twenty-nine days.

EMBALMING, the art of preserving dead bodies from putrefaction. It was much practised by the Egyptians of ancient times, and from them seems to have been borrowed by the Hebrews. It consisted in opening the body, taking out the intestines, and filling the place with odoriferous drugs and spices of a desiccative quality. Joseph gave orders for the embalming of the body of his father Jacob, Gen. l, 1, 2; and Moses informs us that the process took up forty days. Joseph himself also was embalmed, Gen. l, 26. Asa, king of Israel, seems to have been embalmed, 2 Chron. xvi, 13, 14. See Burial.

EMERALD, נפך, Exod. xxviii, 19; Ezek. xxvii, 16; xxviii, 13; σμάραγδος, Rev. xxi, 19; Eccles. xxxii, 6; Tobit xiii, 16; Judith x, 21. This is generally supposed to be the same with the ancient SMARAGDUS. It is one of the most beautiful of all the gems, and is of a bright green colour, without the admixture of any other. Pliny thus speaks of it: "The sight of no colour is more pleasant than green; for we love to view green fields and green leaves; and are still more fond of looking at the emerald, because all other greens are dull in comparison with this. Beside, these stones seem larger at a distance, by tinging the circumambient air. Their lustre is not changed by the sun, by the shade, nor by the light of lamps; but they have always a sensible moderate brilliancy." From the passage in Ezekiel we learn that the Tyrians traded in these jewels in the marts of Syria. They probably had them from India, or the south of Persia. The true oriental emerald is very scarce, and is only found at present in the kingdom of Cambay.

EMERODS. The disease of the Philistines, which is mentioned in 1 Sam. v, 6, 12; vi, 17, is denominated, in the Hebrew, עפלים. This word occurs, likewise, in Deut. xxviii, 27; and it is worthy of remark, that it is every where explained in the KERI, or marginal readings, by the Aramæan word, טחרים; an expression which, in the Syriac dialect, where it occurs under the forms, טהרא and טהורא, means THE FUNDAMENT, and likewise the effort which is made in an evacuation of the system. The authors, therefore, of the reading in the KERI appear to have assented to the opinion of Josephus, and to have understood by this word the dysentery. The corresponding Arabic words mean a swelling, answering somewhat in its nature to the hernia in men: a disease, consequently, very different from the hemorrhoids, which some persons understand to be meant by the word עפלים. Among other objections, it may also be observed, that the mice, which are mentioned, not only in the Hebrew text, 1 Sam. vi, 5, 12; xvi, 18, but also in the Alexandrine and Vulgate versions, 1 Sam. v, 6; vi, 5, 11, 18, are an objection to understanding the hemorrhoids by the word under consideration, since if that were in fact the disease, we see no reason why mice should have been presented as an offering to avert the anger of the God of Israel. Lichtenstein has given this solution: The word, עכברים, which is rendered MICE, he supposes to mean VENOMOUS SOLPUGAS, which belong to the spider class, and yet are so large, and so similar in their form to mice, as to admit of their being denominated by the same word. These venomous animals destroy and live upon scorpions. They also bite men, whenever they can have an opportunity, particularly in the fundament and the verenda. Their bite causes swellings, which are fatal in their consequences, called, in Hebrew, עפלים. The probable supposition, then, is, that solpugas were at this time multiplied among the Philistines by the special providence of God; and that, being very venomous, they were the means of destroying many individuals.

EMIMS, ancient inhabitants of the land of Canaan, beyond Jordan, who were defeated by Chedorlaomer and his allies, Gen. xiv, 5. Moses tells us that they were beaten at Shaveh-Kirjathaim, which was in the country of Sihon, conquered from the Moabites, Josh. xiii, 19–21. The Emims were a warlike people, of a gigantic stature, great and numerous, tall as the Anakims, and were accounted giants as well as they, Deut. ii, 10, 11.

EMMANUEL, or **IMMANUEL**, "God with us." It answers both in the **LXX**, and Matt. i, 23, to the Hebrew עמנואל, from עם, WITH, נו, US, and אל, GOD, Isa. vii, 14; viii, 8.

EMMAUS, a village about eight miles north-west of Jerusalem; on the road to which, two of the disciples were travelling in sorrow and disappointment after the resurrection, when our Lord appeared to them, and held that memorable conversation with them which is recorded by St. Luke, xxiv.

ENDOR, a city in the tribe of Manasseh, where the witch resided whom Saul consulted a little before the battle of Gilboa, Joshua xvii, 11; 1 Sam. xxviii, 13. Mr. Bryant derives Endor from En-Ador, signifying FONS PYTHONIS, "the fountain of light," or oracle of the god Ador: which oracle was probably founded by the Canaanites, and had never been totally suppressed. The ancient world had many such oracles: the most famous of which were that of Jupiter-Ammon in Lybia, and that of Delphi in Greece: and in all of them, the answers to those who consulted them were given from the mouth of a female; who, from the priestess of Apollo at Delphi, has generally received the name of Pythia. That many such oracles existed in Canaan, is evident from the number which Saul himself is said to have suppressed; and such a one, with its Pythia, was this at Endor. At these shrines, either as mock oracles, contrived by a crafty and avaricious priesthood, to impose on the credulity and superstition of its followers; or, otherwise, as is more generally supposed, as the real instruments of infernal power, mankind, having altogether departed from the true God, were permitted to be deluded. That, in this case, the real Samuel appeared is plain both from the affright of the woman herself, and from the fulfilment of his prophecy. It was an instance of God's overruling the wickedness of men, to manifest his own supremacy and justice.

ENGEDI. It is also called Hazazon-Tamar, or CITY OF PALM TREES, 2 Chron. xx, 2, because there was a great quantity of palm trees in the territory belonging to it. It abounded with Cyprus vines, and trees that produced balm. Solomon speaks of the "vineyards of Engedi," Cant. i, 14. This city, according to Josephus, stood near the lake of Sodom, three hundred furlongs from Jerusalem, not far from Jericho, and the mouth of the river Jordan, through which it discharged itself into the Dead Sea. There is frequent mention of Engedi in the Scriptures. It was in the cave of Engedi that David had it in his power to kill Saul, 1 Sam. xxiv. The spot where this transaction took place, was a cavern in the rock, sufficiently large to contain in its recesses the whole of David's men, six hundred in number, unperceived by Saul when he entered. Many similar caves existed in the Holy Land. Such were those at Adullam and Makkedah, and that in which Lot and his daughters dwelt after the destruction of Sodom. Such also is that described by Mr. Maundrell, near Sidon, which contained two hundred smaller caverns. Many of these were natural cavities in the limestone rock, similar to those in Yorkshire and Derbyshire, and in the Mendip hills in Somersetshire; and others, excavations made by the primeval inhabitants, for defence, or for shelter from the sun; and which subsequently served as retreats for robbers, as they are at this day. Josephus has given an interesting account of these caves, and the manner in which the robbers were taken by Herod. And Dr. E. D. Clarke has described similar retreats in the rocks near Bethlehem; others, between Jerusalem and Jericho, are mentioned by Mr. Wilson. Into such caves the Israelites frequently retired for shelter from their enemies, Judg. vi, 2; 1 Sam. xiii, 6; xiv, 11; a circumstance which has afforded some striking and terrific images to the prophets, Isaiah ii, 19; Hosea x, 8; Rev. vi, 15, 16.

ENOCH, the son of Cain, Gen. iv, 17, in honour of whom the first city noticed in Scripture was called Enoch, by his father Cain, who was the builder. It was situated on the east of the province of Eden.

2. Enoch, the son of Jared, and father of Methuselah. He was born A. M. 622, and being contemporary with Adam, he had every opportunity of learning from him the story of the creation, the circumstance of the fall, the terms of the promise, and other important truths. An ancient author affirms, that he was the father of astronomy; and Eusebius hence infers, that he is the same with the Atlas of the Grecian mythology. Enoch's fame rests upon a better basis than his skill in science. The encomium of Enoch is, that he "walked with God." While mankind were living in open rebellion against Heaven, and provoking the divine vengeance daily by their ungodly deeds, he obtained the exalted testimony, "that he pleased God." This he did, not only by the exemplary tenor of his life, and by the attention which he paid to the outward duties of religion, but by the soundness of his faith, and the purity of his heart and life: see Heb. xi, 5, 6. The intent of the Apostle, in the discourse containing this passage, is, to show that there has been but one way of obtaining the divine favour ever since the fall, and that is, by faith, or a firm persuasion and confidence in the atonement to be made for human transgressions by the obedience, sufferings, death, and resurrection of the promised Messiah. The cloud of witnesses which the Apostle has produced of Old Testament worthies, all bore, in their respective generations, their testimony to this great doctrine, in opposition to the atheism or theism, and gross idolatry, which prevailed around them. All the patriarchs are celebrated for their faith in this great truth, and for preserving this principle of religion in the midst of a corrupt generation. Enoch, therefore, is said, by another evangelical writer, to have spoken of the coming of Christ to judgment unto the antediluvian sinners. See Jude 14, 15. This prophecy is a clear, and it is also an awful, description of the day of judgment, when the Messiah shall sit upon his throne of justice, to determine the final condition of mankind, according to their works; and it indicates that the different offices of Messiah both to save and to judge, or as Prophet, Priest, and King, were known to the holy patriarchs. On what the Apostle founded this prediction has been matter of much speculation and inquiry. Some, indeed, have produced a treatise, called "The Book of Enoch," which, as they pretend, contains the cited passage; but its authority is not proved, and internal evidence sufficiently marks its spurious origin. It is, therefore, reasonable to suppose that the prophecy cited by St. Jude was either traditionally handed down, or had been specially communicated to that Apostle. In the departure of Enoch from this world of sin and sorrow, the Almighty altered the ordinary course of things, and gave him a dismissal as glorious to himself, as it was instructive to mankind. To convince them how acceptable holiness is to him, and to show that he had prepared for those that love him a heavenly inheritance, he caused Enoch to be taken from the earth without passing through death. See Elijah.

ENOS, or **ENOSH**, the son of Seth, and father of Cainan. He was born A. M. 235. Moses tells us that then "men began to call upon the name of the Lord," Gen iv, 26; that is, such as abhorred the impiety and immorality which prevailed among the progeny of Cain, began to worship God in public, and to assemble together at stated times for that purpose. Good men, to distinguish themselves from the wicked, began to take the name of sons or servants of God; for which reason Moses, Gen. vi, 1, 2, says that "the sons of God," or the descendants of Enos, "seeing the daughters of men," &c. The eastern people make the following additions to his history:--that Seth, his father, declared him sovereign prince and high priest of mankind, next after himself; that Enos was the first who ordained public alms for the poor, established public tribunals for the administration of justice, and planted, or rather cultivated, the palm tree.

EPHAH, the eldest son of Midian, who gave his name to a city and small extent of land in the country of Midian, situated on the eastern shore of the Dead Sea, Genesis xxv, 4. This country abounded with camels and dromedaries, Isaiah lx, 6, &c.

2. Ephah, a measure both for things dry and liquid, in use among the Hebrews. The ephah for the former contained three pecks and three pints. In liquid measure it was of the same capacity as the bath.

EPHESUS, a much celebrated city of Ionia, in Asia Minor, situated upon the river Cayster, and on the side of a hill. It was the metropolis of the Proconsular Asia, and formerly in great renown among Heathen authors on account of its famous temple of Diana. This temple was seven times set on fire: one of the principal conflagrations happened on the very day that Socrates was poisoned, four hundred years before Christ; the other, on the same night in which Alexander the Great was born, when a person of the name of Erostratus set it on fire, according to his own confession, to get himself a name! It was, however, rebuilt and beautified by the Ephesians, toward which the female inhabitants of the city contributed liberally. In the times of the Apostles it retained much of its former grandeur; but, so addicted were the inhabitants of the city to idolatry and the arts of magic, that the prince of darkness would seem to have, at that time, fixed his throne in it. Ephesus is supposed to have first invented those obscure mystical spells and charms by means of which the people pretended to heal diseases and drive away evil spirits; whence originated the Ἐφέσια γϱάμματα, or EPHESIAN LETTERS, so often mentioned by the ancients.

2. The Apostle Paul first visited this city, A. D. 54; but being then on his way to Jerusalem, he abode there only a few weeks, Acts xviii, 19–21. During his short stay, he found a synagogue of the Jews, into which he went, and reasoned with them upon the interesting topics of his ministry, with which they were so pleased that they wished him to prolong his visit. He however declined that, for he had determined, God willing, to be at Jerusalem at an approaching festival; but he promised to return, which he did a few months afterward, and continued there three years, Acts xix, 10; xx, 31. While the Apostle abode in Ephesus and its neighbourhood, he gathered a numerous Christian church, to which, at a subsequent period, he wrote that epistle, which

forms so important a part of the Apostolic writings. He was then a prisoner at Rome, and the year in which he wrote it must have been 60 or 61 of the Christian æra. It appears to have been transmitted to them by the hands of Tychicus, one of his companions in travel, Ephesians vi, 21. The critics have remarked that the style of the Epistle to the Ephesians is exceedingly elevated; and that it corresponds to the state of the Apostle's mind at the time of writing. Overjoyed with the account which their messenger brought him of the steadfastness of their faith, and the ardency of their love to all the saints, Eph. i, 15; and, transported with the consideration of the unsearchable wisdom of God displayed in the work of man's redemption, and of his amazing love toward the Gentiles, in introducing them, as fellow-heirs with the Jews, into the kingdom of Christ, he soars into the most exalted contemplation of those sublime topics, and gives utterance to his thoughts in language at once rich and varied. The epistle, says Macknight, is written as it were in a rapture. Grotius remarks that it expresses the sublime matters contained in it in terms more sublime than are to be found in any human language; to which Macknight subjoins this singular but striking observation, that no real Christian can read the doctrinal part of the Epistle to the Ephesians, without being impressed and roused by it, as by the sound of a trumpet.

3. Ephesus was one of the seven churches to which special messages were addressed in the book of Revelation. After a commendation of their first works, to which they were commanded to return, they were accused of having left their first love, and threatened with the removal of their candlestick out of its place, except they should repent, Rev. ii, 5. The contrast which its present state presents to its former glory, is a striking fulfilment of this prophecy. Ephesus was the metropolis of Lydia, a great and opulent city, and, according to Strabo, the greatest emporium of Asia Minor. Its temple of Diana, "whom all Asia worshipped," was adorned with one hundred and twenty-seven columns of Parian marble, each of a single shaft, and sixty feet high, and which formed one of the seven wonders of the world. The remains of its magnificent theatre, in which it is said that twenty thousand people could easily have been seated, are yet to be seen. But a few heaps of stones, and some miserable mud cottages, occasionally tenanted by Turks, without one Christian residing there, are all the remains of ancient Ephesus. It is, as described by different travellers, a solemn and most forlorn spot. The Epistle to the Ephesians is read throughout the world; but there is none in Ephesus to read it now. They left their first love, they returned not to their first works. Their "candlestick has been removed out of its place;" and the great city of Ephesus is no more. Dr. Chandler says, "The inhabitants are a few Greek peasants, living in extreme wretchedness, dependence, and insensibility; the representatives of an illustrious people, and inhabiting the wreck of their greatness; some, in the substructions of the glorious edifices which they raised; some, beneath the vaults of the stadium, once the crowded scene of their diversions; and some, by the abrupt precipice, in the sepulchres which received their ashes. Its streets are obscured and overgrown. A herd of goats was driven to it for shelter from the sun at noon; and a noisy flight of crows from the quarries seemed to insult its silence. We heard the partridge call in the area of the theatre and the stadium. The glorious pomp of its Heathen worship is no longer remembered; and Christianity, which was here nursed by Apostles, and fostered by general councils, until it increased to fulness of stature, barely lingers on in an existence hardly visible." "I was at Ephesus," says Mr. Arundell, "in January, 1824; the desolation was then complete: a Turk, whose shed we occupied, his Arab servant, and a single Greek, composed the entire population; some Turcomans excepted, whose black tents were pitched among the ruins. The Greek revolution, and the predatory excursions of the Samiotes, in great measure accounted for this total desertion. There is still, however, a village near, probably the same which Chishull and Van Egmont mention, having four hundred Greek houses."

St. John passed the latter part of his life in Asia Minor, and principally at Ephesus, where he died.

EPHOD, אפוד. This article of dress was worn by laymen as well as by the high priest. The sacred ephod, the one made for the high priest, differed from the others, in being fabricated of cotton, which was coloured with crimson, purple, and blue, and in being ornamented with gold. In the time of Josephus, it was a cubit of the larger size in length, and was furnished with sleeves. The high priest's ephod had a very rich button upon each shoulder, made of a large onyx stone set in gold. This stone was so large, that the names of the twelve tribes of Israel were engraven, six on each stone, Exod. xxviii, 9–12. The word SHOHAM, which we render onyx, is translated, by the Septuagint SMARAGDOS, an emerald; but as we have no certain knowledge either of this, or of any of the twelve stones of the breastplate, we may as well be satisfied with our translation as with any other. To the ephod belonged a curious girdle, of the same rich fabric as the ephod itself. This girdle is said to be upon the ephod, Exod. xxviii, 8; that is, woven with the ephod, as Maimonides understands; and, coming out from the ephod on each side, it was brought under the arms like a sash, and tied upon the breast. Samuel, though a Levite only, and a child, wore a linen ephod, 1 Sam. ii, 18. And David, in the ceremony of removing the ark from the house of Obed-edom to Jerusalem, was girt with a linen ephod, 2 Sam. vi, 14. The Levites were not generally allowed to wear the ephod; but in the time of Agrippa, as we are told by Josephus, a little before the taking of Jerusalem by the Romans, they obtained of that prince permission to wear the linen stole as well as the priests. Spencer and Cunæus are of opinion, that the Jewish kings had a right to wear the ephod, because David, coming to Ziklag, and finding that the Amalekites had plundered the city, and carried away his and the people's wives, ordered Abiathar, the high priest, to bring him the ephod, which being done, David inquired of the Lord, saying, "Shall I pursue after this troop?" 1 Sam. xxx, 8. Whence they infer, that David consulted God by urim and thummim, and consequently put on the ephod. But it is probable the text only means that he ordered the priest to do what he is himself said to have done. The ephod of Gideon is remarkable for having become the occasion of a new kind of idolatry to the Israelites, Judges viii, 27. What this consisted in, is matter of dispute among the learned. Some authors are of opinion that this ephod, as it is called, was an idol; others, that it was only a trophy in memory of the signal victory obtained by Gideon, and that the Israelites paid a kind of divine worship to it; so that Gideon was the innocent cause of their idolatry, in like manner as Moses had been in making the brazen serpent, which was afterward worshipped.

EPHRAIM was the name of Joseph's second son, by Asenath, Potiphar's daughter. He was born in Egypt, A. M. 2294. Ephraim, with his brother Manasseh, was presented by his father Joseph to Jacob on his death bed, Gen. xlviii, 8, &c. Jacob laid his right hand on Ephraim the younger, and his left on Manasseh the elder. Joseph was desirous to change his hands, but Jacob answered, "I know it, my son; Manasseh shall be multiplied, but Ephraim shall be greater." The sons of Ephraim having made an inroad into Palestine, the inhabitants of Gath killed them. Ephraim their father mourned many days for them, and his brethren came to comfort him, 1 Chron. vii, 20, 21. Afterward, he had a son named Beriah, and a daughter Sherah. He had also other sons, Rephah, Resheph, Tela, &c. His posterity multiplied in Egypt to the number of forty thousand five hundred men capable of bearing arms. In the land of promise, Joshua, who was of this tribe, gave them their portion between the Mediterranean west, and the river Jordan east. The ark and tabernacle remained long in this tribe at Shiloh; and after the separation of the ten tribes, the seat of the kingdom was in Ephraim, and hence Ephraim is frequently used to denote the whole kingdom. The district belonging to this tribe is called Ephratah, Psalm cxxxii, 6. Ephraim was led captive beyond the Euphrates, with all Israel, by Salmaneser, king of Assyria, A. M. 3283.

2. Ephraim was also the name of a city, into which Christ retired with his disciples a little before his passion, John xi, 54. It was situated in the tribe of Ephraim near the river Jordan. There was also the wood or forest of Ephraim, situated on the other side Jordan, in which Absalom's army was routed and himself killed, 2 Sam. xviii, 6.

EPHRATH, Caleb's second wife, who was the mother of Hur, 1 Chron. ii, 19. From her, it is believed that the city of Ephratah, otherwise called Bethlehem, where our Lord was born, had its name; and this city is more than once known in Scripture by the name of Ephrath, Gen. xxxv, 16.

EPICUREANS, a sect of philosophers in Greece and Rome. Epicurus was their founder, who lived about B. C. 300. The physical doctrine of Epicurus was as follows: Nothing can ever spring from nothing, nor can any thing ever return to nothing. The universe always existed, and will always remain; for there is nothing into which it can be changed. There is nothing in nature, nor can any thing be conceived, beside body and space. Body is that which possesses the properties of bulk, figure, resistance, and gravity; it is this alone which can touch and be touched. Space, or vacuum, destitute of the properties of body, incapable of action or passion, is the region which is or may be occupied by body, and which affords it an opportunity of moving freely. The existence of bodies is attested by the senses. Space must also exist, in order to allow bodies place in which to move and exist; and of their existence and motion we have the certain proof of perception. Beside body and space, no third nature can be conceived. But the existence of qualities is not precluded, because these have no subsistence except in the body to which they belong. The universe, consisting of body and space, is infinite. Bodies are infinite in multitude; space is infinite in magnitude. The universe is immovable, because there is no place beyond it into which it can move. It is also eternal and immutable, since it is liable to neither increase nor decrease, to production nor decay. Nevertheless, the parts of the universe are in motion, and are subject to change. All bodies consist of parts which are either themselves simple principles, or may be resolved into such. These first principles, or simple atoms, are divisible by no force, and therefore must be immutable.

2. The formation of the world he conceived to have happened in the following manner: A finite number of that infinite multitude of atoms, which, with infinite space, constitute the universe, falling fortuitously into the region of the world, were, in consequence of their innate motion, collected into one rude and indigested mass. In this chaos, the heaviest and largest atoms, or collections of atoms, first subsided, while the smaller, and those which from their form would move most freely, were driven upwards. These latter, after several reverberations, rose into the outer region of the world, and formed the heavens. Those atoms which, by their size and figure, were suited to form fiery bodies, collected themselves into stars; those which were not capable of rising so high in the sphere of the world, being disturbed by the fiery particles, formed themselves into air. At length, from those which subsided, was produced the earth. By the action of air, agitated by heat from the heavenly bodies, upon the mixed mass of the earth, its smoother and lighter particles were separated from the rest, and water was produced, which naturally flowed into the lowest places. In the first combination of atoms, which formed the chaos, various seeds arose, which, being preserved and nourished by moisture and heat, afterward sprung forth in organized bodies of different kinds. The soul is a subtle corporeal substance, composed of the finest atoms, which, by the extreme tenuity of its particles, is able to penetrate the whole body, and to adhere to all its parts. It is composed of four distinct parts: fire, which causes animal heat; an ethereal principle which is moist vapour; air; and a fourth principle, which is the cause of sensation. These four parts are so perfectly combined as to form one subtle substance, which, while it remains in the body, is the cause of all its faculties, motions, and passions, and which cannot be separated from

it, without producing the entire dissolution of the animal system.

3. In the universe there are, according to Epicurus, without contradiction, divine natures; because nature itself has impressed the idea of divinity upon the minds of men. The notion is universal; nor is it established by custom, law, or any human institution; but it is the effect of an innate principle, producing universal consent, and therefore it must be true. This universal notion has probably arisen from images of the gods, which have casually made their way into the minds of men in sleep, and have afterward been recollected. But it is inconsistent with our natural notions of the gods, as happy and immortal beings, to suppose that they encumber themselves with the management of the world, or are subject to the cares and passions which must attend so great a charge. Hence it is inferred, that the gods have no intercourse with mankind, nor any concern with the affairs of the world. Nevertheless, on account of their excellent nature, they are objects of reverence and worship. In their external shape the gods resemble men; and though the place of their residence is unknown to mortals; it is without doubt the mansion of perfect purity, tranquillity, and happiness. Thus he attempted to account for all the appearances of nature, even those which respect animated and intelligent beings, upon the simple principles of matter and motion, without introducing the agency of a supreme intelligence, or admitting any other idea of fate, than that of blind necessity inherent in every atom, by which it moves in a certain direction.

4. The ethics of Epicurus are much less exceptionable than his physics; of which we may judge from the following summary: The end of living, or the ultimate good, which is to be sought for its own sake, according to the universal opinion of mankind, is happiness; which men generally fail of attaining, because they form wrong notions of the nature of happiness, or do not use proper means for attaining it. The happiness which belongs to man, is that state in which he enjoys as many of the good things, and suffers as few of the evils incident to human nature as possible, passing his days in a smooth course of permanent tranquillity. Perfect happiness cannot possibly be possessed without the pleasure that attends freedom from pain, and the enjoyment of the good things of life. Pleasure is in its nature good, and ought to be pursued; and pain is in its nature evil, and should be avoided. Beside, pleasure or pain is the measure of what is good or evil in every object of desire or aversion. However, pleasure ought not in every instance to be pursued, nor pain to be avoided; but reason is to distinguish and compare the nature and degrees of each, that the result may be a wise choice of that which shall appear to be, upon the whole, good. That pleasure is the first good, appears from the inclination which every animal, from its first birth, discovers to pursue pleasure and avoid pain; and is confirmed by the universal experience of mankind, who are incited to action by no other principle, than the desire of avoiding pain, or obtaining pleasure. Of pleasures there are two kinds; one consisting in a state of rest, in which both body and mind are free from pain; the other arising from an agreeable agitation of the senses, producing a correspondent emotion in the soul. Upon the former of these, the enjoyment of life chiefly depends. Happiness may, therefore, be said to consist in bodily ease and mental tranquillity. It is the office of reason to confine the pursuit of pleasure within the limits of nature, so as to attain this happy state; which neither resembles a rapid torrent, nor a standing pool, but is like a gentle stream, that glides smoothly and silently along. This happy state can only be attained by a prudent care of the body, and a steady government of the mind. The diseases of the body are to be prevented by temperance, or cured by medicine, or endured tolerably by patience. Against the diseases of the mind philosophy provides sufficient antidotes; the virtues are its instruments for this purpose; the radical spring of which is prudence, or wisdom, and this instructs men to free their understanding from the clouds of prejudice; to exercise temperance and fortitude in the government of themselves; and to practise justice toward all others. In a happy life, pleasure can never be separated from virtue. The followers of Epicurus, however, degenerated into mere sensualists,--an effect which could only result from a system which denied a supreme God, and excluded from all concern with the affairs of men even those divine natures which it allowed to exist. This sect is mentioned Acts xvii, 18.

EPISCOPACY, Diocesan. The number of Christians in most of the primitive churches was at first small: they could easily, when not prevented by persecution, assemble together; and they thus formed one church or congregation; for, in Scripture, the term CHURCH is never used in the more modern acceptation of the word, but is employed to denote either the whole church of Christ, or a number of disciples meeting for the celebration of divine worship. The converts, however, rapidly increased; and when they could no longer meet in one place, other places would be prepared for them. But, connected as they still were with the parent church, they would choose from its presbyters their own pastors, and view themselves as under the inspection of the president and the presbytery, by whom the affairs of the church had been previously conducted. The pastors would thus remain members of the presbytery, as they had formerly been, and would look up to that one of their number who had been accustomed to preside among them. They were, in fact, for a considerable time, considered as one with the original church: the bishop sent to them the elements of the Lord's Supper as the pledge of unity; and we find it asserted by ancient writers, that there was one altar and one bishop. There were in this way gradually established, first in the towns or cities in which the Apostles had called men to the truth, and then in the contiguous district of country, several congregations: in these pastors officiated, who were authorized by the bishop and presbytery, whose superintendence was extended, so that parochial episcopacy was insensibly but naturally changed into diocesan episcopacy; many of the presbyters sent out by the bishop residing at their churches, but nevertheless composing part of his council, and being summoned to meet with him upon important occasions. This enlargement of the field of inspection rendered the particular superintendence of the bishop more requisite; and was the means both of adding to his influence, and of his being regarded as permanently raised above his brethren.

2. The ministers who were sent to the recently erected churches had probably different powers, according to the numbers to whom they were to officiate, the situation of the churches in respect of the original church, and the tranquillity or persecution which was their lot. In the immediate neighbourhood of the bishop, and where one person was sufficient, he would merely perform the duties that had been assigned to him previous to his mission; but the same reasons that led the Apostles to plant several presbyters in the churches which they founded might render it expedient that more than one, sometimes that a considerable number, should be attached to the newly-formed congregations; more particularly when the number attending was large, and when there was the prospect of their still farther increasing. In such cases, it appears that the bishop gave to one of the presbyters sent, and did so for the same reasons that had at first created inequality among the pastors, more extensive powers than were entrusted to the rest, and made him his representative authorizing him to preside over the others, and to discharge those parts of the ministerial office which, in his own church, he reserved for himself. When this happened, the person so distinguished was termed CHORO-EPISCOPUS: he was more than a presbyter, but he was inferior to the bishop, acted by his directions, and could be controlled by him in the exercise of the privileges which had been granted. Such subordinate bishops continued for a considerable time; but it might, from the beginning, have been foreseen that they would soon aspire to an equality with the original bishops; and they were at length suppressed, under the pretence that, by multiplying the higher order in places of little consequence, the church would detract from the respectability of that order, and lessen the reverence with which it should be regarded.

3. The different congregations or churches which were established in various cities and the adjoining districts were in so far independent of each other, that the bishops and presbyters of each had the rule of their particular church, and of the churches which had sprung from it, and were entitled, by their own authority, to make such regulations as appeared to them to be requisite; and this species of independence continued for a considerable time, every bishop presiding in his congregation, and afterward in his diocess. There was, however, always a common tie by which they were united. Neighbouring churches, actuated by ardent zeal for the interests of divine truth, consulted together upon the best mode of promoting it. We know that the Apostolic churches were enjoined to communicate to other bodies the epistles which they had received; and while persecution continued, it was natural for all who were exposed to it to consider by what means its fury could be avoided.

4. After the bishops were established as superior to presbyters, when any meeting was held respecting religion, or the administration of the church, it was chiefly composed of this higher order, and the president of the synod or council was elected from their number. These meetings were generally assembled in the metropolis, or principal city of the district; and hence the bishop of this city, being frequently called to preside, came, at length, to be regarded as entitled to do so: thus acquiring a superiority over the other bishops, just as they had acquired superiority over the inferior clergy. He was, in consequence, distinguished by a particular name, being denominated, from the city in which he presided, a metropolitan.

EPISCOPALIANS, those who maintain that bishops, presbyters, or priests, and deacons, are three distinct orders in the church; and that the bishops have a superiority over both the others. The episcopal form of church government professes to find in the days of the Apostles the model upon which it is framed. While our Lord remained upon earth, he acted as the immediate governor of his church. Having himself called the Apostles, he kept them constantly about his person, except at one time, when he sent them forth upon a short progress through the cities of Judea, and gave them particular directions how they should conduct themselves. The seventy disciples, whom he sent forth at another time, are never mentioned again in the New Testament. But the Apostles received from him many intimations that their office was to continue after his departure; and as one great object of his ministry was to qualify them for the execution of this office, so, in the interval between his resurrection and his ascension, he explained to them the duties of it, and he invested them with the authority which the discharge of those duties implied. "Go," said he, "make disciples of all nations, baptizing them, teaching them; and lo, I am with you always, even unto the end of the world. As my Father hath sent me, even so send I you. Receive ye the Holy Ghost," Matt. xxviii, 19, 20; John xx, 21, 22. Soon after the ascension of Jesus, his Apostles received those extraordinary gifts of which his promise had given them assurance; and immediately they began to execute their commission, not only as the witnesses of his resurrection, and the teachers of his religion, but as the rulers of that society which was gathered by their preaching. In Acts vi, we find the Apostles ordering the Christians at Jerusalem to "look out seven men of honest report," who might take charge of the daily ministrations to the poor, and to bring the men so chosen to them, that "we," said the Apostles, "may appoint them over this business." The men accordingly were "set before the Apostles; and when they had prayed, they laid their hands on them." Here are the Apostles ordaining deacons. Afterward, we find St. Paul, in his progress through Asia Minor, ordaining in every church elders, πρεσβυτέρους; the name properly expressive of age being transferred, after the practice of the Jews, as a mark of respect, to ecclesiastical rulers, Acts xiv, 23. The men thus ordained by St. Paul appear, from the book of Acts and the Epistles, to have been teachers, pastors, overseers, of the flock of Christ; and to Timothy, who was a minister of the word, the Apostle speaks of "the gift which is in thee by the putting on of my hands," 2 Tim. i, 6. Over the persons to whom he thus conveyed the office of teaching, he exercised jurisdiction; for he sent to Ephesus, to the elders of the church to meet him at Miletus; and there, in a long discourse, gave them a solemn charge, Acts xx, 17–35; and to Timothy and Titus he writes epistles in the style of a superior.

2. As St. Paul unquestionably conceived that there belonged to him, as an Apostle, an authority over other office-bearers of the church, so his epistles contain two examples of a delegation of that authority. He not only directs Timothy, whom he had besought to abide at Ephesus, how to behave himself in the house of God as a minister, but he sets him over other ministers. He empowers him to ordain men to the work of the ministry: "The things that thou hast heard of me among many witnesses, the same commit thou to faithful men, who shall be able to teach others also," 2 Tim. ii, 2. He gives him directions about the ordination of bishops and deacons; he places both these kinds of office-bearers in Ephesus under his inspection, instructing him in what manner to receive an accusation against an elder who laboured in word and doctrine; and he commands him to charge some that they teach no other doctrine but the form of sound words. In like manner he says to Titus, "For this cause left I thee in Crete, that thou shouldest set in order the things that are wanting, and ordain elders in every city, as I had appointed thee," Titus i, 5. He describes to Titus the qualifications of a bishop or elder, making him the judge how far any person in Crete was possessed of these qualifications; he gives him authority over all orders of Christians there; and he empowers him to reject heretics. Here, then, is that Apostle, with whose actions we are best acquainted, seemingly aware that there would be continual occasion in the Christian church for the exercise of that authority over pastors and teachers, which the Apostles had derived from the Lord Jesus; and by these two examples of a delegation, given during his life time, preparing the world for beholding that authority exercised by the successors of the Apostles in all ages. Accordingly, the earliest Christian writers tell us that the Apostles, to prevent contention, appointed bishops and deacons; giving orders, too, that, upon their death, other approved men should succeed in their ministry. We are told that the other Apostles constituted their first-fruits, that is, their first disciples, after they had proved them by the Spirit, bishops and deacons of those who were to believe; and that the Apostle John, who survived the rest, after returning from Patmos, the place of his banishment, went about the neighbouring nations, ordaining bishops, establishing whole churches, and setting apart particular persons for the ministry, as they were pointed out to him by the Spirit.

3. As bishops are mentioned in the earliest times, so ecclesiastical history records the succession of bishops through many ages; and even during the first three centuries, before Christianity was incorporated with the state, every city, where the multitude of Christians required a number of pastors to perform the stated offices, presents to us, as far as we can gather from contemporary writers, an appearance very much the same with that of the church of Jerusalem in the days of the Apostles. The Apostle James seems to have resided in that city. But there is also mention of the elders of the church, who, according to the Scripture representation of elders, must have discharged the ministerial office, but over whom the Apostle James presided. So, in Carthage, where Cyprian was bishop, and in every other Christian city of which we have particular accounts, there was a college of presbyters; and there was one person who had not only presidency, but jurisdiction and authority, over the rest. They were his council in matters relating to the church, and they were qualified to preach, to baptize, and to administer the Lord's Supper; but they could do nothing without his permission and authority. It is a principle in Christian antiquity, εἷς ἐπίσκοπος, μία ἐκκλησία, "one bishop, and one church." The one bishop had the care of all the Christians, who, although they met in separate congregations, constituted one church; and he had the inspection of the pastors, who, having received ordination from the bishop, officiated in the separate congregations, performed the several parts of duty which he prescribed to them, and were accountable to him for their conduct. In continuation of this primitive institution, we find episcopacy in all corners of the church of Christ. Until the time of the reformation, there were, in every Christian state, persons with the name, the rank, and the authority of bishops; and the existence of such persons was not considered as an innovation, but as an establishment, which, by means of catalogues preserved in ecclesiastical writers, may be traced back to the days of the Apostles.

4. Upon the principles which have now been stated, it is understood, according to the episcopal form of government, that there is in the church a superior order of office-bearers, the successors of the Apostles, who possess in their own persons the right of ordination and jurisdiction, and who are called ἐπισκόποι, as being the overseers not only of the people, but also of the clergy; and an inferior order of ministers, called presbyters, the literal translation of the word ϖρεσβυτέροι, which is rendered in our English Bibles ELDERS, persons who receive, from the ordination of the bishop, power to preach and to administer the sacraments, who are set over the people, but are themselves under the government of the bishop, and have no right to convey to others the sacred office, which he gives them authority to exercise under him. According to a phrase used by Charles I, who was by no means an unlearned defender of that form of government to which he was a martyr, the presbyters are EPISCOPI GREGIS; [bishops of the flock;] but the bishops are EPISCOPI GREGIS ET PASTORUM, [bishops of the flock and of the pastors.]

5. The liberal writers on that side, however, do not contend that this form of government is made so binding in the church as not to be departed from, and varied according to circumstances. It cannot be proved, says Dr. Paley, that any form of church government was laid down in the Christian, as it had been in the Jewish, Scriptures, with a view of fixing a constitution for succeeding ages. The truth seems to have

been, that such offices were at first erected in the Christian church as the good order, the instruction, and the exigencies of the society at that time required; without any intention, at least without any declared design, of regulating the appointment, authority, or the distinction, of Christian ministers under future circumstances. To the same effect, also, Bishop Tomline says, "It is not contended that the bishops, priests, and deacons of England are at present precisely the same that bishops, presbyters, and deacons were in Asia Minor, seventeen hundred years ago. We only maintain that there have always been bishops, priests, and deacons, in the Christian church, since the days of the Apostles, with different powers and functions, it is allowed, in different countries and at different periods; but the general principles and duties which have respectively characterized these clerical orders have been essentially the same at all times, and in all places; and the variations which they have undergone have only been such as have ever belonged to all persons in public situations, whether civil or ecclesiastical, and which are indeed inseparable from every thing in which mankind are concerned in this transitory and fluctuating world. I have thought it right to take this general view of the ministerial office, and to make these observations upon the clerical orders subsisting in this kingdom, for the purpose of pointing out the foundation and principles of church authority, and of showing that our ecclesiastical establishment is as nearly conformable, as change of circumstances will permit, to the practice of the primitive church. But, though I flatter myself that I have proved episcopacy to be an Apostolical institution, yet I readily acknowledge that there is no precept in the New Testament which commands that every church should be governed by bishops. No church can exist without some government; but though there must be rules and orders for the proper discharge of the offices of public worship, though there must be fixed regulations concerning the appointment of ministers, and though a subordination among them is expedient in the highest degree, yet it does not follow that all these things must be precisely the same in every Christian country; they may vary with the other varying circumstances of human society, with the extent of a country, the manners of its inhabitants, the nature of its civil government, and many other peculiarities which might be specified. As it has not pleased our almighty Father to prescribe any particular form of civil government for the security of temporal comforts to his rational creatures, so neither has he prescribed any particular form of ecclesiastical polity as absolutely necessary to the attainment of eternal happiness. But he has, in the most explicit terms, enjoined obedience to all governors, whether civil or ecclesiastical, and whatever may be their denomination, as essential to the character of a true Christian. Thus the Gospel only lays down general principles, and leaves the application of them to men as free agents." Bishop Tomline, however, and the high Episcopalians of the church of England, contend for an original distinction in the office and order of bishops and presbyters; which notion is controverted by the Presbyterians, and is, indeed, contradicted by one who may be truly called the founder of the church of England, Archbishop Cranmer, who says, "The bishops and priests were at one time, and were not two things; but both one office in the beginning of Christ's religion." The more rigid Episcopalians admit of no ordination as valid in the church but by the hands of bishops, and those derived in a right line from the Apostles. See Presbyterians.

6. The churches of Rome and of England are the principal Episcopalian churches in the west of Europe; and those of the Greeks and Arminians in the east; but, beside these, there are Episcopalians in Scotland, and in other countries, where, Presbyterianism being the establishment, they are, of course, Dissenters. Thus a Presbyterian is a Dissenter in England, and an Episcopalian a Dissenter in Scotland. There is also an Episcopalian church in the United States of America; but there being no established religion, there are, of course, no Dissenters. The Episcopal church in America is organized very differently from that in England. The following particulars are from the best authorities:--The general convention was formed in 1789, by a delegation from the different states, and meets triennially. They have eleven dioceses, two of which are without bishops, and are at liberty to form more in other states. The above convention consists of an upper and lower house; the former consisting of bishops, in which the senior bishop presides: they have no archbishop: and the lower, of the other clergy, and laymen mingled with them. There are also diocesan conventions annually, in which the bishop presides. The bishops have no salaries as such, but are allowed to hold parishes as other ministers; but it has lately been found more convenient in many states to raise a fund for the support of the bishop, that his time may be more at liberty for visiting the clergy. They have neither patronage nor palaces, and some of their incomes are extremely small. The English Common Prayer Book is adopted, with the omission of the Athanasian Creed, and some other slight alterations. Subscription to the articles is not required by candidates for holy orders. The Methodists in America, also, form an episcopal church; but founded upon the primitive principle that bishops and presbyters are of the same ORDER, although the OVERSIGHT of presbyters may be committed to those who are, by virtue of their office, also called BISHOPS.

[The Methodist Episcopal Church was organized in December, 1784. The fundamental principle on which the episcopacy of this church rests, is here correctly stated. It is proper to add to Mr. Watson's enumeration, that the Roman and Moravian churches in the United States are also episcopal; and that the statement that the bishops of the Protestant Episcopal Church receive no salaries as bishops, is not at present (1832) without exception. Their incomes, too, though doubtless extremely small compared with those of the bishops of the establishment in England, are not so, compared with those of other ministers generally in the United States.

EPISTLES, which occur under the same Hebrew word with books, namely, ספר, are mentioned the more rarely, the farther we go back into antiquity. An epistle is first mentioned, 2 Sam. xi, 14, &c. Afterward, there is more frequent mention of them; and sometimes an epistle is meant, when literally a messenger is spoken of, as in Ezra iv, 15–17. In the east, letters are commonly sent unsealed. In case, however, they are sent to persons of distinction, they are placed in a valuable purse, which is tied, closed over with wax or clay, and then stamped with a signet, Isaiah xxix, 11; Job xxxviii, 14. The most ancient epistles begin and end without either salutation or farewell; but under the Persian monarchy the salutation was very prolix. It is given in an abridged form in Ezra iv, 7–10; v, 7. The Apostles, in their epistles, used the salutation customary among the Greeks; but they omitted the usual farewell at the close, namely, χαίρειν, and adopted a benediction more conformable to the spirit of the Christian religion. St. Paul, when he dictated his letters, wrote the benediction at the close with his own hand, 2 Thess. iii, 17. He was more accustomed to dictate his letters than to write them himself.

The name EPISTLES is given, by way of eminence, to the letters written by the Apostles, or first preachers of Christianity, to particular churches or persons, on particular occasions or subjects. Of these the Apostle Paul wrote fourteen. St. James wrote one general epistle; St. Peter two; St. John three; and St. Jude one.

An epistle has its Hebrew name from its being rolled or folded together. The modern Arabs roll up their letters, and then flatten them to the breadth of an inch, and paste up the end of them, instead of sealing them. The Persians make up their letters in a roll about six inches long, and a bit of paper is fastened round it with gum, and sealed with an impression of ink, which resembles our printers' ink, but is not so thick. Letters, as stated above, were generally sent to persons of distinction in a bag or purse; but to inferiors, or those who were held in contempt, they were sent open, that is, unenclosed. Lady M. W. Montagu says, the BASSA of Belgrade's answer to the English ambassador going to Constantinople was brought to him in a purse of scarlet satin. But, in the case of Nehemiah, an insult was designed to be offered to him by Sanballat, in refusing him the mark of respect usually paid to persons of his station, and treating him contemptuously, by sending the letter open, that is, without the customary appendages when presented to persons of respectability. "Futty Sihng," says Mr. Forbes, "sent a CHOPDAR to me at Dhuboy, with a letter of invitation to the wedding, then celebrating at Brodera at a great expense, and of long continuance. The letter, as usual, from oriental princes, was written on silver paper, flowered with gold, with an additional sprinkling of saffron, enclosed under a cover of gold brocade. The letter was accompanied with a bag of crimson and gold KEEM-CAUB, filled with sweet-scented seeds, as a mark of favour and good omen."

EPOCH, a term in chronology signifying a fixed point of time, from which the succeeding years are numbered. Scaliger says it means "a stop," because "in epochs stop and terminate the measures of times." It now usually denotes a remarkable date; as, the epoch of the destruction of Troy, B. C. 1183, &c. The first epoch is the creation of the world, which, according to the Vulgate Bible, Archbishop Usher fixes in the year 710 of the Julian period, and 4004 years before Jesus Christ. The second is the deluge, which, according to the Hebrew text, happened in the year of the world 1656. Six other epochs are commonly reckoned in sacred history: the building of the tower of Babel, which was, according to Dr. Hales, B. C. 2554; the calling of Abraham, B. C. 2153; the departure of the Israelites out of Egypt, B. C. 1648; the dedication of the temple, B. C. 1027; the end of the Babylonish captivity, B. C. 536; and the birth of Jesus Christ, A. D. 1. In profane history are reckoned five epochs: the founding of the Assyrian empire, B. C. 1267; the era of Nabonassar, or death of Sardanapalus, B. C. 747; the reign of Cyrus at Babylon, B. C. 556; the reign of Alexander the Great over the Persians, B. C. 330; and the beginning of the reign of Augustus, in which our Saviour was born, B. C. 44.

ERA. The term ERA (not ÆRA, as incorrectly written) is Spanish, signifying time, as in the phrase, DE ERA EN ERA, "from time to time." It was first used in the ERA HISPANICA, instituted B. C. 38, in honour of Augustus, when Spain was allotted to him in the distribution of the provinces among the second triumvirate, Augustus, Anthony, and Lepidus. It now usually denotes an indefinite series of years, beginning from some known epoch; and so differs from a period which is a definite series: as the era of the foundation of Rome, the era of the Olympiads, the era of Nabonassar, &c. See Epoch.

ESAR-HADDON, son of Sennacherib, and his successor in the kingdom of Assyria: called Sargon, or Saragon, Isa. xx, 1. He reigned twenty-nine years. He made war with the Philistines, and took Azoth, by Tartan, his general: he attacked Egypt, Cush, and Edom, Isa. xx, xxxiv; designing, probably, to avenge the affront Sennacherib his father had received from Tirhakah, king of Cush, and the king of Egypt, who had been Hezekiah's confederates. He sent priests to the Cuthæans, whom Salmaneser, king of Assyria, had planted in Samaria, instead of the Israelites: he took Jerusalem, and carried King Manasseh to Babylon, of which he had become master, perhaps, because there was no heir to Belesis, king of Bayblon. He is said to have reigned twenty-nine or thirty years at Nineveh, and thirteen years at Babylon; in all forty-two years. He died A. M. 3336.

ESAU, son of Isaac and Rebekah, born A. M. 2168, B. C. 1836. When the time of Rebekah's delivery came, she had twins, Gen. xxv, 24–26: the first-born was hairy, therefore called Esau; that is, a man full grown or of perfect age; but some derive Esau from the Arabic GESCHA or GENCHEVA, which signifies a hair cloth. Esau delighted in hunting, and his father Isaac had a particular affection for him. On one occasion, Esau, returning from the fields greatly fatigued, desired Jacob to give him some red pottage, which he was then preparing. Jacob consented, provided Esau would sell him his birthright. Esau complied, and by oath resigned it to him,

Gen. xxv, 29–34. Esau, when aged forty, married two Canaanitish women, Judith, daughter of Beeri, the Hittite; and Bashemath, daughter of Elon, Gen. xxvi, 34. These marriages were very displeasing to Isaac and Rebekah, because they intermingled the blood of Abraham with that of Canaanite aliens. Isaac being old, and his sight decayed, directed Esau to procure him delicate venison by hunting, that he might give him his chief blessing, Gen. xxvii. The artifice of his mother, however, counteracted his purpose; and she contrived to impose upon Isaac, and to obtain the father's principal blessing for her son Jacob. Esau was indignant on account of this treachery and determined to kill Jacob as soon as their father should die. Rebekah again interposed, and sent Jacob away to her brother Laban, with whom he might be secure. During the period of separation, which lasted several years, Esau married a wife of the family of Ishmael; and, removing to Mount Seir, acquired great power and wealth. When Jacob returned, after long absence, to his father's country, with a numerous family, and large flocks and herds, he dreaded his brother's displeasure; but they had an amicable and affectionate interview. After their father's death, they lived in peace and amity; but, as their possessions enlarged, and there was not sufficient room for them in the land in which they were strangers, Esau returned to Mount Seir, where his posterity multiplied under the denomination of Edomites. (See Edom.) The time of his death is not mentioned; but Bishop Cumberland thinks it probable that he died about the same time with his brother Jacob, at the age of about one hundred and forty-seven years, Gen. xxv-xxxvi.

2. On the most important part of this history, the selling of the birthright, we may observe, (1.) That although it was always the design of God that the blessing connected with primogeniture in the family of Abraham should be enjoyed by Jacob, and to exercise his sovereignty in changing the succession in which the promises of the Abrahamic covenant might descend; yet the conduct of Rebekah and Jacob was reprehensible in endeavouring to bring about the divine design by the unworthy means of contrivance and deceit; and they were punished for their presumption by their sufferings. (2.) That the conduct of Esau in selling his birthright was both wanton and profane. It was wanton, because he, though faint, could be in no danger of not obtaining a supply of food in his father's house; and was therefore wholly influenced by his appetite, excited by the delicacy of Jacob's pottage. It was profane, because the blessings of the birthright were spiritual as well as civil. The church of God was to be established in the line of the first-born; and in that line the Messiah was to appear. These high privileges were despised by Esau, who is therefore made by St. Paul a type of all apostates from Christ, who, like him, profanely despise their birthright as the sons of God. See Birthright.

ESDRAELON, Plain of, in the tribe of Issachar, extends east and west from Scythopolis to Mount Carmel; called, likewise, the Great Plain, the Valley of Jezreel, the Plain of Esdrela. Dr. E. D. Clarke observes, it is by far the largest plain in the Holy Land; extending quite across the country from Mount Carmel and the Mediterranean Sea to the southern extremity of the Sea of Galilee; about thirty miles in length, and twenty in breadth. It is also a very fertile district, abounding in pasture; on which account it has been selected for the purposes of encampment by almost every army that has traversed the Holy Land. Here Barak, descending with his ten thousand men from Mount Tabor, which rises like a cone in the centre of the plain, defeated Sisera, with his "nine hundred chariots of iron, and all the people that were with him, gathered from Harosheth of the Gentiles unto the river of Kishon; and pursued after the chariots and after the host unto Harosheth of the Gentiles; and all the host of Sisera fell upon the edge of the sword; and there was not a man left," Judges iv. Here Josiah, king of Judah, fell, fighting against Necho, king of Egypt, 2 Kings xxiii, 29. And here the Midianites and the Amalekites, who were "like grasshoppers for multitude, and their camels without number as the sand of the sea," encamped, when they were defeated by Gideon, Judges vi. This plain has likewise been used for the same purpose by the armies of every conqueror or invader, from Nabuchodonosor, king of Assyria, to his imitator, Napoleon Buonaparte, who, in the spring of 1799, with a small body of French, defeated an army of several thousand Turks and Mamelukes. Jews, Gentiles, Saracens, Christians, crusaders, and antichristian Frenchmen, Egyptians, Persians, Druses, Turks, and Arabs, warriors out of every nation which is under heaven, have pitched their tents in the Plain of Esdraelon; and have beheld the various banners of their nations wet with the dews of Tabor and of Hermon. And it is to this day generally found to be the place of encampment of large parties of Arabs.

ESDRAS, the name of two apocryphal books which were always excluded the Jewish canon, and are too absurd to be admitted as canonical by the Papists themselves. They are supposed to have been originally written in Greek by some Hellenistical Jews; though some imagine that they were first written in Chaldee, and afterward translated into Greek. It is uncertain when they were composed, though it is generally agreed that the author wrote before Josephus.

ESHBAAL, or **ISHBOSHETH**, the fourth son of Saul. The Hebrews, to avoid pronouncing the word BAAL, "lord," used BOSHETH, "confusion." Instead of Mephi-baal, they said Mephi-bosheth; and, instead of Esh-baal, they said Ish-bosheth, 2 Sam. ii, 8.

ESHCOL, one of Abraham's allies, who dwelt with him in the valley of Mamre, and accompanied him in the pursuit of Chedorlaomer, and the other confederated kings, who pillaged Sodom and Gomorrah, and carried away Lot, Abraham's nephew, Gen. xiv, 24. Also the valley or brook of Eshcol was that in which the Hebrew messengers, who went to spy the land of Canaan, cut a bunch of grapes so large that it was as much as two men could carry. It was situated in the south part of Judah, Num. xiii, 24; xxxii, 9.

ESSENES, or **ESSENIANS**, one of the three ancient sects of the Jews. They appear to have been an enthusiastic sect, never numerous, and but little known; directly opposite to the Pharisees with respect to their reliance upon tradition, and their scrupulous regard to the ceremonial law, but pretending, like them, to superior sanctity of manners. They existed in the time of our Saviour; and though they are not mentioned in the New Testament, they are supposed to be alluded to by St. Paul in his Epistles to the Ephesians and Colossians, and in his first Epistle to Timothy. From the account given of the doctrines and institutions of this sect by Philo and Josephus, we learn that they believed in the immortality of the soul; that they were absolute predestinarians; that they observed the seventh day with peculiar strictness; that they held the Scriptures in the highest reverence, but considered them as mystic writings, and expounded them allegorically; that they sent gifts to the temple, but offered no sacrifices; that they admitted no one into their society till after a probation of three years; that they lived in a state of perfect equality, except that they paid respect to the aged, and to their priests; that they considered all secular employment as unlawful, except that of agriculture; that they had all things in common, and were industrious, quiet, and free from every species of vice; that they held celibacy and solitude in high esteem; that they allowed no change of raiment till necessity required it; that they abstained from wine; that they were not permitted to eat but with their own sect; and that a certain portion of food was allotted to each person, of which they partook together, after solemn ablutions. The austere and retired life of the Essenes is supposed to have given rise to monkish superstition.

The Therapeutæ were a distinct branch of the Essenes. Jahn has thus described the difference between them: The principal ground of difference between the Essenes or Essaëi, and Therapeutæ consisted in this; the former were Jews, who spoke the Aramean; the latter were Greek Jews, as the names themselves intimate, namely, אסיא and Θεραπευταὶ. The Essenes lived chiefly in Palestine; the Therapeutæ, in Egypt. The Therapeutæ were more rigid than the Essenes, since the latter, although they made it a practice to keep at a distance from large cities, lived, nevertheless, in towns and villages, and practised agriculture and the arts, with the exception of those arts which were made more directly subservient to the purposes of war. The Therapeutæ, on the contrary, fled from all inhabited places, dwelt in fields and deserts and gardens, and gave themselves up to contemplation. Both the Essenes and the Therapeutæ held their property in common, and those things which they stood in need of for the support and the comforts of life, were distributed to them from the common stock. The candidates for admission among the Essenes gave their property to the society; but those who were destined for a membership with the Therapeutæ, left theirs to their friends; and both, after a number of years of probation, made a profession which bound them to the exercise of the strictest uprightness. The Romanists pretend, as Dr. Prideaux observes, without any foundation, that the Essenes were Christian monks, formed into a society by St. Mark, who founded the first church at Alexandria. But it is evident, from the accounts of Josephus and Philo, that the Essenes were not Christians, but Jews.

Dr. Neander's account of the Essenes is as follows:--A company of pious men, much experienced in the trials of the outward and of the inward life, had withdrawn themselves out of the strife of theological and political parties, at first apparently (according to Pliny the elder) to the western side of the Dead Sea; where they lived together in intimate connection, partly in the same sort of society as the monks of later days, and partly as mystical orders in all periods have done. From this society, other smaller ones afterward proceeded, and spread themselves over all Palestine. They were called Essenes, Ἐσσηνοὶ or Ἐσσαιοὶ. They employed themselves in the arts of peace, agriculture, pasture, handicraft works, and especially in the art of healing, while they took great delight in investigating the healing powers of nature. It is probable, also, that they imagined themselves under the guidance of a supernatural illumination in their search into nature, and their use of her powers. Their natural knowledge, and their art of healing, appear also to have had a religious, theosophic character, as they professed also to have peculiar prophetical gifts. The Essenes were, no doubt, distinguished from the mass of ordinary Jews by this, that they knew and loved something higher than the outward ceremonial and a dead faith, that they did really strive after holiness of heart, and inward communion with God. Their quiet, pious habits also rendered them remarkable, and by means of these they remained quiet amidst all the political changes, respected by all parties, even by the Heathens; and by their laborious habits and kindness, their obedience toward the higher powers, as ordained of God, their fidelity and love of truth, they were enabled to extend themselves in all directions. In their society every yea and nay had the force of an oath; for every oath, said they, pre-supposes a mutual distrust, which ought not to be the case among a society of honest men. Only in one case was an oath suffered among them, namely, as a pledge for those who after a three years' noviciate were to be received into the number of the initiated. According to the portraiture of them, given by Philo, the Alexandrian, in his separate treatise concerning the "True Freedom of the Virtuous," we should take the Essenes for men of an entirely practical religious turn, far removed from all theosophy and all idle speculation; and we should ascribe to them an inward religious habit of mind, free from all mixture of superstition and reliance on outward things. But the account of Philo does not at all accord with that of Josephus; and the more historical Josephus deserves in general more credit than Philo, who was too apt to indulge in philosophizing and idealism. Beside, Josephus had more opportunity of knowing this sect thoroughly, than Philo; for Philo lived in Egypt, and the Essenes did not extend beyond Palestine. Josephus had here passed the greater part of his life, and had certainly taken all necessary pains to inform himself accurately of the nature of the different sects, among which he was determined, as a youth of sixteen years of age, to make choice, although he can hardly have completely passed through a noviciate in the sect of the Essenes, because he made the round of all the three Jewish sects, in a period of from three to four years. Josephus, also, shows himself completely unprejudiced in this description; while Philo, on the contrary, wished to represent the Essenes to the more cultivated Greeks as models of practical wisdom, and, therefore, he allowed himself to represent much, not as it really was, but as it suited his purpose. We must conclude that the Essenes did also busy themselves with theosophy, and pretended to impart to those of their order disclosures relating to the supernatural world of spirits, because those who were about to be initiated, were obliged to swear that they would never make known to any one the names of the angels then to be communicated to them. The manner in which they kept secret the ancient books of their sect is also a proof of this. And, indeed, Philo himself makes it probable, when he says, that they employed themselves with a φιλοσοφία διά συμβολῶν, a philosophy which was supported by an allegorical interpretation of Scripture, for this kind of allegorizing interpretation was usually the accompaniment of a certain speculative system. According to Philo, they rejected the sacrifice of victims, because they considered, that to consecrate and offer up themselves wholly to God, was the only true sacrifice, the only sacrifice worthy of God. But according to Josephus they certainly considered sacrifice as something peculiarly holy, but they thought that from its peculiar holiness it must have been desecrated by the profane Jews in the temple of Jerusalem, and that it could be worthily celebrated only in their holy community, just as mystic sects of this nature are constantly accustomed to make the OBJECTIVE acts of religion dependent on the SUBJECTIVE condition of those who perform or take part in them. In the troublesome and superstitious observance of the rest of the Sabbath, according to the letter, and not according to the spirit, they went even farther than the other Jews, only with this difference, that they were in good earnest in the matter, while the Pharisees by their casuistry relaxed their rules, or drew them tighter, just as it suited their purpose. The Essenes, not only strenuously abhorred, like the other Jews, contact with the uncircumcised, but, having divided themselves into four classes, the Essenes of a higher grade were averse from contact with those of a lower, as if they were rendered unclean by it, and when any thing of this kind did happen, they purified themselves after it. Like many other Jews, they attributed great value, in general, to lustration by bathing in cold water. To their ascetic notions, the constant and healthy practice in the east of anointing with oil seemed unholy, and if it befel any one of them, he was obliged to purify himself. It was also a great abomination to them to eat any food except such as had been prepared by persons of their own sect. They would die rather than eat of any other. This is a sufficient proof that although the Essenes might possess a certain inward religious life, and a certain practical piety, yet that these qualities with them, as well as with many other mystical sects, as for example, those of the middle ages, were connected with a theosophy, which desired to know things hidden from human reason, ἐμβατευειν εἰς ἁ τις μη ἑωραϰεν, and therefore lost itself in idle imaginations and dreams, and were also mixed up with an outward asceticism, a proud spirit of separation from the rest of mankind, and superstitious observances and demeanours totally at variance with the true spirit of inward religion.

ESTHER. The book of Esther is so called, because it contains the history of Esther a Jewish captive, who by her remarkable accomplishments gained the affection of King Ahasuerus, and by marriage with him was raised to the throne of Persia; and it relates the origin and ceremonies of the feast of Purim, instituted in commemoration of the great deliverance, which she, by her interest, procured for the Jews, whose general destruction had been concerted by the offended pride of Haman. There is great diversity of opinion concerning the author of this book; it has been ascribed to Ezra, to Mordecai, to Joachim, and to the joint labours of the great synagogue; and it is impossible to decide which of these opinions is the most probable. We are told, that the facts here recorded happened in the reign of Ahasuerus king of Persia, "who reigned from India even unto Ethiopia, over a hundred and twenty-seven provinces," Esther i, 1; and this extent of dominion plainly proves that he was one of the successors of Cyrus. That point is indeed allowed by all; but learned men differ concerning the person meant by Ahasuerus, whose name does not occur in profane history; and consequently they are not agreed concerning the precise period to which we are to assign this history. Archbishop Usher supposed, that by Ahasuerus was meant Darius Hystaspes, and Joseph Scaliger contended that Xerxes was meant; but Dean Prideaux has very satisfactorily shown, that by Ahasuerus we are to understand Artaxerxes Longimanus. Josephus also considered Ahasuerus and Artaxerxes as the same person; and we may observe, that Ahasuerus is always translated Artaxerxes in the Septuagint version; and he is called by that name in the apocryphal part of the book of Esther. See Ecbatana, and Ahasuerus.

ETERNITY is an attribute of God. (See GOD.) The self-existent being, says the learned Dr. Clarke, must of necessity be eternal. The ideas of eternity and self-existence are so closely connected, that because something must of necessity be eternal, independently and without any outward cause of its being, therefore it must necessarily be self-existent; and because it is impossible but something must be self-existent, therefore it is necessary that it must likewise be eternal. To be self-existent, is to exist by an absolute necessity in the nature of the thing itself. Now this necessity being absolute, and not depending upon any thing external, must be always unalterably the same; nothing being alterable but what is capable of being affected by somewhat without itself. That being therefore which has no other cause of its existence but the absolute necessity of its own nature, must of necessity have existed from everlasting, without beginning; and must of necessity exist to everlasting, without end.

On the eternal duration of the divine Being, many have held a metaphysical refinement. "The eternal existence of God," it is said, "is not to be considered as successive; the ideas we gain from time are not to be allowed in our conceptions of his duration. As he fills all space with his immensity, he fills all duration with his eternity; and with him eternity is NUNC STANS, a permanent NOW, incapable of the relations of past, present, and future." Such, certainly, is not the view given us of this mysterious subject in the Scriptures; and if it should be said that they speak popularly, and are accommodated to the infirmity of the reason of the body of mankind, we may reply, that philosophy has not, with all its boasting of superior light, carried our views on this attribute of the divine nature at all beyond revelation; and, in attempting it, has only obscured the conceptions of its admirers. "Filling duration with his eternity," is a phrase without any meaning: for how can any man conceive a permanent instant, which coëxists with a perpetually flowing duration? One might as well apprehend a mathematical point coëxtended with a line, a surface, and all dimensions. As this notion has, however, been made the basis of some theological opinions, it may be proper to examine it.

2. Whether we get our idea of time from the motion of bodies without us, or from the consciousness of the succession of our own ideas, or both, is not important to this inquiry. Time, in our conceptions, is divisible. The artificial divisions are years, months, days, minutes, seconds, &c. We can conceive of yet smaller portions of duration; and, whether we have given to them artificial names or not, we can conceive no otherwise of duration, than continuance of being, estimated as to degree, by this artificial admeasurement, and therefore as substantially answering to it. It is not denied but that duration is something distinct from these its artificial measures; yet of this every man's consciousness will assure him, that we can form no idea of duration except in this successive manner. But we are told that the eternity of God is a fixed eternal NOW, from which all ideas of succession, of past and future, are to be excluded; and we are called upon to conceive of eternal duration without reference to past or future, and to the exclusion of the idea of that FLOW under which we conceive of time. The proper abstract idea of duration is, however, simple continuance of being, without any reference to the exact degree or extent of it, because in no other way can it be equally applicable to all the substances of which it is the attribute. It may be finite or infinite, momentary or eternal; but that depends upon the substance of which it is the quality, and not upon its own nature. Our own observation and experience teach us how to apply it to ourselves. As to us, duration is dependent and finite; as to God, it is infinite; but in both cases the originality or dependence, the finiteness or infinity of it, arises, not out of the nature of duration itself, but out of other qualities of the subjects respectively.

3. Duration, then, as applied to God, is no more than an extension of the idea as applied to ourselves; and to exhort us to conceive of it as something essentially different, is to require us to conceive what is inconceivable. It is to demand of us to think without ideas. Duration is continuance of existence; continuance of existence is capable of being longer or shorter; and hence necessarily arises the idea of the succession of the minutest points of duration into which we can conceive it divided. Beyond this the mind cannot go, it forms the idea of duration no other way: and if what we call DURATION be any thing different from this in God, it is not duration, properly so called, according to human ideas; it is something else, for which there is no name among men, because there is no idea, and therefore it is impossible to reason about it. As long as meta-physicians use the term, they must take the idea: if they spurn the idea, they have no right to the term, and ought at once to confess that they can go no farther. Dr. Cudworth defines infinity of duration to be nothing else but perfection, as including in it necessary existence and immutability. This, it is true, is as much a definition of the moon, as of infinity of duration; but it is valuable, as it shows that, in the view of this great man, though an advocate of the NUNC STANS, "the standing now," of eternity, we must abandon the term DURATION, if we give up the only idea under which it can be conceived.

4. It follows from this, therefore, that either we must apply the term DURATION to the divine Being in the same sense in which we apply it to creatures, with the extension of the idea to a duration which has no bounds and limits; or blot it out of our creeds, as a word to which our minds, with all the aid they may derive from the labours of metaphysicians, can attach no meaning. The only objection to successive duration as applied to God, which has any plausibility, is, that it seems to imply change; but this wholly arises from confounding two very distinct things; succession in the duration, and change in the substance. Dr. Cudworth appears to have fallen into this error. He speaks of the duration of an imperfect nature, as sliding from the present to the future, expecting something of itself which is not yet in being; and of a perfect nature being essentially immutable, having a permanent and unchanging duration, never losing any thing of itself once present, nor yet running forward to meet something of itself which is not yet in being. Now, though this is a good description of a perfect and immutable nature, it is no description at all of an eternally-enduring nature. Duration implies no loss in the substance of any being, nor addition to it. A perfect nature never loses any thing of itself, nor expects more of itself than is possessed; but this does not arise from the attribute of its duration, however that attribute may be conceived of, but from its perfection and consequent immutability. These attributes do not flow from the duration, but the continuance of the duration from them. The argument is clearly good for nothing, unless it could be proved that successive duration necessarily implies a change in the nature; but that is contradicted by the experience of finite beings,--their natures are not at all determined by their duration, but their duration by their natures; and they exist for a moment, or for ages, according to the nature which their Maker has impressed upon them. If it be said that, at least, successive duration imports that a being loses past duration, and expects the arrival of future existence, we reply, that this is no imperfection at all. Even finite creatures do not feel it to be an imperfection to have existed, and to look for continued and interminable being. It is true, with the past we lose knowledge and pleasure; and expecting in all future periods

increase of knowledge and happiness, we are reminded by that of our present imperfection; but this imperfection does not arise from our successive and flowing duration, and we never refer it to that. It is not the past which takes away our knowledge and pleasure; nor future duration, simply considered, which will confer the increase of both. Our imperfections arise out of the essential nature of our being, not out of the manner in which our being is continued. It is not the flow of our duration, but the flow of our nature, which produces these effects. On the contrary, we think that the idea of our successive duration, that is of continuance, is an advantage, and not a defect. Let all ideas of continuance be banished from the mind, let there be to us a NUNC SEMPER STANS, during the whole of our being, and we appear to gain nothing,--our pleasures surely are not diminished by the idea of successive duration being added to present enjoyment: that they have been, and still remain, and will continue, on the contrary, greatly heightens them. Without the idea of a flowing duration, we could have no such measure of the continuance of our pleasures; and this we should consider an abatement of our happiness. What is so obvious an excellency in the spirit of man, and in angelic natures, can never be thought an imperfection in God, when joined with a nature essentially perfect and immutable.

5. But it may be said, that "eternal duration, considered as successive, is only an artificial manner of measuring and conceiving of duration; and is no more eternal duration itself than minutes and moments, the artificial measures of time, are time itself." Were this granted, the question would still be, whether there is any thing in duration considered generally, or in time considered specially, which corresponds to these artificial methods of measuring and conceiving of them. The ocean is measured by leagues; and the extension of the ocean, and the measure of it, are distinct; they, nevertheless, answer to each other. Leagues are the nominal divisions of an extended surface; but there is a real extension, which answers to the artificial conception and admeasurement of it. In like manner, days, and hours, and moments, are the measures of time: but there is either something in time which answers to these measures; or not only the measure, but the thing itself, is artificial--an imaginary creation. If any man will contend, that the period of duration which we call TIME is nothing, no farther dispute can be held with him; and he may be left to deny also the existence of matter, and to enjoy his philosophic revel in an ideal world. We apply the same argument to duration generally, whether finite or infinite. Minutes and moments, or smaller portions, for which we have no name, may be artificial things, adopted to aid our conceptions; but conceptions of what? Not of any thing standing still, but of something going on. Of duration we have no other conception; and if there be nothing in nature which answers to this conception, then is duration itself imaginary, and we discourse about nothing. If the duration of the divine Being admits not of past, present, and future, one of these two consequences must follow,--that no such attribute as that of eternity belongs to him,--or that there is no power in the human mind to conceive of it. In either case, the Scriptures are greatly impugned; for "He who WAS, and IS, and IS TO COME," is a revelation of the eternity of God, which is then in no sense true. It is not true, if used literally: and it is as little so, if the language be figurative; for the figure rests on no basis, it illustrates nothing, it misleads. It is, however, to be remembered, that the eternal, supreme cause, must of necessity have such a perfect, independent, unchangeable comprehension of all things, that there can be no one point or instant of his eternal duration, wherein all things that are past, present, and to come, will not be as entirely known and represented to him in one single thought or view, and all things present and future be equally entirely in his power and direction; as if there was really no succession at all, but all things were actually present at once.

6. The Hebrew word for eternity is שלם. This is its proper sense; but, as Gesenius observes, as with us in common life, it is often used in an inaccurate or loose manner to express a very long space of time. So it is applied to the Jewish priesthood; to the Mosaic ordinances; to the possession of the land of Canaan; to the hills and mountains; to the earth, &c. These must, however, be considered as exceptions to predominant and certain usage.

ETHAN, the Ezrahite, one of the wisest men of his time; nevertheless, Solomon was wiser than he, 1 Kings iv, 31. The eighty-ninth psalm bears the name of Ethan the Ezrahite. This Ethan, and Ethan son of Kishi, of the tribe of Levi, and of the family of Merari, are the same person, 1 Chron. vi, 44. He was called likewise Idithun, and appears under this name in the titles to several psalms. He was a principal master of the temple music, 1 Chron. xv, 17, &c.

ETHANIM, one of the Hebrew months, 1 Kings viii, 2. In this month the temple of Solomon was dedicated. After the Jews returned from the captivity, the month Ethanim was called Tisri, which answers to our September.

ETHIOPIA. See Cush.

EUCHARIST, the sacrament of the Lord's Supper. The word, in its original Greek, εὐχαρίςια, properly signifies GIVING THANKS; from the hymns and thanksgivings which accompanied that holy service in the primitive church. See Lord's Supper.

EUNICE, the mother of Timothy, who was a Jewess by birth, but married to a Greek, Timothy's father, 2 Tim. i, 5. Eunice had been converted to Christianity by some other preacher, Acts xvi, 1, 2, and not by St. Paul; for when that Apostle came to Lystra, he found there Eunice and Timothy, already far advanced in grace and virtue.

EUNUCH. The word signifies, one who guards the bed. In the courts of eastern kings, the care of the beds and apartments belonging to princes and princesses, was generally committed to eunuchs; but they had the charge chiefly of the princesses, who lived secluded. The Hebrew SARIS signifies a real eunuch, whether naturally born such, or rendered such. But in Scripture this word often denotes an officer belonging to a prince, attending his court, and employed in the interior of his palace, as a name of office and dignity. In the Persian and Turkish courts, the principal employments are at this day possessed by real eunuchs. Our Saviour speaks of men who "made themselves eunuchs for the kingdom of heaven," Matt. xix, 12; that is, who, from a religious motive, renounced marriage or carnal pleasures.

EUPHRATES, a river of Asiatic Turkey, which rises from the mountains of Armenia, as some have said, in two streams, a few miles to the north-east of Erzeron, the streams uniting to the south-west near that city; and chiefly pursuing a south-west direction to Semisat, where it would fall into the Mediterranean, if not prevented by a high range of mountains. In this part of its course the Euphrates is joined by the Morad, a stream almost doubling in length that of the Euphrates, so that the latter river might more justly be said to spring from Mount Ararat, about one hundred and sixty British miles to the east of the imputed source. At Semisat, the ancient Samosata, this noble river assumes a southerly direction, then runs an extensive course to the south-east, and after receiving the Tigris, falls by two or three mouths into the gulf of Persia, about fifty miles south-east of Bassora; north latitude 29° 50´; east longitude 66° 55´. The comparative course of the Euphrates may be estimated at about one thousand four hundred British miles. This river is navigable for a considerable distance from the sea. In its course it separates Aladulia from Armenia, Syria from Diarbekir, and Diarbekir from Arabia, and passing through the Arabian Irak, joins the Tigris. The Euphrates and Tigris, the most considerable as well as the most renowned rivers of western Asia, are remarkable for their rising within a few miles of each other, running the same course, never being more than one hundred and fifty miles asunder, and sometimes, before their final junction, approaching within fifteen miles of each other, as in the latitude of Bagdad. The space included between the two is the ancient country of Mesopotamia. But the Euphrates is by far the more noble river of the two. Sir R. K. Porter, describing this river in its course through the ruins of Babylon, observes, "The whole view was particularly solemn. The majestic stream of the Euphrates wandering in solitude, like a pilgrim monarch through the silent ruins of his devastated kingdom, still appeared a noble river, even under all the disadvantages of its desert-tracked course. Its banks were hoary with reeds; and the grey osier willows were yet there, on which the captives of Israel hung up their harps, and, while Jerusalem was not, refused to be comforted." The Scripture calls it "the great river," and assigns it for the eastern boundary of that land which God promised to the Israelites, Deut. i, 7; Joshua i, 4.

EUROCLYDON, the Greek name for the north-east wind, very dangerous at sea, of the nature of a whirlwind, which falls of a sudden upon ships, Acts xxvii, 14. The same wind is now called a Levanter.

EUTYCHIANS, a denomination which arose in the fifth century, and were so called from Eutyches, abbot of a certain convent of monks at Constantinople. The Nestorians having explained the two natures in Christ in such a manner as, in the opinion of many, to make them equivalent to two persons, which was an evident absurdity, Eutyches, to avoid this error, fell into the opposite extreme, and maintained that there was only one nature in Jesus Christ, the divine nature, which, according to him, had so entirely swallowed up the human, that the latter could not be distinguished. Hence it was inferred that according to this system our Lord had nothing of humanity but the appearance.

EVANGELISTS, the inspired authors of the Gospels. The word is derived from the Greek, εὐαγτελιον, formed of εὖ, BENE, "well," and ἄγτελος, ANGEL, MESSENGER. The name of evangelists is said by some to have been given in the ancient church to such as preached the Gospel without being attached to any particular church, being either commissioned by the Apostles to instruct the nations, or, of their own accord, abandoning every worldly attachment, consecrated themselves to the sacred office of preaching the Gospel. In which sense these interpreters think it is that St. Philip, who was one of the seven deacons, is called "the evangelist" in Acts xxi, 8; and that St. Paul, writing to Timothy, bids him do the work of an evangelist, 2 Tim. iv, 5. It is, however, to be remarked, that the office in which the evangelists chiefly present themselves to our notice in the New Testament, is that of assistants to the Apostles; or, as they might be termed vice apostles, who acted under their authority and direction. As they were directed to ordain pastors or bishops in the churches, but had no authority given them to ordain successors to themselves in their particular office as evangelists, whatever it might be, they must be considered as but temporary officers in the church, like the Apostles and prophets. The term evangelist is, at present, confined to the writers of the four Gospels.

EVE, the first woman. She was called הוה, Gen. iii, 20, a word that signifies LIFE, because she was to be the mother of all that live. Our translators, therefore, might have called her LIFE, as the Septuagint, who render the Hebrew word by Ζωὴ. Soon after the expulsion of the first pair from paradise, Eve conceived and bare a son; and imagining, as is probable, that she had given birth to the promised seed, she called his name Cain, which signifies POSSESSION, saying, "I have gotten a man from the Lord." She afterward had Abel, and some daughters, and then Seth. The Scriptures name only these three sons of Adam and Eve, but sufficiently inform us, Gen. v, 4, that they had many more, saying, that "Adam lived, after he had begotten Seth, eight hundred years, and begat sons and daughters." See Adam.

EVIL is distinguished into natural and moral. Natural evil is whatever destroys or any way disturbs the perfection of natural beings, such as blindness, diseases, death, &c. Moral evil is the disagreement between the actions of a moral agent, and the rule of those actions, whatever it be. Applied to choice, or acting contrary to the moral or revealed laws of the Deity, it is termed WICKEDNESS, or SIN. Applied to an act contrary to a mere rule of fitness, it is called a FAULT. The question concerning the origin of evil has very much perplexed philosophers and divines, both ancient and modern. Plato, for the solution of this question, maintained, that matter, from its nature, possesses a blind and refractory force, from which arises in it a propensity to disorder and deformity; and that this is the cause of all the imperfection which appears in the works of God, and the origin of evil. Matter, he conceives, resists the will of the supreme Artificer, so that he cannot possibly execute his designs; and this is the cause of the mixture of good and evil, which is found in the material world. "It cannot be," says he, "that evil should be destroyed, for there must always be something contrary to good;" and again, "God wills, as far as it is possible, every thing good, and nothing evil." What that property of matter is which opposes the wise and benevolent intentions of the first Intelligence, Plato has not clearly explained; but he speaks of it as ξύμφυτος ἐπιθυμία, an innate propensity to disorder, and says, that before nature was adorned with its present beautiful forms, it was inclined to confusion and deformity, and that from this habitude arises all the evil which happens in the world. Plutarch supposes the Platonic notion to be, that there is in matter an unconscious, irrational soul; and this supposition has been adopted by several modern writers. But the writings of Plato afford no evidence that he conceived the imperfection of matter to arise from any cause distinct from its nature. Such a notion is incongruous with Plato's general system, and is contrary to the doctrine of the Pythagorean school, to which he was probably indebted for his notions on this subject; for the philosophers of that sect held that motion is the effect of a power essential to matter. Some of the Stoics adopted the notion of the Platonists concerning the origin of evil, and ascribed it to the defective nature of matter, which it is not in the power of the great Artificer to change; asserting, that imperfections appear in the world, not through any defect of skill in its author, but because matter will not admit of the accomplishment of his designs. But it was perceived by others, that this hypothesis was inconsistent with the fundamental doctrine of the Stoics concerning nature. For since, according to their system, matter itself receives all its qualities from God, if its defects be the cause of evil, these defects must be ultimately ascribed to him. No other way of relieving this difficulty remained, than to have recourse to fate, and say, that evil was the necessary consequence of that eternal necessity to which the great whole, comprehending both God and matter, is subject. Thus, when Chrysippus was asked whether diseases were to be ascribed to Divine providence, he replied that it was not the intention of nature that these things should happen; nor were they conformable to the will of the Author of nature and Parent of all good things; but that, in framing the world, some inconveniences had adhered by necessary consequence, to his wise and useful plan. To others the question concerning the origin of evil appeared so intricate and difficult, that, finding themselves unequal to the solution of it, they denied either that there is any God at all, or, at least, any author or governor of the world. The Epicureans belonged to this class; nor does Lucretius allege any other reason for denying the system of the world to be the production of a Deity beside its being so very faulty. Others again judged it to be more rational to assign a double cause of visible effects, than to assign no cause at all; as nothing, indeed, can be more absurd than to admit actions and effects without any agent and cause. These persons perceiving a mixture of good and evil, and being persuaded that so many inconsistencies and disorders could not proceed from a good being, supposed the existence of a malevolent principle, or god, directly contrary to the good one; hence they derived corruption and death, diseases, griefs, mischiefs, frauds, and villanies, while from the good being they deduced nothing but good. This opinion was held by many of the ancients; by the Persian magi, Manicheans, Paulicians, &c.

2. Dr. Samuel Clarke, in his "Demonstration of the Being and Attributes of God," deduces from the possibility and real existence of human liberty an answer to the question, What is the cause and original of evil? For liberty, he says, implying a natural power of doing evil, as well as good; and the imperfect nature of finite beings making it possible for them to abuse this their liberty to an actual commission of evil; and it being necessary to the order and beauty of the whole, and for displaying the infinite wisdom of the Creator, that there should be different and various degrees of creatures, whereof, consequently, some must be less perfect than others; hence there necessarily arises a possibility of evil, notwithstanding that the Creator is infinitely good. In short thus: all that we call evil is either an evil of imperfection, as the want of certain faculties and excellencies which other creatures have; or natural evil, as pain, death, and the like; or moral evil, as all kinds of vice. The first of these is not properly an evil: for every power, faculty, or perfection, which any creature enjoys, being the free gift of God, which he was no more obliged to bestow, than he was to confer being or existence itself, it is plain the want of any certain faculty or perfection in any kind of creatures which never belonged to their nature, is no more an evil to them than their never having been created, or brought into being at all, could properly have been called an evil. The second kind of evil, which we call natural evil, is either a necessary consequence of the former; as death, to a creature on whose nature immortality was never conferred; and then it is no more properly an evil than the former; or else it is counterpoised, in the whole, with as great or greater good, as the afflictions and sufferings of good men, and then also it is not properly an evil; or else, lastly, it is a punishment; and then it is a necessary consequent of the third and last sort of evil, namely, moral evil. And this arises wholly from the abuse of liberty, which God gave to his creatures for other purposes, and which it was reasonable and fit to give them for the perfection and order of the whole creation; only they, contrary to God's intention and command, have abused what was necessary for the perfection of the whole, to the corruption and depravation of themselves. And thus all sorts of evils have entered into the world, without any

diminution to the infinite goodness of its Creator and Governor.

3. This is obviously all the answer which the question respecting the origin of evil is capable of receiving. It brings us to the point to which the Scriptures themselves lead us. And though many questions may yet be asked, respecting a subject so mysterious as the permission of evil by the Supreme Being, this is a part of his COUNSELS of which we can have no cognizance, unless he is pleased to reveal them; and as revelation is silent upon this subject, except generally, that all his acts, his permissive ones as well as others, are "wise, and just, and good," we may rest assured, that beyond what is revealed, human wisdom in the present state can never penetrate.

EXCOMMUNICATION, is the judicial exclusion of offenders from the religious rites and other privileges of the particular community to which they belong. Founded in the natural right which every society possesses to guard its laws and privileges from violation and abuse by the infliction of salutary discipline, proportioned to the nature of the offences committed against them, it has found a place, in one form or another, under every system of religion, whether human or divine. That it has been made an engine for the gratification of private malice and revenge, and been perverted to purposes the most unjustifiable and even diabolical, the history of the world but too lamentably proves; yet this, though unquestionably a consideration which ought to inculcate the necessity of prudence, as well as impartiality and temperance in the use of it, affords no valid argument against its legitimate exercise. From St. Paul's writings we learn that the early excommunication was effected by the offender not being allowed to "eat" with the church, that is, to partake of the Lord's Supper, the sign of communion. In the early ages of the primitive church also, this branch of discipline was exercised with moderation, which, however, gradually gave place to an undue severity. From Tertullian's "Apology" we learn, that the crimes which in his time subjected to exclusion from Christian privileges, were murder, idolatry, theft, fraud, lying, blasphemy, adultery, fornication, and the like: and in Origen's treatise against Celsus, we are informed that such persons were expelled from the communion of the church, and lamented as lost and dead unto God; [UT PERDITOS DEOQUE MORTUOS;] but that on making confession and giving evidence of penitence, they were received back as restored to life. It was at the same time specially ordained, that no such delinquent, however suitably qualified in other respects, could be afterward admitted to any ecclesiastical office. But it does not appear that the infliction of this discipline was accompanied with any of those forms of excommunication, of delivering over to Satan, or of solemn execration, which were usual among the Jews, and subsequently introduced into them by the Romish church. The authors and followers of heretical opinions which had been condemned, were also subject to this penalty; and it was sometimes inflicted on whole congregations when they were judged to have departed from the faith. In this latter case, however, the sentence seldom went farther than the interdiction of correspondence with these churches, or of spiritual communication between their respective pastors. To the same exclusion from religious privileges, those unhappy persons were doomed, who, whether from choice or from compulsion, had polluted themselves, after their baptism, by any act of idolatrous worship; and the penance enjoined on such persons, before they could be restored to communion, was often peculiarly severe. The consequences of excommunication, even then, were of a temporal as well as a spiritual nature. The person against whom it was pronounced, was denied all share in the oblations of his brethren; the ties both of religious and of private friendship were dissolved; he found himself an object of abhorrence to those whom he most esteemed, and by whom he had been most tenderly beloved; and, as far as expulsion from a society held in universal veneration could imprint on his character a mark of disgrace, he was shunned or suspected by the generality of mankind.

2. It was not, however, till churchmen began to unite temporal with spiritual power, that any penal effects of a civil kind became consequent on their sentences of excommunication; and that this ghostly artillery was not less frequently employed for the purposes of lawless ambition and ecclesiastical domination, than for the just punishment of impenitent delinquents, and the general edification of the faithful. But as soon as this union took place, and in exact proportion to the degree in which the papal system rose to its predominance over the civil rights as well as the consciences of men, the list of offences which subjected their perpetrators to excommunication, was multiplied; and the severity of its inflictions, with their penal effects, increased in the same ratio. The slightest injury, or even insult, sustained by an ecclesiastic, was deemed a sufficient cause for the promulgation of an anathema. Whole families, and even provinces, were prohibited from engaging in any religious exercise, and cursed with the most tremendous denunciations of divine vengeance. Nor were kings and emperors secure against these thunders of the church; their subjects were, on many occasions, declared, by a papal bull, to be absolved from allegiance to them; and all who should dare to support them, menaced with a similar judgment. These terrors have passed away; the true Scriptural excommunication ought to be maintained in every church; which is the prohibition of immoral and apostate persons from the use of those religious rites which indicate "the communion of saints," but without any temporal penalty.

EXODUS, from ἐξ, OUT, and ὁδὸς, A WAY, the name of the second book of Moses, and is so called in the Greek version because it relates to the departure of the Israelites out of Egypt. It comprehends the history of about a hundred and forty-five years; and the principal events contained in it are, the bondage of the Israelites in Egypt, and their miraculous deliverance by the hand of Moses; their entrance into the wilderness of Sinai; the promulgation of the law, and the building of the tabernacle. See Pentateuch.

EXPIATION, a religious act, by which satisfaction or atonement is made for the commission of some crime, the guilt done away, and the obligation to punishment cancelled. The chief methods of expiation among the Jews were by sacrifices; and it is important always to recollect that the Levitical sacrifices were of an expiatory character; because as among the Jews sacrifices were unquestionably of divine original, and as the terms taken from them are found applied so frequently to Christ and to his sufferings in the New Testament, they serve to explain that peculiarity under which the Apostles regarded the death of Christ, and afford additional proof that it was considered by them as a sacrifice of expiation, as the grand universal sin-offering for the whole world. For our Lord is announced by John as "the Lamb of God;" and that not with reference to meekness or any other moral virtue; but with an accompanying phrase, which would communicate to a Jew the full sacrificial sense of the term employed, "the Lamb of God, which taketh away the sin of the world." He is called "our Passover, sacrificed for us." He is said to have given "himself for us, an offering and a sacrifice to God, for a sweet-smelling savour." As a priest, it was necessary "he should have somewhat to offer;" and he offered "himself," "his own blood," to which is ascribed the washing away of sin, and our eternal redemption. He is declared to have "put away sin by the sacrifice of himself," to have "by himself purged our sins," to have "sanctified the people by his own blood," to have "offered to God one sacrifice for sins." Add to these, and to innumerable other similar expressions and allusions, the argument of the Apostle in the Epistle to the Hebrews, in which, by proving at length, that the sacrifice of Christ was superior in efficacy to the sacrifices of the law, he most unequivocally assumes, that the death of Christ was a sacrifice and sin-offering; for without that it would no more have been capable of comparison with the sacrifices of the law, than the death of John the Baptist, St. Stephen, or St. James, all martyrs and sufferers for the truth, who had recently sealed their testimony with their blood. This very comparison, we may affirm, is utterly unaccountable and absurd on any hypothesis which denies the sacrifice of Christ; for what relation could his death have to the Levitical immolations and offerings, if it had no sacrificial character? Nothing could, in fact, be more misleading, and even absurd, than to apply those terms which, both among Jews and Gentiles, were in use to express the various processes and means of atonement and piacular propitiation, if the Apostles and Christ himself did not intend to represent his death strictly as an expiation for sin:--misleading, because such would be the natural and necessary inference from the terms themselves, which had acquired this as their established meaning:--and absurd, because if, as Socinians say, they used them metaphorically, there was not even an ideal resemblance between the figure and that which it was intended to illustrate. So totally irrelevant, indeed, will those terms appear to any notion entertained of the death of Christ which excludes its expiatory character, that to assume that our Lord and his Apostles used them as metaphors, is profanely to assume them to be such writers as would not in any other case be tolerated; writers wholly unacquainted with the commonest rules of language, and therefore wholly unfit to be teachers of others, and that not only in religion but in things of inferior importance.

2. The use of such terms, we have said, would not only be wholly absurd, but criminally misleading to the Gentiles, as well as to the Jews, who were first converted to Christianity. To them the notion of propitiatory offerings, offerings to avert the displeasure of the gods, and which expiated the crimes of offenders, was most familiar, and terms corresponding to it were in constant use. The bold denial of this by Dr. Priestley might well bring upon him the reproof of Archbishop Magee, who, after establishing this point from the Greek and Latin writers, observes, "So clearly does their language announce the notion of a propitiatory atonement, that if we would avoid an imputation on Dr. Priestley's fairness, we are driven, of necessity, to question the extent of his acquaintance with those writers." The reader may consult the instances given by this writer, in No. 5 of his "Illustrations," appended to his "Discourses on the Atonement;" and also the tenth chapter of Grotius "*De Satisfactione*," whose learning has most amply illustrated and firmly settled this view of the Heathen sacrifices. The use to be made of this in the argument is, that as the Apostles found the very terms they used with reference to the nature and efficacy of the death of Christ, fixed in an expiatory signification among the Greeks, they could not, in honesty, use them in a distant figurative sense, much less in a contrary one, without giving their readers due notice of their having invested them with a new import. From ἄγος, A POLLUTION, AN IMPURITY, which was to be expiated by sacrifice, are derived ἁγνίζω and ἁγιάζω, which denote the act of expiation; καθαίρω, too, TO PURIFY, CLEANSE, is applied to the effect of expiation; and ἱλάσκομαι denotes the method of propitiating the gods by sacrifice. These, and other words of similar import, are used by the authors of the Septuagint, and by the Evangelists and Apostles; but they give no premonition of using them in any strange and altered sense; and when they apply them to the death of Christ, they must, therefore, be understood to use them in their received meaning. In like manner the Jews had their expiatory sacrifices, and the terms and phrases used in them are, in like manner, employed by the Apostles to characterize the death of their Lord; and they would have been as guilty of misleading their Jewish as their Gentile readers, had they employed them in a new sense, and without warning, which, unquestionably, they never gave.

3. As to the expiatory nature of the sacrifices of the law, it is not required by the argument to show that ALL the Levitical offerings were of this character. There were also offerings for persons and for things prescribed for purification, which were incidental; but even they grew out of the leading notion of expiatory sacrifice, and that legal purification which resulted from the forgiveness of sins. It is enough to prove, that the grand and eminent sacrifices of the Jews were strictly expiatory, and that by them the offerers were released from punishment and death, for which ends they were appointed

by the Lawgiver. When we speak, too, of vicarious sacrifice, we do not mean either, on the one hand, such a substitution as that the victim should bear the same quantum of pain and suffering as the offender himself; or, on the other, that it was put in the place of the offender as a mere symbolical act, by which he confessed his desert of punishment; but A SUBSTITUTION MADE BY DIVINE APPOINTMENT, by which the victim was exposed to sufferings and death instead of the offender, in virtue of which the offender himself was released. With this view, one can scarcely conceive why so able a writer as Archbishop Magee should prefer to use the term, "vicarious IMPORT," rather than the simple and established term, "vicarious;" since the Antinomian notion of substitution may be otherwise sufficiently guarded against, and the phrase "vicarious IMPORT" is certainly capable of being resolved into that figurative notion of mere symbolical action, which, however plausible, does in fact deprive the ancient sacrifices of their TYPICAL, and the oblation of Christ of its REAL, efficacy. Vicarious acting, is acting for another; vicarious suffering, is suffering for another; but the nature and circumstances of that suffering in the case of Christ are to be determined by the doctrine of Scripture at large, and not wholly by the term itself, which is, however, useful for this purpose, (and therefore to be preserved,) that it indicates the sense in which those who use it understand the declaration of Scripture, "Christ died for us," so as that he died not merely for our BENEFIT, but IN OUR STEAD; in other words, that, but for his having died, those who believe in him would personally have suffered that death which is the penalty of every violation of the law of God.

4. That sacrifices under the law were expiatory and vicarious, admits of abundant proof.

The chief objections made to this doctrine are, (1.) That under the law in all capital cases, the offender, upon legal proof or conviction, was doomed to die, and that no sacrifice could exempt him from the penalty. (2.) That in all lower cases to which the law had not attached capital punishment, but pecuniary mulcts, or personal labour or servitude upon their nonpayment, this penalty was to be strictly executed, and none could plead any privilege or exemption on account of sacrifice; and that when sacrifices were ordained with a pecuniary mulct, they are to be regarded in the light of FINE, one part of which was paid to the state, the other to the church. This was the mode of argument adopted by the author of "the Moral Philosopher;" and nothing of weight has been added to these objections since his day. Now, much of this may be granted, without any prejudice to the argument; and, indeed, is no more than the most orthodox writers on this subject have often remarked. The law, under which the Jews were placed, was at once, as to them, both a moral and a political law; and the Lawgiver excepted certain offences from the benefit of pardon, because that would have been exemption from temporal death, which was the state penalty. He therefore would accept no atonement for such transgressions. Blasphemy, idolatry, murder, and adultery, were the "presumptuous sins" which were thus exempted; and the reason will be seen in the political relation of the people to God; for in refusing to exempt them from punishment in this world, respect was had to the order and benefit of society. Running parallel, however, with this political application of the law to the Jews as subjects of the theocracy, we see the authority of the moral law kept over them as men and creatures; and if these "presumptuous sins," of blasphemy and idolatry, of murder and adultery, and a few others, were the only capital crimes considered politically, they were not the only capital crimes considered morally; that is, there were other crimes which would have subjected the offender to death, but for this provision of expiatory oblations. The true question then is, whether such sacrifices were appointed by God, and accepted instead of the personal punishment or life of the offender, which otherwise would have been forfeited, as in the other cases; and if so, if the life of animal sacrifices was accepted instead of the life of man, then the notion that "they were mere mulcts and pecuniary penalties" falls to the ground, and the vicarious nature of most of the Levitical oblations is established. That other offences, beside those above mentioned, were capital, that is, exposed the offender to death, is clear from this, that all offences against the law had this capital character. As death was the sanction of the commandment given to Adam, so every one who transgressed any part of the law of Moses became guilty of death; every man was "accursed," that is, devoted to die, who "continued not in all things written in the book of the law." "The man only that doeth these things shall live by them," was the rule; and it was, therefore, to redeem the offenders from this penalty that sacrifices were appointed. So with reference to the great day of expiation, we read, "For on that day shall the priest make an atonement for you, to cleanse you, that you may be clean from all your sins; and this shall be an everlasting statute unto you, to make an atonement for the children of Israel, for all their sins, once a year," Lev. xvi, 30–34.

5. To prove that this was the intention and effect of the annual sacrifices of the Jews, we need do little more than refer to Lev. xvii, 10, 11: "I will set my face against that soul that eateth blood, and will cut him off from among his people. For the life of the flesh is in the blood; and I have given it to you upon the altar to make an atonement for your souls: for it is the blood that maketh an atonement for the soul." Here the blood which is said to make an atonement for the soul, is the blood of the victims; and to make an atonement for the soul is the same as to be a ransom for the soul, as will appear by referring to Exodus xxx, 12–16; and to be a ransom for the soul is to avert death. "They shall give every man a ransom for his soul unto the Lord, that there be no plague among them," by which their lives might be suddenly taken away. The "soul" is also here used obviously for the life; the blood, or the life of the victims in all sacrifices, was substituted for the life of man, to preserve him from death, and the victims were therefore vicarious.

6. The Hebrew word כפר, rendered ATONEMENT, signifying primarily TO COVER, TO OVERSPREAD, has

been the subject of some evasive criticisms. It comes, however, in the secondary sense to signify atonement or propitiation, because the effect of that is to cover, or, in Scripture meaning, to remit offences. The Septuagint also renders it by ἐξιλάσκομαι, TO APPEASE, TO MAKE PROPITIOUS. It is used, indeed, where the means of atonement are not of the sacrificial kind, but these instances equally serve to evince the Scripture sense of the term, in cases of transgression, to be that of reconciling the offended Deity, by averting his displeasure; so that when the atonement for sin is said to be made by sacrifice, no doubt can remain that the sacrifice was strictly a sacrifice of propitiation. Agreeably to this conclusion we find it expressly declared, in the several cases of piacular oblations for transgression of the divine commands, that the sin for which atonement was made by those oblations should be forgiven.

7. As the notion that the sacrifices of the law were not vicarious, but mere mulcts and fines, is overturned by the general appointment of the blood to be an atonement for the souls, the forfeited lives, of men, so also is it contradicted by particular instances. Let us refer to Leviticus v, 15,16: "If a soul commit a trespass, and sin through ignorance in the holy things of the Lord, he shall make amends for the harm that he hath done in the holy thing, and shall add a fifth part thereto, and shall give it to the priest." Here, indeed, is the proper fine for the trespass; but it is added, "He shall bring for his trespass unto the Lord a ram without blemish, and the priest shall make atonement for him with the ram of the trespass offering, and it shall be forgiven him." Thus, then, so far from the sacrifice being the fine, the fine is distinguished from it, and with the ram only was the atonement made to the Lord for his trespass. Nor can the ceremonies with which the trespass and sin offerings were accompanied agree with any notion but that of their vicarious character. The worshipper, conscious of his trespass, brought an animal, his own property, to the door of the tabernacle. This was not a eucharistical act; not a memorial of mercies received, but of sins committed. He laid his hands upon the head of the animal, the symbolical act of transferring punishment; then slew it with his own hand, and delivered it to the priest, who burned the fat and part of the animal upon the altar; and, having sprinkled part of the blood upon the altar, and, in some cases, upon the offerer himself, poured the rest at the bottom of the altar. And thus, we are told, "The priest shall make an atonement for him, as concerning his sin, and it shall be forgiven him." So clearly is it made manifest by these actions, and by the description of their nature and end, that the animal bore the punishment of the offender, and that by this appointment he was reconciled to God, and obtained the forgiveness of his offences.

8. An equally strong proof that the life of the animal sacrifice was accepted in place of the life of man, is afforded by the fact, that atonement was required by the law to be made, by sin offerings and burnt offerings, for even bodily distempers and disorders. It is not necessary to the argument to explain the distinctions between these various oblations; nor yet to inquire into the reason for requiring propitiation to be made for corporal infirmities which, in many cases, could not be avoided. They were, however, thus connected with sin as the cause of all these disorders; and God, who had placed his residence among the Israelites, insisted upon a perfect ceremonial purity, to impress upon them a sense of his moral purity, and the necessity of purification of mind. Whether these were the reasons, or some others not at all discoverable by us, all such unclean persons were liable to death, and were exempted from it only by animal sacrifices. This appears from the conclusion to all the Levitical directions concerning the ceremonial to be observed in all such cases: "Thus shall ye separate the children of Israel from their uncleanness; that they die not in," or by, "their uncleanness, when they defile my tabernacle which is among them," Lev. xv, 31. So that, by virtue of the sin offerings, the children of Israel were saved from a death which otherwise they would have suffered from their uncleanness, and that by substituting the life of the animal for the life of the offerer. Nor can it be urged that death is, in these instances, threatened only as the punishment of not observing these laws of purification; for the reason given in the passage just quoted shows that the threatening of death was not hypothetical upon their not bringing the prescribed purification, but is grounded upon the fact of "defiling the tabernacle of the Lord which was among them," which is supposed to be done by all uncleanness, as such, in the first instance.

9. As a farther proof of the vicarious character of the principal sacrifices of the Mosaic economy, we may instance those statedly offered for the whole congregation. Every day were offered two lambs, one in the morning, and the other in the evening, "for a continual burnt offering." To these daily victims were to be added, weekly, two other lambs for the burnt offering of every Sabbath. None of these could be considered in the light of fines for offences, since they were offered for no particular persons, and must be considered, therefore, unless resolved into an unmeaning ceremony, piacular and vicarious. To pass over, however, the monthly sacrifices, and those offered at the great feasts, it is sufficient to fix upon those, so often alluded to in the Epistle to the Hebrews, offered on the solemn anniversary of expiation. On that day, to other prescribed sacrifices were to be added another ram for a burnt offering, and another goat, the most eminent of the sacrifices for a sin offering, whose blood was to be carried by the high priest into the inner sanctuary, which was not done by the blood of any other victim, except the bullock, which was offered the same day as a sin offering for the family of Aaron. The circumstances of this ceremony, whereby atonement was to be made "for all the sins" of the whole Jewish people, are so strikingly significant, that they deserve a particular detail. On the day appointed for this general expiation, the priest is commanded to offer a bullock and a goat, as sin offerings, the one for himself, and the other for the people; and, having sprinkled the blood of these in due form before the mercy seat, to lead forth a second goat, denominated "the scape-goat;" and, after laying both his hands upon the head of the scape-goat, and confessing over

him all the iniquities of the people, to put them upon the head of the goat, and to send the animal, thus bearing the sins of the people, away into the wilderness; in this manner expressing, by an action which cannot be misunderstood, that the atonement, which, it is affirmed, was to be effected by the sacrifice of the sin offering, consisted in removing from the people their iniquities by this translation of them to the animal. For it is to be remarked, that the ceremony of the scape-goat is not a distinct one: it is a continuation of the process, and is evidently the concluding part and symbolical consummation of the sin offering: so that the transfer of the iniquities of the people upon the head of the scape-goat, and the bearing them away into the wilderness, manifestly imply, that the atonement effected by the sacrifice of the sin offering consisted in the transfer and consequent removal of those iniquities.

10. How, then, is this impressive and singular ceremonial to be explained? Shall we resort to the notion of mulcts and fines? If so, then this and other stated sacrifices must be considered in the light of penal enactments. But this cannot agree with the appointment of such sacrifices annually in succeeding generations: "This shall be a statute for ever unto you." The law appoints a certain day in the year for expiating the sins both of the high priest himself and of the whole congregation, and that for all high priests and all generations of the congregation. Now, could a law be enacted, inflicting a certain penalty, at a certain time, upon a whole people, as well as upon their high priest, thus presuming upon their actual transgression of it? The sacrifice was also for sins in general; and yet the penalty, if it were one, is not greater than individual persons were often obliged to undergo for single trespasses. Nothing, certainly, can be more absurd than this hypothesis. Shall we account for it by saying that sacrifices were offered for the benefit of the worshipper, but exclude the notion of expiation? But here we are obliged to confine the benefit to reconciliation and the taking away of sins, and that by the appointed means of the shedding of blood, and the presentation of blood in the holy place, accompanied by the expressive ceremony of imposition of hands upon the head of the victim; the import of which act is fixed, beyond all controversy, by the priest's confessing over that victim the sins of all the people, and at the same time imprecating upon its head the vengeance due to them, Lev. xvi, 21. Shall we content ourselves with merely saying that this was a symbol? But the question remains, Of what was it the symbol? To determine this, let the several parts of the symbolic action be enumerated. Here is confession of sin; confession before God at the door of the tabernacle; the substitution of a victim; the figurative transfer of sins to that victim; the shedding of blood, which God appointed to make atonement for the soul; the carrying the blood into the holiest place, the very permission of which clearly marked the divine acceptance; the bearing away of iniquity; and the actual reconciliation of the people to God. If, then, this is symbolical, it has nothing correspondent with it, it never had or can have any thing correspondent to it but the sacrificial death of Jesus Christ, and the communication of the benefits of his passion in the forgiveness of sins to those that believe in him, and in their reconciliation with God. Shall we, finally, say that those sacrifices had respect, not to God to obtain pardon by expiation, but to the offerer, teaching him moral lessons, and calling forth moral dispositions? We answer, that this hypothesis leaves many of the essential circumstances of the ceremonial wholly unaccounted for. The tabernacle and temple were erected for the residence of God, by his own command. There it was his will to be approached, and to these sacred places the victims were required to be brought. Any where else they might as well have been offered, if they had had respect only to the offerer; but they were required to be brought to God, to be offered according to a prescribed ritual, and by an order of men appointed for that purpose. Now truly there is no reason why they should be offered in the sanctuary rather than in any other place, except that they were offered to the Inhabitant of the sanctuary; nor could they be offered in his presence without having respect to him. There were some victims whose blood, on the day of atonement, was to be carried into the inner sanctuary; but for what purpose can we suppose the blood to have been carried into the most secret place of the divine residence, except to obtain the favour of Him in whose presence it was sprinkled? To this we may add, that the reason given for these sacred services is not in any case a mere moral effect to be produced upon the minds of the worshippers: they were "to make atonement," that is, to avert God's displeasure, that the people might not "die."

11. We may find, also, another more explicit illustration in the sacrifice of the passover. The sacrificial character of this offering is strongly marked; for it was an offering brought to the tabernacle; it was slain in the sanctuary; and the blood was sprinkled upon the altar by the priests. It derives its name from the passing over and sparing of the houses of the Israelites, on the door posts of which the blood of the immolated lamb was sprinkled, when the first-born in the houses of the Egyptians were slain; and thus we have another instance of life being spared by the instituted means of animal sacrifice. Nor need we confine ourselves to particular instances. "Almost all things," says an Apostle, who surely knew his subject, "are by the law purged with blood; and without shedding of blood there is no remission." Thus, by their very law, and by constant usage, were the Jews familiarized to the notion of expiatory sacrifice, as well as by the history contained in their sacred books, especially in Genesis, which speaks of the vicarious sacrifices offered by the patriarchs; and in the book of Job, in which that patriarch is said to have offered sacrifices for the supposed sins of his sons; and where Eliphaz is commanded, by a divine oracle, to offer a burnt offering for himself and his friends, "lest God should deal with them after their folly."

12. On the sentiments of the uninspired Jewish writers on this point, the substitution of the life of the animal for that of the offerer, and, consequently, the expiatory nature of their sacrifices, Outram has given many quotations from their writings, which the reader may consult in his work on Sacrifices. Two or three only may be adduced by way of specimen. R. Levi Ben Gerson says, "The imposition of the

hands of the offerers was designed to indicate that their sins were removed from themselves, and transferred to the animal." Isaac Ben Arama: "He transfers his sins from himself, and lays them upon the head of the victim." R. Moses Ben Nachman says, with respect to a sinner offering a victim, "It was just that his blood should be shed, and that his body should be burned; but the Creator, of his mercy, accepted the victim from him, as his substitute and ransom; that the blood of the animal might be shed instead of his blood; that is, that the blood of the animal might be given for his life."

13. Full of these ideas of vicarious expiation, then, the Apostles wrote and spoke, and the Jews of their time heard and read, the books of the New Testament. The Socinian pretence is, that the inspired penmen used the sacrificial terms which occur in their writings figuratively; but we not only reply, as before, that they could not do this honestly, unless they had given notice of this new application of the established terms of the Jewish theology; but, if this be assumed, it leaves us wholly at a loss to discover what that really was which they intended to teach by these sacrificial terms and allusions. They are themselves utterly silent as to this point; and the varying theories of those who reject the doctrine of atonement, in fact, confess that their writings afford no solution of the difficulty. If, therefore, it is blasphemous to suppose, on the one hand, that inspired men should write on purpose to mislead; so, on the other, it is utterly inconceivable that, had they only been ordinary writers, they should construct a figurative language out of terms which had a definite and established sense, without giving any intimation at all that they employed them otherwise than in their received meaning, or telling us why they adopted them at all, and more especially when they knew that they must be interpreted, both by Jews and Greeks, in a sense which, if the Socinians are right, was in direct opposition to that which they intended to convey. See Type, Sacrifice, Propitiation.

Expiation, or Atonement, GREAT DAY OF, was the tenth of Tizri, which nearly answers to our September, O. S. The Hebrews call it KIPPUR, or CHIPPUR, "pardon," or "expiation," because the faults of the year were then expiated. The principal ceremonies of this day have been noticed in the preceding article; but a more particular detail may be useful. The high priest, after he had washed, not only his hands and his feet, as usual at common sacrifices, but his whole body, dressed himself in plain linen, like the other priests, wearing neither his purple robe, nor the ephod, nor the pectoral, because he was to expiate his own sins, together with those of the people. He first offered a bullock and a ram for his own sins, and those of the priests: putting his hands on the heads of these victims, he confessed his own sins and the sins of his house. Afterward, he received from the princes of the people two goats for a sin offering, and a ram for a burnt offering, to be offered in the name of the whole nation. The lot determined which of the two goats should be sacrificed, and which set at liberty. After this, the high priest put some of the sacred fire of the altar of burnt offerings into a censer, threw incense upon it, and entered with it, thus smoking, into the sanctuary. After he had perfumed the sanctuary with this incense, he came out, took some of the blood of the young bullock he had sacrificed, carried that also into the sanctuary, and, dipping his fingers in it, sprinkled it seven times between the ark and the vail, which separated the holy from the sanctuary, or most holy. Then he came out a second time, and, beside the altar of burnt offerings, killed the goat which the lot had determined to be the sacrifice. The blood of this goat he carried into the most holy sanctuary, and sprinkled it seven times between the ark and the vail, which separated the holy from the sanctuary: from thence he returned into the court of the tabernacle, and sprinkled both sides of it with the blood of the goat. During all this, none of the priests or people were admitted into the tabernacle, or into the court. After this, the high priest came to the altar of burnt offerings, wetted the four horns of it with the blood of the goat and young bullock, and sprinkled it seven times with the same blood. The sanctuary, the court, and the altar, being thus purified, the high priest directed the goat which was set at liberty by the lot to be brought to him. He put his hand on the goat's head, confessed his own sins and the sins of the people, and then delivered the goat to a person appointed, who was to carry it to some desert place, and let it loose, or, as others say, throw it down some precipice. This being done, the high priest washed himself all over in the tabernacle; and, putting on other clothes, his pontifical dress, that is, his robe of purple, the ephod, and the pectoral, he sacrificed two rams for burnt offering, one for himself, the other for the people. The great day of expiation was a principal solemnity of the Hebrews, a day of rest and strict fasting.

2. There have been various disputes among the learned respecting the meaning of the word AZAZEL, the name of the scape-goat on which the lot fell; but the most prevailing opinion is, that it is derived from GNEZ, "a goat," and AZEL, "to go away." So Buxtorf and many others explain it; and so it was understood by our translators, who have therefore rendered it "a scape-goat." Both goats were typical of Christ: that which was sacrificed is understood to have denoted his death, by means of which sin was expiated; the other, which was to have the sins of the people confessed over him, and, as it were, put upon him, and then to be sent alive into some desert place, where they could see him no more, was intended to signify the effect of the expiation, namely, the removing of guilt, indicating that it should never more be charged on the pardoned sinner.

3. The rites attending the public service of the day of expiation were chiefly performed by the high priest, whose duties were on this day more arduous than on any other day in the year, or perhaps on all the rest united. He was to kill and offer the sacrifices, and sprinkle their blood with his own hands, Lev. xvi, 11–15; and he was to enter with it into the holy of holies, which he was not permitted to do at any other time, Lev. xvi, 2, &c; Heb. ix, 7. It was thus his peculiar privilege to draw nearer to God, or to the tokens of his special presence, to the ark of the covenant, to the mercy

seat, and to the Shekinah, than was allowed to any other mortal. The services which he performed in the inmost sanctuary were, the burning of incense, and sprinkling the blood of the sacrifices before the mercy seat, which he was to do with his finger seven times, Lev. xvi, 14.

4. The spiritual meaning of all these rites has been particularly explained by the Apostle Paul in Hebrews ix. As the high priest was a type of Christ, his laying aside those vestments which were made "for glory and beauty," Exodus xxviii, 2, and appearing in his common garments, which he did on that day, probably signified our Lord's humiliation, when he emptied himself of the glory which he had with the Father before the world was, and "was made in fashion as a man," Phil. ii, 6, 7. The expiatory sacrifices, offered by the high priest, were typical of the true expiation which Christ made for the sins of his people, when he gave himself for them, that he might redeem them from all iniquity, Titus ii, 14; Heb. i, 3; and the priest's confessing the sins of the people over them, and putting them upon the head of the scape-goat, Lev. xvi, 21, was a lively emblem of the imputation of sin to Christ, who "was made sin for us," 2 Cor. v, 21; for "the Lord hath laid on him the iniquity of us all," Isaiah liii, 6. Farther, the goat's "bearing upon him all the iniquities of the Jews into a land not inhabited," Lev. xvi, 22, represents the effect of Christ's sacrifice in delivering his people from guilt and punishment; and the priest's entering into the holy of holies with the blood of the sacrifice is explained by the Apostle to be typical of Christ's ascension into heaven itself, and his making intercession for his people in virtue of the sacrifice of his death.

EYE, the organ of sight. The Hebrews by a curious and bold metaphor call fountains eyes; and they also give the same name to colours: "And the eye," or colour, "of the manna was as the eye," or colour, "of bdellium," Num. xi, 7. By an "evil eye" is meant, envy, jealousy, grudging, ill-judged parsimony; to turn the eyes on any one, is to regard him and his interests; to find grace in any one's eyes, Ruth ii, 10, is to win his friendship and good will. "The eyes of servants look unto the hands of their masters," Psalm cxxiii, 2, to observe the least motion, and obey the least signal. "Their eyes were opened," Gen. iii, 7, they began to comprehend in a new manner. "The wise man's eyes are in his head," Eccles. ii, 14, he does not act by chance. The eye of the soul, in a moral sense, is the intention, the desire. God threatens to set his eyes on the Israelites for evil, and not for good, Amos ix, 4. Nebuchadnezzar recommends to Nebuzaradan that he would "set his eyes" on Jeremiah, and permit him to go where he pleased, Jer. xxxix, 12; xl, 4. Sometimes expressions of this kind are taken in a quite opposite sense: "Behold, the eyes of the Lord are on the sinful kingdom; and I will destroy it," Amos ix, 8. To be eyes to the blind, or to serve them instead of eyes, is sufficiently intelligible, Job xxix, 15. The Persians called those officers of the crown who had the care of the king's interests and the management of his finances, the king's eyes. Eye service is peculiar to slaves, who are governed by fear only; and is to be carefully guarded against by Christians, who ought to serve from a principle of duty and affection, Eph. vi, 6; Col. iii, 22. The lust of the eyes, or the desire of the eyes, comprehends every thing that curiosity, vanity, &c, seek after; every thing that the eyes can present to men given up to their passions, 1 John ii, 16. "Cast ye away every man the abomination of his eyes," Ezek. xx, 7, 8; let not the idols of the Egyptians seduce you. The height or elevation of the eyes is taken for pride, Eccles. xxiii, 5. St. Paul says that the Galatians would willingly have "plucked out their eyes" for him, Gal. iv, 15; expressing the intensity of their zeal, affection, and devotion to him. The Hebrews call the apple of the eye the black daughter of the eye. To keep any thing as the apple of the eye, is to preserve it with particular care, Deut. xxxii, 10: "He that toucheth you, toucheth the apple of mine eye," Zech. ii, 8; attempts to injure me in the tenderest part, which men instinctively defend. The eye and its actions are occasionally transferred to God: "The eyes of the Lord run to and fro through the whole earth," Zech. iv, 10; 2 Chron. xvi, 9; Psalm xi, 4. "The eyes of the Lord are in every place, beholding the evil and the good," Proverbs xv, 3. "The Lord looked down from heaven," &c. We read, Matthew vi, 22, "The light," or lamp, "of the body is the eye; if therefore thine eye be single," simple, clear, ἁπλοῦς, "thy whole body shall be full of light; but if thine eye be evil," distempered, diseased, "thy whole body shall be darkened." The direct allusion may hold to a lantern, or lamp, λύχνος; if the glass of it be clear, the light will shine through it strongly; but if the glass be soiled, dirty, foul, but little light will pass through it: for if they had not glass lanterns, such as we use, they had others in the east made of thin linen, &c: these were very liable to receive spots, stains, and foulnesses, which impeded the passage of the rays of light from the luminary within. So, in the natural eye, if the cornea be single, and the humours clear, the light will act correctly; but if there be a film over the cornea, or a cataract, or a skin between any of the humours, the rays of light will never make any impression on the internal seat of sight, the retina. By analogy, therefore, if the mental eye, the judgment, be honest, virtuous, sincere, well-meaning, pious, it may be considered as enlightening and directing the whole of a person's actions; but if it be perverse, malign, biassed by undue prejudices, or drawn aside by improper views, it darkens the understanding, perverts the conduct, and suffers a man to be misled by his unwise and unruly passions.

2. The orientals, in some cases, deprive the criminal of the light of day, by sealing up his eyes. A son of the great Mogul was actually suffering this punishment when Sir Thomas Roe visited the court of Delhi. The hapless youth was cast into prison, and deprived of the light by some adhesive plaster put upon his eyes, for the space of three years; after which the seal was taken away, that he might with freedom enjoy the light; but he was still detained in prison. Other princes have been treated in a different manner, to prevent them from conspiring against the reigning monarch, or meddling with affairs of state: they have been compelled to swallow opium and other stupifying drugs, to weaken or benumb their faculties, and render them unfit for business. Influenced by such absurd and cruel policy, Shah Abbas, the celebrated Persian monarch, who died in 1629, ordered a

certain quantity of opium to be given every day to his grandson, who was to be his successor, to stupify him, and prevent him from disturbing his government. Such are probably the circumstances alluded to by the prophet: "They have not known nor understood; for he hath shut their eyes that they cannot see; and their hearts that they cannot understand," Isaiah xliv, 18. The verb טוח, rendered in our version, TO SHUT, signifies "to overlay," "to cover over the surface;" thus, the king of Israel prepared three thousand talents of gold, and seven thousand talents of refined silver, to OVERLAY the walls of the temple, 1 Chron. xxix, 4. But it generally signifies to OVERSPREAD, or daub over, as with mortar or plaster, of which Parkhurst quotes a number of examples; a sense which entirely corresponds with the manner in which the eyes of a criminal are sealed up in some parts of the east. The practice of sealing up the eyes, and stupifying a criminal with drugs, seems to have been contemplated by the same prophet in another passage of his book: "Make the heart of this people fat, and make their ears heavy, and shut their eyes, lest they see with their eyes, and hear with their ears, and understand with their heart, and convert and be healed."

3. Deprivation of sight was a very common punishment in the east. It was at first the practice to sear the eyes with a hot iron; but a discovery that this was not effectual, led to the cruel method of taking them out altogether with a sharp-pointed instrument. The objects of this barbarity were usually persons who aspired to the throne, or who were considered likely to make such an attempt. It was also inflicted on chieftains, whom it was desirable to deprive of power without putting them to death. For this reason the hapless Zedekiah was punished with the loss of sight, because he had rebelled against the king of Babylon, and endeavoured to recover the independence of his throne: "Then he put out the eyes of Zedekiah; and the king of Babylon bound him in chains, and carried him to Babylon, and put him in prison till the day of his death," Jer. lii, 11.

4. Females used to paint their eyes. The substance used for this purpose is called in Chaldee כחל, COHOL; by the **LXX**, ςἰβι. Thus we read of Jezebel, 2 Kings ix, 30, that, understanding that Jehu was to enter Samaria, she decked herself for his reception, and (as in the original Hebrew) "put her eyes in paint." This was in conformity to a custom which prevailed in the earliest ages. As large black eyes were thought the finest, the women, to increase their lustre, and to make them appear larger, tinged the corner of their eyelids with the impalpable powder of antimony or of black lead. This was supposed also to give the eyes a brilliancy and humidity, which rendered them either sparkling or languishing, as suited the various passions. The method of performing this among the women in the eastern countries at the present day, as described by Russel, is by a cylindrical piece of silver or ivory, about two inches long, made very smooth, and about the size of a common probe; this is wet with water, and then dipped into a powder finely levigated, made from what appears to be a rich lead ore, and applied to the eye; the lids are closed upon it while it is drawn through between them. This blacks the inside, and leaves a narrow black rim all round the edge. That this was the method practised by the Hebrew women, we infer from Isaiah iii, 22, where the prophet, in his enumeration of the articles which composed the toilets of the delicate and luxurious daughters of Zion, mentions "the wimples and the crisping pins," or bodkins for painting the eyes. The satirist Juvenal describes the same practice:--

ILLE SUPERCILIUM MADIDA FULIGINE TINCTUM

OBLIQUA PRODUCIT ACU, PINGITQUE TREMENTES

ATTOLLENS OCULOS.

Sat. ii.

"These with a tiring pin their eyebrows dye

Till the full arch give lustre to the eye."

Gifford.

This custom is referred to by Jeremiah, iv, 30:--

"Though thou clothest thyself in scarlet,

Though thou adornest thyself with ornaments of gold,

Though thou distendest thine eyes with paint,

In vain shalt thou set forth thy beauty;

Thy paramours have rejected thee."

And Ezekiel, describing the irregularities of the Jewish nation, under the idea of a debauched woman, says, כחלת עיניך, "Thou didst dress thine eyes with cohol;" which the Septuagint render, Ἐςιβίζ8 τοὺς ὀφθαλμοὺς σου, "Thou didst dress thine eyes with stibium," Ezek. xxiii, 40.

5. The passage, Psalm cxxiii, 2, derives a striking illustration from the customs of the east. The servants or slaves in eastern countries attend their masters or mistresses with the profoundest respect. Maundrell observes, that the servants in Turkey stand round their master and his guests in deep silence and perfect order, watching every motion. Pococke says, that at a visit in Egypt every thing is done with the greatest decency and the most profound silence, the slaves or servants standing at the bottom of the room, with their hands joined before them, watching with the utmost attention every motion of their master, who commands them by signs. De la Motraye says, that the eastern ladies are

waited on even at the least wink of the eye, or motion of the fingers, and that in a manner not perceptible to strangers.

EZEKIEL, like his contemporary Jeremiah, was of the sacerdotal race. He was carried away captive to Babylon with Jehoiachim, king of Judah, B. C. 598, and was placed with many others of his countrymen upon the river Chebar, in Mesopotamia, where he was favoured with the divine revelations contained in his book. He began to prophesy in the fifth year of his captivity, and is supposed to have prophesied about twenty-one years. The boldness with which he censured the idolatry and wickedness of his countrymen is said to have cost him his life; but his memory was greatly revered, not only by the Jews, but also by the Medes and Persians. The book which bears his name may be considered under the five following divisions: the first three chapters contain the glorious appearance of God to the prophet, and his solemn appointment to his office, with instructions and encouragements for the discharge of it. From the fourth to the twenty-fourth chapter inclusive, he describes, under a variety of visions and similitudes, the calamities impending over Judea, and the total destruction of the temple and city of Jerusalem, by Nebuchadnezzar, occasionally predicting another period of yet greater desolation, and more general dispersion. From the beginning of the twenty-fifth to the end of the thirty-second chapter, the prophet foretels the conquest and ruin of many nations and cities, which had insulted the Jews in their affliction; of the Ammonites, the Moabites, the Edomites, and Philistines; of Tyre, of Sidon, and Egypt; all of which were to be punished by the same mighty instrument of God's wrath against the wickedness of man; and in these prophecies he not only predicts events which were soon to take place, but he also describes the condition of these several countries in the remote periods of the world. From the thirty-second to the fortieth chapter, he inveighs against the accumulated sins of the Jews collectively, and the murmuring spirit of his captive brethren; exhorts them earnestly to repent of their hypocrisy and wickedness, upon the assurance that God will accept sincere repentance; and comforts them with promises of approaching deliverance under Cyrus; subjoining intimations of some far more glorious, but distant, redemption under the Messiah, though the manner in which it is to be effected is deeply involved in mystery. The last nine chapters contain a remarkable vision of the structure of a new temple and a new polity, applicable in the first instance to the return from the Babylonian captivity, but in its ultimate sense referring to the glory and prosperity of the universal church of Christ. Jerom observes that the visions of Ezekiel are among the things in Scripture hard to be understood. This obscurity arises, in part at least, from the nature and design of the prophecies themselves; they were delivered amidst the gloom of captivity; and though calculated to cheer the drooping spirits of the Jews, and to keep alive a watchful and submissive confidence in the mercy of God, yet they were intended to communicate only such a degree of encouragement as was consistent with a state of punishment, and to excite an indistinct expectation of future blessings, upon condition of repentance and amendment. It ought also to be observed, that the last twelve chapters of this book bear a very strong resemblance to the concluding chapters of the Revelation. The style of this prophet is characterized by Bishop Lowth as bold, vehement, and tragical; as often worked up to a kind of tremendous dignity. He is highly parabolical, and abounds in figures and metaphorical expressions. He may be compared to the Grecian Æschylus; he displays a rough but majestic dignity; an unpolished though noble simplicity; inferior perhaps in originality and elegance to others of the prophets, but unequalled in that force and grandeur for which he is particularly celebrated. He sometimes emphatically and indignantly repeats his sentiments, fully dilates his pictures, and describes the idolatrous manners of his countrymen under the strongest and most exaggerated representations that the license of eastern style would admit. The middle part of the book is in some measure poetical, and contains even some perfect elegies, though his thoughts are in general too irregular and uncontrolled to be chained down to rule, or fettered by language.

EZION-GEBER. See Elath.

EZRA, the author of the book which bears his name, was of the sacerdotal family, being a direct descendant from Aaron, and succeeded Zerubbabel in the government of Judea. This book begins with the repetition of the last two verses of the second book of Chronicles, and carries the Jewish history through a period of seventy-nine years, commencing from the edict of Cyrus. The first six chapters contain an account of the return of the Jews under Zerubbabel, after the captivity of seventy years; of their reëstablishment in Judea; and of the building and dedication of the temple at Jerusalem. In the last four chapters, Ezra relates his own appointment to the government of Judea by Artaxerxes Longimanus, his journey thither from Babylon, the disobedience of the Jews, and the reform which he immediately effected among them. It is to be observed, that between the dedication of the temple and the departure of Ezra, that is, between the sixth and seventh chapters of this book, there was an interval of about fifty-eight years, during which nothing is here related concerning the Jews, except that, contrary to God's command, they intermarried with Gentiles. This book is written in Chaldee from the eighth verse of the fourth chapter to the twenty-seventh verse of the seventh chapter. It is probable that the sacred historian used the Chaldean language in this part of his work, because it contains chiefly letters and decrees written in that language, the original words of which he might think it right to record; and indeed the people, who were recently returned from the Babylonian captivity, were at least as familiar with the Chaldee as they were with the Hebrew tongue.

Till the arrival of Nehemiah, Ezra had the principal authority in Jerusalem. In the second year of Nehemiah's government, the people being assembled in the temple, at the feast of tabernacles, Ezra was desired to read the law. He read it from morning till noon, and was accompanied by Levites who stood beside him, and kept silence. The next day they desired to know of Ezra how they were to celebrate the feast of tabernacles. This he explained, and continued eight days reading the law in the temple. All this was followed by a solemn renewal of the covenant with the Lord. Josephus says that Ezra was buried at Jerusalem; but the Jews believe that he died in Persia, in a second journey to Artaxerxes. His tomb is shown there in the city of Zamuza. He is said to have lived nearly one hundred and twenty years.

Ezra was the restorer and publisher of the Holy Scriptures, after the return of the Jews from the Babylonian captivity. 1. He corrected the errors which had crept into the existing copies of the sacred writings by the negligence or mistake of transcribers. 2. He collected all the books of which the Holy Scriptures then consisted, disposed them in their proper order, and settled the canon of Scripture for his time. 3. He added throughout the books of his edition what appeared necessary for illustrating, connecting, or completing them; and of this we have an instance in the account of the death and burial of Moses, in the last chapter of Deuteronomy. In this work he was assisted by the same Spirit by which they were at first written. 4. He changed the ancient names of several places become obsolete, and substituted for them new names, by which they were at that time called. 5. He wrote out the whole in the Chaldee character; that language having grown into use after the Babylonish captivity. The Jews have an extraordinary esteem for Ezra, and say that if the law had not been given by Moses, Ezra deserved to have been the legislator of the Hebrews.

FABLE, a fiction destitute of truth. St. Paul exhorts Timothy and Titus to shun profane and Jewish fables, 1 Tim. iv, 7; Titus i, 14; as having a tendency to seduce men from the truth. By these fables some understand the reveries of the Gnostics; but the fathers generally, and after them most of the modern commentators, interpret them of the vain traditions of the Jews; especially concerning meats, and other things, to be abstained from as unclean, which our Lord also styles "the doctrines of men," Matt. xv, 9. This sense of the passages is confirmed by their contexts. In another sense, the word is taken to signify an apologue, or instructive tale, intended to convey truth under the concealment of fiction; as Jotham's fable of the trees, Judges ix, 7–15, no doubt by far the oldest fable extant.

FACE. Moses begs of God to show him his face, or to manifest his glory; he replies, "I will make all my goodness pass before thee," and I will proclaim my name; "but my face thou canst not see; for there shall no man see it and live!" The persuasion was very prevalent in the world, that no man could support the sight of Deity, Genesis xvi, 13; xxxii, 30; Exod. xx, 19; xxiv, 11; Judges vi, 22, 23. We read that God spake mouth to mouth with Moses, even apparently, and not in dark speeches, Numbers xii, 8; "The Canaanites have heard that thou art among thy people, and seen face to face," Numbers xiv, 14. God talked with the Hebrews "face to face out of the midst of the fire," Deut. v, 4. All these places are to be understood simply, that God so manifested himself to the Israelites, that he made them hear his voice as distinctly as if he had appeared to them face to face; but not that they actually saw more than the cloud of glory which marked his presence. The face of God denotes sometimes his anger: "The face of the Lord is against them that do evil." "As wax melteth before the fire, so let the wicked perish before the face of God," Psalm lxviii, 2. To turn the face upon any one, especially when connected with the light or shining of the countenance, are beautiful representations of the divine kindness and condescension. To regard the face of any one, is to have respect of persons, Proverbs xxviii, 21. The Apostle, speaking of the difference between our knowledge of God here and in heaven, says, "Now we see through a glass darkly; but then face to face," 1 Cor. xiii, 12; by which he shows the vast difference between our seeing or knowing God and divine things by an imperfect revelation to faith, and by direct vision. This observation of the Apostle is rendered the more striking, when it is recollected that the Roman glass was not fully transparent as ours, but dull and clouded. Of this, specimens may be seen in the glass vessels taken out of Pompeii.

FAITH, in Scripture, is presented to us under two leading views: the first is that of ASSENT or PERSUASION; the second, that of CONFIDENCE or RELIANCE. The former may be separate from the latter, but the latter cannot exist without the former. Faith, in the sense of an intellectual assent to truth, is, by St. James, allowed to devils. A dead, inoperative faith is also supposed, or declared, to be possessed by wicked men, professing Christianity; for our Lord represents persons coming to him at the last day, saying, "Lord, have we not prophesied in thy name" &c, to whom he will say, "Depart from me, I never knew you." And yet the charge in this place does not lie against the sincerity of their belief, but against their conduct as "workers of iniquity." As this distinction is taught in Scripture, so it is also observed in experience: assent to the truths of revealed religion may result from examination and conviction, while yet the spirit and conduct may remain unrenewed and sinful.

2. The faith which is required of us as a condition of salvation always includes confidence or reliance, as well as assent or persuasion. That faith by which "the elders obtained a good report," was of this character; it united ASSENT to the truth of God's revelations with a noble CONFIDENCE in his promise. "Our fathers trusted in thee, and were not confounded." We have a farther illustration in our Lord's address to his disciples upon the withering away of the fig tree: "Have faith in God." He did not question whether they believed the existence of God, but exhorted them to confidence in his promises, when called by him to contend with mountainous difficulties: "Have faith in God; for verily I say unto you, that whosoever shall say unto this mountain, Be thou removed, and be thou cast into the sea, and shall not doubt in his heart, but shall believe (trust)

that these things which he saith shall come to pass, he shall have whatsoever he saith." It was in reference to his simple confidence in Christ's power that our Lord so highly commended the centurion, and said, "I have not found so great faith, no, not in Israel," Matt. viii, 10. And all the instances of faith in the persons miraculously healed by Christ, were also of this kind: their faith was belief in his claims, and also confidence in his goodness and power.

3. That faith in Christ which in the New Testament is connected with salvation, is clearly of this nature; that is, it combines assent with reliance, belief with trust. "Whatsoever ye ask the Father in my name," that is, in dependence upon my interest and merits, "he shall give it you." Christ was preached both to Jews and Gentiles as the object of their trust, because he was preached as the only true sacrifice for sin; and they were required to renounce their dependence upon their own accustomed sacrifices, and to transfer that dependence to his death and mediation,--and "in his name shall the Gentiles trust." He is said to be set forth as a propitiation, "through faith in his blood;" which faith can neither merely mean assent to the historical fact that his blood was shed by a violent death; nor mere assent to the general doctrine that his blood had an atoning quality; but as all expiatory offerings were TRUSTED IN as the means of propitiation both among Jews and Gentiles, faith or trust was now to be exclusively rendered to the blood of Christ, as the divinely appointed sacrifice for sin, and the only refuge of the true penitent.

4. To the most unlettered Christian this then will be very obvious, that true and saving faith in Christ consists both of assent and trust; but this is not a blind and superstitious trust in the sacrifice of Christ, like that of the Heathens in their sacrifices; nor the presumptuous trust of wicked and impenitent men, who depend on Christ to save them in their sins; but such a trust as is exercised according to the authority and direction of the word of God; so that TO KNOW the Gospel in its leading principles, and to have a cordial BELIEF in it, is necessary to that more specific act of faith which is called RELIANCE, or in systematic language, FIDUCIAL ASSENT. The Gospel, as the scheme of man's salvation, declares that he is under the law; that this law of God has been violated by all; and that every man is under sentence of death. Serious consideration of our ways, confession of the fact, and sorrowful conviction of the evil and danger of sin, will, under the influence of divine grace, follow the cordial belief of the testimony of God; and we shall then turn to God with contrite hearts, and earnest prayers, and supplications for his mercy. This is called "repentance toward God;" and repentance being the first subject of evangelical preaching, and then the injunction to believe the Gospel, it is plain, that Christ is only IMMEDIATELY held out, in this divine plan of our redemption, as the object of trust in order to forgiveness to persons in this state of penitence and under this sense of danger. The degree of sorrow for sin, and alarm upon this discovery of our danger as sinners, is no where fixed to a precise standard in Scripture; only it is supposed every where, that it is such as to lead men to inquire earnestly, "What shall I do to be saved?" and with earnest seriousness to use all the appointed means of grace, as those who feel that their salvation is at issue, that they are in a lost condition, and must be pardoned or perish. To all such persons, Christ, as the only atonement for sin, is exhibited as the object of their trust, with the promise of God, "that whosoever believeth in him shall not perish, but have everlasting life." Nothing is required of such but this actual trust in, and personal apprehension or taking hold of, the merits of Christ's death as a sacrifice for sin; and upon their thus believing they are justified, their "faith is counted for righteousness," or, in other words, they are forgiven.

5. This appears to be the plain Scriptural representation of this doctrine; and we may infer from it, (1.) That the faith by which we are justified is not a mere assent to the doctrines of the Gospel, which leaves the heart unmoved and unaffected by a sense of the evil and danger of sin and the desire of salvation, although it supposes this assent; nor, (2.) Is it that more lively and cordial assent to, and belief in, the doctrine of the Gospel, touching our sinful and lost condition, which is wrought in the heart by the Spirit of God, and from which springeth repentance, although this must precede it; nor, (3.) Is it only the assent of the mind to the method by which God justifies the ungodly by faith in the sacrifice of his Son, although this is an element of it; but it is a hearty concurrence of the will and affections with this plan of salvation, which implies a renunciation of every other refuge, and an actual trust in the Saviour, and personal apprehension of his merits: such a belief of the Gospel by the power of the Spirit of God as leads us to come to Christ, to receive Christ, to trust in Christ, and to commit the keeping of our souls into his hands, in humble confidence of his ability and his willingness to save us.

6. This is that qualifying condition to which the promise of God annexes justification; that without which justification would not take place; and in this sense it is that we are justified by faith; not by the merit of faith, but by faith instrumentally as this condition: for its connection with the benefit arises from the merits of Christ and the promise of God. If Christ had not merited, God had not promised; if God had not promised, justification had never followed upon this faith; so that the indissoluble connection of faith and justification is from God's institution, whereby he hath bound himself to give the benefit upon performance of the condition. Yet there is an aptitude in this faith to be made a condition; for no other act can receive Christ as a Priest propitiating and pleading the propitiation and the promise of God for his sake to give the benefit. As receiving Christ and the gracious promise in this manner, it acknowledgeth man's guilt, and so man renounceth all righteousness in himself, and honoureth God the Father, and Christ the Son, the only Redeemer. It glorifies God's mercy and free grace in the highest degree. It acknowledges on earth, as it will be perpetually acknowledged in heaven, that the whole salvation of sinful man, from the beginning to the last degree thereof, whereof there shall be no end, is from God's freest

love, Christ's merit and intercession, his own gracious promise, and the power of his own Holy Spirit.

7. Faith, in Scripture, sometimes is taken for the truth and faithfulness of God, Rom. iii, 3; and it is also taken for the persuasion of the mind as to the lawfulness of things indifferent, Rom. xiv, 22, 23; and it is likewise put for the doctrine of the Gospel, which is the object of faith, Acts xxiv, 24; Phil. i, 27; Jude 3; for the belief and profession of the Gospel, Rom. i, 8; and for fidelity in the performance of promises.

FALL OF MAN. In addition to what is stated on this subject under the article ADAM, it may be necessary to establish the literal sense of the account given of man's fall in the book of Genesis. This account is, that a garden having been planted by the Creator, for the use of man, he was placed in it, "to dress it, and to keep it;"--that in this garden two trees were specially distinguished, one as "the tree of life," the other as "the tree of the knowledge of good and evil;"--that from eating of the latter Adam was restrained by positive interdict, and by the penalty, "In the day thou eatest thereof thou shalt surely die;"--that the serpent, who was more subtle than any beast of the field, tempted the woman to eat, by denying that death would be the consequence, and by assuring her, that her eyes and her husband's eyes "would be opened," and that they would "be as gods, knowing good and evil;"--that the woman took of the fruit, gave of it to her husband, who also ate;--that for this act of disobedience they were expelled from the garden, made subject to death, and laid under other maledictions.

2. That this history should be the subject of much criticism, not only by infidels, but by those who hold false and perverted views of the Christian system, was to be expected. Taken in its natural and obvious sense, along with the comments of the subsequent Scriptures, it teaches the doctrines of the existence of an evil, tempting, invisible spirit, going about seeking whom he may deceive and devour; of the introduction of moral corruptness into human nature, which has been transmitted to all men; and is connected also with the doctrine of a vicarious atonement for sin; and wherever the fundamental truths of the Christian system are denied, attempts will be made so to interpret this part of the Mosaic history as to obscure the testimony which it gives to them, either explicitly, or by just induction. Interpreters have adopted various and often strange theories; but those whose opinions it seems necessary to notice may be divided into such as deny the literal sense of the relation entirely; such as take the account to be in part literal and in part allegorical; and those who, while they contend earnestly for the literal interpretation of every part of the history, consider some of the terms used, and some of the persons introduced, as conveying a meaning more extensive than the letter, and as constituting several symbols of spiritual things and of spiritual beings.

3. Those who have denied the literal sense entirely, and regarded the whole relation as an instructive MYTHOS, or fable, have, as might be expected, when all restraint of authority was thus thrown off from the imagination, themselves adopted very different theories. Thus we have been taught, that this account was intended to teach the evil of yielding to the violence of appetite and to its control over reason; or the introduction of vice in conjunction with knowledge and the artificial refinements of society; or the necessity of keeping the great mass of mankind from acquiring too great a degree of knowledge, as being hurtful to society; or to consider it as another version of the story of the golden age, and its being succeeded by times more vicious and miserable; or as designed, enigmatically, to account for the origin of evil, or of mankind. This catalogue of opinions might be much enlarged: some of them have been held by mere visionaries; others by men of learning, especially by several of the semi-infidel theologians and Biblical critics of Germany; nor has our own country been exempt from this class of bold expositors. How to fix upon the moral of "the fable" is, however, the difficulty; and the great variety of opinion is a sufficient refutation of the general notion assumed by the whole class, since scarcely can two of them be found who adopt the same views, after they have discarded the literal acceptation.

4. But that the account of Moses is to be taken as a matter of real history, and according to its literal import, is established by two considerations, against which, as being facts, nothing can successfully be urged. The first is, that the account of the fall of the first pair is a part of a continuous history. The creation of the world, of man, of woman; the planting of the garden of Eden, and the placing of man there; the duties and prohibitions laid upon him; his disobedience; his expulsion from the garden; the subsequent birth of his children, their lives, and actions, and those of their posterity, down to the flood; and, from that event, to the life of Abraham, are given in the same plain and unadorned narrative; brief, but yet simple; and with no intimation at all, either from the elevation of the style or otherwise, that a fable or allegory is in any part introduced. As this, then, is the case, and the evidence of it lies upon the very face of the history, it is clear, that if the account of the fall be excerpted from the whole narrative as allegorical, any subsequent part, from Abel to Noah, from Noah to Abraham, from Abraham to Moses, may be excerpted for the same reason, which reason is merely this, that it does not agree with the theological opinions of the interpreter; and thus the whole of the Pentateuch may be rejected history, and converted into fable. Either then the account of the fall must be taken as history, or the historical character of the whole five books of Moses must be unsettled; and if none but infidels will go to the latter consequence, then no one who admits the Pentateuch to be a true history generally, can consistently refuse to admit the story of the fall of the first pair to be a narrative of real events, because it is written in the same style, and presents the same character of a continuous record of events. So conclusive has this argument been felt, that the anti-literal interpreters have endeavoured to evade it, by asserting that the part of the history of Moses in question bears marks of being a separate

fragment, more ancient than the Pentateuch itself, and transcribed into it by Moses, the author and compiler of the whole. This point is examined and satisfactorily refuted in Holden's learned and excellent work, entitled, "Dissertation on the Fall of Man;" but it is easy to show, that it would amount to nothing, if granted, in the mind of any who is satisfied on the previous question of the inspiration of the Holy Scriptures. For let it be admitted that Moses, in writing the pentateuchal history, availed himself of the traditions of the patriarchal ages, a supposition not in the least inconsistent with his inspiration or with the absolute truth of his history, since the traditions so introduced have been authenticated by the Holy Spirit; or let it be supposed, which is wholly gratuitous, that he made use of previously existing documents; and that some differences of style in his books may be traced which serve to point out his quotations, which is a position that some of the best Hebraists have denied; yet two things are to be noted: first, that the inspired character of the books of Moses is authenticated by our Lord and his Apostles, so that they must necessarily be wholly true, and free from real contradictions; and, secondly, that to make it any thing to their purpose who contend that the account of the fall is an older document, introduced by Moses, it ought to be shown that it is not written as truly in the narrative style, even if it could be proved to be, in some respects, a different style, as that which precedes and follows it. Now the very literal character of our translation will enable even the unlearned reader to discover this. Whether it be an embodied tradition, or the insertion of a more ancient document, (though there is no foundation at all for the latter supposition,) it is obviously a narrative, and a NARRATIVE as simple as any which precedes or follows it.

5. The other indisputable fact to which I just now adverted, as establishing the literal sense of the history, is that, as such, it is referred to and reasoned upon in various parts of Scripture: "Knowest thou not this of old, since man (Adam) was placed upon earth, that the triumphing of the wicked is short, and the joy of the hypocrite but for a moment?" Job xx, 4, 5. There is no reason to doubt but that this passage refers to the fall and the first sin of man. The date agrees; for the knowledge here taught is said to arise from facts as old as the first placing of man upon earth, and the sudden punishment of the iniquity corresponds to the Mosaic account: "The triumphing of the wicked is short, his joy but for a moment." "If I covered my transgressions as Adam, by hiding mine iniquity in my bosom," Job xxxi, 33. Magee renders the verse,

"Did I cover, like Adam, my transgression,

By hiding in a lurking place mine iniquity?"

and adds, "I agree with Peters, that this contains a reference to the history of the first man, and his endeavours to hide himself after his transgression." Our margin reads, "after the manner of men;" and also the old versions; but the Chaldee paraphrase agrees with our translation, which is also satisfactorily defended by numerous critics. "What is man, that he should be clean? and he which is born of a woman, that he should be righteous?" Job xv, 14. Why not clean? Did God make woman or man unclean at the beginning? If he did, the expostulation would have been more apposite, and much stronger, had the true cause been assigned, and Job had said, "How canst thou expect cleanness in man, whom thou CREATEDST unclean?" But, as the case now stands, the expostulation has a plain reference to the introduction of vanity and corruption by the sin of the woman, and is an evidence that this ancient writer was sensible of the evil consequences of the fall upon the whole race of man. "Eden" and "the garden of the Lord" are also frequently referred to in the prophets. We have the "tree of life" mentioned several times in the Proverbs and in the Revelation. "God," says Solomon, "made man upright." The enemies of Christ and his church are spoken of, both in the Old and New Testaments, under the names of "the serpent," and "the dragon;" and the habit of the serpent to lick the dust is also referred to by Isaiah.

6. If the history of the fall, as recorded by Moses, were an allegory, or any thing but a literal history, several of the above allusions would have no meaning; but the matter is put beyond all possible doubt in the New Testament, unless the same culpable liberties be taken with the interpretation of the words of our Lord and of St. Paul as with those of the Jewish lawgiver. Our Lord says, "Have ye not read, that he which made them at the beginning, made them male and female; and said, For this cause shall a man leave father and mother, and shall cleave to his wife; and they twain shall be one flesh?" Matt. xix, 4, 5. This is an argument on the subject of divorces, and its foundation rests upon two of the facts recorded by Moses: (1.) That God made at first but two human beings, from whom all the rest have sprung. (2.) That the intimacy and indissolubility of the marriage relation rests upon the formation of the woman from the man; for our Lord quotes the words in Genesis, where the obligation of man to cleave to his wife is immediately connected with that circumstance: "And Adam said, This is now bone of my bones, and flesh of my flesh: she shall be called woman, because she was taken out of man. THEREFORE shall a man leave his father and his mother, and shall cleave unto his wife; and they shall be one flesh." This is sufficiently in proof that both our Lord and the Pharisees considered this early part of the history of Moses as a narrative; for, otherwise, it would neither have been a reason, on his part, for the doctrine which he was inculcating, nor have had any force of conviction as to them. "In Adam," says the Apostle Paul, "all die;" "by one man sin entered into the world." "But I fear lest by any means, as the serpent beguiled Eve through his subtlety, so your minds should be corrupted from the simplicity that is in Christ." In the last passage, the instrument of the temptation is said to be a serpent, ὄφις, which is a sufficient answer to those who would make it any other animal; and Eve is represented as being first seduced, according to the account in Genesis. This St. Paul repeats in 1 Tim. ii, 13, 14: "Adam was first formed, then Eve. And

Adam was not deceived," first or immediately, "but the woman being deceived was in the transgression." And he offers this as the reason of an injunction, "Let the woman learn in silence with all subjection." When, therefore, it is considered, that these passages are introduced, not for rhetorical illustration, or in the way of classical quotation, but are made the basis of grave and important reasonings, which embody some of the most important doctrines of the Christian revelation, and of important social duties and points of Christian order and decorum; it would be to charge the writers of the New Testament with the grossest absurdity, nay, with even culpable and unworthy trifling, to suppose them to argue from the history of the fall as a narrative, when they knew it to be an allegory. And if we are, therefore, compelled to allow that it was understood as a real history by our Lord and his inspired Apostles, those speculations of modern critics, which convert it into a parable, stand branded with their true character of infidel and semi-infidel temerity.

7. The effect of the sin or lapse of Adam was to bring him under the wrath of God; to render him liable to pain, disease, and death; to deprive him of primeval holiness; to separate him from communion with God and that spiritual life which was before imparted by God, and on which his holiness alone depended, from the loss of which a total moral disorder and depravation of his soul resulted; and finally to render him liable to everlasting misery. See Original Sin. For the effect of the fall of Adam upon his posterity, see Justification.

FASTING has been practised in all ages, and among all nations, in times of mourning, sorrow, and affliction. We see no example of fasting, properly so called, before Moses. Since the time of Moses, examples of fasting have been very common among the Jews. Joshua and the elders of Israel remained prostrate before the ark from morning till evening, without eating, after Israel was defeated at Ai, Joshua vii, 6. The eleven tribes which fought against that of Benjamin, fell down on their faces before the ark, and so continued till evening without eating, Judges xx, 26. David fasted while the first child he had by Bathsheba was sick, 2 Sam. xii, 16. The Heathens sometimes fasted: the king of Nineveh, terrified by Jonah's preaching, ordered that not only men, but also beasts, should continue without eating or drinking; should be covered with sackcloth, and each after their manner should cry to the Lord, Jonah iii, 5, 6. The Jews, in times of public calamity, appointed extraordinary fasts, and made even the children at the breast fast, Joel ii, 16. Moses fasted forty days upon Mount Horeb, Exod. xxiv, 18. Elijah passed as many days without eating, 1 Kings xix, 8. Our Saviour fasted forty days and forty nights in the wilderness, Matt. iv, 2. These fasts were miraculous, and out of the common rules of nature.

2. Beside the solemn fast of expiation instituted by divine authority, the Jews appointed certain days of humiliation, called the fasts of the congregation. The calamities for which these were enjoined, were a siege, pestilence, diseases, famine, &c. They were observed on the second and fifth days of the week: they began at sunset, and continued till midnight of the following day. On these days they wore sackcloth next the skin, and rent their clothes; they sprinkled ashes on their heads, and neither washed their hands, nor anointed their heads with oil. The synagogues were filled with suppliants, whose prayers were long and mournful, and their countenances dejected with all the marks of sorrow and repentance.

3. As to the fasts observed by Christians, it does not appear by his own practice, or by his commands to his disciples, that our Lord instituted any particular fast. But when the Pharisees reproached him, that his disciples did not fast so often as theirs, or as John the Baptist's, he replied, "Can ye make the children of the bride-chamber fast while the bridegroom is with them? But the days will come when the bridegroom shall be taken away from them, and then shall they fast in those days," Luke v, 34, 35. Fasting is also recommended by our Saviour in his sermon on the mount; not as a stated, but as an occasional, duty of Christians, for the purpose of humbling their minds under the afflicting hand of God; and he requires that this duty be performed in sincerity, and not for the sake of ostentation, Matt. vi, 16.

4. Although Christians, says Dr. Neander, did not by any means retire from the business of life, yet they were accustomed to devote many separate days entirely to examining their own hearts, and pouring them out before God, while they dedicated their life anew to him with uninterrupted prayers, in order that they might again return to their ordinary occupations with a renovated spirit of zeal and seriousness, and with renewed powers of sanctification. These days of holy devotion, days of prayer and penitence, which individual Christians appointed for themselves, according to their individual necessities, were often a kind of fast-days. In order that their sensual feelings might less distract and impede the occupation of their heart with its holy contemplations, they were accustomed on these days to limit their corporeal wants more than usual, or to fast entirely. In the consideration of this, we must not overlook the peculiar nature of that hot climate in which Christianity was first promulgated. That which was spared by their abstinence on these days was applied to the support of the poorer brethren.

FAT. God forbade the Hebrews to eat the fat of beasts: "All the fat is the Lord's. It shall be a perpetual statute for your generations, throughout all your dwellings, that ye eat neither fat nor blood," Lev. iii, 17. Some interpreters understand these words literally, and suppose fat as well as blood to be forbidden. Josephus says Moses forbids only the fat of oxen, goats, sheep, and their species. This agrees with Lev. vii, 23: "Ye shall eat no manner of fat, of ox, or of sheep, or of goat." This is observed by the modern Jews, who think that the fat of other sorts of clean creatures is allowed them, even that of beasts which have died of themselves, conformably to Lev. vii, 24: "And the fat of the beast that dieth of itself, and the fat of that which is torn with beasts, may be used in any other use; but ye shall in nowise eat of it." Others maintain that the law which forbids the use of fat, should be restrained to fat separated from the flesh, such as that which covers the kidneys and the intestines; and this only in the case of its being offered in sacrifice. This is confirmed by Lev. vii, 25: "Whosoever eateth of the fat of the beast of which men offer an offering made by fire unto the Lord, even the soul that eateth it shall be cut off from his people." In the Hebrew style, fat signifies not only that of beasts, but also the richer or prime part of other things: "He should have fed them with the finest" (in Hebrew the fat) "of the wheat." Fat denotes abundance of good things: "I will satiate the souls of the priests with fatness," Jer. xxxi, 14. "My soul shall be satisfied with marrow and fatness," Psalm lxiii, 5. The fat of the earth implies its fruitfulness: "God give thee of the dew of heaven, and the fatness of the earth, and plenty of corn and wine," Gen. xxvii, 28.

FATHER. This word, beside its common acceptation, is taken in Scripture for grandfather, great-grandfather, or the founder of a family, how remote soever. So the Jews in our Saviour's time called Abraham, Isaac, and Jacob, their fathers. Jesus Christ is called the Son of David, though David was many generations distant from him. By father is likewise understood the institutor of a certain profession. Jabal "was father of such as dwell in tents, and such as have cattle." Jubal "was father of all such as handle the harp and organ," or flute, &c, Gen. iv, 20, 21. Huram is called father of the king of Tyre, 2 Chron. ii, 13; and, 2 Chron. iv, 16, even of Solomon, because he was the principal workman, and chief director of their undertakings. The principal prophets were considered as fathers of the younger, who were their disciples, and are called sons of the prophets, 2 Kings ii, 12. Father is a term of respect given by inferiors to superiors. "My father," said Naaman's attendants to him, "if the prophet had bid thee do some great thing," 2 Kings v, 13; and so the king of Israel addresses the prophet Elisha, 2 Kings vi, 21. Rechab, the founder of the Rechabites, is called their father, Jer. xxxv, 6. A man is said to be a father to the poor and orphans, when he supplies their necessities, and sympathizes with their miseries, as a father would do toward them: "I was a father to the poor," says Job, xxix, 16. God declares himself to be the "Father of the fatherless, and Judge of the widow," Psalm lxviii, 5. God is frequently called our heavenly Father, and simply our Father; eminently the Father, Preserver, and Protector of all, especially of those who invoke him, and serve him: "Is he not thy Father that bought thee?" says Moses, Deut. xxxii, 6. Since the coming of Jesus Christ, we have a new right to call God our Father, by reason of the adoption which our Saviour has merited for us, by clothing himself in our humanity, and purchasing us by his death: "Ye have received the Spirit of adoption, whereby we cry, Abba, Father. The Spirit itself beareth witness with our spirit, that we are the children of God," Romans viii, 15. Job entitles God "the Father of rain," Job xxxviii, 28; he produces it, and causes it to fall. The devil is called the father of the wicked and the father of lies, John viii, 44. He deceived Eve and Adam; he introduced sin and falsehood; he inspires his followers with his spirit and sentiments. The father of Sichem, the father of Tekoah, the father of Bethlehem, &c, signify the chief persons who inhabited these cities; he who built or rebuilt them. Adam is the first father, the father of the living; Abraham is the father of the faithful, the father of the circumcision; called also the "father of many nations," because many people sprung from him; as the Jews, Ishmaelites, Arabs, &c. God is called "the Father of spirits," Heb. xii, 9. He not only creates them, but he justifies, sanctifies, and glorifies them, and thus confers upon them eternal happiness.

FATHERS, a term of honour applied to the first and most eminent writers of the Christian church. Those of the first century are called Apostolical fathers; those of the first three centuries, and till the council of Nice, Ante-Nicene; and those later than that council, Post-Nicene. Learned men are not unanimous concerning the degree of esteem which is due to these ancient fathers. Some represent them as the most excellent guides, while others place them in the very lowest rank of moral writers, and treat their precepts and decisions as perfectly insipid, and, in many respects, pernicious. It appears, however, incontestable, that, in the writings of the primitive fathers are many sublime sentiments, judicious thoughts, and several things well adapted to form a religious temper, and to excite pious and virtuous affections. At the same time, it must be confessed, that, after the earliest age, they abound still more with precepts of an excessive and unreasonable austerity, with stoical and academical dictates, with vague and indeterminate notions, and, what is still worse, with decisions absolutely false, and in evident opposition to the commands of Christ. Though the judgment of antiquity in some disputable points may certainly be useful, yet we ought never to consider the writings of the fathers as of equal authority with the Scriptures. In many cases they may be deemed competent witnesses, but we must not confide in their verdict as judges. As Biblical critics they are often fanciful and injudicious, and their principal value consists in this, that the succession of their writings enables us to prove the existence and authenticity of the sacred books, up to the age of the Apostles.

The following is a list of the entire fathers: Contemporaries of the Apostles, Barnabas, Clement of Rome, Hermas, Ignatius, and Polycarp. Papias, A. D. 116; Justin Martyr, 140; Dionysius of Corinth, 170; Tatian, 172; Hegesippus, 173; Melito, 177; Irenæus, 178; Athenagoras, 178; Miltiades, 180; Theophilus, 181; Clement of Alexandria, 194; Tertullian, 200; Minutius Felix, 210; Ammonius, 220; Origen, 230; Firmilian, 233; Dionysius of Alexandria, 247; Cyprian, 248; Novatus, or Novatian, 251; Arnobius, 306; Lactantius, 306; Alexander of Alexandria, 313; Eusebius, 315; Athanasius, 326; Cyril of Jerusalem, 348; Hilary, 354; Epiphanius, 368; Basil, 370; Gregory of Nazianzum, 370; Gregory of Nyssa, 370; Optatus, 370; Ambrose, 374; Philaster, 380; Jerome, 392; Theodore of Mopsuestia, 394; Ruffin, 397; Augustine, 398; Chrysostom, 398; Sulpitius Severus, 401; Cyril of Alexandria, 412; Theodoret, 423; and Gennadius, 494.

Archbishop Wake, in his *Exposition of the Doctrine of the Church of England* has very satisfactorily shown, that the deference paid by Protestants to the Christian fathers of the first three ages, is neither of such an idolatrous description as is generally represented, nor is their authority ever extolled to an equality with that of the Holy Scriptures. "Though we have appealed," he says, "to the churches of the first ages for new proofs of the truth of our doctrine, it is not that we think that the doctors of those times had more right to judge of our faith than those had that followed them; but it is because after a serious examination we have found, that, as for what concerns THE COMMON BELIEF that is among us, they have believed and practised the same things without adding other opinions or superstitions that destroy them,--wherein they have acted conformably to their and our rule, the Word of God: notwithstanding, it cannot be denied, but that they effectually fell into some wrong opinions, as that of the Millenaries and infant communion," &c. The usefulness and necessity of studying the ancient fathers have been defended by many persons eminent for their learning and piety. Archbishop Usher was one who beyond all men then living knew the vast importance of these studies, and had derived the greatest benefits from them. The following brief advice, in the language of Dr. Parr, his erudite biographer, will convey his sentiments on this very interesting subject: "Indeed he had so great an esteem of the ANCIENT AUTHORS, for the acquiring any solid learning, whether sacred or profane, that his advice to young students, either in divinity or antiquity, was, not to spend too much time in epitomes, but to set themselves to read the ancient authors themselves; as, to begin with the FATHERS, and to read them according to the ages in which they lived, (which was the method he had taken himself,) and, together with them, carefully to peruse the CHURCH HISTORIANS that treated of that age in which those fathers lived: by which means the student would be better able to perceive the reason and meaning of divers passages in their writings, (which otherwise would be obscure,) when he knew the original and growth of those heresies and heterodox opinions against which they wrote, and may also better judge what doctrines, ceremonies, and opinions prevailed in the church in every age, and by what means introduced."

FEAR, a painful apprehension of danger. It is sometimes used for the object of fear; as, "the fear of Isaac," that is, the God whom Isaac feared, Gen. xxxi, 42. God says that he will send his fear before his people, to terrify and destroy the inhabitants of Canaan. Job speaks of the terrors of God, as set in array against him, Job vi, 4; the Psalmist, that he had suffered the terrors of the Lord with a troubled mind, Psalm lxxxviii, 15. Fear is used, also, for reverence: "God is greatly to be FEARED" in the assembly of his saints. This kind of fear, being compatible with confidence and love, is sometimes called filial fear; while "the fear which hath torment," being the result of conscious guilt, and the anticipation of punishment, is removed by that "love" to God which results from a consciousness of our reconciliation to him.

The filial fear of God is a holy affection, or gracious habit, wrought in the soul by God, Jer. xxxii, 40, whereby it is inclined and enabled to obey all God's commandments, even the most difficult, Gen. xxii, 12; Eccl. xii, 13; and to hate and avoid evil, Nehemiah v, 15; Prov. viii, 13; xv, 6. Slavish fear is the consequence of guilt; it is a judicial impression from the sad thoughts of the provoked majesty of the heaven; it is an alarm within that disturbs the rest of a sinner. Fear is put for the whole worship of God: "I will teach you the fear of the Lord," Psalm xxxiv, 11; I will teach you the true way of worshipping and serving God. It is likewise put for the law and word of God: "The fear of the Lord is clean, enduring for ever," Psalm xix, 9. The law is so called, because it is the object, the cause, and the rule of the grace of holy fear.

FEASTS. God appointed several festivals among the Jews. 1. To perpetuate the memory of great events; so, the Sabbath commemorated the creation of the world; the passover, the departure out of Egypt; the pentecost, the law given at Sinai, &c. 2. To keep them under the influence of religion, and by the majesty of that service which he instituted among them, and which abounded in mystical symbols or types of evangelical things, to convey spiritual instruction, and to keep alive the expectation of the Messiah, and his more perfect dispensation. 3. To secure to them certain times of rest and rejoicings. 4. To render them familiar with the law; for, in their religious assemblies, the law of God was read and explained. 5. To renew the acquaintance, correspondence, and friendship of their tribes and families, coming from the several towns in the country, and meeting three times a year in the holy city.

The first and most ancient festival, the Sabbath, or seventh day, commemorated the creation. "The Lord blessed the seventh day, and sanctified it," says Moses, "because that in it he had rested from all his work," Gen. ii, 3. See Sabbath.

The passover was instituted in memory of the Israelites' departure out of Egypt, and of the favour which God showed his people in sparing their first-born, when he destroyed the first-born of the Egyptians, Exod. xii, 14, &c. See Passover.

The feast of pentecost was celebrated on the fiftieth day after the passover, in memory of the law being given to Moses on Mount Sinai, fifty days after the departure out of Egypt. They reckoned seven weeks from the passover to pentecost, beginning at the day after the passover. The Hebrews call it the feast of weeks, and the Christians, pentecost, which signifies the fiftieth day.

The feast of trumpets was celebrated on the first day of the civil year; on which the trumpets sounded, proclaiming the beginning of the year, which was in the month Tisri, answering to our September, O. S. We know no religious cause of its establishment. Moses commands it to be observed as a day of rest, and that particular sacrifices should be offered at that time.

The new moons, or first days of every month, were, in some sort, a consequence of the feasts of trumpets. The law did not oblige people to rest upon this day, but ordained only some particular sacrifices. It appears that, on these days, also, the trumpet was sounded, and entertainments were made, 1 Sam. xx, 5–18.

The feast of expiation or atonement was celebrated on the tenth day of Tisri, which was the first day of the civil year. It was instituted for a general expiation of sins, irreverences, and pollutions of all the Israelites, from the high priest to the lowest of the people, committed by them throughout the year, Lev. xxiii, 27, 28; Num. xxix, 7. See Expiation, DAY OF.

The feast of tents, or tabernacles, on which all Israel were obliged to attend the temple, and to dwell eight days under tents of branches, in memory of their fathers dwelling forty years in tents, as travellers in the wilderness. It was kept on the fifteenth of the month Tisri, the first of the civil year. The first and seventh day of this feast were very solemn. But during the other days of the octave they might work, Lev. xxiii, 34, 35; Num. xxix, 12, 13. At the beginning of the feast, two vessels of silver were carried in a ceremonious manner to the temple, one full of water, the other of wine, which were poured at the foot of the altar of burnt offerings, always on the seventh day of this festival.

Of the three great feasts of the year, the passover, pentecost, and that of the tabernacles, the octave, or seventh day after these feasts, was a day of rest as much as the festival itself; and all the males of the nation were obliged to visit the temple at these three feasts. But the law did not require them to continue there during the whole octave, except in the feast of tabernacles, when they seem obliged to be present for the whole seven days.

Beside these feasts, we find the feast of lots, or PURIM, instituted on occasion of the deliverance of the Jews from Haman's plot, in the reign of Ahasuerus. See Purim.

The feast of the dedication of the temple, or rather of the restoration of the temple, which had been profaned by Antiochus Epiphanes, 1 Mac. iv, 52, &c, was celebrated in winter, and is supposed to be the feast of dedication mentioned in John x, 22. Josephus says, that it was called the feast of lights, probably because this happiness befel them when least expected, and they considered it as a new light risen on them.

In the Christian church, no festival appears to have been expressly instituted by Jesus Christ, or his Apostles. Yet, as we commemorate the passion of Christ as often as we celebrate his Supper, he seems by this to have instituted a perpetual feast. Christians have always celebrated the memory of his resurrection, and observe this feast on every Sunday, which was commonly called the Lord's day, Rev. i, 10. By inference we may conclude this festival to have been instituted by Apostolic authority.

The birth-day of Christ, commonly called Christmas-day, has been generally observed by his disciples with gratitude and joy. His birth was the greatest blessing ever bestowed on mankind. The angels from heaven celebrated it with a joyful hymn; and every man, who has any feeling of his own lost state without a Redeemer, must rejoice and be glad in it. "Unto us a Child is born, unto us a Son is given; and his name shall be called Wonderful, Counsellor, the mighty God, the everlasting Father, the Prince of Peace," Isaiah ix, 6. For this festival, however, there is no authority in Scripture, nor do we know that it was observed in the age of the Apostles.

On Easter Sunday we celebrate our Saviour's victory over death and hell, when, having on the cross made an atonement for the sin of the world, he rose again from the grave, brought life and immortality to light, and opened to all his faithful servants the way to heaven. On this great event rest all our hopes. "If Christ be not risen," says St. Paul, "then is our preaching vain, and your faith is also vain. But now is Christ risen from the dead, and become the first-fruits of them that slept," 1 Cor. xv, 14, 20.

Forty days after his resurrection, our Lord ascended into heaven, in the sight of his disciples. This is celebrated on what is called Ascension-day, or Holy Thursday. Ten days after his ascension, our Lord sent the Holy Spirit to be the comforter and guide of his disciples. This blessing is commemorated on Whit-Sunday, which is a very great festival, and may be profitably observed; for the assistance of the Holy Spirit can alone support us through all temptations, and guide us into all truth.

The pretended success of some in discovering the remains of certain holy men, called "relics," multiplied in the fourth century of the Christian church the festivals and commemorations of the martyrs in a most extravagant manner. These days, instead of being set apart for pious exercises, were spent in indolence, voluptuousness, and criminal pursuits; and were less consecrated to the service of God, than employed in the indulgence of sinful passions. Many of these festivals were instituted on a Pagan model, and perverted to similar purposes.

FELIX, CLAUDIUS. See Claudius.

FERRET, אנקה, from אנק, or CRY OUT, Lev. xi, 30. The ferret is a species of the weasel; but Bochart will have the ANAKAH to be the spotted lizard, called by Pliny STELLIO. Dr. James takes it for the frog, in allusion to the name, which literally signifies THE CRIER, befitting the croaking of that animal; but we shall find the frog mentioned under another name. Dr. Geddes renders it THE NEWT, or rather THE LIZARD OF THE NILE; and it evidently must be of the lizard species. Pliny mentions "the GALLEOTES, covered with red spots, whose cries are sharp," which may be the GEKKO, which is probably the animal here intended. As its name, in the Indies TOCKAI, and in Egypt GEKKO, is formed from its voice, so the Hebrew name ANAKAH, or perhaps ANAKKAH, seems to be formed in like manner; the double k being equally observable in all these appellations. If these remarks are admissible, this lizard is sufficiently identified.

FESTUS. Portius Festus succeeded Felix in the government of Judea, A. D. 60. Felix his predecessor, to oblige the Jews, when he resigned his government, left St. Paul in bonds at Cæsarea, in Palestine, Acts xxiv, 27. Festus, at his first coming to Jerusalem, was entreated by the principal Jews to condemn St. Paul, or to order him up to Jerusalem, they having conspired to assassinate him in the way. Festus answered, that it was not customary with the Romans to condemn any man without hearing him; but said that he would hear their accusations against St. Paul at Cæsarea. From these accusations St. Paul appealed to Cæsar, and by this means secured himself from the prosecution of the Jews, and the wicked intentions of Festus, whom they had corrupted.

FIG TREE, תאנה, Gen. iii, 7; Num. xiii, 23; συκῆ, Matthew vii, 16; xxi, 19; xxiv, 32; Mark xi, 13, 20, 21; xiii, 28; Luke vi, 44; xiii, 6, 7; xxi, 29; John i, 48; James iii, 12; Rev. vi, 13. This tree was very common in Palestine. It becomes large, dividing into many branches, which are furnished with leaves shaped like those of the mulberry, and affords a friendly shade. Accordingly, we read, in the Old Testament, of Juda and Israel dwelling, or sitting securely, every man under his fig tree, 1 Kings iv, 25; Micah iv, 4; Zech. iii, 10; 1 Mac. xiv, 12. And, in the New Testament, we find Nathanael under a fig tree, probably for the purposes of devotional retirement, John i, 49–51. Hasselquist, in his journey from Nazareth to Tiberias, says, "We refreshed ourselves under the shade of a fig tree, where a shepherd and his herd had their rendezvous; but without either house or hut." The fruit which it bears is produced from the trunk and large branches, and not from the smaller shoots, as in most other trees. It is soft, sweet, and very nourishing. Milton is of opinion that the banian tree was that with the leaves of which our first parents made themselves aprons. But his account, as to the matter of fact, wants even probability to countenance it; for the leaves of this are so far from being, as he has described them, of the bigness of an Amazonian target, that they seldom or never exceed five inches in length, and three in breadth. Therefore, we must look for another of the fig kind, that better answers the purpose referred to by Moses, Gen. iii, 7; and as the fruit of the banana tree, is often, by the most ancient authors, called a fig, may we not suppose this to have been the fig tree of paradise? Pliny, describing this tree, says that its leaves were the greatest and most shady of all others; and as the leaves of these are often six feet long, and about two broad, are thin, smooth, and very flexible, they may be deemed more proper than any other for the covering spoken of, especially since they may be easily joined together with the numerous threadlike filaments, which may, without labour, be peeled from the body of the tree. The first ripe fig is still called BOCCÔRE in the Levant, which is nearly its Hebrew name, בכורה, Jer. xxiv, 2. Thus Dr. Shaw, in giving an account of the fruits in Barbary, mentions "the black and white BOCCÔRE, or 'early fig,' which is produced in June, though the KERMES, or KERMOUSE, the 'fig,' probably so called, which they preserve and make up into cakes, is rarely ripe before August." And on Nahum iii, 12, he observes, that "the BOCCÔRES drop as soon as they are ripe, and, according to the beautiful allusion of the prophet, fall into the mouth of the eater upon being shaken." Farther, "It frequently falls out in Barbary," says he; "and we need not doubt of the like in this hotter climate of Judea, that, according to the quality of the preceding season, some of the more forward and vigorous trees will now and then yield a few ripe figs six weeks or more before the full season. Something like this may be alluded to by the Prophet Hosea, when he says, 'I saw your fathers as בכורה, THE FIRST RIPE, in the fig tree, at her first time,' Hosea ix, 10. Such figs were reckoned a great dainty." See Isaiah xxviii, 4. The Prophet Isaiah gave orders to apply a lump of figs to Hezekiah's boil; and immediately after it was cured. God, in effecting this miraculous cure, was pleased to order the use of means not improper for that end.

2. The account of our Saviour's denunciation against the barren fig tree, Matt. xxi, 19; Mark xi, 13, has occasioned some of the boldest cavils of infidelity; and the vindication of it has exercised the ingenuity of several of the most learned critics and commentators. The whole difficulty arises from the circumstance of his disappointment in not finding fruit on the tree, when it is expressly said, that "the time of figs was not yet." While it was supposed that this expression signified, that the time for such trees to bring forth fruit was not yet come, it looked very unaccountable that Christ should reckon a tree barren, though it had leaves, and curse it as such, when he knew that the time of bearing figs was not come; and that he should come to seek figs on this tree, when he knew that figs were not used to be ripe so soon in the year. But the expression does not signify the time of the coming forth of figs, but the time of the gathering in of ripe figs, as is plain from the parallel expressions. Thus, "the time of the fruit," Matt. xxi, 34, most plainly signifies the time of gathering in ripe fruits, since the servants were sent to receive those fruits for their master's use. St. Mark and St. Luke express the same by the word TIME, or SEASON: "At the SEASON he sent a servant," &c; that is, at the season or time of gathering in ripe fruit, Mark xii, 2; Luke xx, 10. In like manner, if any one should say in our language, the season of fruit, the season of apples, the season of figs, every one would understand him to speak of the season or time of gathering in these fruits. When, therefore, St. Mark says, that "the time or season of figs was not yet," he evidently means that the time of gathering ripe figs was not yet past; and, if so, it was natural to expect figs upon all those trees that were not barren; whereas, after the time of gathering figs, no one would expect to find them on a fig tree, and its having none then would be no sign of barrenness. St. Mark, by saying, "For the time of figs was not yet," does not design to give a reason for "his finding nothing but leaves;" but he gives a reason for what he said in the clause before: "He came, if haply he might find any thereon;" and it was a good reason

for our Saviour's coming and seeking figs on the tree, because the time for their being gathered was not come. We have other like instances in the Gospels, and, indeed, in the writings of all mankind, of another clause coming in between the assertion and the proof. Thus, in this very evangelist: "They said among themselves, Who shall roll away the stone from the door of the sepulchre? and when they looked, they saw the stone was rolled away; for it was very great," Mark xvi, 3, 4; where its being very great is not assigned as a reason of its being rolled away, but of the women's wishing for some one to roll it away for them. St. Matthew informs us that the tree was "in the way," that is, in the common road, and therefore, probably, no particular person's property; but if it was, being barren, the timber might be as serviceable to the owner as before. So that here was no real injury; but Jesus was pleased to make use of this innocent miracle to prefigure the speedy ruin of the Jewish nation on account of its unfruitfulness under greater advantages than any other people enjoyed at that day; and, like all the rest of his miracles, it was done with a gracious intention, namely, to alarm his countrymen, and induce them to repent. In the blasting of this barren fig tree, the distant appearance of which was so fair and promising, he delivered one more awful lesson to a degenerate nation, of whose hypocritical exterior and flattering but delusive pretensions it was a just and striking emblem.

FINGER. The finger of God signifies his power, his operation. Pharaoh's magicians discovered the finger of God in the miracle which Moses wrought, Exodus viii, 19. This legislator gave the law written by the finger of God to the Hebrews, Exodus xxxi, 18. Our Saviour says he cast out devils by the finger and Spirit of God, which he intimates was a sign that the kingdom of God was come; that God's spiritual government of his church was begun to be exercised among the Jews, by the Messiah, Luke xi, 20. To put forth one's finger, is a bantering, insulting gesture. "If thou take away from the midst of thee the yoke, and the putting out of the finger," Isaiah lviii, 9; if thou take away from the midst of thee the chain, or yoke, wherewith thou loadest thy debtors; and forbear pointing at them, and using jeering or menacing gestures.

FIRE. God hath often appeared in fire, and encompassed with fire, as when he showed himself in the burning bush; and descended on Mount Sinai, in the midst of flames, thunderings, and lightning, Exodus iii, 2; xix, 18. Hence fire is a symbol of the Deity: "The Lord thy God is a consuming fire," Deut. iv, 24. The Holy Ghost is compared to fire: "He shall baptize you with the Holy Ghost and with fire," Matt. iii, 11. To verify this prediction, he sent the Holy Ghost, which descended upon his disciples, in the form of tongues, or like flames of fire, Acts ii, 3. It is the work of the Holy Spirit to enlighten, purify, and sanctify the soul; and to inflame it with love to God, and zeal for his glory. Fire from heaven fell frequently on the victims sacrificed to the Lord, as a mark of his presence and approbation. It is thought, that God in this manner expressed his acceptance of Abel's sacrifices, Gen. iv, 4. When the Lord made a covenant with Abraham, a fire like that of a furnace passed through the divided pieces of the sacrifices, and consumed them, Gen. xv, 17. Fire fell upon the sacrifices which Moses offered at the dedication of the tabernacle, Lev. ix, 24; and upon those of Manoah, Samson's father, Judges xiii, 19, 20; upon Solomon's, at the dedication of the temple, 2 Chron. vii, 1; and on Elijah's, at Mount Carmel, 1 Kings xviii, 38. The fire which came down from heaven, first upon the altar in the tabernacle, and afterward descended anew upon the altar in the temple of Solomon, at its consecration, was there constantly fed and maintained by the priests, day and night, in the same manner as it had been in the tabernacle. The Jews have a tradition, that Jeremiah, foreseeing the destruction of the temple, took this fire and hid it in a pit; but that at the rebuilding of the temple, being brought again from thence, it revived upon the altar. But this is a fiction: and the generality of them allow, that, at the destruction of the temple, it was extinguished: and in the time of the second temple, nothing was made use of for all their burnt offerings but common fire only. The ancient Chaldeans adored the fire, as well as the old Persians, and some other people of the east. The torments of hell are described by fire, both in the Old and New Testament. Our Saviour makes use of this similitude, to represent the punishment of the damned, Mark ix, 44. He likewise speaks frequently of the eternal fire prepared for the devil, his angels, and reprobates, Matt. xxv, 41. The sting and remorse of conscience is the worm that will never die; and the wrath of God upon their souls and bodies, the fire that shall never go out. There are writers who maintain, that by the worm is to be understood a living and sensible, not an allegorical and figurative, worm; and by fire, a real elementary and material fire. Among the abettors of this opinion are Austin, Cyprian, Chrysostom, Jerom, &c. The word of God is compared to fire: "Is not my word like a fire?" Jer. xxiii, 20. It is full of life and efficacy; like a fire it warms, melts, and heats; and is powerful to consume the dross, and burn up the chaff and stubble. Fire is likewise taken for persecution, dissension, and division: "I am come to send fire on earth," Luke xii, 49; as if it was said, upon my coming and publishing the Gospel, there will follow, through the devil's malice and corruption of men, much persecution to the professors thereof, and manifold divisions in the world, whereby men will be tried, whether they will be faithful or not.

FIRMAMENT. It is said, Gen. i, 7, that God made the firmament in the midst of the waters, to separate the inferior from the superior. The word used on this occasion properly signifies EXPANSION, or something expanded. This expansion is properly the atmosphere, which encompasses the globe on all sides, and separates the water in the clouds from that on the earth.

FIRST-BORN. The first-born, who was the object of special affection to his parents, was denominated by way of eminence, פטר רחם, THE OPENING OF THE WOMB. In case a man married with a widow, who by a previous marriage had become the mother of children, the first-born as respected the second husband was the eldest child by the second marriage. Before the time of Moses, the father might, if he chose, transfer the right of primogeniture to a younger child, but the practice occasioned much contention, Gen. xxv, 31, 32; and a law was enacted, overruling it, Deut. xxi, 15–17. The first-born inherited peculiar rights and privileges. (1.) He received a double portion of the estate. Jacob, in the case of Reuben, his first-born, bestowed his additional portion upon Joseph, by adopting his two sons, Gen. xlviii, 5–8; Deut. xxi, 17. This was done as a reprimand, and a punishment of his incestuous conduct, Genesis xxxv, 22; but Reuben, notwithstanding, was enrolled as the first-born in the genealogical registers, 1 Chron. v, 1. (2.) The first-born was the priest of the whole family. The honour of exercising the priesthood was transferred, by the command of God communicated through Moses, from the tribe of Reuben, to whom it belonged by right of primogeniture, to that of Levi, Num. iii, 12–18; viii, 18. In consequence of God having taken the Levites from among the children of Israel instead of all the first-born to serve him as priests, the first-born of the other tribes were to be redeemed, at a valuation made by the priest not exceeding five shekels, from serving God in that capacity, Numbers xviii, 15, 16; Luke ii, 22, &c. (3.) The first-born enjoyed an authority over those who were younger, similar to that possessed by a father, Gen. xxv, 23, &c; 2 Chron. xxi, 3; Gen. xxvii, 29; Exod. xii, 29: which was transferred in the case of Reuben by Jacob their father to Judah, Gen. xlix, 8–10. The tribe of Judah, accordingly, even before it gave kings to the Hebrews, was every where distinguished from the other tribes. In consequence of the authority which was thus attached to the first-born, he was also made the successor in the kingdom. There was an exception to this rule in the case of Solomon, who, though a younger brother, was made his successor by David at the special appointment of God. It is very easy to see in view of these facts, how the word "first-born" came to express sometimes a great, and sometimes the highest, dignity.

2. First-born is not always to be understood literally; it is sometimes taken for the prime, most excellent, most distinguished of any thing. "The first-born of the poor," Isaiah xiv, 30, signifies the most miserable of the poor; and "the first-born of death," Job xviii, 13, the most terrible of deaths.

3. God ordained that all the Jewish first-born both of men and beasts, for service, should be consecrated to him. The male children only were subject to this law. If a woman's first child were a girl, the father was not obliged to offer any thing for her, or for the children after her, though they were males. If a man had many wives, he was obliged to offer the first-born of each of them to the Lord. The first-born were offered in the temple, and were redeemed for the sum of five shekels. The firstling of a clean beast was offered at the temple, not to be redeemed, but to be killed. An unclean beast, a horse, an ass, or a camel, was either redeemed or exchanged. An ass was redeemed by a lamb, or five shekels; if not redeemed, it was killed.

FIRST-FRUITS, among the Hebrews, were presents made to God of part of the fruits of the harvest, to express the submission, dependence, and thankfulness of the offerers. They were offered at the temple, before the crop was touched; and when the harvest was over, before any private persons used their corn. The first of these first-fruits, offered in the name of the nation, was a sheaf of barley, gathered on the fifteenth of Nisan in the evening, and threshed in a court of the temple. After it was well cleaned, about three pints of it were roasted and pounded in a mortar. Over this was thrown a portion of oil, and a handful of incense. Then the priest took this offering, waved it before the Lord toward the four parts of the world, threw a handful of it into the fire upon the altar, and kept the rest. After this, every one was at liberty to get in his harvest. Beside these first-fruits, every private person was obliged to bring his first-fruits to the temple. The Scripture prescribes neither the time nor the quantity. The rabbins say, that they were obliged to bring at least the sixtieth part of their fruits and harvest. These first-fruits consisted of wheat, barley, grapes, figs, apricots, olives, and dates. They met in companies of four-and-twenty persons to carry their first-fruits in a ceremonious manner. The company was preceded by an ox appointed for the sacrifice, with a crown of olives on his head, and his horns gilded. There was also another sort of first-fruits paid to God, Num. xv, 19, 20, when the bread in every family was kneaded, a portion of it was set apart, and given to the priest or Levite of the place. If there was no priest or Levite, it was cast into the oven, and consumed by the fire. This is one of the three precepts peculiar to the women; because they generally made the bread. The first-fruits and tenths were the most substantial revenue of the priests and Levites. St. Paul says, Christians have the first-fruits of the Spirit, Rom. viii, 23, that is, a greater abundance of God's Spirit, more perfect and more excellent gifts than the Jews. Christ is called the first-fruits of them that slept; for as the first-fruits were earnests to the Jews of the succeeding harvest, so Christ is the first-fruits or the earnest of the general resurrection.

FIR TREE, ברוש, occurs 2 Sam. vi, 5; 1 Kings v, 8, 10; vi, 15, 34; ix, 11; 2 Kings xix, 23; 2 Chron. ii, 8; iii, 5; Psalm civ, 17; Isaiah xiv, 8; xxxvii, 24; xli, 19; lv, 13; lx, 13; Ezek. xxvii, 5; xxxi, 8; Hosea xiv, 8; Nahum ii, 3; Zech. xi, 2. The **LXX** render it so variously as to show that they knew not what particular tree is meant; the Vulgate, generally by ABIETES, the "fir tree." Celsius asserts that it is the cedar; but Millar maintains that it is the fir. The fir tree is an evergreen, of beautiful appearance, whose lofty height, and dense foliage, afford a spacious shelter and shade. The trunk of the tree is very straight. The wood was anciently used for spears, musical instruments, furniture for houses, rafters in building, and for ships. In 2 Sam. vi, 5, it is mentioned that David played on instruments of fir wood; and Dr. Burney, in his "History of Music," observes, "This species of wood, so soft in its nature, and sonorous in its effects, seems to have been preferred by the ancients, as well as moderns, to every other kind for the construction of musical instruments, particularly the bellies of them, on which the tone of them chiefly depends. Those of the harp, lute, guitar, harpsichord, and violin, in present use, are always made of this wood."

FISH, דג, ἰχθὺς, Matt. vii, 10; xvii, 27; Luke v, 6; John xxi, 6, 8, 11, occurs very frequently. This appears to be the general name in Scripture of aquatic animals. Boothroyd, in the note upon Num. xi, 4, says, "I am inclined to think that the word בשר, here rendered FLESH, denotes only the flesh of fish, as it certainly does in Lev. xi, 11; and indeed the next verse seems to support this explication: 'We remember how freely we ate fish.' It was then, particularly, the flesh of fish, for which they longed, which was more relishing than either the beef or mutton of those regions, which, unless when young, is dry and unpalatable. Of the great abundance and deliciousness of the fish of Egypt, all authors, ancient and modern, are agreed." We have few Hebrew names, if any, for particular fishes. Moses says in general, Lev. xi, 9–12, that all sorts of river, lake, and sea fish, might be eaten, if they had scales and fins; others were unclean. St. Barnabas, in his epistle, cites, as from ancient authority, "You shall not eat of the lamprey, the many-feet, [polypes,] nor the cuttle fish." Though fish was the common food of the Egyptians, yet we learn from Herodotus and Chæremon, as quoted by Porphyry, that their priests abstained from fish of all sorts. Hence we may see how distressing to the Egyptians was the infliction which turned the waters of the river into blood, and occasioned the death of the fish, Exod. vii, 18–21. Their sacred stream became so polluted as to be unfit for drink, for bathing, and for other uses of water to which they were superstitiously devoted, and themselves obliged to nauseate what was the usual food of the common people, and held sacred by the priests, Exod. ii, 5; vii, 15; viii, 20.

In Ezekiel xxix, 4, the king of Egypt is compared to the crocodile: "I am against thee, the great dragon that lieth in the midst of his rivers in Egypt. I will put hooks in thy jaws, and I will cause the fish in thy rivers to stick to thy scales, and I will bring thee out of the midst of thy rivers, and all the fish of thy rivers shall stick to thy scales." If the REMORA is as troublesome to the crocodile as it is to some other tenants of the water, it may here be referred to. Forskal mentions the ECHENEIS NEUCRATES [remora] at Gidda, there called KAML EL KERSH, "the louse of the shark," because it often adheres very strongly to this fish; and Hasselquist says that it is found at Alexandria.

The term, ἰχθὺς, A FISH, was, at an early period of the Christian era, adopted as a symbolical word. It was formed from the initial letters of the Greek words, Ἰησοῦς Χριςὸς, Θεοῦ Ὑιὸς, Σωτὴρ, "Jesus Christ, the Son of God, our Saviour." From the use of symbolical terms, the transition was easy to the adoption of symbolical representations, and it therefore soon became common for the Christians to have the letters of the word ιχθυς, or the figures of fishes, sculptured on their monuments for the dead, struck on their medals, engraved on their rings and seals, and even formed on the articles of domestic use.

FITCHES, or **VETCHES**, a kind of tare. There are two words in Hebrew which our translators have rendered FITCHES, קצח and כסמת: the first occurs only in Isaiah xxviii, 25, 27, and must be the name of some kind of seed; but the interpreters differ much in explaining it. Jerom, Maimonides, R. David Kimchi, and the rabbins understand it of the GITH; and rabbi Obdias de Bartenora expressly says that its barbarous or vulgar name is ניילי. The GITH was called by the Greeks μελάνθιον, and by the Latins NIGELLA; and is thus described by Ballester: "It is a plant commonly met with in gardens, and grows to a cubit in height, and sometimes more, according to the richness of the soil. The leaves are small like those of fennel, the flower blue, which disappearing, the ovary shows itself on the top, like that of a poppy, furnished with little horns, oblong, divided by membranes into several partitions, or cells, in which are enclosed seeds of a very black colour, not unlike those of the leek, but of a very fragrant smell." And Ausonius observes, that its pungency is equal to that of pepper:--

EST INTER FRUGES MORSU PIPER
ÆQUIPARENS GIT.

Pliny says it is of use in bakehouses, PISTRINIS, and that it affords a grateful seasoning to the bread. The Jewish rabbins also mention the seeds among condiments, and mixed with bread. For this purpose it was probably used in the time of Isaiah; since the inhabitants of those countries, to this day, have a variety of rusks and biscuits, most of which are strewed on the top with the seeds of sesamum, coriander, and wild garden saffron.

The other word rendered FITCHES in our translation of Ezek. iv, 9, is כסמת; but in Exod. ix, 32, and Isaiah xxviii, 25, "rye." In the latter place the Septuagint has ξέα, and in the two former ὀλύρα; and the Vulgate in Exodus, FAR, and in Isaiah and Ezekiel, VICIA. Saadias, likewise, took it to be something of the leguminous kind, גלבאן, CICIRCULA, (misprinted CIRCULA in the Polyglott version,) or, "a chickling." Aquila has ζέα, and Theodotion, ὀλύρα. Onkelos and Targum have כונהיא and Syriac, כונחא, which are supposed to be the MILLET, or a species of it called PANICUM; Persian, כורכדם, the SPELT; and this seems to be the most probable meaning of the Hebrew word; at least it has the greatest number of interpreters from Jerom to Celsius. There are not, however, wanting, who think it was rye; among whom R. D. Kimchi, followed by Luther, and our English translators: Dr. Geddes, too, has retained it, though he says that he is inclined to think that the SPELT is preferable.

Dr. Shaw thinks that this word may signify RICE. Hasselquist, on the contrary, affirms that rice was brought into cultivation in Egypt under the Caliphs. This, however, may be doubted. One would think from the intercourse of ancient Egypt with Babylon and with India, that this country could not be ignorant of a grain so well suited to its climate.

FLAG, אחו, occurs Gen. xli, 2, 18; Job viii, 11; and סוף, WEEDS, Exod. ii, 3, 5; Isa. xix, 6; John ii, 5. The word ACHU in the first two instances is translated "meadows," and in the latter, "flag." It probably denotes the sedge, or long grass, which grows in the meadows of the Nile, very grateful to the cattle. It is retained in the Septuagint in Genesis, ἐν τῷ ἄχει; and is used by the son of Sirach, Ecclesiasticus xl, 16, ἄχι and ἄχει; for the copies vary.

"We have no radix," says the learned Chapelow, "for אחו, unless we derive it, as Schultens does, from the Arabic ACHI, 'to bind or join together.'" Thus, Parkhurst defines it "a species of plant, sedge, or reed, so called from its fitness for making ropes, or the like, to connect or join things together; as the Latin JUNCUS, a 'bulrush,' A JUNGENDO, from 'joining,' for the same reason;" and he supposes that it is the plant, or reed, growing near the Nile, which Hasselquist describes as having numerous narrow leaves, and growing about eleven feet high, of the leaves of which the Egyptians make ropes.

The word סוף is called by Eben Ezra, "a reed growing on the borders of the river." Bochart, Fuller, Rivetus, Ludolphus, and Junius and Tremellius, render it by JUNCUS, CAREX, or ALGA; and Celsius thinks it the FUCUS or ALGA, "sea weed." Dr. Geddes says there is little doubt of its being the sedge called SARI, which, as we learn from Theophrastus and Pliny, grows on the marshy banks of the Nile, and rises to the height of almost two cubits. This, indeed, agrees very well with Exod. ii, 3, 5, and the thickets of arundinaceous plants, at some small distances from the Red Sea, observed by Dr. Shaw; but the place in Jonah seems to require some submarine plant.

FLAX, פשתה, Exod. ix, 31; Lev. xiii, 47, 48, 52, 59; Deut. xxii, 11; Joshua ii, 6; Judg. xv, 14; Prov. xxxi, 13; Isaiah xix, 9; xlii, 3; xliii, 17; Jer. xiii, 1; Ezek. xl, 3; xliv, 17, 18; Hosea ii, 5, 9; λῖνον Matt. xii, 20; Rev. xv, 6; a plant very common, and too well known to need a description. It is a vegetable upon which the industry of mankind has been exercised with the greatest success and utility. On passing a field of it, one is struck with astonishment when he considers that this apparently insignificant plant may, by the labour and ingenuity of man, be made to assume an entirely new form and appearance, and to contribute to pleasure and health, by furnishing us with agreeable and ornamental apparel. This word Mr. Parkhurst thinks is derived from the verb פשט, TO STRIP, because the substance which we term FLAX is properly the bark or fibrous part of the vegetable, pilled or stripped off the stalks. From time immemorial Egypt was celebrated for the production or manufacture of flax. Wrought into garments, it constituted the principal dress of the inhabitants, and the priests never put on any other kind of clothing. The fine linen of Egypt is celebrated in all ancient authors, and its superior excellence mentioned in the sacred Scriptures. The manufacture of flax is still carried on in that country, and many writers take notice of it. Rabbi Benjamin Tudela mentions the manufactory at Damiata; and Egmont and Heyman describe the article as being of a beautiful colour, and so finely spun that the threads are hardly discernible.

FLEA, פרעש, 1 Sam. xxiv, 14; xxvi, 20. The **LXX**, and another Greek version in the HEXAPLA, render it ψύλλον, and the Vulgate PULEX. It seems, says Mr. Parkhurst, an evident derivative from פרע FREE, and רעש TO LEAP, BOUND, or SKIP, on account of its agility in leaping or skipping. The flea is a little wingless insect, equally contemptible and troublesome. It is thus described by an Arabian author: "A black, nimble, extenuated, hunch-backed animal, which being sensible when any one looks on it, jumps incessantly, now on one side, now on the other, till it gets out of sight." David likens himself to this insect; importing that while it would cost Saul much pains to catch him, he would obtain but very little advantage from it.

FLESH, a term of very ambiguous import in the Scriptures. An eminent critic has enumerated no less than six different meanings which it bears in the sacred writings, and for which, he affirms, there will not be found a single authority in any profane writer: 1. It sometimes denotes the whole body considered as animated, as in Matt. xxvi, 41, "The spirit is willing, but the flesh is weak." 2. It sometimes means a human being, as in Luke iii, 6, "All flesh shall see the salvation of God." 3. Sometimes a person's kindred collectively considered, as in Rom. xi, 14, "If by any means I may provoke them which are my flesh." 4. Sometimes any thing of an external or ceremonial nature, as opposed to that which is internal and moral, as in Gal. iii, 3, "Having begun in the Spirit, are ye now made perfect in the flesh?" 5. The sensitive part of our nature, or that which is the seat of appetite, as in 2 Cor. vii, 1, "Let us cleanse ourselves from all filthiness of the flesh and spirit;" where there can be no doubt that the pollutions of the flesh must be those of the appetites, being opposed to the pollutions of the spirit, or those of the passions. 6. It is employed to denote any principle of vice and moral pravity of whatever kind. Thus among the works of the flesh, Gal. v, 19–21, are numbered not only adultery, fornication, uncleanness, lasciviousness, drunkenness, and revellings, which all relate to criminal indulgence of appetite, but idolatry, witchcraft, hatred, variance, emulations, wrath, strife, seditions, heresies, envyings, and murders, which are manifestly vices of a different kind, and partake more of the diabolical nature than of the beastly.

FLIES. The kinds of flies are exceedingly numerous; some with two, and some with four, wings. They abound in warm and moist regions, as in Egypt, Chaldea, Palestine, and in the middle regions of Africa; and during the rainy seasons are very troublesome. In the Hebrew Scriptures, or in the ancient versions, are seven kinds of insects, which Bochart classes among MUSCÆ, or flies. These are, 1. ערב, Exod. viii, 20; Psa. lxxviii, 45; cv, 31, which those interpreters who, by residing on the spot, have had the best means of identifying, have rendered the DOG-FLY, κυνόμυια, and it is supposed to be the same which in Abyssinia is called the ZIMB. 2. זבוב, 2 Kings i, 2, 3, 6, 16; Eccles. x, 1; Isa. vii, 18. Whether this denotes absolutely a distinct species of fly, or swarms of all sorts, may be difficult to determine. 3. ידברה Judges xiv, 18; Psa. cxviii, 12, rendered BEE. 4. צרעה, σφὴξ, Exodus xxiii, 28; Joshua xxiv, 12; Deut. vii, 20, HORNET. 5. סרבים, οἶςρος, Ezek. ii, 6; Hosea iv, 16. 6. כק, κώνωψ, Matt. xxiii, 24, THE GNAT. 7. כנים, σκνίφες, Exod. viii, 16; Psa. cv, 31, LICE.

2. M. Sonnini, speaking of Egypt, says, "Of insects there the most troublesome are the flies. Both man and beast are cruelly tormented with them. No idea can be formed of their obstinate rapacity when they wish to fix upon some part of the body. It is in vain to drive them away; they return again in the self-same moment; and their perseverance wearies out the most patient spirit. They like to fasten themselves in preference on the corners of the eye, and on the edge of the eyelid; tender parts, toward which a gentle moisture attracts them." The Egyptians paid a superstitious worship to several sorts of flies and insects. If, then, such was the superstitious homage of this people, nothing could be more determinate than the judgment brought upon them by Moses. They were punished by the very things they revered; and though they boasted of spells and charms, yet they could not ward off the evil.

3. "The word ZIMB," says Bruce, "is Arabic, and signifies THE FLY in general." The Chaldee paraphrase is content with calling it simply ZEBUB, which has the same general signification. The Ethiopic version calls it TSALTSALYA, which is the true name of this particular fly in Geez. It is in size very little larger than a bee, of a thicker proportion; and its wings, which are broader, are placed separate like those of a fly. Its head is large; the upper jaw or lip is sharp, and has at the end of it a strong pointed hair, of about a quarter of an inch in length; the lower jaw has two of these hairs: and this pencil of hairs, joined together, makes a resistance to the finger, nearly equal to a strong bristle of a hog. Its legs are serrated on the inside, and the whole covered with brown hair, or down. It has no sting, though it appears to be of the bee kind. As soon as this winged assassin appears, and its buzzing is heard, the cattle forsake their food, and run wildly about the plain till they die, worn out with affright, fatigue, and pain. The inhabitants of Melinda down to Cape Gardefan, to Saba, and the south coast of the Red Sea, are obliged to put themselves in motion, and remove to the next sand in the beginning of the rainy season. This is not a partial emigration; the inhabitants of all the countries, from the mountains of Abyssinia northward, to the confluence of the Nile and Astaboras, are, once in a year, obliged to change their abode, and seek protection in the sands of Beja, till the danger of the insect is over. The elephant and the rhinoceros, which by reason of their enormous bulk, and the vast quantity of food and water they daily need, cannot shift to desert and dry places, are obliged, in order to resist the zimb, to roll themselves in mud and mire, which, when dry, coats them over like armour. It was no trifling judgment, then, with which the prophet threatened the refractory Israelites: "The Lord shall hiss for the fly that is in the uttermost parts of the rivers of Egypt, and for the bee that is in the land of Assyria," Isaiah vii, 18. If the prediction be understood in the literal sense, it represents the ŒSTRA or CINCINELLÆ, as the armies of Jehovah, summoned by him to battle against his offending people; or, if it be taken metaphorically, which is perhaps the proper way of expounding it, the prophet compares the numerous and destructive armies of Babylon to the countless swarms of these flies, whose distant hum is said to strike the quadrupeds with consternation, and whose bite inflicts, on man and beast, a torment almost insupportable. How intolerable a plague of flies can prove, is evident from the fact, that whole districts have been laid waste by them. Such was the fate of Myuns in Ionia, and of Alarnæ. The inhabitants were forced to quit these cities, not being able to stand against the flies and gnats with which they were pestered. Trajan was obliged to raise the siege of a city in Arabia, before which he had sat down, being driven away by the swarms of these insects. Hence different people had deities whose office it was to defend them against flies. Among these may be reckoned Baalzebub, the fly-god of Ekron: HERCULES MUSCARUM ABACTOR, "Hercules, the expeller of flies;" and hence Jupiter had the titles of ἀπόμυιος, μυΐαγρος, μυϊόχορος, because he was supposed to expel flies, and especially to clear his temples of these insects.

4. Solomon observes, "Dead flies cause the apothecary's ointment to stink," Eccles. x, 1. "A fact well known," says Scheuchzer; "wherefore apothecaries take care to prevent flies from coming to their syrups and other fermentable preparations. For in all insects there is an acrid volatile salt, which, mixed with sweet or even alkaline substances, excites them to a brisk intestine motion, disposes them to fermentation, and to putrescence itself; by which the more volatile principles fly off, leaving the grosser behind: at the same time, the taste and odour are changed, the agreeable to fetid, the sweet to insipid." This verse is an illustration, by a very appropriate similitude, of the concluding assertion in the preceding chapter, that "one sinner destroyeth much good," as one dead fly spoils a whole vessel of precious ointment, which, in eastern countries, was considered as very valuable, 2 Kings xx, 13. The application of this proverbial expression to a person's good name, which is elsewhere compared to sweet ointment, Eccles. vii, 1; Cant. i, 3, is remarkably significant. As a fly, though a diminutive creature, can taint and corrupt much precious perfume; so a small mixture of folly and indiscretion will tarnish the reputation of one who, in other respects, is very wise and honourable; and so much the more, because of the malignity and ingratitude of mankind, who are disposed rather to censure one error, than to commend many excellencies, and from whose minds one small miscarriage is sufficient to blot out the memory of all other deserts. It concerns us, therefore, to conduct ourselves unblamably, that we may not by the least oversight or folly blemish our profession, or cause it to be offensive to others.

FLOCK. See Shepherd.

FLOOR, for threshing corn, or threshing floor, is frequently mentioned in Scripture. This was a place in the open air, in which corn was threshed, by means of a cart or sledge, or some other instrument drawn by oxen. The threshing floors among the Jews were only, as they are to this day in the east, round level plats of ground in the open air, where the corn was trodden out by oxen. Thus Gideon's floor appears to have been in the open air, Judges vi, 37; and also that of Araunah the Jebusite, 2 Sam. xxiv, otherwise it would not have been a proper place for erecting an altar, and offering sacrifices. In Hosea xiii, 3, we read of the chaff which is driven by the whirlwind from the floor. This circumstance of the threshing floor's being exposed to the agitation of the wind seems to be the principal reason of its Hebrew name. It appears, therefore, that a threshing floor, which is rendered in our textual translation, "a void place," might well be NEAR the entrance of the gate of Samaria, and a proper situation in which the kings of Israel and Judah might hear the prophets, 1 Kings xxii, 10; 2 Chron. xviii, 9. An instrument sometimes used in Palestine and the east, to force the corn out of the ear, and bruise the straw, was a heavy kind of sledge made of thick boards, and furnished beneath with teeth of stone or iron, Isa. xli, 15. The sheaves being laid in order, the sledge was drawn over the straw by oxen, and at the same time threshed out the corn, and cut or broke the straw into a kind of chaff. An instrument in the east is still used for the same purpose. This sledge is alluded to in 2 Sam. xii, 31; Isa. xxviii, 27; xli, 15; Amos i, 3. Dr. Lowth, in his notes on Isaiah xxviii, 27, 28, observes, that four methods of threshing are mentioned in this passage, by different instruments, the flail, the drag, the wain, and the treading of the cattle. The staff, or flail, was used for the INFIRMIORA SEMINA, the grain that was too tender to be treated in the other methods. The drag consisted of a sort of frame of strong planks, made rough at the bottom with hard stones or iron; it was drawn by horses or oxen over the corn sheaves on the floor, the driver sitting upon it. The wain was nearly similar to this instrument, but had wheels with iron teeth, or edges like a saw. The last method is well known from the law of Moses, which forbids the ox to be muzzled when he treadeth out the corn. Niebuhr, in his Travels, gives the following description of a machine which the people of Egypt use at this day for threshing out their corn: "This machine," says he, "is called NAURIDSJ. It has three rollers which turn on their axles; and each of them is furnished with some irons round and flat. At the beginning of June, Mr. Forskall and I several times saw, in the environs of Dsjise, how corn was threshed in Egypt. Every peasant chose for himself, in the open field, a smooth plat of ground from eighty to a hundred paces in circumference. Hither was brought on camels or asses the corn in sheaves, of which was formed a ring of six or eight feet wide, and two high. Two oxen were made to draw over it again and again the sledge, TRAINEAU, above mentioned; and this was done with the greatest convenience to the driver; for he was seated in a chair fixed on the sledge. Two such parcels or layers of corn are threshed out in a day, and they move each of them as many as eight times, with a wooden fork of five prongs, which they call MEDDRE. Afterward they throw the straw into the middle of the ring, where it forms a heap, which grows bigger and bigger. When the first layer is threshed they replace the straw in the ring, and thresh it as before. Thus the straw becomes every time smaller, till at last it resembles chopped straw. After this, with the fork just described, they cast the whole some yards from thence, and against the wind; which driving back the straw, the corn and the ears not threshed out fall apart from it, and make another heap. A man collects the clods of dirt, and other impurities to which any corn adheres, and throws them into a sieve. They afterward place in a ring the heaps, in which a good many entire ears are still found, and drive over them for four or five hours together ten couple of oxen joined two and two, till by absolute trampling they have separated the grains, which they throw into the air with a shovel to cleanse them."

FO, or **FUH**, as the Chinese now call him, was an Indian prince, who was made a god at thirty years of age, and died at seventy-five. His worshippers form one of the three great sects of China, and it is said to be far the most numerous. The worship of this idol, they pretend, was observed a thousand years before the Christian era, and was introduced from India into China within the first century after. Many temples are reared to this deity, some of which are magnificent; and a number of bonzes, or priests, are consecrated to his service. He is represented shining in light, with his hands hid under his robes, to show that he does all things invisibly. The doctors of this sect, like those of Egypt, Greece, and India, teach a double doctrine; the one public, the other private. According to the former, they say, all the good are recompensed, and the wicked punished, in places destined for each. They enjoin all works of charity; and forbid cheating, impurity, murder, and even the taking of life from any creature whatever. For they believe that the souls of their ancestors transmigrate into irrational creatures; either into such as they liked best, or resembled most in their behaviour; for which reason they never kill any such animals; but, while they live, feed them well, and when they die bury them with respect. As they build temples for Fuh, which are filled with images, so also monasteries for his priests, providing for their maintenance, as the most effectual means to partake of their prayers. These priests pretend to know into what bodies the dead are transmigrated; and seldom fail of representing their case to the surviving friends as miserable, or uncomfortable; that they may extort money from them to procure for the deceased a passage into a better state, or pray them out of purgatory, which forms a part of their system.

The interior doctrine of this sect, which is kept secret from the common people, teaches a philosophical atheism, which admits neither rewards nor punishments after death; and believes not in a providence, or the immortality of the soul; acknowledges no other God than the VOID, or NOTHING; and which makes the supreme happiness of mankind to consist in a total inaction, an entire insensibility, and a perfect quietude. Fuh, though the idol of the common people, is considered as a foreign deity in China, imported by the Boudhists from India: great effects are, however, attached to the perpetual reiteration of his name, and even to meditation upon it. It is supposed to render fate favourable, and life secure; to prevent migration into the bodies of inferior animals; and, in fine, to secure a place in the paradise of Fuh, whose land is yellow gold, whose towers are composed of gems, the bridges of pearls, &c.

FOOL, FOLLY, or **FOOLISHNESS**. The term fool is to be understood sometimes according to its plain, literal meaning, as denoting a person void of understanding; but it is often used figuratively, Psalm xxxviii, 5; lxix, 5. "The fool," that is, the impious sinner, "hath said in his heart, There is no God," Psalm xiv, 1. "I have sinned: do away the iniquity of thy servant; for I have done very foolishly," 1 Chron. xxi, 8. "Fools make a mock at sin," Prov. xiv, 9. See also the language of Tamar to her brother Amnon: "Do not this folly; for whither shall I cause my shame to go? And as for thee, thou shalt be as one of the fools in Israel," 2 Sam. xiii, 13; that is, Thou wilt be accounted a very wicked person. Our Lord seems to have used the term in a sense somewhat peculiar in Matthew v, 22: "Whosoever shall say to his brother, Thou fool, shall be in danger of hell fire." But the whole verse shows the meaning to be, that when any one of his professed disciples indulges a temper and disposition of mind contrary to charity, or that peculiar love which the brethren of Christ are bound by his law to have toward each other, John xiii, 34, not only showing anger against another without a cause, but also treating him with contemptuous language, and that with malicious intent, he shall be in danger of eternal destruction.

FOOT. Anciently it was customary to wash the feet of strangers coming off a journey, because generally they travelled barefoot, or wore sandals only, which did not secure them from dust or dirt. Jesus Christ washed the feet of his Apostles, and thereby taught them to perform the humblest services for one another. Feet, in the sacred writers, often mean inclinations, affections, propensities, actions, motions: "Guide my feet in thy paths." "Keep thy feet at a distance from evil." "The feet of the debauched woman go down to death." "Let not the foot of pride come against me." To be at any one's feet, signifies obeying him, listening to his instructions and commands. Moses says that "the Lord loved his people; all his saints are in thy hand: and they sat down at his feet," Deut. xxxiii, 3. St. Paul was brought up at the feet of Gamaliel. Mary sat at our Saviour's feet, and heard his word, Luke x, 39.

It is said that the land of Canaan is not like Egypt, "where thou sowedst thy seed, and wateredst it with thy FOOT," Deut. xi, 10. Palestine is a country which has rains, plentiful dews, springs, rivulets, brooks, &c, that supply the earth with the moisture necessary to its fruitfulness. On the contrary, Egypt has no river except the Nile: there it seldom rains, and the lands which are not within reach of the inundation continue parched and barren. To supply this want, ditches are dug from the river, and water is distributed throughout the several villages and cantons: there are great struggles who shall first obtain it; and, in this dispute, they frequently come to blows. Notwithstanding these precautions, many places have no water; and, in the course of the year, those places which are nearest the Nile require to be watered again by means of art and labour. This was formerly done by the help of machines, one of which is thus described by Philo: It is a wheel which a man turns by the motion of his feet, by ascending successively the several steps that are within it. This is what Moses means in this place by saying, that, in Egypt, they water the earth with their feet. The water is thus conveyed to cisterns; and when the gardens want refreshment, water is conducted by trenches to the beds in little rills, which are stopped by the FOOT, and turned at pleasure into different directions.

2. To be under any one's feet, to be a footstool to him, signifies the subjection of a subject to his sovereign, of a slave to his master. To lick the dust of one's feet, is an abject manner of doing homage. In Mr. Hugh Boyd's account of his embassy to the king of Candy, in Ceylon, there is a paragraph which singularly illustrates this, and shows the adulation and obsequious reverence with which an eastern monarch is approached. Describing his introduction to the king, he says, "The removal of the curtain was the signal of our obeisances. Mine, by stipulation, was to be only kneeling. My companions immediately began the performance of theirs, which were in the most perfect degree of eastern humiliation. They almost literally licked the dust; prostrating themselves with their faces almost close to the stone floor, and throwing out their arms and legs; then, rising on their knees, they repeated, in a very loud voice, a certain form of words of the most extravagant meaning that can be conceived, that the head of the king of kings might reach beyond the sun; that he might live a thousand years," &c. Nakedness of feet was a sign of mourning. God says to Ezekiel, "Make no mourning for the dead, and put on thy shoes upon thy feet," &c. It was also a mark of respect: "Put off thy shoes from off thy feet; for the place whereon thou standest is holy ground," Exodus iii, 5. The rabbins say that the priests went barefoot in the temple. "If thou turn away thy foot from the Sabbath, from doing thy pleasure on my holy day," Isaiah lviii, 13; if thou forbear walking and travelling on the Sabbath day, and do not then thine own will. We know that journeys were forbidden on the Sabbath day, Matt. xxiv, 20; Acts i, 12. Kissing the feet was often practised as a mark of affection and reverence.

FORNICATION, whoredom, or the act of incontinency between single persons; for if either of the parties be married, the sin is adultery.

FOREHEAD, MARK ON THE, Ezekiel ix, 4. Mr. Maurice, speaking of the religious rites of the Hindoos, says, Before they can enter the great pagoda, an indispensable ceremony takes place, which can only be performed by the hand of a brahmin; and that is, the impression of their foreheads with the TILUK, or mark of different colours, as they may belong either to the sect of Veeshnu, or Seeva. If the temple be that of Veeshnu, their foreheads are marked with a longitudinal line, and the colour used is vermilion. If it be the temple of Seeva, they are marked with a parallel line, and the colour used is turmeric, or saffron. But these two grand sects being again subdivided into numerous classes, both the size and the shape of the TILUK are varied, in proportion to their superior or inferior rank. In regard to the TILUK, I must observe, that it was a custom of very ancient date in Asia to mark their servants in the forehead. It is alluded to in these words of Ezekiel, where the Almighty commands his angels to "go through the midst of the city, and set a mark on the foreheads of the men who sigh for the abominations committed in the midst thereof." The same idea occurs also in Rev. vii, 3. The divers sects of the Hindoos have a distinguishing mark of the sect, by which they are known, on the forehead, of powdered sandal wood, or of the slime of the Ganges. The mark of the Wischnites consists of two nearly oval lines down the nose, which runs from two straight lines on the forehead. The mark of the Schivites consists of two curved lines, like a half moon with a point on the nose. It is made either with the slime of the Ganges, with sandal wood, or the ashes of cow dung.

FOUNTAIN is properly the source or springhead of waters. There were several celebrated fountains in Judea, such as that of Rogel, of Gihon, of Siloam, of Nazareth, &c; and allusions to them are often to be met with in both the Old and New Testament. Dr. Chandler, in his travels in Asia Minor, says, "The reader, as we proceed, will find frequent mention of fountains. Their number is owing to the nature of the country and the climate. The soil, parched and thirsty, demands moisture to aid vegetation; and a cloudless sun, which inflames the air, requires for the people the verdure, with shade and air, its agreeable attendants. Hence fountains are met with, not only in the towns and villages, but in the fields and gardens, and by the sides of the roads, and of the beaten tracks on the mountains. Many of them are the useful donations of humane persons while living, or have been bequeathed as legacies on their decease." As fountains of water were so extremely valuable to the inhabitants of the eastern countries, it is easy to understand why the inspired writers so frequently allude to them, and thence deduce some of their most beautiful and striking similitudes, when they would set forth the choicest spiritual blessings. Thus Jeremiah calls the blessed God, "the fountain of living waters," Jer. ii, 13. As those springs or fountains of water are the most valuable and highly prized which never intermit or cease to flow, but are always sending forth their streams; such is Jehovah to his people: he is a perennial source of felicity. Zechariah, pointing in his days to the atonement which was to be made in the fulness of time, by the shedding of the blood of Christ, describes it as a fountain that was to be opened in which the inhabitants of Jerusalem might wash away all their impurities: "In that day there shall be a fountain opened to the house of David, and to the inhabitants of Jerusalem, for sin and for uncleanness," Zech. xiii, 1. Joel predicted the salvation which was to come out of Zion, under the beautiful figure of "a fountain which should come forth out of the house of the Lord, and water the plain of Shittim," Joel iii, 18. The Psalmist, expatiating on the excellency of the loving-kindness of God, not only as affording a ground of hope to the children of men, but also as the source of consolation and happiness, adds, "Thou shalt make them drink of the river of thy pleasures; for with thee is the fountain of life," Psalm xxxvi, 7–9. In short, the blessedness of the heavenly state is shadowed forth under this beautiful figure; for as "in the divine presence there is fulness of joy, and at God's right hand, pleasures for evermore," Psalm xvi, 11; so it is said of those who came out of great tribulation, that "the Lamb that was in the midst of the throne shall lead them unto living fountains of water, and God shall wipe away all tears from their eyes," Rev. vii, 17.

FOX, שועל, Judges xv, 4; Nehemiah iv, 3; xi, 27; Psalm lxiii, 10; Cant. ii, 15; Lam. v, 11; Ezek. xiii, 4; Matt. viii, 20; Luke ix, 58; xiii, 32. Parkhurst observes that this is the name of an animal, probably so called from its burrowing, or making holes in the earth to hide himself or dwell in. The **LXX** render it by ἀλώπηξ, the Vulgate, VULPES, and our English version, FOX. It is recorded, in Judges xv, 4, 5, that "Samson went and caught three hundred foxes, and took firebrands, and turned tail to tail, and put a firebrand in the midst between two tails; and when he had set the brands on fire, he let them go into the standing corn of the Philistines, and burnt up both the shocks, and also the standing corn, with the vineyards and olives." Dr. Shaw thinks jackals to be the animals here intended; observing, that "as these are creatures by far the most common and familiar, as well as the most numerous of any in the eastern countries, we may well perceive the great possibility there was for Samson to take, or cause to be taken, three hundred of them. The fox, properly so called," he adds, "is rarely to be met with, neither is it gregarious." So Hasselquist remarks: "Jackals are found in great numbers about Gaza; and, from their gregarious nature, it is much more probable that Samson should have caught three hundred of them, than of the solitary quadruped, the fox."

2. At the feast of Ceres, the goddess of corn, celebrated annually at Rome about the middle of April, there was the observance of this custom, to fix burning torches to the tails of a number of foxes, and to let them run through the circus till they were burnt to death. This was done in revenge upon that species of animals, for having once burnt up the fields of corn. The reason, indeed, assigned by Ovid, is too frivolous an origin for so solemn a rite; and the time of its celebration, the seventeenth of April, it seems, was not harvest time, when the fields were covered with corn, VESTITOS MESSIBUS AGROS; for the middle of April was seed time in Italy, as appears from Virgil's Georgics. Hence we must infer that this rite must have taken its rise from some other event than that by which Ovid accounted for it; and Samson's foxes are a probable origin of it. The time agrees exactly, as may be collected from several passages of Scripture. For instance: from the book of Exodus we learn, that before the passover, that is, before the fourteenth day of the month Abib, or March, barley in Egypt

was in the ear, Exod. xii, 18; xiii, 4. And in chapter ix, 31, 32, it is said, that the wheat at that time was not grown up. Barley harvest, then, in Egypt, and so in the country of the Philistines, which bordered upon it, must have fallen about the middle of March. Wheat harvest, according to Pliny, was a month later: "IN EGYPTO HORDEUM SEXTO A SATU MENSE, FRUMENTA SEPTIMO METUNTUR." [In Egypt barley is reaped in the sixth month from the time of its being sown, wheat in the seventh.] Therefore wheat harvest happened about the middle of April; the very time in which the burning of foxes was observed at Rome. It is certain that the Romans borrowed many of their rites and ceremonies, both serious and ludicrous, from foreign nations; and Egypt and Phenicia furnished them with more perhaps than any other country. From one of these the Romans might either receive this rite immediately, or through the hands of their neighbours, the Carthaginians, who were a colony of Phenicians; and so its true origin may be referred back to the story which we have been considering.

Bochart has made it probable that the איים spoken of in Isaiah xiii, 22; xxxiv, 14; and Jer. 1, 39, rendered by our translators "the beasts of the islands," an appellation very vague and indeterminate, are JACKALS; and that the θωὲς of the Greeks, and the BENI ANI of the Arabians are the same animal; and though he takes that to have been their specific name, yet he thinks, that, from their great resemblance to a fox, they might be comprehended under the Hebrew name of a fox, SHUAL; which is indeed almost the same with SCIAGAL SCIUGAL, the Persian names of the jackal. Scaliger and Olearius, quoted by Bochart, expressly call the jackal a fox; and Mr. Sandys speaks of it in the same manner: "The jackals, in my opinion, are no other than foxes, whereof an infinite number," &c. Hasselquist calls it the little eastern fox; and Kæmpfer says that it might not be improperly called the wolf-fox. It is therefore very conceivable that the ancients might comprehend this animal under the general name of fox.

3. To give an idea of his own extreme poverty, the Lord Jesus says, Luke ix, 58, "Foxes have holes, and birds of the air have nests; but the Son of man hath not where to lay his head." And he calls Herod, the tetrarch of Galilee, a fox, Luke xiii, 32; thereby signifying his craft, and the refinements of his policy. In illustration of the pertinency of this allusion, we may quote a remark of Busbequius: "I heard a mighty noise, as if it had been of men who jeered and mocked us. I asked what was the matter; and was answered, 'Only the howlings of certain beasts which the Turks call, CIAGALS, or JACKALS.' They are a sort of wolves, somewhat bigger than foxes, but less than common wolves, yet as greedy and devouring. They go in flocks, and seldom hurt man or beast; but get their food more by craft and stealth than by open force. Thence it is that the Turks call subtle and crafty persons by the metaphorical name of CIAGALS."

FRANKINCENSE, לבונה, Exod. xxx, 34, &c. λίβανος, Matt. ii, 11; Rev. xviii, 13, a dry, resinous substance, of a yellowish white colour, a strong fragrant smell, and bitter, acrid taste. The tree which produces it is not known. Dioscorides mentions it as procured from India. What is here called the pure frankincense is, no doubt, the same with the MASCULA THURA of Virgil, and signifies what is first obtained from the tree.

FRIEND is taken for one whom we love and esteem above others, to whom we impart our minds more familiarly than to others, and that from a confidence of his integrity and good will toward us: thus Jonathan and David were mutually friends. Solomon, in his book of Proverbs, gives the qualities of a true friend. "A friend loveth at all times:" not only in prosperity, but also in adversity; and, "there is a friend that sticketh closer than a brother." He is more hearty in the performance of all friendly offices; he reproves and rebukes when he sees any thing amiss. "Faithful are the wounds of a friend." His sharpest reproofs proceed from an upright, and truly loving and faithful soul. He is known by his good and faithful counsel, as well as by his seasonable rebukes. "Ointment and perfume rejoice the heart, so does the sweetness of a man's friend by hearty counsel:" by such counsel as comes from his very heart and soul, and is the language of his inward and most serious thoughts. The company and conversation of a friend is refreshing and reviving to a person, who, when alone, is sad, dull, and inactive. "Iron sharpeneth iron, so a man sharpeneth the countenance of his friend." The title, "the friend of God," is principally given to Abraham: "Art not thou our God, who gavest this land to the seed of Abraham, thy friend, for ever?" And in Isaiah xli, 8, "But thou Israel art the seed of Abraham, my friend." "And the Scripture was fulfilled, which saith, Abraham believed God, and it was imputed to him for righteousness; and he was called the friend of God," James ii, 23. This title was given him, not only because God frequently appeared to him, conversed familiarly with him, and revealed his secrets to him, "Shall I hide from Abraham that thing which I do?" Gen. xviii, 17; but also because he entered into a covenant of perpetual friendship both with him and his seed. Our Saviour calls his Apostles "friends:" "But I have called you friends;" and he adds the reason of it, "for all things that I have heard of my Father, I have made known unto you," John xv, 15. As men use to communicate their counsels and their whole mind to their friends, especially in things which are of any concern, or may be of any advantage for them to know and understand, so I have revealed to you whatever is necessary for your instruction, office, comfort, and salvation. And this title is not peculiar to the Apostles only, but is common with them to all true believers. The friend of the bridegroom is the brideman; he who does the honours of the wedding, and leads his friend's spouse to the nuptial chamber. John the Baptist, with respect to Christ and his church, was the friend of the bridegroom; by his preaching he prepared the people of the Jews for Christ, John iii, 29. Friend is a word of ordinary salutation, whether to a friend or foe: he is called friend who had not on a wedding garment, Matt. xxii, 12. And our Saviour calls Judas the traitor friend. Some are of opinion that this title is given to the guest by an irony, or antiphrasis; meaning the contrary to what the word importeth; or that he is called so, because he appeared to others to be Christ's friend; or was so in his own esteem and account, though falsely, being a hypocrite. However, this being spoken in the person of him who made the feast, it is generally taken for a usual compellation, and that Christ, following the like courteous custom of appellation and friendly greeting, did so salute Judas, which yet left a sting behind it in his conscience, who knew himself to be the reverse of what he was called. The name of friend is likewise given to a neighbour. "Which of you shall have a friend, and shall go to him at midnight, and say, Friend, lend me three loaves?" Luke xi, 3.

FRIENDS, or **QUAKERS**, a religious society which began to be distinguished about the middle of the seventeenth century. Their doctrines were first promulgated in England, by George Fox, about the year 1647; for which he was imprisoned at Nottingham, in the year 1649, and the year following at Derby. Fox evidently considered himself as acting under a divine commission, and went, not only to fairs and markets, but into courts of justice and "steeple houses," as he called the churches, warning all to obey the Holy Spirit, speaking by him. It is said, that the appellation of Quakers was given them in reproach by one of the magistrates, who, in 1650, committed Fox to prison, on account of his bidding him, and those about him, to QUAKE at the word of the Lord. But they adopted among themselves, and still retain, the kind appellation of Friends.

From their first appearance, they suffered much persecution. In New-England they were treated with peculiar severity, imprisoned, scourged, (women as well as men,) and at Boston four of them were even hanged, among whom was one woman; and this was the more extraordinary and inexcusable, as the settlers themselves had but lately fled from persecution in the parent country! During these sufferings, they applied to King Charles **II**, for relief; who, in 1661, granted a mandamus, to put a stop to them. Neither were the good offices of this prince in their favour confined to the colonies; for in 1672, he released, under the great seal, four hundred of these suffering people who were imprisoned in Great Britain. To what has been alleged against them, on account of James Naylor and his associates, they answer that their extravagancies and blasphemies were disapproved at the time, and the parties disowned; nor was Naylor restored till he had given signs of a sincere repentance, and publicly condemned his errors.

In 1681, Charles **II**, granted to W. Penn the province of Pennsylvania. Penn's treaty with the Indians, and the liberty of conscience which he granted to all denominations, even those which had persecuted his own, do honour to his memory. In the reign of James **II**, the Friends, in common with other English Dissenters, were relieved by the suspension of the penal laws. But it was not till the reign of William and Mary that they obtained any thing like a proper legal protection. An act was passed in the year 1696, which, with a few exceptions, allowed to their affirmation the legal force of an oath, and provided a less oppressive mode for recovering tithes under a certain amount; which provisions, under the reign of George I, were made perpetual. For refusing to pay tithes, &c, however, they are still liable to suffer in the exchequer and ecclesiastical court, both in Great Britain and Ireland.

The true Friends are orthodox, as to the leading doctrines of Christianity, but express themselves in peculiar phrases. They hold special revelations of the Holy Spirit, yet not to the disparagement of the written word, which they regard as the infallible rule of faith and practice. They reject a salaried ministry, and interpret the sacraments mystically. They are advocates of the interior spiritual life of religion, to which, indeed, they have borne constant testimony; and they are distinguished by probity, philanthropy, and a public spirit. [In the United States, the Friends are divided into the Orthodox, (so called,) and Hicksites, or followers of the late Elias Hicks. The latter are considered as having departed from the original doctrines of the Friends, and very far from the leading doctrines of Christianity, as held by Protestant Christians in general.]

FROG, צפרדע; Arabic, AKURRAK; Greek, βάτραχος; Exod. viii, 2–14; Psalm lxxviii, 45; cv, 30; Rev. xvi, 13. When God plagued Pharaoh and his people, the river Nile, which was the object of great admiration to the Egyptians, was made to contribute to their punishment. "The river brought forth frogs abundantly;" but the circumstance of their coming up into the bed chambers, and into the ovens and kneading troughs, needs explanation to us, whose domestic apartments and economy are so different from those of the ancient nations. Their lodgings were not in upper stories, but in recesses on the ground floor; and their ovens were not like ours, built on the side of a chimney, and adjacent to a fireplace, where the glowing heat would frighten away the frogs, but they dug a hole in the ground, in which they placed an earthen pot, which having sufficiently heated, they stuck their cakes to the inside to be baked. To find such places full of frogs when they came to heat them in order to bake their bread, and to see frogs in the beds where they sought repose, must have been both disgusting and distressing in the extreme. Frogs were reckoned unclean by the Hebrews.

FRONTLETS. Leo of Modena thus describes them: The Jews take four pieces of parchment, and write, with an ink made on purpose, and in square letters, these four passages, one on each piece: 1. "Sanctify unto me all the first-born," &c, Exodus xiii, 1–10. 2. "And when the Lord shall bring thee into the land of the Canaanites," &c, verses 11–16. 3. "Hear, O Israel: the Lord our God is one Lord," &c, Deut. vi, 4–9. 4. "If you shall hearken diligently unto my commandments," &c, Deut. xi, 13–21. This they do in obedience to these words of Moses: "These commandments shall be for a sign unto thee upon thine hand, and for a memorial between thine eyes." These four little pieces of parchment are fastened together, and a square formed of them, on which the letter ש is written; then a little square of hard calf's skin is put upon the top, out of which come two leathern strings an inch wide, and a cubit and a half, or thereabouts, in length. This square is put on the middle of the forehead, and the strings being girt about the head, make a knot in the form of the letter ד: they then are brought before, and fall on the breast. It is called TEFFILA-SCHEL-ROSCH, or the TEPHILA of the head. The most devout Jews put it on both at morning and noon-day prayer; but the generality of the Jews wear it only at morning prayer. Only the chanter of the synagogue is obliged to put it on at noon as well as morning.

It is a question, whether the use of frontlets, and other phylacteries, was literally ordained by Moses. They who believe their use to be binding, observe, that the text of Moses speaks as positively of this as of other precepts; he requires the commandments of God to be written on the doors of houses, as a sign on their hands, and as an ornament on their foreheads, Exod. xiii, 16. If there be any obligation to write these commandments on their doors, as the text intimates, there is the same for writing them on their hands and foreheads. On the contrary, others maintain that these precepts should be taken figuratively and allegorically, as denoting that the Jews should very carefully preserve the remembrance of God's law, and observe his commands; that they should always have them before them, and never forget them. Prior to the Babylonish captivity, no traces of them appear in the history of the Jews. The prophets never inveigh against the omission or neglect of them, nor was there any question concerning them in the reformation of manners at any time among the Hebrews. The almost general custom in the east of wearing phylacteries and frontlets, determines nothing for the antiquity or usefulness of this practice. The Caraite Jews, who adhere to the letter of the law, and despise traditions, call the rabbinical Jews bridled asses, because they wear these tephilim and frontlets. See Phylactery.

FRUIT, the product of the earth, as trees, plants, &c. "Blessed shall be the fruit of thy ground and cattle." The fruit of the body signifies children: "Blessed shall be the fruit of thy body." By fruit is sometimes meant reward: "They shall eat of the fruit of their own ways," Prov. i, 31; they shall receive the reward of their bad conduct, and punishment answerable to their sins. The fruit of the lips is the sacrifice of praise or thanksgiving, Heb. xiii, 15. The fruit of the righteous, that is, the counsel, example, instruction, and reproof of the righteous, is a tree of life, is a means of much good, both temporal and eternal; and that not only to himself, but to others also, Prov. xi, 30. Solomon says, in Prov. xii, 14, "A man shall be satisfied with good by the fruit of his mouth;" that is, he shall receive abundant blessings from God as the reward of that good he has done, by his pious and profitable discourses. "Fruits meet for repentance," Matt. iii, 8, is such a conduct as befits the profession of penitence.

2. The fruits of the Spirit are those gracious habits which the Holy Spirit of God produces in those in whom he dwelleth and worketh, with those acts which flow from them, as naturally as the tree produces its fruit. The Apostle enumerates these fruits in Galatians v, 22, 23. The same Apostle, in Eph. v, 9, comprehends the fruits of the sanctifying Spirit in these three things; namely, goodness, righteousness, and truth. The fruits of righteousness are such good works and holy actions as spring from a gracious frame of heart: "Being filled with the fruits of righteousness," Phil. i, 11. Fruit is taken for a charitable contribution, which is the fruit or effect of faith and love: "When I have sealed unto them this fruit," Rom. xv, 28; when I have safely delivered this contribution. When fruit is spoken of good men, then it is to be understood of the fruits or works of holiness and righteousness; but when of evil men, then are meant the fruits of sin, immorality, and wickedness. This is our Saviour's doctrine, Matt. vii, 16–18.

3. Uncircumcised fruit, or impure, of which there is mention in Lev. xix, 23, is the fruit for the first three years of a tree newly planted; it was reputed unclean, and no one was permitted to eat of it in all that time. In the fourth year it was offered to the Lord; after which it was common, and generally eaten. Various reasons are assigned for this precept. As (1.) Because the first-fruits were to be offered to God, who required the best: but in this time the fruit was not come to perfection. (2.) It was serviceable to the trees themselves, which grew the better and faster; being early stripped of those fruits which otherwise would have derived to themselves, and drawn away, much of the strength from the root and tree. (3.) It tended to the advantage of men, both because the fruit was then waterish, undigestible, and unwholesome; and because hereby men were taught to bridle their appetites, a lesson of great use and absolute necessity in a godly life.

FUEL. In preparing their victuals, the orientals are, from the extreme scarcity of wood in many countries, reduced to use cow dung for fuel. At Aleppo, the inhabitants use wood and charcoal in their rooms, but heat their baths with cow dung, the parings of fruit, and other things of a similar kind, which they employ people to gather for that purpose. In Egypt, according to Pitts, the scarcity of wood is so great, that at Cairo they commonly heat their ovens with horse or cow dung, or dirt of the streets; what wood they have, being brought from the shores of the Black Sea, and sold by weight. Chardin attests the same fact: "The eastern people always used cow dung for baking, boiling a pot, and dressing all kinds of victuals that are easily cooked, especially in countries that have but little wood;" and Dr. Russel remarks, in a note, that "the Arabs carefully collect the dung of the sheep and camel, as well as that of the cow; and that the dung, offals, and other matters, used in the bagnios, after having been new gathered in the streets, are carried out of the city, and laid in great heaps to dry, where they become very offensive. They are intolerably disagreeable, while drying, in the town, adjoining to the bagnios; and are so at all times when it rains, though they be stacked, pressed hard together, and thatched at top." These statements exhibit, in a very strong light, the extreme misery of the Jews, who escaped from the devouring sword of Nebuchadnezzar: "They that did feed delicately are desolate in the streets; they that were brought up in scarlet embrace dunghills," Lam. iv,

5. To embrace dunghills, is a species of wretchedness, perhaps unknown to us in the history of modern warfare; but it presents a dreadful and appalling image, when the circumstances to which it alludes are recollected. What can be imagined more distressing to those who lived delicately, than to wander without food in the streets? What more disgusting and terrible to those who had been clothed in rich and splendid garments, than to be forced, by the destruction of their palaces, to seek shelter among stacks of dung, the filth and stench of which it is almost impossible to endure? The dunghill, it appears from Holy Writ, is one of the common retreats of the mendicant. This imparts great force and beauty to a passage in the song of Hannah: "He raiseth up the poor out of the dust, and lifteth the beggar from the dunghill, to set them among princes, and to make them inherit the throne of glory," 1 Sam. ii, 8. The change in the circumstances of that excellent woman, she reckoned as great, (and it was to her as unexpected,) as the elevation of a poor despised beggar from a nauseous and polluting dunghill, rendered tenfold more fetid by the intense heat of an oriental sun, to one of the highest and most splendid stations on earth.

2. Dung is used as fuel in the east only when wood cannot be had; for the latter, and even any other combustible substance, is preferred when it can be obtained. The inhabitants of Aleppo, according to Russel, use thorns and fuel of a similar kind for those culinary purposes which require haste, particularly for boiling, which seems to be the reason that Solomon mentions the "crackling of thorns under a pot," rather than in any other way. The same allusion to the use of thorns for boiling occurs in other parts of the sacred volume: thus, the Psalmist speaks of the wicked, "Before your pots can feel the thorns, he shall take them away as with a whirlwind, both living, and in his wrath." The Jews are sometimes compared in the prophets to "a brand plucked out of the burning," Amos iv, 11; Zech. iii, 2; a figure which Chardin considers as referring to vine twigs, and other brushwood which the orientals frequently use for fuel, and which, in a few minutes, must be consumed if they are not snatched out of the fire; and not to those battens, or large branches, which will lie a long time in the fire before they are reduced to ashes. If this idea be correct, it displays in a stronger and more lively manner the seasonable interposition of God's mercy, than is furnished by any other view of the phrase. The same remark applies to the figure by which the Prophet Isaiah describes the sudden and complete destruction of Rezin, and the son of Remaliah; only in this passage, the firebrands are supposed to be smoking; that is, in the opinion of Harmer, having the steam issuing with force from one end, in consequence of the fire burning violently at the other. The words of the prophet are: "Take heed and be quiet; fear not, neither be faint-hearted, for the two tails of these smoking firebrands, for the fierce anger of Rezin with Syria, and of the son of Remaliah," Isaiah vii, 4. It is not easy to conceive an image more striking than this; the remains of two small twigs burning with violence at one end, as appears by the steaming of the other, are soon reduced to ashes; so shall the kingdoms of Syria and Israel sink into ruin and disappear.

3. The scarcity of fuel in the east obliges the inhabitants to use, by turns, every kind of combustible matter. The withered stalks of herbs and flowers, the tendrils of the vine, the small branches of myrtle, rosemary, and other plants, are all used in heating their ovens and bagnios. We can easily recognise this practice in these words of our Lord: "Consider the lilies of the field, how they grow; they toil not, neither do they spin: and yet I say unto you, that Solomon, in all his glory, was not arrayed like one of these. Wherefore, if God so clothe the grass of the field, which today is, and to-morrow is cast into the oven, shall he not much more clothe you, O ye of little faith?" Matt. vi, 28–30. The grass of the field, in this passage, evidently includes the lilies of which our Lord had just been speaking, and, by consequence, herbs in general; and in this extensive sense the word χόρτος is not unfrequently taken. These beautiful productions of nature, so richly arrayed, and so exquisitely perfumed, that the splendour even of Solomon is not to be compared with theirs, shall soon wither and decay, and be used as fuel to heat the oven and the bagnio. Has God so adorned these flowers and plants of the field, which retain their beauty and vigour but for a few days, and are then applied to some of the meanest purposes of life; and will he not much more clothe you who are the disciples of his own Son, who are capable of immortality, and destined to the enjoyment of eternal happiness?

FULNESS. "The fulness of time" is the time when the Messiah appeared, which was appointed by God, promised to the fathers, foretold by the prophets, expected by the Jews themselves, and earnestly longed for by all the faithful: "When the fulness of the time was come, God sent his Son," Gal. iv, 4. The fulness of Christ is the superabundance of grace with which he was filled: "Of his fulness have all we received," John i, 16. And whereas men are said to be filled with the Holy Ghost, as John the Baptist, Luke i, 15; and Stephen, Acts vi, 5; this differs from the fulness of Christ in these three respects: (1.) Grace in others is by participation, as the moon hath her light from the sun, rivers their waters from the fountain: but in Christ all that perfection and influence which we include in that term is originally, naturally, and of himself. (2.) The Spirit is in Christ infinitely and above measure, John iii, 34; but in the saints by measure according to the gift of God, Eph. iv, 16. The saints cannot communicate their graces to others, whereas the gifts of the Spirit are in Christ as a head and fountain, to impart them to his members. "We have received of his fulness," John i, 16. It is said, that "the fulness of the Godhead dwells in Christ bodily," Col. ii, 2; that is, the whole nature and attributes of God are in Christ, and that really, essentially, or substantially; and also personally, by nearest union; as the soul dwells in the body, so that the same person who is man is God also. The church is called the fulness of Christ, Eph. i, 23. It is the church which makes him a complete and perfect head; for though he has a natural and personal fulness as God, yet, as Mediator, he is not full and complete, without his mystical body, (as a king is not complete without his subjects,) but receives an outward, relative, and mystical fulness from his members.

FUNERAL RITES. See Burial.

FURNACE, a fireplace for melting gold and other metals. "The fining pot is for silver, the furnace for gold," Prov. xvii, 3. It signifies also a place of cruel bondage and oppression, such as Egypt was to the Israelites, who there met with much hardship, rigour, and severity, to try and purge them, Deut. iv, 20; Jer. xi, 4; the sharp and grievous afflictions and judgments, wherewith God tries his people, Ezek. xxii, 18; xx, 22; also a place of torment, as Nebuchadnezzar's fiery furnace, Dan. iii, 6, 11. On the last we may remark, that this mode of putting to death is not unusual in the east in modern times. After speaking of the common modes of punishing with death in Persia, Chardin says, "But there is still a particular way of putting to death such as have transgressed in civil affairs, either by causing a dearth, or by selling above the tax by a false weight, or who have committed themselves in any other manner: they are put upon a spit and roasted over a slow fire, Jer. xxix, 22. Bakers, when they offend, are thrown into a hot oven. During the dearth in 1668, I saw such ovens heated in the royal square in Ispahan, to terrify the bakers, and deter them from deriving advantage from the general distress."

GABBATHA, a place in Pilate's palace, from whence he pronounced sentence of death upon Jesus Christ, John xix, 13. This was probably an eminence, or terrace, paved with marble, for the Hebrew means ELEVATED.

GABRIEL, one of the principal angels of heaven. He was sent to the Prophet Daniel, to explain to him the visions of the ram and goat, and the mystery of the seventy weeks, which had been revealed to him, Dan. viii, 15; ix, 21; xi, 1, &c. The same angel was sent to Zechariah, to declare to him the future birth of John the Baptist, Luke i, 11, &c. Six months after this he appeared to a virgin, whose name was Mary, of the city of Nazareth, as related Luke i, 26, &c.

GAD was the name of the son of Jacob and Zilpah, Leah's servant, Gen. xxx, 9–11. Leah, Jacob's wife, gave him also Zilpah, that by her she might have children. Zilpah brought a son, whom Leah called Gad, saying, "A troop cometh." Gad had seven sons, Ziphion, Haggi, Shuni, Ezbon, Eri, Arodi, and Areli, Genesis xlvi, 16. Jacob, blessing Gad, said, "A troop shall overcome him, but he shall overcome at the last," Gen. xlix, 19; and Moses, in his last song, mentions Gad as "a lion which teareth the arm with the crown of the head," &c, Deut. xxxiii, 20, 21. The tribe of Gad came out of Egypt in number forty-five thousand six hundred and fifty. After the defeat of the kings Og and Sihon, Gad and Reuben desired to have their lot in the conquered country, and alleged their great number of cattle. Moses granted their request, on condition that they would accompany their brethren, and assist in the conquest of the land beyond Jordan. Gad had his inheritance between Reuben south, and Manasseh north, with the mountains of Gilead east, and Jordan west.

2. Gad, a prophet, David's friend, who followed him when persecuted by Saul. The Scripture calls him a prophet and David's seer, 2 Sam. xxiv, 11. The first time we find him with this prince is when he fled into the land of Moab, 1 Sam. xxii, 5, to secure his father and mother in the first year of Saul's persecution. The Prophet Gad warned him to return into the land of Judah. After David had determined to number his people, the Lord sent to him the Prophet Gad, to offer him his choice of three scourges: seven years' famine, or three months' flight before his enemies, or three days' pestilence. Gad also directed David to erect an altar to the Lord, in the threshing floor of Ornan or Araunah, the Jebusite, 2 Sam. xxiv, 13–19; and he wrote a history of David's life, cited in 1 Chron. xxix, 29.

GADARA, a city which gave name to the country of the Gadarenes; situated on a steep rocky hill on the river Hieromax, or Yermuck, about five miles from its junction with the Jordan. It was a place of considerable note in the time of Josephus, and the metropolis of Peræa, or the country beyond Jordan. It was also celebrated for its hot baths. The vicinity was likewise called the country of the Gergesenes, from Gerasa, or Gergesa, another considerable city in the same neighbourhood. Thus the miracle of our Lord performed here is represented by St. Mark to have been done in the country of the Gadarenes, Mark v, 1; and by St. Matthew, in that of the Gergesenes, Matt. viii, 28.

GALATIA, a province of the Lesser Asia, bounded on the west by Phrygia, on the east by the river Haylys, on the north by Paphlagonia, and on the south by Lycaonia. The Galatians are said to have been descended from those Gauls, who, finding their own country too strait for them, left it, after the death of Alexander the Great, in quest of new settlements. Quitting their own country, they migrated eastward along the Danube till they came where the Saave joins that river; then dividing themselves into three bodies, under the conduct of different leaders, one of these bodies entered Pannonia; another marched into Thrace; a third into Illyricum and Macedonia. The party which proceeded into Thrace, crossed the Bosphorus into the Lesser Asia, and hiring themselves to Nicomedes, king of Bithynia, assisted him to subdue his brother Zipetes, with whom he was then at war; and as a reward of their services they received from him a country in the middle of Asia Minor, which from them was afterward called GALLO-GRÆCIA, and, by contraction, Galatia. As their inland situation in a great measure cut them off from all intercourse with more civilized nations, the Galatians long remained a rude and illiterate people. And as a proof of this, it is mentioned by Jerom, that when the Apostle Paul preached the Gospel among them, and for many ages afterward, they continued to speak the language of the country from whence they came out.

2. Paul and Barnabas carried the light of the Gospel into the regions of Galatia at a very early period; and it appears from the epistle which the former subsequently wrote to the churches in that country, that they had at first received it with great joy, Gal. iv, 15. But some Judaizing teachers getting access among them soon after the Apostle's departure, their minds became corrupted from the simplicity that was in Christ Jesus; and, though mostly Gentiles, they were beginning to mingle circumcision, and other Jewish observances, with their faith in Christ, in order to render it more available to their salvation. This occasioned Paul's writing his epistle to those churches; and his object throughout nearly the whole of it is to counteract the pernicious influence of the doctrine of those false teachers particularly as it respected the article of justification, or a sinner's acceptance with God. And in no part of the Apostle's writings is that important doctrine handled in a more full and explicit manner; nor does he any where display, such a firm, determined, and inflexible opposition to all who would corrupt the truth from its simplicity. He begins by expressing his astonishment that they were so soon turned aside "unto another gospel," but instantly checking himself, he recals the word and declares, "it is not another gospel," but a perversion of the Gospel of Christ. "And though we, or an angel from heaven, preach any other gospel unto you than that which we have preached unto you, let him be accursed." There are in his epistle several other things equally pointed and severe, particularly his expostulation on the folly and absurdity of their conduct in subjecting themselves to the Jewish yoke of bondage, Gal. iii, 1. "The erroneous doctrines of the Judaizing teachers," says Dr. Macknight, "and the calumnies they spread for the purpose of discrediting St. Paul's apostleship, no doubt occasioned great uneasiness of mind to him and to the faithful in that age, and did much hurt, at least for a while, among the Galatians. But in the issue these evils have proved of no small service to the church in general; for by obliging the Apostle to produce the evidences of his apostleship, and to relate the history of his life, especially after his conversion, we have obtained the fullest assurance of his being a real Apostle, called to the office by Jesus Christ himself; consequently we are assured that our faith in the doctrines of the Gospel, as taught by him, (and it is he who hath taught the peculiar doctrines of the Gospel most fully,) is not built on the credit of a man, but on the authority of the Spirit of God, by whom St. Paul was inspired in the whole of the doctrine which he has delivered to the world."

GALBANUM, חלבנה, Exod. xxx, 34. Michaëlis makes the word a compound of חלב, MILK or GUM, (for the Syriac uses the noun in both senses,) and [לבן], WHITE, as being the white milk or gum of a plant. It is the thickened sap of an umbelliferous plant, called METOPION, which grows on Mount Amanus, in Syria, and is frequently found in Persia, and in some parts of Africa. It was an ingredient in the holy incense of the Jews.

GALILEANS. In the twelfth year of Christ, about the time that Archelaus was sent away from his government, a secession was made from the sect of the Pharisees, and a new sect arose, called the Galileans. Not long after this time, Judea, which was a Roman province, was added, for civil purposes, to Syria, over which Quirinus was governor. It happened, when the tax was levied by Quirinus, that one Judas, of Galilee, otherwise called Gaulonites, in company with Zaduk, a Sadducee, publicly taught, that such taxation was repugnant to the law of Moses, according to which the Jews, they maintained, had no king but God. The tumults which this man excited were suppressed, Acts v, 37; but his disciples, who were called Galileans, continued to propagate this doctrine, and, farthermore, required of all proselytes that they should be circumcised. It was in reference to this sect that the captious question was proposed in Matt. xxii, 17, &c; namely, whether it was lawful to give tribute to Cæsar. The Galileans, whom Pilate slew in the temple, Luke xiii, 1, 2, appear to have been of this sect. By degrees, the Galileans swallowed up almost all the other sects; and it is highly probable that the zealots, particularly mentioned at the siege of Jerusalem, were of this faction.

GALILEE was one of the most extensive provinces into which the Holy Land was divided. It exceeded Judea in extent, but probably varied in its limits at different times. This province is divided by the rabbins into, 1. The Upper; 2. The Nether; and, 3. The Valley. Josephus divides it into only Upper and Lower; and he says that the limits of Galilee were, on the south, Samaria and Scythopolis, unto the flood of Jordan. Galilee contained four tribes, Issachar, Zebulun, Naphtali, and Asher; a part, also, of Dan, and part of Peræa, that is, beyond the river. Upper Galilee abounded in mountains. Lower Galilee, which contained the tribes of Zebulun and Asher, was sometimes called the Great Field, "the champaign," Deut. xi, 30. The Valley was adjacent to the sea of Tiberias. Josephus describes Galilee as very populous, and containing two hundred and four cities and towns. It was also very rich, and paid two hundred talents in tribute. The natives were brave and good soldiers; but they were seditious, and prone to insolence and rebellion. In the books of Ezra and Nehemiah, the inhabitants of Galilee and Peræa are scarcely mentioned, whether they were Jews returned from Babylon, or a mixture of different nations. The language of these regions differed considerably from that of Judea; as did various customs, in which each followed its own mode. Our Lord so frequently visited Galilee, that he was called a Galilean, Matt. xxvi, 69. The population of Galilee being very great, he had many opportunities of doing good in this country; and, being there out of the power of the priests at Jerusalem, he seems to have preferred it as his abode. Nazareth and Capernaum were in this division. From such a mixture of people, many provincialisms might be expected. Hence, we find Peter detected by his language, probably by his phraseology, as well as his pronunciation, Mark xiv, 70. Upper Galilee had Mount Lebanon and the countries of Tyre and Sidon on the north; the Mediterranean Sea on the west; Abilene, Ituræa, and the country of the

Decapolis, on the east; and Lower Galilee on the south. Its principal city was Cæsarea Philippi. This part of Galilee, being less inhabited by Jews, was thence called Galilee of the Nations, or of the Gentiles. Lower Galilee had the upper division of the same country to the north; the Mediterranean on the west; the sea of Galilee. or lake of Gennesareth, on the east; and Samaria on the south. Its principal cities were Tiberias, Chorazin, Bethsaida, Nazareth, Cana, Capernaum, Nain, Cæsarea of Palestine, and Ptolemais. This district was of all others most honoured with the presence of our Saviour. Here he was conceived; here he was brought back by his mother and reputed father, after their return from Egypt; here he lived with them till he was thirty years of age; and, although after his entrance on his public ministry he frequently visited the other provinces, it was here that he chiefly resided. Here, also, he made his first appearance after his resurrection to his Apostles, who were themselves natives of the same country, and were thence called men of Galilee.

Galilee, SEA OF. This inland sea, or more properly lake, which derives its several names, the lake of Tiberias, the sea of Galilee, and the lake of Gennesareth, from the territory which forms its western and south-western border, is computed to be between seventeen and eighteen miles in length, and from five to six in breadth. The mountains on the east come close to its shore, and the country on that side has not a very agreeable aspect: on the west, it has the plain of Tiberias, the high ground of the plain of Hutin, or Hottein, the plain of Gennesareth, and the foot of those hills by which you ascend to the high mountain of Saphet. To the north and south it has a plain country, or valley. There is a current throughout the whole breadth of the lake, even to the shore; and the passage of the Jordan through it is discernible by the smoothness of the surface in that part. Various travellers have given different accounts of its general aspect. According to Captain Mangles, the land about it has no striking features, and the scenery is altogether devoid of character. "It appeared," he says, "to particular disadvantage to us, after those beautiful lakes we had seen in Switzerland; but it becomes a very interesting object when you consider the frequent allusions to it in the Gospel narrative." Dr. Clarke, on the contrary, speaks of the uncommon grandeur of this memorable scenery. "The lake of Gennesareth," he says, "is surrounded by objects well calculated to heighten the solemn impressions made by such recollections, and affords one of the most striking prospects in the Holy Land. Speaking of it comparatively, it may be described as longer and finer than any of our Cumberland and Westmoreland lakes, although perhaps inferior to Loch Lomond. It does not possess the vastness of the lake of Geneva, although it much resembles it in certain points of view. In picturesque beauty, it comes nearest to the lake of Locarno, in Italy, although it is destitute of any thing similar to the islands by which that majestic piece of water is adorned. It is inferior in magnitude, and in the height of its surrounding mountains, to the Lake Asphaltites." Mr. Buckingham may perhaps be considered as having given the most accurate account, and one which reconciles, in some degree, the differing statements above cited, when, speaking of the lake as seen from Tel Hoom, he says, that its appearance is grand, but that the barren aspect of the mountains on each side, and the total absence of wood, give a cast of dulness to the picture: this is increased to melancholy by the dead calm of its waters, and the silence which reigns throughout its whole extent, where not a boat or vessel of any kind is to be found. The situation of the lake, lying, as it were, in a deep basin between the hills which enclose it on all sides, excepting only the narrow entrance and outlets of the Jordan at either end, protects its waters from long-continued tempests: its surface is in general as smooth as that of the Dead Sea. But the same local features render it occasionally subject to whirlwinds, squalls, and sudden gusts from the mountains, of short duration; especially when the strong current formed by the Jordan is opposed by a wind of this description from the south-east, sweeping from the mountains with the force of a hurricane, it may easily be conceived that a boisterous sea must be instantly raised, which the small vessels of the country would be unable to resist. A storm of this description is plainly denoted by the language of the evangelist, in recounting one of our Lord's miracles: "There came down a storm of wind on the lake, and they were filled with water, and were in jeopardy. Then he arose, and rebuked the wind and the raging of the water; and they ceased, and there was a calm," Luke viii, 23, 24. There were fleets of some force on this lake during the wars of the Jews with the Romans, and very bloody battles were fought between them. Josephus gives a particular account of a naval engagement between the Romans under Vespasian, and the Jews who had revolted during the administration of Agrippa. Titus and Trajan were both present, and Vespasian himself was on board the Roman fleet. The rebel force consisted of an immense multitude, who, as fugitives after the capture of Tarichæa by Titus, had sought refuge on the water. The vessels in which the Romans defeated them were built for the occasion, and yet were larger than the Jewish ships. The victory was followed by so terrible a slaughter of the Jews, that nothing was to be seen, either on the lake or its shores, but the blood and mangled corses of the slain; and the air was infected by the number of dead bodies. Six thousand five hundred persons are stated to have perished in this naval engagement, and in the battle of Tarichæa, beside twelve hundred who were afterward massacred in cold blood, by order of Vespasian, in the amphitheatre at Tiberias, and a vast number who were given to Agrippa as slaves.

GALL, ראש, something excessively bitter, and supposed to be poisonous, Deut. xxix, 18; xxxii, 32; Psalm lxix, 21; Jer. viii, 14; ix, 15; xxiii, 15; Lam. iii, 19; Hosea x, 4; Amos vi, 12. It is evident, from the first-mentioned place, that some herb or plant is meant of a malignant or nauseous kind. It is joined with wormwood, and, in the margin of our Bibles, explained to be "a very poisonful herb." In Psalm lxix, 21, which is justly considered as a prophecy of our Saviour's sufferings, it is said, "They gave me ראש to eat"; which the **LXX** have rendered χολὴν, GALL. And, accordingly, it is recorded in the history, "They gave him vinegar to drink, mingled with gall," ὄξος μετὰ χολῆς, Matt. xxvii, 34. But, in the parallel passage, it is said to be, ἐσμυρνισμένον οἶνον, "wine mingled with myrrh," Mark xv, 23, a very bitter ingredient. From whence it is probable that χολὴ, and perhaps ראש, may be used as a general name for whatever is exceedingly bitter; and, consequently, where the sense requires it, may be put specially for any bitter herb or plant, the infusion of which may be called מי־ראש.

GALLIO was the name of the brother of Seneca, the philosopher. He was at first named Marcus Annæus Novatus; but, being adopted by Lucius Junius Gallio, he took the name of his adoptive father. The Emperor Claudius made him proconsul of Achaia. He was of a mild and agreeable temper. To him his brother Seneca dedicated his books, "Of Anger." He shared in the fortunes of his brothers, as well when out of favour as in their prosperity at court. At length, Nero put him, as well as them, to death. The Jews were enraged at St. Paul for converting many Gentiles, and dragged him to the tribunal of Gallio, who, as proconsul, generally resided at Corinth, Acts xviii, 12, 13. They accused him of teaching "men to worship God contrary to the law." St. Paul being about to speak, Gallio told the Jews, that if the matter in question were a breach of justice, or an action of a criminal nature, he should think himself obliged to hear them; but, as the dispute was only concerning their law, he would not determine such differences, nor judge them. Sosthenes, the chief ruler of the synagogue, was beaten by the Greeks before Gallio's seat of justice; but this governor did not concern himself about it. His abstaining from interfering in a religious controversy did credit to his prudence; nevertheless, his name has oddly passed into a reproachful proverb; and a man regardless of all piety is called "a Gallio," and is said "Gallio-like to care for none of these things." Little did this Roman anticipate that his name would be so immortalized.

GAMALIEL, a celebrated rabbi, and doctor of the Jewish law, under whose tuition the great Apostle of the Gentiles was brought up, Acts xxii, 3. Barnabas and Stephen are also supposed to have been among the number of his pupils. Soon after the day of pentecost, when the Jewish sanhedrim began to be alarmed at the progress the Gospel was making in Jerusalem, and consequently wished to put to death the Apostles, in the hope of checking its farther progress, they were apprehended and brought before the national council, of which Gamaliel seems to have been a leading member. It is very probable that many zealots among them would have despatched the affair in a very summary manner, but their impetuosity was checked by the cool and prudent advice of Gamaliel; for, having requested the Apostles to withdraw for a while, he represented to the sanhedrim that, if the Apostles were no better than impostors, their fallacy would quickly be discovered; but on the other hand, if what they were engaged in was from God, it was vain for them to attempt to frustrate it, since it was the height of folly to contend with the Almighty. The assembly saw the wisdom of his counsel, and very prudently changed the sentence, upon which they were originally bent against the Apostles' lives, into that of corporal punishment.

2. It may here also be remarked, that the sanhedrim could not themselves believe that tale which they had diligently circulated among the people, that the disciples had stolen away the body of Jesus, and then pretended that he had arisen from the dead. If the Jewish council had thought this, it would have been very absurd in Gamaliel to exhort them to wait to see whether "the counsel and work" was of God, that is, whether the Apostles related a fact when they preached the resurrection, and grounded the divine authority of their religion upon that fact. Gamaliel's advice was wholly based upon the admission, that an extraordinary, and to them an inexplicable, event had happened.

GAMES. Games and combats were instituted by the ancients in honour of their gods; and were celebrated with that view by the most polished and enlightened nations of antiquity. The most renowned heroes, legislators, and statesmen, did not think it unbecoming their character and dignity, to mingle with the combatants, or contend in the race; they even reckoned it glorious to share in the exercises, and meritorious to carry away the prize. The victors were crowned with a wreath of laurel in presence of their country; they were celebrated in the rapturous effusions of their poets; they were admired, and almost adored, by the innumerable multitudes which flocked to the games, from every part of Greece, and many of the adjacent countries. They returned to their own homes in a triumphal chariot, and made their entrance into their native city, not through the gates which admitted the vulgar throng, but through a breach in the walls, which were broken down to give them admission; and at the same time to express the persuasion of their fellow citizens, that walls are of small use to a city defended by men of such tried courage and ability. Hence the surprising ardour which animated all the states of Greece to imitate the ancient heroes, and encircle their brows with wreaths, which rendered them still more the objects of admiration or envy to succeeding times, than the victories they had gained, or the laws they had enacted.

2. But the institutors of those games and combats had higher and nobler objects in view than veneration for the mighty dead, or the gratification of ambition or vanity; it was their design to prepare the youth for the profession of arms; to confirm their health; to improve their strength, their vigour, and activity; to inure them to fatigue; and to render them intrepid in close fight, where, in the infancy of the art of war, muscular force commonly decided the victory. This statement accounts for the striking allusions which the Apostle Paul makes in his epistles to these celebrated exercises. Such references were calculated to touch the heart of a Greek, and of every one familiarly acquainted with them, in the liveliest manner, as well as to place before the eye of his mind the most glowing and correct images of spiritual and divine things. No passages in the nervous and eloquent epistles from the pen of St. Paul, have been more admired by the critics and expositors of all times, than those into

which some allusion to these agonistic exercises is introduced; and, perhaps, none are calculated to leave a deeper impression on the Christian's mind, or excite a stronger and more salutary influence on his actions. Certain persons were appointed to take care that all things were done according to custom, to decide controversies that happened among the antagonists, and to adjudge the prize to the victor. Some eminent writers are of opinion that Christ is called the "Author and Finisher of faith," in allusion to these judges. Those who were designed for the profession of ATHLETÆ, or combatants, frequented from their earliest years the academies maintained for that purpose at the public expense. In these places they were exercised under the direction of different masters, who employed the most effectual methods to inure their bodies for the fatigues of the public games, and to form them for the combats. The regimen to which they submitted was very hard and severe. At first, they had no other nourishment than dried figs, nuts, soft cheese, and a gross heavy sort of bread called μάζα; they were absolutely forbidden the use of wine, and enjoined continence. When they proposed to contend in the Olympian games, they were obliged to repair to the public gymnasium at Elis, ten months before the solemnity, where they prepared themselves by continual exercises. No man that had omitted to present himself at the appointed time, was allowed to be a candidate for the prizes; nor were the accustomed rewards of victory given to such persons, if by any means they insinuated themselves, and overcame their antagonists; nor would any apology, though seemingly ever so reasonable, serve to excuse their absence. No person that was himself a notorious criminal, or nearly related to one, was permitted to contend. Farther, to prevent underhand dealings, if any person was convicted of bribing his adversary, a severe fine was laid upon him; nor was this alone thought a sufficient guard against unfair contracts, and unjust practices, but the contenders were obliged to swear they had spent ten whole months in preparatory exercises; and, beside all this, they, their fathers, and their brethren, took a solemn oath, that they would not, by any sinister or unlawful means, endeavour to stop the fair and just proceedings of the games.

3. The spiritual contest, in which all true Christians aim at obtaining a heavenly crown, has its rules also, devised and enacted by infinite wisdom and goodness, which require implicit and exact submission, which yield neither to times nor circumstances, but maintain their supreme authority, from age to age, uninterrupted and unimpaired. The combatant who violates these rules forfeits the prize, and is driven from the field with indelible disgrace, and consigned to everlasting wo. Hence the great Apostle of the Gentiles exhorts his son Timothy strictly to observe the precepts of the Gospel, without which, he can no more hope to obtain the approbation of God, and the possession of the heavenly crown, than a combatant in the public games of Greece, who disregarded the established rules, could hope to receive from the hands of his judge the promised reward: "And if a man also strive for masteries, yet is he not crowned except he strive lawfully," 2 Tim. ii, 5, or according to the established laws of the games. Like the Grecian combatants, the Christian must "abstain from fleshly lusts," and "walk in all the statutes and commandments of the Lord, blameless." Such was St. Paul; and in this manner he endeavoured to act: "But I keep under my body, and bring it into subjection: lest that by any means, when I have preached to others, I myself should be a cast-away," 1 Cor. ix, 27. The latter part of this verse Doddridge renders, "lest after having served as a herald I should be disapproved;" and says in a note, "I thought it of importance to retain the primitive sense of these gymnastic expressions." It is well known to those who are at all acquainted with the original, that the word used means to discharge the office of a herald, whose business it was to proclaim the conditions of the games, and display the prizes, to awaken the emulation and resolution of those who were to contend in them. But the Apostle intimates, that there was this peculiar circumstance attending the Christian contest, that the person who proclaimed its laws and rewards to others, was also to engage in it himself; and that there would be a peculiar infamy and misery in his miscarrying. Ἀδόκιμος, which we render CAST-AWAY, signifies one who is disapproved by the judge of the games, as not having fairly deserved the prize: he therefore loses it; even the prize of eternal life. The rule which the Apostle applies to himself he extends in another passage to all the members of the Christian church: "Those who strive for the mastery are temperate in all things; now they do it to obtain a corruptible crown, but we an incorruptible." Tertullian uses the same thought to encourage the martyrs. He urges constancy upon them, from what the hopes of victory made the ATHLETÆ endure; and repeats the severe and painful exercises they were obliged to undergo, the continual anguish and constraint in which they passed the best years of their lives, and the voluntary privation which they imposed on themselves, of all that was most grateful to their appetites and passions.

4. The ATHLETÆ took care to disencumber their bodies of every article of clothing which could in any manner hinder or incommode them. In the race, they were anxious to carry as little weight as possible, and uniformly stripped themselves of all such clothes as, by their weight, length, or otherwise, might entangle or retard them in the course. The Christian also must "lay aside every weight, and the sin which doth so easily beset" him, Heb. xii, 1. In the exercise of faith and self-denial, he must "cast off the works of darkness," lay aside all malice and guile, hypocrisies, and envyings, and evil speakings, inordinate affections, and worldly cares, and whatever else might obstruct his holy profession, damp his spirits, and hinder his progress in the paths of righteousness.

5. The foot race seems to have been placed in the first rank of public games, and cultivated with a care and industry proportioned to the estimation in which it was held. The Olympic games generally opened with races, and were celebrated at first with no other exercise. The lists or course where the ATHLETÆ exercised themselves in running, was at first but one stadium in length, or about six hundred feet; and from this measure it took its name, and was called the STADIUM, whatever might be its extent. This, in the

language of St. Paul, speaking of the Christian's course, was "the race which was set before them," determined by public authority, and carefully measured. On each side of the stadium and its extremity, ran an ascent or kind of terrace, covered with seats and benches, upon which the spectators were seated, an innumerable multitude collected from all parts of Greece, to which the Apostle thus alludes in his figurative description of the Christian life: "Seeing we are compassed about with so great a cloud of witnesses, let us lay aside every weight," Heb. xii, 1.

The most remarkable parts of the stadium were its entrance, middle, and extremity. The entrance was marked at first only by a line drawn on the sand, from side to side of the stadium. To prevent any unfair advantage being taken by the more vigilant or alert candidates, a cord was at length stretched in front of the horses or men that were to run; and sometimes the space was railed in with wood. The opening of this barrier, was the signal for the racers to start. The middle of the stadium was remarkable, only by the circumstance of having the prizes allotted to the victors set up there. From this custom, Crysostom draws a fine comparison: "As the judges in the races and other games, expose in the midst of the stadium, to the view of the champions, the crowns which they were to receive; in like manner, the Lord, by the mouth of his prophets, has placed the prizes in the midst of the course, which he designs for those who have the courage to contend for them." At the extremity of the stadium was a goal, where the foot races ended; but in those of chariots and horses, they were to run several times round it without stopping, and afterward conclude the race by regaining the other extremity of the lists from whence they started. It is therefore to the foot race the Apostle alludes, when he speaks of the race set before the Christian, which was a straight course, to be run only once, and not, as in the other, several times without stopping.

6. According to some writers, it was at the goal, and not in the middle of the course, that the prizes were exhibited; and they were placed in a very conspicuous situation, that the competitors might be animated by having them always in their sight. This accords with the view which the Apostle gives of the Christian life: "Brethren, I count not myself to have apprehended; but this one thing I do, forgetting those things which are behind, and reaching forth unto those things, which are before, I press toward the mark for the prize of the high calling of God in Christ Jesus," Phil. iii, 13, 14. L'Enfant thinks, the Apostle here alludes to those who stood at the elevated place at the end of the course, calling the racers by their names, and encouraging them by holding out the crown, to exert themselves with vigour. Within the measured and determinate limits of the stadium, the ATHLETÆ were bound to contend for the prize, which they forfeited without hope of recovery, if they deviated ever so little from the appointed course.

7. The honours and rewards granted to the victors were of several kinds. They were animated in their course by the rapturous applauses of the countless multitudes that lined the stadium, and waited the issue of the contest with eager anxiety; and their success was instantly followed by reiterated and long continued plaudits; but these were only a prelude to the appointed rewards, which, though of little value in themselves, were accounted the highest honour to which a mortal could aspire. These consisted of different wreaths of wild olive, pine, parsley, or laurel, according to the different places where the games were celebrated. After the judges had passed sentence, a public herald proclaimed the name of the victor; one of the judges put the crown upon his head, and a branch of palm into his right hand, which he carried as a token of victorious courage and perseverance. As he might be victor more than once in the same games, and sometimes on the same day, he might also receive several crowns and palms. When the victor had received his reward, a herald, preceded by a trumpet, conducted him through the stadium, and proclaimed aloud his name and country; while the delighted multitudes, at the sight of him, redoubled their acclamations and applauses.

8. The crown in the Olympic games was of wild olive; in the Pythian, of laurel; in the Isthmian or Corinthian, of pine tree; and in the Nemæan, of smallage or parsley. Now, most of these were evergreens; yet they would soon grow dry, and crumble into dust. Elsner produces many passages in which the contenders in these exercises are rallied by the Grecian wits, on account of the extraordinary pains they took for such trifling rewards; and Plato has a celebrated passage, which greatly resembles that of the Apostle, but by no means equals it in force and beauty: "Now they do it to obtain a corruptible crown, but we an incorruptible." The Christian is thus called to fight the good fight of faith, and to lay hold of eternal life; and to this he is more powerfully stimulated by considering that the ancient ATHLETÆ took all their care and pains only for the sake of obtaining a garland of flowers, or a wreath of laurel, which quickly fades and perishes, possessed little intrinsic value, and only served to nourish their pride and vanity, without imparting any solid advantage to themselves or others; but that which is placed in the view of the spiritual combatants, to animate their exertions, and reward their labours, is no less than a crown of glory which never decays; "an inheritance incorruptible, undefiled, and that fadeth not away, reserved in heaven for them," 1 Pet. i, 4; v, 4. But the victory sometimes remained doubtful, in consequence of which a number of competitors appeared before the judges, and claimed the prize. The candidates who were rejected on such occasions by the judge of the games, as not having fairly merited the prize, were called by the Greeks ἀδοκιμοί, or DISAPPROVED, which we render CAST AWAY, in a passage already quoted from St. Paul's First Epistle to the Corinthians: "But I keep under my body, and bring it into subjection, lest that by any means, when I have preached to others, I myself should be, ἀδόκιμος, cast away," rejected by the Judge of all the earth, and disappointed of my expected crown. What has been observed concerning the spirit and ardour with which the competitors engaged in the race, and concerning the prize they had in view to reward their arduous contention, will illustrate the following sublime passage of the same sacred

writer in his Epistle to the Philippians: "Not as though I had already attained, either were already perfect; but I follow after, if that I may apprehend that for which also I am apprehended of Christ Jesus. Brethren, I count not myself to have apprehended: but this one thing I do, forgetting those things which are behind, and reaching forth unto those things which are before, I press toward the mark, for the prize of the high calling of God in Christ Jesus," Phil. iii, 12–14. The affecting passage, also, of the same Apostle, in the Second Epistle of Timothy, written a little before his martyrdom, is beautifully allusive to the above-mentioned race, to the crown that awaited the victory, and to the Hellanodics or judges who bestowed it: "I have fought a good fight, I have finished my course, I have kept the faith. Henceforth there is laid up for me a crown of righteousness, which the Lord, the righteous Judge, shall give me at that day: and not to me only, but to all them also that love his appearing," 2 Tim. iv, 8.

GARDENS. In the language of the Hebrews, every place where plants and trees were cultivated with greater care than in the open field, was called a garden. The idea of such an enclosure was certainly borrowed from the garden of Eden, which the bountiful Creator planted for the reception of our first parents. Beside, the gardens of primitive nations were commonly, if not in every instance, devoted to religious purposes. In these shady retreats were celebrated, for a long succession of ages, the rites of Pagan superstition. Thus Jehovah calls the apostate Jews, "a people that provoketh me continually to anger to my face, that sacrificeth in gardens," Isa. lxv, 3. And in a preceding chapter, the prophet threatens them in the name of the Lord: "They shall be ashamed of the oaks which ye have desired, and ye shall be confounded for the gardens which ye have chosen." The oriental gardens were either open plantations, or enclosures defended by walls or hedges. Some fences in the Holy Land, in later times, are not less beautiful than our living fences of white thorn; and perfectly answer the description of ancient Jewish prophets, who inform us that the hedges in their times consisted of thorns, and that the spikes of these thorny plants were exceedingly sharp. Doubdan found a very fruitful vineyard, full of olives, fig trees, and vines, about eight miles south-west from Bethlehem, enclosed with a hedge; and that part of it adjoining to the road, strongly formed of thorns and rose bushes, intermingled with pomegranate trees of surpassing beauty and fragrance. A hedge composed of rose bushes and wild pomegranate shrubs, then in full flower, mingled with other thorny plants, adorned in the varied livery of spring, must have made at once a strong and beautiful fence. The wild pomegranate tree, the species probably used in fencing, is much more prickly than the other variety; and when mingled with other thorny bushes, of which they have several kinds in Palestine, some of whose prickles are very long and sharp, must form a hedge very difficult to penetrate. These facts illustrate the beauty and force of several passages in the sacred volume: thus, in the Proverbs of Solomon, "The way of the slothful man is as a hedge of thorns," Prov. xv, 19; it is obstructed with difficulties, which the sloth and indolence of his temper represent as galling or insuperable; but which a moderate share of resolution and perseverance would easily remove or surmount. In the prophecies of Hosea, God threatens his treacherous and idolatrous people with many painful embarrassments and perplexities, which would as effectually retard or obstruct their progress in the paths of wickedness, as a hedge of thorny plants stretching across the traveller's way, the prosecution of his journey: "Therefore, behold, I will hedge up thy way with thorns, and make a wall, that she shall not find her paths," Hosea ii, 6. In the days of Micah, the magistrates of Judah had become exceedingly corrupt: "The best of them is a brier; the most upright is sharper than a thorn hedge;" to appear before their tribunal, or to have any dealings with them, was to involve one's self in endless perplexities, and to be exposed to galling disappointments, if not to certain destruction. They resembled those thorny plants which are twisted together, whose spines point in every direction, and are so sharp and strong that they cannot be touched without danger, and so entangling that when the traveller has with much pain and exertion freed himself from one, he is instantly seized by another. "But the sons of Belial," said the king of Israel, "shall be all of them as thorns thrust away, because they cannot be taken with hands: but the man that shall touch them must be fenced with iron, and the staff of a spear; and they shall be utterly burned with fire in the same place," 2 Sam. xxiii, 6, 7. Other enclosures had fences of loose stones, or mud walls, some of them very low, which often furnished a retreat to venomous reptiles. To this circumstance the royal preacher alludes, in his observations of wisdom and folly: "He that diggeth a pit, shall fall into it: and whoso breaketh a hedge, a serpent shall bite him," Eccles. x, 8. The term which our translators render HEDGE in this passage, they might with more propriety have rendered WALL, as they had done in another part of the writings of Solomon: "I went by the field of the slothful, and by the vineyard of the man void of understanding; and lo, it was all grown over with thorns, and nettles had covered the face thereof, and the stone wall thereof was broken down," Proverbs xxiv, 30.

2. The land of promise has been, from the earliest ages, an unenclosed country, with a few spots defended by a hedge of thorny plants, or a stone wall built without any cement. At Aleppo, most of the vineyards are fenced with stone walls; for in many parts of Syria a hedge would not grow for want of moisture. But, as their various esculent vegetables are now not unfrequently planted in the open fields, both in Syria and Palestine, so Chardin seems to suppose they were often unfenced in ancient times; and, on this account, those lodges and booths, to which Isaiah refers, in the first chapter of his prophecy, were built. In Hindostan they follow the same custom. At the commencement of the rainy season, the peasants plant abundance of melons, cucumbers, and gourds, which are then the principal food of the inhabitants. They are planted in the open fields and extensive plains, and are therefore liable to the depredations of men and beasts. In the centre of the field is an artificial mount, with a hut on the top, sufficiently large to shelter a single person from the inclemency of the weather. There, amid heavy rains and

tempestuous winds, a poor solitary being is stationed day and night to protect the crop. From thence he gives an alarm to the nearest village. Few situations can be more unpleasant than a hovel of this kind, exposed for three or four months to wind, lightning, and rain. To such a cheerless station the prophet no doubt alludes, in that passage where he declares the desolations of Judah: "The daughter of Zion is left as a cottage in a vineyard, as a lodge in a garden of cucumbers," Isa. i, 8. If such watch houses were necessary in those gardens which were defended by walls or hedges, some of which, indeed, it was not difficult to get over, they must have been still more necessary in those which were perfectly open.

3. The oriental garden displays little method, or design; the whole being commonly no more than a confused medley of fruit trees, with beds of esculent plants, and even plots of wheat and barley sometimes interspersed. The garden belonging to the governor of Eleus, a Turkish town on the western border of the Hellespont, which Dr. Chandler visited, consisted only of a very small spot of ground, walled in, and containing only two vines, a fig and a pomegranate tree, and a well of excellent water. And, it would seem, the garden of an ancient Israelite could not boast of greater variety; for the grape, the fig, and the pomegranate, are almost the only fruits which it produced. This fact may perhaps give us some insight into the reason of the sudden and irresistible conviction which flashed on the mind of Nathanael, when our Saviour said to him, "When thou wast under the fig tree, I saw thee." The good man seems to have been engaged in devotional exercises in a small retired garden, walled in, and concealed from the scrutinizing eyes of men. The place was so small, that he was perfectly certain no man but himself was there; and so completely defended, that none could break through, or look over, the fence; and, by consequence, that no eye was upon him, but the all-seeing eye of God; and, therefore, since Christ saw him there, Nathanael knew he could be no other than the Son of God, and the promised Messiah.

GARLICK, שום. As this word occurs only in Numbers xi, 5, some doubts have arisen respecting the plant intended. From its being coupled with leeks and onions, there can be but little doubt that the garlick is meant. The Talmudists frequently mention the use of this plant among the Jews, and their fondness for it. That garlicks grew plenteously in Egypt, is asserted by Dioscorides: there they were much esteemed, and were both eaten and worshipped:--

"Then gods were recommended by their taste.

Such savoury deities must needs be good,

Which served at once for worship and for food."

GARMENT. See Habits.

GATE is often used in Scripture to denote a place of public assembly, where justice was administered, Deut. xvii, 5, 8; xxi, 19; xxii, 15; xxv, 6, 7, &c. One instance of these judgments appears in that given at the gate of Bethlehem, between Boaz and a relation of Naomi, on the subject of Ruth, chap. iv, 2; another in Abraham's purchase of a field to bury Sarah, Gen. xxiii, 10, 18. The gate of judgment is a term still common to the Arabians to express a court of justice, and even introduced by the Saracens into Spain. "I had several times," says Jacob, "visited the Alhambra, the ancient palace and fortress of the Moorish kings: it is situated on the top of a hill, overlooking the city, and is surrounded by a wall of great height and thickness. The entrance is through an archway, over which is carved a key, the symbol of the Mohammedan monarchs. This gate, called the gate of judgment, according to eastern forms, was the place where the kings administered justice." In Morocco, the gate is still the place where judgment is held. "All complaints," says Host, "are brought, in the first instance, to the cadi, or governor, who, for that purpose, passes certain hours of the day in the gate of the city, partly for the sake of the fresh air, and partly to see all those who go out; and, lastly, to observe a custom which has long prevailed, of holding judgment there. The gate is contrived accordingly, being built like a square chamber, with two doors, which are not directly opposite to each other, but on two adjoining sides, with seats on the other sides. In this manner David sat between two gates," 2 Sam. xviii, 24. Gate sometimes signifies power, dominion, almost in the same sense as the Turkish emperor's palace is called the PORTE. God promises Abraham that his posterity shall possess the gates of their enemies, their towns, their fortresses, Genesis xxii, 17. Jesus Christ says to Peter, "Thou art Peter; and on this rock will I build my church, and the gates of hell shall not prevail against it," Matt. xvi, 18. This may mean either the powers of hell, or invisible spirits; or simply death,--the church shall be replenished by living members from generation to generation, so that death shall never annihilate it.

Solomon says, "He that exalteth his gate seeketh destruction." The Arabs are accustomed to ride into the houses of those they design to harass. To prevent this, Thevenot tells us that the door of the house in which the French merchants live at Rama was not three feet high, and that all the doors of that town are equally low. Agreeably to this account, the Abbé Mariti, speaking of his admission into a monastery near Jerusalem, says, "The passage is so low, that it will scarcely admit a horse; and it is shut by a gate of iron, strongly secured in the inside. As soon as we entered, it was again made fast with various bolts and bars of iron: a precaution extremely necessary in a desert place, exposed to the incursions, and insolent attacks of the Arabs." Mr. Drummond says, that in the country about Roudge, in Syria, "the poor miserable Arabs are under the necessity of hewing their houses out of the rock, and cutting very small doors or openings to them, that they may not be made stables for the Turkish horse, as they pass and repass." And thus, long before him, Sandys, at Gaza, in Palestine: "We lodged under an arch in a little court, together with our asses; the door exceeding low, as are all that belong unto Christians, to withstand the sudden entrance of the insolent Turks." "To exalt the gate," would consequently be to court destruction. Morier says, "A poor man's door is scarcely three feet in height; and this is a precautionary measure to hinder the servants of the great from entering it on horseback; which, when any act of oppression is intended, they would make no scruple to do. But the habitation of a man in power is known by his gate, which is generally elevated in proportion to the vanity of its owner. A lofty gate is one of the insignia of royalty: such is the ALLAN CAPI, at Ispahan, and BOB HOMAYAN, or the SUBLIME PORTE, at Constantinople. It must have been the same in ancient days; the gates of Jerusalem, Zion, &c, are often mentioned in the Scripture, with the same notion of grandeur annexed to them."

GATH, the fifth of the Philistine cities. It was a place of strength in the time of the prophets Amos and Micah, and is placed by Jerom on the road between Eleutheropolis and Gaza. It appears to have been the extreme boundary of the Philistine territory in one direction, as Ekron was on the other. Hence the expression, "from Ekron even unto Gath," 1 Sam. vii, 14.

GAULAN, or **GOLAN**, a city beyond Jordan, from which the small province called Gaulonitis took its name. It was given to the half tribe of Manasseh, on the other side Jordan, Deut. iv, 43; and became a city of refuge, Joshua xxi, 27.

GAZA, a city of the Philistines, made by Joshua part of the tribe of Judah. It was one of the five principalities of the Philistines, situated toward the southern extremity of the promised land, 1 Sam. vi, 17, between Raphia and Askelon. The advantageous situation of Gaza was the cause of the numerous revolutions which it underwent. It first of all belonged to the Philistines, and then to the Hebrews. It recovered its liberty in the reigns of Jotham and Ahaz, and was reconquered by Hezekiah, 2 Kings xviii, 8. It was subject to the Chaldeans, who conquered Syria and Phenicia. Afterward, it fell into the hands of the Persians. It must have been a place of considerable strength. For two months it baffled all the efforts of Alexander the Great, who was repeatedly repulsed, and wounded in the siege; which he afterward revenged in a most infamous manner on the person of the gallant defender Betis, whom, while yet alive, having ordered his ankles to be bored, he dragged round the walls, tied to his chariot wheels, in the barbarous parade of imitating the less savage treatment of the corpse of Hector by Achilles.

Dr. Wittman gives the following description of his visit to Gaza: "In pursuing our route toward this place, the view became still more interesting and agreeable: the groves of olive trees extending from the place where we had halted to the town, in front of which a fine avenue of these trees was planted. Gaza is situated on an eminence, and is rendered picturesque by the number of fine minarets which rise majestically above the buildings, and by the beautiful date trees which are interspersed. The suburbs of Gaza are composed of wretched mud huts; but within side the town the buildings make a much better appearance than those we had generally met with in Syria. The streets are of a moderate breadth. Many fragments of statues, columns, &c, of marble were seen in the walls and buildings in different parts of the town. The suburbs and environs of Gaza are rendered infinitely agreeable by a number of large gardens, cultivated with the nicest care, which lie in a direction north and south of the town; while others of the same description run to a considerable distance westward. These gardens are filled with a great variety of choice fruit trees, such as the fig, the mulberry, the pomegranate, the apricot, the peach, and the almond; together with a few lemon and orange trees. The numerous plantations of olive and date trees which are interspersed contribute greatly to the picturesque effect of the scene exhibited by the surrounding plains. These, on our arrival, were overspread with flowers, the variegated colours of which displayed every tint and every hue. Among these were the chrysanthemum, scarlet ranunculus, lupin, pheasant-eye, tulip, china-aster, dwarf-iris, lintel, daisy, &c, all of them growing wild and abundantly, with the exception of the lupin, which was cultivated in patches, regularly ploughed and sowed, with a view to collect the seeds, which the inhabitants employ at their meals, more especially to thicken their ragouts. The few corn fields, which lay at a distance, displayed the promise of a rich golden harvest; and the view of the sea, distant about a league, tended to diversify still more the animated features of this luxuriant scene." This and similar descriptions of modern travellers, which are occasionally introduced into this work, are given both as interesting in themselves, and to show that relics of the ancient beauty and fertility of the Holy Land are still to be found in many parts of it.

GEMARA. This word signifies COMPLEMENT, PERFECTION. The rabbins call the Pentateuch the law, without any addition. Next to this they have the Talmud, which is divided into two parts: the first is only an application of the law to particular cases, with the decision of the ancient rabbins, and is called MISHNAH, or "second law:" the other part, which is a more extensive application of the same law, is a collection of determinations by rabbins, later than the MISHNAH. This last is termed GEMARA, "perfection," "finishing," because they consider it as a conclusive explanation of the law, to which no farther additions can be made. There are two GEMARAS, or two Talmuds, that of Jerusalem, and that of Babylon. The former was compiled, according to the Jews, about the end of the second or third century, by a celebrated rabbin, called Jochanan; but father Morinus maintains that the GEMARA was not finished till about the seventh century. Dr. Prideaux says that it was completed about A. D. 300. The Jews have little value for this Jerusalem Talmud, on account of its obscurity. The Babylonish GEMARA is, as the rabbins say, more modern. It was begun by a Jewish doctor, named Asa, and continued by Marmar and Mar, his sons or disciples. The Jews believe that the GEMARA contains nothing but the word of God, preserved in the tradition of the elders, and transmitted, without alteration, from Moses to rabbi Judah, the holy, and the other compilers of the Talmud; who did not reduce it to writing till they were afraid it would be corrupted by the several transmigrations and persecutions to which their nation was subjected.

GENEALOGY, γενεαλογία, signifies a list of a person's ancestors. The common Hebrew expression for it is SEPHER-TOLEDOTH, "the Book of Generations." No nation was ever more careful to preserve their genealogies than the Jews. The sacred writings contain genealogies extended three thousand five hundred years backward. The genealogy of our Saviour is deduced by the evangelists from Adam to Joseph and Mary, through a space of four thousand years and upward. The Jewish priests were obliged to produce an exact genealogy of their families, before they were admitted to exercise their function. Wherever placed, the Jews were particularly careful not to marry below themselves; and to prevent this, they kept tables of genealogy in their several families, the originals of which were lodged at Jerusalem, to be occasionally consulted. These authentic monuments, during all their wars and persecutions, were taken great care of, and from time to time renewed. But, since the last destruction of their city, and the dispersion of the people, their ancient genealogies are lost. But to this the Jews reply, that either Elias, or some other inspired priest or prophet, shall come, and restore their genealogical tables before the Messiah's appearance; a tradition, which they ground on a passage in Nehemiah vii, 64, 65, to this effect: the genealogical register of the families of certain priests being lost, they were not able to make out their lineal descent from Aaron; and therefore, "as polluted, were put from the priesthood;" the "Tirshatha said unto them, that they should not eat of the most holy things, till there stood up a priest with Urim and Thummim." From hence the Jews conclude, that such a priest will stand up, and restore and complete the genealogies of their families: though others suppose these words to import, that they should never exercise their priesthood any more; and that, "till there shall stand up a priest with Urim and Thummim," amounts to the same as the Roman proverb, AD GRÆCAS CALENDAS, [never,] since the Urim and Thummim were now absolutely and for ever lost.

GENERATION. Beside the common acceptation of this word, as signifying descent, it is used for the history and genealogy of any individual, as "The book of the generations of Adam," Genesis v, 1, the history of Adam's creation, and of his posterity. "The generations of the heavens and of the earth," Genesis ii, 4, is a recital of the creation of heaven and earth. "The book of the generation of Jesus Christ, the Son of David," Matthew i, 1, is the genealogy of Jesus Christ, and the history of his life. The ancients sometimes computed by generations: "In the fourth generation thy descendants shall come hither again," Genesis xv, 16. "Joseph saw Ephraim's children of the third generation," Genesis 1, 23. "A bastard shall not be admitted into the congregation, till the tenth generation," Deut. xxiii, 2. Among the ancients, when the duration of generations was not exactly described by the age of four men succeeding one another from father to son, it was fixed by some at a hundred years, by others at a hundred and ten, by others at thirty-three, thirty, twenty-five, and even at twenty years; being neither uniform nor settled: only, it is remarked, that a generation is longer as it is more ancient.

GENESIS, a canonical book of the Old Testament, so called from the Greek γενεσις, GENESIS, or GENERATION, because it contains an account of the origin of all visible things, and of the genealogy of the first patriarchs. In the Hebrew it is called בראשית, which signifies, IN THE BEGINNING, because it begins with that word. See Pentateuch.

GENNESARETH, Land of, or **GENNESAR**, a small district of Galilee, supposed to have been so called from its pleasantness, and extending about four miles along the north-western shore of the sea of Galilee, or Gennesareth, so called from this same region. It is more probable, however, that Gennesareth is nothing more than a word moulded from Cinnereth, the ancient name of a city and adjoining tract in this very situation, as well as of the lake itself. This part of Galilee is described by Josephus as possessing a singular fertility, with a delightful temperature of the air, and abounding in the fruits of different climates.

GENTILE. The Hebrews called the Gentiles גויים, ἔθνη, THE NATIONS, that is, those who have not received the faith or law of God. All who are not Jews, and circumcised, are GOIIM. Those who were converted, and embraced Judaism, they called proselytes. Since the Gospel, the true religion is not confined to any one nation or country, as heretofore, God, who had promised by his prophets to call the Gentiles to the faith, with a superabundance of grace, has fulfilled his promise; so that the Christian church is now composed principally of Gentile converts; and the Jews, too proud of their particular privileges, and abandoned to their reprobate sense of things, have disowned Jesus Christ, their Messiah and Redeemer, for whom, during so many ages, they had looked so impatiently. In the writings of St. Paul, the Gentiles are generally denoted as Greeks, Rom. i, 14, 16; ii, 9, 10; iii; x, 12; 1 Cor. i, 22–24; Gal. iii, 28. St. Luke, in the Acts, expresses himself in the same manner, Acts vi, 1; xi, 20; xviii, &c.

2. St. Paul is commonly called the Apostle of the Gentiles, 1 Tim. ii, 7, or Greeks; because he, principally, preached Jesus Christ to them; whereas Peter, and the other Apostles, preached generally to the Jews, and are called Apostles of the circumcision, Gal. ii, 8. The prophets declared very particularly the calling of the Gentiles. Jacob foretold that the Messiah, he who was to be sent, the Shiloh, should gather the Gentiles to himself. Solomon, at the dedication of his temple, prays for "the stranger" who should there entreat God. The Psalmist says, that the Lord would give the Gentiles to the Messiah for his inheritance; that Egypt and Babylon shall know him; that Ethiopia shall hasten to bring him presents; that the kings of Tarshish, and of the isles, the kings of Arabia and Sheba, shall be tributary to him, Psalm ii, 8; lxvii, 4; lxxii, 9, 10. Isaiah abounds with prophecies of

the like nature, on which account he has justly been distinguished by the name of "the prophet of the Gentiles."

Gentiles, Court of the. Josephus says there was, in the court of the temple, a wall, or balustrade, breast-high, with pillars at particular distances, and inscriptions on them in Greek and Latin, importing that strangers were forbidden from entering farther; here their offerings were received, and sacrifices were offered for them, they standing at the barrier; but they were not allowed to approach to the altar. Pompey, nevertheless, went even into the sanctuary, but behaved with strict decorum; and the next day he commanded the temple to be purified, and the customary sacrifices to be offered. A little before the last rebellion of the Jews, some mutineers would have persuaded the priests to accept no victim not presented by a Jew; and obliged them to reject those which were offered by command of the emperor, for the Roman people. The wisest in vain remonstrated with them on the danger this would bring on their country; urged that their ancestors had never rejected the presents of Gentiles; and that the temple was mostly adorned with the offerings of such people; at the same time, the most learned priests, who had spent their whole lives in the study of the law, testified that their forefathers had always received the sacrifices of strangers.

From the above particulars, we learn the meaning of what the Apostle Paul calls "the middle wall of partition," between Jews and Gentiles broken down by the Gospel.

GERAR, a royal city of the Philistines, situate not far from the angle where the south and west sides of Palestine meet.

GERIZIM, a mount near Shechem, in Ephraim, a province of Samaria. Shechem lay at the foot of two mountains, Ebal and Gerizim. Gerizim was fruitful, Ebal was barren. God commanded that the Hebrews, after passing the Jordan, should be so divided, that six tribes might be stationed on Mount Gerizim, and six on Mount Ebal. The former was to pronounce blessings on those who observed the law of the Lord; the others, curses against those who should violate it, Deut. xi, 29; xxvii, 12. As to the original of the temple upon Gerizim, we must take Josephus's relation of it. Manasseh, the grandson of Eliashib, the high priest, and brother to Jaddus, high priest of the Jews, having been driven from Jerusalem in the year of the world 3671, and not enduring patiently to see himself deprived of the honour and advantages of the priesthood, Sanballat, his father-in-law, addressed himself to Alexander the Great, who was then carrying on the siege of Tyre; and having paid him homage for the province of Samaria, whereof he was governor, he farther offered him eight thousand of his best troops, which disposed Alexander to grant what he desired for his son-in-law, and for many other priests, who being married, as well as he, contrary to the law, chose rather to forsake their country than their wives, and had joined Manasseh in Samaria. When Antiochus Epiphanes began to persecute the Jews, A. M. 3836; B. C. 186, the Samaritans entreated him that their temple upon Gerizim, which hitherto had been dedicated to an unknown and nameless god, might be consecrated to Jupiter the Grecian, which was easily consented to by Antiochus. The temple of Gerizim subsisted some time after the worship of Jupiter was introduced into it; but it was destroyed by John Hircanus Maccabæus, and was not rebuilt till Gabinius was governor of Syria; who repaired Samaria, and called it by his own name. It is certain, that, in our Saviour's time, this temple was in being; and that the true God was worshipped there, since the woman of Samaria, pointing to Gerizim, said to him, "Our fathers worshipped in this mountain, and ye say, that in Jerusalem is the place where men ought to worship," John iv, 20. We are assured, that Herod the Great, having rebuilt Samaria, and called it Sebaste, in honour of Augustus, would have obliged the Samaritans to worship in the temple which he had erected there, but they constantly refused.

GETHSEMANE. See Olives, MOUNT OF.

GIANT, נפל, Greek, γίγας, A MONSTER, A TERRIBLE MAN, a chief who beats and bears down other men. Scripture speaks of giants before the flood: "Nephilim, mighty men who were of old, men of renown," Gen. vi, 4. Aquila translates nephilim, ἐπιπίπτοντες, MEN WHO ATTACK, who fall with impetuosity on their enemies, which renders very well the force of the term. Symmachus translates it βιαίοι, VIOLENT MEN, cruel, whose only rule of action is violence. Scripture sometimes calls giants Rephaim: Chedorlaomer beat the Rephaim at Ashteroth-Karnaim. The Emim, ancient inhabitants of Moab, were of a gigantic stature, that is, Rephaim. The Rephaim and the Perizzites are connected as old inhabitants of Canaan. The Rephaim in some parts of Scripture signify spirits in the invisible world, in a state of misery. Job says that the ancient Rephaim groan under the waters; and Solomon, that the ways of a loose woman lead to the Rephaim; that he who deviates from the ways of wisdom, shall dwell in the assembly of Rephaim, that is, in hell, Prov. ii, 18; iv, 18; xxi, 16, &c; Gen. xiv, 5; Deut. ii, 11, 20; iii, 11, 13; Joshua xii, 4; xiii, 12; Job xxvi, 5. The Anakim, or the sons of Anak, were the most famous giants of Palestine. They dwelt at Hebron and thereabouts. The Israelites sent to view the promised land reported, that, in comparison, they themselves were but grasshoppers, Num. xiii, 33.

2. As to the existence of giants, several writers, both ancient and modern, have thought that the giants of Scripture were men famous for violence and crime, rather than for strength or stature. But it cannot be denied, that there have been races of men of a stature much above that common at present; although their size has often been absurdly magnified. The ancients considered persons whose stature exceeded seven feet as gigantic. Living giants have certainly been seen who were somewhat taller; but the existence of those who greatly surpassed it, or were double the height, has been inferred only from remains discovered in the earth, but not from the ocular testimony of credible witnesses. Were we to admit what has been reported on the subject, there would be no bounds to the dimensions of giants; the earth would seem

unsuitable for them to tread upon. History, however, acquaints us that, in the reign of Claudius, a giant named Galbara, ten feet high was brought to Rome from the coast of Africa. An instance is cited by Goropius, an author with whom we are otherwise unacquainted, of a female of equal stature. A certain Greek sophist, Proæresius, is said to have been nine feet in height. Julius Capitolinus affirms that Maximinian, the Roman emperor was eight feet and a half; there was a Swede, one of the life guards of Frederick the Great, of that size. M. Le Cat speaks of a giant exhibited at Rouen, measuring eight feet and some inches; and we believe some have been seen in this country, within the last thirty years, whose stature was not inferior. In Plott's "History of Staffordshire," there is an instance of a man of seven feet and a half high, and another, in Thoresby's account of Leeds, of seven feet five inches high. Examples may be found elsewhere of several individuals seven feet in height, below which, after the opinion of the ancients, we may cease to consider men gigantic. Entire families sometimes, though rarely, occur of six feet four, or six feet six inches high. From all this we may conclude, that there may have possibly been seen some solitary instances of men who were ten feet in height; that those of eight feet are extremely uncommon, and that even six feet and a half far exceeds the height of men in Europe. We may reasonably understand that the gigantic nations of Canaan were above the average size of other people, with instances among them of several families of gigantic stature. This is all that is necessary to suppose, in order to explain the account of Moses; but the notion that men have gradually degenerated in size has no foundation. There is no evidence whatever, that the modern tribes of mankind have thus degenerated. The catacombs of ancient Egypt and Palestine; the cenotaph, if it be truly such, in the great pyramid; the tomb of Alexander the Great, are all calculated for bodies of ordinary dimensions. The truth is still more satisfactorily established from the mummies which are yet withdrawn from their receptacles in Egypt, and the caverns of the Canary Islands. In the most ancient sepulchres of Britain, those apparently anterior to the introduction of Christianity, no remains are discovered which indicate the larger stature of the inhabitants than our own. In every part of the world domestic implements and personal ornaments, many centuries old, are obtained from tombs, from bogs and mosses, or those cities overwhelmed by volcanic eruptions, which would be ill adapted to a gigantic race of ancestors.

GIBEON, the capital city of the Gibeonites, who took advantage of the oaths of Joshua, and of the elders of Israel, procured by an artful representation of their belonging to a very remote country, Joshua ix. Joshua and the elders had not the precaution to consult God on this affair, but inconsiderately made a league with these people. They soon discovered their mistake, and, without revoking their promise of saving their lives, they condemned them to labour in carrying wood and water for the tabernacle; and to other works, as slaves and captives; in which state of servitude they remained, till the entire dispersion of the Jewish nation, A. M. 2553; B. C. 1451. Three days after the Gibeonites had surrendered to the Hebrews, the kings of Canaan being informed of it, five of them came and besieged the city of Gibeon. The Gibeonites sent to Joshua, and desired speedy help. Joshua attacked the five kings early in the morning, put them to flight, and pursued them to Bethoron, Josh. x, 3, &c. The Gibeonites were descended from the Hivites, the old inhabitants of the country, and possessed four cities: Cephirah, Beeroth, Kirjath-jearim, and Gibeon, their capital; all afterward given to Benjamin, except Kirjath-jearim, which fell to Judah. The Gibeonites continued subject to those burdens which Joshua imposed on them, and were very faithful to the Israelites. Nevertheless, Saul destroyed a great number of them, 2 Sam. xxi, 1; but God, in the reign of David, sent a great famine, which lasted three years, A. M. 2983; B. C. 1021; and the prophets told David that this calamity would continue while Saul's cruelty remained unavenged. David asked the Gibeonites what satisfaction they desired. They answered, "Seven of Saul's sons we will put to death, to avenge the blood of our brethren." The Gibeonites crucified them. From this time there is no mention of the Gibeonites as a distinct people. But they were probably included among the Nethinim, appointed for the service of the temple, 1 Chron. ix, 2. Afterward, those of the Canaanites who were subdued, and had their lives spared, were added to the Gibeonites. We see in Ezra viii, 20; ii, 58; 1 Kings ix, 20, 21, that David, Solomon, and the princes of Judah, gave many such to the Lord; these Nethinim being carried into captivity with Judah and the Levites, many of them returned with Ezra, Zerubbabel, and Nehemiah, and continued, as before, in the service of the temple, under the priests and Levites. We neither know when, nor by whom, nor on what occasion, the tabernacle and altar of burnt sacrifices, made by Moses in the wilderness, were removed to Gibeon; but this we certainly know, that, toward the end of David's reign, and in the beginning of Solomon's, they were there, 1 Chron. xxi, 29, 30. David, seeing an angel of the Lord at Araunah's threshing floor, was so terrified, that he had not time or strength to go so far as Gibeon to offer sacrifice; but Solomon, being seated on the throne, went to sacrifice at Gibeon, 1 Kings iii, 4.

GIDEON, the son of Joash, of the tribe of Manasseh; the same with Jerubbaal, the seventh judge of Israel. He dwelt in the city of Ophra, and was chosen by God in a very extraordinary manner to deliver the Israelites from the oppression of the Midianites, under which they had laboured for the space of seven years. See Judges vi, 14–27; viii, 1–24, &c.

GIER EAGLE, רחם, Lev. xi, 18; Deut. xiv, 17. As the root of this word signifies TENDERNESS and AFFECTION, it is supposed to refer to some bird remarkable for its attachment to its young; hence some have thought that the pelican is to be understood; and Bochart endeavours to prove that the golden vulture is meant; but there can be no doubt that it is the PERCNOPTERUS of the ancients, the ACH-BOBBA of the Arabians, particularly described by Bruce under the name of RACHAMAH. He says, "We know from Horus Apollo, that the RACHMA, or she vulture, was sacred to Isis, and adorned the statue of the goddess; that it was the emblem of parental affection; and that it was the hieroglyphic for an affectionate mother." He farther says, that "this female vulture, having hatched her young ones, continues with them one hundred and twenty days, providing them with all necessaries; and, when the stock of food fails them, she tears off the fleshy part of her thigh, and feeds them with that and the blood which flows from the wound."

Hasselquist thus describes the Egyptian vulture: "The appearance of the bird is as horrid as can well be imagined. The face is naked and wrinkled, the eyes are large and black, the beak black and crooked, the talons large, and extended ready for prey, and the whole body polluted with filth. These are qualities enough to make the beholder shudder with horror. Notwithstanding this, the inhabitants of Egypt cannot be enough thankful to Providence for this bird. All the places round Cairo are filled with the dead bodies of asses and camels; and thousands of these birds fly about and devour the carcasses, before they putrify and fill the air with noxious exhalations." No wonder that such an animal should be deemed unclean.

GIFT OF TONGUES, an ability given to the Apostles and others of readily and intelligibly speaking a variety of languages which they had never learned. This was a glorious and decisive attestation to the Gospel, as well as a suitable, and, indeed, in their circumstances, a necessary qualification for the mission for which the Apostles and their coadjutors were designed. Nor is there any reason, with Dr. Middleton, to understand it as merely an occasional gift, so that a person might speak a language most fluently one hour, and be entirely ignorant of it the next; which neither agrees with what is said of the abuse of it, nor would it have been sufficient to answer the end proposed, Acts ii. Some appear to have been gifted with one tongue, others with more. To St. Paul this endowment was vouchsafed in a more liberal degree, than to many others; for, as to the Corinthians, who had received the gift of tongues, he says, "that he spake with tongues more than they all."

GIFTS. The practice of making presents is very common in oriental countries. The custom probably had its origin among those men who first sustained the office of kings or rulers, and who, from the novelty and perhaps the weakness attached to their situation, chose, rather than make the hazardous attempt of exacting taxes, to content themselves with receiving those presents which might be freely offered, 1 Sam. x, 27. Hence it passed into a custom, that whoever approached the king should come with a gift. This was the practice and the expectation. The custom of presenting gifts was subsequently extended to other great men; to men who were inferior to the king, but who were, nevertheless, men of influence and rank; it was also extended to those who were equals, when they were visited, Proverbs xviii, 16. Kings themselves were in the habit of making presents, probably in reference to the custom in question and the feelings connected with it, to those individuals, their inferiors in point of rank, whom they wished to honour, and also to those who, like themselves, were clothed with the royal authority. These presents, namely, such as were presented by the king as a token of the royal esteem and honour, are almost invariably denominated in the Hebrew, שחד and ברכה, 1 Kings xv, 19; 2 Kings xvi, 8; xviii, 14; Isaiah xxxvi, 16. The more ancient prophets did not deem it discreditable to them to receive presents, nor unbecoming their sacred calling, except when, as was sometimes the case, they refused by way of expressing their dissatisfaction or indignation, 2 Kings v, 15; viii, 9. In later times, when false prophets, in order to obtain money, prophesied without truth and without authority, the true prophets, for the purpose of keeping the line of distinction as broad as possible, rejected every thing that looked like reward. Gifts of this kind, that have now been described, are not to be confounded with those which are called שחד, and which were presented to judges, not as a mark of esteem and honour, but for purposes of bribery and corruption. The former was considered an honour to the giver, but a gift of the latter kind has been justly reprobated in every age, Exod. xxii, 8; Deut. x, 17; xvi, 19; xxvii, 25; Psalm xv, 5; xxvi, 10; Isaiah i, 23; v, 23; xxxiii, 15. The giver was not restricted as to the kind of present which he should make. He might present not only silver and gold, but clothes and arms, also different kinds of food, in a word any thing which could be of benefit to the recipient, Gen. xliii, 11; 1 Sam. ix, 7; xvi, 20; Job xiii, 11. It was the custom anciently, as it is at the present time in the east, for an individual when visiting a person of high rank, to make some presents of small value to the servants or domestics of the person visited, 1 Sam. xxv, 27. It was the usual practice among kings and princes to present to their favourite officers in the government, to ambassadors from foreign courts, to foreigners of distinction, and to men eminent for their learning, garments of greater or less value, Genesis xiv, 22, 23; Esther viii, 15. The royal wardrobe, in which a large number of such garments was kept, is denominated in Hebrew בגדים 2 Chronicles xxxiv, 22. It was considered an honour of the highest kind, if a king or any person in high authority thought it proper, as a manifestation of his favour, to give away to another the garment which he had previously worn himself, 1 Sam. xviii, 4. In the east, at the present day, it is expected, that every one who has received a garment from the king will immediately clothe himself in it, and promptly present himself and render his homage to the giver; otherwise he runs the hazard of exciting the king's displeasure, Matt. xxii, 11, 12. It was sometimes the case, that the king, when he made a feast, presented vestments to all the guests who were invited, with which they clothed themselves before they sat down to it, 2 Kings x, 22; Gen. xlv, 22; Rev. iii, 5. In oriental countries, the presents which are made to kings and princes are to this day carried on beasts of burden, are attended with a body of men, and are escorted with much pomp. It matters not how light or how small the present may be, it must either be carried on the back of a beast of burden, or by a man, who must support it with both his hands, Judges iii, 18; 2 Kings viii, 9.

GIHON, the name of one of the four rivers the source of which was in paradise, Genesis ii, 13. (See EDEN.) Reland, Calmet, &c, think that Gihon is the Araxes, which has its source, as well as the Tigris and Euphrates, in the mountains of Armenia, and, running with almost incredible rapidity, falls into the Caspian Sea. Gihon was also the name of a fountain to the west of Jerusalem, at which Solomon was anointed king by the high priest Zadok, and the Prophet Nathan, 1 Kings i, 33.

GILBOA, Mount, a ridge of mountains on the north of Bethshan, or Scythopolis, forming in that part the boundary of the plain of Jordan to the west. It is memorable from the defeat of Saul by the Philistines; when his three sons were slain, and he himself died by his own hand, his armourbearer refusing to kill him, 1 Sam. xxxi.

GILEAD, the name given to the monument erected by Laban and Jacob, in testimony of a mutual covenant and agreement, Gen. xxxi, 47, 48. Hence the hill upon which it was erected, was called Mount Gilead, Cant. iv, 1; vi, 5; Jer. 1, 19. The mountains of Gilead were part of that ridge of mountains which extend from Mount Lebanon southward, on the east of the Holy land; they gave their name to the whole country which lies on the east of the sea of Galilee, and included the mountainous region called in the New Testament Trachonitis. The Scripture speaks of the balm of Gilead, Jer. viii, 22; xlvi, 11; li, 8. The merchants who bought Joseph came from Gilead, and were carrying balm into Egypt, Gen. xxxvii, 25. See Balm.

GILGAL, a celebrated place situated on the west of Jordan, where the Israelites encamped some time after their passage over that river, and where Joshua pitched twelve stones taken out of Jordan as a memorial. A considerable city was afterward built there, which became renowned for many events recorded in the history of the Jews. Gilgal was about a league from Jordan, and at an equal distance from Jericho. It received its name from the circumstance of the Hebrews being there circumcised; for when by divine command that rite had been performed upon them, the Lord said, "This day have I rolled away from off you the reproach of Egypt," Joshua v, 2–4, &c.--The word Gilgal signifies ROLLING. Here the ark was long stationed, and consequently the place was much resorted to by the Israelites. It seems to have been the place in which Jeroboam or some of the kings of Israel instituted idolatrous worship; and hence the allusions to it by the prophets, Hosea iv, 15; Amos iv, 4. It is probable that there were idols at Gilgal as early as the days of Ehud, who was one of the judges; for it is said that, having delivered his presents to the king, "Ehud went away, but returned again from the quarries that were by Gilgal," Judges iii, 19. The margin of our Bibles reads, "the graven images," or idols set up by the Moabites, the viewing of which, it is thought, stirred up Ehud to revenge the affront thereby offered to the God of Israel. At this same place, the people met to confirm the kingdom to Saul, 1 Sam. xi, 14, 15. It was at Gilgal, too, that Saul incurred the divine displeasure, in offering sacrifice before Samuel arrived, 1 Sam. xiii; and there also it was that he received the sentence of his rejection for disobeying the divine command, and sparing the king of Amalek with the spoils which he had reserved, 1 Sam. xv.

It has been supposed that the setting up of stones, as at Gilgal and other places, gave rise to the rude stone circular temples of the Druids, and other Heathens. The idea, however, appears fanciful, and there is an essential difference between stones erected for memorials, and those used to mark sacred, or supposed sacred, places for worship.

GIRDLE. The girdle is an indispensable article in the dress of an oriental: it has various uses; but the principal one is to tuck up their long flowing vestments, that they may not incommode them in their work, or on a journey. The Jews, according to some writers, wore a double girdle, one of greater breadth, with which they girded their tunic when they prepared for active exertions: the other they wore under their shirt, around their loins. This under girdle they reckon necessary to distinguish between the heart and the less honourable parts of the human frame. The upper girdle was sometimes made of leather, the material of which the girdle of John the Baptist was made; but it was more commonly fabricated of worsted, often very artfully woven into a variety of figures, and made to fold several times about the body; one end of which being doubled back, and sewn along the edges, serves them for a purse, agreeably to the acceptation of ζώνη, in the Scriptures, which is translated PURSE, in several places of the New Testament, Matt. x, 9; Mark vi, 8. The ancient Romans, in this, as in many other things, imitated the orientals; for their soldiers, and probably all classes of the citizens, used to carry their money in their girdles. Whence, in Horace, QUI ZONAM PERDIDIT, means one who had lost his purse; and Aulus Gellius, C. Gracchus is introduced, saying, "Those girdles which I carried out full of money when I went from Rome, I have, at my return from the province, brought again empty." The Turks make a farther use of these girdles, by fixing their knives and poinards in them; while the writers and secretaries suspend in them their ink-horns; a custom as old as the Prophet Ezekiel, who mentions "a person clothed in white linen, with an ink-horn upon his loins," Ezek. ix, 2. That part of the ink-holder which passes between the girdle and the tunic, and receives their pens, is long and flat; but the vessel for the ink, which rests upon the girdle, is square, with a lid to clasp over it.

2. To loose the girdle and give it to another was, among the orientals, a token of great confidence and affection. Thus, to ratify the covenant which Jonathan made with David, and to express his cordial regard for his friend, among other things, he gave him his girdle. A girdle curiously and richly wrought was among the ancient Hebrews a mark of honour, and sometimes bestowed as a reward of merit; for this was the recompense which Joab declared he meant to bestow on the man who put Absalom to death: "Why didst thou not smite him there to the ground? and I would have given thee ten shekels of silver, and a girdle," 2 Samuel xviii, 11. The reward was certainly meant to correspond with the importance of

the service which he expected him to perform, and the dignity of his own station as commander in chief: we may, therefore, suppose that the girdle promised was not a common one of leather, or plain worsted, but of costly materials and richly adorned; for people of rank and fashion in the east wear very broad girdles, all of silk, and superbly ornamented with gold and silver, and precious stones, of which they are extremely proud, regarding them as the tokens of their superior station and the proof of their riches. "To gird up the loins" is to bring the flowing robe within the girdle, and so to prepare for a journey, or for some vigorous exercise.

GLASS, ὕαλος. This word occurs Rev. xxi, 18, 21; and the adjective ὑάλινος, Rev. iv, 6; xv, 2. Parkhurst says that in the later Greek writers, and in the New Testament, ὕαλος denotes the artificial substance, GLASS; and that we may either with Mintert derive it from ἕλη, SPLENDOUR, or immediately from the Hebrew הל, TO SHINE. There seems to be no reference to glass in the Old Testament. The art of making it was not known. Our translators have rendered the Hebrew word מראת, in Exodus xxxviii, 8, and Job xxxvii, 18, "looking-glass." But the making mirrors of glass coated with quicksilver, is an invention quite modern. The word LOOKING-GLASS occurs in our version of Ecclesiasticus xii, 11, "Never trust thine enemy; for like as iron rusteth, so is his wickedness. Though he humble himself, and go crouching, yet take good heed and beware of him, and thou shalt be unto him as if thou hadst washed a looking-glass, and thou shalt know that his rust hath not been altogether wiped away." This passage proves, by its mention of rust, that mirrors were then made of polished metal. The word ἔσοπτρον, or MIRROR, occurs in 1 Cor. xiii, 12, and James i, 23. Dr. Pearce thinks that in the former place it signifies any of those transparent substances which the ancients used in their windows, and through which they saw external objects obscurely. But others are of opinion that the word denotes a mirror of polished metal; as this, however, was liable to many imperfections, so that the object before it was not seen clearly or fully, the meaning of the Apostle is, that we see things as it were by images reflected from a mirror, which shows them very obscurely and indistinctly. In the latter place, a mirror undoubtedly is meant; "For if any be a hearer of the word, and not a doer, he is like unto a man beholding his natural face in a glass: for he beholdeth himself, and goeth his way, and straightway he forgetteth what manner of man he was:" but in the former, 1 Cor. xiii, 12, semi-transparent glass such as that which we see in the ancient glass vases of the Romans is obviously intended. Specimens of Roman glass may be seen in collections of antiquities, and some have been dug up at Pompeii; but in all it is cloudy and dull, and objects can only be seen through it with indistinctness. From this we may fully perceive the force of the Apostle's words, "now we see through a glass darkly."

GLEAN. To glean is properly to gather ears of corn, or grapes, left by the reapers, &c. The Jews were not allowed to glean their fields, but were to leave this to the poor, Lev. xix, 10; xxiii, 22; Deut. xxiv, 21; Ruth ii, 3.

GLORIFY, to make glorious or honourable, or to cause to appear so, John xii, 28; xiii, 31, 32; xv, 8; xvii, 4, 5; xxi, 19; Acts iii, 13. In this view it particularly refers to the resurrection of Christ, and his ascension to the right hand of God, John vii, 39; xii, 16. It also expresses that change which shall pass upon believers at the general resurrection, and their admission into heaven.

GLORY, splendour, magnificence. The glory of God in the writings of Moses, denotes, generally, the divine presence; as when he appeared on Mount Sinai; or, the bright cloud which declared his presence, and descended on the tabernacle of the congregation, Exod. xxiv, 9, 10, 16, 17. Moses, with Aaron, Nadab, Abihu, and seventy elders of Israel, went up to Mount Sinai, and "saw the glory of the Lord." Now "the glory of the Lord was, as it were, a burning fire on the mountain; and under his feet was, as it were, the brightness of the sapphire stone, resembling heaven itself in clearness." The glory of the Lord appeared to Israel in the cloud also, when he gave them manna and quails, Exod. xvi, 7, 10. Moses having earnestly begged of God to show his glory to him, God said, "Thou canst not see my face, for there shall no man see me and live. And the Lord said, There is a place by me, and thou shalt stand upon a rock: and it shall come to pass, while my glory passeth by, that I will put thee in the cleft of the rock, and will cover thee with my hand while I pass by: and I will take away my hand, and thou shalt see my back parts:" (the train, the fainter rays of the glory:) "but my face shall not be seen," Exod. xxxiii, 18. The ark of God is called the glory of Israel; and the glory of God, 1 Samuel iv, 21, 22; Psalm xxvi, 8. The priestly ornaments are called "garments of glory," Exod. xxviii, 2, 40; and the sacred vessels, "vessels of glory," 1 Macc. ii, 9, 12. Solomon "in all his glory," in all his lustre, in his richest ornaments, was not so beautifully arrayed as a lily, Matt. vi, 29; Luke xii, 27. When the prophets describe the conversion of the Gentiles, they speak of the "glory of the Lord" as filling the earth; that is, his knowledge shall universally prevail, and he shall be every where worshipped and glorified. The term "glory" is used also of the Gospel dispensation by St. Paul; and to express the future felicity of the saints in heaven. When the Hebrews required an oath of any man, they said, "Give glory to God:" confess the truth, give him glory, confess that God knows the most secret thoughts, the very bottom of your hearts, Joshua vii, 19; John ix, 24.

GNAT, κώνωψ, Matt. xxiii, 24, a small-winged insect, comprehending a genus of the order of DIPTERA. In those hot countries, as Servius remarks, speaking of the east, gnats and flies are very apt to fall into wine, if it be not carefully covered; and passing the liquor through a strainer, that no gnat or part of one might remain, became a proverb for exactness about little matters. This may help us to understand that passage, Matt. xxiii, 24, where the proverbial expression of carefully straining out a little fly from the liquor to be drunk, and yet swallowing a camel, intimates, that the scribes and Pharisees affected to scruple little things, and yet disregarded those of the greatest moment.

GNOSTICS, from γνῶσις, "knowledge," men of science and wisdom, ILLUMINATI; men who, from blending the philosophy of the east, or of Greece, with the doctrines of the Gospel, boasted of deeper knowledge in the Scriptures and theology than others. It was, therefore, not so properly a distinct sect as a generic term, comprehending all who, forsaking the simplicity of the Gospel, pretended to be "wise above what is written," to explain the New Testament by the dogmas of the philosophers, and to derive from the sacred writings mysteries which never were contained in them. The origin of the Gnostic heresy, as it is called, has been variously stated. The principles of this heresy were, however, much older than Christianity; and many of the errors alluded to in the apostolic epistles are doubtless of a character very similar to some branches of the Gnostic system. (See CABBALA.) Cerinthus, against whom St. John wrote his Gospel; the Nicolaitans, mentioned in the Revelation, and the Ebionites, (described under that article,) were all early Gnostics, although the system was not then so completely formed as afterward. Dr. Burton, in his Bampton Lectures, has thus sketched the Gnostic system:--In attempting to give an account of these doctrines, I must begin with observing what we shall see more plainly when we trace the causes of Gnosticism, that it was not by any means a new and distinct philosophy, but made up of selections from almost every system. Thus we find in it the Platonic doctrine of ideas, and the notion that every thing in this lower world has a celestial and immaterial archetype. We find in it evident traces of that mystical and cabalistic jargon which, after their return from captivity, deformed the religion of the Jews; and many Gnostics adopted the oriental notion of two independent coëternal principles, the one the author of good, the other of evil. Lastly, we find the Gnostic theology full of ideas and terms which must have been taken from the Gospel; and Jesus Christ, under some form or other, of ÆON, emanation, or incorporeal phantom, enters into all their systems, and is the means of communicating to them that knowledge which raised them above all other mortals, and entitled them to their peculiar name. The genius and very soul of Gnosticism was mystery: its end and object was to purify its followers from the corruptions of matter, and to raise them to a higher scale of being, suited only to those who were become perfect by knowledge.

2. We have a key to many parts of their system, when we know that they held matter to be intrinsically evil, of which, consequently, God could not be the author. Hence arose their fundamental tenet, that the creator of the world, or Demiurgus, was not the same with the supreme God, the Author of good, and the Father of Christ. Their system allowed some of them to call the creator God; but the title most usually given to him was Demiurgus. Those who embraced the doctrine of two principles supposed the world to have been produced by the evil principle; and, in most systems, the creator, though not the father of Christ, was looked upon as the God of the Jews, and the author of the Mosaic law. Some, again, believed that angels were employed in creating the world; but all were agreed in maintaining that matter itself was not created, that it was eternal, and remained inactive, till

DISPOSITAM, QUISQUIS FUIT ILLE DEORUM,

CONGERIEM SECUIT, SECTAMQUE IN MEMBRA REDEGIT.

Ovid.

[Some God, whoever he was, separated and arranged the mass, and reduced it, when separated, into elements.]

The supreme God had dwelt from all eternity in a PLEROMA of inaccessible light; and beside the name of first Father, or first Principle, they called him also Bythus, as if to denote the unfathomable nature of his perfections. This being, by an operation purely mental, or by acting upon himself, produced two other beings of different sexes, from whom, by a series of descents, more or less numerous according to different schemes, several pairs of beings were formed, who were called ÆONS, from the periods of their existence before time was, or EMANATIONS, from the mode of their production. These successive ÆONS or emanations appear to have been inferior each to the preceding; and their existence was indispensable to the Gnostic scheme, that they might account for the creation of the world without making God the author of evil. These ÆONS lived through countless ages with their first father; but the system of emanations seems to have resembled that of concentric circles; and they gradually deteriorated, as they approached nearer and nearer to the extremity of the PLEROMA. Beyond this PLEROMA was matter, inert and powerless, though coëternal with the supreme God, and like him without beginning. At length, one of the ÆONS passed the limits of the PLEROMA, and, meeting with matter, created the world, after the form and model of an ideal world which existed in the PLEROMA or in the mind of the supreme God. Here it is that inconsistency is added to absurdity in the Gnostic scheme. For, let the intermediate ÆONS be as many as the wildest imagination could devise, still God was the remote, if not the proximate, cause of creation. Added to which, we are to suppose that the Demiurgus formed the world without the knowledge of God; and that, having formed it, he rebelled against him. Here, again, we find a strong resemblance to the oriental doctrine of two principles, good and evil, or light and darkness. The two principles were always at enmity with each other. God must have been conceived to be more powerful than matter, or an emanation from God could not have shaped and moulded it into form: yet God was not able to reduce matter into its primeval chaos, nor to destroy the evil which the Demiurgus had produced. What God could not prevent, he was always endeavouring to cure: and here it is that the Gnostics borrowed so largely from the Christian scheme. The names, indeed, of several of their ÆONS were evidently taken from terms which they found in the Gospel. Thus we meet with LOGOS, MONOGENES, ZOE, ECCLESIA, all of them successive emanations from the supreme God, and all dwelling in the PLEROMA. At length, we meet with Christ and the Holy Ghost, as two of the last ÆONS which were put forth. Christ was sent into the world to remedy the evil which the creative ÆON or Demiurgus had caused. He was to emancipate men from the tyranny of matter, or of the evil principle; and, by revealing to them the true God, who was hitherto unknown, to fit them, by a perfection and sublimity of knowledge, to enter the divine PLEROMA. To give this knowledge, was the end and object of Christ's coming upon earth; and hence the inventors and believers of the doctrine assumed to themselves the name of Gnostics. In all their notions concerning Christ, we still find them struggling with the same difficulty of reconciling the author of good with the existence of evil. Christ, as being an emanation from God, could have no real connection with matter: yet, the Christ of the Gnostics was held out to be the same with him who was revealed in the Gospel; and it was notorious that he was revealed as the Son of Mary, who appeared in a human form. The methods which they took to extricate themselves from the difficulty, were principally two: they either denied that Christ had a real body at all, and held that he was an unsubstantial phantom; or, granting that there was a man called Jesus, the son of human parents, they believed that one of the ÆONS, called Christ, quitted the PLEROMA, and descended upon Jesus at his baptism.

3. We have seen that the God who was the father or progenitor of Christ, was not considered to be the creator of the world. Neither was he the God of the Old Testament, and the giver of the Mosaic law. This notion was supported by the same argument which infidels have often urged, that the God of the Jews is represented as a God of vengeance and of cruelty; but it was also a natural consequence of their fundamental principle, that the author of good cannot in any manner be the author of evil. In accordance with this notion, we find all the Gnostics agreed in rejecting the Jewish Scriptures, or, at least, in treating them with contempt. Since they held that the supreme God was revealed for the first time to mankind by Christ, he could not have been the God who inspired the prophets; and yet, with that strange inconsistency which we have already observed in them, they appealed to these very Scriptures in support of their own doctrines. They believed the prophets to have been inspired by the same creative ÆON, or the same principle of evil, which acted originally upon matter; and if their writings had come down to us, we should perhaps find them arguing, that, though the prophets were not inspired by the supreme God, they still could not help giving utterance to truth.

4. Their same abhorrence of matter, and their same notion concerning that purity of knowledge which Christ came upon earth to impart, led them to reject the Christian doctrines of a future resurrection and a general judgment. They seem to have understood the Apostles as preaching literally a resurrection of the body; and it is certain that the fathers insisted upon this very strongly as an article of belief. But to imagine that the body, a mass of created and corruptible matter, could ever enter into heaven, into that PLEROMA which was the dwelling of the supreme God, was a notion which violated the fundamental principle of the Gnostics. According to their scheme, no resurrection was necessary, much less a final judgment. The Gnostic, the man who had attained to perfect knowledge, was gradually emancipated from the grossness of matter; and, by an imperceptible transition, which none but a Gnostic could comprehend, he was raised to be an inhabitant of the divine PLEROMA. If we would know the effect which the doctrines of the Gnostics had upon their moral conduct, we shall find that the same principle led to two very opposite results. Though the fathers may have exaggerated the errors of their opponents, it seems undeniable, that many Gnostics led profligate lives, and maintained upon principle that such conduct was not unlawful. Others, again, are represented as practising great austerities, and endeavouring, by every means, to mortify the body and its sensual appetites. Both parties were actuated by the same common notion, that matter is inherently evil. The one thought that the body, which is compounded of matter, ought to be kept in subjection; and hence they inculcated self-denial, and the practice of moral virtue: while others, who had persuaded themselves that knowledge was every thing, despised the distinctions of the moral law, which was given, as they said, not by the supreme God, but by an inferior ÆON, or a principle of evil, who had allied himself with matter.

5. With respect to the origin of this system the same author observes: There is no system of philosophy which has been traced to a greater number of sources than that which we are now discussing; and the variety of opinions seems to have arisen from persons either not observing the very different aspects which Gnosticism assumed, or from wishing to derive it from one exclusive quarter. Thus, some have deduced it from the eastern notion of a good and evil principle, some from the Jewish Cabbala, and others from the doctrines of the later Platonists. Each of these systems is able to support itself by alleging very strong resemblances; and those persons have taken the most natural and probably the truest course, who have concluded that all these opinions contributed to build up the monstrous system, which was known by the name of Gnosticism.

GOAT, עז. There are other names or appellations given to the goat, as, 1. השופ, 1 Kings xx, 27, which means the RAM-GOAT, or leader of the flock. 2. עתודים, a word which never occurs but in the plural, and means, THE BEST PREPARED, or choicest of the flock; and metaphorically PRINCES, as, Zech. x, 3, "I will visit the goats, saith the Lord," that is, I will begin my vengeance with the princes of the people. "Hell from beneath is moved for thee, to meet thee at thy coming; it stirreth up the dead for thee, even all the great goats of the earth," Isaiah xiv, 9; all the kings, all the great men. And Jeremiah, speaking of the princes of the Jews, says, "Remove out of the midst of

Babylon, and be as the he-goats before the flocks," Jer. 1, 8. 3. צפיר, a name for the goat, of Chaldee origin, and found only in Ezra vi, 17; viii, 35; Daniel viii, 5, 21. 4. עזאזל, from עז, A GOAT, and אזל, TO WANDER ABOUT, Leviticus xvi, 8, "the scape-goat." 5. שער, HAIRY, or SHAGGY, whence שעירים, "THE SHAGGY ONES." In Lev. xvii, 7, it is said, "And they shall no more offer their sacrifices unto devils," (SEIRIM, "hairy ones,") "after whom they have gone a whoring." The word here means idolatrous images of goats, worshipped by the Egyptians. It is the same word that is translated SATYRS, in Isaiah xiii, 21; where the **LXX** render it δαιμόνια, DEMONS. But here they have ματαιοίς, TO VAIN THINGS or IDOLS, which comes to the same sense. What gives light to so obscure a passage is what we read in Maimonides, that the Zabian idolaters worshipped demons under the figure of goats, imagining them to appear in that form, whence they called them by the names of SEIRIM; and that this custom, being spread among other nations, gave occasion to this precept. In like manner we learn from Herodotus, that the Egyptians of Mendes held goats to be sacred animals, and represented the god Pan with the legs and head of that animal. From those ancient idolaters the same notion seems to have been derived by the Greeks and Romans, who represented their Pan, their fauns, satyrs, and other idols, in the form of goats: from all which it is highly probable, that the Israelites had learned in Egypt to worship certain demons, or sylvan deities, under the symbolical figure of goats. Though the phrase, "after whom they have gone a whoring," is equivalent in Scripture to that of committing idolatry, yet we are not to suppose that it is not to be taken in a literal sense in many places, even where it is used in connection with idolatrous acts of worship. It is well known that Baal-peor and Ashtaroth were worshipped with unclean rites, and that public prostitution formed a grand part of the worship of many deities among the Egyptians, Moabites, Canaanites, &c.

The goat was one of the clean beasts which the Israelites might both eat and offer in sacrifice. The kid, גדי is often mentioned as a food, in a way that implies that it was considered as a delicacy. The אקו, or WILD GOAT, mentioned Deut. xiv, 5, and no where else in the Hebrew Bible, is supposed to be the TRAGELAPHUS, or "goat-deer." Schultens conjectures that this animal might have its name, OB FUGACITATEM, from its shyness, or running away. The word יעל, occurs 1 Sam. xxiv, 3; Job xxxix, 1; Psalm civ, 18; Prov. v, 19: and various have been the sentiments of interpreters on the animal intended by it. Bochart insists that it is the IBEX, or "rock-goat." The root whence the name is derived, signifies TO ASCEND, TO MOUNT; and the ibex is famous for clambering, climbing, and leaping, on the most craggy precipices. The Arab writers attribute to the JAAL very long horns, bending backward; consequently it cannot be the chamois. The horns of the JAAL are reckoned among the valuable articles of traffic, Ezek. xxvii, 15. The ibex is finely shaped, graceful in its motions, and gentle in its manners. The female is particularly celebrated by natural historians for tender affection to her young, and the incessant vigilance with which she watches over their safety; and also for ardent attachment and fidelity to her mate.

GOD, an immaterial, intelligent, and free Being; of perfect goodness, wisdom, and power; who made the universe, and continues to support it, as well as to govern and direct it, by his providence. Philologists have hitherto considered the word God as being of the same signification with good; and this is not denied by M. Hallenberg. But he thinks that both words originally denoted UNITY; and that the root is אחד, UNUS; whence the Syriac CHAD and GADA; the Arabic AHD and GAHD; the Persic CHODA and CHUDA; the Greek ἀγαθὸς and γάθος; the Teutonic GUD; the German GOTT; and our Saxon GOD. The other names of God, this author thinks, are referable to a similar origin.

2. By his immateriality, intelligence, and freedom, God is distinguished from Fate, Nature, Destiny, Necessity, Chance, ANIMA MUNDI, and from all the other fictitious beings acknowledged by the Stoics, Pantheists, Spinosists, and other sorts of Atheists. The knowledge of God, his nature, attributes, word, and works, with the relations between him and his creatures, makes the subject of the extensive science called theology. In Scripture God is defined by, "I am that I am; Alpha and Omega; the Beginning and End of all things." Among philosophers, he is defined a Being of infinite perfection; or in whom there is no defect of any thing which we conceive may raise, improve, or exalt his nature. He is the First Cause, the First Being, who has existed from the beginning, has created the world, or who subsists necessarily, or of himself.

3. The plain argument, says Maclaurin, in his "Account of Sir I. Newton's Philosophical Discoveries," for the existence of the Deity, obvious to all, and carrying irresistible conviction with it, is from the evident contrivance and fitness of things for one another, which we meet with throughout all parts of the universe. There is no need of nice or subtle reasonings in this matter; a manifest contrivance immediately suggests a contriver. It strikes us like a sensation; and artful reasonings against it may puzzle us, but it is without shaking our belief. No person, for example, that knows the principles of optics, and the structure of the eye, can believe that it was formed without skill in that science; or that the ear was formed without the knowledge of sounds; or that the male and female in animals were not formed for each other, and for continuing the species. All our accounts of nature are full of instances of this kind. The admirable and beautiful structure of things for final causes, exalts our idea of the Contriver; the unity of design shows him to be one. The great motions in the system performed with the same facility as the least, suggest his almighty power, which gave motion to the earth and the celestial bodies with equal ease as to the minutest particles. The subtilty of the motions and actions in the internal parts of bodies, shows that his influence penetrates the inmost recesses of things, and that he is equally active and present every where. The simplicity of the

laws that prevail in the world, the excellent disposition of things, in order to obtain the best ends, and the beauty which adorns the works of nature, far superior to any thing in art, suggest his consummate wisdom. The usefulness of the whole scheme, so well contrived for the intelligent beings that enjoy it, with the internal disposition and moral structure of these beings themselves, shows his unbounded goodness. These are arguments which are sufficiently open to the views and capacities of the unlearned, while at the same time they acquire new strength and lustre from the discoveries of the learned. The Deity's acting and interposing in the universe, show that he governs as well as formed it; and the depth of his counsels, even in conducting the material universe, of which a great part surpasses our knowledge, keeps up an inward veneration and awe of this great Being, and disposes us to receive what may be otherwise revealed to us concerning him. It has been justly observed, that some of the laws of nature now known to us must have escaped us if we had wanted the sense of seeing. It may be in his power to bestow upon us other senses, of which we have at present no idea; without which it may be impossible for us to know all his works, or to have more adequate ideas of himself. In our present state, we know enough to be satisfied of our dependency upon him, and of the duty we owe to him, the Lord and Disposer of all things. He is not the object of sense; his essence, and, indeed, that of all other substances, are beyond the reach of all our discoveries; but his attributes clearly appear in his admirable works. We know that the highest conceptions we are able to form of them, are still beneath his real perfections; but his power and dominion over us, and our duty toward him, are manifest.

4. Though God has given us no innate ideas of himself, says Mr. Locke, yet, having furnished us with those faculties our minds are endowed with, he hath not left himself without a witness; since we have sense, perception, and reason, and cannot want a clear proof of him as long as we carry ourselves about us. To show, therefore, that we are capable of knowing, that is, of being certain that there is a God, and how we may come by this certainty, I think we need go no farther than ourselves, and that undoubted knowledge we have of our own existence. I think it is beyond question, that man has a clear perception of his own being; he knows certainly that he exists, and that he is something. In the next place, man knows, by an intuitive certainty, that bare nothing can no more produce any real being, than it can be equal to two right angles. If, therefore, we know there is some real Being, it is an evident demonstration, that from eternity there has been something; since what was not from eternity had a beginning; and what had a beginning must be produced by something else. Next it is evident, that what has its being from another must also have all that which is in, and belongs to, its being from another too; all the powers it has must be owing to, and derived from, the same source. This eternal source, then, of all being must be also the source and original of all power; and so this eternal Being must be also the most powerful. Again: man finds in himself perception and knowledge: we are certain, then, that there is not only some Being, but some knowing, intelligent Being, in the world. There was a time, then, when there was no knowing Being, or else there has been a knowing Being from eternity. If it be said there was a time when that eternal Being had no knowledge, I reply, that then it is impossible there should have ever been any knowledge; it being as impossible that things wholly void of knowledge, and operating blindly, and without any perception, should produce a knowing Being, as it is impossible that a triangle should make itself three angles bigger than two right ones. Thus from the consideration of ourselves, and what we infallibly find in our own constitutions, our reason leads us to the knowledge of this certain and evident truth, that there is an eternal, most powerful, and knowing Being, which, whether any one will call God, it matters not. The thing is evident; and from this idea, duly considered, will easily be deduced all those other attributes we ought to ascribe to this eternal Being. From what has been said, it is plain to me, that we have a more certain knowledge of the existence of a God, than of any thing our senses have not immediately discovered to us. Nay, I presume I may say that we more certainly know that there is a God, than that there is any thing else without us. When I say we KNOW, I mean, there is such a knowledge within our reach, which we cannot miss, if we will but apply our minds to that as we do to several other inquiries. It being then unavoidable for all rational creatures to conclude that something has existed from eternity, let us next see what kind of thing that must be. There are but two sorts of beings in the world that man knows or conceives; such as are purely material without sense or perception, and sensible, perceiving beings, such as we find ourselves to be. These two sorts we shall call cogitative and incogitative beings; which to our present purpose are better than material and immaterial. If, then, there must be something eternal, it is very obvious to reason that it must be a cogitative being; because it is as impossible to conceive that bare incogitative matter should ever produce a thinking, intelligent being, as that nothing should of itself produce matter. Let us suppose any parcel of matter eternal, we shall find it in itself unable to produce any thing. Let us suppose its parts firmly at rest together, if there were no other being in the world, must it not eternally remain so, a dead inactive lump? Is it possible to conceive that it can add motion to itself, or produce any thing? Matter, then, by its own strength cannot produce in itself so much as motion. The motion it has must also be from eternity, or else added to matter by some other being, more powerful than matter. But let us suppose motion eternal too, yet matter, incogitative matter, and motion could never produce thought: knowledge will still be as far beyond the power of nothing to produce. Divide matter into as minute parts as you will, vary its figure and motion as much as you please, it will operate no otherwise upon other bodies of proportionable bulk, than it did before this division. The minutest particles of matter knock, impel, and resist one another, just as the greater do; so that if we suppose nothing eternal, matter can never begin to be; if we suppose bare matter without motion eternal, motion can never begin to be; if we suppose only matter and motion to be eternal, thought can never begin to be; for it is impossible to

conceive that matter, either with or without motion, could have originally in and from itself, sense, perception, and knowledge, as is evident from hence, that then sense, perception, and knowledge must be a property eternally inseparable from matter, and every particle of it. Since, therefore, whatsoever is the first eternal Being must necessarily be cogitative; and whatsoever is first of all things must necessarily contain in it, and actually have, at least all the perfections that can ever after exist, it necessarily follows, that the first eternal Being cannot be matter. If, therefore, it be evident that something must necessarily exist from eternity, it is also evident that that something must necessarily be a cogitative Being. For it is as impossible that incogitative matter should produce a cogitative Being, as that nothing, or the negation of all being, should produce a positive Being or matter.

This discovery of the necessary existence of an eternal mind sufficiently leads us to the knowledge of God. For it will hence follow, that all other knowing beings that have a beginning must depend upon him, and have no other ways of knowledge or extent of power than what he gives them; and therefore if he made those, he made also the less excellent pieces of this universe, all inanimate bodies, whereby his omniscience, power, and providence will be established, and from thence all his other attributes necessarily follow.

5. In the Scriptures no attempt is made to prove the existence of a God; such an attempt would have been entirely useless, because the fact was universally admitted. The error of men consisted, not in denying a God, but in admitting too many; and one great object of the Bible is to demonstrate that there is but one. No metaphysical arguments, however, are employed in it for this purpose. The proof rests on facts recorded in the history of the Jews, from which it appears that they were always victorious and prosperous so long as they served the only living and true God, Jehovah, the name by which the Almighty made himself known to them, and uniformly unsuccessful when they revolted from him to serve other gods. What argument could be so effectual to convince them that there was no god in all the earth but the God of Israel? The sovereignty and universal providence of the Lord Jehovah are proved by predictions delivered by the Jewish prophets, pointing out the fate of nations and of empires, specifying distinctly their rise, the duration of their power, and the causes of their decline; thus demonstrating that one God ruled among the nations, and made them the unconscious instruments of promoting the purposes of his will. In the same manner, none of the attributes of God are demonstrated in Scripture by reasoning; they are simply affirmed and illustrated by facts; and instead of a regular deduction of doctrines and conclusions from a few admitted principles, we are left to gather them from the recorded feelings and devotional expressions of persons whose hearts were influenced by the fear of God. These circumstances point out a marked singularity in the Scriptures, considered as a repository of religious doctrines. The writers, generally speaking, do not reason, but exhort and remonstrate; they do not attempt to fetter the judgment by the subtleties of argument, but to rouse the feelings by an appeal to palpable facts. This is exactly what might have been expected from teachers acting under a divine commission, and armed with undeniable facts to enforce their admonitions.

6. In three distinct ways do the sacred writers furnish us with information on this great and essential subject, the existence and the character of God; from the NAMES by which he is designated; from the ACTIONS ascribed to him; and from the ATTRIBUTES with which he is invested in their invocations and praises; and in those lofty descriptions of his nature which, under the inspiration of the Holy Spirit, they have recorded for the instruction of the world. These attributes will be considered under their respective heads; but the impression of the general view of the divine character, as thus revealed, is too important to be omitted.

7. The NAMES of God as recorded in Scripture convey at once ideas of overwhelming greatness and glory, mingled with that awful mysteriousness with which, to all finite minds, and especially to the minds of mortals, the divine essence and mode of existence must ever be invested. Though One he is אלהים, Elohim, Gods, PERSONS ADORABLE. He is יהוה, Jehovah, self-EXISTING; אל, El, STRONG, POWERFUL; אהיה, Ehieh, I AM, I WILL BE, SELF-EXISTENCE, INDEPENDENCY, ALL-SUFFICIENCY, IMMUTABILITY, ETERNITY; שדי, Sha ddai, ALMIGHTY, ALL-SUFFICIENT; אדן, Adon, SUPPORTER, LORD, JUDGE. These are among the adorable appellatives of God which are scattered throughout the revelation that he has been pleased to make of himself: but on one occasion he was pleased more particularly to declare his NAME, that is, such of the qualities and attributes of the divine nature as mortals are the most interested in knowing; and to unfold, not only his natural, but also those of his moral attributes by which his conduct toward his creatures is regulated. "And the Lord passed by and proclaimed, The Lord, the Lord God, merciful and gracious, long-suffering, and abundant in goodness and truth, keeping mercy for thousands, forgiving iniquity, transgression, and sin, and that will by no means clear the guilty; visiting the iniquity of the fathers upon the children, and upon the children's children, unto the third and fourth generation," Exodus xxxiv. This is the most ample and particular description of the character of God, as given by himself in the sacred records; and the import of the several titles by which he has thus in his infinite condescension manifested himself, has been thus exhibited. He is not only Jehovah, SELF-EXISTENT, and El, THE STRONG OR MIGHTY GOD; but he is, says Dr. A. Clarke, "רחום, Rochum, THE MERCIFUL BEING, who is full of tenderness and compassion; חנון, Chanun, THE GRACIOUS ONE, he whose nature is goodness itself, the loving God. פים ארך, Erec Apayim, LONG-SUFFERING, the Being who, because of his tenderness, is not easily irritated, but suffers long and is kind; דב Rab, THE GREAT

OR MIGHTY ONE: חסד, Chesed, THE BOUNTIFUL BEING, he who is exuberant in his beneficence; אמת, Emeth, THE TRUTH, or TRUE ONE, he alone who can neither deceive nor be deceived; נצר חסד, Notser Chesed, THE PRESERVER OF BOUNTIFULNESS, he whose beneficence never ends, keeping mercy for thousands of generations, showing compassion and mercy while the world endures; נשא עון ופשע וחטאה, Nose avon vapesha vechataah, HE WHO BEARS AWAY INIQUITY, TRANSGRESSION, AND SIN; properly the REDEEMER, the PARDONER, the FORGIVER, the Being whose prerogative it is to forgive sin, and save the soul; נקה לא ינקה, Nakeh lo yinnakeh, THE RIGHTEOUS JUDGE, who distributes justice with an impartial hand; and פקד עין, Paked avon, &c, HE WHO VISITS INIQUITY, he who punishes transgressors, and from whose justice no sinner can escape; the God of retributive and vindictive justice."

8. The second means by which the Scriptures convey to us the knowledge of God, is by the ACTIONS which they ascribe to him. They contain, indeed, the important record of his dealings with men in every age which is comprehended within the limit of the sacred history; and, by prophetic declaration, they also exhibit the principles on which he will govern the world to the end of time: so that the whole course of the divine administration may be considered as exhibiting a singularly illustrative comment upon those attributes of his nature which, in their abstract form, are contained in such declarations as those which have been just quoted. The first act ascribed to God is that of creating the heavens and the earth out of nothing; and by his fiat alone arranging their parts, and peopling them with living creatures. By this were manifested--his ETERNITY AND SELF-EXISTENCE, as he who creates must be before all creatures, and he who gives being to others can himself derive it from none:--his ALMIGHTY POWER, shown both in the act of creation and in the number and vastness of the objects so produced:--his WISDOM, in their arrangement, and in their fitness to their respective ends:--and his GOODNESS, as the whole tended to the happiness of SENTIENT beings. The foundations of his natural and moral government are also made manifest by his creative acts. In what he made out of nothing he had an absolute right and prerogative: it awaited his ordering, and was completely at his disposal; so that to alter or destroy his own work, and to prescribe the laws by which the intelligent and rational part of his creatures should be governed, are rights which none can question. Thus on the one hand his character of LORD or GOVERNOR is established, and on the other our duty of lowly HOMAGE and absolute OBEDIENCE.

9. Agreeably to this, as soon as man was created, he was placed under a rule of conduct. Obedience was to be followed with the continuance of the divine favour; transgression, with death. The event called forth new manifestations of the character of God. His tender MERCY, in the compassion showed to the fallen pair; his JUSTICE, in forgiving them only in the view of a satisfaction to be hereafter offered to his justice by an innocent representative of the sinning race; his LOVE to that race, in giving his own Son to become this Redeemer, and in the fulness of time to die for the sins of the whole world; and his HOLINESS, in connecting with this provision for the pardon of man the means of restoring him to a sinless state, and to the obliterated image of God in which he had been created. Exemplifications of the divine MERCY are traced from age to age, in his establishing his own worship among men, and remitting the punishment of individual and national offences in answer to prayer offered from penitent hearts, and in dependence upon the typified or actually offered universal sacrifice:--of his CONDESCENSION, in stooping to the cases of individuals; in his dispensations both of providence and grace, by showing respect to the poor and humble; and, principally, by the incarnation of God in the form of a servant, admitting men into familiar and friendly intercourse with himself, and then entering into heaven to be their patron and advocate, until they should be received unto the same glory, "and so be for ever with the Lord:"--of his strictly RIGHTEOUS GOVERNMENT, in the destruction of the old world, the cities of the plain, the nations of Canaan, and all ancient states, upon their "filling up the measure of their iniquities;" and, to show that "he will by no means clear the guilty;" in the numerous and severe punishments inflicted even upon the chosen seed of Abraham, because of their transgressions:--of his LONG-SUFFERING, in frequent warnings, delays, and corrective judgments inflicted upon individuals and nations, before sentence of utter excision and destruction:--of FAITHFULNESS and TRUTH, in the fulfilment of promises, often many ages after they were given, as in the promises to Abraham respecting the possession of the land of Canaan by his seed, and in all the "promises made to the fathers" respecting the advent, vicarious death, and illustrious offices of the "Christ," the Saviour of the world:--of his IMMUTABILITY, in the constant and unchanging laws and principles of his government, which remain to this day precisely the same, in every thing universal, as when first promulgated, and have been the rule of his conduct in all places as well as through all time:--of his PRESCIENCE of future events, manifested by the predictions of Scripture:--and of the depth and stability of his COUNSEL, as illustrated in that plan and purpose of bringing back a revolted world to obedience and felicity, which we find steadily kept in view in the Scriptural history of the acts of God in former ages; which is still the end toward which all his dispensations bend, however wide and mysterious their sweep; and which they will finally accomplish, as we learn from the prophetic history of the future, contained in the Old and New Testaments.

Thus the course of divine operation in the world has from age to age been a manifestation of the divine character, continually receiving new and stronger illustrations until the completion of the Christian revelation by the ministry of Christ and his inspired followers, and still placing itself in brighter light and more impressive aspects as the scheme of human redemption runs on to its consummation. From all the acts of God as recorded in the Scriptures, we are taught that he alone is God; that he is present every where to sustain and govern all things; that his wisdom is infinite, his counsel settled, and his power irresistible; that he is holy, just, and good; the Lord and the Judge, but the Father and the Friend, of man.

10. More at large do we learn what God is, from the declarations of the inspired writings. As to his SUBSTANCE, that "God is a Spirit." As to his DURATION, that "from everlasting to everlasting he is God;" "the King, eternal, immortal, invisible." That, after all the manifestations he has made of himself, he is, from the infinite perfection and glory of his nature, INCOMPREHENSIBLE: "Lo, these are but parts of his ways, and how little a portion is heard of him!" "Touching the Almighty, we cannot find him out." That he is UNCHANGEABLE: "The Father of Lights, with whom there is no variableness, neither shadow of turning." That "he is the fountain of life," and the only independent Being in the universe: "Who only hath immortality." That every other being, however exalted, has its existence from him: "For by him were all things created, which are in heaven and in earth, whether they are visible or invisible." That the existence of every thing is upheld by him, no creature being for a moment independent of his support: "By him all things consist;" "upholding all things by the word of his power." That he is OMNIPRESENT: "Do not I fill heaven and earth with my presence, saith the Lord?" That he is OMNISCIENT: "All things are naked and open before the eyes of him with whom we have to do." That he is the absolute Lord and OWNER of all things: "The heavens, even the heaven of heavens, are thine, and all the parts of them:" "The earth is thine, and the fulness thereof, the world and them that dwell therein:" "He doeth according to his will in the armies of heaven, and among the inhabitants of the earth." That his PROVIDENCE extends to the minutest objects: "The hairs of your head are all numbered:" "Are not two sparrows sold for a farthing? and one of them shall not fall on the ground without your Father." That he is a Being of unspotted PURITY and perfect RECTITUDE: "Holy, holy, holy, Lord God of hosts!" "A God of truth, and in whom is no iniquity:" "Of purer eyes than to behold iniquity." That he is JUST in the administration of his government: "Shall not the Judge of the whole earth do right?" "Clouds and darkness are round about him; judgment and justice are the habitation of his throne." That his WISDOM is unsearchable: "O the depth of the wisdom and knowledge of God! How unsearchable are his judgments, and his ways past finding out!" And, finally, that he is GOOD and MERCIFUL: "Thou art good, and thy mercy endureth for ever:" "His tender mercy is over all his works:" "God, who is rich in mercy, for his great love wherewith he loved us, even when we were dead in sins, hath quickened us together with Christ:" "God was in Christ, reconciling the world unto himself, not imputing their trespasses unto them:" "God hath given to us eternal life, and this life is in his Son."

11. Under these deeply awful but consolatory views, do the Scriptures present to us the supreme object of our worship and trust; and they dwell upon each of the above particulars with inimitable sublimity and beauty of language, and with an inexhaustible variety of illustration. Nor can we compare these views of the divine nature with the conceptions of the most enlightened of Pagans, without feeling how much reason we have for everlasting gratitude, that a revelation so explicit, and so comprehensive, should have been made to us on a subject which only a revelation from God himself could have made known. It is thus that Christian philosophers, even when they do not use the language of the Scriptures, are able to speak on this great and mysterious doctrine, in language so clear, and with conceptions so noble; in a manner too so equable, so different from the sages of antiquity, who, if at any time they approach the truth when speaking of the divine nature, never fail to mingle with it some essentially erroneous or grovelling conception. "By the Word of God," says Dr. Barrow, "we mean a Being of infinite wisdom, goodness, and power, the Creator and the Governor of all things, to whom the great attributes of eternity and independency, omniscience and immensity, perfect holiness and purity, perfect justice and veracity, complete happiness, glorious majesty, and supreme right of dominion belong; and to whom the highest veneration, and most profound submission and obedience are due." "Our notion of Deity," says Bishop Pearson, "doth expressly signify a Being or Nature of infinite perfection; and the infinite perfection of a being or nature consists in this, that it be absolutely and essentially necessary; an actual Being of itself; and potential, or causative of all beings beside itself, independent from any other, upon which all things else depend, and by which all things else are governed." "God is a Being," says Lawson, "and not any kind of being; but a substance, which is the foundation of other beings. And not only a substance, but perfect. Yet many beings are perfect in their kind, yet limited and finite. But God is absolutely, fully, and every way infinitely perfect; and therefore above spirits, above angels, who are perfect comparatively. God's infinite perfection includes all the attributes, even the most excellent. It excludes all dependency, borrowed existence, composition, corruption, mortality, contingency, ignorance, unrighteousness, weakness, misery, and all imperfections whatever. It includes necessity of being, independency, perfect unity, simplicity, immensity, eternity, immortality; the most perfect life, knowledge, wisdom, integrity, power, glory, bliss, and all these in the highest degree. We cannot pierce into the secrets of this eternal Being. Our reason comprehends but little of him, and when it can proceed no farther, faith comes in, and we believe far more than we can understand; and this our belief is not contrary to reason; but reason itself dictates unto us, that we must believe far more of God than it can inform us of." To these we may add an admirable passage from Sir Isaac Newton: "The word God frequently signifies LORD; but every lord is not God; it is the dominion of a spiritual Being or Lord that constitutes God; true dominion, true God; supreme, the Supreme; feigned, the false god. From such true dominion it

follows, that the true God is living, intelligent, and powerful; and from his other perfections, that he is supreme, or supremely perfect; he is eternal and infinite; omnipotent and omniscient; that is, he endures from eternity to eternity; and is present from infinity to infinity. He governs all things that exist, and knows all things that are to be known; he is not eternity or infinity, but eternal and infinite; he is not duration or space, but he endures and is present; he endures always, and is present every where; he is omnipresent, not only virtually, but also substantially; for power without substance cannot subsist. All things are contained and move in him, but without any mutual passion; he suffers nothing from the motions of bodies; nor do they undergo any resistance from his omnipresence. It is confessed, that God exists necessarily, and by the same necessity he exists always and every where. Hence also he must be perfectly similar, all eye, all ear, all arm, all the power of perceiving, understanding, and acting; but after a manner not at all corporeal, after a manner not like that of men, after a manner wholly to us unknown. He is destitute of all body, and all bodily shape; and therefore cannot be seen, heard, or touched; nor ought he to be worshipped under the representation of any thing corporeal. We have ideas of the attributes of God, but do not know the substance of even any thing; we see only the figures and colours of bodies, hear only sounds, touch only the outward surfaces, smell only odours, and taste tastes; and do not, cannot, by any sense, or reflex act, know their inward substances; and much less can we have any notion of the substance of God. We know him by his properties and attributes."

12. Many able works in proof of the existence of God have been written, the arguments of which are too copious for us even to analyze. It must be sufficient to say that they all proceed, as it is logically termed, either À PRIORI, from cause to effect, or, which is the safest and most satisfactory mode, À POSTERIORI, from the effect to the cause. The irresistible argument from the marks of DESIGN with which all nature abounds, to one great intelligent, designing Cause, is by no writers brought out in so clear and masterly a manner as by Howe, in his "Living temple," and Paley, in his "Natural Theology."

GODS, in the plural, is used of the false deities of the Heathens, many of which were only creatures to whom divine honours and worship were superstitiously paid. The Greeks and Latins, it is observable, did not mean, by the name GOD, an all-perfect being, whereof eternity, infinity, omnipresence, &c, were essential attributes: with them the word only implied an excellent and superior nature; and, accordingly, they give the appellation GODS to all beings of a rank or class, higher or more perfect than that of men, and especially to those who were inferior agents in the divine administration, all subject to the one Supreme. Thus men themselves, according to their system, might become gods after death, inasmuch as their souls might attain to a degree of excellence superior to what they were capable of in life. The first idols, or false gods, that are said to have been adored were the stars, sun, moon, &c, on account of the light, heat, and other benefits which we derive from them. (See IDOLATRY.) Afterward the earth came to be deified, for furnishing fruits necessary for the subsistence of men and animals: then fire and water became objects of divine worship, for their usefulness to human life. In process of time, and by degrees, gods became multiplied to infinity; and there was scarce any thing but the weakness or caprice of some devotee or other, elevated into the rank of deity: things useless or even destructive not excepted. The principal of the ancient gods, whom the Romans called DII MAJORUM GENTIUM, and Cicero celestial gods, Varro select gods, Ovid NOBILES DEOS, others CONSENTES DEOS, were Jupiter, Juno, Vesta, Minerva, Ceres, Diana, Venus, Mars, Mercury, Neptune, Vulcan, and Apollo. Jupiter is considered as the god of heaven; Neptune, as god of the sea; Mars, as the god of war; Apollo, of eloquence, poetry, and physic; Mercury, of thieves; Bacchus, of wine; Cupid, of love, &c. A second sort of gods, called demi-gods, SEMI-DII, DII MINORUM GENTIUM, INDIGETES, or gods adopted, were men canonized and deified. As the greater gods had possession of heaven by their own right, these secondary deities had it by merit and donation, being translated into heaven because they had lived as gods upon earth.

2. The Heathen gods may be all reduced to the following classes: (1.) Created spirits, angels, or demons, whence good and evil gods; Genii, Lares, Lemures, Typhones, guardian gods, infernal gods, &c. (2.) Heavenly bodies; as, the sun, moon, and other planets; also, the fixed stars, constellations, &c. (3.) Elements; as air, earth, ocean, Ops, Vesta; the rivers, fountains, &c. (4.) Meteors. Thus the Persians adored the wind: thunder and lightning were honoured under the name of Geryon; and several nations of India and America have made themselves gods of the same. Castor, Pollux, Helena, and Iris, have also been preferred from meteors to be gods; and the like has been practised in regard to comets: witness that which appeared at the murder of Cæsar. (5.) They erected minerals or fossils into deities. Such was the Bætylus. The Finlanders adored stones; the Scythians, iron; and many nations, silver and gold. (6.) Plants have been made gods. Thus leeks and onions were deities in Egypt; the Sclavi, Lithuanians, Celtæ, Vandals, and Peruvians, adored trees and forests; the ancient Gauls, Britons, and Druids, paid a particular devotion to the oak; and it was no other than wheat, corn, seed, &c, that the ancients adored under the names of Ceres and Proserpina. (7.) They took themselves gods from among the waters. The Syrians and Egyptians adored fishes; and what were the Tritons, the Nereids, Syrens, &c, but fishes? Several nations have adored serpents; particularly the Egyptians, Prussians, Lithuanians, Samogitians, &c. (8.) Insects, as flies and ants, had their priests and votaries. (9.) Among birds, the stork, raven, sparrowhawk, ibis, eagle, grisson, and lapwing have had divine honours; the last in Mexico, the rest in Egypt and at Thebes. (10.) Four-footed beasts have had their altars; as the bull, dog, cat, wolf, baboon, lion, and crocodile, in Egypt and elsewhere; the hog in the island of Crete; rats and mice in the Troas, and at Tenedos; weasels at Thebes; and the porcupine throughout all Zoroaster's school. (11.) Nothing was more

common than to place men among the number of deities; and from Belus or Baal, to the Roman emperors before Constantine, the instances of this kind are innumerable: frequently they did not wait so long as their deaths for the apotheosis. Nebuchadnezzar procured his statue to be worshipped while living; and Virgil shows that Augustus had altars and sacrifices offered to him; as we learn from other hands that he had priests called AUGUSTALES, and temples at Lyons, Narbona, and several other places, and he must be allowed the first of the Romans in whose behalf idolatry was carried to such a pitch. The Ethiopians deemed all their kings gods: the Velleda of the Germans, the Janus of the Hungarians, and the Thaut, Woden, and Assa of the northern nations, were indisputably men. (12.) Not men only, but every thing that relates to man, has also been deified; as labour, rest, sleep, youth, age, death, virtues, vices, occasion, time, place, numbers, among the Pythagoreans; the generative power, under the name of Priapus. Infancy alone had a cloud of deities; as, Vagetanus, Levana, Rumina, Edufa, Potina, Cuba, Cumina, Carna, Ossilago, Statulinus, Fabulinus, &c. They also adored the gods Health, Fever, Fear, Love, Pain, Indignation, Shame, Impudence, Opinion, Renown, Prudence, Science, Art, Fidelity, Felicity, Calumny, Liberty, Money, War, Peace, Victory, Triumph, &c. Lastly, Nature, the universe, or τὸ πᾶν, was reputed a great god.

3. Hesiod has a poem under the title of Θεογονία, that is, "The Generation of the Gods," in which he explains their genealogy and descent, sets forth who was the first and principal, who next descended from him, and what issue each had: the whole making a sort of system of Heathen theology. Beside this popular theology, each philosopher had his system, as may be seen from the "Timæus" of Plato, and Cicero "*De Natura Deorum.*" Justin Martyr, Tertullian, Arnobius, Minutius Felix, Lactantius, Eusebius, St. Augustine, and Theodoret, show the vanity of the Heathen gods. It is very difficult to discover the real sentiments of the Heathens with respect to their gods: they are exceedingly intricate and confused, and even frequently contradictory. They admitted so many superior and inferior gods, who shared the empire, that every place was full of gods. Varro reckons up no less than thirty thousand adored within a small extent of ground, and yet their number was every day increasing. In modern oriental Paganism they amount to many millions, and are, in fact, innumerable.

4. The name of God, in Hebrew, ELOHIM, is very ambiguous in Scripture. The true God is often called so, as are sometimes angels, judges, and princes, and sometimes idols and false gods; for example: "God created the heaven and the earth," Gen. i, 1. The Hebrew ELOHIM denotes, in this place, the true God. "He who sacrificeth unto any god, (ELOHIM,) shall be put to death," Exodus xxii, 20. And again: "Among the gods there is none like unto thee," Psalm lxxxvi, 8. Princes, magistrates, and great men are called gods in the following passages: "If a slave is desirous to continue with his master, he shall be brought to the judges," Exod. xxi, 6, in the original, to the GODS. Again: "If the thief be not found, then the master of the house shall be brought unto the judges," Exod. xxii, 8, in the original, to the gods; and in the twenty-eighth verse of the same chapter, "Thou shalt not speak evil of the gods;" that is, of the judges or great men. The Psalmist says that the Lord "judgeth among the gods," Psalm lxxxii, 1. And again, God says to Moses, "I have made thee a god to Pharaoh," Exod. vii, 1. The pious Israelites had so great an aversion and such an extreme contempt for strange gods, that they scorned even to mention them; they disguised and disfigured their names by substituting in the room of them some term of contempt; for example, instead of ELOHIM, they called them ELILIM, "nothings, gods of no value;" instead of MEPHIBAAL, MERIBAAL, and JERUBAAL, they said "Mephibosheth, Meribosheth, and Jeribosheth." BAAL signifies master, husband; and BOSHETH, something to be ashamed of, something apt to put one in confusion. God forbade the Israelites to swear by strange gods, and to pronounce the names of them in their oaths, Exod. xxiii, 13.

GODLINESS, strictly taken, signifies right worship, or devotion; but, in general, it imports the whole of practical religion, 1 Tim. iv, 8; 2 Peter i, 6.

GOEL, גאל, the avenger of blood. The inhabitants of the east, it is well known, are now, what they anciently were, exceedingly revengeful. If, therefore, an individual should unfortunately happen to lay violent hands upon another person and kill him, the next of kin is bound to avenge the death of the latter, and to pursue the murderer with unceasing vigilance until he have caught and killed him, either by force or by fraud. The same custom exists in Arabia, and it appears to have been alluded to by Rebecca: when she learned that Esau was threatening to kill his brother Jacob, she endeavoured to send the latter out of the country, saying, "Why should I be bereft of you both in one day?" Gen. xxvii, 15. She could not be afraid of the magistrate for punishing the murderer, for the patriarchs were subject to no superior in Palestine; and Isaac was much too partial to Esau for her to entertain any expectation that he would condemn him to death for it. It would therefore appear that she dreaded lest he should fall by the hand of the blood avenger, perhaps of some Ishmaelite. The office, therefore, of the GOEL was in use before the time of Moses; and it was probably filled by the nearest of blood to the party killed, as the right of redeeming a mortgage field is given to him. To prevent the unnecessary loss of life through a sanguinary spirit of revenge, the Hebrew legislator made various enactments concerning the blood avenger. In most ages and countries, certain reputed sacred places enjoyed the privileges of being asylums; Moses, therefore, taking it for granted that the murderer would flee to the altar, commanded that when the crime was deliberate and intentional, he should be torn even from the altar, and put to death, Exod. xxi, 14. But in the case of unintentional murder, the man-slayer was enjoined to flee to one of the six cities of refuge, which were appropriated for his residence. The roads to these cities, it was enacted, should be kept in such a state that the unfortunate individual might meet with no impediment whatever in his way, Deut. xix, 3. If the GOEL overtook the fugitive before he reached an asylum, and put him to death, he was not considered as guilty of blood; but if the man-slayer had reached a place of refuge, he was immediately protected, and an inquiry was instituted whether he had a right to such protection and asylum, that is, whether he had caused his neighbour's death undesignedly, or was a deliberate murderer. In the latter case he was judicially delivered to the GOEL, who might put him to death in whatever way he chose; but in the former case the homicide continued in the place of refuge until the high priest's death, when he might return home in perfect security. If, however, the GOEL found him without the city, or beyond its suburbs, he might slay him without being guilty of blood, Numbers xxxv, 26, 27. Farther, to guard the life of man, and prevent the perpetration of murder, Moses positively prohibited the receiving of a sum of money from a murderer in the way of compensation, Numbers xxxv, 31. It would seem that if no avenger of blood appeared, or if he were dilatory in the pursuit of the murderer, it became the duty of the magistrate himself to inflict the sentence of the law; and thus we find that David deemed this to be his duty in the case of Joab, and that Solomon, in obedience to his father's dying entreaty, actually discharged it by putting that murderer to death, 1 Kings ii, 5; vi, 28–34. There is a beautiful allusion to the blood avenger in Heb. vi, 17, 18.

The following extracts will prove how tenaciously the eastern people adhere to the principle of revenging the death of their relations and friends:--"Among the Circassians," says Pallas, "all the relatives of the murderers are considered as guilty. This customary infatuation to revenge the blood of relations generates most of the feuds, and occasions great bloodshed among all the tribes of Caucasus; for unless pardon be purchased, or obtained by intermarriage between the two families, the principle of revenge is propagated to all succeeding generations. If the thirst of vengeance is quenched by a price paid to the family of the deceased, this tribute is called THLIL-UASA, or, 'the price of blood;' but neither princes nor usdens accept such compensation, as it is an established law among them to demand blood for blood." "The Nubians," observes Light, "possess few traces among them of government, or law, or religion. They know no master, although the cashief claims a nominal command of the country. They look for redress of injuries to their own means of revenge, which, in cases of blood, extends from one generation to another, till blood is repaid by blood. On this account they are obliged to be ever on the watch, and armed: and in this manner even their daily labours are carried on; the very boys are armed." "If one Nubian," remarks Burckhardt, "happen to kill another, he is obliged to pay the debt of blood to the family of the deceased, and a fine to the governors of six camels, a cow, and seven sheep, or they are taken from his relations. Every wound inflicted has its stated fine, consisting of sheep and DHOURRA, but varying in quantity, according to the parts of the body wounded." "When a man or woman is murdered," says Malcolm, "the moment the person by whom the act was perpetrated is discovered, the heir-at-law to the deceased demands vengeance for the blood. Witnesses are examined, and if the guilt be established, the criminal is delivered into his hands, to deal with as he chooses. It is alike legal for him to forgive him, to accept a sum of money as the price of blood, or to put him to death. It is only a few years ago that the English resident at Abusheher saw three persons delivered into the hands of the relations of those whom they had murdered. They led their victims bound to the burial ground, where they put them to death; but the part of the execution that appeared of the most importance, was to make the infant children of the deceased stab the murderers with knives, and imbrue their little hands in the blood of those who had slain their father. The youngest princes of the blood that could hold a dagger were made to stab the assassins of Aga Mahomed Khan. When they were executed, the successor of Nadir Shah sent one of the murderers of that monarch to the females of his harem, who, we are told, were delighted to become his executioners."

GOG AND MAGOG. Moses speaks of Magog, son of Japheth, but says nothing of Gog, Gen. x, 2. According to Ezekiel, Gog was prince of Magog, Ezek. xxxviii, 2, 3, &c; xxxix, 1, 2, &c. Magog signifies the country or people, and Gog the king of that country; the general name of the northern nations of Europe and Asia, or the districts north of the Caucasus, or Mount Taurus. The prophecy of Ezekiel, xxxix, 1–22, seems to be revived in the Apocalypse, where the hosts of Gog and Magog are represented as coming to invade "the beloved city," and perishing with immense slaughter likewise in Armageddon, "the mount of Mageddo," or Megiddo, Rev. xvi, 14–16; xx, 7–10.

GOLD, זהב, Gen. xxiv, 22, and very frequently in all other parts of the Old Testament; χρυσος, Matt. xxiii, 16, 17, &c; the most perfect and valuable of the metals. In Job xxviii, 15–18, 19, gold is mentioned five times, and four of the words are different in the original: 1. סגור, which may mean "gold in the mine," or "shut up," as the root signifies, "in the ore." 2. כתם, KETHEM, from כתם, CATHAM, "to sign," "seal," or "stamp;" gold made current by being coined; standard gold, exhibiting the stamp expressive of its value. 3. זהב, wrought gold, pure, highly polished gold. 4. פז, denoting solidity, compactness, and strength; probably gold formed into different kinds of plate, or vessels. Jerom, in his comment on Jer. x, 9, writes "SEPTEM DOMINIBUS APUD HEBRÆOS APPELLATUR AURUM." The seven names, which he does not mention, are as follows, and thus distinguished by the Hebrews: 1. ZAHAB, gold in general. 2. ZAHAB TOB, good gold, of a more valuable kind, Gen. ii, 12. 3. ZAHAB OPHIR, gold of Ophir, 1 Kings ix, 28, such as was brought by the navy of Solomon. 4. ZAHAB MUPHAZ, solid gold, pure, wrought gold, translated, 1 Kings x, 18, "the best gold." 5. ZAHAB SHACHUT, beaten gold, 2 Chron. ix, 15. 6. ZAHAB SEGOR, shut up gold; either as mentioned above, gold in the ore, or as the rabbins explain it, "gold shut up in the treasuries," gold in bullion. 7. ZAHAB PARVAIM, 2 Chron. iii, 6. To these Buxtorf adds three others: 1. כתם, pure gold of the circulating medium. 2. צרל, gold in the treasury. 3. חרצז, choice, fine gold. Arabia had formerly its golden mines. "The gold of Sheba," Psalm lxxii, 15, is, in the Septuagint and Arabic versions, "the gold of Arabia." Sheba was the ancient name of Arabia Felix. Mr. Bruce, however, places it in Africa, at Azab. The gold of Ophir, so often mentioned, must be that which was procured in Arabia, on the coast of the Red Sea. We are assured by Sanchoniathon, as quoted by Eusebius, and by Herodotus, that the Phenicians carried on a considerable traffic with this gold even before the days of Job, who speaks of it, xxii, 24.

GOLIATH, a famous giant of the city of Gath, who was slain by David, 1 Sam. xvii, 4, 5, &c. See Giants.

GOMER, the eldest son of Japheth, by whom a great part of Asia Minor was first peopled, and particularly that extensive tract which was called Phrygia, including the subdivisions of Mysia, Galatia, Bithynia, Lycaonia, &c. The colonies of Gomer extended into Germany, Gaul, (in both of which traces of the name are preserved,) and Britain, which was undoubtedly peopled from Gaul. Among the descendants of the ancient inhabitants of this island, namely, the Welsh, the words KUMERO and KUMERAEG, the names of the people and the language, sufficiently point out their origin. In fact, under the names of Cimmerii, Cimbri, Cymrig, Cumbri, Umbri, and Cambri, the tribes of Gomerians extended themselves from the Euxine to the Atlantic, and from Italy to the Baltic; having added to their original names those of Celts, Gauls, Galatæ, and Gaels, superadded.

GOMORRAH, one of the five cities of the Pentapolis, consumed by fire, Genesis xix, 24, &c. See Dead Sea.

GOSHEN. This was the most fertile pasture ground in the whole of Lower Egypt; thence called Goshen, from GUSH, in Arabic, signifying "a heart," or whatsoever is choice or precious. There was also a Goshen in the territory of the tribe of Judah, so called for the same reason, Joshua x, 41. Hence Joseph recommended it to his family as "the best of the land," Gen. xlvii, 11, and "the fat of the land," Gen. xlv, 18. The land of Goshen lay along the most easterly branch of the Nile, and on the east side of it; for it is evident that, at the time of the exode, the Israelites did not cross the Nile. In ancient times, the fertile land was considerably more extensive, both in length and breadth, than at present, in consequence of the general failure of the eastern branches of the Nile; the main body of the river verging more and more to the west continually, and deepening the channels on that side.

GOSPEL, a history of the life, actions, death, resurrection, ascension, and doctrine of Jesus Christ. The word is Saxon, and of the same import with the Latin term EVANGELIUM, or the Greek εὐαγγέλιον, which signifies "glad tidings," or "good news;" the history of our Saviour being the best history ever published to mankind. This history is contained in the writings of St. Matthew, St. Mark, St. Luke, and St. John, who from thence are called evangelists. The Christian church never acknowledged any more than these four Gospels as canonical: notwithstanding which, several apocryphal gospels are handed down to us, and others are entirely lost. The four Gospels contain each of them the history of our Saviour's life and ministry; but we must remember, that no one of the evangelists undertook to give an account of all the miracles which Christ performed, or of all the instructions which he delivered. They are written with different degrees of conciseness; but every one of them is sufficiently full to prove that Jesus was the promised Messiah, the Saviour of the world, who had been predicted by a long succession of prophets, and whose advent was expected at the time of his appearance, both by Jews and Gentiles.

2. That all the books which convey to us the history of events under the New Testament were written and immediately published by persons contemporary with the events, is most fully proved by the testimony of an unbroken series of authors, reaching from the days of the evangelists to the present times; by the concurrent belief of Christians of all denominations; and by the unreserved confession of avowed enemies to the Gospel. In this point of view the writings of the ancient fathers of the Christian church are invaluable. They contain not only frequent references and allusions to the books of the New Testament, but also such numerous professed quotations from them, that it is demonstratively certain that these books existed in their present state a few years after the conclusion of Christ's ministry upon earth. No unbeliever in the apostolic age, in the age immediately subsequent to it, or, indeed, in any age whatever, was ever able to disprove the facts recorded in these books; and it does not appear that in the early times any such attempt was made. The facts, therefore, related in the New Testament must be admitted to have really happened. But if all the circumstances of the history of Jesus, that is, his miraculous conception in the womb of the virgin, the time at which he was born, the place where he was born, the family from which he was descended, the nature of the doctrines which he preached, the meanness of his condition, his rejection, death, burial, resurrection, and ascension, with many other minute particulars; if all these various circumstances in the history of Jesus exactly accord with the predictions of the Old Testament relative to the promised Messiah, in whom all the nations of the earth were to be blessed, it follows that Jesus was that Messiah. And again: if Jesus really performed the miracles as related in the Gospels, and was perfectly acquainted with the thoughts and designs of men, his divine mission cannot be doubted. Lastly: if he really foretold his own death and resurrection, the descent of the Holy Ghost, its miraculous effects, the sufferings of the Apostles, the call of the Gentiles, and the destruction of Jerusalem, it necessarily follows that he spake by the authority of God himself. These, and many other arguments, founded in the more than human character of Jesus, in the rapid propagation of the Gospel, in the excellence of its precepts and doctrines, and in the constancy, intrepidity, and fortitude of its early professors, incontrovertibly establish the truth

and divine origin of the Christian religion, and afford to us, who live in these latter times, the most positive confirmation of the promise of our Lord, that "the gates of hell shall not prevail against it."

3. The Gospels recount those wonderful and important events with which the Christian religion and its divine Author were introduced into the world, and which have produced so great a change in the principles, the manners, the morals, and the temporal as well as spiritual condition of mankind. They relate the first appearance of Christ upon earth, his extraordinary and miraculous birth, the testimony borne to him by his forerunner, John the Baptist, the temptation in the wilderness, the opening of his divine commission, the pure, the perfect, and sublime morality which he taught, especially in his inimitable sermon on the mount, the infinite superiority which he showed to every other moral teacher, both in the matter and manner of his discourses, more particularly by crushing vice in its very cradle, in the first risings of wicked desires and propensities in the heart, by giving a decided preference to the mild, gentle, passive, conciliating virtues, before that violent, vindictive, high-spirited, unforgiving temper, which has been always too much the favourite character of the world; by requiring us to forgive our very enemies, and to do good to them that hate us; by excluding from our devotions, our alms, and all our virtues, all regard to fame, reputation, and applause; by laying down two great general principles of morality, love to God, and love to mankind, and deducing from thence every other human duty; by conveying his instructions under the easy, familiar, and impressive form of parables; by expressing himself in a tone of dignity and authority unknown before; by exemplifying every virtue that he taught in his own unblemished and perfect life and conversation; and, above all, by adding those awful sanctions, which he alone, of all moral instructers, had the power to hold out, eternal rewards to the virtuous, and eternal punishments to the wicked. The sacred narratives then represent to us the high character that he assumed; the claim he made to a divine original; the wonderful miracles he wrought in proof of his divinity; the various prophecies which plainly marked him out as the Messiah, the great Deliverer of the Jews; the declarations he made that he came to offer himself a sacrifice for the sins of all mankind; the cruel indignities, sufferings, and persecutions to which, in consequence of this great design, he was exposed; the accomplishment of it, by the painful and ignominious death to which he submitted, by his resurrection after three days from the grave, by his ascension into heaven, by his sitting there at the right hand of God, and performing the office of a Mediator and Intercessor for the sinful sons of men, till he shall come a second time in his glory to sit in judgment on all mankind, and decide their final doom of happiness or misery for ever. These are the momentous, the interesting, truths on which the Gospels principally dwell.

4. We find in the ancient records a twofold order, in which the evangelists are arranged. They stand either thus, Matthew, John, Luke, Mark; or thus, Matthew, Mark, Luke, John. The first is made with reference to the character and the rank of the persons, according to which the Apostles precede their assistants and attendants (ἀκολουθοις, COMITIBUS.) It is observed in the oldest Latin translations and in the Gothic; sometimes also in the works of Latin teachers; but among all the Greek **MSS.** only in that at Cambridge. But the other, namely, Matthew, Mark, Luke, and John, is, in all the old translations of Asia and Africa, in all catalogues of the canonical books, and in Greek **MSS.** in general, the customary and established one as it regarded not personal circumstances, but as it had respect to chronological; which is to us a plain indication what accounts concerning the succession of the evangelists, the Asiatic, and Greek churches, and also those of Africa, had before them, when the Christian books were arranged in collections. It is a considerable advantage, says Michaëlis, that a history of such importance as that of Jesus Christ has been recorded by the pens of separate and independent writers, who, from the variations which are visible in these accounts, have incontestably proved that they did not unite with a view of imposing a fabulous narrative on mankind. That St. Matthew had never seen the Gospel of St. Luke, nor St. Luke the Gospel of St. Matthew, is evident from a comparison of their writings. The Gospel of St. Mark, which was written later, must likewise have been unknown to St. Luke; and that St. Mark had ever read the Gospel of St. Luke, is at least improbable, because their Gospels so frequently differ. It is a generally received opinion, that St. Mark made use of St. Matthew's Gospel in the composition of his own; but this is an unfounded hypothesis. The Gospel of St. John, being written after the other three, supplies what they had omitted. Thus have we four distinct and independent writers of one and the same history; and, though trifling variations may seem to exist in their narratives, yet these admit of easy solutions; and in all matters of consequence, whether doctrinal or historical, there is such a manifest agreement between them as is to be found in no other writings whatever. Though we have only four original writers of the life of Jesus, the evidence of the history does not rest on the testimony of four men. Christianity had been propagated in a great part of the world before any of them had written, on the testimony of thousands and tens of thousands, who had been witnesses of the great facts which they have recorded; so that the writing of these particular books is not to be considered as the cause, but rather the effect, of the belief of Christianity; nor could those books have been written and received as they were, namely, as authentic histories, of the subject of which all persons of that age were judges, if the facts they have recorded had not been well known to be true.

5. The term Gospel is often used in Scripture to signify the whole Christian doctrine: hence, "preaching the Gospel" is declaring all the truths, precepts, promises, and threatenings of Christianity. This is termed, "the Gospel of the grace of God," because it flows from God's free love and goodness, Acts xx, 24; and when truly and faithfully preached, is accompanied with the influences of the divine Spirit. It is called, "the Gospel of the kingdom," because it treats of the kingdom of grace, and shows the way to the kingdom of

glory. It is styled, "the Gospel of Christ," because he is the Author and great subject of it, Romans i, 16; and "the Gospel of peace and salvation," because it publishes peace with God to the penitent and believing, gives, to such, peace of conscience and tranquillity of mind, and is the means of their salvation, present and eternal. As it displays the glory of God and of Christ, and ensures to his true followers eternal glory, it is entitled, "the glorious Gospel," and, "the everlasting Gospel," because it commenced from the fall of man, is permanent throughout all time, and produces effects which are everlasting.

GOVERNMENT OF THE HEBREWS. The posterity of Jacob, while remaining in Egypt, maintained, notwithstanding the augmentation of their numbers, that patriarchal form of government which is so prevalent among the nomades. Every father of a family exercised a father's authority over those of his own household. Every tribe obeyed its own PRINCE, נשיא, who was originally the first-born of the founder of the tribe, but who, in process of time, appears to have been elected. As the people increased in numbers, various heads of families united together, and selected some individual from their own body, who was somewhat distinguished, for their leader. Perhaps the choice was made merely by tacit consent; and, without giving him the title of ruler in form, they were willing, while convinced of his virtues, to render submission to his will. Such a union of families was denominated "the house of the father;" and "the house of the father of the families," Num. iii, 24, 30, 35. In other instances, although the number varied, being sometimes more and sometimes less than a thousand, it was denominated, אלפים אלף, A THOUSAND. "Now therefore present yourselves before the Lord by your tribes, and by your THOUSANDS;" "the thousands of Judah;" "the thousands of Israel," &c, 1 Sam. x, 19; xxiii, 23; Judges vi, 15; Num. xxvi, 5–50. The heads of these united families were designated "heads of thousands," Num. i, 16; x, 4. They held themselves in subjection to the "princes of the tribes." Both the princes and heads of families are mentioned under the common names of זקנים, SENIORS or SENATORS, and שבטים ראשי HEADS OF TRIBES. Following the law of reason, and the rules established by custom, they governed with a paternal authority the tribes and united families; and, while they left the minor concerns to the heads of individual families, aimed to superintend and promote the best interests of the community generally. Originally, it fell to the princes of the tribes themselves to keep genealogical tables: subsequently, they employed scribes especially for this purpose, who, in the progress of time, acquired so great authority, that under the name of שוטרים, translated, in the English version, OFFICERS, they were permitted to exercise a share in the government of the nation. It was by magistrates of this description that the Hebrews were governed while they remained in Egypt; and the Egyptian kings made no objection to it, Exod. iii, 16; v, 1, 14, 15, 19.

2. The posterity of Abraham, Isaac, and Jacob were set apart and destined to the great object of preserving and transmitting the true religion, Gen. xviii, 16–20; xvii, 9–14; xii, 3; xxii, 18; xxviii, 14. Having increased in numbers, it appeared very evident that they could not live among nations given to idolatry without running the hazard of becoming infected with the same evil. They were, therefore, in the providence of God, assigned to a particular country, the extent of which was so small, that they were obliged, if they would live independently of other nations, to give up in a great measure the life of shepherds, and devote themselves to agriculture. Farther: very many of the Hebrews during their residence in Egypt had fallen into idolatrous habits. These were to be brought back again to the knowledge of the true God, and all were to be excited to engage in those undertakings which should be found necessary for the support of the true religion. All the Mosaic institutions aim at the accomplishment of these objects. The fundamental principle, therefore, of those institutions was this,--that the true God, the Creator and Governor of the universe, and none other, ought to be worshipped. To secure this end the more certainly, God became king to the Hebrews. Accordingly, the land of Canaan, which was destined to be occupied by them, was declared to be the land of Jehovah, of which he was to be the king, and the Hebrews merely the hereditary occupants. God promulgated, from the clouds of Mount Sinai, the prominent laws for the government of his people, considered as a religious community, Exod. xx. These laws were afterward more fully developed and illustrated by Moses. The rewards which should accompany the obedient, and the punishments which should be the lot of the transgressor, were at the same time announced, and the Hebrews promised by a solemn oath to obey, Exodus xxi-xxiv; Deut. xxvii-xxx.

3. In order to keep the true nature of the community fully and constantly in view, all the ceremonial institutions had reference to God, not only as the Sovereign of the universe, but as the King of the people. The people were taught to feel that the tabernacle was not only the temple of Jehovah, but the palace of their King; that the priests were the royal servants, and were bound to attend not only to sacred but to secular affairs, and were to receive, as their salary, the first tithes, which the people, as subjects, were led to consider a part of that revenue which was due to God, their immediate Sovereign. Other things of a less prominent and important nature had reference to the same great end. Since, therefore, God was the Sovereign, in a civil point of view as well as others, of Palestine and its inhabitants, the commission of idolatry by any inhabitant of that country, even a foreigner, was a defection from the true King. It was, in fact, treason; was considered a crime equal in aggravation to that of murder; and was, consequently, attended with the severest punishment. Whoever invited or exhorted to idolatry was considered seditious, and was obnoxious to the same punishment. Incantations also, necromancy, and other practices of this nature, were looked upon as arts of a kindred aspect with idolatry itself; and the same punishment was to be inflicted upon the perpetrators of them as upon idolaters. The same rigour of inquiry after the perpetrators of idolatry was enforced, that was exhibited in respect to

other crimes of the deepest aggravation; and the person who knew of the commission of idolatry in another was bound by the law to complain of the person thus guilty before the judge, though the criminal sustained the near relationship of a wife or a brother, a daughter or a son.

4. Many things in the administration of the government remained the same under the Mosaic economy, as it had been before. The authority which they had previously possessed, was continued in the time of Moses and after his time, to the princes of the tribes, to the heads of families and combinations of families, and to the genealogists, Num. xi, 16; Deut. xvi, 18; xx, 5; xxxi, 28. Yet Moses, by the advice of Jethro, his father-in-law, increased the number of rulers by the appointment of an additional number of judges; some to judge over ten, some over fifty, some over a hundred, and some over a thousand, men, Exodus xviii, 13–26. These judges were elected by the suffrages of the people from those who, by their authority and rank, might be reckoned among the rulers or princes of the people. The inferior judges, that is, those who superintended the judicial concerns of the smaller numbers, were subordinate to the superior judges, or those who judged a larger number; and cases, accordingly, of a difficult nature went up from the inferior to the superior judges. Those of a very difficult character, so much so as to be perplexing to the superior judges, were appealed to Moses himself, and in some cases from Moses to the high priest. The judges, of whom we have now spoken, sustained a civil as well as a judicial authority, and were included in the list of those who are denominated the elders and princes of Israel: that is to say, supposing they were chosen from the elders and princes, they did not forfeit their seat among them by accepting a judicial office; and, on the contrary, the respectability attached to their office, supposing they were not chosen from them, entitled them to be reckoned in their number, Deut. xxxi, 28; Joshua viii, 33; xxiii, 2; xxiv, 1. The various civil officers that have been mentioned, namely, judges, heads of families, genealogists, elders, princes of the tribes, &c, were dispersed, as a matter of course, in different parts of the country. Those of them, accordingly, who dwelt in the same city, or the same neighbourhood, formed the COMITIA, senate or legislative assembly of their immediate vicinity, Deut. xix, 12; xxv, 8, 9; Judges viii, 14; ix, 3–46; xi, 5; 1 Sam. viii, 4; xvi, 4. When all that dwelt in any particular tribe were convened, they formed the legislative assembly of the tribe; and when they were convened in one body from all the tribes, they formed in like manner the legislative assembly of the nation, and were the representatives of all the people, Joshua xxiii, 1, 2; xxiv, 1. The priests, who were the learned class of the community, and beside were hereditary officers in the state, being set apart for civil as well as religious purposes, had, by the divine command, a right to a sitting in this assembly, Exod. xxxii, 29; Num. xxxvi, 15; viii, 5–26. Being thus called upon to sustain very different and yet very important offices, they became the subjects of that envy which would naturally be excited by the honour and the advantages attached to their situation. In order to confirm them in the duties which devolved upon them, and to throw at the greatest distance the mean and lurking principle just mentioned, God, after the sedition of Korah, Dathan, and Abiram, sanctioned the separation of the whole tribe, which had been previously made to the service of religion and the state, by a most evident and striking miracle, Num. xvi, 1–7.

5. Each tribe was governed by its own rulers, and consequently to a certain extent constituted a civil community, independent of the other tribes, Judges xx, 11–46; 2 Sam. ii, 4; Judges i, 21. If any affair concerned the whole or many of the tribes, it was determined by them in conjunction in the legislative assembly of the nation, Judges xi, 1–11; 1 Chron. v, 10, 18, 19; 2 Sam. iii, 17; 1 Kings xii, 1–24. If one tribe found itself unequal to the execution of any proposed plan, it might connect itself with another, or even a number of the other tribes, Judges i, 1–3, 22; iv, 10; vii, 23, 24; viii, 1–3. But, although in many things each tribe existed by itself, and acted separately, yet in others they were united, and formed but one community: for all the tribes were bound together, so as to form one church and one civil community, not only by their common ancestors, Abraham, Isaac, and Jacob; not only by the common promises which they had received from those ancestors; not only by the need in which they stood of mutual counsel and assistance; but also by the circumstance that God was their common King, and that they had a common tabernacle for his palace, and a common sacerdotal and Levitical order for his ministers. Accordingly, every tribe exerted a sort of inspection over the others, as respected their observance of the law. If any thing had been neglected, or any wrong had been done, the particular tribe concerned was amenable to the others; and, in case justice could not be secured in any other way, might be punished with war, Joshua xxii, 9–34; Judges xx, 1, &c.

6. When we remember that God was expressly chosen the King of the people, and that he enacted laws and decided litigated points of importance, Numbers xvii, 1–11; xxvii, 1–11; xxxvi, 1–10; when we remember also that he answered and solved questions proposed, Num. xv, 32–41; Joshua vii, 16–22; Judges i, 1, 2; xx, 18, 27, 28; 1 Sam. xiv, 37; xxiii, 9–12; xxx, 8; 2 Sam. ii, 1; that he threatened punishment, and that, in some instances, he actually inflicted it upon the hardened and impenitent, Num. xi, 33–35; xii, 1–15; xvi, 1–50; Lev. xxvi, 3–46; Deut. xxvi-xxx; when, finally, we take into account, that he promised prophets, who were to be, as it were, his ambassadors, Deut. xviii, and afterward sent them according to his promise, and that, in order to preserve the true religion, he governed the whole people by a striking and peculiar providence, we are at liberty to say, that God was, in fact, the Monarch of the people, and that the government was a theocracy. But, although the government of the Jews was a theocracy, it was not destitute of the usual forms which exist in civil governments among men. God, it is true, was the King, and the high priest, if we may be allowed so to speak, was his minister of state; but still the political affairs were in a great measure under the disposal of the elders, princes, &c. It was to them that Moses gave the divine commands, determined expressly their powers; and submitted their requests to the decision of God, Num. xiv,

5; xvi, 4, &c; xxvii, 5; xxxvi, 5, 6. It was in reference to the great power possessed by these men, who formed the legislative assembly of the nation, that Josephus pronounced the government to be aristocratical. But from the circumstance that the people possessed so much influence, as to render it necessary to submit laws to them for their ratification, and that they even took upon themselves sometimes to propose laws or to resist those which were enacted; from the circumstance also that the legislature of the nation had not the power of laying taxes, and that the civil code was regulated and enforced by God himself, independently of the legislature, Lowman and Michaëlis are in favour of considering the Hebrew government a democracy. In support of their opinion such passages are exhibited as the following, Exodus xix, 7, 8; xxiv, 3–8; Deut. xxix, 9–14; Joshua ix, 18, 19; xxiii, 1, &c; xxiv, 2, &c; 1 Samuel x, 24; xi, 14, 15; Num. xxvii, 1–8; xxxvi, 1–9. The truth seems to lie between these two opinions. The Hebrew government, putting out of view its theocratical feature, was of a mixed form, in some respects approaching to a democracy, in others assuming more of an aristocratical character.

7. From what has been said, it is clear, that the Ruler and supreme Head of the political community in question was God, who, with the design of promoting the good of his subjects, condescended to exhibit his visible presence in the tabernacle, wherever it travelled and wherever it dwelt. If, in reference to the assertion, that God was the Ruler of the Jewish state, it should be inquired what part was sustained by Moses, the answer is, that God was the Ruler, the people were his subjects, and Moses was the mediator or internuncio between them. But the title most appropriate to Moses, and most descriptive of the part he sustained, is that of legislator of the Israelites and their deliverer from the Egyptians. If the same question should be put in respect to Joshua, the answer would be, that he was not properly the successor of Moses, and that, so far from being the ruler of the state, he was designated by the ruler to sustain the subordinate office of military leader of the Israelites in their conquest of the land of Canaan.

8. But, although the Hebrew state was so constituted, that beside God, the invisible King, and his visible servant, the high priest, there was no other general ruler of the commonwealth, yet it is well known that there were rulers of a high rank, appointed at various times, called ושפט, a word which not only signifies a JUDGE in the usual sense of the term, but any governor, or administrator of public affairs, 1 Sam. viii, 20; Isaiah xi, 4; 1 Kings iii, 9. The power lodged in these rulers, who are called judges in the Scriptures, seems to have been in some respects paramount to that of the general COMITIA of the nation, and we find that they declared war, led armies, concluded peace; and that this was not the whole, if indeed it was the most important part, of their duties. For many of the judges, for instance, Jair, Ibzan, Elon, Abdon, Eli, and Samuel, ruled the nation in peace. They might appropriately enough be called the supreme executive, exercising all the rights of sovereignty, with the exception of enacting laws, and imposing taxes. They were honoured, but they bore no external badges of distinction; they were distinguished, but they enjoyed no special privileges themselves, and communicated none to their posterity. They subserved the public good without emolument, that the state might be prosperous, that religion might be preserved, and that God alone might be King in Israel. It ought to be observed, however, that not all the judges ruled the whole nation: some of them presided over only a few separate tribes.

9. God, in the character of King, had governed the Israelites for sixteen ages. He ruled them, on the terms which he himself, through the agency of Moses, had proposed to them, namely, that if they observed their allegiance to him, they should be prosperous; if not, adversity and misery would be the consequence, Exod. xix, 4, 5; xxiii, 20–33; Lev. xxvi, 3–46; Deut. xxviii-xxx. We may learn from the whole book of Judges, and from the first eight chapters of Samuel, how exactly the result, from the days of Joshua down to the time of Samuel, agreed with these conditions. But in the time of Samuel, the government, in point of form, was changed into a monarchy. The election of king, however, was committed to God, who chose one by lot: so that God was still the Ruler, and the king the vicegerent. The terms of the government, as respected God, were the same as before, and the same duties and principles were inculcated on the Israelites as had been originally, 1 Sam. viii, 7; x, 17–23; xii, 14, 15, 20–22, 24, 25. In consequence of the fact, that Saul did not choose at all times to obey the commands of God, the kingdom was taken from him and given to another, 1 Sam. xiii, 5–14; xv, 1–31. David, through the agency of Samuel, was selected by Jehovah for king, who thus gave a proof that he still retained, and was disposed to exercise, the right of appointing the ruler under him, 1 Samuel xvi, 1–3. David was first made king over Judah; but as he received his appointment from God, and acted under his authority, the other eleven tribes submitted to him, 2 Sam. v, 1–3; 1 Chron. xxviii, 4–6. David expressly acknowledged God as the Sovereign, and, as having a right to appoint the immediate ruler of the people, 1 Chron. xxviii, 7–10; he religiously obeyed his statutes, the people adhered firmly to God, and his reign was prosperous. The paramount authority of God, as the King of the nation, and his right to appoint one who should act in the capacity of his vicegerent, are expressly recognized in the books of Kings and Chronicles.

10. On the subversion of the Babylonian empire by Cyrus, the founder of the Persian monarchy, (B. C. 543,) he authorized the Jews, by an edict, to return into their own country, with full permission to enjoy their laws and religion, and caused the city and temple of Jerusalem to be rebuilt. In the following year, part of the Jews returned under Zerubbabel, and renewed their sacrifices: but the reërection of the city and temple being interrupted for several years by the treachery and hostility of the Samaritans or Cutheans, the avowed enemies of the Jews, the completion and dedication of the temple did not take place until the year B. C. 511, six years after the accession of Cyrus. The rebuilding of

Jerusalem was accomplished, and the reformation of their ecclesiastical and civil polity was effected, by the two divinely inspired and pious governors, Ezra and Nehemiah; but the theocratic government does not appear to have been restored. The new temple was not, as formerly, God's palace; and the cloud of his presence did not take possession of it. After their death the Jews were governed by their high priests, in subjection however to the Persian kings, to whom they paid tribute, Ezra iv, 13; vii, 24, but with the full enjoyment of their other magistrates, as well as their liberties, civil and religious. Nearly three centuries of uninterrupted prosperity ensued, until the reign of Antiochus Epiphanes, king of Syria, when they were most cruelly oppressed, and compelled to take up arms in their own defence. Under the able conduct of Judas, surnamed Maccabeus, and his valiant brothers, the Jews maintained a religious war for twenty-six years with five successive kings of Syria; and after destroying upward of two hundred thousand of their best troops, the Maccabees finally established the independence of their own country and the aggrandizement of their family. This illustrious house, whose princes united the regal and pontifical dignity in their own persons, administered the affairs of the Jews during a period of one hundred and twenty-six years; until, disputes arising between Hyrcanus **II**, and his brother Aristobulus, the latter was defeated by the Romans under Pompey, who captured Jerusalem, and reduced Judea to dependence, B. C. 59.

GOVERNOR. Judea having been reduced into a province by the Romans, they sent governors thither, who were subject not only to the emperors, but also to the governors of Syria, whereof Judea made a part.

GOURD, קיקון, Jonah iv, 6, 7, 9, 10. Michaëlis, in his remarks on this subject, says, "Celsius appears to me to have proved that it is the KIKI of the Egyptians." He refers it to the class of the RICINUS, the great CATAPUCUS. According to Dioscorides, it is of rapid growth, and bears a berry from which an oil is expressed. In the Arabic version of this passage, which is to be found in Avicenna, it is rendered, "from thence is pressed the oil which they call oil of KIKI, which is the oil of Alkeroa." So Herodotus says: "The inhabitants of the marshy grounds in Egypt make use of an oil, which they term the KIKI, expressed from the Sillicyprian plant. In Greece this plant springs spontaneously, without any cultivation; but the Egyptians sow it on the banks of the river and of the canals; it there produces fruit in great abundance, but of a very strong odour. When gathered, they obtain from it, either by friction or pressure, an unctuous liquid, which diffuses an offensive smell, but for burning it is equal in quality to the oil of olives." This plant rises with a strong herbaceous stalk to the height of ten or twelve feet; and is furnished with very large leaves, not unlike those of the plane tree. Rabbi Kimchi says that the people of the east plant them before their shops for the sake of the shade, and to refresh themselves under them. Niebuhr says, "I saw, for the first time at Basra, the plant El-KEROA, mentioned in Michaëlis's 'Questions.' It has the form of a tree. The trunk appeared to me rather to resemble leaves than wood; nevertheless, it is harder than that which bears the Adam's fig. Each branch of the keroa has but one large leaf, with six or seven foldings in it. This plant was near to a rivulet, which watered it amply. At the end of October, 1765, it had risen in five months' time about eight feet, and bore at once flowers and fruit, ripe and unripe. Another tree of this species, which had not had so much water, had not grown more in a whole year. The flowers and leaves of it which I gathered withered in a few minutes; as do all plants of a rapid growth. This tree is called at Aleppo, PALMA CHRISTI. An oil is made from it called OLEUM DE KEROA; OLEUM CICINUM; OLEUM FICUS INFERNALIS. The Christians and Jews of Mosul (Nineveh) say, it was not the KEROA whose shadow refreshed Jonah, but a sort of gourd, EL-KERA, which has very large leaves, very large fruit, and lasts but about four months." The epithet which the prophet uses in speaking of the plant, "son of the night it was, and, as a son of the night it died," does not compel us to believe that it grew in a single night, but, either by a strong oriental figure that it was of rapid growth, or akin to night in the shade it spread for his repose. The figure is not uncommon in the east, and one of our own poets has called the rose "child of the summer." Nor are we bound to take the expression "on the morrow," as strictly importing the very next day, since the word has reference to much more distant time, Exod. xiii, 14; Deut. vi, 20; Joshua iv, 6. It might be simply taken as AFTERWARD. But the author of "Scripture Illustrated" justly remarks, "As the history in Jonah expressly says, THE Lord prepared this plant, no doubt we may conceive of it as an extraordinary one of its kind, remarkably rapid in its growth, remarkably hard in its stem, remarkably vigorous in its branches, and remarkable for the extensive spread of its leaves and the deep gloom of their shadow; and, after a certain duration, remarkable for a sudden withering, and a total uselessness to the impatient prophet."

2. We read of the wild gourd in 2 Kings iv, 39; that Elisha, being at Gilgal during a great famine, bade one of his servants prepare something for the entertainment of the prophets who were in that place. The servant, going into the field, found, as our translators render it, some WILD GOURDS, gathered a lapful of them, and, having brought them with him, cut them in pieces and put them into a pot, not knowing what they were. When they were brought to table, the prophets, having tasted them, thought they were mortal poison. Immediately, the man of God called for flour, threw it into the pot, and desired them to eat without any apprehensions. They did so, and perceived nothing of the bitterness whereof they were before sensible. This plant or fruit is called in Hebrew פקיעות and פקעים. There have been various opinions about it. Celsius supposes it the COLOCYNTH. The leaves of the plant are large, placed alternate; the flowers white, and the fruit of the gourd kind, of the size of a large apple, which, when ripe, is yellow, and of a pleasant and inviting appearance, but, to the taste intolerably bitter, and proves a drastic purgative. It seems that the fruit, whatever it might have been, was early thought proper for an ornament in architecture. It furnished a model

for some of the carved work of cedar in Solomon's temple, 1 Kings vi, 18; vii, 24.

GRACE. This word is understood in several senses: for beauty, graceful form, and agreeableness of person, Prov. i, 9; iii, 22. For favour, friendship, kindness, Gen. vi, 8; xviii, 3; Rom. xi, 6; 2 Tim. i, 9. For pardon, mercy, undeserved remission of offences, Eph. ii, 5; Col. i, 6. For certain gifts of God, which he bestows freely, when, where, and on whom, he pleases; such are the gifts of miracles, prophecy, languages, &c, Rom. xv, 15; 1 Cor. xv, 10; Eph. iii, 8, &c. For the Gospel dispensation, in contradistinction to that of the law, Rom. vi, 14; 1 Peter v, 12. For a liberal and charitable disposition, 2 Cor. viii, 7. For eternal life, or final salvation, 1 Peter i, 13. In theological language grace also signifies divine influence upon the soul; and it derives the name from this being the effect of the great grace or favour of God to mankind. Austin defines inward actual grace to be the inspiration of love, which prompts us to practise according to what we know, out of a religious affection and compliance. He says, likewise, that the grace of God is the blessing of God's sweet influence, whereby we are induced to take pleasure in that which he commands, to desire and to love it; and that if God does not prevent us with this blessing, what he commands, not only is not perfected, but is not so much as begun in us. Without the inward grace of Jesus Christ, man is not able to do the least thing that is good. He stands in need of this grace to begin, continue, and finish all the good he does, or rather, which God does in him and with him, by his grace. This grace is free; it is not due to us: if it were due to us, it would be no more grace; it would be a debt, Rom. xi, 6; it is in its nature an assistance so powerful and efficacious, that it surmounts the obstinacy of the most rebellious human heart, without destroying human liberty. There is no subject on which Christian doctors have written so largely, as on the several particulars relating to the grace of God. The difficulty consists in reconciling human liberty with the operation of divine grace; the concurrence of man with the influence and assistance of the Almighty. And who is able to set up an accurate boundary between these two things? Who can pretend to know how far the privileges of grace extend over the heart of man, and what that man's liberty exactly is, who is prevented, enlightened, moved, and attracted by grace?

GRAPE, ענב, the fruit of the vine. There were fine vineyards and excellent grapes in the promised land. The bunch of grapes which was cut in the valley of Eshcol, and was brought upon a staff between two men to the camp of Israel at Kadeshbarnea, Num. xiii, 23, may give us some idea, of the largeness of the fruit in that country. It would be easy to produce a great number of witnesses to prove that the grapes in those regions grow to a prodigious size. By Calmet, Scheuchzer, and Harmer, this subject has been exhausted. Doubdan assures us, that in the valley of Eshcol were clusters of grapes to be found of ten or twelve pounds. Moses, in the law, commanded that when the Israelites gathered their grapes, they should not be careful to pick up those that fell, nor be so exact as to leave none upon the vines: what fell, and what were left behind, the poor had liberty to glean, Lev. xix, 10; Deut. xxiv, 21, 22. For the same beneficent purpose the second vintage was reserved: this, in those warm countries, was considerable, though never so good nor so plentiful as the former. The wise son of Sirach says, "I waked up last of all, as one that gleaneth after grape gatherers. By the blessing of the Lord, I profited, and filled my wine-press like a gatherer of grapes," Ecclus. xxxiii, 16. It is frequent in Scripture to describe a total destruction by the similitude of a vine, stripped in such a manner, that there was not a bunch of grapes left for those who came to glean. The prophecy, "He shall wash his clothes in wine, and his garments in the blood of the grape," Gen. xlix, 11, means that he shall reside in a country where grapes were in abundance. The vineyards of Engedi and of Sorek, so famous in Scripture, were in the tribe of Judah; and so was the valley of Eshcol, whence the spies brought those extraordinary clusters. "It appears," says Manti, "that the cultivation of the vine was never abandoned in this country. The grapes, which are white, and pretty large, are, however, not much superior in size to those of Europe. This peculiarity seems to be confined to those in this neighbourhood; for at the distance of only six miles to the south, is the rivulet and valley called Escohol, celebrated in Scripture for its fertility, and for producing very large grapes. In other parts of Syria, also, I have seen grapes of such an extraordinary size, that a bunch of them would be a sufficient burden for one man. It is not at all surprising, therefore, that when the spies, sent by Moses to reconnoitre the promised land, returned to give him an account of its fertility, it required two of them to carry a bunch of grapes, which they brought with them suspended from a pole placed upon their shoulders." Many eye witnesses assure us, that in Palestine the vines, and bunches of grapes, are almost of an incredible size. "At Beidtdjin," says Schultz, a "village near Ptolemais, we took our supper under a large vine, the stem of which was nearly a foot and a half in diameter, the height about thirty feet, and covered with its branches and shoots (for the shoots must be supported) a hut of more than fifty feet long and broad. The bunches of these grapes are so large that they weigh from ten to twelve pounds, and the grapes may be compared to our plumbs. Such a bunch is cut off and laid on a board, round which they seat themselves, and each helps himself to as many as he pleases." Forster, in his Hebrew Dictionary, (under the word Eshcol,) says, that he knew at Nurnburg, a monk of the name of Acacius, who had resided eight years in Palestine, and had also preached at Hebron, where he had seen bunches of grapes which were as much as two men could conveniently carry.

The wild grapes, באשים, are the fruit of the wild or bastard vine; sour and unpalatable, and good for nothing but to make verjuice. In Isaiah v, 2–4, the Lord complains that he had planted his people as a choice vine, excellent as that of Sorek; but that its degeneracy had defeated his purpose, and disappointed his hopes: when he expected that it should bring forth choice fruit, it yielded only such as was bad; not merely useless and unprofitable grapes, but clusters offensive and noxious. By the force and intent of the allegory, says Bishop Lowth, "good grapes" ought to be opposed "to fruit of a dangerous and pernicious quality," as, in the application of it, to judgment is opposed tyranny, and to righteousness oppression. Hasselquist is inclined to believe that the prophet here means the SOLANUM INCANUM, "hoary nightshade," because it is common in Egypt and Palestine, and the Arabian name agrees well with it. The Arabs call it ANEB EL DIB, "wolf's grapes." The prophet could not have found a plant more opposite to the vine than this; for it grows much in the vineyards, and is very pernicious to them. It is likewise a vine. Jeremiah uses the same image, and applies it to the same purpose, in an elegant paraphrase of this part of Isaiah's parable, in his flowing and plaintive manner: "I planted thee a Sorek, a scion perfectly genuine. How then art thou changed, and become to me the degenerate shoot of a strange vine!" Jer. ii, 21. From some sort of poisonous fruits of the grape kind, Moses, Deut. xxxii, 32, 33, has taken those strong and highly poetical images with which he has set forth the future corruption and extreme degeneracy of the Israelites, in an allegory which has a near relation, both in its subject and imagery, to this of Isaiah:--

"Their vine is from the vine of Sodom,

And from the fields of Gomorrah.

Their grapes are grapes of gall;

And their clusters are bitter.

Their wine is the poison of dragons,

And the deadly venom of aspics."

GRASS, דשא, Gen. i, 11, the well known vegetable upon which flocks and herds feed, and which decks our fields, and refreshes our sight with its grateful verdure. Its feeble frame and transitory duration are mentioned in Scripture as emblematic of the frail condition and fleeting existence of man. The inspired poets draw this picture with such inimitable beauty as the laboured elegies on mortality of ancient and modern times have never surpassed. See Psalm xc, 6, and particularly Isaiah xl, 6–8: "The voice said, Cry! And he said, What shall I cry? All flesh is grass, and all the goodliness thereof is as the flower of the field. The grass withereth, the flower fadeth, because the Spirit of the Lord bloweth upon it. Verily this people is grass. The grass withereth, the flower fadeth; but the word of our God shall stand for ever." As, in their decay, the herbs of the fields strikingly illustrate the shortness of human life, so, in the order of their growth, from seeds dead and buried, they give a natural testimony to the doctrine of a resurrection. The Prophet Isaiah, and the Apostle Peter, both speak of bodies rising from the dead, as of so many seeds springing from the ground to renovated existence and beauty, although they do not, as some have absurdly supposed, consider the resurrection as in any sense analogous to the process of vegetation, Isaiah xxvi, 19; 1 Peter i, 24, 25.

It is a just remark of Grotius, that the Hebrews ranked the whole vegetable system under two classes, עץ, and עשב. The first is rendered ξύλον, or δένδρον, TREE: to express the second, the **LXX** have adopted χόρτος, as their common way to translate one Hebrew word by one Greek word, though not quite proper, rather than by a circumlocution. It is accordingly used in their version of Genesis i, 11, where the distinction first occurs, and in most other places. Nor is it with greater propriety rendered GRASS in English than χόρτος in Greek. The same division occurs in Matt. vi, 30, and Rev. viii, 7, where our translators have in like manner had recourse to the term GRASS. Dr. Campbell prefers and uses the word HERBAGE, as coming nearer the meaning of the sacred writer. Under the name HERB is comprehended every sort of plant which has not, like trees and shrubs, a perennial stalk. That many, if not all, sorts of shrubs were included by the Hebrews under the denomination, TREE, is evident from Jotham's apologue of the trees choosing a king, Judges ix, 7, where the bramble is mentioned as one. See Hay.

GRASSHOPPER, חגב, Lev. xi, 22; Num. xiii, 33; 2 Chron. vii, 13; Eccles. xii, 5; Isaiah xl, 22; 2 Esdras iv, 24; Wisdom xvi, 9; Eccles. xliii, 17. Bochart supposes that this species of the locust has its name from the Arabic verb HAJABA, "to veil," because, when they fly, as they often do, in great swarms, they eclipse even the light of the sun. "But I presume," says Parkhurst, "this circumstance is not peculiar to any particular kind of locust: I should rather, therefore, think it denotes the CUCULLATED species, so denominated by naturalists from the CUCULLUS, "cowl" or "hood," with which they are furnished, and which distinguishes them from the other kinds. In Scheuchzer may be seen several of this sort; and it will appear that this species nearly resemble our grasshopper." Our translators render the Hebrew word LOCUST in the prayer of Solomon at the dedication of the temple, 2 Chron. vii, 13, and with propriety. But it is rendered GRASSHOPPER, in Eccles. xii, 5, where Solomon, describing the infelicities of old age, says, "The grasshopper shall be a burden." "To this insect," says Dr. Smith, "the preacher compares a dry, shrunk, shrivelled, crumpling, craggy old man; his backbone sticking out, his knees projecting forward, his arms backward, his head downward, and the apophyses or bunching parts of the bones in general enlarged. And from this exact likeness, without all doubt, arose the fable of Tithonus, who, living to extreme old age, was at last turned into a grasshopper." Dr. Hodgson, referring it to the custom of eating locusts, supposes it to imply that luxurious gratification will become insipid; and Bishop Reynolds, that the lightest pressure of so small a creature shall be uncomfortable to the aged, as not being able to bear any weight. Other commentators suppose the reference to the chirping noise of the grasshopper, which must be disagreeable to the aged and infirm, who naturally love quiet, and are commonly unable to bear much noise. It is probable that here, also, a kind of locust is meant; and these creatures are proverbially loquacious. They make a loud, screaking, and disagreeable noise with their wings. If one begins, others join, and the hateful concert becomes universal. A pause then ensues, and, as it were, on a signal given, it again commences; and in this manner they continue squalling for two or three hours without intermission. The Prophet Isaiah contrasts the grandeur and power of God, and every thing reputed great in this world, by a very expressive reference to this insect: Jehovah sitteth on the circle of the earth, and the inhabitants are to him as grasshoppers, Isaiah xl, 22. What atoms and inanities are they all before him, who sitteth on the circle of the immense heavens, and views the potentates of the earth in the light of grasshoppers, those poor insects that wander over the barren heath for sustenance, spend the day in insignificant chirpings, and take up their contemptible lodging at night on a blade of grass! See Locust.

GRECIA, or **GREECE**, both names occurring in the English Scriptures. The boundaries of the country which received this name differed under the different governments which ruled over it. Thus the Greece of the Old Testament is not exactly the same as that of the New: the former including Macedonia, Thessaly, Epirus, Hellas or Greece Proper, and the Peloponnesus or Morea; while the latter excludes Macedonia, Thessaly, and Epirus. But the Romans, in the time of the Apostles, had, in fact, made two divisions of these countries. The first, which was that of Macedonia, included also Thessaly and Epirus; and the other, that of Achaia, all the rest of Greece, which is, properly speaking, the Greece of the New Testament. But the term GREEK admits of a larger interpretation, and applies not only to the inhabitants of Greece Proper, but to those of Asia Minor, Syria, and Egypt, over nearly the whole of the former of which countries, and great part of the two latter, Grecian colonies and the Grecian language had extended themselves. In fact, in the two books of the Maccabees, and in those of the New Testament, the word GREEK commonly implies a Gentile.

2. The Scripture has but little reference to Greece till the time of Alexander, whose conquests extended into Asia, where Greece had hitherto been of no importance. Yet that some intercourse was maintained with these countries from Jerusalem, may be inferred from the desire of Baasha to shut up all passage between Jerusalem and Joppa, which was its port, by the building of Ramah; and the anxiety of Asa to counteract his scheme, 1 Kings xv, 2, 17. Greece was certainly intended by the Prophet Daniel under the symbol of the single-horned goat; and it is probable that when he calls Greece Chittim, he spoke the language of the Hebrew nation, rather than that of the Persian court. After the establishment of the Grecian dynasties in Asia, Judea could not but be considerably affected by them; and the books of the Maccabees afford proofs of this. The Roman power, superseding the Grecian establishments, yet left traces of Greek language, customs, &c, to the days of the Herods, when the Gospel history commences. By the activity of the Apostles, and especially by that of St. Paul, the Gospel was propagated in those countries which used the Grecian dialects: hence, we are interested in the study of this language. Moreover as Greece, like all other countries, had its peculiar manners, we are not able to estimate properly an epistle written to those who dwell where they prevailed, without a competent acquaintance with the manners themselves, with the sentiments and reasonings of those who practised them, and with the arguments employed in their defence by those who adhered to them.

GREEK LANGUAGE. It was because of the wide diffusion of this language that the New Testament was written in Greek. Its diction is not, however, that of the classical Greek, but it was chosen, no doubt, with a view to greater usefulness. In the age which succeeded Alexander the Great, the Greek language underwent an internal change of a double nature. In part, a prosaic language of books was formed, ἡ κοινὴ διαλεκτὸς, which was built on the Attic dialect, but was intermixed with not a few provincialisms; but a language of popular intercourse was also formed, in which the various dialects of the different Grecian tribes, heretofore separate, were more or less mingled together, while the Macedonian dialect was peculiarly prominent. The latter language constitutes the basis of the diction employed by the **LXX**, the writers of the Apocrypha, and of the New Testament. The style of the New Testament has a considerable affinity with that of the Septuagint version which was executed at Alexandria, although it approaches somewhat nearer to the idiom of the Greek language; but the peculiarities of the Hebrew phraseology are discernible throughout: the language of the New Testament being formed by a mixture of oriental idioms and expressions with those which are properly Greek. Hence it has, by some philologers, been termed HEBRAIC GREEK, and (from the Jews having acquired the Greek language, rather by practice than by grammar, among the Greeks, in whose countries they resided in large communities) HELLENISTIC GREEK. The propriety of this appellation was severely contested toward the close of the seventeenth, and in the early part of the eighteenth, century; and numerous publications were written on both sides of the question, with considerable asperity, which, together with the controversy, are now almost forgotten. The dispute, however interesting to the philological antiquarian, is after all a mere "strife of words;" and as the appellation of Hellenistic or Hebraic Greek is sufficiently correct for the purpose of characterizing the language of the New Testament, it is now generally adopted. A large proportion, however, of the phrases and constructions of the New Testament is pure Greek; that is to say, of the same degree of purity as the Greek which was spoken in Macedonia, and that in which Polybius wrote his Roman history. It should farther be noticed, that there occur in the New Testament, words that express both doctrines and practices which were utterly unknown to the Greeks; and also words bearing widely different interpretations from those which are ordinarily found in Greek writers. It contains examples of all the dialects occurring in the Greek language, as the Æolic, Bœtic, Doric, Ionic, and especially of the Attic; which, being most generally in use on account of its elegance, pervades every book of the New Testament.

2. A variety of solutions has been given to the question, why the New Testament was written in Greek. The true reason is, that it was the language most generally understood both by writers and readers; being spoken and written, read and understood, throughout the Roman empire, and particularly in the eastern provinces. To the universality of the Greek language, Cicero, Seneca, and Juvenal bear ample testimony: and the circumstances of the Jews having long had political, civil, and commercial relations with the Greeks, and being dispersed through various parts of the Roman empire, as well as their having cultivated the philosophy of the Greeks, of which we have evidence in the New Testament, all sufficiently account for their being acquainted with the Greek language. And if the eminent Jewish writers, Philo and Josephus, had motives for preferring to write in Greek, there is no reason, at least there is no general presumption, why the first publishers of the Gospel might not use the Greek language. It is indeed probable, that many of the common people were acquainted with it; though it is also certain the Christian churches being in many countries composed chiefly of that class of persons, some did not understand Greek. But in every church, says Macknight, there were persons endowed with the gift of tongues, and of the interpretation of tongues, who could readily turn the Apostles' Greek epistles into the language of the church to which they were sent. In particular, the president or the spiritual man, who read the Apostle's Greek letter to the Hebrews in their public assemblies, could without any hesitation render it into the Hebrew language, for the edification of those who did not understand Greek. And with respect to the Jews in the provinces, Greek being the native language of most of them, this epistle was much better calculated for their use, written in the Greek language, than if it had been written in the Hebrew, which few of them understood. Farther, it was proper that all the apostolical epistles should be written in the Greek language, because the different doctrines of the Gospel being delivered and explained in them, the explanation of these doctrines could with more advantage be compared so as to be better understood, being expressed in one language, than if, in the different epistles, they had been expressed in the language of the churches and persons to whom they were sent. Now what should that one language be, in which it was proper to write the Christian revelation, but the Greek, which was then generally understood, and in which there were many books extant; that treated of all kinds of literature, and on that account were likely to be preserved, and by the reading of which Christians, in after ages, would be enabled to understand the Greek of the New Testament? This advantage none of the provincial dialects used in the Apostles' days could pretend to. Being limited to particular countries, they were soon to be disused; and few (if any) books being written in them which merited to be preserved, the meaning of such of the Apostles' letters as were composed in the provincial languages could not easily have been ascertained.

GREEK CHURCH. As the Gospel spread in the first ages both east and west, the first Christian churches were so denominated. From the languages respectively used in their devotions, they were also called the Greek and Latin or Roman churches. For the first seven centuries these churches preserved a friendly communion with each other, notwithstanding they disagreed as to the time of keeping Easter, and some other points. But about the middle of the eighth century, disputes arose, which terminated in a schism, that continues to this day. It arose out of a controversy respecting the use of images in the churches. It happened that at this time both churches were under prelates equally dogmatical and ambitious. The patriarch of Constantinople insisted on putting down the use of all images and pictures, not only in his own church, but at Rome also, which the pope resented with equal violence and asperity. They mutually excommunicated each other; and the pope of Rome excommunicated not only the patriarch of Constantinople, but the emperor also. The controversy respecting images engendered another, no less bitter, respecting the procession of the Holy Ghost both from the Father and the Son, which the Greeks flatly denied, and charged the Romans with interpolating the word FILIOQUE into the ancient creeds. These controversies occupied the eighth and ninth centuries, after which some intervals of partial peace occurred; but in the eleventh century, the flame broke out afresh, and a total separation took place. At that time, the Patriarch Michael Cerularius, who was desirous to free himself from the papal authority, published an invective against the Latin church, and accused its members of maintaining various errors. Pope Leo retorted the charge, and sent legates from Rome to Constantinople. The Greek patriarch refused to see them; upon which they excommunicated him and his adherents, publicly, in the church of St. Sophia, A. D. 1054. The Greek patriarch excommunicated those legates, with all their adherents and followers, in a public council; and procured an order of the emperor for burning the act of excommunication which they had pronounced against the Greeks. Thus the separation was completed, and at this day a very considerable part of the world profess the religion of the Greek or eastern church. The Nicene and Athanasian creeds, with the exception of the words above-mentioned, are the symbols of their faith.

2. The principal points which distinguish the Greek church from the Latin, are as follows: they maintain that the Holy Ghost proceeds from the Father only, and not from the Father and Son. They disown the authority of the pope, and deny that the church of Rome is the only true catholic church. They do not affect the character of infallibility, and utterly disallow works of supererogation, and indulgences. They admit of prayers and services for the dead, as an ancient and pious custom; but they will not admit the doctrine of purgatory, nor determine any thing dogmatically concerning the state of departed souls. In baptism they practise triune

immersion, or dip three times; but some, as the Georgians, defer the baptism of their children till they are three, four, or more years of age. The chrism, or baptismal unction, immediately follows baptism. This chrism, solemnly consecrated on Maunday Thursday, is called the unction with ointment, and is a mystery peculiar to the Greek communion, holding the place of confirmation in that of the Roman: it is styled, "the seal of the gift of the Holy Ghost." They administer the Lord's Supper in both kinds, dipping the bread in the cup of wine, in which a small portion of warm water is also inserted. They give it both to the clergy and laity, and to children after baptism. They exclude confirmation and extreme unction out of the number of sacraments; but they use the holy oil, which is not confined to persons in the close of life, like extreme unction, but is administered, if required, to all sick persons. Three priests, at least, are required to administer this sacrament, each priest, in his turn, anointing the sick person, and praying for his recovery. They deny auricular confession to be a divine command; but practise confession attended with absolution, and sometimes penance. Though they believe in transubstantiation, or rather consubstantiation, they do not worship the elements. They pay a secondary kind of adoration to the virgin and other saints. They do not admit of images or figures in bas-relief, or embossed work; but use paintings and silver shrines. They admit matrimony to be a sacrament, and celebrate it with great formality. Their secular clergy, under the rank of bishops, are allowed to marry once, and laymen twice; but fourth marriages they hold in abomination. They observe a great number of holy days, and keep four fasts in the year more solemn than the rest, of which Good Friday is the chief.

3. The service of the Greek church is too long and complicated to be particularly described in this work; the greater part consists in psalms and hymns. Five orders of priesthood belong to the Greek church; namely, bishops, priests, deacons, sub-deacons, and readers; which last includes singers, &c. The episcopal order is distinguished by the titles of metropolitan, archbishops, and bishops. The head of the Greek church, the patriarch of Constantinople, is elected by twelve bishops, who reside nearest that famous capital. This prelate calls councils by his own authority to govern the church. The other patriarchs are those of Jerusalem, Antioch, and Alexandria, all nominated by the patriarch of Constantinople, who enjoys a most extensive jurisdiction. For the administration of ecclesiastical affairs, a synod, convened monthly, is composed of the heads of the church resident in Constantinople. In this assembly, the patriarch of Constantinople presides, with those of Antioch and Jerusalem, and twelve archbishops. In regard to discipline and worship, the Greek church has the same division of the clergy into regular and secular, the same spiritual jurisdiction of bishops and their officials, the same distinction of ranks and offices, with the church of Rome.

4. The Greek church comprehends a considerable part of Greece, the Grecian isles, Wallachia, Moldavia, Egypt, Abyssinia, Nubia, Lybia, Arabia, Mesopotamia, Syria, Cilicia, and Palestine; Alexandria, Antioch, and Jerusalem; the whole of the Russian empire in Europe; great part of Siberia in Asia, Astrachan, Casan, and Georgia.

GRIND. See Mill.

GROVE. It is proper to observe, that in order the more effectually to guard the Israelites from idolatry, the blessed God, in instituting the rites of his own worship, went directly counter to the practice of the idolatrous nations. Thus, because they worshipped in groves, he expressly forbade "the planting a grove of trees near his altar," Deut. xvi, 21. Nor would he suffer his people to offer their sacrifices on the tops of hills and mountains, as the Heathens did, but ordered that they should be brought to one altar in the place which he appointed, Deut. xii, 13, 14. And as for the groves, which the Canaanites had planted, and the idols and altars which they had erected on the tops of high mountains and hills for the worship of their gods, the Israelites are commanded utterly to destroy them, Deut. xii, 2, 3. The groves and high places do not seem to have been different, but the same places, or groves planted on the tops of hills, probably round an open area, in which the idolatrous worship was performed, as may be inferred from the following words of the Prophet Hosea: "They sacrifice upon the tops of mountains, and burn incense upon the hills, under oaks, and poplars, and elms," Hosea iv, 13. The use of groves for religious worship is generally supposed to have been as ancient as the patriarchal ages; for we are informed, that "Abraham planted a grove in Beersheba, and called there on the name of the Lord," Gen. xxi, 33. However, it is not expressly said, nor can it by this passage be proved, that he planted the grove for any religious purpose; it might only be designed to shade his tent. And this circumstance perhaps is recorded to intimate his rural way of living, as well as his religious character; that he dwelt in a tent, under the shade of a grove, or tree, as the word אשל, ESHEL, may more properly be translated; and in this humble habitation led a very pious and devout life. The reason and origin of planting sacred groves is variously conjectured; some imagining it was only hereby intended to render the service more agreeable to the worshippers, by the pleasantness of the shade; whereas others suppose it was to invite the presence of the gods. The one or the other of these reasons seems to be intimated in the fore-cited passage of Hosea: "They burn incense under oaks, and poplars, and elms, because the shade thereof is good," Hosea iv, 13. Others conceive their worship was performed in the midst of groves, because the gloom of such a place is apt to strike a religious awe upon the mind; or else, because such dark concealments suited the lewd mysteries of their idolatrous worship. Another conjecture, which seems as probable as any, is, that this practice began with the worship of demons, or departed souls. It was an ancient custom to bury the dead under trees, or in woods. "Deborah was buried under an oak, near Bethel," Genesis xxxv, 8; and the bones of Saul and Jonathan under a tree at Jabesh, 1 Samuel xxxi, 13. Now an imagination prevailing among the Heathen, that the souls of the deceased hover about their graves, or at least delight to visit their dead bodies, the idolaters, who paid divine honours to the souls of their departed heroes, erected images and altars for their worship in the same groves where they were buried; and from thence it grew into a custom afterward to plant groves, and build temples, near the tombs of departed heroes, 2 Kings xxiii, 15, 16, and to surround their temples and altars with groves and trees; and these sacred groves being constantly furnished with the images of the heroes or gods that were worshipped in them, a grove and an idol came to be used as convertible terms, 2 Kings xxiii, 6.

HABAKKUK, the author of the prophecy bearing his name, Habakkuk i, 1, &c. Nothing is certainly known concerning the tribe or birth place of Habakkuk. He is said to have prophesied about B. C. 605, and to have been alive at the time of the destruction of Jerusalem by Nebuchadnezzar. It is generally believed that he remained and died in Judea. The principal predictions contained in this book are, the destruction of Jerusalem, and the captivity of the Jews by the Chaldeans or Babylonians; their deliverance from the oppressor "at the appointed time;" and the total ruin of the Babylonian empire. The promise of the Messiah is confirmed; the overruling providence of God is asserted; and the concluding prayer, or rather hymn, recounts the wonders which God had wrought for his people, when he led them from Egypt into Canaan, and expresses the most perfect confidence in the fulfilment of his promises. The style of Habakkuk is highly poetical, and the hymn in the third chapter is perhaps unrivalled for sublimity, simplicity, and power.

HABITS. The dress of oriental nations, to which the inspired writers often allude, has undergone almost no change from the earliest times. Their stuffs were fabricated of various materials; but wool was generally used in their finer fabrics; and the hair of goats, camels, and even of horses, was manufactured for coarser purposes, especially for sackcloth, which they wore in time of mourning and distress. Sackcloth of black goat's hair was manufactured for mournings; the colour and the coarseness of which being reckoned more suitable to the circumstances of the wearer, than the finer and more valuable texture which the hair of white goats supplied. This is the reason why a clouded sky is represented, in the bold figurative language of Scripture, as covered with sackcloth and blackness, the colour and dress of persons in affliction. In Egypt and Syria, they wore also fine linen, cotton, and byssus, probably fine muslin from India, in Hebrew בוץ, the finest cloth known to the ancients. In Canaan, persons of distinction were dressed in fine linen of Egypt; and according to some authors, in silk, and rich cloth, shaded with the choicest colours, or, as the Vulgate calls it, with feathered work, embroidered with gold. The beauty of their clothes consisted in the fineness and colour of the stuffs; and it seems, the colour most in use among the Israelites, as well as among the Greeks and Romans, was white, not imparted and improved by the dyer's art, but the native colour of the wool. The general use of this colour seems to be recognized by Solomon in his direction: "Let thy garments be always white," Eccles. ix, 8. But garments in the native colour of the wool were not confined to the lower orders; they were also in great esteem among persons of superior station, and are particularly valued in Scripture, as the emblem of knowledge and purity, gladness and victory, grace and glory. The priests of Baal were habited in black; a colour which appears to have been peculiar to themselves, and which few others in those countries, except mourners, would choose to wear. Blue was a colour in great esteem among the Jews, and other oriental nations. The robe of the ephod, in the gorgeous dress of the high priest, was made all of blue; it was a prominent colour in the sumptuous hangings of the tabernacle; and the whole people of Israel were required to put a fringe of blue upon the border of their garments, and on the fringe a riband of the same colour. The palace of Ahasuerus, the king of Persia, was furnished with curtains of this colour, on a pavement of red, and blue, and white marble; a proof that it was not less esteemed in Persia than on the Jordan. And from Ezekiel we learn, that the Assyrian nobles were habited in robes of this colour: "She doated on the Assyrians, her neighbours, which were clothed with blue, captains and rulers, all of them desirable young men."

2. The Jewish nobles and courtiers, upon great and solemn occasions, appeared in scarlet robes, dyed, not as at present with madder, with cochineal, or with any modern tincture, but with a shrub, whose red berries give an orient tinge to the cloth. Crimson or vermilion, a colour, as the name imports, from the blood of the worm, was used in the temple of Solomon, and by many persons of the first quality; sometimes they wore purple, the most sublime of all earthly colours, says Mr. Harmer, having the gaudiness of red, of which it retains a shade, softened with the gravity of blue. This was chiefly dyed at Tyre, and was supposed to take the tincture from the liquor of a shell fish, anciently found in the adjacent sea; though Mr. Bruce, in his Travels, inclines to the opinion, that the murex, or purple fish at Tyre, was only a concealment of their knowledge of cochineal, as, if the whole city of Tyre had applied to nothing else but fishing, they would not have coloured twenty yards of cloth in a year. The children of wealthy and noble families were dressed in vestments of different colours. This mark of distinction may be traced to the patriarchal age; for Joseph was arrayed, by his indulgent and imprudent father, in a coat of many colours. A robe of divers colours was anciently reserved for the kings' daughters who were virgins; and in one of these was Tamar, the virgin daughter of David, arrayed, when she was met by her brother.

3. In these parts of the world, the fashion is in a state of almost daily fluctuation, and different fashions are not unfrequently seen contending for the superiority; but in the east, where the people are by no means given to change, the form of their garments continues nearly the same from one

age to another. The greater part of their clothes are long and flowing, loosely cast about the body, consisting only of a large piece of cloth, in the cutting and sewing of which very little art or industry is employed. They have more dignity and gracefulness than ours, and are better adapted to the burning climates of Asia. From the simplicity of their form, and their loose adaptation to the body, the same clothes might be worn, with equal ease and convenience, by many different persons. The clothes of those Philistines whom Samson slew at Askelon required no altering to fit his companions; nor the robe of Jonathan, to answer his friend. The arts of weaving and fulling seem to have been distinct occupations in Israel, from a very remote period, in consequence of the various and skilful operations which were necessary to bring their stuffs to a suitable degree of perfection; but when the weaver and the fuller had finished their part, the labour was nearly at an end; no distinct artizan was necessary to make them into clothes; every family seems to have made their own. Sometimes, however, this part of the work was performed in the loom; for they had the art of weaving robes with sleeves all of one piece: of this kind was the coat which our Saviour wore during his abode with men. The loose dresses of these countries, when the arm is lifted up, expose its whole length: to this circumstance the Prophet Isaiah refers: "To whom is the arm of the Lord revealed?" that is, uncovered: who observes that he is about to exert the arm of his power?

4. The chosen people were not allowed to wear clothes of any materials or form they chose; they were forbidden by their law to wear a garment of woollen and linen. This law did not prevent them from wearing many different substances together, but only these two; nor did the prohibition extend to the wool of camels and goats, (for the hair of these animals they called by the same name,) but only to that of sheep. It was lawful for any man who saw an Israelite dressed in such a garment to fall upon him and put him to death. In the opinion of Maimonides, this was principally intended as a preservative from idolatry; for the Heathen priests of those times wore such mixed garments of woollen and linen, in the superstitious hope, it was imagined, of having the beneficial influence of some lucky conjunction of the planets or stars, to bring down a blessing upon their sheep and their flax. The second restraint referred to the sexes, of which one was not to wear the dress appropriated to the other. This practice is said to be an abomination to the Lord; which plainly intimates that the law refers to some idolatrous custom, of which Moses and the prophets always spoke in terms of the utmost abhorrence. Nothing, indeed, was more common among the Heathen, in the worship of some of their false deities, than for the males to assist in women's clothes, and the females in the dress appropriated to men; in the worship of Venus, in particular, the women appeared before her in armour, and the men in women's apparel; and thus the words literally run in the original Scriptures, "Women shall not put on the armour of a man, nor a man the stole of a woman." Maimonides says he found this precept in an old magical book, "That men ought to stand before the star of Venus in the flowered garments of women, and women to put on the armour of men before the star of Mars." But whatever there may be in these observations, it is certain that, if there were no distinction of sexes made by their habits, there would be danger of involving mankind in all manner of licentiousness and impurity.

5. The ancient Jews very seldom wore any covering upon the head, except when they were in mourning, or worshipping in the temple, or in the synagogue. To pray with the head covered, was, in their estimation, a higher mark of respect for the majesty of heaven, as it indicated the conscious unworthiness of the suppliant to lift up his eyes in the divine presence. To guard themselves from the wind or the storm, or from the still more fatal stroke of the sun-beam, to which the general custom of walking bare headed particularly exposed them, they wrapped their heads in their mantles, or upper garments. But during their long captivity in Babylon, the Jews began to wear turbans, in compliance with the customs of their conquerors; for Daniel informs us, that his three friends were cast into the fiery furnace with their hats, or, as the term should be rendered, their turbans. It is not, however, improbable, that the bulk of the nation continued to follow their ancient custom; and that the compliance prevailed only among those Jews who were connected with the Babylonish court; for many ages after that, we find Antiochus Epiphanes introducing the habits and fashions of the Grecians among the Jews; and as the history of the Maccabees relates, he brought the chief young men under his subjection, and made them wear a hat, or turban. Their legs were generally bare; and they never wore any thing upon the feet, but soles fastened in different ways, according to the taste or fancy of the wearer.

HADAD, son to the king of East Edom, was carried into Egypt by his father's servants, when Joab, general of David's troops, extirpated the males of Edom. Hadad was then a child. The king of Egypt gave him a house, lands, and every necessary subsistence, and married him to the sister of Tahpenes, his queen. By her he had a son, named Genubath, whom Queen Tahpenes educated in Pharaoh's house with the king's children. Hadad being informed that David was dead, and that Joab was killed, desired leave to return into his own country. Pharaoh wished to detain him, but at last permitted his return to Edom. Here he began to raise disturbances against Solomon; but the Scripture does not mention particulars. Josephus says, that Hadad did not return to Edom till long after the death of David, when Solomon's affairs began to decline, by reason of his impieties. He also observes, that, not being able to engage the Edomites to revolt, because of the strong garrisons which Solomon had placed there, Hadad got together such people as were willing, and carried them to Razon, then in rebellion against Hadadezer, king of Syria. Razon received Hadad with joy, and assisted him in conquering part of Syria, where he reigned, and from whence he insulted Solomon's territories.

HAGAR. After ten years' residence in the land of Canaan, Abram, by the persuasion of his wife, who had been barren heretofore, and now despaired of bearing children herself when she was seventy-five years old, took, as a second wife, or concubine, her handmaid, Hagar, an Egyptian. When Hagar conceived, she despised her mistress, who dealt hardly with her, Abram giving her up to his wife's discretion; so that she fled toward Egypt from the face of her mistress, but was stopped in her flight by the angel of the Lord, who foretold that she should bear a son called Ishmael, because the Lord heard her affliction, and that his race should be numerous, warlike, and unconquered; a prediction, as seen under the article ARABIA, remarkably fulfilled to the present day. Abram was eighty-six years old when Hagar bare Ishmael. When Isaac was weaned, Ishmael, the son of Hagar, who was now about fifteen years of age, offended Sarah by some mockery or ill treatment of Isaac; the original word signifies elsewhere, "to skirmish," or "fight," 2 Samuel ii, 14; and St. Paul represents Ishmael as "persecuting" him, Gal. iv, 29. Sarah therefore complained to Abraham, and said, "Cast out this bond-woman and her son, for the son of this bond-woman shall not be heir with my son Isaac. And the thing was very grievous in Abraham's sight, because of his son Ishmael;" but God approved of Sarah's advice, and again excluded Ishmael from the special covenant of grace: "For in Isaac shall thy seed be called: nevertheless, the son of the bond-woman will I make a nation also, because he is thy seed." God renewed this promise also to Hagar, during her wanderings in the wilderness of Beersheba, when she despaired of support: "Arise, lift up the lad, and hold him in thine hands, for I will make him a great nation. And God was with the lad, and he grew, and dwelt in the wilderness of Paran, and became an archer. And his mother took him a wife out of the land of Egypt." See Abraham and Ishmael.

We do not know when Hagar died. The rabbins say she was Pharaoh's daughter; but Chrysostom asserts that she was one of those slaves which Pharaoh gave to Abraham, Gen. xii, 16. The Chaldee paraphrasts, and many of the Jews, believe Hagar and Keturah to be the same person; but this is not credible. Philo thinks that Hagar embraced Abraham's religion, which is very probable. The Mussulmans and Arabians, who are descended from Ishmael, the son of Hagar, speak mightily in her commendation. They call her in eminency, Mother Hagar, and maintain that she was Abraham's lawful wife; the mother of Ishmael, his eldest son; who, as such, possessed Arabia, which very much exceeds, say they, both in extent and riches, the land of Canaan, which was given to his younger son Isaac.

HAGARENES, the descendants of Ishmael: called also Ishmaelites and Saracens, or Arabians, from their country. Their name, Saracens, is not derived, as some have thought, from Sarah, Abraham's wife, but from the Hebrew SARAK, which signifies "to rob" or "to steal;" because they mostly carry on the trade of thieving: or from Sahara, the desert; Saracens, inhabitants of the desert. But some writers think Hagarene imports SOUTH, conformably to the Arabic; hence Hagar, that is, the southern woman; and Mount Sinai is called Hagar, that is, the southern mountain, Gal. iv, 25. But there seems also to have been a particular tribe who bore this name more exclusively, as the Hagarenes are sometimes mentioned in Scripture distinct from the Ishmaelites, Psalm lxxxiii, 6; 1 Chron. v, 19.

HAGGAI was one of the Jews who returned with Zerubbabel to Jerusalem in consequence of the edict of Cyrus; and it is believed that he was born during the captivity, and that he was of the sacerdotal race. His prophecy consists of four distinct revelations, all which took place in the second year of Darius, king of Persia, B. C. 520. The prophet reproves the people for their delay in building the temple of God, and represents the unfruitful seasons which they had experienced as a divine punishment for this neglect. He exhorts them to proceed in the important work; and by way of encouragement predicts, that the glory of the second temple, however inferior in external magnificence, shall exceed that of the first; which was accomplished by its being honoured with the presence of the Saviour of mankind. He farther urges the completion of the temple by promises of divine favour, and under the type of Zerubbabel he is supposed by some to foretel the great revolutions which shall precede the second advent of Christ. The style of Haggai is in general plain and simple; but in some passages it rises to a considerable degree of sublimity.

HAIR. The eastern females wear their hair, which the prophet emphatically calls the "instrument of their pride," very long, and divided into a great number of tresses. In Barbary, the ladies all affect to have their hair hang down to the ground, which, after they have collected into one lock, they bind and plait with ribands. Where nature has been less liberal in its ornaments, the defect is supplied by art, and foreign is procured to be interwoven with the natural hair. The Apostle's remark on this subject corresponds entirely with the custom of the east, as well as with the original design of the Creator: "Does not even nature itself teach you, that, if a man have long hair, it is a shame unto him? But if a woman have long hair, it is a glory to her; for her hair is given her for a covering," 1 Cor. xi, 14. The men in the east, Chardin observes, are shaved; the women nourish their hair with great fondness, which they lengthen by tresses, and tufts of silk down to the heels. But among the Hebrews the men did not shave their heads; they wore their natural hair, though not long; and it is certain that they were, at a very remote period, initiated in the art of cherishing and beautifying the hair with fragrant ointments. The head of Aaron was anointed with a precious oil, compounded after the art of the apothecary; and in proof that they had already adopted the practice, the congregation were prohibited, under pain of being cut off, to make any other like it, after the composition of it, Exod. xxx, 32, 33. The royal Psalmist alludes to the same custom in the twenty-third Psalm: "Thou anointest my head with oil." We may infer from the direction of Solomon, that the custom had at least become general in his time: "Let thy garments be always white, and let thy head lack no ointment," Eccles. ix, 8. After the hair is plaited and perfumed, the eastern ladies proceed to dress their heads, by tying above the lock into which they collect it, a triangular piece of linen, adorned with various figures in needlework. This, among persons of better fashion, is covered with a SARMAH, as they call it, which is made in the same triangular shape, of thin flexible plates of gold or silver, carefully cut through, and engraven in imitation of lace, and might therefore answer to השהרנים, the moonlike ornament mentioned by the prophet in his description of the toilette of a Jewish lady, Isaiah iii, 18. Cutting off the hair was a sign of mourning, Jer. vii, 29; but sometimes in mourning they suffered it to grow long. In ordinary sorrows they neglected their hair; and in violent paroxysms they plucked it off with their hands.

John Baptist was clothed in a garment made of camel's hair, not with a camel's skin, as painters and sculptors represent him, but with coarse camlet made of camel's hair. The coat of the camel in some places yields very fine silk, of which are made stuffs of very great price; but in general this animal's hair is hard, and scarcely fit for any but coarse habits, and a kind of hair cloth. Some are of opinion that camlet derives its name from the camel, being originally composed of the wool and hair of camels; but at present there is no camel's hair in the composition of it, as it is commonly woven and sold among us.

HAM, or **CHAM**, חם, son of Noah, and brother to Shem and Japheth, is believed to have been Noah's youngest son. Ham, says Dr. Hales, signifies BURNT or BLACK, and this name was peculiarly significant of the regions allotted to his family. To the Cushites, or children of his eldest son, Cush, were allotted the hot southern regions of Asia, along the coasts of the Persian Gulf, Susiana or Chusistan, Arabia, &c; to the sons of Canaan, Palestine and Syria; to the sons of Misraim, Egypt and Libya, in Africa. The Hamites, in general, like the Canaanites of old, were a sea-faring race, and sooner arrived at civilization and the luxuries of life than their simpler pastoral and agricultural brethren of the other two families. The first great empires of Assyria and Egypt were founded by them; and the republics of Tyre, Sidon, and Carthage, were early distinguished for their commerce: but they sooner also fell to decay; and Egypt, which was one of the first, became the last and "basest of the kingdoms," Ezek. xxix, 15; and has been successively in subjection to the Shemites, and Japhethites; as have also the settlements of the other branches of the Hamites. See Canaan.

HAMAN, son of Hammedatha, the Amalekite, of the race of Agag; or, according to other copies, son of Hamadath the Bugean or Gogean, that is, of the race of Gog; or it may be read, Haman the son of Hamadath, which Haman was Bagua or Bagoas, eunuch, that is, officer to the king of Persia. We have no proof of Haman's being an Amalekite; but Esther iii, 1, reads of the race of Agag. In the apocryphal Greek, Esther ix, 24, and the Latin, Esther xvi, 10, he is called a Macedonian, ANIMO ET GENTE MACEDO. King Ahasuerus, having taken him into favour, promoted him above all the princes of his court, who bent the knee to him (probably prostrated themselves wholly before him, as to a deity) when he entered the palace: this Mordecai the Jew declined, for which slight, Haman plotted the extirpation of the whole Jewish nation; which was providentially prevented. He was hanged on a gibbet fifty cubits high, which he had prepared for Mordecai; his house was given to Queen Esther; and his employments to Mordecai. His ten sons were likewise executed. See Esther.

HAMATH, a city of Syria, capital of a province of the same name, lying upon the Orontes, Joshua xiii, 5; Judges iii, 3; 2 Kings xiv, 25; 2 Chron. vii, 8. The king of Hamath cultivated a good understanding with David, 2 Sam. viii, 9. This city was taken by the kings of Judah, and afterward retaken by the Syrians, and recovered from them by Jeroboam the Second, 2 Kings xiv, 28.

HAND sometimes denotes the vengeance of God: "The hand of the Lord was heavy upon them of Ashdod," after they had taken the ark, 1 Samuel v, 6, 7. To pour water on any one's hands, signifies to serve him, 2 Kings iii, 11. To wash one's hands, denotes innocence: Pilate washed his hands to denote his being innocent of the blood of Jesus, Matthew xxvii, 24. To kiss one's hand, is an act of adoration, 1 Kings xix, 18. "If I beheld the sun when it shined, and my mouth hath kissed my hand," Job xxxi, 27. To fill one's hands, is to take possession of the priesthood, to perform the functions of that office; because in this ceremony, those parts of the victim which were to be offered, were put into the hand of the newly created priest, Judges xvii, 5, 12; 1 Kings xiii, 33. To lean upon any one's hand, is a mark of familiarity and superiority. The king of Israel had a confident on whom he thus leaned, 2 Kings vii, 17. The king of Syria leaned on the hand or arm of Naaman when he went up to the temple of Rimmon, 2 Kings v, 18. To lift up one's hand, is a way of taking an oath which has been in use among all nations. To give one's hand, signifies to grant peace, to swear friendship, to promise entire security, to make alliance, 2 Kings x, 15. The Jews say, they were obliged to give the hand to the Egyptians and Assyrians, that they might procure bread, 2 Macc. xiii, 22; that is, to surrender to them, to submit. To stretch out one's hand, signifies to chastise, to exercise severity or justice, Ezek. xxv, 7. God delivered his people with a high hand, and arm stretched out; by performing many wonders, and inflicting many chastisements, on the Egyptians. To stretch out one's hand, sometimes denotes mercy: "I have spread out my hands," entreated, "all the day unto a rebellious people," Isaiah lxv, 2. Hand is also frequently taken for the power and impression of the Holy Spirit felt by a prophet: "The hand of the Lord was on Elijah," 1 Kings xviii, 46. It is said that God gave his law by the hand of Moses, that he spoke by the hand of prophets, &c; that is, by their means, by them, &c. The right hand denotes power, strength. The Scripture generally imputes to God's right hand all the effects of his omnipotence: "Thy right hand, O Lord, hath dashed in pieces the enemy," Exodus xv, 6. The Son of God is often represented as sitting at the right hand of his heavenly Father: "The Lord said to my Lord, Sit thou at my right hand," Psalm cx, 1; thou hast done thy work upon earth, now take possession of that sovereign kingdom and glory which by right belongeth unto thee; do thou rule with authority and honour, as thou art Mediator. The right hand commonly denotes the south, as the left does the north; for the Hebrews speak of the quarters of the world, in respect of themselves, having their faces turned to the east, their backs to the west, their right hands to the south, and their left to the north. For example: "Doth not David hide himself with us in strong holds, in the woods, in the hill of Hachilah, which is on the south of Jeshimon?" in Hebrew, "on the RIGHT HAND of Jeshimon." The accuser was commonly at the right hand of the accused: "Let Satan stand at his right hand," Psalm cix, 6. And in Zech. iii, 1, Satan was at the right hand of the high priest Joshua, to accuse him. Often, in a contrary sense, to be at one's right hand signifies to defend, to protect, to support him: "I have set the Lord always before me; because he is at my right hand, I shall not be moved," Psalm xvi, 8. To turn from the law of God, neither to the right hand nor to the left, is a frequent Scripture expression, the meaning of which is, that we must not depart from it at all. Our Saviour, in Matt, vi, 3, to show with what privacy we should do good works, says that our left hand should not know what our right hand does. Above all things, we should avoid vanity and ostentation in all the good we undertake to do, and should not think that thereby we merit any thing. Laying on hands, or imposition of hands, is understood in different ways both in the Old and New Testament. It is often taken for ordination and consecration of priests and ministers, as well among the Jews as Christians, Num. viii, 10; Acts vi, 6; xiii, 3; 1 Tim. iv, 14. It is sometimes also made use of to signify the establishment of judges and magistrates, on whom it was usual to lay hands when they were entrusted with these employments. Thus, when Moses constituted Joshua his successor, God appointed him to lay his hands upon him, Numbers xxvii, 18. Jacob laid his hands on Ephraim and Manasseh, when he gave them his last blessing, Gen. xlviii, 14. The high priest stretched out his hands to the people, as often as he recited the solemn form of blessing, Lev. ix, 22. The Israelites, who presented sin offerings at the tabernacle, confessed their sins while they laid their hands upon them, Lev. i, 4. This testified that the person acknowledged himself worthy of death, that he laid his sins upon the sacrifice, that he trusted in Christ for the expiation of his sins, and that he devoted himself to God. Witnesses laid their hands upon the head of the accused person, as it were to signify that they charged upon him the guilt of his blood, and freed themselves from it, Deut. xiii, 9; xvii, 7. Our Saviour laid his hands upon the children that were presented to him, and blessed them, Mark x, 16. And the Holy Ghost was conferred on those who were baptized by the laying on of the hands of the Apostles, Acts viii, 17; xix, 6.

HANNAH. See Samuel.

HARAN, the eldest son of Terah, and brother to Abraham and Nahor. He was the father of Lot, Milcah, and Iscah, Gen. xi, 26, &c. Haran died before his father Terah.

2. Haran, otherwise called Charran, in Mesopotamia, a city celebrated for having been the place to which Abraham removed first, after he left Ur, Gen. xi, 31, 32, and where Terah was buried. Thither it was likewise that Jacob repaired to Laban, when he fled from Esau, Gen. xxvii, 43; xxviii, 10, &c. Haran was situated in the north-western part of Mesopotamia on a river of the same name running into the Euphrates. Mr. Kinneir says, that Haran, which is still so called, or rather Harran, is now peopled by a few families of wandering Arabs, who have been led thither by a plentiful supply of good water from several small streams. It is situated in 36° 52′ north latitude, and 39° 5′ east longitude; in a flat and sandy plain. Some think that it was built by Terah, or by Haran, his eldest son.

HARE, ארנבת, Arabic ARNEB, Lev. xi, 6; Deut. xiv, 7. This name is derived, as Bochart and others suppose, from ארה, TO CROP, and ניב, THE PRODUCE OF THE GROUND; these animals being remarkable for devouring young plants and herbage. This animal resembles the rabbit, but is larger, and somewhat longer in proportion to its thickness. The hare in Syria, says Dr. Russel, is distinguished into two species, differing considerably in point of size. The largest is the Turkman hare, and chiefly haunts the plains; the other is the common hare of the desert: both are abundant. The difficulty as to this animal is, that Moses says the ARNABETH chews the cud, which our hares do not: but Aristotle takes notice of the same circumstance, and affirms that the structure of its stomach is similar to that of ruminating animals. The animal here mentioned may then be a variety of the species.

HAROSHETH OF THE GENTILES, a city supposed to be situated near Hazor, in the northern parts of Canaan, called afterward Upper Galilee, or Galilee of the Gentiles, for the same reason that this place probably obtained that title, namely, from being less inhabited by Jews, and being near the great resorts of the Gentiles, Tyre and Sidon. This is said to have been the residence of Sisera, the general of the armies of Jabin, king of Canaan, who reigned at Hazor.

HARP, a stringed musical instrument. The Hebrew word KINAOR, which is translated "harp" in our English version, very probably denoted all stringed instruments. By the Hebrews, the harp was called the PLEASANT harp; and it was employed by them, not only in their devotions, but also at their entertainments and pleasures. It is probable, that the harp was nearly the earliest, if not the earliest, instrument of music. David danced when he played on the harp: the Levites did the same. Hence it appears, that it was light and portable, and that its size was restricted within limits which admitted of that service, and of that manner of using it.

HART, איל, Deut. xii, 15; xiv, 5; Psalm xlii, 1; Isaiah xxxv, 6, the stag, or male deer. Dr. Shaw considers its name in Hebrew as a generic word including all the species of the deer kind; whether they are distinguished by round horns, as the stag; or by flat ones, as the fallow deer; or by the smallness of the branches, as the roe. Mr. Good observes that the hind and roe, the hart and the antelope, were held, and still continue to be, in the highest estimation in all the eastern countries, for the voluptuous beauty of their eyes, the delicate elegance of their form, or their graceful agility of action. The names of these animals were perpetually applied, therefore, to persons, whether male or female, who were supposed to be possessed of any of their respective qualities. In 2 Sam. i, 19, Saul is denominated "the roe of Israel;" and in the eighteenth verse of the ensuing chapter, we are told that "Asahel was as light of foot as a wild roe:" a phraseology perfectly synonymous with the epithet SWIFT-FOOTED, which Homer has so frequently bestowed upon his hero Achilles. Thus again: "Her princes are like harts which find no pasture; they are fled without strength before their pursuers," Lam. i, 6. "The Lord Jehovah is my strength; he will make my feet like hinds' feet; he will cause me to tread again on my own hills," Hab. iii, 19. See Hind.

HARVEST. Three months intervened between the seed time and the first reaping, and a month between this and the full harvest. Barley is in full ear all over the Holy Land, in the beginning of April; and about the middle of the same month, it begins to turn yellow, particularly in the southern districts; being as forward near Jericho in the latter end of March, as it is in the plains of Acre a fortnight afterward. The reaping continues till the middle of Sivan, or till about the end of May or beginning of June, which, as the time of wheat harvest, finishes this part of the husbandman's labours.

2. The reapers in Palestine and Syria make use of the sickle in cutting down their crops, and, according to the present custom in this country, "fill their hand" with the corn, and those who bind up the sheaves, their "bosom," Psalm cxxix, 7; Ruth ii, 5. When the crop is thin and short, which is generally the case in light soils, and with their imperfect cultivation, it is not reaped with the sickle, but plucked up by the root with the hand. By this mode of reaping, they leave the most fruitful fields as naked as if nothing had ever grown on them; and as no hay is made in the east, this is done, that they may not lose any of the straw, which is necessary for the sustenance of their cattle. The practice of plucking up with the hand is perhaps referred to in these words of the Psalmist, to which reference has already been made: "Let them be as the grass upon the house tops, which withereth afore it groweth up; wherewith the mower filleth not his hand, nor he that bindeth sheaves his bosom." The tops of the houses in Judea are flat, and, being covered with plaster of terrace, are frequently grown over with grass. As it is but small and weak, and from its elevation exposed to the scorching sun, it is soon withered. A more beautiful and striking figure, to display the weak and evanescent condition of wicked men, cannot easily be conceived.

3. The reapers go to the field very early in the morning, and return home betimes in the afternoon. They carry provisions along with them, and leathern bottles, or dried bottle gourds, filled with water. They are followed by their own children, or by others, who glean with much success, for a great quantity of corn is scattered in the reaping, and in their manner of carrying it. The greater part of these circumstances are discernible in the manners of the ancient Israelites. Ruth had not proposed to Naomi, her mother-in-law, to go to the field, and glean after the reapers; nor had the servant of Boaz, to whom she applied for leave, so readily granted her request, if gleaning had not been a common practice in that country. When Boaz inquired who she was, his overseer, after informing him, observes, that she came out to the field in the morning; and that the reapers left the field early in the afternoon, as Dr. Russel states, is evident from this circumstance, that Ruth had time to beat out her gleanings before evening. They carried water and provisions with them; for Boaz invited her to come and drink of the water which the young men had drawn; and at meal-time, to eat of the bread, and dip her morsel in the vinegar. And so great was the simplicity of manners in that part of the world, and in those times, that Boaz himself, although a prince of high rank in Judah, sat down to dinner in the field with his reapers, and helped Ruth with his own hand. Nor ought we to pass over in silence the mutual salutation of Boaz and his reapers, when he came to the field, as it strongly marks the state of religious feeling in Israel at the time, and furnishes another proof of the artless, the happy, and unsuspecting simplicity, which characterized the manners of that highly favoured people. "And, behold, Boaz came from Bethlehem, and said unto the reapers, The Lord be with you. And they answered him, The Lord bless thee," Ruth ii, 4.

4. It appears from the beautiful history of Ruth, that, in Palestine, the women lent their assistance in cutting down and gathering in the harvest; for Boaz commands her to keep fast by his maidens. The women in Syria shared also in the labours of the harvest; for Dr. Russel informs us, they sang the ZIRALEET, or song of thanks, when the passing stranger accepted their present of a handful of corn, and made a suitable return. It was another custom among the Jews to set a confidential servant over the reapers, to see that they executed their work properly, that they had suitable provisions, and to pay them their wages: the Chaldees call him RAB, the master, ruler, or governor of the reapers. Such was the person who directed the labours of the reapers in the field of Boaz. The right of the poor in Israel to glean after the reapers was secured by a positive law, couched in these words: "And when ye reap the harvest of your land, thou shalt not wholly reap the corners of thy land; neither shalt thou gather the gleanings of thy harvest. And thou shalt not glean thy vineyard, neither shalt thou gather every grape of thy vineyard: thou shalt leave them to the poor and the stranger: I am the Lord your God," Lev. xix, 9. It is the opinion of some writers, that, although the poor were allowed the liberty of gleaning, the Israelitish proprietors were not obliged to admit them immediately into the field, as soon as the reapers had cut down the corn, and bound it up in sheaves, but when it was carried off: they might choose, also, among the poor, whom they thought most deserving, or most necessitous. These opinions receive some countenance from the request which Ruth presented to the servant of Boaz, to permit her to glean "among the sheaves;" and from the charge of Boaz to his young men, "Let her

glean even among the sheaves;" a mode of speaking which seems to insinuate that though they could not legally hinder Ruth from gleaning in the field, they had a right, if they chose to exercise it, to prohibit her from gleaning among the sheaves, or immediately after the reapers.

HATE. To hate is not always to be understood rigorously, but frequently signifies merely a less degree of love. "If a man have two wives, one beloved and another hated," Deut. xxi, 15; that is, less beloved. Our Saviour says that he who would follow him must hate father and mother; that is, he must love them less than Christ, less than his own salvation, and not prefer them to God. "Jacob have I loved, and Esau have I hated;" that is, have deprived of the privileges of his primogeniture, through his own profanity; and visited him with severe judgment on account of his sins.

HAURAN. The tract of country of this name is mentioned only twice in Scripture, Ezek. xlvii, 16, 18. It was probably of small extent in the time of the Jews; but was enlarged under the Romans, by whom it was called Auranitis. At present it extends from about twenty miles south of Damascus to a little below Bozra, including the rocky district of El Ledja, the ancient Trachonitis, and the mountainous one of the Djebel Haouran. Within its limits are also included, beside Trachonitis, Ituræa or Ittur, now called Djedour, and part of Batanæa or Bashan. It is represented by Burckhardt as a volcanic region, consisting of a porous tufa, pumice, and basalt, with the remains of a crater on the Tel Shoba, on its eastern side. It produces, however, crops of corn, and has many patches of luxuriant herbage, which are frequented in the summer by the Arab tribes for pasturage. It abounds, also, with many interesting remains of cities, scattered over its surface, with Grecian inscriptions. The chief of these are Bozra, Ezra, Medjel, Shoba, Shakka, Souerda, Kanouat, Hebran, Zarle, Oerman, and Aatyl; with Messema, Berak, and Om Ezzeitoun, in the Ledja.

HAVILAH, the son of Cush, Genesis x, 7. There must have been other, and perhaps many, Havilahs beside the original one, a part of the numerous and wide-spread posterity of Cush. By one and the first of these, it is probable that the western shores of the Persian Gulf were peopled; by another, the country of Colchis; and by another, the parts about the southern border of the Dead Sea and the confines of Judea, the country afterward inhabited by the Amalekites.

HAWK, נץ, from the root נצה, TO FLY, because of the rapidity and length of flight for which this bird is remarkable, Lev. xi, 16; Deut. xiv, 15; Job xxxix, 26. NAZ is used generically by the Arabian writers to signify both falcon and hawk; and the term is given in both these senses by Meninski. There can be little doubt that such is the real meaning of the Hebrew word, and that it imports various species of the falcon family, as jer-falcon, goshawk, and sparrow-hawk. As this is a bird of prey, cruel in its temper, and gross in its manners, it was forbidden as food, and all others of its kind, in the Mosaic ritual. The Greeks consecrated the hawk to Apollo; and among the Egyptians no animal was held in so high veneration as the ibis and the hawk. Most of the species of hawk, we are told; are birds of passage. The hawk, therefore, is produced, in Job xxxix, 26, as a specimen of that astonishing instinct which teaches birds of passage to know their times and seasons, when to migrate out of one country into another for the benefit of food, or a warmer climate, or both. The common translation does not give the full force of the passage: "Doth the hawk fly by thy wisdom?" The real meaning is, "Doth she know, through thy skill or wisdom, the precise period for taking flight, or migrating and stretching her wings toward a southern or warmer climate?" The passage is well rendered by Sandys:--

"Doth the wild haggard tower into the sky,

And to the south by thy direction fly?"

Her migration is not conducted by the wisdom and prudence of man, but by the superintending and upholding providence of the only wise God.

HAY, חציר. In the two places where this word occurs, Prov. xxvii, 25, and Isaiah xv, 16, our translators have very improperly rendered it "hay." But in those countries they made no hay; and, if they did, it appears from inspection that hay could hardly be the meaning of the word in either of those texts. The author of "Fragments," in continuation of Calmet, has the following remarks: "There is a gross impropriety in our version of Prov. xxvii, 25: 'The hay appeareth, and the tender grass showeth itself, and the herbs of the mountains are gathered.' Now, certainly, if the tender grass is but just beginning to show itself, the hay, which is grass cut and dried after it has arrived at maturity, ought by no means to be associated with it, still less ought it to be placed before it. And this leads me to observe, that none of the dictionaries which I have seen seem to me to give the accurate import of the word, which, I apprehend, means THE FIRST SHOOTS, THE RISING, BUDDING, SPIRES OF GRASS. So, in the present passage, חציר גלה, 'the tender shoots of the grass rise up; and the buddings of grass,' grass in its early state, as is the peculiar import of רשא, 'appear; and the tufts of grass,' proceeding from the same root, 'collect themselves together, and, by their union, begin to clothe the mountain tops with a pleasing verdure.'" Surely, the beautiful progress of vegetation, as described in this passage, must appear too poetical to be lost; but what must it be to an eastern beholder! to one who had lately witnessed all surrounding sterility, a grassless waste!

HAZAEL. Elisha coming to Damascus, the capital of Syria, Benhadad, the reigning monarch, being then indisposed, sent Hazael, who was one of his principal officers, to wait upon the prophet, and consult him as to the issue of his disorder, 2 Kings viii, 7–13. The prophet told Hazael that certainly his master might recover, because his complaint was not mortal; yet he was very well assured that he would not recover; and, looking him steadfastly in the face, Elisha burst into tears. Surprised at this conduct, Hazael inquired the cause. "Because I know," said the prophet, "the evil that thou wilt do to the children of Israel: their strong holds wilt thou set on fire, and their young men wilt thou slay with the sword, and wilt dash their infants against the stones, and rip up their women with child." Hazael indignantly exclaimed, "Is thy servant a dog, that he should do this great thing?" Elisha merely answered, "The Lord hath showed me that thou shalt be king over Syria," 2 Kings viii, 7–13. On his return home, Hazael concealed from his master Benhadad the prophet's answer, and inspired him with hopes of recovery; but on the following day, he took effectual means to prevent it, by stifling the king with a thick cloth dipped with water; and, as Benhadad had no son, and Hazael was a man much esteemed in the army, he was, without difficulty declared his successor, A. M. 3120. Hazael soon inflicted upon Israel all the cruelties which Elisha had foretold. For when Jehu broke up the siege of Ramoth-Gilead, and came with his army to Samaria, Hazael took advantage of his absence to fall upon his territories beyond Jordan, destroying all the land of Gilead, Gad, Reuben, and Manasseh, from Aroer to Bashan, 2 Kings x, 32. Some years passed after this before Hazael undertook any thing against the kingdom of Judah, it being remote from Damascus; but in the reign of Joash, the son of Jehoahaz, A. M. 3165, he besieged the city of Gath, and, having taken it, marched against Jerusalem, 2 Kings xii, 17, 18. But Joash, conscious of his inferiority, bribed him at the price of all the money he could raise, to evacuate Judea, with which he for the moment complied; yet, in the following year, the army of Hazael returned, entered the territories of Judah, and the city of Jerusalem, slew all the princes of the people, and sent a valuable booty to their royal master, 2 Kings xiii, 22; 2 Chron. xxiv, 23.

HEAD. This word has several significations, beside its natural one, which denotes the head of a man. It is sometimes used in Scripture for the whole man: "Blessings are upon the head of the just," Prov. x, 6; that is, upon their persons. God says of the wicked, "I will recompense their way upon their head," Ezek. ix, 10. It signifies a chief or capital city: "The head of Syria is Damascus," Isaiah vii, 8. It denotes a chief or principal members in society: "The Lord will cut off from Israel head and tail. The ancient and honourable he is the head," Isaiah ix, 14, 15. "The seed of the woman shall bruise the head of the serpent," Gen. iii, 15; that is, Christ Jesus, the blessed seed of the woman, shall overthrow the power, policy, and works of the devil. The river in paradise was divided into four heads or branches. In times of grief, the mourners covered their heads: they cut and plucked off their hair. Amos, speaking of unhappy times, says, "I will bring baldness upon every head," Amos viii, 10. In prosperity, they anointed their heads with sweet oils: "Let thy head lack no" perfumed "ointment," Eccles. ix, 8. To shake the head at any one, expresses contempt: "The virgin, the daughter of Zion, hath despised thee, and laughed thee to scorn; the daughter of Jerusalem hath shaken her head at thee," Isaiah xxxvii, 22. Head is taken for one that hath rule and preëminence over others. Thus God is the head of Christ; as Mediator, from him he derives all his dignity and authority. Christ is the only spiritual head of the church, both in respect of eminence and influence; he communicates life, motion, and strength to every believer. Also the husband is the head of his wife, because by God's ordinance he is to rule over her, Gen. iii, 16; also in regard to preëminence of sex, 1 Peter iii, 7, and excellency of knowledge, 1 Cor. xiv, 35. The Apostle mentions this subordination of persons in 1 Cor. xi, 3: "But I would have you know, that the head of every man is Christ, and the head of the woman is the man, and the head of Christ is God." "The stone which the builders rejected was made the head of the corner," Psalm cxviii, 22. It was the first in the angle, whether it were disposed at the top of that angle to adorn and crown it, or at the bottom to support it. This, in the New Testament, is applied to Christ, who is the strength and beauty of the church, to unite the several parts of it, namely both Jews and Gentiles together.

HEAR, HEARING. This word is used in several senses in Scripture. In its obvious and literal acceptation, it denotes the exercise of that bodily sense of which the ear is the organ; and as hearing is a sense by which instruction is conveyed to the mind, and the mind is excited to attention and to obedience, so the ideas of attention and obedience are also grafted on the expression or sense of hearing. God is said, speaking after the manner of men, to hear prayer, that is, to attend to it, and comply with the requests it contains: "I love the Lord, because he hath heard," hath attended to, hath complied with, "the voice of my supplication," Psalm cxvi, 1. On the contrary, God is said not to hear, that is, not to comply with, the requests of sinners, John ix, 31. Men are said to hear, when they attend to, or comply with, the request of each other, or when they obey the commands of God: "He who is of God heareth," obeyeth, practiseth, "God's words," John viii, 47. "My sheep hear my voice," and show their attention to it, by following me, John x, 27. "This is my beloved Son: hear ye him," Matt. xvii, 5. This seems to be an allusion to Deut. xviii, 15, 18, 19: "The Lord shall raise up unto you a prophet; him shall ye hear;" which is also expressly applied in Acts iii, 22. The other senses which may be attached to the word "hear," seem to rise from the preceding, and may be referred to the same ideas.

HEART. The Hebrews regarded the heart as the source of wit, understanding, love, courage, grief, and pleasure. Hence are derived many modes of expression. "An honest and good heart," Luke viii, 15, is a heart studious of holiness, being prepared by the Spirit of God to receive the word with due affections, dispositions, and resolutions. We read of a broken heart, a clean heart, an evil heart, a liberal heart. To "turn the heart of the fathers to the children, and the heart of the children to their fathers," Mal. iv, 6, signifies to cause them to be perfectly reconciled, and that they should be of the same mind. To want heart, sometimes denotes to want understanding and prudence: "Ephraim is like a silly dove, without heart," Hosea vii, 11. "O fools, and slow of heart," Luke xxiv, 25; that is, ignorant, and without understanding.

"This people's heart is waxed gross, lest they should understand with their heart," Matt. xiii, 15; their heart is become incapable of understanding spiritual things; they resist the light, and are proof against all impressions of truth. "The prophets prophesy out of their own heart," Ezekiel xiii, 2; that is, according to their own imagination, without any warrant from God.

The heart is said to be dilated by joy, contracted by sadness, broken by sorrow, to grow fat, and be hardened by prosperity. The heart melts under discouragement, forsakes one under terror, is desolate in affliction, and fluctuating in doubt. To speak to any one's heart is to comfort him, to say pleasing and affecting things to him. The heart expresses also the middle part of any thing: "Tyre is in the heart of the seas," Ezekiel xxvii, 4; in the midst of the seas. "We will not fear though the mountains be carried into the heart (middle) of the sea," Psalm xlvi, 2.

The heart of man is naturally depraved and inclined to evil, Jer. xvii, 9. A divine power is requisite for its renovation, John iii, 1–11. When thus renewed, the effects will be seen in the temper, conversation, and conduct at large. Hardness of heart is that state in which a sinner is inclined to, and actually goes on in, rebellion against God.

HEATH, ערער, Jer. xvii, 6; xlviii, 6. "He shall be like the heath in the desert. He shall not see when good cometh; but shall inhabit the parched places in the wilderness, a salt land." The **LXX** and Vulgate render OROR, "the tamarisk;" and this is strengthened by the affinity of the Hebrew name of this tree with the Turkish ŒRŒR. Taylor and Parkhurst render it, "a blasted tree stripped of its foliage." If it be a particular tree, the tamarisk is as likely as any. Celsius thinks it to be the juniper; but from the mention of it as growing in a salt land, in parched places, the author of "Scripture Illustrated" is disposed to seek it among the LICHENS, a species of plants which are the last production of vegetation under the frozen zone, and under the glowing heat of equatorial deserts; so that it seems best qualified to endure parched places, and a salt land. Hasselquist mentions several kinds seen by him in Egypt, Arabia, and Syria. In Jer. xlviii, 6, the original word is ערועד, which the Septuagint translators have read ערוד, for they render it ὄνος ἄγριος, WILD ASS; and, as this seems best to agree with the flight recommended in the passage, it is to be preferred. See Wild Ass.

HEAVEN, the place of the more immediate residence of the Most High, Gen. xiv, 19. The Jews enumerated three heavens: the first was the region of the air, where the birds fly, and which are therefore called "the fowls of heaven," Job xxxv, 11. It is in this sense also that we read of the dew of heaven, the clouds of heaven, and the wind of heaven. The second is that part of space in which are fixed the heavenly luminaries, the sun, moon, and stars, and which Moses was instructed to call "the firmament or expanse of heaven," Gen. i, 8. The third heaven is the seat of God and of the holy angels; the place into which Christ ascended after his resurrection, and into which St. Paul was caught up, though it is not like the other heavens perceptible to mortal view.

2. It is an opinion not destitute of probability, that the construction of the tabernacle, in which Jehovah dwelt by a visible symbol, termed "the cloud of glory," was intended to be a type of heaven. In the holiest place of the tabernacle, "the glory of the Lord," or visible emblem of his presence, rested between the cherubims; by the figures of which, the angelic host surrounding the throne of God in heaven was typified; and as that holiest part of the tabernacle was, by a thick vail, concealed from the sight of those who frequented it for the purposes of worship, so heaven, the habitation of God, is, by the vail of flesh, hidden from mortal eyes. Admitting the whole tabernacle, therefore, in which the worship of God was performed according to a ritual of divine appointment, to be a representation of the universe, we are taught by it this beautiful lesson, that the whole universe is the temple of God; but that in this vast temple there is "a most holy place," where the Deity resides and manifests his presence to the angelic hosts and redeemed company who surround him. This view appears to be borne out by the clear and uniform testimony of Scripture; and it is an interesting circumstance, that heaven, as represented by "the holiest of all," is heaven as it is presented to the eye of Christian faith, the place where our Lord ministers as priest, to which believers now come in spirit, and where, they are gathered together in the disembodied state. Thus, for instance, St. Paul tells the believing Hebrews, "Ye are come unto Mount Zion, and unto the city of the living God, the heavenly Jerusalem, and to an innumerable company of angels, to the general assembly and church of the first-born, which are written," or are enrolled, "in heaven, and to God the Judge of all, and to the spirits of just men made perfect, and to Jesus the Mediator of the new covenant, and to the blood of sprinkling, that speaketh better things than the blood of Abel," Heb. xii, 22–24. Here we are presented with the antitype of almost every leading circumstance of the Mosaic dispensation. Instead of the land of Canaan, we have heaven; for the earthly Jerusalem, we have the heavenly, the city of the living God; in place of the congregation of Israel after the flesh, we have the general assembly and church of the first-born, that is, all true believers "made perfect;" for just men in the imperfect state of the old dispensation, we have just men made perfect in evangelical knowledge and holiness; instead of Moses, the mediator of the old covenant, we have Jesus the Mediator of the new and everlasting covenant; and instead of the blood of slaughtered animals, which was sprinkled upon the Israelites, the tabernacle, and all the vessels of the sanctuary, to make a typical atonement, we have the blood of the Son of God, which was shed for the remission of the sins of the whole world; that blood which doth not, like the blood of Abel, call for vengeance but for mercy, which hath made peace between heaven and earth, effected the true and complete atonement for sin, and which therefore communicates peace to the conscience of every sinner that believes the Gospel.

3. Among the numerous refinements of modern times that is one of the most remarkable which goes to deny the locality of heaven. "It is a state," say many, "not a place." But if that be the case, the very language of the Scriptures, in regard to this point, is calculated to mislead us. For that God resides in a particular part of the universe, where he makes his presence known to his intelligent creatures by some transcendent, visible glory, is an opinion that has prevailed among Jews and Christians, Greeks and Romans, yea, in every nation, civilized or savage, and in every age; and, since it is confirmed by revelation, why should it be doubted? Into this most holy place, the habitation of the Deity, Jesus, after his resurrection, ascended; and there, presenting his crucified body before the manifestation of the divine presence, which is called "the throne of the Majesty in the heavens," he offered unto God the sacrifice of himself, and made atonement for the sins of his people. There he is sat down upon his throne, crowned with glory and honour, as king upon his holy hill of Zion, and continually officiates as our great High Priest, Advocate, and Intercessor, within the vail. There is his Father's house, into which he is gone before, to prepare mansions of bliss for his disciples; it is the kingdom conferred upon him as the reward of his righteousness, and of which he has taken possession as their forerunner, Acts i, 11; Heb. vi, 19, 20.

4. Some of the ancients imagined that the habitation of good men, after the resurrection, would be the sun; grounding this fanciful opinion on a mistaken interpretation of Psalm xix, 4, which they rendered, with the **LXX** and Vulgate, "He has set his tabernacle in the sun." Others, again, have thought it to lie beyond the starry firmament, a notion less improbable than the former. Mr. Whiston supposes the air to be the mansion of the blessed, at least for the present; and he imagines that Christ is at the top of the atmosphere, and other spirits nearer to or more remote from him according to the degree of their moral purity, to which he conceives the specific gravity of their inseparable vehicles to be proportionable. Mr. Hallet has endeavoured to prove that they will dwell upon earth, when it shall be restored to its paradisaical state. The passages of Scripture, however, on which he grounds his hypothesis, are capable of another and very different interpretation. After all, we may observe, that the place of the blessed is a question of comparatively little importance; and we may cheerfully expect and pursue it, though we cannot answer a multitude of curious questions, relating to various circumstances that pertain to it. We have reason to believe that heaven will be a social state, and that its happiness will, in some measure, arise from mutual communion and converse, and the expressions and exercises of mutual benevolence. All the views presented to us of this eternal residence of good men are pure and noble; and form a striking contrast to the low hopes, and the gross and sensual conceptions of a future state, which distinguish the Pagan and Mohammedan systems. The Christian heaven may be described to be a state of eternal communion with God, and consecration to hallowed devotional and active services; from which will result an uninterrupted increase of knowledge, holiness, and joy, to the glorified and immortalized assembly of the redeemed.

HEBER, or **EBER**, the father of Peleg, and the son of Salah, who was the grandson of Shem, one of Noah's sons, was born A. M. 1723; B. C. 2281. From him some have supposed that Abraham and his descendants derived the appellation of Hebrews. But others have suggested, with greater probability, that Abraham and his family were thus called, because they came from the other side of the Euphrates into Canaan; Heber signifying in the Hebrew language ONE THAT PASSES, or, A PASSAGE, that is, of the river Euphrates. According to this opinion, Hebrew signifies much the same as foreigner among us, or one that comes from beyond sea. Such were Abraham and his family among the Canaanites; and his posterity, learning and using the language of the country, still retained the appellation originally given them, even when they became possessors and settled inhabitants.

2. Heber the Kenite, of Jethro's family, husband to Jael, who killed Sisera, Judges iv, 17, &c.

HEBREW OF THE HEBREWS, an appellation which the Apostle Paul applies to himself, Phil. iii, 5, concerning the meaning of which there has been some difference of opinion. Godwin, in his "Moses and Aaron," understands by this expression, a Hebrew both by father's and mother's side. But if it meant no more than this, there was little occasion for the Apostle's using it immediately after having declared that he was "of the stock of Israel, and the tribe of Benjamin," which, on Godwin's supposition, is the same as a Hebrew of the Hebrews; for the Jews were not allowed to marry out of their own nation. Beside, it is not likely that St. Paul would have mentioned it as a distinguishing privilege and honour, that his parents were not proselytes. It is more probable that a Hebrew of the Hebrews signifies a Hebrew both by nation and language, which many of Abraham's posterity, in those days, were not; or one of the Hebrew Jews who performed their public worship in the Hebrew tongue; for such were reckoned more honourable than the Jews born out of Judea, and who spoke the Greek tongue. See Hellenists.

HEBREW LANGUAGE, called also absolutely Hebrew, is the language spoken by the Hebrews, and in which all the books of the Old Testament are written; whence it is also called the holy or sacred language. It is said to have been preserved in the midst of the confusion at Babel, in the family of Heber, or Eber, who, as it is alleged, was not concerned in the building of Babel, and, consequently, did not share in the punishment inflicted on the actual transgressors. The Jews, in general, have been of opinion, that the Hebrew was the language of Heber's family, from whom Abraham sprung. On the other hand, it has been maintained that Heber's family, in the fourth generation after the dispersion, lived in Chaldea, where Abraham was born, Gen. xi, 27, 28, and that there is no reason to think they used a different language from their neighbours around them. It appears, moreover, that the Chaldee, and not the Hebrew, was the language of Abraham's country, and of his kindred, Gen. xxiv, 4; xxxi, 46, 47; and it is probable that Abraham's native language was Chaldee, and that the Hebrew was the language of the Canaanites, which Abraham and his posterity learned by travelling among them. It is surprising that this adoption of the Phenician language by the patriarchs should have escaped the notice of several intelligent readers of the Bible. Jacob and Laban, it is clear, by the names they gave to the cairn, or memorial of stones, spoke two different dialects; and it is nearly equally evident, that the language of Laban was the dialect of Ur of the Chaldees, the original speech of the Hebrew race. As the patriarchs disused the true Hebrew dialect, it is manifest that they had conformed to the speech of Canaan; and that this conformity was complete, is proved by the identity between all the remains of Canaanitish names. At the same time, it must be remarked, that the Phenician and the Chaldean were merely different dialects of the same primitive language which had been spoken by the first ancestors of mankind.

2. There is no work in all antiquity written in pure Hebrew, beside the books of the Old Testament; and even some parts of those are in Chaldee. The Hebrew appears to be the most ancient of all the languages in the world; at least it is so with regard to us, who know of no older. Dr. Sharpe adopts the opinion, that the Hebrew was the original language; not indeed that the Hebrew is the unvaried language of our first parents, but that it was the general language of men at the dispersion; and, however it might have been improved and altered from the first speech of our first parents, it was the original of all the languages, or almost all the languages, rather dialects, that have since arisen in the world. Arguments have also been deduced from the nature and genius of the Hebrew language, in order to prove that it was the original language, neither improved nor debased by foreign idioms. The words of which it is composed are short, and admit of very little flexion. The names of places are descriptive of their nature, situation, accidental circumstances, &c. The compounds are few, and inartificially conjoined; and it is less burdened with those artificial affixes which distinguish other cognate dialects, such as the Chaldean, Syrian, Arabian, Phenician, &c.

The period, from the age of Moses to that of David, has been considered the golden age of the Hebrew language, which declined in purity from that time to the reign of Hezekiah or Manasseh, having received several foreign words, particularly Aramean, from the commercial and political intercourse of the Jews and Israelites with the Assyrians and Babylonians. This period has been termed the silver age of the Hebrew language. In the interval between the reign of Hezekiah and the Babylonish captivity, the purity of the language was neglected, and so many foreign words were introduced into it, that this period has not inaptly been designated its iron age. During the seventy years' captivity, though it does not appear that the Hebrews entirely lost their native tongue, yet it underwent so considerable a change from their adoption of the vernacular languages of the countries where they had resided, that afterward, on their return from exile, they spoke a dialect of Chaldee mixed with Hebrew words. On this account it was, that, when the Scriptures were read, it was found necessary to interpret them to the people in the Chaldean language; as, when Ezra the scribe brought the book of the law of Moses before the congregation, the Levites are said to have caused the people to understand the law, because "they read in the book, in the law of God, distinctly, and gave the sense, and caused them to understand the reading," Nehem. viii, 8. Some time after the return from the great captivity, Hebrew ceased to be spoken altogether; though it continued to be cultivated and studied by the priests and Levites, as a learned language, that they might be enabled to expound the law and the prophets to the people, who, it appears from the New Testament, were well acquainted with their general contents and tenor: this last mentioned period has been called the leaden age of the language.

The present Hebrew characters, or letters, are twenty-two in number, and of a square form; but the antiquity of these letters is a point that has been most severely contested by many learned men. From a passage in Eusebius's Chronicle, and another in St. Jerom, it was inferred by Joseph Scaliger, that Ezra, when he reformed the Jewish church, transcribed the ancient characters of the Hebrews into the square letters of the Chaldeans; and that this was done for the use of those Jews who, being born during the captivity, knew no other alphabet than that of the people among whom they had been educated. Consequently, the old character, which we call the Samaritan, fell into total disuse. This opinion Scaliger supported by passages from both the Talmuds, as well as from rabbinical writers, in which it is expressly affirmed that such characters were adopted by Ezra. But the most decisive confirmation of this point is to be found in the ancient Hebrew coins, which were struck before the captivity, and even previously to the revolt of the ten tribes. The characters engraven on all of them are manifestly the same with the modern Samaritan, though with some trifling variations in their forms, occasioned by the depredations of time.

HEBREWS, sometimes called Israelites, from their progenitor, Jacob, surnamed Israel, and in modern times Jews, as the descendants of Judah, the name of this leading tribe being given to all. See Jews.

Hebrews, Epistle to the. Though the genuineness of this epistle has been disputed both in ancient and modern times, its antiquity has never been questioned. It is generally allowed that there are references to it, although the author is not mentioned, in the remaining works of Clement of Rome, Ignatius, Polycarp, and Justin Martyr; and that it contains, as was first noticed by Chrysostom and Theodoret, internal evidence of having been written before the destruction of Jerusalem, Heb. viii, 4; ix, 25; x, 11, 37; xiii, 10. The earliest writer now extant who quotes this epistle as the work of St. Paul is Clement of Alexandria, toward the end of the second century; but, as he ascribes it to St. Paul repeatedly and without hesitation, we may conclude that in his time no doubt had been entertained upon the subject, or, at least, that the common tradition of the church attributed it to St. Paul. Clement is followed by Origen, by Dionysius and Alexander, both bishops of Alexandria, by Ambrose, Athanasius, Hilary of Poitiers, Jerom, Chrysostom, and Cyril, all of whom consider this epistle as written by St. Paul; and it is also ascribed to him in the ancient Syriac version, supposed to have been made at the end of the first century. Eusebius says, "Of St. Paul there are fourteen epistles manifest and well known; but yet there are some who reject that to the Hebrews, urging for their opinion that it is contradicted by the church of the Romans, as not being St. Paul's." In Dr. Lardner we find the following remark: "It is evident that this epistle was generally received in ancient times by those Christians who used the Greek language, and lived in the eastern parts of the Roman empire." And in another place he says, "It was received as an epistle of St. Paul by many Latin writers in the fourth, fifth, and sixth centuries." The earlier Latin writers take no notice of this epistle, except Tertullian, who ascribes it to Barnabas. It appears, indeed, from the following expression of Jerom, that this epistle was not generally received as canonical Scripture by the Latin church in his time: "LICET EAM LATINA CONSUETUDO INTER CANONICAS SCRIPTURAS NON RECIPIAT." [Although the usage of the Latin church does not receive it among the canonical Scriptures.] The same thing is mentioned in other parts of his works. But many individuals of the Latin church acknowledged it to be written by St. Paul, as Jerom himself, Ambrose, Hilary, and Philaster; and the persons who doubted its genuineness were those the least likely to have been acquainted with the epistle at an early period, from the nature of its contents not being so interesting to the Latin churches, which consisted almost entirely of Gentile Christians, ignorant, probably, of the Mosaic law, and holding but little intercourse with Jews.

2. The moderns, who, upon grounds of internal evidence, contend against the genuineness of this epistle, rest principally upon the two following arguments, the omission of the writer's name, and the superior elegance of the style in which it is written. It is indeed certain that all the acknowledged epistles of St. Paul begin with a salutation in his own name, and that, in the Epistle to the Hebrews, there is nothing of that kind; but this omission can scarcely be considered as conclusive against positive testimony. St. Paul might have reasons for departing, upon this occasion, from his usual mode of salutation, which we at this distant period cannot discover. Some have imagined that he omitted his name, because he knew that it would not have much weight with the Hebrew Christians, to whom he was in general obnoxious, on account of his zeal in converting the Gentiles, and in maintaining that the observance of the Mosaic law was not essential to salvation: it is, however, clear, that the persons to whom this epistle was addressed knew from whom it came, as the writer refers to some acts of kindness which he had received from them, and also expresses a hope of seeing them soon, Hebrews x, 34; xiii, 18, 19, 23. As to the other argument, it must be owned that there does not appear to be such superiority in the style of this epistle, as should lead to the conclusion that it was not written by St. Paul. Those who have thought differently have mentioned Barnabas, St. Luke, and Clement, as authors or translators of this epistle. The opinion of Jerom was, that the sentiments are the Apostle's, but the language and composition that of some one else, who committed to writing the Apostle's sense, and, as it were, reduced into commentaries the things spoken by his master. Dr. Lardner says, "My conjecture is, that St. Paul dictated the epistle in Hebrew, and another, who was a great master of the Greek language, immediately wrote down the Apostle's sentiments in his own elegant Greek; but who this assistant of the Apostle was, is altogether unknown." But surely the writings of St. Paul, like those of other authors, may not all have the same precise degree of merit; and if, upon a careful perusal and comparison, it should be thought that the Epistle to the Hebrews is written with greater elegance than the acknowledged compositions of this Apostle; it should also be remembered that the apparent design and contents of this epistle suggest the idea of more studied composition, and yet, that there is nothing in it which amounts to a marked difference of style: on the other hand, there is the same concise, abrupt, and elliptical mode of expression, and it contains many phrases and sentiments which are found in no part of Scripture, except in St. Paul's Epistles. We may farther observe, that the manner in which Timothy is mentioned in this epistle makes it probable that it was written by St. Paul. Compare Heb. xiii, 23, with 2 Cor. i, 1, and Col. i, 1. It was certainly written by a person who had suffered imprisonment in the cause of Christianity; and this is known to have been the case of St. Paul, but of no other person to whom this epistle has been attributed. Upon the whole, both the external and internal evidence appear to preponderate so greatly in favour of St. Paul's being the author of this epistle, that it cannot but be considered as written by that Apostle.

3. "They of Italy salute you," is the only expression in the epistle which can assist us in determining from whence it was written. The Greek words are, οἱ ἀπὸ τῆς Ἰταλίας which should have been translated, "Those from Italy salute you;" and the only inference to be drawn from them seems to be, that St. Paul, when he wrote this epistle, was at a place where some Italian converts were. This inference is not incompatible with the common opinion, that this epistle was written from Rome, and therefore we consider it as written from that city. It is supposed to have been written toward the end of St. Paul's first imprisonment at Rome, or immediately after it, because the Apostle expresses an intention of visiting the Hebrews shortly: we therefore place the date of this epistle in the year 63.

4. Clement, of Alexandria, Eusebius, and Jerom, thought that this epistle was originally written in the Hebrew language; but all the other ancient fathers who have mentioned this subject speak of the Greek as the original work; and as no one pretends to have seen this epistle in Hebrew, as there are no internal marks of the Greek being a translation, and as we know that the Greek language was at this time very generally understood at Jerusalem, we may

accede to the more common opinion, both among the ancients and moderns, and consider the present Greek as the original text. It is no small satisfaction to reflect, that those who have denied either the genuineness or the originality of this epistle have always supposed it to have been written or translated by some fellow labourer or assistant of St. Paul, and that almost every one admits that it carries with it the sanction and authority of the inspired Apostle.

5. There has been some little doubt concerning the persons to whom this epistle was addressed; but by far the most general and most probable opinion is, that it was written to those Christians of Judea who had been converted to the Gospel from Judaism. That it was written, notwithstanding its general title, to the Christians of one certain place or country, is evident from the following passages: "I beseech you the rather to do this, that I may be restored to you the sooner," Heb. xiii, 19. "Know ye that our brother Timothy is set at liberty, with whom, if he come shortly, I will see you," Heb. xiii, 23. And it appears from the following passage in the Acts, "When the number of the disciples was multiplied, there arose a murmuring of the Grecians against the Hebrews," Acts vi, 1, that certain persons were at this time known at Jerusalem by the name of Hebrews. They seem to have been native Jews, inhabitants of Judea, the language of which country was Hebrew, and therefore they were called Hebrews, in contradistinction to those Jews who, residing commonly in other countries, although they occasionally came to Jerusalem, used the Greek language, and were therefore called Grecians.

6. The general design of this epistle was to confirm the Jewish Christians in the faith and practice of the Gospel, which they might be in danger of deserting, either through the persuasion or persecution of the unbelieving Jews, who were very numerous and powerful in Judea. We may naturally suppose, that the zealous adherents to the law would insist upon the majesty and glory which attended its first promulgation, upon the distinguished character of their legislator, Moses, and upon the divine authority of the ancient Scriptures; and they might likewise urge the humiliation and death of Christ as an argument against the truth of his religion. To obviate the impression which any reasoning of this sort might make upon the converts to Christianity, the writer of this epistle begins with declaring to the Hebrews, that the same God who had formerly, upon a variety of occasions, spoken to their fathers by means of his prophets, had now sent his only Son for the purpose of revealing his will; he then describes, in most sublime language, the dignity of the person of Christ, Heb. i; and thence infers the duty of obeying his commands, the divine authority of which was established by the performance of miracles, and by the gifts of the Holy Ghost; he points out the necessity of Christ's incarnation and passion, Heb. ii; he shows the superiority of Christ to Moses, and warns the Hebrews against the sin of unbelief, Heb. iii; he exhorts to steadfastness in the profession of the Gospel, and gives an animated description of Christ as our high priest, Heb. iv-vii; he shows that the Levitical priesthood and the old covenant were abolished by the priesthood of Christ, and by the new covenant, Heb. viii; he points out the efficacy of the ceremonies and sacrifices of the law, and the sufficiency of the atonement made by the sacrifice of Christ, Heb. ix, x; he fully explains the nature, merit, and effects of faith, Heb. xi; and in the last two chapters he gives a variety of exhortations and admonitions, all calculated to encourage the Hebrews to bear with patience and constancy any trials to which they might be exposed. He concludes with the valedictory benediction usual in St. Paul's Epistles: "Grace be with you all. Amen." The most important articles of our faith are explained, and the most material objections to the Gospel are answered with great force, in this celebrated epistle. The arguments used in it, as being addressed to persons who had been educated in the Jewish religion, are principally taken from the ancient Scriptures; and the connection between former revelations and the Gospel of Christ, is pointed out in the most perspicuous and satisfactory manner.

7. In addition, it may be observed, that Mr. Stuart, an American critic, has published an ample investigation of several of the points referred to in the above remarks, and the following are the RESULTS:--

(1.) As to the place in which the persons lived to whom the epistle is addressed, I have now examined all the objections against the opinion, that the Epistle to the Hebrews was directed to Palestine, which I have met with, and which seem to be of sufficient magnitude to deserve attention. I am unable to perceive that they are very weighty; and surely they come quite short of being conclusive. On the other hand, the positive proof, I acknowledge, is only of a circumstantial nature, and falls short of the weight which direct and unequivocal testimony in the epistle itself would possess. But uniting the whole of it together; considering the intimate knowledge of Jewish rites, the strong attachment to their ritual, and the special danger of defection from Christianity in consequence of it, which the whole texture of the epistle necessarily supposes, and combining these things with the other circumstances above discussed, I cannot resist the impression, that the universal opinion of the ancient church respecting the persons to whom this epistle was addressed, was well founded, being built upon early tradition and the contents of the epistle; and that the doubts and difficulties thrown in the way by modern and recent critics, are not of sufficient importance to justify us in relinquishing the belief that Palestine Christians were addressed by the epistle to the Hebrews. Thousands of facts, pertaining to criticism and to history, are believed and treated as realities, which have less support than the opinion that has now been examined.

(2.) As to the author, we now come to the result of this investigation. In the Egyptian and eastern churches, there were, it is probable, at a pretty early period, some who had doubts whether St. Paul wrote the Epistle to the Hebrews; but no considerable person or party is definitely known to us, who entertained these doubts; and it is manifest, from Origen and Eusebius, that there was not, in that quarter, any important opposition to the general and constant tradition of the church, that Paul did write it. Not a single witness of any considerable respectability is named, who has given his voice, in this part of the church, for the negative of the question which we are considering. What Jerom avers, appears to be strictly true, namely, AB ECCLESIIS ORIENTIS ET AB OMNIBUS RETRÒ ECCLESIASTICIS GRÆCI SERMONIS SCRIPTORIBUS, QUASI APOSTOLI PAULI SUSCIPI. In the western churches a diversity of opinion prevailed; although the actual quantity of negative testimony, that can be adduced, is not great. Yet the concessions of Jerom and Augustine leave no room to doubt the fact, that the predominant opinion of the western churches, in their times, was in the negative. In early times, we have seen that the case was different, when Clement of Rome wrote his epistle, and when the old Latin version was brought into circulation. What produced a change of opinion in the west, we are left to conjecture. The scanty critical and literary records of those times afford us no means for tracing the history of it. But this is far from being a singular case. Many other changes in the opinions of the churches have taken place, which we are, for a similar reason, as little able to trace with any certainty or satisfaction. Storr has endeavoured to show, that Marcion occasioned this revolution, when he came from the east to Rome, and brought with him a collection of the sacred books, in which the Epistle to the Hebrews was omitted. But it is very improbable, that an extravagant man, excommunicated by the Roman church itself, should have produced such a revolution there in sentiment. Others have with more probability, attributed it to the zealous disputes at Rome against the Montanist party, whom the Epistle to the Hebrews was supposed particularly to favour. The Montanists strenuously opposed the reception again into the bosom of the church of those persons who had so lapsed as to make defection from the Christian faith. The passages in Heb. vi, 4–8, and x, 26–31, at least seem strongly to favour the views which they maintained. The church at Rome carried the dispute against the Montanists very high; and Ernesti and many other critics have been led to believe, that the Epistle to the Hebrews was ultimately rejected by them, because the Montanists relied on it as their main support. As a matter of fact, this cannot be established by direct historical evidence. But, in the absence of all testimony in respect to this subject, it must be allowed as not improbable, that the Epistle to the Hebrews may have, in this way, become obnoxious to the Roman church. Many such instances might be produced from the history of the church. The Ebionites, the Manicheans, the Alogi, and many ancient and modern sects, have rejected some part of the canon of Scripture, because it stood opposed to their party views. The Apocalypse was rejected by many of the oriental churches, on account of their opposition to the Chiliasts, who made so much use of it. And who does not know, that Luther himself rejected the Epistle of James, because he viewed it as thwarting his favourite notions of justification; yea, that he went so far as to give it the appellation of EPISTOLA STRAMINEA? [an epistle of straw.] It cannot be at all strange, then, that the Romish church, exceedingly imbittered by the dispute with the Montanists, should have gradually come to call in question the apostolic origin of the epistle; because it was to their adversaries a favourite source of appeal, and because, unlike St. Paul's other epistles, it was anonymous. That all, even of the Montanists, however, admitted the apostolic origin of our epistle, does not seem to be true. Tertullian, who took a very active part in favour of this sect, had, as we have already seen, doubts of such an origin, or rather, he ascribed it to Barnabas. But whatever might have been the cause that the epistle in question was pretty generally rejected by the churches of the west, the fact that it was so cannot be reasonably disputed. A majority of these churches, from the latter half of the second century to the latter half of the fourth, seem to have been generally opposed to receiving this epistle as St. Paul's; although there were some among them who did receive it. It remains, then, to balance the testimony thus collected together and compared. The early testimony is, of course, immeasurably the most important. And there seems to me sufficient evidence, that this was as general and as uniform for the first century after the apostolic age as in respect to many other books of the New Testament; and more so, than in respect to several. I cannot hesitate to believe, that the weight of evidence from tradition is altogether preponderant in favour of the opinion, that St. Paul was the author of our epistle.

(3.) As to the language in which the epistle was originally written, there has been a difference of opinion among critics, both in ancient and modern times. Clement of Alexandria says that St. Paul wrote to the Hebrews in the Hebrew language, and that St. Luke carefully translated it into Greek. Eusebius in the same manner says, that Paul wrote to the Hebrews in his vernacular language, and that, according to report, either Luke or Clement translated it. So Jerom, also, SCRIPSERAT UT HEBRÆUS HEBRÆIS HEBRAICÈ; [as a Hebrew he had written to the Hebrews in Hebrew;] and then he adds that this epistle was translated into Greek, so that the colouring of the style was made diverse, in this way, from that of St. Paul's. Of the same opinion, in respect to this, was Clement, of Alexandria; and Origen, as we have seen above, supposes that the thoughts contained in the epistle were St. Paul's, while the diction or costume of it must be attributed to the person who wrote down the sentiments of the Apostle. By the Hebrew language, no one can reasonably doubt, that these fathers meant the Jerusalem dialect, which was spoken in the days of the Apostles, and not the ancient Hebrew, which had long ceased to be a vernacular language. It is quite plain also, that these fathers were led to the conclusion, that the Epistle to the Hebrews was originally written in the dialect of Palestine, from their belief, so universal in ancient times, of its having been addressed to some church, or to the churches, in that country. It was very natural to draw such a conclusion; for would not an epistle addressed to Hebrews in all probability be more acceptable, if written in their own vernacular language? Moreover, St. Paul was well acquainted with that language, for he was brought up at Jerusalem, and "at the feet of Gamaliel;" and when he had visited that city, he had addressed the Jewish multitude, who were excited against him, in their native tongue, Acts xxii, 1, 2. Why should it not be supposed, that if, as is probable, this epistle was originally directed to Palestine, it was written in the dialect of that country? So the fathers above quoted evidently thought and reasoned; although other fathers have said nothing on this point, and do not appear to have coincided in opinion with those to whom I have just referred. Among the moderns, also, several critics have undertaken to defend the same opinion; and particularly Michaëlis, who has discussed the subject quite at length, in his introduction to this epistle. I do not think it necessary minutely to examine his arguments. To my own mind they appear altogether unsatisfactory. Some of them are built on an exegesis most palpably erroneous, and which, if admitted, would deduce a very strange meaning from the words of the epistle. Yet, assuming such a meaning, he thence concludes, that the original writer must have expressed a different idea, and that the translator mistook his meaning. He then undertakes to conjecture what the original Hebrew must have been. In other cases, he deduces his arguments from considerations wholly À PRIORI; as if these were admissible in a question of mere fact. He has not adduced a single instance of what he calls WRONG TRANSLATION, which wears the appearance of any considerable probability. On the other hand, Bolton, a sharp-sighted critic, and well acquainted with the Aramean language, who has gone through with the New Testament, and found almost every where marks, as he thinks, of translation from Aramean documents, confesses, that, in respect to this epistle, he finds not a single vestige of incorrect translation from an Aramean original, and no marks that there ever was such an original. This testimony is of considerable importance in respect to the question before us, as it comes from a critic who spent many years on the study of that which is most intimately connected with the very subject under consideration, namely, the detection of the Aramean originals of the various parts of the New Testament.

(4.) The principal arguments in favour of a Hebrew original are deduced from two sources: That Hebrews are addressed in our epistle, to whom the Hebrew language would have been more acceptable and intelligible, and many of whom, indeed, could not understand Greek, certainly could not read it: That the diversity of style in the Epistle to the Hebrews is so great, when compared with that of St. Paul's epistles, that, unless we suppose the Greek costume did in fact come from another hand, we must be led to the conclusion that St. Paul did not write it. Both of these topics have been already discussed. I merely add here, therefore, that in case the writer of the epistle designed it should have a wide circulation among the Jews, to write in Greek was altogether the most feasible method of accomplishing this. Beside, if St. Paul did address it to the church at Cæsarea, it is altogether probable that he wrote in Greek, as Greek was the principal language of that city. Even if he did not, it was not necessary that he should write in Hebrew; for in every considerable place in Palestine, there were more or less who understood the Greek language. Whoever wishes to see this last position established beyond any reasonable doubt, may read Hug's "Introduction to the New Testament," vol. ii, pp. 32–50. When St. Paul wrote to the Romans, he did not write in Latin; yet there was no difficulty in making his epistle understood, for the knowledge of Greek was very common in Rome. If St. Paul understood the Latin language, which is no where affirmed, and he had not resided when he wrote this epistle, in any of the countries where it was commonly used, still he understood Greek so much better that he would of course prefer writing in it. For a similar reason, if no other could be given, one may regard it as more probable, that he would write the Epistle to the Hebrews in the Greek language. At the time of writing it, he had been abroad twenty-five years at least, in Greek countries, and had been in Palestine, during all that period, only a few days. The Jews abroad, whom he every where saw, spoke Greek, not Hebrew. In Greek he preached and conversed. Is it any wonder, then, that, after twenty-five years' incessant labour or preaching, conversing, and writing, in this language, he should have preferred writing in it? Indeed, can it be probable, that, under circumstances like these, he still possessed an equal facility of writing in his native dialect of Palestine? I cannot think it strange, therefore, that although the Epistle to the Hebrews was in all probability directed to some part of Palestine, yet it was written by St. Paul in Greek, and not in Hebrew. But, whatever may be the estimation put upon arguments of this nature, there are internal marks of its having been originally composed in Greek, which cannot well be overlooked.

HEBRON, one of the most ancient cities in the world; for it was built seven years before Zoan, the capital of Lower Egypt, Numbers xiii, 22. Now, as the Egyptians gloried much in the antiquity of their cities, and their country was indeed one of the first that was peopled after the dispersion of Babel, it may be from hence concluded that it was one of the most ancient. Some think it was founded by Arba, one of the oldest giants in Palestine; for which reason it was called Kirjath-arba, or Arba's city, Joshua xiv, 15; which name was afterward changed to that of Hebron, Joshua xv, 13. Arba was the father of Anak; and from Anak the giants, called Anakim, took their name, who were still dwelling at Hebron when Joshua conquered the land of Canaan. When it was first called Hebron, is uncertain; some think, not till it was conquered by Caleb, and that he called it so from his son of that name. But Calmet is of opinion that the name of Hebron is more ancient; and that Caleb, to do honour to his son, named him after this ancient and celebrated place. Hebron was situated upon an eminence, twenty miles southward from Jerusalem, and twenty miles north from Beersheba. Abraham, Sarah, and Isaac were buried near Hebron, in the cave of Machpelah, or the double cave, which Abraham bought of Ephron, Genesis xxiii, 7–9. Hebron was the allotment of Judah. The Lord assigned it for the inheritance of Caleb, Joshua xiv, 13; x, 3, 23, 37. Joshua first took Hebron, and killed the king, whose name was Hoham. But afterward Caleb again made a conquest of it, assisted by the troops of his tribe, and the valour of Othniel, Judges i, 12, 13. It was appointed to be a dwelling for priests, and declared to be a city of refuge, Joshua xxi, 13. David, after the death of Saul, fixed the seat of his government there, 2

Sam. ii, 2–5. At Hebron, Absalom began his rebellion, 2 Sam. xv, 7, 8, &c. During the captivity of Babylon, the Edomites having invaded the southern parts of Judea, made themselves masters of Hebron; hence Josephus sometimes makes it a part of Edom. Here Zacharias and Elizabeth are believed to have dwelt; and it is supposed to have been the birth place of John the Baptist. Hebron is now called El Khalil; though not a town of large dimensions, it has a considerable population. According to Ali Bey, it contains about four hundred families of Arabs; but he does not notice either the Jews, who are numerous, or the Turks. He describes it as situated on the slope of a mountain, and having a strong castle. Provisions, he says, are abundant, and there is a considerable number of shops. The streets are winding, and the houses unusually high. The country is well cultivated, to a considerable extent. Hebron is computed to be twenty-seven miles south-west of Jerusalem.

HEIFER, a young cow, used in sacrifice at the temple, Num. xix, 1–10. Moses and Aaron were instructed to deliver the divine command to the children of Israel that they should procure "a red heifer, without spot," that is, one that was entirely red, without one spot of any other colour; "free from blemish, and on which the yoke had never yet come," that is, which had never yet been employed in ploughing the ground or in any other work; for according to the common sense of all mankind, those animals which had been made to serve other uses, became unfit to be offered to God,--a sentiment which we find in Homer and other Heathen writers. The animal was to be delivered to the priest, who was to lead her forth out of the camp, and there to slay her: the priest was then to take of the blood with his finger, and sprinkle it seven times before the tabernacle, and afterward to burn the carcass: then to take cedar wood and hyssop, and scarlet wood, and cast them into the flames. The ashes were to be gathered up, and preserved in a secure and clean place, for the use of the congregation, by the sprinkling of which ashes in water, it became a water of separation, by means of which a typical or ceremonial purification for sin was effected, Heb. ix, 13.

HELIOPOLIS. See On.

HELL. This is a Saxon word, which is derived from a verb which signifies TO HIDE or CONCEAL. A late eminent Biblical critic, Dr. Campbell, has investigated this subject with his usual accuracy; and the following is the substance of his remarks. In the Hebrew Scriptures the word SHEOL frequently occurs, and uniformly, he thinks, denotes the state of the dead in general, without regard to the virtuous or vicious characters of the persons, their happiness or misery. In translating that word, the **LXX** have almost invariably used the Greek term ἅιδης, HADES, which means the receptacle of the dead, and ought rarely to have been translated HELL, in the sense in which we now use it, namely, as the place of torment. To denote this latter object, the New Testament writers always make use of the Greek word γέεννα, which is compounded of two Hebrew words, GE HINNOM, that is, "The Valley of Hinnom," a place near Jerusalem, in which children were cruelly sacrificed by fire to Moloch, the idol of the Ammonites, 2 Chron. xxxiii, 6. This place was also called TOPHET, 2 Kings xxiii, 10, alluding, as is supposed, to the noise of drums, (TOPH signifying a drum,) there raised to drown the cries of helpless infants. As in process of time this place came to be considered an emblem of hell, or the place of torment reserved for the punishment of the wicked in a future state, the name TOPHET came gradually to be used in this sense, and at length to be confined to it. In this sense, also, the word GEHENNA, a synonymous term, is always to be understood in the New Testament, where it occurs about a dozen times. The confusion that has arisen on this subject has been occasioned not only by our English translators having rendered the Hebrew word SHEOL and the Greek word GEHENNA frequently by the term HELL; but the Greek word HADES, which occurs eleven times in the New Testament, is, in every instance, except one, translated by the same English word, which it ought never to have been. In the following passages of the Old Testament it seems, however, that a future world of wo is expressed by SHEOL: "They," the wicked, "spend their days in wealth, and in a moment go down to SHEOL," Job xxi, 13. "The wicked shall be turned into SHEOL, and all the nations that forget God," Psalm ix, 17, 18. "Her feet go down to death, her steps take hold on SHEOL," Prov. v, 5. "But he knoweth not that the ghosts are there, and that her guests are in the depths of sheol," Prov. ix, 18. "Thou shalt beat him with a rod, and shalt deliver his soul from SHEOL," Prov. xxiii, 14. Thus, as Stuart observes, in his "Essay on Future Punishment," while the Old Testament employs SHEOL, in most cases to designate the grave, the region of the dead, the place of departed spirits, it employs it also, in some cases, to designate along with this idea the adjunct one of the place of misery, place of punishment, region of wo]. In this respect it accords fully with the New Testament use of HADES. For though HADES signifies the grave, and often the invisible region of separate spirits, without reference to their condition, yet, in Luke xvi, 23, "In hades ἐν τῷ ᾅδῃ, he lifted up his eyes, being in torments," it is clearly used for a place and condition of misery. The word HELL is also used by our translators for GEHENNA, which means the world of future punishment, "How shall ye escape the damnation of hell, κρίσεως τῆς γεέννης?"

Hell, GATES OF. See Gates.

HELLENISTS. On this appellation, Dr. Jennings observes, There is a very remarkable appellation which the Apostle Paul, after glorying in his being "of the stock of Israel, and of the tribe of Benjamin," applies to himself, namely, that he was "a Hebrew of the Hebrews," Phil. iii, 5. By this expression Godwin understands a Hebrew both by father's and mother's side. But if this be all that the phrase imports, there seems to be very little occasion for the Apostle's using it immediately after having declared, that he was "of the stock of Israel, and the tribe of Benjamin;" which, on Godwin's supposition, is the same as a Hebrew of the Hebrews; for the Jews were not allowed to marry out of their own nation; or if they sometimes married proselytes, yet their number was comparatively so small among them, especially while they were under oppression, as they were at that time by the Romans, that methinks Paul would hardly have mentioned it as a distinguishing privilege and honour, that neither of his parents were proselytes. It is therefore a much more probable sense, that a Hebrew of the Hebrews signifies a Hebrew both by nation and language, which multitudes of Abraham's posterity, in those days, were not; or one of the Hebrew Jews, who performed their public worship in the Hebrew tongue; for such were reckoned more honourable than the Hellenistic Jews, who in their dispersion having, in a manner, lost the Hebrew, used the Greek language IN SACRIS, and read the Scripture out of the Septuagint version. We meet with this distinction among the converted Jews, in the Acts of the Apostles: "In those days, when the number of the disciples was multiplied, there arose a murmuring of the Grecians or Hellenists against the Hebrews," Acts vi, 1. This is what St. Paul probably meant by his being a Hebrew, as distinguished from an Israelite: "Are they Hebrews? So am I. Are they Israelites? So am I," 2 Corinthians xi, 22. In one sense, these were convertible terms, both signifying Jews by nation and religion; but in the sense just mentioned, there were many, in those days, who were Israelites, but not Hebrews. St. Paul was both, not only an Israelite by birth, but a Hebrew, and not a Hellenistic Jew. Godwin expresses himself inaccurately, when he says that those who lived in Palestine, and who, as using the Hebrew text in their public worship, were opposed to the Ἑλληνιςαί, are called Hebrews, or Jews. For, though Hebrew and Jew are convertible terms, when opposed to Gentiles, as denoting the seed of Abraham, and professors of the Mosaic religion, see Jer. xxxiv, 9; yet, as opposed to the Ἑλληνιςαὶ, they are not convertible terms, there being Hebrew Jews and Hellenistic Jews; for it is said, that when "they, who were scattered by the persecution that arose about Stephen, travelled into several countries, preaching the word to none but Jews only," yet they spoke, ϖρος τοὺς Ἑλληνιςὰς, to the Hellenists or Grecians, Acts xi, 19, 20. In order to confirm the sense which is here given of the word Ἑλληνιςαὶ, in opposition to the appellation Hebrews, it is proper we should take notice of the distinction between the Ἕλληνες and Ἑλληνιςαὶ. The former were Greeks by nation, and as such distinguished from Jews, Acts xvi, 1; xix, 10; and the Greek empire having been rendered by Alexander in a manner universal, and their language being then the most common and general, the appellation Greeks is sometimes given to the whole Heathen world, or to all who were not Jews, Rom. i, 16; ii, 9. These Greeks, called Ἑλληνικοὶ by Josephus, are always styled Ἕελληνες in the New Testament. On which account Grotius, understanding by the Ἑλληνιςαὶ, or "Grecians, to whom some of those who were dispersed on the persecution which arose about Stephen, preached the Lord Jesus," Acts xi, 19, 20, Greeks by nation, concludes there is a mistake in the text, and alters it according to the Syriac and Vulgate versions: "CERTÈ LEGENDUM," [it ought certainly to be read,] saith he, "ϖρος τοὺς Ἕλληνας." So indeed the Alexandrian manuscript reads, but it is supported by no other copy. And this is decisive against it--that from the words immediately preceding, it is evident that these Grecians were by nation Jews, and not Greeks; it being expressly said, that those who were scattered on the persecution "preached the Gospel to the Jews only." As for the Ἕλληνες, or Greeks mentioned in St. John's Gospel, as being come to Jerusalem at the passover to worship in the temple, John xii, 20, and likewise those mentioned in the Acts, as worshipping along with the Jews in the synagogues, Acts xiv, 1; xviii, 4; they were doubtless Greeks by birth and nation, yet proselytes to the Jewish religion. There is a distinction made between Jews and proselytes, Acts ii, 10; but none between Hebrews and proselytes, because a proselyte might be either a Hebrew or a Hellenist, according to the language in which he performed public worship. That the Hellenists or Grecians, were Jews, is farther argued from the account we have, that when at Jerusalem St. Paul "disputed against the Grecians, they went about to slay him," Acts ix, 29, as the Jews at Damascus had done before, Acts ix, 23. Now had these Grecians been strangers of a different nation, it cannot be imagined they durst have attempted to kill a Jew, among his own countrymen, in the capital, and without a formal accusation of him before any of their tribunals. Upon the whole, the Ἑλληνιςαὶ, or Grecians being Jews who used the Greek tongue in their sacred exercises, the Hebrew Jews and Grecian Jews were distinguished in those days, in like manner as the Portuguese and Dutch Jews are among us, not so much by the place of their birth, (many being born in England, others abroad,) as by the language they use in their public prayers and sermons.

Among the wonderful dealings of God, says Dr. Neander, by which the coming of Christianity was prepared, must be placed the spreading of the Jews among the Greeks and Romans. Those among them who belonged to the Pharisees gave themselves much trouble to obtain proselytes; and the loss of respect for the old popular religion, and the unsatisfied religious wants of multitudes, farthered their views. Reverence for the national God of the Jews, as a mighty Being, and reverence for the secret sanctuary of the splendid temple of Jerusalem, had long gained admittance among the Heathen. Jewish goetæ (enchanters, jugglers, &c) permitted themselves to make use of a thousand acts of delusion, in which they were very skilful, to make an impression of astonishment on the minds of those around them. Confidence in Judaism had in consequence made such wide progress, especially in large capital towns, that the Roman writers in the time of the first emperors openly complain of it; and Seneca, in his book upon superstition, said of the Jews, "The conquered have given laws to the conquerors." The Jewish proselyte-makers, "blind leaders of the blind," who had themselves no conception of the real nature, of religion, could give to others no insight into it. They often allowed their converts to take up a kind of dead monotheism, and merely exchange one kind of superstition for another; they taught them, that, by the mere outward worship of one God, and outward ceremonials, they were sure of the grace of God, without requiring any change of life; and they gave to them only new means of silencing their conscience, and new support in the sins which they were unwilling to renounce: and hence our Saviour reproached these proselyte-makers, that they made their converts ten times more the children of hell, than they themselves were. But we must here accurately distinguish between the two classes of proselytes. The proselytes in the strict sense of the word, the proselytes of righteousness, who underwent circumcision and took upon themselves the whole of the ceremonial law, were very different from the proselytes of the gate, who only bound themselves to renounce idolatry, to the worship of the one God, and to abstinence from all Heathenish excess, as well as from every thing which appeared to have any connection with idolatry. The former often embraced all the fanaticism and superstition of the Jews, and allowed themselves to be blindly led by their Jewish teachers. The more difficult it had been to them to subject themselves to the observance of the Jewish ceremonial law, necessarily so irksome to a Greek or a Roman, the less could they find it in their hearts to believe, that all this had been in vain, that they had obtained no advantage by it, and that they must renounce their presumed holiness. What Justin Martyr says to the Jews, holds good of these proselytes: "The proselytes not only do not believe, but they calumniate the name of Christ twice as much as you, and they wish to murder and torture us who believe on him, because they are desirous to resemble you in every thing." The proselytes of the gate, on the contrary, had taken many of the most admirable truths out of Judaism. Without becoming entirely Jews, they had become acquainted with the Holy Scriptures of the Jews, they had heard of the promised messenger from God, of the King armed with power from God, of whom a report had been spread, as Suetonius says in the life of Vespasian, over the whole of the east. Much of that which they had heard from their Jewish teachers, whose writings they had read, had remained dark to them, and they were still to seek in them. By the notions which they had received from the Jews, of one God, of the divine government of the world, of God's judgment, and of the Messiah, they were more prepared for the Gospel than other Heathens; and because they still thought that they had too little, because they had no determined religious system, and were curious after more instruction in divine things, and because they had not received many of the prejudices which swayed the Jews, they were more fitted to receive the Gospel than many of the Jews. From the very beginning they must have been attentive to the preaching of the Gospel, which secured to them, without making them Jews, a full share in the fulfilment of those promises of which the Jews had spoken to them. To these proselytes of the gate, (the φοβούμενοι τὸν Θεὸν, the εὐσεβεῖς of the New Testament,) passed, therefore, according to the Acts, the preaching of the Gospel, when it had been rejected by the blinded Jews; and here the seed of the divine word found a fitting soil in hearts desirous of holiness. There were, however, doubtless, among the proselytes of the gate, some who, wanting in proper earnestness in their search after religious truth, only desired, in every case, an easy road to heaven, which did not require any self-denial; and who, in order to be sure of being on the safe side, whether power and truth lay with the Jews or the Heathens, sometimes worshipped in the synagogue of Jehovah, sometimes in the temples of the gods, and who, therefore, fluttered in suspense between Judaism and Heathenism.

HEMLOCK, רוש and ראש, Deut. xxix, 18; xxxii, 32; Psalm lxix, 21; Jer. viii, 14; ix, 15; xxiii, 15; Lam. iii, 5, 19; Hosea x, 4; Amos vi, 12. In the two latter places our translators have rendered the word HEMLOCK in the others, GALL. Hiller supposes it the CENTAUREUM, described by Pliny; but Celsius shows it to be the hemlock. It is evident, from Deut. xxix, 18, that some herb or plant is meant of a malignant or nauseous kind, being there joined with WORMWOOD, and in the margin of our Bibles explained to be "a poisonful herb." In like manner see Jer. viii, 14; ix, 15; and xxiii, 15. In Hosea x, 4, the comparison is to a bitter herb, which, growing among grain, overpowers the useful vegetable, and substitutes a pernicious weed. "If," says the author of "Scripture Illustrated," "the comparison be to a plant growing in the furrows of the field, strictly speaking, then we are much restricted in our plants likely to answer this character; but if we may take the ditches around, or the moist or sunken places within the field also, which I partly suspect, then we may include other plants; and I do not see why hemlock may not be intended. Scheuchzer inclines to this rather than WORMWOOD or AGROSTES, as the **LXX** have rendered it. The prophet appears to mean a vegetable which should appear wholesome, and resemble those known to be salutary, as judgment, when just, properly is; but experience would demonstrate its malignity, as unjust judgment is when enforced. Hemlock is poisonous, and water-hemlock especially; yet either of these may be mistaken, and some of their parts, the root particularly, may deceive but too fatally."

HEN, ὄρνις, 2 Esdras i, 30; Matt. xxiii, 37; Luke xiii, 34. In these last two passages our Saviour exclaims, "O Jerusalem, Jerusalem, how often would I have gathered thy children together, even as a hen gathereth her chickens under her wings, and ye would not!" The metaphor here used is a very beautiful one. When the hen sees a bird of prey coming, she makes a noise to assemble her chickens, that she may cover them with her wings from the danger. The Roman eagle was about to fall upon the Jewish state; our Lord invited them to himself in order to guard them from threatened calamities: they disregarded his invitations and warnings, and fell a prey to their adversaries. The affection of the hen to her brood is so strong as to have become proverbial. There is a beautiful Greek epigram in the Anthologia, which affords a very fine illustration of the affection of this bird in another view. It has been thus translated:--

"Beneath her fostering wing the hen defends

Her darling offspring, while the snow descends;

And through the winter's day unmoved defies

The chilling fleeces and inclement skies;

Till vanquish'd by the cold and piercing blast,

True to her charge she perishes at last."

Plutarch, in his book *De Philostorgiâ*, represents this parental attachment and care in a very pleasing manner: "Do we not daily observe with what care the hen protects her chickens; giving some shelter under her wings, supporting others upon her back, calling them around her, and picking out their food; and if any animal approaches that terrifies them, driving it away with a courage and strength truly wonderful?"

HENOTICON, a decree or edict of the Emperor Zeno, which was dated at Constantinople in the year 482, and by which he intended to unite all the parties in religion under one faith. For this reason the decree was called HENOTICON, which signifies "union" or "uniting." It is generally agreed that it was published by the advice of Acacius, bishop of Constantinople, who wished to reconcile the contending parties. This decree repeated and confirmed all that had been enacted in the councils of Nice, Constantinople, Ephesus, and Chalcedon, against the Arians, Nestorians, and Eutychians, without particularly mentioning the council of Chalcedon. The HENOTICON was approved by all those of the two contending parties who were remarkable for their candour and moderation; but it was opposed by the violent and obstinate, who complained that it was injurious to the honour and authority of the most holy council of Chalcedon. Hence arose new contests and new divisions not less deplorable than those which this decree was intended to suppress. The Catholics opposed it with all their strength; and it was condemned in form by Pope Felix **II**.

HERESY, HÆRESIS, αἵρεσις, from αἱρέω, I CHOOSE, signifies an error in some essential point of Christian faith, publicly avowed, and obstinately maintained; or, according to the legal definition, "SENTENTIA RERUM DIVINARUM HUMANO SENSU EXCOGITATA, PALAM DOCTA, ET PERTINACITER DEFENSA." [An opinion of divine things invented by human reason, openly taught, and obstinately defended.] Among the ancients, the word HERESY appears to have had nothing of that odious signification which has been attached to it by ecclesiastical writers in later times. It only signified a peculiar opinion, dogma, or sect, without conveying any reproach; being indifferently used, either of a party approved, or of one disapproved, by the writer. In this sense they spoke of the heresy of the Stoics, of the Peripatetics, Epicureans, &c, meaning the sect or peculiar system of these philosophers. In the historical part of the New Testament, the word seems to bear very nearly the same signification, being employed indiscriminately to denote a sect or party, whether good or bad. Thus we read of the sect or heresy of the Sadducees, of the Pharisees, of the Nazarenes, &c. See Acts v, 17; xv, 5; xxiv, 5; xxvi, 5; xxviii, 22. In the two former of these passages, the term HERESY seems to be adopted by the sacred historian merely for the sake of distinction, without the least appearance of any intention to convey either praise or blame. In Acts xxvi, 4, 5, St. Paul, in defending himself before King Agrippa, uses the same term, when it was manifestly his design to exalt the party to which he had belonged, and to give their system the preference over every other system of Judaism, both with regard to soundness of doctrine and purity of morals.

2. It has been suggested that the acceptation of the word αἵρεσις in the epistles is different from what it has been observed to be in the historical books of the New Testament. In order to account for this difference, it may be observed that the word SECT has always something relative in it; and therefore, although the general import of the term be the same, it will convey a favourable or an unfavourable idea, according to the particular relation which it bears in the application. When it is used along with the proper name, by way of distinguishing one party from another, it conveys neither praise nor reproach. If any thing reprehensible or commendable be meant, it is suggested, not by the word αἵρεσις itself, but by the words with which it stands connected in construction. Thus we may speak of a strict sect, or a lax sect; or of a good sect, or a bad sect. Again: the term may be applied to a party formed in a community, when considered in reference to the whole. If the community be of such a nature as not to admit of such a subdivision, without impairing or corrupting its constitution, a charge of splitting into sects, or forming parties, is equivalent to a charge of corruption in that which is most essential to the existence and welfare of the society. Hence arises the whole difference in the word, as it is used in the historical part of the New Testament, and in the epistles of St. Peter and St. Paul; for these are the only Apostles who employ it. In the history, the reference is always of the first kind; in the epistles, it is always of the second. In these last, the Apostles address themselves only to Christians, and either reprehend them for, or warn them against, forming sects among themselves, to the prejudice of charity, to the production of much mischief within their community, and of great scandal to the unconverted world without. In both applications, however, the radical import of the word is the same; and even in the latter it has no necessary reference to doctrine, true or false. During the early ages of Christianity, the term HERESY gradually lost the innocence of its original meaning, and came to be applied, in a reproachful sense, to any corruption of what was considered as the orthodox creed, or even to any departure from the established rites and ceremonies of the church.

3. The heresies chiefly alluded to in the apostolical epistles are, first, those of the Judaizers, or rigid adherents to the Mosaic rites, especially that of circumcision; second, those of converted Hellenists, or Grecian Jews, who held the Greek eloquence and philosophy in too high an estimation, and corrupted, by the speculations of the latter, the simplicity of the Gospel; and third, those who endeavoured to blend Christianity with a mixed philosophy of magic, demonology,

and Platonism, which was then highly popular in the world. With respect to the latter, the remarks of Hug will tend to illustrate some passages in the writings of St. Paul:--Without being acquainted with the notions of those teachers who caused the Apostle so much anxiety and so much vexation, a considerable part of these treatises must necessarily remain dark and unintelligible. From the criteria by which the Apostle points them out, at one time some deemed that they recognised the Gnostics; others perceived none but the Essenes; and every one found arguments for his assertions from the similarity of the doctrines, opinions, and morals. It would, however, be as difficult to prove that the Gnostic school had at that time indeed perfectly developed itself, as it is unjust to charge the Essenes with that extreme of immorality of which St. Paul accused these seducers, since the contemporaries and acquaintances of this Jewish sect mention them with honour and respect, and extol its members as the most virtuous men of their age. The similarity of the principles and opinions, which will have been observed in both parties compared with St. Paul's declarations, flows from a common source, from the philosophy of that age, whence both the one and the other have derived their share. We shall therefore go less astray, if we recede a step, and consider the philosophy itself, as the general modeller of these derivative theories. It found its followers among Judaism as well as among the Heathens; it both introduced its speculative preparations into Christianity, and endeavoured to unite them or to adjust them to it, as well as they were able, by which means Christianity would have become deformed and unlike to itself, and would have been merged in the ocean of philosophical reveries, unless the Apostles had on this occasion defended it against the follies of men. An oriental, or, as it is commonly called, a Babylonian or Chaldean, doctrinal system had already long become known to the Greeks, and even to the Romans, before Augustus, and still more so in the Augustan age, and was in the full progress of its extension over Asia and Europe. It set up different deities and intermediate spirits in explanation of certain phenomena of nature, for the office of governing the world, and for the solution of other metaphysical questions, which from time immemorial were reckoned among the difficult propositions of philosophy. The practical part of this system was occupied with the precepts by means of which a person might enter into communication with these spirits or demons. But the result which they promised to themselves from this union with the divine natures, was that of acquiring, by their assistance, superhuman knowledge, that of predicting future events, and of performing supernatural works. These philosophers were celebrated under the name of magi and Chaldeans; who, for the sake of better accommodating themselves to the western nations, modified their system after the Greek forms, and then, as it appears, knew how to unite it with the doctrine of Plato, from whence afterward arose the Neo-Platonic and in Christendom the Gnostical school. These men forced their way even to the throne. Tiberius had received instruction in their philosophy, and was very confident that by means of an intelligence with the demons, it was possible to learn and perform extraordinary things. Nero caused a great number of them to be brought over from Asia, not unfrequently at the expense of the provinces. The supernatural spirits would not always appear, yet he did not discard his belief of them. The magi and Chaldeans were the persons who were consulted on great undertakings, who, when conspiracies arose, predicted the issue; who invoked spirits, prepared offerings, and in love affairs were obliged to afford aid from their art. Even the force of the laws, to which recourse was frequently necessary to be had at Rome, tended to nothing but the augmentation of their authority. As they found access and favour with people of all classes in the capital, so did they also in the provinces. Paul found a magus at the court of the proconsul at Paphos, Acts xiii, 6. Such was that Simon in Samaria, Acts viii, 10, who was there considered as a higher being of the spiritual class. The expression is remarkable, as it is a part of the technical language of the Theurgists; they called him Δύναμις τοῦ Θεοῦ μεγάλη, "The great power of God." So also Pliny calls some of the demons and intermediate spirits, by whose coöperation particular results were effected, POTESTATES. [Powers.] Justin Martyr, the fellow countryman of Simon, has preserved to us some technical expressions of his followers. He says that they ascribed to him the high title ὑπεράνω πάσης ἀρχῆς, καὶ ἐξουσίας, καὶ δυνάμεως. [Far above all principality, and power, and might.] Of these classes of spirits, which appear under such different appellations, the superior were those who ruled; but the inferior, who had more of a material substance, and who, on that account, were able to connect themselves immediately with matter, were those who executed the commands of the superior. By an intelligence with the superior spirits a person might have the subaltern at his service and assistance; for the more powerful demons thus commanded the inferior to execute certain commissions in the material world: Ἐν τῷ ἄρχοντι τῶν δαιμονίων, "By the prince of the devils," Matt. xii, 24.

4. The Syrian philosopher, Jamblichus, of Chalcis, has furnished us with a circumstantial representation of this system and its several varieties, in his book on the mysteries of the Chaldeans and Egyptians:--The nature of the gods is a pure, spiritual, and perfect unity. With this highest and perfect immateriality no influence on matter is conceivable, consequently, no creation and dominion of the world. Certain subordinate deities must therefore be admitted, which are more compounded in their nature, and can act upon gross matter. These are the "creators of the world," δημίουργοι, and the "rulers of the world," κοσμοκράτορες. The superior deities are, however, the real cause of all that exists; and from their fulness, from their πλήρωμα, it derives its existence. The succession from the highest deities down to the lowest is not by a sudden descent, but by a continually graduating decrease from the highest, pure, and spiritual natures, down to those which are more substantial and material, which are the nearest related to the gross matter of the creation, and which consequently possess the property of acting upon it. In proportion to their purer quality, or coarser composition, they occupy different places as their

residence, either in a denser atmosphere, or in higher regions. The highest among these classes of spirits are called ἄρχαι, or, ἀρχικὸν ἀιτιόν. Others among the "divine natures," θείαι οὐσίαι, are "intermediate beings," μέσαι. Those which occupy themselves with the laws of the world are also called ἄρχοντες, and "the ministering spirits" are δύναμεις and ἄγγελοι. The archangels are not generally recognised in this theory; this class is said to have been of a later origin, and to have been first introduced by Porphyry. (See ARCHANGEL.) If we take here also into consideration the ἐξουσίαι, of which Justin has before spoken, we shall have enumerated the greater part of the technical appellations of this demonology. But to arrive at a union with the higher orders of the spiritual world, in which alone the highest bliss of man consists, it is necessary, before all things, to become disengaged from the servitude of the body, which detains the soul from soaring up to the purely spiritual. Matrimony, therefore, and every inclination to sexual concupiscence, must be renounced before the attainment of this perfection. Hence, the offerings and initiations of the magi cannot, without great injury, be even communicated to those who have not as yet emancipated themselves from the LIBIDO PROCREANDI, and the propensities to corporeal attachments. To eat meat, or to partake in general of any slain animal, nay, to even touch it, contaminates. Bodily exercises and purifications, though not productive of the gifts of prophecy, are nevertheless conducive to them. Though the gods only attend to the pure, they nevertheless sometimes mislead men to impure, actions. This may perhaps proceed from the totally different ideas of that which is good and righteous, which subsist between them and mankind.

5. This philosophy of which the elements had already existed a long time in the east, formed itself, in its progress to the west, into a doctrinal system, which found there far more approbation and celebrity than it ever had deserved. It was principally welcome in those countries, to which the epistles of the Apostle are directed. When St. Paul had preached at Ephesus, a quantity of magical and theurgical books were brought forward by their possessors and burned before his eyes, Acts xix, 19. This city had long since been celebrated for them, and the Ἐφέσια ἀλεξιφάρμακα, and Ἐφέσια γράμματα, were spells highly extolled by the ancients for the purpose of procuring an authority over the demons. As late even as the fourth century, the synod at Laodicea was obliged to institute severe laws against the worship of angels, against magic, and against incantations. These opinions had taken such a deep root in the mind, that some centuries did not suffice for the extinction of the recollection of them. Now, there are passages in the Apostle which strikingly characterize this theory. He calls the doctrinal system of his opponents φιλοσοφία οὐ κατὰ Χριϛὸν, "a philosophy incompatible with Christianity," Col. ii, 8; θρησκειά τῶν ἀγγέλων, "a worship of angels," Col. ii, 18; διδασκαλίαι δαιμονίων, "a demonology," 1 Tim. iv, 1. He calls it still farther γοητεία, 2 Tim. iii, 13. This is the peculiar expression by which the ancients denoted magical arts and necromantic experiments; γόης is, according to Hesychius, μάγος, κόλαξ, ϖερίεργος, and γοητεύει, ἀπατᾶ μαγεύει, φαρμακεύει, ἐξᾴιδει. λ. St. Paul compares these teachers to Jannes and Jambres, 2 Timothy iii, 8. These two persons are, according to the ancient tradition, the magicians who withstood Moses by their arts. They were from time immemorial names so notorious in the magical science, that they did not remain unknown even to the Neo-Platonics. When the Apostle enjoins the Ephesians to array themselves in the arms of faith, and courageously to endure the combat, Ephes. vi, 12, he says that it is the more necessary, because their combat is not against human force, οὐ ϖρὸς [not against] ἅιμα καὶ σάρκα, "flesh and blood," but against superhuman natures. Where he mentions these, he enumerates in order the names of this magico-spiritual world, ἀρχὰς, ἐξουσίας, particularly the κοσμοκράτορας, "principalities," "powers," "rulers;" and likewise fixes their abode in the upper aërial regions, εἰς τὸν ἀέρα ἐν τοῖς ἐπουρανίοις. In like manner, in the Epistle to the Colossians, for the sake of representing to them Christianity in an exalted and important light, and of praising the divine nature of Jesus, he says, that all that exists is his creation, and is subjected to him, not even the spiritual world excepted. He then selects the philosophic appellations to demonstrate that this supposititious demonocracy is wholly subservient to him; whether they be θρόνοι, or κυριότητες, ἀρχαὶ ἐξουσίαι, [thrones, dominions, principalities, powers,] Col. i, 16. Finally, to destroy completely and decisively the whole doctrinal system, he demonstrates, that Christ, through the work of redemption, has obtained the victory over the entire spiritual creation, that he drags in triumph the ἀρχὰς [principalities] and ἐξουσίας [powers] as vanquished, and that henceforth their dominion and exercise of power have ceased, Col. ii, 15. But what he says respecting the seared consciences of these heretics, respecting their deceptions, their avarice, &c, is certainly more applicable to this class of men, than to any other. None throughout all antiquity are more accused of these immoralities, than those pretended confidents of the occult powers. If he speaks warmly against any distinction of meats, against abstinence from matrimony, this also applies to them; and if he rejects bodily exercises, it was because they recommended them, because they imposed baths, lustrations, continence, and long preparations, as the conditions by which alone the connection with the spirits became possible. These, then, are the persons who passed before the Apostle's mind, and who, when they adopted Christianity, established that sect among the professors of Jesus, which gave to it the name of Gnostics, and which, together with the different varieties of this system, is accused by history of magical arts. Other adherents of this system among the Heathens, to which the Syrian philosophers, as well as some Egyptian, such as Plotinus and his scholars, belonged, formed the sect of Neo-Platonism.

6. But in the above remarks of this learned German, some considerations are wanting, necessary to the right understanding of several of the above passages quoted from St. Paul. The philosophic system above mentioned was built

on the Scripture doctrine of good and evil angels, and so had a basis of truth, although abused to a gross superstition, and even idolatry. It was grounded, too, upon the notion of different orders among both good and evil spirits, with subordination and government; which also is a truth of which some intimation is given in Scripture. The Apostle then could use all these terms without giving any sanction to the errors of the day. He knew that the spiritual powers they had converted into subordinate deities, were either good or evil angels in their various ranks, and he uproots the whole superstition, by showing that the "thrones and dominions" of heaven are submissive created servants of Christ; and that the evil spirits, the rulers of "the darkness of this world," are put under his feet.

HERMON, a celebrated mountain in the Holy Land, often spoken of in Scripture. It was in the northern boundary of the country, beyond Jordan, and in the territories which originally belonged to Og, king of Bashan, Joshua xii, 5; xiii, 5. The Psalmist connects Tabor and Hermon together, upon more than one occasion, Psalm lxxxix, 12; cxxxiii, 3; from which it may be inferred that they lay contiguous to each other. This is agreeable to the account that is given us by travellers. Mr. Maundrell, in his journey from Aleppo, says that in three hours and a half from the river Kishon, he came to a small brook near which was an old village and a good kane, called Legune; not far from which his company took up their quarters for the night, and from whence they had an extensive prospect of the plain of Esdraëlon. At about six or seven hours' distance eastward, stood, within view, Nazareth, and the two mountains Tabor and Hermon. He adds that they were sufficiently instructed by experience what the holy Psalmist means by the dew of Hermon; their tents being as wet with it as if it had rained all night, Psalm cxxxiii, 3.

HEROD, surnamed the Great, king of the Jews, second son of Antipater the Idumean, born B. C. 71. At the age of twenty-five he was made by his father governor of Galilee, and distinguished himself by the suppression of a band of robbers, with the execution of their leader, Hezekiah, and several of his comrades. As he had performed this act of heroism by his own authority, and had executed the culprits without the form of trial, he was summoned before the sanhedrim, but, through the strength of his party and zeal of his friends, he escaped any censure. In the civil war between the republican and Cæsarian parties, Herod joined Cassius, and was made governor of Cœlo-Syria; and when Mark Antony arrived victorious in Syria, Herod and his brother found means to ingratiate themselves with him, and were appointed as tetrarchs in Judea; but in a short time an invasion of Antigonus, who was aided by the Jews, obliged Herod to make his escape from Jerusalem, and retire first to Idumea, and then to Egypt. He at length arrived at Rome, and obtained the crown of Judea upon occasion of a difference between the two branches of the Asmodean family. Hyrcanus had been for a considerable time prince and high priest of the Jewish nation; but while the Roman empire was in an unsettled state, after the death of Julius Cæsar, Antigonus, son of Aristobulus, brother of Hyrcanus, made himself master of the city and all Judea. In this state Herod found things when he came to Rome, and the most that he then aimed at was to obtain the kingdom for Aristobulus, his wife's brother; but the senate of Rome, moved by the recommendations of Mark Antony, conferred the kingdom of Judea upon Herod himself. Having met with this unexpected success at Rome, he returned without delay to Judea, and in about three years got possession of the whole country. He had, however, to fight his way to the throne, which, as we have seen, was in the possession of Antigonus. Though aided by the Roman army, he was obliged to lay siege to Jerusalem, which held out for six months, when it was carried by assault, and a vast slaughter was made of the inhabitants, till the intercession and bribes of Herod put an end to it. Antigonus was taken prisoner and put to death, which opened the way to Herod's quiet possession of the kingdom. His first cares were to replenish his coffers, and to repress the faction still attached to the Asmodean race, and which regarded him as a usurper. He was guilty of many extortions and cruelties in the pursuit of these objects. Shortly after this, an accusation was lodged against Herod before Mark Antony by Cleopatra, who had been influenced to the deed by his mother-in-law, Alexandra. He was summoned to answer to the charges exhibited against him before the triumvir; and on this occasion he gave a most remarkable display of the conflict of opposite passions in a ferocious heart. Doatingly fond of his wife, Mariamne, and not being able to bear the thought of her falling into the hands of another, he exacted a solemn promise from Joseph, whom he appointed to govern in his absence, that should the accusation prove fatal to him he would put the queen to death. Joseph disclosed the secret to Mariamne, who, abhorring such a savage proof of his love, from that moment conceived the deepest and most settled aversion to her husband. Herod, by great pecuniary sacrifices, made his peace with Antony, and returned in high credit. Some hints were thrown out respecting Joseph's familiarity with Mariamne during his absence; he communicated his suspicions to his wife, who, recriminating, upbraided him with his cruel order concerning her. His rage was unbounded; he put Joseph to death for communicating the secret entrusted to him alone, and he threw his mother-in-law, Alexandra, into prison.

2. In the war between Antony and Octavius, Herod raised an army for the purpose of joining the former; but he was obliged first to engage Malchus, king of Arabia, whom he defeated and obliged to sue for peace. After the battle of Actium, his great object was to make terms with the conqueror; and, as a preliminary step, he put to death Hyrcanus, the only surviving male of the Asmodeans; and, having secured his family, he embarked for Rhodes, where Augustus at that time was. He appeared before the master of the Roman world in all the regal ornaments excepting his diadem, and with a noble confidence related the faithful services he had performed for his benefactor, Antony, concluding that he was ready to transfer the same gratitude to a new patron, from whom he should hold his crown and

kingdom. Augustus was struck with the magnanimity of the defence, and replaced the diadem on the head of Herod, who remained the most favoured of the tributary sovereigns. When the emperor afterward travelled through Syria, in his way to and from Egypt, he was entertained with the utmost magnificence by Herod; in recompense for which he restored to him all his revenues and dominions, and even considerably augmented them. His good fortune as a prince, was poisoned by domestic broils, and especially by the insuperable aversion of Mariamne, whom at length he brought to trial, convicted, and executed. She submitted to her fate with all the intrepidity of innocence, and was sufficiently avenged by the remorse of her husband, who seems never after to have enjoyed a tranquil hour.

3. His rage being quenched, Herod endeavoured to banish the memory of his evil acts from his mind by scenes of dissipation; but the charms of his once loved Mariamne haunted him wherever he went: he would frequently call aloud upon her name, and insist upon his attendants bringing her into his presence, as if willing to forget that she was no longer among the living. At times he would fly from the sight of men, and on his return from solitude, which was ill suited to a mind conscious of the most ferocious deeds, he became more brutal than ever, and in fits of fury spared neither foes nor friends. Alexandra, whose malignity toward her daughter has been noticed, was an unpitied victim to his rage. At length he recovered some portion of self-possession, and employed himself in projects of regal magnificence. He built at Jerusalem a stately theatre and amphitheatre, in which he celebrated games in honour of Augustus, to the great displeasure of the zealous Jews, who discovered an idolatrous profanation in the theatrical ornaments and spectacles. Nothing, it is said, gave them so much offence as some trophies which he had set round his theatre in honour of Augustus, and in commemoration of his victories, but which the Jews regarded as images devoted to the purposes of idol worship. For this and other acts of the king a most serious conspiracy was formed against him, which he, fortunately for himself, discovered; and he exercised the most brutal revenge on all the parties concerned in it. He next built Samaria, which he named Sebaste, and adorned it with the most sumptuous edifices; and for his security he built several fortresses throughout the whole of Judea, of which the principal was called Cæsarea, in honour of the emperor. In his own palace, near the temple of Jerusalem, he lavished the most costly materials and curious workmanship; and his palace Herodion, at some miles' distance from the capital, by the beauty of its situation, and other appropriate advantages, drew round it the population of a considerable city.

4. To supply the place of his lost Mariamne, he married a new wife of the same name, the beautiful daughter of a priest, whom he raised to the high rank of the supreme pontificate. He sent his two sons, by the first Mariamne, to be educated at Rome, and so ingratiated himself with Augustus and his ministers, that he was appointed imperial procurator for Syria. To acquire popularity among the Jews, and to exhibit an attachment to their religion, he undertook the vast enterprise of rebuilding the temple of Jerusalem, which he finished in a noble style of magnificence in about a year and a half. During the progress of this work he visited Rome, and brought back his sons, who had attained to man's estate. These at length conspired against their father's person and government, and were tried, convicted, and executed. Another act deserving of notice, performed by Herod, was the dedication of his new city of Cæsarea, at which time he displayed such profuse magnificence, that Augustus said his soul was too great for his kingdom. Notwithstanding the execution of his sons, he was still a slave to conspiracies from his other near relations. In the thirty-third year of his reign, our Saviour was born. This event was followed, according to the Gospel of St. Matthew, by the massacre of the children of Bethlehem. About this time, Antipater, returning from Rome, was arrested by his father's orders, charged with treasonable practices, and was found guilty of conspiring against the life of the king. This and other calamities, joined to a guilty conscience, preying upon a broken constitution, threw the wretched monarch into a mortal disease, which was doubtless a just judgment of Heaven on the many foul enormities and impieties of which he had been guilty. His disorder was attended with the most loathsome circumstances that can be imagined. A premature report of his death caused a tumult in Jerusalem, excited by the zealots, who were impatient to demolish a golden eagle which he had placed over the gate of the temple. The perpetrators of this rash act were seized, and by order of the dying king, put to death. He also caused his son Antipater to be slain in prison, and his remains to be treated with every species of ignominy. He bequeathed his kingdom to his son Archelaus, with tetrarchies to his two other sons. Herod, on his dying bed, had planned a scheme of horrible cruelty which was to take place at the instant of his own death. He had summoned the chief persons among the Jews to Jericho, and caused them to be shut up in the hippodrome, or circus, and gave strict orders to his sister Salome to have them all massacred as soon as he should have drawn his last breath: "for this," said he, "will provide mourners for my funeral all over the land, and make the Jews and every family lament my death, who would otherwise exhibit no signs of concern." Salome and her husband, Alexas, chose rather to break their oath extorted by the tyrant, than be implicated in so cruel a deed; and accordingly, as soon as Herod was dead, they opened the doors of the circus, and permitted every one to return to his own home. Herod died in the sixty-eighth year of his age. His memory has been consigned to merited detestation, while his great talents, and the active enterprise of his reign, have placed him high in the rank of sovereigns.

Herod Antipas. See Antipas.

HERODIANS, a sect among the Jews at the time of Jesus Christ, mentioned Matt. xxii, 16; Mark iii, 6; viii, 15; xii, 13; but passed over in silence both by Josephus and Philo. The critics and commentators on the New Testament are very much divided with regard to the Herodians; some making them to be a political party, and others a religious sect. The former opinion is favoured by the author of the Syriac version, who calls them the domestics of Herod; and also by Josephus's having passed them over in silence, though he professes to give an account of the several religious sects of the Jews. The latter opinion is countenanced by our Lord's caution against "the leaven of Herod," which implies that the Herodians were distinguished from the other Jews by some doctrinal tenets. M. Basnage supposes, that one thing meant by the leaven of the Herodians might be a conformity to Roman customs in some points which were forbidden the Jews: if this was the case, it is not strange that they are not mentioned by Josephus among the Jewish sects. St. Jerom, in his Dialogue against the Luciferians, takes the name to have been given to such as owned Herod for the Messiah; and Tertullian, Epiphanius, Chrysostom, and Theophylact, among the ancients; and Grotius, and other moderns, are of the same sentiment. But the same St. Jerom, in his Comment on St. Matthew, treats this opinion as ridiculous; and indeed it must be highly improbable. He maintains that the Pharisees gave this appellation, by way of derision, to Herod's soldiers, who paid tribute to the Romans; agreeably to which the Syriac interpreters render the word by the domestics of Herod, that is, his courtiers. M. Simon, in his notes on the twenty-second chapter of St. Matthew, advances a more probable opinion. The name Herodian, he imagines to have been given to such as adhered to Herod's party and interest, and were for preserving the government in his family, about which there were, at that time, great divisions among the Jews. F. Hardouin will have the Herodians and Sadducees to have been the same; nor is it at all improbable that the Herodians were chiefly of the sect of the Sadducees; since that which is called by St. Mark "the leaven of Herod," is by St. Matthew styled "the leaven of the Sadducees."

2. Dr. Prideaux is of opinion that they derived their name from Herod the Great, and that they were distinguished from the other Jews by their concurrence with Herod's scheme of subjecting himself and his dominions to the Romans, and likewise by complying with many of their Heathen usages and customs. In their zeal for the Roman authority they were diametrically opposite to the Pharisees, who esteemed it unlawful to submit or pay taxes to the Roman emperor; an opinion which they grounded on their being forbidden by the law to set a stranger over them, who was not one of their own nation, as their king. The conjunction of the Herodians, therefore, with the Pharisees, against Christ, is a memorable proof of the keenness of their resentment and malice against him; especially when we consider that they united together in proposing to him an ensnaring question, on a subject which was the ground of their mutual dissension; namely, whether it was lawful to pay tribute to Cæsar. And provided he answered in the negative, the Herodians would accuse him of treason against the state; and should he reply in the affirmative, the Pharisees were as ready to excite the people against him, as an enemy of their civil liberties and privileges. Herod had introduced several Heathen idolatrous usages; for, as Josephus says, he built a temple to Cæsar, near the head of the river Jordan; he erected a magnificent theatre at Jerusalem, instituted Pagan games, and placed a golden eagle over the gate of the temple of Jehovah; and he furnished the temples, which he reared in several places out of Judea, with images for idolatrous worship, in order to ingratiate himself with the emperor and the people of Rome; though to the Jews he pretended that he did it against his will, and in obedience to the imperial command. The Herodians probably complied with, acquiesced in, or approved these idolatrous usages. This symbolizing with idolatry upon views of interest and worldly policy, was probably that leaven of Herod, against which our Saviour cautioned his disciples.

HERON, אנפה, Lev. xi, 19; Deut. xiv, 18. This word has been variously understood. Some have rendered it the kite, others the woodcock, others the curlieu, some the peacock, others the parrot, and others the crane. The root, אנפ, signifies TO BREATHE SHORT through the nostrils, TO SNUFF, as in anger; hence to be angry; and it is supposed that the word is sufficiently descriptive of the heron, from its very irritable disposition. Bochart, however, thinks it the mountain falcon; the same that the Greeks call ἀνόπαια, mentioned by Homer; and this bears a strong resemblance to the Hebrew name.

HESHBON, a celebrated city beyond Jordan, twenty miles eastward of that river, according to Eusebius. It was given to the tribe of Reuben, Josh. xiii, 17. It was probably made over to Gad, since we meet with it among the cities which were given to the Levites, Joshua xxi, 39.

HETERODOX, formed of the Greek ἑτερόδοξος, a compound of ἕτερος, ALTER, and δόξα, OPINION, something that is contrary to the faith or doctrine established in the true church. Thus, we say, a heterodox opinion, a heterodox divine, &c. The word stands in opposition to orthodox.

HETEROUSH, **HETEROUSIANS**, composed of ἕτερος, and οὐσία, SUBSTANCE, a sect or branch of Arians, the followers of Aëtius, and from him denominated Aëtians. They were called Heterousii, because they held, not that the Son of God was of a substance like, or similar to, that of the Father, which was the doctrine of another branch of Arians, thence called Homoousians, Homoousii; but that he was of another substance different from that of the Father.

HETH, the father of the Hittites, was the eldest son of Canaan, Gen. x, 15, and dwelt southward of the promised land, probably about Hebron. Ephron, who was an inhabitant of that city, was of the race of Heth; and in the time of Abraham the whole city were of the family of Heth.

HEXAPLA, formed of ἕξ, SIX, and ἁπλόω, I OPEN, or UNFOLD, a Bible disposed in six columns, containing the text, and divers versions of it, compiled and published by Origen, with a view of securing the sacred text from future corruptions, and to correct those that had been already introduced. Eusebius relates that Origen after his return from Rome under Caracalla, applied himself to learn Hebrew, and began to collect the several versions that had been made of the sacred writings, and of these to compose his *Tetrapla*, and *Hexapla*: others, however, will not allow him to have begun till the time of Alexander, after he had retired into Palestine, about the year 231. To conceive what this *Hexapla* was, it must be observed that, beside the translation of the sacred writings called the Septuagint, made under Ptolemy Philadelphus, above 280 years B. C., the Scripture had been since translated into Greek by other interpreters. The first of those versions, or, reckoning the Septuagint, the second, was that of Aquila, a proselyte Jew, the first edition of which he published in the twelfth year of the Emperor Adrian, or about A. D. 128; the third was that of Symmachus, published as is commonly supposed, under Marcus Aurelius, but, as some say, under Septimius Severus, about the year 200; the fourth was that of Theodotion, prior to that of Symmachus, under Commodus, or about the year 175: these Greek versions, says Dr. Kennicott, were made by the Jews from their corrupted copies of the Hebrew, and were designed to stand in the place of the **LXX**, against which they were prejudiced, because it seemed to favour the Christians. The fifth was found at Jericho, in the reign of Caracalla, about the year 217; and the sixth was discovered at Nicopolis, in the reign of Alexander Severus, about the year 228: lastly, Origen himself recovered part of a seventh, containing only the Psalms. Now, Origen, who had held frequent disputations with the Jews in Egypt and Palestine, observing that they always objected against those passages of Scripture quoted against them, and appealed to the Hebrew text, the better to vindicate those passages and confound the Jews, by showing that the **LXX** had given the sense of the Hebrew, or rather, to show, by a number of different versions, what the real sense of the Hebrew was, undertook to reduce all these several versions into a body, along with the Hebrew text, so as they might be easily confronted, and afford a mutual light to each other. He made the Hebrew text his standard; and, allowing that corruptions might have happened, and that the old Hebrew copies might and did read differently, he contented himself with marking such words or sentences as were not in his Hebrew text, nor the later Greek versions, and to add such words or sentences as were omitted in the **LXX**, prefixing an asterisk to the additions, and an obelisk to the others. In order to this he made choice of eight columns: in the first he gave the Hebrew text in Hebrew characters; in the second, the same text in Greek characters: the rest were filled with the several versions above mentioned; all the columns answering verse for verse, and phrase for phrase; and in the Psalms there was a ninth column for the seventh version. This work Origen called Ἑξαπλα, *Hexapla*, that is, SEXTUPLE, or a work of six columns, as only regarding the first six Greek versions. Indeed, St. Epiphanius, taking in likewise the two columns of the text, calls the work *Octapla*, as consisting of eight columns. This celebrated work, which Montfaucon imagines consisted of fifty large volumes, perished long ago, probably with the library at Cæsarea, where it was preserved, in the year 653; though several of the ancient writers have preserved us portions of it, particularly St. Chrysostom on the Psalms, Philoponus in his *Hexameron*, &c. Some modern writers have earnestly endeavoured to collect fragments of the *Hexapla*, Flaminius Nobilius, Drusius, and especially Montfaucon, in two folio volumes, printed at Paris in 1713. In his edition, Montfaucon has prefixed prolegomena, explaining the form and detailing the history of the *Hexapla*.

The object of Origen being to correct the differences found in the then existing copies of the Old Testament, he carefully noted all the alterations which he discovered; and for the information of those who might consult his work, he made use of the following marks: 1. Where any passages appeared in the Septuagint, that were not found in the Hebrew, he designated them by an OBELUS ÷ with two bold points **:** annexed. This mark was also used to denote words not extant in the Hebrew, but added by the Septuagint translators, either for the sake of elegance, or for the purpose of illustrating the sense. 2. To passages wanting in the copies of the Septuagint, and supplied by himself from the other Greek versions, he prefixed an asterisk ⁜ with two bold points **:** also annexed, in order that his additions might be immediately perceived. These supplementary passages, we are informed by Jerom, were for the most part taken from Theodotion's translation; not unfrequently from that of Aquila; sometimes, though rarely, from the version of Symmachus; and sometimes from two or three together. But, in every case, the initial letter of each translator's name was placed immediately after the asterisk, to indicate the source whence such supplementary passage was taken. And in lieu of the very erroneous Septuagint version of Daniel, Theodotion's translation of that book was inserted entire. 3. Farther: not only the passages wanting in the Septuagint were supplied by Origen with the asterisks, as above noticed, but also where that version does not appear accurately to express the Hebrew original, having noted the former reading with an OBELUS **:**, he added the correct rendering from one of the other translators, with an asterisk subjoined. Concerning the shape and uses of the LEMNISCUS and HYPOLEMNISCUS, two other marks used by Origen, there is so great a difference of opinion among learned men, that it is difficult to determine what they were. Dr. Owen, after Montfaucon, supposes them to have been marks of better and more accurate renderings. These several marks of distinction have been carefully observed, so far as they have been recovered from various quarters, in the very accurate edition of the Septuagint commenced by our learned countryman, Dr. Holmes, and continued by his able successor, the Rev. J. Parsons, B. D.

For nearly fifty years was Origen's stupendous work buried in a corner of the city of Tyre, probably on account of the very great expense of transcribing forty or fifty volumes, which far exceeded the means of private individuals; and here, perhaps, it might have perished in oblivion, if Eusebius and Pamphilus had not discovered it, and deposited it in the library of Pamphilus the martyr at Cæsarea, where Jerome saw it about the middle of the fourth century. As we have no account whatever of Origen's autograph after this time, it is most probable that it perished in the year 653, on the capture of that city by the Arabs; and a few imperfect fragments, collected from manuscripts of the Septuagint and the catenæ of the Greek fathers, are all that now remain of a work, which, in the present improved state of sacred literature, would most eminently have assisted in the interpretation and criticism of the Old Testament. The Syro-Estrangelo translation of Origen's edition of the Greek Septuagint was executed in the former part of the seventh century; the author of it is not known. This version exactly corresponds with the text of the Septuagint, especially in those passages in which the latter differs from the Hebrew. A manuscript of this translation is in the Ambrosian library at Milan; it contains the OBELUS and other marks of Origen's Hexapla; and a subscription at the end states it to have been literally translated from the Greek copy, corrected by Eusebius himself, with the assistance of Pamphilus, from the books of Origen, which were deposited in the library at Cæsarea. From this version Norberg edited the prophecies of Jeremiah and Ezekiel in 1787; and Bugati, the book of Daniel, 1788.

HEZEKIAH, king of Judah, was the son of Ahaz, and born in the year of the world 3251. At the age of five-and-twenty he succeeded his father in the government of the kingdom of Judah, and reigned twenty-nine years in Jerusalem, namely, from the year of the world 3277 to 3306, 2 Kings xviii, 1, 2; 2 Chron. xxix, 1. The reign of his father Ahaz had been most unpropitious for his subjects. A war had raged between the kingdoms of Israel and Judah, in which Pekah, king of Israel, overthrew the army of Ahaz, destroying a hundred and twenty thousand of his men; after which he carried away two hundred thousand women and children as captives into his own country: they were, however, released and sent home again, at the remonstrance of the Prophet Oded. As idolatry had been established in Jerusalem and throughout Judea, by the command of Ahaz, and the service of the temple either intermitted, or converted into an idolatrous worship, the first object of his son Hezekiah, on his accession to the throne, was to restore the legal worship of God, both in Jerusalem and throughout Judea. He cleansed and repaired the temple, and held a solemn passover. He improved the city, repaired the fortifications, erected magazines of all sorts, and built a new aqueduct. In the fourth year of his reign, Salmanezer, king of Assyria, invaded the kingdom of Israel, took Samaria, and carried away the ten tribes into captivity, replacing them by different people sent from his own country. But Hezekiah was not deterred by this alarming example from refusing to pay that tribute to the Assyrians which had been imposed on Ahaz: this brought on the invasion of Sennacherib, in the fourteenth year of the reign of Hezekiah, of which we have a very particular account in the writings of the Prophet Isaiah, who was then living, Isaiah xxxvi.

Immediately after the termination of this war, Hezekiah "was sick unto death," owing, as the sacred historian strongly intimates, to his heart being improperly elevated on occasion of this miraculous deliverance, and not sufficiently acknowledging the hand of God in it, 2 Kings xx; Isaiah xxxviii. Isaiah was sent to bid him set his house in order, for he should die and not live. Hezekiah had instant recourse to God by prayer and supplications for his recovery; and the prophet had scarcely proceeded out of the threshold, when the Lord commanded him to return to Hezekiah, and to say to him, "Thus saith the Lord, I have heard thy prayer, and I have seen thy tears: I will heal thee: on the third day thou shalt go up to the house of the Lord, and I will add unto thy days fifteen years." And to confirm to him the certainty of all these tokens of the divine regard, the shadow of the sun on the dial of Ahaz, at his request, went backward ten degrees. After his recovery, he composed an ode of thanksgiving to the God of all his mercies, which the Prophet Isaiah has recorded in his writings, Isaiah xxxviii, 10, 11. Yet, as an instance of human fickleness and frailty, we find Hezekiah, with all his excellencies, again forgetting himself, and incurring the divine displeasure. The king of Babylon having been informed of his sickness and recovery, sent ambassadors to congratulate him on his restoration: an honour with which the heart of Hezekiah was greatly elated; and, to testify his gratitude, he made a pompous display to them of all his treasures, his spices, and his rich vessels; and concealed from them nothing that was in his palace. In all this the pride of Hezekiah was gratified; and to humble him, Isaiah was sent to declare to him that his conduct was displeasing to God, and that a time should come when all the treasures of which he had made so vain a display should be removed to Babylon, and even his sons be made eunuchs to serve in the palace of the king of Babylon. Hezekiah bowed submissively to the will of God, and acknowledged the divine goodness toward him, in ordaining peace and truth to continue during the remainder of his reign. He accordingly passed the latter years of his life in tranquillity, and contributed greatly to the prosperity of his people and kingdom. He died in the year of the world 3306, leaving behind him a son, Manasseh, who succeeded him in the throne: a son every way unworthy of such a father.

HIDDEKEL. See Eden.

HIGH PLACES. The prophets reproach the Israelites for nothing with more zeal than for worshipping upon the high places. The destroying of these high places is a commendation given only to few princes in Scripture; and many, though zealous for the observance of the law, had not courage to prevent the people from sacrificing upon these eminences. Before the temple was built, the high places were not absolutely contrary to the law, provided God only was there adored, and not idols. They seem to have been tolerated under the judges; and Samuel offered sacrifices in several places where the ark was not present. Even in David's time they sacrificed to the Lord at Shiloh, Jerusalem, and Gibeon. But after the temple was built at Jerusalem, and the ark had a fixed settlement, it was no longer allowed to sacrifice out of Jerusalem. The high places were much frequented in the kingdom of Israel. The people sometimes went upon those mountains which had been sanctified by the presence of patriarchs and prophets, and by appearances of God, to worship the true God there. This worship was lawful, except as to its being exercised where the Lord had not chosen. But they frequently adored idols upon these hills, and committed a thousand abominations in groves, and caves, and tents; and hence arose the zeal of pious kings and prophets to suppress the high places. Dr. Prideaux thinks it probable that the PROSEUCHÆ, open courts, built like those in which the people prayed at the tabernacle and the temple, were the same as those called high places in the Old Testament. His reason is, that the PROSEUCHÆ had groves in or near them, in the same manner as the high places.

HIN, הין, a liquid measure, as of oil, or of wine, Exodus xxix, 40; xxx, 24; Lev. xxiii. According to Josephus, it contained two Attic CONGII, and was therefore the sixth part of an ephah. He says that they offered with an ox half a hin of oil; in English measure, six pints, twenty-five thousand five hundred and ninety-eight solid inches. With a ram they offered the third part of a hin, or three pints, ten thousand four hundred and sixty-nine solid inches: with a lamb, the fourth part of a hin, or two pints, fifteen thousand and seventy-one solid inches.

HIND, אילה, Gen. xlix, 21; 2 Sam. xxii, 34; Job xxxix, 1; Psalm xviii, 33; xxix, 9; Prov. v, 19; Cant. ii, 7; iii, 5; Jer. xiv, 5; Hab. iii, 19; the mate or female of the stag. It is a lovely creature, and of an elegant shape. It is noted for its swiftness and the sureness of its step as it jumps among the rocks. David and Habakkuk both allude to this character of the hind. "The Lord maketh my feet like hinds' feet, and causeth me to stand on the high places," Psalm xviii, 33; Hab. iii, 19. The circumstance of their standing on the high places or mountains is applied to these animals by Xenophon. Our translators make Jacob, prophesying of the tribe of Naphtali, say, "Naphtali is a hind let loose: he giveth goodly words," Gen. xlix, 21. There is a difficulty and incoherence here which the learned Bochart removes by altering a little the punctuation of the original; and it then reads, "Naphtali is a spreading tree, shooting forth beautiful branches." This, indeed, renders the simile uniform; but another critic has remarked that "the allusion to a tree seems to be purposely reserved by the venerable patriarch for his son Joseph, who is compared to the boughs of a tree; and the repetition of the idea in reference to Naphtali is every way unlikely. Beside," he adds, "the word rendered 'let loose,' imports an active motion, not like that of the branches of a tree, which, however freely they wave, are yet attached to the parent stock; but an emission, a dismission, or sending forth to a distance: in the present case, a roaming, roaming at liberty. The verb 'he giveth' may denote shooting forth. It is used of production, as of the earth, which shoots forth, yields, its increase, Lev. xxvi, 4. The word rendered 'goodly' signifies NOBLE, GRAND, MAJESTIC; and the noun translated 'words' radically signifies DIVERGENCES, what is spread forth." For these reasons he proposes to read the passage, "Naphtali is a deer roaming at liberty; he shooteth forth spreading branches," or "majestic antlers." Here the distinction of imagery is preserved, and the fecundity of the tribe and the fertility of their lot intimated. In our version of Psalm xxix, 9, we read, "The voice of the Lord maketh the hinds to calve, and discovereth the forests." Mr. Merrick, in an ingenious note on the place, attempts to justify the rendering; but Bishop Lowth, in his "Lectures on the Sacred Poetry of the Hebrews," observes that this agrees very little with the rest of the imagery, either in nature or dignity; and that he does not feel himself persuaded, even by the reasonings of the learned Bochart on this subject: whereas the oak, struck with lightning, admirably agrees with the context. The Syriac seems, for אילות, HINDS, to have read אלות, OAKS, or rather, perhaps, TEREBINTHS. The passage may be thus versified:--

"Hark! his voice in thunder breaks,

And the lofty mountain quakes;

Mighty trees the tempests tear,

And lay the spreading forests bare!"

HINNOM, Valley of, called also Tophet, and by the Greeks Gehenna, a small valley on the south-east of Jerusalem, at the foot of Mount Zion, where the Canaanites, and afterward the Israelites, sacrificed their children to the idol Moloch, by making them "pass through the fire," or burning them. To drown the shrieks of the victims thus inhumanly sacrificed, musical instruments, called in the Hebrew TUPH, tympana or timbrels, were played; whence the spot derived the name of Tophet. GE HINNOM, or "The Valley of Hinnom," from which the Greeks framed their Gehenna, is sometimes used in Scripture to denote hell or hell fire. See Hell.

HIRAM, king of Tyre, and son of Abibal, is mentioned by profane authors as distinguished for his magnificence, and for adorning the city of Tyre. When David was acknowledged king by all Israel, Hiram sent ambassadors with artificers, and cedar, to build his palace. Hiram also sent ambassadors to Solomon, to congratulate him on his accession to the crown Solomon desired of him timber and stones for building the temple, with labourers. These Hiram promised, provided Solomon would furnish him with corn and oil. The two princes lived on the best terms with each other.

HIRELING. Moses requires that the hireling should be paid as soon as his work is over: "The wages of him that is hired shall not abide with thee all night unto the morning," Lev. xix, 19. A hireling's days or year is a kind of proverb, signifying a full year, without abating any thing of it: "His days are like the days of a hireling," Job vii, 1; the days of man are like those of a hireling; as nothing is deducted from them, so nothing, likewise is added to them. And again: "Till he shall accomplish as a hireling his day," Job xiv, 6; to the time of death, which he waits for as the hireling for the end of the day. The following passage from Morier's Travels in Persia, illustrates one of our Lord's parables: "The most conspicuous building in Hamadan is the Mesjid Jumah, a large mosque now falling into decay, and before it a maidan or square, which serves as a market place. Here we observed, every morning before the sun rose, that a numerous band of peasants were collected with spades in their hands, waiting, as they informed us, to be hired for the day to work in the surrounding fields. This custom, which I have never seen in any other part of Asia, forcibly struck me as a most happy illustration of our Saviour's parable of the labourers in the vineyard in Matt. xx; particularly when, passing by the same place late in the day, we still found others standing idle, and remembered his words, 'Why stand ye here all the day idle?' as most applicable to their situation; for in putting the very same question to them, they answered us, 'Because no man hath hired us.'"

HITTITES, the descendants of Heth, Gen. xv, 20.

HIVITES, a people descended from Canaan, Gen. x, 17. They are also mentioned, Deut. ii, 23. The inhabitants of Shechem, and the Gibeonites, were Hivites, Joshua xi, 19; Gen. xxxiv, 2. Mr. Bryant supposes the Hivites to be the same as the Ophites, or ancient worshippers of the sun under the figure of a serpent; which was, in all probability, the deity worshipped at Baal-Hermon.

HOLY GHOST, the third person in the Trinity. The orthodox doctrine is, that as Christ is God by an eternal FILIATION, so the Spirit is God by PROCESSION from the Father and the Son. "And I believe in the Holy Ghost," says the Nicene Creed, "the Lord and Giver of life, who PROCEEDETH from the Father and the Son, who, with the Father and the Son together, is worshipped and glorified." And with this agrees the Athanasian Creed, "The Holy Ghost is of the Father and of the Son, neither made, nor created, nor begotten, but PROCEEDING." In the Articles of the English church it is thus expressed: "The Holy Ghost, PROCEEDING from the Father and the Son, is of one substance, majesty, and glory with the Father and the Son, very and eternal God." The Latin church introduced the term SPIRATION, from SPIRO, "to breathe," to denote the manner of this procession: on which Dr. Owen remarks, "As the vital breath of a man has a continual emanation from him, and yet is never separated utterly from his person, or forsaketh him, so doth the Spirit of the Father and the Son proceed from them by a continual divine emanation, still abiding one with them." On this refined view little can be said which has clear Scriptural authority; and yet the very term by which the Third Person in the Trinity is designated, WIND or BREATH, may, as to the Third Person, be designed, like the term SON applied to the Second, to convey, though imperfectly, some intimation of that manner of being by which both are distinguished from each other, and from the Father; and it was a remarkable action of our Lord, and one certainly which does not discountenance this idea, that when he imparted the Holy Ghost to his disciples, "He BREATHED on them, and saith unto them, Receive ye the Holy Ghost," John xx, 22.

2. But, whatever we may think as to the doctrine of SPIRATION, the PROCESSION of the Holy Ghost rests on more direct Scriptural authority, and is thus stated by Bishop Pearson: "Now this procession of the Spirit, in reference to the Father, is delivered expressly in relation to the Son, and is contained virtually in the Scriptures. 1. It is expressly said, that the Holy Ghost proceedeth from the Father, as our Saviour testifieth, 'When the Comforter is come, whom I will send unto you from the Father, even the Spirit of truth, which proceedeth from the Father, he shall testify of me,' John xv, 26. And this is also evident from what hath been already asserted; for being the Father and the Spirit are the same God, and, being so the same in the unity of the nature of God, are yet distinct in the personality, one of them must have the same nature from the other; and because the Father hath been already shown to have it from none, it followeth that the Spirit hath it from him. 2. Though it be not expressly spoken in the Scripture, that the Holy Ghost proceedeth from the Father and Son, yet the substance of the same truth is virtually contained there; because those very expressions which are spoken of the Holy Spirit in relation to the Father, for that reason, because he proceedeth from the Father, are also spoken of the same Spirit in relation to the Son; and therefore there must be the same reason presupposed in reference to the Son, which is expressed in reference to the Father. Because the Spirit proceedeth from the Father, therefore it is called 'the Spirit of God,' and 'the Spirit of the Father.' 'It is not ye that speak, but the Spirit of your Father which speaketh in you,' Matt. x, 20. For by the language of the Apostle, 'the Spirit of God' is the Spirit which is of God, saying, 'The things of God knoweth no man, but the Spirit of God. And we have received not the spirit of the world, but the Spirit which is of God,' 1 Cor. ii, 11, 12. Now the same Spirit is also called 'the Spirit of the Son:' for 'because we are sons, God hath sent forth the Spirit of his Son into our hearts,' Gal. iv, 6. 'The Spirit of Christ:' 'Now if any man have not the Spirit of Christ, he is none of his,' Romans viii, 9; 'Even the Spirit of Christ which was in the prophets,' 1 Peter i, 11. 'The Spirit of Jesus Christ,' as the Apostle speaks: 'I know that this shall turn to my salvation through your prayer, and the supply of the Spirit of Jesus Christ,' Phil. i, 19. If then the Holy Ghost be called 'the Spirit of the Father,' because he proceedeth from the Father, it followeth that, being called also 'the Spirit of the Son,' he proceedeth also from the Son. Again: because the Holy Ghost proceedeth from the Father, he is therefore sent by the Father, as from him who hath, by the original communication, a right of mission; as, 'the Comforter, which is the Holy Ghost, whom the Father will send,' John xiv, 26. But the same Spirit which is sent by the Father, is also sent by the Son, as he saith, 'When the Comforter is come, whom I will send unto you.' Therefore the Son hath the same right

of mission with the Father, and consequently must be acknowledged to have communicated the same essence. The Father is never sent by the Son, because he received not the Godhead from him; but the Father sendeth the Son, because he communicated the Godhead to him: in the same manner, neither the Father nor the Son is ever sent by the Holy Spirit; because neither of them received the divine nature from the Spirit: but both the Father and the Son sendeth the Holy Ghost, because the divine nature, common to the Father and the Son, was communicated by them both to the Holy Ghost. As therefore the Scriptures declare expressly, that the Spirit proceedeth from the Father; so do they also virtually teach, that he proceedeth from the Son."

3. Arius regarded the Spirit not only as a creature, but as created by Christ, κτίσμα κτίςματος, THE CREATURE OF A CREATURE. Some time afterward, his personality was wholly denied by the Arians, and he was considered as the EXERTED ENERGY of God. This appears to have been the notion of Socinus, and, with occasional modifications, has been adopted by his followers. They sometimes regard him as an attribute; and at others, resolve the passages in which he is spoken of into a periphrasis, or circumlocution, for God himself; or, to express both in one, into a figure of speech.

4. In establishing the proper personality and deity of the Holy Ghost, the first argument may be drawn from the frequent association, in Scripture, of a Person under that appellation with two other Persons, one of whom, the Father, is by all acknowledged to be divine; and the ascription to each of them, or to the three in union, of the same acts, titles, and authority, with worship, of the same kind, and, for any distinction that is made, of an equal degree. The manifestation of the existence and divinity of the Holy Spirit may be expected in the law and the prophets, and is, in fact, to be traced there with certainty. The Spirit is represented as an agent in creation, "moving upon the face of the waters;" and it forms no objection to the argument, that creation is ascribed to the Father, and also to the Son, but is a great confirmation of it. That creation should be effected by all the three Persons of the Godhead, though acting in different respects, yet so that each should be a Creator, and, therefore, both a Person and a divine Person, can be explained only by their unity in one essence. On every other hypothesis this Scriptural fact is disallowed, and therefore no other hypothesis can be true. If the Spirit of God be a mere influence, then he is not a Creator, distinct from the Father and the Son, because he is not a Person; but this is refuted both by the passage just quoted, and by Psalm xxxiii, 6: "By the Word of the Lord were the heavens made; and all the host of them by the breath (Heb. SPIRIT) of his mouth." This is farther confirmed by Job xxxiii, 4: "The Spirit of God hath made me, and the BREATH of the Almighty hath given me life;" where the second clause is obviously exegetic of the former: and the whole text proves that, in the patriarchal age, the followers of the true religion ascribed creation to the Spirit, as well as to the Father; and that one of his appellations was, "the BREATH of the Almighty." Did such passages stand alone, there might, indeed, be some plausibility in the criticism which resolves them into a personification; but, connected as they are with the whole body of evidence, as to the concurring doctrine of both Testaments, they are inexpugnable. Again: If the personality of the Son and the Spirit be allowed, and yet it is contended that they were but instruments in creation, through whom the creative power of another operated, but which creative power was not possessed by them; on this hypothesis, too, neither the Spirit nor the Son can be said to create, any more than Moses created the serpent into which his rod was turned, and the Scriptures are again contradicted. To this association of the three Persons in creative acts, may be added a like association in acts of preservation, which has been well called a CONTINUED CREATION, and by that term is expressed in the following passage: "These wait all upon thee, that thou mayest give them their meat in due season. Thou hidest thy face, they are troubled; thou takest away their breath, they die, and return to dust: thou sendest forth thy Spirit, they are created; and thou renewest the face of the earth," Psalm civ, 27–30. It is not surely here meant, that the Spirit by which the generations of animals are perpetuated, is WIND; and if he be called an attribute, WISDOM, POWER, or both united, where do we read of such attributes being "sent," "sent forth from God?" The personality of the Spirit is here as clearly marked as when St. Paul speaks of God "sending forth the Spirit of his Son," and when our Lord promises to "send" the Comforter; and as the upholding and preserving of created things is ascribed to the Father and the Son, so here they are ascribed, also, to the Spirit, "sent forth from" God to "create and renew the face of the earth."

5. The next association of the three Persons we find in the INSPIRATION of the prophets: "God spake unto our fathers by the prophets," says St. Paul, Heb. i, 1. St. Peter declares that these "holy men of God spake as they were moved by the Holy Ghost," 2 Peter i, 21; and also that it was "the Spirit of Christ which was in them," 1 Peter i, 11. We may defy any Socinian to interpret these three passages by making the Spirit an influence or attribute, and thereby reducing the term Holy Ghost into a figure of speech. "God," in the first passage, is, unquestionably, God the Father; and the "holy men of God," the prophets, would then, according to this view, be moved by the INFLUENCE of the Father; but the influence, according to the third passage, which was the source of their inspiration, was the Spirit, or the INFLUENCE of "Christ." Thus the passages contradict each other. Allow the trinity in unity, and you have no difficulty in calling the Spirit, the Spirit of the Father, and the Spirit of the Son, or the Spirit of either; but if the Spirit be an influence, that influence cannot be the influence of two persons,--one of them God, and the other a creature. Even if they allowed the pre-existence of Christ, with Arians, these passages are inexplicable by the Socinians; but, denying his prëexistence, they have no subterfuge but to interpret, "the Spirit of Christ," THE SPIRIT WHICH PROPHESIED OF CHRIST, which is a purely gratuitous paraphrase; or "the

spirit of an anointed one, or prophet;" that is, the prophet's own spirit, which is just as gratuitous and as unsupported by any parallel as the former. If, however, the Holy Ghost be the Spirit of the Father and of the Son, united in one essence, the passages are easily harmonized. In conjunction with the Father and the Son, he is the source of that prophetic inspiration under which the prophets spoke and acted. So the same Spirit which raised Christ from the dead, is said by St. Peter to have preached by Noah while the ark was preparing;--in allusion to the passage, "My Spirit shall not always strive (contend, debate) with man." This, we may observe, affords an eminent proof, that the writers of the New Testament understood the phrase, "the Spirit of God," as it occurs in the Old Testament, PERSONALLY. For, whatever may be the full meaning of that difficult passage in St. Peter, Christ is clearly declared to have preached by the Spirit in the days of Noah; that is, he, by the Spirit, inspired Noah to preach. If, then, the Apostles understood that the Holy Ghost was a Person, a point which will presently be established, we have, in the text just quoted from the book of Genesis, a key to the meaning of those texts in the Old Testament where the phrases, "My Spirit," "the Spirit of God," and "the Spirit of the Lord," occur; and inspired authority is thus afforded us to interpret them as of a Person; and if of a Person, the very effort made by Socinians to deny his personality, itself, indicates that that Person must, from the lofty titles and works ascribed to him, be inevitably divine. Such phrases occur in many passages of the Hebrew Scriptures; but, in the following, the Spirit is also eminently distinguished from two other Persons: "And now the Lord God, and his Spirit, hath sent me," Isaiah xlviii, 16; or, rendered better, "hath sent me and his Spirit," both terms being in the accusative case. "Seek ye out of the book of the Lord, and read: for my mouth it hath commanded, and his Spirit it hath gathered them," Isaiah xxxiv, 16. "I am with you, saith the Lord of Hosts, according to the word that I covenanted with you when ye came out of Egypt, so my Spirit remaineth among you: fear ye not. For thus saith the Lord of Hosts, I will shake all nations, and the Desire of all nations shall come," Hag. ii, 4–7. Here, also, the Spirit of the Lord is seen collocated with the Lord of Hosts and the Desire of all nations, who is the Messiah.

6. Three Persons, and three only, are associated also, both in the Old and New Testament, as objects of supreme worship; and form the one "name" in which the religious act of solemn benediction is performed, and to which men are bound by solemn baptismal covenant. In the plural form of the name of God, each received equal adoration. This threefold personality seems to have given rise to the standing form of triple benediction used by the Jewish high priest. The very important fact, that, in the vision of Isaiah, the Lord of hosts, who spake unto the prophet, is, in Acts xxviii, 25, said to be the Holy Ghost, while St. John declares that the glory which Isaiah saw was the glory of Christ, proves, indisputably, that each of the three Persons bears this august appellation; it gives also the reason for the threefold repetition, "Holy, holy, holy!" and it exhibits the prophet and the very seraphs in deep and awful adoration before the Triune Lord of hosts. Both the prophet and the seraphim were, therefore, worshippers of the Holy Ghost and of the Son, at the very time and by the very acts in which they worshipped the Father; which proves that, as the three Persons received equal homage in a case which does not admit of the evasion of pretended superior and inferior worship, they are equal in majesty, glory, and essence.

7. As in the tabernacle form of benediction, the Triune Jehovah is recognised as the source of all grace and peace to his creatures; so also we have the apostolic formula: "The grace of our Lord Jesus Christ, and the love of God, and the communion of the Holy Spirit be with you all. Amen." Here the personality of the three is kept distinct; and the prayer is, that Christians may have a common participation of the Holy Spirit, that is, doubtless, as he was promised by our Lord to his disciples, as a Comforter, as the Source of light and spiritual life, as the Author of regeneration. Thus the Spirit is acknowledged, equally with the Father and the Son, to be the Source and the Giver of the highest spiritual blessings; while this solemn ministerial benediction is, from its specific character, to be regarded as an act of prayer to each of the three Persons, and therefore is at once, an acknowledgment of the divinity and personality of each. The same remark applies to Revelation i, 4, 5: "Grace be unto you, and peace, from Him which was, and which is, and which is to come; and from the seven spirits which are before his throne," (an emblematical reference, probably to the golden branch with its seven lamps,) "and from Jesus Christ." The style of this book sufficiently accounts for the Holy Spirit being called "the seven spirits;" but no created spirit or company of created spirits is ever spoken of under that appellation: and the place assigned to the seven spirits, between the mention of the Father and the Son, indicates, with certainty, that one of the sacred Three, so eminent, and so exclusively eminent in both dispensations, is intended.

8. The form of baptism next presents itself with demonstrative evidence on the two points before us, the personality and divinity of the Holy Spirit. It is the form of covenant by which the sacred Three become our one or only God, and we become his people: "Go ye, therefore, and teach all nations, baptizing them in the name of the Father, and of the Son, and of the Holy Ghost." In what manner is this text to be disposed of, if the personality of the Holy Ghost is denied? Is the form of baptism to be so understood as to imply that baptism is in the name of one GOD, one CREATURE, and one ATTRIBUTE? The grossness of this absurdity refutes it, and proves that here, at least, there can be no personification. If all the Three, therefore, are persons, are we to have baptism in the name of one God and two creatures? This would be too near an approach to idolatry, or, rather, it would be idolatry itself; for, considering baptism as an act of dedication to God, the acceptance of God as our God, on our part, and the renunciation of all other deities and all other religions, what could a Heathen convert conceive of the two creatures so distinguished from all other creatures in heaven and in earth, and so associated with God himself as to form together the ONE NAME, to

which, by that act, he was devoted, and which he was henceforward to profess and honour, but that they were equally divine, unless special care were taken to instruct him that but one of the Three was God, and the two others but creatures? But of this care, of this cautionary instruction, though so obviously necessary upon this theory, no single instance can be given in all the writings of the Apostles.

9. But other arguments are not wanting to prove both the personality and the divinity of the Holy Spirit. With respect to the former, (1.) The mode of his subsistence in the sacred Trinity proves his personality. He proceeds from the Father and the Son, and cannot, therefore, be either. To say that an attribute proceeds and comes forth, would be a gross absurdity. (2.) Many passages of Scripture are wholly unintelligible and even absurd, unless the Holy Ghost is allowed to be a person. For as those who take the phrase as ascribing no more than a figurative personality to an attribute, make that attribute to be the ENERGY or POWER OF GOD, they reduce such passages as the following to utter unmeaningness: "God anointed Jesus with the Holy Ghost and with power;" that is, with the power of God and with power. "That ye may abound in hope through the power of the Holy Ghost;" that is, through the power of power. "In demonstration of the Spirit and of power;" that is, in demonstration of power and of power.

(3.) Personification of any kind is, in some passages in which the Holy Ghost is spoken of, impossible. The reality which this figure of speech is said to present to us, is either some of the attributes of God, or else the doctrine of the Gospel. Let this theory, then, be tried upon the following passages: "He shall not speak of himself; but whatsoever he shall hear, that shall he speak." What attribute of God can here be personified? And if the doctrine of the Gospel be arrayed with personal attributes, where is there an instance of so monstrous a prosopopœia as this passage would exhibit?--the doctrine of the Gospel not speaking "of himself," but speaking "whatsoever he shall hear!"--"The Spirit maketh intercession for us." What attribute is capable of interceding, or how can the doctrine of the Gospel intercede? Personification, too, is the language of poetry, and takes place naturally only in excited and elevated discourse; but if the Holy Spirit be a personification, we find it in the ordinary and cool strain of mere narration and argumentative discourse in the New Testament, and in the most incidental conversations. "Have ye received the Holy Ghost since ye believed? We have not so much as heard whether there be any Holy Ghost." How impossible is it here to extort, by any process whatever, even the shadow of a personification of either any attribute of God, or of the doctrine of the Gospel! So again: "The Spirit said unto Philip, Go near, and join thyself to this chariot." Could it be any attribute of God which said this, or could it be the doctrine of the Gospel? Finally, that the Holy Ghost is a person, and not an attribute, is proved by the use of masculine pronouns and relatives in the Greek of the New Testament, in connection with the neuter noun Πνεῦμα, SPIRIT, and also by many distinct personal acts being ascribed to him, as, "to come," "to go," "to be sent," "to teach," "to guide," "to comfort," "to make intercession," "to bear witness," "to give gifts," "dividing them to every man as he WILL," "to be vexed," "grieved," and "quenched." These cannot be applied to the mere fiction of a person, and they therefore establish the Spirit's true personality.

10. Some additional arguments to those before given to establish the divinity of the Holy Ghost may also be adduced. The first is taken from his being the subject of blasphemy: "The blasphemy against the Holy Ghost shall not be forgiven unto men," Matt. xii, 31. This blasphemy consisted in ascribing his miraculous works to Satan; and that he is capable of being blasphemed proves him to be as much a person as the Son; and it proves him to be divine, because it shows that he may be sinned against, and so sinned against that the blasphemer shall not be forgiven. A person he must be, or he could not be blasphemed: a divine person he must be, to constitute this blasphemy a sin against him in the proper sense, and of so malignant a kind as to place it beyond the reach of mercy. He is called God: "Why hath Satan filled thine heart to lie unto the Holy Ghost? Why hast thou conceived this in thine heart? Thou hast not lied unto men, but unto God," Acts v, 3, 4. Ananias is said to have lied particularly "unto the Holy Ghost," because the Apostles were under his special direction in establishing the temporary regulation among Christians that they should have all things in common: the detection of the crime itself was a demonstration of the divinity of the Spirit, because it showed his omniscience, his knowledge of the most secret acts. In addition to the proof of his divinity thus afforded by this history, he is also called God: "Thou hast not lied unto men, but unto God." He is also called the Lord: "Now the Lord is that Spirit," 2 Cor. iii, 17. He is ETERNAL: "The eternal Spirit," Heb. ix, 14. OMNIPRESENCE is ascribed to him: "Your body is the temple of the Holy Ghost," 1 Cor. vi, 19. "As many as are led by the Spirit of God, they are the sons of God," Rom. viii, 14. For, as all true Christians are his temples, and are led by him, he must be present to them at all times and in all places. He is OMNISCIENT: "The Spirit searcheth all things, yea, the deep things of God," 1 Cor. ii, 10. Here the Spirit is said to search or know "all things" absolutely; and then, to make this more emphatic, that he knows even "the deep things of God," things hidden from every creature, the depths of his essence, and the secrets of his counsels; for, that this is intended, appears from the next verse, where he is said to know "the things of God," as the spirit of a man knows the things of a man. SUPREME MAJESTY is also attributed to him, so that to "lie" to him, to "blaspheme" him, to "vex" him, to do him "despite," are sins, and as such render the offender liable to divine punishment. How impracticable then is it to interpret the phrase, "the Holy Ghost," as a periphrasis for God himself! A Spirit, which is the Spirit OF God, which is so often distinguished FROM the Father, which "sees" and "hears" the Father, which searches "the deep things" of God, which is "sent" by the Father, which "proceedeth" from him, and who has special prayer addressed to him at the same time as

the Father, cannot, though "one with him," be the Father; and that he is not the Son is acknowledged on both sides. As a divine person, our regards are therefore justly due to him as the object of worship and trust, of prayer and blessing.

11. Various are the gracious offices of the Holy Spirit in the work of our redemption. He it is that first quickens the soul, dead in trespasses and sins, to spiritual life; it is by him we are "born again," and made new creatures; he is the living root of all the Christian graces, which are therefore called "the fruits" of the Spirit; and by him all true Christians are aided in the "infirmities" and afflictions of this present life. Eminently, he is promised to the disciples as "the Comforter," which is more fully explained by St. Paul by the phrase "the Spirit of adoption;" so that it is through him that we receive a direct inward testimony to our personal forgiveness and acceptance through Christ, and are filled with peace and consolation. This doctrine, so essential to the solid and habitual happiness of those who believe in Christ, is thus clearly explained in a sermon on that subject by the Rev. John Wesley:--

"(1.) But what is the witness of the Spirit? The original word, μαρτυρία, may be rendered either, as it is in several places, THE WITNESS, or, less ambiguously, THE TESTIMONY, or, THE RECORD: so it is rendered in our translation: 'This is the record,' the testimony, the sum of what God testifies in all the inspired writings, 'that God hath given unto us eternal life, and this life is in his Son,' 1 John v, 11. The testimony now under consideration is given by the Spirit of God to and with our spirit. He is the person testifying. What he testifies to us is, 'that we are the children of God.' The immediate result of this testimony is, 'the fruit of the Spirit;' namely, 'love, joy, peace, long suffering, gentleness, goodness.' And without these, the testimony itself cannot continue. For it is inevitably destroyed, not only by the commission of any outward sin, or the omission of known duty, but by giving way to any inward sin: in a word, by whatever grieves the Holy Spirit of God. (2.) I observed many years ago, It is hard to find words in the language of men to explain the deep things of God. Indeed, there are none that will adequately express what the Spirit of God works in his children. But, perhaps, one might say, (desiring any who are taught of God to correct, soften, or strengthen the expression,) by the 'testimony of the Spirit,' I mean, an inward impression on the soul, whereby the Spirit of God immediately and directly witnesses with my spirit, that I am a child of God; that 'Jesus Christ hath loved me, and given himself for me;' that all my sins are blotted out, and I, even I, am reconciled to God. (3.) After twenty years' farther consideration, I see no cause to retract any part of this. Neither do I conceive how any of these expressions may be altered, so as to make them more intelligible. I can only add, that if any of the children of God will point out any other expressions which are more clear, or more agreeable to the word of God, I will readily lay these aside. (4.) Meantime, let it be observed, I do not mean hereby, that the Spirit of God testifies this by any outward voice; no, nor always by an inward voice, although he may do this sometimes. Neither do I suppose, that he always applies to the heart, though he often may, one or more texts of Scripture. But he so works upon the soul by his immediate influence, and by a strong, though inexplicable, operation, that the stormy wind and troubled waves subside, and there is a sweet calm: the heart resting as in the arms of Jesus, and the sinner being clearly satisfied that all his 'iniquities are forgiven, and his sins covered.' (5.) Now what is the matter of dispute concerning this? Not, whether there be a witness or testimony of the Spirit. Not, whether the Spirit does testify with our spirit, that we are the children of God. None can deny this, without flatly contradicting the Scriptures, and charging a lie upon the God of truth. Therefore, that there is a testimony of the Spirit, is acknowledged by all parties. (6.) Neither is it questioned, whether there is an indirect witness or testimony, that we are the children of God. This is nearly, if not exactly, the same with 'the testimony of a good conscience toward God;' and is the result of reason or reflection on what we feel in our own souls. Strictly speaking, it is a conclusion drawn partly from the word of God, and partly from our own experience. The word of God says, Every one who has the fruit of the Spirit is a child of God. Experience or inward consciousness tells me, that I have the fruit of the Spirit; and hence I rationally conclude, Therefore I am a child of God. This is likewise allowed on all hands, and so is no matter of controversy. (7.) Nor do we assert, that there can be any real testimony of the Spirit, without the fruit of the Spirit. We assert, on the contrary, that the fruit of the Spirit immediately springs from this testimony; not always indeed in the same degree even when the testimony is first given; and much less afterward: neither joy nor peace is always at one stay. No, nor love: as neither is the testimony itself always equally strong and clear. (8.) But the point in question is, whether there be any direct testimony of the Spirit at all; whether there be any other testimony of the Spirit, than that which arises from a consciousness of the fruit. I believe there is, because that is the plain, natural meaning of the text, 'The Spirit itself beareth witness with our spirit, that we are the children of God.' It is manifest here are two witnesses mentioned, who together testify the same thing, the Spirit of God, and our own spirit. The late bishop of London, in his sermon on this text, seems astonished that any one can doubt of this, which appears upon the very face of the words. Now, 'the testimony of our own spirit,' says the bishop, 'is one which is the consciousness of our own sincerity;' or, to express the same thing a little more clearly, the consciousness of the fruit of the Spirit. When our spirit is conscious of this, of love, joy, peace, long suffering, gentleness, goodness, it easily infers from these premises, that we are the children of God. It is true, that great man supposes the other witness to be 'the consciousness of our own good works.' This, he affirms, is 'the testimony of God's Spirit.' But this is included in the testimony of our own spirit: yea, and in sincerity, even according to the common sense of the word. So the Apostle: 'Our rejoicing is this, the testimony of our conscience, that in simplicity and godly sincerity we have our conversation in the world;' where it is plain, sincerity refers to our words and actions, at least, as much as to our inward dispositions. So that this is not another witness, but the very same that he mentioned before: the consciousness of our good works being only one branch of the consciousness of our sincerity. Consequently, here is only one witness still. If therefore, the text speaks of two witnesses, one of these is not the consciousness of our good works, neither of our sincerity; all this being manifestly contained in 'the testimony of our spirit.' What, then, is the other witness? This might easily be learned, if the text itself were not sufficiently clear, from the verse immediately preceding: 'Ye have received, not the spirit of bondage, but the Spirit of adoption, whereby we cry, Abba, Father.' It follows, 'The Spirit itself beareth witness with our spirit, that we are the children of God.' This is farther explained by the parallel text, Gal. iv, 6: 'Because ye are sons, God hath sent forth the Spirit of his Son into your hearts, crying, Abba, Father.' Is not this something immediate and direct, not the result of reflection or argumentation? Does not this Spirit cry, 'Abba, Father,' in our hearts, the moment it is given? antecedently to any reflection upon our sincerity, yea, to any reasoning whatsoever? And is not this the plain, natural sense of the words, which strikes any one as soon as he hears them? All these texts, then, in their most obvious meaning, describe a direct testimony of the Spirit. That the testimony of the Spirit of God, must, in the very nature of things, be antecedent to the testimony of our own spirit, may appear from this single consideration: We must be holy in heart and life, before we can be conscious that we are so. But we must love God before we can be holy at all, this being the root of all holiness. Now, we cannot love God, till we know he loves us: 'We love him, because he first loved us.' And we cannot know his love to us, till his Spirit witnesses it to our spirit. Since, therefore, the testimony of his Spirit must precede the love of God and all holiness, of consequence it must precede our consciousness thereof."

12. The precedence of the direct witness of the Spirit of God to the indirect witness of our own, and the dependence of the latter upon the former, are also clearly stated by other divines of great authority. Calvin, on Romans viii, 16, says, "St. Paul means that the Spirit of God gives such a testimony to us, that he being our guide and teacher, our spirit concludes our adoption of God to be certain. For our own mind, of itself, independent of the preceding testimony of the Spirit, [NISI PRÆUNTE SPIRITÛS TESTIMONIO,] could not produce this persuasion in us. For while the Spirit witnesses that we are the sons of God, he at the same time inspires this confidence into our minds, that we are bold to call God our Father." On the same passage Dr. John Owen says, "The Spirit itself beareth witness with our spirits that we are the sons of God; the witness which our own spirits do give unto our adoption is the work and effect of the Holy Spirit in us; if it were not, it would be false, and not confirmed by the testimony of the Spirit himself, who is the Spirit of truth. 'And none knoweth the things of God but the Spirit of God,' 1 Cor. ii, 11. If he declare not our sonship in us and to us, we cannot know it. How doth he then bear witness to our spirits? What is the distinct testimony? It must be some such act of his as evidenceth itself to be from him immediately, unto them that are concerned in it, that is, those unto whom it is given." Poole on the same passage remarks, "The Spirit of adoption doth not only excite us to call upon God as our Father, but it doth ascertain and assure us, as before, that we are his children. And this it doth not by an outward voice, as God the Father to Jesus Christ, nor by an angel, as to Daniel and the Virgin Mary, but by an inward and secret suggestion, whereby he raiseth our hearts to this persuasion, that God is our Father, and we are his children. This is not the testimony of the graces and operations of the Spirit, but of the Spirit itself." Bishop Pearson, in his elaborate work on the Creed, and Dr. Barrow, in his Sermons, are equally explicit in stating this Scriptural doctrine.

HOMOIOUSIANS, a branch of the high Arians, who maintained that the nature of the Son, though not the same, was similar to that of the Father.

HOMOOUSIANS, or **HOMOUSIASTS**, was, on the other hand, a name applied to the Athanasians, who held the Son to be HOMOUSIOS, or consubstantial with the Father, that is, of the same nature and substance.

HONEY, דבש. It is probable, that it was in order to keep the Jews at a distance from the customs of the Heathen, who were used to offer honey in their sacrifices, that God forbade it to be offered to him, that is to say, burnt upon the altar, Lev. ii, 11; but at the same time he commanded that the first-fruits of it should be presented. These first-fruits and offerings were designed for the support and sustenance of the priests, and were not consumed upon the altar. In hot weather, the honey burst the comb, and ran down the hollow trees or rocks, where, in the land of Judea, the bees deposited great store of it. This, flowing spontaneously, was the best and most delicious, as it was quite pure, and clear from all dregs and wax. The Israelites called it יערה, WOOD HONEY. It is therefore improperly rendered "honeycomb," 1 Sam. xiv, 27; Cant. v, 1; in both which places it means the honey that has distilled from the trees, as distinguished from the domestic, which was eaten with the comb. Hasselquist says, that between Acra and Nazareth, great numbers of wild bees breed, to the advantage of the inhabitants; and Maundrell observes of the great plain near Jericho, that he perceived in it, in many places, a smell of honey and wax as strong as if he had been in an apiary. Milk and honey were the chief dainties of the earlier ages, and continue to be so of the Bedoween Arabs now. So butter and honey are several times mentioned in Scripture as among the most delicious refreshments, 2 Sam. xvii, 29; Job xx, 17; Cant. iv, 11; Isaiah vii, 15. Thus Irby and Mangles, in their Travels, relate, "They gave us some honey and butter together, with bread to dip in it, Narsah desiring one of his men to mix the two ingredients for us, as we were awkward at it. The Arab, having stirred the mixture up well with his fingers, showed his dexterity at consuming, as well as mixing, and recompensed himself for his trouble by eating half of it." The WILD HONEY, μέλι ἄγριον, mentioned to have been a part of the food of John the Baptist, Matt. iii, 4, was probably such as he got in the rocks and hollows of trees. Thus, "honey out of the stony rock," Psalm lxxxi, 16; Deut. xxxii, 13.

HOPHNI. See Eli.

HOPKINSIANS, or **HOPKINSONIANS**, so called from the Rev. Samuel Hopkins, D.D., pastor of the first Congregational church at Newport, Rhode Island, North America, about A. D. 1770. Dr. Hopkins, in his sermons and tracts, made several additions to the sentiments previously advanced by the celebrated President Edwards, of New-Jersey College. The following is a summary of their distinguishing tenets:--

1. That all true virtue or real holiness consists in disinterested benevolence. The object of benevolence is universal being, including God, and all intelligent creatures. It wishes and seeks the good of every individual, so far as is consistent with the greatest good of the whole, which is comprised in the glory of God, and the perfection and happiness of his kingdom. The law of God is the standard of all moral rectitude or holiness. This is reduced into love to God and to our neighbour; and universal good will comprehends all the love to God, our neighbour, and ourselves, required in the divine law, and therefore must be the whole of holy obedience. Let any person reflect on what are the particular branches of true piety, and he will find that disinterested affection is the distinguishing characteristic of each. For instance, all which distinguishes pious fear from the fear of the wicked consists in love. Holy gratitude is nothing but good will to God and man, ourselves included, excited by a view of the good will and kindness of God. Justice, truth, and faithfulness, are comprised in universal benevolence. So are temperance and chastity; for an undue indulgence of our appetites and passions is contrary to benevolence, as tending to hurt ourselves or others, and so opposite to the general good, and the divine command. In short, all virtue is nothing but love to God and our neighbour, made perfect in all its genuine exercises and expressions.

2. That all sin consists in selfishness. By this is meant an interested affection, by which a person sets himself up as the supreme or only object of regard; and nothing is lovely in his view, unless suited to promote his private interest. This self-love is, in its whole nature, and every degree of it, enmity against God: it is not subject to the law of God, and it is the only affection that can oppose it. It is the foundation of all spiritual blindness, and the source of all idolatry and false religion. It is the foundation of all covetousness and sensuality; of all falsehood, injustice, and oppression; as it excites mankind, by undue methods, to invade the property of others. Self-love produces all the violent passions, envy, wrath, clamour, and evil speaking; and every thing contrary to the divine law is briefly comprehended in this fruitful source of iniquity, self-love.

3. That there are no promises of regenerating grace made to the actions of the unregenerate. For as far as men act from self-love, they act from a bad end; for those who have no true love to God really fulfil no duty when they attend on the externals of religion. Also, that inability, which consists in disinclination, never renders any thing improper to be the subject of a command.

4. That the impotency of sinners, with respect to believing in Christ, is not natural, but moral; for it is a plain dictate of common sense, that natural impossibility excludes all blame. But an unwilling mind is universally considered as a crime, and not as an excuse; and is the very thing wherein our wickedness consists.--Also,

5. That in order to faith in Christ, a sinner must approve in his heart of the divine conduct, even though God should cast him off for ever; which, however, neither implies love to misery, nor hatred of happiness. But as a particle of water is small, in comparison of a generous stream, so the man of humility feels small before the great family of his fellow creatures. He values his soul; but, when he compares it to the great soul of mankind, he almost forgets and loses sight of it: for the governing principle of his heart is, to estimate things according to their worth. When, therefore, he indulges an humble comparison with his Maker, he feels lost in the infinite fulness and brightness of divine love, as a ray of light is lost in the sun, and a particle of water in the ocean. It inspires him with the most grateful feelings of heart, that he has opportunity to be in the hand of God, as clay in the hand of the potter; and as he considers himself in this humble light, he submits the nature and size of his future vessel entirely to God. As his pride is lost in the dust, he looks up with pleasure toward the throne of God, and rejoices, with all his heart, in the rectitude of the divine administration. He also considers that, if the law be good, death is due to those who have broken it; and "the Judge of all the earth cannot but do right," Gen. xviii, 25. It would bring everlasting reproach upon his government to spare us, considered merely as in ourselves. When this is felt in our hearts, and not till then, we shall be prepared to look to the free grace of God, through Christ's redemption.

6. That the infinitely wise and holy God has exerted his omnipotent power, in such a manner as he purposed should be followed with the existence and entrance of moral evil in the system: for it must be admitted, on all hands, that God has a perfect knowledge, foresight, and view of all possible existences and events. If that system and scene of operation, in which moral evil should never have existence, was actually preferred in the divine mind, certainly the Deity is infinitely disappointed in the issue of his own operations. Dr. Hopkins maintains, therefore, that "God was the author, origin, and positive cause of Adam's sin:" yea, "that he is the origin and cause of moral evil, as really as he is of the existence of any thing that he wills."

7. That the introduction of sin is, upon the whole, for the general good. For the wisdom and power of the Deity are displayed in carrying on designs of the greatest good: and the existence of moral evil has, undoubtedly, occasioned a more

full, perfect, and glorious discovery of the infinite perfections of the divine nature, than could otherwise have been made to the view of creatures.

8. That repentance is before faith in Christ. By this, is not intended, that repentance is before a speculative conviction of the being and perfections of God, and of the person and character of Christ; but only, that true repentance is previous to a saving faith in Christ, by which the believer is united to Christ, and entitled to the benefits of his mediation and atonement. So Christ commanded, "Repent ye, and believe the Gospel;" and Paul preached "repentance toward God, and faith in our Lord Jesus Christ."

9. That though men became sinners by Adam, according to a divine constitution, yet they were and are accountable for no sins but personal: for, (1.) Adam's act, in eating the forbidden fruit, was not the act of his posterity; therefore they did not sin at the same time that he did. (2.) The sinfulness of that act could not be transferred to them afterward; because the sinfulness of an act can no more be transferred from one person to another, than an act itself. (3.) Therefore Adam's act, in eating the forbidden fruit, was not the cause, but only the occasions of his posterity being sinners. Adam sinned, and now God brings his posterity into the world sinners.

10. That though believers are justified through Christ's righteousness, yet his righteousness is not transferred to them. For personal righteousness cannot be transferred from one person to another, nor personal sin; otherwise the sinner would become innocent, and Christ the sinner. The Scripture, therefore, represents believers as receiving only the benefits of Christ's righteousness in justification, or their being pardoned and accepted for Christ's righteousness' sake; and this is the proper Scripture notion of imputation. Jonathan's righteousness was imputed to Mephibosheth, when David showed kindness to him for his father Jonathan's sake, 2 Samuel ix, 7.

11. The Hopkinsians warmly advocate the doctrine of the divine decrees, not only particular election, but also reprobation; they hold also the total depravation of human nature, the special influences of the Spirit of God in regeneration, justification by faith alone, the final perseverance of the saints, and the consistency between entire freedom and absolute dependence; and therefore claim it as their just due, since the world will make distinctions, to be called Hopkinsian Calvinists. Calvinists, however, have demurred against several of these propositions, and a long and warm controversy was occasioned by them in the United States; to a few points of which we shall advert.--(1.) Selfishness, as confining our affections and exertions to ourselves, is confessedly a vice; but that self is not to be excluded from our affections, is evident even from the terms of the divine law,--"Thou shalt love thy neighbour as thyself." And the Scriptures teach us, that "no man hateth his own flesh." Such a "disinterested benevolence," therefore, as implies no peculiar anxiety for our personal salvation and happiness, can never be required of us. A good man may and must be convinced, that God would be just in his final condemnation, considered out of Christ; but it is impossible to acquiesce in such a prospect; it is making holiness to consist in being satisfied with remaining for ever unholy, which is as impious as it is contradictory; and the strong and strange things which some Hopkinsonians have said on this subject, can only be accounted for from the love of paradox. (2.) The other principal point on which Calvinists dissent, is the making God "the author and efficient cause of sin." It is true that the Doctor says elsewhere, that "in causing or originating sin, there is no sin;" this, however, is a position so dangerous, so unsupported, and so contrary to the common sense of mankind, that we may well shrink from it; and should risk no speculation that can implicate the divine character, or furnish an excuse for sin. "Is God unrighteous who taketh vengeance?" saith the Apostle. "God forbid! for how then shall God judge the world?" Rom. iii, 5, 6. Those who feel interested in the controversy, may be fully gratified in the "Contrast between Calvinism and Hopkinsianism," by Ezra Styles Ely, A. M., (New-York, 1811,) and other American publications. In this country the controversy is but little known; but we may remark that the theory of Hopkins appears to be an attempt to unite some points of mystic theology with the Calvinism commonly received, and that where it differs from the latter system, it relieves no difficulty.

HOR. This mountain, in its general acceptation, is probably the same with Mount Seir, Hor being the name by which that mountainous tract was denominated before it was exchanged for Seir. But one particular mountain of this region retained the name of Hor long after; as it was a mountain of this name, "by the coast of the land of Edom," that Aaron was commanded to ascend, in order to die there, Num. xx, 23. This mountain, or at least the one to which tradition assigns the tomb of Aaron, was visited by Burckhardt; from whose account it appears to form a conspicuous object in the chain of the Djebel Shera, or Mount Seir, rising abruptly from the valley of El Araba, or desert of Zin, about fifty miles north of Akaba, or Ezion-Geber.

HOREB, a mountain in Arabia Petræa, a part of which, or near to which, was Sinai. At Horeb God appeared to Moses in the burning bush, Exod. iii, 1, &c. Hither Elijah retired to avoid the persecution of Jezebel, 1 Kings xix, 8. Sinai and Horeb seem to be two parts of the same mountain; hence the law is sometimes said to be given there.

HORN. By horns the Hebrews sometimes understood an eminence, or angle, a corner, or a rising. By horns of the altar of burnt offerings, many understand the angles of that altar; but there were also horns, or eminences, at the corners of that altar, Exod. xxvii, 2; xxx, 2. Horn also signifies glory, brightness, rays. God's "brightness was as the light, he had horns coming out of his hand," Hab. iii, 4; that is, refulgent beams issuing from the hollow of it. As the ancients frequently used horns to hold liquors, vessels containing oil and perfumes are often called horns, whether made of horn or not. "Fill thine horn with oil," says the Lord to Samuel, "and anoint David," 1 Sam. xvi, 1. Zadok took a horn of oil out of the tabernacle, and anointed Solomon, 1 Kings i, 39. Job called one of his daughters Kerenhappuch, horn of antimony, or horn to put antimony (STIBIUM) in, which the women of the east still use at this day, Job xliii, 14. The principal defence and strength of horned beasts consist in their horns; and hence the Scripture mentions the horn as a symbol of strength. The Lord exalted the horn of David, the horn of his people; he breaketh the horn of the ungodly; he cutteth off the horn of Moab; he cutteth off the horn of Israel; he promiseth to make the horn of Israel to bud forth; to reëstablish the honour of it, and restore its former vigour. Moses compares Joseph to a young bull, and says that he has horns like those of a unicorn. Kingdoms and great powers are often in Scripture described by the symbol of horns. In Daniel vii, viii, horns represent the power of the Persians, of the Greeks, of Syria, of Egypt, or of Pagan and Papal Rome. The prophet represents three animals as having many horns, one of which grew from the other. This emblem is a natural one, since in the east are rams which have many horns.

HORNET, הצרעה, Exod. xxiii, 28; Deut. vii, 20; Joshua xxiv, 12. The hornet, in natural history, belongs to the species CRABO, of the genus VESPA or wasp. It is a most voracious insect, and is exceedingly strong for its size, which is generally an inch in length, and sometimes more. In each of the instances where this creature is mentioned in Scripture, it is as sent among the enemies of the Israelites, to drive them out of the land. Some explain the word metaphorically, as "I will send my terror as the hornet," &c. But Bochart contends that it is to be taken in its proper literal meaning, and has accumulated examples of several other people having been chased from their habitations by insects of different kinds. Ælian records that the Phaselites, who dwelt about the mountains of Solyma, were driven out of their country by wasps. As these people were Phenicians or Canaanites, it is probable that the event to which he refers is the same as took place in the days of Joshua. How distressing and destructive a multitude of these fierce and severely stinging insects might be, any person may conjecture. No armour, no weapons could avail against them. A few thousands of them would be sufficient to overthrow the best disciplined army and put it into confusion and rout. From Joshua xxiv, 12, we find that two kings of the Amorites were actually driven out of the land by these hornets, so that the Israelites were not obliged to use either sword or bow in the conquest. One of these, according to the Jewish commentaries of R. Nachman, was the nation of the Girgashites, who retired into Africa, fearing the power of God. And Procopius, in his history of the Vandals, mentions an ancient inscription in Mauritania Tingitana, stating, that the inhabitants had fled thither from the face of Joshua, the son of Nun. This account accords with Scripture, in which, though the Girgashites are included in the general list of the seven devoted nations either to be driven out or destroyed by the Israelites, Gen. xv, 20, 21; Deut. vii, 1; Josh. iii, 10; xxiv, 11; yet they are omitted in the list of those to be utterly destroyed, Deut. xx, 17; and among whom, in neglect of the divine decree, the Israelites lived and intermarried, Judges iii, 1–6. That the name of the Girgashites, however, was not extirpated, we may collect from the Gergesenes, in our Saviour's time, inhabiting the same country, Matt. viii, 28. Other tribes of the Hivites, Canaanites, and Hittites, were also expelled by the hornet gradually; not in one year, lest the land should become desolate, and the wild beasts multiply to the prejudice of the Israelites, Exod. xxiii, 28–30.

The "arms of Jove," to which Virgil refers, (*Æneid* viii, 355–358,) in describing the flight of Saturn from the east, were the hornets sent by the God of Israel, Iahoh, or by contraction Io, to which also his description of the Asilus exactly corresponds:--

PLURIMUS--VOLITANS, (CUI NOMEN ASILO

ROMANUM EST; οἶστρον, GRAII VERTERE VOCANTES,)

ASPER, ACERBA SONANS, QUO TOTA EXTERRITA SYLVIS

DIFFUGIUNT ARMENTA.

Georg. iii, 145.

"About the Alburnian groves, with holly green,

Of winged insects mighty swarms are seen;

This flying plague, to mark its quality,

Œstros the Grecians call; ASYLUS, we:

A fierce loud buzzing breeze; their stings draw blood,

And drive the cattle gadding through the wood.

Seized with unusual pains, they loudly cry."

Dryden.

Dr. Hales is of opinion, that the Latin ASILUS and Greek οιστρον, were probably only different pronunciations of the same oriental term, הצרעה, HATSIRAAH, as this fly is called by Moses and Joshua. The vindictive power that presided over this dreadful scourge was worshipped at Ekron, in Palestine, through fear, the reigning motive of Pagan superstition, under the title of BAAL-ZEBUB, "master or lord of the hornet," whence BEELZEBUB, in the New Testament, "the prince of demons," Matt. xii, 24. Isaiah, denouncing a wo against Abyssinia, describes it as "the land of the winged cymbal," (TSALTSAL CANAPHIM,) Isaiah xviii, 1; by the same analogy that TSALTSAL signifies "a locust," Deut. xxviii, 42; A STREPERÂ VOCE SIC DICTAM. [So called from its streperous sound.] Bruce, in his Travels in Abyssinia, has given an accurate description of this tremendous fly, which in Arabic is called ZIMB, and by the Abyssinians TSALTSAL-YA, "the cymbal of the Lord," from its sonorous buzzing. And in his Appendix he has given a drawing of it, magnified, for distinctness' sake, something above twice the natural size: after which he observes, "He has no sting, though he seems to me to be rather of the bee kind; but his motion is more rapid and sudden than that of the bee, (VOLITANS,) and resembles that of the gad-fly in England. There is something particular in the sound or buzzing of this insect; it is a jarring noise, together with a humming, (ACERBA SONANS,) which induces me to believe it proceeds, in part at least, from a vibration made with the three hairs at his snout." Bruce does not cite or refer to Virgil's description, though his account furnishes the most critical and exact explanation of it. Such undesigned coincidences are most satisfactory and convincing; they show that the poet and the naturalist both copied from nature. And the terror impressed by this insect on all the cattle, QUO TOTA EXTERRITA SYLVIS DIFFUGIUNT, [affrighted at which the entire herds flee to the thickets,] according to Virgil, is thus illustrated by Bruce: "As soon as this plague appears, and their buzzing is heard, all the cattle forsake their food, and run wildly about the plain till they die, worn out with fatigue, fright, and hunger. No remedy remains but to leave the black earth, where they breed, and hasten down to the sands of Atbara; and there they remain while the periodical rains last, this cruel enemy (ASPER) never daring to pursue them farther. The camel, emphatically called by the Arabs the ship of the desert, though his size is immense as is his strength, and his body covered with a thick skin, defended with strong hair, still is not able to sustain the violent punctures the fly makes with his pointed proboscis. He must lose no time in removing to the sands of Atbara; for when once attacked by this fly, his body, head, and legs, break out into large bosses, which swell, break, and putrefy, to the certain destruction of the creature. I have found some of these tubercles upon almost every elephant and rhinoceros that I have seen, and attribute them to this cause. All the inhabitants of the sea coast are obliged to put themselves in motion, and remove to the next sand, in the beginning of the rainy season, to prevent all their stock of cattle from being destroyed. Nor is there any alternative, or means of avoiding this, though a hostile band was in the way, capable of spoiling them of half their substance, as was actually the case when we were at Sennaar. Of such consequence is the weakest instrument in the hand of Providence." See Flies and Beelzebub.

HORSE, סוס. Horses were very rare among the Hebrews in the early ages. The patriarchs had none; and after the departure of the Israelites from Egypt, God expressly forbade their ruler to procure them: "He shall not multiply horses to himself, nor cause the people to return to Egypt, to the end that he should multiply horses: forasmuch as the Lord hath said, Ye shall henceforth return no more that way," Deut. xvii, 16. As horses appear to have been generally furnished by Egypt, God prohibits these, 1. Lest there should be such commerce with Egypt as might lead to idolatry. 2. Lest the people might depend on a well appointed cavalry, as a means of security, and so cease from trusting in the promised aid and protection of Jehovah. 3. That they might not be tempted to extend their dominion by means of cavalry, and so get scattered among the surrounding idolatrous nations, and thus cease in process of time, to be that distinct and separate people which God intended they should be, and without which the prophecies relative to the Messiah could not be known to have their due and full accomplishment. In the time of the Judges we find horses and war chariots among the Canaanites, but still the Israelites had none; and hence they were generally too timid to venture down into the plains, confining their conquests to the mountainous parts of the country. In the reign of Saul, it would appear, that horse breeding had not yet been introduced into Arabia; for, in a war with some of the Arabian nations, the Israelites got plunder in camels, sheep, and asses, but no horses. David's enemies brought against him a strong force of cavalry into the field; and in the book of Psalms the horse commonly appears only on the side of the enemies of the people of God; and so entirely unaccustomed to the management of this animal had the Israelites still continued, that, after a battle, in which they took a considerable body of cavalry prisoners, 2 Sam. viii, 4, David caused most of the horses to be cut down, because he did not know what use to make of them. Solomon was the first who established a cavalry force. Under these circumstances, it is not wonderful that the Mosaic law should take no notice of an animal which we hold in such high estimation. To Moses, educated as he was in Egypt, and, with his people, at last chased out by Pharaoh's cavalry, the use of the horse for war and for travelling was well known; but as it was his object to establish a nation of husbandmen, and not of soldiers for the conquest of foreign lands, and as Palestine, from its situation, required not the defence of cavalry, he might very well decline introducing among his people the yet unusual art of horse breeding. Solomon, having married a daughter of Pharaoh, procured a breed of horses from Egypt; and so greatly did he multiply them, that he had four hundred stables, forty thousand stalls, and twelve thousand horsemen, 1 Kings iv, 26; 2 Chron. ix, 25. It seems that the Egyptian horses were in high repute, and were much used in war. When the Israelites were disposed to place too implicit confidence in the assistance of cavalry, the prophet remonstrated in these terms: "The Egyptians are men, and not God; and their horses are flesh, not spirit," Isaiah xxxi, 3.

HORSE-LEECH, עלוקה, from a root which signifies TO ADHERE, STICK CLOSE, or HANG FAST, Prov. xxx, 15. A sort of worm that lives in water, of a black or brown colour, which fattens upon the flesh, and does not quit it till it is entirely full of blood. Solomon says, "The horse-leech hath two daughters, Give, give." This is so apt an emblem of an insatiable rapacity and avarice, that it has been generally used by different writers to express it. Thus Plautus makes one say, speaking of the determination to get money, "I will turn myself into a horse-leech, and suck out their blood;" and Cicero, in one of his letters to Atticus, calls the common people of Rome horse-leeches of the treasury. Solomon, having mentioned those that devoured the property of the poor as the worst of all the generations which he had specified, proceeds to state the insatiable cupidity with which they prosecuted their schemes of rapine and plunder. As the horse-leech had two daughters, cruelty and thirst of blood, which cannot be satisfied, so the oppressor of the poor has two dispositions, rapacity and avarice, which never say they have enough, but continually demand additional gratifications.

HOSANNA, "Save, I beseech thee," or, "Give salvation," a well known form of blessing, Matthew xxi, 9, 15; Mark xi, 9, 10; John xii, 13.

HOSEA, son of Beeri, the first of the minor prophets. He is generally considered as a native and inhabitant of the kingdom of Israel, and is supposed to have begun to prophesy about B. C. 800. He exercised his office sixty years; but it is not known at what periods his different prophecies now remaining were delivered. Most of them are directed against the people of Israel, whom he reproves and threatens for their idolatry and wickedness, and exhorts to repentance, with the greatest earnestness, as the only means of averting the evils impending over their country. The principal predictions contained in this book, are the captivity and dispersion of the kingdom of Israel; the deliverance of Judah from Sennacherib; the present state of the Jews; their future restoration, and union with the Gentiles in the kingdom of the Messiah; the call of our Saviour out of Egypt, and his resurrection on the third day. The style of Hosea is peculiarly obscure; it is sententious, concise, and abrupt; the transitions of persons are sudden; and the connexive and adversative particles are frequently omitted. The prophecies are in one continued series, without any distinction as to the times when they were delivered, or the different subjects to which they relate. They are not so clear and detailed, as the predictions of those prophets who lived in succeeding ages. When, however, we have surmounted these difficulties, we shall see abundant reason to admire the force and energy with which this prophet writes, and the boldness of the figures and similitudes which he uses.

2. Hosea, or Hoshea, son of Elah, was the last king of Israel. Having conspired against Pekah, son of Remaliah, king of Israel, he killed him, A. M. 3265; B. C. 739. However, the elders of the land seem to have taken the government into their hands; for Hoshea was not in possession of the kingdom till nine years after, 2 Kings xv, 30; xvii, 1. Hoshea did evil in the sight of the Lord, but not equal to the kings of Israel who preceded him; that is, say the Jewish doctors, he did not restrain his subjects from going to Jerusalem to worship, if they would; whereas the kings of Israel, his predecessors, had forbidden it, and had placed guards on the road to prevent it. Salmaneser, king of Assyria, being informed that Hoshea meditated a revolt, and had concerted measures with So, king of Egypt, to shake off the Assyrian yoke, marched against him, and besieged Samaria. After a siege of three years, in the ninth year of Hoshea's reign, the city was taken, and was reduced to a heap of ruins, A. M. 3282. The king of Assyria removed the Israelites of the ten tribes to countries beyond the Euphrates, and thus terminated the kingdom of the ten tribes.

HOSPITALITY. Instances of ancient hospitality occur frequently in the Old Testament. So in the case of Abraham, Gen. xviii, where he invites the angels who appeared in the form of men to rest and refreshment, "And he stood by them under the tree, and they did eat." "Nothing is more common in India," says Mr. Ward, "than to see travellers and guests eating under the shade of trees. Even feasts are never held in houses. The house of a Hindoo serves for the purposes of sleeping and cooking, and of shutting up the women; but is never considered as a sitting or a dining room." "On my return to the boat," says Belzony, "I found the aga and all his retinue seated on a mat, under a cluster of palm trees, close to the water. The sun was then setting, and the shades of the western mountains had reached across the Nile, and covered the town. It is at this time the people recreate themselves in various scattered groups, drinking coffee, smoking their pipes, and talking of camels, horses, asses, dhourra, caravans, or boats." "The aga having prepared a dinner for me," says Mr. Light, "invited several of the natives to sit down. Water was brought in a skin by an attendant, to wash our hands. Two fowls roasted were served up on wheaten cakes, in a wooden bowl, covered with a small mat, and a number of the same cakes in another: in the centre of these were liquid butter, and preserved dates. These were divided, broken up, and mixed together by some of the party, while others pulled the fowls to pieces: which done, the party began to eat as fast as they could: getting up, one after the other, as soon as their hunger was satisfied." "Hospitality to travellers," says Mr. Forbes, "prevails throughout Guzerat: a person of any consideration passing through the province is presented, at the entrance of a village, with fruit, milk, butter, fire wood, and earthen pots for cookery; the women and children offer him wreaths of flowers. Small bowers are constructed on convenient spots, at a distance from a well or lake, where a person is maintained by the nearest villages, to take care of the water jars, and supply all travellers gratis. There are particular villages, where the inhabitants compel all travellers to accept of one day's provisions: whether they be many or few, rich or poor, European or native, they must not refuse the offered bounty."

"So when angelic forms to Syria sent

Sat in the cedar shade, by Abraham's tent,

A spacious bowl th' admiring patriarch fills

With dulcet water from the scanty rills;

Sweet fruits and kernels gathers from his hoard,

With milk and butter piles the plenteous board;

While on the heated hearth his consort bakes

Fine flour well kneaded in unleavened cakes,

The guests ethereal quaff the lucid flood,

Smile on their hosts, and taste terrestrial food;

And while from seraph lips sweet converse springs,

They lave their feet, and close their silver wings."

Darwin.

HOURS. See Day.

HOUSES. The following description of oriental houses will serve to illustrate several passages of Scripture. From the gate of the porch, one is conducted into a quadrangular court, which, being exposed to the weather, is paved with stone, in order to carry off the water in the rainy season. The principal design of this quadrangle, is to give light to the house, and admit the fresh air into the apartments; it is also the place where the master of the house entertains his company, who are seldom or never honoured with admission into the inner apartments. This open space bears a striking resemblance to the IMPLUVIUM, or CAVA ÆDIUM, of the Romans, which was also an uncovered area, from whence the chambers were lighted. For the accommodation of the guests, the pavement is covered with mats or carpets; and as it is secured against all interruption from the street, is well adapted to public entertainments. It is called, says Dr. Shaw, the middle of the house, and literally answers to τὸ μέσον of the evangelist, into which the man afflicted with the palsy was let down through the ceiling, with his couch, before Jesus, Luke v, 19. Hence, he conjectures that our Lord was at this time instructing the people in the court of one of these houses; and it is by no means improbable, that the quadrangle was to him and his Apostles a favourite situation, while they were engaged in disclosing the mysteries of redemption. To defend the company from the scorching sun-beams, or "windy storm and tempest," a veil was expanded upon ropes from one side of the parapet wall to the other, which might be unfolded or folded at pleasure. The court is for the most part surrounded with a cloister, over which, when the house has a number of stories, a gallery is erected of the same dimensions with the cloister, having a balustrade, or else a piece of carved or latticed work, going round about, to prevent people from falling from it into the court. The doors of the enclosure round the house are made very small; but the doors of the houses very large, for the purpose of admitting a copious stream of fresh air into their apartments. The windows which look into the street are very high and narrow, and defended by lattice work; as they are only intended to allow the cloistered inmate a peep of what is passing without, while he remains concealed behind the casement. This kind of window the ancient Hebrews called ARUBAH, which is the same term that they used to express those small openings through which pigeons passed into the cavities of the rocks, or into those buildings which were raised for their reception. Thus the prophet asks: "Who are these that fly as a cloud, and as the doves, ארבתיהם-אל, to their small or narrow windows." The word is derived from a root which signifies to lie in wait for the prey; and is very expressive of the concealed manner in which a person examines through that kind of window an external object. Irwin describes the windows in Upper Egypt as having the same form and dimensions; and says expressly, that one of the windows of the house in which they lodged, and through which they looked into the street, more resembled a pigeon hole than any thing else. But the sacred writers mention another kind of window, which was large and airy; it was called חלון, and was large enough to admit a person of mature age being cast out of it; a punishment which that profligate woman Jezebel suffered by the command of Jehu, the authorized extirminator of her family. These large windows admit the light and the breeze into spacious apartments of the same length with the court, but which seldom or never communicate with one another. In the houses of the fashionable and the gay, the lower part of the walls is adorned with rich hangings of velvet or damask, tinged with the liveliest colours, suspended on hooks, or taken down at pleasure. A correct idea of their richness and splendour may be formed from the description, which the inspired writer has given of the hangings in the royal garden at Shushan, the ancient capital of Persia: "Where were white, green, and blue hangings, fastened with cords of fine linen and purple, to silver rings and pillars of marble," Esther i, 6. The upper part of the walls is adorned with the most ingenious wreathings and devices, in stucco and fret-work. The ceiling is generally of wainscot, painted with great art, or else thrown into a variety of pannels with gilded mouldings. In the days of Jeremiah the prophet, when the profusion and luxury of all ranks in Judea were at their height, their chambers were ceiled with fragrant and costly wood, and painted with the richest colours. Of this extravagance the indignant seer loudly complains: "Wo unto him that saith, I will build me a wide house and large chambers, and cutteth him out windows: and it is ceiled with cedar, and painted with vermilion," Jer. xxii, 14. The floors of these splendid apartments were laid with painted tiles, or slabs of the most beautiful marble. A pavement of this kind is mentioned in the book of Esther; at the sumptuous entertainment which Ahasuerus made for the princes and nobles of his vast empire, "the beds," or couches, upon which they reclined, "were of gold and silver, upon a pavement of red and blue, and white and black marble." Plaster of terrace is often vised for the same purpose; and the floor is always covered with carpets, which are for the most part of the richest materials. Upon these carpets, a range of narrow beds, or mattresses, is often placed along the sides of the wall, with velvet or damask bolsters, for the greater ease and convenience of the company. To these luxurious indulgences the prophets occasionally seem to allude: Ezekiel was commanded to pronounce a "wo to the women that sew pillows to all armholes," Ezek. xiii, 18; and Amos denounces the judgments of his God against them "that lie upon beds of ivory, and stretch themselves upon their couches, and eat the lambs out of the flock, and the calves out of the midst of the stall," Amos vi, 4. At one end of each chamber is a little gallery, raised three or four feet above the floor, with a balustrade in front, to which they go up by a few steps. Here they place their beds; a situation frequently alluded to in the Holy Scriptures. Thus Jacob addressed his undutiful son, in his last benediction: "Thou wentest up to thy father's bed,--he went up to my couch," Gen. xlix, 4. The allusion is again involved in the declaration of Elijah to the king of Samaria: "Now, therefore, thus saith the Lord, Thou shalt not come down from that bed on which thou art gone up, but shalt surely die," 2 Kings i, 4, 16. And the Psalmist sware unto the Lord, and vowed unto the mighty God of Jacob, "Surely I will not come into the tabernacle of my house, nor go up into my bed, until I find out a place for the Lord," Psalm cxxxii, 3. This arrangement may likewise illustrate the circumstance of Hezekiah's "turning his face to the wall, when he prayed," that the greatness of his sorrow, and the fervour of his devotion, might, as much as possible, be concealed from his attendants, 2 Kings xx.

The roof is always flat, and often composed of branches of wood laid across rude beams; and, to defend it from the injuries of the weather, to which it is peculiarly exposed in the rainy season, it is covered with a strong plaster of terrace. It is surrounded by a wall breast-high, which forms the partition with the contiguous houses, and prevents one from falling into the street on the one side, or into the court on the other. This answers to the battlements which Moses commanded the people of Israel to make for the roof of their houses, for the same reason. "When thou buildest a new house, then thou shalt make a battlement, מעקה, for thy roof, that thou bring not blood upon thine house, if any man fall from thence," Deut. xxii, 8. Instead of the parapet wall, some terraces are guarded, like the galleries, with balustrades only, or latticed work. Of the same kind, probably, was the lattice or net, as the term שבכה seems to import, through which Ahaziah, the king of Samaria, fell down into the court, 2 Kings i, 2. This incident proves the necessity of the law which was graciously dictated from Sinai, and furnishes a beautiful example of God's paternal care and goodness; for the terrace was a place where many offices of the family were performed, and business of no little importance was occasionally transacted. Rahab concealed the spies on the roof, with the stalks of flax which she had laid in order to dry, Joshua ii, 6; the king of Israel, according to the custom of his country, rose from his bed, and walked upon the roof of his house, to enjoy the refreshing breezes of the evening, 2 Sam. xi, 2; upon the top of the house the prophet conversed with Saul, about the gracious designs of God, respecting him and his family, 1 Sam. ix, 25; to the same place Peter retired to offer up his devotions, Acts x, 9; and in the feast of tabernacles, under the government of Nehemiah, booths were erected, as well upon the terraces of their houses, as in their courts, and in the streets of the city, Neh. viii, 16. In Judea, the inhabitants sleep upon the tops of their houses during the heats of summer, in arbours made of the branches of trees, or in tents of rushes. When Dr. Pococke was at Tiberias, in Galilee, he was entertained by the sheik's steward, and with his company supped upon the top of the house for coolness, according to their custom, and lodged there likewise, in a sort of closet of about eight feet square, formed of wicker-work, plastered round toward the bottom, but without any door, each person having his cell. In like manner, the Persians take refuge during the day in subterraneous chambers, and pass the night on the flat roofs of their houses.

The expression, "to dig through houses," occurs, Job xxiv, 16. "Thieves," says Mr. Ward, "in Bengal very frequently dig through the mud walls, and under the clay floors of houses, and, entering unperceived, plunder them while the inhabitants are asleep." Our Lord's parable of the foolish man who built his house on the sand derives illustration from the following passages in Ward's "View," and Belzoni's "Travels:" "The fishermen in Bengal build their huts in the dry season on the beds of sand, from which the river has retired. When the rains set in, which they often do very suddenly, accompanied by violent north-west winds, the water pours down in torrents from the mountains. In one night multitudes of these huts are frequently swept away, and the place where they stood is the next morning undiscoverable." "It so happened, that we were to witness one of the greatest calamities that have occurred in Egypt in the recollection of any one living. The Nile rose this season three feet and a half above the highest mark left by the former inundation, with uncommon rapidity, and carried off several villages, and some hundreds of their inhabitants. I never saw any picture that could give a more correct idea of a deluge than the valley of the Nile in this season. The Arabs had expected an extraordinary inundation this year, in consequence of the scarcity of water the preceding season; but they did not apprehend it would rise to such a height. They generally erect fences of earth and reeds around their villages, to keep the water from their houses; but the force of this inundation baffled all their efforts. Their cottages, being built of earth, could not stand one instant against the current; and no sooner did the water reach them, than it levelled them with the ground. The rapid stream carried off all that was before it; men, women, children, cattle, corn, every thing was washed away in an instant, and left the place where the village stood without any thing to indicate that there had ever been a house on the spot."

House is taken for family: "The Lord plagued Pharaoh and his house," Gen. xii, 17. "What is my house, that thou hast brought me hitherto?" 2 Sam. vii, 18. So Joseph was of the house of David, Luke i, 27; ii, 4; but more especially he was of his royal lineage, or family; and, as we conceive, in the direct line or eldest branch of the family; so that he was next of kin to the throne, if the government had still continued in possession of the descendants of David. House is taken for kindred: it is a Christian's duty to provide first for those of his own house, 1 Tim. v, 8, his family, his relatives.

HUSBANDRY. In the primitive ages of the world, agriculture, as well as the keeping of flocks, was a principal employment among men Gen. ii, 15; iii, 17–19; iv, 2. It is an art which has ever been a prominent source, both of the necessaries and the conveniences of life. Those states and nations, especially Babylon and Egypt, which made the cultivation of the soil their chief business, arose in a short period to wealth and power. To these communities just mentioned, which excelled in this particular all the others of antiquity, may be added that of the Hebrews, who learned the value of the art while remaining in Egypt, and ever after that time were famous for their industry in the cultivation of the earth. Moses, following the example of the Egyptians, made agriculture the basis of the state. He accordingly apportioned to every citizen a certain quantity of land, and gave him the right of tilling it himself, and of transmitting it to his heirs. The person who had thus come into possession could not alienate the property for any longer period than the year of the coming jubilee: a regulation which prevented the rich from coming into possession of large tracts of land, and then leasing them out in small parcels to the poor: a practice which anciently prevailed, and does to this day, in the east. It was another law of Moses, that the vender of a piece of land, or his nearest relative, had a right to redeem the land sold, whenever they chose, by paying the amount of profits up to the year of jubilee, Ruth iv, 4; Jer. xxxii, 7. Another law enacted by Moses on this subject was, that the Hebrews, as was the case among the Egyptians after the time of Joseph, should pay a tax of two-tenths of their income unto God, whose servants they were to consider themselves to be, and whom they were to obey as their King and Lord, Lev. xxvii, 30; Deut. xii, 17–19; xiv, 22–29; Gen. xxviii, 22. The custom of marking the boundaries of lands by stones, although it prevailed a long time before, Job xxiv, 2, was confirmed and perpetuated in the time of Moses by an express law; and a curse was pronounced against him who without authority removed them. These regulations having been made in respect to the tenure, incumbrances, &c, of landed property, Joshua divided the whole country which he had occupied, first among the respective tribes, and then among individual Hebrews, running it out with the aid of a measuring line, Joshua xvii, 5, 14; Amos vii, 17; Micah ii, 5; Psalm lxxviii, 55; Ezek. xl, 3. The word, חבל, A LINE, is accordingly used by a figure of speech, for the heritage itself, Psalm xvi, 6: "The LINES have fallen to me in pleasant places, yea I have a goodly heritage." Though Moses was the friend of the agriculturist, he by no means discouraged the keeper of the flock.

The occupation of the husbandman was held in honour, not only for the profits which it brought, but from the circumstance that it was supported and protected by the fundamental laws of the state. All who were not set apart for religious duties, such as the priests and the Levites, whether inhabitants of the country, or of towns and cities, were considered by the laws, and were, in fact, agriculturists. The rich and the noble, it is true, in the cultivation of the soil, did not always put themselves on a level with their servants; but none were so rich or so noble as to disdain to put their hand to the plough, 1 Sam. xi, 7; 1 Kings xix, 19; 2 Chron. xxvi, 10. The priests and Levites were indeed engaged in other employments, yet they could not withhold their honour from an occupation which supplied them with their income. The esteem in which agriculture was held diminished as luxury increased; but it never wholly came to an end. Even after the captivity, when many of the Jews had become merchants and mechanics, the esteem and honour attached to this occupation still continued, especially under the dynasty of the Persians, who were agriculturists from motives of religion.

The soil of Palestine is very fruitful, if the dews and vernal and autumnal rains are not withheld. The country, in opposition to Egypt, is eulogized for its rains in Deut. xi, 10. The Hebrews, notwithstanding the richness of the soil, endeavoured to increase its fertility in various ways. They not only divested it of stones, but watered it by means of canals, communicating with the rivers or brooks; and thereby imparted to their fields the richness of gardens, Psalm i, 3; lxv, 10; Prov. xxi, 1; Isa. xxx, 25; xxxii, 2, 20. Springs, therefore, fountains, and rivulets, were held in as much honour and worth by husbandmen as by shepherds, Joshua xv, 9; Judges i, 15; and we accordingly find that the land of Canaan was extolled for those fountains of water of which Egypt was destitute. The soil was enriched, also, in addition to the method just mentioned, by means of ashes; to which the straw, the stubble, the husks, the brambles, and grass, that overspread the land during the sabbatical year, were reduced by fire. The burning over the surface of the land had also another good effect, namely, that of destroying the seeds of the noxious herbs, Isa. vii, 23; xxxii, 13; Prov. xxiv, 31. Finally, the soil was manured with dung.

The Hebrew word, דגן, which is translated variously by the English words, GRAIN, CORN, &c, is of general signification, and comprehends in itself different kinds of grain and pulse, such as wheat, millet, spelt, wall-barley, barley, beans, lentils, meadow-cumin, pepperwort, flax, cotton; to these may be added various species of the cucumber, and perhaps rice. Rye and oats do not grow in the warmer climates; but their place is, in a manner, supplied by barley. Barley, mixed with broken straw, affords the fodder for beasts of burden, which is called כליל. Wheat, חטה, which, by way of eminence, is called דגן, grew in Egypt in the time of Joseph, as it now does in Africa, on several branches from one stalk, each one of which produced an ear, Gen. xii, 47. This sort of wheat does not flourish in Palestine: the wheat of Palestine is of a much better kind.

HUSKS, κεράτιον, Luke xv, 16; the husks of leguminous plants, so named from their resemblance to κέρας, A HORN; but Bochart thinks that the κερατία were the CERETONIA, the husks or fruit of the carob tree, a tree very common in the Levant. We learn from Columella, that these pods afforded food for swine; and they are mentioned as what the prodigal desired to eat, when reduced to extreme hunger.

HUTCHINSONIANS, the followers of John Hutchinson, Esq., a learned and respectable layman, who was born at Spennythorn, in Yorkshire, in 1674. In 1724, he published the first part of that curious work, "Moses's *Principia*," in which he ridiculed Dr. Woodward's "Natural History of the Earth," and exploded the doctrine of gravitation established in Sir Isaac Newton's "*Principia*." In the second part of this work, published in 1727, he maintained, in opposition to the Newtonian system, that a PLENUM is the principle of the Scripture philosophy. In this work he also intimated that the idea of a Trinity is to be taken from the grand agents in the natural system, fire, light, and spirit. From this time he continued to publish a volume every year or two till his death; and a correct and elegant edition of his works, including the **MSS**. which he left was published in 1748, in 12 vols. 8vo. Mr. Hutchinson thought that the Hebrew Scriptures comprise a perfect system of natural philosophy, theology, and religion. He entertained so high an opinion of the Hebrew language, that he thought the Almighty must have employed it to communicate every species of knowledge, human and divine; and that, accordingly, every species of knowledge is to be found in the Old Testament. Both he and his followers laid a great stress on the evidence of Hebrew etymology. After Origen, and other eminent commentators, he asserted that the Scriptures are not to be understood and interpreted in a literal but in a typical sense, and according to the radical import of the Hebrew expressions; that even the historical parts, and particularly those relating to the Jewish ceremonies and Levitical law, are to be considered in this light; and he also asserted that, agreeably to this mode of interpretation, the Hebrew Scriptures would be found amply to testify concerning the nature and offices of Jesus Christ. His plan was to find natural philosophy in the Bible, where hitherto it had been thought no such thing was to be met with, or ever intended. His editors tell us, he found, upon examination, that the Hebrew Scriptures nowhere ascribe motion to the body of the sun, nor fixedness to the earth; that they describe the created system to be a PLENUM without any vacuum at all, and reject the assistance of gravitation, attraction, or any such occult qualities, for performing the stated operations of nature, which are carried on by the mechanism of the heavens, in their threefold condition of fire, light, and spirit, or air, the material agents set to work at the beginning; that the heavens, thus framed by almighty Wisdom, are an instituted emblem and visible substitute of JEHOVAH ALEIM, the eternal Three, the coëqual and co-adorable Trinity in Unity; that the unity of substance in the heavens points out the unity of essence and the distinction of conditions, the personality in Deity, without confounding the persons or dividing the substance; and that, from their being made emblems, they are called in Hebrew SHEMIM, the names, representatives, or substitutes, expressing by their names that they are emblems, and, by their conditions or offices, what it is they are emblems of. He also found that the Hebrew Scriptures have some capital words, which he has proved, or endeavoured to prove, contain, in their radical meaning, the greatest and most comfortable truths. Thus, the word ELOHIM, which we call God, or, as he reads it, ALEIM, he refers to the oath or conditional execration, by which the eternal covenant of grace among the persons in Jehovah was and is confirmed. The word BERITH, which our translation renders "covenant," signifies, "he or that which purifies" and so the Purifier or purification FOR, not WITH, man. The cherubim, which have been thought "angels placed as a guard to deter Adam from breaking into Eden again," he explains to have been a hieroglyphic of divine construction, or a sacred image, to describe, as far as figures could go, the ALEIM and man taken in, or humanity united to deity. In like manner, he treats several other words of similar, though not quite so solemn, import. Hence he drew this conclusion, "that all the rites and ceremonies of the Jewish dispensation were so many delineations of Christ, in what he was to be, to do, and to suffer; and that the early Jews knew them to be types of his actions and sufferings, and, by performing them as such, were in so far Christians, both in faith and practice." His followers maintain, that the cherubim, and the glory around them, with the divine presence in them, were not only emblematical figures, representing the persons of the ever blessed Trinity, as engaged in covenant for the redemption of man, but also that they were intended "to keep or preserve the way of the tree of life, to show man the way to life eternal, and keep him from losing or departing from it." That Melchizedec was an eminent type of Christ, there can be little doubt; but that he was actually the second person of the Trinity, in a human form, is a tenet of the Hutchinsonians, though not entirely peculiar to them. Mr. Hutchinson supposes that "the air exists in three conditions, fire, light, and spirit; the two latter are the finer and grosser parts of the air in motion: from the earth to the sun, the air is finer and finer till it becomes pure light near the confines of the sun, and fire in the orb of the sun, or solar focus." From the earth toward the circumference of this system, in which he includes the fixed stars, the air becomes grosser and grosser till it becomes stagnant, in which condition it is at the utmost verge of this system; from whence, in his opinion, the expression of "outer darkness," and "blackness of darkness," used in the New Testament, seems to be taken. These are some of the principal outlines of this author's doctrines, which have been patronized by several eminent divines, both of the church and among the Dissenters.

2. The followers of Mr. Hutchinson have not erected themselves into a sect or separate community. Among them may be reckoned some eminent and respectable divines, both in England and Scotland; but their numbers seem at present to be rather on the decrease. Of those who, in their day, were ranked in the list of Hutchinsonians, perhaps the most eminent were the following: Mr. Julius Bate, and Mr. Parkhurst, the lexicographers; Mr. Holloway, author of "Originals," and "Letter and Spirit;" Dr. Hodges, provost of Oriel College, Oxford; Mr. Henry Lee, author of "Sophron, or Nature's Characteristics of the Truth;" Dr. Wetherell, late

master of University College, Oxford; Mr. Romaine; Bishop Horne; and Mr. William Jones, the bishop's learned friend and biographer.

HYMN, a song, or ode, composed in honour of God. The Jewish hymns were accompanied with trumpets, drums, and cymbals, to assist the voices of the Levites and people. The word is used as synonymous with canticle, song, or psalm, which the Hebrews scarcely distinguish, having no particular term for a hymn, as distinct from a psalm or canticle. St. Paul requires Christians to edify one another with "psalms, and hymns, and spiritual songs." St. Matthew says, that Christ, having supped, sung a hymn, and went out. He recited the hymns or psalms which the Jews were used to sing after the passover; which they called the HALAL; that is, the Hallelujah Psalms.

HYPERBOLE. This figure, in its representation of things or objects, either magnifies or diminishes them beyond or below their proper limits: it is common in all languages, and is of frequent occurrence in the Scriptures. Thus, things which are lofty are said to reach up to heaven, Deut. i, 28; ix, 1; Psalm cvii, 26. So things which are beyond the reach or capacity of man are said to be in "heaven," in the "deep," or "beyond the sea," Deut. xxx, 12; Rom. x, 6, 7. So a great quantity or number is commonly expressed by the "sand of the sea," the "dust of the earth," and the "stars of heaven," Genesis xiii, 16; xli, 49; Judges vii, 12; 1 Sam. xiii, 5; 1 Kings iv, 29; 2 Chron. i, 9; Jer. xv, 8; Heb. xi, 12. In like manner we meet with "smaller than grasshoppers," Num. xiii, 33, to denote extreme diminutiveness; "swifter than eagles," 2 Sam. i, 23, to intimate extreme celerity; the "earth trembled," the "mountains melted," Judges v, 4, 5; the "earth rent," 1 Kings i, 40. "I make my bed to swim;" "rivers of tears run down mine eyes." So we read of "angels' food," Psalm vi, 6; cxix, 136; lxxviii, 25; the "face of an angel," Acts vi, 15; and the "tongue of an angel," 1 Cor. xiii, 1. See also Gal. i, 8; iv, 14. We read "sigh with the breaking of thy loins," Ezek. xxi, 6, that is, most deeply. So we read that "the stones would cry out," and "they shall not leave in thee one stone upon another," Luke xix, 40, 44; that is, there shall be a total desolation.

HYPOCRITE, a word from the Greek, which signifies one who feigns to be what he is not; who puts on a masque or character, like actors in tragedies and comedies. It is generally applied to those who assume appearances of a virtue, without possessing it in reality. Our Saviour accused the Pharisees of hypocrisy. In the Old Testament, the Hebrew word CANEPH, which is rendered "hypocrite," "counterfeit," signifies also a profane wicked man, a man polluted, corrupted, a man of impiety, a deceiver. It was ingeniously said by Basil, that the hypocrite did not put off the old man, but put the new man upon it.

HYPOSTATICAL UNION; the union of the divine and human natures of Christ in one person. This is the doctrine generally received in the church of Christ; but there have been some who have denied this, who yet acknowledge our Lord's divinity. Nestorius, who had been taught to distinguish accurately between the divine and human nature of Christ, was offended with some expressions commonly used by Christians in the beginning of the fifth century, which seemed to destroy that distinction, and particularly with their calling the Virgin Mary θεότοκος, as if it were possible for the Godhead to be born. His zeal provoked opposition; in the eagerness of controversy he was led to use unguarded expressions; and he was condemned by the third of the general councils, the council of Ephesus, in the year 431. It is a matter of doubt whether the opinions of Nestorius, if he had been allowed by his adversaries fairly to explain them, would have appeared inconsistent with the doctrine established by the council of Ephesus, that Christ is one person, in whom two natures were most closely united. But whatever was the extent of the error of Nestorius, from him is derived that system concerning the incarnation of Christ, which is held by a large body of Christians in Chaldea, Assyria, and other regions of the east, and which is known in the ecclesiastical history of the west by the name of the Nestorian heresy. The object of the Nestorians is to avoid every appearance of ascribing to the divinity of Christ the weakness of humanity; and therefore they distinguish between Christ, and God who dwelt in Christ as in a temple. They say, that from the moment of the virgin's conception, there commenced an intimate and indissoluble union between Christ and God, that these two persons presented in Jesus Christ one ϖρόσωπον, or aspect, but that the union between them is merely a union of will and affection, such in kind as that which subsists between two friends, although much closer in degree. Opposite to the Nestorian opinion is the Eutychian, which derives its name from Eutyches, an abbot of Constantinople, who, about the middle of the fifth century, in his zeal to avoid the errors of Nestorius, was carried to the other extreme. Those who did not hold the Nestorian opinions had been accustomed to speak of the "one incarnate nature" of Christ. But Eutyches used this phrase in such a manner as to appear to teach that the human nature of Christ was absorbed in the divine, and that his body had no real existence. This opinion was condemned in the year 451, by the council of Chalcedon, the fourth general council, which declared, as the faith of the catholic church, that Christ is one person; that in this unity of person there are two natures, the divine and the human; and that there is no change, or mixture, or confusion of these two natures, but that each retains its distinguishing properties. The decree of Chalcedon was not universally submitted to. But many of the successors of Eutyches, wishing to avoid the palpable absurdity which was ascribed to him, of supposing that one nature was absorbed by another, and anxious at the same time to preserve that unity which the Nestorians divided, declared their faith to be, that in Christ there is one nature, but that this nature is twofold or compounded. From this tenet the successors of Eutyches derive the name of Monophysites; and from Jacob Baradæus, who in the following century was a zealous and successful preacher, of the system of the Monophysites, they are more commonly known by the name of Jacobites. The Monophysites, or Jacobites, are found chiefly near the Euphrates and Tigris;

they are much less numerous than the Nestorians; and, although they profess to have corrected the errors which were supposed to adhere to the Eutychian heresy, they may be considered as having formed their peculiar opinions upon the general principles of that system. The Monothelites, an ancient sect, of whom a remnant is found in the neighbourhood of Mount Libanus, disclaim any connection with Eutyches, and agree with the Catholics in ascribing two natures to Christ; but they have received their name from their conceiving that Christ, being one person, can only have one will: whereas the Catholics, considering both natures as complete, think it essential to each to have a will, and say that every inconvenience which can be supposed to arise from two wills in one person, is removed by the perfect harmony between that will which belongs to the divine, and that which belongs to the human nature of Christ.

HYSSOP, אזוב, Exod. xii, 22; Lev. xiv, 4, 6, 49, 51, 52; Num. xix, 6, 18; 1 Kings iv, 33; Psalm li, 7; Matt, xxvii, 48; Mark xv, 36; ὑσσωπὸς, John xix, 29; Heb. ix, 19. It grows plentifully on the mountains near Jerusalem. It is of a bitter taste; and, from being considered as possessing detersive and cleansing qualities, derived probably its Hebrew name. The original word has been variously translated; and Celsius has devoted forty-two pages to remove difficulties, occasioned by the discordant opinions of the Talmudical writers, and to ascertain the plant intended. That it is the hyssop seems most probable: the passage in Heb. ix, 19, sufficiently identifies it. Under the law, it was commonly used in purifications as a sprinkler. When the children of Israel came out of Egypt, they were commanded to take a bunch of hyssop, to dip it in the blood of the paschal lamb, and sprinkle it on the lintel and the two side-posts of the door. It was also used in sprinkling the leper. The hyssop is extremely well adapted to such purposes, as it grows in bunches, and puts out many suckers from a single root.

ICONIUM, the chief city of Lycaonia, in Asia Minor. An assault being meditated at the place by the unbelieving Jews and Gentiles upon the Apostles Paul and Barnabas, who, by preaching in the synagogue, had converted many Jews and Greeks, they fled to Lystra; where the designs of their enemies were put in execution, and St. Paul miraculously escaped with his life, Acts xiv. The church planted at this place by St. Paul continued to flourish, until, by the persecutions of the Saracens, and afterward of the Seljukian Turks, who made it the capital of one of their sultanies, it was nearly extinguished. But some Christians of the Greek and Armenian churches, with a Greek archbishop, are yet found in the suburbs of this city, who are not permitted to reside within the walls. Iconium is now called Cogni, and is still a considerable city; being the capital of the extensive province of Caramania, as it was formerly of Lycaonia, and the seat of a Turkish beglerberg, or viceroy. It is the place of chief strength and importance in the central parts of Asiatic Turkey, being surrounded by a strong wall of four miles in circumference; but, as is the case with most eastern cities, much of the enclosed space is waste. It is situated about a hundred and twenty miles inland from the Mediterranean, on the lake Trogilis. Mr. Kinneir says, Iconium, the capital of Lycaonia, is mentioned by Xenophon, and afterward by Cicero and Strabo; but does not appear to have been a place of any consideration until after the taking of Nice by the crusaders in 1099, when the Seljukian sultans of Roum chose it as their residence. These sultans rebuilt the walls, and embellished the city: they were, however, expelled in 1189 by Frederic Barbarossa, who took it by assault; but after his death they reëntered their capital, where they reigned in splendour till the irruption of Tchengis Khan, and his grandson, Holukow, who broke the power of the Seljukians. Iconium, under the name of Cogni, or Konia, has been included in the dominions of the grand seignior ever since the time of Bajazet, who finally extirpated the Ameers of Caramania. The modern city has an imposing appearance from the number and size of its mosques, colleges, and other public buildings; but these stately edifices are crumbling into ruins, while the houses of the inhabitants consist of a mixture of small huts built of sun-dried bricks, and wretched hovels thatched with reeds. The city, according to the same authority, contains about eighty thousand inhabitants, principally Turks, with only a small proportion of Christians. It is represented as enjoying a fine climate, and pleasantly situated among gardens and meadows; while it is nearly surrounded, at some distance, with mountains which rise to the regions of perpetual snow. It was formerly the capital of an extensive government, and the seat of a powerful pasha, who maintained a military force competent to the preservation of peace and order, and the defence of his territories. But it has now dwindled into insignificance, and exhibits upon the whole a mournful scene of desolation and decay.

ICONOCLASTES, image breakers; or Iconomachi, image opposers, were names given to those who rejected the use of images in churches, and, on certain occasions, vented their zeal in destroying them. The great opposition to images began under Bardanes, a Greek emperor, in the beginning of the eighth century; and was revived again, a few years after, under Leo, the Isaurian, who issued an edict against image worship, which occasioned a civil war in the islands of the Archipelago, and afterward in Italy; the Roman pontiffs and Greek councils alternately supporting it. At length images were rejected by the Greek church, which however retains pictures in churches, though her members do not worship them; but the Latin church, more corrupt, not only retained images, but made them the medium, if not the object, of their worship, and are therefore ICONODULI, or ICONOLATRÆ, image worshippers.

IDDO, a prophet of the kingdom of Judah, who wrote the actions of Rehoboam's and Abijah's reigns, 2 Chron. xii, 15. It seems by 2 Chron. xiii, 22, that he had entitled his work, MIDRASCH, or, "Inquiries." We know nothing particularly concerning the life of this prophet. It is probable that he likewise wrote some prophecies against Jeroboam, the son of Nebat, 2 Chron. ix, 29, wherein part of Solomon's life was included. Josephus, and many others after him, are of opinion that it was Iddo who was sent to Jeroboam, while he was at Bethel, and was there dedicating an altar to the golden calves; and that it was he who was killed by a lion, 1 Kings xiii.

IDOLATRY, from εἰδωλολατρεία, composed of εἶδος, IMAGE, and λατρεύειν, TO SERVE, the worship and adoration of false gods; or the giving those honours to creatures, or the works of man's hands, which are only due to God. Several have written of the origin and causes of idolatry: among the rest, Vossius, Selden, Godwyn, Tenison, and Faber; but it is still a doubt who was the first author of it. It is generally allowed, however, that it had not its beginning till after the deluge; and many are of opinion, that Belus, who is supposed to be the same with Nimrod, was the first man that was deified. But whether they had not paid divine honours to the heavenly bodies before that time, cannot be determined; our acquaintance with those remote times being extremely slender. The first mention we find made of idolatry is where Rachel is said to have taken the idols of her father; for though the meaning of the Hebrew word תרפים, be disputed, yet it is pretty evident they were idols. Laban calls them his gods, and Jacob calls them strange gods, and looks on them as abominations. The original idolatry by image worship is by many attributed to the age of Eber, B. C. 2247, about a hundred and one years after the deluge, according to the Hebrew chronology; four hundred and one years according to the Samaritan; and five hundred and thirty-one years according to the Septuagint; though most of the fathers place it no higher than that of Serug; which seems to be the more probable opinion, considering that for the first hundred and thirty-four years of Eber's life all mankind dwelt in a body together; during which time it is not reasonable to suppose that idolatry broke in upon them; then some time must be allowed after the dispersion of the several nations, which were but small at the beginning, to increase and settle themselves; so that if idolatry was introduced in Eber's time, it must have been toward the end of his life, and could not well have prevailed so universally, and with that obstinacy which some authors have imagined. Terah, the father of Abraham, who lived at Ur, in Chaldea, about B. C. 2000, was unquestionably an idolater; for he is expressly said in Scripture to have served other gods. The authors of the Universal History think, that the origin and progress of idolatry are plainly pointed out to us in the account which Moses gives of Laban's and Jacob's parting, Gen. xxxi, 44, &c. From the custom once introduced of erecting monuments in memory of any solemn covenants, the transition was easy into the notion, that some deity took its residence in them, in order to punish the first aggressors; and this might be soon improved by an ignorant and degenerate world, till not only birds, beasts, stocks, and stones, but sun, moon, and stars, were called into the same office; though used, perhaps, at first, by the designing part of mankind, as scare-crows, to overawe the ignorant.

Sanchoniathon, who wrote his "Phenician Antiquities," apparently with a view to apologize for idolatry, traces its origin to the descendants of Cain, the elder branch, who began with the worship of the sun, and afterward added a variety of other methods of idolatrous worship: proceeding to deify the several parts of nature, and men after their death; and even to consecrate the plants shooting out of the earth, which the first men judged to be gods, and worshipped as those that sustained the lives of themselves and of their posterity. The Chaldean priests, in process of time, being by their situation early addicted to celestial observations, instead of conceiving as they ought to have done concerning the omnipotence of the Creator and Mover of the heavenly bodies, fell into the impious error of esteeming them as gods, and the immediate governors of the world, in subordination, however, to the Deity, who was invisible except by his works, and the effects of his power. Concluding that God created the stars and great luminaries for the government of the world, partakers with himself and as his ministers, they thought it but just and natural that they should be honoured and extolled, and that it was the will of God they should be magnified and worshipped. Accordingly, they erected temples, or SACELLA, to the stars, in which they sacrificed and bowed down before them, esteeming them as a kind of mediators between God and man. Impostors afterward arose, who gave out, that they had received express orders from God himself concerning the manner in which particular heavenly bodies should be represented, and the nature and ceremonies of the worship which was to be paid them. When they proceeded to worship wood, stone, or metal, formed and fashioned by their own hands, they were led to apprehend, that these images had been, in some way or other, animated or informed with a supernatural power by supernatural means; though Dr. Prideaux imagines, that, being at a loss to know how to address themselves to the planets when they were below the horizon, and invisible, they recurred to the use of images. But it will be sufficient to suppose, that they were persuaded that each star or planet was actuated by an intelligence; and that the virtues of the heavenly body were infused into the image that represented it. It is certain, that the SENTIENT nature and divinity of the sun, moon, and stars, was strenuously asserted by the philosophers, particularly by Pythagoras and his followers, and by the Stoics, as well as believed by the common people, and was, indeed, the very foundation of the Pagan idolatry. The heavenly bodies were the first deities of all the idolatrous nations, were esteemed eternal, sovereign, and supreme; and distinguished by the title of the natural gods. Thus we find that the primary gods of the Heathens in general were Saturn, Jupiter, Mars, Apollo, Mercury, Venus, and Diana; by which we can understand no other than the sun and moon, and the five greatest luminaries next to these. Plutarch expressly censures the Epicureans for asserting that the sun and moon, whom all men worshipped, are void of intelligence.

Sanchoniathon represents the most ancient nations, particularly the Phenicians and Egyptians, as acknowledging only the natural gods, the sun, moon, planets, and elements; and Plato declares it as his opinion, that the first Grecians likewise held these only to be gods, as many of the barbarians did in his time. Beside these natural gods, the Heathens believed that there were certain spirits who held a middle rank between the gods and men on earth, and carried on all intercourse between them; conveying the addresses of men to the gods, and the divine benefits to men. These spirits were called demons. From the imaginary office ascribed to them, they became the grand objects of the religious hopes and fears of the Pagans, of immediate dependence and divine worship. In the most learned nations, they did not so properly share, as engross, the public devotion. To these alone sacrifices were offered, while the celestial gods were worshipped only with a pure mind, or with hymns and praises. As to the nature of these demons, it has been generally believed, that they were spirits of a higher origin than the human race; and, in support of this opinion, it has been alleged, that the supreme deity of the Pagans is called the greatest demon; that demons are described as beings placed between the gods and men; and that demons are expressly distinguished from heroes, who were the departed souls of men. Some, however, have combatted this opinion, and maintained, on the contrary, that by demons, such as were the more immediate objects of the established worship among the ancient nations, particularly the Egyptians, Greeks, and Romans, we are to understand beings of an earthly origin, or such departed human souls as were believed to become demons.

Although the Hindoo inhabitants of the East Indies deny the charge of idolatry, using the same description of arguments as are so inconclusively urged by superstitious Europeans in defence of image worship, it is still evident that the mass of the Hindoos are addicted to gross idolatry. The gods of Rome were even less numerous, certainly less whimsical and monstrous, than those at Benares. In Moore's Hindoo Pantheon are given exact portraits of many scores of deities worshipped, with appropriate ceremonies, and under various forms and names, by different sects of that grossly superstitious race. Some of these portraits are of images colossal to a degree perhaps unequalled by any existing statues; others are exceedingly diminutive. Some are metallic casts, and some apparently extremely ancient, which exhibit every gradation of art from the rudest imaginable specimen, up to a very respectable portion of skill, so as to approach to elegance of form, and to ease and expression of attitude.

The principal causes which have been assigned for idolatry are, the indelible idea which every man has of God, and the evidence which he gives of it to himself; an inviolable attachment to the senses, and a habit of judging and deciding by them, and them only; the pride and vanity of the human mind, which is not satisfied with simple truth, but mingles and adulterates it with fables; men's ignorance of antiquity, or of the first times, and the first men, of whom they had but very dark and confused knowledge by tradition, they having left no written monuments, or books; the ignorance and change of languages; the style of the oriental writings, which is figurative and poetical, and personifies every thing; the scruples and fears inspired by superstition; the flattery and fictions of poets; the false relations of travellers; the imaginations of painters and sculptors; a smattering of physics, that is, a slight acquaintance with natural bodies and appearances, and their causes; the establishment of colonies, and the invention of arts, mistaken by barbarous people; the artifices of priests; the pride of certain men, who affected to pass for gods; the love and gratitude borne by the people to certain of their great men and benefactors; and, finally, the historical events of the Scriptures ill understood. "One great spring and fountain of all idolatry," says Sir William Jones, "was the veneration paid by men to the sun, or vast body of fire, which 'looks from his sole dominion like the god of this world;' and another, the immoderate respect shown to the memory of powerful or virtuous ancestors and warriors, of whom the sun and the moon were wildly supposed to be the parents." But the Scriptural account of the matter refers the whole to wilful ignorance and a corrupt heart: "They did not like to retain God in their knowledge." To this may be added, what indeed proceeds from the same sources, the disposition to convert religion into outward forms; the endeavour to render it more impressive upon the imagination through the senses; the substitution of sentiment for real religious principle; and the license which this gave to inventions of men, which in process of time became complicated and monstrous. That debasement of mind, and that alienation of the heart from God, and the gross immoralities and licentious practices which have ever accompanied idolatry, will sufficiently account for the severity with which it is denounced, both in the Old and New Testaments.

The veneration which the Papists pay to the Virgin Mary, and other saints and angels, and to the bread in the sacrament, the cross, relics, and images, affords ground for the Protestants to charge them with being idolaters, though they deny that they are so. It is evident that they worship these persons and things, and that they justify the worship, but deny the idolatry of it, by distinguishing subordinate from supreme worship. This distinction is justly thought by Protestants to be futile and nugatory, and certainly has no support from Holy Writ.

Under the government of Samuel, Saul, and David, there was little or no idolatry in Israel. Solomon was the first Hebrew king, who, in complaisance to his foreign wives, built temples and offered incense to strange gods. Jeroboam, the son of Nebat, who succeeded him in the greater part of his dominions, set up golden calves at Dan and Bethel. Under the reign of Ahab, this disorder was at its height, occasioned by Jezebel, the wife of Ahab, who did all she could to destroy the worship of the true God, by driving away and persecuting his prophets. God, therefore, incensed at the sins and idolatry of the ten tribes, abandoned those tribes to the kings of Assyria and Chaldea, who transplanted them beyond the Euphrates, from whence they never returned. The people of Judah were no less corrupted. The prophets give an awful description of their idolatrous practices. They were punished after the same manner, though not so severely, as the ten tribes; being led into captivity several times, from which at last they returned, and were settled in the land of Judea, after which we hear no more of their idolatry. They have been, indeed, ever since that period, distinguished for their zeal against it. See Image.

IDUMÆA is properly the Greek name for the land of Edom, which lay to the south of Judea, and extended from the Dead Sea to the Elanitic Gulf of the Red Sea, where were the ports of Elath and Ezion-Gaber. But the Idumæa of the New Testament applies only to a small part adjoining Judea on the south, and including even a portion of that country; which was taken possession of by the Edomites, or Idumæans, while the land lay unoccupied during the Babylonish captivity. The capital of this country was Hebron, which had formerly been the metropolis of the tribe of Judah. These Idumæans were so reduced by the Maccabees, that, in order to retain their possessions, they consented to embrace Judaism; and their territory became incorporated with Judea; although, in the time of our Saviour, it still retained its former name of Idumæa, Mark iii, 8. The proper Idumæans, or those who remained in the ancient land of Edom, became in process of time mingled with the Ishmaelites; the two people thus blended, being, from Nabaioth, or Nabath, the son of Ishmael, termed Nabathæans; under which names they are frequently mentioned in history. See Edom.

ILLYRICUM, a province lying to the north and north-west of Macedonia, along the eastern coast of the Adriatic Gulf, or Gulf of Venice. It was distinguished into two parts: Liburnia to the north, where is now Croatia, and Dalmatia to the south, which still retains the same name, and to which, as St. Paul informs Timothy, Titus went, 2 Tim. iv, 10. St. Paul says, that he preached the Gospel from Jerusalem round about to Illyricum, Rom. xv, 19.

IMAGE, in a religious sense, is an artificial representation of some person or thing used as an object of adoration, and is synonymous with idol. Nothing can be more clear, full, and distinct, than the expressions of Scripture prohibiting the making and worship of images, Exod. xx, 4, 5; Deut. xvi, 22. No sin is so strongly and repeatedly condemned in the Old Testament as that of idolatry, to which the Jews, in the early part of their history, were much addicted, and for which they were constantly punished. St. Paul was greatly affected, when he saw that the city of Athens was "wholly given to idolatry," Acts xvii, 16; and declared to the Athenians, that they ought not "to think that the Godhead is like unto gold, or silver, or stone, graven by art and man's device," Acts xvii, 29. He condemns those who "changed the glory of the incorruptible God into an image made like unto corruptible man, and to birds, and four-footed beasts, and creeping things," Romans i, 23.

That the first Christians had no images, is evident from this circumstance,--that they were reproached by the Heathens, because they did not use them; and we find almost every ecclesiastical writer of the first four centuries arguing against the Gentile practice of image worship, from the plain declarations of Scripture, and from the pure and spiritual nature of God. The introduction of images into places of Christian worship, dates its origin soon after the times of Constantine the Great; but the earlier Christians reprobated every species of image worship in the strongest language. It is sometimes pretended by the Papists, that they do not worship the images, but God through the medium of images; or, that the worship which they pay to images is inferior to that which they pay to the Deity himself. These distinctions would be scarcely understood by the common people; and formerly an enlightened Heathen or Jew would probably have urged the same thing. The practice is in direct opposition to the second commandment, and notwithstanding every sophistical palliation, it has always led to a transfer of human trust from God to something else. Hence idolatry, in general, is condemned in Scripture; and all use of images in the worship of God, making or bowing to any likeness, is absolutely forbidden. See Iconoclastes and Idolatry.

IMMATERIALITY, abstraction from matter; or what we understand by pure spirit.

IMMORTAL. That which will endure to all eternity, as having in itself no principle of alteration or corruption. God is absolutely immortal,--he cannot die. Angels are immortal; but God, who made them, can terminate their being. Man is immortal in part, that is, in his spirit; but his body dies. Inferior creatures are not immortal; they die wholly. Thus the principle of immortality is differently communicated according to the will of him who can render any creature immortal, by prolonging its life; who can confer immortality on the body of man, together with his soul; and will do so at the resurrection. God only is absolutely perfect, and, therefore, absolutely immortal. See Soul.

IMPOSITION OF HANDS. An ecclesiastical action, by which, among Episcopalians, a bishop lays his hands on the head of a person, in ordination, confirmation, or in uttering a blessing. In Presbyterian churches, the imposition is by the hands of the presbytery. This practice is also frequently observed by the Independents and others at their ordinations, when all the ministers present place their hands on the head of him whom they are ordaining, while one of them prays for a blessing on him and his future labours. This they retain as an ancient practice, justified by the example of the Apostles, when no extraordinary gifts were conveyed. However, Christians are not agreed as to the propriety of this ceremony; nor do they all consider it as an essential part of ordination.

Imposition of hands was a Jewish ceremony, introduced, not by any divine authority, but by custom; it being the practice among that people, whenever they prayed to God for any person, to lay their hands on his head. Our Saviour observed the same custom, both when he conferred his blessing on children, and when he cured the sick. The Apostles likewise laid hands on those upon whom they bestowed the Holy

Ghost, but it was a form accompanied by PRAYER, through which only the blessing was obtained. And the Apostles themselves sometimes underwent the imposition of hands afresh, when they entered upon any new design. In the ancient church, imposition of hands was practised on persons when they married; which custom the Abyssinians still observe. But this ceremony of laying on of hands is now restrained, by custom, chiefly to that imposition which is practised at the ordination of ministers.

[In the Methodist Episcopal Church, a bishop is constituted by the election of the general conference, and the laying on of the hands of three bishops, or at least of one bishop and two elders; unless it happen that, by death or otherwise, there be no bishop remaining in the church: in this case, the general conference is empowered to elect a bishop, and the elders, or any three of them appointed by the general conference for that purpose, to ordain him. An elder is constituted by the election of an annual conference, and the laying on of the hands of a bishop and of two or more elders. A deacon, by the election of an annual conference, and the laying on of the hands of a bishop.]

IMPUTED RIGHTEOUSNESS. See Justification.

INCENSE. THUS; so called by the dealers of drugs in Egypt from THUR, or THOR, the name of a harbour in the north bay of the Red Sea, near Mount Sinai; thereby distinguishing it from the gum arabic, which is brought from Suez, another port in the Red Sea, not far from Cairo. It differs also in being more pellucid and white. It burns with a bright and strong flame, not easily extinguished. It was used in the temple service as an emblem of prayer, Psalm cxli, 2; Rev. viii, 3, 4. Authors give it, or the best sort of it, the epithets white, pure, pellucid; and so it may have some connection with a word, derived from the same root, signifying unstained, clear, and so applied to moral whiteness and purity, Psalm li, 7; Dan. xii, 10. This gum is said to distil from incisions made in the tree during the heat of summer. What the form of the tree is which yields it, we do not certainly know. Pliny one while says, it is like a pear tree; another, that it is like a mastic tree; then, that it is like the laurel; and, in fine, that it is a kind of turpentine tree. It has been said to grow only in the country of the Sabeans, a people in Arabia Felix; and Theophrastus and Pliny affirm that it is found in Arabia. Dioscorides, however, mentions an Indian as well as an Arabian frankincense. At the present day it is brought from the East Indies, but not of so good a quality as that from Arabia. The "sweet incense," mentioned Exodus xxx, 7, and elsewhere, was a compound of several drugs, agreeably to the direction in the thirty-fourth verse. To offer incense was an office peculiar to the priests. They went twice a day into the holy place; namely, morning and evening, to burn incense there. Upon the great day of expiation, the high priest took incense, or perfume, pounded and ready for being put into the censer, and threw it upon the fire, the moment he went into the sanctuary. One reason of this was, that so the smoke which rose from the censer might prevent his looking with too much curiosity on the ark and mercy-seat. God threatened him with death upon failing to perform this ceremony, Lev. xvi, 13. Generally incense is to be considered as an emblem of the "prayers of the saints," and is so used by the sacred writers.

INCEST, an unlawful conjunction of persons related within the degrees of kindred prohibited by God. In the beginning of the world, and again, long after the deluge, marriages between near relations were allowed. In the time of Abraham and Isaac, these marriages were permitted, and among the Persians much later: it is even said to be esteemed neither criminal nor ignominious among the remains of the old Persians at this day. Some authors believe that marriages between near relations were permitted, or, at least, tolerated, till the time of Moses, who first prohibited them among the Hebrews; and that among other people they were allowed even after him. Others hold the contrary; but it is hard to establish either of these opinions, for want of historical documents. The degrees of consanguinity within which marriage was prohibited are stated in Lev. xviii, 6–18. Most civilized people have looked on incests as abominable crimes. St. Paul, speaking of the incestuous man of Corinth, says, "It is reported commonly, that there is fornication among you, and such fornication as is not so much as named among the Gentiles, that one should have his father's wife," 1 Cor. v, 1. In order to preserve chastity in families, and between persons of different sexes, brought up and living together in a state of unreserved intimacy, it is necessary, by every method possible, to inculcate an abhorrence of incestuous conjunctions; which abhorrence can only be upholden by the absolute reprobation of all commerce of the sexes between near relations. Upon this principle, the marriage, as well as other cohabitations, of brothers and sisters, of lineal kindred, and of all who usually live in the same family, may be said to be forbidden by the law of nature. Restrictions which extend to remoter degrees of kindred than what this reason makes it necessary to prohibit from intermarriage, are founded in the authority of the positive law which ordains them, and can only be justified by their tendency to diffuse wealth, to connect families, or to promote some political advantage. The Levitical law, which is received in this country, and from which the rule of the Roman law differs very little, prohibits marriages between relations within three degrees of kindred; computing the generations, not from, but through, the common ancestor, and accounting affinity the same as consanguinity. The issue, however, of such marriages are not bastardized, unless the parents be divorced during their life time.

INCHANTMENTS. The law of God condemns inchantments and inchanters. Several terms are used in Scripture to denote inchantments: 1. לחש, which signifies TO MUTTER, TO SPEAK WITH A LOW VOICE, like magicians in their evocations and magical operations, Psalm lviii, 6. 2. לטים, SECRETS, whence Moses speaks of the inchantments wrought by Pharaoh's magicians. 3. כשף, meaning those who practise juggling, legerdemain, tricks, and witchery, deluding people's eyes and senses, 2 Chron.

xxxiii, 6. 4. חבר, which signifies, properly, TO BIND, ASSEMBLE, ASSOCIATE, REUNITE: this occurs principally among those who charm serpents, who tame them, and make them gentle and sociable, which before were fierce, dangerous, and untractable, Deut. xviii, 11. We have examples of each of these ways of inchanting. It was common for magicians, sorcerers, and inchanters, to speak in a low voice, to whisper: they are called VENTRILOQUI, because they spake, as one would suppose, from the bottom of their stomachs. They affected secrecy and mysterious ways, to conceal the vanity, folly, or infamy of their pernicious art. Their pretended magic often consisted in cunning tricks only, in sleight of hand, or some natural secrets, unknown to the ignorant. They affected obscurity and night, or would show their skill only before the uninformed or mean persons, and feared nothing so much as serious examinations, broad day-light, and the inspection of the intelligent. Respecting the inchantments practised by Pharaoh's magicians, (see Exod. viii, 18, 19,) in order to imitate the miracles which were wrought by Moses, it must be said either that they were mere illusions, whereby they imposed on the spectators; or that, if they performed such miracles, and produced real changes of their rods, and the other things said to be performed by them, it must have been by a supernatural power which God had permitted Satan to give them, but the farther operation of which he afterward thought proper to prevent.

INDEPENDENTS, a denomination of Protestants in England and Holland, originally called Brownists. They derive their name from their maintaining that every particular congregation of Christians has, according to the New Testament, a full power of ecclesiastical jurisdiction over its members, independent of the authority of bishops, synods, presbyteries, or any other ecclesiastical assemblies. This denomination appeared in England in the year 1616. John Robinson, a Norfolk divine, who, being banished from his native country for non-conformity, afterward settled at Leyden, was considered as their founder and father. He possessed sincere piety, and no inconsiderable share of learning. Perceiving defects in the denomination of the Brownists, to which he belonged, he employed his zeal and diligence in correcting them and in new modelling the society. Though the Independents considered their own form of ecclesiastical government as of divine institution, and as originally introduced by the authority of the Apostles, nay, by the Apostles themselves; yet they did not always think it necessary to condemn other denominations, but often acknowledged that true religion might flourish in those communities which were under the jurisdiction of bishops, or the government of presbyteries. They approved, also, of a regular and educated ministry; nor is any person among them now permitted to speak in public before he has submitted to a proper examination of his capacity and talents, and has been approved of by the church to which he belonged. Their grounds of separation from the established church are different from those of other puritans. Many of the latter objected chiefly to certain rites, ceremonies, vestments, or forms, or to the government of the church; while yet they were disposed to arm the magistrate in support of the truth, and regretted and complained that they could not on these accounts conform to it. But Robinson and his companions not only rejected the appointments of the church on these heads, but denied its authority to enact them; contending, that every single congregation of Christians was a church, and independent of all legislation, save that of Christ; standing in need of no such provision or establishment as the state can bestow, and incapable of soliciting or receiving it. Hence they sought not to reform the church, but chose to dissent from it. They admitted there were many godly men in its communion, and that it was reformed from the grossest errors of the man of sin; but thought it still wanted some things essential to a true church of Christ; in particular, a power of choosing its own ministers, and a stricter discipline among its members. The creed of the Independents is uniformly Calvinistic, though with considerable shades of difference; and many in Scotland and Ireland have symbolized with the Sandemanians, or the Scottish Baptist denominations. The Congregationalist and Independent have been generally considered as convertible and synonymous: many, however, in the present day, prefer the former appellation, considering it desirable, in many cases, to unite, for mutual advice and support, more closely than the term INDEPENDENT seems to warrant.

INDULGENCES. In the primitive church very severe penalties were inflicted on those who had been guilty of any sins, whether public or private; and, in particular, they were forbidden to partake, for a certain time, of the sacrament of the Lord's Supper, or to hold any communion with the church. General rules were formed upon these subjects; but as it was often found expedient to make a discrimination in the degrees of punishment, according to the different circumstances of the offenders, and especially when they showed marks of contrition and repentance, power was given to bishops, by the council of Nice, to relax or remit those punishments as they should see reason. Every favour of this kind was called an indulgence or pardon. After the bishops had enjoyed this privilege for some centuries, and had begun to abuse it, the popes discovered that in their own hands it might be rendered a powerful instrument to promote both their ambition and their avarice. They could not but perceive that if they could persuade men they had the power of granting pardon for sin, it would give them a complete influence over their consciences; and if they could at the same time prevail upon them to purchase these pardons for money, it must add greatly to the wealth of the Roman see. In the eleventh century, therefore, when the dominion of the popes was rising to its zenith, and their power was almost irresistible, they took to themselves the exclusive prerogative of dispensing indulgences, which they carried to a most unwarrantable length. Instead of confining them, according to their original institution, to the ordinary purposes of ecclesiastical discipline, they extended them to the punishment of the wicked in the world to come; instead of shortening the duration of earthly penance, they pretended that they could deliver men from the pains of purgatory; instead of allowing them gratuitously, and upon just grounds, to the penitent offender, they sold them in the most open and corrupt manner to the profligate and abandoned, who still continued in their vices. They did not scruple to call these indulgences a plenary remission of all sins, past, present, and future, and to offer them as a certain and immediate passport from the troubles of this world to the eternal joys of heaven. To give some sort of colour and support to this infamous traffic, they confidently asserted that the superabundant merits of Christ, and of his faithful servants, formed a fund of which the pope was the sole manager; and that he could, at his own discretion, dispense those merits, as the sure means of procuring pardon from God, in any proportions, for any species of wickedness, and to any person he pleased. The bare statement of this doctrine is a sufficient refutation of it; and it is scarcely necessary to add, that it has no foundation whatever in Scripture. It is an arrogant and impious usurpation of a power which belongs to God alone; and it has an obvious tendency to promote licentiousness and sin of every description, by holding out an easy and certain method of absolution. The popes derived very large sums from the sale of these indulgences; and it is well known that the gross abuses practised in granting them were among the immediate and principal causes of bringing about the reformation. They continue still to be sold at Rome, and are to be purchased by any who are weak enough to buy them. The sums required for indulgences were first published by Anthony Egane, a Franciscan friar, in 1673; and the original pamphlet was republished by Baron Maseres, in 1809, in his last volume of "Occasional Essays."

INK. The ink of the ancients was not so fluid as ours. Demosthenes reproaches Æschines with labouring in the grinding of ink, as painters do in the grinding of their colours. The substance also found in an inkstand at Herculaneum, looks like a thick oil or paint, with which the manuscripts there have been written in a relievo visible in the letters, when you hold a leaf to the light in a horizontal direction. Such vitriolic ink as has been used on the old parchment manuscripts would have corroded the delicate leaves of the papyrus, as it has done the skins of the most ancient manuscripts of Virgil and Terence, in the Vatican library; the letters are sunk into the parchment, and some have eaten quite through it, in consequence of the corrosive acid of the vitriolic ink, with which they were written. The inkhorn is also mentioned in Scripture: "And one man among them was clothed with linen, with a writer's inkhorn by his side," Ezek. ix, 2. The eastern mode and apparatus for writing differs so materially from those with which we are conversant, that it is necessary particularly to describe them. D'Arvieux informs us that "the Arabs of the desert, when they want a favour of their emir, get his secretary to write an order agreeable to their desire, as if the favour were granted, this they carry to the prince, who, after having read it, sets his seal to it with ink, if he grants it; if not, he returns the petitioner his paper torn, and dismisses him. These papers are without date, and have only the emir's flourish or cypher at the bottom, signifying the poor, the abject Mohammed, son of Turabeye." Pococke says, that "they make the impression of their name with their seal, generally of cornelian, which they wear on their finger, and which is blacked when they have occasion to seal with it." The custom of placing the inkhorn by the side, Olearius says, continues in the east to this day. Dr. Shaw informs us, that, among the Moors in Barbary, "the HOJAS, that is, the writers or secretaries, suspend their inkhorns in their girdles; a custom as old as the Prophet Ezekiel, ix, 2." And in a note he adds, "that part of these inkhorns (if an instrument of brass may be so called) which passes between the girdle and the tunic, and holds their pens, is long and flat; but the vessel for the ink which rests upon the girdle is square, with a lid to clasp over it." So Mr. Hanway: "Their writers carry their ink and pens about them in a case, which they put under their sash."

INN. The inns or caravanserais of the east, in which travellers are accommodated, are not all alike, some being simply places of rest, by the side of a fountain, if possible, and at a proper distance on the road. Many of these places are nothing more than naked walls; others have an attendant, who subsists either by some charitable donation, or the benevolence of passengers; others are more considerable establishments, where families reside, and take care of them, and furnish the necessary provisions. "Caravanserais," says Campbell, "were originally intended for, and are now pretty generally applied to, the accommodation of strangers and travellers, though, like every other good institution, sometimes perverted to the purposes of private emolument, or public job. They are built at proper distances through the roads of the Turkish dominions, and afford to the indigent or weary traveller an asylum from the inclemency of the weather, are in general built of the most solid and durable materials, have commonly one story above the ground floor, the lower of which is arched, and serves for warehouses to store goods, for lodgings, and for stables, while the upper is used merely for lodgings; beside which they are always accommodated with a fountain, and have cooks' shops and other conveniences to supply the wants of lodgers. In Aleppo, the caravanserais are almost exclusively occupied by merchants, to whom they are, like other houses, rented." "In all other Turkish provinces," observes Antes, "particularly those in Asia, which are often thinly inhabited, travelling is subject to numberless inconveniences, since it is necessary not only to carry all sorts of provisions along with one, but even the very utensils to dress them in, beside a tent for shelter at night and in bad weather, as there are no inns, except here and there a caravanserai, where nothing but bare rooms, and those often very bad, and infested with all sorts of vermin, can be procured." "There are no inns anywhere," says Volney, "but the cities, and commonly the villages, have a large building called a kan or kervanserai, which serves as an asylum for all travellers. These houses of reception are always built without the precincts of towns, and consist of four wings round a square court, which serves by way of enclosure for the beasts of burden. The lodgings are cells, where you find nothing but bare walls, dust, and sometimes scorpions. The keeper of this kan gives the traveller the key and a mat, and he provides himself the rest; he must therefore carry with him his bed, his kitchen utensils, and even his provisions, for frequently not even bread is to be found in the villages. On this account the orientals contrive their equipage in the most simple and portable form. The baggage of a man who wishes to be completely provided, consists in a carpet, a mattress, a blanket, two sauce pans with lids contained within each other, two dishes, two plates, and a coffee pot, all of copper, well tinned, a small wooden box for salt and pepper, a round leathern table, which he suspends from the saddle of his horse, small leathern bottles or bags for oil, melted butter, water, and brandy, if the traveller be a Christian, a tinder box, a cup of cocoa nut, some rice, dried raisins, dates, Cyprus cheese, and, above all, coffee berries, with a roaster and wooden mortar to pound them." The Scriptures use two words to express a caravanserai, in both instances translated inn: "There was no room for them in the inn," καταλύματι, Luke ii, 7; the place of untying, that is, of beasts for rest. "And brought him to the inn," πανδοχεῖον, Luke x, 34, whose keeper is called in the next verse πανδοχεὺς. This word properly signifies "a receptacle open to all comers." "The serai or principal caravansary at Surat," observes Forbes, "was much neglected. Most of the eastern cities contain one, at least, for the reception of strangers; smaller places, called choultries, are erected by charitable persons, or munificent princes, in forests, plains, and deserts, for the accommodation of travellers. Near them is generally a well, and a cistern for the cattle; a brahmin, or fakeer, often resides there to furnish the pilgrim with food, and the few necessaries he may stand in need of. In the deserts of Persia and Arabia, these buildings are invaluable; in those pathless plains, for many miles together, not a tree, a bush, nor even a blade of grass, is to be seen; all is one undulating mass of sand, like waves on the trackless ocean. In these ruthless wastes, where no rural village or cheerful hamlet, no inn or house of refreshment, is to be found, how noble is the charity that rears the hospitable roof, that plants the shady grove, and conducts the refreshing moisture into reservoirs!"

INSPIRATION, the conveying of certain extraordinary and supernatural notices or thoughts into the soul; or it denotes any supernatural influence of God upon the mind of a rational creature, whereby he is formed to a degree of intellectual improvement, to which he could not have attained in his present circumstances in a natural way. In the first and highest sense, the prophets, evangelists, and Apostles are said to have spoken and written by divine inspiration. This inspiration of the Old Testament Scriptures is so expressly attested by our Lord and his Apostles, that among those who receive them as a divine revelation the only question relates to the inspiration of the New Testament. On this subject it has been well observed:--

1. That the inspiration of the Apostles appears to have been necessary for the purposes of their mission; and, therefore, if we admit that Jesus came from God, and that he sent them forth to make disciples, we shall acknowledge that some degree of inspiration is highly probable. The first light in which the books of the New Testament lead us to consider the Apostles, is, as the historians of Jesus. After having been his companions during his ministry, they came forth to bear witness of him; and as the benefit of his religion was not to be confined to the age in which he or they lived, they left in the four Gospels a record of what he did and taught. Two of the four were written by the Apostles Matthew and John. St. Mark and St. Luke, whose names are prefixed to the other two, were probably of the seventy whom our Lord sent out in his life time; and we learn from the most ancient Christian historians, that the Gospel of St. Mark was revised by St. Peter, and the Gospel of St. Luke by St. Paul, and that both were afterward approved by St. John; so that all the four may be considered as transmitted to the church with the sanction of apostolical authority. Now, if we recollect the condition of the Apostles, and the nature of their history, we shall perceive that, even as historians, they stood in need of some measure of inspiration. Plato might feel himself at liberty to feign many things of his master Socrates, because it mattered little to the world whether the instruction that was conveyed to them proceeded from the one philosopher or from the other. But the servants of a divine teacher, who appeared as his witnesses, and professed to be the historians of his life, were bound by their office to give a true record. And their history was an imposition upon the world, if they did not declare exactly and literally what they had seen and heard. This was an office which required not only a love of the truth, but a memory more retentive and more accurate than it was possible for the Apostles to possess. To relate, at the distance of twenty years, long moral discourses, which were not originally written, and which were not attended with any striking circumstances that might imprint them upon the mind; to preserve a variety of parables, the beauty and significancy of which depended upon particular expressions; to record long and minute prophecies, where the alteration of a single phrase might have produced an inconsistency between the event and the prediction; and to give a particular detail of the intercourse which Jesus had with his friends and with his enemies;--all this is a work so very much above the capacity of unlearned men, that, had they attempted to execute it by their own natural powers, they must have fallen into such absurdities and contradictions as would have betrayed them to every discerning eye. It was therefore highly expedient, and even necessary, for the faith of future ages, that, beside those opportunities of information which the Apostles enjoyed, and that tried integrity which they possessed, their understanding and their memory should be assisted by a supernatural influence, which might prevent them from mistaking the meaning of what they had heard, which might restrain them from putting into the mouth of Jesus any words which he did not utter, or omitting what was important, and which might thus give us perfect security, that the Gospels are as faithful a copy as if Jesus himself had left in writing those sayings and those actions which he wished posterity to remember.

But we consider the Apostles in the lowest view, when we speak of them as barely the historians of their Master. In their epistles they assume a higher character, which renders inspiration still more necessary. All the benefit which they derived from the public and the private instructions of Jesus before his death had not so far opened their minds as to qualify them for receiving the whole counsel of God. And he who knows what is in man declares to them, the night on which he was betrayed, "I have yet many things to say unto you, but you cannot bear them now," John xv, 12. The purpose of many of his parables, the full meaning even of some of his plain discourses, had not been attained by them. They had marvelled when he spake to them of earthly things. But many heavenly things of his kingdom had not been told them; and they who were destined to carry his religion to the ends of the earth themselves needed, at the times of their receiving this commission, that some one should instruct them in the doctrine of Christ. It is true that, after his resurrection, Jesus opened their understandings, and explained to them the Scriptures; and he continued upon earth forty days, speaking to them of the things pertaining to the kingdom of God. It appears, however, from the history which they have recorded in the book of Acts, that some farther teaching was necessary for them, Acts i. Immediately before our Lord ascended, their minds being still full of the expectation of a temporal kingdom, they say unto him, "Lord, wilt thou at this time restore the kingdom to Israel?" It was not till some time after they received the gift of the Holy Ghost, that they understood that the Gospel had taken away the obligation to observe the ceremonies of the Mosaic law; and the action of St. Peter in baptizing Cornelius, a devout Heathen, gave offence to some of the Apostles and brethren in Judea when they first heard it, Acts xi. Yet, in their epistles, we find just notions of the spiritual nature of the religion of Jesus as a kingdom of righteousness, the subjects of which are to receive remission of sins, and sanctification through his blood, and just notions also of the extent of this religion as a dispensation the spiritual blessings of which are to be communicated to all, in every land, who receive it in faith and love. These notions appear to us to be the explication both of the ancient predictions, and of many particular expressions that occur in the discourses of our Lord. But it is manifest that they had not been acquired by the Apostles during the teaching of Jesus. They are so adverse to every thing which men educated in Jewish prejudices had learned and had hoped, that they could not be the fruit of their own reflections; and therefore they imply the teaching of that Spirit who gradually impressed them upon the mind, guiding the Apostles gently, as they were able to follow him, into all the truth connected with the salvation of mankind. As inspiration was necessary to give the minds of the Apostles possession of the system that is unfolded in their epistles, so many parts of that system are removed to such a distance from human discoveries, and are liable to such misapprehension, that unless we suppose a continued superintendence of the Spirit by whom it was taught, succeeding ages would not have a sufficient security that those who were employed to deliver it had not been guilty of gross mistakes in some most important doctrines.

Inspiration will appear still farther necessary, when we recollect that the writings of the Apostles contain several predictions of things to come. St. Paul foretels, in his epistles, the corruptions of the church of Rome, and many other circumstances which have taken place in the history of the Christian church; and the Revelation is a book of prophecy, of which part has been already fulfilled, while the rest will no doubt be explained by the events which are to arise in the course of Providence. But prophecy is a kind of writing which implies the highest degree of inspiration. When predictions, like those in Scripture, are particular and complicated, and the events are so remote and so contingent as to be out of the reach of human sagacity, it is plain that the writers of the predictions do not speak according to the measure of information which they had acquired by natural means, but are merely the instruments through which the Almighty communicates, in such measure and such language as he thinks fit, that knowledge of futurity which is denied to man. And although the full meaning of their own predictions was not understood by themselves, they will be acknowledged to be true prophets when the fulfilment comes to reflect light upon that language, which, for wise purposes, was made dark at the time of its being put into their mouth.

Thus the nature of the writings of the Apostles suggests the necessity of their having been inspired. They could not be accurate historians of the life of Jesus without divine inspiration, nor safe expounders of his doctrine, nor prophets of distant events.

2. Inspiration was promised by our Lord to his Apostles. It is not unfair reasoning to adduce promises contained in the Scriptures themselves, as proofs of their divine inspiration. It were, indeed, reasoning in a circle, to bring the testimony of the Scriptures in proof of the divine mission of Jesus. But that being established by sufficient evidence, and the books of the New Testament having been proved to be the authentic genuine records of the persons whose names they bear, we are warranted to argue, from the declarations contained in them, what is the measure of inspiration which Jesus was pleased to bestow upon his servants. He might have been a divine teacher, and they might have been his Apostles, although he had bestowed none at all. But his character gives us security that they possessed all that he promised. We read in the Gospels that Jesus ordained twelve that they should be with him, and that he might send them forth to preach, Mark iii, 14. And as this was the purpose for which they were first called, so it was the charge left them at his departure. "Go," said he, "preach the Gospel to every creature: make disciples of all nations," Mark xvi, 16; Matt. xxviii, 19. His constant familiar intercourse with them was intended to qualify them for the execution of this charge; and the promises made to them have a special reference to the office in which they were to be employed. When he sent them, during his life, to preach in the cities of Israel, he said, "But when they deliver you up, take no thought how or what ye shall speak; for it shall be given you in that same hour what ye shall speak. For it is not ye that speak, but the Spirit of your Father which speaketh in you," Matt. x, 19, 20. And when he spake to them in his prophecy of the destruction of Jerusalem, of the persecution which they were to endure after his death, he repeats the same promise: "For I will give

you a mouth and wisdom, which all your adversaries shall not be able to gainsay nor resist," Luke xxi, 15. It is admitted that the words in both these passages refer properly to that assistance which the inexperience of the Apostles was to derive from the suggestions of the Spirit, when they should be called to defend their conduct and their cause before the tribunals of the magistrates. But the fulfilment of this promise was a pledge, both to the Apostles and to the world, that the measure of inspiration necessary for the more important purpose implied in their commission would not be withheld; and, accordingly, when that purpose came to be unfolded to the Apostles, the promise of the assistance of the Spirit was expressed in a manner which applies it to the extent of their commission. In the long affectionate discourse recorded by St. John, when our Lord took a solemn farewell of the disciples, after eating the last passover with them, he said, "And I will pray the Father, and he shall give you another Comforter, that he may abide with you for ever; even the Spirit of truth, whom the world cannot receive, because it seeth him not, neither knoweth him. But ye know him; for he dwelleth with you, and shall be in you. The Comforter, which is the Holy Ghost, whom the Father will send in my name, he shall teach you all things, and bring all things to your remembrance, whatsoever I have said unto you. I have yet many things to say unto you, but you cannot bear them now. Howbeit, when he, the Spirit of truth, is come, he will guide you into all truth; for he shall not speak of himself, but whatsoever he shall hear that shall he speak; and he will show you things to come," John xiv, 16, 17, 26; xvi, 12, 13. Here are all the degrees of inspiration which we have seen to be necessary for the Apostles: the Spirit was to bring to their remembrance what they had heard; to guide them into the truth, which they were not then able to bear; and to show them things to come; and all this they were to derive, not from occasional illapses, but from the perpetual inhabitation of the Spirit. That this inspiration was vouchsafed to them, not for their own sakes, but in order to qualify them for the successful discharge of their office as the messengers of Christ, and the instructers of mankind, appears from several expressions of that prayer which immediately follows the discourse containing the promise of inspiration; particularly from these words: "Neither pray I for these alone, but for them also which shall believe on me through their word; that they all may be one, as thou, Father, art in me, and I in thee; that they may be one in us; that the world may believe that thou hast sent me," John xvii, 20, 21. In conformity to this prayer, so becoming him who was not merely the friend of the Apostles, but the light of the world, is that charge which he gives them immediately before his ascension: "Go ye, therefore, and teach all nations, baptizing them in the name of the Father, and of the Son, and of the Holy Ghost; teaching them to observe all things whatsoever I have commanded you: and, lo, I am with you alway, even unto the end of the world," Matt. xxviii, 19, 20; I am with you alway, not by my bodily presence; for immediately after he was taken out of their sight; but I am with you by the Holy Ghost, whom I am to send upon you not many days hence, and who is to abide with you for ever.

The promise of Jesus, then, implies, according to the plain construction of the words, that the Apostles, in executing their commission, were not to be left wholly to their natural powers, but were to be assisted by that illumination and direction of the Spirit which the nature of the commission required; and we may learn the sense which our Lord had of the importance and effect of this promise from one circumstance, that he never makes any distinction between his own words and those of his Apostles, but places the doctrines and commandments which they were to deliver upon a footing with those which he had spoken: "He that heareth you, heareth me; and he that despiseth you, despiseth me; and he that despiseth me, despiseth him that sent me," Luke x, 16. These words plainly imply that Christians have no warrant to pay less regard to any thing contained in the epistles than to that which is contained in the Gospels; and teach us that every doctrine and precept clearly delivered by the Apostles comes to the Christian world with the same stamp of the divine authority as the words of Jesus, who spake in the name of him that sent him.

The Author of our religion having thus made the faith of the Christian world to hang upon the teaching of the Apostles, gave the most signal manifestation of the fulfilment of that promise which was to qualify them for their office, by the miraculous gifts with which they were endowed on the day of pentecost, and by the abundance of those gifts which the imposition of their hands was to diffuse through the church. One of the twelve, indeed, whose labours in preaching the Gospel were the most abundant and the most extensive, was not present at this manifestation; for St. Paul was not called to be an Apostle till after the day of pentecost. But it is very remarkable that the manner of his being called was expressly calculated to supply this deficiency. As he journeyed to Damascus, about noon, to bring the Christians who were there bound to Jerusalem, there shone from heaven a great light round about him. And he heard a voice, saying, "I am Jesus whom thou persecutest. And I have appeared unto thee for this purpose, to make thee a minister and a witness both of these things which thou hast seen, and of those things in the which I will appear unto thee; and now I send thee to the Gentiles to open their eyes," Acts xxvi, 12–18. In reference to this manner of his being called, St. Paul generally inscribes his epistles with these words: "Paul, an Apostle of Jesus Christ, by the will" or "by the commandment of God;" and he explains very fully what he meant by the use of this expression, in the beginning of his Epistle to the Galatians, where he gives an account of his conversion: "Paul, an Apostle, not of men, neither by man, but by Jesus Christ, and God the Father, who raised him from the dead. I neither received the Gospel of man, neither was I taught it, but by the revelation of Jesus Christ. When it pleased God, who separated me from my mother's womb, and called me by his grace, to reveal his Son in me, that I might preach him among the Heathen: immediately I conferred not with flesh and blood, neither went I up to Jerusalem to them which were Apostles before me; but I went into Arabia," Gal. i, 1, 12, 15–17. All that we said of the necessity of inspiration, and of the import of the promise which Jesus made to the other

Apostles, receives very great confirmation from this history of St. Paul, who, being called to be an Apostle after the ascension of Jesus, received the Gospel by immediate revelation from heaven, and was thus put upon a footing with the rest, both as to his designation, which did not proceed from the choice of man, and as to his qualifications, which were imparted, not by human instruction, but by the teaching of the Author of Christianity. The Lord Jesus who appeared to him might furnish St. Paul with the same advantages which the other Apostles had derived from his presence on earth, and might give him the same assurance of the inhabitation of the Spirit that the promises, which we have been considering, had imparted to those.

3. Inspiration was claimed by the Apostles; and their claim may be considered as the interpretation of the promise of their Master. We shall not find the claim to inspiration formally advanced in the Gospels. This omission has sometimes been stated by those superficial critics, whose prejudices serve to account for their haste, as an objection against the existence of inspiration. But if you attend to the reason of the omission, you will perceive that it is only an instance of that delicate propriety which pervades all the New Testament. The Gospels are the record of the great facts which vouch the truth of Christianity. These facts are to be received upon the testimony of men who had been eye-witnesses of them. The foundation of Christian faith being laid in an assent to these facts, it would have been preposterous to have introduced in support of them that influence of the Spirit which preserved the minds of the Apostles from error. For there can be no proof of the inspiration of the Apostles, unless the truth of the facts be previously admitted. The Apostles, therefore, bring forward the evidence of Christianity in its natural order, when they speak in the Gospels as the companions and eye-witnesses of Jesus, claiming that credit which is due to honest men who had the best opportunities of knowing what they declared. This is the language of St. John: "Many other signs did Jesus in the presence of his disciples. But these are written that ye may believe; and this is the disciple which testifieth these things," John xx, 30, 31; xxi, 24. The Evangelist Luke appears to speak differently in the introduction to his Gospel, Luke i, 1–4; and opposite opinions have been entertained respecting the information conveyed by that introduction.

There is a difference of opinion, first, with regard to the time when St. Luke wrote his Gospel. It appears to some to be expressly intimated that he wrote after St. Matthew and St. Mark, because he speaks of other Gospels then in circulation; and it is generally understood that St. John wrote his after the other three. But the manner in which St. Luke speaks of these other Gospels does not seem to apply to those of St. Matthew and St. Mark. He calls them many, which implies that they were more than two, and which would confound these two canonical Gospels with imperfect accounts of our Lord's life, which we know from ancient writers were early circulated, but were rejected after the four Gospels were published. It is hardly conceivable that St. Luke would have alluded to the two Gospels of St. Matthew and St. Mark without distinguishing them from other very inferior productions; and therefore it is probable that when he used this mode of expression, no accounts of our Lord's life were then in existence but those inferior productions. There appears, also, to very sound critics, to be internal evidence that St. Luke wrote first. He is much more particular than the other evangelists in his report of our Lord's birth, and of the meetings with his Apostles after his resurrection. They might think it unnecessary to introduce the same particulars into their Gospels after St. Luke. But if they wrote before him, the want of these particulars gives to their Gospels an appearance of imperfection which we cannot easily explain.

The other point suggested by this introduction, upon which there has been a difference of opinion, is, whether St. Luke, who was not an Apostle, wrote his Gospel from personal knowledge, attained by his being a companion of Jesus, or from the information of others. Our translation certainly favours the last opinion; and it is the more general opinion, defended by very able critics. Dr. Randolph, in the first volume of his works, which contains a history of our Saviour's life, supports the first opinion, and suggests a punctuation of the verses, and an interpretation of one word, according to which that opinion may be defended. Read the second and third verses in connection: Καθὼς ϖαρέδοσαν ἡμῖν ὁι απ' ἀρχῆς αὐτόπται καὶ ὑπηρέται γενόμενοι τοῦ λογοῦ Ἔδοξε κἀιμοὶ, ϖαρακολουθηκότι ἄνωθεν ϖᾶσιν ἀκριβως καθεξῆς σοι γράψαι, κράτιστε Θεόφιλε, "Even as they who were eye-witnesses and ministers of the word from the beginning delivered them to us, it seemed good to me also, having accurately traced," &c. By ἡμῖν is understood the Christian world, who had received information, both oral and written, from those that had been αὐτόπται καὶ ὑπηρέται, "eye-witnesses and ministers." Κἀιμοὶ means St. Luke, who proposed to follow the example of those αὐτόπται in writing what he knew; and he describes his own knowledge by the word ϖαρακολουθηκότι, which is more precise than the circumlocution, by which it is translated, "having had understanding of all things." Perfect understanding may be derived from various sources; but ϖαρακολουθέω properly means, "I go along with as a companion, and derive knowledge from my own observation." And it is remarkable that the word is used in this very sense by the Jewish historian, Josephus, who published his history not many years after St. Luke wrote, and who, in his introduction, represents himself as worthy of credit, because he had not merely inquired of those who knew, but ϖαρηκολουθηκότα τοις γεγόνοσιν, which he explains by this expression: Πολλῶν μὲν αὐτουργὸς ϖραξέων, and to state in the third verse that he, ϖλεῖςων δ' αὐτόπτης γενόμενος, AN ACTOR IN MANY THINGS, AND AN EYE-WITNESS OF MOST. If this interpretation is not approved of, then, according to the sense of those verses which is most commonly adopted, St. Luke will be understood to give in the second verse an account of that ground upon which the knowledge of the Christian world with regard to these things rested, the reports of the "eye-witnesses and ministers," having collected and collated these reports, and employed the most careful and minute investigation, he had resolved to write an account of the life of Jesus. Here he does not claim inspiration: he does not even say that he was an eye-witness. But he says that, having, like others, heard the report of eye-witnesses, he had accurately examined the truth of what they said, and presented to the Christian world the fruit of his researches.

The foundation is still the same as in St. John's Gospel, the report of those in whose presence Jesus did and said what is recorded. To this report is added, (1.) The investigation of St. Luke, a contemporary of the Apostles, the companion of St. Paul in a great part of his journeyings, and honoured by him with this title, "Luke, the beloved physician," Col. iv, 14. (2.) The approbation of St. Paul, who is said, by the earliest Christian writers, to have revised this Gospel written by his companion, so that it came abroad with apostolical authority. (3.) The universal consent of the Christian church, which, although jealous of the books that were then published, and rejecting many that claimed the sanction of the Apostles, has uniformly, from the earliest times, put the Gospel of St. Luke upon a footing with those of St. Matthew and St. Mark: a clear demonstration that they who had access to the best information knew that it had been revised by an Apostle.

As, then, the authors of the Gospels appear under the character of eye-witnesses, attesting what they had seen, there would have been an impropriety in their resting the evidence of the essential facts of Christianity upon inspiration. But after the respect which their character and their conduct procured to their testimony, and the visible confirmation which it received from heaven, had established the faith of a part of the world, a belief of their inspiration became necessary. They might have been credible witnesses of facts, although they had not been distinguished from other men. But they were not qualified to execute the office of Apostles without being inspired. And therefore, as soon as the circumstances of the church required the execution of that office, the claim which had been conveyed to them by the promise of their Master, and which is implied in the apostolical character, appears in their writings. They instantly exercised the authority derived to them from Jesus, by planting ministers in the cities where they had preached the Gospel, by setting every thing pertaining to these Christian societies in order, by controlling the exercise of those miraculous gifts which they had imparted, and by correcting the abuses which happened even in their time. But they demanded from all who had received the faith of Christ submission to the doctrines and commandments of his Apostles, as the inspired messengers of Heaven. "But God hath revealed it," not THEM, as our translators have supplied the accusative, "revealed the wisdom of God, the dispensation of the Gospel unto us by his Spirit; for the Spirit searcheth all things, yea, the deep things of God. Now we have received not the spirit of the world, but the Spirit which is of God; that we might know the things which are freely given us of God; which things, also, we speak, not in the words which man's wisdom teacheth, but which the Holy Ghost teacheth," 1 Cor. ii, 10, 12, 13. "If any man think himself to be a prophet, or spiritual, let him acknowledge that the things that I write unto you are the commandments of the Lord," 1 Cor. xiv, 37; that is, Let no eminence of spiritual gifts be set up in opposition to the authority of the Apostles, or as implying any dispensation from submitting to it. "For this cause, also, thank we God without ceasing, because when ye received the word of God which ye heard of us, ye received it not as the word of men, but, as it is in truth, the word of God," 1 Thess. ii, 13. St. Peter, speaking of the epistles of St. Paul, says, "Even as our beloved brother Paul, also, according to the wisdom given unto him, hath written unto you," 2 Peter iii, 15. And St. John makes the same claim of inspiration for the other Apostles, as well as for himself: "We are of God: he that knoweth God, heareth us: he that is not of God, heareth not us," 1 John iv, 6.

The claim to inspiration is clearly made by the Apostles in those passages where they place their own writings upon the same footing with the books of the Old Testament; for St. Paul, speaking of the ἱερα γράμματα, "HOLY SCRIPTURES," a common expression among the Jews, in which Timothy had been instructed from his childhood, says, "All Scripture is given by inspiration of God," 2 Tim. iii, 16. St. Peter, speaking of the ancient prophets, says, "The Spirit of Christ was in them," 1 Peter i, 11; and, "The prophecy came not in old time by the will of man; but holy men of God spake as they were moved by the Holy Ghost," 2 Peter i, 21. And the quotations of our Lord and his Apostles from the books of the Old Testament are often introduced with an expression in which their inspiration is directly asserted: "Well spake the Holy Ghost by Esaias;" "By the mouth of thy servant David thou hast said," &c, Acts i, 16; iv, 25; xxviii, 25. But with this uniform testimony to that inspiration of the Jewish Scriptures, which was universally believed among that people, we are to conjoin this circumstance, that St. Paul and St. Peter in different places rank their own writings with the books of the Old Testament. St. Paul commands that his epistles should be read in the churches, where none but those books which the Jews believed to be inspired were ever read, Col. iv, 16. He says that Christians "are built upon the foundation of the Apostles and prophets," ἐπὶ τῷ θεμελίῳ τῶν ἀποςόλων καὶ ϖροφητῶν, Eph. ii, 20: a conjunction which would have been highly improper, if the former had not been inspired as well as the latter; and St. Peter charges the Christians to "be mindful of the words which were spoken before by the holy prophets, and of the commandment of us the Apostles," 2 Peter iii, 2. The nature of the book of Revelation led the Apostle John to assert most directly his personal inspiration; for he says that "Jesus sent and signified by his angel to his servant John the things that were to come to pass;" and that the divine Person, like the Son of man, who appeared to him when he was in the Spirit, commanded him to write in a book what he saw. And in one of the visions there recorded, when the dispensation of the Gospel was presented to St. John under the figure of a great city, the New Jerusalem, descending out of heaven, there is one part of the image which is a beautiful expression of that authority in settling the form of the Christian church, and teaching articles of faith, which the Apostles derived from their inspiration: "The wall of the city had twelve foundations, and in them the names of the twelve Apostles of the Lamb," Rev. i, 1, 10–19; xxi, 14.

These are only a few of the many passages to the same purpose which occur in reading the New Testament. But it is manifest, even from them, that the manner in which the Apostles speak of their own writings is calculated to mislead every candid reader, unless they really wrote under the direction of the Spirit of God. So gross and daring an imposture is absolutely inconsistent not only with their whole character, but also with those gifts of the Holy Ghost of which there is unquestionable evidence that they were possessed; and which, being the natural vouchers of the assertion made by them concerning their own writings, cannot be supposed, upon the principles of sound theism, to have been imparted for a long course of years to persons who continued during all that time asserting such a falsehood, and appealing to those gifts for the truth of what they said.

4. The claim of the Apostles derives much confirmation from the reception which it met with among the Christians of their days. It appears from an expression of St. Peter, that at the time when he wrote his second epistle, the epistles of St. Paul were classed with "the other Scriptures," the books of the Old Testament; that is, were accounted inspired writings, 2 Peter iii, 16. It is well known to those who are versed in the early history of the church, with what care the first Christians discriminated between the apostolical writings and the compositions of other authors however much distinguished by their piety, and with what reverence they received those books which were known by their inscription, by the place from which they proceeded, or the manner in which they were circulated, to be the work of an Apostle. In Lardner's "Credibility of the Gospel History," will be found the most particular information upon this subject; and it will be perceived that the whole history of the supposititious writings which appeared in early times, conspires in attesting the veneration in which the authority of the Apostles was held by the Christian church. We learn from Justin Martyr, that, before the middle of the second century, "the memoirs of the Apostles, and the compositions of the prophets," were read together in the Christian assemblies. We know, that from the earliest times, the church has submitted to the writings of the Apostles as the infallible standard of faith and practice; and we find the ground of this peculiar respect expressed by the first Christian writers as well as by their successors, who speak of the writings of the Apostles as "divine writings from the inspiration of the Holy Ghost."

To this general argument we may add that right views on the subject of the inspiration of the sacred writers are also necessary, because even some Christian writers have spoken obscurely and unsatisfactorily on the subject, dividing inspiration into different kinds, and assigning each to different portions of the holy volume. By inspiration we are to understand, that the sacred writers composed their works under so plenary and immediate an influence of the Holy Spirit, that God may be said to speak by those writers to man, and not merely that they spoke to men in the name of God, and by his authority; and there is a considerable difference between the two propositions. Each supposes an authentic revelation from God; but the former view secures the Scriptures from all error both as to the SUBJECTS spoken, and the MANNER of expressing them. This, too, is the doctrine taught in the Scriptures themselves, which declare not only that the prophets and Apostles spake in the name of God, but that God spake by them as his instruments. "The Holy Ghost by the mouth of David SPAKE." "Well SPAKE the Holy Ghost by Esaias the prophet." "The prophecy came not of old time, by the will of man; but holy men of God SPAKE as they were moved by the Holy Ghost." For this reason, not only that the MATTER contained in the book of "the Law, the Prophets, and the Psalms," (the usual phrase by which the Jews designated the whole Old Testament,) was true; but that the books were WRITTEN under divine inspiration, they are called collectively by our Lord and by his Apostles, "THE SCRIPTURES," in contradistinction to all other writings;--a term which the Apostle Peter, as stated above, applies also to the writings of St. Paul, and which therefore verifies them as standing on the same level with the books of the Old Testament as to their inspiration: "Even as our beloved brother Paul also, according to the wisdom given unto him, hath written unto you; as also in all his epistles, speaking of these things, in which are some things hard to be understood, which they that are unlearned and unstable wrest, as they do also the other Scriptures, unto their own destruction." The Apostles also, as we have seen, expressly claim an inspiration, not only as to the subjects on which they wrote, but as to the words in which they expressed themselves. Farther, our Lord promised to them the Holy Spirit "to guide them into all truth;" and that he was not to fulfil his office by suggesting thoughts only, but words, is clear from Christ's discourse with them on the subject of the persecutions they were to endure for "his name's sake:" "And when they bring you into the synagogues, and unto magistrates and powers, take ye no thought how or what thing ye shall answer, or what ye shall say; for the Holy Ghost shall teach you in the same hour what ye ought to say; for it is not ye that speak; but the Spirit of your Father which speaketh in you." This inspiration of words is also asserted by St. Paul as to himself and his brethren, when he says to the Corinthians, "Which things also we speak, not in the words which man's wisdom teacheth; but which the Holy Ghost teacheth." Thus we find that the claim which the sacred writers make on this subject is, that they were in truth what they have been aptly called, "the penmen of the Holy Ghost;" and that the words in which they clothed "the wisdom given unto them" were words "taught" by the Holy Spirit.

But it may be asked, How are we to account for that difference of style which is observable in each? that manner, too, so natural to each, and so distinct in all? with those reasonings, recollections of memory, and other indications of the working of the mind of each writer in its own character and temperament? Some persons, indeed, observing this, have concluded their style and manner to be entirely human, while their thoughts were either wholly divine, or so superintended by the Holy Ghost as to have been adopted by him, and therefore, although sometimes natural, to be of equal authority as if they had been exclusively of divine suggestion. This, indeed, would be sufficient to oblige our implicit credence to their writings, as being from God; but it falls below the force of the passages above cited, and which attribute to a divine agency their words also. The matter may be rightly conceived by considering, that an inspiration of words took place either by suggesting those most fit to express the thoughts, or by overruling the selection of such words from the common as if they had been exclusively of divine suggestion. This, indeed, would be sufficient to oblige our implicit credence to their writings, as being from God; but it falls below the force of the passages above cited, and which attribute to a divine agency the store acquired by, and laid up in, the mind of each writer, which is quite compatible with the fact, that a peculiarity and appropriateness of manner might still be left to them separately. To suppose that an inspiration of terms, as well as thoughts, could not take place without producing one uniform style and manner, is to suppose that the minds of the writers would thus become entirely passive under the influence of the Holy Spirit; whereas it is easily conceivable that the verbiage, style, and manner of each, was not so much displaced, as elevated, enriched, and controlled by the Holy Spirit; and that there was a previous fitness, in all these respects, in all the sacred penmen, for which they were chosen to be the instruments under the aid and direction of the Holy Ghost, of writing such portions of the general revelation as the wisdom of God assigned to each of them. On the other hand, while it is so conceivable that the words and manner of each might be appropriated to his own design by the inspiration of the Holy Ghost, it by no means follows that both were not greatly altered, as well as controlled, although they still retained a general similarity to the uninfluenced style and manner of each, and still presented a characteristic variety. As none of their writings on ordinary occasions, and when uninspired, have come down to us, we cannot judge of the degree of this difference; and therefore no one can with any just reason affirm that their writings are "the word of God as to the doctrine, but the word of man as to the channel of conveyance." Certain it is, that a vast difference may be remarked between the writings of the Apostles, and those of the most eminent fathers of the times nearest to them; and that not only as to precision and strength of thought, but also as to language. This circumstance is at least strongly presumptive, that although the style of inspired men was not stripped of the characteristic peculiarity of the writers, it was greatly exalted and influenced.

But the same FORCE of inspiration, so to speak, was not probably exerted upon each of the sacred writers, or upon the same writer throughout his writings, whatever might be its subject. There is no necessity that we should so state the case, in order to maintain what is essential to our faith,--the plenary inspiration of each of the sacred writers. In miracles there was no needless application of divine power. Traditional history and written chronicles, facts of known occurrence, and opinions which were received by all, are often inserted or referred to by the sacred writers. There needed no miraculous operation upon the memory to recall what the memory was furnished with, or to reveal a fact which the writers previously and perfectly knew: but their plenary inspiration consisted in this, that they were kept from all lapses of memory, or inadequate conceptions, even on these subjects; and on all others the degree of communication and influence, both as to doctrine, facts, and the terms in which they were to be recorded for the edification of the church, was proportioned to the necessity of the case, but so that the whole was authenticated or dictated by the Holy Spirit with so full an influence, that it became truth without mixture of error, expressed in such terms as he himself ruled or suggested. This, then, seems the true notion of plenary inspiration, that for the revelation, insertion, and adequate enunciation of truth, it was full and complete.

The principal objections to this view of the inspiration of words are well answered by Dr. Woods, an American divine, in a recent publication, from which, as the subject has been lately debated in this country, the following extracts will be acceptable, although there is in them a repetition of some of the preceding observations:--

"One argument which has been urged against the supposition that divine inspiration had a respect to language, is, that the language employed by the inspired writers exhibits no marks of a divine interference, but is perfectly conformed to the genius and taste of the writers. The fact here alleged is admitted. But how does it support the opinion of those who allege it? Is it not evident, that God may exercise a perfect superintendency over inspired writers as to the language they shall use, and yet that each one of them shall write in his own style, and in all respects according to his own taste? May not God give such aid to his servants, that, while using their own style, they will certainly be secured against all mistakes, and exhibit the truth with perfect propriety? It is unquestionable, that Isaiah, and St. Paul, and St. John might be under the entire direction of the Holy Spirit, even as to language, and, at the same time, that each one of them might write in his own manner; and that the peculiar manner of each might be adopted to answer an important end; and that the variety of style, thus introduced into the sacred volume, might be suited to excite a livelier interest in the minds of men, and to secure to them a far greater amount of good, than could ever have been derived from any one mode of writing. The great variety existing among men as to their natural talents, and their peculiar manner of thinking and writing may, in this way, be turned to account in the work of revelation, as well as in the concerns of common life. Now, is it not clearly a matter of fact, that God has made use of this variety, and given the Holy Spirit to men, differing widely from each other in regard to natural endowments, and knowledge, and style, and employed them, with all their various gifts, as agents in writing the Holy Scriptures? And what colour of reason can we have to suppose, that the language which they used was less under the divine direction on account of this variety, than if it had been perfectly uniform throughout?

"To prove that divine inspiration had no respect to the language of the sacred writers, it is farther alleged, that even the same doctrine is taught and the same event described in a different manner by different writers. This fact I also admit. But how does it prove that inspiration had no respect to language? Is not the variety alleged a manifest advantage, as to the impression which is likely to be made upon the minds of men? Is not testimony, which is substantially the same, always considered as entitled to higher credit, when it is given by different witnesses in different language, and in a different order? And is it not perfectly reasonable to suppose, that, in making a revelation, God would have respect to the common principles of human nature and human society, and would exert his influence and control over inspired men in such a manner, that, by exhibiting the same doctrines and facts in different ways, they should make a more salutary impression, and should more effectually compass the great ends of a revelation? All I have to advance on this part of the subject may be summed up in these two positions: 1. The variety of manner apparent among different inspired writers, even when treating of the same subjects, is far better suited to promote the object of divine revelation, than a perfect uniformity. 2. It is agreeable to our worthiest conceptions of God and his administration, that he should make use of the best means for the accomplishment of his designs; and, of course, that he should impart the gift of inspiration to men of different tastes and habits as to language, and should lead them, while writing the Scriptures, to exhibit all the variety of manner naturally arising from the diversified character of their minds.

"But there is another argument, perhaps the most plausible of all, against supposing that inspiration had any respect to language; which is, that the supposition of a divine influence in this respect is wholly unnecessary; that the sacred writers, having the requisite information in regard to the subjects on which they were to write, might, so far as language is concerned, be left entirely to their own judgment and fidelity. But this view of the subject is not satisfactory. For whatever may be said as to the judgment and fidelity of those who wrote the Scriptures, there is one important circumstance which cannot be accounted for, without supposing them to have enjoyed a guidance above that of their own minds; namely, that they were infallibly preserved from every mistake or impropriety in the manner of writing. If we should admit that the divine superintendence and guidance afforded to the inspired writers had no relation at all to the manner in which they exhibited either doctrines or facts; how easily might we be disturbed with doubts, in regard to the propriety of some of their representations? We should most certainly consider them as liable to all the inadvertencies and mistakes, to which uninspired men are commonly liable; and we should think ourselves perfectly justified in undertaking to charge them with real errors and faults as to style, and to show how their language might have been improved; and, in short, to treat their writings just as we treat the writings of Shakspeare and Addison. 'Here,' we might say, 'Paul was unfortunate in the choice of words; and here his language does not express the ideas which he must have intended to convey.' 'Here the style of St. John was inadvertent; and here it was faulty: and here it would have been more agreeable to the nature of the subject, and would have more accurately expressed the truth, had it been altered thus.' If the language of the sacred writers did not in any way come under the inspection of the Holy Spirit, and if they were left, just as other writers are, to their own unaided faculties in regard to every thing which pertained to the manner of writing; then, evidently, we might use the same freedom in animadverting upon their style, as upon the style of other writers. But who could treat the volume of inspiration in this manner, without impiety and profaneness? And rather than make any approach to this, who would not choose to go to an excess, if there could be an excess, in reverence for the word of God?

"On this subject, far be it from me to indulge a curiosity which would pry into things not intended for human intelligence. And far be it from me to expend zeal in supporting opinions not warranted by the word of God. But this one point I think it specially important to maintain; namely, that the sacred writers had such direction of the Holy Spirit, that they were secured against all liability to error, and enabled to write just what God pleased; so that what they wrote is, in truth, the word of God, and can never be subject to any charge of mistake either as to matter or form. Whether this perfect correctness and propriety as to language resulted from the divine guidance directly or indirectly, is a question of no particular consequence. If the Spirit of God directs the minds of inspired men, and gives them just conceptions relative to the subjects on which they are to write; and if he constitutes and maintains a connection, true and invariable, between their conceptions and the language they employ to express them, the language must, in this way, be as infallible, and as worthy of God, as though it were dictated directly by the Holy Spirit. But to assert that the sacred writers used such language as they chose, or such as was natural to them, without any special divine superintendence, and that, in respect to style, they are to be regarded in the same light, and equally liable to mistakes, as other writers, is plainly contrary to the representations which they themselves make, and is suited to diminish our confidence in the word of God. For how could we have entire confidence in the representations of Scripture, if, after God had instructed the minds of the sacred writers in the truth to be communicated, he gave them up to all the inadvertencies and errors to which human nature in general is exposed, and took no effectual care that their manner of writing should be according to his will?

"Let us then briefly examine the subject, as it is presented in the Holy Scriptures, and see whether we find sufficient reason to affirm that inspiration had no relation whatever to language. 1. The Apostles were the subjects of such a divine inspiration as enabled them to speak 'with other tongues:' here inspiration related directly to language. 2. It is the opinion of most writers, that, in some instances, inspired men had not in their own minds a clear understanding of the things which they spake or wrote. One instance of this, commonly referred to, is the case of Daniel, who heard and repeated what the angel said, though he did not understand it, Dan. xii, 7–9. This has also been thought to be in some measure the case with the prophets referred to, 1 Peter i, 10–12. And is there not reason to think this may have been the case with many of the prophetic representations contained in the Psalms, and many of the symbolical rites of the Mosaic institute? Various matters are found in the Old Testament, which were not intended so much for the benefit of the writers, or their contemporaries, as for the benefit of future ages. And this might have been a sufficient reason why they should be left without a clear understanding of the things which they wrote. In such cases, if the opinion above stated is correct, inspired men were led to make use of expressions, the meaning of which they did not fully understand. And, according to this view, it would seem that the teaching of the Spirit which they enjoyed, must have related rather to the words than to the sense. 3. Those who deny that the divine influence afforded to the sacred writers had any respect to language, can find no support in the texts which most directly relate to the subject of inspiration. And it is surely in such texts, if any where, that we should suppose they would find support. The passage, 2 Peter i, 21, is a remarkable one. It asserts that 'holy men of God spake as they were moved by the Holy Ghost.' There is surely nothing here which limits the divine influence to the conceptions of their minds. They were moved by the Holy Ghost to SPEAK or WRITE. 'All Scripture is divinely inspired,' 2 Tim. iii, 16. Does this text afford any proof that the divine influence granted to the inspired penmen was confined to their inward conceptions, and had no respect whatever to the manner in which they expressed their conceptions? What is SCRIPTURE? Is it divine truth CONCEIVED IN THE MIND, or divine truth WRITTEN? In Heb. i, 1, it is said that 'God spake to the fathers by the prophets.' Does this afford any proof that the divine guidance which the prophets enjoyed related exclusively to the conceptions of their own minds, and had no respect to the manner in which they communicated those conceptions? Must we not rather think the meaning to be, that God influenced the prophets to utter or make known important truths? And how could they do this, except by the use of proper words?

"I have argued in favour of the inspiration of the Apostles, from their commission. They were sent by Christ to teach the truths of religion in his stead. It was an arduous work; and in the execution of it they needed and enjoyed much divine assistance. But forming right conceptions of Christianity in their own minds, was not the great work assigned to the Apostles. If the divine assistance reached only to this, it reached only to that which concerned them as private men, and which they might have possessed though they had never been commissioned to teach others. As Apostles, they were to preach the Gospel to all who could be brought to hear it, and to make a record of divine truth for the benefit of future ages. Now is it at all reasonable to suppose, that the divine assistance afforded them had no respect to their main business, and that, in the momentous and difficult work of communicating the truths of religion, either orally or by writing, they were left to themselves, and so exposed to all the errors and inadvertencies of uninspired men? But our reasoning does not stop here. For that divine assistance which we might reasonably suppose would have been granted to the Apostles in the work of teaching divine truth, is the very thing which Christ promised them in the texts before cited. I shall refer only to Matt. x, 19, 20, 'When they shall deliver you up, take no thought how or what ye shall speak; for it shall be given you in the same hour what ye shall speak. For it is not ye that speak, but the Spirit of your Father that speaketh in you.' This promise, as Knapp understands it, implies, that divine assistance should extend not only to WHAT they should say, but to the MANNER in which they should say it. It is not, however, to be understood as implying, that the Apostles were not rational and voluntary agents in the discharge of their office. But it implies that, in consequence of the influence of the Spirit to be exercised over them, they should say what God would have them to say, without any liability to mistake, either as to matter or manner. From the above-cited promise, taken in connection with the instances of its accomplishment which are recorded in the Acts of the Apostles, it becomes evident that God may exert his highest influence upon his servants, so as completely to guide them in thought and in utterance, in regard to subjects which lie chiefly within the province of their natural faculties. For in those speeches of the Apostles which are left on record, we find that most of the things which they declared, were things which, for aught that appears, they might have known, and might have expressed to others, in the natural exercise of their own faculties. This principle being admitted, and kept steadily in view, will relieve us of many difficulties in regard to the doctrine of inspiration. The passage, 1 Cor. ii, 12, 13, already cited as proof of the inspiration of the Apostles, is very far from favouring the opinion that inspiration had no respect whatever to their language, or that it related exclusively to their thoughts. 'Which things we speak, not in the words which man's wisdom teacheth, but which the Holy Ghost teacheth.' The Apostle avoided the style and the manner of teaching which prevailed among the wise men of Greece, and made use of a style which corresponded with the nature of his subject, and the end he had in view. And this, he tells us, he did, under the guidance of the Holy Spirit. His language, or manner of teaching, was the thing to which the divine influence imparted to him particularly referred. Storr and Flatt give the following interpretation of this text: Paul, they say, asserts that the doctrines of Christianity were revealed to him by the almighty agency of God himself; and, finally, that the inspiration of the divine Spirit extended even to his words, and to all his exhibitions of revealed truths. They add, that St. Paul clearly distinguishes between the doctrine itself, and the manner in which it is communicated."

INTERMEDIATE STATE. Beside questions concerning the nature of the happiness of heaven, there have also arisen questions concerning the state of the soul in the interval between death and the general resurrection. If we believe, with Dr. Priestley, that the soul is not a substance distinct from the body, we must believe with him that the whole of the human machine is at rest after death, till it be restored to its functions at the last day; but if we are convinced of the immateriality of the soul, we shall not think it so entirely dependent in all its operations upon its present companion, but that it may exist and act in an unembodied state. And if once we are satisfied that a state of separate existence is possible, we shall easily attach credit to the interpretation commonly given of the various expressions in Scripture, which intimate that the souls of good men are admitted to the presence of God immediately after death, although we soon find that a bound is set to our speculations concerning the nature of this intermediate state. But when we leave philosophical probability, and come to the doctrine of Scripture, the only ground of certainty on all such subjects, a great number of passages are so explicit, that no ingenuity of interpretation has been sufficient to weaken their evidence on this point. One branch of the opinions that have been held concerning an intermediate state is the Popish doctrine of purgatory; a doctrine which appears upon the slightest inspection of the texts that have been adduced in support of it to derive no evidence from Scripture; which originated in the error of the church of Rome in assigning to personal suffering a place in the justification of a sinner; and which is completely overturned by the doctrine of justification by faith, and by the general strain of Scripture, which represents this life as a state of probation, upon our conduct during which our everlasting condition depends. The holy Lazarus is carried by angels into Abraham's bosom; and the rich and careless sinner lifts up his eyes in hell, and is separated from the place of bliss by an impassable gulf. This at once disproves the doctrine of purgatory, and demonstrates an intermediate conscious state of happiness and misery.

IRON, ברזל; occurs first in Gen. iv, 22, and afterward frequently; and the Chaldee פרזל, in Dan. ii, 33, 41, and elsewhere often in that book; σίδηρος, Rev. xviii, 12, and the adjectives, Acts xii, 10; Rev. ii, 27; ix, 9; xii, 5; xix, 15; a well known and very serviceable metal. The knowledge of working it was very ancient, as appears from Genesis iv, 22. We do not, however, find that Moses made use of iron in the fabric of the tabernacle in the wilderness, or Solomon in any part of the temple at Jerusalem. Yet, from the manner in which the Jewish legislator speaks of iron, the metal, it appears, must have been in use in Egypt before his time. He celebrates the great hardness of it, Lev. xxvi, 19; Deut. xxviii, 23, 48; takes notice that the bedstead of Og, king of Bashan, was of iron, Deut. iii, 11; he speaks of mines of iron, Deut. viii, 9; and he compares the severity of the servitude of the Israelites in Egypt to the heat of a furnace for melting iron, Deut. iv, 20. We find, also, that swords, Num. xxxv, 16, axes, Deut. xix, 5, and tools for cutting stones, Deut. xxvii, 5, were made of iron. By the "northern iron," Jer. xv, 12, we may probably understand the hardened iron, called in Greek χάλυψ, from the Chalybes, a people bordering on the Euxine sea, and consequently lying on the north of Judea, by whom the art of tempering steel is said to have been discovered. Strabo speaks of this people by the name of Chalybes, but afterward Chaldæi; and mentions their iron mines. These, however, were a different people from the Chaldeans, who were united with the Babylonians.

ISAAC, the son of Abraham and Sarah, was born in the year of the world 2108. His name, which signifies LAUGHTER, was given him by his mother, because when it was told her by an angel that she should have a son, and that at a time of life when, according to the course of nature, she was past child-bearing, she privately laughed, Gen. xviii, 10–12. And when the child was born she said, "God hath made me to laugh, so that all that hear will laugh with me," Gen. xxi, 6. The life of Isaac, for the first seventy-five years of it, is so blended with that of his illustrious father, that the principal incidents of it have been already noticed under the article ABRAHAM. His birth was attended with some extraordinary circumstances: it was the subject of various promises and prophecies; an event most ardently desired by his parents, and yet purposely delayed by Divine Providence till they were both advanced in years, no doubt for the trial of their faith, and that Isaac might more evidently appear to be the gift of God, and "the child of promise." At an early period of life he was the object of the profane contempt of Ishmael, the son of the bond woman, by whom he was persecuted; and as in the circumstances attending his birth there was something typical of the birth of Abraham's greater Son, the Messiah, the promised Seed; so, in the latter instance, we contemplate in him a resemblance of real Christians, who, as Isaac was, are "the children of promise," invested in all the immunities and blessings of the new covenant; but, as then, "he that was born after the flesh persecuted him that was born after the Spirit, even so it is now," Gal. iv, 29.

When Isaac had arrived at a state of manhood, he was required to give a signal proof of his entire devotedness to God. Abraham was commanded to offer up his beloved son in sacrifice, Genesis xxii, 1. This remarkable transaction, so far as Abraham was concerned in it, has already been considered under the article ABRAHAM. But, if from this trial of the faith of the parent we turn our attention to the conduct of Isaac, the victim destined for the slaughter, we behold an example of faith and of dutiful obedience equally conspicuous with that of his honoured parent. Isaac submitted, as it should seem, without resistance, to be bound and laid on the altar, exposing his body to the knife that was lifted up to destroy him. How strikingly calculated is this remarkable history to direct our thoughts to a more exalted personage, whom Isaac prefigured; and to a more astonishing transaction represented by that on Mount Moriah! Behold Jesus Christ, that Seed of Abraham, in whom all the families of the earth were to be blessed, voluntarily going forth, in obedience to the command of his heavenly Father, and laying down his life, as a sacrifice for the sins of the world.

In the progress of Isaac's history, we find him, in the time of his greatest activity and vigour, a man of retired habits and of remarkable calmness of mind. He appears to have been affectionately attached to his mother Sarah, and, even at the age of forty, was not insusceptible of great sorrow on occasion of her death. But he allows his father to choose for him a suitable partner in life; and Rebekah was selected from among his own kindred, in preference to the daughters of Canaan, in the midst of whom he dwelt. In a few years afterward, he who had mourned for his mother, was called to weep over his father's grave; and in that last act of filial duty, it is pleasing to find the two rival brothers, Isaac and Ishmael, meeting together for the interment of Abraham. The occasion, indeed, was well calculated to allay all existing jealousies and contentions, and cause every family broil to cease, Gen. xxv, 9. After the death of Abraham, "God blessed his son Isaac;" but, though the latter had now been married twenty years, Rebekah was childless. "Isaac entreated the Lord for his wife, because she was barren; and the Lord was entreated of him, and Rebekah his wife conceived," Gen. xxv, 21. God also promised to multiply Isaac's seed, and his promise was fulfilled. Two children were born to him at one time, concerning whom the divine purpose was declared to the mother, and no doubt to the father also, that "the elder should serve the younger." A famine which came upon the country in the days of Isaac, obliged him to remove his family and flocks and retire to Gerar, in the country of the Philistines, of which Abimelech was at that time king. The possessions of Isaac multiplied so prodigiously, that the inhabitants of the country became envious of him, and even Abimelech, to preserve peace among them, was under the necessity of requesting him to retire, because he was become too powerful. He accordingly withdrew, and pitched his tent in the valley of Gerar, where he digged new wells, and, after a time, returned to Beersheba, where he fixed his habitation, Genesis xxvi, 1–23. Here the Lord appeared to him, and renewed to him the covenant which he had made with Abraham, promising to be his God, and to make him a blessing to others. Abimelech now sought his friendship, and, to form an alliance with him, paid him a visit; on which occasion Isaac displayed his magnificence by a sumptuous entertainment, A. M. 2240.

When he was a hundred and thirty-seven years of age, and his sight had so failed him that he could not distinguish one of his sons from the other, Jacob craftily obtained from him the blessing of primogeniture. Yet Isaac survived many years after this, to him, distressing occurrence. He sent Jacob into Mesopotamia, there to take a wife of his own family, Genesis xxviii, 1, 2, and to prevent his marrying among the Canaanites as his brother Esau had done. And when Jacob returned, after a lapse of twenty years, Isaac was still living, and continued to live twenty-three years longer. He then died at the age of a hundred and eighty years, and was buried with Abraham by his sons Esau and Jacob, Gen. xxxv, 29. See Esau and Jacob.

ISAIAH. Though fifth in the order of time, the writings of the Prophet Isaiah are placed first in order of the prophetical books, principally on account of the sublimity and importance of his predictions, and partly also because the book which bears his name is larger than all the twelve minor prophets put together. Concerning his family and descent, nothing certain has been recorded, except what he himself tells us, Isaiah, i, 1, namely, that he was the son of Amos, and discharged the prophetic office "in the days of Uzziah, Jotham, Ahaz, and Hezekiah, kings of Judah," who successively flourished between A. M. 3194 and 3305. There is a current tradition that he was of the blood royal; and some writers have affirmed that his father Amoz or Amos was the son of Joash, and consequently brother of Uzziah, king of Judah. Jerom, on the authority of some rabbinical writers, says, that the prophet gave his daughter in marriage to Manasseh, king of Judah; but this opinion is scarcely credible, because Manasseh did not commence his reign until about sixty years after Isaiah had begun to discharge his prophetic functions. He must, indeed, have exercised the office of a prophet during a long period of time, if he lived to the reign of Manasseh; for the lowest computation, beginning from the year in which Uzziah died, when he is by some supposed to have received his first appointment to that office, brings it to sixty-one years. But the tradition of the Jews, which has been adopted by most Christian commentators, that he was put to death by Manasseh, is very uncertain; and Aben Ezra, one of the most celebrated Jewish writers, is rather of opinion that he died before Hezekiah; which Bishop Lowth thinks most probable. It is, however, certain, that he lived at least to the fifteenth or sixteenth year of Hezekiah; which makes the least possible term of the duration of his prophetic office to be about forty-eight years. The name of Isaiah, as Vitringa has remarked after several preceding commentators, is in some measure descriptive of his high character, since it signifies the SALVATION OF JEHOVAH; and was given with singular propriety to him, who foretold the advent of the Messiah, through whom "all flesh shall see the salvation of God," Isa. xl, 5; Luke iii, 6; Acts iv, 12. Isaiah was contemporary with the Prophets Amos, Hosea, Joel, and Micah.

Isaiah is uniformly spoken of in the Scriptures as a prophet of the highest dignity: Bishop Lowth calls him the prince of all the prophets, and pronounces the whole of his book to be poetical, with the exception of a few detached passages. It is remarkable, that his wife is styled a prophetess in Isaiah viii, 3; whence the rabbinical writers have concluded that she possessed the spirit of prophecy: but it is very probable that the prophets' wives were called prophetesses, as the priests' wives were termed priestesses, only from the quality of their husbands. Although nothing farther is recorded in the Scriptures concerning the wife of Isaiah, we find two of his sons mentioned in his prophecy, who were types or figurative pledges; and their names and actions were intended to awaken a religious attention in the persons whom they were commissioned to address and to instruct. Thus, Shear-jashub signifies, "a remnant shall return," and showed that the captives who should be carried to Babylon should return thence after a certain time, Isaiah vii, 3; and Maher-shalal-hash-baz, which denotes, "make speed (or RUN SWIFTLY) to the spoil," implied that the kingdoms of Israel and Syria would in a short time be ravaged, Isaiah viii, 1, 3. Beside the volume of prophecies, which we are now to consider, it appears from 2 Chron. xxvi, 22, that Isaiah wrote an account of "the acts of Uzziah," king of Judah: this has perished with some other writings of the prophets, which, as probably not written by inspiration, were never admitted into the canon of Scripture. There are also two apocryphal books ascribed to him, namely, The Ascension of Isaiah, and The Apocalypse of Isaiah; but these are evidently forgeries of a later date, and the Apocalypse has long since perished.

The scope of Isaiah's predictions is threefold, namely, 1. To detect, reprove, aggravate, and condemn, the sins of the Jewish people especially, and also the iniquities of the ten tribes of Israel, and the abominations of many Gentile nations and countries; denouncing the severest judgments against all sorts and degrees of persons, whether Jews or Gentiles. 2. To invite persons of every rank and condition, both Jews and Gentiles, to repentance and reformation, by numerous promises of pardon and mercy. It is worthy of remark, that no such promises are intermingled with the denunciations of divine vengeance against Babylon, although they occur in the threatenings against every other people. 3. To comfort all the truly pious, in the midst of all the calamities and judgments denounced against the wicked, with prophetic promises of the true Messiah, which seem almost to anticipate the Gospel history, so clearly do they foreshow the divine character of Christ.

Isaiah has, with singular propriety, been denominated the evangelical prophet, on account of the number and variety of his prophecies concerning the advent and character, the ministry and preaching, the sufferings and death, and the extensive permanent kingdom, of the Messiah. So explicit and determinate are his predictions, as well as so numerous, that he seems to speak rather of things past than of events yet future; and he may rather be called an evangelist than a prophet. No one, indeed, can be at a loss in applying them to the mission and character of Jesus Christ, and to the events which are cited in his history by the writers of the New Testament. This prophet, says Bishop Lowth, abounds in such transcendent excellencies, that he may be properly said to afford the most perfect model of prophetic poetry. He is at once elegant and sublime, forcible and ornamented; he unites energy with copiousness, and dignity with variety. In his sentiments there is uncommon elevation and majesty; in his imagery, the utmost propriety, elegance, dignity, and diversity; in his language, uncommon beauty and energy; and, notwithstanding the obscurity of his subjects, a surprising degree of clearness and simplicity. To these we may add, that there is such sweetness in the poetical composition of his sentences, whether it proceed from art or genius, that, if the Hebrew poetry at present is possessed of any remains of its native grace and harmony, we shall chiefly find them in the writings of Isaiah: so that the saying of Ezekiel may most justly be applied to this prophet:--

"Thou art the confirmed exemplar of measures,

Full of wisdom, and perfect in beauty."

Ezekiel xxviii, 12.

Isaiah also greatly excels in all the graces of method, order, connection, and arrangement: though in asserting this we must not forget the nature of the prophetic impulse, which bears away the mind with irresistible violence, and frequently in rapid transitions from near to remote objects, from human to divine. We must likewise be careful in remarking the limits of particular predictions, since, as they are now extant, they are often improperly connected, without any marks of discrimination; which injudicious arrangement, on some occasions, creates almost insuperable difficulties.

Bishop Lowth has selected the thirty-fourth and thirty-fifth chapters of this prophet, as a specimen of the poetic style in which Isaiah delivers his predictions, and has illustrated at some length the various beauties which eminently distinguish the simple, regular, and perfect poem contained in those chapters. But the grandest specimen of his poetry is presented in the fourteenth chapter, which is one of the most sublime odes occurring in the Bible, and contains the noblest personifications to be found in the records of poetry. The prophet, after predicting the liberation of the Jews from their severe captivity in Babylon, and their restoration to their own country, verses 1–3, introduces a chorus of them, expressing their surprise and astonishment at the sudden downfall of Babylon, and the great reverse of fortune that had befallen the tyrant, who, like his predecessors, had oppressed his own, and harassed the neighbouring kingdoms. These oppressed kingdoms, or their rulers, are represented under the image of the fir trees and the cedars of Libanus, which is frequently used to express any thing in the political or religious world that is supereminently great and majestic: the whole earth shouts for joy; the cedars of Libanus utter a severe taunt over the fallen tyrant, and boast their security now he is no more, verses 4–8. This is followed, verse 9, by one of the boldest and most animated personifications of hades, or the regions of the dead, that was ever executed in poetry. Hades excites his inhabitants, the shades of princes, and the departed spirits of monarchs. These illustrious shades rise at once from their couches as from their thrones; and, advancing to the entrance of the cavern to meet the king of Babylon, they insult and deride him on being reduced to the same low state of impotence and dissolution with themselves, verses 10, 11. The Jews now resume the speech, verse 12; they address the king of

Babylon as the morning star fallen from heaven, as the first in splendour and dignity, in the political world fallen from his high state: they introduce him as uttering the most extravagant vaunts of his power and ambitious designs in his former glory; these are strongly contrasted, in the close, with his present low and abject condition, verses 13–15. Immediately follows a different scene, and a most happy image, to diversify the same subject, and give it a new turn and additional force. Certain persons are introduced, who light upon the corpse of the king of Babylon, cast out and lying naked upon the bare ground, among the common slain, just after the taking of the city, covered with wounds, and so disfigured, that it is some time before they know him. They accost him with the severest taunts, and bitterly reproach him with his destructive ambition, and his cruel usage of the conquered; which have deservedly brought upon him this ignominious treatment, so different from what those of his high rank usually meet with, and which shall cover his posterity with disgrace, verses 16–20. To complete the whole, God is introduced, declaring the fate of Babylon; the utter extirpation of the royal family, and the total desolation of the city; the deliverance of his people, and the destruction of their enemies; confirming the irreversible decree by the awful sanction of his oath, verses 21–27. How forcible, says Bishop Louth, is this imagery, how diversified, how sublime! How elevated the diction, the figures, the sentiments! The Jewish nation, the cedars of Lebanon, the ghosts of departed kings, the Babylonish monarch, the travellers who find his corpse, and last of all Jehovah himself, are the characters which support this beautiful lyric drama. One continued action is kept up, or rather, a series of interesting actions are connected together in an incomparable whole: this, indeed, is the principal and distinguished excellence of the sublimer ode, and is displayed in its utmost perfection in this poem of Isaiah, which may be considered as one of the most ancient, and certainly one of the most finished, specimens of that species of composition which has been transmitted to us. The personifications here are frequent, yet not confused; bold, yet not improbable; a free, elevated, and truly divine spirit pervades the whole; nor is there any thing wanting in this ode to defeat its claim to the character of perfect pathos and sublimity. There is not a single instance in the whole compass of Greek and Roman poetry which, in every excellence of composition, can be said to equal or even to approach it.

ISCARIOT, the name of that disciple who betrayed our Saviour. He was so called, probably, as belonging to Karioth, or Cerioth; that is, a man of Kerioth, Matt. x, 4.

ISHBOSHETH, a son of King Saul, and his successor in the throne. He was acknowledged king by a part of the tribes of Israel, A. M. 2949, while David reigned at Hebron, over the tribe of Judah, 2 Sam. ii, 8, 9, &c; iii. He reigned two years in peace, but the remaining eight years were spent in perpetual wars between his troops and those of David, till in the end he perished, and with him ended the royal dignity of the house of Saul.

ISHMAELITES, the descendants of Ishmael, the son of Abraham by Hagar, his Egyptian bond-maid. Ishmael was born B. C. 1910, and his name, founded on a circumstance which afforded relief to his mother, when she was wandering from her master's house toward Egypt, her native country, is derived from the Hebrew מעאליש, formed of שמע, TO HEAR, and אל, GOD, and denoting, "the Lord hath hearkened." The heavenly messenger who appeared to Hagar in the wilderness, and instructed her by what name to call her future son, predicted also that he and his posterity would prove fierce and warlike, engaged in repeated hostilities, and yet able to maintain their independence. Hagar, deriving encouragement from this circumstance, returned to the house of Abraham, and was soon delivered of her promised son. The father regarded Ishmael as the heir of his wealth, till Sarah had the promise of her son Isaac. After the birth of Isaac, Abraham was persuaded by his wife to dismiss Hagar and her son; and the patriarch probably provided for their subsistence in some distant situation, where they could not encroach on the patrimony of Isaac. Having wandered for some time in the wilderness of Beersheba, they proceeded farther to the wilderness of Paran, which bordered on Arabia; and here Ishmael arrived at maturity, and became an expert archer, or a hunter and warrior. In process of time his mother procured for him a wife out of Egypt, by whom he had twelve sons, who eventually established themselves as the heads of so many distinct Arabian tribes. Accordingly, the descendants of Ishmael are mentioned in history under the general name of Arabians and Ishmaelites. Of Ishmael's personal history, we merely learn from the sacred writings, that he joined with his brother Isaac in paying the last tribute of respect to the remains of their father; and that he died at the age of a hundred and thirty-seven years, B. C. 1773, Gen. xxv, 9, 18. His descendants, according to the Scripture account, spread themselves "from Havilah to Shur, that is, before Egypt, as thou goest toward Assyria." From this brief statement, we may conjecture how far their territory extended; for Havilah, according to the generality of writers, was situated near the confluence of the Tigris and Euphrates, and Shur, on the isthmus which separates Arabia from Egypt, now called the Isthmus of Suez. From thence we may well imagine, that they spread themselves on both sides so far as to have taken possession of the greatest part of Arabia; and, indeed, Josephus does not scruple to style their progenitor the founder of the Arabian nation. See Arabia.

ISHTOB, a country situated at the northern extremity of the mountains of Gilead, toward Mount Libanus, 2 Sam. x, 6. See Tob.

ISRAEL, a prince of God, or prevailing, or wrestling with God. This is the name which the angel gave Jacob, after having wrestled with him all night at Mahanaim, or Peniel, Genesis xxxii, 1, 2, 28, 29, 30; Hosea xii, 4. By the name of Israel is sometimes understood the person of Jacob, sometimes the whole people of Israel, the whole race of Jacob; sometimes the kingdom of Israel, or ten tribes, distinct from the kingdom of Judah; and finally, the spiritual Israel, the true church of God.

ISRAELITES, the descendants of Israel, who were first called Hebrews by reason of Abraham, who came from the other side of the Euphrates; and afterward Israelites, from Israel, the father of the twelve tribes; and, lastly, Jews, particularly after their return from the captivity of Babylon; because the tribe of Judah was then much stronger and more numerous than the other tribes, and foreigners had scarcely any knowledge but of this tribe. See Jews.

ISSACHAR, the fifth son of Jacob and Leah, Gen. xxx, 14–18. He had four sons, Tola, Phovah, Job, and Shimron. We know nothing particular of his life. The tribe of Issachar had its portion in one of the best parts of the land of Canaan, along the great plain or valley of Jezreel, with the half tribe of Manasseh to the south, that of Zebulun to the north, the Mediterranean to the west, and Jordan, with the extremity of the sea of Tiberias, to the east.

ITHAMAR, Aaron's fourth son, Exod. vi, 23. There is no probability that he ever exercised the high priesthood. He and his sons continued in the rank of simple priests, till this dignity came into his family in the person of Eli.

ITURÆA, so called from Itur, or Jetur, one of the sons of Ishmael, who settled in it, but whose posterity were either driven out or subdued by the Amorites; when it is supposed to have formed a part of the kingdom of Bashan, and subsequently of the half tribe of Manasseh east of Jordan; but as it was situated beyond the southern spur of Mount Hermon, called the Djebel Heish, this is doubtful. It lay on the north-eastern side of the land of Israel, between it and the territory of Damascus, or Syria; and is supposed to have been the same country at present known by the name of Djedour, on the east of the Djebel Heish, between Damascus and the lake of Tiberias. The Ituræans being subdued by Aristobulus, the high priest and governor of the Jews, B. C. 106, were forced by him to embrace the Jewish religion; and were at the same time incorporated into the state. Philip, one of the sons of Herod the Great, was tetrarch, or governor, of this country when John the Baptist commenced his ministry.

IVORY. שנבים; from שז, A TOOTH, and הבים, ELEPHANTS; ἐλεφάντινος, Rev. xviii, 12. The first time that ivory is mentioned in Scripture is in the reign of Solomon. If the forty-fifth Psalm was written before the Canticles, and before Solomon had constructed his royal and magnificent throne, then that contains the first mention of this commodity. It is spoken of as used in decorating those boxes of perfume, whose odours were employed to exhilarate the king's spirits. It is probable that Solomon, who traded to India, first brought thence elephants and ivory to Judea. "For the king had at sea a navy of Tharshish, with the navy of Hiram: once in three years came the navy of Tharshish, bringing gold and silver, and ivory," 1 Kings x, 22; 2 Chron. ix, 21. It seems that Solomon had a throne decorated with ivory, and inlaid with gold; the beauty of these materials relieving the splendour, and heightening the lustre of each other, 1 Kings x, 18. Cabinets and wardrobes were ornamented with ivory, by what is called marquetry, Psalm xlv, 8.

QUALE PER ARTEM

INCLUSUM BUXO AUT ORICIA TEREBINTHO

LUCET EBUR.

Virgil.

"So shines a gem, illustrious to behold,

On some fair virgin's neck, enchased in gold:

So the surrounding ebon's darker hue

Improves the polish'd ivory to the view."

Pitt.

These were named "houses of ivory," probably because made in the form of a house, or palace; as the silver ναοὶ of Diana, mentioned Acts xix, 24, were in the form of her temple at Ephesus; and as we have now ivory models of the Chinese pagodas, or temples. In this sense we may understand what is said of the ivory house which Ahab made, 1 Kings xxii, 39; for the Hebrew word translated "HOUSE is used," as Dr. Taylor well observes, for "a place, or case, wherein any thing lieth, is contained, or laid up." Ezekiel gives the name of house to chests of rich apparel, Ezek. xxvii, 24. Dr. Durell, in his note on Psalm xlv, 8, quotes places from Homer and Euripides, where the same appropriation is made. Hesiod makes the same. As to dwelling houses, the most, I think, we can suppose in regard to them is, that they might have ornaments of ivory, as they sometimes have of gold, silver, or other precious materials, in such abundance as to derive an appellation from the article of their decoration; as the Emperor Nero's palace, mentioned by Suetonius, was named AUREA, or "golden," because LITA AURO, "overlaid with gold." This method of ornamental buildings, or apartments, was very ancient among the Greeks. Homer mentions ivory as employed in the palace of Menelaus at Lacedæmon:--

Χαλκοῦ τε στεροπὴν, καδδώματα ἠχήεντα

Χρυσοῦ τ', ἠλέκτρȣ τε, καὶ ἀργύρȣ ἠ δ' ἐλέφαντος.

Odyss. iv, 72.

"Above, beneath, around the palace, shines

The sumless treasure of exhausted mines;

The spoils of elephants the roof inlay,

And studded amber darts a golden ray."

Bacchylides, cited by Athenæus, says, that, in the island of Ceos, one of the Cyclades, the houses of the great men "glister with gold and ivory."

AN ALPHABETICAL
TABLE OF THE PROPER NAMES AND THEIR MEANINGS

- AARON, *Ay´-ron*, lofty, mountainous.
- Abad´don, the destroyer.
- Abagtha, *Ab-ag´-tha*, father of the wine press.
- Abana, *Ab-ay´-nah*, stony.
- Abarim, *Ab´-a-rim*, passages.
- Ab´aron, strength.
- Ab´ba, father.
- Ab´da, a servant.
- Ab´di, my servant.
- Abdiel, *Ab´-de-el*, a servant of God.
- Ab´don, a servant.
- Abed-nego, *A-bed´-ne-go*, servant of light.
- A´bel, vanity, vapour, mourning.
- Abel-beth-maachah, *Ay´-bel-beth-ma-ay´-kah*, mourning of the house of Maachah.
- A´bel-ma´im, the mourning of the waters.
- Abel-meholah, *Ay´-bel-me-ho´-lah*, mourning of weakness, of sickness.
- Abel-mizraim, *Ay´-bel-miz-ra´-im*, the mourning of the Egyptians.
- A´bel-shit´tim, mourning of the thorns.
- A´bez, an egg, muddy.
- Abi, *A´-be*, my father.
- Abiah, *Ab-i´-ah*, the Lord is my father.
- Abi´ahil, the father of light or praise.
- Abi-albon, *Ab-e-al´-bon*, intelligent father.
- Ab´iam, the father of the sea.
- Abi-as´aph, a gathering or consuming father.
- Abiathar, *Ab-i´-a-thar*, excellent father.
- A´bib, green fruits, ears of corn.
- Abi´dah, father of knowledge.
- Abi´dan, father of judgment.
- Abiel, *Ab´-e-el*, God my father.
- Abiezer, *Ab-e-e´-zer*, father of help.
- Abi-ezrite, *Ab-e-ez´-rite*.
- Abigail, *Ab´-e-gal*, the joy of the father.
- Abi´-gibeon, the father of the cup, father of Gibeon.
- Abihail, *Ab-e-hay´-il*, the father of strength.
- Abi´hu, he is my father, or his father.
- Abi´hud, the father of praise or confession.
- Abijah, *Ab-i´-jah*, the will of the Lord.
- Abi´jam, father of the sea.
- Abilene, *Ab-e-le´-ne*, the father of the apartment, or of mourning.
- Abimael, *Ab-be-may´-el*, a father sent from God, my father comes from God.
- Abimelech, *Ab-im´-me-lek*, father of the king.
- Abinadab, *Ab-in´-na-dab*, father of willingness, my father is a prince.
- Abinoam, *Ab-in´-no-am*, father of beauty or comeliness, my father is beautiful.
- Abiram, *Ab-i´-ram*, a high father, father of
- fraud.
- Abishag, *Ab´-be-shag*, ignorance of the father.
- Abishai, *Ab-bish´-a-i*, the present of my father, the father of the sacrifice.
- Abishalom, *Ab-bish´-a-lom*, the father of peace, the recompence of the father.
- Abishua, *Ab-bish´-u-a*, father of salvation or of magnificence.
- Abishur, *Ab´-be-shur*, the father of the wall or of uprightness.
- Abital, *Ab´-be-tal*, the father of the dew.
- Abitub, *Ab´-be-tub*, father of goodness.

- Abiud, *Ab´-be-ud*, father of praise.
- Ab´ner, father of light, the son of the father.
- A´braham, the father of a great multitude.
- A´bram, a high father, the father of elevation.
- Ab´salom, father of peace.
- Accad, *Ak´-ad*, a pitcher, a sparkle.
- Accho, *Ak´-ko*, close, pressed together.
- Aceldama, *A-kel´-da-mah*, the field of blood.
- Achaia, *A-kay´-yah*, grief, trouble.
- Achaicus, *A-kay´-e-kus*, a native of Achaia.
- Achan, Achar, *A´-kan*, *A´-kar*, he that troubles and bruises.
- Achbor, *Ak´-bor*, a rat, bruising.
- Achim, *A´-kim*, preparing, confirming, revenging.
- Achir, *A´-ker*, the brother's light.
- Achish, *A´-kish*, thus it is, how is this?
- Achmetha, *Ak´-me-thah.*
- Achor, *A´-kor*, trouble.
- Achsah, *Ak´-sah*, adorned, bursting of the veil.
- Achshaph, *Ak´-shaph*, poison, tricks, one that breaks, the brim of any thing.
- Achzib, *Ak´-zib*, liar, one that runs.
- Adadah, *Ad´-a-dah*, the testimony of the assembly.
- Adah, *Ay´-dah*, an assembly.
- Adaiah, *Ad-a´-yah*, the witness of the Lord.
- Adaliah, *Ad-a-ly´-ah*, one that draws water, poverty, cloud, death.
- Ad´am, earthy, taken out of red earth.
- Adamah, *Ad´-da-mah*, red earth.
- Adami, *Ad´-da-my*, my man, red, earthy.
- A´dar, high, eminent.
- Adbeel, *Ad´-be-el*, a vapour, a cloud of God, a vexer of God.
- Ad´di, my witness, adorned, passage, prey.
- Ad´don, basis, foundation, the Lord.
- Adiel, *Ad´-i-el*, the witness of the Lord.
- Adin, *Ad´-din*, adorned, dainty.
- Adithaim, *Ad-e-thay´-im*, assemblies, testimonies.
- Adlai, *Ad-lay´-i*, my witness, my ornament.
- Ad´mah, earthy, red earth.
- Admatha, *Ad´-ma-thah*, a cloud of death, a mortal vapour.
- Ad´nah, rest, testimony, eternal.
- Adona´i, my Lord.
- Adoni-bezek, *Ad´-o-ne-bee´-zek*, the lightning of the Lord, the Lord of Bezek.
- Adonijah, *Ad-o-ny´-jah*, the Lord is my master.
- Adonikam, *Ad-o-ny´-kam*, the Lord is raised, my Lord hath raised me.
- Adoniram, *Ad-o-ny´-ram*, my Lord is most high, the Lord of might and elevation.
- Adoni-zedek, *Ad´-o-ne-zee´-dek*, justice of the Lord.
- Adoraim, *Ad-o-ray´-im*, strength or power of the sea.
- Adoram, *Ad-o´-ram*, their beauty, their power, their praise.
- Adrammelech, *Ad-ram´-me-lek*, the cloak or glory of the king.
- Adramyttium, *Ad-ra-mit´-te-um*, the court of death.
- Adria, *Ay´-dre-ah*, the name of a city, which gives name to the Adriatic Sea, now the Gulf of Venice.
- A´driel, the flock of God.
- Adullam, *Ad-ul´-lam*, their testimony, their prey, their ornament.
- Adum´mim, earthly or bloody things.
- Æ´neas, praised.
- Agabus, *Ag´-ga-bus*, a locust, the feast of the father.
- Agag, *Ay´-gag*, roof, floor.
- A´gagite, of the race of Agag.
- Aga´pæ, love feasts.
- Agar, see Hagar.
- Agi´e, a valley, deepness.
- Agrippa, *A-grip´-pah*, one who at his birth causes great pain.
- A´gur, a stranger, gathering.
- A´hab, the brother of the father.
- Aha´rah, a sweet brother, an odoriferous meadow.
- Ahar´hel, another host, another sorrow, the sleep of the brother.

- Ahasba´i, trusting in me, brother compassing. In Syriac, a brother of age.
- Ahasuerus, *A-has-u-e´-rus*, prince, chief.
- Ahava, *A-hay´-vah*, essence, generation.
- A´haz, one that takes and possesses.
- Ahaziah, *A-ha-zy´-ah*, possession, vision of the Lord.
- Ahi, my brother, my brethren.
- Ahiah, *A-hy´-ah*, brother of the Lord.
- Ahiam, *A-hy´am*, brother of the mother, brother of the nation.
- Ahian, *A-hy´-an*, brother of wine.
- Ahie´zer, brother of assistance.
- Ahi´hud, brother of vanity, a brother of praise.
- Ahijah, THE SAME as Ahiah.
- Ahikam, *A-hy´-kam*, a brother that raises up.
- Ahi´lud, a brother born.
- Ahim´aaz, brother of the council.
- Ahi´man, a brother prepared.
- Ahimelech, *A-him´-me-lek*, my brother is a king.
- Ahimoth, *A´-he-moth*, brother of death.
- Ahin´adab, a willing brother, a brother of a vow, brother of the prince.
- Ahinoam, *A-hin´-no-am*, the beauty and comeliness of the brother.
- Ahi´o, his brother, his brethren.
- Ahior. See Achior.
- Ahira, *A-hy´-rah*, brother of iniquity or of the shepherd.
- Ahiram, *A-hy´-ram*, brother of craft, protection.
- Ahisamach, *A-his´-sa-mak*, brother of strength or of support.
- Ahishabar, *A-his´-sa-bar*, brother of the morning or dew, brother of blackness.
- Ahi´shar, brother of a prince.
- Ahithophel, *A-hit´-to-fel*, brother of ruin or folly.
- Ahi´tub, brother of goodness.
- Ah´lab, which is of milk, is fat.
- Ah´lai, beseeching, sorrowing, beginning, brother to me.
- Aho´ah, a thistle, a thorn, a fish hook, brotherhood.
- Aho´hi, a living brother, my thistle or thorn.
- Aho´lah, his tabernacle, his tent.
- Aholiab, *A-ho´-le-ab*, the tent or tabernacle of the father.
- Aholibah, *A-ho´-le-bah*, my tent and my tabernacle in her.
- Aholibamah, *A-ho´-le-bay´-mah*, my tabernacle is exalted.
- Ahran. See Charan.
- Ahu´mar, a meadow of waters, brother of waters.
- Ahu´zam, their taking possession, vision.
- Ahuz´zah, possession, apprehension, vision.
- Ai, or Hai, *Ay´-i*, mass, heap.
- Ai´ah, a raven, a vulture, alas, where is it?
- Ai´ath, an hour.
- Ai´n, an eye, a fountain.
- Aioth, THE SAME AS Ai.
- Ajalon, *Ad´-ja-lon*, a chain, strength, a stag.
- Ak´kub, the print of the foot where any creature hath gone, supplantation.
- Alammelech, *Al-am´-me-lek*, God is king.
- Al´cimus, strong, of strength.
- Al´emeth, a hiding, youth, worlds, upon the dead.
- Al´emis, strength.
- Alexan´der, one that assists men, one that turns away evil.
- Alexandria, *Al-ex-an´-dre-a*, the city of Alexander.
- Alleluia, *Al-le-lu´-yah*, praise the Lord.
- A´lian, high.
- Al´lon, an oak.
- Allon-bachuth, *Al´-lon-bak´-kuth*, the oak of weeping.
- Almo´dad, measure of God.
- Al´mon, hidden.
- Al´mon-dib´lathaim, a hiding, a heap of fig trees.
- Alpha, *Al´-fah*, the first letter of the Greek alphabet, marked A.
- Alpheus, *Al-fe´-us*, a thousand, chief.
- A´mad, a people of witness, people everlasting.
- Am´alek, a people that licks up or uses ill.
- Amal´ekites, people descended from Amalek.

- A´mam, mother, fear of them, people.
- Amana, *Am-ay´-nah*, integrity and truth.
- Amariah, *Am-a-ry´-ah*, the Lord says, the excellency of the Lord.
- Amasa, *Am-ay´-sah*, a forgiving people, the burden of the people.
- Amaziah, *Am-a-zy´-ah*, the strength of the Lord.
- A´mi. See Amam.
- Am´mah, my people.
- Ammi, the same as Ammah.
- Ammihud, *Am´-me-hud*, people of praise.
- Amminadab, *Am-min´-na-dab*, prince of the people, a people that vows.
- Ammishaddai, *Am-me-shad´-day-i*, the people of the Almighty.
- Am´mon, the son of my people.
- Am´monites, a people descended from Benammi, son of Lot.
- Am´non, faithful and true, foster father.
- Amon, *Ay´-mon*, faithful, true.
- Am´orite, bitter, a rebel, a babbler.
- Amos, *Ay´-mos*, loading, weighty.
- Amoz, *Ay´-moz*, strong, robust.
- Amphipolis, *Am-fip´-po-lis*, a city encompassed by the sea.
- Amplias, *Am´-ple-as*, large, extensive.
- Am´ram, an exalted people, handfuls of corn.
- Amraphel, *Am´-ra-fel*, one that speaks of hidden things or of ruin.
- Am´zi, strong, mighty.
- A´nab, a grape, a knot.
- Anah, *Ay´-nah*, one who answers or sings, poor, afflicted.
- Anak, *Ay´-nak*, a collar, an ornament.
- Anakims, *An´-ak-ims*. See Anak.
- Anammelech, *An-am´-me-lek*, answer, song of the king.
- A´nan, a cloud, a prophecy.
- Ananias, *An-a-ny´-as*, the cloud of the Lord.
- Anathoth, *An´-a-thoth*, answer, affliction.
- Andrew, *An´drue*, a stout and strong man.
- Andronicus, *An-dron´-ne-kus*, a man excelling others.
- Aner, *Ay´-ner*, answer, song, affliction.
- An´na, gracious, merciful.
- An´nas, one that answers, that afflicts.
- An´tichrist, an adversary to Christ.
- Antioch, *An´-te-ok*, instead of a chariot.
- An´tipas, against all.
- Antipatris, *An-te-pay´-tris*, against his own father.
- Apelles, *A-pel´-lees*, to exclude, to separate.
- Aphek, *Ay´-fek*, a stream, vigour.
- Apollonia, *Ap-po-lo´-ne-ah*, perdition.
- Apol´los, one that destroys and lays waste.
- Apollyon, *A-pol´-le-on*, one that exterminates or destroys.
- Apphia, *Af´-e-ah*, that is fruitful.
- Appii-forum, *Ap´-pe-i-fo´-rum*, a town so called from Appius Claudius, whose statue was erected there.
- Aquila, *Ak´-we-lah*, an eagle.
- Ar, awaking, uncovering.
- Ara´bia, evening, a place wild and desert; mixtures, because this country was inhabited by different kinds of people.
- Ara´bian, an inhabitant of Arabia.
- A´rad, a wild ass, a dragon.
- A´ram, magnificence, one that deceives.
- Ararat, *Ar´-ra-rat*, the curse of trembling.
- Araunah, *A-raw´-nah*, ark, song, curse.
- Ar´ba, the city of the four.
- Archelaus, *Ar-ke´-lay-us*, the prince of the people.
- Archippus, *Ar-kip´-pus*, governor of horses.
- Arcturus, *Ark-tew´-rus*, a gathering together.
- Ard, one that commands.
- Areli, *Ar-e´-lie*, the light or vision of God.
- Areopagite, *A-re-op´-a-gyte*, belonging to the council called Areopagus.
- Areopagus, *A-re-op´-a-gus*, the hill of Mars; a place where the magistrates of Athens held their supreme council; from ἀρεῖος, "of Mars," and πάγος, "a hill."
- Aretas, *A-re´-tas*, one that is agreeable or virtuous.
- Ar´gob, a turf of earth, curse of the well.

- Ariel, *Ay´-re-el*, the altar, light, lion of God.
- Arimathea, *Ar-re-ma-the´-ah*, a lion dead to the Lord. Ramath, or Ramah, a city where Samuel dwelt.
- Arioch, *Ar´-e-ok*, long, your drunkenness, your lion.
- Aristarchus, *A-ris-tar´-kus*, the best prince.
- Aristobulus, *A-ris-tob´-bu-lus*, a good counsellor.
- Armageddon, *Ar-ma-ged´-don*, the mountain of Megiddo, of the gospel, of fruits.
- Armenia, *Ar-me´-ne-ah*, a province which is supposed to take its name from Aram.
- Ar´non, rejoicing, their ark.
- Ar´oer, heath, tamarisk, the nakedness of the skin or of the enemy.
- Ar´pad, the light of redemption, that lies down.
- Arphaxad, *Ar-fak´s-ad*, one that heals or releases.
- Artaxerxes, *Ar-taks-erk´s-es*, in Hebrew, Artachsasta, the silence of light.
- Artemas, *Ar´-te-mas*, whole, sound.
- Asa, *Ay´-sah*, physician, cure.
- Asahel, *As´-a-el*, the work or creature of God.
- Asaiah, *As´-a-i-ah*, the Lord hath wrought.
- Asaph, *Ay´-saf*, one that assembles together.
- Asenath, *As´-e-nath*, peril, misfortune.
- A´shan, vapour, smoke.
- Ash´dod, inclination, a wild open place.
- Ash´er, blessedness.
- As´hiel, the work of God.
- Ashima, *Ash´-e-mah*, crime, position, fire of the sea.
- Ashkenaz, *Ash´-ke-naz*, a fire that distils or spreads.
- Ashtaroth, *Ash´-ta-roth*, flocks, riches.
- Ash´ur, one that is happy.
- Ash´vath, making vestments.
- Asia, *Ay´-she-a*, muddy, boggy.
- As´kelon, weight, balance, fire of infamy.
- Asnap´per, unhappiness, fruitless.
- Assir, prisoner, fettered.
- As´sos, approaching.
- Assyria, *As-sir´-re-a.*
- Assyrian, *As-sir´-re-an.*
- Asyncritus, *A-sin´-kre-tus*, incomparable.
- A´tad, a thorn.
- Ata´roth, crowns, counsel of making full.
- Athaliah, *Ath-a-ly´-ah*, the time of the Lord.
- Athenians, *Ath-ee´-ne-ans*, inhabitants of Athens.
- Ath´ens, so called from Athene, Minerva.
- Attalia, *At-ta-ly´-ah*, that increases or sends.
- A´ven, iniquity, force, riches.
- Augus´tus, increased, majestic.
- Azariah, *Az-a-ry´-ah*, assistance, he that hears the Lord.
- Azekah, *Az-ee´-kah*, strength of walls.
- Az´gad, a strong army, a gang of robbers.
- Aznoth-tabor, *Az´-noth-tay´-bor*, the ears of Tabor, of choice, purity, contrition.
- Azo´tus, THE SAME AS Ashdod.
- A´zur, he that assists, that is assisted.

- Baal, *Bay´-al*, he that rules and subdues.
- Baalah, *Bay´-al-ah*, her idol, a spouse; the name of a city.
- Baal-berith, *Bay´-al-be´-rith*, idol of the covenant.
- Baal-gad, *Bay´-al-gad´*, the idol of the troop, the Lord is master of the troop.
- Baal-hamon, *Bay´-al-hay´-mon*, one that rules a multitude, a populous place.
- Baal-hazer, *Bay´-al-hay´-zer*, lord of court, possessor of grace.
- Ba´al-Her´mon, the possessor of destruction, of a thing devoted to God.
- Ba´ali, my idol, or master.
- Ba´alim, idols, masters.
- Ba´alis, a rejoicing, proud lord.
- Baal-meon, *Bay´-al-me´-on*, the idol, the master of the house.
- Baal-peor, *Bay´-al-pe´-or*, master of the opening.
- Baal-perazim, *Bay´-al-per´-a-zim*, master, or god of divisions.
- Baal-shalisha, *Bay´-al-shal´-e-shah*, the third idol, the third husband.
- Baal-tamar, *Bay´-al-tay´-mar*, master of the palm tree.

- Baal-zebub, *Bay´-al-ze´-bub*, the master of flies.
- Baal-zephon, *Bay´-al-ze´-fon*, the idol of the north, secret.
- Baanah, *Bay´-a-nah*, in the answer, in affliction.
- Baa´rah, a flame, purging.
- Baashah, *Ba-ay´-shah*, in the work, he that demands, who lays waste.
- Ba´bel, confusion, mixture.
- Babylon, *Bab´-be-lon*. See Babel.
- Babylonians, *Bab-be-lo´-ne-ans*.
- Babylonish, *Bab-be-lo´-nish*.
- Baca, *Bay´-kah*, mulberry tree.
- Bahurim, *Ba-hew´-rim*, choice, warlike.
- Ba´jith, a house.
- Balaam, *Bay´-lam*, the old age or ancient of the people, without the people.
- Bala´dan, one without rule or judgment, ancient in judgment.
- Ba´lak, who lays waste, who laps.
- Ba´mah, an eminence.
- Barabbas, *Bar-ab´-bas*, son of the father or of confusion.
- Barachel, *Bar´-a-kel*, who blesses God.
- Barachias, *Bar´-a-ky-as*, the same as Barachel.
- Ba´rak, thunder, in vain.
- Bar-je´sus, son of Jesus.
- Bar-jo´na, son of Jona or of a dove.
- Bar´nabas, the son of the prophet or of consolation.
- Bar´sabas, son of return, of rest, of swearing.
- Barthol´omew, a son that suspends the waters.
- Bartimeus, *Bar-te-me´-us*, the son of Timeus or of the honourable.
- Baruch, *Bay´-ruk*, who is blessed, who bends the knee.
- Barzillai, *Bar-zil´-la-i*, made of iron, son of contempt.
- Ba´shan, in the tooth, in the change or sleep.
- Bashemath, *Bash´-e-math*, perfumed, in desolation.
- Bath-sheba, *Bath-she´-bah* or *Bath´-she-bah*, the seventh daughter, the daughter of an oath.
- Bathshu´a, the daughter of salvation.
- Be´dad, alone, in friendship.
- Be´dan, only, in the judgment.
- Beel-zebub, *Be-el´-ze-bub*. See Baal-zebub.
- Beer, *Be´-er*, a well, the name of a city.
- Beer-lahai-roi, *Be´-er-la-hay´-e-roy*, the well of him that liveth and seeth me.
- Beer-sheba, *Be´-er-she´-bah*, the well of an oath, of satiety, the seventh well.
- Be´kah, half a shekel.
- Bel, ancient, nothing, subject to change.
- Belial, *Bee´-le-al*, wicked, the devil.
- Belshaz´zar, master of the treasure.
- Belteshaz´zar, who lays up treasures in secret, secretly endures pain and pressure.
- Benaiah, *Ben-ay´-yah*, son of the Lord, the Lord's building.
- Ben-am´mi, the son of my people.
- Benha´dad, the son of Hadad, of noise.
- Ben´jamin, the son of the right hand.
- Ben´jamite, a descendant of Benjamin.
- Benoni, *Ben-o´-ny*, son of my grief.
- Be´or, burning, mad, beast.
- Berachah, *Ber´-a-kah*, blessing.
- Beræa, *Be-ree´-ah*, heavy, from βάρος.
- Be´rith, covenant.
- Bernice, *Ber-ny´-se*, one that brings victory.
- Be´sor, glad news, incarnation.
- Be´tah, confidence.
- Bethabara, *Beth-ab´-ba-rah*, the house of passage, of anger.
- Beth´any, the house of song, of affliction, of obedience, the grace of the Lord.
- Beth-a´ven, the house of vanity, of strength.
- Beth-birei, *Beth-bir´-re-i*, the house of my Creator.
- Beth´-car, the house of the lamb, of knowledge.
- Beth-da´gon, the house of corn, of the fish, of the god Dagon.
- Beth-diblathaim, *Beth-dib-la-thay´-im*, the house of dry figs.
- Beth´el, the house of God.
- Bethelite, *Beth´-el-ite*, an inhabitant of Bethel.

- Be´ther, division, in the turtle, in the trial.
- Bethes´da, the house of effusion, of pity.
- Beth-e´zel, a neighbour's house.
- Beth-gamul, *Beth-gay´-mul*, the house of recompense, of the weaned, of the camel.
- Beth-haccerem, *Beth-hak´-ke-rem*, the house of the vineyard.
- Beth-ho´ron, the house of wrath, of the hole, of liberty.
- Bethjesh´imoth, the house of desolation.
- Beth´-lehem, the house of bread, of war.
- Beth-lehem-ephratah, *Beth´-le-hem-eff-ray´-tah* or *eff´-ra-tah*.
- Beth´-lehem-ju´dah.
- Beth´-lehemite, an inhabitant of Bethlehem.
- Beth-pe´or, the house of gaping.
- Bethphage, *Beth´-fa-je*, the house of the mouth, of early figs.
- Bethsaida, *Beth-say´-dah*, the house of fruits, of hunters.
- Beth´-shan, the house of the tooth, of change, of sleep.
- Beth-she´mesh, the house of the sun.
- Bethuel, *Beth-ew´-el*, filiation of God.
- Beulah, *Bew´-lah*, married.
- Bezaleel, *Bez-a-lee´-el*, in the shadow of God.
- Be´zek, lightning, in chains.
- Bichri, *Bick´-ry*, first-born, in the ram.
- Bid´kar, in compunction, in sharp pain.
- Big´than, giving meat.
- Bil´dad, old friendship.
- Bil´hah, who is old, troubled, confused.
- Bir´sha, in evil, son that beholds.
- Bithiah, *Be-thy´-ah*, daughter of the Lord.
- Bith´ron, division, in his examination, daughter of the song, of anger, of liberty.
- Bithynia, *Be-thin´-e-ah*, violent precipitation.
- Blas´tus, one that sprouts and brings forth.
- Boanerges, *Bo-a-ner´-jes*, the sons of thunder; James and John, the sons of Zebedee.
- Bo´az, or Bo´oz, in strength, in the goat.
- Bochim, *Bo´-kim*, the place of weeping, of mulberry trees.
- Bo´zez, mud, in the flower.
- Boz´rah, in tribulation or distress.
- Bul, changeable, perishing.
- Buz, despised, plundered.
- Buzi, *Bew´-zye*, my contempt.
- Buzite, *Bew´-zyte*, a descendant from Buz.

- Cabul, *Kay´-bul*, displeasing, dirt.
- Cæsar, *See´-sar*, one cut out.
- Cæsarea, *Ses-a-ree´-a*, a bush of hair.
- Caiaphas, *Kay´-a-fas*, a searcher.
- Cain, *Kay´n*, possession.
- Cainan, *Kay´-nan*, possessor, one that laments.
- Ca´lah, good opportunity, as the verdure.
- Ca´leb, a dog, a crow, a basket.
- Caleb-ephratah, *Kay´-leb-ef-ray´-tah* or *ef´-ra-tah*, a place so called by a conjunction of the names of Caleb and his wife Ephratah.
- Calneh, *Kal´-nay*, our consummation, all we, as murmuring.
- Cal´no, our consummation, quite himself.
- Cal´vary, the place of a skull.
- Ca´mon, his resurrection.
- Ca´na, zeal, possession, nest, cane.
- Canaan, *Kay´-nan*, a merchant, a trader. The son of Ham, who gave name to the land of Canaan.
- Canaanite, *Kay´-nan-ite*, an inhabitant of Canaan.
- Candace, *Kan-day´-se*, who possesses contrition.
- Capernaum, *Ka-per´-na-um*, the field of repentance, city of comfort.
- Caphtor, *Kaf´-tor*, a sphere, a buckle, a hand, doves, those that seek and inquire.
- Cappadocia, *Kap-pa-do´-she-a*, in Hebrew, Caphtor.
- Carcas, *Kar´-kas*, the covering of a lamb.
- Carchemish, *Kar´-ke-mish*, a lamb, as taken away.
- Car´mel, a circumcised lamb, harvest, vineyard of God.
- Carmelite, *Kar´-me-lyte*, an inhabitant of Mount Carmel.

- Car´mi, my vineyard, the knowledge or the lamb of the waters.
- Car´pus, fruit, fruitful.
- Casiphia, *Ka-se-fy´-a*, money, covetousness.
- Cas´tor, a beaver.
- Cedron, *See´-dron* or *Kee´-dron*, black, sad.
- Cenchrea, *Senk´-re-a*, millet, small pulse.
- Cephas, *See´-fas* or *Kee´-fas*, a rock or stone.
- Ce´sar. See Cæsar.
- Cesarea, *Ses-a-ree´-a*. See Cæsarea.
- Chalcol, *Kal´-kol*, who nourishes, sustains the whole.
- Chaldea, *Kal-dee´-a*, as demons, as robbers.
- Chaldean, *Kal-dee´-an*, an inhabitant of Chaldea.
- Chaldees, *Kal-deez´*, the same as Chaldeans.
- Charran, *Kar´-ran*, a singing, the heat of wrath.
- Chebar, *Ke´-bar*, strength or power.
- Chedorlaomer, *Ke´-dor-la-o´-mer*, as a generation of servitude.
- Chemarims, *Kem´-a-rims*, the name of Baal's priests.
- Chemosh, *Ke´-mosh*, as handling, as taking away.
- Chenania, *Ke-na-ny´-ah*, preparation, rectitude of the Lord.
- Cherethims, *Ker´-eth-ims*, who cuts, tears away.
- Cherethites, *Ker´-eth-ites*. See Cherethims.
- Cherith, *Ke´-rith*, cutting, piercing, slaying.
- Chesed, *Ke´-sed*, as a devil, a destroyer.
- Chileab, *Kil´-le-ab*, totality or perfection of the father.
- Chilion, *Kil´-le-on*, finished, complete.
- Chilmad, *Kil´-mad*, as teaching or learning.
- Chimham, *Kim´-ham*, as they, like to them.
- Chios, *Ky´-os*, open, opening.
- Chisleu, *Kis´-lu*, rashness, confidence.
- Chittim, *Chit´-tim*, those that bruise, gold, staining.
- Chiun, *Ky´-un*, an Egyptian god, whom some think to be Saturn.
- Chloe, *Klo´-e*, green herb.
- Chorazin, *Ko-ray´-zin*, the secret, here is a mystery.
- Chushan-rishathaim, *Kew´-shan-rish-a-thay´-im*, Ethiopian, blackness of iniquities.
- Chuza, *Kew´-zah*, the prophet, Ethiopian.
- Cilicia, *Sil-ish´-e-a*, which rolls or overturns.
- Clauda, *Klaw´-dah*, a broken voice, a lamentable voice.
- Claudia, *Klaw´-de-ah*, lame.
- Cle´ment, mild, good, merciful.
- Cleophas, *Klee´-o-fas*, the whole glory.
- Colosse, *Ko-los´-see*, punishment, correction.
- Coniah, *Ko-ny´-ah*, the strength or stability of the Lord.
- Co´rinth, which is satisfied, beauty.
- Corin´thians, inhabitants of Corinth.
- Corne´lius, a horn.
- Coz´bi, a liar, as sliding away.
- Crescens, *Kres´-sens*, growing, increasing.
- Crete, *Kree´t*, carnal, fleshly.
- Cretes, *Kree´ts*, inhabitants of Crete.
- Cretians, *Kree´-she-ans*, the same as Cretes.
- Crispus, *Kris´-pus*, curled.
- Cush, Ethiopian, black.
- Cush´an, Ethiopia, blackness, heat.
- Cush´i, the same as Cushan.
- Cyprus, *Sy´-prus*, fair, fairness.
- Cyrene, *Sy-re´-ne*, a wall, coldness, meeting, a floor.
- Cyreneans, *Sy-re´-ne-ans*, people of Cyrene.
- Cyrenius, *Sy-re´-ne-us*, who governs.
- Cyrus, *Sy´-rus*, as miserable, as heir, the belly.

- Dabbasheth, *Dab´-ba-sheth*, flowing with honey, causing infamy.
- Daberath, *Dab´-be-rath*, word, thing, bee, submissive.
- Da´gon, corn, a fish.
- Dalmanutha, *Dal-ma-new´-thah*, a bucket, leanness, branch.
- Dalmatia, *Dal-may´-she-a*, deceitful lamps, vain brightness.
- Damaris, *Dam´-a-ris*, a little woman.
- Damas´cus, a sack full of blood, similitude of burning.

- Dan, judgment, he that judges.
- Dan´iel, judgment of God.
- Da´ra, generation, house of the shepherd, companion, race of wickedness.
- Darius, *Da-ry´-us*, he that inquires and informs himself.
- Da´than, laws, rites.
- Da´vid, beloved, dear.
- Deb´orah, a word, a bee.
- Decapolis, *De-kap´-po-lis*, a Greek word compounded of δέκα, TEN, and πόλις, a CITY, because this country contained ten cities.
- De´dan, their breasts, friendship, uncle.
- Dedanim, *Ded´-an-im*, descendants of Dedan.
- Del´ilah, poor, head of hair, bucket.
- De´mas, popular.
- Demetrius, *De-me´-tre-us*, belonging to Ceres, to corn.
- Der´be, a sting.
- Deuel, *De-ew´-el*, the knowledge of God.
- Diana, *Dy-ay´-nah*, luminous, perfect.
- Di´bon, understanding, abundance of building.
- Di´bon-gad, abundance of sons, happy and powerful.
- Didymus, *Did´-e-mus*, a twin.
- Di´mon, where it is red.
- Di´nah, judgment, who judges.
- Din´habah, she gives judgment.
- Dionysius, *Dy-o-nish´-e-us*, divinely touched; from δῖος, DIVINE, and νεύω, I MOVE.
- Diotrephes, *Di-ot´-re-feez*, nourished by Jupiter; from δῖος, of JUPITER, and τρἐφος, A FOSTER-CHILD.
- Do´eg, who acts with uneasiness, a fisherman.
- Dor, generation, habitation.
- Dor´cas, the female of a roe-buck.
- Do´than, the law, custom.
- Drusilla, *Drew-sil´-lah*, watered by the dew; from δρόσος, THE DEW.
- Dumah, *Dew´-mah*, silence, resemblance.
- Dura, *Dew´-rah*, generation, habitation.

- Easter, *Ee´s-ter*, the passover, a feast of the Jews.
- E´bal, a heap, collection of old age.
- E´bed, a servant or labourer.
- Ebed-melech, *Ee´-bed-me´-lek*, the king's servant.
- Eben-ezer, *Eb-en-ee´-zer*, the stone of help.
- E´ber, one that passes, anger, wrath.
- Ebiasaph, *E-by´-a-saf*, a father that gathers together.
- Ed, witness.
- E´den, pleasure, delight.
- E´dom, red, earthy, red earth.
- E´domite, a descendant of Esau, of Edom.
- Edrei, *Ed´-re-i*, a very great mass, cloud, death of the wicked.
- Eg´lah, heifer, chariot, round.
- Eglaim, *Eg-lay´-im*, drops of the sea.
- Eg´lon, the same as Eglah.
- E´gypt, in Hebrew, Mizraim; that binds or straitens, that troubles or oppresses.
- Egyp´tian, an inhabitant of Egypt.
- E´hud, he that praises.
- Ek´ron, barrenness, torn away.
- Ek´ronites, inhabitants of Ekron.
- E´lah, an oak, oath, imprecation.
- E´lam, a young man, a virgin, secret, an age.
- E´lamites, descendants of Elam.
- E´lath, a hind, strength, an oak.
- El-beth´el, the God of Bethel.
- El´dad, loved or favoured of God.
- Elealeh, El-e-ay´-leh ascension or burnt-offering of God.
- Eleazar, *El-e-ay´-zar*, the help or court of God.
- El-elohe-israel, *El-el-ho´-he-is´-ra-el*, God, the God of Israel.
- Elha´nan, grace, gift, or mercy of God.
- E´li, *E´li*, my God, my God.
- E´li, the offering or lifting up.
- Eli´ab, God my father.
- Eliada, *E-ly´-a-da* or *E-le-ay´-da*, the knowledge of God.

- Eliakim, *E-ly´-a-kim*, the resurrection of God, God the avenger.
- Eli´am, the people of God.
- Eli´as. See Elijah.
- Eliashib, *E-ly´-a-shib*, the God of conversion.
- Eliathah, *E-ly´-a-thah*, thou art my God, my God comes.
- Eliezer, *E-le-ee´-zer*, help or court of my God.
- Elihoreph, *E-le-ho´-ref*, the God of winter, of youth.
- Eli´hu, he is my God himself.
- Eli´jah, God the Lord, the strong Lord.
- Eli´ka, pelican of God.
- E´lim, the rams, the strong, the stags, the valleys.
- Elimelech, *E-lim´-me-lek*, my God is king.
- Elioenai, *El-e-o´-en-a-i*, toward him are my eyes, my fountains, toward him is my poverty or misery.
- Eliphalet, *E-lif´-fa-let*, the God of deliverance.
- Eliphaz, *E-ly´-faz*, the endeavour of God.
- Elisabeth, *E-liz´-a-beth*, God hath sworn, the fulness of God.
- Eli´sha, salvation of God.
- Eli´shah, son of Javan; it is God, God that gives help.
- Elishamah, *E-lish´-a-mah*, God hearing.
- Elisheba, *E-lish´-e-ba*. See Elisabeth.
- Elishua, *El-e-shew´-ah*, God is my salvation.
- Eliud, *E-ly´-ud*, God is my praise.
- Eli´zur, God is my strength, my rock.
- Elka´nah, God the jealous, the reed of God.
- Elmo´dam, the God of measure, of the garment.
- Elna´than, God has given.
- E´lon, oak, grove, strong.
- E´lul, cry, outcry.
- Eluzai, *E-lu´-za-i*, God is my strength.
- Elymas, *El´-e-mas*, in Arabic, a magician.
- E´mims, fears of terrors, people.
- Emmaus, *Em-may´-us* or *Em´-ma-us*, people despised.
- Em´mor, an ass.
- E´nam, a fountain or well, the eyes of them.
- En´dor, fountain or eye of generation.
- Ene´as, laudable; from αἰνέω, "I praise."
- En-eglaim, *En-eg-lay´-im*, the eye of the calves, of the chariots, of roundness.
- En-gedi, *En-ge´-dy*, fountain of the goat, of happiness.
- En-mish´pat, fountain of judgment.
- Enoch, *Ee´-nok*, dedicated, disciplined, well regulated.
- Enon, *Ee´-non*, cloud, his fountain.
- Enos, *Ee´-nos*, fallen man, subject to all kind of evil.
- Ex-rogel, *En-ro´-gel*, the fuller's fountain.
- En-shemesh, *En-she´-mesh*, fountain of the sun.
- Epaphras, *Ep´-pa-fras*, covered with foam.
- Epaphroditus, *E-paf-ro-dy´-tus*, agreeable, handsome.
- Epenetus, *E-pe-nee´-tus*, laudable, worthy of praise.
- Ephah, *Ee´-fah*, weary, to fly as a bird.
- Ephes-dammim, *E´-fez-dam´-mim*, the effusion or drop of blood.
- Ephesians, *E-fee´-se-ans*, the people of Ephesus.
- Ephesus, *Ef´-fe-sus*, desirable; chief city of Asia Minor.
- Ephphatha, *Ef´-fa-tha*, be opened.
- Ephraim, *Ee´-fra-im*, that brings forth fruit or grows.
- E´phraimite, a descendant of Ephraim.
- Ephratah, *Eff-ray´-tah*, abundance, bearing fruit.
- Ephrath, *Eff´-rath*, See Ephratah.
- Ephrathite, *Eff´-rath-ite*, an inhabitant of Ephratah, or a descendant from Ephraim.
- Ephron, *Ef´-ron*, dust.
- Epicureans, *Ep-e-kew-re´-ans*, who gives assistance; from the Greek ἐπικȣρέω, I help.
- Er, watch, enemy.
- Eras´tus, lovely, amiable.
- E´rech, length, health.
- Esaias, *E-zay´-e-as*. See Isaia.
- Esar-haddon, *E´-sar-had-´don*, that binds, joy, or closes the point.
- E´sau, he that does or finishes.
- E´sek, contention.
- Esh-ba´al, the fire of the idol.

- Esh´col, a bunch of grapes.
- Eshtaol, *Esh´-ta-ol*, stout, strong woman.
- Eshtemoa, *Esh-te-mo´-a*, which is heard, the bosom of a woman.
- Es´li, near me, he that separates.
- Es´rom, the dart of joy, division of the song.
- Esther, *Ess´-ter*, secret, hidden.
- E´tam, their bird or covering.
- E´tham, their strength or sign.
- E´than, strong, the gift of the island.
- Ethanim, *Eth´-an-im*, strong, valiant.
- Ethbaal, *Eth-bay´-al*, toward the idol, he that rules.
- Ethiopia, *Ee-the-o´-pe-a*, in Hebrew, Cush, blackness; in Greek it signifies heat, from ἄιθω, I BURN, and ὄψις, FACE.
- Ethiopians, *Ee-the-o´-pe-ans*, Africans.
- Eubulus, *Yew´-bu-lus*, a prudent counsellor.
- Eunice, *Yew-ny´-se*, good victory.
- Euodias, *Yew-o´-de-as*, sweet scent.
- Euphrates, *Yew-fray´-tes*, that makes fruitful.
- Euroc´lydon, the north-east wind.
- Eutychus, *Yew´-te-kus*, happy, fortunate.
- Eve, living, enlivening.
- Evil-merodach, *Ee´-vil-me-ro´-dak*, or *mer´-o-dak*, the fool of Merodach, despising the bitterness of the fool.
- Ezekiel, *E-zee´-ke-el*, the strength of God.
- E´zel, going abroad, distillation.
- Ezion-Geber, *E´-ze-on-ge´-ber*, the wood of the man, counsel of the man, of the strong.
- Ez´ra, a helper.

- Fe´lix, happy, prosperous.
- Fes´tus, festival, joyful.
- Fortuna´tus, happy, prosperous.

- Gaal, *Gay´al*, contempt, abomination.
- Gaash, *Gay´-ash*, tempest, overthrow.
- Gabbatha, *Gab´-ba-tha*, high, elevated. In Greek, LITHOSTROTOS, paved with stones.
- Ga´briel, God is my strength.
- Gad, a band, happy, armed and prepared.
- Gadarenes, *Gad-a-ree´ns*, surrounded, walled.
- Gad´di, my happiness, my troop, a kid.
- Gaddiel, *Gad´-de-el*, goat of God, the Lord is my army.
- Gadites, *Gad´-dites*, descendants of Gad.
- Gaius, *Gay´-e-us*, lord, an earthly man.
- Galatia, *Gal-ay´-she-a*, white, of the colour of milk.
- Galatians, *Gal-ay´-she-ans*, born in Galatia.
- Galbanum, *Gal´-ba-num*, a gum, sweet spice.
- Galeed, *Gal´-e-ed*, the heap of witness.
- Galilee, *Gal´-le-lee*, wheel, revolution, heap.
- Galileans, *Gal-le-lee´-ans*, inhabitants of Galilee.
- Gal´lim, who heap up, cover, roll.
- Gal´lio, he that sucks or lives upon milk.
- Gama´liel, recompense, camel, weaned of God.
- Gam´madims, soldiers placed in the towers of Tyrus; men who came from Gammade, a town of Phenicia.
- Ga´tam, their lowing, their touch.
- Gath, a press.
- Gath-rim´mon, the press of the granite, exalted press.
- Ga´za, strong, a goat.
- Ge´ba, a hill, a cup.
- Ge´bal, bound, limit.
- Ge´bim, grasshoppers, height.
- Gedaliah, *Ged-a-ly´-ah*, God is my greatness, fringe of the Lord.
- Gehazi, *Ge-hay´-zye*, valley of sight, of the breast.
- Gemari´ah, accomplishment of the Lord.
- Gennesaret, *Gen-ness´-a-ret*, or *Jen-ness´-a-ret*, the garden or protection of the prince.
- Genubath, *Gen´-u-bath*, theft, garden or protection of the daughter.
- Ge´ra, pilgrimage, dispute.
- Ge´rah, the twentieth part of a shekel.
- Ge´rar. See Gera.
- Gergesenes, *Ger´-ge-seens*, those who come from pilgrimage or from fight.
- Gerizim, *Ger´-re-zim*, cutters.

- Ger´shom, a stranger there, a traveller of reputation.
- Ger´shon, his banishment, the change of pilgrimage.
- Ge´shur, the sight of the valley, the vale of the ox or the wall.
- Geshurites, *Gesh´-u-rytes*, inhabitants of Geshur.
- Ge´ther, the vale of trial, of searching, the press of inquiry.
- Gethsemane, *Geth-sem´-a-ne*, a very fat valley.
- Giah, *Gy´-ah*, to guide, draw out, a sigh.
- Gibeah, *Gib´-e-ah*, a hill.
- Gib´eon, hill, cup, that which is without.
- Gib´eonites, people of Gibeon.
- Gid´eon, he that bruises, cutting off iniquity.
- Gihon, *Gy´-hon*, valley of grace, impetuous.
- Gilboah, *Gil´-bo-ah*, revolution of inquiry.
- Gilead, *Gil´-le-ad*, the mass of testimony.
- Gileadites, *Gil´-le-ad-ites*, the inhabitants of Gilead.
- Gil´gal, wheel, revolution, heap.
- Giloh, *Gy´-loh*, he that rejoices, overturns, or discovers.
- Gilonite, *Gy´-lo-nite*.
- Girgashite, *Gir´-ga-shite*, who arrives from pilgrimage.
- Gittite, *Git´-tite*, a wine press.
- Gob, cistern, grasshopper, eminence.
- Gog, roof, covering.
- Go´lan, passage, revolution.
- Gol´gotha, a heap of skulls.
- Goli´ath, revolution, discovery, heap.
- Go´mer, to finish, accomplish, a consumer.
- Gomor´rah, a rebellious people.
- Go´shen, approaching, drawing near.
- Go´zan, fleece, pasture, nourishing the body.
- Grecia, *Gree´-she-a*, Greece, the country of the Greeks.
- Grecians, *Gree´-she-ans*, Greeks, the inhabitants of Greece.
- Gur, the young of a beast, dwelling, fear.
- Gurba´al, the whelp of the governor.
- Habakkuk, *Hab´-a-kuk*, he that embraces, a wrestler.
- Hachaliah, *Hak-a-ly´-ah*, who waits for the Lord.
- Hachilah, *Hak´-e-lah*, my trust is in her.
- Ha´dad, joy, noise.
- Hadadezer, *Hay´-dad-ee´-zer*, the beauty of assistance.
- Hadad-rimmon, *Hay´-dad-rim´-mon*, the voice of height, the invocation of Rimmon, a god of the Syrians.
- Hadas´sah, a myrtle, joy.
- Hado´ram, their beauty, power, praise.
- Hadrach, *Hay´-drak*, point, joy of tenderness, your chamber.
- Ha´gar, a stranger, that fears.
- Hagarenes, *Hay´-gar-eens*, of the family of Hagar.
- Hagarites, *Hay´-gar-ites*. See Hagarenes.
- Haggai, *Hag´-ga-i*, feast, solemnity.
- Hag´gith, rejoicing.
- Hak´katan, little.
- Halleluiah, *Hal-le-lu´-yah*, praise the Lord.
- Ham, hot, brown.
- Ha´man, noise, tumult, he that prepares.
- Ha´math, anger, heat, a wall.
- Hammedatha, *Ham-med´-a-thah*, or *Ham-me-day´-thah*, he that troubles the law.
- Ha´mon-gog, the multitude of Gog.
- Ha´mor, an ass, clay, wine.
- Ha´mul, godly, merciful.
- Hamu´tal, the shadow of his heat, the heat of the dew.
- Hanameel, *Han-am´-e-el*, or *Han-am-ee´-el*, grace or pity from God.
- Hananeel, *Han-an-ee´-el*, mercy of God.
- Hanani, *Han-ay´-ny*, my grace or mercy.
- Hanani´ah, grace or mercy of the Lord.
- Han´nah, gracious, merciful, taking rest.
- Ha´noch, dedicated.
- Ha´nun, gracious, merciful, he that rests.
- Ha´ran, mountainous country, which is enclosed.
- Harbo´nah, his destruction or dryness.
- Ha´rod, astonishment, fear.

- Harosheth, *Har-o´-sheth*, agriculture, silence, vessel of earth, forest.
- Hashmo´nah, diligence, enumeration, embassy, present.
- Ha´tach, he that strikes.
- Havilah, *Hav´-e-lah*, that suffers pain, brings forth, declares to her.
- Havoth-jair, *Hay´-voth-jay´-ir*, villages that enlighten.
- Hazael, *Haz´-a-el*, that sees God.
- Hazarmaveth, *Hay´-zar-may´-veth*, court or dwelling of death.
- Hazelelponi, Hay´-zel-el-po´-ny, shade, sorrow of the face.
- Hazeroth, *Haz-ee´-roth*, villages, court.
- Ha´zor, court, hay.
- He´ber, one that passes, anger.
- He´brews, descended from Heber.
- He´bron, society, friendship, enchantment.
- Hegai, or Hege, *Heg´-a-i*, meditation, word, separation.
- He´lam, their army, trouble, or expectation.
- Hel´bon, milk, fatness.
- Heldai, *Hel´-da-i*, or *Hel-day´-i*, the world.
- He´li, ascending, climbing up.
- Hel´kath-haz´urim, the field of strong men, of rocks.
- He´man, their trouble, their tumult, much.
- Hen, grace, quiet.
- Hepher, *Hee´-fer*, a digger or delver.
- Hephzi-bah, *Hef´-ze-bah*, my pleasure.
- Her´mes, MERCURY, gain, refuge.
- Hermogenes, *Her-moj´-e-nes*, begotten of Mercury, of lucre.
- Her´mon, anathema, destruction.
- Her´monites, the inhabitants of Hermon.
- Herod, *Her´-rod*, the glory of the skin.
- Herodians, *He-ro´-de-ans.*
- Hero´dias, the wife of Herod.
- Herodion, *He-ro´-de-on*, song of Juno.
- Hesh´bon, invention, industry, thought, he that hastens to understand.
- Heth, trembling, fear.
- Heth´lon, fearful dwelling, his covering.
- Hezeki´ah, strong in the Lord.
- Hez´ron, the dart of joy, division of the song.
- Hiddai, *Hid´-da-i*, praise, cry.
- Hiddekel, *Hid´-de-kel*, a sharp voice.
- Hi´el, the life of God.
- Hierapolis, *Hy-er-ap´-po-lis*, holy city.
- Higgaion, *Hig-gay´-e-on*, meditation.
- Hilki´ah, God is my portion, the Lord's gentleness.
- Hil´lel, praising folly, Lucifer.
- Hin´nom, there they are, their riches.
- Hi´ram, exaltation of life, their whiteness, he that destroys.
- Hit´tites, who are broken or fear.
- Hi´vites, wicked, bad, wickedness.
- Ho´bab, favoured and beloved.
- Ho´bah, love, friendship, secrecy.
- Hog´lah, his festival, his dance.
- Hophni, *Hoff´-ni*, he that covers, my fist.
- Hor, who conceives, shows.
- Ho´reb, desert, destruction, dryness.
- Hor-hagidgad, *Hor-ha-gidd´-gad*, hill of felicity.
- Hor´mah, devoted to God, destruction.
- Horonaim, *Hor-o-nay´-im*, anger, raging.
- Horonite, *Hor´-o-nyte*, anger, fury, liberty.
- Hosea, and Hoshea, *Ho-zee´-a*, and *Ho-shee´-a*, Saviour.
- Hul, infirmity, bringing forth children.
- Hul´dah, the world, a prophetess.
- Hur, liberty, whiteness, cavern.
- Hushai, *Hew´-sha-i*, their haste, sensuality, or silence.
- Huz´zab, molten.
- Hymeneus, *Hy-men-ee´-us*, nuptial, marriage.

- Ib´har, election, he that is chosen.
- Ichabod, *Ik´-a-bod*, where is the glory?
- Iconium, *I-ko´-ne-um*, from ἵκω, "I come."
- Id´do, his hand, power, praise, witness.

- Idumea, *Id-ew-mee´-a*, red, earthy.
- Igdali´a, the greatness of the Lord.
- I´jon, look, eye, fountain.
- Illyricum, *Il-lir´-re-kum*, joy, rejoicing.
- Im´lah, plenitude, repletion, circumcision.
- Imman´uel, a name given to our Lord Jesus Christ, signifying, God with us.
- Im´rah, a rebel, changing.
- India, *In´-de-a*, praise, law.
- Iphedeiah, *If-fe-dy´-ah*, or *If-fe-dee´-ah*, the redemption of the Lord.
- I´ra, city, watch, spoil, heap of vision.
- I´rad, wild ass, heap of descents, of empire.
- Irijah, *I-ry´-jah*, the fear, vision, or protection of the Lord.
- Isaac, *I´-zak*, laughter.
- Isaiah, *I-zay´-yah*, or *I-zay´-e-ah*, the salvation of the Lord.
- Iscah, *Is´-kah*, he that anoints, or covers.
- Iscariot, *Is-kar´-re-ot*, is thought to signify a native of the town of Iscarioth.
- Ish´bak, empty, forsaken, abandoned.
- Ishbi-benob, *Ish´-by-bee´-nob*, he that sits in the prophecy, conversion.
- Ish-bosheth, *Ish´-bo-sheth*, a man of shame.
- Ishmael, *Ish´-ma-el*, God who hears.
- Ishmaelites, *Ish´-ma-el-ites*, the posterity of Ishmael.
- Israel, *Is´-ra-el*, a prince with God, prevailing with God, that wrestleth with God.
- Israelites, *Is´-ra-el-ites*, the posterity of Israel, or Jacob.
- Issachar, *Is´-sa-kar*, price, reward.
- Italian, *I-tal´-e-an*, belonging to Italy.
- Italy, *It´-ta-le*, a Latin word that has its original from VITULUS, or VITULA, "a calf," or from a king called ITALUS.
- Ith´amar, island of the palm tree, wo to the palm or change.
- Ithiel, *Ith´-e-el*, God with me, sign.
- Ithream, *Ith´-re-am*, excellence of the people.
- Iturea, *It-u-ree´-a*, which is guarded, a country of mountains.
- I´vah, iniquity.

TABLES OF THE WEIGHTS, MEASURES, AND MONEY,

MENTIONED IN THE BIBLE.

JEWISH WEIGHTS, REDUCED TO ENGLISH TROY WEIGHT.

	lbs.	ozs.	pen.	gr.
The Gerah, the twentieth part of a Shekel	0	0	0	12
The Bekah, half a Shekel	0	0	5	0
The Shekel	0	0	10	0
The Maneh, sixty Shekels	2	6	0	0
The Talent, fifty Maneh, or three thousand Shekels	125	0	0	0

According to the bishop of Peterborough's calculations, the Gerah is nearly equal to 11 grains Troy; the Bekah, to about $4\frac{3}{4}$ pennyweights; and the Shekel, to about $9\frac{1}{8}$ pennyweights.

TABLES OF SCRIPTURE MEASURES OF LENGTH, REDUCED TO ENGLISH MEASURE.

SHORT MEASURES.

								English feet.	Inches.
Digit								0	0.912
4	Palm							0	3.684
12	3	Span						0	10.944
24	6	3	Cubit					1	9.888
96	24	6	2	Fathom				7	3.552
144	36	12	6	1.5	Ezekiel's reed			10	11.328
192	48	16	8	2	1.3	Arabian pole		14	7.104
1920	480	160	80	20	13.3	10	Schœnus's meas'ng line	145	11.04

LONG MEASURES.

						English miles.	Paces.	Feet.
Cubit						0	0	1.824
400	Stadium or Furlong					0	145	4.6
2000	5	Sabbath day's journey				0	729	3.0
4000	10	2	Eastern mile			1	403	1.0
12000	30	6	3	Parasang		4	153	3.0
96000	240	48	24	8	A day's journey	33	172	4.0

⁂ 5 Feet=1 Pace; 1056=1 mile.

According to the bishop of Peterborough, a Parasang is equal to 4 miles, 116 paces.

FOR TABLES OF TIME SEE THE ARTICLES "MONTHS" AND "DAY."

TABLES OF SCRIPTURE MEASURES OF CAPACITY.

MEASURES FOR LIQUIDS, REDUCED TO ENGLISH WINE MEASURE.

						Gallons.	Pints.
Caph						0	0.625
1.3	Log					0	0.833
5.3	4	Cab				0	3.333
16	12	3	Hin			1	2
32	24	6	2	Seah		2	4
96	72	18	6	3	Bath or Epha	7	4

960	720	180	60	20	10	Chomer, Homer, Kor, or Coros	75	5

The Omer was one-tenth of an Epha, and contained 6 pints; the Metretes of Syria, translated in John ii, 6, "firkins," 7⅛ pints; and the eastern Cotyla, half a pint. This Cotyla, says the bishop of Peterborough, contains just 10 ounces Averdupois of rain water; the Omer, 100 ounces; the Epha, 1000; and the Chomer, 10,000 ounces. So by these weights all these measures of capacity may be expeditiously recovered to a near exactness.

MEASURES FOR THINGS DRY, REDUCED TO ENGLISH CORN MEASURE.

							Pecks.	Gals.	Pints.
Gachal							0	0	0.1416
20	Cab						0	0	2.8333
36	1.8	Omer or Gomer					0	0	5.1
120	6	3.3	Seah				1	0	1
360	18	10	3	Epha			3	0	3
1800	90	50	15	5	Letech		16	0	0
3600	180	100	30	10	2	Chomer Homer, &c.	32	0	0

TABLES OF MONEY.

JEWISH MONEY, REDUCED TO THE ENGLISH STANDARD.

					£.	s.	d.
				Gerah	0	0	1.3687
10				Bekah	0	1	1.6875
20	2			Shekel	0	2	3.375
1200	120	50		Maneh, or Mina Hebraica	5	14	0.75
60,000	6000	3000	60	Talent	342	3	9

Solidus Aureus, or Sextula, was worth

Siclus Aureus, or Gold Shekel

Talent of Gold

The bishop of Peterborough makes the Mina Hebraica to contain 60 Shekels, and to weigh 27 oz. 7½ dwts.; which, at 5S. per ounce, will amount to 6L. 16S. 10½D.; and the Talent of Silver to contain 50 Minæ, which, at 5S., will equal the amount in this table, 342L. 3S. 9D.

ROMAN MONEY, MENTIONED IN THE NEW TESTAMENT, REDUCED TO THE ENGLISH STANDARD.

	£.	s.	d.	far.
Mite (Assarium)	0	0	0	¾
Farthing, (Quadrans,) about	0	0	0	1½
Penny, or Denarius (Silver)	0	0	7	3
Pound, or Mina	3	2	6	0

According to the bishop of Peterborough, the Roman Mite is one-third of our farthing; Quadrans, three-fourths of a farthing; the Assarium, a farthing and a half; and the Assis three farthings.

⁂ IN THE PRECEDING TABLES, SILVER IS VALUED AT 5S., AND GOLD AT £4. PER OUNCE.

EGYPTIAN EMPIRE
1450 B.C.
English Miles
PONTUS EUXINUS
Caucasus
Hittites
Taurus
MARE INTERNUM
Kefti
Damascus
Jerusalem
Memphis
Deserta
Libyca
Tehenu
ARABIA
KUSH
Nubæans
Meroe Insula
Minæans
Nineveh
Calah
Assur
Naharina
Mesopotamia
Babylon
Sippar
Borsippa
Sumer
Sinai
Thebæ
Syene
Khartum
Napata
Abydos
Hermopolis
Khuaten
Gaza
Aradus
Hamath
Kadesh
Sidon
Tyrus
Megiddo
Carchemish
Sardes
Athenæ
Rhodus
Alashia
Asiy
Tigris
Euphrates
Nile
Semneh
Kummeh
Napata
Meroe
Kash
Arabs
Ægyptus Inferior
Ægyptus Superior
Sinus Arabicus
Punt
Halys
Araxes
Cyrus
Mare Ægæum

CANAAN
AFTER THE CONQUEST,
as divided amongst the tribes
Scale of English Miles.
THE GREAT SEA
PHOENICIA
ZIDON
TYRE
DAMASCUS
Mt. Hermon
Pharpar
DAN
ASHER
NAPHTALI
Geshuri
ARGOB
BASHAN
MANASSEH
Mt. Carmel
ZEBULON
Mt. Tabor
ISSACHAR
Megiddo
Dor
MANASSEH
GAD
Saleah
Tirzah
Mt. Ebal
Mt. Gerizim
EPHRAIM
SHECHEM
RAMOTH GILEAD
Joppa
DAN
BENJAMIN
JERUSALEM
Bethlehem
Jericho
Rabbath Ammon
Ammonites
HESHBON
Mt. Nebo
REUBEN
Ashdod
Ashkelon
Gaza
Philistia
JUDAH
HEBRON
SEA OF THE PLAIN OR SALT SEA
MOAB
Beersheba
Gerar
SIMEON
Hormah
Wilderness of Zin
EDOM
Wilderness of Paran

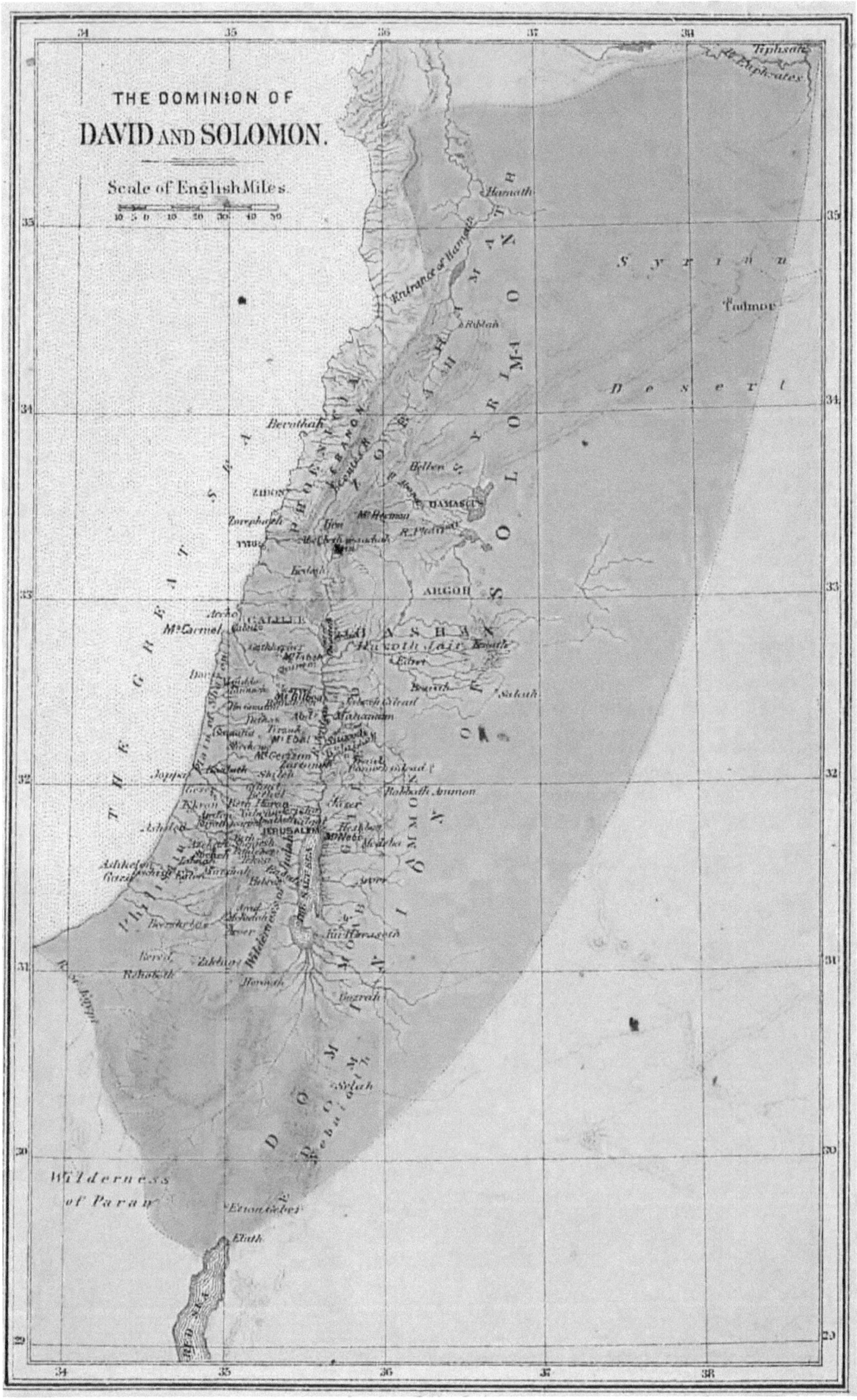
THE DOMINION OF
DAVID AND SOLOMON.
Scale of English Miles.
Hamath
Syria
Tadmor
Riblah
Desert
Berothah
Hermon
DAMASCUS
ARGOB
BASHAN
Mt. Carmel
Joppa
JERUSALEM
Rabbath Ammon
Kir Haraseth
Bozrah
Selah
Ezion Geber
Elath
Wilderness
of Paran
RED SEA

THE KINGDOMS
OF
JUDAH AND ISRAEL
Scale of English Miles
THE GREAT SEA
PHOENICIA
ZOBAH
SYRIA
ZIDON
Zarephath
TYRE
DAMASCUS
Mt. Hermon
R. Pharpar
R. Abana
Helbon
Dan
Kedesh
ARGOB
Accho
Mt. Carmel
GALILEE
BASHAN
KINGDOM OF ISRAEL
Edrei
Bozrah
Salcah
Dor
Plain of Sharon
Jabesh Gilead
Mahanaim
Beth Gamul
Dothan
Samaria
Mt. Ebal
Shechem
Mt. Gerizim
R. Jordan
GILEAD
Penuel
Ramoth Gilead
Joppa
Shiloh
Bethel
Rabbath Ammon
AMMON
Jazer
Heshbon
Mt. Nebo
Medeba
Ashdod
Ashkelon
JERUSALEM
Bethlehem
Gaza
Hebron
Engedi
THE SALT SEA
MOAB
R. Arnon
Ar
Aroer
PHILISTIA
Gerar
Beersheba
Arad
Moladah
Ziklag
Hormah
Bozrah
KINGDOM OF JUDAH
Wilderness of Judah
River of Egypt
Selah

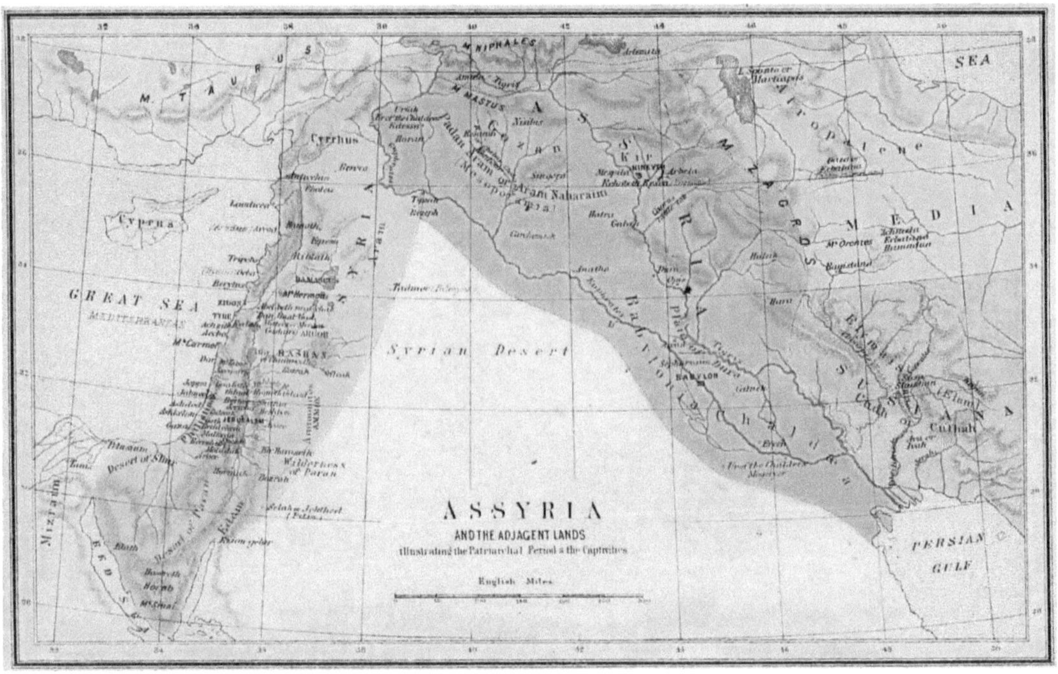
M. TAURUS
SEA
Cyrrhus
Cyprus
GREAT SEA
MEDITERRANEAN
Syrian Desert
MEDIA
BABYLON
Mizraim
ASSYRIA
AND THE ADJACENT LANDS
Illustrating the Patriarchal Period & the Captivities
English Miles
PERSIAN GULF

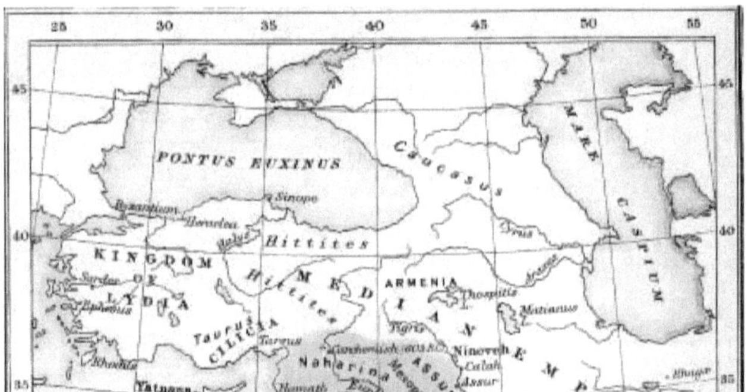
PONTUS EUXINUS
Sinope
Caucasus
MARE CASPIUM
Hittites
KINGDOM OF LYDIA
ARMENIA
Nineveh
MARE INTERNUM
Sidon
Tyrus
Damascus
Jerusalem
BABYLON
Susa
Persepolis
SINUS PERSICUS
Memphis
Arabs
ARABIA
KUSH
Meroe
Minæans
Sabæans
BABYLONIAN EMPIRE
560 B.C.
English Miles

Printed in Poland
by Amazon Fulfillment
Poland Sp. z o.o., Wrocław

31411276R00282